OBSCENITY AND FREEDOM OF EXPRESSION, ed. by Haig A. Bosmajian. Burt Franklin (dist. by Lenox Hill Publ. and Dist. Corp.), 1976. 348p bibl index 75-23138. 27.50 ISBN 0-89102-034-9. C.I.P.

Despite the somewhat cryptic word "Obscenity" which appears starkly alone on its spine, this excellent book is not an anthology of prurient snippets, but rather a compilation, by a professor at the University of Washington, of the leading court decisions, from 1868 to 1973, that have shaped the American obscenity law. The rulings are arranged according to the medium involved: Part I covers books, periodicals, and pamphlets; Part II, films and photographs; Part III, drama, dance, and night club performances, etc. Within each category, arrangement is chronological. The decisions are printed in their complete form, including dissents. A brief introduction provides a useful summary of the evolution of obscenity law, while the annotated bibliography surveys the state of the secondary literature. As a subject of litigation the question of obscenity appears destined to remain forever unresolved, and this compilation is thus already four years out of date. But for the period covered, it remains a most valuable guide. When supplemented by the numerous historical and sociological s that cast light on the social background from which these rulings emerged, *Obscenity*

Continued

OBSCENITY AND FREEDOM OF EXPRESSION

and freedom of expression should prove highly useful not only to graduates and undergraduates, but to their teachers as well — indeed, to anyone interested in this fascinating aspect of American law and American culture.

OBSCENITY
AND
FREEDOM OF EXPRESSION

OBSCENITY
AND
FREEDOM OF EXPRESSION

Compiled and Edited by

Haig A. Bosmajian
University of Washington

BURT FRANKLIN & CO., INC.
NEW YORK

OBSCENITY AND FREEDOM OF EXPRESSION

©1976 Burt Franklin & Co., Inc.
235 East 44th St.
New York, New York
10017

Library of Congress Cataloging in Publication Data
Main entry under title:

Obscenity and freedom of expression.

Bibliography: p.
1. Obscenity (Law)—United States—Cases.
I. Bosmajian, Haig A.
KF9444.A703 345'.73'0274 75-23138
ISBN 0-89102-034-9

CONTENTS

INTRODUCTION

A Historical Survey of Obscenity Tests

Obscenity, like beauty and a number of other things in life, lies in the eye of the beholder. In the words of Supreme Court Justice John Harlan, "one man's vulgarity is another's lyric."[1] In his *Ginzburg* dissent Justice Potter Stewart, after declaring that "the Constitution protects coarse expression as well as refined, and vulgarity no less than elegance," wrote: "A book worthless to me may convey something of value to my neighbor."[2] The film "The Art of Marriage," said the Minnesota Supreme Court majority in 1972, aroused "vicarious sexual pleasure"; a dissenting judge on the same court asserted: "If there is anything remotely romantic or erotic about it, I confess it has eluded me. It is about as sexually provocative as a documentary on techniques for artificially inseminating cattle."[3] Justice William O. Douglas has, on more than one occasion, reiterated the idea that "what is good literature, what has educational value, what is refined public information, what is art, varies with individuals as it does from one generation to another."[4] In his *Ginzburg* dissent, Douglas put it still another way: "Some like Chopin, others like 'rock and roll' . . . . Man was not made in a fixed mould . . . . Each of us is a very temporary transient with likes and dislikes that cover the spectrum."[5] In a 1946 post office censorship case, Douglas said that "what seems to one trash may have for others fleeting or even enduring values."[6]

In June 1973, the United States Supreme Court upheld the convictions of several individuals who had violated various federal and state obscenity statutes, Justices Burger, Blackmun, Powell, Rehnquist, and White constituting the majority; Justice Douglas, along with Justices Brennan, Marshall, and Stewart, dissented in all five cases. In his *Miller* dissent, Douglas wrote: "The Court is at large because we deal with tastes and standards of literature. What shocks me may be sustenance for my neighbor. What causes one person to boil up in rage over one pamphlet or movie may reflect only his neurosis, not shared by others."[7] In his *U.S. v. 12 200-Ft. Reels of Super 8mm. Film* dissent, Douglas again pointed out: "Most of the items that come this way denounced as 'obscene' are in my view trash. I would find few, if any, that had by my standards any redeeming social value. But what may be trash to me may be prized by others."[8]

Even Chief Justice Warren Burger, not one to tolerate obscene materials, recognized in *Miller* the personal and cultural relativity of obscenity when he wrote: "It is neither realistic nor constitutionally sound to read the First Amendment as requiring that the people of Maine or Mississippi accept public depiction of conduct found tolerable in Las Vegas, or New York City . . . . People in different States vary in their tastes and attitudes, and this diversity is not to be strangled by the absolutism of imposed uniformity."[9] But instead of concluding, as do Justices Douglas, Marshall, and others, that the consequence of such a concept of relativity should be less censorship, Burger uses the concept to place into the hands of "local communities" the power to suppress and ban nationally distributed books, films, and periodicals. In effect, the Chief Justice agrees with D.H. Lawrence's statement that "what is pornography for one man is the laughter of genius to another"; but then the Chief Justice proceeds to give to those persons who do not hear "the laughter of genius" the power to prohibit the material from those in the community who might hear it.

This diversity has not meant, however, that the "local community" has the power to silence speakers whose political and religious expressions are offensive to the community. When the majority of the Court of Appeals of New York held in 1951 that the film *The Miracle* was sacrilegious and not protected by the First Amendment, Judge Fuld dissented, pointing out that "it has been aptly observed that one man's heresy is another's orthodoxy, one's 'sacrilege,' another's consecrated belief."[10] When the case of *The Miracle* reached the United States Supreme Court, Judge Fuld's position was vindicated and the high court decided that "under the First and Fourteenth Amendments a state may not ban a film on the basis of a censor's conclusion that it is 'sacrilegious.'"[11] In his concurring opinion in this case, Justice Felix Frankfurter wrote: "In *Cantwell v. Connecticut* . . . Mr. Justice Roberts, speaking for the whole Court, said: 'In the realm of religious faith, and in that of political belief sharp differences arise. In both fields the tenets of one man may seem the rankest error to his neighbor.' Conduct and beliefs dear to one may seem the rankest 'sacrilege' to another."[12] In 1943, when the Supreme Court decided that children of the Jehovah's Witness faith could not be compelled to take part in the daily flag salute ceremony in the schoolhouse, Justice Robert Jackson said for the majority that "if there is any fixed star in our constitutional constellation, it is that no official, high or petty, can prescribe what shall be orthodox in politics, nationalism, religion, or other matters of opinion or force citizens to confess by word or act their faith therein."[13]

The courts have said, in effect, that in political and religious matters the citizenry has the right to freely speak, to freely pick and choose. The First Amendment does not say that "local communities" may prohibit speech which is politically or religiously offensive; the First Amendment applies equally to all the people across the land, those who live in Maine and Mississippi as well as those who live in Nevada and New York. The message of the First Amendment is that the people have the unabridged right and must be trusted to distinguish between dangerous and legitimate political doctrines, between traditional and nontraditional religious beliefs, between what is tasteful and distasteful in politics and religion. Justice Douglas has declared that he would place that same trust in the people in matters of literature. In his 1957 *Roth* dissent, Douglas wrote: "I have the same confidence in the ability of our people to reject noxious literature as I have in their capacity to sort out the true from the false in theology, economics, politics, or any other field."[14]

Historically, Justice Douglas's confidence in the people "to reject noxious literature" has not generally been shared by governmental officials, jurists, and legislators. Until Gutenberg, the limited number of books available to the populace and the low literacy amongst the masses precluded any widespread reading of books. But with the coming of printing and increased literacy, the church and state began to take a greater interest in the regulation of the printing and distribution of religious, political, and literary works. As long as literary and political works were available only to the rich and learned, censorship was minimal; it was only when the state felt it necessary to protect the morality of an increasingly literate citizenry that anti-obscenity laws and decisions appear in significantly greater number.

Charles Rembar has observed that "censorship is ancient, but censorship for obscenity is not." The law of obscenity, he points out, began relatively late "because there were not many books until late in history. Literary censorship is an elitist notion: obscenity is something from which the masses should be shielded. We never hear a prosecutor, or a condemning judge . . . declare his moral fibre has been injured by the book in question. It is always someone else's moral fibre for which anxiety is felt. It is always 'they' who will be damaged"[15] The nineteenth-century English Society for the Suppression of Vice was dubbed by Sydney Smith in 1809 as "a society for suppressing the vices of persons whose incomes do not exceed £500 a year."[16] The infamous Star Chamber of the seventeenth century concerned itself with pamphlets and books which attacked church and state, not obscene publications. In his 1973 *United States v. 12 200-Ft. Reels* dissent, Justice Douglas, after asserting that there is no "basis in the legal history antedating the First Amendment for the creation of an obscenity exception," said:

> The advent of the printing press spurred censorship in England, but the ribald and the obscene were not, at first, within the scope of that which was officially banned, The censorship of the Star Chamber and the licensing of books under the Tudors and Stuarts was aimed at the blasphemous or heretical, the editious or treasonous. At that date, the government made no effort to prohibit the dissemination of obscenity. Rather, obscene literature was considered to raise a moral question properly cognizable only by ecclesiastical, and not the common law, courts.[17]

Ecclesiastical vs. Civil Courts

It was an ecclesiastical court which in 1584 brought a charge "against William Trene and Elizabeth his wife. Detected, for that they have made a filthie ryme, of the most parte of the inhabitantes of this parishe."[18] In 1639, one Susan Seamer was brought before the church court "for her common and fearfull swearing and cursing. We present the same Susan for her most shameful and ordinary filthy and impure speeches and obscene songs and immodest be-

haviour, such as we shame to relate."'[9] The following "crime" and excommunication was recorded in 1623: "Aginst Alice Sundell. Presented for abuseing herself [i.e., misbehaving] in the Churchyeard by easing herself in open shew. She appears and admits the charge [the fame only, the offence she denies]. His lordship orders her to produce three testifiers, men worthy of credit among her neighbors. She fails to produce them. She is order to admit the offence in the presence of the minister, churchwardens and six or eight others. She fails to certify accordingly and is excommunicated."[20] In 1708, an English temporal court said in *Queen v. Read* that "an obscene book, as that intitled 'The Fifteen Plagues of a Maidenhead,' is not indictable, but punishable only in the spiritual court."[21]It is clear from this latter case, writes Alec Craig, "that at the beginning of the eighteenth century a bawdy book could be published in England with impunity."[22]

But it was a temporal court which fined Edmund Curl in 1727 and ordered him to stand in the pillory for publishing an "obscene little book" titled *Venus in the Cloister: or, The Nun in her Smock.* The Lord Chief Justice declared: "I think this is a case of very great consequence, though if it was not for the case of *The Queen v. Read,* I should make no great difficulty of it. Certainly the Spiritual Court has nothing to do with it, if in writing: and if it reflects on religion, virtue, or morality, if it tends to disturb the civil order of society, I think it is a temporal offence."[23] The significance of Curl's case, writes Alec Craig, is that "his prosecution authoritatively established the publication of an obscene libel as a misdemeanour at common law. A misdemeanour is an offence less grave than a felony, and is tried on indictment normally with a jury. No Act of Parliament had been passed. The law was judge-made law."[24] Obscenity combined with blasphemy led the House of Lords to declare in 1763 John Wilkes' *An Essay on Woman* constituted "a most scandalous, obscene, and impious libel, a gross profanation of many parts of the Holy Scriptures, and a most wicked and blasphemous attempt to ridicule and vilify the person of our Blessed Saviour."[25]

The Hicklin Decision

It was eleven years after the passage of the Obscene Publications Act of 1857 that the most far-reaching decision on obscenity was handed down. In 1857, the House of Lords and the House of Commons passed what became known as "Lord Campbell's Act," Lord Campbell being a major force in the passage of the Act, which provided that magistrates or justices of the peace could give authority by special warrant to any constable or police officer to enter, search for, and seize "any obscene books, papers, writings, prints, pictures, drawings, or other representations" kept "in any house, shop, room, or other place within the limits of the jurisdiction of any such magistrate or justices, for the purpose of sale or distribution, exhibition for purposes of gain, lending upon hire, or being otherwise published for purposes of gain . . . ."[26] Lord Campbell's Act was used in 1867 when it was ordered that one Henry Scott's two hundred fifty copies of a pamphlet titled *The Confessional Unmasked; shewing the depravity of the Romish priesthood, the iniquity of the Confessional, and the questions put to females in confession* be seized and destroyed. Scott appealed, and Recorder Benjamin Hicklin ordered the seized pamphlets be returned to Scott "subject to the opinion of the Court of Queen's Bench." Hicklin stated that while the material was "obscene," the purpose of Scott was to expose the evils of Catholicism, not to corrupt the moral of youth, and hence the Recorder found for Scott. The higher court, however, disagreed with Hicklin and in overruling him Lord Chief Justice Cockburn gave us the now famous "Hicklin test" which more accurately should be called the "Cockburn test": "The test of obscenity is this, whether the tendency of the matter charged as obscenity is to deprave and corrupt those whose minds are open to such immoral influences, and into whose hands a publication of this sort may fall."[27] Having defined "obscenity," Judge Cockburn continued: "Now, with regard to this work, it is quite certain that it would suggest to the minds of the young of either sex, or even to persons of more advanced years, thoughts of a most impure and libidinous character. The very reason why this work is put forward to expose the practices of the Roman Catholic confessional is the tendency of questions, involving practices and propensities of a certain description, to do mischief to the minds of those to whom such questions are addressed, by suggesting thoughts and desires which otherwise would not have occurred to their minds."[28] Therefore, said the judge, "apart from the ulterior object which the publisher of this work had in view, the work itself is, in every sense of the term, an obscene publication, and that, consequently, as the law of England does not allow of any obscene publication, such publication is indictable."[29] Scott's conceivably honest and laudable motives and intent in distributing the pamphlets, said the Lord Chief Justice, could not save the materials: "It seems to me that the effect of this work is mischievous and against the law, and is not to be justified because the immediate object of the publication is not to deprave the public mind, but, it may be, to destroy and extirpate Roman Catholicism. I think the old and honest maxim, that you shall not do evil that good may come, is applicable in law as well as in morals; and we have a certain and positive evil produced for the purpose of effecting an uncertain, remote, and very doubtful good."[30]

First American Cases

The *Hicklin* test was imported into the United States and was used immediately to prohibit the publication and distribution of a variety of books and periodicals. Before the adoption of *Hicklin,* however, there were very few obscenity cases tried in the courts of this country. As Justice Douglas has noted, "Julius Goebel, our leading expert on colonial law, does not so much as allude to punishment of obscenity."[31] The first obscentiy conviction in the United States came in *Commonwealth of Pennsylvania v. Sharpless* (1815) in which the court upheld the conviction of one Jesse Sharpless who had been charged as follows:

The Grand Inquest of the Commonwealth of Pennsylvania, inquiring for the city of Philadelphia, upon their oaths and affirmations respectively do present, that Jesse Sharpless, late of the same city yeoman . . . [and five other persons], being evil disposed persons, and designing, contriving, and intending the morals, as well of youth as of divers other citizens of this commonwealth, to debauch and corrupt, and to raise and create in their minds inordinate and lustful desires, on the first day of March, in the year one thousand eight hundred and fifteen, at the city aforesaid, and within the jurisdiction of this Court, in a certain house there exhibit, and show for money, to persons, to the inquest aforesaid unknown, a certain lewd, wicked, scandalous, infamous, and obscene painting, representing a man in an obscene, impudent, and indecent posture with a woman, to the

manifest corruption and subversion of youth, and other citizens of this commonwealth, to the evil examples of all others in like case offending, and against the peace and dignity of the commonwealth of Pennsylvania.[32]

Judge Yeates, in finding against Sharpless, wrote: "The question then in this part of the case is narrowed to a single point; — Whether the exhibition of a lewd, wicked, scandalous, infamous, and obscene painting, representing, &c. to certain individuals in a private house for money, is dispunishable by the sound principles of common law? On this question I cannot hesitate. It is settled, that the publication of a libel to any *one* person renders the act complete. . . . No man is permitted to corrupt the morals of the people. Secret poison cannot be thus disseminated."[33]

While the Pennsylvania court upheld the Sharpless conviction for exhibition of an obscene painting, the Massachusetts Supreme Court in 1821 upheld the conviction of Peter Holmes for publishing John Cleland's *Memoirs of a Woman of Pleasure,* more commonly known as *Fanny Hill* and which one-hundred-and-forty-five years later was declared not obscene by the United States Supreme Court. The 1821 indictment against Holmes contained five counts, including:

The second count alleged that the defendant, "being a scandalous and evil disposed person, and contriving, devising and intending, the morals as well of youth as of other good citizens of said Commonwealth to debauch and corrupt, and to raise and create in their minds inordinate and lustful desires, with force and arms, at &c. on &c. knowingly, unlawfully, wickedly, maliciously and scandalously, did utter, publish and deliver to A.B. a certain lewd, wicked, scandalous, infamous and obscene printed book, entitled &c. which said printed book is so lewd, wicked and obscene, that the same would be offensive to the court here, and improper to be placed upon the records thereof; wherefore the jurors aforesaid do not set forth the same in this indictment: to the manifest corruption and subversion of the youth and other good citizens of said Commonwealth in their manners and conversation; in contempt of law; to the evil and pernicious example of others in like case offending, and against the peace" &c.

The fifth count charged the publishing and delivering to C.D. the print contained in the same book, describing the print, and averring the same evil intent and tendency.[34]

In upholding Holmes' conviction, the court declared that "the offence of libel is an offence at common law, of which the Court of Sessions [which had indicted Holmes] originally had jurisdiction, without doubt."[35]

Until 1865, when Congress passed legislation declaring that no obscene materials shall be admitted into the mails, "there had been no federal anti-obscenity law except an obscure prohibition against importation of pictorial matter which had crept into the customs law in 1842, without any discussion or explanation. Indeed, there were, as of 1865, only a few anti-obscenity statutes in the country; the vast network of legislative prohibitions which exists today was the product of nineteenth century lawmaking still to come."[36] While the 1865 legislation prohibited the mailing of obscene matter, no definition of "obscenity" was provided.

First Federal Legislation & The Hicklin Test

In March 1873, largely due to the efforts and pressures originating from anti-obscenity crusader Anthony Comstock and his Society for the Suppression of Vice, Congress passed a piece of legislation which became 18 U.S.C. § 1461, legislation which was to be used for over a century to prohibit the mailing of "obscene" books, pamphlets, newspapers, and periodicals. Among the works which were at one time banned from the mails are Aristophenes' *Lysistrata,* D.H. Lawrence's *Lady Chatterley's Lover,* Lillian Smith's *Strange Fruit,* James Joyce's *Ulysses,* and James Jones's *From Here to Eternity.* The *Roth* decision of 1957 dealt, in part, with Roth's violation of 18 U.S.C. § 1481. Again in 1966, the United States Supreme Court upheld the conviction of Ralph Ginzburg for violating this federal obscenity statute.

Eleven years after *Regina v. Hicklin* and six years after passage of the "Comstock Act," a New York court found one D.M. Bennett guilty of violating the Act by mailing to "G. Brackett" a copy of *Cupid's Yokes; G.* Brackett, who requested the book be mailed to him, turned out to be Anthony Comstock. A Circuit Court upheld the conviction asserting *Hicklin* as the proper test of obscenity: "In saying that the 'test of obscenity, within the meaning of the statute,' is, as to 'whether the tendency of the matter is to deprave and corrupt the morals of those whose minds are open to such influences, and into whose hands a publication of this sort may fall,' the court [lower court] substantially said, that the matter must be regarded as obscene, if it would have a tendency to suggest impure and libidinous thoughts in the minds of those open to the influence of such thoughts, and thus deprave and corrupt their morals, if they should read such matter. It was not an erroneous statement of the test of obscenity, nor did the court give an erroneous definition of obscenity . . . . "[37]

In 1883, the conviction of a sender of an "obscene" letter was upheld in *United States v. Britton.* The Court concluded, seeimingly having no trouble defining the term "obscene," that "Congress has passed this law, having in mind the meaning of common terms, and has used there, to-wit, 'obscene,' 'indecent,' 'lewd,' and 'lascivious,' in defining what kind of matter is non-mailable, and it meant, by the use of these common and plain words, that nothing should circulate in the mail which would disseminate immorality in any form to the people. Therefore, I am led to the irresistible conclusion that the mailing of this letter is a violation of the law . . . . Every violation of this law should be heeded, and thus there will be secured to the people a pure, decent, and undefiled mail."[38] The *Britton* court cited *Bennett's* reliance on the *Hicklin* test and quoting from *Bennett* said: "It is not a question of whether it would corrupt the morals of every person . . . . It is within the law if it would suggest impure and libidinous thoughts in the minds of the young and the inexperienced."[39]

In 1884, the *Hicklin* test was used to uphold the conviction of August Muller for selling "indecent and obscene" photographs. In finding against Muller, the court stated that "the test of an obscene book was stated in *Regina v. Hicklin* . . . to be whether the tendency of the matter charged as obscenity is to deprave and corrupt those whose minds are open to such immoral influences, and who might come into contact with it."[40] The court declared that this test could properly be applied to paintings and statues as well as to books. The court contended, as did the *Hicklin* court, that the intent of the persons distributing the "obscene" materials did not protect them even if the intent may have been lawful. "In *Regina v. Hicklin,*" said the *Muller* court, ',the question was whether a certain book was obscene and liable to seizure for that reason under an English statute. It appeared that it was published to expose the alleged immoralities of private confession in the Ro-

man Catholic Church. But the court having found the passages purporting to be extracts from the writings of Roman Catholics were obscene in fact, it was held that the intent of the publication, however innocent, was no answer to the proceeding."[41]

Erosion of Hicklin

While *Hicklin* continued to be used as the obscenity test in the courts of the United States as the nineteenth century came to an end [see *infra, United States v. Wightman* (1886), *United States v. Bebout* (1886), *United States v. Clarke* (1889)], this test imported from England was beginning to be questioned as a proper determinant of obscenity. One of the characteristics of *Hicklin* was that a book could be condemned and prohibited on the basis of isolated passages being labelled "obscene." In 1894, the New York Supreme Court, deciding that some rare and expensive editions of *The Arabian Nights,* the works of Rabelais, Ovid's *Art of Love, The Decameron* by Boccaccio, and other classic works were not obscene, stated that "to condemn a standard literary work, because of a few of its episodes, would compel the exclusion from circulation of a very large proportion of the works of fiction of the most famous writers of the English language."[42] The concept of condemning a book as "obscene" on the basis of isolated passages came under more vigorous attack in 1922 when a New York court, in deciding *Halsey v. The New York Society for the Suppression of Vice,* found the English translation of Theophile Gautier's *Mademoiselle de Maupin* to be not obscene, said that "no work may be judged from a selection of such paragraphs alone. Printed by themselves they might, as a matter of law, come within the prohibition of the statute. So might a similar selection from Aristophenes or Chaucer or Boccaccio or even from the Bible. The book, however, must be considered broadly as a whole."[43]

While some judges were arguing that a book was not to be determined obscene and prohibited on the basis of isolated passages, others were attacking the idea that the effect of the material on the most susceptible persons should determine obscenity. *Hicklin* was being slowly eroded. In 1913, Judge Learned Hand spoke in *United States v. Kennerley* of the outdated English test: "I question whether in the end men will regard that as obscene which is honestly relevant to the adequate expression of innocent ideas, and whether they will not believe that truth and beauty are too precious to society at large to be mutilated in the interests of those most likely to pervert them to base uses. Indeed, it seems hardly likely that we are even today so lukewarm in our interest in letters or serious discussion as to be content to reduce our treatment of sex to the standard of a child's library in the supposed interest of a salacious few, or that shame will for long prevent us from adequate portrayal of some of the most serious and beautiful sides of human nature."[44] In this 1913 opinion, Judge Hand spoke of the "average conscience" being a better basis for determining obscenity than the most susceptible person, an "average conscience" which twenty years later became the "average person" rule used by Judge John Woolsey to give First Amendment protection to James Joyce's *Ulysses,* a rule which the United States Supreme Court finally adopted as part of its *Roth* test a half century after Judge Learned Hand's *Kennerley* opinion. Hand had written: "To put thought in leash to the average conscience of the time is perhaps tolerable, but to fetter it by the necessities of the lowest and least capable seems a fatal policy."[45]

Hicklin, however, persisted. In 1929, a New York court used the *Hicklin* test to decide that Radclyffe Hall's *The Well of Loneliness* was obscene and not protected, the judge concluding: "I am convinced that "The Well of Loneliness" tends to debauch public morals, that its subject-matter is offensive to public decency, and that it is calculated to deprave and corrupt minds open to its immoral influences and who might come in contact with it, and applying the rules and recognized standards of interpretation as laid down by our courts, I refuse to hold as matter of law that the book in question is not violative of the statute."[46] A year later, a Massachusetts court refused to give Theodore Drieser's *An American Tragedy* First Amendment protection, and in upholding the conviction of Donald Friede for selling Dreiser's book, the court stated: "The seller of a book which contains passages offensive to the statute has no right to assume that children to whom the book might come would not read the obnoxious passages or that if they should read them would continue to read on until the evil effects of the obscene passages were weakened or dissipated with the tragic denouement of a tale."[47]

These applications of *Hicklin* did not, however, stop inroads into the 1868 English obscenity test. In his 1930 *United States v. Dennett* opinion, Judge Augustus Hand gave protection to a sex information pamphlet titled *Sex Side of Life*, a pamphlet which had received wide acceptance from various religious, educational, and civic groups. In finding the publication not obscene, Judge Hand looked at the publication as a whole, not at the isolated words or passages or the "incidental tendency to arouse sex impulses": "Any incidental tendency to arouse sex impulses which such a pamphlet may perhaps have is apart from and subordinate to its main effect."[48]

In 1933, a New York judge took *God's Little Acre* as a whole in determining that the Caldwell book was not obscene, but a year-and-a-half before the famous *Ulysses* decision, Judge Greenspan wrote of *God's Little Acre*: "The book as a whole is very clearly not a work of pornography. It is not necessary for the court to decide whether it is an important work of literature. Its subject-matter constitutes a legitimate field for literary effort and the treatment is also legitimate. The court must consider the book as a whole even though some paragraphs standing by themselves might be objectionable."[49] Judge Greenspan cited the 1922 statement in *Halsey* asserting that a book "must be considered broadly as a whole" and the test is whether "not in certain passages but in its main purpose and construction" the book is obscene.[50]

The Decline of Hicklin

By the time Judge Woolsey wrote his *Ulysses* opinion in which he said that a book had to be judged by its effects on the average person, not on the young or abnormal and that a book had to be judged as a whole and not on isolated passages, the underpinnings of Hicklin were considerably weakened. In his now classic opinion, Judge Woolsey contended that "reading 'Ulysses' in its entirety, as a book must be read on such a test as this, did not tend to excite sexual impulses or lustful thoughts, but that its net effect . . . was only that of a somewhat tragic and very powerful commentary on the inner lives of men and women." In addition to asserting that the work had to be considered as a whole, Judge Woolsey argued that the law was con-

cerned with the effects of a book "on a person with average sex instincts,"[51] not on the most susceptible person. The government appealed, and Judges Learned Hand and Augustus Hand of the Circuit Court of Appeals upheld the Woolsey decision, and in doing so cited Judge Andrews, who had said eleven years earlier in *Halsey* that "the effect of the book as a whole is the test." The cousins Hand said: "The question in each case is whether a publication taken as a whole has a libidinous effect. The book before us has such portentous length, is written with such evident truthfulness in its depiction of certain types of humanity, and is so little erotic in its result, that it does not fall within the forbidden class."[52] But the word and the spirit of *Hicklin* appeared in Judge Manton's *Ulysses* dissent: "Who can doubt the obscenity of this book after reading of the pages referred to, which are too indecent to add as a footnote to this opinion? Its characterization as obscene should be quite unanimous by all who read it." Judge Manton's commitment to *Hicklin* was clearly revealed when he wrote that "the tendency of the matter to deprave and corrupt the morals of those whose minds are open to such influence and into whose hands the publication of this sort may fall, has become the test thoroughly entrenched in the federal courts."[53] The government decided not to appeal to the United States Supreme Court, and the two to one decision stood, making available to the American public a book which was soon to become a classic in literature.

Although books and films were being banned across the country between the 1933 *Ulysses* decision and the 1957 *Roth* decision, the demise of *Hicklin* brought First Amendment protection to materials which, in the last quarter of the nineteenth century and the first quarter of the twentieth, would have been declared obscene and hence suppressed. By 1940, Judge Learned Hand could refer to the 1868 English test as "the old and abandoned standard of *Regina v. Hicklin*."[54] Also in 1940, the United States Court of Appeals for the District of Columbia, in finding six books entitled *Nudism in Modern Life* not obscene, referred to the obsolete *Hicklin*: " . . . the rule was applied to those portions of the book charged to be obscene rather than to the book as a whole. But more recently this standard has been repudiated, and for it has been substituted the test that a book must be considered as a whole in its effect, not upon any particular class, but upon all those whom it is likely to reach."[55]

As O. John Rogge has pointed out, "in the two decades between Judge Woolsey's ruling in *Ulysses* and the Supreme Court's announcement of its prurient interest test in *Roth v. United States* and *Alberts v. California,* there was one opinion deserving of mention, that of Judge Curtis Bok, later a member of the Pennsylvania Supreme Court, in *Commonwealth v. Gordon.*"[56] Judge Bok concluded in that 1949 decision that Erskine Caldwell's *God's Little Acre,* James T. Farrell's Studs Lonigan Trilogy and *A World I Never Made,* William Faulkner's *Sanctuary* and *Wild Palms,* Calder Wallingham's *End as a Man,* and Harold Robbins' *Never Love a Stranger* were not obscene. In his well documented and well written opinion, Judge Bok stated in a resume of the opinion:

> Section 524 [of the Penal Code], for all its verbiage, is very bare. The full weight of the legislative prohibition dangles from the word "obscene" and its synonyms. Nowhere are these words defined; nowhere is the danger to be expected of them stated; nowhere is a standard of judgment set forth. I assume that "obscenity" is expected to have a familiar and inherent meaning, both as to what it is and as to what it does.

It is my purpose to show that it has no such inherent meaning; that different meanings given to it at different times are not
constant, either historically or legally; and that it is not constitutionally indictable unless it takes the form of sexual impurity,
i.e., "dirt for dirt's sake" and can be traced to actual criminal
behavior, either actual or demonstrably imminent.[57]

While Judge Bok gave First Amendment protection to
the variety of books involved in *Commonwealth v. Gordon,* other courts in the 1940s were still declaring obscene
such works as D.H. Lawrence's *Lady Chatterley's Lover*
and Lillian Smith's *Strange Fruit.* [see infra, *People v. Dial
Press, Inc.* (1944) and *Commonwealth v. Isenstadt* (1945)]

Film and The First Amendment

During the first half of the twentieth century, the courts
had to deal not only with "obscene" written communication, but also with "obscenity" in the movies. The medium
of the film brought with it First Amendment questions
hitherto unknown to the courts. The films posed such
questions as: Are movies a form of communication? Do
films come under the protection of the First Amendment?
In the first film censorship case (1907), one dealing with
Chicago's refusal to issue permits for the showing of *The
James Boys* and *Night Riders,* the Illinois Supreme Court
said nothing about the First Amendment and proceeded to
defend Chicago's ordinance requiring permits issued by the
chief of police before films could be shown. The court's
opinion reflected some class consciousness and discrimination:

> The purpose of the ordinance is to secure decency and moral-
> ity in the moving picture business, and that purpose falls within
> the police power . . . . The ordinance applies to five and ten cent
> theaters such as the complainants operate, and which, on ac-
> count of the low price of admission, are frequented and patron-
> ized by a large number of children, as well as by those of limited
> means who do not attend the productions of plays and dramas
> given in the regular theaters. The audiences include those classes
> whose age, education, and situation in life specially entitle them
> to protection against the evil influence of obscene and immoral
> representations. The welfare of society demands that every ef-
> fort of municipal authorities to afford such protection shall be
> sustained, unless it is clear that some constitutional right is inter-
> fered with.[58]

When in 1915 the United States Supreme Court handed
down its first film censorship decision, a unanimous Court
decided that the First Amendment did not apply to films.
Justice Joseph McKenna declared in *Mutual Film Corp. v.
Ohio*: "It cannot be put out of view that the exhibition of
moving pictures is a business pure and simple, originated
and conducted for profit, like other spectacles, not to be
regarded, nor intended to be regarded by the Ohio constitution, we think, as part of the press of the country or as
organs of public opinion."[59]

Thirty-seven years passed before the United States Supreme Court decided another film censorship case, and
during those thirty-seven years "not only had censorial
excesses become commonplace and in obvious need of correction, but two other developments made it hard to ignore motion pictures as a medium of speech. The first of
these was the technical and artistic advance of the medium
itself. The other was an expanding constitutional theory of
free speech in which the absence of the movies was increasingly conspicuous."[60]

In *Burnstyn v. Wilson* the high court finally decided in
1952 that films were included in the First Amendment

guarantees. The Court said: "It cannot be doubted that
motion pictures are a significant medium for the communication of ideas. They may affect public attitudes and behavior in a variety of ways, ranging from direct espousal of
a political or social doctrine to the subtle shaping of
thought which characterizes all artistic expression. The importance of motion pictures as an organ of public opinion
is not lessened by the fact that they are designed to entertain as well as to inform."[61] The Court held unconstitutional a New York statute which forbade the showing of
"sacrilegious" motion picture films: "Since the term 'sacrilegious' is the sole standard under attack here, it is not
necessary for us to decide, for example, whether a state
may censor motion pictures under a clearly drawn statute
and applied to prevent the showing of obscene films. That
is a very different question from the one now before us.
We hold only that under the First and Fourteenth Amendments a state may not ban a film on the basis of a censor's
conclusion that it is 'sacrilegious.' "[62]

One year later, in 1953, the Court of Appeals of New
York refused to give First Amendment protection to the
film *La Ronde* which had been determined by New York
not to be entitled to licensing for public exhibition upon
the ground that it was "immoral" and "would tend to
corrupt morals." The clear and present danger test which
had been used by Judge Bok in 1949 to protect the novels
involved in *Commonwealth v. Gordon* was brought to
bear, diluted with the bad tendency test, in 1953 to deny
protection to the film *La Ronde*: "That a motion picture
which panders to base human emotions is a breeding
ground for sensuality, depravity, licentiousness and sexual
immorality can hardly be doubted. That these vices represent a 'clear and present danger' to the body social seems
manifestly clear. The danger to youth is self-evident."[63]
The New York court saw "obvious" conclusions which
were not so clearly evident to other courts and justices:
"Although vulgar pornography is avoided, suggestive dialogue and action are present throughout and not merely
incidentally, depicting promiscuity as the natural and normal relation between the sexes, whether married or unmarried. Can we disagree with the judgment that such a
picture will tend to corrupt morals? To do so would close
our eyes to the obvious facts of life."

In his concurring opinion to ban *La Ronde,* Judge Desmond demonstrated that in 1953 *Hicklin* was still taken
seriously by some judges: "The point is not that it [the
film] depicts immoral conduct—it glorifies and romanticizes it, and conveys the idea that it is universal and inevitable. Are we as a court to say as matter of law that it does
not thus 'tend to corrupt morals'? This court should hold
that the State of New York may prevent the publication of
such matter, the obvious tendency of which is 'to deprave
or corrupt those minds open to such immoral influences,
and who might come into contact with it.' "[64]

Judges Dye and Fuld of the New York Court of Appeals
disagreed with the court's finding against *La Ronde,* Judge
Dye pointing out in his dissent that "the term 'immoral,'
as used in this pre- censorship statute, without more, affords little help in advising the citizen of what constitutes
a violating offense." Further, he saw no clear and present
danger: "Since reasonable men may differ on the import
and effect of 'La Ronde,' it follows that there is not a
'clear and present danger' sufficiently imminent to override the protection of the United States Constitution."[65]

The United States Supreme Court reversed the New

York court's judgment one year later, in 1954, with Justices Douglas and Black stating in a concurring opinion: "Motion pictures are of course a different medium of expression than the public speech, the radio, the stage, the novel, or the magazine. But the First Amendment draws no distinction between the various methods of communicating ideas. On occasion one may be more powerful or effective than another . . . . The First and the Fourteenth Amendments say that Congress and the States shall make 'no law' which abridges freedom of speech or of the press. In order to sanction a system of censorship I would have to say that 'no Law' does not mean what it says, that 'no law' is qualified to mean 'some' laws. I cannot take that step."[66] As the selections in the section on film in this book indicate, motion pictures have continued to be objects of censorship, including such films as *Lady Chatterley's Lover, I Am Curious—Yellow, Deep Throat,* and *Carnal Knowledge.*

The Roth Test

While for a century the state and lower federal courts across the land had been deciding questions of obscenity, the United States Supreme Court did not meet head on the question of whether obscenity was protected by the First Amendment until its *Roth* decision in 1957. Justice Douglas presents in footnote four of his 1968 *Ginsberg* dissent some reasons for the Supreme Court's relatively late consideration of this important constitutional question: " . . . the issue 'whether obscenity is utterance within the area of protected speech and press' was only 'squarely presented' to this Court for the first time in 1957. Roth v. United States, 354 U.S. 476, 481. This is indeed understandable, for the state legislatures have borne the main burden in enacting laws dealing with 'obscenity'; and the strictures of the First Amendment were not applied to them through the Fourteenth until comparatively late in our history. In *Gitlow v. New York,* 268 U.S. 652, decided in 1925, the Court assumed that the right of free speech was among the freedoms protected against state infringement by the Due Process Clause of the Fourteenth Amendment."[67] In *Roth* the Supreme Court rejected the *Hicklin* test and presented its "new" test for obscenity: "Whether to the average person, applying contemporary community standards, the dominant theme of the material taken as a whole appeals to prurient interest."[68] The Court declared that "obscenity is not within the area of constitutionally protected speech"; that "sex and obscenity are not synonymous"; that "obscene material is material which deals with sex in a manner appealing to prurient interest"; that "the federal obscenity statute punishing the use of the mails for obscene materials is a proper exercise of the postal powers delegated to Congress." At the same time that the Court upheld the convictions of Roth and Alberts, Roth for his violation of a federal obscenity statute, and Alberts for his violation of a California obscenity statute, it enunciated what became known as the *Roth* test, a test which was to influence obscenity decisions for years to come.

Justice Douglas, with whom Justice Black concurred, wrote a strong dissent beginning with: "When we sustain these convictions, we make the legality of a publication turn on the purity of thought which a book or tract instills in the mind of the reader. I do not think we can approve that standard and be faithful to the command of the First Amendment, which by its terms is a restraint on Congress, and which by the Fourteenth is a restraint on the States." Douglas was concerned that it was the arousal of sexual thoughts, and not human action and conduct, which the Court was attempting to control. "The absence of dependable information on the effect of obscene literature on human conduct should make us wary," wrote Douglas after reviewing some studies which were inconclusive about the relationship between anti-social sexual behavior and exposure to sex literature. Douglas concluded his dissent: "I would give the broad sweep of the First Amendment full support. I have the same confidence in the ability of our people to reject noxious literature as I have in their capacity to sort out the true from the false in theology, economics, politics, or any other field."[69]

There were no dissenting opinions when four months earlier the Court reversed the conviction of a Detroit bookseller who had been convicted of violating a Michigan statute which "made it an offense for him to make available for the general reading public . . . a book that the trial judge found to have a potentially deleterious influence on youth."[70] Justice Frankfurter, delivering the opinion of the Court, wrote:

> It is clear on the record that appellant was convicted because Michigan . . . made it an offense for him to make available for the general reading public (and he in fact sold to a police officer) a book that the trial judge found to have a potentially deleterious influence on youth. The State insists that, by thus quarantining the general reading public against books not too rugged for grown men and women in order to shield juvenile innocence, it is exercising its power to promote the general welfare. Surely, this is to burn the house to roast the pig . . . .
> We have before us legislation not reasonably restricted to the evil with which it is said to deal. The incidence of this enactment is to reduce the adult population of Michigan to reading only what is fit for children.[71]

This decision of February 25, 1957 was a prelude to the June 24, 1957 *Roth* decision. In *Butler v. Michigan,* the Supreme Court rejected the "most susceptible person" element of *Hicklin,* and then in *Roth,* the Court rejected *Hicklin* outright.

The *Roth* test brought with it the problems of deciding who constituted the "average person"; what constituted "contemporary community standards," "prurient interest," and "redeeming social importance." While "redeeming social importance" did not appear in the definition itself, Justice Brennan stated in the Court's opinion that "all ideas having even the slightest redeeming social importance— unorthodox ideas, controversial ideas, even ideas hateful to the prevailing climate of opinion—have the full protection of the guaranties . . . . But implicit in the history of the First Amendment is the rejection of obscenity as utterly without redeeming social importance."[72]

The decade following *Roth* saw the Court deciding a number of obscenity cases, but the question of what constituted obscenity and whether it was protected by the First Amendment remained only partially answered in the scores of concurring and dissenting opinions written by different justices who had their different views on obscenity and speech. On March 21, 1966, the Court reached some kind of a record when, in deciding three obscenity cases, fourteen different opinions were written by seven different justices. Justice Harlan wrote in 1967 that "the subject of obscenity has produced a variety of views among the members of the Court unmatched in any other course of constitutional adjudications."[73] In a footnote to this assertion, Harlan notes with documentation that "in the 13 obscenity cases since *Roth* in which a signed opinion was written for the Court, there have been a total of 55 separate opinions among the Justices."

The various phrases and terms in the *Roth* test from the outset caused problems and in fact were reinterpreted as the years passed.

Average person

It was twenty-four years before *Roth* that Judge Woolsey, in protecting *Ulysses*, said: "Whether a particular book would tend to excite such [sex] impulses and thoughts must be tested by the Court's opinion as to its effect on a person with average sex instincts— what the French would call *l'homme moyen sensuel*—who plays in this branch of legal inquiry, the same role of hypothetical reagent as does the 'reasonable man' in the law of torts . . . ."[74] Some light is thrown on the *Roth* court's conception of the "average person" when it expressed satisfaction with the *Roth* trial judge's instructing the jury as follows: " . . . the test is not whether it would arouse sexual desires or sexual impure thoughts in those comprising a particular segment of the community, the young, the immature or the highly prudish or would leave another segment, the scientific or highly educated or the so-called worldly-wise and sophisticated indifferent and unmoved."[75]

In 1966, however, the Supreme Court decided in *Mishkin v. New York* that materials could be suppressed, not for their effects on the "average person" in the community, but on a specified group for whom the materials were prepared or to whom the materials were directed. Edward Mishkin had argued that the books he had prepared and distributed could not be considered "obscene" since they did not appeal to the prurient interest of the "average person." The Mishkin materials dealt with sadism, masochism, fetishism, and homosexuality, and hence, it was argued, not likely to appeal to the "average person's" prurient interest. Justice Brennan, however, in upholding Mishkin's conviction, said: "Where the material is designed for and primarily disseminated to a clearly defined deviant sexual group rather than the public at large, the prurient-appeal requirement of the *Roth* test is satisfied if the dominant theme of the material taken as a whole appeals to the prurient interest in sex of the members of that group."[76] Apparently concerned that some persons might see this as a throwback to *Hicklin*, Justice Brennan explained: "We adjust the prurient- appeal requirement to social realities by permitting the appeal of this type of material to be assessed in terms of the sexual interests of its intended and probable recipient group: and since our holding requires that the recipient group be defined with more specificity than in terms of sexually immature persons, it also avoids the inadequacy of the most-susceptible-person facet of the *Hicklin* test."[77]

Contemporary Community Standards

While the Justices spoke in *Roth* of "contemporary community standards," they by no means defined what that "community" constituted. Was the Court speaking of a national community, a state community, a county, a city, a borough? In 1962, the Court decided to give First Amendment protection to several magazines titled *Manual, Trim,* and *Grecian Guild Pictorial,* magazines consisting mostly of photographs of nude or near nude male models accompanied with the names of the models and photog-

raphers. Justice Harlan announced the judgment of the Court and said in an opinion in which Justice Stewart joined: "We think that the proper test under this federal statute, reaching as it does to all parts of the United States whose population reflects many different ethnic and cultural backgrounds, is a national standard of decency. We need not decide whether Congress could constitutionally prescribe a lesser geographical framework for judging this issue which would not have the intolerable consequence of denying some sections of the country access to material, there deemed acceptable, which in others might be considered offensive to prevailing community standards of decency."[78] In 1964, Justice Brennan delivered an opinion in *Jacobellis v. Ohio*, in which Justice Goldberg joined, arguing that a proper reading of *Roth* meant that the community was to be defined as a "national community." Brennan wrote: "We thus reaffirm the position taken in *Roth* to the effect that the constitutional status of an allegedly obscene work must be determined on the basis of a national standard. It is, after all, a national Constitution we are expounding."[79] Then Chief Justice Earl Warren argued in his dissenting opinion that in *Roth* the Court meant to define "community" to mean "community": "It is my belief that when the Court said in *Roth* that obscenity is to be defined by reference to 'community standards,' it meant community standards—not a national standard as is sometimes argued. I believe there is no provable 'national standard' and perhaps there should be none."[80]

While the federal courts and some state courts have relied on the "national standard," a few states have defined the community as the city or the area in which the sale of the material occurred. In 1968, the California Supreme Court, in giving First Amendment protection to topless dancing, opted for the "State of California" as the "community." The California court devoted a significant part of its opinion to a discussion of "community standards" and explained why in the topless dancing case the state was the appropriate community, whereas in other cases a national standard would be called for:

> The strongest argument in support of a national community, that a non-national standard would produce the "intolerable consequence of denying some sections of the country access to material, there deemed acceptable, which in others might be considered offensive to prevailing community standards of decency . . . ," does not apply with any force to the instant fact situation. Evaluation of "speech" that is designed for nationwide dissemination, such as books or films, according to a non-national community standard might well unduly deter expression in the first instance and thus run afoul of First Amendment guarantees. But we need not, in the instant case, reconcile this contention with the practical problems of producing evidence of national standards. Iser's dancing is purely local in nature, a subject matter obviously not intended for nationwide dissemination. Since the decision as to whether to stage a "topless" dance rests solely on local considerations, the problem that unduly restrictive local standards may interfere with dissemination of and "access to [such] material" as books or film does not arise in the instant case.[81]

Books and films, however, were the materials which the United States Supreme Court found obscene and not protected "speech" using a non-national community standard on June 21, 1973. Chief Justice Warren Burger, speaking for the majority in *Miller v. California,* said: "Under a national Constitution, fundamental First Amendment limitations on the powers of the States do not vary from community to community, but this does not mean that there are, or should or can be, fixed, uniform national standards of precisely what appeals to the 'prurient interest' or is 'patently offensive.' "[82] After citing from Justice Warren's *Jacobellis* dissent, Burger declared that "it is neither realistic nor constitutionally sound to read the First Amendment as requiring that the people of Maine or Mississippi accept public depiction of conduct found tolerable in Las Vegas or New York City."[83] In his *Miller* dissent, Justice Douglas, arguing for First Amendment protection for "offensive" speech, countered: "The idea that the First Amendment permits government to ban publications that are 'offensive' to some people puts an ominous gloss on freedom of the press. That test would make it possible to ban any paper or any journal or magazine in some benighted place . . . . The idea that the First Amendment permits punishment for ideas that are 'offensive' to the particular judge or jury sitting in judgment is astounding. No greater leveler of speech or literature has ever been designed. To give the power to the censor, as we do today, is to make a sharp and radical break with the traditions of a free society. The First Amendment was not fashioned as a vehicle for dispensing tranquilizers to the people."[84]

Prurient Interest

In *Roth,* the Court defined "prurient interest" as that which has "a tendency to excite lustful thoughts"; "prurient interest," the majority said, was "a shameful or morbid interest in nudity, sex, or excretion . . . . " The Court asserted that material charged as obscene had to be taken as a whole in determining its prurient interest appeal. Sex and obscenity, said the Court, "are not synonymous."

Two years after *Roth,* the high court had to decide whether the State of New York could legally censor the film *Lady Chatterley's Lover.* New York had refused to grant a license for the exhibition of the film on the ground that "the whole theme of this motion picture is immoral under said law, for that theme is the presentation of adultery as a desirable, acceptable and proper pattern of behavior." In finding for the film, the United States Supreme Court pointed out in 1959 that obscenity and "sexual immorality" are not the same thing. What New York had done, said Justice Stewart, was "to prevent the exhibition of a motion picture because that picture advocates an idea—that adultery under certain circumstances may be proper behavior. Yet the First Amendment's basic guarantee is of freedom to advocate ideas. The State, quite simply, has thus struck at the very heart of constitutionally protected liberty."[85]

In finding Ralph Ginzburg's publications *Liaison, The Housewife's Handbook on Selective Promiscuity,* and *Eros* unprotected speech, the United States District Court in Pennsylvania said in 1963 that "pruriency is required and is defined as an itching, longing morbid or shameful sexual desire . . . . When material creates in the reader shame and guilt feelings simultaneously with sexual arousal, the result is usually obscenity. The material listed above clearly qualifies. There is no notable distinction between the aforesaid, taking each one as a whole, and the admittedly obscene material which was in evidence for comparison purposes."[86] In affirming the District Court's judgments against Ginzburg, the United States Court of Appeals stated in 1964 that "from our own close reading and scrutiny of *Eros,* its basic material predominantly appeals to prurient interest; it is on its face offensive to present day national community standards, and it has no artistic or social value." *Liaison* and *Handbook* were similarly declared ob-

scene because the court found that the appeal of the publications was "directed to the prurient interest of the average person in the national community." When the United States Supreme Court found against Ginzburg in 1966, it did so on the basis of the manner in which the publications were advertised. "The deliberate representation of petitioners' publications as erotically arousing," said the Court, "stimulated the reader to accept them as prurient; he looks for titillation, not for saving intellectual content . . . . Where the purveyor's sole emphasis is on the sexually provocative aspects of his publications, that fact may be decisive in the determination of obscenity. Certainly in a prosecution which, as here, does not necessarily imply suppression of the materials involved, the fact that they originate or are used as a subject of pandering is relevant to the application of the Roth test."[87] The court has said, in effect, that if the alleged obscene material cannot be shown to be obscene under the *Roth* test, the manner in which the material is advertised (i.e., pandering) can determine whether it will be held to appeal to prurient interest. In his *Ginzburg* dissent, Justice Black attacked the criterion of "prurient interest": "It seems quite apparent to me that human beings, serving either as judges or jurors, could not be expected to give any sort of decision on this element which would even remotely promise any kind of uniformity in the enforcement of this law. What conclusion an individual, be he judge or juror, would reach about whether the material appeals to 'prurient interest in sex' would depend largely in the long run not upon testimony of witnesses such as can be given in ordinary criminal cases where conduct is under scrutiny, but would depend to a large extent upon the judge's or juror's personality, habits, inclinations, attitudes, and other individual characteristics. In one community or in one courthouse a matter would be condemned as obscene under this so-called criterion but in another community, maybe only a few miles away, or in another courthouse in the same community, the material could be given a clean bill of health."[88]

Redeeming Social Value

In *Roth,* Justice Brennan, in delivering the opinion of the Court, said that "all ideas having even the slightest redeeming social importance . . . have the full protection of the guaranties, unless excludable because they encroach upon the limited area of more important interests. But implicit in the history of the First Amendment is the rejection of obscenity as utterly without redeeming social importance."

In 1965, when the Supreme Judicial Court of Massachusetts found John Cleland's *Memoirs of a Woman of Pleasure* obscene, it asserted that there was no doubt that the dominant theme of the book appeals to prurient interests. The Massachusetts court also found the book to be "utterly without social importance": "We are mindful that there was expert testimony, much of which was strained, to the effect that *Memoirs* is a structural novel with literary merit; that the book displays a skill in characterization and a gift for comedy; that it plays a part in the history of the development of the English novel; and that it contains a moral, namely, that sex with love is superior to sex in a brothel. But the fact that the testimony may indicate this book has some minimal literary value does not mean it is of any social importance. We do not interpret the 'social importance' test as requiring that a book which appeals to prurient interest and is patently offensive must be unqualifiedly worthless before it can be deemed obscene."[89] The United States Supreme Court disagreed, and in giving First Amendment protection to *Fanny Hill,* Justice Brennan wrote: "The Supreme Judicial Court erred in holding that a book need not be 'unqualifiedly worthless before it can be deemed obscene.' A book cannot be proscribed unless it is found to be *utterly* [the Court's emphasis] without redeeming social value. This is so even though the book is found to possess the requisite prurient appeal and to be patently offensive."[90] To find material obscene, said Brennan, three elements were required to coalesce: " . . . it must be established that (a) the dominant theme of the material taken as a whole appeals to prurient interest in sex; (b) the material is patently offensive because it affronts contemporary community standards relating to the description or representation of sexual matters; and (c) the material is utterly without redeeming social value." In the case of *Memoirs,* no such coalescing took place. The *Memoirs* test protected a publication which, while it may have appealed to prurient interest and may have been patently offensive to community standards, was saved because of its redeeming social value. Leon Friedman, attorney and writer, in 1966 optimistically saw progress in the *Memoirs* test: "In the *Fanny Hill* case the Supreme Court established a rule that can stay with us for many years to come. By making clear that no book, picture or printed matter of any kind can be proscribed unless it is utterly and completely without redeeming social value, the Court has made an intelligent step forward."[91]

Erosion of Roth

Seven years later, on June 21, 1973, Chief Justice Burger, speaking for the majority of the Court in *Miller v. California,* rejected the "redeeming social value" test: "We do not adopt as a constitutional standard the '*utterly* without redeeming social value' test of *Memoirs v. Massachusetts* . . . ; that concept has never commanded the adherence of more than three Justices at one time."[92] The Court then added one of its own guidelines for determining obscenity: "(c) whether the work, taken as a whole, lacks serious literary, artistic, political or scientific value."[93]

In the Home

While the Court had said quite pointedly in *Roth* that obscenity is not in the area of protected speech, in 1969 the high court decided in *Stanley v. Georgia* that the private possession and viewing of obscene materials within one's own home are constitutionally protected. "Prurient interest," "redeeming social value," and "patently offensive" were not relevant in the privacy of one's own home. The entire Court decided for Stanley, who had been convicted for knowingly possessing in his home obscene matter in violation of Georgia law. Justice Marshall dealt with the question of the *Roth* declaration of no First Amendment protection for obscenity and the *Stanley* declaration of protection of obscene materials by pointing out that *Roth* and subsequent obscenity cases "dealt with the power of the State and Federal Governments to prohibit or regulate certain public actions taken or intended to be taken with respect to obscene matter."[94] The Court emphasized in *Stanley* the right of individuals to read or view what they wished within the confines of their home: "Whatever may be the justifications for other statutes regulating obscenity, we do not think they reach into the privacy of one's own home. If the First Amendment means

anything, it means that a State has no business telling a man, sitting alone in his own house, what books he may read or what films he may watch. Our whole constitutional heritage rebels at the thought of giving government the power to control men's minds." But the states' power to "regulate" obscenity remained: "We hold that the First and Fourteenth Amendments prohibit making mere possession of obscene material a crime. *Roth* and the cases following that decision are not impaired by today's holding. As we have said, the States retain broad power to regulate obscenity; that power simply does not extend to mere possession by the individual in the privacy of his own home."[95]

Two years after *Stanley,* the Court reiterated the power of the State or Federal Governments to restrict the sale, distribution, and transportation of obscene materials. In *United States v. Thirty Seven Photographs,* the Court found against Milton Luros, who had upon his return from Europe brought back with him thirty seven photographs in his luggage. The photographs were declared obscene by the customs agents and the Supreme Court decided that "obscene materials may be removed from the channels of commerce when discovered in the luggage of a returning foreign traveler even though intended solely for his private use. That the private user under *Stanley* may not be prosecuted for possession of obscenity in his home does not mean that he is entitled to import it from abroad free from the power of Congress to exclude noxious articles from commerce. *Stanley's* emphasis was on the freedom of thought and mind in the privacy of the home. But a port of entry is not a traveler's home."[96]

In his *Thirty Seven Photographs* dissent, Justice Black argued that this decision of the Court did not square with *Stanley:* "It would seem to me that if a citizen had a right to possess 'obscene' material in the privacy of his home he should have the right to receive it voluntarily through the mail. Certainly when a man legally purchases such material abroad he should be able to bring it with him through customs to read later in his home. The mere act of importation for private use can hardly be more offensive to others than is private perusal in one's home. The right to read and view any literature and pictures at home is hollow indeed if it does not include the right to carry that material privately in one's luggage when entering the country." Justice Black rather sardonically declared: "Since the plurality opinion offers no plausible reason to distinguish private possession of 'obscenity' from importation for private use, I can only conclude that at least four members of the Court would overrule *Stanley.* Or perhaps in the future that case will be recognized as good law only when a man writes salacious books in his attic, prints them in his basement, and reads them in his living room."[97]

On May 3, 1971, the same day that *Thirty Seven Photographs* was decided, the high court reversed a District Court judgment for Norman Reidel, who had been indicted for mailing a booklet titled *The True Facts About Imported Pornography.* The District Court had dismissed the indictment, relying heavily on *Stanley.* The government took the case to the Supreme Court, which asserted through the majority opinion that "nothing in *Stanley* questioned the validity of *Roth* insofar as the distribution of obscene material was concerned. Clearly the Court had no thought of questioning the validity of §1461 as applied to those who, like Reidel, are routinely disseminating obscenity through the mails and who have no claim, and could make none, about unwanted governmental intrusions into the privacy of their home."[98] While Justice Marshall concurred in the Court's *Reidel* judgment, he dissented in *Thirty Seven Photographs,* pointing out that "although claimant [Luros] stipulated that he intended to use some of the photographs to illustrate a book which would be later distributed commercially, the seized items were then in his purely private possession and threatened neither children nor anyone else. In my view, the Government has ample opportunity to protect its valid interests if and when commercial distribution should take place."[99]

One month after the Court decided *Thirty Seven Photographs* and *Reidel,* it gave protection to a kind of "obscene" speech with which it had previously not been confronted: nonerotic "obscenity." Paul Cohen had been convicted for violating a California statute for his wearing in public a jacket on the back of which appeared the words "Fuck the Draft." Cohen had appeared in the Los Angeles courthouse corridor wearing the jacket which carried his clearly visible message informing the public of his feelings against the draft and, he said, against the Vietnam war. While the word "fuck" had appeared in Cohen's "speech," the United States Supreme Court, speaking through Justice Harlan, decided that this was not an obscenity case: "Whatever else may be necessary to give rise to the States' broader power to prohibit obscene expression, such expression must be, in some significant way erotic . . . . It cannot plausibly be maintained that this vulgar allusion to the Selective Service System would conjure up such psychic stimulation in anyone likely to be confronted with Cohen's crudely defaced jacket."[100] Justices Blackmun, Black, and Burger dissented, claiming that "Cohen's absurd and immature antic . . . was mainly conduct and little speech."[101]

In subsequent cases dealing with "obscene" words and phrases in political speech, the Court divided clearly, with the Nixon appointees consistently refusing to give such "obscenities" First Amendment protection. On June 26, 1972, the Court vacated three judgments and remanded for reconsideration in *Rosenfeld v. New Jersey, Lewis v. City of New Orleans,* and *Brown v. Oklahoma,* all dealing with convictions based upon "obscene" language spoken before individuals and audiences. In all three cases, the Nixon appointees, Burger, Blackmun, Powell, and Rehnquist, dissented, arguing that the "obscene" language involved was not protected speech. Justice Powell left the Nixon camp, and joined the majority (Brennan, Douglas, Marshall, Stewart, and White) in *Brown* because "the papers filed in this case indicate that the language for which appellant was prosecuted was used in a political meeting to which appellant had been invited to present the Black Panther viewpoint. In these circumstances language of the character charged might well have been anticipated by the audience."[102] Brown had spoken to a large audience gathered in the University of Tulsa chapel, and during a question period, he referred to some policemen as "motherfucking fascist pig cops" and to a particular police officer as that "black motherfucking pig." He had been convicted of violating an Oklahoma statute that prohibited the utterance of "any obscene or lascivious language or word in any public place, or in the presence of females."

While Powell left the Nixon ranks in finding for Brown, he wrote a dissenting opinion in *Rosenfeld,* joined by Burger and Blackmun. Rosenfeld had been convicted of violating a New Jersey statute prohibiting the utterance of "loud and offensive or profane or indecent language in any public street or other meeting place". Rosenfeld had used the term "motherfucking" at a public school board meeting to describe teachers, the school board, the town, and the United States. The meeting was attended by about one-hundred-fifty people, approximately forty of whom were children and twenty-five women.[103] In his arguments to deny First Amendment protection to Rosenfeld, Justice Powell wrote that the exception to First Amendment protection "extends to the willful use of scurrilous language calculated to offend the sensibilities of an unwilling audience." Powell saw the use of such language an erosion on civilized society: "One of the hallmarks of a civilized society is the level and quality of discourse. We have witnessed in recent years a disquieting deterioration in standards of taste and civility in speech . . . . The shock and sense of affront, and sometimes the injury to mind and spirit, can be as great from words as from some physical attacks."[104] Justice Burger also saw the toleration of such language as a contributing factor to the retrogression of liberty and civilization. In his dissent, Burger, joined by Blackmun and Rehnquist, declared: "In Rosenfeld's case . . . civilized people attending such a meeting with wives and children would not likely have an instantaneous violent response, but it does not unduly tax the imagination to think that some justifiably outraged parent whose family were exposed to the foul mouthings of the speaker would 'meet him outside' and, either alone or with others, resort to the 19th century's vigorous modes of dealing with such people. I cannot see these holdings as an 'advance' in human liberty but rather a retrogression to what men have struggled to escape for a long time." The "retrogression" of which Burger speaks is not clearly defined.

On March 3, 1973, the United States Supreme Court decided in *Papish v. The Board of Curators of the University of Missouri* that graduate student Papish, who had been expelled from the University of Missouri for distributing an underground newspaper which had on its cover a policeman raping the Statue of Liberty and the Goddess of Justice and which had an article titled "M----- f----- Acquitted," had been illegally expelled, and the Court ordered that she be reinstated as a student at the University. The Court said that "the mere dissemination of ideas—no matter how offensive to good taste—on a state university campus may not be shut off in the name alone of 'conventions of decency.' Other precedents of this Court make it equally clear that neither the political cartoon nor the headline story involved in this case can be labelled as constitutionally obscene or otherwise unprotected."[105] Justice Burger, along with Blackmun and Rehnquist, dissented, arguing that "a university is not merely an arena for the discussion of ideas by students and faculty; it is also an institution where individuals learn to express themselves in acceptable and civil terms."[106]

But since the famous 1969 *Tinker* decision in which the United States Supreme Court found for three school children who had been suspended from school for wearing black armbands to protest the war in Vietnam, lower courts have heeded Justice Fortas's position in *Tinker* that "First Amendment rights, applied in light of the special characteristics of the school environment, are available to teachers and students. It can hardly be argued that either students or teachers shed their constitutional rights to freedom of speech or expression at the schoolhouse gate."[107]

In 1973, the United States Court of Appeals, Seventh

District, decided that the inclusion of "earthy" words in the unofficial student newspaper *Corn Cob Curtain* distributed at Indianapolis high schools did not constitute "obscenity." The court said: "In the first place, the issues of the *Corn Cob Curtain* in the record are very far from obscene in the legal sense. A few earthy words relating to bodily functions and sexual intercourse are used in the copies of the newspaper in the record. Usually they appear as expletives or at some similar level . . . . These issues contain no material which is in any significant way erotic, sexually explicit, or which could plausibly be said to appeal to the prurient interest of adult or minor."[108]

In a case involving a high school teacher who had been suspended for assigning to his senior English class an *Atlantic* magazine article on dissent and protest which included "a vulgar term for an incestuous son," the federal court found for the teacher, declaring: "We do not question the good faith of the defendants [Ipswich, Massachusetts Public School Committee] in believing that some parents have been offended. With the greatest of respect to such parents, their sensibilities are not the full measure of what is a proper education."[109] And in 1973, the California Supreme Court found for a teacher who had been "terminated" by the Governing Board of the Torrance School District in California because he had read to his tenth grade English class a short story which "contained language . . . deemed objectionable by South High's principal—including a slang expression for an incestuous son."[110] In finding for the teacher, a Catholic priest on leave of absence from the Church, the California court said: "Lindros was obviously trying to teach his students that in writing creative compositions the author must attempt to put those words in the mouths of his characters that belong there. The blasphemous epithet must fit the emotional outburst of the speaker. To isolate the epithet and to condemn the teacher is to miss the function of expressive writing. In sum, we could not impose upon teachers of writing, as a matter of law, that they must tell and teach their students that in depicting the jargon of the ghetto, the slum, or the barrack room, characters must speak in the pedantry of Edwardian English."[111]

Justices Burger, Blackmun, and Rehnquist, however, have used the argument that to allow the use of "obscenity" in our schools will lead to a disenchantment of the citizenry and legislators with education. In addition to writing his own *Papish* dissent, Burger joined with Blackmun in the Rehnquist dissent in which the latter argued for upholding the expulsion of Papish on the basis of the negative effects her "speech" and slow progress toward her degree would have on taxpayers and legislators: "The system of tax supported public universities which has grown up in this country is one of its truly great accomplishments; if they are to continue to grow and thrive to serve an expanding population, they must have something more than the grudging support of taxpayers and legislators. But one can scarcely blame the latter, if told by the Court that their only function is to supply tax money for the operation of the University, the 'disenchantment' may reach such a point that they doubt the game is worth the candle."[112] But as the *Keefe* court stated: "with the greatest of respect to such parents, their sensibilities are not the full measure of what is a proper education." Under the restrictive conditions espoused by Burger, Blackmun, and Rehnquist an educational institution cannot fully perform its important function of discovering the truth and following

it wherever it may lead. The path to truth and creativity is not always paved with the most "acceptable" and "civil" language. As the California Supreme Court declared in *Lindros*, characters in creative writing do not all speak the "pedantry of Edwardian English."

Broadcasting

While the courts have spoken on obscenity in the schoolhouse and on the use of obscenity in books, films, periodicals, drama, and dance, they have had little to say about obscenity on radio and television. In the area of radio broadcasting, the Federal Communications Act provides that "nothing in this Act shall be understood or construed to give the Commission the power of censorship over the radio communications or signals transmitted by any radio station, and no regulation or condition shall be promulgated or fixed by the Commission which shall interfere with the right of free speech by means of radio communication."[113] However, while the FCC asserts this protection of freedom of speech, the United States Criminal Code (18 U.S.C. § 1464) provides that "whoever utters any obscene, indecent, or profane language by means of radio communications shall be fined not more than $10,000 or imprisoned not more than two years or both." In 1934, the FCC was given the power to grant broadcast licenses "if public convenience, interest, or necessity will be served thereby."[114] While the courts have decided obscenity cases related to the other media, it has been the FCC which has handled cases arising out of the use of obscenity on radio. The FCC itself has noted: "The legal considerations applicable to 18 U.S.C. § 1464 are not clear, because of the dearth of court decisions dealing with this section."[115] In 1970, FCC Commissioner Nicholas Johnson pointed out in a case in which the Commission fined a station for broadcasting "obscene" material that there was a lack of precedents and research in this area of speech: "Groups in this country interested in civil liberties and speech freedoms should understand that the Commission today enters a new and untested area of federal censorship—censorship over the words, thoughts and ideas that can be conveyed over the most powerful medium of communication known to man: the *broadcasting* medium. To my knowledge, there are no judicial precedents, no law review articles, no FCC decisions, and no scholarly thinking that even attempt to define the standards of permissible free speech for the broadcasting medium."[116]

In a 1970 decision to penalize a radio station for broadcasting the words "fuck" and "shit" (used in a phrase such as "political change is so fucking slow"), the FCC said that "there is no precedent, judicial or administrative, for this case."[117] In a 1962 case the FCC refused to renew the license of a Kingstree, South Carolina radio station partly on the basis of broadcasted "obscenity," and while bringing *Roth* to bear in its decision, the FCC was uncomfortable about applying the *Roth* test to radio broadcasting: "The field of broadcast regulation is perhaps an area as ill adapted as any for employment of the *Roth* test. First, it must be remembered that, unlike the acquisition of books and pictures, broadcast material is available at the flick of a switch to young and old alike, to the sensitive and the indifferent, to the sophisticated and the credulous. Further, broadcast material is delivered on a route commonly owned by the public on a vehicle especially licensed to serve them and is received on property owned by the consignee. In short, there is a universality of utility and a public stake present in broadcasting wholly lacking in the kind of thing that was involved in *Roth*."[118] The FCC rejected the radio station's contention that the *Roth* test needed to be applied to determine whether the broadcast materials were protected by the First Amendment. The Commission examiner concluded "that even under the *Roth* test the Walker broadcasts here at issue are obscene and indecent and, a fortiori, coarse, vulgar, suggestive, and susceptible of indecent double meaning. Without employing the *Roth* test, he holds the material in question obscene and indecent on its face."[119]

In a case involving the renewal of licenses for station KPFA-FM (Berkeley), KPFB (Educational FM, Berkeley), and WBAI-FM (New York), the FCC considered the complaints it had received about the broadcasting of some poems by Lawrence Ferlinghetti, *The Zoo Story* by Edward Albee, *Live and Let Live* (a discussion of homosexuality by eight homosexuals), *Ballad of the Despairing Husband* read by the author, Robert Creely, and some readings from *The Kid,* an unfinished novel by Edward Pomerantz. In deciding to grant the license renewals, the FCC declared: "We recognize that as shown by the complaints here, such provocative programming as here involved may offend some listeners. But this does not mean that those offended have the right, through the Commission's licensing power, to rule such programming off the airwaves. Were this the case, only the wholly inoffensive, the bland, could gain access to the radio microphone or TV camera. No such drastic curtailment can be countenanced under the Constitution, the Communications Act, or the Commission's policy . . . . "[120] While concurring with the Commission's action in granting renewals to the Pacifica Foundation stations involved in this case, Commissioner Robert E. Lee was moved to say in a concurring statement: "The airing of a program dealing with sexual aberrations is not to my mind, per se, a violation of good taste nor contrary to the public interest. When these subjects are discussed by physicians and sociologists, it is conceivable that the public would benefit. But a panel of eight homosexuals discussing their experiences and past history does not approach the treatment of a delicate subject one could expect by a responsible broadcaster. A microphone in a bordello, during slack hours, could give us similar information on a related subject. Such programs obviously designed to be lurid and to stir the public curiosity, have little place on the air." Commissioner Lee concluded: "I do not hold myself to be either a moralist or a judge of taste. Least of all do I have a clear understanding of what may constitute obscenity in broadcasting."[121]

In 1970, the FCC granted the Seattle FM station KRAB a one-year renewal of its license instead of the usual three-year renewal on the basis of complaints of obscene language being aired over KRAB. The Seattle station filed a petition asking the FCC to reconsider and to grant the full three year renewal, which it did in 1971. In so doing, the FCC stated: "We cannot emphasize too strongly that while KRAB did broadcast a few programs that included some language offensive to some people, they did not do so with any intent to give offense, to pander, to sensationalize, to shock, or to break down community standards . . . . We conclude that KRAB's programming, in total, is outstanding and meritorious. We conclude that the few instances in which KRAB did broadcast obscene language, either willing or unwillingly, do not justify denying grant of a full term three year renewal of its license."[122]

Public Performances

Just as the 1960s and 1970s brought before the courts (and the FCC) an increasing number of cases dealing with "obscenity" in political discourse, more cases were brought before the courts on matters relating to "obscenity" in live theatrical and nightclub performances. In June 1964, the Illinois Supreme Court upheld the conviction of nightclub entertainer Lenny Bruce for an "obscene" performance before an adult nightclub audience. A few months later, however, the same court reluctantly decided that the lower court judgment against Bruce had to be reversed in light of the United States Supreme Court's decision in *Jacobellis v. Ohio* (1964). The Illinois Supreme Court declared: "While we would not have thought that constitutional guarantees necessitate the subjection of society to the gradual deterioration of its moral fabric which this type of presentation promotes, we must concede that some of the topics commented on by defendant are of social importance. Under *Jacobellis* the entire performance is thereby immunized, and we are constrained to hold that the judgment of the circuit court of Cook county must be reversed and defendant discharged."[123] The question of whether topless dancing was "speech" protected by the First Amendment came to the California Supreme Court which said in *In re Giannini* that "a performance of such a dance, like other forms of expression or communication prima facie enjoys protection under the First Amendment of the Constitution of the United States; it loses such protection upon a showing of its obscenity." "To show such obscenity," continued the California court, "the prosecution must introduce evidence that, applying contemporary community standards, the questioned dance appealed to the prurient interest of the audience and affronted the standards of decency accepted in the community." The court concluded that "the convictions must be set aside because the prosecution failed to introduce any evidence of community standards, either that Iser's [the dancer's] conduct appealed to prurient interest or offended contemporary standards of decency."[124]

The theatrical production *Hair* met different fates in different courts. In 1971, the United States District Court, N.D. Georgia, ordered the Atlanta Civic Center be made available to Southeastern Promotions, Ltd., which had requested a reservation of the Civic Center but had been denied its use because *Hair* "was not the proper type of entertainment for a public auditorium." District Judge Edenfield wrote: "Stripped of window-dressing and distracting side issues, the naked question in this case is whether municipal officials, solely by reason of their authority to manage a municipal civic center and auditorium, have the unfettered right to censor and monitor the types of speech, and to prescribe the types of productions, which may be performed in such a public auditorium. They do not."[125]

The *Hair* production was considered as a whole, in its entirety. Judge Edenfield explained: "The court cannot accept the proposition that stage productions may be dissected into 'speech' and 'nonspeech' components as those terms have been used by the Supreme Court. The nonverbal elements in a theatrical production are the very ones which distinguish this form of art from literature. It may be true that First Amendment protections vary in different media, but a musical play must be deemed a unitary form of constitutionally protected expression. The court concludes that the entire musical play 'Hair' is speech and entitled to First Amendment protection."[126]

In Tennessee, another District Court decided in 1972 not to give *Hair* First Amendment protection, asserting that "the theatrical production of 'Hair' contains conduct, apart from speech or symbolic speech, which would render it in violation of both the public nudity ordinances of the City of Chattanooga and the obscenity ordinances and statutes of the City and of the State of Tennessee. The defendants accordingly acted within their lawful discretion in declining to lease the Municipal Auditorium or the Tivoli Theater unto the plaintiff."[127] In defending its ban on *Hair*, the court pointed to the destructiveness of "undisciplined sex": "Undisciplined sex is one of the most destructive forces in any society and has historically been so recognized. It is destructive of many human values and institutions, not the least of which is the family, which in turn has served as the foundation for every civilization yet known to man. Regulation of public and undisciplined sexual conduct is clearly within the police power of the state."[128]

In 1972, the United States Supreme Court, for the first time, decided a case involving the prohibition of "explicitly sexual live entertainment and films at bars and other establishments licensed to dispense liquor by the drink." Justice Rehnquist, speaking for the majority in *California v. LaRue,* stated that the rules adopted by the California Department of Alcoholic Beverage Control prohibiting such entertainment and films "at bars and other establishments licensed to dispense liquor by the drink" were constitutional. Rehnquist said: " . . . we would poorly serve both the interests for which the State may validly seek vindication and the interests protected by the First and Fourteenth Amendments were we to insist that the sort of Bacchanalian revelries which the Department sought to prevent by these liquor regulations were the constitutional equivalent of a performance by a scantily clad ballet troupe in a theater."[129] In his dissent, Douglas argued that it was not clear how broadly or how narrowly the California regulations would be applied: "It is conceivable that a licensee might produce in a garden served by him a play—Shakespearian perhaps or one in a more modern setting—in which, for example, 'fondling' in the sense of the Rules appears. I cannot imagine that any such performance could constitutionally be punished or restrained, even though the police power of a State is now buttressed by the Twenty-First Amendment . . . . Certainly a play which passes muster under the First Amendment is not made illegal because it is performed in a beer garden."[130] Justice Marshall, also dissenting, saw the regulations as overbroad and unconstitutional, pointing out that California's regulatory scheme did not conform to the standards which the Supreme Court had previously established for the control of obscenity: "Instead of the contextual test approved in *Roth* and *Memoirs* these regulations create a system of *per se* rules to be applied regardless of context: Certain acts simply may not be depicted and certain parts of the body may under no circumstances be revealed. The regulations thus treat on the same level a serious movie such as 'Ulysses' and a crudely made 'stag film.' They ban not only obviously pornographic photographs, but also great sculpture from antiquity."[131]

Contemporary Community Standards

By June 21, 1973, when the United States Supreme Court handed down five decisions upholding the convictions of several individuals who had been found guilty of violating state and federal obscenity statutes, the division of the Court on First Amendment and obscenity matters was clearly establihsed. The Nixon appointees consistently denied First Amendment protection to a variety of books, films, and speech. Justices Brennan, Douglas, Marshall, and Stewart consistently dissented. This is how the Court lined up, with Justice White voting with the Nixon appointees, in all five June 21, 1973 cases. Rejecting the *Memoirs* "utterly without redeeming social value" test and rejecting the "national standards" test, the majority said: "The basic guidelines for the trier of fact must be (a) whether 'the average person, applying contemporary community standards' would find that the work, taken as a whole, appeals to the prurient interest . . . (b) whether the work depicts or describes, in a patently offensive way, sexual conduct specifically defined by the applicable state law, and (c) whether the work, taken as a whole, lacks serious literary, artistic, political, or scientific value. We do not adopt as a constitutional standard the 'utterly without redeeming social value' test of *Memoirs v. Massachusetts . . . .* "[132]

In rejecting the "national standards" test, the Chief Justice said: "We conclude that neither the State's alleged failure to offer evidence of 'national standards,' nor the trial court's charge that the jury consider state community standards, were constitutional errors. Nothing in the First Amendment requires that a jury must consider hypothetical and unascertainalbe 'national standards' when attempting to determine whether certain materials are obscene as a matter of fact."[133] While the majority found acceptable as "community standards" the standards of the State of California in the *Miller* case, the Burger opinion did not clearly define what was meant by "community standards." Under *Miller,* a state, a county, a city could conceivably prohibit the showing of the films *Carnal Knowledge, I Am Curious—Yellow,* and *The Stewardesses,* prohibit the presentation of the plays *Hair, Oh! Calcutta,* and *The Beard,* and ban the sale of *Last Exit to Brooklyn, The Happy Hooker,* and *Slaughterhouse Five.* Under *Miller,* a local community could decide that these films, plays, and books appeal to the prurient interest of the average persons in that community.

One justification for the suppression of such films, plays, and books according to Burger and the majority in the five obscenity cases of June 21, 1973 is that "there is at least an arguable correlation between obscene material and crime." The Chief Justice stated in *Paris Adult Theatre I v. Slaton* that "the Hill-Link Minority Report of the Commission on Obscenity and Pornography indicates that there is at least an arguable correlation between obscene material and crime."[134] The Court majority agreed that "although there is no conclusive proof of a connection between antisocial behavior and obscene material, the legislature of Georgia could quite reasonably determine that such a connection does or might exist."[135] [While Burger and the majority spoke of "arguable correlations" and connections which "might exist," they failed to cite the Commission's majority which stated that "if a case is to be made against 'pornography in 1970, it will have to be made on grounds other than demonstrated effects of a damaging personal or social nature. Empirical research designed to clarify the question has found no reliable evidence to date that exposure to explicit sexual materials plays a significant role in the causation of delinquent or criminal sexual behavior among youth or adults."[136]]

Other justices on the Court and in the lower courts have disagreed with the Nixon appointees' position and have agreed with the Commission's conclusions, arguing that an empirical link between obscenity and criminal activity has not been proven and therefore censorship of many of the films, books, and dramatic productions is and has been unwarranted. In his 1957 *Roth* dissent, Justice Douglas had declared: "If we were certain that impurity of sexual thoughts impelled to action, we would be on less dangerous ground in punishing the distributors of this sex literature. But it is by no means clear that obscene literature, as so defined, is a significant factor in influencing substantial deviations from community standards . . . . The absence of dependable information on the effect of obscene literature on human conduct should make us wary. It should put us on the side of protecting society's interest in literature, except and unless it can be said that the particular publication has an impact on action that the government can control."[137] Justice Marshall made much the same point in his dissent in *California v. LaRue*: "The State defends its rules as necessary to prevent sex crimes, drug abuse, prostitution, and a wide variety of other evils. These are precisely the same interests which have been asserted time and again before this Court as justification for laws banning frank discussion of sex and which we have consistently rejected. In fact, the empirical link between sex-related entertainment and the criminal activity popularly associated with it has never been proved and, indeed, has now been largely discredited . . . . Yet even if one were to concede that such a link existed, it would hardly justify a broadscale attack on First Amendment freedoms."[138]

When United States Court of Appeals Judge Jerome Frank expressed in *United States v. Roth* (1966) his misgivings with the federal statute on mailing obscene materials, he stated that "the troublesome aspect of the federal obscenity statute . . . is that (a) no one can now show that, with any reasonable probability obscene publications tend to have any effects on the behavior of normal, average adults, and (b) that under that statute, as judicially interpreted, punishment is apparently inflicted for provoking, in such adults, undesirable thoughts, feelings, or desires—not overt dangerous or anti-social conduct, either actual or probable."[139]

Judge Frank, in an Appendix to his opinion, wrote in a section devoted to the effects of obscenity on normal persons: "Suppose we assume *arguendo*, that sexual thoughts or feelings, stirred by the 'obscene,' probably will often issue into overt conduct. Still it does not at all follow that that conduct will be anti-social . . . . Doubtless, Congress could validly provide punishment for mailing any publications if there were some moderately substantial reliable data showing that reading or seeing those publications probably conduces to seriously harmful sexual conduct on the part of normal adult human beings. But we have no such data."[140]

In his June 21, 1973 opinions, Chief Justice Burger used several analogies to support the majority decisions to prohibit the sale and distribution of "obscene" materials, analogies which helped to justify the suppression of the materials on the basis of the claimed causal connection between obscenity and antisocial behavior. But the analogies have been questioned. In *Miller* the Chief Justice compared obscenity with heroin: "One can concede that the 'sexual revolution' of recent years may have had useful byproducts in striking layers of prudery from a subject long irrationally

kept from needed ventilation. But it does not follow that no regulation of patently offensive 'hard core' materials is needed or permissible; civilized people do not allow unregulated access to heroin because it is a derivative of medicinal morphine."[141] In *Paris Adult Theatre* Burger compared obscenity with sewage, garbage, and controls over securities claims: " . . . neither the First Amendment nor 'free will' precludes States from having 'blue sky' laws to regulate what sellers of securities may write or publish about their wares . . . . Such laws are to protect the weak, the uninformed, the unsuspecting, and the gullible from the exercise of their own volition. Nor do modern societies leave disposal of garbage and sewage up to the individual 'free will,' but impose regulation to protect both public health and the appearance of public places."[142] Later in *Paris*, in comparing the control of obscenity with the control of drugs, Burger wrote: "The fantasies of a drug addict are his own and beyond the reach of government, but government regulation of drug sales is not prohibited by the Constitution."[143]

One year before *Miller*, the Chief Justice had presented another analogy having serious implications for freedom of expression. While he reasserted in *Miller* the need to take the work as a whole in determining obscenity, in his footnote no. 2 in *Rabe v. Washington* Justice Burger contended that in a specified circumstance an artistic work need not be judged in its entirety. Comparing obscenity with libel, in a case dealing with the showing of a film titled *Carmen Baby* at a drive-in theater that had a screen visible to passing motorists and nearby residents, Burger noted: "For me, the First Amendment must be treated in this context as it would in a libel action: if there is some libel in a book, article, or speech we do not average the tone and tenor of the whole; the libelous part is not protected."[144]

It was almost a century earlier that Circuit Judge Blatchford said in *United States v. Bennett* (1879) that a publication titled *Cupid's Yokes, or the Binding Forces of Conjugal Life* could be found to be obscene if there were some obscenity in the book; the obscene parts were not protected: "If you find that the tendency of the passages marked in this book is to deprave and corrupt the morals of those whose minds are open to such influences and into whose hands a publication of this sort may fall, it is your duty to convict the defendant, notwithstanding the fact that there may be many worse books in every library in the city."[145] With the United States Supreme Court's five 5-4 obscenity decisions of June 21, 1973, with the arguments that "the weak, the uninformed, the unsuspecting, and the gullible" must be protected, with suggestions that isolated expletives need to be prohibited to maintain civility in society, with the seeming acceptance of the claim that there is a causal relationship between "obscenity" and "depravity and antisocial behavior," along with suggestions that a book or film can be suppressed not on the basis of the work as a whole but on the basis of isolated passages, the highest court in the land has reached a point which has overtones of a turn back towards the spirit, if not the word, of *Hicklin*.

A century of thousands of pages of statutes, court opinions, articles, and books on obscenity has brought us as far as *Miller*, and *Miller* brings with it all the problems, trappings, and flaws which have accompanied all preceding obscenity tests. A century of futile attempts to legally define "obscenity" and prohibit its distribution and viewing should tell us something about the futility of the task. All through his 1973 *Paris* dissent, Justice Brennan, who had delivered the Court's 1957 *Roth* opinion, has pointed to the elusiveness of a workable definition of "obscenity"; he begins his dissent: "This case requires the Court to confront once again the vexing problem of reconciling state efforts to suppress sexually oriented expression with the protections of the First Amendment, as applied to the States through the Fourteenth Amendment. No other aspect of the First Amendment has, in recent years, demanded so substantial a commitment of our time, generated such disharmony of views, and remained so resistant to the formulation of stable and manageable standards. I am convinced that the approach initiated 15 years ago in *Roth v. United States* ... and culminating in the Court's decision today, cannot bring stability to this area of the law without jeopardizing fundamental First Amendment values, and I have concluded that the time has come to make a significant departure from that approach."[146] Justice Brennan, with Justices Stewart and Marshall joining, concluded that "at least in the absence of distribution to juveniles or obtrusive exposure to unconsenting adults, the First and Fourteenth Amendments prohibit the state and federal governments from attempting wholly to suppress sexually oriented materials on the basis of their allegedly 'obscene' contents."[147] Justice Douglas, in his own *Paris* dissent, commended Brennan "for seeking a new path through the thicket which the Court entered when it undertook to sustain the constitutionality of obscenity laws and to place limits on their application."[148] Douglas reiterated his persistent position in opposition to anti-obscenity statutes and obscenity tests: "Art and literature reflect tastes; and tastes, like musical appreciation, are hardly reducible to precise definitions. That is one reason I have always felt that 'obscenity' was not an exception to the First Amendment. For matters of taste, like matters of belief, turn on the idiosyncracies of the individuals. They are too personal to define and too emotional and vague to apply . . . . " In the concluding paragraph to his dissent, Douglas stressed that freedom of speech is one of the distinguishing characteristics of our nation: "When man was first in the jungle he took care of himself. When he entered a societal group, controls were necessarily imposed. But our society—unlike most in the world—presupposes that freedom and liberty are in a frame of reference that make the individual, not the government, the keeper of his tastes, beliefs, and ideas. That is the philosophy of the First Amendment; and it is the article of faith that sets us apart from most nations of the world." (See Appendix)

Haig A. Bosmajian—

NOTES

1. *Cohen v. California,* 403 U.S. 15 (1971).

2. *Ginzberg v. United States,* 383 U.S. 463 (1966).

3. *State v. Lebewitz,* 202 N.W.2d 648 (1972).

4. *Hannegan v. Esquire, Inc.,* 327 U.S. 146 (1946).

5. *Ginzberg v. United States,* 383 U.S. 463 (1966).

6. *Hannegan v. Esquire, Inc.,* 327 U.S. 146 (1946).

7. *Miller v. California,* 413 U.S. 15 (1973).

8. *United States v. 12 200-Ft. Reels of Super 8mm. Film,* 413 U.S. 123 (1973).

9. *Miller v. California,* 413 U.S. 15 (1973).

10. *Joseph Burstyn, Inc. v. Wilson,* 101 N.E.2d 665 (1951).

11. *Joseph Burstyn, Inc. v. Wilson,* 343 U.S. 495 (1952).

12. *Ibid.*

13. *West Virginia State Board of Education v. Barnette,* 319 U.S. 624 (1943).

14. *Roth v. United States,* 354 U.S. 476 (1957).

15. Charles Rembar, "The Outrageously Immoral Fact," in *Censorship and Freedom of Expression,* ed. Harry Clor (Chicago: Rand McNally & Co., 1971), p. 30.

16. Alec Craig, *The Banned Books of England and Other Countries* (London: George Allen & Unwin Ltd., 1962), p. 38.

17. *United States v. 12 200-Ft. Reels of Super 8mm. Film,* 413 U.S. 123 (1973).

18. Paul Hair, *Before the Bawdy Court* (London: Paul Elek Books, 1972), p. 195.

19. *Ibid.,* p. 119.

20. *Ibid.,* p. 222.

21. *Queen v. Read,* 11 Mod. Rep. 142 (1708).

22. Craig, p. 26.

23. *Dominus Rex v. Curl,* 2 Stra. 788 (1727).

24. Craig, p. 32.

25. George R. Scott, "Into Whose Hands" (London: Gerald G. Swan, 1945), p. 87.

26. *Ibid.,* pp. 55-56.

27. *Regina v. Hicklin,* L.R. 3 Q.B. 360 (1868).

28. *Ibid.*

29. *Ibid.*

30. *Ibid.*

31. *United States v. 12 200-Ft. Reels of Super 8mm. Film,* 413 U.S. 123 (1973).

32. *Commonwealth of Pennsylvania v. Sharpless,* 2 Serg. & R. 91 (1815).

33. *Ibid.*

34. *Commonwealth of Massachusetts v. Holmes,* 17 Mass. 336 (1821).

35. *Ibid.*

35. James Paul, "The Post Office and Non-Mailability of Obscenity: An Historical Note," *UCLA Law Review,* VIII (January 1961), 48.

37. *United States v. Bennett,* 16 Blatchf. 338 (1879).

38. *United States v. Britton,* 17 F. 731 (1883).

39. *Ibid.*

40. *People v. Muller,* 96 N.Y. 408 (1884).

41. *Ibid.*

42. *In re Worthington,* 30 N.Y.S. 361 (1894).

43. *Halsey v. The New York Society for the Suppression of Vice,* 136 N.E. 219 (1922).

44. *United States v. Kennerley,* 209 F. 119 (1913).

45. *Ibid.*

46. *People v. Friede,* 223 N.Y.S. 565 (1929).

47. *Commonwealth v. Friede,* 171 N.E. 472 (1930).

48. *United States v. Dennett,* 39 F.2d 564 (1930).

49. *People v. Viking Press,* 264 N.Y.S. 534 (1933).

50. *Ibid.*

51. *United States v. One Book Called "Ulysses",* 5 F.Supp. 182 (1933).

52. *United States v. One Book Entitled "Ulysses",* 72 F.2d 705 (1934).

53. *Ibid.*

54. *United States v. Rebhuhn,* 190 F.2d 512 (1940).

55. *Parmelee v. United States,* 113 F.2d 729 (1940).

56. O. John Rogge, "The High Court of Obscenity," *University of Colorado Law Review,* XLI (February-May 1969), 16.

57. *Commonwealth v. Gordon*, 66 D.&C. 101 (1949).

58. *Block v. Chicago*, 87 N.E. 1011 (1907).

59. *Mutual Film Corp. v. Ohio*, 236 U.S. 230 (1915).

60. Richard Randall, *Censorship of the Movies* (Madison, Wisc.: University of Wisconsin Press, 1968), p. 25.

61. *Burstyn v. Wilson*, 343 U.S. 495 (1952).

62. *Ibid.*

63. *Commercial Pictures Corp. v. Board of Regents of University of State of New York*, 113 N.E.2d 502 (1953).

64. *Ibid.*

65. *Ibid.*

66. *Commercial Pictures Corp. v. Regents of University of State of New York*, 346 U.S. 587 (1954).

67. *Ginsberg v. New York*, 390 U.S. 629 (1968).

68. *Roth v. United States*, 354 U.S. 476 (1957).

69. *Ibid.*

70. *Butler v. Michigan*, 352 U.S. 380 (1957).

71. *Ibid.*

72. *Roth v. United States*, 354 U.S. 476 (1957).

73. *Interstate Circuit v. Dallas*, 390 U.S. 676 (1968).

74. *United States v. One Book Called "Ulysses"*, 5 F.Supp. 182 (1933).

75. *Roth v. United States*, 354 U.S. 476 (1957).

76. *Mishkin v. New York*, 383 U.S. 502 (1966).

77. *Ibid.*

78. *Manual Enterprises v. Day*, 370 U.S. 478 (1962).

79. *Jacobellis v. Ohio*, 378 U.S. 184 (1964).

80. *Ibid.*

81. *In re Giannini*, 446 P.2d 535 (1968).

82. *Miller v. California*, 413 U.S. 15 (1973).

83. *Ibid.*

84. *Ibid.*

85. *Kingsley International Picture Corp. v. Regents of the University of the State of New York*, 360 U.S. 684 (1959).

86. *United States v. Ginzburg*, 224 F.Supp. 129 (1963).

87. *Ginzburg v. United States*, 383 U.S. 461 (1966).

88. *Ibid.*

89. *Attorney General v. A Book Named "John Cleland's Memoirs of A Woman of Pleasure"*, 206 N.E.2d 403 (1965).

90. *A Book Named "John Cleland's Memoirs of A Woman of Pleasure" v. Attorney General*, 383 U.S. 413 (1966).

91. Leon Friedman, "The Ginzburg Decision and the Law," *American Scholar*, XXXVI (Winter 1966-1967), 91.

92. *Miller v. California*, 413 U.S. 15 (1973).

93. *Ibid.*

94. *Stanley v. Georgia*, 394 U.S. 557 (1969).

95. *Ibid.*

96. *United States v. Thirty Seven Photographs*, 402 U.S. 363 (1971).

97. *Ibid.*

98. *United States v. Reidel*, 402 U.S. 351 (1971).

99. *United States v. Thirty Seven Photographs*, 402 U.S. 363 (1971).

100. *Cohen v. California*, 403 U.S. 15 (1971).

101. *Ibid.*

102. *Brown v. Oklahoma*, 408 U.S. 914 (1972).

103. It is noteworthy that besides being definitionally thrown in with children, the insane, habitual drunkards, and slaves in relation to contractual obligations and liquor restrictions, women have been and still are identified with children in matters dealing with obscenity.

104. *Rosenfeld v. New Jersey*, 408 U.S. 901 (1972).

105. *Papish v. University of Missouri Curators*, 410 U.S. 667 (1973).

106. *Ibid.*

107. *Tinker v. Des Moines School District*, 393 U.S. 503 (1969).

108. *Jacobs v. Board of School Commissioners*, 490 F.2d 601 (1973).

109. *Keefe v. Geanakos*, 418 F.2d 359 (1969).

110. *Lindros v. Governing Board of Torrance U. Scho. Dist.*, 510 P.2d 361 (1973).

111. *Ibid.*

112. *Papish v. University of Missouri Curators*, 410 U.S. 667 (1973).

113. Title III, Section 326, Federal Communications Act.

114. Title III, Section 307, Federal Communications Act.

115. Palmetto Broadcasting Co., 33 F.C.C. 250 (1962).

116. *In re* WUHY-FM, F.C.C. 70-346 (1970).

117. *Ibid.*

118. Palmetto Broadcasting Co., 33 F.C.C. 250 (1962).

119. *Ibid.*

120. Pacifica Foundation, 36 F.C.C. 147 (1964).

121. *Ibid.*

122. The Jack Straw Memorial Foundation, 29 F.C.C.2d 334 (1971).

123. *People v. Bruce*, 202 N.E.2d 497 (1964).

124. *In re Giannini*, 446 P.2d 535 (1968).

125. *Southeastern Promotions, Ltd. v. City of Atlanta, Ga.*, 334 F.Supp. 634 (1971).

126. *Ibid.*

127. *Southeastern Promotions, Inc. v. Conrad*, 341 F.Supp. 465 (1972).

128. *Ibid.*

129. *California v. LaRue*, 409 U.S.109 (1972).

130. *Ibid.*

131. *Ibid.*

132. *Miller v. California*, 413 U.S. 15 (1973).

133. *Ibid.*

134. *Paris Adult Theatre I v. Slaton*, 413 U.S. 49 (1973).

135. *Ibid.*

136. *The Report of the Commission on Obscenity and Pornography*, (New York: Bantam Books, 1970), p. 59.

137. *Roth v. United States*, 354 U.S. 476 (1957).

138. *United States v. LaRue*, 409 U.S. 109 (1972).

139. *United States v. Roth*, 237 F.2d 796 (1956).

140. *Ibid.*

141. *Miller v. California*, 413 U.S. 15 (1973).

142. *Paris Adult Theatre I v. Slaton*, 413 U.S. 49 (1973).

143. *Ibid.*

144. *Rabe v. Washington*, 405 U.S. 49 (1972).

145. *United States v. Bennett*, 16 Blatchf. 338 (1879).

146. *Paris Adult Theatre I v. Slaton*, 413 U.S. 49 (1973).

147. *Ibid.*

148. *Ibid.*

BOOKS, PERIODICALS, PAMPHLETS, AND OBSCENITY

BOOKS, PERIODICALS, PAMPHLETS, AND OBSCENITY

THE CONFESSIONAL UNMASKED; SHEWING THE DEPRAVITY OF THE ROMISH PRIESTHOOD, THE INIQUITY OF THE CONFESSIONAL, AND THE QUESTIONS PUT TO FEMALES IN CONFESSION IS DECLARED OBSCENE IN 1868 AND THE HICKLIN TEST FOR OBSCENITY IS ESTABLISHED AS LAW

Queen v. Hicklin, L.R. 3 Q.B. (1868)

AT the quarter sessions for the borough of Wolverhampton on the 27th of May, 1867, Henry Scott appealed against an order made by two justices of the borough under 20 & 21 Vict. c. 83 (1), whereby the justices ordered certain books which had been seized in the dwelling-house of the appellant, within their jurisdiction, to be destroyed, as being obscene books within the meaning of the statute.

The appellant is a metal broker, residing in the town of Wolverhampton, and a person of respectable position and character. He is a member of a body styled "The Protestant Electoral Union," whose objects are, inter alia, " to protest against those teachings and practices which are un-English, immoral, and blasphemous, to maintain the Protestantism of the Bible and the liberty of England," and " to promote the return to Parliament of men who will assist them in these objects, and particularly will expose and defeat the deep-laid machinations of the Jesuits, and resist grants of money for Romish purposes." In order to promote the objects and principles of this society, the appellant purchased from time to time, at the central office of the society in London, copies of a pamphlet, entitled " The Confessional Unmasked ; shewing the depravity of the Romish priesthood, the iniquity of the Confessional, and the questions put to females in confession ;" of which pamphlets he sold between two and three thousand copies at the price he gave for them, viz., 1s. each, to any person who applied for them.

A complaint was thereupon made before two justices of the borough, by a police officer acting under the direction of the Watch Committee of the borough, and the justices issued their warrant under the above statute, by virtue of which warrant 252 of the pamphlets were seized on the premises of the appellant, and ordered by the justices to be destroyed.

The pamphlet (1) consists of extracts taken from the works of certain theologians who have written at various times on the doctrines and discipline of the Church of Rome, and particularly on the practice of auricular confession. On one side of the page are printed passages in the original Latin, correctly extracted from the works of those writers, and opposite to each extract is placed a free translation of such extract into English. The pamphlet also contains a preface and notes and comments, condemnatory of the tracts and principles laid down by the authors from whose works the extracts are taken. About one half of the pamphlet relates to casuistical and controversial questions which are not obscene, but

the remainder of the pamphlet is obscene in fact as relating to impure and filthy acts, words, and ideas. The appellant did not keep or sell the pamphlets for purposes of gain, nor to prejudice good morals, though the indiscriminate sale and circulation of them is calculated to have that effect ; but he kept and sold the pamphlets, as a member of the Protestant Electoral Union, to promote the objects of that society, and to expose what he deems to be errors of the Church of Rome, and particularly the immorality of the Confessional.

The recorder was of opinion that, under these circumstances, the sale and distribution of the pamphlets would not be a misdemeanor, nor, consequently, be proper to be prosecuted as such, and that the possession of them by the appellant was not unlawful within the meaning of the statute. He therefore quashed the order of the justices, and directed the pamphlets seized to be returned to the appellant, subject to the opinion of the Court of Queen's Bench.

If the Court should be of opinion, upon the facts stated, that the sale and distribution of the pamphlets by the appellant would be a misdemeanor, and proper to be prosecuted as such, the order of the justices for destroying the pamphlets so seized was to be enforced ; if not, the order was to be quashed.

Kydd, for the appellant. The decision of the recorder was right, the intention of the appellant being innocent, the publication of this pamphlet was not an indictable misdemeanor ; and therefore the justices had no jurisdiction to order the copies to be destroyed. The book is controversial.

[COCKBURN, C.J. The recorder has found that the work, at least the latter half of it, is obscene, and there can be no doubt of it ; and the question is, that being so, are the magistrates deprived of jurisdiction to destroy this obscene work, because the real object of the appellant in distributing it was not to do harm, but good ?]

The criminal intention must be shewn before the justices have jurisdiction ; but here that intent is expressly negatived. Thus in *Woodfall's Case* (1), Lord Mansfield told the jury, " That, where an act, in itself indifferent, if done with a particular intent becomes criminal, then the intent must be proved and found ; but when the act is in itself unlawful, . . the proof of justification or excuse lies on the defendant ; and in failure thereof, the law implies a criminal intent." But the question of intent is for the jury, per Lord Ellenborough in *Rex* v. *Lambert* (2) ; although the law was formerly otherwise : *Rex* v. *Shebbeare* (3) ; see also, however, per Holt, C.J., in *Tutchin's Case.* (4) In *Fowler* v. *Padget* (5) it was held that a debtor leaving his house did not commit an act of bankruptcy, though creditors were delayed, unless there was an intention to delay, and Lord Kenyon observed, " It is a principle of natural justice and of our law, that actus non facit reum nisi mens sit rea. The intent and the act must both concur to constitute the crime." In *Reg.* v. *Sleep* (6) in which an indictment was laid under 9 & 10 Wm. 3, c. 41, s. 2, for having been in possession of naval stores, and the jury negatived that the prisoner knew that the stores were marked with the broad arrow, Cockburn, C.J., said, " It is a principle of our law that to constitute an offence there must be a guilty mind, and that principle must be imported into the statute, although the Act itself does not in terms make a guilty mind necessary to the commission of the offence." *Reg.* v. *Dodsworth* (7), and *Reg.* v. *Allday* (8), are to the same effect. In *Buckmaster* v. *Reynolds* (9), Erle, C.J., says, "A man cannot be said to be guilty of a delict unless to some extent his mind goes with the act. Here it seems that the respondent acted on the belief that he had a right to enter the room, and that he had no intention to do a wrongful act." The mere use of obscene words, or the occurrence of obscene passages, does not make the work obscene. Thus Milton, in his celebrated defence of himself (1), justifies by examples the use of language adequate to the occasion, though it may be obscene. On this principle it is that the defence of unlicensed printing has always been based. The opposite principle is that of the Church of Rome. Thus in Hallam's Literature of Europe, part ii., c. 8, s. 70, it is said, "Rome struck a fatal blow at literature in the index expurgatorius of prohibited books.... The first list of books prohibited by the church was set forth by Paul IV. in 1559. His index includes all bibles in modern languages, enumerating forty-eight editions, chiefly printed in countries still within the obedience of the church." If mere obscenity, without reference to the object, is indictable, Collier's View of the Immorality of the English Stage, written with the best motives and published with the best results, would have been indictable. The same may be said of David Clarkson's works, just now republished in Edinburgh, with a preface by Dr. Miller. What can be more obscene than many pictures publicly exhibited, as the Venus in the Dulwich gallery?

[LUSH, J. It does not follow that because such a picture is exhibited in a public gallery, that photographs of it might be sold in the streets with impunity.]

What can be more obscene than Bayle's Dictionary, or many of the works of the standard authors in English poetry, from Chaucer to Byron?—Dryden's translation, for instance, of the sixth satire of Juvenal? Or Savage's St. Valentine's Day? And yet of Savage, the great moralist Dr. Johnson (2), says, alluding to the attempt to prosecute him in the King's Bench for his "Progress of a Divine," as being an obscene libel: "It was urged in his defence, that obscenity was criminal when it was intended to promote the practice of vice; but that Mr. Savage had only introduced obscene ideas with the view of exposing them to detestation, and of amending the age by showing the deformity of wickedness. This plea was admitted, and Sir Philip Yorke, who then presided in that court, dismissed the information, with encomiums upon the purity and excellence of Mr. Savage's writings." So here, the object of the compiler, as expressed in his preface and his comments throughout the pamphlet, is to expose the obscenity and grossness of the Romish practice of the confessional. In *Murray* v. *Benbow* (1) shortly noticed with other cases in Phillips on Copyright, pp. 23-25, Lord Eldon, C., refused an injunction to restrain the sale of a pirated edition of Lord Byron's Cain, on the ground that it was a profane libel. Lord Eldon's judgment is given in the prefatory notes to Cain in the collected editions of Byron's works by Moore. And the learned judge expressly puts the distinction of the author's motive. Thus, alluding to Paradise Lost and Regained, he says: "It appears to me that the great object of the author was to promote the cause of Christianity. There are undoubtedly a great many passages in it, of which, if that were not the object, it would be very improper by law to vindicate the publication; but, taking it altogether, it is clear that the object and effect was not to bring disrepute, but to promote the reverence, of our religion."

[BLACKBURN, J. "Object and effect;" concede the object here to be good, what was the effect?]

Starkie, in his Law of Slander and Libel, vol. ii., p. 147, 2nd edit., treating of blasphemy as a crime, says: "A malicious and

mischievous intention, or what is equivalent to such an intention, in law, as well as morals, a state of apathy and indifference to the interests of society, is the broad boundary between right and wrong. If it can be collected from the circumstances of the publication, from a display of offensive levity, from contumelious and abusive expressions applied to sacred persons or subjects, that the design of the author was to occasion that mischief to which the matter which he publishes immediately tends, to destroy or even to weaken man's sense of religious or moral obligations, to insult those who believe by casting contumelious abuse and ridicule upon their doctrines, or to bring the established religion and form of worship into disgrace and contempt, the offence against society is complete."

[BLACKBURN, J. The argument to meet the present case must go the length, that the object being good, or at all events innocent, would justify the publication of anything however indecent, however obscene, and however mischievous.

LUSH, J. And by any means such as giving away obscene extracts like these as tracts.

COCKBURN, C.J. A medical treatise, with illustrations necessary for the information of those for whose education or information the work is intended, may, in a certain sense, be obscene, and yet not the subject for indictment; but it can never be that these prints may be exhibited for any one, boys and girls, to see as they pass. The immunity must depend upon the circumstances of the publication.]

The animus must always be looked at. Thus in *Moxon's Case* (1), which was a prosecution of the publisher of Shelley's works for blasphemy, Lord Denman, C.J., in summing up, is reported to have said: "The purpose of the passage cited from 'Queen Mab' was, he thought, to cast reproach and insult upon what in Christian minds were the peculiar objects of veneration. It was not, however, sufficient that mere passages of such an offensive character should exist in a work, in order to render the publication of it an act of criminality. It must appear that no condemnation of such passages appeared in the context." Such condemnation does appear in page after page of this pamphlet. Alderson, B., distinctly recognized the right of every one to attack the errors of any sect of religion. In *Gathercole's Case* (2), that learned Judge told the jury, "A person may, without being liable to prosecution for it, attack Judaism, Mohammedanism, or even any sect of the Christian religion (except the established religion of the country) .... The defendant here has a right to entertain his opinions, to express them, and to discuss the subject of the Roman Catholic religion and its institutions." Lord Mansfield expressed himself to the same effect in a speech in the House of Lords, which is cited by Lord Campbell in his life of Lord Mansfield. (3)

The 20 & 21 Vict. c. 83, s. 1. does not make the mere possession or sale of an obscene work sufficient, and the question is therefore quo animo was the publication; and the mere committing of the act is not sufficient, as in 3 & 4 Wm. 4, c. 15, s. 2, or 5 & 6 Vict. c. 93, s. 3. Here the publication of this pamphlet, though obscene, was with an honest intention of exposing the Roman Confessional, an object honestly carried out by correct quotations of the original Latin, correctly translated. The recorder has found that this was the intention, and he therefore rightly decided that the publication was not a misdemeanor.

A. S. Hill, Q.C., for the respondents. The preamble of the statute, taken with the enacting part, shows what the intention of the legislature was, and the question is whether the pamphlet was of such a character as to make the publication of it a misdemeanor.

[COCKBURN, C.J. The section says, "for the purposes of gain."]

The word "gain" does not occur in the clause, "for the purpose of sale or distribution." If the work be of an obscene character, it may be questioned whether intention has anything to do with the matter. But, if intention is necessary, it must be inferred that the appellant intended the natural consequences of his act, which the recorder finds are to prejudice good morals, and the motive of such a publication cannot justify it. Thus, an indictment lies for carrying a child with an infectious disease in the public streets, though there was no intention to do injury to the passengers: *Rex* v. *Vantandillo.* (1) In *Rex* v. *Topham* (2), Lord Kenyon says: "It was argued, that even supposing there was sufficient evidence of publication, there was no evidence of a criminal intent in the defendant. To this I can answer in the words of Lord Mansfield in *Rex* v. *Woodfall* (1), that ' where the act is in itself unlawful (as in this case), the proof of justification or excuse lies on the defendant; and in failure thereof, the law implies a criminal intent;'" and this passage is again cited with approbation by Lord Ellenborough in *Rex* v. *Phillips.* (2)

[BLACKBURN, J. Lord Ellenborough propounded the same principle in *Rex* v. *Dixon.* (3)]

The ruling of Alderson B., in *Gathercole's Case* (4), part of which was cited for the appellant, is also in point. "This indictment charges the defendant with intending to injure the character of the prosecutors; and every man, if he be a rational man, must be considered to intend that which must necessarily follow from what he does." In Starkie, on Slander and Libel, vol. ii. p. 158, 2nd ed., it is said, "Ever since the decision in *Curl's Case* (5), it seems to have been settled, that any publication tending to the destruction of the morals of society is punishable by indictment. ... Although many vicious and immoral acts are not indictable, yet, if they tend to the destruction of morality in general, if they do or may affect the mass of society, they become offences of a public nature." *Reg.* v. *Read* (6) was to the contrary; it was there held that an indictment would not lie for publishing an obscene libel, unless it libelled some one; and the note added by Fortescue is remarkable, and much in point. "N.B. There was the case of the *King* v. *Curl* in B. R., which was an indictment for printing and publishing a libel called *The Nun in her Smock*, which contained several bawdy expressions, but did contain no libel against any person whatsoever; the Court gave judgment against the defendant, but contrary to my opinion; and I quoted this case. And, indeed, I thought it rather to be published on purpose to expose the Romish priests, the father confessors, and the popish religion."

[The Court then adjourned; on the Judges' return into court.]

COCKBURN, C.J. We have considered this matter, and we are of opinion that the judgment of the learned recorder must be reversed, and the decision of the magistrates affirmed. This was a proceeding under 20 & 21 Vict. c. 83, s. 1, whereby it is provided that, in respect of obscene books, &c., kept to be sold or distributed, magistrates may order the seizure and condemnation of such works, in case they are of opinion that the publication of them would have been the subject-matter of an indictment at law, and that such a prosecution ought to have been instituted. Now, it is found here as a fact that the work which is the subject-matter of the present proceeding was, to a considerable extent, an obscene publication, and, by reason of the obscene matter in it, calculated to produce a pernicious effect in depraving and debauching the minds of the persons into whose hands it might come. The magistrates must have been of opinion that the work was indictable, and that the publication of it was a fit and proper subject for indictment. We must take the latter finding of the magistrates to have been adopted by the learned recorder when he reversed their decision, because it is not upon that ground that he reversed it; he leaves that ground untouched, but he reversed the magistrates' decision upon the ground that, although this work was an obscene publication, and although its tendency upon the public mind was that suggested upon the part of the information, yet that the immediate intention

of the appellant was not so to affect the public mind, but to expose the practices and errors of the confessional system in the Roman Catholic Church. Now, we must take it, upon the finding of the recorder, that such was the motive of the appellant in distributing this publication; that his intention was honestly and bonâ fide to expose the errors and practices of the Roman Catholic Church in the matter of confession; and upon that ground of motive the recorder thought an indictment could not have been sustained, inasmuch as to the maintenance of the indictment it would have been necessary that the intention should be alleged and proved, namely, that of corrupting the public mind by the obscene matter in question. In that respect I differ from the recorder. I think that if there be an infraction of the law the intention to break the law must be inferred, and the criminal character of the publication is not affected or qualified by there being some ulterior object in view (which is the immediate and primary object of the parties) of a different and of an honest character. It is quite clear that the publishing an obscene book is an offence against the law of the land. It is perfectly true, as has been pointed out by Mr. Kydd, that there are a great many publications of high repute in the literary productions of this country the tendency of which is immodest, and, if you please, immoral, and possibly there might have been subject-matter for indictment in many of the works which have been referred to. But it is not to be said, because there are in many standard and established works objectionable passages, that therefore the law is not as alleged on the part of this prosecution, namely, that obscene works are the subject-matter of indictment; and I think the test of obscenity is this, whether the tendency of the matter charged as obscenity is to deprave and corrupt those whose minds are open to such immoral influences, and into whose hands a publication of this sort may fall. Now, with regard to this work, it is quite certain that it would suggest to the minds of the young of either sex, or even to persons of more advanced years, thoughts of a most impure and libidinous character. The very reason why this work is put forward to expose the practices of the Roman Catholic confessional is the tendency of questions, involving practices and propensities of a certain description, to do mischief to the minds of those to whom such questions are addressed, by suggesting thoughts and desires which otherwise would not have occurred to their minds. If that be the case as between the priest and the person confessing, it manifestly must equally be so when the whole is put into the shape of a series of paragraphs, one following upon another, each involving some impure practices, some of them of the most filthy and disgusting and unnatural description it is possible to imagine. I take it therefore, that, apart from the ulterior object which the publisher of this work had in view, the work itself is, in every sense of the term, an obscene publication, and that, consequently, as the law of England does not allow of any obscene publication, such publication is indictable. We have it, therefore, that the publication itself is a breach of the law. But, then, it is said for the appellant, "Yes, but his purpose was not to deprave the public mind; his purpose was to expose the errors of the Roman Catholic religion especially in the matter of the confessional." [Be it so. The question then presents itself in this simple form: May you commit an offence against the law in order that thereby you may effect some ulterior object which you have in view, which may be an honest and even a laudable one? My answer is, emphatically, no. The law says, you shall not publish an obscene work. An obscene work is here published, and a work the obscenity of which is so clear and decided, that it is impossible to suppose that the man who published it must not have known and seen that the effect upon the minds of many of those into whose hands it would come would be of a mischievous and demoralizing character. Is he justified in doing that which clearly would be wrong, legally as well as morally, because he thinks that some greater good may be accomplished? In order to prevent the spread and progress of Catholicism in this country, or possibly to extirpate it in another, and to prevent the state from affording any assistance to the Roman Catholic Church in Ireland, is he justified in doing that which has necessarily the immediate tendency of demoralizing the public mind wherever this publication is circulated? It seems to me that to adopt the affirmative of that proposition would be to uphold something which, in my sense of what is right and wrong, would be very reprehensible. It appears to me the only good that is to be accomplished is of the most uncertain character. This work, I am told, is sold at the corners of streets, and in all directions, and of course it falls into the hands of persons of all classes, young and old, and the minds of those hitherto pure are exposed to the danger of contamination and pollution from the impurity it contains. And for what? To prevent them, it is said, from becoming Roman Catholics, when the probability is, that nine hundred and ninety-nine out of every thousand into whose hands this work would fall would never be exposed to the chance of being converted to the Roman Catholic religion. It seems to me that the effect of this work is mischievous and against the law, and is not to be justified because the immediate object of the publication is not to deprave the public mind, but, it may be, to destroy and extirpate Roman Catholicism. I think the old sound and honest maxim, that you shall not do evil that good may come, is applicable in law as well as in morals; and here we have a certain and positive evil produced for the purpose of effecting an uncertain, remote, and very doubtful good. I think, therefore, the case for the order is made out, and although I quite concur in thinking that the motive of the parties who published this work, however mistaken, was an honest one, yet I cannot suppose but what they had that intention which constitutes the criminality of the act, at any rate that they knew perfectly well that this work must have the tendency which, in point of law, makes it an obscene publication, namely, the tendency to corrupt the minds and morals of those into whose hands it might come. The mischief of it, I think, cannot be exaggerated. But it is not upon that I take my stand in the judgment I pronounce. I am of opinion, as the learned recorder has found, that this is an obscene publication. I hold that, where a man publishes a work manifestly obscene, he must be taken to have had the intention which is implied from that act; and that, as soon as you have an illegal act thus established, quoad the intention and quoad the act, it does not lie in the mouth of the man who does it to say, "Well, I was breaking the law, but I was breaking it for some wholesome and salutary purpose." The law does not allow that; you must abide by the law, and if you would accomplish your object, you must do it in a legal manner, or let it alone; you must not do it in a manner which is illegal. I think, therefore, that the recorder's judgment must be reversed, and the order must stand.

BLACKBURN, J. I am of the same opinion. The question arises under the 20 & 21 Vict. c. 83, an act for "the more effectually preventing the sale of obscene books," and so forth; and the provision in the first section is this:—[The learned judge read the section.] Now, what the magistrate or justices are to be satisfied of is that the belief of the complainant is well founded, and also "that any of such articles so published for any of the purposes aforesaid, are of such a character and description," that is to say of such an obscene character and description, that the publication of them would be a misdemeanor, and that the publication in the manner alleged would be proper to be prosecuted; and having satisfied themselves in respect of those things, the magistrates may proceed to order the seizure of the works. And then the justices in petty sessions are also in effect to be satisfied of the same three things; first, that the articles complained of have been kept for any of the purposes aforesaid, and that they are of the character stated in the warrant, that is, that they are of such a character that it would be a misdemeanor to publish them; and that it would not only be a misdemeanor to publish them, but that it would be proper to be prosecuted as such; and then, and then only, are they to order them to be destroyed. I think with respect to the last clause, that the object of the legislature was to guard against the vexatious prosecution of publishers of old and recognized standard works, in which there may be some obscene or mischievous matter. In the case of *Reg.* v. *Moxon* (1), and in many of the instances cited by Mr. Kydd, a book had been published which, in its nature, was such as to be called obscene or mischievous, and it might be held to be a misdemeanor to publish it; and on that account an indictable offence. In *Moxon's Case* (1), the publication of Shelley's "Queen Mab" was found by the jury to be an indictable offence; I hope I may not be understood to agree with what the jury found, that the publication of "Queen Mab" was sufficient to make it an indictable offence. I believe, as everybody knows, that it was a prosecution instituted merely for the purpose of vexation and annoyance. So whether the publication of the whole works of Dryden is or is not a misdemeanor, it would not be a case in which a prosecution would be proper; and I think the legislature put in that provision in order to prevent proceedings in such cases. It appears that the work in question was published, and the magistrates in petty sessions were satisfied that it was a proper subject for indictment, and their finding as to that accords with the view we entertain. Then there was an appeal to the recorder in quarter sessions to reverse their decision, which appeal was successful. The learned recorder, in stating the grounds on which he reversed their decision, says, "About one half of the pamphlet relates to casuistical and controversial questions which are not obscene, but the latter half of the pamphlet is obscene in fact, as containing passages which relate to impure and filthy acts, words and ideas. The appellant did not keep or sell the pamphlets for purposes of gain, nor to prejudice good morals, though the indiscriminate sale and circulation of them is calculated to have that effect; but he kept and sold the pamphlet as a member of the Protestant Electoral Union, to promote the objects of that society, and to expose what he deemed to be errors in the church of Rome, and particularly the immorality of the confessional." The recorder then says he was of opinion that the sale and distribution of the pamphlet would not be a misdemeanor, nor consequently be proper to be prosecuted as such, and upon that ground he quashed the magistrates' order, leaving to this Court the question whether he was right or not. Upon that I understand the recorder to find the facts as follows: He finds that one half of the book was in fact obscene, and he finds that the effect of it would be such, that the sale and circulation of it was calculated to prejudice good morals. He does not find that he differs from the justices at all in matter of fact as to that, but he finds that the publication would not be indictable at all as a misdemeanor, and consequently that it would not be proper to prosecute it as a misdemeanor; and his reason for thinking it was not indictable as a misdemeanor is this, that the object of the person publishing was not to injure public morality, but with a view to expose the errors of the Church of Rome, and particularly the immorality, as he thought it, of the confessional; and, consequently upon those grounds, the recorder held it was not indictable. Then comes the question whether, upon those grounds, the publication was not indictable, and I come to the conclusion that the recorder was wrong, and that it would be indictable. I take the rule of law to be, as stated by Lord Ellenborough in *Rex* v. *Dixon* (1), in the shortest and clearest manner: "It is a universal principle that when a man is charged with doing an act" (that is a wrongful act, without any legal justification) "of which the probable consequence may be highly injurious, the intention is an inference of law resulting from the doing the act." And although the appellant may have had another object in view, he must be taken to have intended that which is the natural consequence of the act. If he does an act which is illegal, it does not make it legal that he did it with some other object. That is not a legal excuse, unless the object was such as under the circumstances rendered the particular act lawful. That is illustrated by the same case of *Rex* v. *Dixon.* (2) The question in that particular case was, whether or not an indictment would lie against a man who unlawfully and wrongfully gave to children unwholesome bread, but without intent to do them harm. The defendant was a contractor to supply bread to a military asylum, and he supplied the children with bread which was unwholesome and deleterious, and although it was not shewn or suggested that he intended to make the children suffer, yet Lord Ellenborough held that it was quite sufficient that he had done an unlawful act in giving them bread which was deleterious, and that an indictment could be sustained, as he must be taken to intend the natural consequences of his act. So in the case in which a person carried a child which was suffering from a contagious disease, along the public road to the danger of the health of all those who happened to be in that road, it was held to be a misdemeanor, without its being alleged that the defendant intended that anybody should catch the disease: *Rex* v. *Vantandillo.* (1) Lord Ellenborough said that if there had been any necessity, as supposed, for the defendant's conduct, this would have been matter of defence. If, on the other hand, the small-pox hospital were on fire, and a person in endeavouring to save the infected inmates from the flames, took some of them into the crowd, although some of the crowd would be liable to catch the small-pox, yet, in that case, he would not be guilty of a wrongful act, and he does not do it with a wrong intention, and he would have a good defence, as Lord Ellenborough said, under not guilty. To apply that to the present case, the recorder has found that one half of this book is obscene, and nobody who looks at the pamphlet can for a moment doubt that really one half of it is obscene, and that the indiscriminate circulation of it in the way in which it appears to have been circulated, must be calculated necessarily to prejudice the morals of the people. The object was to produce the effect of exposing and attacking the Roman Catholic religion, or practices rather, and particularly the Roman Catholic confessional, and it was not intended to injure public morals; but that in itself would be no excuse whatever for the illegal act. The occasion of the publication of libellous matter is never irrelevant, and is for the jury, and the jury have to consider, taking into view the occasion on which matter is written which might injure another, is it a fair and proper comment, or is it not more injurious than the circumstances warranted? But on the other hand it has never been held that the occasion being lawful can justify any libel, however gross. I do not say there is anything illegal in taking the view that the Roman Catholics are not right. Any Protestant may say that without saying anything illegal. Any Roman Catholic may say, if he pleases, that Protestants are altogether wrong, and that Roman Catholics are right. There is nothing illegal in that. But I think it never can be said that in order to enforce your views, you may do something contrary to public morality; that you are at liberty to publish obscene publications, and distribute them amongst every one—schoolboys and every one else—when the inevitable effect must be to injure public morality, on the ground that you have an innocent object in view, that is to say, that of attacking the Roman Catholic religion, which you have a right to do. It seems to me that never could be made a defence to an act of this sort, which is in fact a public nuisance. If the thing is an obscene publication, then, notwithstanding that the wish was, not to injure public morality, but merely to attack the Roman Catholic religion and practices, still I think it would

be an indictable offence. The question, no doubt, would be a question for the jury; but I do not think you could so construe this statute as to say, that whenever there is a wrongful act of this sort committed, you must take into consideration the intention and object of the party in committing it, and if these are laudable, that that would deprive the justices of jurisdiction. The justices must themselves be satisfied that the publication, such as the publication before them, would be a misdemeanor on account of its obscenity, and that it would be proper to indict. The recorder has found that the pamphlet is obscene, and he supports the justices in every finding, except in what he has reversed it upon. He finds the object of the appellant in publishing the work was not to prejudice good morals, and consequently he thinks it would not be indictable at all. But I do not understand him for a moment to say, that if he had not thought there was a legal object in view, it would not have been a misdemeanor at all, and that therefore it would have been vexatious or improper to indict it; nor do I think that anybody who looks at this book would for a moment have a doubt upon the matter. That being so, on the question of whether or not on the facts that the recorder has found it would be a misdemeanor and indictable as such, I come to the conclusion that it is a misdemeanor, and that an indictment would lie; and I say the justices were right, and consequently the recorder's decision is reversed, and the order of justices is confirmed.

MELLOR, J. I confess I have with some difficulty, and with some hesitation, arrived very much at the conclusion at which my Lord and my learned Brothers have arrived. My difficulty was mainly, whether or not this publication was, under the finding of the recorder, within the act having reference to obscene publications. I am not certainly in a condition to dissent from the view which my Lord and my Brothers have taken as to the recorder's finding, and if that view be correct then I agree with what has been said by my Lord and my Brother Blackburn. The nature of the subject itself, if it may be discussed at all (and I think it undoubtedly may), is such that it cannot be discussed without to a certain extent producing authorities for the assertion that the confessional would be a mischievous thing to be introduced into this kingdom; and therefore it appears to me very much a question of degree, and if the matter were left to the jury it would depend very much on the opinion which the jury might form of that degree in such a publication as the present. Now, I take it for granted that the magistrates themselves were perfectly satisfied that this work went far beyond anything which was necessary or legitimate for the purpose of attacking the confessional. I take it that the finding of the recorder is (as I suppose was the finding of the justices below) that though one half of the book consists of casuistical and controversial questions, and so on, and which may be discussed very well without detriment to public morals, yet that the other half consists of quotations which are detrimental to public morals. On looking at this book myself, I cannot question the finding either of the recorder or of the justices. It does appear to me that there is a great deal here which there cannot be any necessity for in any legitimate argument on the confessional and the like, and agreeing in that view, I certainly am not in a condition to dissent from my Lord and my Brother Blackburn, and I know my Brother Lush agrees entirely with their opinion. Therefore, with the expression of hesitation I have mentioned, I agree in the result at which they have arrived.

LUSH, J. I agree entirely in the result at which the rest of the Court have arrived, and I adopt the arguments and the reasonings of my Lord Chief Justice and my Brother Blackburn.

Order of justices affirmed.

Attorney for appellant: *C. Bassett.*
Attorney for respondents: *Needham.*

HICKLIN APPLIED IN 1886: ONE YEAR OF HARD LABOR FOR SENDING "OBSCENE" MATERIALS THROUGH THE MAIL

United States v. Bebout, 28 F. 522 (1886)

WELKER, J., (*charging jury.*) The defendants are indicted under section 3893 of the Revised Statutes, which provides that "every obscene, lewd, or lascivious book, pamphlet, picture, paper, writing, print, or other publication, of an indecent character, * * * are hereby declared to be non-mailable matter, and shall not be conveyed in the mails, nor delivered from any post-office, nor by any letter-carrier; and any person who shall knowingly deposit, or cause to be deposited, for mailing or delivery, anything declared by this section to be non-mailable, * * * shall be found guilty of a misdemeanor," and punished as therein stated.

This indictment contains two counts: The first one charges that the defendants did, on the seventeenth January, 1886, unlawfully and knowingly deposit, and cause to be deposited, for mailing and delivery, in the mail of the United States, in the post-office of the city of Toledo, a certain obscene, lewd, and lascivious paper, called the Sunday Democrat, and directed to E. P. Willey; containing therein the obscene, lewd, and lascivious words, figures, and illustrations following; and setting out a copy of the article therein published. The second count charges a like violation of the statute, but calls the publication a certain publication of an indecent character.

The defendants have entered a plea of not guilty,—a general denial of the allegations of the indictment. You are to start on this investigation of these charges with the humane presumptions of the law that the defendants are innocent of the charges alleged against them, and to require the government to establish, beyond a fair and reasonable doubt, everything necessary to constitute the offense, and to establish the guilt of the defendants.

Three things must be established by the government to authorize a conviction of the defendants: *First*, that the paper containing the objectionable matter was deposited by them, or that they caused it to be deposited, at Toledo, in the post-office, for mailing; *second*, that the defendants knew that the paper contained the matter described; and, *third*, that the publication was obscene, lewd, lascivious, or indecent. The failure to make out either one will entitle the defendants to an acquittal.

It must be shown to your satisfaction, and beyond a reasonable doubt, that the paper containing the matter set out in the indictment was deposited, directly or indirectly, by the defendants, in the post-office at Toledo, for mailing or delivery, as charged. If it was deposited by their agent for that purpose, or some person acting directly under their orders, it would be the same as if done by themselves. If it was deposited by a person not their agent, and not acting under their orders or authority, then the defendants would not be guilty of the offense. It will, then, be important for you to examine carefully the evidence on this point, and ascertain who did deposit the paper described in the indictment; under whose direction and authority he was acting when he did it; what relation the defendants sustained to the printing company who employed them; what was the scope of their duties respectively; who constituted the company; the relation the person who in fact did deposit the paper had to the corporation, or to the defendants; and all the circumstances disclosed in the evidence; and from all this determine.

If you are satisfied by the proof, beyond such fair and reasonable doubt, that the defendants did so deposit the paper, or cause the same to be so deposited, then, to authorize a conviction of the defendants, it must be shown that they knew at the time that the paper contained the article or objectionable matter set out in the indictment. This knowledge is essential to constitute the offense. If they did not know that the matter described was in the paper, then the offense is not made out, and they are entitled to an acquittal. This knowledge may be shown by direct or circumstantial evidence. To determine this knowledge, you will also consider all the evidence and the circumstances shown in the proof. All reasonable doubts on this point must be solved by you in favor of the defendants.

Next, was the publication obscene, lewd, lascivious, or indecent? Words used in the statute are to be understood in their usual and common signification. The dictionary defines these words as follows: "Obscene: Expressing or presenting to the mind or view something which delicacy, purity, and decency forbid to be expressed." "Lewd: Given to the unlawful indulgence of lust; eager for sexual indulgence." "Lascivious: Loose; wanton; lewd; lustful; tending to produce voluptuous or lewd emotions." "Indecent: Not decent; unfit to be seen or heard."

There is a test which has often been applied and approved of by the courts, in this class of cases, to determine whether the publication is obscene or indecent within the meaning of the statute before referred to. It is whether the tendency of the matter is to deprave and corrupt the morals of those whose minds are open to such influences, and into whose hands a publication of this sort may fall. Under these definitions, whether the matter set out in the indictment was obscene or indecent is a question of fact for you to determine. The defendants are entitled to the benefit of all reasonable doubts in this part of the case as in others; and all such doubts should be solved in their favor. The statute does not make the publication of obscene and indecent matter an offense. It consists in using the United States mails for its circulation. It is not designed or intended to prohibit the publication of obscene matter, but only to prohibit and prevent its circulation through the mails. Nor does the statute make a purpose or intent to deprave or demoralize the public, or injure individuals, an ingredient to constitute the offense. Nor does the truth or falsity of the publication make any part of the offense; the only inquiry being, was the publication obscene or indecent, and was it placed in the mails for circulation in violation of the statute? You will bear in mind that you are only trying these defendants for such use of the mail, and not for the publication of the matter charged to be obscene and indecent; nor for any attempt to black-mail any citizen or individual, or injury resulting to any person by reason of the publication.

These defendants are indicted and tried together; but you may convict one, and acquit the other, or convict or acquit both, as the evidence may justify. The act of the one, or statement of either, separately made, does not bind the other. The knowledge of one is not the knowledge of the other. Each one can only be held responsible for his own acts and knowledge, and not that of the other. In all things in which they acted jointly, each would be responsible for such joint action.

The defendants being competent for that purpose, having offered themselves as witnesses, you will judge their testimony, and its reliability, as you do that of the other witnesses; and it is proper for you to consider the evidence offered by the government as to general character for truth and veracity, and give their testimony, as also that of all the witnesses, such weight and effect as you may think the same is entitled to receive.

Take the case, and make such findings as will satisfy you that you have rightfully decided the questions submitted to you, and return your verdict accordingly.

The jury found a verdict of guilty as to A. J. Bebout, and not guilty as to A. S. Bebout. A motion for new trial was overruled, and A. J. Bebout sentenced to one year at hard labor in the penitentiary of the state of Ohio, and payment of costs of prosecution.

NOTE.

See, also, Bates v. U. S., 10 Fed. Rep. 92, and note, 97.
That the prohibition applies also to the mailing of sealed letters, see U. S. v. Gaylord, 17 Fed. Rep. 438; U. S. v. Hanover, Id. 444; U. S. v. Britton, Id. 731; U. S. v. Thomas, 27 Fed. Rep. 682, and note; U. S. v. Morris, 18 Fed Rep. 900, in which Justice DEADY overrules his contrary decision in U. S. v. Loftis, 12 Fed. Rep. 671.
In U. S. v. Williams, 3 Fed. Rep. 484, it was held that the provision does not apply to sealed letters; and the same doctrine was last year repeated in U. S. v. Comerford, 25 Fed. Rep. 902.
In Indiana, the offense is punishable under the state law also. See Thomas v. State, 2 N. E. Rep. 808.

"COARSE" AND "VULGAR" ARE NOT THE SAME AS "OBSCENE" AND "LEWD"

United States v. Wightman, 29 F. 636 (1886)

ACHESON, J. In the view I take of this case, it is not necessary for me to express any opinion upon the unsettled question (*U. S. v. Chase,* 27 Fed. Rep. 807) whether the words, "every obscene, lewd, or lascivious book, pamphlet, picture, paper, writing, print, or other publication of an indecent character," as used in the first clause of section 3893 of the Revised Statutes defining non-mailable matter, etc., include an obscene letter inclosed in a sealed envelope, bearing nothing but the address of the person to whom the letter is written; for I have reached the conclusion that neither of the letters which are the subject of this indictment, either in language or import, is "obscene, lewd, or lascivious," within the purview of the statute. According to the well-considered case of *U. S. v. Bennett,* 16 Blatchf. 362, the test of obscenity is whether the tendency of the matter is to deprave and corrupt the morals of those whose minds are open to such influences. This, it seems to me, correctly indicates the purport of the word "obscene," as employed in this statute. Like the terms "lewd" and "lascivious," with which it is associated, it implies something tending to suggest libidinous thoughts, or excite impure desires. Now, I do not think that either of the letters under consideration has any such corrupting or debauching tendency. Both letters are exceedingly coarse and vulgar, and one of them is grossly libelous, —imputing to the person addressed an atrocious crime,—but none of these characteristics, nor all combined, are sufficient to bring the letters within the inhibition and penalty of the statute. *U. S. v. Smith,* 11 Fed. Rep. 663.

I may add that the word "indecent," in the first clause of section 3893, seems to be confined to the "other publication" declared to be nonmailable. But, at any rate, the term as there employed has been held to mean that which "tends to obscenity," or "matter having that form of indecency which is calculated to promote the general corruption of morals." *U. S. v. Bennett, supra.*

The opinion of the court, then, being that the letters in question do not contain anything of an "obscene, lewd, or lascivious" character, within the meaning of the statute, judgment must be arrested; and it is so ordered.

NOTE.

Obscene Publications. The test which determines the obscenity or indecency of a publication is the tendency of the matter to deprave and corrupt the morals of those whose minds are open to such influences, and into whose hands such a publication may fall. U. S. v. Bebout, 28 Fed. Rep. 522; U. S. v. Britton, 17 Fed. Rep. 731. A letter which, if it should fall into the hands of an inexperienced or susceptible person, would excite impure thoughts and indecent ideas, is obscene and indecent. U. S. v. Britton, *supra.* An illustrated pamphlet, purporting to be a work on the subject of the treatment of spermatorrhea and impotency, and consisting partially of extracts from standard books upon medicine and surgery, but of an indecent and obscene character, and intended for general circulation, held to come within the provisions of section 3893 of the Revised Statutes. U. S. v. Chesman, 19 Fed. Rep. 497.

As to the application of the statute to the mailing of sealed letters, see U. S. v. Bebout, 28 Fed. Rep. 522, and note.

HICKLIN APPLIED IN 1889: "DR. CLARKE'S TREATISE ON VENEREAL, SEXUAL, NERVOUS, AND SPECIAL DISEASES" IS LEWD AND OBSCENE

United States v. Clarke, 38 F. 732 (1889)

Thayer, J., (*charging jury.*) The admission having been made during the course of the trial that the defendant caused the pamphlet and two other papers referred to in the indictment and offered in evidence to be deposited in the St. Louis post-office for mailing to the several persons to whom they were addressed, the sole question that remains for you to consider and determine is whether the pamphlet and papers are obscene, lewd, or lascivious. If they were obscene, lewd, or lascivious, then they were non-mailable matter, and an offense was committed in causing them to be deposited in the post-office for mailing. Now the question arises, what is an obscene, lewd, or lascivious publication within the meaning of the statute? I propose to define those terms as well as possible, and leave you to determine in the light of such definitions, and all the circumstances of the case, whether they fall within the definitions I shall give.

The word "obscene" ordinarily means something that is offensive to chastity, something that is foul or filthy, and for that reason is offensive to pure-minded persons. That is the meaning of the word in the concrete. But when used, as in the statute under which this indictment is framed, to describe the character of a book, pamphlet, or paper, it means a book, pamphlet, or paper containing immodest and indecent matter, the reading whereof would have a tendency to deprave and corrupt the minds of those into whose hands the publication might fall whose minds are open to such immoral influences. *U. S. v. Bennett,* 16 Blatchf. 338; *Queen v. Hicklin,* L. R. 3 Q. B. 371. A lewd book, pamphlet, or paper, within the meaning of the statute, is one that describes dissolute and unchaste acts, scenes, or incidents, or one, the reading whereof, by reason of its contents, is calculated to excite lustful and sensual desires (that is to say, a desire for the gratification of the animal passions) in those whose minds are open to such influences. The word "lascivious" is very nearly synonymous with the word "lewd;" so nearly so that I will not undertake to draw a distinction between the two words. For the purposes of this case it may be said that if the pamphlet and papers involved are not lewd or obscene in the sense that I have defined those terms, then they are not lascivious, and you need give yourselves no further concern about the exact meaning of that word. In view of what has been said it follows that, if you are satisfied beyond a reasonable doubt that the pamphlet and papers, in question in this case, contain such immodest, indecent, or filthy matter that the reading thereof would tend to deprave and corrupt the minds of those persons into whose hands the same might fall whose minds are open to such influences, then you should find the defendant guilty. Or if you are satisfied beyond a reasonable doubt that the subject-matter of the pamphlet and papers is of such character as would tend to excite lustful and sensual desires in the minds of those persons into whose hands they might come, whose minds are open to influences of that sort, then you should find the defendant guilty. If you find that the pamphlet is obscene or lewd, and that the other papers are not, or, *vice versa,* that the papers are obscene or lewd and the pamphlet is not, you can return a verdict against the defendant on some counts, and in his favor in others, according as you find the character of the several publications to be.

These are as precise definitions and directions as it is possible for me to give. The case is one that addresses itself largely to your good judgment, common sense, and knowledge of human nature, and the weaknesses of human nature. You must consider carefully the contents of the pamphlet and papers in the first instance, and then the effect that the reading of such contents would naturally have on that class of persons into whose hands the publications might fall, whose thoughts, emotions, or desires are liable to be influenced or directed by reading matter such as the publications contain. There is to be found in every community a class of people who are so intelligent or so mature that their minds are not liable to be affected by reading matter, however obscene, lewd, or indecent it may be. Then there is another large class to be found in every community—the young and immature, the ignorant, and those who are sensually inclined—who are liable to be influenced to their harm by reading indecent and obscene publications. The statute under which this indictment is framed was designed to protect the latter class from harm, and it is a wholesome statute. Hence, in judging of the tendency of the publications to deprave and corrupt the mind, or to excite lustful or sensual desires, (which are the tests of obscenity and lewdness,) you should consider the effect that the publications would have on the minds of that class of persons whom the statute aims to protect, and the liability of the publications to get into the hands of that class of persons, rather than the effect such publications would have on people of a high order of intelligence, and those who have reached mature years, who by reason of their intelligence or years are steeled against such influences. As I said before, you must bring your common sense and knowledge of human nature and its weaknesses to the consideration and determination of these questions.

Now, gentlemen, there are a few incidental matters which I feel bound to notice in view of what has occurred during the trial. In the first place, you must not allow the fact that defendant advertises his calling quite extensively in the newspapers to prejudice your view of the case. You have nothing whatever to do with a question of professional ethics of that sort. The defendant has a right to advertise his calling if he so desires, and that is not an offense in the eye of the law. If the publications which he deposited in the mail are neither obscene, lewd, nor lascivious in your opinion, he is entitled to a verdict of acquittal; and you must not allow your attention to be diverted from the real matter in issue, or your minds to be prejudiced, by any extraneous considerations of the kind to which I have last alluded. The question whether defendant is a licensed physician under the laws of the state is immaterial. In the second place, gentlemen, I desire to say that I have no doubt that under the statute under which this indictment is framed standard medical works (and by that I mean works that are studied and consulted by physicians, and are kept in medical and public libraries) may lawfully be sent through the mail to persons who buy or call for them for the purpose of seeking information on the subjects of which they treat. But I feel bound to say that, in my opinion, there is no evidence in this case that would warrant you in finding that the publications complained of in the indictment are standard medical works or publications. Furthermore, gentlemen, I have no doubt that persons may lawfully communicate through the mails with their physicians by describing symptoms of their physical ailments, habits, and practices, and asking professional advice in relation thereto; and I have no doubt that in response to such inquiries a physician may lawfully advise a patient through the mails with respect to the subject-matter of such communications. But I feel bound to say that, in my opinion, there is no evidence that would warrant you in finding that the publications complained of in this case, were sent by a physician to his patient in response to a request for such publications as were sent, and that the mailing of them to the parties named in the indictment was justified as being a communication by a doctor to his patient. Therefore, gentlemen, you will decide the issue with respect to the obscene and lewd character of the publications, unembarrassed by any consideration of the two defenses last alluded to, which might be appropriate in certain cases, but are not applicable to this case.

There is another fact to which it is necessary to allude. The defendant's counsel, for the purpose of enforcing his view that the publications complained of are neither obscene or lewd, has read in the course of his argument certain passages from certain well-known authors,—from Shakespeare, Sterne, Suetonius,—and even from the Bible. The passages read, taken in connection with their context, may be, or may not be, obscene or indecent. You are not trying that question, and you are not called upon in this case to determine, nor will your verdict in this case (whether it is guilty or not guilty) decide whether the Bible, Shakespeare, Sterne, and Suetonius must be excluded from the mails. I trust you will not allow any consideration of the possible tendency of your verdict to exclude other standard literary works from the mails, to prevent you from passing an honest judgment upon the question you have to decide in this case,—whether the pamphlet and papers complained of are obscene or lewd, and tend to corrupt and deprave the minds of readers. Of course, so far as your experience goes of the effect that Shakespeare's writings, or any other author's writings, have had on the world, notwithstanding certain passages that they contain, you have the right to resort to that experience in determining what will be the probable effect of the publications involved in this case, providing you think such comparison, or a reference to such experience, will be of any service, and will aid you in reaching a correct conclusion. I think this is all that is necessary to be said in this case. I ask you to consider the case fairly, and decide the issue that I have defined as to the character of these publications, according to your honest judgment of the effect that such publications will have on the minds of those that read them.

The jury impaneled in this cause, after retiring, returned into court, and submitted to the court the following question, to-wit:

"If the jury find any portion of the book, pamphlet, or circular obscene, lewd, etc., would such finding be sufficient grounds for them to condemn the whole book, pamphlet, or circular?   W. S. HUMPHREYS, Foreman."

Thereupon the court further instructed the said jury as follows, to-wit:

"If the effect of the pamphlet and papers as a whole would be to deprave and corrupt the minds of those into whose hands they might come whose minds are open to such influences, or to excite lustful or sensual desires, then the pamphlets and circulars should be found to be obscene and lewd, whether such effect on the minds of readers is produced by single passages or portions of the pamphlets and circulars, or by many passages or portions."

The jury returned a verdict of guilty on all counts.

A SLIGHT EROSION OF *HICKLIN*: RARE AND COSTLY EDITIONS OF ARABIAN NIGHTS, OVID'S *ART OF LOVE*, BOCCACCIO'S *DECAMERON*, AND OTHER VOLUMES NOT OBSCENE

In re Worthington Co., 30 N.Y.S. 361 (1894)

O'BRIEN, J.   After consultation with some of my brethren, we have concluded that the following views should be expressed concerning the merits of this motion: This is an application made by the receiver of the Worthington Company for instructions concerning the final disposition of certain books which were found among the assets of that company, and which are now in his custody, and respecting which it is alleged by certain parties that they are unfit for general circulation, and come under the designation of "immoral literature," and as such should be excluded from sale.   That these books constitute valuable assets of this receivership cannot be doubted, and the question before the court for decision on this motion is whether or not they are of such a character as should be condemned and their sale prohibited.   The books in question consist of Payne's edition of the Arabian Nights, Fielding's novel, Tom Jones, the works of Rabelais, Ovid's Art of Love, the Decameron of Boccaccio, the Heptameron of Queen Margaret of Navarre, the Confessions of J. J. Rousseau, Tales from the Arabic, and Alladin.   Most of the volumes that have been submitted to the inspection of the court are of choice editions, both as to the letter-press and the bindings, and are such, both as to their commercial value and subject-matter, as to prevent their being generally sold or purchased, except by those who would desire them for their literary merit, or for their worth as specimens of fine book-making.   It is very difficult to see upon what theory these world-renowned classics can be regarded as specimens of that pornographic literature which it is the office of the Society for the Suppression of Vice to suppress, or how they can come under any stronger condemnation than that high standard literature which consists of the works of Shakespeare, of Chaucer, of Laurence Sterne, and of other great English writers, without making reference to many parts of the Old Testament Scriptures, which are to be found in almost every household in the land.   The very artistic character, the high qualities of style, the absence of those glaring and crude pictures, scenes, and descriptions which affect the common and vulgar mind, make a place for books of the character in question, entirely apart from such gross and obscene writings as it is the duty of the public authorities to suppress.   It would be quite as unjustifiable to condemn the writings of Shakespeare and Chaucer and Laurence Sterne, the early English novelists, the playwrights of the Restoration, and the dramatic literature which has so much enriched the English language, as to place an interdict upon these volumes, which have received the admiration of literary men for so many years.   What has become standard literature of the English language—has been wrought into the very structure of our splendid English literature—is not to be pronounced at this late day unfit for publication or circulation, and stamped with judicial disapprobation, as hurtful to the community.   The works under consideration are the product of the greatest literary genius.   Payne's Ara-

bian Nights is a wonderful exhibition of Oriental scholarship, and the other volumes have so long held a supreme rank in literature that it would be absurd to call them now foul and unclean.   A seeker after the sensual and degrading parts of a narrative may find in all these works, as in those of other great authors, something to satisfy his pruriency.   But to condemn a standard literary work, because of a few of its episodes, would compel the exclusion from circulation of a very large proportion of the works of fiction of the most famous writers of the English language.   There is no such evil to be feared from the sale of these rare and costly books as the imagination of many even well-disposed people might apprehend. They rank with the higher literature, and would not be bought nor appreciated by the class of people from whom unclean publications ought to be withheld.   They are not corrupting in their influence upon the young, for they are not likely to reach them.   I am satisfied that it would be a wanton destruction of property to prohibit the sale by the receiver of these works,—for if their sale ought to be prohibited the books should be burned,—but I find no reason in law, morals, or expediency why they should not be sold for the benefit of the creditors of the receivership.   The receiver is therefore allowed to sell these volumes.

LETTERS MAILED TO CONVEY INFORMATION ABOUT THE AVAILABILITY OF "OBSCENE" MATERIALS: "THE LAW WAS ACTUALLY VIOLATED BY THE DEFENDANT; HE PLACED LETTERS IN THE POST-OFFICE WHICH CONVEYED INFORMATION AS TO WHERE OBSCENE MATTER COULD BE OBTAINED, AND HE PLACED THEM THERE WITH A VIEW OF GIVING SUCH INFORMATION TO THE PERSON WHO SHOULD ACTUALLY RECEIVE THOSE LETTERS, NO MATTER WHAT HIS NAME; AND THE FACT THAT THE PERSON WHO WROTE UNDER THESE ASSUMED NAMES AND RECEIVED HIS LETTERS WAS A GOVERNMENT DETECTIVE IN NO MANNER DETRACTS FROM HIS GUILT."

Grimm v. United States, 156, U.S. 604 (1895)

MR. JUSTICE BREWER, after stating the case, delivered the opinion of the court.

The sufficiency of the indictment is the first question presented.   It is insisted that the possession of obscene, lewd, or lascivious pictures constitutes no offence under the statute. This is undoubtedly true, and no conviction was sought for the mere possession of such pictures.   The gravamen of the complaint is that the defendant wrongfully used the mails for transmitting information to others of the place where such pictures could be obtained, and the allegation of possession is merely the statement of a fact tending to interpret the letter which he wrote and placed in the post-office.

It is said that the letter is not in itself obscene, lewd, or lascivious.   This also may be conceded.   But however innocent on its face it may appear, if it conveyed, and was intended to convey, information in respect to the place or person where, or of whom, such objectionable matters could be obtained, it is within the statute.

Again, it is objected that it is not sufficient to simply allege that the pictures, papers, and prints were obscene, lewd, and lascivious; that the pleader should either have incorporated them into the indictment or given a full description of them so that the court could, from the face of the pleading, see whether they were in fact obscene.   We do not think this objection is well taken.   The charge is not of sending obscene matter through the mails, in which case some description might be necessary, both for identification of the offence and to enable the court to determine whether the matter was obscene, and, therefore, non-mailable. Even in such cases it is held that it is unnecessary to spread the obscene matter in all its filthiness upon the record; it is enough to so far describe it that its obnoxious character may be discerned. There the gist of the offence is the placing a certain objectionable article in the mails, and, therefore, that article should be identified and disclosed; so, here, the gist of the offence is the mailing of a letter giving information, and, therefore, it is proper that such letter should be stated so as to identify the offence. But it does not follow that everything referred to in the letter, or concerning which information is given therein, should be spread at length on the indictment. On the contrary, it is sufficient to allege its character and leave further disclosures to the introduction of evidence. It may well be that the sender of such a letter has no single picture or other obscene publication or print in his mind, but, simply knowing where matter of an obscene character can be obtained, uses the mails to give such information to others. It is unnecessary that unlawful intent as to any particular picture be charged or proved. It is enough that in a certain place there could be obtained pictures of that character, either already made and for sale or distribution, or from some one willing to make them, and that the defendant, aware of this, used the mails to convey to others the like knowledge.

A final matter complained of grows out of these facts: It appears that the letters to defendant — the one signed "Herman Huntress," described in the second count, and one signed "William W. Waters," described in the fourth count — were written by Robert W. McAfee; that there were no such persons as Huntress and Waters; that McAfee was and had been for years a post-office inspector in the employ of the United States, and at the same time an agent of the Western Society for the Suppression of Vice; that for some reasons not disclosed by the evidence McAfee suspected that defendant was engaged in the business of dealing in obscene pictures, and took this method of securing evidence thereof; that after receiving the letters written by defendant, he, in name of Huntress and Waters, wrote for a supply of the pictures, and received from defendant packages of pictures which were conceded to be obscene. Upon these facts it is insisted that the conviction cannot be sustained, because the letters of defendant were deposited in the mails at the instance of the government, and through the solicitation of one of its officers; that they were directed and mailed to fictitious persons; that no intent can be imputed to defendant to convey information to other than the persons named in the letters sent by him, and that as they were fictitious persons there could in law be no intent to give information to any one. This objection was properly overruled by the trial court. There has been much discussion as to the relations of detectives to crime, and counsel for defendant relies upon the cases of *United States* v. *Whittier*, 5 Dillon, 35; *United States* v. *Matthews*, 35 Fed. Rep. 890; *United States* v. *Adams*, 59 Fed. Rep. 674; *Saunders* v. *People*, 38 Michigan, 218, in support of the contention that no conviction can be sustained under the facts in this case.

It is unnecessary to review these cases, and it is enough to say that we do not think they warrant the contention of counsel. It does not appear that it was the purpose of the post-office inspector to induce or solicit the commission of a crime, but it was to ascertain whether the defendant was engaged in an unlawful business. The mere facts that the letters were written under an assumed name, and that he was a government official — a detective, he may be called — do not of themselves constitute a defence to the crime actually committed. The official, suspecting that the defendant was engaged in a business offensive to good morals, sought information directly from him, and the defendant, responding thereto, violated a law of the United States by using the mails to convey such

information, and he cannot plead in defence that he would not have violated the law if inquiry had not been made of him by such government official. The authorities in support of this proposition are many and well considered. Among others reference may be made to the cases of *Bates* v. *United States*, 10 Fed. Rep. 92, and the authorities collected in a note of Mr. Wharton, on page 97; *United States* v. *Moore*, 19 Fed. Rep. 39; *United States* v. *Wight*, 38 Fed. Rep. 106, in which the opinion was delivered by Mr. Justice Brown, then District Judge, and concurred in by Mr. Justice Jackson, then Circuit Judge; *United States* v. *Dorsey*, 40 Fed. Rep. 752; *Commonwealth* v. *Baker*, 155 Mass. 287, in which the court held that one who goes to a house alleged to be kept for illegal gaming, and engages in such gaming himself for the express purpose of appearing as a witness for the government against the proprietor, is not an accomplice, and the case is not subject to the rule that no conviction should be had on the uncorroborated testimony of an accomplice; *People* v. *Noelke*, 94 N. Y. 137, in which the same doctrine was laid down as to the purchaser of a lottery ticket, who purchased for the purpose of detecting and punishing the vendor; *State* v. *Jansen*, 22 Kansas, 498, in which the court, citing several authorities, discusses at some length the question as to the extent to which participation by a detective affects the liability of a defendant for a crime committed by the two jointly; *State* v. *Stickney*, 53 Kansas, 308. But it is unnecessary to multiply authorities. The law was actually violated by the defendant; he placed letters in the post-office which conveyed information as to where obscene matter could be obtained, and he placed them there with a view of giving such information to the person who should actually receive those letters, no matter what his name; and the fact that the person who wrote under these assumed names and received his letters was a government detective in no manner detracts from his guilt.

These are all the questions presented by counsel. We see no error in the rulings of the trial court, and the judgment is, therefore,

Affirmed.

HICKLIN TEST IS SERIOUSLY CHALLENGED IN 1913 BY JUDGE LEARNED HAND

United States v. Kennerley, 209 F. 119 (1913)

HAND, District Judge (after stating the facts as above). It seems to have been thought in U. S. v. Bennett, 16 Blatch. 338, 351, Fed. Cas. No. 14,571, that in an indictment of this sort the question whether the case must go to the jury could be raised in advance of the trial by inspection of the book, after it had been made a part of the record, by bill of particulars. However, in Dunlop v. U. S., 165 U. S. 486, 491, 17 Sup. Ct. 375, 376 (41 L. Ed. 799), the Supreme Court said that the book does not ever become a part of the record, and that therefore, "if the indictment be not demurrable upon its face, it would not become so by the addition of a bill of particulars." The same rule is laid down in U. S. v. Clarke (D. C.) 38 Fed. 500. It is a little questionable in my mind whether Mr. Boyle's consent that the book should be considered as a part of the indictment really effects any more than if it had been produced by bill of particulars. However, as the result from any point of view is the same, I have considered the case as though the book had been set out in extenso.

Whatever be the rule in England, in this country the jury must determine under instructions whether the book is obscene. The court's only power is to decide whether the book is so clearly innocent that the jury should not pass upon it at all. U. S. v. Clarke (D. C.) 38 Fed. 500; U. S. v. Smith (D. C.) 45 Fed. 478. The same question arises as would arise upon motion to direct a verdict at the close of the case. Swearingen v. U. S., 161 U. S. 446, 16 Sup. Ct. 562, 40 L. Ed. 765, did not decide that the court is finally to interpret the words, but that matter was left open, because the instructions in any case misinterpreted the statute. The question here is, therefore, whether the jury might find the book obscene under proper instructions. Lord Cockburn laid down a test in Reg. v. Hicklin, L. R. 3 Q. B. 36, in these words:

"Whether the tendency of the matter charged as obscenity is to deprave and corrupt those whose minds are open to such immoral influences and into whose hands a publication of this sort may fall."

That test has been accepted by the lower federal courts until it would be no longer proper for me to disregard it. U. S. v. Bennett, 16 Blatch. 338, Fed. Cas. No. 14,571; U. S. v. Clarke (D. C.) 38 Fed. 500; U. S. v. Harmon (D. C.) 45 Fed. 414; U. S. v. Smith (D. C.) 45 Fed. 478. Under this rule, such parts of this book as pages 169 and 170 might be found obscene, because they certainly might tend to corrupt the morals of those into whose hands it might come and whose minds were open to such immoral influences. Indeed, it would be just those who would be most likely to concern themselves with those parts alone, forgetting their setting and their relevancy to the book as a whole.

While, therefore, the demurrer must be overruled, I hope it is not improper for me to say that the rule as laid down, however consonant it may be with mid-Victorian morals, does not seem to me to answer to the understanding and morality of the present time, as conveyed by the words, "obscene, lewd, or lascivious." I question whether in the end men will regard that as obscene which is honestly relevant to the adequate expression of innocent ideas, and whether they will not believe that truth and beauty are too precious to society at large to be mutilated in the interests of those most likely to pervert them to base uses. Indeed, it seems hardly likely that we are even to-day so lukewarm in our interest in letters or serious discussion as to be content to reduce our treatment of sex to the standard of a child's library in the supposed interest of a salacious few, or that shame will for long prevent us from adequate portrayal of some of the most serious and beautiful sides of human nature. That such latitude gives opportunity for its abuse is true enough; there will be, as there are, plenty who will misuse the privilege as a cover for lewdness and a stalking horse from which to strike at purity, but that is true to-day and only involves us in the same question of fact which we hope that we have the power to answer.

Yet, if the time is not yet when men think innocent all that which is honestly germane to a pure subject, however little it may mince its words, still I scarcely think that they would forbid all which might corrupt the most corruptible, or that society is prepared to accept for its own limitations those which may perhaps be necessary to the weakest of its members. If there be no abstract definition, such as I have suggested, should not the word "obscene" be allowed to indicate the present critical point in the compromise between candor and shame at which the community may have arrived here and now? If letters must, like other kinds of conduct, be subject to the social sense of what is right, it would seem that a jury should in each case establish the standard much as they do in cases of negligence. To put thought in leash to the average conscience of the time is perhaps tolerable, but to fetter it by the necessities of the lowest and least capable seems a fatal policy.

Nor is it an objection, I think, that such an interpretation gives to the words of the statute a varying meaning from time to time. Such words as these do not embalm the precise morals of an age or place; while they presuppose that some things will always be shocking to the public taste, the vague subject-matter is left to the gradual development of general notions about what is decent. A jury is especially the organ with which to feel the content comprised within such words at any given time, but to do so they must be free to follow the colloquial connotations which they have drawn up instinctively from life and common speech.

Demurrer overruled.

VULGAR AND INDECENT PARAGRAPHS MAKE NOT A BOOK OBSCENE; CONSIDERED BROADLY AND AS A WHOLE, *MADEMOISELLE DE MAUPIN* IS NOT OBSCENE

Halsey v. New York Soc. for Suppression of Vice, 136 N.E. 219 (1922)

ANDREWS, J. On November 17, 1917, in the city of New York, the plaintiff sold to an agent of the defendant, one Sumner, an English translation of Mademoiselle de Maupin. Mr. Sumner submitted the book to City Magistrate House who, however, took no action. He then,

on November 22d, presented a marked copy to Magistrate Simms, with a letter calling attention to certain pages which he thought deserved examination. On the 28th he also presented a verified complaint to this magistrate charging that the book was obscene and indecent, referring not only to the marked pages, but to the entire work. Thereupon an order was issued stating that it appeared "from the within depositions and statements that the crime therein mentioned has been committed," and holding the plaintiff to answer. The plaintiff was arrested at the direction of Sumner, and arraigned. He waived examination, was held for the action of the Court of Special Sessions, tried and acquitted. The record of that trial is not before us, but it was conceded that the copy of Mademoiselle de Maupin had been sold by the plaintiff, and the acquittal was for the reason, apparently, that the book was not obscene or indecent. This action to recover damages for malicious prosecution was then begun. At the close of the evidence the case was submitted to the jury, which found a verdict for the plaintiff. The Appellate Division (194 App. Div. 961, 185 N.Y. Supp. 931) has affirmed the judgment entered thereon.

The entire book was offered in evidence. We are asked to say from its bare perusal that probable cause existed for the belief on the part of Sumner that the plaintiff was guilty by its sale of a violation of section 1141 of the Penal Law (Consol. Law, c. 40).

In an action for malicious prosecution, one of the elements of the plaintiff's case is lack of probable cause. Whether or not this fact has been established may be for the jury to determine. Or it may become a question of law for the court. It is for the jury either when the circumstances upon which the answer depends are disputed or where conflicting inferences may fairly be drawn from them. Burns v. Wilkinson, 228 N.Y. 113, 120 N.E.513; Galley v. Brennan, 216 N.Y. 118, 110 N.E. 179.

Theophile Gautier is conceded to be among the greatest French writers of the nineteenth century. When some of his earlier works were submitted to Sainte-Beuve, that distinguished critic was astonished by the variety and richness of his expression. Henry James refers to him as a man of genius (North American Review, April, 1873). Arthur Symons (Studies in Prose and Verse), George Saintsbury (A Short History of French Literature), James Breck Perkins (Atlantic Monthly, March, 1887), all speak of him with admiration. They tell of his command of style, his poetical imagery, his artistic conceptions, his indescribable charm, his high and probably permanent place in French literature. They say that in many respects he resembles Thackeray. This was the man who in 1836 published "Mademoiselle de Maupin." It is a book of over 400 pages. The moment it was issued it excited the criticism of many, but not all, of the great Frenchmen of the day. It has since become a part of French literature. No review of French writers of the last 100 years fails to comment upon it. With the author's felicitous style, it contains passages of purity and beauty. It seems to be largely a protest against what the author, we believe mistakenly, regards as the prudery of newspaper criticism. It contains many paragraphs, however, which, taken by themselves, are undoubtedly vulgar and indecent.

No work may be judged from a selection of such paragraphs alone. Printed by themselves they might, as a matter of law, come within the prohibition of the statute. So might a similar selection from Aristophanes or Chaucer or Boccaccio, or even from the Bible. The book, however, must be considered broadly, as a whole. So considered, critical opinion is divided. Some critics, while admitting that the novel has been much admired, call it both "pornographic and dull." The Nation, Nov. 2, 1893. Mr. Perkins writes that—

"There is much in Mademoiselle de Maupin that is unpleasant and is saved only by beauty of expression from being vulgar. Though Gautier's style reached in this novel its full perfection, it is far from his best work, and it is unfortunate that it is probably the one best known."

An article in the June, 1868, issue of the Atlantic Monthly says that this is Gautier's representative romance. James calls it his one disagreeable performance, but "in certain lights the book is almost ludicrously innocent, and we are at a loss what to think of those critics who either hailed or denounced it as a serious profession of faith." Finally, in A Century of French Fiction, Benjamin W. Wells, professor of modern languages in the University of the South, says:

"Mademoiselle de Maupin is an exquisite work of art, but it spurns the conventions of received morality with a contempt that was to close the Academy to Gautier forever. With a springboard of fact in the Seventeenth century to start from, he conceives a wealthy and energetic girl of 20, freed from domestic restraints, and resolved to acquire, by mingling as man among men, more knowledge of the other sex than the conventions of social intercourse would admit. He transfers the adventures from the real world to a sort of forest of Arden, where the Rosalind of Shakespeare might meet a Watteau shepherdess and a melancholy Jacques. Thus he helps us over the instinctive repulsion that we feel for the situation. Various forms of love reaching out for an unattainable ideal occupy the body of the book, and when once the actors learn to know themselves and each other Gautier parts them forever. In its ethics the book is opposed to the professed morality of nearly all, and doubtless to the real morality of most, but, as Sainte-Beuve said of it, 'Every physician of the soul, every moralist, should have it on some back shelf of his library,' and those who, like Mithridates, no longer react to such poisons will find in Mlle. de Maupin much food for the purest literary enjoyment."

We have quoted estimates of the book as showing the manner in which it affects different minds. The conflict among the members of this court itself points a finger at the dangers of a censorship intrusted to men of one profession, of like education and similar surroundings. Far better than we is a jury drawn from those of varied experiences, engaged in various occupations, in close touch with the currents of public feeling, fitted to say whether the defendant had reasonable ground to believe that a book such as this was obscene or indecent. Here is the work of a great author, written in admirable style, which has become a part of classical literature. We may take judicial notice that it has been widely sold, separately and as a part of every collection of the works of Gautier. It has excited admiration as well as opposition. We know that a book merely obscene soon dies. Many a Roman poet wrote a Metamorphoses. Ovid survives. So this book also has lived for a hundred years. On the other hand, it does contain indecent paragraphs. We are dealing, too, with a translation where the charm of style may be attenuated. It is possible that the morality of New York City to-day may be on a higher plane than that of Paris in 1836—that there

is less vice, less crime. We hope so.

We admit freely that a book may be thoroughly indecent, no matter how great the author or how fascinating the style. It is also true that well-known writers have committed crimes; yet it is difficult to trace the connection between this fact and the question we are called upon to decide. Dr. Dodd was hanged for forgery, yet his sermons were not indecent. Oscar Wilde was convicted of personal wrongdoing, and confined in Reading gaol. It does not follow that all his plays are obscene. It is also true that the work before us bears the name of no publisher. That the house which issued it was ashamed of its act is an inference not perhaps justified by any evidence before us.

Regarding all these circumstances, so far as they are at all material, we believe it is for the jury, not for us, to draw the conclusion that must be drawn. Was the book as a whole of a character to justify the reasonable belief that its sale was a violation of the Penal Law? The jury has said that it was not. We cannot say as a matter of law that they might not reach this decision. We hold that the question of probable cause was properly submitted to them.

We have examined various other questions called to our attention. The jury was told that malice was to be presumed if there was no probable cause for the prosecution. This is not an accurate statement of the law. Under such circumstances malice may be presumed. It is not an inference which the jury is required to draw. Stewart v. Sonneborn, 98 U. S. 187, 193, 25 L. Ed. 116. The attention of the trial judge, however, was not called to this error by any exception. Nor do other exceptions as to the exclusion of evidence and as to the refusal of various requests to charge justify a reversal of the judgment appealed from.

The judgment must therefore be affirmed, with costs.

CRANE, J. (dissenting.) Section 1141 of the Penal Law provides that a person who sells any obscene, lewd, lascivious, indecent, or disgusting book is guilty of a misdemeanor.

On the 28th day of November, 1917, the defendant filed an information in the Magistrate's Court of the city of New York charging the plaintiff with the violation of this section in having sold a book entitled "Mademoiselle de Maupin" by Theophile Gautier. The accused, having waived examination before the magistrate, was held for the Special Sessions, where he was thereafter tried and found not guilty. He thereupon commenced this action charging this defendant with having maliciously prosecuted him, in that it caused his arrest without any probable cause to believe him guilty of having sold an indecent book; in other words, charging the defendant with having no reasonable grounds to believe "Mademoiselle de Maupin" an indecent publication.

There have been two trials of this action. On the first trial the judge charged the jury as a matter of law that there was no probable cause to believe this book indecent. On appeal this was reversed, on the ground that probable cause in this case was a question of fact for the jury, and not for the court. Halsey v. New York Society for the Suppression of Vice, 191 App. Div. 245, 180 N.Y. Supp. 836.

The question of probable cause, when there is no conflict in the evidence, no disputed facts, nor any doubt upon the evidence of inferences to be drawn from it, is one of law for the court, and not of fact for the jury. Heyne v.

Blair, 62 N.Y. 19; Hazzard v. Flury, 120 N.Y. 223, 24 N.E. 194; Wass v. Stephens, 128 N.Y. 123, 28 N.E. 21.

In Carl v. Ayers, 53 N.Y. 14, 17, the court, speaking through ANDREWS, J., said:

"A person making a criminal accusation may act upon appearances, and if the apparent facts are such that a discreet and prudent person would be led to the belief that a crime had been committed by the person charged, he will be justified, although it turns out that he was deceived and that the party accused was innocent. Public policy requires that a person shall be protected, who in good faith and upon reasonable grounds causes an arrest upon a criminal charge, and the law will not subject him to liability therefor. But a groundless suspicion, unwarranted by the conduct of the accused, or by facts known to the accuser, when the accusation is made, will not exempt the latter from liability to an innocent person for damages for causing his arrest."

When facts and circumstances are undisputed, probable cause is a question of law for the court which it is error to submit to the jury. Brown v. Selfridge, 224 U.S. 189, 193, 32 Sup. Ct. 444, 56 L. Ed. 727; Anderson v. How, 116 N.Y. 336, 22 N.E. 695; Burt v. Smith, 181 N.Y. 1, 73 N.E. 495, 2 Ann. Cas. 576; Rawson v. Leggett, 184 N.Y. 504, 77 N.E. 662.

In Besson v. Southard, 10 N.Y. 236, 240, we find the law stated as follows:

"If the facts which are adduced as proof of a want of probable cause are controverted, if conflicting testimony is to be weighed, or if the credibility of witnesses is to be passed upon, the question of probable cause should go to the jury, with proper instructions as to the law. But where there is no dispute about facts, it is the duty of the court, on the trial, to apply the law to them."

As an instance where the court found on the facts that there was probable cause and dismissed the malicious prosecution complaint, see Murray v. Long, 1 Wend. 140. So, also, in Burlingame v. Burlingame, 8 Cow. 141, where concededly there was a mistake in making the arrest. See Driggs v. Burton, 44 Vt. 124; Gilbertson v. Fuller, 40 Minn. 413, 42 N.W. 203; Bell v. Atlantic City R. Co., 58 N.J. Law, 227, 33 Atl. 211; Stone v. Crocker, 24 Pick. (Mass.) 81; Bell v. Keepers, 37 Kan. 64, 14 Pac. 542.

In Blachford v. Dod, 2 Barn. & Adol. 179, the facts were these: An attorney was indicted for sending a threatening letter. Being acquitted he brought suit for malicious prosecution, and was nonsuited. The court said:

"Here the question of probable cause depends on a document coming from the plaintiff himself, viz. the letter sent and written by him to the defendant; and the only question is, whether we are justified in point of law in giving to that letter the construction that it contained a threat of charging the defendants with endeavoring to obtain goods under false pretenses. * * * I concur, therefore, in thinking that the letter, independently of the summons, showed a reasonable and probable cause."

See page 187.

The construction of the letter and its meaning, and whether from its contents there was probable cause, was held to be a question of law for the court.

"It was for the judge to construe the written instrument."

If it were always for a jury to determine what reasonable men would do on undisputed facts, there would never be a question of law for the court—the rule would be meaningless. It was for the trial court, and it is now for us, to say whether or not, as a matter of law, the defendant had probable cause to believe the plaintiff guilty of selling an obscene book. At the very outset a marked distinction must be drawn. It cannot be too strongly emphasized that we are not determining whether Mademoiselle de Maupin be an indecent book. All we are called upon to determine is whether or not, recognizing the latitude afforded all works of literature and of art, and that tastes may differ, a reasonable, cautious, and prudent man would be justified in believing that this publication was obscene and lewd not in certain passages, but in its main purpose and construction. When the plaintiff was charged with having violated section 1141 of the Penal Law (that is, charged with a misdemeanor) it necessarily became a question of fact for the triers of fact, Special Sessions or jury, to determine his guilt—to determine whether the book sold was indecent and immoral. People v. Eastman, 188 N.Y. 478, 481, N.E. 459, 11 Ann. Cas. 302.

In a criminal case the questions of fact are always for the jury. In People v. Muller, 96 N.Y. 408, 411 (48 Am. Rep. 635), Judge ANDREWS said:

"The test of an obscene book was stated in Regina v. Hicklin, L. R. 3 Q. B. 360, to be, whether the tendency of the matter charged as obscenity is to deprave or corrupt those whose minds are open to such immoral influences, and who might come into contact with it."

The Special Sessions, as the triers of fact, have found the plaintiff not guilty; that is, have found that Mademoiselle de Maupin was not such an indecent book as had the tendency spoken of in the Muller Case. When it came, however, to the trial of this action, another question was presented, and that was whether the defendant here and the complainant in the criminal case had reason to believe that the book had this tendency—that is whether reasonable men would have been justified in believing the book lascivious, corrupting to morals—even though in the mind of a jury they were mistaken. This reasoning clearly shows that the jury, or triers of fact, in a criminal case have a different question to pass upon than those disposing of the malicious prosecution case. In the latter case when the facts are all conceded, and no different inferences are to be drawn from them, probable cause is a question of law for the court. In this case we have the book. The inferences to be drawn from it are all one way. Vice and lewdness are treated as virtues.

The book was submitted to the magistrate a week before the issuance of the warrant for the plaintiff's arrest. The plaintiff appeared, waived examination, and was held for trial before the Special Sessions. Schultz v. Greenwood Cemetery, 190 N.Y. 276, 83 N.E. 41.

What is probable cause? We have quoted above what this court said about it in Carl v. Ayers, supra, and we cannot add to it. It is such a state of facts presented to the complainant as would incline or move reasonable minded men of the present-day and of this generation to believe the accused guilty of the crime charged. Would reasonable, careful, prudent men, acting with caution, and environed with the conditions of life as they exist to-day, and not in some past age, be justified in believing Mademoiselle de Maupin a filthy and indecent book, and published for no useful purpose, but simply from a desire to cater to the lowest and most sensual part of human nature? In order to justify my conclusion that the defendant had probable cause to believe this book such an one as mentioned in section 1141 of the Penal Law, it is not necessary to spread upon our pages all the indecent and lascivious part of this work. People v. Eastman, supra, 188 N.Y. 481, 81 N.E. 459, 11 Ann. Cas. 302. Some facts, however, may be mentioned to give point and direction to this inquiry.

In the first place the Society for the Suppression of Vice was confronted with the fact that the publisher, whoever he was, does not put his name to the book. The book consists of certain letters purported to be written by a young man of 22 as a sort of a satire on virtue and in praise of the sensual passions, adultery and fornication. It counsels vice. He tells his friend of his love for certain women, describes them, and relates the scenes leading up to immoral practices and to intercourse. To have a mistress in the eyes of this young man is the first qualification of a gentleman, and adultery to him appears to be the most innocent thing in the world. He writes: "I deem it quite a simple matter that a young girl should prostitute herself."

No doubt many books of fine literature known as standard works have passages in them which may shock the moral sensibilities of some people of this day, but they appear as expressions of the times, and not to my knowledge as in praise of vice and derision of virtue. Most works, wherever prostitution appears, condemn or confess it as a vice or admit its evil effects and influences. The purport of this book seems to be to impress upon the readers that vice and voluptuousness are natural to society, are not wrongs, but proper practices to be indulged in by the young. Tyomies Pub. Co. v. United States, 211 Fed. 385, 128 C.C.A. 47.

Theophile Gautier published Mlle. De Maupin in 1835. The people of his time condemned it, and by reason of its lasciviousness and bad taste he was forever barred from the French Academy. He acquired a reputation as a writer, but it was not because of this book. The New International Encyclopedia has this to say about Gautier and his Mlle. De Maupin:

"Theophile Gautier, 1811-1872. Gautier's next book, Mlle. De Maupin (1835), a curious attempt at self-analysis, was a frank expression of Hedonism. Its art is fascinating, but it treats the fundamental postulates of morality with a contempt that closed the Academy to him for life."

In the Encyclopedia Britannica we read the following:

"His first novel of any size, and in many respects his most remarkable work, was Mlle. De Maupin. Unfortunately this book, while it establishes his literary reputation on an imperishable basis, was *unfitted* by its subject, and in parts by its treatment, *for general perusal,* and created even in France a prejudice against its author which he was very far from really deserving." Article by George Saintsbury, (Italics mine.)

In the Encyclopedia Americana may be read:

"Gautier's whole philosophy is a philosophy of paradox, his ideal of life hardly more than a picturesque viciousness. His besetting sin was a desire to say something clever and wicked to shock the Philistines (see Mlle. De Maupin). The Academy was forever closed to him."

When the people of France and Gautier's time condemned his book as being vicious and unfit for general perusal, are we going to say that the defendant in this case did not have probable cause to believe the same thing when the translation was published in America by a publisher who was ashamed to put his name to it? Many things have moved in the past century, and with the teachings of church, synagogue, and college, we, at least,

have the right to expect that the general tone of morality in America in 1922 is equal to that of France in 1835. It may be true that Gautier's style is fascinating and his imagination rich, but neither style, imagination, nor learning can create a privileged class, or permit obscenity because it is dressed up in a fashion difficult to imitate or acquire. American literature has been fairly clean. That the policy of this state is to keep it so is indicated by section 1141 of the Penal Law. The Legislature has declared in this section that no obscene, lewd, lascivious, or disgusting book shall be sold. Language could not be plainer.

If the things said by Gautier in this book of Mlle. De Maupin were stated openly and frankly in the language of the street, there would be no doubt in the minds of anybody, I take it, that the work would be lewd, vicious, and indecent. The fact that the disgusting details are served up in a polished style, with exquisite settings and perfumed words, makes it all the more dangerous and insidious, and none the less obscene and lascivious. Gautier may have a reputation as a writer, but his reputation does not create a license for the American market. Oscar Wilde had a great reputation for style, but went to jail just the same. Literary ability is no excuse for degeneracy.

Sufficient to say that a reading of this book convinces me that as a matter of law the Society for the Suppression of Vice had probable cause to believe the defendant, plaintiff, guilty of violating section 1141 of the Penal Law in selling this book, and that the complaint in this case should have been dismissed.

HISCOCK, C. J., and CARDOZO, POUND, and McLAUGHLIN, JJ., concur with ANDREWS, J.

CRANE, J., reads dissenting opinion, in which HOGAN, J., concurs.

Judgment affirmed.

MOTHER'S SEX EDUCATION PAMPHLET "SEX SIDE OF LIFE" IS NOT OBSCENE

United States v. Dennett, 39 F.2d 564 (1930)

Mary W. Dennett was convicted of mailing obscene matter in contravention of section 211 of the United States Criminal Code (18 USCA § 334), and she appeals. Reversed.

The statute under which the defendant was convicted reads as follows: "Every obscene, lewd, or lascivious, and every filthy book, pamphlet, picture, paper, letter, writing, print, or other publication of an indecent character, and every article or thing designed, adapted, or intended for preventing conception or producing abortion, or for any indecent or immoral use; * * * is hereby declared to be nonmailable matter and shall not be conveyed in the mails or delivered from any post office or by any letter carrier. Whoever shall knowingly deposit, or cause to be deposited, for mailing or delivery, anything declared by this section to be nonmailable, or shall knowingly take, or cause the same to be taken, from the mails for the purpose of circulating or disposing thereof, or of aiding in the circulation or disposition thereof, shall be fined not more than $5,000, or imprisoned not more than five years, or both."

The defendant is the mother of two boys. When they had reached the respective ages of eleven and fourteen, she concluded that she ought to teach them about the sex side of life. After examining about sixty publications on the subject and forming the opinion that they were inadequate and unsatisfactory, she wrote the pamphlet entitled "Sex of Life," for the mailing of which she was afterwards indicted.

The defendant allowed some of her friends, both parents and young people, to read the manuscript which she had written for her own children, and it finally came to the notice of the owner of the Medical Review of Reviews, who asked if he might read it and afterwards published it. About a year afterwards she published the article herself at twenty-five cents a copy when sold singly, and at lower prices when ordered in quantities. Twenty-five thousand of the pamphlets seem to have been distributed in this way.

At the trial, the defendant sought to prove the cost of publication in order to show that there could have been no motive of gain on her part. She also offered to prove that she had received orders from the Union Theological Seminary, Young Men's Christian Association, the Young Women's Christian Association, the Public Health Departments of the various states and from no less than four hundred welfare and religious organizations, as well as from clergymen, college professors, and doctors, and that the pamphlet was in use in the public schools at Bronxville, N.Y. The foregoing offers were rejected on the ground that the defendant's motive in distributing the pamphlet was irrelevant, and that the only issues were whether she caused the pamphlet to be mailed and whether it was obscene.

The pamphlet begins with a so-called "Introduction for Elders" which sets forth the general views of the writer and is as follows:

"In reading several dozen books on sex matters for the young with a view to selecting the best for my own children, I found none that I was willing to put into their hands, without first guarding them against what I considered very misleading and harmful impressions, which they would otherwise be sure to acquire in reading them. That is the excuse for this article.

"It is far more specific than most sex information written for young people. I believe we owe it to children to be specific if we talk about the subject at all.

"From a careful observation of youthful curiosity and a very vivid recollection of my own childhood, I have tried to explain frankly the points about which there is the greatest inquiry. These points are not frankly or clearly explained in most sex literature. They are avoided, partly from embarrassment, but more, apparently, because those who have undertaken to instruct the children are not really clear in their own minds as to the proper status of the sex relation.

"I found that from the physiological point of view, the question was handled with limitations and reservations. From the point of natural science it was often handled with plans for perpetuating the plant and animal species, and the effort to have the child carry over into human life some sense of that beauty has come from a most commendable instinct to protect the child from the natural shock of the revelation of so much that is unesthetic and revolting in human sex life. The nearness of the sex organs to the excretory organs, the pain and messiness of childbirth are elements which certainly need some compensating antidote to prevent their making too disagreeable and disproportionate an impress on the child's mind.

"The results are doubtless good as far as they go, but they do not go nearly far enough. What else is there to call upon to help out? Why, the one thing which has been persistently neglected by practically all the sex writers,—the emotional side of sex experience. Parents and teachers have been afraid of it and distrustful of it. In not a single one of all the books for young people that I have thus far read has there been the frank unashamed declaration that the climax of sex emotion is an unsurpassed joy, something which rightly belongs to every normal human being, a joy to be proudly and serenely experienced. Instead there has been all too evident an inference that sex emotion is a thing to be ashamed of, that yielding to it is indulgence which must be curbed as much as possible, that all thought and understanding of it must be rigorously postponed, at any rate till after marriage.

"We give to young folks, in their general education, as much as they can grasp of science and ethics and art, and yet in their sex education, which rightly has to do with all of these, we have said, 'Give them only the bare physiological facts, lest they be prematurely stimulated.' Others of us, realizing that the bare physiological facts are shocking to many a sensitive child, and must somehow be softened with something pleasant, have said, 'Give them the facts, yes, but see to it that they are so related to the wonders of evolution and the beauties of the natural world that the shock is minimized.' But none of us has yet dared to say, 'Yes, give them the facts, give them the nature study, too, but also give them some conception of sex life as a vivifying joy, as a vital art, as a thing to be studied and developed with reverence for its big meaning, with understanding of its far-reaching reactions, psychologically and spiritually, with temperant restraint, good taste and the highest idealism.' We have contented ourselves by assuming that marriage makes sex relations respectable. We have not yet said that it is sentimentality, the child being led from a semi-esthetic study of the reproduction of flowers and animals to the acceptance of a similar idea for human beings. From the moral point of view it was handled least satisfactorily of all, the child being given a jumble of conflicting ideas, with no means of correlating them—fear of venereal disease, one's duty to suppress 'animal passion,' the sacredness of marriage, and so forth. And from the emotional point of view, the subject was not handled at all.

"This one omission seems to me to be the key to the whole situation, and it is the basis of the radical departure I have made from the precedents in most sex literature for children.

"Concerning all four points of view just mentioned, there are certain departures from the traditional method that have seemed to me worth making.

"On the physiological side I have given, as far as possible, the proper terminology for the sex organs and functions. Children have had to read the expurgated literature which has been specially prepared for them in poetic or colloquial terms, and then are needlessly mystified when they hear things called by their real names.

"On the side of natural science, I have emphasized our unlikeness to the plants and animals rather than our likeness, for while the points we have in common with the lower orders make an interesting section in our general education, it is knowing about the vital points in which we differ that helps us to solve the sexual problems of maturity; and the child needs that knowledge precisely as he needs knowledge of everything which will fortify him for wise decisions when he is grown.

"On the moral side, I have tried to avoid confusion and dogmatism in the following ways: by eliminating fear of venereal disease as an appeal for strictly limited sex relations, stating candidly that venereal disease is becoming curable; by barring out all mention of 'brute' or 'animal' passion, terms frequently used in pleas for chastity and self control, as such talk is an aspersion on the brute and has done children much harm in giving them the impression that there is an essential baseness in the sex relation; by inviting the inference that marriage is 'sacred' by virtue of its being a reflection of human ideality rather than because it is a legalized institution.

"Unquestionably the stress which most writers have laid upon the beauty of nature's only beautiful sex relations that can make marriage lovely.

"Young people are just as capable of being guided and inspired in their thought about sex emotion as in their taste and ideals in literature and ethics, and just as they imperatively need to have their general taste and ideals cultivated as a preparation for mature life, so do they need to have some understanding of the marvelous place which sex emotion has in life.

"Only such an understanding can be counted on to give them the self control that is born of knowledge, not fear, the reverence that will prevent premature or trivial connections, the good taste and finesse that will make their sex life when they reach maturity a vitalizing success."

After the foregoing introduction comes the part devoted to sex instruction entitled, "An Explanation for Young People." It proceeds to explain sex life in detail both physiologically and emotionally. It describes the sex organs and their operation and the way children are begotten and born. It negatives the idea that the sex impulse is in itself a base passion, and treats it as normal and its satisfaction as a great and justifiable joy when accompanied by love between two human beings. It warns against perversion, venereal disease, and prostitution, and argues for continence and healthy mindedness and against promiscuous sex relations.

The pamphlet in discussing the emotional side of the human sex relation, says:

"It means that a man and a woman feel that they *belong* to each other in a way that they belong to no one else; it makes them wonderfully happy to be together; they find they want to live together, work together, play together, and to have children together, that is, to marry each other; and their dream is to be happy together all their lives. * * * The idea of sex relations between people who do not love each other, who do not feel any sense of belonging to each other, will always be revolting to highly developed sensitive people."

"People's lives grow finer and their characters better, if they have sex relations only with those they love. And those who make the wretched mistake of yielding to the sex impulse alone when there is no love to go with it, usually live to despise themselves for their weakness and their bad taste. They are always ashamed of doing it, and they try to keep it secret from their families and those they respect. You can be sure that whatever people are ashamed to do is something that can never bring them real happiness. It is true that one's sex relations are the most personal and private matters in the world, and they belong just to us and to no one else, but while we may be shy and reserved about them, *we are not ashamed.*

"When two people really love each other, they don't care who knows it. They are proud of their happiness. But no man is ever proud of his connection with a prostitute and no prostitute is ever proud of her business.

"Sex relations belong to love, and love is never a *business.* Love is the nicest thing in the world, but it can't be bought. And the sex side of it is the biggest and most important side of it, so it is the one side of us that we must be absolutely sure to keep in good order and perfect health, if we are going to be happy ourselves or make any one else happy."

The government proved that the pamphlet was mailed to Mrs. C. A. Miles, Grottoes, Va.

Upon the foregoing record, of which we have given a summary, the trial judge charged the jury that the motive of the defendant in mailing the pamphlet was immaterial, that it was for them to determine whether it was obscene, lewd, or lascivious within the meaning of the statute, and that the test was "whether its language has a tendency to deprave and corrupt the morals of those whose minds are open to such things and into whose hands it may fall; arousing and implanting in such minds lewd and obscene thought or desires."

The court also charged that, "even if the matter sought to be shown in the pamphlet complained of were true, that fact would be immaterial, if the statements of such facts were calculated to deprave the morals of the readers by inciting sexual desires and libidinous thoughts."

The jury returned a verdict of guilty upon which the defendant was sentenced to pay a fine of $300, and from the judgment of conviction she has taken this appeal.

Greenbaum, Wolff & Ernst, of New York City (Morris L. Ernst, Newman Levy, and Alexander Lindey, all of New York City, of counsel), for appellant.

Howard W. Ameli, U. S. Atty., of Brooklyn, N.Y. (Herbert H. Kellogg, James E. Wilkinson, and Emanuel Bublick, Asst. U. S. Attys., all of Brooklyn, N.Y., of counsel), for the United States.

Before SWAN, AUGUSTUS N. HAND, and CHASE, Circuit Judges.

AUGUSTUS N. HAND, Circuit Judge (after stating the facts as above).

It is doubtless true that the personal motive of the defendant in distributing her pamphlet could have no bearing on the question whether she violated the law. Her own belief that a really obscene pamphlet would pay the price for its obscenity by means of intrinsic merits would leave her as much as ever under the ban of the statute. Regina v. Hicklin, L. R. 3 Q. B. 360; United States v. Bennett, Fed. Case No. 14,571; Rosen v. United States, 161 U. S. at page 41, 16 S. Ct. 434, 480, 40 L. Ed. 606.

It was perhaps proper to exclude the evidence offered by the defendant as to the persons to whom the pamphlet was sold, for the reason that such evidence, if relevant at all, was part of the government's proof. In other words, a publication might be distributed among doctors or nurses or adults in cases where the distribution among small children could not be justified. The fact that the latter might obtain it accidently or surreptitiously, as they might see some medical books which would not be desirable for them to read, would hardly be sufficient to bar a publication otherwise proper. Here the pamphlet appears to have been mailed to a married woman. The tract may fairly be said to be calculated to aid parents in the instruction of their children in sex matters. As the record stands, it is a reasonable inference that the pamphlet was to be given to children at the discretion of adults and to be distributed through agencies that had the real welfare of the adolescent in view. There is no reason to suppose that it was to be broadcast among children who would have no capacity to understand its general significance. Even the court in Regina v. Hicklin, L. R. 3 Q. B. at p. 367, which laid down a more strict rule than the New York Court of Appeals was inclined to adopt in People v. Eastman, 188 N.Y. 478, 81 N. E. 459, 11 Ann. Cas. 302, said that "the circumstances of the publication" may determine whether the statute has been violated.

But the important consideration in this case is not the correctness of the rulings of the trial judge as to the admissibility of evidence, but the meaning and scope of those words of the statute which prohibit the mailing of an *"obscene, lewd or lascivious * * * pamphlet."* It was for the trial court to determine whether the pamphlet could reasonably be thought to be of such a character before submitting any question of the violation of the statute to the jury. Knowles v. United States (C. C. A.) 170 F. 409; Magon v. United States (C. C. A.) 248 F. 201. And the test most frequently laid down seems to have been whether it would tend to deprave the morals of those into whose hands the publication might fall by suggesting lewd thoughts and exciting sensual desires. Dunlop v. United States, 165 U. S. at page 501, 17 S. Ct. 375 41 L. Ed. 799; Rosen v. United States, 161 U. S. 29, 16 S. Ct. 434, 480, 40 L. Ed. 606.

It may be assumed that any article dealing with the sex side of life and explaining the functions of the sex organs is capable in some circumstances of arousing lust. The sex impulses are present in every one, and without doubt cause much of the weal and woe of human kind. But it can hardly be said that, because of the risk of arousing sex impulses, there should be no instruction of the young in sex matters, and that the risk of imparting instruction outweighs the disadvantages of leaving them to grope about in mystery and morbid curiosity and of requiring them to secure such information, as they may be able to obtain, from ill-informed and often foul-minded companions, rather than from intelligent and high-minded sources. It may be argued that suggestion plays a large part in such matters, and that on the whole the less sex questions are dwelt upon the better. But it by no means follows that such a desideratum is attained by leaving adolescents in a state of inevitable curiosity, satisfied only by the casual gossip of ignorant playmates.

The old theory that information about sex matters should be left to chance has greatly changed, and, while there is still a difference of opinion as to just the kind of instruction which ought to be given, it is commonly thought in these days that much was lacking in the old mystery and reticence. This is evident from the current literature on the subject, particularly such pamphlets as "Sex Education," issued by the Treasury Department United States Public Health Service in 1927.

The statute we have to construe was never thought to bar from the mails everything which *might* stimulate sex impulses. If so, much chaste poetry and fiction, as well as many useful medical works would be under the ban. Like everything else, this law must be construed reasonably with a view to the general objects aimed at. While there can be no doubt about its constitutionality, it must not be assumed to have been designed to interfere with serious instruction regarding sex matters unless the terms in which the information is conveyed are clearly indecent.

We have been referred to no decision where a truthful exposition of the sex side of life, evidently calculated for instruction and for the explanation of relevant facts, has been held to be obscene. In Dysart v. United States, 272 U. S. 655, 47 S. Ct. 234, 71 L. Ed. 461, it was decided that the advertisement of a lying-in retreat to enable unmarried women to conceal their missteps, even though written in a coarse and vulgar style, did not fall within prohibition of the statute, and was not "obscene" within the meaning of the law.

The defendant's discussion of the phenomena of sex is written with sincerity of feeling and with an idealization of the marriage relation and sex emotions. We think it tends to rationalize and dignify such emotions rather than to arouse lust. While it may be thought by some that portions of the tract go into unnecessary details that would better have been omitted, it may be fairly answered that the curiosity of many adolescents would not be satisfied without full explanation, and that no more than that is really given. It also may reasonably be thought that accurate information, rather than mystery and curiosity, is better in the long run and is less likely to occasion lascivious thoughts than ignorance and anxiety. Perhaps instruction other than that which the defendant suggests would be better. That is a matter as to which there is bound to be a wide difference of opinion, but, irrespective of this, we hold that an accurate exposition of the relevant facts of the sex side of life in decent language and in manifestly serious and disinterested spirit cannot ordinarily be regarded as obscene. Any incidental tendency to arouse sex impulses which such a pamphlet may perhaps have is apart from and subordinate to its main effect. The tendency can only exist in so far as it is inherent in any sex instruction, and it would seem to be outweighed by the elimination of ignorance, curiosity, and morbid fear. The direct aim and the net result is to promote understanding and self-control.

No case was made for submission to the jury, and the judgment must therefore be reversed.

THE BOOK *MARRIED LOVE,* WHICH "IS A CONSIDERED ATTEMPT TO EXPLAIN TO MARRIED PEOPLE HOW THEIR MUTUAL SEX LIFE MAY BE MADE HAPPIER," IS NOT OBSCENE.

United States v. One Obscene Book Entitled "Married Love", 48 F.2d 821 (1931)

WOOLSEY, District Judge.

I dismiss the libel in this case.

I. The first point with which I shall deal is as to the contention that the section of the Tariff Act under which this libel was brought, title 19, U. S. C., § 1305 (19 USCA § 1305), is unconstitutional as impinging on the right of the freedom of the press. I think there is nothing in this contention. The section does not involve the suppression of a book before it is published, but the exclusion of an already published book which is sought to be brought into the United States.

After a book is published, its lot in the world is like that of anything else. It must conform to the law and, if it does not, must be subject to the penalties involved in its failure to do so. Laws which are thus disciplinary of publications, whether involving exclusion from the mails or from this country, do not interfere with freedom of the press.

II. Passing to the second point, I think that the matter here involved is res adjudicata by reason of the decision hereinafter mentioned.

This is a proceeding in rem against a book entitled "Married Love," written by Dr. Marie C. Stopes and sent from England by the London branch of G.P. Putnam's Sons to their New York office.

The libel was filed under the provisions of Title 19, U.S.C., § 1305 (19 USCA § 1305), which provides, so far as is here relevant, as follows:

"§ 1305. *Immoral Articles—Importation Prohibited.* (a) *Prohibition of importation.* All persons are prohibited from importing into the United States from any foreign country * * * any obscene book, pamphlet, paper, writing, advertisement, circular, print, pictures, drawing, or other representation, figure, or image on or of paper or other material, or any cast, instrument, or other article which is obscene or immoral, or any drug or medicine or any article whatever for the prevention of conception or for causing unlawful abortion. * * * No such articles, whether imported separately or contained in packages with other goods entitled to entry, shall be admitted to entry; and all such articles * * * shall be subject to seizure and forfeiture as hereinafter provided: * * * *Provided further,* that the secretary of the Treasury may, in his discretion, admit the so-called classics or books of recognized and established literary or scientific merit, but may, in his discretion, admit such classics or books only when imported for noncommercial purposes."

Then it goes on:

"Upon the appearance of any such book or matter at any customs office, the same shall be seized and held by the collector to await the judgment of the district court as hereinafter provided. * * * Upon the seizure of such book or matter the collector shall transmit information thereof to the district attorney of the district in which is situated the office at which such seizure has taken place, who shall institute proceedings in the district court for the forfeiture, confiscation, and destruction of the book or matter seized. Upon the adjudication that such book or matter thus seized is of the character the entry of which is by this section prohibited, it shall be ordered destroyed and shall be destroyed. Upon adjudication that such book or matter thus seized is not of the character the entry of which is by this section prohibited, it shall not be excluded from entry under the provisions of this section.

"In any such proceeding any party in interest may upon demand have the facts at issue determined by a jury and any party may have an appeal or the right of review as in the case of ordinary actions or suits."

The book before me now has had stricken from it all matters dealing with contraceptive instruction and, hence, does not come now within the prohibition of the statute against imports for such purposes, even if a book dealing with such matters falls within the provisions of this section—which I think it probably does not—and the case falls to be dealt with entirely on the question of whether the book is obscene or immoral.

Another copy of this same book, without the excision of the passages dealing with contraceptive matters, was before Judge Kirkpatrick, United States District Judge for the Eastern District of Pennsylvania, on a forfeiture libel under the Tariff Act of 1922, and he ruled that the book was not obscene or immoral, and directed a verdict for the claimant.[1]

Although the government took an exception to this ruling at the time of the trial, it did not mature this exception by an appeal, and the case therefore stands as a final decision of a coordinate court in a proceeding in rem involving the same book that we have here. The answer in this case is amended and pleads res adjudicata on the ground of the proceedings had before Judge Kirkpatrick which involved exactly the same question as that now before me.

The only difference between the Philadelphia case and this case is that another copy of the same book has been here seized and libeled.

I think that the proper view of the meaning of the word "book" in title 19, U. S. C., § 1305 (19 USCA § 1305), is not merely a few sheets of paper bound together in cloth or otherwise, but that a book means an assembly or concourse of ideas expressed in words, the subject-matter which is embodied in the book, which is sought to be excluded, and not merely the physical object called a book which can be held in one's hands.

Assuming it is proper so to view the meaning of the word "book" in the statute under consideration, Judge Kirkpatrick's decision at Philadelphia in a proceeding in rem against this book is a bar to another similar proceeding such as this in this district.

I hold that Judge Kirkpatrick's decision established the book "Married Love" as having an admissible status at any point around the customs' barriers of the United States. In this connection, see Gelston v. Hoyt, 3 Wheat. 246, 312 to page 316, 4 L. Ed. 381; Waples on Proceedings in Rem, §§ 87, 110, 111, 112, and cases therein cited.

It is perfectly obvious, I think, that, if a vessel had been libeled on a certain count for forfeiture at Philadelphia, and there acquitted of liability to forfeiture, on her coming around to New York she could not properly be libeled again on the same count. That is the real situation in the present case. Cf. United States v. 2180 Cases of Champagne, 9 F.(2d) 710, 712, 713 (C. C. A.2).

III. However, in case the Circuit Court of Appeals, to which I presume this case will eventually be taken, should disagree with my construction of the word "book," and should consider that it was a copy of the book that was subject to exclusion, and not merely the book regarded as an embodiment of ideas, or should disagree with my application of the admiralty law to a situation of this kind, I will now deal with the case on the merits.

In Murray's Oxford English Dictionary the word

"obscene" is defined as follows:

"Obscene–1. Offensive to the senses, or to taste or refinement; disgusting, repulsive, filthy, foul, abominable, loathsome. Now somewhat arch.

"2. Offensive to modesty or decency; expressing or suggesting unchaste or lustful ideas; impure, indecent, lewd."

In the same Dictionary the word "immoral" is defined as follows:

"Immoral–The opposite of moral; not moral.

"1. Not consistent with, or not conforming to, moral law or requirement; opposed to or violating morality; morally evil or impure; unprincipled, vicious, dissolute. (Of persons, things, actions, etc.)

"2. Not having a moral nature or character; non-moral."

The book "Married Love" does not, in my opinion, fall within these definitions of the words "obscene" or "immoral" in any respect.

Dr. Stopes treats quite as decently and with as much restraint of the sex relations as did Mrs. Mary Ware Dennett in "The Sex Side of Life, An Explanation for Young People," which was held not to be obscene by the Circuit Court of Appeals for this circuit in United States v. Dennett, 39 F.(2d) 564.

The present book may fairly be said to do for adults what Mrs. Dennett's book does for adolescents.

The Dennett Case, as I read it, teaches that this court must determine, as a matter of law in the first instance, whether the book alleged to be obscene falls in any sense within the definition of that word. If it does, liability to forfeiture becomes a question for the jury under proper instructions. If it does not, the question is one entirely for the court.

"Married Love" is a considered attempt to explain to married people how their mutual sex life may be made happier.

To one who had read Havelock Ellis, as I have, the subject-matter of Dr. Stope's book is not wholly new, but it emphasizes the woman's side of sex questions. It makes also some apparently justified criticisms of the inopportune exercise by the man in the marriage relation of what are often referred to as his conjugal or marital rights, and it pleads with seriousness, and not without some eloquence, for a better understanding by husbands of the physical and emotional side of the sex life of their wives.

I do not find anything exceptionable anywhere in the book, and I cannot imagine a normal mind to which this book would seem to be obscene or immoral within the proper definition of these words or whose sex impulses would be stirred by reading it.

Whether or not the book is scientific in some of its theses is unimportant. It is informative and instructive, and I think that any married folk who read it cannot fail to be benefited by its counsels of perfection and its frank discussion of the frequent difficulties which necessarily arise in the more intimate aspects of married life, for as Professor William G. Sumner used aptly to say in his lectures on the Science of Society at Yale, marriage, in its essence, is a status of antagonistic co-operation.

In such a status, necessarily, centripetal and centrifugal forces are continuously at work, and the measure of its success obviously depends on the extent to which the centripetal forces are predominant.

The book before me here has as its whole thesis the strengthening of the centripetal forces in marriage, and instead of being inhospitably received, it should, I think, be welcomed within our borders.

NOTES

1. No opinion was filed.

ULYSSES IS NOT OBSCENE

United States v. One Book Called "Ulysses", 5 F.Supp. 182 (1933)

WOOLSEY, District Judge.

The motion for a decree dismissing the libel herein is granted, and, consequently, of course, the government's motion for a decree of forfeiture and destruction is denied.

Accordingly a decree dismissing the libel without costs may be entered herein.

I. The practice followed in this case is in accordance with the suggestion made by me in the case of United States v. One Book, Entitled "Contraception" (D.C.) 51 F.(2d) 525, and is as follows:

After issue was joined by the filing of the claimant's answer to the libel for forfeiture against "Ulysses," a stipulation was made between the United States Attorney's office and the attorneys for the claimant providing:

1. That the book "Ulysses" should be deemed to have been annexed to and to have become part of the libel just as if it had been incorporated in its entirety therein.

2. That the parties waived their right to a trial by jury.

3. That each party agreed to move for decree in its favor.

4. That on such cross-motions the court might decide all the questions of law and fact involved and render a general finding thereon.

5. That on the decision of such motions the decree of the court might be entered as if it were a decree after trial.

It seems to me that a procedure of this kind is highly appropriate in libels such as this for the confiscation of books. It is an especially advantageous procedure in the instant case because, on account of the length of "Ulysses" and the difficulty of reading it, a jury trial would have been an extremely unsatisfactory, if not an almost impossible method of dealing with it.

II. I have read "Ulysses" once in its entirety and I have read those passages of which the government particularly complains several times. In fact, for many weeks, my spare time has been devoted to the consideration of the decision which my duty would require me to make in this matter.

"Ulysses" is not an easy book to read or to understand. But there has been much written about it, and in order properly to approach the consideration of it it is advisable to read a number of other books which have now become its satellites. The study of "Ulysses" is, therefore, a heavy task.

III. The reputation of "Ulysses" in the literary world, however, warranted my taking such time as was necessary to enable me to satisfy myself as to the intent with which the book was written, for, of course, in any case where a book is claimed to be obscene it must first be determined, whether the intent with which it was written was what is called, according to the usual phrase, pornographic, that is, written for the purpose of exploiting obscenity.

If the conclusion is that the book is pornographic, that is the end of the inquiry and forfeiture must follow.

But in "Ulysses," in spite of its unusual frankness, I do not detect anywhere the leer of the sensualist. I hold, therefore, that it is not pornographic.

IV. In writing "Ulysses," Joyce sought to make a serious experiment in a new, if not wholly novel, literary genre. He takes persons of the lower middle class living in Dublin in 1904 and seeks, not only to describe what they did on a certain day early in June of that year as they went about the city bent on their usual occupations, but also to tell what many of them thought about the while.

Joyce has attempted—it seems to me, with astonishing success—to show how the screen of consciousness with its ever-shifting kaleidoscopic impressions carries, as it were on a plastic palimpsest, not only what is in the focus of each man's observation of the actual things about him, but also in a penumbral zone residua of past impressions, some recent and some drawn up by association from the domain of the subconscious. He shows how each of these impressions affects the life and behavior of the character which he is describing.

What he seeks to get is not unlike the result of a double or, if that is possible, a multiple exposure on a cinema film, which would give a clear foreground with a background visible but somewhat blurred and out of focus in varying degrees.

To convey by words an effect which obviously lends itself more appropriately to a graphic technique, accounts, it seems to me, for much of the obscurity which meets a reader of "Ulysses." And it also explains another aspect of the book, which I have further to consider, namely, Joyce's sincerity and his honest effort to show exactly how the minds of his characters operate.

If Joyce did not attempt to be honest in developing the technique which he has adopted in "Ulysses" the result would be psychologically misleading and thus unfaithful to his chosen technique. Such an attitude would be artistically inexcusable.

It is because Joyce has been loyal to his technique and has not funked its necessary implications, but has honestly attempted to tell fully what his characters think about, that he has been the subject of so many attacks and that his purpose has been so often misunderstood and misrepresented. For his attempt sincerely and honestly to realize his objective has required him incidentally to use certain words which are generally considered dirty words and has led at times to what many think is a too poignant preoccupation with sex in the thoughts of his characters.

The words which are criticized as dirty are old Saxon words known to almost all men and, I venture, to many women, and are such words as would be naturally and habitually used, I believe, by the types of folk whose life, physical and mental, Joyce is seeking to describe. In respect of the recurrent emergence of the theme of sex in the minds of his characters, it must always be remembered that his locale was Celtic and his season spring.

Whether or not one enjoys such a technique as Joyce uses is a matter of taste on which disagreement or argument is futile, but to subject that technique to the standards of some other technique seems to me to be little short of absurd.

Accordingly, I hold that "Ulysses" is a sincere and honest book, and I think that the criticisms of it are entirely disposed of by its rationale.

V. Furthermore, "Ulysses" is an amazing tour de force when one considers the success which has been in the main achieved with such a difficult objective as Joyce set for himself. As I have stated, "Ulysses" is not an easy book to read. It is brilliant and dull, intelligible and obscure, by turns. In many places it seems to me to be disgusting, but although it contains, as I have mentioned above, many words usually considered dirty, I have not found anything that I consider to be dirt for dirt's sake. Each word of the book contributes like a bit of mosaic to the detail of the picture which Joyce is seeking to construct for his readers.

If one does not wish to associate with such folk as Joyce describes, that is one's own choice. In order to avoid indirect contact with them one may not wish to read "Ulysses"; that is quite understandable. But when such a great artist in words, as Joyce undoubtedly is, seeks to draw a true picture of the lower middle class in a European city, ought it to be impossible for the American public legally to see that picture?

To answer this question it is not sufficient merely to find, as I have found above, that Joyce did not write "Ulysses" with what is commonly called pornographic intent, I must endeavor to apply a more objective standard to his book in order to determine its effect in the result, irrespective of the intent with which it was written.

VI. The statute under which the libel is filed only denounces, in so far as we are here concerned, the importation into the United States from any foreign country of "any obscene book." Section 305 of the Tariff Act of 1930, title 19 United States Code, § 1305 (19 USCA § 1305). It does not marshal against books the spectrum of condemnatory adjectives found, commonly, in laws dealing with matters of this kind. I am, therefore, only required to determine whether "Ulysses" is obscene within the legal definition of that word.

The meaning of the word "obscene" as legally defined by the courts is: Tending to stir the sex impulses or to lead to sexually impure and lustful thoughts. Dunlop v. United States, 165 U. S. 486, 501, 17 S. Ct. 375, 41 L. Ed. 799; United States v. One Obscene Book Entitled "Married Love" (D. C.) 48 F.(2d) 821, 824; United States v. One Book, Entitled "Contraception" (D. C.) 51 F.(2d) 525, 528; and compare Dysart v. United States, 272 U. S. 655, 657, 47 S. Ct. 234, 71 L. Ed. 461; Swearingen v. United States, 161 U. S. 446, 450, 16 S. Ct. 562, 40 L. Ed. 765; United States v. Dennett, 39 F.(2d) 564, 568, 76 A. L. R. 1092 (C. C. A.2); People v. Wendling, 258 N. Y. 451, 453, 180 N. E. 169, 81 A. L. R. 799.

Whether a particular book would tend to excite such impulses and thoughts must be tested by the court's opinion as to its effect on a person with average sex instincts—what the French would call l'homme moyen sensuel—who plays, in this branch of legal inquiry, the same role of hypothetical reagent as does the "reasonable man" in the law of torts and "the man learned in the art" on questions of invention in patent law.

The risk involved in the use of such a reagent arises from the inherent tendency of the trier of facts, however fair he may intend to be, to make his reagent too much subservient to his own idiosyncrasies. Here, I have attempted to avoid this, if possible, and to make my reagent herein more objective than he might otherwise be, by adopting the following course:

After I had made my decision in regard to the aspect of "Ulysses," now under consideration, I checked my impressions with two friends of mine who in my opinion answered to the above-stated requirement for my reagent.

These literary assessors—as I might properly describe them—were called on separately, and neither knew that I was consulting the other. They are men whose opinion on literature and on life I value most highly. They had both read "Ulysses," and, of course, were wholly unconnected with this cause.

Without letting either of my assessors know what my decision was, I gave to each of them the legal definition of obscene and asked each whether in his opinion "Ulysses" was obscene within that definition.

I was interested to find that they both agreed with my opinion: That reading "Ulysses" in its entirety, as a book must be read on such a test as this, did not tend to excite sexual impulses or lustful thoughts, but that its net effect on them was only that of a somewhat tragic and very powerful commentary on the inner lives of men and women.

It is only with the normal person that the law is concerned. Such a test as I have described, therefore, is the only proper test of obscenity in the case of a book like "Ulysses" which is a sincere and serious attempt to devise a new literary method for the observation and description of mankind.

I am quite aware that owing to some of its scenes "Ulysses" is a rather strong draught to ask some sensitive, though normal, persons to take. But my considered opinion, after long reflection, is that, whilst in many places the effect of "Ulysses" on the reader undoubtedly is somewhat emetic, nowhere does it tend to be an aphrodisiac.

"Ulysses" may, therefore, be admitted into the United States.

JUDGES AUGUSTUS HAND AND LEARNED HAND UPHOLD JUDGE WOOLSEY'S DECISION THAT *ULYSSES* IS NOT OBSCENE

United States v. One Book Entitled Ulysses, 72 F.2d 705 (1934)

AUGUSTUS N. HAND, Circuit Judge.

This appeal raises sharply the question of the proper interpretation of section 305 (a) of the Tariff Act of 1930 (19 USCA §1305 (a). That section provides that "all persons are prohibited from importing into the United States from any foreign country * * * any obscene book, pamphlet, paper, writing, advertisement, circular, print, picture, drawing, or other representation, figure, or image on or of paper or other material, * * * " and directs that, upon the appearance of any such book or matter at any

customs office, the collector shall seize it and inform the district attorney, who shall institute proceedings for forfeiture. In accordance with the statute, the collector seized Ulysses, a book written by James Joyce, and the United States filed a libel for forfeiture. The claimant, Random House, Inc., the publisher of the American edition, intervened in the cause and filed its answer denying that the book was obscene and was subject to confiscation and praying that it be admitted into the United States. The case came on for trial before Woolsey, J., who found that the book, taken as a whole, "did not tend to excite sexual impulses or lustful thoughts but that its net effect was only that of a somewhat tragic and very powerful commentary on the inner lives of men and women." He accordingly granted a decree adjudging that the book was "not of the character the entry of which is prohibited under the provision of section 305 of the Tariff Act of 1930 * * * *and * * * dismissing the libel," from which this appeal has been taken.

James Joyce, the author of Ulysses, may be regarded as a pioneer among those writers who have adopted the "stream of consciousness" method of presenting fiction, which has attracted considerable attention in academic and literary circles. In this field Ulysses is rated as a book of considerable power by persons whose opinions are entitled to weight. Indeed it has become a sort of contemporary classic, dealing with a new subject-matter. It attempts to depict the thoughts and lay bare the souls of a number of people, some of them intellectuals and some social outcasts and nothing more, with a literalism that leaves nothing unsaid. Certain of its passages are of beauty and undoubted distinction, while others are of a vulgarity that is extreme and the book as a whole has a realism characteristic of the present age. It is supposed to portray the thoughts of the principal characters during a period of about eighteen hours.

We may discount the laudation of Ulysses by some of its admirers and reject the view that it will permanently stand among the great works of literature, but it is fair to say that it is a sincere portrayal with skillful artistry of the "stream of consciousness" of its characters. Though the depiction happily is not of the "stream of consciousness" of all men and perhaps of only those of a morbid type, it seems to be sincere, truthful, relevant to the subject, and executed with real art. Joyce, in the words of Paradise Lost, has dealt with "things unattempted yet in prose or rime"—with things that very likely might better have remained "unattempted"—but his book shows originality and is a work of symmetry and excellent craftsmanship of a sort. The question before us is whether such a book of artistic merit and scientific insight should be regarded as "obscene" within section 305 (a) of the Tariff Act.

That numerous long passages in Ulysses contain matter that is obscene under any fair definition of the word cannot be gainsaid; yet they are relevant to the purpose of depicting the thoughts of the characters and are introduced to give meaning to the whole, rather than to promote lust or portray filth for its own sake. The net effect even of portions most open to attack, such as the closing monologue of the wife of Leopold Bloom, is pitiful and tragic, rather than lustful. The book depicts the souls of men and women that are by turns bewildered and keenly apprehensive, sordid and inspiring, ugly and beautiful, hateful and loving, In the end one feels, more than anything else, pity and sorrow for the confusion, misery, and degredation of humanity. Page after page of the book is, or seems to be, incomprehensible. But many passages show the trained hand of an artist, who can at one moment adapt to perfection the style of an ancient chronicler, and at another become a veritable personification of Thomas Carlyle. In numerous places there are found originality, beauty, and distinction. The book as a whole is not pornographic, and, while in not a few spots it is coarse, blasphemous, and obscene, it does not, in our opinion, tend to promote lust. The erotic passages are submerged in the book as a whole and have little resultant effect. If these are to make the book subject to confiscation, by the same test Venus and Adonis, Hamlet, Romeo and Juliet, and the story told in the Eighth Book of the Odyssey by the bard Demodocus of how Ares and Aphrodite were entrapped in a net spread by the outraged Hephaestus amid the laughter of the immortal gods, as well as many other classics, would have to be suppressed. Indeed, it may be questioned whether the obscene passages in Romeo and Juliet were as necessary to the development of the play as those in the monologue of Mrs. Bloom are to the depiction of the latter's tortured soul.

It is unnecessary to add illustrations to show that, in the administration of statutes aimed at the suppression of immoral books, standard works of literature have not been barred merely because they contained *some* obscene passages, and that confiscation for such a reason would destroy much that is precious in order to benefit a few.

It is settled, at least so far as this court is concerned, that works of physiology, medicine, science, and sex instruction are not within the statute, though to some extent and among some persons they may tend to promote lustful thoughts. United States v. Dennett, 39 F.(2d) 564, 76 A. L. R. 1092. We think the same immunity should apply to literature as to science, where the presentation, when viewed objectively, is sincere, and the erotic matter is not introduced to promote lust and does not furnish the dominant note of the publication. The question in each case is whether a publication taken as a whole has a libidinous effect. The book before us has such portentous length, is written with such evident truthfulness in its depiction of certain types of humanity, and is so little erotic in its result, that it does not fall within the forbidden class.

In Halsey v. New York Society for Suppression of Vice, 234 N.Y. 1, 136 N. E. 219, 220, the New York Court of Appeals dealt with Mademoiselle de Maupin, by Theophile Gautier, for the sale of which the plaintiff had been prosecuted under a New York statute forbidding the sale of obscene books, upon the complaint of the defendant. After acquittal, the plaintiff sued for malicious prosecution, and a jury rendered a verdict in his favor. The Court of Appeals refused to disturb the judgment because the book had become a recognized French classic and its merits on the whole outweighed its objectionable qualities, though, as Judge Andrews said, it contained many paragraphs which, "taken by themselves," were "undoubtedly vulgar and indecent." In referring to the obscene passages, he remarked that: "No work may be judged from a selection of such paragraphs alone. Printed by themselves they might, as a matter of law, come within the prohibition of the statute. So might a similar selection from Aristophanes or Chaucer or Boccaccio, or even from the Bible. The book, however, must be considered broadly, as a whole." We think Judge Andrews was clearly right,

and that the effect of the book as a whole is the test.

In the New York Supreme Court, Judge Morgan J. O'Brien declined to prohibit a receiver from selling Arabian Nights, Rabelais, Ovid's Art of Love, the Decameron of Boccaccio, the Heptameron of Queen Margaret of Navarre, or the Confessions of Rousseau. He remarked that a rule which would exclude them would bar "a very large proportion of the works of fiction of the most famous writers of the English language." In re Worthington Co. (Sup.) 30 N. Y. S. 361, 362, 24 L. R. A. 110. The main difference between many standard works and Ulysses is its far more abundant use of coarse and colloquial words and presentation of dirty scenes, rather than in any excess of prurient suggestion. We do not think that Ulysses, taken as a whole, tends to promote lust, and its criticised passages do this no more than scores of standard books that are constantly bought and sold. Indeed a book of physiology in the hands of adolescents may be more objectionable on this ground than almost anything else.

But it is argued that United States v. Bennett, Fed. Cas. No. 14,571, stands in the way of what has been said, and it certainly does. There a court, consisting of Blatchford, C. J., and Benedict and Choate, D.JJ., held that the offending paragraphs in a book could be taken from their context and the book judged by them alone, and that the test of obscenity was whether the tendency of these passages in themselves was "to deprave the minds of those open to such influences and into whose hands a publication of this character might come." The opinion was founded upon a dictum of Cockburn, C. J., in Regina v. Hicklin, L. R. 3 Q. B. 360, where half of a book written to attack alleged practices of the confession was obscene and contained, as Mellor, J., said, "a great deal * * * which there cannot be any necessity for in any legitimate argument on the confessional. * * *" It is said that in Rosen v. United States, 161 U. S. 29, 16 S. Ct. 434, 480, 40 L. Ed. 606, the Supreme Court cited and sanctioned Regina v. Hicklin, and United States v. Bennett. The subject-matter of Rosen v. United States was, however, a pictorial representation of "females, in different attitudes of indecency." The figures were partially covered "with lamp black, that could be easily erased with a piece of bread." Page 31 of 161 U. S., 16 S. Ct. 434. The pictures were evidently obscene, and plainly came within the statute prohibiting their transportation. The citation of Regina v. Hicklin and United States v. Bennett, was in support of a ruling that allegations in the indictment as to an obscene publication need only be made with sufficient particularity to inform the accused of the nature of the charge against him. No approval of other features of the two decisions was expressed, nor were such features referred to. Dunlop v. United States, 165 U. S. 486, 489, 17 S. Ct. 375, 41 L. Ed. 799, also seems to be relied on by the government, but the publication there was admittedly obscene and the decision in no way sanctioned the rulings in United States v. Bennett which we first mentioned. The rigorous doctrines laid down in that case are inconsistent with our own decision in United States v. Bennett (C.C.A.) 39 F.(2d) 564, 76 A.L.R. 1692, as well as with Konda v. United States (C.C.A.) 166 F.91, 92, 22 L.R.A. (N.S.) 304; Clark v. United States (C.C.A.) 211 F.916; Halsey v. N.Y. Society for Suppression of Vice, 234 N.Y. 1, 4, 136 N.E. 219; and St. Hubert Guild v. Quinn, 64 Misc. 336, 339, 118 N.Y.S. 582, and, in our opinion, do not represent the law. They would exclude much of the great works of literature and involve an impracticability that cannot be imputed to Congress and would in the case of many books containing obscene passages inevitably require the court that uttered them to restrict their applicability.

It is true that the motive of an author to promote good morals is not the test of whether a book is obscene, and it may also be true that the applicability of the statute does not depend on the persons to whom a publication is likely to be distributed. The importation of obscene books is prohibited generally, and no provision is made permitting such importation because of the character of those to whom they are sold. While any construction of the statute that will fit all cases is difficult, we believe that the proper test of whether a given book is obscene is its dominant effect. In applying this test, relevancy of the objectionable parts to the theme, the established reputation of the work in the estimation of approved critics, if the book is modern, and the verdict of the past, if it is ancient, are persuasive pieces of evidence; for works of art are not likely to sustain a high position with no better warrant for their existence than their obscene content.

It may be that Ulysses will not last as a substantial contribution to literature, and it is certainly easy to believe that, in spite of the opinion of Joyce's laudators, the immortals will still reign, but the same thing may be said of current works of art and music and of many other serious efforts of the mind. Art certainly cannot advance under compulsion to traditional forms, and nothing in such a field is more stifling to progress than limitation of the right to experiment with a new technique. The foolish judgments of Lord Eldon about one hundred years ago, proscribing the works of Byron and Southey, and the finding by the jury under a charge by Lord Denman that the publication of Shelley's "Queen Mab" was an indictable offense are a warning to all who have to determine the limits of the field within which authors may exercise themselves. We think that Ulysses is a book of originality and sincerity of treatment and that it has not the effect of promoting lust. Accordingly it does not fall within the statute, even though it justly may offend many.

Decree affirmed.

MANTON, Circuit Judge.

I dissent. This libel, filed against the book Ulysses prays for a decree of forfeiture, and it is based upon the claim that the book's entry into the United States is prohibited by section 305 (a) of the Tariff Act of 1930 (19 USCA 1305 (a). On motion of appellee, the court below entered an order dismissing the libel, and the collector of customs was ordered to release the book. The motion was considered on the pleadings and a stipulation entered into by the parties.

The sole question presented is whether or not the book is obscene within section 305 (a) which provides:

"All persons are prohibited from importing into the United States from any foreign country * * * any obscene book, pamphlet, paper, writing, advertisement, circular, print, picture, drawing, or other representation, figure, or image on or of paper or other material. * * *

"Upon the appearance of any such book or matter at any customs office, the same shall be seized and held by the collector to await the judgment of the district court as hereinafter provided. * * * Upon the seizure of such book or matter the collector shall transmit information thereof to the district attorney of the district in which is situated

the office at which such seizure has taken place, who shall institute proceedings in the district court for the forfeiture, confiscation, and destruction of the book or matter seized. * * *

"In any such proceeding any party in interest may upon demand have the facts at issue determined by a jury and any party may have an appeal or the right of review as in the case of ordinary actions or suits."

The parties agreed as to the facts in the stipulation. There is no conflicting evidence; the decision to be made is dependent entirely upon the reading matter found on the objectionable pages of the book (pages 173, 213, 214, 359, 361, 423, 424, 434, 467, 488, 498, 500, 509, 522, 526, 528, 551, 719, 724-727, 731, 738, 739, 745, 746, 754-756, 761, 762, 765, Random House Edition). The book itself was the only evidence offered.

In a suit of this kind upon stipulation, the ultimate finding based solely on stipulated facts is reviewable on appeal to determine whether the facts support the finding. Lumbermen's Trust Co. v. Town of Ryegate, 61 F.(2d) 14 (C. C. A. 9); Order of United Commercial Travelers of America v. Shane, 64 F.(2d) 55 (C. C. A. 8). Moreover, the procedure in this suit in rem conforms to that obtaining in suits in admiralty (Coffey v. United States, 117 U. S. 233, 6 S. Ct. 717, 29 L. Ed. 890) where the appellate courts may review the facts. The Africa Maru, 54 F.(2d) 265 (C. C. A. 2); The Perry Setzer, 299 F.586 (C. C. A. 2).

Who can doubt the obscenity of this book after a reading of the pages referred to, which are too indecent to add as a footnote to this opinion? Its characterization as obscene should be quite unanimous by all who read it.

In the year 1868 in Regina v. Hicklin L. R., 3 Q. B. 359, at page 369, Cockburn C. J., stated that "the test of obscenity is this, whether the tendency of the matter charged as obscenity is to deprave and corrupt those whose minds are open to such immoral influences, and into whose hands a publication of this sort may fall."

In 1879, in United States v. Bennett, Fed. Cas. No. 14,571 Judge Blatchford, later a justice of the Supreme Court, in this circuit, sitting with Judges Choate and Benedict, approved the rule of the Hicklin Case and held a charge to a jury proper which embodied the test of that case. The Bennett Case clearly holds the test of obscenity, within the meaning of the statute, is "whether the tendency of the matter is to deprave and corrupt the morals of those whose minds are open to such influences, and into whose hands a publication of this sort may fall." The court held that the object of the use of the obscene words was not a subject for consideration.

Judge Blatchford's decision met with approval in Rosen v. United States, 151 U. S. 29, 16 S. Ct. 434, 438, 480, 40 L. Ed. 606. The court had under consideration an indictment charging the accused with depositing obscene literature in the mails. There instructions to the jury requested that conviction could not be had although the defendant may have had knowledge or notice of the contents of the letter "unless he knew or believed that such paper could be properly or justly characterized as obscene, lewd, and lascivious." The court said the statute was not to be so interpreted. "The inquiry under the statute is whether the paper charged to have been obscene, lewd, and lascivious was in fact of that character; and if it was of that character, and was deposited in the mail by one who knew or had notice at the time of its contents, the offense is complete, although the defendant himself did not regard the paper as one that the statute forbade to be carried in the mails. Congress did not intend that the question as to the character of the paper should depend upon the opinion or belief of the person who, with knowledge or notice of its contents, assumed the responsibility of putting it in the mails of the United States. The evils that congress sought to remedy would continue and increase in volume if the belief of the accused as to what was obscene, lewd, and lascivious were recognized as the test for determining whether the statute has been violated. Every one who uses the mails of the United States for carrying papers or publications must take notice of what, in this enlightened age, is meant by decency, purity, and chastity in social life, and what must be deemed obscene, lewd, and lascivious."

Further the Supreme Court approved the test of the Hicklin Case. On page 43 of 151 U. S., 16 S. Ct. 434, 439, the court states: "That was what the court did when it charged the jury that 'the test of obscenity is whether the tendency of the matter is to deprave and corrupt the morals of those whose minds are open to such influence, and into whose hands a publication of this sort may fall.' 'Would it,' the court said, 'suggest or convey lewd thoughts and lascivious thoughts to the young and inexperienced?' In view of the character of the paper, as an inspection of it will instantly disclose, the test prescribed for the jury was quite as liberal as the defendant had any right to demand."

Again the Supreme Court in Dunlop v. United States, 165 U. S. 486, 17 S. Ct. 375, 380, 41 L. Ed. 799, reviewed a charge in a criminal case upon the subject of obscene publications as follows: "Now, what is (are) obscene, lascivious, lewd, or indecent publications is largely a question of your own conscience and your own opinion; but it must come—before it can be said of such literature or publication—it must come up to this point: that it must be calculated with the ordinary reader to deprave him, deprave his morals, or lead to impure purposes. * * * It is your duty to ascertain, in the first place, if they are calculated to deprave the morals; if they are calculated to lower that standard which we regard as essential to civilization; if they are calculated to excite those feelings which, in their proper field, are all right, but which, transcending the limits of that proper field, play most of the mischief in the world."

In approving the charge, the court said: "The alleged obscene and indecent matter consisted of advertisements by women, soliciting or offering inducements for the visits of men, usually 'refined gentlemen,' to their rooms, sometimes under the disguise of 'Baths' and 'Massage,' and oftener for the mere purpose of acquaintance. It was in this connection that the court charged the jury that, if the publications were such as were calculated to deprave the morals, they were within the statute. There could have been no possible misapprehension on their part as to what was meant. There was no question as to depraving the morals in any other direction than that of impure sexual relations. The words were used by the court in their ordinary signification, and were made more definite by the context and by the character of the publications which have been put in evidence. The court left to the jury to say whether it was within the statute, and whether persons of ordinary intelligence would have any difficulty of divining the intention of the advertiser."

Thus the court sustained a charge having a test as to whether or no the publications depraved the morals of the ordinary reader or tended to lower the standards of civilization. The tendency of the matter to deprave and corrupt the morals of those whose minds are open to such influence and into whose hands the publication of this sort may fall, has become the test thoroughly entrenched in the federal courts. United States v. Bebout (D. C.) 28 F. 522; United States v. Wightman (D. C.) 29 F. 636; United States v. Clarke (D. C.) 38 F. 732; United States v. Smith (D. C.) 45 F. 476; Burton v. United States, 142 F. 57 (C. C. A. 8); United States v. Dennett, 39 F.(2d) 564, 76 A. L. R. 1092 (C. C. A. 2). What is the probable effect on the sense of decency of society, extending to the family made up of men, women, young boys, and girls, was said to be the test in United States v. Harmon (D. C.) 45 F.414, 417.

Ulysses is a work of fiction. It may not be compared with books involving medical subjects or description of certain physical or biological facts. It is written for alleged amusement of the reader only. The characters described in the thoughts of the author may in some instances be true, but, be it truthful or otherwise, a book that is obscene is not rendered less so by the statement of truthful fact. Burton v. United States, supra. It cannot be said that the test above has been rejected by United States v. Dennett (C. C. A.) 39 F.(2d) 564, 76 A. L. R. 1092, nor can that case be taken to mean that the book is to be judged as a whole. If anything, the case clearly recognizes that the book may be obscene because portions thereof are so, for pains are taken to justify and show not to be obscene portions to which objection is made. The gist of the holding is that a book is not to be declared obscene if it is "an accurate exposition of the relevant facts of the sex side of life in decent language and in manifestly serious and disinterested spirit." A work of obvious benefit to the community was never intended to be within the purview of the statute. No matter what may be said on the side of letters, the effect on the community can and must be the sole determining factor. "Laws of this character are made for society in the aggregate, and not in particular. So, while there may be individuals and societies of men and women of peculiar notions or idiosyncrasies, whose moral sense would neither be depraved nor offended, * * * yet the exceptional sensibility, or want of sensibility, of such cannot be allowed as a standard." United States v. Harmon, supra.

In United States v. Kennerley (D.C.) 209 F.119, the Bennett Case was followed despite the dictum objecting to a test which protected the "salacious" few. By the very argument used, to destroy a test which protects those most easily influenced, we can discard a test which would protect only the interests of the other comparatively small groups of society. If we disregard the protection of the morals of the susceptible, are we to consider merely the benefits and pleasures derived from letters by those who pose as the more highly developed and intelligent? To do so would show an utter disregard for the standards of decency of the community as a whole and an utter disregard for the effect of a book upon the average less sophisticated member of society, not to mention the adolescent. The court cannot indulge any instinct it may have to foster letters. The statute is designed to protect society at large, of that there can be no dispute; notwithstanding the deprivation of benefits to a few, a work must be condemned if it has a depraving influence.

And are we to refuse to enforce the statute Congress has enacted because of the argument that obscenity is only the superstition of the day—the modern counterpart of ancient witchcraft"? Are we to be persuaded by the statement, set forth in the brief, made by the judge below in an interview with the press, "Education, not law, must solve problems of taste and choice (of books)," when the statute is clear and our duty plain?

The prevailing opinion states that classics would be excluded if the application of the statute here argued for prevailed. But the statute, Tariff Act 1930, § 305 (a), 19 USCA § 1305 (a), provides as to classics that they may be introduced into the commerce of the United States provided "that the Secretary of the Treasury * * * in his discretion, admit the so-called classics or books of recognized and established literary or scientific merit, but may, in his discretion, admit such classics or books only when imported for non-commercial purposes." The right to admission under this proviso was not sought nor is it justified by reason thereof in the prevailing opinion.

Congress passed this statute against obscenity for the protection of the great mass of our people; the unusual literator can, or thinks he can, protect himself. The people do not exist for the sake of literature, to give the author fame, the publisher wealth, and the book a market. On the contrary, literature exists for the sake of the people, to refresh the weary, to console the sad, to hearten the dull and downcast, to increase man's interest in the world, his joy of living, and his sympathy in all sorts and conditions of men. Art for art's sake is heartless and soon grows artless; art for the public market is not art at all, but commerce; art for the people's service is a noble, vital, and permanent element of human life.

The public is content with the standard of salability; the prigs with the standard of preciosity. The people need and deserve a moral standard; it should be a point of honor with men of letters to maintain it. Masterpieces have never been produced by men given to obscenity or lustful thoughts—men who have no Master. Reverence for good work is the foundation of literary character. A refusal to initiate obscenity or to load a book with it is an author's professional chastity.

Good work in literature has its permanent mark; it is like all good work, noble and lasting. It requires a human aim—to cheer, console, purify, or ennoble the life of people. Without this aim, literature has never sent an arrow close to the mark. It is by good work only that men of letters can justify their right to a place in the world.

Under the authoritative decisions and considering the substance involved in this appeal, it is my opinion that the decree should be reversed.

THE FIRST LADY CHATTERLEY IS "CLEARLY OBSCENE"

People v. Dial Press, 48 N.Y.S.2d 480 (1944)

CHARLES G. KEUTGEN, City Magistrate.

The complaint in this case charges the defendant corporation, the Dial Press, Incorporated, with publishing and having in its possession with intent to sell an obscene book entitled "The First Lady Chatterly" by D. H. Lawrence.

The defendant demanded a hearing in this court. At the hearing, it was proved by sufficient evidence that the defendant had a considerable number of copies of the book in its possession with intent to sell and the defendant admitted that it published this book. A copy of the book was received in evidence.

The statute which the defendant is accused of violating, Section 1141 of the Penal Law, is of complex verbiage. So much of it as is necessary for the decision in this case is as follows:

"1. A person who * * * has in his possession with intent to sell * * * any obscene, lewd, lascivious, filthy, indecent or disgusting book * * * or who * * * publishes * * * any such book * * *

"Is guilty of a misdemeanor."

In the application of this statute, the People contend that I may not resort to the statement of the rule given by the U. S. Circuit Court of Appeals in the Second Circuit for the reason that the case which that court was dealing with came under the Customs Law, Tariff Act 1930. § 305(a), 19 U.S.C.A. § 1305(a), which forbade the importation of an obscene book without using the other words quoted.

I have plodded through the definitions in two dictionaries of the several words used and I have come to the conclusion that each of these words is synonomous with the others and that the real intent and meaning of each of these words and all of them is that the ban is against the publication of a book which contravenes the moral law and which tends to subvert respect for decency and morality. I am therefore guided by the rule as stated in United States v. One Book Entitled Ulysses by James Joyce, 2 Cir., 72 F.2d 705, and I feel authorized to accept that rule, more particularly because the courts of the State of New York, in making decisions, have acted upon that rule, although they have not said the rule in so many words. I refer particularly to: People v. Pesky, 230 App.Div. 200, 243 N.Y.S. 193, affirmed 254 N.Y. 373, 173 N.E. 227; People v. Berg, 241 App.Div. 543, 272 N.Y.S. 586, affirmed 269 N.Y. 514, 199 N.E. 513.

The rule that I gather from these cases is that the whole book must be read and that upon the reading of the entire book, the question to be answered is whether or not the effect of the whole volume is obscene, that is, contrary to the moral law and tending to subvert respect for decency and morality.

The defendant has contended that the literary merit of the particular volume may be considered. For several reasons, it seems to me that the literary merit or demerit of the volume cannot be the criterion. Judges are not trained to be, nor are they, competent literary critics. If judgment in such a case as this will depend upon the determination of the author's skill as a writer, the judicial officer responsible for the enforcement of the statute would have to surrender his own judgment and base his opinion on the opinions of experts who have no responsibility in the premises. More than this, it is easy to imagine a book, let us say, by another Oscar Wilde, clever, scintillating, even brilliant in its writing and utterly foul and disgusting in its central theme and dominating effect.

Considering the book which is here before the court, as a whole, it purports to tell a story. The scene is laid in the English Midlands within an hour by auto of Sheffield. The period is 1920 to 1921 and the time in which the story runs is less than a year, from the late fall of 1920 to the pheasant season of 1921.

The author's own summary of the situation of his heroine, Lady Constance Chatterly, cannot be improved upon in respect to brevity and therefore is quoted—this is taken from page three of the volume:

"She married Clifford Chatterly in 1917 when he was home on leave. They had a month of honeymoon, and he went back to France. In 1918, he was very badly wounded, brought home a wreck. She was 23 years old.

"After two years, he was restored to comparative health. But the lower part of his body was paralyzed forever."

And further on page six:

"He could never be a husband to her. She lived with him like a married nun, a sister of Christ. It was more than that, too. For of course, they had had a month of real marriage. And Clifford knew that in her nature was a heavy, craving physical desire. He knew."

There follows what cannot be called a love story without distorting that term. The author proceeds to recount a series of acts of sexual intercourse which take place between the heroine and her husband's gamekeeper, one Oliver Parkin, which result in the lady's becoming pregnant. The story ends at the point where she is three months pregnant and is making up her mind to leave her husband and flee to the physical delights of life with Parkin. Hung lightly over this story, like the diaphanous veil over the naked body of a dancer, there are certain dialogues between Constance and Parkin regarding the difference in social caste between them. These are of minor importance. They call attention only to the one thing which restrains the heroine from going to live with Parkin earlier, the thought that she will have to give up the luxury of her husband's home. No moral considerations whatever enter into her thinking and she repeatedly proclaims that she is proud of what she is doing.

The author's central theme and the dominant effect of the whole book is that it is dangerous to the physical and mental health of a young woman to remain continent (pp. 12, 22, 23, 24, 26, 27, 32, 33, 35, 36) and that the most important thing in her life, more important than any rule of law or morals, is the gratification of her sexual desire (pp. 191 to 193, and the last paragraph, page 320).

The book is clearly obscene and the defendant will be held for the Court of Special Sessions.

STRANGE FRUIT IS DECLARED OBSCENE IN MASSACHUSETTS

Commonwealth v. Isenstadt, 62 N.E.2d 840 (1945)

QUA, Justice.

The defendant has been found guilty by a judge of the Superior Court sitting without jury upon two complaints charging him respectively with selling and with having in his possession for the purpose of sale, exhibition, loan, or circulation a book published under the title "Strange Fruit," which is "obscene, indecent, or impure, or manifestly tends to corrupt the morals of youth." G.L.(Ter.Ed.) c. 272, §28, as amended by St.1934, c. 231, and St.1943, c. 239. The section (except the part describing the penalty) is reproduced in the footnote.[1]

The complaints are in disjunctive form, but this point was not taken. The defendant could therefore be convicted if he committed any one of the several offenses set forth in so far as such offenses are susceptible of differentiation. G.L.(Ter.Ed.) c. 278, §17. Commonwealth v. McKnight, 283 Mass. 35, 38, 39, 186 N.E. 42; Commonwealth v. McMenimon, 295 Mass. 467, 470, 471, 4 N.E.2d 246.

We do not pretend ignorance of the controversy which has been carried on in this Commonwealth, sometimes with vehemence, over so called "literary censorship."[2] With this background in mind it may not be out of place to recall that it is not our function to assume a "liberal" attitude or a "conservative" attitude. As in other cases of statutory construction and application, it is our plain but not necessarily easy duty to read the words of the statute in the sense in which they were intended, to accept and enforce the public policy of the Commonwealth as disclosed by its policymaking body, whatever our own personal opinions may be, and to avoid judicial legislation in the guise of new constructions to meet real or supposed new popular viewpoints, preserving always to the Legislature alone its proper prerogative of adjusting the statutes to changed conditions.

We are fully aware of the uselessness of all interpretations of the crucial words of this statute which merely define each of those words by means of the others or of still other words of practically the same signification. We do not now attempt by any single formula to furnish a test for all types of publications, including scientific and medical treatises, religious and educational works, newspapers and periodicals, and classical and recent literature, as well as phonograph records, prints, pictures, paintings, images, statuary and sculpture, artistic or otherwise, all of which are within the literal words of the statute and might conceivably fall within its prohibitions. In this case we are dealing with a recent work of fiction—a novel. We shall, in general, confine our observations to the case in hand, without necessarily binding ourselves to apply all that is here said to entirely different forms of writing or to representations by picture or image.

We deal first with a number of pertinent propositions advanced in the able briefs filed in behalf of the defendant. We agree with some of them.

(1) We agree that since the amendment of the section as it appeared in the General Laws by St.1930, c. 162, the book is to be treated as a whole in determining whether it violates the statute.[3] It is not to be condemned merely because it may contain somewhere between its covers some expressions which, taken by themselves alone, might be obnoxious to the statute. Halsey v. New York Soc. for Suppression of Vice, 234 N.Y. 1, 4, 136 N.E. 219; United States v. One Book Entitled "Ulysses", 2 Cir., 72 F.2d 705, 707. United States v. Levine, 2 Cir., 83 F.2d 156. But this does not mean that every page of the book must be of the character described in the statute before the statute can apply to the book. It could never have been intended that obscene matter should escape proscription simply by joining to itself some innocent matter. A reasonable construction can be attained only by saying that the book is within the statute if it contains prohibited matter in such quantity or of such nature as to flavor the whole and impart to the whole any of the qualities mentioned in the statute, so that the book as a whole can fairly be described by any of the adjectives or descriptive expressions contained in the statute. The problem is to be solved, not by counting pages, but rather by considering the impressions likely to be created. For example, a book might be found to come within the prohibition of the statute although only a comparatively few passages contained matter objectionable according to the principles herein explained if that matter were such as to offer a strong salacious appeal and to cause the book to be bought and read on account of it.

(2) We agree with the weight of authority that under each of the prohibitions contained in the statute the test of unlawfulness is to be found in the effect of the book upon its probable readers and not in any classification of its subject matter or of its words as being in themselves innocent or obscene.[4] A book is "obscene, indecent or impure" within the statutory prohibition if it has a substantial tendency to deprave or corrupt its readers by inciting lascivious thoughts or arousing lustful desire. It also violates the statute if it "manifestly tends to corrupt the morals of youth." The latter prohibition is expressly limited to the kind of effect specified—the corruption of morals. Under this branch of the statute it is not enough that a book may tend to coarsen or vulgarize youth if it does not manifestly tend to corrupt the morals of youth. People v. Wendling, 258 N.Y. 451, 453, 180 N.E. 169, 81 A.L.R. 799.

Although in their broadest meaning the statutory words "Obscene, indecent or impure" might signify offensive to refinement, propriety and good taste, we are convinced that the Legislature did not intend by those words to set up any standard merely of taste, even if under the Constitution it could do so. Taste depends upon convention, and sometimes upon irrational taboo. It varies "with the period, the place, and the training, environment and characteristics of persons." Reddington v. Reddington, 317 Mass. 760, 765, 59 N.E.2d 775, 778. A penal statute requiring conformity to some current standard of propriety defined only by the statutory words quoted above would make the standard an uncertain one, shifting with every new judge or jury. It would be like a statute penalizing a citizen for failing to act in every situation in a gentlemanly manner. Such a statute would be unworkable if not unconstitutional, for in effect it would "[license] the jury to create its own standard in each case," ex post facto. Herndon v. Lowry, 301 U.S. 242, 263, 57 S.Ct. 732, 741, 81 L.Ed. 1066. Such a test must be rejected. The prohibitions of the statute are concerned with sex and sexual desire. The statute does not forbid realistically coarse scenes or vulgar words merely because they are coarse or vulgar, although such scenes or words may be considered so far as they bear upon the test already stated of the effect of the book upon its readers.

(3) Since effect is the test, it follows that a book is to be judged in the light of the customs and habits of thought of the time and place of the alleged offence. Although the fundamentals of human nature change but slowly, if indeed they change at all, customs and habits of thought do vary with time and place. That which may give rise to impure thought and action in a highly conventional society may pass almost unnoticed in a society habituated to greater freedom. United States v. Kennerly, D.C., 209 F. 119, 121; Parmelee v. United States, 72 App.D.C. 203, 113 F.2d 729, 731, 732. To recognize this is not to change the law. It is merely to acknowledge the facts upon which the application of the law has always depended. And of the operation of this principle it would seem that a jury of the time and place, representing a cross section of the people, both old and young, should commonly be a suitable arbiter. United States v. Clarke, D.C., 38 F. 500; United States v. Kennerly, D.C., 209 F. 119, 121.

(4) So, too, we think it proper to take into account what we may call the probable "audience" of the book, just as the effect of a lecture might depend in large degree upon the character of those to whom it is addressed. At one extreme may be placed a highly technical medical work, sold at a great price and advertised only among physicians. At the other extreme may be placed a rather well known type of the grossest pornography obviously prepared for persons of low standards and generally intended for juvenile consumption and distributed where it is most likely to reach juvenile eyes. Most questioned books will fall between these extremes. Moreover, the statute was designed for the protection of the public as a whole. Putting aside for the moment the reference in the statute itself to that which manifestly tends to corrupt the morals of youth, a book placed in general circulation is not to be condemned merely because it might have an unfortunate effect upon some few members of the community who might be peculiarly susceptible. The statute is to be construed reasonably. The fundamental right of the public to read is not to be trimmed down to the point where a few prurient persons can find nothing upon which their hypersensitive imaginations may dwell. United States v. Kennerly, D.C., 209 F. 119, 120. The thing to be considered is whether the book will be appreciably injurious to society in the respects previously stated because of its effect upon those who read it, without segregating either the most susceptible or the least susceptible, remembering that many persons who form

part of the reading public and who cannot be called abnormal are highly susceptible to influences of the kind in question and that most persons are susceptible to some degree, and without forgetting youth as an important part of the mass, if the book is likely to be read by youth. United States v. Harmon, D.C., 45 F. 414, 417; United States v. Levine, 2 Cir., 83 F.2d 156; Parmelee v. United States, 72 App. D.C. 203, 113 F.2d 729, 731. The jury must ask themselves whether the book will in some appreciable measure do the harm the legislature intended to prevent. This is not a matter of mathematics. The answer cannot be found by saying, for example, that only about one third of probable readers would be adversely affected and then classifying that one third as "abnormal" and concluding that as the book does not adversely affect "normal" persons it is not within the statute. A book that adversely affects a substantial proportion of its readers may well be found to lower appreciably the average moral tone of the mass in the respects hereinbefore described and to fall within the intended prohibition.[5] It seems to us that the statute cannot be construed as meaning less than this without impairing its capacity to give the protection to society which the legislature intended it should give.

(5) We cannot accept the proposition which seems to have been accorded hospitality in a few of the more recent cases in another jurisdiction and which perhaps has been suggested rather than argued in the present case, to wit, that even a work of fiction, taken as a whole, cannot be obscene, indecent or impure if it is written with a sincere and lawful purpose and possesses artistic merit, and if sincerity and artistry are more prominent features of the book than obscenity.[6] In dealing with such a practical matter as the enforcement of the statute here involved there is no room for the pleasing fancy that sincerity and art necessarily dispel obscenity. The purpose of the statute is to protect the public from that which is harmful. The public must be taken as it is. The mass of the public may have no very serious interest in that which has motivated the author, and it can seldom be said that the great majority of the people will be so rapt in admiration of the artistry of a work as to overlook its salacious appeal. Sincerity and literary art are not the antitheses of obscenity, indecency, and impurity in such manner that one set of qualities can be set off against the other and judgment rendered according to an imaginary balance supposed to be left over on one side or the other. The same book may be characterized by all of these qualities. Indeed, obscenity may sometimes be made even more alluring and suggestive by the zeal which comes from sincerity and by the added force of artistic presentation. We are not sure that it would be impossible to produce even a serious treatise on gynecology in such a manner as to make it obscene. Certainly a novel can be so written. even though the thoughtful reader can also find in it a serious message. Sincerity and art can flourish without pornography, and seldom, if ever, will obscenity be needed to carry the lesson. See United States v. Kennerly, D.C., 209 F. 119, 120, 121; United States v. Dennett, 2 Cir., 19 F.2d 564, 569, 76 A.L.R. 1092. The statute contains no exception of works of sincerity and art, or of works in which those elements predominate, if the proscribed elements predominate, if the proscribed elements are also present in such manner and degree as to remain characteristic of the book as a whole. If it is thought that modern conditions require that such an exception be

made, the Legislature and not this court should make it. This subject was the principal point of the decision in Commonwealth v. Buckley, 200 Mass. 346, 86 N.E. 910, 22 L.R.A.,N.S., 225, 128 Am.St.Rep. 425, where apt illustration is used. We adhere to the reasoning of that case. See furhter, Commonwealth v. Friede, 271 Mass. 318, 322, 323, 171 N.E. 472, 69 A.L.R. 640; Halsey v. New York Soc. for Suppression of Vice, 234 N.Y. 1, 6, 136 N.E. 219; and People v. Pesky, 230 App.Div. 200, 243 N.Y.S. 193, citing Commonwealth v. Buckley, supra.

In taking this position, to which we believe ourselves compelled by the words of the statute, the necessity of enforcing it to accomplish its purposes, and our own previous construction of it, we do not go so far as to say that sincerity of purpose and literary merit are to be entirely ignored. These elements may be considered in so far as they bear upon the question whether the book, considered as a whole, is or is not obscene, indecent, or impure. It is possible that, even in the mind of the general reader, overpowering sincerity and beauty may sometimes entirely obscure or efface the evil effect of occasional questionable passages, especially with respect to the classics of literature that have gained recognized place as part of the great heritage of humanity. The question will commonly be one of fact in each case, and if, looking at the book as a whole, the bad is found to persist in substantial degree alongside the good, as the law now stands, the book will fall within the statute.

A brief description of the book "Strange Fruit" now seems necessary. The scene is laid in a small town in Georgia. A white boy, Tracy Dean, who lacks the forcefulness to get ahead in the world, and an educated but compliant colored girl, Nonnie Anderson, fall genuinely in love, but because of race inhibitions and pressures they cannot marry. Nonnie supplies to Tracy the sympathy and the nourishment of his self-esteem which his other associations deny him. Illicit intercourse occurs, resulting in pregnancy. Tragedy follows in the form of the murder of Tracy committed by Nonnie's outraged brother and the lynching of an innocent colored man for that crime. Distributed through this book (consisting of two hundred fifty pages in the edition submitted with the record) are four scenes of sexual intercourse, including one supposed to have been imagined. The immediate approaches to these acts and the descriptions of the acts themselves vary in length from a few lines to several pages. They differ in the degree of their suggestiveness. Two of them might be thought highly emotional, with strongly erotic connotations. In addition to these there is a fifth scene in an old abandoned cabin in which there are amatory attitudes, kissing, a loosened blouse, exposed breasts, and circumstances suggesting but perhaps not necessarily requiring an act of intercourse. In still another scene Tracy in a confused drunken frenzy "saw somebody" (himself) tear off Nonnie's clothes "until there was nothing between his hands and her body," "press her down against the floor," "press her body hard—saw him try and fail, try and fail, try and fail," but he "couldn't." In addition to the scenes just mentioned there are distributed fairly evenly throughout the book approximately fifty instances where the author introduces into the story such episodes as indecent assaults upon little girls, an instance of, and a soliloquy upon, masturbation by boys, and references to acts of excretion, to "bobbing" or "pointed" breasts, to "nice little rumps, hard * * *

light, bouncy * * *", to a group of little girls "giggling mightily" upon discovering a boy behind a bush and looking at his "bared genitals." We need not recite more of these. The instances mentioned will indicate the general character of the others. Some of these minor incidents might be dismissed as of little or no consequence if there were fewer of them, but when they occur on an average on every fifth page from beginning to end of the book it would seem that a jury or a judge performing the function of a jury might find that they had a strong tendency to maintain a salacious interest in the reader's mind and to whet his appetite for the next major episode.

The principal question in the case is whether, consistently with the principles hereinbefore stated, we can say as matter of law that an honest jury, or an honest trial judge taking the place of a jury with the consent of the defendant, as in this case, would not be acting as reasonable men in concluding beyond a reasonable doubt that this book, taken as a whole, possesses the qualities of obscenity, indecency, or impurity. The test is not what we ourselves think of the book, but what in our best judgment a trier of the facts might think of it without going beyond the bounds of honesty and reason. This distinction, difficult for laymen to grasp, is familiar enough to all lawyers. It is constantly applied by appellate courts and must be preserved if jury trial is to be preserved.

It is urged that this book was written with a serious purpose; that its theme is a legitimate one; that it possesses great literary merit; and that it has met with a generally favorable reception by reviewers and the reading public. We agree that it is a serious work. It brings out in bold relief the depth and the complexity of the race problem in the South, although, so far as we can see, it offers no remedy. We agree that the theme of a love which because of social conditions and conventions cannot be sanctioned by marriage and which leads to illicit relations is a permissible theme. That such a theme can be handled with power and realism without obscenity seems sufficiently demonstrated in George Eliot's "Adam Bede," which we believe is universally recognized as an English classic. We assume that the book before us is a work of literary merit. We are also prepared to assume for the purposes of this opinion that it has been favorably received by reviewers generally and widely sold to the public, although we do not find it necessary to decide whether the opinions of reviewers and the extent of sale are such well known facts that we ought to take judicial notice of them, if the result of the case depended upon our doing so. We hold, however, that the matters mentioned in this paragraph are not decisive of the issue before us.

Regarding the book as a whole, it is our opinion that a jury of honest and reasonable men could find beyond a reasonable doubt that it contains much that, even in this post-Victorian era, would tend to promote lascivious thoughts and to arouse lustful desire in the minds of substantial numbers of that public into whose hands this book, obviously intended for general sale, is likely to fall; that the matter which could be found objectionable is not necessary to convey any sincere message the book may contain and is of such character and so pervades the work as to give to the whole a sensual and licentious quality calculated to produce the harm which the statute was intended to prevent; and that that quality could be found to persist notwithstanding any literary or artistic merit. We are therefore of opinion that the book could be found to be obscene, indecent, and impure within the meaning of the statute. We think that not only the legislators of 1835 who inserted the substance of the present wording in the statute but also the legislators of later years down to 1943 who amended the statute without greatly altering its substance would be surprised to learn that this court had held that a jury or a judge trying the facts could not even consider whether a book which answers the description already given of "Strange Fruit" falls within the statute.

For the same reasons we are of opinion that an honest and reasonable judge or jury could find beyond a reasonable doubt that this book "manifestly tends to corrupt the morals of youth." The statute does not make fitness for juvenile reading the test for all literature regardless of its object and of the manner of its distribution. Yet it cannot be supposed that the Legislature intended to give youth less protection than that given to the community as a whole by the general proscription of that which is "obscene, indecent or impure." Rather it would seem that something in the nature of additional protection of youth was intended by proscribing anything that manifestly tends to corrupt the morals of youth, even though it may not be obscene, indecent, or impure in the more general sense. At any rate, we think that almost any novel that is obscene, indecent or impure in the general sense also "manifestly tends to corrupt the morals of youth," if it is likely to fall into the hands of youth. The judge could find that the book in question would be read by many youths. Many adolescents are avid readers of novels.

It is contended that the conviction of the defendant violates the Fourteenth Amendment to the Constitution of the United States. See Near v. State of Minnesota, 283 U.S. 697, 707, 51 S.Ct. 625, 75 L.Ed. 1357; De Jonge v. State of Oregon, 299 U.S. 353, 364, 57 S.Ct. 255, 81 L.Ed. 278. If, however, we are right in holding that an honest and reasonable jury could have found the defendant guilty, it seems to us that no substantial constitutional question remains. The State must have power to protect its citizens, and especially its youth, against obscenity in its various forms, including that which is written or printed. Statutes to this end have long existed. The distribution of obscene printed matter was a crime at common law. Commonwealth v. Holmes, 17 Mass. 336. Our own statute was held constitutional in Commonwealth v. Allison, 227 Mass. 57, 62, 116 N.E. 265, 266, where this court said. "The subject-matter is well within one of the most obvious and necessary branches of the police power of the state." State v. McKee, 73 Conn., 18, 45 A. 409, 49 L.R.A. 542, 84 Am.St.Rep. 124. In Near v. Minnesota, 283 U.S. 697, at page 716, 51 S.Ct. 625, at page 631, 75 L.Ed. 1357, Chief Justice Hughes, after asserting the right of Government in time of war to prevent the publication of the sailing dates of transports or of the number and location of troops, added this, "On similar grounds, the primary requirements of decency may be enforced against obscene publications." See Gitlow v. People of State of New York, 268 U.S. 652, 667, 45 S.Ct. 625, 69 L.Ed. 1138; Fox v. State of Washington, 236 U.S. 273, 35 S.Ct. 383, 59 L.Ed. 573. And in Chaplinsky v. State of New Hampshire, 315 U.S. 568, at pages 571, 572, 62 S.Ct. 766, at page 769. 86 L.Ed. 1031, the court said that the use of certain well defined and narrowly limited classes of speech, including "the lewd and obscene" may be prevented and punished. If the so called "clear and

present danger" doctrine enunciated in such cases as Schenck v. United States, 249 U.S. 47, 52, 39 S.Ct. 247, 249, 63 L.Ed. 470; Herndon v. Lowry, 301 U.S. 242, 57 S.Ct. 732, 81 L.Ed. 1066; Bridges v. State of California, 314 U.S. 252, 62 S.Ct. 190, 86 L.Ed. 192, and Thomas v. Collins, 323 U.S. 516, 65 S.Ct. 315, applies to cases like the present, it would seem that danger of corruption of the public mind is a sufficient danger, and that actual publication and sale render that danger sufficiently imminent to satisfy the doctrine.

The defendant complains of the exclusion of testimony offered by him through three witnesses—a writer and teacher of literature, a child psychiatrist, and a professor of theology who was the editor of "Zion's Herald" and who had also been pastor of a church, had taught in a junior college and had been director of a boy's camp—tending to show as matter of expert opinion that the book was sincerely written; that it would elevate rather than corrupt morals; that it would not create lustful or lecherous desires in any one; that it is "perfectly consistent with the regular flow of literature now publicly sold in the Commonwealth * * *"; and that books containing material more likely to corrupt the morals of youth are sold daily without prosecution.

We cannot regard this exclusion as error. The principal matter about which expert opinion was sought was nothing more than the reaction of normal human beings to a kind of stimulation which is well within the experience of all mankind. Since the inquiry relates to the probable effect upon the general public who may read the book, there is reason to believe that a jury, being composed of men drawn from the various segments of that public, would be as good a judge of the effect as experts in literature or psychiatry, whose points of view and mental reactions in such matters are likely to be entirely different from those of the general public. If expert testimony is to be admitted in this instance it is difficult to see why it would not likewise be competent in a vast number of civil and criminal cases where issues of fact depend upon the emotions and reactions of normal persons in the conditions to which they are exposed. If such evidence becomes competent it will follow that an immense number of cases now submitted without hesitation to the good sense of juries and of trial judges performing the functions of juries cannot be adequately tried without an expensive array of experts on both sides. Experience in those fields in which expert testimony is now admittedly necessary does not lead us to look with favor upon such a sweeping extension. Without prejudging the indefinite future, we are not convinced that the time has come for it. In this we agree with People v. Muller, 96 N.Y. 408, 48 Am.Rep. 635, and St. Hubert Guild v. Quinn, 64 Misc. 336, 341, 342, 118 N.Y.S. 582. See Commonwealth v. Buckley, 200 Mass. 346, 352, 86 N.E. 910, 22 L.R.A.,N.S., 225, 128 Am.St.Rep. 425; United States v. Harmon, D.C., 45 F. 414, 418. Compare Parmelee v. United States, 72 App.D.C. 203, 113 F.2d 729, 732. In so far as the excluded evidence was expected to show that other books of the same kind, or worse, were being sold without prosecution it was obviously incompetent. Commonwealth v. Buckley, 200 Mass. 346, 349, 350, 351, 354, 86 N.E. 910, 22 L.R.A.,N.S., 225, 128 Am.St.Rep. 425 (request 26). See Commonwealth v. Friede, 271 Mass. 318, 322, 171 N.E. 472, 69 A.L.R. 640.

What has already been said covers all of the defendant's

requests for rulings that were refused, excepting numbers fourteen and sixteen. Request fourteen was rightly refused on the ground stated by the judge that it makes the effect upon youth the sole test of applicability of the statute. Request sixteen asked the judge "as a matter of law" to "take into consideration the attitude of the community in accepting or rejecting the book. * * * ." Since there was no evidence bearing upon the "attitude of the community," this seems to be a request that the judge take judicial notice of that "attitude." We do not feel called upon to prolong this opinion by entering upon a discussion as to whether "attitude of the community" in any of its possible aspects might have any bearing upon any of the issues before the judge. Some courts seem to have favored the taking of judicial notice of literary reviews and criticisms. Halsey v. New York Soc. for Suppression of Vice, 234 N.Y. 1, 136 N.E. 219; United States v. One Book Entitled "Ulysses", 2 Cir., 72 F.2d 705, 708. In one case it was said that published reviews of qualified critics might reasonably be allowed "in evidence," which was said to be "quite another thing * * * from expert witnesses at the trial." United States v. Levine, 2 Cir., 83 F.2d 156, 158. Whether these decisions are consistent with our own rules, we need not determine. Neither need we determine whether the views of literary critics show the "attitude of the community" or merely that of a very specialized part of the community, or whether they bear upon anything more than the literary value of the work. For purposes of the present case we are satisfied that the defendant could not compel the judge to commit himself to a ruling upon such vague and sweeping generalities as "attitude of the community" and "accepting or rejecting the book." These seem to us to be composite conclusions which, if they could have been determined at all, could have been determined only by weighing subsidiary facts, some of which might perhaps be susceptible of judicial notice and others of which might well require proof by competent evidence. We cannot say that at the time of the trial the generalization, "attitude of the community in accepting or rejecting" this new book, had become in any aspect an established fact so notorious and indisputable that the judge could be compelled against his own judgment to ascertain it without evidence. Wigmore on Evidence, 3d Ed., §§ 2568, 2568a.

In closing this opinion it is proper to call attention to St.1945, c. 278, which is to take effect October 1, 1945, and which makes substantial changes in the law and adds a new procedure directed against the book itself by which a judicial determination can be had whether or not a book is obscene, indecent, or impure. This statute should go far to remedy complaints that the present law has operated unjustly in that sales people or clerks in stores may be convicted for selling a book when the seller does not know and perhaps as a practical matter cannot know whether or not he is violating the law.

Exceptions overruled.

LUMMUS, Justice (dissenting).

The opinion seems to me to construe the statute rightly. My dissent is only from the conclusion that the evidence warranted a finding of guilty.

It must be conceded that the book in question is blemished by coarse words and scenes, none of which appear irrelevant to the plot. Yet in them I can find no erotic allurement such as the opinion makes necessary for a conviction. On the contrary, their coarseness is repellent.

The book is a serious study of the relations of different races in a small southern town. It is a grim tragedy, not relieved even by humor. Virtue is not derided, neither is vice made attractive. In the book, the wages of sin is literally death. The reader is left depressed, unable to solve a tragic problem.

The opinion rests its support of the conviction upon the statutory words "manifestly tends to corrupt the morals of youth," as well as upon the other prohibition of the statute. It asserts that "Many adolescents are avid readers of novels." The record contains no evidence to warrant that assertion, or to show that any adolescent ever read the book or would read it under normal conditions. Neither is there, in my judgment, any common knowledge upon which in the absence of evidence a court might conclude that under normal conditions the book would be read by any substantial number of adolescents. Of course, conditions that exist after prosecution for obscenity has been brought or publicly threatened, are abnormal and furnish no test of what the opinion calls the "probable audience" of the book. The market for any novel can be artificially stimulated and widened through curiosity aroused by actual or threatened prosecution in this Commonwealth, frequently to the satisfaction and profit of the publisher elsewhere.

Such knowledge as I have leads me to believe that without such artificial stimulation novels of the class into which the book in question falls are read by few girls and by practically no boys. The great mass of readers are mature women. Plainly the book was not written for juveniles. They would find it dull reading. Under normal conditions I think the book could do no substantial harm to the morals of youth, for few juveniles would ever see it, much less read it. And if by chance some should wade through it, I think it could not reasonably be found to have any erotic allurement, even for youth.

NOTES

1. "Whoever imports, prints, publishes, sells or distributes a book, pamphlet, ballad, printed paper, phonographic record or other thing which is obscene, indecent or impure, or manifestly tends to corrupt the morals of youth, or an obscene, indecent or impure print, picture, figure, image or description, manifestly tending to corrupt the morals of youth, or introduces into a family, school or place of education, or buys, procures, receives or has in his possession any such book, pamphlet, ballad, printed paper, phonographic record, obscene, indecent or impure print, picture, figure, image or other thing, either for the purpose of sale, exhibition, loan or circulation or with intent to introduce the same into a family, school or place of education, shall * * * be punished * * * ." The germ of this statute is to be found in Prov.Sts.1711–12, c. 6 § 19, 1 Prov. Laws. 682. It assumes a form approximating its present form in Rev.Sts. c. 130, § 10. Changes introduced by St.1862, c. 168, § 1; St.1880, c. 97; Pub.Sts. c. 207, § 15; St.1890, c. 70; St.1894, c. 433; R.L. c. 212, § 20; St.1904, c. 120, § 1; St.1913, c. 259; St.1934, c. 231; and St.1943, c. 239, require no comment in this case. Reference will be made later to St.1930, c. 162, and to St.1945, c. 278. The statute last mentioned adds an entirely new procedure.

2. See "Massachusetts Censorship," by S. S. Grant and S. E. Angoff, 10 Boston Univ.L.Rev. 147; "Judicial

Censorship of Obscene Literature," by L. M. Alpert, 52 Harv.L.Rev. 40.

3. Before this amendment the section read. "Whoever * * * sells * * * a book * * * *containing obscene, indecent or impure language,* or manifestly tending to corrupt the morals of youth * * * ." After the amendment it read. "Whoever * * * sells * * * a book * * * *which is obscene, indecent or impure,* or manifestly tends to corrupt the morals of youth * * * ." (Italics ours.) See Commonwealth v. Friede, 271 Mass. 318, 321, 322, 171 N. E. 472, 69 A.L.R. 640.

4. The Queen v. Hicklin, L.R. 3 Q.B. 360, 371; Commonwealth v. Allison, 227 Mass. 57, 61, 116 N.E. 265; Commonwealth v. Friede, 271 Mass. 318, 321, 171 N.E. 472, 69 A.L.R. 640; Rosen v. United States, 161 U.S. 29, 43, 16 S.Ct. 434, 480, 40 L.Ed. 606; Dunlop v. United States, 165 U.S. 486, 500, 17 S.Ct. 375, 41 L.Ed. 799; Dysart v. United States, 272 U.S. 655, 47 S.Ct. 234, 71 L.Ed. 461; United States v. Bennett, Fed.Cas.No.14,571; 16 Blatchf. 338, 364–366; United States v. Males, D.C., 51 F. 41; Knowles v. United States, 8 Cir., 170 F. 409, 412; United States v. Kennerly, D.C., 209 F. 119; Griffin v. United States, 1 Cir., 248 F. 6, 8, 9; Krause v. United States, 4 Cir., 29 F.2d 248, 250; United States v. Dennett, 2 Cir., 39 F.2d 564, 568, 76 A.L.R. 1092; Duncan v. United States, 9 Cir., 48 F.2d 128, 132; People v. Brainard, 192 App.Div. 816, 820, 821, 183 N.Y.S. 452. See also People v. Wendling, 258 N.Y. 451, 180 N. E. 169, 81 A.L.R. 799.

5. It is for this reason, if not for others, that we think it was not error to deny the defendant's fifteenth request for ruling, which reads, "As a matter of law the defendant cannot be found to be guilty of violating the provisions of General Laws (Ter.Ed.) chap. 272, sec. 28 as amended, unless it is found that the manifest tendency of the book is to corrupt the morals of the normal youth or adult as compared to the abnormal." This request seeks to classify rigidly all persons with respect to susceptibility as "normal" or "abnormal" and overlooks the possible harmful effect upon a substantial proportion of readers who may be less than a majority and therefore overlooks the possible harm to the mass.

6. See United States v. One Book Entitled "Ulysses", 2 Cir., 72 F.2d 705, 707, 708; United States v. Levine, 2 Cir., 83 F.2d 156, 158; Parmelee v. United States, 72 App.D.C. 203, 113 F.2d 729, 736.

UNITED STATES SUPREME COURT, 1948: "WE DO NOT ACCEDE TO APPELLEE'S SUGGESTION THAT THE CONSTITUTIONAL PROTECTION FOR A FREE PRESS APPLIES ONLY TO THE EXPOSITION OF IDEAS. THE LINE BETWEEN THE INFORMING AND THE ENTERTAINING IS TOO ELUSIVE FOR THE PROTECTION OF THAT BASIC RIGHT . . . . WHAT IS ONE MAN'S AMUSEMENT TEACHES ANOTHER'S DOCTRINE."

Winters v. New York, 333 U.S. 507 (1948)

MR. JUSTICE REED delivered the opinion of the Court.

Appellant is a New York City bookdealer, convicted, on information,[1] of a misdemeanor for having in his possession with intent to sell certain magazines charged to violate subsection 2 of § 1141 of the New York Penal Law. It reads as follows:

"§ 1141. Obscene prints and articles
   1. A person . . . who,
   2. Prints, utters, publishes, sells, lends, gives away, distributes or shows, or has in his possession with intent to sell, lend, give away, distribute or show, or otherwise offers for sale, loan, gift or distribution, any book, pamphlet, magazine, newspaper or other printed paper devoted to the publication, and principally made up of criminal news, police reports, or accounts of criminal deeds. or pictures. or stories of deeds of bloodshed. lust or crime; . . .

   ·   ·   ·   ·   ·   ·

   Is guilty of a misdemeanor, . . ."

Upon appeal from the Court of Special Sessions, the trial court, the conviction was upheld by the Appellate Division of the New York Supreme Court, 268 App. Div. 30, 48 N. Y. S. 2d 230, whose judgment was later upheld by the New York Court of Appeals. 294 N. Y. 545, 63 N. E. 2d 98.

The validity of the statute was drawn in question in the state courts as repugnant to the Fourteenth Amendment to the Constitution of the United States in that it denied the accused the right of freedom of speech and press, protected against state interference by the Fourteenth Amendment. *Gitlow* v. *New York,* 268 U. S. 652, 666; *Pennekamp* v. *Florida,* 328 U. S. 331, 335. The principle of a free press covers distribution as well as publication. *Lovell* v. *City of Griffin,* 303 U. S. 444, 452. As the validity of the section was upheld in a final judgment by the highest court of the state against this constitutional challenge, this Court has jurisdiction under Judicial Code § 237 (a). This appeal was argued at the October 1945 Term of this Court and set down for reargument before a full bench at the October 1946 Term. It was then reargued and again set down for further reargument at the present term.

The appellant contends that the subsection violates the right of free speech and press because it is vague and indefinite. It is settled that a statute so vague and indefinite, in form and as interpreted. as to permit within the scope of its language the punishment of incidents fairly within the protection of the guarantee of free speech is void, on its face, as contrary to the Fourteenth Amendment. *Stromberg* v. *California,* 283 U. S. 359, 369; *Herndon* v. *Lowry,* 301 U. S. 242, 258. A failure of a statute limiting freedom of expression to give fair notice of what acts will be punished and such a statute's inclusion of prohibitions against expressions, protected by the principles of the First Amendment, violates an accused's rights under procedural due process and freedom of speech or press. Where the alleged vagueness of a state statute had been cured by an opinion of the state court, confining a statute punishing the circulation of publications "having a tendency to encourage or incite the commission of any crime" to "encouraging an actual breach of law," this Court affirmed a conviction under the stated limitation of meaning. The accused publication was read as advocating the commission of the crime of indecent exposure. *Fox* v. *Washington*, 236 U. S. 273, 277.

We recognize the importance of the exercise of a state's police power to minimize all incentives to crime, particularly in the field of sanguinary or salacious publications with their stimulation of juvenile delinquency. Although we are dealing with an aspect of a free press in its relation to public morals, the principles of unrestricted distribution of publications admonish us of the particular importance of a maintenance of standards of certainty in the field of criminal prosecution for violation of statutory prohibitions against distribution. We do not accede to appellee's suggestion that the constitutional protection for a free press applies only to the exposition of ideas. The line between the informing and the entertaining is too elusive for the protection of that basic right. Everyone is familiar with instances of propaganda through fiction. What is one man's amusement, teaches another's doctrine. Though we can see nothing of any possible value to society in these magazines, they are as much entitled to the protection of free speech as the best of literature. Cf. *Hannegan* v. *Esquire*, 327 U. S. 146, 153, 158. They are equally subject to control if they are lewd, indecent, obscene or profane. *Ex parte Jackson*, 96 U. S. 727, 736; *Chaplinsky* v. *New Hampshire*, 315 U. S. 568.

The section of the Penal Law, § 1141 (2), under which the information was filed is a part of the "indecency" article of that law. It comes under the caption "Obscene prints and articles." Other sections make punishable various acts of indecency. For example, § 1141 (1), a section not here in issue but under the same caption, punishes the distribution of obscene, lewd, lascivious, filthy, indecent or disgusting magazines.[2] Section 1141 (2) originally was aimed at the protection of minors from the distribution of publications devoted principally to criminal news and stories of bloodshed, lust or crime.[3] It was later broadened to include all the population and other phases of production and possession.

Although many other states have similar statutes, they, like the early statutes restricting paupers from changing residence, have lain dormant for decades. *Edwards* v. *California*, 314 U. S. 160, 176. Only two other state courts, whose reports are printed, appear to have construed language in their laws similar to that here involved. In *Strohm* v. *Illinois*, 160 Ill. 582, 43 N. E. 622, a statute to suppress exhibiting to any minor child publications of this character was considered. The conviction was upheld. The case, however, apparently did not involve any problem of free speech or press or denial of due process for uncertainty under the Fourteenth Amendment.

In *State* v. *McKee*, 73 Conn. 18, 46 A. 409, the court considered a conviction under a statute which made criminal the sale of magazines "devoted to the publication, or principally made up of criminal news, police reports, or pictures and stories of deeds of bloodshed, lust, or crime." The gist of the offense was thought to be a "selection of immoralities so treated as to excite attention and interest sufficient to command circulation for a paper devoted mainly to the collection of such matters." Page 27. It was said, apropos of the state's constitutional provision as to free speech, that the act did not violate any constitutional provision relating to the freedom of the press. It was held, p. 31, that the principal evil at which the statute was directed was "the circulation of this massed immorality." As the charge stated that the offense might be committed "whenever the objectionable matter is a leading feature of the paper or when special attention is devoted to the publication of the prohibited items," the court felt that it failed to state the full meaning of the statute and reversed. As in the *Strohm* case, denial of due process for uncertainty was not raised.

On its face, the subsection here involved violates the rule of the *Stromberg* and *Herndon* cases, *supra*, that statutes which include prohibitions of acts fairly within the protection of a free press are void. It covers detective stories, treatises on crime, reports of battle carnage, *et cetera*. In recognition of this obvious defect, the New York Court of Appeals limited the scope by construction. Its only interpretation of the meaning of the pertinent subsection is that given in this case. After pointing out that New York statutes against indecent or obscene publications have generally been construed to refer to sexual impurity, it interpreted the section here in question to forbid these publications as "indecent or obscene" in a different manner. The Court held that collections of criminal deeds of bloodshed or lust "can be so massed as to become vehicles for inciting violent and depraved crimes against the person and in that case such publications are indecent or obscene in an admissible sense, ..." 294 N. Y. at 550. "This idea," its opinion goes on to say, "was the principal reason for the enactment of the statute." The Court left open the question of whether "the statute extends to accounts of criminal deeds not characterized by bloodshed or lust" because the magazines in question "are nothing but stories and pictures of criminal deeds of bloodshed and lust." As the statute in terms extended to other crimes, it may be supposed that the reservation was on account of doubts as to the validity of so wide a prohibition. The court declared: "In short, we have here before us accumulations of details of heinous wrongdoing which plainly carried an appeal to that portion of the public who (as many recent records remind us) are disposed to take to vice for its own sake." Further, the Court of Appeals, 294 N. Y. at 549, limited the statute so as not to "outlaw all commentaries on crime from detective tales to scientific treatises" on the ground that the legislature did not intend such literalness of construction. It thought that the magazines the possession of which caused the filing of the information were indecent in the sense just explained. The Court had no occasion to and did not weigh the character of the magazine exhibits by the more frequently used scales of § 1141 (1), printed in note 2. It did not interpret § 1141 (2) to punish distribution of indecent or obscene publications, in the usual sense, but that the present magazines were indecent and obscene because they "massed" stories of bloodshed and lust to incite crimes. Thus interpreting § 1141 (2) to include the expanded concept of indecency and obscenity stated in its opinion, the Court of Appeals met appellant's contention of invalidity from indefiniteness and uncertainty of the subsection by saying, 294 N. Y. at 551,

"In the nature of things there can be no more precise test of written indecency or obscenity than the continuing and changeable experience of the community as to what types of books are likely to bring about the corruption of public morals or other analogous injury to the public order. Consequently, a question as to whether a particular publication is indecent or obscene in that sense is a question of the times which must be determined as matter of fact, unless the appearances are thought to be necessarily harmless from the standpoint of public order or morality."

The opinion went on to explain that publication of any crime magazine would be no more hazardous under this interpretation than any question of degree and concluded, p. 552,

"So when reasonable men may fairly classify a publication as necessarily or naturally indecent or obscene, a mistaken view by the publisher as to its character or tendency is immaterial."

The Court of Appeals by this authoritative interpretation made the subsection applicable to publications that, besides meeting the other particulars of the statute, so massed their collection of pictures and stories of bloodshed and of lust "as to become vehicles for inciting violent and depraved crimes against the person." Thus, the statute forbids the massing of stories of bloodshed and lust in such a way as to incite to crime against the person. This construction fixes the meaning of the statute for this case. The interpretation by the Court of Appeals puts these words in the statute as definitely as if it had been so amended by the legislature. *Hebert* v. *Louisiana,* 272 U. S. 312, 317; *Skiriotes* v. *Florida,* 313 U. S. 69, 79. We assume that the defendant, at the time he acted, was chargeable with knowledge of the scope of subsequent interpretation. Compare *Lanzetta* v. *New Jersey,* 306 U. S. 451. As lewdness in publications is punishable under § 1141 (1) and the usual run of stories of bloodshed, such as detective stories, are excluded, it is the massing as an incitation to crime that becomes the important element.

Acts of gross and open indecency or obscenity, injurious to public morals, are indictable at common law, as violative of the public policy that requires from the offender retribution for acts that flaunt accepted standards of conduct. 1 Bishop, Criminal Law (9th ed.), § 500; Wharton, Criminal Law (12th ed.), § 16. When a legislative body concludes that the mores of the community call for an extension of the impermissible limits, an enactment aimed at the evil is plainly within its power, if it does not transgress the boundaries fixed by the Constitution for freedom of expression. The standards of certainty in statutes punishing for offenses is higher than in those depending primarily upon civil sanction for enforcement. The crime "must be defined with appropriate definiteness." *Cantwell* v. *Connecticut,* 310 U. S. 296; *Pierce* v. *United States,* 314 U. S. 306, 311. There must be ascertainable standards of guilt. Men of common intelligence cannot be required to guess at the meaning of the enactment.[4] The vagueness may be from uncertainty in regard to persons within the scope of the act, *Lanzetta* v. *New Jersey,* 306 U. S. 451, or in regard to the applicable tests to ascertain guilt.[5]

Other states than New York have been confronted with similar problems involving statutory vagueness in connection with free speech. In *State* v. *Diamond,* 27 New Mexico 477, 202 P. 988, a statute punishing "any act of any kind whatsoever which has for its purpose or aim the destruction of organized government, federal, state or municipal, or to do or cause to be done any act which is antagonistic to or in opposition to such organized government, or incite or attempt to incite revolution or opposition to such organized government" was construed. The court said, p. 479: "Under its terms no distinction is made between the man who advocates a change in the form of our government by constitutional means, or advocates the abandonment of organized government by peaceful methods, and the man who advocates the overthrow of our government by armed revolution, or other form of force and violence." Later in the opinion the statute was held void for uncertainty, p. 485:

"Where the statute uses words of no determinative meaning, or the language is so general and indefinite as to embrace not only acts commonly recognized as reprehensible, but also others which it is unreasonable to presume were intended to be made criminal, it will be declared void for uncertainty."

Again in *State* v. *Klapprott,* 127 N. J. L. 395, 22 A. 2d 877, a statute was held invalid on an attack against its constitutionality under state and federal constitutional provisions that protect an individual's freedom of expression. The statute read as follows, p. 396:

"Any person who shall, in the presence of two or more persons, in any language, make or utter any speech, statement or declaration, which in any way incites, counsels, promotes, or advocates hatred, abuse, violence or hostility against any group or groups of persons residing or being in this state by reason of race, color, religion or manner of worship, shall be guilty of a misdemeanor."

The court said, pp. 401–2:

"It is our view that the statute, *supra,* by punitive sanction, tends to restrict what one may say lest by one's utterances there be incited or advocated hatred, hostility or violence against a group 'by reason of race, color, religion or manner of worship.' But additionally and looking now to strict statutory construction, is the statute definite, clear and precise so as to be free from the constitutional infirmity of the vague and indefinite? That the terms 'hatred,' 'abuse,' 'hostility,' are abstract and indefinite admits of no contradiction. When do they arise? Is it to be left to a jury to conclude beyond reasonable doubt when the emotion of hatred or hostility is aroused in the mind of the listener as a result of what a speaker has said? Nothing in our criminal law can be invoked to justify so wide a discretion. The criminal code must be definite and informative so that there may be no doubt in the mind of the citizenry that the interdicted act or conduct is illicit."

This Court goes far to uphold state statutes that deal with offenses, difficult to define, when they are not entwined with limitations on free expression.[6] We have the same attitude toward federal statutes.[7] Only a definite conviction by a majority of this Court that the conviction violates the Fourteenth Amendment justifies reversal of the court primarily charged with responsibility to protect persons from conviction under a vague state statute.

The impossibility of defining the precise line between permissible uncertainty in statutes caused by describing crimes by words well understood through long use in the criminal law—obscene, lewd, lascivious, filthy, indecent or disgusting—and the unconstitutional vagueness that leaves a person uncertain as to the kind of prohibited conduct—massing stories to incite crime—has resulted in three arguments of this case in this Court. The legislative bodies in draftsmanship obviously have the same difficulty as do the judicial in interpretation. Nevertheless despite the difficulties, courts must do their best to determine whether or not the vagueness is of such a character "that men of common intelligence must necessarily guess at its meaning." *Connally* v. *General Constr. Co.*, 269 U. S. 385, 391. The entire text of the statute or the subjects dealt with may furnish an adequate standard.[8] The present case as to a vague statute abridging free speech involves the circulation of only vulgar magazines. The next may call for decision as to free expression of political views in the light of a statute intended to punish subversive activities.

The subsection of the New York Penal Law, as now interpreted by the Court of Appeals, prohibits distribution of a magazine principally made up of criminal news or stories of deeds of bloodshed or lust, so massed as to become vehicles for inciting violent and depraved crimes against the person. But even considering the gloss put upon the literal meaning by the Court of Appeals' restriction of the statute to collections of stories "so massed as to become vehicles for inciting violent and depraved crimes against the person . . . not necessarily . . . sexual passion," we find the specification of publications, prohibited from distribution, too uncertain and indefinite to justify the conviction of this petitioner. Even though all detective tales and treatises on criminology are not forbidden, and though publications made up of criminal deeds not characterized by bloodshed or lust are omitted from the interpretation of the Court of Appeals, we think fair use of collections of pictures and stories would be interdicted because of the utter impossibility of the actor or the trier to know where this new standard of guilt would draw the line between the allowable and the forbidden publications. No intent or purpose is required—no indecency or obscenity in any sense heretofore known to the law. "So massed as to incite to crime" can become meaningful only by concrete instances. This one example is not enough. The clause proposes to punish the printing and circulation of publications that courts or juries may think influence generally persons to commit crimes of violence against the person. No conspiracy to commit a crime is required. See *Musser* v. *Utah*, 333 U. S. 95. It is not an effective notice of new crime. The clause has no technical or common law meaning. Nor can light as to the meaning be gained from the section as a whole or the Article of the Penal Law under which it appears. As said in the *Cohen Grocery Company* case, *supra*, p. 89:

> "It leaves open, therefore, the widest conceivable inquiry, the scope of which no one can foresee and the result of which no one can foreshadow or adequately guard against."

The statute as construed by the Court of Appeals does not limit punishment to the indecent and obscene, as formerly understood. When stories of deeds of bloodshed, such as many in the accused magazines, are massed so as to incite to violent crimes, the statute is violated. It does not seem to us that an honest distributor of publications could know when he might be held to have ignored such a prohibition. Collections of tales of war horrors, otherwise unexceptionable, might well be found to be "massed" so as to become "vehicles for inciting violent and depraved crimes." Where a statute is so vague as to make criminal an innocent act, a conviction under it cannot be sustained. *Herndon* v. *Lowry*, 301 U. S. 242, 259.

To say that a state may not punish by such a vague statute carries no implication that it may not punish circulation of objectionable printed matter, assuming that it is not protected by the principles of the First Amendment, by the use of apt words to describe the prohibited publications. Section 1141, subsection 1, quoted in note 2, is an example. Neither the states nor Congress are prevented by the requirement of specificity from carrying out their duty of eliminating evils to which, in their judgment, such publications give rise.

Reversed.

MR. JUSTICE FRANKFURTER, joined by MR. JUSTICE JACKSON and MR. JUSTICE BURTON, dissenting.

By today's decision the Court strikes down an enactment that has been part of the laws of New York for more than sixty years,[1] and New York is but one of twenty States having such legislation. Four more States have statutes of like tenor which are brought into question by this decision, but variations of nicety preclude one from saying that these four enactments necessarily fall within the condemnation of this decision. Most of this legislation is also more than sixty years old. The latest of the statutes which cannot be differentiated from New York's law, that of the State of Washington, dates from 1909. It deserves also to be noted that the legislation was judicially applied and sustained nearly fifty years ago. See *State* v. *McKee*, 73 Conn. 18, 46 A. 409. Nor is this an instance where the pressure of proximity or propaganda led to the enactment of the same measure in a concentrated region of States. The impressiveness of the number of States which have this law on their statute books is reinforced by their distribution throughout the country and the time range of the adoption of the measure.[2] Cf. Hughes, C. J., in *West Coast Hotel Co.* v. *Parrish*, 300 U. S. 379, 399.

These are the statutes that fall by this decision:[3]

1. Gen. Stat. Conn. (1930) c. 329, § 6245, derived from L. 1885, c. 47, § 2.*

2. Ill. Ann. Stat. (Smith-Hurd) c. 38, § 106, derived from Act of June 3, 1889, p. 114, § 1 (minors).

3. Iowa Code (1946) § 725.8, derived from 21 Acts, Gen. Assembly, c. 177, § 4 (1886) (minors).

4. Gen. Stats. Kans. (1935) § 21–1102, derived from L. 1886, c. 101, § 1.

5. Ky. Rev. Stat. (1946) § 436.110, derived from L. 1891–93, c. 182, § 217 (1893) (similar).

6. Rev. Stat. Maine (1944) c. 121, § 27, derived from Acts and Resolves 1885, c. 348, § 1 (minors).

7. Ann. Code Md. (1939) Art. 27, § 496, derived from L. 1894, c. 271, § 2.

8. Ann. Laws Mass. (1933) c. 272, § 30, derived from Acts and Resolves 1885, c. 305 (minors).

9. Mich. Stat. Ann. (1938) § 28.576, derived from L. 1885, No. 138.

10. Minn. Stat. (1945) § 617.72, derived from L. 1885, c. 268, § 1 (minors).

11. Mo. Rev. Stat. (1939) § 4656, derived from Act of April 2, 1885, p. 146, § 1 (minors).

12. Rev. Code Mont. (1935) § 11134, derived from Act of March 4, 1891, p. 255, § 1 (minors).

13. Rev. Stat. Neb. (1943) § 28–924, derived from L. 1887, c. 113, § 4 (minors).

14. N. Y. Consol. L. (1938) Penal Law, Art. 106, § 1141 (2), derived from L. 1884, c. 380.

15. N. D. Rev. Code (1943) § 12–2109, derived from L. 1895, c. 84, § 1 (similar).

16. Ohio Code Ann. (Throckmorton, 1940) § 13035, derived from 82 Sess. L. 184 (1885) (similar).

17. Ore. Comp. L. Ann. (1940) § 23–924, derived from Act of Feb. 25, 1885, p. 126 (similar).

18. Pa. Stat. Ann. (1945) Tit. 18, § 4524, derived from L. 1887, P. L. 38, § 2.

19. Rev. Stat. Wash. (Remington, 1932) § 2459 (2), derived from L. 1909, c. 249, § 207 (2).

20. Wis. Stat. (1945) § 351.38 (4), derived from L. 1901, c. 256.

The following statutes are somewhat similar, but may not necessarily be rendered unconstitutional by the Court's decision in the instant case:

1. Colo. Stat. Ann. (1935) c. 48, § 217, derived from Act of April 9, 1885, p. 172, § 1.

2. Ind. Stat. Ann. (1934) § 2607, derived from L. 1895, c. 109.

3. S. D. Code (1939) § 13.1722 (4), derived from L. 1913, c. 241, § 4.

4. Tex. Stat. (Vernon, 1936), Penal Code, Art. 527, derived from L. 1897, c. 116.

This body of laws represents but one of the many attempts by legislatures to solve what is perhaps the most persistent, intractable, elusive, and demanding of all problems of society—the problem of crime, and, more particularly, of its prevention. By this decision the Court invalidates such legislation of almost half the States of the Union. The destructiveness of the decision is even more far-reaching. This is not one of those situations where power is denied to the States because it belongs to the Nation. These enactments are invalidated on the ground that they fall within the prohibitions of the "vague contours" of the Due Process Clause. The decision thus operates equally as a limitation upon Congressional authority to deal with crime, and, more especially, with juvenile delinquency. These far-reaching consequences result from the Court's belief that what New York, among a score of States, has prohibited, is so empty of meaning that no one desirous of obeying the law could fairly be aware that he was doing that which was prohibited.

Fundamental fairness of course requires that people be given notice of what to avoid. If the purpose of a statute is undisclosed, if the legislature's will has not been revealed, it offends reason that punishment should be meted out for conduct which at the time of its commission was not forbidden to the understanding of those who wished to observe the law. This requirement of fair notice that there is a boundary of prohibited conduct not to be overstepped is included in the conception of "due process of law." The legal jargon for such failure to give forewarning is to say that the statute is void for "indefiniteness."

But "indefiniteness" is not a quantitative concept. It is not even a technical concept of definite components. It is itself an indefinite concept. There is no such thing as "indefiniteness" in the abstract, by which the sufficiency of the requirement expressed by the term may be ascertained. The requirement is fair notice that conduct may entail punishment. But whether notice is or is not "fair" depends upon the subject matter to which it relates. Unlike the abstract stuff of mathematics, or the quantitatively ascertainable elements of much of natural science, legislation is greatly concerned with the multiform psychological complexities of individual and social conduct. Accordingly, the demands upon legislation, and its responses, are variable and multiform. That which may appear to be too vague and even meaningless as to one subject matter may be as definite as another subject-matter of legislation permits, if the legislative power to deal with such a subject is not to be altogether denied. The statute books of every State are full of instances of what may look like unspecific definitions of crime, of the drawing of wide circles of prohibited conduct.

In these matters legislatures are confronted with a dilemma. If a law is framed with narrow particularity, too easy opportunities are afforded to nullify the purposes of the legislation. If the legislation is drafted in terms so vague that no ascertainable line is drawn in advance between innocent and condemned conduct, the purpose of the legislation cannot be enforced because no purpose is defined. It is not merely in the enactment of tax measures that the task of reconciling these extremes—of avoiding throttling particularity or unfair generality—is one of the most delicate and difficult confronting legislators. The reconciliation of these two contradictories is necessarily an empiric enterprise largely depending on the nature of the particular legislative problem.

What risks do the innocent run of being caught in a net not designed for them? How important is the policy of the legislation, so that those who really like to pursue innocent conduct are not likely to be caught unaware? How easy is it to be explicitly particular? How necessary is it to leave a somewhat penumbral margin but sufficiently revealed by what is condemned to those who do not want to sail close to the shore of questionable conduct? These and like questions confront legislative draftsmen. Answers to these questions are not to be found in any legislative manual nor in the work of great legislative draftsmen. They are not to be found in the opinions of this Court. These are questions of judgment, peculiarly within the responsibility and the competence of legislatures. The discharge of that responsibility should not be set at naught by abstract notions about "indefiniteness."

The action of this Court today in invalidating legislation having the support of almost half the States of the

Union rests essentially on abstract notions about "indefiniteness." The Court's opinion could have been written by one who had never read the issues of "Headquarters Detective" which are the basis of the prosecution before us, who had never deemed their contents as relevant to the form in which the New York legislation was cast, had never considered the bearing of such "literature" on juvenile delinquency, in the allowable judgment of the legislature. Such abstractions disregard the considerations that may well have moved and justified the State in not being more explicit than these State enactments are. Only such abstract notions would reject the judgment of the States that they have outlawed what they have a right to outlaw, in the effort to curb crimes of lust and violence, and that they have not done it so recklessly as to occasion real hazard that other publications will thereby be inhibited, or also be subjected to prosecution.

This brings our immediate problem into focus. No one would deny, I assume, that New York may punish crimes of lust and violence. Presumably also, it may take appropriate measures to lower the crime rate. But he must be a bold man indeed who is confident that he knows what causes crime. Those whose lives are devoted to an understanding of the problem are certain only that they are uncertain regarding the role of the various alleged "causes" of crime. Bibliographies of criminology reveal a depressing volume of writings on theories of causation. See, e. g., Kuhlman, A Guide to Material on Crime and Criminal Justice (1929) Item Nos. 292 to 1211; Culver, Bibliography of Crime and Criminal Justice (1927–1931) Item Nos. 877–1475, and (1932–1937) Item Nos. 799–1560. Is it to be seriously questioned, however, that the State of New York, or the Congress of the United States, may make incitement to crime itself an offense? He too would indeed be a bold man who denied that incitement may be caused by the written word no less than by the spoken. If "the Fourteenth Amendment does not enact Mr. Herbert Spencer's Social Statics," (Holmes, J., dissenting in *Lochner* v. *New York*, 198 U. S. 45, 75), neither does it enact the psychological dogmas of the Spencerian era. The painful experience which resulted from confusing economic dogmas with constitutional edicts ought not to be repeated by finding constitutional barriers to a State's policy regarding crime, because it may run counter to our inexpert psychological assumptions or offend our presuppositions regarding incitements to crime in relation to the curtailment of utterance. This Court is not ready, I assume, to pronounce on causative factors of mental disturbance and their relation to crime. Without formally professing to do so, it may actually do so by invalidating legislation dealing with these problems as too "indefinite."

Not to make the magazines with which this case is concerned part of the Court's opinion is to play "Hamlet" without Hamlet. But the Court sufficiently summarizes one aspect of what the State of New York here condemned when it says "we can see nothing of any possible value to society in these magazines." From which it jumps to the conclusion that, nevertheless, "they are as much entitled to the protection of free speech as the best of literature." Wholly neutral futilities, of course, come under the protection of free speech as fully as do Keats' poems or Donne's sermons. But to say that these magazines have "nothing of any possible value to society" is only half the truth. This merely denies them goodness. It disregards their mischief. As a result of appropriate judicial determination, these magazines were found to come within the prohibition of the law against inciting "violent and depraved crimes against the person," and the defendant was convicted because he exposed for sale such materials. The essence of the Court's decision is that it gives publications which have "nothing of any possible value to society" constitutional protection but denies to the States the power to prevent the grave evils to which, in their rational judgment, such publications give rise. The legislatures of New York and the other States were concerned with these evils and not with neutral abstractions of harmlessness. Nor was the New York Court of Appeals merely resting, as it might have done, on a deep-seated conviction as to the existence of an evil and as to the appropriate means for checking it. That court drew on its experience, as revealed by "many recent records" of criminal convictions before it, for its understanding of the practical concrete reasons that led the legislatures of a score of States to pass the enactments now here struck down.

The New York Court of Appeals thus spoke out of extensive knowledge regarding incitements to crimes of violence. In such matters, local experience, as this Court has said again and again, should carry the greatest weight against our denying a State authority to adjust its legislation to local needs. But New York is not peculiar in concluding that "collections of pictures or stories of criminal deeds of bloodshed or lust unquestionably can be so massed as to become vehicles for inciting violent and depraved crimes against the person." 294 N. Y. at 550. A recent murder case before the High Court of Australia sheds light on the considerations which may well have induced legislation such as that now before us, and on the basis of which the New York Court of Appeals sustained its validity. The murder was committed by a lad who had just turned seventeen years of age, and the victim was the driver of a taxicab. I quote the following from the opinion of Mr. Justice Dixon: "In his evidence on the *voir dire* Graham [a friend of the defendant and apparently a very reliable witness] said that he knew Boyd Sinclair [the murderer] and his moods very well and that he just left him; that Boyd had on a number of occasions outlined plans for embarking on a life of crime, plans based mainly on magazine thrillers which he was reading at the time. They included the obtaining of a motor car and an automatic gun." *Sinclair* v. *The King*, 73 Comm. L. R. 316, 330.

"Magazine thrillers" hardly characterizes what New York has outlawed. New York does not lay hold of publications merely because they are "devoted to and principally made up of criminal news or police reports or accounts of criminal deeds, regardless of the manner of treatment." So the Court of Appeals has authoritatively informed us. 294 N. Y. at 549. The aim of the publication must be incitation to "violent and depraved crimes against the person" by so massing "pictures and stories of criminal deeds of bloodshed or lust" as to encourage like deeds in others. It would be sheer dogmatism in a field not within the professional competence of judges to deny to the New York legislature the right to believe that the intent of the type of publications which it has proscribed is to cater to morbid and immature minds—whether chronologically or permanently immature. It would be sheer dogmatism to deny that in some instances, as in the case of young Boyd Sinclair, deeply embedded, unconscious impulses may be discharged into destructive and often fatal action.

If legislation like that of New York "has been enacted upon a belief of evils that is not arbitrary we cannot measure their extent against the estimate of the legislature." *Tanner* v. *Little*, 240 U. S. 369, 385. The Court fails to give enough force to the influence of the evils with which the New York legislature was concerned "upon conduct and habit, not enough to their insidious potentialities." *Rast* v. *Van Deman & Lewis Co.*, 240 U. S. 342, 364. The other day we indicated that, in order to support its constitutionality, legislation need not employ the old practice of preambles, nor be accompanied by a memorandum of explanation setting forth the reasons for the enactment. See *Woods* v. *Cloyd W. Miller Co.*, 333 U. S. 138, 144. Accordingly, the New York statute, when challenged for want of due process on the score of "indefiniteness," must be considered by us as though the legislature had thus spelled out its convictions and beliefs for its enactment:

> Whereas, we believe that the destructive and adventurous potentialities of boys and adolescents, and of adults of weak character or those leading a drab existence are often stimulated by collections of pictures and stories of criminal deeds of bloodshed or lust so massed as to incite to violent and depraved crimes against the person; and
>
> Whereas, we believe that such juveniles and other susceptible characters do in fact commit such crimes at least partly because incited to do so by such publications, the purpose of which is to exploit such susceptible characters; and
>
> Whereas, such belief, even though not capable of statistical demonstration, is supported by our experience as well as by the opinions of some specialists qualified to express opinions regarding criminal psychology and not disproved by others; and
>
> Whereas, in any event there is nothing of possible value to society in such publications, so that there is no gain to the State, whether in edification or enlightenment or amusement or good of any kind; and
>
> Whereas, the possibility of harm by restricting free utterance through harmless publications is too remote and too negligible a consequence of dealing with the evil publications with which we are here concerned;
>
> Be it therefore enacted that—

Unless we can say that such beliefs are intrinsically not reasonably entertainable by a legislature, or that the record disproves them, or that facts of which we must take judicial notice preclude the legislature from entertaining such views, we must assume that the legislature was dealing with a real problem touching the commission of crime and not with fanciful evils, and that the measure was adapted to the serious evils to which it was addressed. The validity of such legislative beliefs or their importance ought not to be rejected out of hand.

Surely this Court is not prepared to say that New York cannot prohibit traffic in publications exploiting "criminal deeds of bloodshed or lust" so "as to become vehicles for inciting violent and depraved crimes against the person." Laws have here been sustained outlawing utterance far less confined. A Washington statute, directed against printed matter tending to encourage and advocate disrespect for law, was judged and found not wanting on these broad lines:

> "We understand the state court by implication at least to have read the statute as confined to encouraging an actual breach of law. Therefore the argument that this act is both an unjustifiable restriction of liberty and too vague for a criminal law must fail. It does not appear and is not likely that the statute will be construed to prevent publications merely because they tend to produce unfavorable opinions of a particular statute or of law in general. In this present case the disrespect for law that was encouraged was disregard of it—an overt breach and technically criminal act. It would be in accord with the usages of English to interpret disrespect as manifested disrespect, as active disregard going beyond the line drawn by the law. That is all that has happened as yet, and we see no reason to believe that the statute will be stretched beyond that point.
>
> "If the statute should be construed as going no farther than it is necessary to go in order to bring the defendant within it, there is no trouble with it for want of definiteness." *Fox* v. *Washington*, 236 U. S. 273, 277.

In short, this Court respected the policy of a State by recognizing the practical application which the State court gave to the statute in the case before it. This Court rejected constitutional invalidity based on a remote possibility that the language of the statute, abstractly considered, might be applied with unbridled looseness.

Since Congress and the States may take measures against "violent and depraved crimes," can it be claimed that "due process of law" bars measures against incitement to such crimes? But if they have power to deal with incitement, Congress and the States must be allowed the effective means for translating their policy into law. No doubt such a law presents difficulties in draftsmanship where publications are the instruments of incitement. The problem is to avoid condemnation so unbounded that neither the text of the statute nor its subject matter affords "a standard of some sort" (*United States* v. *Cohen Grocery Co.*, 255 U. S. 81, 92). Legislation must put people on notice as to the kind of conduct from which to refrain. Legislation must also avoid so tight a phrasing as to leave the area for evasion ampler than that which is condemned. How to escape, on the one hand, having a law rendered futile because no standard is afforded by which conduct is to be judged, and, on the other, a law so particularized as to defeat itself through the opportunities it affords for evasion, involves an exercise of judgment which is at the heart of the legislative process. It calls for the accommodation of delicate factors. But this accommodation is for the legislature to make and for us to respect, when it concerns a subject so clearly within the scope of the police power as the control of crime. Here we are asked to declare void the law which expresses the balance so struck by the legislature, on the ground that the legislature has not expressed its policy clearly enough. That is what it gets down to.

What were the alternatives open to the New York legislature? It could of course conclude that publications such as those before us could not "become vehicles for inciting violent and depraved crimes." But surely New York was entitled to believe otherwise. It is not for this Court to impose its belief, even if entertained, that no "massing of print and pictures" could be found to be effective means for inciting crime in minds open to such stimulation. What gives judges competence to say that while print and pictures may be constitutionally outlawed because judges deem them "obscene," print and pictures which in the judgment of half the States of the Union operate as incitements to crime enjoy a constitutional prerogative? When on occasion this Court has presumed to act as an authoritative faculty of chemistry, the result has not been fortunate. See *Burns Baking Co.* v. *Bryan,* 264 U. S. 504, where this Court ventured a view of its own as to what is reasonable "tolerance" in breadmaking. Considering the extent to which the whole domain of psychological inquiry has only recently been transformed and how largely the transformation is still in a pioneer stage, I should suppose that the Court would feel even less confidence in its views on psychological issues. At all events, it ought not to prefer its psychological views—for, at bottom, judgment on psychological matters underlies the legal issue in this case—to those implicit in an impressive body of enactments and explicitly given by the New York Court of Appeals, out of the abundance of its experience, as the reason for sustaining the legislation which the Court is nullifying.

But we are told that New York has not expressed a policy, that what looks like a law is not a law because it is so vague as to be meaningless. Suppose then that the New York legislature now wishes to meet the objection of the Court. What standard of definiteness does the Court furnish the New York legislature in finding indefiniteness in the present law? Should the New York legislature enumerate by name the publications which in its judgment are "inciting violent and depraved crimes"? Should the New York legislature spell out in detail the ingredients of stories or pictures which accomplish such "inciting"? What is there in the condemned law that leaves men in the dark as to what is meant by publications that exploit "criminal deeds of bloodshed or lust" thereby "inciting violent and depraved crimes"? What real risk do the Conan Doyles, the Edgar Allen Poes, the William Rougheads, the ordinary tribe of detective story writers, their publishers, or their booksellers run?

Insofar as there is uncertainty, the uncertainty derives not from the terms of condemnation, but from the application of a standard of conduct to the varying circumstances of different cases. The Due Process Clause does not preclude such fallibilities of judgment in the administration of justice by men. Our penal codes are loaded with prohibitions of conduct depending on ascertainment through fallible judges and juries of a man's intent or motive—on ascertainment, that is, from without of a man's inner thoughts, feelings and purposes. Of course a man runs the risk of having a jury of his peers misjudge him. Mr. Justice Holmes has given the conclusive answer to the suggestion that the Due Process Clause protects against such a hazard: "the law is full of instances where a man's fate depends on his estimating rightly, that is, as the jury subsequently estimates it, some matter of degree. If his judgment is wrong, not only may he incur a fine or a short imprisonment, as here; he may incur the penalty of death." *Nash* v. *United States,* 229 U. S. 373, 377. To which it is countered that such uncertainty not in the standard but in its application is not objectionable in legislation having a long history, but is inadmissible as to more recent laws. Is this not another way of saying that when new circumstances or new insights lead to new legislation the Due Process Clause denies to legislatures the power to frame legislation with such regard for the subject matter as legislatures had in the past? When neither the Constitution nor legislation has formulated legal principles for courts, and they must pronounce them, they find it impossible to impose upon themselves such a duty of definiteness as this decision exacts from legislatures.

The Court has been led into error, if I may respectfully suggest, by confusing want of certainty as to the outcome of different prosecutions for similar conduct, with want of definiteness in what the law prohibits. But diversity in result for similar conduct in different trials under the same statute is an unavoidable feature of criminal justice. So long as these diversities are not designed consequences but due merely to human fallibility, they do not deprive persons of due process of law.

In considering whether New York has struck an allowable balance between its right to legislate in a field that is so closely related to the basic function of government, and the duty to protect the innocent from being punished for crossing the line of wrongdoing without awareness, it is relevant to note that this legislation has been upheld as putting law-abiding people on sufficient notice, by a court that has been astutely alert to the hazards of vaguely phrased penal laws and zealously protective of individual rights against "indefiniteness." See, *e. g.,* *People* v. *Phyfe,* 136 N. Y. 554, 32 N. E. 978; *People* v. *Briggs,* 193 N. Y. 457, 86 N. E. 522; *People* v. *Shakun,* 251 N. Y. 107, 167 N. E. 187; *People* v. *Grogan,* 260 N. Y. 138, 183 N. E. 273. The circumstances of this case make it particularly relevant to remind, even against a confident judgment of the invalidity of legislation on the vague ground of "indefiniteness," that certitude is not the test of certainty. If men may reasonably differ whether the State has given sufficient notice that it is outlawing the exploitation of criminal potentialities, that in itself ought to be sufficient, according to the repeated pronouncements of this Court, to lead us to abstain from denying power to the States. And it deserves to be repeated that the Court is not denying power to the States in order to leave it to the Nation. It is denying power to both. By this decision Congress is denied power, as part of its effort to grapple with the problems of juvenile delinquency in Washington, to prohibit what twenty States have seen fit to outlaw. Moreover, a decision like this has a destructive momentum much beyond the statutes of New York and of the other States immediately involved. Such judicial nullification checks related legislation which the States might deem highly desirable as a matter of policy, and this Court might not find unconstitutional.

Almost by his very last word on this Court, as by his first, Mr. Justice Holmes admonished against employing "due process of law" to strike down enactments which, though supported on grounds that may not commend themselves to judges, can hardly be deemed offensive to reason itself. It is not merely in the domain of economics that the legislative judgment should not be subtly supplanted by the judicial judgment. "I cannot believe that the Amendment was intended to give us *carte blanche* to embody our economic or moral beliefs in its prohibitions." So wrote Mr. Justice Holmes in summing up his protest for nearly thirty years against using the Fourteenth Amendment to cut down the constitutional rights of the States. *Baldwin* v. *Missouri,* 281 U. S. 586, 595 (dissenting).

Indeed, Mr. Justice Holmes is a good guide in deciding this case. In three opinions in which, speaking for the Court, he dealt with the problem of "indefiniteness" in relation to the requirement of due process, he indicated the directions to be followed and the criteria to be applied. Pursuit of those directions and due regard for the criteria require that we hold that the New York legislature has not offended the limitations which the Due Process Clause has placed upon the power of States to counteract avoidable incitements to violent and depraved crimes.

Reference has already been made to the first of the trilogy, *Nash* v. *United States, supra.* There the Court repelled the objection that the Sherman Law "was so vague as to be inoperative on its criminal side." The opinion rested largely on a critical analysis of the requirement of "definiteness" in criminal statutes to be drawn from the Due Process Clause. I have already quoted the admonishing generalization that "the law is full of instances where a man's fate depends on his estimating rightly, that is. as the jury subsequently estimates it, some matter of degree." 229 U. S. at 377. Inasmuch as "the common law as to restraint of trade" was "taken up" by the Sherman Law, the opinion in the *Nash* case also drew support from the suggestion that language in a criminal statute which might otherwise appear indefinite may derive definiteness from past usage. How much definiteness "the common law of restraint of trade" has imparted to "the rule of reason," which is the guiding consideration in applying the Sherman Law, may be gathered from the fact that since the *Nash* case this Court has been substantially divided in at least a dozen cases in determining whether a particular situation fell within the undefined limits of the Sherman Law.[4] The Court's opinion in this case invokes this doctrine of "permissible uncertainty" in criminal statutes as to words that have had long use in the criminal law, and assumes that "long use" gives assurance of clear meaning. I do not believe that the law reports permit one to say that statutes condemning "restraint of trade" or "obscenity" are much more unequivocal guides to conduct than this statute furnishes, nor do they cast less risk of "estimating rightly" what judges and juries will decide than does this legislation.

The second of this series of cases. *International Harvester Co.* v. *Kentucky,* 234 U. S. 216, likewise concerned anti-trust legislation. But that case brought before the Court a statute quite different from the Sherman Law. However indefinite the terms of the latter, whereby "it throws upon men the risk of rightly estimating a matter of degree," it is possible by due care to keep to the line of safety. But the Kentucky statute was such that no

amount of care would give safety. To compel men, wrote Mr. Justice Holmes "to guess on peril of indictment what the community would have given for them [commodities] if the continually changing conditions were other than they are, to an uncertain extent; to divine prophetically what the reaction of only partially determinate facts would be upon the imaginations and desires of purchasers, is to exact gifts that mankind does not possess." 234 U. S. at 223–224. The vast difference between this Kentucky statute and the New York law, so far as forewarning goes, needs no laboring.

The teaching of the *Nash* and the *Harvester* cases is that it is not violative of due process of law for a legislature in framing its criminal law to cast upon the public the duty of care and even of caution, provided that there is sufficient warning to one bent on obedience that he comes near the proscribed area. In his last opinion on this subject, Mr. Justice Holmes applied this teaching on behalf of a unanimous Court, *United States* v. *Wurzbach,* 280 U. S. 396, 399. The case sustained the validity of the Federal Corrupt Practices Act. What he wrote is too relevant to the matter in hand not to be fully quoted:

"It is argued at some length that the statute, if extended beyond the political purposes under the control of Congress. is too vague to be valid. The objection to uncertainty concerning the persons embraced need not trouble us now. There is no doubt that the words include representatives. and if there is any difficulty, which we are far from intimating, it will be time enough to consider it when raised by someone whom it concerns. The other objection is to the meaning of 'political purposes.' This would be open even if we accepted the limitations that would make the law satisfactory to the respondent's counsel. But we imagine that no one not in search of trouble would feel any. Whenever the law draws a line there will be cases very near each other on opposite sides. The precise course of the line may be uncertain. but no one can come near it without knowing that he does so, if he thinks, and if he does so it is familiar to the criminal law to make him take the risk. *Nash* v. *United States,* 229 U. S. 373."

Only a word needs to be said regarding *Lanzetta* v. *New Jersey,* 306 U. S 451. The case involved a New Jersey statute of the type that seek to control "vagrancy." These statutes are in a class by themselves, in view of the familiar abuses to which they are put. See Note, 47 Col. L. Rev. 613, 625. Definiteness is designedly avoided so as to allow the net to be cast at large, to enable men to be caught who are vaguely undesirable in the eyes of police and prosecution, although not chargeable with any particular offense. In short. these "vagrancy statutes" and laws against "gangs" are not fenced in by the text of the statute or by the subject matter so as to give notice of conduct to be avoided.

And so I conclude that New York. in the legislation before us, has not exceeded its constitutional power to control crime. The Court strikes down laws that forbid publications inciting to crime, and as such not within the constitutional immunity of free speech, because in effect it does not trust State tribunals. nor ultimately this Court, to safeguard inoffensive publications from condemnation under this legislation. Every legislative limitation upon utterance, however valid, may in a particular case serve as an inroad upon the freedom of speech which the Constitution protects. See, *e. g., Cantwell* v. *Connecticut,* 310 U. S. 296, and Mr. Justice Holmes' dissent in *Abrams* v. *United States,* 250 U. S. 616, 624. The decision of the Court is concerned solely with the validity of the statute, and this opinion is restricted to that issue.

COURT'S OPINION NOTES

[1] The counts of the information upon which appellant was convicted charged, as the state court opinions show, violation of subsection 2 of § 1141. An example follows:

"Fourth Count

"And I, the District Attorney aforesaid, by this information, further accuse the said defendant of the Crime of Unlawfully Possessing Obscene Prints, committed as follows:

"The said defendant, on the day and in the year aforesaid, at the city and in the county aforesaid, with intent to sell, lend, give away and show, unlawfully did offer for sale and distribution, and have in his possession with intent to sell, lend, give away and show, a certain obscene, lewd, lascivious, filthy, indecent and disgusting magazine entitled 'Headquarters Detective, True Cases from the Police Blotter, June 1940', the same being devoted to the publication and principally made up of criminal news, police reports, and accounts of criminal deeds, and pictures and stories of deeds of bloodshed, lust and crime."

[2] "§ 1141. . . . 1. A person who sells, lends, gives away, distributes or shows, or offers to sell, lend, give away, distribute, or show, or has in his possession with intent to sell, lend, distribute or give away, or to show, or advertises in any manner, or who otherwise offers for loan, gift, sale or distribution, any obscene, lewd, lascivious, filthy, indecent or disgusting book, magazine, pamphlet, newspaper, story paper, writing, paper, picture, drawing, photograph, figure or image, or any written or printed matter of an indecent character; . . .

.　　.　　.　　.　　.

"Is guilty of a misdemeanor, ..."

[3] Ch. 380, New York Laws, 1884; ch. 692, New York Laws, 1887; ch. 925, New York Laws, 1941.

[4] *Connally* v. *General Construction Co.,* 269 U. S. 385, 391–92: "But it will be enough for present purposes to say generally that the decisions of the court upholding statutes as sufficiently certain, rested upon the conclusion that they employed words or phrases having a technical or other special meaning, well enough known to enable those within their reach to correctly apply them, . . . or a well-settled common law meaning, notwithstanding an element of degree in the definition as to which estimates might differ, . . . or, as broadly stated by Mr. Chief Justice White in *United States* v. *Cohen Grocery Co.,* 255 U. S. 81, 92, 'that, for reasons found to result either from the text of the statutes involved or the subjects with which they dealt, a standard of some sort was afforded.' "

[5] *United States* v. *Cohen Grocery Co.,* 255 U. S. 81, 89–93; *Champlin Refining Co.* v. *Corporation Commission,* 286 U. S. 210, 242; *Smith* v. *Cahoon,* 283 U. S. 553, 564.

[6] *Omaechevarria* v. *Idaho,* 246 U. S. 343; *Waters-Pierce Oil Co.* v. *Texas,* 212 U. S. 86.

[7] *United States* v. *Petrillo,* 332 U. S. 1; *Gorin* v. *United States,* 312 U. S. 19.

[8] *Hygrade Provision Co.* v. *Sherman,* 266 U. S. 497, 501; *Mutual Film Corp.* v. *Ohio Industrial Commission,* 236 U. S. 230, 245–46; *Screws* v. *United States,* 325 U. S. 91, 94–100.

JUSTICE FRANKFURTER'S OPINION NOTES

[1] The original statute, N. Y. L. 1884, c. 380, has twice since been amended in minor details. N. Y. L. 1887, c. 692; N. Y. L. 1941, c. 925. In its present form, it reads as follows:
"§ 1141. Obscene prints and articles
"1. A person . . . who,

.　　.　　.　　.

"2. Prints, utters, publishes, sells, lends, gives away, distributes or

shows, or has in his possession with intent to sell, lend, give away, distribute or show, or otherwise offers for sale, loan, gift or distribution, any book, pamphlet, magazine, newspaper or other printed paper devoted to the publication, and principally made up of criminal news, police reports, or accounts of criminal deeds, or pictures, or stories of deeds of bloodshed, lust or crime; . . .

.　　.　　.　　.　　.

"Is guilty of a misdemeanor . . . ."
That this legislation was neither a casual enactment nor a passing whim is shown by the whole course of its history. The original statute was passed as the result of a campaign by the New York Society for the Suppression of Vice and the New York Society for the Prevention of Cruelty to Children. See 8th Ann. Rep., N. Y. Soc. for the Suppression of Vice (1882) p. 7; 9th *id.* (1883) p. 9; 10th *id.* (1884) p. 8; 11th *id.* (1885) pp. 7–8. The former organization, at least, had sought legislation covering many more types of literature and conduct. See 8th *id.* (1882) pp. 6–9; 9th *id.* (1883) pp. 9–12. On the other hand, in 1887, the limitation of the statute to sales, etc., to children was removed. N. Y. L. 1887, c. 692. More recently, it has been found desirable to add to the remedies available to the State to combat this type of literature. A 1941 statute conferred jurisdiction upon the Supreme Court, at the instance of the chief executive of the community, to enjoin the sale or distribution of such literature. N. Y. L. 1941, c. 925, § 2, N. Y. Code Crim. Proc. § 22–a. (The additional constitutional problems that might be raised by such injunctions, cf. *Near* v. *Minnesota,* 283 U. S. 697, are of course not before us.)

[2] We have no statistics or other reliable knowledge as to the incidence of violations of these laws, nor as to the extent of their enforcement. Suffice it to say that the highest courts of three of the most industrialized States—Connecticut, Illinois, and New York—have had this legislation before them.

[3] This assumes a similar construction for essentially the same laws.

*Since this opinion was filed, Conn. L. 1935, c. 216, repealing this provision, has been called to my attention.

[4] See, *e. g., United States* v. *United Shoe Machinery Co.,* 247 U. S. 32; *United States* v. *United States Steel Corp.,* 251 U. S. 417; *United States* v. *Reading Co.,* 253 U. S. 26; *American Column & Lumber Co.* v. *United States,* 257 U. S. 377; *Maple Flooring Mfrs. Assn.* v. *United States,* 268 U. S. 563; *Cement Mfrs. Protective Assn.* v. *United States,* 268 U. S. 588; *United States* v. *Trenton Potteries Co.,* 273 U. S. 392; *Interstate Circuit, Inc.* v. *United States,* 306 U. S. 208; *United States* v. *Socony-Vacuum Oil Co.,* 310 U. S. 150; *United States* v. *South-Eastern Underwriters Assn.,* 322 U. S. 533; *Associated Press* v. *United States,* 326 U. S. 1; *United States* v. *Line Material Co.,* 333 U. S. 287.

SANCTUARY, WILD PALMS, GOD'S LITTLE ACRE, A WORLD I NEVER MADE, END AS A MAN, AND THE *STUDS LONIGAN TRILOGY* GET FIRST AMENDMENT PROTECTION FROM JUDGE CURTIS BOK: "WHO CAN DEFINE THE CLEAR AND PRESENT DANGER TO THE COMMUNITY THAT ARISES FROM READING A BOOK?"

Commonwealth v. Gordon, 66 D. & C. 101 (1949)

BOK, J., March 18, 1949.—This is a trial without jury, all defendants having signed waivers on all indictments.

The evidence consists of nine books and an oral stipulation at bar that defendants are booksellers and that they possessed the books with the intent to sell them on the dates and at the times and places set forth in the indictments. This constituted in full the Commonwealth's evidence, to which defendants have demurred.

I have read the books with thoughtful care and find that they are not obscene, as alleged. The demurrers are therefore sustained.

The Statute

The indictments are drawn under section 524 of The Penal Code of June 24, 1939, P. L. 872, 18 PS §4524, which reads as follows:

"Whoever sells, lends, distributes, exhibits, gives away, or shows or offers to sell, lend, distribute, exhibit, or give away or show, or has in his possession with intent to sell, lend, distribute or give away or to show, or knowingly advertises in any manner, any obscene, lewd, lascivious, filthy, indecent or disgusting book, magazine, pamphlet, newspaper, storypaper, paper, writing, drawing, photograph, figure or image, or any written or printed matter of an indecent character, or any article or instrument of indecent or immoral use or purporting to be for indecent or immoral use or purpose, or whoever designs, copies, draws, photographs, prints, utters, publishes, or in any manner manufactures or prepares any such book, picture, drawing, magazine, pamphlet, newspaper, storypaper, paper, writing, figure, image, matter, article or thing, or whoever writes, prints, publishes or utters, or causes to be printed, published or uttered, any advertisement or notice of any kind giving information, directly or indirectly, stating or purporting to do so, where, how, of whom, or by what means any, or what purports to be, any obscene, lewd, lascivious, filthy, disgusting or indecent book, picture, writing, paper, figure, image, matter, article or thing named in this section can be purchased, obtained or had, or whoever prints, utters, publishes, sells, lends, gives away, or shows, or has in his possession with intent to sell, lend, give away, or show, or otherwise offers for sale, loan or gift, or distribution, any pamphlet, magazine, newspaper or other printed paper devoted to the publication and principally made up of criminal news, police reports or accounts of criminal deeds, or pictures of stories of deeds of bloodshed, lust or crime, or whoever hires, employs, uses or permits any minor or child to do or assist in doing any act or thing mentioned in this section, is guilty of a misdemeanor, and upon conviction, shall be sentenced to imprisonment not exceeding one (1) year, or to pay a fine not exceeding five hundred dollars ($500), or both."

The particular and only charge in the indictments is that defendants possessed some or all of the books with the intent to sell them.

Section 524, quoted above, is based upon the earlier Acts of May 6, 1887, P. L. 84, and May 12, 1897, P. L. 63, 18 PS §§780, 781 and 782, which are similar in scope and not essentially different in wording. The earliest and only other act is the Criminal Code of March 31, 1860, P. L. 382, sec. 40, 18 PS §779, which made it an offense to "publish or sell any filthy and obscene libel".

It should be noted at once that the wording of section 524 requires consideration of the indicted material as a whole; it does not proscribe articles or publications that merely contain obscene matter. This is now true in all jurisdictions that have dealt with the subject: the Federal courts, Swearingen v. United States, 161 U. S. 446 (1896); United States v. Ulysses, 72 F.(2d) 705 (1934); Walker v. Popenoe, 149 F.(2d) 511 (1945); Massachusetts, Commonwealth v. Isenstadt, 318 Mass. 543 (1945); New York, Halsey v. New York Society, 234 N. Y. 1, 136 N. E. 219 (1922); England, Regina v. Hicklin, L. R. 3 Q. B. 360 (1868).

It is also the rule in Pennsylvania. In Commonwealth v. New, 142 Pa. Superior Ct. 358 (1940), the court said:

"We have no fault to find with the statement that in determining whether a work is obscene, it must be construed as a whole and that *regard shall be had for its place in the arts*." (Italics supplied.)

Résumé of the Opinion

Section 524, for all its verbiage, is very bare. The full weight of the legislative prohibition dangles from the word "obscene" and its synonyms. Nowhere are these words defined; nowhere is the danger to be expected of them stated; nowhere is a standard of judgment set forth. I assume that "obscenity" is expected to have a familiar and inherent meaning, both as to what it is and as to what it does.

It is my purpose to show that it has no such inherent meaning; that different meanings given to it at different times are not constant, either historically or legally; and that it is not constitutionally indictable unless it takes the form of sexual impurity, i. e., "dirt for dirt's sake" and can be traced to actual criminal behavior, either actual or demonstrably imminent.

Résumé of the Books

1, 2 and 3. The Studs Lonigan trilogy ("Young Lonigan", "The Young Manhood of Studs Lonigan", "Judgment Day"), by James T. Farrell; Vanguard Press, 1932-1935.

This is the story of the moral and physical disintegration of a young man living in Chicago between the years 1916 and 1932. Nothing that he attempted ever quite came off, and his failures became more and more incisive. He left school to hang around the streets with others of his kind; he was too young to enlist for war service; he loved Lucy since they were in school together, but avoided her for four years and finally alienated her by making drunken advances to her; he worked for his father as a painter, but, on a casual tip, invested his savings in a dubious stock, which failed; he fell half-heartedly in love with Catherine, and they were engaged to be married, but she became pregnant by him before the ceremony; looking for a job on a stormy day a few weeks before the wedding, he caught cold and died of pneumonia and a weakened heart.

The background of the semi-slum district in which Lonigan was born and lived was the outward counterpart of his own nature, and both together were too much for such decency of soul as he had. His drift downhill was relentless and inevitable. On the theory that no literature is vital that cannot be vulgarized, this trilogy may rank as an epic, for our criminal courts and prisons and many of our streets are peopled by Studs Lonigans. The characters in these books act and speak the kind of life that bred them, and Mr. Farrell has brought to the surface the groundswell of thought and inclination that move more people than, if they were honest, would admit to them.

It is not a pleasant story, nor are the characters gentle and refined. There is rape and dissipation and lust in these books, expressed in matching language, but they do not strike me as being out of proportion. The books as a whole create a sustained arc of a man's life and era, and the obvious effort of the author is to be faithful to the scene he depicts.

No one would want to be Studs Lonigan.

4. "A World I Never Made", by James T. Farrell; The Vanguard Press, New York, 1936.

This book could well be the beginning of another series, for it takes a minor character from the Lonigan books, Danny O'Neill, and shows him as a child. The milieu is the same—Chicago in 1911—but there is a discernible effort to show Danny's struggle uphill against the same factors that pushed Lonigan down.

This is the one book of the nine that does not end tragically; it merely stops in midstream, but the people who surround Danny do and say the same things that appear in the Lonigan series. Unlike the latter, this book is plastered with the short Saxon words of common vulgarity; they are consistent with the characters who use them and with the quality of the lives and actions that are the subject of the author's scrutiny.

I am not of a mind, nor do I have the authority, to require an author to write about one kind of people and not about another, nor do I object to his effort to paint a complete picture of those whom he has chosen. Certainly I will not say that it is not a good thing to look deeply into life and people, regardless of the shadows that are to be found there.

5. "Sanctuary", by William Faulkner; Random House, 1931.

This is a powerful and dreadful story about a gay but virginal girl of 17 who accidentally falls into the hands of a sadistic man called Popeye, who is sexually impotent. He kills a half-witted boy who is informally guarding the girl, and ravishes her with a corncob. He then keeps her imprisoned in a house of prostitution and takes pleasure in watching her have intercourse with a man whom he kills when she tries to escape with him. Terrified of Popeye, she testifies that another man committed the murder, and is taken from court by her father, who has finally been able to locate her. Popeye is later apprehended on another charge of murder and is convicted.

There are no vulgar Saxon words in the book, but the situations are stark and unrelieved. It makes one shudder to think of what can happen by misadventure.

6. "Wild Palms", by William Faulkner; Random House, 1939.

This book concerns a wife who left her husband and children to seek integrity of experience, in terms of vitality, with her lover; "hunger is in the heart", she says, when the next meal seems uncertain, "not in the stomach". They wander about the country together, living as they must or as they wish, and she finally becomes pregnant. Her lover, a former doctor, attempts to abort her but mishandles it and she dies. He pleads guilty and is sentenced to 50 years in prison. He refuses a gift of cyanide from the woman's husband, saying: "Between grief and nothing I will take grief".

The redeeming feature of this tale is that an acid loneliness comes through, the awful loneliness that pervades lost people, even in company. No one could envy these two miserable creatures.

7. "God's Little Acre", by Erskine Caldwell; Random House, 1933.

An able companion to the same author's "Tobacco Road", it is the story of a poor and illiterate farmer's family in Georgia. The central figure is the father, who for 15 years has dug holes in his farm in search of gold. God's Little Acre is a part of the farm which he mentally moves about in order to keep it from getting in the way of his search for treasure; his idea is to give all that comes from it to the church, but he never works it. His daughters and sons and their wives get variously tangled up in sexual affairs which are taken as being in the nature of things. One brother kills another over his wife. The final and despairing cry of the father, who has always tried to keep peace, is, "Blood on my land!"

It is a frank and turbulent story, but it is an obvious effort to be faithful to the locality and its people.

8. "End As a Man", by Calder Willingham; The Vanguard Press, 1947.

Life in a southern military academy. A drinking party and crooked poker game finally result in the expulsion of several cadets, including the wily and unmoral ringleader. The retired general in charge of the academy is the stereotype of military martinet, whose conception of the narrow and rigid discipline necessary to produce "a man" is set in bold relief against the energy of growing boys. The result is a fair picture of the frustration inherent in an overdose of discipline and in the license and disobedience that is largely engendered by it.

No one would care to send his son to such an institution.

This is perhaps the foulest book of the lot, so far as language is concerned, but it is the language of vulgarity and not of erotic allurement.

9. "Never Love a Stranger", by Harold Robbins; Knopf, 1948.

The story of a boy brought up in an orphanage who finds that he has an uncle and is Jewish. After losing touch with his uncle he has various experiences and is finally down and out because he can find no work. He then becomes head of New York City's gambling racket, which he ultimately leaves in order to marry a childhood friend. She dies in childbirth and he is killed in the war; his friends take over the child, who will presumably have a better chance in life than he had.

It is a swift story that covers a great deal of ground, its point being to portray a hard and lonely man who could not fully trust or give himself to anyone. Its last and least convincing part is also the least open to attack for obscenity; the rest, particularly the section dealing with New York City during the depression of the early 1930's, is very moving, not because there are sexual incidents but because the lines of the story are deep and authentic.

General Comment

Three of these books have already been judicially cleared in New York City.

"A World I Never Made" was before Magistrate Curran in 1937, under the caption of Bamberger v. The Vanguard Press, Inc., docket no. 329. The opinion was impromptu and is in the perceptive magistrate's best style.

"God's Little Acre" was the subject of People v. Viking Press, Inc., 147 N. Y. Misc. 813 (1933). In the course of his opinion Magistrate Greenspan said:

"The Courts have strictly limited the applicability of the statute to works of pornography and they have consistently declined to apply it to books of genuine literary value. If the statute were construed more broadly than in the manner just indicated, its effect would be to prevent altogether the realistic portrayal in literature of a large and important field of life. . . . The Court may not require the author to put refined language into the mouths of primitive people." (Italics supplied.)

Magistrate Strong held "End As a Man" not obscene in People v. Vanguard Press, 192 N. Y. Misc. 127 (1947), and observed:

"The speech of the characters must be considered in relation to its setting and the theme of the story. It seems clear that use of foul language will not of itself bring a novel or play within the condemnation of the statute."

After clearance by the magistrates, these books could have been brought before the grand jury, but no such indictments were attempted.

As I have indicated above, all but one of these books are profoundly tragic, and that one has its normal quota of frustration and despair. No one could envy or wish to emulate the characters that move so desolately through these pages. Far from inciting to lewd or lecherous desires, which are sensorially pleasurable, these books leave one either with a sense of horror or of pity for the degradation of mankind. The effect upon the normal reader, "l'homme moyen sensuel" (there is no such deft precision in English), would be anything but what the vice hunters fear it might be. We are so fearful for other people's morals; they so seldom have the courage of our own convictions.

It will be asked whether one would care to have one's young daughter read these books. I suppose that by the time she is old enough to wish to read them she will have learned the biologic facts of life and the words that go with them. There is something seriously wrong at home if those facts have not been met and faced and sorted by then; it is not children so much as parents that should receive our concern about this. I should prefer that my own three daughters meet the facts of life and the literature of the world in my library than behind a neighbor's barn, for I can face the adversary there directly. If the young ladies are appalled by what they read, they can close the book at the bottom of page one; if they read further, they will learn what is in the world and in its people, and no parents who have been discerning with their children need fear the outcome. Nor can they hold it back, for life is a series of little battles and minor issues, and the burden of choice is on us all, every day, young and old. Our daughters must live in the world and decide what sort of women they are to be, and we should be willing to prefer their deliberate and informed choice of decency rather than an innocence that continues to spring from ignorance. If that choice be made in the open sunlight, it is more apt than when made in shadow to fall on the side of honorable behavior.

The lesson to be learned from such books as these is not so facile as that the wages of sin is death, or, in Hollywood's more modern version, that the penalty of sinning is suffering. That is not enough to save a book from proper censorship. The tragedy of these books is not in death but in the texture of the slope that leads to death—in the inner suffering that comes at times from crimes against oneself as much as from crimes against society. That has been the green pastures of storytellers ever since the Greek dramatists, especially when the pressures on a character are not, as they are not always, of his own making or within his control. Sin is too apt a word to take in the full reach of circumstance, and I venture to say that in human experience suffering does not automatically follow sinning. Our laws have a good deal to do with that guarded notion. It is necessary to know what our laws are up to, and it is my conviction that, outside the police power, the laws of Anglo-Saxon countries are made less as absolute mandates than as clinical experiments. Democratic nations prefer checks and balances to absolute authority, and it is worthy of notice that the jury system exists only in those countries where the law is not considered to have been drawn, as Cicero put it, from the forehead of the gods, but rather from the will of the people, who wish to keep an eye on it. The eighteenth amendment to the Constitution is a case in point.

Such sumptuary laws, and some economic ones, differ from obscenity statutes only in the degree of danger to society inherent in the appetite in question. The need for decency is as old as the appetites, but it is not expressed in uniform law or custom. The ancient Hebrews had a rigid moral code which, for example, excluded bastards from the congregation up to the tenth generation, for the combined reasons of preserving their ancient tradition of tribe and family and of increasing the number of effective warriors. The Greeks, more cosmopolitan in a country whose sterile soil could not support many people comfortably, approved pederasty and a restricted form of concubinage in order to keep the population down. Standards of sexual behavior, as well as of the need to censor it, have shifted from age to age, from country to country, and from economy to economy. The State of New Mexico has no obscenity statute. South Carolina has no divorce law.

Censorship, which is the policeman of decency, whether religious, patriotic, or moral, has had distinct fashions, depending on which great questions were agitating society at the time. During the Middle Ages, when the church was supreme, the focus of suppression was upon heresy and blasphemy. When the State became uppermost, the focus of suppression was upon treason and sedition. The advent of technology made Queen Victoria realize, perhaps subconsciously, that loose morals would threaten the peace of mind necessary to the development of invention and big business; the focus moved to sexual morality. We are now emerging into an era of social ideology and psychology, and the focus is turning to these. The right to speak out and to act freely is always at a minimum in the area of the fighting faiths.

The censorship of books did not become a broad public issue until after the invention of printing in the fifteenth century. The earliest real example of it was the first Index Librorum Prohibitorum of the Catholic Church in 1559, and the church was broadly tolerant of sexual impurity in the books that it considered; its main object was the suppression of heresy. I think it is a fair general statement that from ancient times until the Comstockian laws of 1873 the only form of written obscenity that was censored was "dirt for dirt's sake".

I do not regard the above as apart from the decisional purpose of this case. The words of the statute—"obscene, lewd, lascivious, filthy, indecent, or disgusting" —restrict rather than broaden the meaning of a highly penal statute. The effect of this plethora of epithets is to merge them into one prevailing meaning—that of sexual impurity alone, and this has been universally held: People v. Eastman, 188 N. Y. 478 (1907); People v. Wendling, 258 N. Y. 451 (1932); Commonwealth v. Isenstadt, supra (318 Mass. 543 (1945)); Attorney General v. "Forever Amber", (Mass.) 81 N. E. (2d) 663 (1948); United States v. Ulysses, supra, (72 F.(2d) 705 (1934)).

In Swearingen v. United States, 161 U. S. 446 (1896), a case involving the mailing of obscene matter, the court said:

"The offence aimed at, in that portion of the statute we are now considering, was the use of the mails to circulate or deliver matter to corrupt the morals of the people. The words 'obscene', 'lewd', and 'lascivious', as used in the statute, signify that form of immorality which has relation to sexual impurity, and have the same meaning as is given them at common law in prosecutions for obscene libel. As the statute is highly penal, it should not be held to embrace language unless it is fairly within its letter and spirit."

This view has been adopted in Pennsylvania, for the court said in Commonwealth v. New, supra (142 Pa. Superior Ct. 358 (1940)):

"The test for obscenity most frequently laid down seems to be whether the writing would tend to deprave the morals of those into whose hands the publication might fall by suggesting lewd thoughts and exciting sensual desires."

The statute is therefore directed only at sexual impurity and not at blasphemy or coarse and vulgar behavior of any other kind. The word in common use for the purpose of such a statute is "obscenity". The great point of this case is to find out what that word means.

Nowhere in the statute is there a definition of it or a formula given for determining when it exists. Its derivation, ob and scena, suggests that anything done offstage, furtively, or lefthandedly, is obscene. The act does not penalize anyone who seeks to change the prevailing moral or sexual code, nor does it state that the writing must be such as to corrupt the morals of the public or of youth; it merely proscribes books that are obscene and leaves it to the authorities to decide whether or not they are. This cannot be done without regard to the nature and history of obscenity. It is unlike the fundamental laws of property, of crimes like murder, rape, and theft, or even of negligence, whose meaning has remained relatively constant. That of obscenity has frequently changed, almost from decade to decade within the past century; "Ulysses" was condemned by the State courts in New York just 10 years before it was cleared by Judge Woolsey in the District Court for the Southern District of New York. I must determine what this elusive word means now.

Something might be said at the outset about the familiar four-letter words that are so often associated with sexual impurity. These are, almost without exception, of honest Anglo-Saxon ancestry, and were not invented for purely scatological effect. The one, for example, that is used to denote the sexual act is an old agricultural word meaning "to plant", and was at one time a wholly respectable member of the English vocabulary. The distinction between a word of decent etymological history and one of smut alone is important; it shows that fashions in language change as expectably as do the concepts of what language connotes. It is the old business of semantics again, the difference between word and concept.

But there is another distinction. The decisions that I shall cite have sliced off vulgarity from obscenity. This has had the effect of making a clear division between the words of the bathroom and those of the bedroom: the former can no longer be regarded as obscene, since they have no erotic allurement, and the latter may be so regarded, depending on the circumstances of their use. This reduces the number of potentially offensive words sharply.

With such changes as these, the question is whether the legal mace should fall upon words or upon concepts —language or ideas.

Obscenity is not like sedition, blasphemy, or open lewdness, against which there are also criminal statutes. These offenses not only have acquired precise meaning but are defined specifically in the act. Sedition (Act of June 24, 1939, P. L. 872, section 207, 18 PS §4207), which includes writing and publication, is carefully defined in eight subheadings. Blasphemy (same act, section 523, 18 PS §4523) is stated as speaking "loosely and profanely of Almighty God, Christ Jesus, the Holy Spirit, or the Scriptures of Truth". Open lewdness (same act, section 519, 18 PS §4519) is "any notorious act of public indecency, tending to debauch the morals or manners of the people". Other crimes, involving restriction on free speech and having their scope or purpose set forth with particularity in The Penal Code, include blackmail (section 801), libel (section 412), anonymous communications (section 414), false letters of recommendation (section 856), false advertising (section 857), advertising without publisher's consent (section 858), and fortune telling (section 870).

No such definition of standard or legislative intention occurs in section 524, and I am convinced that without a declaration of the legislature's intention as to what obscenity means or of what the lawmakers sought to prevent, there is no constant or reliable indication of it to be found in human experience.

The argument is often made that anyone can tell by instinct what is obscene and what is not, even if it is hard to put the difference into words. The same might be said of sedition, blasphemy, and open lewdness, but the legislature was careful to specify. With regard to obscenity, however, the argument does not hold water. When he was an editor, Walter Hines Page deleted the word "chaste" because it was suggestive, and the play "Sappho" was banned in New York City because a man carried the leading lady up a flight of stairs. A librarian once charged Mark Twain's "Tom Sawyer" and "Huckleberry Finn" with corrupting the morals of children. In 1907 Richard Strauss's "Salome" was banned in Boston. Charlotte Bronte's "Jane Eyre", when first published, was called "too immoral to be ranked as decent literature". Hawthorne's "Scarlet Letter" was referred to as "a brokerage of lust". George Eliot's "Adam Bede" was called "the vile outpourings of a lewd woman's mind". Others to suffer similarly were Elizabeth Barrett Browning's "Aurora Leigh", Hardy's "Tess" and "Jude", DuMaurier's "Trilby", and Shaw's "Mrs. Warren's Profession". Walt Whitman lost his job in the United States Department of the Interior because of "Leaves of Grass".

It is presumed that Mr. Page and the others who attacked this imposing array of classics could tell by instinct what was decent and what was not. The idea that instinct can be resorted to as a process of moral stare decisis reduces to absurdity.

It is a far cry from the examples just cited to what society accepts as innocuous now. The stage, literature, painting, sculpture, photography, fashions of dress, and even the still pudibund screen tolerate things that would have made Anthony Comstock turn blue. In its issue of April 11, 1938, Life magazine ran a series of factual and dignified pictures called "The Birth of a Baby". It was attacked in the courts but was exonerated. Dr. Kinsey's report on the sexual behavior of men is now current. Truth and error, as Milton urged in his "Areopagitica", are being allowed to grapple, and we are the better for it.

In addition to the books whose banning is the subject of cases cited later in this opinion, I suggest a short list of modern books that have not been banned, so far as I can find out. All of these books contain sexual material, and all of them can be found in the Boston Public Library. I defy anyone to provide a rational basis for the distinction between these two sets of books. My list includes: Fanny Hurst's "Back Street"; Arthur Koestler's "Arrival and Departure"; Erich Maria Remarque's "All Quiet on The Western Front" and "Arch of Triumph"; Eugene O'Neill's "Anna Christie" and "Hairy Ape"; John Dos Passos's "U. S. A."; Ernest Hemingway's "For Whom the Bell Tolls"; Somerset Maugham's "Of Human Bondage"; Charles Morgan's "The Fountain" and "The Voyage"; Richard Wright's "Black Boy".

It is no answer to say that if my point about the books just listed be sound, then by analogy the law against murder is useless because all murderers are not caught. The inherent evil of murder is apparent, but by what apparent, inherent standard of evil is obscenity to be judged, from book to book? It is my purpose to provide such a standard, but it will reduce to a minimum the operation of any norm of indefinite interpretation.

Before leaving this point, research discloses a curious but complete confusion between the post office and the customs over what constitutes obscenity. No unanimity of opinion unites these two governmental services in a common standard. Books have cleared the port only to find the mails closed to them: others, printed here, have circulated freely while foreign copies were stopped at the ports. One would expect greater uniformity than this if obscenity could be unmistakably detected.

There is a bale of literature on obscenity and the history of censorship, i. e., suppression of the right of free expression. It is best represented by two books by Morris L. Ernst, Esq., entitled "To The Pure" (Viking Press, 1929) and "The Censor Marches On" (Doubleday, Doran & Co., 1940), with William Seagle and Alexander Lindey, respectively, colloborating. In addition to the brilliant and scholarly text, there is a large bibliography and appendices. These two books should be required reading, of at least equal importance with legal authority, in deciding a censorship case.

An interesting volume on literary censorship is "Banned Books", by Anne Lyon Haight (R. R. Bowker Co., New York, 1935), which lists the principal suppressions of books, for various reasons, at various times and in various places, from Caligula's attempt to suppress "The Odessey" in A. D. 35 to the lifting of the ban on "Ulysses" in 1934.

The legal authorities on obscenity may be found well collected in 76 A. L. R. 1099, and 81 A. L. R. 801.

It is my conclusion that the books before me are obvious efforts to show life as it is. I cannot be convinced that the deep drives and appetites of life are very much different from what they have always been, or that censorship has ever had any effect on them, except as the law's police power to preserve the peace in censorship. I believe that the consensus of preference today is for disclosure and not stealth, for frankness and not hypocrisy, and for public and not secret distribution. That in itself is a moral code.

It is my opinion that frank disclosure cannot legally be censored, even as an exercise of the police power, unless it is sexually impure and pornographic, as I shall define those words. They furnish the only possible test for obscenity and its effect.

These books are not, in my view, sexually impure and pornographic.

The Pennsylvania Cases

I venture a long and detailed opinion because this is the first case in Pennsylvania that deals with current literature in book form. Our authorities on the censoring of obscenity are so few that they can all be referred to.

The earliest case is that of Commonwealth v. Sharpless, 2 S. & R. 91 (1815), in which defendant was convicted of exhibiting an indecent picture. The case has importance because of the holding by Tilghman, C. J., that since there was no act of assembly on the matter, the case had to be decided on common-law principles, which he found covered such an indictment. The chief justice did not doubt that the publication of an indecent book was also indictable at common law, and cited the English case of Rex v. Curl, 2 Str. 788, 93 E. R. 849 (1727).

The Sharpless case can be taken as authority that obscenity was a common-law offense in England at the time of the American Revolution and hence became part of the common law of Pennsylvania. The status of the common law on many points often depends on the date to which one opens the books, and it should be observed that obscenity was not a part of English common law until Rex v. Curl, supra: in Regina v. Read, Fortescue, 98, 92 E. R. 777 (1707), only 20 years earlier, the lords wished that there were a law to punish the publication of "The Fifteen Plagues of a Maidenhead", but decided that they couldn't make one—it was a matter for the ecclesiastical courts.

In Rex v. Wilkes, 4 Burr. 2527, 98 E. R. 327 (1770), defendant was indicted and convicted of printing an obscene libel entitled "An Essay on Women". Jurisdiction was assumed, for there was no discussion of it nor was any objection made to the indictment: the reported proceedings have to do with procedural matters and with the propriety of a sentence of outlawry for a misdemeanor.

It is on these two cases—Rex v. Curl and Rex v. Wilkes—and on Blackstone that indictable obscenity as a part of the English common law depends.

Blackstone, who began his Vinerian lectures on October 25, 1758, after labors "of so many years" in collecting his material, says, in Book IV of the Commentaries, pp. 150 and 151, that libels in their largest and most extensive sense signify any writings, pictures, or the like, of an immoral or illegal tendency, and are punishable in the interest of the preservation of peace and good order. It is interesting to note that he goes on at once to make the point that freedom of the press is not involved, since the right exists to publish anything, but only the abuse of it, established by trial after publication, is punishable.

While Blackstone had only Rex v. Curl (1727) to support him as authority, he is regarded as authority himself, and it must therefore be held that obscene publication was indictable at common law.

It is important to observe that there are few, if any, obscene book cases in the English reports between the time of Rex v. Curl, in 1727, and Regina v. Hicklin, in 1868; that in Pennsylvania no act was passed against obscenity until 1860, and that no case involving an obscene book appeared until Commonwealth v. Landis, infra, in 1870. Commonwealth v. Sharpless, in 1815, mentioned books by dictum only.

This removes from the doctrine of indictable obscenity much of the veneration that is usually given to common-law doctrines because of their hoary age. The plain fact is that the period of the Renaissance, in both countries, was a lusty one, and that concern over sexual purity did not begin to arise until Victorianism really took hold in the middle 1850's. One need only recall that the father of the post office, Benjamin Franklin, wrote and presumably mailed his "Letter of Advice to Young Men on the Proper Choosing of a Mistress"; that Thomas Jefferson worried about the students at his new University of Virginia having a respectable brothel; that Alexander Hamilton's adultery while holding public office created no great scandal, or that the morals of Southern chivalry provided us with mulattos until the abolition of slavery at least made the matter one of free choice on both sides.

The formulation of the common-law proscription of obscene publication did not, therefore, amount to very much. It is a good example of a social restriction that became law and was allowed to slumber until a change of social consciousness should animate it. It is the prevailing social consciousness that matters quite as much as the law. Between 1870 and 1930 the obscenity law was on the social anvil: since then society has found other irons in the fire and has lost its interest in what Shaw has called Comstockery.

The next Pennsylvania case was Commonwealth v. Landis, 8 Phila. 453 (1870), in which defendant was convicted of selling a book called "Secrets of Generation". This case is interesting because it holds that it was for the jury to say whether the book was obscene, and that "that which offends modesty, and is indecent and lewd, and tends to the creation of lascivious desires, is obscene". Not only is this the first book case in the State, but it is the first example of showing the effort by both legislature and courts to define the libidinous synonyms in terms of each other: obscenity is filthiness, filthiness is indecency, indecency is lewdness, lewdness is lasciviousness, and lasciviousness is obscenity. The opinion also states "that to justify a publication of the character of this book they (the jury) must be satisfied that the publication was made for a legitimate and useful purpose, and that it was not made from any motive of mere gain or with a corrupt desire to debauch society". It ends with a warning that a book, obscene in itself, might be used either for a proper purpose, such as medical instruction, or for an improper one, such as general publication, and that in the latter case the utterer would have to answer.

In Commonwealth v. Havens, 6 Pa. C. C. 545 (1889), the constitutionality of the Act of May 6, 1887, was upheld, on the one ground advanced, that its title was broad enough. The case involved "The National Police Gazette" and "The Illustrated Police News". A conviction resulted. The court restricted the evidence to the specific advertisements complained of and refused to allow testimony as to what their real purpose was. Their inherent indecency was the only issue. The test of obscenity finally approved by the opinion was: "Would the articles or the pictures here . . . suggest impure and libidinous thoughts in the young and inexperienced?"

In re Arentsen, 26 W. N. C. 359 (1890), dealt with Count Leo Tolstoy's "Kreutzer Sonata". This case also holds that selling an obscene book was a common-law offense, and Judge Thayer cited Regina v. Hicklin, L. R. 3 Q. B. 360 (1868), of which more hereafter. Defendant was acquitted because the book was found to condemn marriage, not in favor of free love but of complete celibacy.

In Commonwealth v. Dowling, 14 Pa. C. C. 607 (1894), defendant was convicted of selling immoral newspapers to minors. The case is of little interest, except for the affirmance of one of defendant's points for charge: "The law does not undertake to punish bad English, vulgarity, or bad taste, and no matter how objectionable the jury may consider the papers referred to on those grounds, they have no right to convict on account of them."

In Commonwealth v. Magid & Dickstein, 91 Pa. Superior Ct. 513 (1927), the subject matter was indecent pictures. The court stated that the purpose of the Acts of 1887 and 1897 was "to shield minors and young children from obscene and indecent books and pictures."

In Commonwealth v. Kutler, 93 Pa. Superior Ct. 119 (1928), and Commonwealth v. Kufel, 142 Pa. Superior Ct. 273 (1940), the only question was whether defendants were the ones who sold certain pamphlets, the obscene character of which was conceded.

In Commonwealth v. New, supra (142 Pa. Superior Ct. 358 (1940)), the matter involved was certain pictures in a magazine called "Tipster". The test of obscenity adopted by the court shows a virtual abandonment of the harsh rule of Regina v. Hicklin, infra, and is stated thus: "Whether the writing would tend to deprave the morals of those into whose hands the publication might fall by suggesting lewd thoughts and exciting sensual desires." The purpose of the act is again stated to be the prevention of "appealing to those of depraved tastes or to the curiosity of adolescents".

In Commonwealth v. Mercur, 90 Pitts. L. J. 318 (1942), the court applied the "as a whole" rule of Commonwealth v. New, supra, and held that certain pictures appearing in a book of instruction for photographers called "U. S. Camera 1942", did not render the volume obscene.

This exhausts the Pennsylvania cases.

It is therefore clear that section 524 of our act has not yet been applied to serious current literature. There has not been the opportunity to form a modern test for obscenity in Pennsylvania as there has been in the lower Federal courts, and in the highest appellate courts of New York and Massachusetts.

Despite the scarcity of literary obscenity cases in this State, the trend has been away from and beyond the English common law. The range in growth of doctrine is from the dictum in the Sharpless case, that the common-law rule of obscene libel would apply to a book, to the opinion in the New case, that a book must be considered as a whole and regard be given to its place in the arts. The English appellate courts have not gone so far, as will be seen.

The first articulate test appears in the leading English case of Regina v. Hicklin, L. R. 3 Q. B. 360 (1868), and the American jurisdictions have had to face it before they could disregard it and forge the modern rule. In Pennsylvania, the rule for which it has become famous was cited with approval in Commonwealth v. Havens, supra (6 Pa. C. C. 545 (1889)), and again in In re Arentsen, supra (26 W. N. C. 359 (1890)), but the modern American rule has not yet been squarely adopted here.

The English Cases

Regina v. Hicklin is an example of judge-made law quite at variance with the parliamentary intent behind the act on which it was based. Lord Campbell's act provided for search and seizure warrants that would enable the police to take and destroy obscene publications. The report of the debates in Hansard show the lords' difficulties in deciding what an obscene publication might be. Lord Campbell, who was lord chief justice at the time, explained that the act was to apply exclusively to works written for the purpose of corrupting the morals of youth and of a nature calculated to shock the common feelings of decency in any well regulated mind. He was ready to make whatever was then indictable a test of obscenity in his new act. He made it clear that any work that even pretended to be literature or art, classic or modern, had little to fear.

All of this was nullified by Lord Chief Justice Cockburn in the Hicklin case, where the subject matter was a pamphlet entitled "The Confessional Unmasked", and containing a diatribe against the Catholic Church; its purpose was to show the depravity of the priesthood and the character of the questions put to women in the confessional. This is the now famous rule of the case:

"I think the test of obscenity is this, whether the tendency of the matter charged as obscenity is to deprave and corrupt those whose minds are open to such immoral influences, and into whose hands a publication of this sort may fall."

Strictly applied, this rule renders any book unsafe, since a moron could pervert to some sexual fantasy to which his mind is open the listings in a seed catalogue. Not even the Bible would be exempt; Annie Besant once compiled a list of 150 passages in Scripture that might fairly be considered obscene—it is enough to cite the story of Lot and his daughters, Genesis 19, 30-38. Portions of Shakespeare would also be offensive, and of Chaucer, to say nothing of Aristophanes, Juvenal, Ovid, Swift, Defoe, Fielding, Smollett, Rousseau, Maupassant, Voltaire, Balzac, Baudelaire, Rabelais, Swinburne, Shelley, Byron, Boccaccio, Marguerite de Navarre, Hardy, Shaw, Whitman, and a host more.

As will be seen later, the classics—whatever that may mean precisely—are considered exempt from censorship, but many of them were hounded in England, despite Lord Campbell's assurances, as a result of the rule of the Hicklin case.

The next English case—passing Regina v. Read, Rex v. Curl, and Rex v. Wilkes, which have been examined above—was Steele v. Brannan, L. R. 7 C. P. 261 (1872), which involved the report of the trial of one George Mackey for selling a pamphlet called "The Confessional Unmasked". The report set forth the pamphlet in full, and the court held not only the publication was not privileged as a report of legal proceedings but that it was obscene, despite its purpose to expose what the author considered dangerous religious practices. The court followed Regina v. Hicklin, without quoting the rule, and placed its point of emphasis upon the effect of the pamphlet "on the young and inexperienced".

The next case was Bradlaugh v. Regina, L. R. 3 Q. B. 607 (1878), in which a conviction for publishing a book called "Fruits of Philosophy" was reversed. The point was whether the allegedly obscene matter should be included in the indictment instead of being referred to by name only. The Court of Error held that it should be, and expressly avoided passing upon the character of the book.

The lower court case of Regina v. Thomson, 64 J. P. 456 (1900), in which the jury found defendant not guilty in an issue of whether or not the "Heptameron", by Queen Margaret of Navarre, was obscene, is interesting because of the charge of Bosanquet, C. S. It is the first mention that I have found in the English reports of the idea that fashions in obscenity change. After mentioning that in the Middle Ages things were discussed which would not be tolerated now, if given general publicity, Sergeant Bosanquet left it to the jury to say "whether the book is a fit book to put into people's hands in these days at the end of the nineteenth century". The jury felt that it was.

Sergeant Bosanquet was referred to with respect in Rex v. Barraclough, L. R. 1 K. B. 201 (1906), but the opinions, while mentioning Regina v. Hicklin indirectly, decided a point under a new act of Parliament as to what the indictment should contain. A conviction for publishing an obscene typewritten document that libeled one Edith Woodhead was upheld.

In Rex v. Montalk, 23 Cr. App. Rep. 182 (1932), a conviction for publishing a typewritten libel was sustained, the lord chief justice citing Regina v. Hicklin in a very brief opinion. In the court below, the recorder charged the jury that if it was of the opinion "that this can be for the public good as an advancement of literature, in my opinion that would be a defense". The libel was not a book but a series of verses on half a dozen sheets of paper.

This exhausts the reported English cases that are in point. They show continued adherence to the Hicklin rule, but the paucity of authority is noteworthy. It is as if the English public does not want to risk the severity of the common law, and it is clear proof to me of the clinical nature of the laws that are made to cover social situations. While the higher English courts were kept relatively idle on the question, private censorship in England has been very active; the most effective censor of the Victorian era was Mudie's circulating library. It was the time of the three-decker novel—ponderous, dull, and pure as the driven snow. When Mudie's power was finally broken, smaller circulating libraries continued to wield the same sort of influence and to reflect the general desire of the public for no disturbing material of an emotional nature. England was the pioneer in the advance of the Industrial Age, and the nation of shopkeepers was unwilling to be diverted from making money by sidetrips into erotica; what individuals did in the dark was their affair, but bad morals could not profitably become a matter of public concern.

The rule of Regina v. Hicklin suited the English, and presumably still does—not as a satisfying standard but as an effective policeman to take over and tone down the situation when the social experiment threatens to get out of hand.

Censorship should be the proper activity of the community rather than of the law, and the community has never been lazy upholding what it believes to be inherently decent at the moment. With a legal policeman handy, the market place is the best crucible in which to distil an instinctive morality. We have the evidence of Milton that there is no authoritative example of the suppression of a book in ancient times solely because of obscenity, but this does not mean that private criticism was not alert. Plato thought that Homer should be expurgated before Greek children should be allowed to read him. In Plutarch's opinion the comedies of Aristophanes were coarse and vulgar.

This is healthy, for it is the struggle of free opinion: it is not suppression by law. In the English community the people argue and Hicklin stands guard in case of trouble. The American method is different: the rule has been modernized.

The American Cases

1. The Federal Courts. There are two important opinions involving James Joyce's "Ulysses". Judge Woolsey's, in the district court, is reported as United States v. One Book Entitled Ulysses, 5 F. Supp. 182 (S. D. N. Y., 1933), and Judge Hand's, affirming Judge Woolsey, is reported in 72 F.(2d) 705 (C. C. A. 2d, 1934).

Judge Woolsey's decision may well be considered the keystone of the modern American rule, as it brings out clearly that indictable obscenity must be "dirt for dirt's sake". He said:

"It is because Joyce has been loyal to his technique and has not funked its necessary implications, but has honestly attempted to tell fully what his characters think about, that he has been the subject of so many attacks and that his purpose has been so often misunderstood and misrepresented. For his attempt sincerely and honestly to realize his objective has required him incidentally to use certain words which are generally considered dirty words and has led at times to what many think is a too poignant pre-occupation with sex in the thoughts of his characters.

"The words which are criticized as dirty are old, Saxon words known to almost all men and, I venture, to many women, and are such words as would be naturally and habitually used, I believe, by the types of folk whose life, physical and mental, Joyce is seeking to describe. . . . As I have stated, 'Ulysses' is not an easy book to read. It is brilliant and dull, intelligible and obscure, by turns. In many places it seems to me to be disgusting, but although it contains, as I have mentioned above, many words usually considered dirty, I have not found anything that I consider to be dirt for dirt's sake. Each word of the book contributes like a bit of mosaic to the detail of the picture which Joyce is seeking to construct for his readers.

"If one does not wish to associate with such folk as Joyce describes, that is one's own choice. In order to avoid indirect contact with them one may not wish to read 'Ulysses'; that is quite understandable. But when such a great artist in words, as Joyce undoubtedly is, seeks to draw a true picture of the lower middle class in a European city, ought it to be impossible for the American public legally to see that picture?"

In affirming Judge Woolsey, Judge Hand said, in the circuit court of appeals:

"That numerous long passages in Ulysses contain matter that is obscene under any fair definition of the word cannot be gainsaid; yet they are relevant to the purpose of depicting the thoughts of the characters and are introduced to give meaning to the whole, rather than to promote lust or portray filth for its own sake. The net effect even of portions most open to attack, such as the closing monologue of the wife of Leopold Bloom, is pitiful and tragic, rather than lustful. The book depicts the souls of men and women that are by turns bewildered and keenly apprehensive, sordid and aspiring, ugly and beautiful, hateful and loving. In the end one feels, more than anything else, pity and sorrow for the confusion, misery, and degradation of humanity. . . . The book as a whole is not pornographic, and, while in not a few spots it is coarse, blasphemous, and obscene, it does not, in our opinion, tend to promote lust. The erotic passages are submerged in the book as a whole and have little resultant effect."

In the circuit court Judge Manton dissented, and his opinion reviews the earlier Federal cases which he asserts approve the rule of Regina v. Hicklin: the prinicpal ones are U. S. v. Bennett, Fed. Cas. no. 14,571 (1879); Rosen v. U. S., 161 U. S. 29, 16 S. Ct. 434, 40 L. Ed. 606 (1896): Dunlop v. U. S., 165 U. S. 486, 17 S. Ct. 375, 41 L. Ed. 799 (1897).

These cases were individually and carefully distinguished by Judge Hand in the majority opinion, who held them not to represent the law:

"But it is argued that United States v. Bennett, Fed. Cas. No. 14,571, stands in the way of what has been said, and it certainly does. There a court, consisting of Blatchford, C. J., and Benedict and Choate, D.J.J., held that the offending paragraphs in a book could be taken from their context and the book judged by them alone, and that the test of obscenity was whether the tendency of these passages in themselves was 'to deprave the minds of those open to such influences and into whose hands a publication of this character might come.' The opinion was founded upon a dictum of Cockburn, C. J., in Regina v. Hicklin, L. R. 3 Q. B. 360, where half of a book written to attack the alleged practices of the confession was obscene and contained, as Mellor, J., said 'a great deal . . . which there cannot be any necessity for in any legitimate argument on the confessional. . . .' It is said that in Rosen v. United States, 161 U. S. 29, 16 S. Ct. 434, 480, 40 L. Ed. 606, the Supreme Court cited and sanctioned Regina v. Hicklin, and United States v. Bennett. The subject matter of Rosen v. United States was, however, a pictorial representation of 'females, in different attitudes of indecency'. The figures were partially covered 'with lamp black that could be easily erased with a piece of bread.' p. 31 of 161 U. S., 16 S. Ct. 434. The pictures were evidently obscene, and plainly came within the statute prohibiting their transportation. The citation of Regina v. Hicklin and United States v. Bennett, was in support of a ruling that allegations in the indictment as to an obscene publication need only be made with suffieient particularity to inform the accused of the nature of the charge against him. No approval of other features of the two decisions was expressed, nor were such features referred to. Dunlop v. United States, 165 U. S. 486, 489, 17 S. Ct. 375, 41 L. Ed. 799, also seems to be relied on by the government, but the publication there was admittedly obscene and the decision in no way sanctioned the rulings in United States v. Bennett, which we first mentioned. The rigorous doctrines laid down in that case are inconsistent with our own decision in United States v. Dennett, (C. C. A.) 39 F. (2d) 564, 76 A. L. R. 1092, as well as with Konda v. United States, (C. C. A.) 166 F. 91, 92, 22 L. R. A. (N. S.) 304; Clark v. United States, (C. C. A.) 211 F. 916, 922; Halsey v. New York Society for the Suppression of Vice, 234 N. Y. 1, 4, 136 N. E. 219; and St. Hubert Guild v. Quinn, 64 Misc. 336, 339, 118 N. Y. S. 582, and, in our opinion, do not represent the law. They would exclude much of the great works of literature and involve an impracticability that cannot be imputed to Congress and would in the case of many books containing obscene passages inevitably require the court that uttered them to restrict their applicability."

It is quite clear that the harsh rule of Regina v. Hicklin has been supplanted by the modern test of obscenity, namely, whether the matter in question has a substantial tendency to deprave or corrupt by inciting lascivious thoughts or arousing lustful desire in the ordinary reader. This has been stated in various ways.

It has been said that the matter charged, to be obscene, must "suggest impure or libidinous thoughts", must "invite to lewd and lascivious practices and conduct", must "be offensive to chastity", must "incite dissolute acts", must "create a desire for gratification of animal passions", must "encourage unlawful indulgences of lust", must "attempt to satisfy the morbid appetite of the salacious", must "pander to the prurient taste". See, United States v. Journal Co., Inc., 197 Fed. 415 (D. C., Va., 1912), United States v. Klauder, 240 Fed. 501 (D. C., N. Y., 1917), United States v. Durant, 46 Fed. 753 (D. C., S. C., 1891), United States

v. Moore, 104 Fed. 78 (D. C., Ky., 1900), United States v. Reinheimer, 233 Fed. 545 (D. C., Pa. 1916), United States v. Clarke, 38 Fed. 732 (D. C., Mo., 1889), Dysart v. United States, 4 F.(2d) 765, reversed, 272 U. S. 655 (1926), United States v. Wroblenski, 118 Fed. 495 (D. C., Wis., 1902), United States v. O'Donnell, 165 Fed. 218 (D. C., N. Y., 1908), United States v. Smith, 11 Fed. 663, (D. C., Ky., 1882), United States v. Wightman, 29 Fed. 636 (D. C., Pa., 1886), United States v. Wyatt, 122 Fed. 316 (D. C., Del., 1903), Hanson v. United States, 157 Fed. 749 (C. C. A. 7th, 1907), United States v. Davidson, 244 Fed. 523 (D. C., N. Y., 1917), Dunlop v. United States, 165 U. S. 486 (1897), United States v. Males, 51 Fed. 41 (D. C., Ind., 1892), and MacFadden v. United States, 165 Fed. 51 (C. C. A. 3d, 1908).

In Walker v. Popenoe, 149 F.(2d) 511 (1945), it was held:

"The effect of a publication on the ordinary reader is what counts. The Statute does not intend that we shall 'reduce our treatment of sex to the standard of a child's library in the supposed interest of a salacious few' ".

This test, however, should not be left to stand alone, for there is another element of equal importance—the tenor of the times and the change in social acceptance of what is inherently decent. This element is clearly set forth in United States v. Kennerley, 209 Fed. 119 (D. C., N. Y., 1913), where Judge Hand said:

"If there be no abstract definition, such as I have suggested, should not the word 'obscene' be allowed to indicate the present critical point in the compromise between candor and shame at which the community may have arrived here and now? . . . Nor is it an objection, I think, that such an interpretation gives to the words of the statute a varying meaning from time to time. Such words as these do not embalm the precise morals of an age or place; while they presuppose that some things will always be shocking to the public taste, the vague subject matter is left to the gradual development of general notions about what is decent."

In his The Paradoxes of Legal Science, Mr. Justice Cardozo said: "Law accepts as the pattern of its justice the morality of the community whose conduct it assumes to regulate" (p. 37). In Towne v. Eisner, 245 U. S., 418, 425, 62 L. Ed. 372, 376 (1918) Mr. Justice Holmes said: "A word is not a crystal, transparent and unchanged, it is the skin of a living thought and may vary greatly in color and content according to the circumstances and the time in which it is used." And in the same vein, Professor Wormser wrote in The Development of the Law, 23 Columbia Law Review, 701, 702 (1923): "Increasingly—ever increasingly—the community is beginning to require of the law that it justify its own administration of its resources before the bar of public opinion. And in order to justify itself before this critical bar, the law must be brought to evidence the mores of the times, to which it must conform, or it will fail to fulfill its function as the judicial expression of the community passion for justice and right dealing."

2. The New York Courts. The modern test was applied in People v. Wendling, 258 N. Y. 451, (1932), which involved the dramatization of the song "Frankie and Johnnie". In holding that the courts are not censors of morals and manners, Judge Pound said:

"The language of the play is coarse, vulgar and profane; the plot cheap and tawdry. As a dramatic composition it serves to degrade the stage where vice is thought by some to lose 'half its evil by losing all its grossness.' 'That it is "indecent" from every consideration of propriety is entirely clear' (People v. Eastman, 188 N. Y. 478, 480), but the court is not a censor of plays and does not attempt to regulate manners. One may call a spade a spade without offending decency, although modesty may be shocked thereby. (People v. Muller, 96 N. Y. 408, 411). The question is not whether the scene is laid in a low dive where refined people are not found or whether the language is that of the bar room rather than the parlor. The question is whether the tendency of the play is to excite lustful and lecherous desire. (People v. Eastman, supra; People v. Muller, supra)."

Since the New York cases are generally in line with the modern Federal rule above stated, it is necessary only to cite the principal one: Halsey v. N. Y. Society for the Suppression of Vice, 234 N. Y. 1 (1922), which involved Theophile Gautier's "Mademoiselle de Maupin"; People v. Brainard, 192 App. Div. (N. Y.) 816 (1920), where the subject was "Madeleine", the anonymous autobiography of a prostitute.

3. The Massachusetts Courts. Boston has long been the center of book suppression in this country. Before 1930 the Massachusetts obscenity statute forbade the sale of any book "containing obscene, indecent language". The Supreme Court upheld convictions for the sale of Dreiser's "An American Tragedy" and D. H. Lawrence's "Lady Chatterly's Lover". After a general wave of censorship that swept over Boston in 1929 and resulted in the suppression of 68 books, the law was changed to proscribe the sale of "a book which is obscene, indecent," etc.

The result was the modern rule, but the Massachusetts courts were still severe with individual books. Commonwealth v. Isenstadt, 318 Mass. 543 (1945), upheld a conviction for the sale of "Strange Fruit", and while it announced the modern rule to great extent, it refused to sanction the idea that sincerity of purpose and artistic merit would necessarily dispel obscenity. But it clearly held that the time and custom of the community are important elements. The court said:

"Since effect is the test, it follows that a book is to be judged in the light of the customs and habits of thought of the time and place of the alleged offense. Although the fundamentals of human nature change but slowly, if indeed they change at all, customs and habits of thought do vary with time and place. That which may give rise to impure thought and action in a highly conventional society may pass almost unnoticed in a society habituated to greater freedom."

In the very recent case of Attorney General v. Book Named "Forever Amber", decided October 11, 1948, and reported in 81 N. E. (2d) 663, the court repeated the stand it took in Commonwealth v. Isenstadt, supra, but it goes further on the question of sincerity and artistic purpose when the court said:

"It (the book) undoubtedly has historical purpose, and in this is adequately accurate in achievement. . . . The paramount impression is of an unfortunate country and its people as yet unfreed of the grasp of the Stuarts. . . . As to the individual characters, the reader is left with an estimate of an unattractive, hedonistic group, whose course of conduct is abhorrent and whose mode of living can be neither emulated nor envied."

The Modern Test of Obscenity

From all of these cases the modern rule is that obscenity is measured by the erotic allurement upon the average modern reader; that the erotic allurement of a book is measured by whether it is sexually impure— i. e., pornographic, "dirt for dirt's sake", a calculated incitement to sexual desire—or whether it reveals an effort to reflect life, including its dirt, with reasonable accuracy and balance; and that mere coarseness or vulgarity is not obscenity.

Forging such a rule from the precedents does not fully reach the heart of the matter, for I am sure that the books before me could be declared obscene or not obscene under either the Hicklin or the modern rule. Current standards create both the book and the judgment of it.

The evil of an indefinite statute like our section 524, however, is that it is also too loose. Current standards of what is obscene can swing to extremes if the entire question is left open, and even in the domestic laboratories of the States such freedom cannot safely be allowed. It is no longer possible that free speech be guaranteed Federally and denied locally; under modern methods of instantaneous communication such a discrepancy makes no sense. If speech is to be free anywhere, it must be free everywhere, and a law that can be used as a spigot that allows speech to flow freely or to be checked altogether is a general threat to free opinion and enlightened solution. What is said in Pennsylvania may clarify an issue in California, and what is suppressed in California may leave us the worse in Pennsylvania. Unless a restriction on free speech be of National validity, it can no longer have any local validity whatever. Some danger to us all must appear before any of us can be muzzled.

In the field of written obscenity this principle has met oblique acceptance with regard to what is called "the classics", which are now exempt from legal censorship. Just how old a work must be before it can enjoy this immunity is uncertain, but what we know as classics are the books by remarkable people that have withstood the test of time and are accepted as having lasting value; they have become historical samples, which itself is important. This importance could not be as great if the screening process were not free.

Current literature, good, bad, or indifferent, goes into the hopper without any background for judgment; it is in the idiom of the moment and is keyed to the tempo of modern life. I do not believe that such considerations should result in removing any of the output from the hopper before the process of screening can begin. What is pure dirt to some may be another's sincere

effort to make clear a point, and there is not much difference, from the historical angle, between censoring books before publication and suppressing them afterwards, before there has been a reasonable chance to judge them. Blackstone's neat distinction may satisfy an exact legal mind, but it has no meaning for history. The unworthy books will die soon enough, but the great work of genius has a hard enough time to make its way even in the free market of thought. James Joyce, whose work is difficult to understand, even after years of study, has evolved a new form of communication, by his method of using words, that will some day be a shorthand for complexity. The public was deprived for years of this work of genius because someone found objectionable passages in it.

I can find no universally valid restriction on free expression to be drawn from the behavior of "l'homme moyen sensuel", who is the average modern reader. It is impossible to say just what his reactions to a book actually are. Moyen means, generally, average, and average means a median between extremes. If he reads an obscene book when his sensuality is low, he will yawn over it or find that its suggestibility leads him off on quite different paths. If he reads the Mechanics' Lien Act while his sensuality is high, things will stand between him and the page that have no business there. How can anyone say that he will infallibly be affected one way or another by one book or another? When, where, how, and why are questions that cannot be answered clearly in this field. The professional answer that is suggested is the one general compromise—that the appetite of sex is old, universal, and unpredictable, and that the best we can do to keep it within reasonable bounds is to be our brother's keeper and censor, because we never know when his sensuality may be high. This does not satisfy me, for in a field where even reasonable precision is utterly impossible, I trust people more than I do the law. Had legal censorship been as constant throughout the centuries as the law of murder, rape, theft, and negligence, a case for the compromise could be made out; as it is, legal censorship is not old, it is not popular, and it has failed to strengthen the private censor in each individual that has kept the race as decent as it has been for several thousand years. I regard legal censorship as an experiment of more than dubious value.

I am well aware that the law is not ready to discard censorship altogether. The English keep their policeman handy, just in case, and the modern rule is a more efficient policeman. Its scope, however, must be defined with regard to the universal right of free speech, as limited only by some universally valid restriction required by a clear and present danger. For this we must consider the Constitution and the cases lately decided under it.

Constitutional Questions

The fourteenth amendment to the Federal Constitution prohibits any State from encroaching upon freedom of speech and freedom of the press to the same extent that the first amendment prevents the Federal Congress from doing so: Pennekamp v. Florida, 328 U. S. 331 (1946); Chaplinsky v. New Hampshire, 315

U. S. 568 (1942) ; Thornhill v. Alabama, 310 U. S. 88 (1940) ; Winters v. New York, 333 U. S. 507, 68 S. Ct. 665 (1948).

The principle of a free press covers distribution as well as publication: Lovell v. City of Griffin, 303 U. S. 444, 58 S. Ct. 666 (1938).

These guarantees occupy a preferred position under our law to such an extent that the courts, when considering whether legislation infringes upon them, neutralize the presumption usually indulged in favor of constitutionality: Thomas v. Collins, 323 U. S. 516, 530 (1945) ; Thornhill v. Alabama, 310 U. S. 88 (1940) ; United States v. Carolene Products Co., 304 U. S. 144, 152, note 4 (1938). See also Spayd v. Ringing Rock Lodge, 270 Pa. 67 (1921).

And article 1, sec. 7 of the Pennsylvania Constitution states that:

"The free communication of thoughts and opinions is one of the invaluable rights of man, and every citizen may freely speak, write and print on any subject, being responsible for the abuse of that liberty."

When the first amendment came before the Supreme Court for interpretation in Reynolds v. United States, 98 U. S. 145 (1878), the court declared that government had no authority whatsoever in the field of thought or opinion: only in the area of conduct or action could it step in. Chief Justice Waite said: (p. 164)

"Congress was deprived of all legislative power over mere opinion, but was left free to reach actions which were in violation of social duties or subversive of good order."

Quoting from Jefferson's bill for establishing religious freedom, the Chief Justice stated:

" 'That to suffer the Civil magistrate to intrude his powers into the field of opinion, and to restrain the profession or propagation of principles on supposition of their *ill tendency*, is a dangerous fallacy which at once destroys all religious liberty . . . it is time enough for the rightful purposes of civil government for its officers to interfere *when principles break out into overt acts against peace and good order.' In these two sentences is found the true distinction between what properly belongs to the church and what to the State."* (Italics supplied.)

The now familiar "clear and present danger" rule, first stated by Mr. Justice Holmes in Schenck v. United States, 249 U. S. 47 (1918), represents a compromise between the ideas of Jefferson and those of the judges, who had in the meantime departed from the forthright views of the great statesman. Under that rule the publisher of a writing may be punished if the publication in question creates a clear and present danger that there will result from it some substantive evil which the legislature has a right to proscribe and punish.

The famous illustration in the Schenck case was:

"The most stringent protection of free speech would not protect a man in falsely shouting fire in a theater and causing a panic. It does not even protect a man from an injunction against uttering words that may have all the effect of force."

Mr. Justice Brandeis added, in Whitney v. California, 274 U. S. 357 (1927), the idea that free speech may not be curbed where the community has the chance to answer back. He said:

"Those who won our independence by revolution were not cowards. They did not fear political change. They did not exalt order at the cost of liberty. To courageous, self-reliant men, with confidence in the power of free and fearless reasoning applied through the processes of popular government, *no danger flowing from speech can be deemed clear and present, unless the incidence of the evil apprehended is so imminent that it may befall before there is opportunity for full discussion.* If there be time to expose through discussion the falsehood and fallacies, to avert the evil by the processes of education, *the remedy to be applied is more speech, not enforced silence. Only an emergency can justify repression.* Such must be the rule if authority is to be reconciled with freedom. Such, in my opinion, is the command of the Constitution. It is therefore always open to Americans to challenge a law abridging free speech and assembly by showing that there was no emergency justifying it. (Italics supplied.)

"Moreover, even imminent danger cannot justify resort to prohibition of these functions essential to effective democracy, unless the evil apprehended is relatively serious. Prohibition of free speech and assembly is a measure so stringent that it would be inappropriate as the means for averting a relatively trivial harm to society. A police measure may be unconstitutional merely because the remedy, although effective as means of protection, is unduly harsh or oppressive. Thus, a State might, in the exercise of its police power, make any trespass upon the land of another a crime, regardless of the results or of the intent or purpose of the trespasser. It might, also, punish an attempt, a conspiracy, or an incitement to commit the trespass. But it is hardly conceivable that this Court would hold constitutional a statute which punished as a felony the mere voluntary assembly with a society formed to teach that pedestrians had the moral right to cross unenclosed, unposted, waste lands and to advocate their doing so, even if there was imminent danger that advocacy would lead to a trespass. The fact that speech is likely to result in some violence or in destruction of property is not enough to justify its suppression. There must be the probability of serious injury to the State. Among free men, the deterrents ordinarily to be applied to prevent crime are education and punishment for violations of the law, not abridgment of the rights of free speech and assembly."

It is true that subsequent to the decision of the court in the Schenck case, Justices Holmes and Brandeis fought what for a time appeared to be a losing battle. To them the "clear and present danger" rule was a rule of the criminal law, and they applied it only to prohibit speech which incited to punishable conduct. See the dissenting opinion in Gitlow v. New York, 268 U. S. 652 (1925), where they say:

"If the publication of this document had been laid as *an attempt* to induce an uprising against government at once and not at some indefinite time in the future it would have presented a different question. The object would have been one with which the law might deal, subject to the doubt whether there was any danger that the publication could produce any result, or in other words, whether it was not futile and too remote from possible consequences. *But the indictment alleges the publication and nothing more.*" (Italics supplied.)

The history of the Supreme Court, since its decision in Gitlow v. New York, has been marked by gradual progress along the path staked out by Justices Holmes and Brandeis, culminating finally in the complete acceptance of their views.

This progress may be traced in the following decisions: Stromberg v. California, 283 U. S. 359 (1931); DeJonge v. Oregon, 299 U. S. 353 (1937); Herndon v. Lowry, 301 U. S. 242 (1937); Palko v. Connecticut, 302 U. S. 319 (1937); Lovell v. Griffin, 303 U. S. 444 (1938); Cantwell v. Connecticut, 310 U. S. 296 (1940); Thornhill v. Alabama, 310 U. S. 88 (1940); Bridges v. California, 314 U. S. 252 (1941); Board of Education v. Barnette, 319 U. S. 624 (1943); Schneiderman v. United States, 320 U. S. 118 (1943); United States v. Ballard, 322 U. S. 78 (1944); Thomas v. Collins, 323 U. S. 516 (1945); Pennekamp v. Florida, 328 U. S. 331 (1946); Musser v. Utah, 333 U. S. 95 (1948).

As was said in Martin v. Struthers, 319 U. S. 141 (1943):

"The right of freedom of speech and press has broad scope. The authors of the First Amendment knew that novel and unconventional ideas might disturb the complacent, but they chose to encourage a freedom which they believed essential if vigorous enlightenment was ever to triumph over slothful ignorance. This freedom embraces the right to distribute literature, Lovell v. Griffin (citation), and necessarily protects the right to receive it."

There are other milestones in the judicial reëstablishment of freedom of speech and freedom of the press. We cite the language of the Supreme Court in some of those cases:

In Herndon v. Lowry, 301 U. S. 242 (1937), the court said:

"The power of a state to abridge freedom of speech and of assembly is the exception rather than the rule and the penalizing even of utterances of a defined character must find its justification in a reasonable apprehension of danger to organized government. The judgment of the legislature is not unfettered."

In DeJonge v. Oregon, 299 U. S. 353 (1937), the court said:

"These rights may be abused by using speech or press or assembly *in order to incite to violence and crime.* The people through their legislatures may protect themselves against that abuse. But the legislative intervention can find constitutional justification only by dealing with the abuse. The rights themselves must not be curtailed." (Italics supplied.)

In Thornhill v. Alabama, 310 U. S. 88 (1940), the court said:

"Every expression of opinion on matters that are important has the potentiality of inducing action in the interests of one rather than another group in society. But the group in power at any moment may not impose penal sanctions on peaceful and truthful discussion of matters of public interest merely on a

showing that others may thereby be persuaded to take action inconsistent with its interests. Abridgement of the liberty of such discussion can be justified only where the clear danger of substantive evils arises *under circumstances affording no opportunity to test the merits of ideas by competition for acceptance in the market of public opinion.*" (Italics supplied.)

The nature of the evil which the legislature has the power to guard against by enacting an obscenity statute is not clearly defined. As Jefferson saw it, the legislature was restricted to punishing criminal acts and not publications. To Holmes and Brandeis the bookseller could be punished if his relation to the criminal act was such that he could be said to have incited it. In neither view could the bookseller be punished if his books merely "tended" to result in illegal acts and much less if his books "tended" to lower the moral standards of the community. A much closer relationship was required. The legislature may validly prevent criminal acts and legislate to protect the moral standards of the community. But the threat must in either case be more than a mere tendency. The older cases which upheld obscenity statutes on the "tendency" theory would appear to be invalid in the light of the more recent expressions of the Supreme Court.

Thus the opinion of the Supreme Court in Bridges v. California, 314 U. S. 252 (1941) says: (p. 273)

"In accordance with what we have said on the 'clear and present danger' cases, neither 'inherent tendency' nor 'reasonable tendency' is enough to justify a restriction of free expression."

In Pennekamp v. Florida, 328 U. S. 331 (1946), a case in which the resulting evil was said to be that of improperly influencing the administration of justice, the Supreme Court said, in discussing the Bridges case:

"In the Bridges Case the clear and present danger rule was applied to the stated issue of whether the expressions there under consideration prevented 'fair judicial trials free from coercion or intimidation.' Page 259. There was, of course, no question as to the power to punish for disturbances and disorder in the courtroom. Page 266. The danger to be guarded against is the 'substantive evil' sought to be prevented. Pages 261, 262, 263. In the Bridges Case that 'substantive evil' was primarily the 'disorderly and unfair administration of justice.' Pages 270, 271, 278."

In addition to being substantive, the evil which the legislature seeks to control must be substantial: Bridges v. California, supra. The evil consequence must be serious and the imminence high; the proof must be clear, that is to say, "a solidity of evidence should be required": Pennekamp v. Florida, supra. Or, as was said in a contempt of court case (Craig v. Harney, 331 U. S. 367 (1947)):

"The fires which it kindles must constitute an imminent, not merely a likely, threat to the administration of Justice. The danger must not be remote or even probable; *it must immediately imperil.*" (Italics supplied.)

These principles have not been applied specifically to an obscenity statute by any recent opinion of the United States Supreme Court, but as Mr. Justice Rutledge said orally when the "Hecate County" case, Doubleday & Co., Inc. v. People of New York, 93 L. Ed. 37 (an obscenity case), was recently argued before the court:

"Before we get to the question of clear and present danger, we've got to have something which the State can forbid as dangerous. We are talking in a vacuum until we can establish that there is some occasion for the exercise of the State's power."

"Yes, you must first ascertain the substantive evil at which the statute is aimed, and then determine whether the publication of this book constitutes a clear and present danger."

"*It is up to the State to demonstrate that there was a danger, and until they demonstrate that, plus the clarity and imminence of the danger, the constitutional prohibition would seem to apply.*" (Italics supplied.) (Quoted in 17 U. S. Law Week (Supreme Court Sections 3118)).

This appears to me much closer to a correct solution of obscenity cases than several general dicta by the Supreme Court to the effect that obscenity is indictable just because it is obscenity. For example, in Near v. Minnesota, 283 U. S. 697 (1931), Chief Justice Hughes remarked: "On similar grounds, the primary requirements of decency may be enforced against obscene publications."

It seems impossible, in view of the late decisions under the first amendment, that the word "obscene" can any longer stand alone, lighted up only by a vague and mystic sense of impurity, unless it is interpreted by other solid factors such as clear and present danger, pornography, and divorcement from mere coarseness of vulgarity.

In Chaplinsky v. New Hampshire, 315 U. S. 568 (1942), however, Mr. Justice Murphy said this: (p. 571)

"There are certain well-defined and narrowly limited classes of speech, the prevention and punishment of which have never been thought to raise any constitutional problem. These include the lewd and obscene, the profane, the libellous, and the insulting or 'fighting' words—those which by their very utterance inflict injury or tend to incite an immediate breach of the peace."

It is not clear to me, nor, I venture to assert, would it be to the Supreme Court, if faced directly by an appropriate case of literary obscenity, what words inflict injury by their very utterance or how such injury is inflicted. As for the notion of an obscene book tending to incite to an immediate breach of the peace, the proper point of emphasis is the breach of the peace. That is different from saying that obscenity automatically tends to a breach of the peace, for the idea is unreal.

The latest dictum on this subject is in Kovacs v. Cooper, decided on January 31, 1949, and reported in 17 U. S. Law Week 4163, where Mr. Justice Reed said:

"But in the *Winters* case (Winters v. New York, 333 U. S. 507 (1948)) we pointed out that prosecutions might be brought under statutes punishing the distribution of 'obscene, lewd, lascivious, filthy, indecent

and disgusting' magazines. P. 511. We said, p. 518:

" 'The impossibility of defining the precise line between permissible uncertainty in statutes caused by describing crimes by words well understood through long use in the criminal law—obscene, lewd, lascivious, filthy, indecent or disgusting—and the unconstitutional vagueness that leaves a person uncertain as to the kind of prohibited conduct—massing stories to incite crime—has resulted in three arguments of this case in this Court.' "

The difficulty here is that insofar as they apply to literature, obscenity and its imposing string of synonyms do *not* have a fixed meaning through long use in the criminal law—or to put it the other way, that they have a very narrow and restricted meaning quite at variance with the assumption that obscenity debauches public morals by a mysterious and self-executing process that can be feared but not proved.

Certainly the books before me do not command, or urge, or incite, or even encourage persons to commit sexual misconduct of a nature that the legislature has the right to prevent or punish. Nor are they an imminent threat to the morality of the community as a whole. The conduct described in them is at most offensive. It does not incite to unlawfulness of any kind. These facts are important in view of the following language of Justice Rutledge, speaking for Justices Murphy, Douglas and himself (the other members of the court did not reach the question) in Musser v. Utah, 333 U. S. 95 (1948):

"The Utah statute was construed to proscribe any agreement to advocate the practice of polygamy. Thus the line was drawn between discussion and advocacy.

"The Constitution requires that the statute be limited more narrowly. *At the very least the line must be drawn between advocacy and incitment, and even the state's* power to punish incitement may vary with the nature of the speech, whether persuasive or coercive, the nature of the wrong induced, whether violent or merely offensive to the mores, and the degree of probability that the substantive evil actually will result." (Italics supplied.)

Freedom of expression is the touchiest and most important right we have; it is asserted frequently and vigorously, for the democratic process rests fundamentally on the need of people to argue, exhort, and clarify. Thomas v. Collins, supra (323 U. S. 516) speaks of ". . . the preferred place given in our scheme to the great, the indispensable democratic freedoms secured by the First Amendment", and went on to say, at page 530:

"For these reasons any attempt to restrict those liberties must be justified by clear public interest, threatened not doubtfully or remotely, but by clear and present danger. The rational connection between the remedy provided and the evil to be curbed, which in other contexts might support legislation against attack on due process grounds, will not suffice. These rights rest on firmer foundation. Accordingly, whatever occasion would restrain orderly discussion and persuasion, at appropriate time and place, *must have clear support in public danger, actual or impending.*

Only the gravest abuses, endangering paramount interest, give occasion for permissible limitation." (Italics supplied.)

The "preferred position" cases have been collected in Mr. Justice Frankfurter's concurring opinion in Kovacs v. Cooper, supra (decided January 31, 1949: 17 U. S. L. W. 4163). They are: Herndon v. Lowry, supra (301 U. S. 242) ; United States v. Carolene Products Co., 304 U. S. 144 (1948) ; Thornhill v. Alabama, 310 U. S. 88 (1940) ; Schneider v. State, 308 U. S. 147 (1939) ; Bridges v. California, supra (314 U. S. 252) ; Murdock v. Pennsylvania, 319 U. S. 105 (1943) ; Prince v. Massachusetts, 321 U. S. 158 (1944) ; Follett v. McCormick, 321 U. S. 573 (1944) ; Marsh v. Alabama, 326 U. S. 501 (1946) ; Pennekamp v. Florida, supra (328 U. S. 331) ; West Virginia State Board v. Barnette, 319 U. S. 624 (1943) ; Thomas v. Collins, supra (323 U. S. 516) ; Saia v. New York, 334 U. S. 558 (1948).

Mr. Justice Frankfurter sounds the warning that the phrase "preferred position" should not be allowed to become a rigid formula, lest another one grow beside it—that any legislative restriction on free speech be considered "presumptively invalid". The warning is well taken, for there are too many kinds of restriction as well as vehicles of free speech to warrant such rigidity. The Kovacs and Sara cases involve loud speakers and sound trucks, which are perilously close to nuisances and even to threats to public health. There are many instances where the police power may be used, at the expense of free expression, where the threat to order or health is directly and imminently demonstrable. The point is to see and understand the danger, and to keep particular cases within or without the justifiable area of the police power.

Short of books that are sexually impure and pornographic, I can see no rational legal catalyst that can detect or define a clear and present danger inherent in a writing or that can demonstrate what result ensues from reading it. All that is relied upon, in a prosecution, is an indefinable fear for other people's moral standards—a fear that I regard as a democratic anomaly.

Finally, the Supreme Court, in Winters v. New York, supra (333 U. S. 507), held subdivision 2 of section 1141 of New York's Penal Law unconstitutional because it was vague and allowed punishment of matters within the protection of free speech. The court said:

"The appellant contends that the subsection violates the right of free speech and press because it is vague and indefinite. *It is settled that a statute so vague and indefinite, in form and as interpreted, as to permit within the scope of its language the punishment of incidents fairly within the protection of the guarantee of free speech is void, on its face, as contrary to the Fourteenth Amendment.* Stromberg v. California, 283 US 359, 369; Herndon v. Lowry, 301 US 242, 258. A failure of a statute limiting freedom of expression to give fair notice of what acts will be punished and such a statute's inclusion of prohibitions against expressions, protected by the principles of the First Amendment, violates an accused's rights under procedural due process and freedom of speech or press." (Italics supplied.)

I am clear that the books before me are within the protection of the first and fourteenth amendments of the Federal Constitution, and of article 1, sec. 7 of the Pennsylvania Constitution. They bear obvious internal evidence of an effort to portray certain segments of American life, including parts that more refined people than the characters may deplore, but which we know exist. The vulgarity and obscenity in them are inherent in the characters themselves and are obviously not set forth as erotic allurement or as an excuse for selling the volumes. Nor can it be said that they have the effect of inciting to lewdness, or of inciting to any sexual crime, or that they are sexually impure and pornographic, i. e., "dirt for dirt's sake".

Definition of Obscenity as Sexual Impurity

Sexual impurity in literature (pornography, as some of the cases call it) I define as any writing whose dominant purpose and effect is erotic allurement—that is to say, a calculated and effective incitement to sexual desire. It is the effect that counts, more than the purpose, and no indictment can stand unless it can be shown. This definition is in accord with the cases that have restricted the meaning of obscenity and its synonyms to that of sexual impurity, and with those cases that have made erotic allurement the test of its effect.

This excludes from pornography medical or educational writings, whether in technical or layman's language, and whether used only in schools or generally distributed, whose dominant purpose and effect is exegetical and instructional rather than enticing. It leaves room for interpretation of individual books, for as long as censorship is considered necessary, it is as impossible as it is inadvisable to find a self-executing formula.

Sex education has been before the courts in many cases. In United States v. "Married Love", 48 F. (2d) 821 (1931), Judge Woolsey said:

"It makes also some apparently justified criticisms of the inopportune exercise by the man in the marriage relation of what are often referred to as his conjugal or marital rights, and it pleads with seriousness, and not without some eloquence, for a better understanding by husbands of the physical and emotional side of the sex life of their wives. I do not find anything exceptionable anywhere in the book, and I cannot imagine a normal mind to which this book would seem to be obscene or immoral within the proper definition of these words, or whose sex impulses would be stirred by reading it."

Judge Woolsey held similarly in United States v. "Contraception", 51 F. (2d) 525 (1931). Both of the above books were by Dr. Marie C. Stopes.

The case of United States v. Dennett, 39 F. (2d) 564 (C. C. A. 2d, 1930), involved a pamphlet written by a woman for the education of her children. Sections of it appear in the reporter's summary of the case, and show that it gave full and frank information, together with the view that the sexual impulse is not a base passion but as a great joy when accompanied by love between two human beings. In reversing a conviction, Judge Hand said:

"It also may reasonably be thought that accurate information, rather than mystery and curiosity, is better in the long run and is less likely to occasion lascivious thoughts than ignorance and anxiety. Perhaps instruction other than that which the defendant suggests would be better. That is a matter as to which there is bound to be a wide difference of opinion, but, irrespective of this, we hold that an accurate exposition of the relevant facts of the sex side of life in decent language and in manifestly serious and disinterested spirit cannot ordinarily be regarded as obscene. Any incidental tendency to arouse sex impulses which such a pamphlet may perhaps have, is apart from and subordinate to its main effect. The tendency can only exist in so far as it is inherent in any sex instruction, and it would seem to be outweighed by the elimination of ignorance, curiosity, and morbid fear. The direct aim and the net result is to promote understanding and self-control."

The definition of sexual impurity given above brings literary obscenity into workable analogy with sedition, blasphemy, open lewdness, and the other examples set forth earlier, as those terms are used in our Penal Code, except for one remaining point. Sedition, blasphemy, and open lewdness, by definition, carry their own threat of danger to the public peace. The deep and peculiar nature of religious faith is such that people are entitled to protection against those who call their gods in vain; religion has too recently and for too long been one of the greatest of the fighting faiths to assume that disorder will not follow from public irreverence. He who is publicly lewd is in himself an open and immediate invitation to morally criminal behavior. The pressing danger inherent in sedition speaks for itself.

A book, however sexually impure and pornographic, is in a different case. It cannot be a present danger unless its reader closes it, lays it aside, and transmutes its erotic allurement into overt action. That such action must inevitably follow as a direct consequence of reading the book does not bear analysis, nor is it borne out by general human experience; too much can intervene and too many diversions take place. It must be constantly borne in mind that section 524 does not include the element of debauching public morals or of seeking to alter the prevailing moral code. It only proscribes what *is* obscene, and that term is meaningless unless activated by precise dangers within legal limits. Since section 524 provides no standard, the danger and the limits must be found elsewhere, and the only clear and discernible ones are those having to do with the police power and the preservation of the peace.

The Clear and Present Danger

I have pointed out above that any test of the effect of obscenity is bound to be elusive. Section 524 is therefore vague, indefinite, and unconstitutional unless some exact definition can be found for the "clear and present danger" to be prevented that will satisfy the constitutional protection of free speech. There are various types of cases in which definition is clear because the need is clear. The police power operates in pure food cases because people can sicken and die from eating bad food; in traffic cases because people can be injured or killed unless there is regulation; in weights and measures cases because of the ease with which the consumer can be cheated, and in conventional crimes because of the threat to persons and property. The list could be extended.

Mr. Justice Holmes's example in Schenck v. United States is no test for the case before me; the public does not read a book and simultaneously rush by the hundreds into the streets to engage in orgiastic riots. Mr. Justice Brandeis's discussion in Whitney v. California is a better yardstick, for in the field of the printed word the community has full opportunity to answer back. How can it be said that there is a "clear and present danger"—granted that anyone can say what it is—when there is both time and means for ample discussion?

These words of Jefferson should not be forgotten:

"I deplore . . . the putrid state into which our newspapers have passed, and the malignity, the vulgarity, and the mendacious spirit of those who write them. . . . These ordures are rapidly depraving the public taste.

"It is, however, an evil for which there is no remedy: our liberty depends on the freedom of the press, and that cannot be limited without being lost."

Who can define the clear and present danger to the community that arises from reading a book? If we say it is that the reader is young and inexperienced and incapable of resisting the sexual temptations that the book may present to him, we put the entire reading public at the mercy of the adolescent mind and of those adolescents who do not have the expected advantages of home influence, school training, or religious teaching. Nor can we say into how many such hands the book may come. Adults, or even a gifted minor, may be capable of challenging the book in public and thus of forwarding the education and enlightenment of us all by free discussion and correction. If the argument be applied to the general public, the situation becomes absurd, for then no publication is safe. How is it possible to say that reading a certain book is bound to make people behave in a way that is socially undesirable? And beyond a reasonable doubt, since we are dealing with a penal statute?

We might remember the words of Macaulay:

"We find it difficult to believe that in a world so full of temptations as this, any gentleman, whose life would have been virtuous if he had not read Aristophanes and Juvenal, will be made vicious by reading them."

Substitute the names of the books before me for "Aristophanes and Juvenal", and the analogy is exact.

The only clear and present danger to be prevented by section 524 that will satisfy both the Constitution and the current customs of our era is the commission or the imminence of the commission of criminal behavior resulting from the reading of a book. Publication alone can have no such automatic effect.

The Rule of Decision

Thus limited, the constitutional operation of section 524 of our act rests on narrow ground.

The modern test of obscenity, as I have stated it above (page 136), furnishes a means of determining whether a book, taken as a whole, is sexually impure, as I have defined that term (page 151, ante).

I hold that section 524 may not constitutionally be applied to any writing unless it is sexually impure and pornographic. It may then be applied, as an exercise of the police power, only where there is a reasonable and demonstrable cause to believe that a crime or misdemeanor has been committed or is about to be committed as the perceptible result of the publication and distribution of the writing in question: the opinion of anyone that a tendency thereto exists or that such a result is self-evident is insufficient and irrelevant. The causal connection between the book and the criminal behavior must appear beyond a reasonable doubt. The criminal law is not, in my opinion, "the custos morum of the King's subjects", as Regina v. Hicklin states: it is only the custodian of the peace and good order that free men and women need for the shaping of their common destiny.

There is no such proof in the instant case.

For that reason, and also because of the character of the books themselves, I hold that the books before me are not sexually impure and pornographic, and are therefore not obscene, lewd, lascivious, filthy, indecent, or disgusting. The sustaining of the demurrers follows.

POSTMASTER'S PROHIBITION OF THREE "OBSCENE" BOOKS FROM THE MAILS HELD CONSTITUTIONAL, WITH JUDGE JEROME FRANK CONCURRING IN AN OPINION IN WHICH HE DECLARES HIS "HOPE THAT THE SUPREME COURT WILL REVIEW OUR DECISION, THUS DISSIPATING THE FOGS WHICH SURROUND THIS SUBJECT."

Roth v. Goldman, 172 F.2d 788 (1949)

PER CURIAM.

This injunction action serves to bring up for review the validity of five orders of the Postmaster General, entered after administrative proceedings and hearings, excluding from the mails three books published by plaintiff under various trade names. The vagaries of censorship are perhaps suggested by the fact that only one of these books was excluded as "obscene, lewd, or lascivious," 18 U.S.C.A. §§ 334, 339 [now §§ 1461, 1342], 39 U.S.C.A. § 255, while all material concerning the others was held unmailable because of the steps taken to secure mail orders for them by fraudulently advertising them to be salacious when they were not. 39 U.S.C.A. §§ 259, 732. The orders involving these latter books actually cause us the less difficulty just because the standards of fraud are at least somewhat clearer than those of obscenity. There can be little doubt of the misleading character of the condemned advertising or of the sufficiency of the evidence to sustain these administrative findings.

The other order, based upon a finding of obscenity as to a single book, naturally presents more of a problem because of the imprecise judicial meaning of the statutory terms and the many doubts now held as to the feasibility of administrative or judicial review of book publishing mores and standards. Involved here is a collection of some ninety-six "waggish tales," supposed to have been brought down to us from another era and another clime, and sold through the mails at the special discount of $10 from the listed $20 per volume. Our task is not made easier, however, when we discover them to be American-made or shared smoking room jests and stories, obscene or offensive enough by any refined standards and only saved, if at all, by reason of being both dull and well known. It is urged that such material is not of the sort to stimulate lust. Waiving the question how a court may test such a claim, we may suggest the curious dilemma involved in a view that the duller the book, the more its lewdness is to be excused or at least accepted. If under existing decisions, however, there be some reason to suppose that only books which are dull and without substantial literary merit will be suppressed, it may be answered that within limits it perhaps is not unreasonable to stifle compositions that clearly have little excuse for being beyond their provocative obscenity and to allow those of literary distinction to survive. But in any event, decision under the law here applicable is committed in the first instance to an administrative official; and under normal rules, therefore, judicial review channelled within the confines of a plea for an injunction should not be overextensive. Certainly material such as this does not afford much stimulus or basis for a finding of abuse of administrative discretion or power.

Affirmed.

FRANK, Circuit Judge (concurring).

This is the first case in which I have sat where the validity of an administrative order suppressing a book allegedly obscene has been contested. Because of my judicial inexperience in this field, I yield in this case to the more experienced judgment of my colleagues. But I do so with much puzzlement, and with the hope that the Supreme Court will review our decision, thus dissipating the fogs which surround this subject. For, as I shall try to show, those fogs are indeed thick, and I find no clear light penetrating them either in my colleagues' opinion in this suit or elsewhere.

My private tastes are such that I think the American people will suffer no great loss if deprived of the opportunity to read Waggish Tales from the Czechs. But far more is here involved than this particular book: Our decision will become a precedent—in a circuit which includes America's great publishing center—affecting the exercise of the right of free press guaranteed by the First Amendment. Our decision may put in peril other writings, of a higher order of excellence, which any man who happens at the moment to be Postmaster General happens to find offensive.

For my colleagues allow small room for court review, saying that the determination of obscenity "is committed in the first instance to an administrative official; and, under normal rules, therefore, judicial review channeled within the confines of a plea for an injunction[1] should not be overextensive." That ruling vests immense administrative censorship authority in one fallible man, makes him an almost despotic arbiter of literary products. If one day he bans a mediocre book, another day he may do the same to a work of genius. Originality is not so common that we should lightly contemplate its potential stifling. And censorship does more than to keep finished books from being sold: it keeps many from ever being written. Tolstoy and other Russians of the Czarist era have told how fear of the censor impeded their creative writing. An American author's imagination may be severely cramped if he must write with one eye on the Postmaster General; authors must cope with publishers who, uncertain about that official's judgment, may refuse to accept the manuscripts of contemporary or future Shelleys or Whitmans.

Such a condition is compatible with the ideologies of Hitlers,[2] Czars and Commissars. It does not accord with democratic ideals which repudiate thought-control. "Freedom of thought," it has been wisely said, " * * * is worthless unless it goes with freedom of expression. Thought is impossible without expression; thought is expression; an unexpressed thought, like an unlaid egg, comes to nothing. Given this freedom, then, other freedoms follow."[3] The "right of expression beyond the conventions of the day," wrote Mr. Justice Frankfurter three years ago, is "the very basis of a free society."[4] It would seem desirable that, in this industrial age, when economic pursuits will, perforce, become increasingly regulated by government, the realm of art should remain free, unregimented, the domain of unrestricted competition, free enterprise, and unhampered individual initiative at its maximum.[5] De gustibus non disputandum represents a cherished democratic maxim. Governmental control of the individual's taste may insidiously expand into menacing widespread anti-democratic practices. "Man," warned Goethe, "is easily accustomed to slavery and learns quickly to be obedient when his freedom is taken from him."

In that vein, President Franklin Roosevelt said: "The arts cannot thrive except where men are free to be themselves and to be in charge of the discipline of their own energies and ardors. The conditions for democracy and for art are one and the same. What we call liberty in politics results in freedom in the arts. * * * American artists * * * have no compulsion to be limited in method or manner of expression."[6] Disturbed by the way my colleagues' ruling runs counter to that ideal, I think it not inappropriate to ask some questions.

1. In the light of the First Amendment, it is not, I think, frivolous to ask a question about the constitutional power of Congress to authorize an official to bar from the mails, and probably thus largely to suppress, any book or writing he finds obscene. For Mr. Justice Holmes, dissenting, with Mr. Justice Brandeis' concurrence, in Leach v. Carlile, 258 U.S. 138, 140, 141, 42 S.Ct. 227, 229, 66 L.Ed. 511, asserted the unconstitutionality of one of the very suppression statutes before us in this case,[7] for the reason that the First Amendment was "intended to prevent restraints"[8] except those needed "for the safety of the nation."[9] Mr. Justice Frankfurter, concurring in Hannegan v. Esquire, Inc., 327 U.S. 146, 160, 66 S.Ct. 456, 90 L.Ed. 586, cited with approval the dissent in Leach v. Carlile. The majority of the Court in the Esquire case, speaking

through Mr. Justice Douglas, remarked, 327 U.S. 156, 66 S.Ct. 461, that "grave constitutional questions are immediately raised once it is said that the use of the mails is a privilege which may be extended or withheld on any grounds whatsoever."[10] It is germane here that several times the Supreme Court has with seeming approval referred to the distinction first proposed by Mr. Justice Stone in United States v. Carolene Products Co., 304 U.S. 144, 152 note, 58 S.Ct. 778, 783, 82 L.Ed. 1234: "There may be a narrower scope for operation of the presumption of constitutionality when legislation appears on its fact to be within a specific prohibition of the Constitution, such as those of the first ten Amendments. * * * " See Thomas v. Collins, 323 U.S. 516, 529, 530, 65 S.Ct. 315, 89 L.Ed. 430; cf. Thornhill v. Alabama, 310 U.S. 88, 95, 60 S.Ct. 736, 84 L.Ed. 1093; Schneider v. State, 308 U.S. 147, 161, 60 S.Ct. 146, 84 L.Ed. 155; Herndon v. Lowry, 301 U.S. 242, 258, 57 S.Ct. 732, 81 L.Ed. 1006; Bridges v. California, 314 U.S. 252, 262, 263, 62 S.Ct. 190, 86 L.Ed. 192, 159 A.L.R. 1346; Skinner v. Oklahoma, 316 U.S. 535, 543, 544, 62 S.Ct. 1110, 86 L.Ed. 1655; Kovacs v. Cooper, 69 S.Ct. 448, 458. Some there are who doubt the wisdom of that distinction,[11] but members of an inferior court, like ours, may not judicially act on such doubts. Mr. Justice Frankfurter, concurring in the recent Kovacs case, objected to what he described as the oversimplified and dogmatic formulation of the distinction; yet he said that, since "without freedom of expression, thought becomes checked and atrophied," he would adhere to the views of Mr. Justice Holmes who "was far more ready to find legislative invasion [of the Constitution] where free inquiry was involved than in the debatable area of economics."

If we were dealing here with that part of the statute providing not for administrative suppression of an obscene book but for criminal punishment of one who had already published it, the question might be different (although in a case a few weeks ago, four Supreme Court Justices, out of the eight who participated, may perhaps have held even such punitive legislation, enacted by a State, violative of the constitutional right of free press and free speech[12]).

The "safety of the Nation" exception would today, I think, be given a broader interpretation than Holmes'. It would, for example, include readily demonstrable social mischiefs such as commercial fraud and the like.[13] It would doubtless justify suppression of a book if there were a "clear and present danger" that its words would bring about grave "substantive evils" adversely affecting the public interest.[14] In terms of that exception, it may be urged that the reading of obscene books demonstrably entails such socially dangerous effects on normal persons[15] as to empower Congress, notwithstanding the First Amendment, to direct suppression of those writings.

I think that no sane man thinks socially dangerous the arousing of normal sexual desires. Consequently, if reading obscene books has merely that consequence, Congress, it would seem, can constitutionally no more suppress such books than it can prevent the mailing of many other objects, such as perfumes, for example, which notoriously produce that result. But the constitutional power to suppress obscene publications might well exist if there were ample reason to believe that reading them conduces to socially harmful sexual conduct on the part of normal human beings. However, convincing proof of that fact has never been assembled. It may be exceedingly difficult to obtain. Perhaps in order to be trustworthy, such proof ought to be at least as extensive and intensive as the Kinsey Report.[16] Macaulay, replying to demands for suppression of obscene books, said: "We find it difficult to believe that in a world so full of temptations as this, any gentleman, whose life would have been virtuous if he had not read Aristophanes and Juvenal, will be made vicious by reading them." Substitute "Waggish Tales from the Czech" for "Aristophanes and Juvenal," and those remarks become relevant here.

Psychological studies in the last few decades suggest that all kinds of stimuli—for instance, the odor of lilacs or old leather, the sight of an umbrella or a candle, or the touch of a piece of silk or cheese-cloth—may be provocative of irregular sexual behavior in apparently normal men,[17]—for all we know, far more provocative than the reading of obscene books. Perhaps further research will disclose that, for most men,[18] such reading diverts from, rather than stimulates to, anti-social conduct[19] (which, I take it, is what is meant by expressions, used in the cases, such as "sexual impurity," "corrupt and debauch the minds and morals"[20]).

Some dictionary definitions of "obscene"—as "disgusting," "loathesome," "repulsive"—may suggest that there is serious social danger, constitutionally justifying suppression, in the shock of obscene writings to normal susceptibilities. But there are indications that Thomas Jefferson[21] and James Madison,[22] no mean authorities when it comes to interpreting the First Amendment, recognized no such limitations on the free-press right.

It is not altogether impossible, then, that the Supreme Court, following the lead of Mr. Justice Holmes and Mr. Justice Brandeis, will strike down this suppression statute.[23] But I do not venture so to prophesy.

2. If, however, it be true that "grave constitutional questions are immediately raised" by a statute authorizing an official to suppress books,[24] one would suppose that such a statute, verging as it does on unconstitutionality, should at least contain unusual safeguards against arbitrary official incursions on the rights guaranteed by the First Amendment, and should be strictly interpreted[25] so as to preclude doubts about its validity. To avoid unconstitutionality it might seem that the statute should provide some fairly precise standard to guide the officials' action, a standard far more precise than is necessary in those statutes, providing for administrative action, which do not come close to the very edge of constitutional power. If anyone regards as precise the standard in the obscenity statute, he cannot have read the pertinent cases. For see: At one time, the courts held that the existence of obscenity turned on the subjective intention of the author, regardless of the book's probable effect on readers. This test has now been abandoned; now the courts consider solely the author's "objective" intention, which equates with the book's effect on others.[26] In other words, an author does not violate an obscenity statute if he writes and publishes a dainty ditty which he alone, of all men, believes obscene; his private, unsuccessfully communicated, thought and purposes are not a wrong.[27] Also, at one time, a writing was held obscene if it would probably have a socially undesirable effect on the abnormal; but now the test has shifted and become that of the way the words will probably affect normal persons.[28] A standard so difficult for our ablest judges to interpret is hardly precise.[29] Nor are there any Supreme Court decisions which clarify it.

3. Let us assume, however, that we have a standard sufficiently precise to render the statute constitutional if it be interpreted to mean that a book is obscene which will probably have socially undesirable effects on normal readers. Even so, it is arguable that with a statute which, at best, skirts unconstitutionality, the finding of fact that such will be the probable results must be supported by evidence of an unusually clear and convincing kind—in other words, it is arguable that the evidence ought to be of a far stronger character than is required as the basis of ordinary administrative action. But, in the case at bar, the sole evidence to support the finding consists of the book itself.

However, although the Supreme Court has never passed on this question, the lower courts have held that direct proof of such harmful effects is not necessary. Perhaps because the primitive state of our psychological knowledge makes convincing proof of any such effects almost unobtainable, the lower courts have, instead, taken the current mores, "the social sense of what is right," the "average conscience of the time," i.e., what at the time is the attitude of the community in general.[30] Maybe, then, the Postmaster General's finding will suffice, if based upon a not irrational determination of the contemporary public attitude towards books like this. But here he made no express finding about that attitude.

We thus do not know how he arrived at his conclusion as to obscenity. To sustain his order, we must, at a minimum, read into the record an implied administrative determination that the book is at odds with the "average conscience of the time." He has not told us how he ascertained that average conscience.[31] In effect, we are asked to infer that he invoked something like judicial notice. That, however, can mean no more than a guess as to public opinion. And the recent Presidential election teaches that such a guess, even when assisted by so-called public-opinion polls, may go badly astray.

Because the state of our knowledge of psychology and the inadequacy of our procedures for determining public opinion make this question less susceptible of expert, objective, and explainable administrative determination than most questions passed on by administrative bodies, and noting again how closely this suppression statute approaches unconstitutionality, I would think that a reviewing court should scrutinize with more than ordinary care such an administrative determination with respect to public opinion. Engaged in such scrutiny, the judges must fall back on their own judicial notice, must by that means decide whether the official's guess is rational enough to be supportable. But where will the judges gather the facts to inform their judicial notice? Those whose views most judges know best are other lawyers. It would seem not improper to take judicial notice that tales such as those the Postmaster General here found obscene are freely told at many gatherings of prominent lawyers in meetings of Bar Associations or of alumni of our leading law-schools.[32] I doubt whether we ought arrogantly, undemocratically, to conclude that lawyers are a race apart, or an intellectual elite (like Plato's totalitarian "guardians" or "guards"[33]) with a "sense of what is right" for themselves, which has no relation to what is right for the vast multitude of other Americans, whom (a la Plato) they may look upon as children.

The truth of the matter is that we do not know, with anything that approximates reliability, the "average"

American public opinion on the subject of obscenity. Perhaps we never will have such knowledge. For many years we have heard talk of "social science," and some may believe that from that source we may obtain the needed enlightenment. But, if "science" connotes a fairly high degree of accuracy, most studies of society, although by no means useless for all purposes,[34] are further away from the "scientific" than were alchemy or astrology.[35] Maybe some day we will attain scientific data about community opinion. One wonders whether free speech and free press may validly be suppressed when their suppression turns on the dubious data now available.

4. I can think of no better way, in the present state of our ignorance, to decide the rationality of the finding that this book is obscene than to compare it with other books now accessible to all American readers. On that basis, I have considerable difficulty in believing the Postmaster General's finding correct. For anyone can obtain for the asking, from almost any public library, a copy of Balzac's Droll Stories, translated into English.[36] That easy accessibility of that book might well serve as a persuasive indicator of current public judgments about the type of acceptable—i.e., not obscene—writing. Within the past few days, I have re-read Droll Stories. For the life of me, I cannot see, nor understand how anyone else could see, anything in that book less obscene than in Waggish Tales which the Postmaster General has suppressed.

This court, per Judge A. N. Hand, has held that the passages alleged to be obscene in Joyce's Ulysses played a subordinate role.[37] The same cannot possibly be said of Droll Stories, which one deceased conservative critic described as "tales in which the lusts of the flesh are unleashed, satisfied and left to run riot amid a bacchanalia of flushed Priapi."[38] Were that critic the Postmaster General, and were he to set up his own opinion of obscenity in disregard of the most readily available manifestations of American attitudes (i.e., public-library usages), he would suppress the Balzac book.

It will not do to differentiate Waggish Tales on the ground that Droll Stories is a "classic" which comported with the mores prevailing at the time and place of its publication. Balzac's own comments on this work show his awareness that it would, as it did, offend many of his contemporaries,[39] such as George Sand who called it indecent. More important, where we seek to discover the attitude prevailing in this country today, the question is not what those living in Balzac's day thought of that book but how the "average" American now regards it. Wherefore (perhaps because I am without experience or am overly obtuse), I do not understand just how the "average conscience of the time"[40] test of obscenity can be reconciled with the notion that a "classic"—defined as a work which has an "accepted place in the arts"—is not obscene,[41] no matter what its contents and regardless of whether it is in tune with that current "average conscience."

Nor will it do to say that Droll Stories possesses unusual artistry which I chance to think Waggish Tales lacks. For this argument cuts just the other way: If a book is dominantly obscene, the greater the art, the greater the harmful impact on its "average" reader. If superior artistry—or what my colleagues call "literary distinction"— were to confer immunity from official control, then someone would have to determine which books have that quality. The Postmaster General's function would then be

that of literary critic, with the reviewing judges as super-critics. Jurisprudence would merge with aesthetics. Authors and publishers would consult the legal digests for legal-artistic precedents. We might some day have a legal Restatement of the Canons of Literary Taste. I cannot believe Congress had anything so grotesque in mind.

In sum, as Droll Stories appears obviously acceptable to the American public, and by that test is not obscene, no more, one would incline to think, is Waggish Tales.

6. I agree that the fraud orders concerning the circulars which advertise Self Defense For Women and Bumarap must stand, for the evidence—the circulars themselves—support the findings on which those orders are based.[42] But, as they rest on the ground that a person commits a fraud who advertises a book as if its dominant theme resembled that of Waggish Tales when in fact it does not, these orders tend to show that a considerable number of the reading public, and especially those who would buy and would probably read Waggish Tales,[43] want books like it. If so, then these orders strongly indicate that that book is not out of line with our present mores, and thus those orders may well be inconsistent with the finding that Waggish Tales is obscene.

I repeat, however, that, since, as a novice, I am unwilling in this case to oppose my views to those of my more experienced colleagues, I concur in their decision, but with bewilderment.

NOTES

1. I am unaware of any means of review under this statute other than a suit for injunction.
2. Cf. Timasheff, The Legal Regimentation of Culture in National Socialist Germany, 11 Fordham L.Rev. (1942) 1.
3. Kallen, The Liberal Spirit (1948) 133.
4. Frankfurter, J., concurring in Hannegan v. Esquire, Inc., 327 U.S. 146, 159, 160, 66 S.Ct. 456, 463, 90 L.Ed. 586.
The Justice substantially reiterated those views the other day in his concurring opinion in Kovacs v. Cooper, 69 S.Ct. 448.
5. See Frank, Fate and Freedom (1945) 194-202.
6. Message at dedicating exercises of the New York Museum of Modern Art, May 8, 1939.
7. 39 U.S.C.A. § 259 (Rev.St.3929).
8. See Patterson v. Colorado, 205 U.S. 454, 462, 27 S.Ct. 556, 51 L.Ed. 879, 10 Ann.Cas. 689, per Holmes J.: Grosjean v. American Press, 297 U.S. 233, 249, 56 S.Ct. 444, 80 L.Ed. 660; Lovell v. Griffin, 303 U.S. 444, 451, 452, 58 S.Ct. 666, 82 L.Ed. 949.
9. Holmes, J., there said: "I do not suppose that anyone would say that the freedom of written speech is less protected by the First Amendment than the freedom of spoken words. Therefore I cannot understand by what authority Congress undertakes to authorize anyone to determine in advance, on the grounds before us, that certain words shall not be uttered. Even those who interpret the Amendment most strictly agree that it was intended to prevent previous restraints. We have not before us any question as to how far Congress may go for the safety of the nation."
10. The Court cited "the dissents of Mr. Justice Brandeis and Mr. Justice Holmes in United States ex rel. Milwaukee Social Democratic Publishing Co. v. Burleson, 255 U.S. 407, 421, 423, 430–432, 437, 438, 41 S.Ct. 352, 357,

358, 360, 361, 363, 65 L.Ed. 704."

11. See discussion in Clark, The Dilemma of American Judges, 35 Am. Bar Ass'n. J. (l949), 8, 10, 11.

12. See Doubleday & Co., Inc., v. New York, 335 U.S. 848, 69 S.Ct. 79, affirming, by a divided Court and without any opinions, 297 N.Y. 687, 77 N.E.2d 6. Mr. Justice Frankfurter took no part in the decision.

13. Donaldson v. Read Magazine, 333 U.S. 178, 68 S.Ct. 591.

14. See Bridges v. California, 314 U.S. 252, 261–263, 62 S.Ct. 190, 86 L.Ed. 192, 159 A.L.R. 1346; Thornhill v. Alabama, 310 U.S. 88, 104, 105, 60 S.Ct. 736, 84 L.Ed. 1093; Herndon v. Lowry, 301 U.S. 242, 258, 57 S.Ct. 732, 81 L.Ed. 1066; Thomas v. Collins, 323 U.S. 516, 529, 530, 65 S.Ct. 315, 89 L.Ed. 430.

15. As noted below, the courts in the obscenity cases now refer to the reactions of normal persons.

16. "Interestingly enough," we are told, "New Mexico has no obscenity law, and does not seem to feel handicapped by the lack of one. As a footnote to sexual behavior, it would be instructive to discover * * * whether the sexual pattern of the people of New Mexico is substantially different from that of other people who have enjoyed the 'protection' of State censorship of printed materials on grounds of obscenity." Ernst and Loth, American Sexual Behavior and The Kinsey Report (1948) 129.

17. "The psychiatrist and psychologist fail to find any sharp distinction between * * * apparently abnormal traits, on the one hand, and similar, though less marked, traits in normal people. The psychoneurotic and insane are, so to speak, 'more so.'" Gardner Murphy, in the Introduction to An Outline of Abnormal Psychology (1929).

See also West, Conscience and Society (1945), a book by a psychiatrist well versed in matters legal, which contains discussions, cautiously phrased, helpful to lawyers interested in the pull of the unconscious motivations of normal human beings; see especially pp. 158, 161-165, 219, 222, 231.

Of course, psychiatry is not an infallible science but an art still in its period of adolescence, and, with many psychiatrists, tainted by a superfluous deterministic philosophy. See Frank, Law and The Modern Mind (1930) 21 note, 359-360; Frank, Fate and Freedom (1945) 64-69; cf. Hall, Principles of Criminal Law, (1947) Ch. 14.

18. Alpert, Censorship and The Press, 52 Harv.L.Rev. (1938) 40, 72: "Over ten years ago the Bureau of Social Hygiene of New York City sent questionnaires to ten thousand college and normal school women graduates. Twelve hundred answers were received; and of those seventy-two persons who replied that the source of their sex information came from books, mentioning specific volumes, not one specified a 'dirty' book as the source. Instead, the books listed were: the Bible, the Dictionary, the Encyclopaedia, novels from Dickens to Henry James, Shakespeare, circulars for venereal diseases, medical books, and Motley's Rise of the Dutch Republic. In answer to the question of what things were most stimulating sexually, of the 409 replies, 9 said 'Music,' 18 said 'Pictures,' 29 said 'Dancing,' 40 said 'Drama,' 95 said 'Books,' and 218 noted very simply 'Man.' "

19. Alpert writes of the American Youth Commission study of the conditions and attitudes of young people in Maryland between the ages of sixteen and twenty-four, as reported in 1938: "For this study Maryland was deliberately picked as a 'typical' state, and, according to the Commission, the 13,528 young people personally interviewed in Maryland can speak for the two hundred and fifty thousand young people in Maryland and the twenty millions in the United States. The chief source of sex "education" for the youth of all ages and all religious groups was found to be the youth's contemporaries. * * * Sixty-six percent of the boys and forty percent of the girls reported that what they knew about sex was more or less limited to what their friends of their own age had told them. After "contemporaries" and the youth's home, the source that is next in importance is the school, from which about 8 percent of the young people reported they had received most of their sex information. A few, about 4 percent, reported they owed most to books, while less than 1 percent asserted that they had acquired most of their information from movies. Exactly the same proportion specified the church as the chief source of their sex information.' These statistical results are not offered as conclusive; but that they do more than cast doubt upon the assertion that 'immoral' books corrupt and deprave must be admitted. These statistical results placed in the scale against the weight of the dogma upon which the law is founded lift the counterpan high. Add this: that 'evil manners' are as easily acquired without books as with books; that crowded slums, machine labor, barren lives, starved emotions, and unreasoning minds are far more dangerous to morals than any so-called obscene literature. True, this attack is tangential, but a social problem is here involved, and the weight of this approach should be felt. The counterpan is lifted a trifle higher". Id. at 74.

20. See Swearingen v. United States, 161 U.S. 446, 451, 16 S.Ct. 562, 564, 40 L.Ed. 765; Dysart v. United States, 272 U.S. 655, 657, 47 S.Ct. 234, 71 L.Ed. 461. In the Swearingen case, 161 U.S. at page 450, 16 S.Ct. at page 563, 40 L.Ed. 765, the Court said that the words "obscene, lewd or lascivious" are "used in the statute, as describing one and the same offense."

21. In Jefferson's Second Inaugural Address, March 4, 1805, he referred to articles published in the press, during his first administration, "charged with whatsoever its licentiousness could devise or dare." He said that libel suits were the proper redress, adding that "the press * * * needs no other legal restraint, * * * and no other line can be drawn between the inestimable liberty of the press and its demoralizing licentiousness. If there be still improprieties which this rule would not restrain, its supplement must be sought in the censorship of public opinion."

Previously, in 1776, in his draft of a proposed Constitution for Virginia, he had included this statement: "Printing-presses shall be free, except so far as by commission of private injury cause may be given of private action."

See Berman, Thomas Jefferson Among The Artists (1947) 250-251: "He violently opposed censorship of books, coming to the defense of the bookseller Dufief when the latter was threatened with prosecution for selling De Becourt's Sur la Creation du Monde, saying that he was 'really mortified to be told that, in the United States of America * * * a question about the sale of a book can be carried before the civil magistrate.' So, too, he uncompromisingly defended the freedom of the press, even though he himself was the victim of as unscrupulous, as venal and mendacious a press as ever in our history assailed the character of a great public figure. Where the press is free, and every man able to read, all is safe,' he told Col. Yancey [1816] * * * 'The force of public opinion cannot be resisted, when permitted to be freely expressed. * * * Were it left to me whether we should have a government without newspapers or newspapers without a government, I should not hesitate a moment to prefer the latter.' " [1809].

22. Madison, writing of guaranties of press freedom in State Constitutions, said: "Some degree of abuse is inseparable from the proper use of anything. It has accordingly been decided by the practice of the States, that it is better to leave a few of its noxious branches to their luxuriant growth, than, by pruning them away, to injure the vigor of those yielding the proper fruits." Works, Vol. 4, p. 544.

23. There are dicta that may perhaps be to the contrary. See Near v. Minnesota, 283 U.S. 697, 716, 51 S.Ct. 625, 75 L.Ed. 1357; Chaplinsky v. New Hampshire, 315 U.S. 568, 571, 572, 62 S.Ct. 766, 86 L.Ed. 1031; Winters v. New York, 333 U.S. 507, 510, 68 S.Ct. 665.

24. Hannegan v. Esquire, Inc., 327 U.S. 146, 156, 66 S.Ct. 456, 90 L.Ed. 586.

25. Cf. Swearingen v. United States, 161 U.S. 446, 451, 16 S.Ct. 562, 40 L.Ed. 765.

26. See United States v. One Book Entitled Ulysses, 2 Cir., 72 F.2d 705, 709; Parmelee v. United States, 72 App.D.C. 203, 113 F.2d 729.

27. It might conceivably be argued that it would be a defense if what he wrote had evil effects but he thought his words wholly demure.

28. See Judge L. Hand in United States v. Kennerley, D.C., 209 F. 119, 120; United States v. Levine, 2 Cir., 83 F.2d 156; Parmelee v. United States, 72 App.D.C. 203, 113 F.2d 729.

29. George Bernard Shaw, testifying in 1909 before a Parliamentary committee, was asked whether he thought there "should be power of prosecution if incitements to sexual vice take place on the stage." He replied, "No, I could not admit that, because if you prosecute for incentives to sexual vice, you immediately make it possible to prosecute a manager because the principal actress has on a pretty hat or is a pretty woman. I strongly protest against anything that is not quite definite. You may make any law you like defining what is an incentive to sexual vice, but to lay down a general law of that kind with regard to unspecified incentives to sexual vice is going too far, when the mere fact of a woman washing her face and putting on decent clothes, or anything of the kind, may possibly cause somebody in the street who passes to admire her and to say, 'I have been incited to sexual vice.' These generalizations are too dangerous." Pearson, G.B.S. (1942) 255.

30. See United States v. Kennerley, D.C. 1913, 209 F. 119, 121, a criminal obscenity case.

Judge L. Hand there said that a jury is especially equipped to determine the "social sense of what is right" at "any given time." He repeated that idea in United States v. Levine, 2 Cir., 1936, 83 F.2d 156, 157. I have my doubts. For any particular single jury may not at all represent the "average" views of the community, especially on such a subject.

Moreover, eleven years after deciding the Levine case, Judge Learned Hand, in Repouille v. United States, 2 Cir.,

165 F.2d 152, 153, rejected a jury's verdict as a guide to the prevailing moral standards with respect to the "good moral character" of the very man there before the court. That case did not relate to obscenity, but, according to Judge Hand, the applicable test was "the generally accepted moral conventions current at the time."

31. Perhaps his order, on that account, fails to comply with the Administrative Procedure Act, 5 U.S.C.A. § 1007(b); but I pass that point.

32. One thinks of the lyrics sung at many such gatherings by a certain respected and conservative member of the faculty of a great law-school which considers itself the most distinguished and which is the Alma Mater of many judges sitting on upper courts.

To revert for a moment to the question of the socially dangerous effects of obscenity, it is relevant that no noticeably depraved behavior has been discovered among lawyers as a group.

33. That the correct translation is "guards," see Fite, The Platonic Legend (1934) 14.

As to Plato's totalitarian, anti-democratic teachings, see, e.g., Fite, loc.cit., passim.

Let it not be forgotten that Plato would have banished all poets from his ideal state, and that in the Laws he advocated rigid censorship.

34. Cf. Frank, Book Review, 15 Un. of Chi.L.Rev. (1947) 462; Frank, Fate and Freedom (1945) 40-41.

35. Cf. Frank, A Plea for Lawyer-Schools, 56 Yale L.J. (1947) 1303, 1330-1342; Frank, Fate and Freedom (1945) passim.

36. Apparently in 1930, a United States Customs ban on Droll Stories, theretofore existing, was lifted and never reimposed. See Haight, Banned Books (1935) 47.

37. United States v. One Book Entitled Ulysses, 2 Cir., 72 F.2d 705, 708.

38. Quoted by Jacques Le Clercq, in translator's Preface to Heritage Press ed. (1932).

39. In the foreword to the first ten tales, he wrote: "There are countless people in France attacked by that British cant Lord Byron so often complained of. These people, whose cheeks blush at a pithy frankness which once moved kings and princesses to laughter, have draped our hallowed physiognomy in mourning; they have persuaded the gayest, wittiest nation in the world to laugh decorously and underhand * * * ".

40. Judge L. Hand in United States v. Kennerley, D.C., 209 F. 120.

41. Judge L. Hand in United States v. Levine, 2 Cir., 83 F.2d 156, 157.

Perhaps Judge Hand meant merely that the fact that a book is a "classic" is some evidence that it is attuned to the "average conscience." Then, however, the character of a classic—like Droll Stories or the Decameron—should represent the standard of non-obscenity by which other books (like Waggish Tales) are to be judged.

42. Here, again, however, there may be a doubt as to compliance with the Administrative Procedure Act.

43. It has been said that "what counts is its effect * * * upon all those whom it [a book] is likely to reach"; United States v. Levine, 2 Cir., 83 F.2d 156, 157.

GOD'S LITTLE ACRE IS "OBSCENE, INDECENT, AND IMPURE"

Attorney General v. Book Named "God's Little Acre," 93 N.E.2d 819 (1950)

SPALDING, Justice.

The Attorney General under the provisions of G.L.(Ter.Ed.) c. 272, §§28C-28G, as inserted by St.1945, c. 278, §1, seeks by this petition to have the novel "God's Little Acre" by Erskine Caldwell adjudicated obscene, indecent, or impure. In an answer filed by persons interested in the book it was admitted that it was being sold and distributed in this Commonwealth. From a final decree in favor of the book the Attorney General appealed. The case comes here on a report of the evidence, including a copy of the book itself, and findings of fact by the trial judge.

While conceding "that if one were seeking so called racy, off-color or suggestive paragraphs, they can be found in the book," the judge was of opinion that the "book as a whole would not stimulate sexual passions or desires in a person with average sex instincts," and concluded that he did not believe that it would have "a substantial tendency to deprave or corrupt its readers by inciting lascivious thoughts or arousing lustful desires."

The tests to be applied in determining whether a book is obscene, indecent, or impure are fully set forth in the recent case of Commonwealth v. Isenstadt, 318 Mass. 543, 62 N.E.2d 840. They were quoted with approval and applied in Attorney General v. Book Named "Forever Amber," 323 Mass. 302, 81 N.E.2d 663. They need not be restated. Comprehensive and complete as are these tests, their application in a given case is by no means easy. Indeed it is not indulging in hyperbole to say that no more difficult or delicate task confronts a court than that arising out of the interpretation and application of statutes of this sort. On the one hand, an interpretation ought not to be given to the statute in question which would trim down the fundamental right of the public to read "to the point where a few prurient persons can find nothing upon which their hypersensitive imaginations may dwell." Commonwealth v. Isenstadt, 318 Mass. 543, 551-552, 62 N.E. 2d 840, 845: On the other hand, care must be taken that it be not construed in such a way as to render it incapable of accomplishing the objects intended by the Legislature.

We turn to the story itself. It has to do with life of a poor white farmer and his family on a run down farm in Georgia. The father, Ty Ty Walden, is a pathetic figure with the mentality of a moron. Believing that there is gold on his land, he and two of his sons dig for it incessantly, leaving the raising of cotton to two colored share croppers. Ty Ty, who is pious, dedicates one acre of his land to God and intends to turn over the proceeds of that acre to the church. But he is so busy digging for gold that he never gets around to raising anything on it, and he relocates it from time to time to meet the exigencies of his digging. Ty Ty's sons, daughters, and daughter-in-law become involved in numerous sexual affairs. These lead to quarrels among the brothers, and as the story closes one brother kills another and departs with his shotgun, presumably to kill himself. Ty Ty, who had always tried to keep peace in the family, in despair resumes his digging for gold.

Viewing the book as a whole we find ourselves unable to agree with the conclusion of the trial judge that the book was not obscene, indecent, or impure as those words have been defined in our decisions. The book abounds in sexual episodes and some are portrayed with an abundance of realistic detail. In some instances the author's treatment of sexual relations descends to outright pornography. Nothing would be gained by spreading these portions of the book on the pages of this opinion.

Evidence was introduced at the hearing below by literary critics, professors of English literature, and a professor of sociology touching the "literary, cultural or educational character" of the book. See §28F. In general the literary experts regarded the book as a sincere and serious work possessing literary merit. The sociologist was of opinion that the book was of value as a sociological document in its portrayal of life of the so-called "poor whites" in the south. The judge, who had the advantage of hearing these witnesses, has indicated in his findings that he accorded considerable weight to their testimony. We accept his findings on this aspect of the case. But the fact that under §28F evidence may be received as to the literary, cultural or educational character" of the book does not change the substantive law as to what is obscene, indecent, or impure. Those provisions were undoubtedly inserted to clarify doubts as to the sort of expert evidence that may be received in cases of this type. See Commonwealth v. Isenstadt, 318 Mass. 543, at pages 558-559, 62 N.E.2d 840. In reaching the conclusion that the book offends against the statute we have taken into consideration the expert testimony described above. In the Isenstadt case we recognized that sincerity of purpose and literary merit were not to be entirely ignored and could "be considered in so far as they bear upon the question whether the book, considered as a whole, is or is not obscene, indecent, or impure." 318 Mass. at page 554, 62 N.E.2d at page 846. But as we said in that case, "In dealing with such a practical matter as the enforcement of the statute here involved there is no room for the pleasing fancy that sincerity and art necessarily dispel obscenity. * * * Sincerity and art can flourish without pornography, and seldom, if ever, will obscenity be needed to carry the lesson." 318 Mass. at page 553, 62 N.E.2d 846.

Our attention has been directed to two decisions in other jurisdictions in which the book in question has been held not to be obscene under statutes somewhat similar to ours. One of them, People v. Viking Press, Inc., 147 Misc. 813, 264 N.Y.S. 534, is an opinion by a city magistrate. The other case, Commonwealth v. Gordon, 66 Pa.Dist. & Co.R. 101, was decided by a court of first instance in Pennsylvania and was affirmed by the Superior Court on appeal in a per curiam decision, 166 Pa.Super. 120, 70 A.2d 389. A discussion of these decisions would not be profitable. It is enough for present purposes to say that the interpretations placed on the statutes there involved differ materially from that which this court has placed on our statute.

The contention that a decree adjudicating the book as obscene, indecent, or impure would be an abridgment of the rights of freedom of the press guaranteed by the Fourteenth Amendment to the Constitution of the United States requires no discussion. A similar contention was made without success in Commonwealth v. Isenstadt, 318

Mass. 543, 557–558, 62 N.E.2d 840. What was said there is applicable here.

It follows that the decree below is reversed and a new decree is to be entered adjudicating that the book in question is obscene, indecent, and impure.

So ordered.

TROPIC OF CANCER AND *TROPIC OF CAPRICORN* ARE OBSCENE

Besig v. United States, 208 F.2d 142 (1953)

STEPHENS, Circuit Judge.

Two books entitled respectively "Tropic of Cancer" and "Tropic of Capricorn", which were written by Henry Miller and were printed in Paris, were intercepted at an American port of entry and libeled under Section 1305(a) of Title 19 U.S.C.A.[1] as obscene. The district court found them to be obscene and ordered them destroyed. Besig, the owner of the books, is here appealing upon the ground that neither of the two books, which are commonly referred to together as "The Tropics", is obscene.

Since all of the evidence is in writing, we review and weigh the evidence, though with due regard to the conclusions of the trial court.[2]

We note in the margin[3] the Funk & Wagnalls New Standard Dictionary and Webster's New International Dictionary definitions of the word "obscene".

The word "obscene" is not uncommon and is used in English and American speech and writings as the word symbol for indecent, smutty, lewd or salacious reference to parts of the human or animal body or to their functions or to the excrement therefrom. Each of The Tropics is written in the composite style of a novel-autobiography, and the author as a character in the book carries the reader as though he himself is living in disgrace, degradation, poverty, mean crime, and prostitution of mind and body. The vehicle of description is the unprintable word of the debased and morally bankrupt. Practically everything that the world loosely regards as sin is detailed in the vivid, lurid, salacious language of smut, prostitution, and dirt. And all of it is related without the slightest expressed idea of its abandon. Consistent with the general tenor of the books, even human excrement is dwelt upon in the dirtiest words available. The author conducts the reader through sex orgies and perversions of the sex organs, and always in the debased language of the bawdy house. Nothing has the grace of purity or goodness. These words of the language of smut, and the disgraceful scenes, are so heavily larded throughout the books that those portions which are deemed to be of literary merit do not lift the reader's mind clear of their sticky slime. And it is safe to say that the "literary merit" of the books carries the reader deeper into it. For this reason, The Tropics are far more dangerous than "Confessions of a Prostitute" which was the subject of our opinion in Burstein v. United States, 9 Cir., 1949, 178 F.2d 665. There, the scenes depicted are obscene because of the scene itself which in its stark ugliness might well repel many. The Tropics lure on with the cleverness of scene, skilfulness of recital, and the use of worse than gutter words. All of this is sought to be justified through the sophistry, as the trial judge, Honorable Louis E. Goodman, put it, of "confession and avoidance".[4] It is claimed that they truthfully describe a base status of society in the language of its own iniquities. And that, since we live in an age of realism, obscene language depicting obscenity in action ceases to be obscenity.

Whether the moral conventions should be flaunted in the cause of frankness, art, or realism, we have no occasion to decide. That question is for the policy branches of the government. Nor do we understand that we have the legal power to hold that the statute authorizing the seizure of obscene books is inapplicable to books in which obscenity is an integral part of a literary work. So that obscenity, though a part of a composition of high literary merit, is not excepted from operation of the statute, whether written in the style of the realists, surrealists, or plain shock writers. The civilization of our times holds to the premise that dirt in stark nakedness is not generally and at all times acceptable. And the great mass of the people still believe there is such a thing as decency. Indecency is easily recognizable. Such is the premise of the statute. The Congress has chosen to enact a censorship which would not have been possible except for the self-styled prophets of truth who offend so grievously.

It is of course true that the ears of some may be so accustomed to words which are ordinarily regarded as obscene that they take no offense at them, but the law is not tempered to the hardened minority of society. The statute forbidding the importation of obscene books is not designed to fit the normal concept of morality of society's dregs, nor of the different concepts of morality throughout the world, nor for all time past and future, but is designed to fit the normal American concept in the age in which we live. It is no legitimate argument that because there are social groups composed of moral delinquents in this or in other countries, that their language shall be received as legal tender along with the speech of the great masses who trade ideas and information in the honest money of decency.

Adequate provision is made in the statute in the interests of classics and the technical, by the following proviso:

"*Provided further,* That the Secretary of the Treasury may, in his discretion, admit the so-called classics or books of recognized and established literary or scientific merit, but may, in his discretion, admit such classics or books only when imported for noncommercial purposes." Title 19 U.S.C.A. § 1305 (a). No action under this proviso has been taken by the Secretary of the Treasury, nor has appellant requested any action under or pursuant to it.

It is claimed that these books (The Tropics) are not for the immature of mind, and that adults read them for their literary and informative merits, but, whether true or untrue, we cannot measure their importability by such a yardstick. The Congress probably saw the impracticability of preventing the use of the books by the young and the pure. And of course they knew that salacious print in the hands of adults, even in the hands of those whose sun is near the western horizon, may well incite to disgusting practices and to hideous crime.

We agree that the book as a book must be obscene to justify its libel and destruction, but neither the number of the "objectionable" passages nor the proportion they bear to the whole book are controlling. If an incident, integrated with the theme or story of a book, is word-painted in such lurid and smutty or pornographic language that dirt appears as the primary purpose rather than the relation of a fact or adequate description of the incident, the book itself is obscene. We are not well acquainted with Aristophanes or his times, but we know they were different from ours. We have chanced upon Chaucer and we know his times were different from ours. Boccaccio is lurid. The Bible is not free from the recounting of immoral practices. But the translators, from the languages in which The Bible was originally written, did not word-paint such practices in the lurid-Miller-morally-corrupt manner. Dirty word description of the sweet and sublime, especially of the mystery of sex and procreation, is the ultimate of obscenity. We have referred to Aristophanes, Chaucer, Boccaccio, and The Bible only because those works were taken as examples by the author of the opinion in the case of United States v. One Book Entitled Ulysses, 2 Cir., 1934, 72 F.2d 705, 707, a case cited by appellant to illustrate his point that " 'No work may be judged from a selection of such paragraphs alone. * * * ' " Appellant also cites United States v. Levine, 2 Cir., 1936, 83 F.2d 156, 157. Whether those cases were rightly decided we do not say, but the point is not relevant because we have adjudged each book as an integrated whole.

Appellant argues that the test we used in Burstein v. United States, 9 Cir., 1949, 178 F.2d 665, 667, as to what is obscene, is unworkable because it approves the rule that language is obscene when it may be termed "dirt for dirt's sake". He finds the opinion self-contradictory" when we say that obscene matter "is offensive to the common sense of decency and modesty of the community," and later in the opinion say "[t]he true test to determine whether a writing is * * * obscene * * * is whether its language has a tendency to deprave or corrupt the morals of those whose minds are open to such influences and into whose hands it may fall by allowing or implanting in such minds obscene, lewd, or lascivious thoughts or desires." Appellant thinks our opinion is "unclear as to whether the test of obscenity is that it *repels* or that it *seduces.*"

We observe no contradiction in any of these expressions. They aptly describe the quality of language which the word "obscene" is meant to suggest. Of course, language can be so nasty as to repel and of course to seduce as well. Appellant's argument tempts us to quote Pope's[5] quatrain about the Monster Vice which, when too prevalent, is embraced.

Appellant thinks the district court committed error in deciding contrary to the great weight of opinion evidence as to the quality of Mr. Miller's writings. The point has no merit. Opinion evidence is useful, but not controlling.[6] We have carefully read and analyzed the voluminous affidavits and exhibits contained in the record. To a large extent they are opinions of authors who resent any limitation on their writings. Their opinions are relevant and competent evidence, but their views are advisory only as to the norm of the meaning of the word "obscene". We share the general antipathy to censorship and we are aware that individual tastes and special occasions and different times and different peoples differ as to what is offensive language. Yet we risk the assertion that there is an underlying, perhaps universal, accord that there is a phase

of respectable delicacy related to sex, and that those compositions which purposefully flaunt such delicacy in language generally regarded as indecent come under the ban of the statute.

We think Judge Learned Hand was in the best of his famous form in his happy use of words in United States v. Kennerley, D.C.S.D.N.Y.1913, 209 F. 119, 121: "If there be no abstract definition, such as I have suggested, should not the word 'obscene' be allowed to indicate the present critical point in the compromise between candor and shame at which the community may have arrived here and now? If letters must, like other kinds of conduct, be subject to the social sense of what is right, it would seem that a jury should in each case establish the standard much as they do in cases of negligence. To put thought in leash to the average conscience of the time is perhaps tolerable, but to fetter it by the necessities of the lowest and least capable seems a fatal policy. Nor is it an objection, I think, that such an interpretation gives to the words of the statute a varying meaning from time to time. Such words as these do not embalm the precise morals of an age or place; while they presuppose that some things will always be shocking to the public taste, the vague subject-matter is left to the gradual development of general notions about what is decent. * * * "

The point that the Constitutional guarantee of freedom of speech or of the printing press, (or, we may add, of the radio and television,) is violated, is without merit. The point is made and the only argument to sustain it is simply that the books, since they have some literary merit, are not obscene. We have decided otherwise.

The judgment is affirmed.

NOTES

1. Title 19 U.S.C.A. § 1305(a): "All persons are prohibited from importing into the United States from any foreign country any book, pamphlet, paper, writing, advertisement, circular, print, picture, or drawing containing any matter advocating or urging treason or insurrection against the United States, or forcible resistance to any law of the United States, or containing any threat to take the life of or inflict bodily harm upon any person in the United States, or any obscene book, pamphlet, paper, writing, advertisement, circular, print, picture, drawing, or other representation, figure, or image on or of paper or other material, or any cast, instrument, or other article which is obscene or immoral, or any drug or medicine or any article whatever for the prevention of conception or for causing unlawful abortion, or any lottery ticket, or any printed paper that may be used as a lottery ticket, or any advertisement of any lottery. No such articles, whether imported separately or contained in packages with other goods entitled to entry, shall be admitted to entry; and all such articles and, unless it appears to the satisfaction of the collector that the obscene or other prohibited articles contained in the package were inclosed therein without the knowledge or consent of the importer, owner, agent, or consignee, the entire contents of the package in which such articles are contained, shall be subject to seizure and forfeiture as hereinafter provided: Provided, That the drugs hereinbefore mentioned, when imported in bulk and not put up for any of the purposes hereinbefore specified, are excepted from the operation of this subdivision: Provided

further, That the Secretary of the Treasury may, in his discretion, admit the so-called classics or books of recognized and established literary or scientific merit, but may, in his discretion, admit such classics or books only when imported for non-commercial purposes.

"Upon the appearance of any such book or matter at any customs office, the same shall be seized and held by the collector to await the judgment of the district court as hereinafter provided; and no protest shall be taken to the United States Customs Court from the decision of the collector. Upon the seizure of such book or matter the collector shall transmit information thereof to the district attorney of the district in which is situated the office at which such seizure has taken place, who shall institute proceedings in the district court for the forfeiture, confiscation, and destruction of the book or matter seized. Upon the adjudication that such book or matter thus seized is of the character the entry of which is by this section prohibited, it shall be ordered destroyed and shall be destroyed. Upon adjudication that such book or matter thus seized is not of the character the entry of which is by this section prohibited, it shall not be excluded from entry under the provisions of this section.

"In any such proceeding any party in interest may upon demand have the facts at issue determined by a jury and any party may have an appeal or the right of review as in the case of ordinary actions or suits." Title 19 U.S.C.A. § 1305(a).

2. See Orvis v. Higgins, 2 Cir., 1950, 180 F.2d 537, 539; Equitable Life Assurance Soc. v. Irelan, 9 Cir., 1941, 123 F.2d 462, 464; Rule 52(a), Federal Rules of Civil Procedure, 28 U.S.C.A.

3. Funk & Wagnalls New Standard Dictionary defines the word "obscene" as follows: "1. Offensive to chastity, delicacy, or decency; expressing or presenting to the mind or view something that decency, delicacy and purity forbid to be exposed; offensive to morals; indecent; impure. 2. [Poet.] Offensive to the senses; foul; disgusting. 3. Of evil omen."

Webster's New International Dictionary, 2nd ed. unabridged, 1940: "1. Offensive to taste; foul; loathsome; disgusting; 2.a. Offensive to chastity of mind or to modesty; expressing or presenting to the mind or view something that delicacy, purity, and decency forbid to be exposed; lewd; indecent; as obscene language, dances, images, b. Characterized by or given to obscenity; as, an obscene mind or person. 3. Inauspicious; ill-omened;–a Latinism. Obs."

4. United States v. Two Obscene Books, D. C.1951, 99 F.Supp. 760, 762. Also see United States v. Two Obscene Books, D.C.1950, 92 F.Supp. 934.

5. Alexander Pope (1688–1744), English poet, from his poem entitled "Essay on Man": "Vice is a Monster of so frightful mien As to be hated needs but to be seen. Yet seen too oft, familiar with her face, We first endure, then pity, then embrace."

THE SUPREME COURT REJECTS MICHIGAN'S STATUTE WHICH REDUCES "THE ADULT POPULATION OF MICHIGAN TO READING ONLY WHAT IS FIT FOR CHILDREN"

Butler v. Michigan, 352 U.S. 380 (1957)

MR. JUSTICE FRANKFURTER delivered the opinion of the Court.

This appeal from a judgment of conviction entered by the Recorder's Court of the City of Detroit, Michigan, challenges the constitutionality of the following provision, § 343, of the Michigan Penal Code:

"Any person who shall import, print, publish, sell, possess with the intent to sell, design, prepare, loan, give away, distribute or offer for sale, any book, magazine, newspaper, writing, pamphlet, ballad, printed paper, print, picture, drawing, photograph, publication or other thing, including any recordings, containing obscene, immoral, lewd or lascivious language, or obscene, immoral, lewd or lascivious prints, pictures, figures or descriptions, tending to incite minors to violent or depraved or immoral acts, manifestly tending to the corruption of the morals of youth, or shall introduce into any family, school or place of education or shall buy, procure, receive or have in his possession, any such book, pamphlet, magazine, newspaper, writing, ballad, printed paper, print, picture, drawing, photograph, publication or other thing, either for the purpose of sale, exhibition, loan or circulation, or with intent to introduce the same into any family, school or place of education, shall be guilty of a misdemeanor."

Appellant was charged with its violation for selling to a police officer what the trial judge characterized as "a book containing obscene, immoral, lewd, lascivious language, or descriptions, tending to incite minors to violent or depraved or immoral acts, manifestly tending to the corruption of the morals of youth." Appellant moved to dismiss the proceeding on the claim that application of § 343 unduly restricted freedom of speech as protected by the Due Process Clause of the Fourteenth Amendment in that the statute (1) prohibited distribution of a book to the general public on the basis of the undesirable influence it may have upon youth; (2) damned a book and proscribed its sale merely because of some isolated passages that appeared objectionable when divorced from the book as a whole; and (3) failed to provide a sufficiently definite standard of guilt. After hearing the evidence, the trial judge denied the motion, and, in an oral opinion, held that ". . . the defendant is guilty because he sold a book in the City of Detroit containing this language [the passages deemed offensive], and also because the Court feels that even viewing the book as a whole, it [the objectionable language] was not necessary to the proper development of the theme of the book nor of the conflict expressed therein." Appellant was fined $100.

Pressing his federal claims, appellant applied for leave to appeal to the Supreme Court of Michigan. Although the State consented to the granting of the application "because the issues involved in this case are of great public interest, and because it appears that further clarification of the language of . . . [the statute] is necessary," leave to appeal was denied. In view of this denial, the appeal is here from the Recorder's Court of Detroit. We noted probable jurisdiction. 350 U. S. 963.

Appellant's argument here took a wide sweep. We need not follow him. Thus, it is unnecessary to dissect the remarks of the trial judge in order to determine whether he construed § 343 to ban the distribution of books merely because certain of their passages, when viewed in isolation, were deemed objectionable. Likewise, we are free to put aside the claim that the Michigan law falls within the doctrine whereby a New York obscenity statute was found invalid in *Winters* v. *New York*, 333 U. S. 507.

It is clear on the record that appellant was convicted because Michigan, by § 343, made it an offense for him to make available for the general reading public (and he in fact sold to a police officer) a book that the trial judge found to have a potentially deleterious influence upon youth. The State insists that, by thus quarantining the general reading public against books not too rugged for grown men and women in order to shield juvenile innocence, it is exercising its power to promote the general welfare. Surely, this is to burn the house to roast the pig. Indeed, the Solicitor General of Michigan has, with characteristic candor, advised the Court that Michigan has a statute specifically designed to protect its children against obscene matter "tending to the corruption of the morals of youth." * But the appellant was not convicted for violating this statute.

We have before us legislation not reasonably restricted to the evil with which it is said to deal. The incidence of this enactment is to reduce the adult population of Michigan to reading only what is fit for children. It thereby arbitrarily curtails one of those liberties of the individual, now enshrined in the Due Process Clause of the Fourteenth Amendment, that history has attested as the indispensable conditions for the maintenance and progress of a free society. We are constrained to reverse this conviction.

Reversed.

Mr. Justice Black concurs in the result.

*Section 142 of Michigan's Penal Code provides:
"Any person who shall sell, give away or in any way furnish to any minor child any book, pamphlet, or other printed paper or other thing, containing obscene language, or obscene prints, pictures, figures or descriptions tending to the corruption of the morals of youth, or any newspapers, pamphlets or other printed paper devoted to the publication of criminal news, police reports, or criminal deeds, and any person who shall in any manner hire, use or employ such child to sell, give away, or in any manner distribute such books, pamphlets or printed papers, and any person having the care, custody or control of any such child, who shall permit him or her to engage in any such employment, shall be guilty of a misdemeanor."
Section 143 provides:
"Any person who shall exhibit upon any public street or highway, or in any other place within the view of children passing on any public street or highway, any book, pamphlet or other printed paper or thing containing obscene language or obscene prints, figures, or descriptions, tending to the corruption of the morals of youth, or any newspapers, pamphlets, or other printed paper or thing devoted to the publication of criminal news, police reports or criminal deeds, shall on conviction thereof be guilty of a misdemeanor."

THE *ROTH* TEST IS ENUNCIATED: THE TEST OF OBSCENITY IS "WHETHER TO THE AVERAGE PERSON, APPLYING CONTEMPORARY COMMUNITY STANDARDS, THE DOMINANT THEME OF THE MATERIAL TAKEN AS A WHOLE APPEALS TO PRURIENT INTEREST"

Roth v. United States, 354 U.S. 476 (1957)

Mr. Justice Brennan delivered the opinion of the Court.

The constitutionality of a criminal obscenity statute is the question in each of these cases. In *Roth*, the primary constitutional question is whether the federal obscenity statute [1] violates the provision of the First Amendment that "Congress shall make no law . . . abridging the freedom of speech, or of the press . . . ." In *Alberts,* the primary constitutional question is whether the obscenity provisions of the California Penal Code [2] invade the freedoms of speech and press as they may be incorporated in the liberty protected from state action by the Due Process Clause of the Fourteenth Amendment.

Other constitutional questions are: whether these statutes violate due process,[3] because too vague to support conviction for crime; whether power to punish speech and press offensive to decency and morality is in the States alone, so that the federal obscenity statute violates the Ninth and Tenth Amendments (raised in *Roth*); and whether Congress, by enacting the federal obscenity statute, under the power delegated by Art. I, § 8, cl. 7, to establish post offices and post roads, pre-empted the regulation of the subject matter (raised in *Alberts*).

Roth conducted a business in New York in the publication and sale of books, photographs and magazines. He used circulars and advertising matter to solicit sales. He was convicted by a jury in the District Court for the Southern District of New York upon 4 counts of a 26-count indictment charging him with mailing obscene circulars and advertising, and an obscene book, in violation of the federal obscenity statute. His conviction was affirmed by the Court of Appeals for the Second Circuit.[4] We granted certiorari.[5]

Alberts conducted a mail-order business from Los Angeles. He was convicted by the Judge of the Municipal Court of the Beverly Hills Judicial District (having waived a jury trial) under a misdemeanor complaint which charged him with lewdly keeping for sale obscene and indecent books, and with writing, composing and publishing an obscene advertisement of them, in violation of the California Penal Code. The conviction was affirmed by the Appellate Department of the Superior Court of the State of California in and for the County of Los Angeles.[6] We noted probable jurisdiction.[7]

The dispositive question is whether obscenity is utterance within the area of protected speech and press.[8] Although this is the first time the question has been squarely presented to this Court, either under the First Amendment or under the Fourteenth Amendment, expressions found in numerous opinions indicate that this

Court has always assumed that obscenity is not protected by the freedoms of speech and press. *Ex parte Jackson*, 96 U. S. 727, 736–737; *United States v. Chase*, 135 U. S. 255, 261; *Robertson v. Baldwin*, 165 U. S. 275, 281; *Public Clearing House v. Coyne*, 194 U. S. 497, 508; *Hoke v. United States*, 227 U. S. 308, 322; *Near v. Minnesota*, 283 U. S. 697, 716; *Chaplinsky v. New Hampshire*, 315 U. S. 568, 571–572; *Hannegan v. Esquire, Inc.*, 327 U. S. 146, 158; *Winters v. New York*, 333 U. S. 507, 510; *Beauharnais v. Illinois*, 343 U. S. 250, 266.[9]

The guaranties of freedom of expression [10] in effect in 10 of the 14 States which by 1792 had ratified the Constitution, gave no absolute protection for every utterance. Thirteen of the 14 States provided for the prosecution of libel,[11] and all of those States made either blasphemy or profanity, or both, statutory crimes.[12] As early as 1712, Massachusetts made it criminal to publish "any filthy, obscene, or profane song, pamphlet, libel or mock sermon" in imitation or mimicking of religious services. Acts and Laws of the Province of Mass. Bay, c. CV, § 8 (1712), Mass. Bay Colony Charters & Laws 399 (1814). Thus, profanity and obscenity were related offenses.

In light of this history, it is apparent that the unconditional phrasing of the First Amendment was not intended to protect every utterance. This phrasing did not prevent this Court from concluding that libelous utterances are not within the area of constitutionally protected speech. *Beauharnais v. Illinois*, 343 U. S. 250, 266. At the time of the adoption of the First Amendment, obscenity law was not as fully developed as libel law, but there is sufficiently contemporaneous evidence to show that obscenity, too, was outside the protection intended for speech and press.[13]

The protection given speech and press was fashioned to assure unfettered interchange of ideas for the bringing about of political and social changes desired by the people. This objective was made explicit as early as 1774 in a letter of the Continental Congress to the inhabitants of Quebec:

> "The last right we shall mention, regards the freedom of the press. The importance of this consists, besides the advancement of truth, science, morality, and arts in general, in its diffusion of liberal sentiments on the administration of Government, its ready communication of thoughts between subjects, and its consequential promotion of union among them, whereby oppressive officers are shamed or intimidated, into more honourable and just modes of conducting affairs." 1 Journals of the Continental Congress 108 (1774).

All ideas having even the slightest redeeming social importance—unorthodox ideas, controversial ideas, even ideas hateful to the prevailing climate of opinion—have the full protection of the guaranties, unless excludable because they encroach upon the limited area of more important interests.[14] But implicit in the history of the First Amendment is the rejection of obscenity as utterly without redeeming social importance. This rejection for that reason is mirrored in the universal judgment that obscenity should be restrained, reflected in the international agreement of over 50 nations,[15] in the obscenity laws of all of the 48 States,[16] and in the 20 obscenity laws enacted by the Congress from 1842 to 1956.[17] This is the same judgment expressed by this Court in *Chaplinsky v. New Hampshire*, 315 U. S. 568, 571–572:

> ". . . There are certain well-defined and narrowly limited classes of speech, the prevention and punishment of which have never been thought to raise any Constitutional problem. *These include the lewd and obscene . . . . It has been well observed that such utterances are no essential part of any exposition of ideas, and are of such slight social value as a step to truth that any benefit that may be derived from them is clearly outweighed by the social interest in order and morality. . . .*" (Emphasis added.)

We hold that obscenity is not within the area of constitutionally protected speech or press.

It is strenuously urged that these obscenity statutes offend the constitutional guaranties because they punish incitation to impure sexual *thoughts*, not shown to be related to any overt antisocial conduct which is or may be incited in the persons stimulated to such *thoughts*. In *Roth*, the trial judge instructed the jury: "The words 'obscene, lewd and lascivious' as used in the law, signify that form of immorality which has relation to sexual impurity and has a tendency to excite lustful *thoughts*." (Emphasis added.) In *Alberts*, the trial judge applied the test laid down in *People v. Wepplo*, 78 Cal. App. 2d Supp. 959, 178 P. 2d 853, namely, whether the material has "a substantial tendency to deprave or corrupt its readers by inciting lascivious *thoughts* or arousing lustful desires." (Emphasis added.) It is insisted that the constitutional guaranties are violated because convictions may be had without proof either that obscene material will perceptibly create a clear and present danger of antisocial conduct,[18] or will probably induce its recipients to such conduct.[19] But, in light of our holding that obscenity is not protected speech, the complete answer to this argument is in the holding of this Court in *Beauharnais v. Illinois, supra*, at 266:

> "Libelous utterances not being within the area of constitutionally protected speech, it is unnecessary, either for us or for the State courts, to consider the issues behind the phrase 'clear and present danger.' Certainly no one would contend that obscene speech, for example, may be punished only upon a showing of such circumstances. Libel, as we have seen, is in the same class."

However, sex and obscenity are not synonymous. Obscene material is material which deals with sex in a manner appealing to prurient interest.[20] The portrayal of sex, *e. g.*, in art, literature and scientific works,[21] is not itself sufficient reason to deny material the constitutional protection of freedom of speech and press. Sex, a great and mysterious motive force in human life, has indisputably been a subject of absorbing interest to mankind through the ages; it is one of the vital problems of human interest and public concern. As to all such problems, this Court said in *Thornhill v. Alabama*, 310 U. S. 88, 101–102:

"The freedom of speech and of the press guaranteed by the Constitution embraces at the least the liberty to discuss publicly and truthfully *all matters of public concern* without previous restraint or fear of subsequent punishment. The exigencies of the colonial period and the efforts to secure freedom from oppressive administration developed a broadened conception of these liberties as adequate to supply the public need for *information and education with respect to the significant issues of the times. . . .* Freedom of discussion, if it would fulfill its historic function in this nation, must embrace *all issues about which information is needed or appropriate to enable the members of society to cope with the exigencies of their period."* (Emphasis added.)

The fundamental freedoms of speech and press have contributed greatly to the development and well-being of our free society and are indispensable to its continued growth.[22] Ceaseless vigilance is the watchword to prevent their erosion by Congress or by the States. The door barring federal and state intrusion into this area cannot be left ajar; it must be kept tightly closed and opened only the slightest crack necessary to prevent encroachment upon more important interests.[23] It is therefore vital that the standards for judging obscenity safeguard the protection of freedom of speech and press for material which does not treat sex in a manner appealing to prurient interest.

The early leading standard of obscenity allowed material to be judged merely by the effect of an isolated excerpt upon particularly susceptible persons. *Regina* v. *Hicklin*, [1868] L. R. 3 Q. B. 360.[24] Some American courts adopted this standard[25] but later decisions have rejected it and substituted this test: whether to the average person, applying contemporary community standards, the dominant theme of the material taken as a whole appeals to prurient interest.[26] The *Hicklin* test, judging obscenity by the effect of isolated passages upon the most susceptible persons, might well encompass material legitimately treating with sex, and so it must be rejected as unconstitutionally restrictive of the freedoms of speech and press. On the other hand, the substituted standard provides safeguards adequate to withstand the charge of constitutional infirmity.

Both trial courts below sufficiently followed the proper standard. Both courts used the proper definition of obscenity. In addition, in the *Alberts* case, in ruling on a motion to dismiss, the trial judge indicated that, as the trier of facts, he was judging each item as a whole as it would affect the normal person,[27] and in *Roth*, the trial judge instructed the jury as follows:

". . . The test is not whether it would arouse sexual desires or sexual impure thoughts in those comprising a particular segment of the community, the young, the immature or the highly prudish or would leave another segment, the scientific or highly educated or the so-called worldly-wise and sophisticated indifferent and unmoved. . . .

"The test in each case is the effect of the book, picture or publication considered as a whole, not upon any particular class, but upon all those whom it is likely to reach. In other words, you determine its impact upon the average person in the community. The books, pictures and circulars must be judged as a whole, in their entire context, and you are not to consider detached or separate portions in reaching a conclusion. You judge the circulars, pictures and publications which have been put in evidence by present-day standards of the community. You may ask yourselves does it offend the common conscience of the community by present-day standards.

.   .   .   .   .

"In this case, ladies and gentlemen of the jury, you and you alone are the exclusive judges of what the common conscience of the community is, and in determining that conscience you are to consider the community as a whole, young and old, educated and uneducated, the religious and the irreligious—men, women and children."

It is argued that the statutes do not provide reasonably ascertainable standards of guilt and therefore violate the constitutional requirements of due process. *Winters* v. *New York*, 333 U. S. 507. The federal obscenity statute makes punishable the mailing of material that is "obscene, lewd, lascivious, or filthy . . . or other publication of an indecent character."[28] The California statute makes punishable, *inter alia*, the keeping for sale or advertising material that is "obscene or indecent." The thrust of the argument is that these words are not sufficiently precise because they do not mean the same thing to all people, all the time, everywhere.

Many decisions have recognized that these terms of obscenity statutes are not precise.[29] This Court, however, has consistently held that lack of precision is not itself offensive to the requirements of due process. ". . . [T]he Constitution does not require impossible standards"; all that is required is that the language "conveys sufficiently definite warning as to the proscribed conduct when measured by common understanding and practices. . . ." *United States* v. *Petrillo*, 332 U. S. 1, 7–8. These words, applied according to the proper standard for judging obscenity, already discussed, give adequate warning of the conduct proscribed and mark ". . . boundaries sufficiently distinct for judges and juries fairly to administer the law . . . . That there may be marginal cases in which it is difficult to determine the side of the line on which a particular fact situation falls is no sufficient reason to hold the language too ambiguous to define a criminal offense. . . ." *Id.*, at 7. See also *United States* v. *Harriss*, 347 U. S. 612, 624, n. 15; *Boyce Motor Lines, Inc.* v. *United States*, 342 U. S. 337, 340; *United States* v. *Ragen*, 314 U. S. 513, 523–524; *United States* v. *Wurzbach*, 280 U. S. 396; *Hygrade Provision Co.* v. *Sherman*, 266 U. S. 497; *Fox* v. *Washington*, 236 U. S. 273; *Nash* v. *United States*, 229 U. S. 373.[30]

In summary, then, we hold that these statutes, applied according to the proper standard for judging obscenity, do not offend constitutional safeguards against convictions based upon protected material, or fail to give men in acting adequate notice of what is prohibited.

Roth's argument that the federal obscenity statute unconstitutionally encroaches upon the powers reserved by the Ninth and Tenth Amendments to the States and to the people to punish speech and press where offensive to decency and morality is hinged upon his contention that obscenity is expression not excepted from the sweep of the provision of the First Amendment that *"Congress shall make no law . . . abridging the freedom of speech, or of the press . . . ."* (Emphasis added.) That argument falls in light of our holding that obscenity is not expression protected by the First Amendment.[31] We therefore hold that the federal obscenity statute punishing the use of the mails for obscene material is a proper exercise of the postal power delegated to Congress by Art. I, § 8, cl. 7.[32] In *United Public Workers v. Mitchell,* 330 U. S. 75, 95–96, this Court said:

> ". . . The powers granted by the Constitution to the Federal Government are subtracted from the totality of sovereignty originally in the states and the people. Therefore, when objection is made that the exercise of a federal power infringes upon rights reserved by the Ninth and Tenth Amendments, the inquiry must be directed toward the granted power under which the action of the Union was taken. If granted power is found, necessarily the objection of invasion of those rights, reserved by the Ninth and Tenth Amendments, must fail. . . ."

Alberts argues that because his was a mail-order business, the California statute is repugnant to Art. I, § 8, cl. 7, under which the Congress allegedly pre-empted the regulatory field by enacting the federal obscenity statute punishing the mailing or advertising by mail of obscene material. The federal statute deals only with actual mailing; it does not eliminate the power of the state to punish "keeping for sale" or "advertising" obscene material. The state statute in no way imposes a burden or interferes with the federal postal functions. ". . . The decided cases which indicate the limits of state regulatory power in relation to the federal mail service involve situations where state regulation involved a direct, physical interference with federal activities under the postal power or some direct, immediate burden on the performance of the postal functions. . . ." *Railway Mail Assn. v. Corsi,* 326 U. S. 88, 96.

The judgments are

Affirmed.

MR. CHIEF JUSTICE WARREN, concurring in the result.

I agree with the result reached by the Court in these cases, but, because we are operating in a field of expression and because broad language used here may eventually be applied to the arts and sciences and freedom of communication generally, I would limit our decision to the facts before us and to the validity of the statutes in question as applied.

Appellant Alberts was charged with wilfully, unlawfully and lewdly disseminating obscene matter. Obscenity has been construed by the California courts to mean having a substantial tendency to corrupt by arousing lustful desires. *People v. Wepplo,* 78 Cal. App. 2d Supp. 959, 178 P. 2d 853. Petitioner Roth was indicted for unlawfully, wilfully and knowingly mailing obscene material that was calculated to corrupt and debauch the minds and morals of those to whom it was sent. Each was accorded all the protections of a criminal trial.

Among other things, they contend that the statutes under which they were convicted violate the constitutional guarantees of freedom of speech, press and communication.

That there is a social problem presented by obscenity is attested by the expression of the legislatures of the forty-eight States as well as the Congress. To recognize the existence of a problem, however, does not require that we sustain any and all measures adopted to meet that problem. The history of the application of laws designed to suppress the obscene demonstrates convincingly that the power of government can be invoked under them against great art or literature, scientific treatises, or works exciting social controversy. Mistakes of the past prove that there is a strong countervailing interest to be considered in the freedoms guaranteed by the First and Fourteenth Amendments.

The line dividing the salacious or pornographic from literature or science is not straight and unwavering. Present laws depend largely upon the effect that the materials may have upon those who receive them. It is manifest that the same object may have a different impact, varying according to the part of the community it reached. But there is more to these cases. It is not the book that is on trial; it is a person. The conduct of the defendant is the central issue, not the obscenity of a book or picture. The nature of the materials is, of course, relevant as an attribute of the defendant's conduct, but the materials are thus placed in context from which they draw color and character. A wholly different result might be reached in a different setting.

The personal element in these cases is seen most strongly in the requirement of *scienter.* Under the California law, the prohibited activity must be done "wilfully and lewdly." The federal statute limits the crime to acts done "knowingly." In his charge to the jury, the district judge stated that the matter must be "calculated" to corrupt or debauch. The defendants in both these cases were engaged in the business of purveying textual or graphic matter openly advertised to appeal to the erotic interest of their customers. They were plainly engaged in the commercial exploitation of the morbid and shameful craving for materials with prurient effect. I believe that the State and Federal Governments can constitutionally punish such conduct. That is all that these cases present to us, and that is all we need to decide.

I agree with the Court's decision in its rejection of the other contentions raised by these defendants.

MR. JUSTICE HARLAN, concurring in the result in No. 61, and dissenting in No. 582.

I regret not to be able to join the Court's opinion. I cannot do so because I find lurking beneath its disarming generalizations a number of problems which not only leave me with serious misgivings as to the future effect of today's decisions, but which also, in my view, call for different results in these two cases.

I.

My basic difficulties with the Court's opinion are threefold. First, the opinion paints with such a broad brush that I fear it may result in a loosening of the tight reins which state and federal courts should hold upon the enforcement of obscenity statutes. Second, the Court fails to discriminate between the different factors which, in my opinion, are involved in the constitutional adjudication of state and federal obscenity cases. Third, relevant distinctions between the two obscenity statutes here involved, and the Court's own definition of "obscenity," are ignored.

In final analysis, the problem presented by these cases is how far, and on what terms, the state and federal governments have power to punish individuals for disseminating books considered to be undesirable because of their nature or supposed deleterious effect upon human conduct. Proceeding from the premise that "no issue is presented in either case, concerning the obscenity of the material involved," the Court finds the "dispositive question" to be "whether obscenity is utterance within the area of protected speech and press," and then holds that "obscenity" is not so protected because it is "utterly without redeeming social importance." This sweeping formula appears to me to beg the very question before us. The Court seems to assume that "obscenity" is a peculiar *genus* of "speech and press," which is as distinct, recognizable, and classifiable as poison ivy is among other plants. On this basis the *constitutional* question before us simply becomes, as the Court says, whether "obscenity," as an abstraction, is protected by the First and Fourteenth Amendments, and the question whether a *particular* book may be suppressed becomes a mere matter of classification, of "fact," to be entrusted to a factfinder and insulated from independent constitutional judgment. But surely the problem cannot be solved in such a generalized fashion. Every communication has an individuality and "value" of its own. The suppression of a particular writing or other tangible form of expression is, therefore, an *individual* matter, and in the nature of things every such suppression raises an individual constitutional problem, in which a reviewing court must determine for *itself* whether the attacked expression is suppressable within constitutional standards. Since those standards do not readily lend themselves to generalized definitions, the constitutional problem in the last analysis becomes one of particularized judgments which appellate courts must make for themselves.

I do not think that reviewing courts can escape this responsibility by saying that the trier of the facts, be it a jury or a judge, has labeled the questioned matter as "obscene," for, if "obscenity" is to be suppressed, the question whether a particular work is of that character involves not really an issue of fact but a question of constitutional *judgment* of the most sensitive and delicate kind. Many juries might find that Joyce's "Ulysses" or Bocaccio's "Decameron" was obscene, and yet the conviction of a defendant for selling either book would raise, for me, the gravest constitutional problems, for no such verdict could convince me, without more, that these books are "utterly without redeeming social importance." In short, I do not understand how the Court can resolve the constitutional problems now before it without making its own independent judgment upon the character of the material upon which these convictions were based. I am very much afraid that the broad manner in which the Court has decided these cases will tend to obscure the peculiar responsibilities resting on state and federal courts in this field and encourage them to rely on easy labeling and jury verdicts as a substitute for facing up to the tough individual problems of constitutional judgment involved in every obscenity case.

My second reason for dissatisfaction with the Court's opinion is that the broad strides with which the Court has proceeded has led it to brush aside with perfunctory ease the vital constitutional considerations which, in my opinion, differentiate these two cases. It does not seem to matter to the Court that in one case we balance the power of a State in this field against the restrictions of the Fourteenth Amendment, and in the other the power of the Federal Government against the limitations of the First Amendment. I deal with this subject more particularly later.

Thirdly, the Court has not been bothered by the fact that the two cases involve different statutes. In California the book must have a "tendency to deprave or corrupt its readers"; under the federal statute it must tend "to stir sexual impulses and lead to sexually impure thoughts." [1] The two statutes do not seem to me to present the same problems. Yet the Court compounds confusion when it superimposes on these two statutory definitions a third, drawn from the American Law Institute's Model Penal Code, Tentative Draft No. 6: "A thing is obscene if, considered as a whole, its predominant appeal is to prurient interest." The bland assurance that this definition is the same as the ones with which we deal flies in the face of the authors' express rejection of the "deprave and corrupt" and "sexual thoughts" tests:

> "Obscenity [in the Tentative Draft] is defined in terms of material which appeals predominantly to prurient interest in sexual matters and which goes beyond customary freedom of expression in these matters. We reject the prevailing test of tendency to arouse lustful thoughts or desires because it is unrealistically broad for a society that plainly tolerates a great deal of erotic interest in literature, advertising, and art, and because regulation of thought or desire, unconnected with overt misbehavior, raises the most acute constitutional as well as practical difficulties. We likewise reject the common definition of obscene as that which 'tends to corrupt or debase.' If this means anything different from tendency to arouse lustful thought and desire, it suggests that change of character or actual misbehavior follows from contact with obscenity. Evidence of such consequences is lacking . . . . On the other hand, 'appeal to prurient interest' refers to qualities of the material itself: the capacity to attract individuals eager for a forbidden look . . . ." [2]

As this passage makes clear, there is a significant distinction between the definitions used in the prosecutions before us, and the American Law Institute formula. If, therefore, the latter is the correct standard, as my Brother BRENNAN elsewhere intimates,[3] then these convictions should surely be reversed. Instead, the Court merely assimilates the various tests into one indiscriminate potpourri.

I now pass to the consideration of the two cases before us.

II.

I concur in the judgment of the Court in No. 61, *Alberts* v. *California*.

The question in this case is whether the defendant was deprived of liberty without due process of law when he was convicted for selling certain materials found by the judge to be obscene because they would have a "tendency to deprave or corrupt its readers by exciting lascivious thoughts or arousing lustful desire."

In judging the constitutionality of this conviction, we should remember that our function in reviewing state judgments under the Fourteenth Amendment is a narrow one. We do not decide whether the policy of the State is wise, or whether it is based on assumptions scientifically substantiated. We can inquire only whether the state action so subverts the fundamental liberties implicit in the Due Process Clause that it cannot be sustained as a rational exercise of power. See Jackson, J., dissenting in *Beauharnais* v. *Illinois*, 343 U. S. 250, 287. The States' power to make printed words criminal is, of course, confined by the Fourteenth Amendment, but only insofar as such power is inconsistent with our concepts of "ordered liberty." *Palko* v. *Connecticut*, 302 U. S. 319, 324–325.

What, then, is the purpose of this California statute? Clearly the state legislature has made the judgment that printed words *can* "deprave or corrupt" the reader—that words can incite to antisocial or immoral action. The assumption seems to be that the distribution of certain types of literature will induce criminal or immoral sexual conduct. It is well known, of course, that the validity of this assumption is a matter of dispute among critics, sociologists, psychiatrists, and penologists. There is a large school of thought, particularly in the scientific community, which denies any causal connection between the reading of pornography and immorality, crime, or delinquency. Others disagree. Clearly it is not our function to decide this question. That function belongs to the state legislature. Nothing in the Constitution requires California to accept as truth the most advanced and sophisticated psychiatric opinion. It seems to me clear that it is not irrational, in our present state of knowledge, to consider that pornography can induce a type of sexual conduct which a State may deem obnoxious to the moral fabric of society. In fact the very division of opinion on the subject counsels us to respect the choice made by the State.

Furthermore, even assuming that pornography cannot be deemed ever to cause, in an immediate sense, criminal sexual conduct, other interests within the proper cognizance of the States may be protected by the prohibition placed on such materials. The State can reasonably draw the inference that over a long period of time the indiscriminate dissemination of materials, the essential character of which is to degrade sex, will have an eroding effect on moral standards. And the State has a legitimate interest in protecting the privacy of the home against invasion of unsolicited obscenity.

Above all stands the realization that we deal here with an area where knowledge is small, data are insufficient, and experts are divided. Since the domain of sexual morality is pre-eminently a matter of state concern, this Court should be slow to interfere with state legislation calculated to protect that morality. It seems to me that nothing in the broad and flexible command of the Due Process Clause forbids California to prosecute one who sells books whose dominant tendency might be to "deprave or corrupt" a reader. I agree with the Court, of course, that the books must be judged as a whole and in relation to the normal adult reader.

What has been said, however, does not dispose of the case. It still remains for us to decide whether the state court's determination that this material should be suppressed is consistent with the Fourteenth Amendment; and that, of course, presents a federal question as to which we, and not the state court, have the ultimate responsibility. And so, in the final analysis, I concur in the judgment because, upon an independent perusal of the material involved, and in light of the considerations discussed above, I cannot say that its suppression would so interfere with the communication of "ideas" in any proper sense of that term that it would offend the Due Process Clause. I therefore agree with the Court that appellant's conviction must be affirmed.

III.

I dissent in No. 582, *Roth* v. *United States*.

We are faced here with the question whether the federal obscenity statute, as construed and applied in this case, violates the First Amendment to the Constitution. To me, this question is of quite a different order than one where we are dealing with state legislation under the Fourteenth Amendment. I do not think it follows that state and federal powers in this area are the same, and that just because the State may suppress a particular utterance, it is automatically permissible for the Federal Government to do the same. I agree with Mr. Justice Jackson that the historical evidence does not bear out the claim that the Fourteenth Amendment "incorporates" the First in any literal sense. See *Beauharnais* v. *Illinois*, *supra*. But laying aside any consequences which might flow from that conclusion, cf. Mr. Justice Holmes in *Gitlow* v. *New York*, 268 U. S. 652, 672,⁴ I prefer to rest my views about this case on broader and less abstract grounds.

The Constitution differentiates between those areas of human conduct subject to the regulation of the States and those subject to the powers of the Federal Government. The substantive powers of the two governments, in many instances, are distinct. And in every case where we are called upon to balance the interest in free expression against other interests, it seems to me important that we should keep in the forefront the question of whether those other interests are state or federal. Since under our constitutional scheme the two are not necessarily equivalent, the balancing process must needs often produce different results. Whether a particular limitation on speech or press is to be upheld because it subserves a paramount governmental interest must, to a large extent, I think, depend on whether that government has, under the Constitution, a direct substantive interest, that is, the power to act, in the particular area involved.

The Federal Government has, for example, power to restrict seditious speech directed against it, because that Government certainly has the substantive authority to protect itself against revolution. Cf. *Pennsylvania* v.

Nelson, 350 U. S. 497.   But in dealing with obscenity we are faced with the converse situation, for the interests which obscenity statutes purportedly protect are primarily entrusted to the care, not of the Federal Government, but of the States.   Congress has no substantive power over sexual morality.   Such powers as the Federal Government has in this field are but incidental to its other powers, here the postal power, and are not of the same nature as those possessed by the States, which bear direct responsibility for the protection of the local moral fabric.[5] What Mr. Justice Jackson said in *Beauharnais, supra,* 343 U. S., at 294–295, about criminal libel is equally true of obscenity:

> "The inappropriateness of a single standard for restricting State and Nation is indicated by the disparity between their functions and duties in relation to those freedoms.   Criminality of defamation is predicated upon power either to protect the private right to enjoy integrity of reputation or the public right to tranquillity.   Neither of these are objects of federal cognizance except when necessary to the accomplishment of some delegated power . . . .   When the Federal Government puts liberty of press in one scale, it has a very limited duty to personal reputation or local tranquillity to weigh against it in the other.   But state action affecting speech or press can and should be weighed against and reconciled with these conflicting social interests."

Not only is the federal interest in protecting the Nation against pornography attenuated, but the dangers of federal censorship in this field are far greater than anything the States may do.   It has often been said that one of the great strengths of our federal system is that we have, in the forty-eight States, forty-eight experimental social laboratories.   "State statutory law reflects predominantly this capacity of a legislature to introduce novel techniques of social control.   The federal system has the immense advantage of providing forty-eight separate centers for such experimentation."[6]   Different States will have different attitudes toward the same work of literature.   The same book which is freely read in one State might be classed as obscene in another.[7]   And it seems to me that no overwhelming danger to our freedom to experiment and to gratify our tastes in literature is likely to result from the suppression of a borderline book in one of the States, so long as there is no uniform nation-wide suppression of the book, and so long as other States are free to experiment with the same or bolder books.

Quite a different situation is presented, however, where the Federal Government imposes the ban.   The danger is perhaps not great if the people of one State, through their legislature, decide that "Lady Chatterley's Lover" goes so far beyond the acceptable standards of candor that it will be deemed offensive and non-sellable, for the State next door is still free to make its own choice.   At least we do not have one uniform standard.   But the dangers to free thought and expression are truly great if the Federal Government imposes a blanket ban over the Nation on such a book.   The prerogative of the States to differ on their ideas of morality will be destroyed, the ability of States to experiment will be stunted.   The fact

that the people of one State cannot read some of the works of D. H. Lawrence seems to me, if not wise or desirable, at least acceptable.   But that no person in the United States should be allowed to do so seems to me to be intolerable, and violative of both the letter and spirit of the First Amendment.

I judge this case, then, in view of what I think is the attenuated federal interest in this field, in view of the very real danger of a deadening uniformity which can result from nation-wide federal censorship, and in view of the fact that the constitutionality of this conviction must be weighed against the First and not the Fourteenth Amendment.   So viewed, I do not think that this conviction can be upheld.   The petitioner was convicted under a statute which, under the judge's charge,[8] makes it criminal to sell books which "tend to stir sexual impulses and lead to sexually impure thoughts."   I cannot agree that any book which tends to stir sexual impulses and lead to sexually impure thoughts necessarily is "utterly without redeeming social importance."   Not only did this charge fail to measure up to the standards which I understand the Court to approve, but as far as I can see, much of the great literature of the world could lead to conviction under such a view of the statute.   Moreover, in no event do I think that the limited federal interest in this area can extend to mere "thoughts."   The Federal Government has no business, whether under the postal or commerce power, to bar the sale of books because they might lead to any kind of "thoughts."[9]

It is no answer to say, as the Court does, that obscenity is not protected speech.   The point is that this statute, as here construed, defines obscenity so widely that it encompasses matters which might very well be protected speech.   I do not think that the federal statute can be constitutionally construed to reach other than what the Government has termed as "hard-core" pornography.   Nor do I think the statute can fairly be read as directed only at *persons* who are engaged in the business of catering to the prurient minded, even though their wares fall short of hard-core pornography.   Such a statute would raise constitutional questions of a different order.   That being so, and since in my opinion the material here involved cannot be said to be hard-core pornography, I would reverse this case with instructions to dismiss the indictment.

MR. JUSTICE DOUGLAS, with whom MR. JUSTICE BLACK concurs, dissenting.

When we sustain these convictions, we make the legality of a publication turn on the purity of thought which a book or tract instills in the mind of the reader. I do not think we can approve that standard and be faithful to the command of the First Amendment, which by its terms is a restraint on Congress and which by the Fourteenth is a restraint on the States.

In the *Roth* case the trial judge charged the jury that the statutory words "obscene, lewd and lascivious" describe "that form of immorality which has relation to sexual impurity and has a tendency to excite lustful thoughts."   He stated that the term "filthy" in the statute pertains "to that sort of treatment of sexual matters in such a vulgar and indecent way, so that it tends to arouse a feeling of disgust and revulsion." He went on to say that the material "must be calculated to corrupt and debauch the minds and morals" of "the average person in the community," not those of any particular class. "You judge the circulars, pictures and publications which have been put in evidence by present-day standards of the community. You may ask yourselves does it offend the common conscience of the community by present-day standards."

The trial judge who, sitting without a jury, heard the *Alberts* case and the appellate court that sustained the judgment of conviction, took California's definition of "obscenity" from *People* v. *Wepplo,* 78 Cal. App. 2d Supp. 959, 961, 178 P. 2d 853, 855. That case held that a book is obscene "if it has a substantial tendency to deprave or corrupt its readers by inciting lascivious thoughts or arousing lustful desire."

By these standards punishment is inflicted for thoughts provoked, not for overt acts nor antisocial conduct. This test cannot be squared with our decisions under the First Amendment. Even the ill-starred *Dennis* case conceded that speech to be punishable must have some relation to action which could be penalized by government. *Dennis* v. *United States,* 341 U. S. 494, 502–511. Cf. Chafee, The Blessings of Liberty (1956), p. 69. This issue cannot be avoided by saying that obscenity is not protected by the First Amendment. The question remains, what is the constitutional test of obscenity?

The tests by which these convictions were obtained require only the arousing of sexual thoughts. Yet the arousing of sexual thoughts and desires happens every day in normal life in dozens of ways. Nearly 30 years ago a questionnaire sent to college and normal school women graduates asked what things were most stimulating sexually. Of 409 replies, 9 said "music"; 18 said "pictures"; 29 said "dancing"; 40 said "drama"; 95 said "books"; and 218 said "man." Alpert, Judicial Censorship of Obscene Literature, 52 Harv. L. Rev. 40, 73.

The test of obscenity the Court endorses today gives the censor free range over a vast domain. To allow the State to step in and punish mere speech or publication that the judge or the jury thinks has an *undesirable* impact on thoughts but that is not shown to be a part of unlawful action is drastically to curtail the First Amendment. As recently stated by two of our outstanding authorities on obscenity, "The danger of influencing a change in the current moral standards of the community, or of shocking or offending readers, or of stimulating sex thoughts or desires apart from objective conduct, can never justify the losses to society that result from interference with literary freedom." Lockhart & McClure, Literature, The Law of Obscenity, and the Constitution, 38 Minn. L. Rev. 295, 387.

If we were certain that impurity of sexual thoughts impelled to action, we would be on less dangerous ground in punishing the distributors of this sex literature. But it is by no means clear that obscene literature, as so defined, is a significant factor in influencing substantial deviations from the community standards.

"There are a number of reasons for real and substantial doubts as to the soundness of that hypothesis. (1) Scientific studies of juvenile delinquency demonstrate that those who get into trouble, and are the greatest concern of the advocates of censorship, are far less inclined to read than those who do not become delinquent. The delinquents are generally the adventurous type, who have little use for reading and other non-active entertainment. Thus, even assuming that reading sometimes has an adverse effect upon moral conduct, the effect is not likely to be substantial, for those who are susceptible seldom read. (2) Sheldon and Eleanor Glueck, who are among the country's leading authorities on the treatment and causes of juvenile delinquency, have recently published the results of a ten year study of its causes. They exhaustively studied approximately 90 factors and influences that might lead to or explain juvenile delinquency, but the Gluecks gave no consideration to the type of reading material, if any, read by the delinquents. This is, of course, consistent with their finding that delinquents read very little. When those who know so much about the problem of delinquency among youth—the very group about whom the advocates of censorship are most concerned—conclude that what delinquents read has so little effect upon their conduct that it is not worth investigating in an exhaustive study of causes, there is good reason for serious doubt concerning the basic hypothesis on which obscenity censorship is defended. (3) The many other influences in society that stimulate sexual desire are so much more frequent in their influence, and so much more potent in their effect, that the influence of reading is likely, at most, to be relatively insignificant in the composite of forces that lead an individual into conduct deviating from the community sex standards. The Kinsey studies show the minor degree to which literature serves as a potent sexual stimulant. And the studies demonstrating that sex knowledge seldom results from reading indicates [sic] the relative unimportance of literature in sex thoughts as compared with other factors in society." Lockhart & McClure, *op. cit. supra,* pp. 385–386.

The absence of dependable information on the effect of obscene literature on human conduct should make us wary. It should put us on the side of protecting society's interest in literature, except and unless it can be said that the particular publication has an impact on action that the government can control.

As noted, the trial judge in the *Roth* case charged the jury in the alternative that the federal obscenity statute outlaws literature dealing with sex which offends "the common conscience of the community." That standard is, in my view, more inimical still to freedom of expression.

The standard of what offends "the common conscience of the community" conflicts, in my judgment, with the command of the First Amendment that "Congress shall make no law . . . abridging the freedom of speech, or of the press." Certainly that standard would not be an acceptable one if religion, economics, politics or philosophy were involved. How does it become a constitutional standard when literature treating with sex is concerned?

Any test that turns on what is offensive to the community's standards is too loose, too capricious, too destructive of freedom of expression to be squared with the First Amendment. Under that test, juries can censor, suppress, and punish what they don't like, provided the matter relates to "sexual impurity" or has a tendency "to excite lustful thoughts." This is community censorship in one of its worst forms. It creates a regime where in the battle between the literati and the Philistines, the Philistines are certain to win. If experience in this field teaches anything, it is that "censorship of obscenity has almost always been both irrational and indiscriminate." Lockhart & McClure, *op. cit. supra,* at 371. The test adopted here accentuates that trend.

I assume there is nothing in the Constitution which forbids Congress from using its power over the mails to proscribe *conduct* on the grounds of good morals. No one would suggest that the First Amendment permits nudity in public places, adultery, and other phases of sexual misconduct.

I can understand (and at times even sympathize) with programs of civic groups and church groups to protect and defend the existing moral standards of the community. I can understand the motives of the Anthony Comstocks who would impose Victorian standards on the community. When speech alone is involved, I do not think that government, consistently with the First Amendment, can become the sponsor of any of these movements. I do not think that government, consistently with the First Amendment, can throw its weight behind one school or another. Government should be concerned with antisocial conduct, not with utterances. Thus, if the First Amendment guarantee of freedom of speech and press is to mean anything in this field, it must allow protests even against the moral code that the standard of the day sets for the community. In other words, literature should not be suppressed merely because it offends the moral code of the censor.

The legality of a publication in this country should never be allowed to turn either on the purity of thought which it instills in the mind of the reader or on the degree to which it offends the community conscience. By either test the role of the censor is exalted, and society's values in literary freedom are sacrificed.

The Court today suggests a third standard. It defines obscene material as that "which deals with sex in a manner appealing to prurient interest." * Like the standards applied by the trial judges below, that standard does not require any nexus between the literature which is prohibited and action which the legislature can regulate or prohibit. Under the First Amendment, that standard is no more valid than those which the courts below adopted.

I do not think that the problem can be resolved by the Court's statement that "obscenity is not expression protected by the First Amendment." With the exception of *Beauharnais* v. *Illinois,* 343 U. S. 250, none of our cases has resolved problems of free speech and free press by placing any form of expression beyond the pale of the absolute prohibition of the First Amendment. Unlike the law of libel, wrongfully relied on in *Beauharnais,* there is no special historical evidence that literature dealing with sex was intended to be treated in a special manner by those who drafted the First Amendment. In fact, the first reported court decision in this country involving obscene literature was in 1821. Lockhart & McClure, *op. cit. supra,* at 324, n. 200. I reject too the implication that problems of freedom of speech and of the press are to be resolved by weighing against the values of free expression, the judgment of the Court that a particular form of that expression has "no redeeming social importance." The First Amendment, its prohibition in terms absolute, was designed to preclude courts as well as legislatures from weighing the values of speech against silence. The First Amendment puts free speech in the preferred position.

Freedom of expression can be suppressed if, and to the extent that, it is so closely brigaded with illegal action as to be an inseparable part of it. *Giboney* v. *Empire Storage Co.,* 336 U. S. 490, 498; *Labor Board* v. *Virginia Power Co.,* 314 U. S. 469, 477–478. As a people, we cannot afford to relax that standard. For the test that suppresses a cheap tract today can suppress a literary gem tomorrow. All it need do is to incite a lascivious thought or arouse a lustful desire. The list of books that judges or juries can place in that category is endless.

I would give the broad sweep of the First Amendment full support. I have the same confidence in the ability of our people to reject noxious literature as I have in their capacity to sort out the true from the false in theology, economics, politics, or any other field.

COURT'S OPINION NOTES

[1] The federal obscenity statute provided, in pertinent part:
"Every obscene, lewd, lascivious, or filthy book, pamphlet, picture, paper, letter, writing, print, or other publication of an indecent character; and—

.   .   .   .   .

"Every written or printed card, letter, circular, book, pamphlet, advertisement, or notice of any kind giving information, directly or indirectly, where, or how, or from whom, or by what means any of such mentioned matters, articles, or things may be obtained or made, . . . whether sealed or unsealed . . .

.   .   .   .   .

"Is declared to be nonmailable matter and shall not be conveyed in the mails or delivered from any post office or by any letter carrier.
"Whoever knowingly deposits for mailing or delivery, anything declared by this section to be nonmailable, or knowingly takes the same from the mails for the purpose of circulating or disposing thereof, or of aiding in the circulation or disposition thereof, shall be fined not more than $5,000 or imprisoned not more than five years, or both." 18 U. S. C. § 1461.
The 1955 amendment of this statute, 69 Stat. 183, is not applicable to this case.

[2] The California Penal Code provides, in pertinent part:
"Every person who wilfully and lewdly, either:

.   .   .   .   .

"3. Writes, composes, stereotypes, prints, publishes, sells, distributes, keeps for sale, or exhibits any obscene or indecent writing, paper, or book; or designs, copies, draws, engraves, paints, or otherwise prepares any obscene or indecent picture or print; or molds, cuts, casts, or otherwise makes any obscene or indecent figure; or,
"4. Writes, composes, or publishes any notice or advertisement of any such writing, paper, book, picture, print or figure; . . .

.   .   .   .   .

"6. . . . is guilty of a misdemeanor. . . ." West's Cal. Penal Code Ann., 1955, § 311.

[3] In *Roth,* reliance is placed on the Due Process Clause of the

Fifth Amendment, and in *Alberts*, reliance is placed upon the Due Process Clause of the Fourteenth Amendment.

[4] 237 F. 2d 796.

[5] 352 U. S. 964. Petitioner's application for bail was granted by Mr. Justice Harlan in his capacity as Circuit Justice for the Second Circuit. 1 L. Ed. 2d 34, 77 Sup. Ct. 17.

[6] 138 Cal. App. 2d Supp. 909, 292 P. 2d 90. This is the highest state appellate court available to the appellant. Cal. Const., Art. VI, § 5; see *Edwards v. California*, 314 U. S. 160.

[7] 352 U. S. 962.

[8] No issue is presented in either case concerning the obscenity of the material involved.

[9] See also the following cases in which convictions under obscenity statutes have been reviewed: *Grimm v. United States*, 156 U. S. 604; *Rosen v. United States*, 161 U. S. 29; *Swearingen v. United States*, 161 U. S. 446; *Andrews v. United States*, 162 U. S. 420; *Price v. United States*, 165 U. S. 311; *Dunlop v. United States*, 165 U. S. 486; *Bartell v. United States*, 227 U. S. 427; *United States v. Limehouse*, 285 U. S. 424.

[10] Del. Const., 1792, Art. I, § 5; Ga. Const., 1777, Art. LXI; Md. Const., 1776, Declaration of Rights, § 38; Mass. Const., 1780, Declaration of Rights, Art. XVI; N. H. Const., 1784, Art. I, § XXII; N. C. Const., 1776, Declaration of Rights, Art. XV; Pa. Const., 1776, Declaration of Rights, Art. XII; S. C. Const., 1778, Art. XLIII; Vt. Const., 1777, Declaration of Rights, Art. XIV; Va. Bill of Rights, 1776, § 12.

[11] Act to Secure the Freedom of the Press (1804), 1 Conn. Pub. Stat. Laws 355 (1808); Del. Const., 1792, Art. I, § 5; Ga. Penal Code, Eighth Div., § VIII (1817), Digest of the Laws of Ga. 364 (Prince 1822); Act of 1803, c. 54, II Md. Public General Laws 1096 (Poe 1888); *Commonwealth v. Kneeland*, 37 Mass. 206, 232 (1838); Act for the Punishment of Certain Crimes Not Capital (1791), N. H. Laws 1792, 253; Act Respecting Libels (1799), N. J. Rev. Laws 411 (1800); *People v. Croswell*, 3 Johns. (N. Y.) 337 (1804); Act of 1803, c. 632, 2 Laws of N. C. 999 (1821); Pa. Const., 1790, Art. IX, § 7; R. I. Code of Laws (1647), Proceedings of the First General Assembly and Code of Laws 44–45 (1647); R. I. Const., 1842, Art. I, § 20; Act of 1804, 1 Laws of Vt. 366 (Tolman 1808); *Commonwealth v. Morris*, 1 Brock. & Hol. (Va.) 176 (1811).

[12] Act for the Punishment of Divers Capital and Other Felonies, Acts and Laws of Conn. 66, 67 (1784); Act Against Drunkenness, Blasphemy, §§ 4, 5 (1737), 1 Laws of Del. 173, 174 (1797); Act to Regulate Taverns (1786), Digest of the Laws of Ga. 512, 513 (Prince 1822); Act of 1723, c. 16, § 1, Digest of the Laws of Md. 92 (Herty 1799); General Laws and Liberties of Mass. Bay, c. XVIII, § 3 (1646), Mass. Bay Colony Charters & Laws 58 (1814); Act of 1782, c. 8, Rev. Stat. of Mass. 741, § 15 (1836); Act of 1798, c. 33, §§ 1, 3, Rev. Stat. of Mass. 741, § 16 (1836); Act for the Punishment of Certain Crimes Not Capital (1791), N. H. Laws 1792, 252, 256; Act for the Punishment of Profane Cursing and Swearing (1791), N. H. Laws 1792, 258; Act for Suppressing Vice and Immorality, §§ VIII, IX (1798), N. J. Rev. Laws 329, 331 (1800); Act for Suppressing Immorality, § IV (1788), 2 Laws of N. Y. 257, 258 (Jones & Varick 1777–1789); *People v. Ruggles*, 8 Johns. (N. Y.) 290 (1811); Act . . . for the More Effectual Suppression of Vice and Immorality, § III (1741), 1 N. C. Laws 52 (Martin Rev. 1715–1790); Act to Prevent the Grievous Sins of Cursing and Swearing (1700), II Statutes at Large of Pa. 49 (1700–1712); Act for the Prevention of Vice and Immorality, § II (1794), 3 Laws of Pa. 177, 178 (1791–1802); Act to Reform the Penal Laws, §§ 33, 34 (1798), R. I. Laws 1798, 584, 595; Act for the More Effectual Suppressing of Blasphemy and Prophaneness (1703), Laws of S. C. 4 (Grimké 1790); Act, for the Punishment of Certain Capital, and Other High Crimes and Misdemeanors, § 20 (1797), 1 Laws of Vt. 332, 339 (Tolman 1808); Act, for the Punishment of Certain Inferior Crimes and Misdemeanors, § 20 (1797), 1 Laws of Vt. 352, 361 (Tolman 1808); Act for the Effectual Suppression of Vice, § 1 (1792), Acts of General Assembly of Va. 286 (1794).

[13] Act Concerning Crimes and Punishments, § 69 (1821), Stat. Laws of Conn. 109 (1824); *Knowles v. State*, 3 Day (Conn.) 103 (1808); Rev. Stat. of 1835, c. 130, § 10, Rev. Stat. of Mass. 740 (1836); *Commonwealth v. Holmes*, 17 Mass. 335 (1821); Rev. Stat. of 1842, c. 113, § 2, Rev. Stat. of N. H. 221 (1843); Act for Suppressing Vice

and Immorality, § XII (1798), N. J. Rev. Laws 329, 331 (1800); *Commonwealth v. Sharpless*, 2 S. & R. (Pa.) 91 (1815).

[14] *E. g.*, *United States v. Harriss*, 347 U. S. 612; *Breard v. Alexandria*, 341 U. S. 622; *Teamsters Union v. Hanke*, 339 U. S. 470; *Kovacs v. Cooper*, 336 U. S. 77; *Prince v. Massachusetts*, 321 U. S. 158; *Labor Board v. Virginia Elec. & Power Co.*, 314 U. S. 469; *Cox v. New Hampshire*, 312 U. S. 569; *Schenck v. United States*, 249 U. S. 47.

[15] Agreement for the Suppression of the Circulation of Obscene Publications, 37 Stat. 1511; Treaties in Force 209 (U. S. Dept. State, October 31, 1956).

[16] Hearings before Subcommittee to Investigate Juvenile Delinquency of the Senate Committee on the Judiciary, pursuant to S. Res. 62, 84th Cong., 1st Sess. 49–52 (May 24, 1955).

Although New Mexico has no general obscenity statute, it does have a statute giving to municipalities the power "to prohibit the sale or exhibiting of obscene or immoral publications, prints, pictures, or illustrations." N. M. Stat. Ann., 1953, §§ 14–21–3, 14–21–12.

[17] 5 Stat. 548, 566; 11 Stat. 168; 13 Stat. 504, 507; 17 Stat. 302; 17 Stat. 598; 19 Stat. 90; 25 Stat. 187, 188; 25 Stat. 496; 26 Stat. 567, 614–615; 29 Stat. 512; 33 Stat. 705; 35 Stat. 1129, 1138; 41 Stat. 1060; 46 Stat. 688; 48 Stat. 1091, 1100; 62 Stat. 768; 64 Stat. 194; 64 Stat. 451; 69 Stat. 183; 70 Stat. 699.

[18] *Schenck v. United States*, 249 U. S. 47. This approach is typified by the opinion of Judge Bok (written prior to this Court's opinion in *Dennis v. United States*, 341 U. S. 494) in *Commonwealth v. Gordon*, 66 Pa. D. & C. 101, aff'd, *sub nom. Commonwealth v. Feigenbaum*, 166 Pa. Super. 120, 70 A. 2d 389.

[19] *Dennis v. United States*, 341 U. S. 494. This approach is typified by the concurring opinion of Judge Frank in the *Roth* case, 237 F. 2d, at 801. See also Lockhart & McClure, Literature, The Law of Obscenity, and the Constitution, 38 Minn. L. Rev. 295 (1954).

[20] *I. e.*, material having a tendency to excite lustful thoughts. Webster's New International Dictionary (Unabridged, 2d ed., 1949) defines *prurient*, in pertinent part, as follows:

". . . Itching; longing; uneasy with desire or longing; of persons, having itching, morbid, or lascivious longings; of desire, curiosity, or propensity, lewd. . . ."

Pruriency is defined, in pertinent part, as follows:

". . . Quality of being prurient; lascivious desire or thought. . . ."

See also *Mutual Film Corp. v. Industrial Comm'n*, 236 U. S. 230, 242, where this Court said as to motion pictures: ". . . They take their attraction from the general interest, eager and wholesome it may be, in their subjects, but a *prurient interest may be excited and appealed to*. . . ." (Emphasis added.)

We perceive no significant difference between the meaning of obscenity developed in the case law and the definition of the A. L. I., Model Penal Code, § 207.10 (2) (Tent. Draft No. 6, 1957), *viz.*:

". . . A thing is obscene if, considered as a whole, its predominant appeal is to prurient interest, i. e., a shameful or morbid interest in nudity, sex, or excretion, and if it goes substantially beyond customary limits of candor in description or representation of such matters. . . ." See Comment, *id.*, at 10, and the discussion at page 29 *et seq.*

[21] See, *e. g.*, *United States v. Dennett*, 39 F. 2d 564.

[22] Madison's Report on the Virginia Resolutions, 4 Elliot's Debates 571.

[23] See note 14, *supra.*

[24] But see the instructions given to the jury by Mr. Justice Stable in *Regina v. Martin Secker Warburg*, [1954] 2 All Eng. 683 (C. C. C.).

[25] *United States v. Kennerley*, 209 F. 119; *MacFadden v. United States*, 165 F. 51; *United States v. Bennett*, 24 Fed. Cas. 1093; *United States v. Clarke*, 38 F. 500; *Commonwealth v. Buckley*, 200 Mass. 346, 86 N. E. 910.

[26] *E. g.*, *Walker v. Popenoe*, 80 U. S. App. D. C. 129, 149 F. 2d 511; *Parmelee v. United States*, 72 App. D. C. 203, 113 F. 2d 729; *United States v. Levine*, 83 F. 2d 156; *United States v. Dennett*, 39 F. 2d 564; *Khan v. Feist, Inc.*, 70 F. Supp. 450, aff'd, 165 F. 2d 188; *United States v. One Book Called "Ulysses,"* 5 F. Supp. 182, aff'd, 72 F. 2d 705; *American Civil Liberties Union v. Chicago*, 3 Ill. 2d 334, 121 N. E. 2d 585; *Commonwealth v. Isenstadt*, 318 Mass. 543, 62 N. E.

2d 840; *Missouri* v. *Becker*, 364 Mo. 1079, 272 S. W. 2d 283; *Adams Theatre Co.* v. *Keenan*, 12 N. J. 267, 96 A. 2d 519; *Bantam Books, Inc.* v. *Melko*, 25 N. J. Super. 292, 96 A. 2d 47; *Commonwealth* v. *Gordon*, 66 Pa. D. & C. 101, aff'd, *sub nom. Commonwealth* v. *Feigenbaum*, 166 Pa. Super. 120, 70 A. 2d 389; cf. *Roth* v. *Goldman*, 172 F. 2d 788, 794–795 (concurrence).

[27] In *Alberts*, the contention that the trial judge did not read the materials in their entirety is not before us because not fairly comprised within the questions presented. U. S. Sup. Ct. Rules, 15 (1)(c)(1).

[28] This Court, as early as 1896, said of the federal obscenity statute: ". . . Every one who uses the mails of the United States for carrying papers or publications must take notice of what, in this enlightened age, is meant by decency, purity, and chastity in social life, and what must be deemed obscene, lewd, and lascivious." *Rosen* v. *United States*, 161 U. S. 29, 42.

[29] E. g., *Roth* v. *Goldman*, 172 F. 2d 788, 789; *Parmelee* v. *United States*, 72 App. D. C. 203, 204, 113 F. 2d 729, 730; *United States* v. *4200 Copies International Journal*, 134 F. Supp. 490, 493; *United States* v. *One Unbound Volume*, 128 F. Supp. 280, 281.

[30] It is argued that because juries may reach different conclusions as to the same material, the statutes must be held to be insufficiently precise to satisfy due process requirements. But, it is common experience that different juries may reach different results under any criminal statute. That is one of the consequences we accept under our jury system. Cf. *Dunlop* v. *United States*, 165 U. S. 486, 499–500.

[31] For the same reason, we reject, in this case, the argument that there is greater latitude for state action under the word "liberty" under the Fourteenth Amendment than is allowed to Congress by the language of the First Amendment.

[32] In *Public Clearing House* v. *Coyne*, 194 U. S. 497, 506–508, this Court said:

"The constitutional principles underlying the administration of the Post Office Department were discussed in the opinion of the court in *Ex parte Jackson*, 96 U. S. 727, in which we held that the power vested in Congress to establish post offices and post roads embraced the regulation of the entire postal system of the country; that Congress might designate what might be carried in the mails and what excluded . . . . It may . . . refuse to include in its mails such printed matter or merchandise as may seem objectionable to it upon the ground of public policy . . . . For more than thirty years not only has the transmission of obscene matter been prohibited, but it has been made a crime, punishable by fine or imprisonment, for a person to deposit such matter in the mails. The constitutionality of this law we believe has never been attacked. . . ."

JUSTICE HARLAN'S OPINION NOTES

[1] In *Alberts* v. *California*, the state definition of "obscenity" is, of course, binding on us. The definition there used derives from *People* v. *Wepplo*, 78 Cal. App. 2d Supp. 959, 178 P. 2d 853, the question being whether the material has "a substantive tendency to deprave or corrupt its readers by exciting lascivious thoughts or arousing lustful desire."

In *Roth* v. *United States*, our grant of certiorari was limited to the question of the constitutionality of the statute, and did not encompass the correctness of the definition of "obscenity" adopted by the trial judge as a matter of statutory construction. We must therefore assume that the trial judge correctly defined that term, and deal with the constitutionality of the statute as construed and applied in this case.

The two definitions do not seem to me synonymous. Under the federal definition it is enough if the jury finds that the book as a whole leads to certain thoughts. In California, the further inference must be drawn that such thoughts will have a substantive "tendency to deprave or corrupt"—i. e., that the thoughts induced by the material will affect character and action. See American Law Institute, Model Penal Code, Tentative Draft No. 6, § 207.10 (2), Comments, p. 10.

[2] *Ibid.*

[3] See dissenting opinion of MR. JUSTICE BRENNAN in *Kingsley*

Books, Inc. v. *Brown*, No. 107, *ante*, p. 447.

[4] "The general principle of free speech, it seems to me, must be taken to be included in the Fourteenth Amendment, in view of the scope that has been given to the word 'liberty' as there used, although perhaps it may be accepted with a somewhat larger latitude of interpretation than is allowed to Congress by the sweeping language that governs or ought to govern the laws of the United States."

[5] The hoary dogma of *Ex parte Jackson*, 96 U. S. 727, and *Public Clearing House* v. *Coyne*, 194 U. S. 497, that the use of the mails is a privilege on which the Government may impose such conditions as it chooses, has long since evaporated. See Brandeis, J., dissenting, in *Milwaukee Social Democratic Publishing Co.* v. *Burleson*, 255 U. S. 407, 430–433; Holmes, J., dissenting, in *Leach* v. *Carlile*, 258 U. S. 138, 140; *Cates* v. *Haderline*, 342 U. S. 804, reversing 189 F. 2d 369; *Door* v. *Donaldson*, 90 U. S. App. D. C. 188, 195 F. 2d 764.

[6] Hart, The Relations Between State and Federal Law, 54 Col. L. Rev. 489, 493.

[7] To give only a few examples: Edmund Wilson's "Memoirs of Hecate County" was found obscene in New York, see *Doubleday & Co.* v. *New York*, 335 U. S. 848; a bookseller indicted for selling the same book was acquitted in California. "God's Little Acre" was held to be obscene in Massachusetts, not obscene in New York and Pennsylvania.

[8] While the correctness of the judge's charge is not before us, the question is necessarily subsumed in the broader question involving the constitutionality of the statute as applied in this case.

[9] See American Law Institute, Model Penal Code, Tentative Draft No. 6, § 207.10, Comments, p. 20: "As an independent goal of penal legislation, repression of sexual thoughts and desires is hard to support. Thoughts and desires not manifested in overt antisocial behavior are generally regarded as the exclusive concern of the individual and his spiritual advisors."

JUSTICE DOUGLAS'S OPINION NOTE

*The definition of obscenity which the Court adopts seems in substance to be that adopted by those who drafted the A. L. I., Model Penal Code. § 207.10 (2) (Tentative Draft No. 6, 1957).

"Obscenity is defined in terms of material which appeals predominantly to prurient interest in sexual matters and which goes beyond customary freedom of expression in these matters. We reject the prevailing tests of tendency to arouse lustful thoughts or desires because it is unrealistically broad for a society that plainly tolerates a great deal of erotic interest in literature, advertising, and art, and because regulation of thought or desire, unconnected with overt misbehavior, raises the most acute constitutional as well as practical difficulties." *Id.*, at 10.

"THE QUESTION WHICH IS BEFORE ME FOR DECISION, THEREFORE, IS WHETHER § 305(a) OF THE TARIFF ACT OF 1930, IN PROHIBITING THE IMPORTATION OF 'OBSCENE' MATERIAL PROHIBITS THE IMPORTATION OF MATERIAL WHICH MAY BE ASSUMED TO APPEAL TO THE PRURIENT INTEREST OF THE 'AVERAGE PERSON,' IF THE ONLY PERSONS WHO WILL HAVE ACCESS TO THE MATERIAL WILL STUDY IT FOR THE PURPOSES OF SCIENTIFIC RESEARCH, AND IF, AS TO THOSE WHO ALONE WILL HAVE ACCESS TO THE MATERIAL, THERE IS NO REASONABLE PROBABILITY THAT IT WILL APPEAL TO THEIR PRURIENT INTEREST."

United States v. *31 Photographs, Etc.*, 156 F.Supp. 350 (1957)

PALMIERI, District Judge.

The United States Attorney has filed a libel under the provisions of § 305(a) of the Tariff Act of 1930,[1] seeking the forfeiture, confiscation, and destruction of certain photographs, books, and other articles which the claimant, Institute for Sex Research, Inc., at Indiana University, seeks to import into the United States. The libel is based upon the allegation that the libelled material is "obscene and immoral"[2] within the meaning of § 305(a). The claimant seeks the release of the material to it, maintaining that the attempted importation is not in violation of § 305(a) and that, if § 305(a) is interpreted so as to prohibit the importation of the libelled material, the section violates the provisions of certain articles of the Constitution of the United States. Since I believe that § 305(a) does not permit the exclusion of the material, I do not reach the latter contention. Thus, the question of "academic freedom," much bruited in the oral argument by claimant, does not arise in this case.

Both the Government and the claimant have moved for summary judgment. The Government's motion is supported by the photographs, books, and articles themselves. For the purposes of this decision, I assume that the libelled material is of such a nature that, "to the average person, applying contemporary community standards, the dominant theme of the material taken as a whole appeals to prurient interest."[3] The claimant's motion is supported by affidavits sworn to by the President of the Institute, the Institute's Director of Field Research, the President of Indiana University, and various physicians, psychologists, psychiatrists, penologists, and academicians. Among these is an affidavit sworn to by the Hon. James V. Bennett, Director of the Bureau of Prisons, United States Department of Justice. Mr. Bennett states in his affidavit that the Institute has made substantial contributions to the study of problems of sexual adjustment encountered among prison inmates. He also states that understanding of pathological sexuality and sexual offenders has been enhanced by the study of the erotic productions of these deviated persons. An affidavit has also been filed by claimant's attorney, setting forth certain prior proceedings in this matter. Finally, the Trustees of Indiana University have submitted a brief, *amicus curiae,* in support of claimant's position. The President of the University, in his affidavit, has described the Institute as "[i]n essence * * * for all practical purposes * * * a special research department of the University." The Government has neither served affidavits setting forth any facts in opposition to those contained in the affidavits served by the claimant,[4] nor has it served an affidavit from which it would appear that it cannot "present by affidavit facts essential to justify [its] opposition."[5]

There is, therefore, no genuine issue as to the following facts, which are the only ones I find relevant to a decision of the issues before me:

1. That the claimant seeks to import the libelled material "for the sole purpose of furthering its study of human sexual behavior as manifested in varying forms of expression and activity and in different national cultures and historical periods."[6]

2. That the libelled material will not be available to members of the general public, but "will be held under security conditions * * * for the sole use of the Institute staff members or of qualified scholars engaged in bona fide research * * * "[7] and

3. That, as to those who will have access to the material sought to be imported, there is no reasonable probability that it will appeal to their prurient interest.[8]

In limine, it is well to set forth the posture of this case as I have it before me for decision. Claimant applied, in 1952, to the Secretary of the Treasury for permission to import the material under the second proviso of § 305(a).[9] The Secretary declined to exercise his discretion for this purpose. In a letter advising claimant's attorneys of this decision, the Acting Secretary of the Treasury stated that a limited exception to the prohibition of § 305(a) had been established by certain cases, but that the exception was "limited to a narrow category of articles and * * * applicable to only a specialized practice of medicine." The Acting Secretary stated that he did not feel that administrative extension of this exception would be justified and that the Department of Justice would be requested to bring forfeiture proceedings "in order to resolve the pertinent questions of law and furnish judicial guidance for our future actions."[10] The claimant has not, however, sought review of the Secretary's action, and my decision on the Government's libel implies nothing as to the correctness of his action.

The question which is before me for decision, therefore, is whether § 305(a) of the Tariff Act of 1930, in prohibiting the importation of "obscene" material prohibits the importation of material which may be assumed to appeal to the prurient interest of the "average person," if the only persons who will have access to the material will study it for the purposes of scientific research, and if, as to those who alone will have access to the material, there is no reasonable probability that it will appeal to their prurient interest. In short, the question presented for decision is the meaning of the word "obscene" in § 305(a) of the Tariff Act of 1930.[11]

Material is obscene if it makes a certain appeal to the viewer. It is not sufficient that the material be "merely coarse, vulgar, or indecent in the popular sense of those terms." United States v. Males, D.C.D.Ind.1892, 51 F. 41, 43.[12] Its appeal must be to "prurient interest." "Obscene material is material which deals with sex in a manner appealing to prurient interest." Roth v. United States, 1957, 354 U.S. 476, 487, 77 S.Ct. 1304, 1310, 1 L.Ed.2d 1498 (footnote omitted).

But the search for a definition does not end there.[13] To whose prurient interest must the work appeal? While the rule is often stated in terms of the appeal of the material to the "average person," Roth v. United States, 1957, 354 U.S. 476, 489, 77 S.Ct. 1304, 1 L.Ed.2d 1498,[14] it must be borne in mind that the cases applying the standard in this manner do so in regard to material which is to be distributed to the public at large. I believe, however, that the more inclusive statement of the definition is that which judges the material by its appeal to "all those whom it is likely to reach." United States v. Levine, 2 Cir., 1936, 83 F.2d 156, 157.[15] Viewed in this light, the "average man" test is but a particular application of the rule, often found in the cases only because the cases often deal with material which is distributed to the public at large.

Of course, this rule cuts both ways. Material distributed to the public at large may not be judged by its appeal to the most sophisticated,[16] nor by its appeal to the most susceptible.[17] And I believe that the cases establish that material whose use will be restricted to those in whose hands it will not have a prurient appeal is not to be judged by its appeal to the populace at large.

In Commonwealth v. Landis, Q.S.1870, 8 Phila., Pa., 453, defendant had been convicted of publishing an obscene libel.[18] The court approved a charge to the jury in which it was stated that the publication would be justified if "made for a legitimate and useful purpose, and * * * not made from any motive of mere gain or with a corrupt desire to debauch society." Q.S.1870, 8 Phila., Pa., 453, 454. While scientific and medical publications "in proper hands for useful purposes" may contain illustrations exhibiting the human form, the court held that such publications would be obscene libels "if wantonly exposed in the open markets, with a wanton and wicked desire to create a demand for them." Id. at pages 454–455. Finally, the court held that the human body might be exhibited before a medical class for purposes of instruction, "but that if the same human body were exposed in front of one of our medical colleges to the public indiscriminately, even for the purpose of operation, such an exhibition would be held to be indecent and obscene." Id. at page 455.[19]

In United States v. Chesman, C.C.E.D. Mo.1881, 19 F. 497, the court found offensive, matter which was taken from books upon medicine and surgery. The court held that such matter "would be proper enough for the general use of members and students of the profession." But, the court continued, "[t]here are many things contained in the standard works upon these subjects which, if printed in pamphlet form and spread broadcast among the community, being sent through the mail to persons of all classes, including boys and girls, would be highly indecent and obscene." C.C.E.D.Mo.1881, 19 F. 497–8.[20]

And in United States v. Clarke, D.C.E.D.Mo.1889, 38 F. 500, it is said that "[E]ven an obscene book, or one that, in view of its subject-matter, would ordinarily be classed as such, may be sent through the mail, or published, to certain persons, for certain purposes." D.C.E.D.Mo.1889, 38 F. 500, 502.[21]

In United States v. Smith, D.C.E.D. Wis.1891, 45 F. 476, the court stated that a determination of obscenity depended upon circumstance. "The public exposure of the person is most obscene, yet the necessary exhibition of the person to a physician is not only innocent, but is a proper act, dictated by positive duty. Instruction touching the organs of the body, under proper circumstances, is not reprehensible; but such instruction to a mixed assemblage of the youth of both sexes might be most demoralizing." D.C.E.D.Wis.1891, 45 F. 476, 478.

In upholding the exclusion from evidence of testimony tending to show that the book in issue was intended for doctors and married couples, the Court of Appeals for the Eighth Circuit has said: "The book itself was in evidence. It was not a communication from a doctor to his patient, nor a work designed for the use of medical practitioners only." Burton v. United States, 8 Cir., 1906, 142 F. 57, 63.

The Court of Appeals for this Circuit, in holding that proof of those to whom the pamphlet was sold is part of the Government's case, said: "In other words, a publication might be distributed among doctors or nurses or adults in cases where the distribution among small children could not be justified. The fact that the latter might obtain it accidently or surreptitiously, as they might see some medical books which would not be desirable for them to read, would hardly be sufficient to bar a publication otherwise proper. * * * Even the court in Regina v. Hicklin, L.R. 3 Q.B. at p. 367 * * * said that 'the circumstances of the publication' may determine whether the statute has been violated." United States v. Dennett, 2 Cir., 1930, 39 F.2d 564, 568, 76 A.L.R. 1092.

Finally, a situation very similar to the one at bar was decided in United States v. One Unbound Volume, etc., D.C.D.Md.1955, 128 F.Supp. 280. Claimant had attempted to import a collection of prints which depicted statues, vases, lamps, and other antique artifacts which were decorated with or displayed erotic activities, features, or symbols, and which portrayed acts of sodomy and other forms of perverted sexual practice. While finding that the study of erotica in ancient times was a recognized field of archeology, the court, after referring to the fact that the claimant was a microchemist and, at best, an amateur archeologist, significantly added: "I do not believe the present state of the taste and morals of the community would approve the public exhibition of a collection of objects similar to those shown on the prints, nor the public exhibition or sale of the prints themselves, although in my opinion most normal men and women in this country would approve the ownership of such a publication by a museum, library, college or other educational institution, where its use could be controlled." D.C.D.Md.1955, 128 F.Supp. 280, 282.[22]

The cases upholding importation of contraceptives and books dealing with contraception when sought to be brought into the country for purposes of scientific and medical research[23] are further indications that the statute is to be interpreted as excluding or permitting material depending on the conditions of its use.[24] It is true that these cases held, on analogy to what is now 18 U.S.C. § 1461 (Supp. IV) that only contraceptives intended for "unlawful" use were banned.[25] The circumstances of the use were thus held relevant. But "contraception" is a word describing a physical act, devoid of normative connotations until modified by an adjective such as "unlawful." "Obscene," on the other hand, describes that quality of an article which causes it to have a certain appeal to the interests of the beholder.

The intent of the importer, therefore, relevant to the contraceptive cases only because "unlawful" use alone was proscribed, is relevant in an obscenity case[26] because of the very nature of the determination (as to the appeal of the material to the viewer) which must be made before the article may be deemed "obscene."

The customs barrier which is sought to be imposed by this suit must be viewed in the light of the great variety of goods permitted to enter our ports. For instance, despite the legitimate concern of the community with the distribution and sale of narcotic drugs, their importation is not completely prevented.[27] It is carefully regulated so as to insure their confinement to appropriate channels.[28] Viruses, serums, and toxins are another example. Their potential harm would be incalculable if they were placed in unknowing or mischievous hands. But proposed importations of bacilli of dangerous and highly contagious diseases do not lead us to shut our ports in panic. Rather, we place our faith in the competence of those who are entrusted with their proper use.[29] So, here, while the material would not be importable for general circulation, its closely regulated use by an unimpugned institution of learning and research removes it from the ban of the statute. The successive judicial interpretations of the statute here involved point as clearly to this result as does the express Congressional permission for the importation of potentially harmful biologic products. The work of serious scholars need find no impediment in this law.

The Government, in certain portions of its Memorandum of Law, talks of, and I find two cases[30] which have described material as being "obscene *per se.*" But I cannot understand this to mean that the material was held to have a prurient appeal without reference to any beholder. I take it to mean that in the cases under decision there was not shown to be anyone to whom the appeal would be other than prurient, or that in a case of widespread distribution the material was of such a nature that its appeal to the average person must be held, as a matter of law, to be prurient.[31] It should be obvious that obscenity must be judged by the material's appeal to somebody. For what is obscenity to one person is but a subject of scientific inquiry to another. And, of course, the substitution, required by Roth,[32] of the "average person" test (in cases of widespread distribution) for the test according to the effect upon one of particular susceptibility, is a matter of determining the person according to whom the appeal of the material is to be judged. Once it is admitted that the material's appeal to some person, or group of persons, must be used as the standard by which to gauge obscenity, I believe that the cases teach that, in a case such as this, the appeal to be probed is that to the people for whom, and for whom alone, the material will be available.

It is possible, instead of holding that the material is not obscene in the hands of the persons who will have access to it, to speak of a conditional privilege in favor of scientists and scholars, to import material which would be obscene in the hands of the average person.[33] I find it unnecessary to choose between these theories. In the first place, under either theory the material may not be excluded in this case. Moreover, I believe that the two theories are but opposite sides of one coin. For it is the importer's scientific interest in the material which leads to the conditional privilege, and it is this same interest which requires the holding that the appeal of the material to the scientist is not to his prurient interest and that, therefore, the material is not obscene as to him.[34]

There remain to be mentioned two objections which the Government raises to the course of decision I follow today. The first is that the second proviso of § 305(a) of the Tariff Act of 1930[35] provides the sole means by which this material may be imported. Of course, under the theory that the nature of the material is to be judged by its appeal to those who will see it, the libelled material is simply not obscene and the second proviso has no application, providing, as it does, for a method by which certain obscene matter may be imported.[36] And if the correct theory be that there is a conditional privilege in favor of scientists and scholars to import material, for their study alone, which would be obscene in the hands of the general public, I am not convinced that Congress, by enacting the second proviso to § 305(a) in 1930[37] intended to establish the Secretary's discretion as the sole means by which scientists could import such materials. Indeed, the cases decided since 1930 have not so held.[38]

The Government also raises a *concursus horribilium,* maintaining that there are no workable criteria by which the section may be administered if it is interpreted as I do today. It is probably sufficient unto this case to point out

that there is no dispute in this proceeding as to the fact that there is no reasonable likelihood that the material will appeal to the prurient interest of those who will see it. But I will add that I fail to see why it should be more difficult to determine the appeal of libelled matter to a known group of persons than it is to determine its appeal to an hypothetical "average man."[39] The question is not whether the materials are necessary, or merely desirable for a particular research project. The question is not whether the fruits of the research will be valuable to society.[40] The Tariff Act of 1930 provides no warrant for either customs officials or this court to sit in review of the decisions of scholars as to the bypaths of learning upon which they shall tread. The question is solely whether, as to those persons who will see the libelled material, there is a reasonable probability that it will appeal to their prurient interest.[41]

For those who would seek to pander materials such as those libelled in this case, I need hardly express my contempt. Nor need I add that the theory of this decision, rightly interpreted, affords no comfort to those who would import materials such as these for public sale or private indulgence. The cry against the circulation of obscenity raised by the law-abiding community is a legitimate one; and one with which Congress, the State legislatures, and the courts have been seriously concerned.[42] When that case arises in which the Government determines that it should go to trial upon the facts, a showing that multiple copies of a particular piece of matter are sought to be imported by the same person should raise an extremely strong inference against any claim that the material is sought for allegedly scientific purposes. And, while I express no definitive opinion on this point, since it is unnecessary to the decision before me, it would seem that any individual, not connected with an institution recognized to be conducting bona fide research into these matters, will not easily establish that he seeks importation for a reason other than gratification of his prurient interest. See United States v. One Unbound Volume, etc., D.C.D. Md. 1955, 128 F.Supp. 280.

Nor do I envision the establishment of myriad and spurious "Institutes for Sex Research" as screens for the importation of pornographic material for public sale. In addition to what has already been said, it should be pointed out that the *bona fides* of any such Institute and of the research or study to which it claims to be dedicated will be a threshold inquiry in each case. The accumulation of an inventory, as I mentioned above, will tend to negate the assertion of a legitimate interest. And those whose business it is to pander such material will be unlikely to convince anyone that they are serious candidates for the mantle of scientific researcher.

There being no dispute in this case as to the fact that there is no reasonable probability that the libelled material will appeal to the prurient interest of those who will see it, it is proper that the motion of the libellant for an order that the libelled material be forfeited, confiscated and destroyed, be denied; and that the motion of the claimant for summary judgment dismissing the libel and releasing the libelled material to it, be granted.

Settle order on notice.

NOTES

1. 46 Stat. 688 (1930). 19 U.S.C.A. § 1305 (a). This

section provides, in pertinent part, as follows: "All persons are prohibited from importing into the United States from any foreign country * * * any obscene book, pamphlet, paper, writing, advertisement, circular, print, picture, drawing, or other representation, figure, or image on or of paper or other material, or any cast, instrument, or other article which is obscene or immoral * * * No such articles * * * shall be admitted to entry; and all such articles * * * shall be subject to seizure and forfeiture as hereinafter provided * * * ." The section further provides for the admission of certain classics or books in the discretion of the Secretary of the Treasury. See note 9, infra. The Secretary has refused to exercise his discretion to admit in this case. See note 10, infra.

2. My discussion is framed in terms of whether the libelled material is "obscene." I do not believe that the word "immoral" adds to the class of material excluded from importation by the word "obscene," and the Government has not contended that it does. See 71 Cong. Rec. 4457 (1929). Cf. Commercial Pictures Corp. v. Regents of University of State of New York 1954. 346 U.S. 587, 74 S.Ct. 286, 98 L.Ed. 329.

3. Roth v. United States, 1957, 354 U.S. 476, 489, 77 S. Ct. 1304, 1305, 1311, 1 L.Ed.2d 1498.

4. Fed.R.Civ.P. 56(c), 28 U.S.C.A.

5. Fed.R.Civ.P. 56(f). The Government's position on oral argument and subsequently has been that while it does not wish to submit affidavits, it does not concede the truth of the facts set forth in claimant's affidavits. Of course, a motion for summary judgment cannot be defeated by a simple declaration that the opponent does not concede the facts which are clearly established by the movant's affidavits. "But where the moving party properly shoulders his burden, the opposing party must either come forward with some proof that raises a genuine factual issue, or, in accordance with Rule 56(f), show reasons satisfactory to the court why it is presently not forthcoming." 6 Moore's Federal Practice, par. 56.15[5] (2nd Ed. 1953. Cf. Engl v. Aetna Life Ins. Co., 2 Cir., 1943, 139 F.2d 469. I am aware, of course, of my discretion to refuse summary judgment even though the Government has stood mute, see 6 Moore's Federal Practice, par. 56.-15[6] (2nd Ed. 1953); but I see no reason to do so in this case.

6. Affidavit of Paul H. Gebhard, president of the Institute, page 10.

7. Id. at page 13.

8. Affidavit of Walter C. Alvarez, M.D., page 5. See, also, the affidavit of Karl M. Bowman, M.D., page 7.

9. Affidavit of Harriet F. Pilpel, member of the firm which is acting as claimant's attorney, page 3. The proviso reads: *Provided further,* That the Secretary of the Treasury may, in his discretion, admit the so-called classics or books of recognized and established literary or scientific merit, but may, in his discretion, admit such classics or books only when imported for noncommercial purposes." 46 Stat. 688 (1930), 19 U.S.C.A. § 1305(a). I discuss the contention that this provision exhausts the possibilities of allowing the importation of the libelled material infra at page 359 of 156 F.Supp.

10. Pilpel affidavit, supra note, 9, page 4, and Exhibit A. It appears, from the reference of the Secretary to United States v. One Package, 2 Cir., 1936, 86 F.2d 737, that the articles to which the Secretary referred were contraceptives. But the second proviso of § 305 (a) allows the Secretary to "admit the so-called classics or books of

recognized and established literary or scientific merit." See Note 9, supra.

11. In arriving at my conclusion on this aspect of the case I have relied upon a number of cases arising under what is now 18 U.S.C. § 1461 (Supp. IV) prohibiting use of the mails for the transportation of, *inter alia,* obscene matter. The provisions now found in 19 U.S.C.A. § 1305(a) and 18 U.S.C. §1461 (Supp. IV) "were part of a continuous scheme to suppress immoral articles and obscene literature and should so far as possible be construed together and consistently." United States v. One Package, 2 Cir., 1936, 86 F.2d 737, 739. The Government urges, however, that the audience to which the material is directed is relevant in a criminal prosecution under 18 U.S.C. § 1461 (Supp. IV) since it bears on the question of criminal intent, but not in a libel under 19 U.S.C.A. § 1305(a) since intent is not there a factor. To the extent, if any, that the One Package decision does not answer this contention, it is answered by the requirement of Roth that obscenity statutes be construed as narrowly as is possible to effectuate their purpose though impinging on other interests. "The fundamental freedoms of speech and press have contributed greatly to the development and well-being of our free society and are indispensable to its continued growth. Ceaseless vigilance is the watchword to prevent their erosion by Congress or by the States. The door barring federal and state intrusion into this area cannot be left ajar; it must be kept tightly closed and opened only the slightest crack necessary to prevent encroachment upon more important interests." Roth v. United States. 1957, 354 U.S. 476, 488, 77 S.Ct. 1304, 1311, 1 L.Ed. 2d 1498 (footnotes omitted). And see footnote 40, infra, and text at footnote 26, infra.

12. See also Swearingen v. United States, 1896. 161 U.S. 446, 450-451. 16 S.Ct. 562, 40 L.Ed. 765; Duncan v. United States, 9 Cir., 48 F.2d 128, certiorari denied 1931, 283, U.S. 863, 51 S.Ct. 656, 75 L. Ed. 1468; United States v. Wroblenski, D.C.E.D. Wis.1902, 118 F. 495; cf. United States v. Limehouse, 1932, 285 U.S. 424, 52 S.Ct. 412,76 L.Ed. 843.

13. See Judge Frank's discussion of the appropriateness of judicial definitions of obscenity, prior to the Supreme Court's decision in the Roth case. United States v. Roth, 2 Cir., 1956, 237 F.2d 796, 801 et seq. (concurring opinion), affirmed 1957, 354 U.S. 476, 77 S.Ct. 1304, 1 L. Ed. 2d 1498.

14. See also United States v. One Book Entitled Ulysses. etc., 2 Cir., 1934, 72 F. 2d 705, 708; Walker v. Popenoe, 1945, 80 U.S.App.D.C. 129, 149 F.2d 511, 512 ("ordinary reader"), I understand the statement in Ulysses that permission to import does not depend upon "the character of those to whom [the materials] are sold." 2 Cir., 1934. 72 F.2d 705, 708, to mean that in a case of material distributed to the general public, the claimant may not show that there are some members of the public as to whom the material will not have a prurient appeal.

15. The Chief Justice, concurring in Roth, said that "Present [obscenity] laws depend largely upon the effect that the materials may have upon those who receive them. It is manifest that the same object may have a different impact, varying according to the part of the community it reached." Roth v. United States, 1957, 354 U.S., 476, 495. 77 S.Ct. 1304, 1314, 1 L.Ed.2d 1498. And the charge of the trial judge in Roth, approved by the Court, stated the test in terms of "all those whom [the material] is

likely to reach." Id. 354 U.S. at page 490, 77 S.Ct. at page 1312. And see United States v. Dennett, 2 Cir., 1930, 39 F.2d 564, 568, 76 A.L.R. 1092 ("those into whose hands the publication might fall"); One, inc., v. Olesen, 9 Cir., 1957, 241 F. 2d 772, 775, petition for certiorari filed, 26 U.S.L.Week 3046 (U.S., July 18, 1957, 78 S.Ct. 364) ("effect * * * upon the reader"); Parmelee v. United States, 1940, 72 App.D.C. 203, 113 F.2d 729,731 ("all those whom it is likely to reach"); United States v. Two Obscene Books, D.C.N.D.Cal.1951, 99 F.Supp. 760, 762, affirmed sub nom. Besig v. United States, 9 Cir., 1953, 208 F.2d 142 ("those whose minds are open to such influences and into whose hands [the material] may fall * * * ."); United States v. Goldstein, D.C.D.N.J.1947, 73 F.Supp. 875, 877 ("those into whose hands the publication might fall"); United States v. Males, D.C.D.Ind.1892, 51 F. 41, 43 ("those into whose hands it may fall"); United States v. Clarke, D.C.E.D.Mo.1889, 38 F. 500, 502 (same). Cf. United States v. 4200 Copies International Journal, etc., D.C.E.D.Wash.1955, 134 F.Supp. 490, 494, affirmed sub. nom. Mounce v. United States, 9 Cir., 1957, 247 F.2d 148, petition for certiorari granted 78 S.Ct. 267.

16. See the charge to the jury quoted in Roth v. United States, 1957, 354 U.S. 476, 490, 77 S.Ct. 1304, 1 L.Ed.2d 1498.

17. Butler v. State of Michigan, 1957, 352 U.S. 380, 77 S.Ct. 524. 1 L.Ed.2d 412; Volnaski v. United States, 6 Cir., 1957, 246 F. 2d 842.

18. The book was entitled "Secrets of Generation." Commonwealth v. Gordon, Phila. Q.S.1949, 66 Pa.Dist. & Co.R. 101, 121.

19. The history of the early ban upon the use of the human body for the purposes of anatomical study and the eventual removal of the restriction so long as books and treatises exhibiting the human body were restricted to practitioners and students is recounted in Parmelee v. United States, 1940, 72 App.D.C. 203, 113 F.2d 729, 734-735.

20. I understand the statement in Chesman, D.C.E.D.Mo. 1881, 19 F. 497, 498, that "[T]he law is violated, without regard to the character of the person to whom [the publications] are directed" to apply to cases of widespread distribution, such as was present in Chesman, and in the sense set forth in note 14, supra. It is interesting to note that the court in Parmelee v. United States, 1940, 72 App.D.C. 203, 113 F.2d 729, said that "No reasonable person at the present time would suggest even that limitation [that texts containing representations of the human body be restricted to use among practitioners and students] upon the circulation and use of medical texts, treatises and journals. In many homes such books can be found today; in fact standard dictionaries, generally, contain anatomical illustrations. It is apparent, therefore, that civilization has advanced far enough, at last, to permit picturization of the human body for scientific and educational purposes." 1940, 72 App.D.C. 203, 113 F.2d 729, 735.

21. And see the charge to the jury in the same case, United States v. Clarke, D.C.E.D.Mo. 1889, 38 F. 732. "It is settled, at least so far as this court is concerned, that works on physiology, medicine, science, and sex instruction are not within the statute, though to some extent and among some persons they may tend to promote lustful thoughts." United States v. One Book Entitled Ulysses, etc., 2 Cir., 1934, 72 F.2d 705, 707.

22. See also Burstein v. United States, 9 Cir., 1949, 178 F.2d 665. Cf. Klaw v. Schaffer, D.C.S.D.N.Y.1957, 151 F.Supp. 534, 539, note 6, appeal pending.

23. United States v. One Package, 2 Cir., 1936, 86 F.2d 737; United States v. Nicholas, 2 Cir., 1938, 97 F.2d 510; Davis v. United States, 6 Cir., 1933, 62 F.2d 473; Consumers Union of United States, Inc., v. Walker, 1944, 79 U.S.App.D.C. 229, 145 F.2d 33; see also, Youngs Rubber Corp. v. C.I. Lee & Co., 2 Cir., 1930, 45 F.2d 103, 108; cf. Bours v. United States, 7 Cir., 1915, 229 F. 960.

24. "[W]e are satisfied that this statute [19 U.S.C.A. § 1305(a)] * * * embraced only such articles as Congress would have denounced as immoral if it had understood all the conditions under which they were to be used." United States v. One Package, 2 Cir., 1936, 86 F.2d 737, 739. In the Roth case, the Supreme Court stated: "We perceive no significant difference between the meaning of obscenity developed in the case law and the definition of the A.L.I., Model Penal Code, § 207.10(2) (Tent. Draft No. 6, 1957) * * * ." Roth v. United States, 1957, 354 U.S. 476, 487, note 20, 77 S.Ct. 1304, 1 L.Ed.2d 1498. Section 207.10(4) (c) of the Draft provides that non-criminal dissemination of obscenity includes: "dissemination to institutions or individuals having scientific or other special justification for possessing such material."

25. United States v. One Package, 2 Cir., 1936, 86 F.2d 737.

26. At least in a case such as this, where the importer and those who will have access to the material are the same or of the same class and proven to have the same reaction to the material.

27. 35 Stat. 614 (1909), as amended, 21 U.S.C.A. § 173.

28. 21 C.F.R., Part 302 (1955).

29. The importation of such products for animal use is regulated by 37 Stat. 832 (1913), 21 U.S.C.A. § 151 et seq. Their importation for human use is regulated by 58 Stat. 702 (1944), 42 U.S.C.A. § 262. The former is more strictly regulated. See 9 C.F.R., Part 102 (1949); and compare 19 C.F.R. § 12.17 (1953), with 19 C.F.R. § 12.21 (1953).

30. United States v. Rebhuhn. 2 Cir., 109 F.2d 512, certiorari denied 1940. 310 U.S. 629, 60 S.Ct. 976, 84 L.Ed. 1399; United States v. Newman, 2 Cir., 1944, 143 F.2d 389. But the court in Rebhuhn also said: "Most of the books could lawfully have passed through the mails, if directed to those who would be likely to use them for the purposes for which they were written, though that was not true of one or two: for example, of that entitled, 'Sex Life in England', which was a collection of short and condensed erotic bits, culled from various sources, and plainly put together as pornography. * * * [W]e will assume * * * that the works themselves had a place, though a limited one, in anthropology and in psychotherapy. They might also have been lawfully sold to laymen who wished seriously to study the sexual practices of savage or barbarous peoples, or sexual aberrations; in other words, most of them were not obscene per se. In several decisions we have held that the statute does not in all circumstances forbid the dissemination of such publications, and that in the trial of an indictment the prosecution must prove that the accused has abused a conditional privilege, which the law gives him. [Citing Dennett, Ulysses, and Levine.] However, in the case at bar, the prosecution succeeded upon that issue, when it showed

that the defendants had indiscriminately flooded the mails with advertisements, plainly designed merely to catch the prurient, though under the guise of distributing works of scientific or literary merit. We do not mean that the distributor of such works is charged with a duty to insure that they shall reach only proper hands, nor need we say what care he must use, for these defendants exceeded any possible limits; the circulars were no more than appeals to the salaciously disposed, and no sensible jury could have failed to pierce the fragile screen, set up to cover that purpose." 2 Cir., 1940, 109 F. 2d 512, 514–515.

31. See footnotes 14, 20, supra.

32. Roth v. United States, 1957, 354 U.S. 476, 488–489, 77 S.Ct. 1304, 1 L.Ed. 2d 1498.

33. See note 30, supra.

34. It may be that the drafters of Tentative Draft No. 6 of the A.L.I. Model Penal Code have adopted both theories. § 207.10(4) (c) of the Draft, quoted in note 24, supra, creates a limited exception to the prohibition of dissemination of obscenity in favor of "institutions or individuals having scientific or other special justification for possessing such material." And § 207.10(2) of the Draft sets forth the class as to which the material's appeal shall be judged as follows: "Obscenity shall be judged with reference to ordinary adults, except that it shall be judged with reference to children or other specially susceptible audience if it appears from the character of the material or the circumstances of its dissemination to be specially designed for or directed to such an audience." It is possible to understand the term "specially susceptible" to include not only those who are specially more susceptible, but also those who are specially less susceptible. See Comment 9 to the Draft and page 38, note 59.

35. Quoted in note 9, supra.

36. I do not believe that my decision leaves the second proviso without function, for it appears to provide the only means by which classics, and works of scientific and literary merit, although obscene in the hands of the general public, may be distributed to the general public.

37. The Congressional debates on § 305 (a), 72 Cong. Rec. 5414-33, 5487-5520 (1930), 71 Cong. Rec. 4432-4439, 4445-4472 (1929), are largely illustrative of the members who spoke on literature which may contain salacious passages. While bits may be culled from these debates which appear to deal with the problem at issue here, I believe that a fair reading of the debates as a whole indicates that Congress was concerned with the widespread distribution of obscene matter, and with the manner in which the ban on such distribution was to be enforced.

38. See note 30, supra. And see Parmelee v. United States, 1940, 72 App.D.C. 203, 113 F.2d 729, 737: "It cannot reasonably be contended that the purpose of the pertinent statute is to prevent scientific research and education. * * * So to interpret it would be to abandon the field, in large measure, to the charlatan and the fakir." (Footnote omitted.) And see the excerpt from Ulysses quoted in note 21, supra.

39. Cf. Roth v. Goldman, 2 Cir., 172 F.2d 788, 792 (concurring opinion by Judge Frank), certiorari denied 1949, 337 U.S. 938, 69 S.Ct. 1514, 93 L.Ed. 1743.

40. "All ideas having even the slightest redeeming social importance—unorthodox ideas, controversial ideas, even ideas hateful to the prevailing climate of opinion—have the full protection of the [Constitutional] guaranties, unless excludable because they encroach upon the limited area of more important interests. But implicit in the history of the First Amendment is the rejection of obscenity as utterly without redeeming social importance.

" * * * Sex, a great and mysterious motive force in human life, has indisputably been a subject of absorbing interest to mankind through the ages; it is one of the vital problems of human interest and public concern." Roth v. United States, 1957, 354 U.S. 476, 484, 487, 77 S.Ct. 1304, 1 L.Ed.2d 1498 (footnote omitted). I believe that the statement above quoted concerning the rejection of obscenity must be interpreted in the light of the widespread distribution of the material in Roth. While I do not reach the constitutional issues posed by claimant in this case I may note that, since it is taken as proved in this case that the libelled material will not, in all probability, appeal to the prurient interest of those into whose hands it will come, I cannot conceive of any interest which Congress might have intended to protect by prohibiting the importation of the material by the claimant.

41. The Government also maintains that the holding in United States v. One Obscene Book Entitled "Married Love," D.C.S.D.N.Y.1931, 48 F.2d 821, that a decision that a book is importable under § 305(a) is res judicata in a subsequent libel, precludes my holding that material is to be judged by its appeal to those who will see it. But the successive importations in that case were both for the purpose of distributing the book to the public at large. I see no reason for extending the rationale of the cited case beyond the situation in which the successive importations are for the purpose of distributing the material to the same person or class of persons.

42. See Roth v. United States, 1957, 354 U.S. 476, 485, 77 S.Ct. 1304, 1 L.Ed.2d 1498.

"LADY CHATTERLEY'S LOVER IS NOT OBSCENE. THE DECISION OF THE POSTMASTER GENERAL THAT IT IS OBSCENE AND THEREFORE NON-MAILABLE IS CONTRARY TO LAW AND CLEARLY ERRONEOUS."

Grove Press, Inc. v. Christenberry, 175 F.Supp. 488 (1959)

FREDERICK van PELT BRYAN, District Judge.

These two actions against the Postmaster of New York, now consolidated, arise out of the denial of the United States mails to the recently published Grove Press unexpurgated edition of "Lady Chatterley's Lover" by D. H. Lawrence.

Plaintiffs seek to restrain the Postmaster from enforcing a decision of the Post Office Department that the unexpurgated "Lady Chatterley's Lover", and circulars announcing its availability, are non-mailable under the statute barring obscene matter from the mails (18 U.S.C. § 1461).[1] They also seek a declaratory judgment to the effect (1) that the novel is not "obscene, lewd, lascivious, indecent or filthy" in content or character, and is not non-mailable under the statute or, in the alternative, (2) that if the novel be held to fall within the purview of the statute, the statute is to that extent invalid and violates plaintiffs' rights in contravention of the First and Fifth Amendments.

Grove Press, Inc., one of the plaintiffs, is the publisher of the book. Readers' Subscription, Inc., the other plaintiff, is a book club which has rights to distribute it.

Defendant has moved and plaintiffs have cross-moved for summary judgment, pursuant to Rule 56, F.R.Civ.P., 28 U.S.C. There are no disputed issues of fact. The cases are before me for final determination on the pleadings, the decision of the Postmaster General, the record before him and supplemental affidavits.[2]

On April 30, 1959 the New York Postmaster withheld from dispatch some 20,000 copies of circulars deposited for mailing by Readers' Subscription, which announced the availability of the new Grove edition of Lady Chatterley. At about the same time he also detained a number of copies of the book which had been deposited for mailing by Grove Press.

On May 8, 1959 letters of complaint issued by the General Counsel of the Post Office Department were served on Grove and Readers' Subscription alleging that there was probable cause to believe that these mailings violated 18 U.S.C. § 1461, and advising them of a departmental hearing. The respondents filed answers denying these allegations and a hearing was held before the Judicial Officer of the Post Office Department on May 14, 1959.[3]

The General Counsel, as complainant, introduced the Grove edition and the circulars which had been detained and rested.

The respondents offered (1) testimony as to their reputation and standing in the book publishing and distribution fields and their purpose in publishing and distributing the novel; (2) reviews of the book in leading newspapers and literary periodicals throughout the country; (3) copies of editorials and comments in leading newspapers concerning publication of the book and its anticipated impact; (4) news articles dealing with the banning of the book by the Post Office; and (5) expert testimony by two leading literary critics, Malcolm Cowley and Alfred Kazin, as to the literary stature of the work and its author, contemporary acceptance of literature dealing with sex and sex relations and their own opinions as to the effect of the book on its readers. The editorials and comments and the news articles were excluded.

The Judicial Officer before whom the hearing was held did not decide the issues. On May 28 he issued an order referring the proceedings to the Postmaster General "for final departmental decision."[4]

On June 11, 1959 the Postmaster General rendered a departmental decision finding that the Grove edition "is obscene and non-mailable pursuant to 18 U.S.Code § 1461," and that the Readers' Subscription circulars "give information where obscene material, namely, the book in issue in this case, may be obtained and are non-mailable * * * ."

This litigation, which had been commenced prior to the decision, was then brought on for hearing.

I

The basic question here is whether the unexpurgated "Lady Chatterley's Lover" is obscene within the meaning of 18 U.S.C. § 1461,[5] and is thus excluded from the protections afforded freedom of speech and the press by the First Amendment.

However, the defendant takes the position that this question is not before me for decision. He urges that the determination by the Postmaster General that this novel is obscene and non-mailable is conclusive upon the court unless it is found to be unsupported by substantial evidence and is clearly wrong. He argues, therefore, that I may not determine the issue of obscenity *de novo*.

Thus, an initial question is raised as to the scope of the court's power of review. In the light of the issues presented, the basis of the Postmaster General's decision, and the record before him, this question is not of substance.

(1) Prior to Roth v. United States, 354 U.S. 476, 77 S.Ct. 1304, 1 L.Ed.2d 1498, the Supreme Court had "always assumed that obscenity is not protected by the freedoms of speech and press." However, until then the constitutional question had not been directly passed upon by the court. In Roth the question was squarely posed.

The court held, in accord with its long-standing assumption, that "obscenity is not within the area of constitutionally protected speech or press."[6]

The court was faced with a dilemma. On the one hand it was required to eschew any impingement upon the cherished freedoms of speech and the press guaranteed by the Constitution and so essential to a free society. On the other hand it was faced with the recognized social evil presented by the purveyance of pornography.

The opinion of Mr. Justice Brennan for the majority makes it plain that the area which can be excluded from constitutional protection without impinging upon the free speech and free press guarantees is narrowly limited. He says (354 U.S. at page 484, 77 S.Ct. at page 1309):

"All ideas having even the slightest redeeming social importance—unorthodox ideas, controversial ideas, even ideas hateful to the prevailing climate of opinion—have the full protection of the guarantees, unless excludable because they encroach upon the limited area of more important interests."

He gives stern warning that no publication advancing such ideas can be suppressed under the guise of regulation of public morals or censorship of public reading matter. As he says (354 U.S. at page 488, 77 S.Ct. at page 1311):

"The fundamental freedoms of speech and press have contributed greatly to the development and well-being of our free society and are indispensable to its continued growth. Ceaseless vigilance is the watchword to prevent their erosion by Congress or by the States. The door barring federal and state intrusion into this area cannot be left ajar; it must be kept tightly closed and opened only the slightest crack necessary to prevent encroachment upon more important interests."

It was against the background of these constitutional requirements that the Court laid down general standards for judging obscenity, recognizing that it was "vital that [such] standards * * * safeguard the protection of freedom of speech and press for material which does not treat sex" in an obscene manner. The standards were "whether to the average person, applying contemporary community standards, the dominant theme of the material taken as a whole appeals to prurient interest."

The Court did not attempt to apply these standards to a specific set of facts. It merely circumscribed and limited the excluded area in general terms.

Plainly application of these standards to specific

material may involve no little difficulty as the court was well aware. Cases involving "hard core" pornography, or what Judge Woolsey referred to as "dirt for dirt's sake,"[7] purveyed furtively by dealers in smut, are relatively simple. But works of literary merit present quite a different problem, and one which the majority in Roth did not reach as such.[8]

Chief Justice Warren, concurring in the result, said of this problem (354 U.S. at page 476, 77 S.Ct. at page 1314):

" * * * The history of the application of laws designed to suppress the obscene demonstrates convincingly that the power of government can be invoked under them against great art or literature, scientific treatises, or works exciting social controversy. Mistakes of the past prove that there is a strong countervailing interest to be considered in the freedoms guaranteed by the First and Fourteenth Amendments."

And Mr. Justice Harlan, dissenting, also deeply concerned, had this to say (354 U.S. at pages 497, 498, 77 S.Ct. at page 1315):

" * * * The suppression of a particular writing or other tangible form of expression is * * * an *individual* matter, and in the nature of things every such suppression raises an individual constitutional problem, in which a reviewing court must determine for *itself* whether the attacked expression is suppressible within constitutional standards. Since those standards do not readily lend themselves to generalized definitions, the constitutional problem in the last analysis becomes one of particularized judgments which appellate courts must make for themselves.

"I do not think that reviewing courts can escape this responsibility by saying that the trier of the facts, be it a jury or a judge, has labeled the questioned matter as 'obscene,' for, if 'obscenity' is to be suppressed, the question whether a particular work is of that character involves not really an issue of fact but a question of constitutional *judgment* of the most sensitive and delicate kind."

Mr. Justice Frankfurter, concurring in Kingsley International Pictures Corp. v. Regents, 79 S.Ct. 1362, 1369 expressed a similar view. He pointed out that in determining whether particular works are entitled to the constitutional protections of freedom of expression "We cannot escape such instance-by-instance, case-by-case * * * [constitutional adjudication] in all the variety of situations that come before this Court." And Mr. Justice Harlan, in the same case, also concurring in the result, speaks of "the necessity for individualized adjudication. In the very nature of things the problems in this area are ones of individual cases * * *." These views are not inconsistent with the decisions of the majority determining both Roth and Kingsley upon broader constitutional grounds.

It would seem that the Court itself made such "individualized" or "case by case" adjudications as to the obscenity of specific material in at least two cases following Roth. In One, Inc. v. Olesen, 355 U.S. 371, 78 S.Ct. 364, 2 L.Ed.2d 352 and Sunshine Book Co. v. Summerfield, 355 U.S. 372, 78 S.Ct. 365, 2 L.Ed.2d 352, the courts below had found in no uncertain terms that the material was obscene within the meaning of Section 1461.[9] In each case the Supreme Court in a one sentence per curiam opinion granted certiorari and reversed on the authority of Roth.

One, Inc. v. Olesen, and Sunshine Book Co. v. Summerfield, involved determinations by the Post Office barring material from the mails on the ground that it was obscene. In both the District Court had found that the publication was obscene and that the determination of the Post Office should be upheld. In both the Court of Appeals had affirmed the findings of the District Court.

Yet in each the Supreme Court, without discussion, summarily reversed on the authority of Roth. As Judge Desmond of the New York Court of Appeals said of these cases—"Presumably, the court having looked at those books simply held them not to be obscene."[10]

It is no less the duty of this court in the case at bar to scrutinize the book with great care and to determine for itself whether it is within the constitutional protections afforded by the First Amendment, or whether it may be excluded from those protections because it is obscene under the Roth tests.

(2) Such review is quite consistent with the Administrative Procedure Act (5 U.S.C.A. § 1001 et seq.), assuming that the act is applicable here.

This is not a case where the agency determination under review is dependent on "a fair estimate of the worth of the testimony of witnesses or its informed judgment on matters within its special competence or both." See Universal Camera Corp. v. National Labor Board, 340 U.S. 474, 490, 71 S.Ct. 456, 95 L.Ed. 456. Cf. O'Leary v. Brown-Pacific-Maxon, 340 U.S. 504, 71 S.Ct. 470, 95 L.Ed. 483; Gooding v. Willard, 2 Cir., 209 F. 2d 913.

There were no disputed facts before the Postmaster General. The facts as to the mailings and the detainer were stipulated and the only issue before him was whether "Lady Chatterley's Lover" was obscene.

The complainant relied on the text of the novel and nothing more to establish obscenity. Respondents' evidence was wholly uncontradicted, and, except for the opinions of the critics Cowley and Kazin as to the effect of the book upon its readers, it scarcely could have been. The complainant conceded that the book had literary merit. The views of the critics as to the place of the novel and its author in twentieth century English literature have not been questioned.

As the Postmaster General said, he attempted to apply to the book "the tests which, it is my understanding, the courts have established for determining questions of obscenity." Thus, all he did was to apply the statute, as he interpreted it in the light of the decisions, to the book. His interpretation and application of the statute involved questions of law, not questions of fact.

The Postmaster General has no special competence or technical knowledge on this subject which qualifies him to render an informed judgment entitled to special weight in the courts. There is no parallel here to determinations of such agencies as the Interstate Commerce Commission, the Securities and Exchange Commission, the National Labor Relations Board, the Federal Communications Commission, the Federal Power Commission, or many others on highly technical and complicated subject matter upon which they have specialized knowledge and are particularly qualified to speak.

No doubt the Postmaster General has similar qualifications on many questions involving the administration of the Post Office Department, the handling of the mails, postal rates and other matters. See Bates & Guild Co. v. Payne, 194 U.S. 106, 24 S.Ct. 595,

48 L.Ed. 894. But he has no special competence to determine what constitutes obscenity within the meaning of Section 1461, or that "contemporary community standards are not such that this book should be allowed to be transmitted in the mails" or that the literary merit of the book is outweighed by its pornographic features, as he found. Such questions involve interpretation of a statute, which also imposes criminal penalties, and its application to the allegedly offending material. The determination of such questions is peculiarly for the courts, particularly in the light of the constitutional questions implicit in each case.[11]

It has been suggested that the court cannot interfere with the order of the Postmaster General unless it finds that he abused his discretion. But it does not appear that the Postmaster General has been vested with "discretion" finally to determine whether a book is obscene within the meaning of the statute.

It is unnecessary to pass on the questions posed by the plaintiffs as to whether the Postmaster General has any power to impose prior restraints upon the mailing of matter allegedly obscene and whether the enforcement of the statute is limited to criminal proceedings, though it seems to me that these questions are not free from doubt.[12]

Assuming power in the Postmaster General to withhold obscene matter from dispatch in the mails temporarily, a grant of discretion to make a final determination as to whether a book is obscene and should be denied to the public should certainly not be inferred in the absence of a clear and direct mandate. As the Supreme Court pointed out under comparable circumstances in Hannegan v. Esquire, Inc., 327 U.S. 146, 151, 66 S.Ct. 456, 459, 90 L.Ed. 586, to vest such power in the Postmaster General would, in effect, give him the power of censorship and that "is so abhorrent to our traditions that a purpose to grant it should not be easily inferred."

No such grant of power to the Postmaster General has been called to my attention and I have found none.[13] Whatever administrative functions the Postmaster General has go no further than closing the mails to material which is obscene within the meaning of the statute. This is not an area in which the Postmaster General has any "discretion" which is entitled to be given special weight by the courts.[14]

The Administrative Procedure Act makes the reviewing court responsible for determining all relevant questions of law, for interpreting and applying all constitutional and statutory provisions and for setting aside agency action not in accordance with law. 5 U.S.C.A. § 1009. The question presented here falls within this framework.

Thus, the question presented for decision is whether "Lady Chatterley's Lover" is obscene within the meaning of the statute and thus excludable from constitutional protections. I will now consider that question.

II

This unexpurgated edition of "Lady Chatterley's Lover" has never before been published either in the United States or England, though comparatively small editions were published by Lawrence himself in Italy and authorized for publication in France, and a number of pirated copies found their way to this country.

Grove Press is a reputable publisher with a good list which includes a number of distinguished writers and serious works. Before publishing this edition Grove consulted recognized literary critics and authorities on English literature as to the advisability of publication. All were of the view that the work was of major literary importance and should be made available to the American public.

No one is naive enough to think that Grove Press did not expect to profit from the book. Nevertheless the format and composition of the volume, the advertising and promotional material and the whole approach to publication, treat the book as a serious work of literature. The book is distributed through leading bookstores throughout the country. There has been no attempt by the publisher to appeal to prurience or the prurient minded.

The Grove edition has a preface by Archibald MacLeish, former Librarian of Congress, Pulitzer Prize winner, and one of this country's most distinguished poets and literary figures, giving his appraisal of the novel. There follows an introduction by Mark Schorer, Professor of English Literature at the University of California, a leading scholar of D. H. Lawrence and his work. The introduction is a critique of the novel against the background of Lawrence's life, work and philosophy. At the end of the novel there is a bibliographical note as to the circumstances under which it was written and first published. Thus, the novel is placed in a setting which emphasizes its literary qualities and its place as a significant work of a major English novelist.

Readers' Subscription has handled the book in the same vein. The relatively small number of Readers' Subscription subscribers is composed largely of people in academic, literary and scholarly fields. Its list of books includes works of high literary merit, including books by and about D. H. Lawrence.

There is nothing of "the leer of the sensualist"[15] in the promotion or methods of distribution of this book. There is no suggestion of any attempt to pander to the lewd and lascivious minded for profit. The facts are all to the contrary.

Publication met with unanimous critical approval. The book was favorably received by the literary critics of such diverse publications as the New York Times, the Chicago Tribune, the San Francisco Call Bulletin, the New York Post, the New York Herald Tribune, Harpers and Time, to mention only some. The critics were not agreed upon their appraisal. Critical comment ranged from acclaim on the one hand to more restrained views that this was not the best of Lawrence's writing, and was dated and in parts "wooden". But as MacLeish says in the preface,

" * * * in spite of these reservations no responsible critic would deny the book a place as one of the most important works of fiction of the century, and no reader of any kind could undertake to express an opinion about the literature of the time or about the spiritual history that literature expresses without making his peace in one way or another with D. H. Lawrence and with this work."

Publication of the Grove edition was a major literary event. It was greeted by editorials in leading newspapers throughout the country unanimously approving the publication and viewing with alarm possible attempts to ban the book.

It was against this background that the New York Postmaster impounded the book and the Postmaster General barred it. The decision of the Postmaster General, in a brief four pages, relied on three cases, Roth v. United States, supra; United States v. One Book Called "Ulysses", D.C.S.D.N.Y., 5 F.Supp. 182, affirmed 2 Cir., 72 F.2d 705, and Besig v. United States, 9 Cir., 208 F.2d 142. While he quotes from Roth the Postmaster General relies principally on Besig, which was not reviewed by the Supreme Court. It may be noted that the Ninth Circuit relied heavily on Besig in One Book, Inc. v. Olesen, supra, which was summarily reversed by the Supreme Court on the authority of Roth.

He refers to the book as "currently withheld from the mails in the United States and barred from the mails by several other major nations." His only discussion of its content is as follows:

"The contemporary community standards are not such that this book should be allowed to be transmitted in the mails.

"The book is replete with descriptions in minute detail of sexual acts engaged in or discussed by the book's principal characters. These descriptions utilize filthy, offensive and degrading words and terms. Any literary merit the book may have is far outweighed by the pornographic and smutty passages and words, so that the book, taken as a whole, is an obscene and filthy work.

"I therefore see no need to modify or reverse the prior rulings of this Department and the Department of the Treasury with respect to this edition of this book."[16]

This seems to be the first time since the notable opinions of Judge Woolsey and Judge Augustus Hand in United States v. One Book Called "Ulysses", supra, in 1934 that a book of comparable literary stature has come before the federal courts charged with violating the federal obscenity statutes. That case held that James Joyce's "Ulysses" which had been seized by the Customs under Section 305 of the Tariff Act of 1930, 19 U.S.C.A. § 1305, was not obscene within the meaning of that statute. It thoroughly discussed the standards to be applied in determining this question.

The essence of the Ulysses holding is that a work of literary merit is not obscene under federal law merely because it contains passages and language dealing with sex in a most candid and realistic fashion and uses many four-letter Anglo-Saxon words. Where a book is written with honesty and seriousness of purpose, and the portions which might be considered obscene are relevant to the theme, it is not condemned by the statute even though "it justly may offend many." "Ulysses" contains numerous passages dealing very frankly with sex and the sex act and is free in its use of four-letter Anglo-Saxon words. Yet both Judge Woolsey in the District Court, and Judge Hand in the Court of Appeals, found that it was a sincere and honest book which was not in any sense "dirt for dirt's sake."[17] They both concluded that "Ulysses" was a work of high literary merit, written by a gifted and serious writer, which did not have the dominant effect of promoting lust or prurience and therefore did not fall within the interdiction of the statute.

Roth v. United States, supra, decided by the Supreme Court in 1957, twenty-three years later, unlike the Ulysses case, did not deal with the application of the obscenity statutes to specific material. It laid down general tests circumscribing the area in which matter is excludable from constitutional protections because it is obscene, so as to avoid impingement on First Amendment guarantees.[18]

The court distilled from the prior cases (including the Ulysses case, which it cited with approval) the standards to be applied[19]—"whether to the average person, applying contemporary community standards, the dominant theme of the material taken as a whole appeals to prurient interest."

The court saw no significant difference between this expression of the standards and those in the American Law Institute Model Penal Code[20] to the effect that

" * * * A thing is obscene if, considered as a whole, its predominant appeal is to prurient interest, i.e., a shameful or morbid interest in nudity, sex, or excretion, and if it goes substantially beyond customary limits of candor in description or representation of such matters * * * ."

These standards are not materially different from those applied in Ulysses to the literary work considered there. Since the Roth case dealt with these standards for judging obscenity in general terms and the Ulysses case dealt with application of such standards to a work of recognized literary stature, the two should be read together.

A number of factors are involved in the application of these tests.

As Mr. Justice Brennan pointed out in Roth, sex and obscenity are by no means synonymous and "[t]he portrayal of sex, e. g., in art, literature and scientific works, is not in itself sufficient reason to deny material the constitutional protection of freedom of speech and press." As he said, sex has been "a subject of absorbing interest to mankind through the ages; it is one of the vital problems of human interest and public concern." The subject may be discussed publicly and truthfully without previous restraint or fear of subsequent punishment as long as it does not fall within the narrowly circumscribed interdicted area.

Both cases held that, to be obscene, the dominant effect of the book must be an appeal to prurient interest—that is to say, shameful or morbid interest in sex. Such a theme must so predominate as to submerge any ideas of "redeeming social importance" which the publication contains.

It is not the effect upon the irresponsible, the immature or the sensually minded which is controlling. The material must be judged in terms of its effect on those it is likely to reach who are conceived of as the average man of normal sensual impulses,[21] or, as Judge Woolsey says, "what the French would call l'homme moyen sensuel." [5 F.Supp.184.]

The material must also exceed the limits of tolerance imposed by current standards of the community with respect to freedom of expression in matters concerning sex and sex relations. Moreover, a book is not to be judged by excerpts or individual passages but must be judged as a whole.

All of these factors must be present before a book can be held obscene and thus outside constitutional protections.

Judged by these standards, "Lady Chatterley's Lover" is not obscene. The decision of the Postmaster General that it is obscene and therefore non-mailable is contrary to law and clearly erroneous. This is emphasized when the book is considered against its background and in the light of its stature as a significant work of a distinguished English novelist.

D. H. Lawrence is one of the most important novelists writing in the English language in this century. Whether he is, as some authorities say, the greatest English novelist since Joseph Conrad, or one of a number of major figures, makes little difference. He was a writer of great gifts and of undoubted artistic integrity.

The text of this edition of "Lady Chatterley's Lover" was written by Lawrence toward the close of his life and was his third version of the novel, originally called "Tenderness".

The book is almost as much a polemic as a novel.

In it Lawrence was expressing his deep and bitter dissatisfaction with what he believed were the stultifying effects of advancing industrialization and his own somewhat obscure philosophic remedy of a return to "naturalness". He attacks what he considered to be the evil effects of industrialization upon the wholesome and natural life of all classes in England. In his view this was having disastrous consequences on English society and on the English countryside. It had resulted in devitalization of the upper classes of society and debasement of the lower classes. One result, as he saw it, was the corrosion of both the emotional and physical sides of man as expressed in his sexual relationships which had become increasingly artificial and unwholesome.

The novel develops the contrasts and conflicts in characters under these influences.

The plot is relatively simple.

Constance Chatterly is married to a baronet, returned from the first world war paralyzed from the waist down. She is physically frustrated and dissatisfied with the artificiality and sterility of her life and of the society in which she moves. Her husband, immersed in himself, seeks compensation for his own frustrations in the writing of superficial and brittle fiction and in the exploitation of his coal mining properties, a symbol of the creeping industrial blight. Failing to find satisfaction in an affair with a man in her husband's circle, Constance Chatterley finds herself increasingly restless and unhappy. Her husband half-heartedly urges her to have a child by another man whom he will treat as his heir. Repelled by the suggestion that she casually beget a child, she is drawn to Mellors, the gamekeeper, sprung from the working class who, having achieved a measure of spiritual and intellectual independence, is a prototype of Lawrence's natural man. They establish a deeply passionate and tender relationship which is described at length and in detail. At the conclusion she is pregnant and plans to obtain a divorce and marry the gamekeeper.

This plot serves as a vehicle through which Lawrence develops his basic theme of contrast between his own philosophy and the sterile and debased society which he attacks. Most of the characters are prototypes. The plot and theme are meticulously worked out with honesty and sincerity.

The book is replete with fine writing and with descriptive passages of rare beauty. There is no doubt of its literary merit.

It contains a number of passages describing sexual intercourse in great detail with complete candor and realism. Four-letter Anglo-Saxon words are used with some frequency.

These passages and this language understandably will shock the sensitive minded. Be that as it may, these passages are relevant to the plot and to the development of the characters and of their lives as Lawrence unfolds them. The language which shocks, except in a rare instance or two, is not inconsistent with character, situation or theme.

Even if it be assumed that these passages and this language taken in isolation tend to arouse shameful, morbid and lustful sexual desires in the average reader, they are an integral, and to the author a necessary[22] part of the development of theme, plot and character. The dominant theme, purpose and effect of the book as a whole is not an appeal to prurience or the prurient minded. The book is not "dirt for dirt's sake".[23] Nor do these passages and this language submerge the dominant theme so as to make the book obscene even if they could be considered and found to be obscene in isolation.

What the Postmaster General seems to have done is precisely what the Supreme Court in Roth and the courts in the Ulysses case said ought not to be done. He has lifted from the novel individual passages and language, found them to be obscene in isolation and therefore condemned the book as a whole. He has disregarded the dominant theme and effect of the book and has read these passages and this language as if they were separable and could be taken out of context. Thus he has "weighted" the isolated passages which he considered obscene against the remainder of the book and concluded that the work as a whole must be condemned.

Writing about sex is not in itself pornographic, as the Postmaster General recognized. Nor does the fact that sex is a major theme of a book condemn the book as obscene. Neither does the use of "four letter" words, despite the offense they may give. "Ulysses" was found not to be obscene despite long passages containing similar descriptions and language. As Judge Woolsey said there (5 F.Supp. at pages 183, 184):

"The words which are criticized as dirty are old Saxon words known to almost all men and, I venture, to many women, and are such words as would be naturally and habitually used, I believe, by the types of folk whose life, physical and mental, Joyce is seeking to describe."

Such words "are, almost without exception of honest Anglo-Saxon ancestry and were not invented for purely scatological effect."[24]

The tests of obscenity are not whether the book or passages from it are in bad taste or shock or offend the sensibilities of an individual, or even of a substantial segment of the community. Nor are we concerned with whether the community would approve of Constance Chatterley's morals. The statute does not purport to regulate the morals portrayed or the ideas expressed in a novel, whether or not they are contrary to the accepted moral code, nor could it constitutionally do so. Kingsley International Pictures v. Regents, supra.

Plainly "Lady Chatterley's Lover" is offensive to the Postmaster General, and I respect his personal views. As a matter of personal opinion I disagree with him for I do not personally find the book offensive.

But the personal views of neither of us are controlling here. The standards for determining what constitutes obscenity under this statute have been laid down. These standards must be objectively applied regardless of personal predilections.

There has been much discussion of the intent and purpose of Lawrence in writing Lady Chatterley. It is suggested that the intent and purpose of the author has no relevance to the question as to whether his work is obscene and must be disregarded.

No doubt an author may write a clearly obscene book in the mistaken belief that he is serving a high moral purpose. The fact that this is the author's purpose does not redeem the book from obscenity.

But the sincerity and honesty of purpose of an author as expressed in the manner in which a book is written and in which his theme and ideas are developed has a great deal to do with whether it is of literary and intellectual merit. Here, as in the Ulysses case, there is no question about Lawrence's honesty and sincerity of purpose, artistic integrity and lack of intention to appeal to prurient interest.

Thus, this is an honest and sincere novel of literary merit and its dominant theme and effect, taken as a whole, is not an appeal to the prurient interest of the average reader.

This would seem to end the matter. However, the Postmaster General's finding that the book is non-mailable because it offends contemporary community standards bears some discussion.

I am unable to ascertain upon what the Postmaster General based this conclusion. The record before him indicates general acceptance of the book throughout the country and nothing was shown to the contrary. The critics were unanimous. Editorial comment by leading journals of opinion welcomed the publication and decried any attempts to ban it.

It is true that the editorial comment was excluded by the Judicial Officer at the hearing. But it seems to me that this was error. These expressions were relevant and material on the question of whether the book exceeded the limits of freedom of expression in matters involving sex and sex relations tolerated by the community at large in these times.

The contemporary standards of the community and the limits of its tolerance cannot be measured or ascertained accurately. There is no poll available to determine such questions. Surely expressions by leading newspapers, with circulations of millions, are some evidence at least as to what the limits of tolerance by present day community standards are, if we must embark upon a journey of exploration into such uncharted territory.

Quite apart from this, the broadening of freedom of expression and of the frankness with which sex and sex relations are dealt with at the present time require no discussion. In one best selling novel after another frank descriptions of the sex act and "four-letter" words appear with frequency. These trends appear in all media of public expression, in the kind of language used and the subjects discussed in polite society, in pictures, advertisements and dress, and in other ways familiar to all. Much of what is now accepted would have shocked the community to the core a generation ago. Today such things are generally tolerated whether we approve or not.

I hold that, at this stage in the development of our society, this major English novel, does not exceed the outer limits of the tolerance which the community as a whole gives to writing about sex and sex relations.

One final word about the constitutional problem implicit here.

It is essential to the maintenance of a free society that the severest restrictions be placed upon restraints which may tend to prevent the dissemination of ideas.[25] It matters not whether such ideas be expressed in political pamphlets or works of political, economic or social theory or criticism, or through artistic media. All such expressions must be freely available.

A work of literature published and distributed through normal channels by a reputable publisher stands on quite a different footing from hard core pornography furtively sold for the purpose of profiting by the titillation of the dirty minded. The courts have been deeply and properly concerned about the use of obscenity statutes to suppress great works of art or literature. As Judge Augustus Hand said in Ulysses (72 F.2d at page 708):

" * * * The foolish judgments of Lord Eldon about one hundred years ago, proscribing the works of Byron and Southey, and the finding by the jury under a charge by Lord Denman that the publication of Shelley's 'Queen Mab' was an indictable offense are a warning to all who have to determine the limits of the field within which authors may exercise themselves."

To exclude this book from the mails on the grounds of obscenity would fashion a rule which could be applied to a substantial portion of the classics of our literature. Such a rule would be inimical to a free society. To interpret the obscenity statute so as to bar "Lady Chatterley's Lover" from the mails would render the statute unconstitutional in its application, in violation of the guarantees of freedom of speech and the press contained in the First Amendment.

It may be, as the plaintiffs urge, that if a work is found to be of literary stature, and not "hard core" pornography, it is *a fortiori* within the protections of the First Amendment. But I do not reach that question here. For I find that "Lady Chatterley's Lover" is not obscene within the meaning of 18 U.S.C. § 1461, and is entitled to the protections guaranteed to freedoms of speech and press by the First Amendment. I therefore hold that the order of the Postmaster General is illegal and void and violates plaintiffs' rights in contravention of the Constitution.

NOTES

1. The relevant portions of § 1461 provide: "Every obscene, lewd, lascivious, indecent, filthy or vile article * * * and

"Every written or printed * * * circular. * * * or notice of any kind giving information * * * where, or how, or from whom * * * any of such * * * articles * * * may be obtained * * *.

"Is declared to be nonmailable matter and shall not be conveyed in the mails or delivered from any post office or by any letter carrier."

The statute provides penalties for violation of up to five years imprisonment and a maximum fine of $5,000 for a first offense and up to ten years' imprisonment and a maximum $10,000 fine for subsequent offenses.

2. Plaintiffs originally moved for a preliminary injunction but that motion is moot in the present posture of the case.

3. The Judicial Officer heard the case pursuant to a stipulation between the parties which had the effect of obviating the requirement that the case be heard by an independent Hearing Examiner. See Borg-Johnson Electronics, Inc. v. Christenberry, D.C.S.D.N.Y., 169 F.Supp. 746.

4. This referral was made pursuant to paragraph III (b) 23 F.R. 2817, which provides certain "Decisions and orders of the Judicial Officer * * * shall be the final departmental decision * * * except that the Judicial Officer may refer any proceeding to * * * the Postmaster General * * * for final decision." The order of the Judicial Officer making the referral said:

"The complainant alleges that the book 'Lady Chatterley's Lover' is obscene and nonmailable under 18 U.S.C. 1461 and that the circular of Readers' Subscription, Inc. gives information as to where obscenity may be obtained.

The complainant admits that the novel has literary merit but claims that the obscene passages outweigh the literary merit.

"The book at issue, which is the unexpurgated version has for many years been held to be nonmailable by the Post Office Department and non-importable by the Bureau of Customs of the Department of the Treasury. To hold the book to be mailable matter would require a reversal of rulings of long standing by this Department and to cast doubt on the rulings of a coordinate executive department."

5. I use the word "obscene" as covering the words "obscene, lewd, lascivious, indecent, filthy or vile" as used in the statute in so far as they may be applicable to this book.

6. The court expressly limited its grant of certiorari to constitutional questions concerning the validity of Section 1461 on its face, and thus was not concerned with the specific facts of the case. Roth v. United States, 352 U.S. 964, 77 S.Ct. 1304, 1309, 1 L.Ed.2d 319.

7. United States v. One Book Called "Ulysses", D.C.S.D.N.Y., 5 F.Supp. 182, 184, affirmed, 2 Cir., 72 F.2d 705.

8. "No issue is presented * * * concerning the obscenity of the material involved." Footnote 8, 354 U.S. at page 481, 77 S.Ct. at page 1307.

9. One, Inc. v. Olesen, 9 Cir., 241 F.2d 772; Sunshine Book Co. v. Summerfield, D.C.D.C., 128 F.Supp 564; 101 U.S. App.D.C. 358, 249 F.2d 114.

10. Concurring in Kingsley Intern., Pictures Corp. v. Regents, 4 N.Y.2d 349, 368, 175 N.Y.S.2d 39, 54, 151 N.E.2d 197.

11. Professor Davis notes in Administrative Law Treatise, (1958) Vol. 4 § 30.07, "Substitution of judicial for administrative judgment is often rather clearly desirable, * * * [on questions] which (1) transcend the single field of the particular agency, (2) call for interpretation of the common law * * * (4) are affected substantially by constitutional considerations, whether or not a constitutional issue is directly presented, * * * (6) bring into question judge-made law previously developed in the course of statutory interpretation * * *." These criteria are all present here.

12. These questions have never been decided by the Supreme Court. The sharply divided Court of Appeals for the District of Columbia Circuit, sitting *en banc* found that the Postmaster General had such power in Sunshine Book Co. v. Summerfield, supra. But I find the dissenting opinion persuasive.

13. Even under 39 U.S.C.A. §§ 259a and 259b, which give the Postmaster General power to withhold incoming mail from a purveyor of obscenity "upon evidence satisfactory" to him, an application to the District Court is required within twenty days for a determination, inter alia. as to whether the detention is reasonable or necessary. This is in contrast to Section 1461, included in the Criminal Code, where no such statutory scheme is provided.

14. The defendant cites language to indicate that the question of whether material is obscene is committed to agency discretion. One line of cases deals with "fraud orders". (39 U.S.C.A. § 259.) Fraud is almost always a question of fact and Section 259 provides that the Postmaster General may deny the mails "upon evidence satisfactory to him." Such cases as Gottlieb v. Schaffer,

D.C.S.D.N.Y., 141 F.Supp. 7, which apply the substantial evidence test to agency findings of fact under these circumstances are clearly distinguishable. See, also, Donaldson v. Read Magazine, Inc., 333 U.S. 178, 68 S.Ct. 591, 92 L.Ed. 628.

Other cases cited deal with matters requiring expert judgment in the administration of the mails. E. g., Smith v. Hitchcock, 226 U.S. 53, 33 S.Ct. 6, 57 L.Ed. 119.

Cases cited involving obscenity while referring to "administrative discretion" considered the facts. In Glanzman v. Christenberry, D.C.S.D.N.Y.1958, 175 F.Supp. 485, Judge Dimock found the material clearly obscene. It was "unnecessary to seek support in the rule that an administrative determination must stand unless clearly wrong." In Anderson v. Patten, D.C.S.D.N.Y., 247 F. 382, the material, the subject matter and the treatment were salacious. In Roth v. Goldman, 2 Cir., 172 F.2d 788, 789 the materials had "little excuse for being beyond their provocative obscenity * * * ."

Monart, Inc. v. Christenberry, D.C.S.D.N.Y., 168 F.Supp. 654, was concerned only with the power of the Post Office.

These cases do not hold that a Post Office determination of obscenity is entitled to special weight.

15. Woolsey, D.J. in United States v. One Book Called "Ulysses", supra [5 F.Supp. 183].

16. The "rulings" referred to, apparently made even before the Ulysses case, were not produced at the hearing and it does not appear that they have ever seen the light of day. There is nothing in the record as to their content, the grounds on which they were based, whether whatever parties may have been involved were given a hearing, or what standards were applied. Nor is there any indication as to what "major nations" have banned the book or whether in such countries there are any constitutional or other legal protections afforded speech and press.

17. As Judge Woolsey said (5 F.Supp. at page 184): "Each word of the book contributes like a bit of mosaic to the detail of the picture which Joyce is seeking to construct for his readers."

18. There was no question but that the material involved in Roth was hard core pornography and that the defendants were engaged "in the commercial exploitation of the morbid and shameful craving for materials with prurient effect." (354 U.S. at page 496, 77 S.Ct. at page 1315.)

19. For a comprehensive review of the prior material see Judge Frank's provocative concurring opinion in the Court of Appeals which points to problems in this field still unresolved. United States v. Roth, 2 Cir., 237 F.2d 796, 801.

20. § 207.10(2), Tent.Draft No. 6, 1957.

21. See Volanski v. United States, 6 Cir., 246 F.2d 842.

22. See D. H. Lawrence, "Sex Literature and Censorship." (Twayne Publishers, 1953), p. 89. Essay "A Propos of Lady Chatterley's Lover."

23. As Mr. Justice Frankfurter pointed out in Kingsley International Pictures Corp. v. Regents, supra, Lawrence "knew there was such a thing as pornography, dirt for dirt's sake, or, to be more accurate, dirt for money's sake. This is what D. H. Lawrence wrote:

" 'But even I would censor genuine pornography, rigorously. It would not be very difficult. In the first place, genuine pornography is almost always underworld, it doesn't come into the open. In the second, you can recognize it by the insult it offers invariably, to sex, and to the human spirit.

" 'Pornography is the attempt to insult sex, to do dirt on it. This is unpardonable. Take the very lowest instance, the picture post-card sold underhand, by the underworld, in most cities. What I have seen of them have been of an ugliness to make you cry. The insult to the human body, the insult to a vital human relationship! Ugly and cheap they make the human nudity, ugly and degraded they make the sexual act, trivial and cheap and nasty.' (D. H. Lawrence, Pornography and Obscenity, p. 13.)" Collected in Lawrence "Sex Literature and Censorship", supra, p. 69 [79 S.Ct. 1367].

24. Judge Bok in Commonwealth v. Gordon, 66 Pa.Dist. & Co.R. 101, 114.

25. It should be noted that if the book is obscene within § 1461 and thus barred from the mails it is a crime to ship it by express or in interstate commerce generally under 18 U.S.C. §§ 1462, 1465, and it would be subject to seizure by the customs authorities if imported for sale. 19 U.S.C.A. § 1305.

JOHN CLELAND'S *MEMOIRS OF A WOMAN OF PLEASURE (FANNY HILL)* HAS "REDEEMING SOCIAL IMPORTANCE" AND IS NOT OBSCENE

Memoirs v. Massachusetts, 383 U.S. 413 (1966)

MR. JUSTICE BRENNAN announced the judgment of the Court and delivered an opinion in which THE CHIEF JUSTICE and MR. JUSTICE FORTAS join.

This is an obscenity case in which *Memoirs of a Woman of Pleasure* (commonly known as *Fanny Hill*), written by John Cleland in about 1750, was adjudged obscene in a proceeding that put on trial the book itself, and not its publisher or distributor. The proceeding was a civil equity suit brought by the Attorney General of Massachusetts, pursuant to General Laws of Massachusetts, Chapter 272, §§ 28C–28H, to have the book declared obscene.[1] Section 28C requires that the petition commencing the suit be "directed against [the] book by name" and that an order to show cause "why said book should not be judicially determined to be obscene" be published in a daily newspaper and sent by registered mail "to all persons interested in the publication." Publication of the order in this case occurred in a Boston daily newspaper, and a copy of the order was sent by registered mail to G. P. Putnam's Sons, alleged to be the publisher and copyright holder of the book.

As authorized by § 28D, G. P. Putnam's Sons intervened in the proceedings in behalf of the book, but it did not claim the right provided by that section to have the issue of obscenity tried by a jury. At the hearing before a justice of the Superior Court, which was conducted, under § 28F, "in accordance with the usual course of proceedings in equity," the court received the book in evidence and also, as allowed by the section, heard the testimony of experts[2] and accepted other evidence, such

as book reviews, in order to assess the literary, cultural, or educational character of the book. This constituted the entire evidence, as neither side availed itself of the opportunity provided by the section to introduce evidence "as to the manner and form of its publication, advertisement, and distribution."[3] The trial justice entered a final decree, which adjudged *Memoirs* obscene and declared that the book "is not entitled to the protection of the First and Fourteenth Amendments to the Constitution of the United States against action by the Attorney General or other law enforcement officer pursuant to the provisions of . . . § 28B, or otherwise."[4] The Massachusetts Supreme Judicial Court affirmed the decree. 349 Mass. 69, 206 N. E. 2d 403 (1965). We noted probable jurisdiction. 382 U. S. 900. We reverse.[5]

I.

The term "obscene" appearing in the Massachusetts statute has been interpreted by the Supreme Judicial Court to be as expansive as the Constitution permits: the "statute covers all material that is obscene in the constitutional sense." *Attorney General* v. *The Book Named "Tropic of Cancer,"* 345 Mass. 11, 13, 184 N. E. 2d 328, 330 (1962). Indeed, the final decree before us equates the finding that *Memoirs* is obscene within the meaning of the statute with the declaration that the book is not entitled to the protection of the First Amendment.[6] Thus the sole question before the state courts was whether *Memoirs* satisfies the test of obscenity established in *Roth* v. *United States*, 354 U. S. 476.

We defined obscenity in *Roth* in the following terms: "[W]hether to the average person, applying contemporary community standards, the dominant theme of the material taken as a whole appeals to prurient interest." 354 U. S., at 489. Under this definition, as elaborated in subsequent cases, three elements must coalesce: it must be established that (a) the dominant theme of the material taken as a whole appeals to a prurient interest in sex; (b) the material is patently offensive because it affronts contemporary community standards relating to the description or representation of sexual matters; and (c) the material is utterly without redeeming social value.

The Supreme Judicial Court purported to apply the *Roth* definition of obscenity and held all three criteria satisfied. We need not consider the claim that the court erred in concluding that *Memoirs* satisfied the prurient appeal and patent offensiveness criteria; for reversal is required because the court misinterpreted the social value criterion. The court applied the criterion in this passage:

"It remains to consider whether the book can be said to be 'utterly without social importance.' We are mindful that there was expert testimony, much of which was strained, to the effect that Memoirs is a structural novel with literary merit; that the book displays a skill in characterization and a gift for comedy; that it plays a part in the history of the development of the English novel; and that it contains a moral, namely, that sex with love is superior to sex in a brothel. But the fact that the testimony may indicate this book has some minimal literary value does not mean it is of any social importance. We do not interpret the 'social importance' test as requiring that a book which appeals to prurient interest and is patently offensive must be unqualifiedly worthless before it can be deemed obscene." 349 Mass., at 73, 206 N. E. 2d, at 406.

The Supreme Judicial Court erred in holding that a book need not be "unqualifiedly worthless before it can be deemed obscene." A book cannot be proscribed unless it is found to be *utterly* without redeeming social value. This is so even though the book is found to possess the requisite prurient appeal and to be patently offensive. Each of the three federal constitutional criteria is to be applied independently; the social value of the book can neither be weighed against nor canceled by its prurient appeal or patent offensiveness.[7] Hence, even on the view of the court below that *Memoirs* possessed only a modicum of social value, its judgment must be reversed as being founded on an erroneous interpretation of a federal constitutional standard.

II.

It does not necessarily follow from this reversal that a determination that *Memoirs* is obscene in the constitutional sense would be improper under all circumstances. On the premise, which we have no occasion to assess, that *Memoirs* has the requisite prurient appeal and is patently offensive, but has only a minimum of social value, the circumstances of production, sale, and publicity are relevant in determining whether or not the publication or distribution of the book is constitutionally protected. Evidence that the book was commercially exploited for the sake of prurient appeal, to the exclusion of all other values, might justify the conclusion that the book was utterly without redeeming social importance. It is not that in such a setting the social value test is relaxed so as to dispense with the requirement that a book be *utterly* devoid of social value, but rather that, as we elaborate in *Ginzburg* v. *United States, post,* pp. 470–473, where the purveyor's sole emphasis is on the sexually provocative aspects of his publications, a court could accept his evaluation at its face value. In this proceeding, however, the courts were asked to judge the obscenity of *Memoirs* in the abstract, and the declaration of obscenity was neither aided nor limited by a specific set of circumstances of production, sale, and publicity.[8] All possible uses of the book must therefore be considered, and the mere risk that the book might be exploited by panderers because it so pervasively treats sexual matters cannot alter the fact—given the view of the Massachusetts court attributing to *Memoirs* a modicum of literary and historical value—that the book will have redeeming social importance in the hands of those who publish or distribute it on the basis of that value.

Reversed.

Mr. Justice Black and Mr. Justice Stewart concur in the reversal for the reasons stated in their respective dissenting opinions in *Ginzburg* v. *United States, post,* p. 476 and p. 497, and *Mishkin* v. *New York, post,* p. 515 and p. 518.

APPENDIX TO OPINION OF MR. JUSTICE BRENNAN.

State Statute.

Massachusetts General Laws, Chapter 272.

Section 28B. Whoever imports, prints, publishes, sells, loans or distributes, or buys, procures, receives, or has in his possession for the purpose of sale, loan or distribution, a book, knowing it to be obscene, indecent or impure, or whoever, being a wholesale distributor, a jobber, or publisher sends or delivers to a retail storekeeper a book, pamphlet, magazine or other form of printed or written material, knowing it to be obscene, indecent or impure, which said storekeeper had not previously ordered in writing, specifying the title and quantity of such publication he desired, shall be punished by imprisonment in the state prison for not more than five years or in a jail or house of correction for not more than two and one half years, or by a fine of not less than one hundred dollars nor more than five thousand dollars, or by both such fine and imprisonment in jail or the house of correction.

Section 28C. Whenever there is reasonable cause to believe that a book which is being imported, sold, loaned or distributed, or is in the possession of any person who intends to import, sell, loan or distribute the same, is obscene, indecent or impure, the attorney general, or any district attorney within his district, shall bring an information or petition in equity in the superior court directed against said book by name. Upon the filing of such information or petition in equity, a justice of the superior court shall, if, upon a summary examination of the book, he is of opinion that there is reasonable cause to believe that such book is obscene, indecent or impure, issue an order of notice, returnable in or within thirty days, directed against such book by name and addressed to all persons interested in the publication, sale, loan or distribution thereof, to show cause why said book should not be judicially determined to be obscene, indecent or impure. Notice of such order shall be given by publication once each week for two successive weeks in a daily newspaper published in the city of Boston and, if such information or petition be filed in any county other than Suffolk county, then by publication also in a daily newspaper published in such other county. A copy of such order of notice shall be sent by registered mail to the publisher of said book, to the person holding the copyrights, and to the author, in case the names of any such persons appear upon said book, fourteen days at least before the return day of such order of notice. After the issuance of an order of notice under the provisions of this section, the court shall, on motion of the attorney general or district attorney, make an interlocutory finding and adjudication that said book is obscene, indecent or impure, which finding and adjudication shall be of the same force and effect as the final finding and adjudication provided in section twenty-eight E or section twenty-eight F, but only until such final finding and adjudication is made or until further order of the court.

Section 28D. Any person interested in the sale, loan or distribution of said book may appear and file an answer on or before the return day named in said notice or within such further time as the court may allow, and may claim a right to trial by jury on the issue whether said book is obscene, indecent or impure.

Section 28E. If no person appears and answers within the time allowed, the court may at once upon motion of the petitioner, or of its own motion, no reason to the contrary appearing, order a general default and if the court finds that the book is obscene, indecent or impure, may make an adjudication against the book that the same is obscene, indecent and impure.

SECTION 28F. If an appearance is entered and answer filed, the case shall be set down for speedy hearing, but a default and order shall first be entered against all persons who have not appeared and answered, in the manner provided in section twenty-eight E. Such hearing shall be conducted in accordance with the usual course of proceedings in equity including all rights of exception and appeal. At such hearing the court may receive the testimony of experts and may receive evidence as to the literary, cultural or educational character of said book and as to the manner and form of its publication, advertisement, and distribution. Upon such hearing, the court may make an adjudication in the manner provided in said section twenty-eight E.

SECTION 28G. An information or petition in equity under the provisions of section twenty-eight C shall not be open to objection on the ground that a mere judgment, order or decree is sought thereby and that no relief is or could be claimed thereunder on the issue of the defendant's knowledge as to the obscenity, indecency or impurity of the book.

SECTION 28H. In any trial under section twenty-eight B on an indictment found or a complaint made for any offence committed after the filing of a proceeding under section twenty-eight C, the fact of such filing and the action of the court or jury thereon, if any, shall be admissible in evidence. If prior to the said offence a final decree had been entered against the book, the defendant, if the book be obscene, indecent or impure, shall be conclusively presumed to have known said book to be obscene, indecent or impure, or if said decree had been in favor of the book he shall be conclusively presumed not to have known said book to be obscene, indecent or impure, or if no final decree had been entered but a proceeding had been filed prior to said offence, the defendant shall be conclusively presumed to have had knowledge of the contents of said book.

MR. JUSTICE DOUGLAS, concurring in the judgment.

Memoirs of a Woman of Pleasure, or, as it is often titled, *Fanny Hill*, concededly is an erotic novel. It was first published in about 1749 and has endured to this date, despite periodic efforts to suppress it.[1] The book relates the adventures of a young girl who becomes a prostitute in London. At the end, she abandons that life and marries her first lover, observing:

"Thus, at length, I got snug into port, where, in the bosom of virtue, I gather'd the only uncorrupt sweets: where, looking back on the course of vice I had run, and comparing its infamous blandishments with the infinitely superior joys of innocence, I could not help pitying, even in point of taste, those who, immers'd in gross sensuality, are insensible to the so delicate charms of VIRTUE, than which even PLEASURE has not a greater friend, nor than VICE a greater enemy. Thus temperance makes men lords over those pleasures that intemperance enslaves them to: the one, parent of health, vigour, fertility, cheerfulness, and every other desirable good of life; the other, of diseases, debility, barrenness,

self-loathing, with only every evil incident to human nature.

". . . The paths of Vice are sometimes strew'd with roses, but then they are for ever infamous for many a thorn, for many a cankerworm: those of Virtue are strew'd with roses purely, and those eternally unfading ones." [2]

In 1963, an American publishing house undertook the publication of *Memoirs*. The record indicates that an unusually large number of orders were placed by universities and libraries; the Library of Congress requested the right to translate the book into Braille. But the Commonwealth of Massachusetts instituted the suit that ultimately found its way here, praying that the book be declared obscene so that the citizens of Massachusetts might be spared the necessity of determining for themselves whether or not to read it.

The courts of Massachusetts found the book "obscene" and upheld its suppression. This Court reverses, the prevailing opinion having seized upon language in the opinion of the Massachusetts Supreme Judicial Court in which it is candidly admitted that *Fanny Hill* has at least "some minimal literary value." I do not believe that the Court should decide this case on so disingenuous a basis as this. I base my vote to reverse on my view that the First Amendment does not permit the censorship of expression not brigaded with illegal action. But even applying the prevailing view of the *Roth* test, reversal is compelled by this record which makes clear that *Fanny Hill* is not "obscene." The prosecution made virtually no effort to prove that this book is "utterly without redeeming social importance." The defense, on the other hand, introduced considerable and impressive testimony to the effect that this was a work of literary, historical, and social importance.[3]

We are judges, not literary experts or historians or philosophers. We are not competent to render an independent judgment as to the worth of this or any other book, except in our capacity as private citizens. I would pair my Brother CLARK on *Fanny Hill* with the Universalist minister I quote in the Appendix. If there is to be censorship, the wisdom of experts on such matters as literary merit and historical significance must be evaluated. On this record, the Court has no choice but to reverse the judgment of the Massachusetts Supreme Judicial Court, irrespective of whether we would include *Fanny Hill* in our own libraries.

Four of the seven Justices of the Massachusetts Supreme Judicial Court conclude that *Fanny Hill* is obscene. 349 Mass. 69, 206 N. E. 2d 403. Four of the seven judges of the New York Court of Appeals conclude that it is not obscene. *Larkin* v. *Putnam's Sons*, 14 N. Y. 2d 399, 200 N. E. 2d 760. To outlaw the book on such a voting record would be to let majorities rule where minorities were thought to be supreme. The Constitution forbids abridgment of "freedom of speech, or of the press." Censorship is the most notorious form of abridgment. It substitutes majority rule where minority tastes or viewpoints were to be tolerated.

It is to me inexplicable how a book that concededly has social worth can nonetheless be banned because of the manner in which it is advertised and sold. However florid its cover, whatever the pitch of its advertisements, the contents remain the same.

Every time an obscenity case is to be argued here, my office is flooded with letters and postal cards urging me to protect the community or the Nation by striking down the publication. The messages are often identical even down to commas and semicolons. The inference is irresistible that they were all copied from a school or church blackboard. Dozens of postal cards often are mailed from the same precinct. The drives are incessant and the pressures are great. Happily we do not bow to them. I mention them only to emphasize the lack of popular understanding of our constitutional system. Publications and utterances were made immune from majoritarian control by the First Amendment, applicable to the States by reason of the Fourteenth. No exceptions were made, not even for obscenity. The Court's contrary conclusion in *Roth*, where obscenity was found to be "outside" the First Amendment, is without justification.

The extent to which the publication of "obscenity" was a crime at common law is unclear. It is generally agreed that the first reported case involving obscene conduct is *The King* v. *Sir Charles Sedley*.[4] Publication of obscene literature, at first thought to be the exclusive concern of the ecclesiastical courts,[5] was not held to constitute an indictable offense until 1727.[6] A later case involved the publication of an "obscene and impious libel" (a bawdy parody of Pope's "Essay on Man") by a member of the House of Commons.[7] On the basis of these few cases, one cannot say that the common-law doctrines with regard to publication of obscenity were anything but uncertain. "There is no definition of the term. There is no basis of identification. There is no unity in describing what is obscene literature, or in prosecuting it. There is little more than the ability to smell it." Alpert, Judicial Censorship of Obscene Literature, 52 Harv. L. Rev. 40, 47 (1938).

But even if the common law had been more fully developed at the time of the adoption of the First Amendment, we would not be justified in assuming that the Amendment left the common law unscathed. In *Bridges* v. *California*, 314 U. S. 252, 264, we said:

> "[T]o assume that English common law in this field became ours is to deny the generally accepted historical belief that 'one of the objects of the Revolution was to get rid of the English common law on liberty of speech and of the press.' Schofield, *Freedom of the Press in the United States*, 9 Publications Amer. Sociol. Soc., 67, 76.

> "More specifically, it is to forget the environment in which the First Amendment was ratified. In presenting the proposals which were later embodied in the Bill of Rights, James Madison, the leader in the preparation of the First Amendment, said: 'Although I know whenever the great rights, the trial by jury, freedom of the press, or liberty of conscience, come in question in that body [Parliament], the invasion of them is resisted by able advocates, yet their Magna Charta does not contain any one provision for the security of those rights, respecting which the people of America are most alarmed. The freedom of the press and rights of conscience, those choicest privileges of the people, are unguarded in the British Constitution.' "

And see *Grosjean* v. *American Press Co.*, 297 U. S. 233, 248–249.

It is true, as the Court observed in *Roth*, that obscenity laws appeared on the books of a handful of States at the time the First Amendment was adopted.[8] But the First Amendment was, until the adoption of the Fourteenth, a restraint only upon federal power. Moreover, there is an absence of any *federal* cases or laws relative to obscenity in the period immediately after the adoption of the First Amendment. Congress passed no legislation relating to obscenity until the middle of the nineteenth century.[9] Neither reason nor history warrants exclusion of any particular class of expression from the protection of the First Amendment on nothing more than a judgment that it is utterly without merit. We faced the difficult questions the First Amendment poses with regard to libel in *New York Times* v. *Sullivan*, 376 U. S. 254, 269, where we recognized that "libel can claim no talismanic immunity from constitutional limitations." We ought not to permit fictionalized assertions of constitutional history to obscure those questions here. Were the Court to undertake that inquiry, it would be unable, in my opinion, to escape the conclusion that no interest of society with regard to suppression of "obscene" literature could override the First Amendment to justify censorship.

The censor is always quick to justify his function in terms that are protective of society. But the First Amendment, written in terms that are absolute, deprives the States of any power to pass on the value, the propriety, or the morality of a particular expression. Cf. *Kingsley Int'l Pictures Corp.* v. *Regents*, 360 U. S. 684, 688–689; *Joseph Burstyn, Inc.* v. *Wilson*, 343 U. S. 495. Perhaps the most frequently assigned justification for censorship is the belief that erotica produce antisocial sexual conduct. But that relationship has yet to be proven.[10] Indeed, if one were to make judgments on the basis of speculation, one might guess that literature of the most pornographic sort would, in many cases, provide a substitute—not a stimulus—for antisocial sexual conduct. See Murphy, The Value of Pornography, 10 Wayne L. Rev. 655, 661 and n. 19 (1964). As I read the First Amendment, judges cannot gear the literary diet of an entire nation to whatever tepid stuff is incapable of triggering the most demented mind. The First Amendment demands more than a horrible example or two of the perpetrator of a crime of sexual violence, in whose pocket is found a pornographic book, before it allows the Nation to be saddled with a regime of censorship.[11]

Whatever may be the reach of the power to regulate *conduct*, I stand by my view in *Roth* v. *United States*, *supra*, that the First Amendment leaves no power in government over *expression of ideas*.

APPENDIX TO OPINION OF MR. JUSTICE DOUGLAS, CONCURRING.

DR. PEALE AND FANNY HILL.

An Address by
Rev. John R. Graham, First Universalist Church of Denver.

December 1965.

. . . . . .

At the present point in the twentieth century, it seems

to me that there are two books which symbolize the human quest for what is moral. *Sin, Sex and Self-Control* by Dr. Norman Vincent Peale, the well-known clergyman of New York City, portrays the struggle of contemporary middle-class society to arrive at a means of stabilizing behavior patterns. At the same time, there is a disturbing book being sold in the same stores with Dr. Peale's volume. It is a seventeenth century English novel by John Cleland and it is known as *Fanny Hill: The Memoirs of a Woman of Pleasure.*

Quickly, it must be admitted that it appears that the two books have very little in common. One was written in a day of scientific and technological sophistication, while the other is over two hundred years old. One is acclaimed in the pulpit, while the other is protested before the United States Supreme Court. *Sin, Sex and Self-Control* is authored by a Christian pastor, while *Fanny Hill* represents thoughts and experiences of a common prostitute. As far as the general public seems to be concerned, one is moral and the other is hopelessly immoral. While Dr. Peale is attempting to redeem the society, most people believe that *Fanny Hill* can only serve as another instance in an overall trend toward an immoral social order. Most parents would be pleased to find their children reading a book by Dr. Peale, but I am afraid that the same parents would be sorely distressed to discover a copy of *Fanny Hill* among the school books of their offspring.

Although one would not expect to find very many similarities between the thoughts of a pastor and those of a prostitute, the subject matter of the two books is, in many ways, strangely similar. While the contents are radically different, the concerns are the same. Both authors deal with human experience. They are concerned with people and what happens to them in the world in which they live each day. But most significantly of all, both books deal with the age-old question of "What is moral?" I readily admit that this concern with the moral is more obvious in Dr. Peale's book than it is in the one by John Cleland. The search for the moral in *Fanny Hill* is clothed in erotic passages which seem to equate morality with debauchery as far as the general public is concerned. At the same time, Dr. Peale's book is punctuated with such noble terms as "truth," "love," and "honesty."

These two books are not very important in themselves. They may or may not be great literature. Whether they will survive through the centuries to come is a question, although John Cleland has an historical edge on Norman Vincent Peale! However, in a symbolic way they do represent the struggle of the moral quest and for this reason they are important.

Dr. Peale begins his book with an analysis of contemporary society in terms of the moral disorder which is more than obvious today. He readily admits that the traditional Judeo-Christian standards of conduct and behavior no longer serve as strong and forceful guides. He writes:

> "For more than forty years, ever since my ordination, I had been preaching that if a person would surrender to Jesus Christ and adopt strong affirmative attitudes toward life he would be able to live abundantly and triumphantly. I was still absolutely convinced that this was true. But I was also bleakly aware that the whole trend in the seventh decade of the twentieth century seemed to be away from the principles and practices of religion—not toward them." (Page 1.)

Dr. Peale then reflects on the various changes that have taken place in our day and suggests that although he is less than enthusiastic about the loss of allegiance to religion, he is, nevertheless, willing to recognize that one cannot live by illusion.

After much struggle, Dr. Peale then says that he was able to develop a new perspective on the current moral dilemma of our times. What first appeared to be disaster was really opportunity. Such an idea, coming from him, should not be very surprising, since he is more or less devoted to the concept of "positive thinking!" He concludes that our society should welcome the fact that the old external authorities have fallen. He does not believe that individuals should ever be coerced into certain patterns of behavior.

According to Dr. Peale, we live in a day of challenge. Our society has longed for a time when individuals would be disciplined by self-control, rather than being motivated by external compunction. Bravely and forthrightly, he announces that the time has now come when self-control can and must replace external authority. He is quick to add that the values contained in the Judeo-Christian tradition and "the American way of life" must never be abandoned for they emanate from the wellsprings of "Truth." What has previously been only an external force must now be internalized by individuals.

In many ways, Dr. Peale's analysis of the social situation and the solution he offers for assisting the individual to stand against the pressures of the times, come very close to the views of Sigmund Freud. He felt that society could and would corrupt the individual and, as a result, the only sure defense was a strong super-ego or conscience. This is precisely what Dr. Peale recommends.

Interestingly enough John Cleland, in *Fanny Hill*, is concerned with the same issues. Although the question of moral behavior is presented more subtly in his book, the problem with which he deals is identical. There are those who contend that the book is wholly without redeeming social importance. They feel that it appeals only to prurient interests.

I firmly believe that *Fanny Hill* is a moral, rather than an immoral, piece of literature. In fact, I will go as far as to suggest that it represents a more significant view of morality than is represented by Dr. Peale's book *Sin, Sex and Self-Control.* As is Dr. Peale, Cleland is concerned with the nature of the society and the relationship of the individual to it. *Fanny Hill* appears to me to be an allegory. In the story, the immoral becomes the moral and the unethical emerges as the ethical. Nothing is more distressing than to discover that what is commonly considered to be evil may, in reality, demonstrate characteristics of love and concern.

There is real irony in the fact that Fanny Hill, a rather naive young girl who becomes a prostitute, finds warmth, understanding and the meaning of love and faithfulness amid surroundings and situations which the society, as a whole, condemns as debased and depraved. The world outside the brothel affirms its faith in the dignity of man, but people are often treated as worthless and unimportant creatures. However, within the world of prostitution, Fanny Hill finds friendship, understanding, respect and is treated as a person of value. When her absent lover returns, she is not a lost girl of the gutter. One perceives that she is a whole and healthy person who has discovered the ability to love and be loved in a brothel.

I think Cleland is suggesting that one must be cautious about what is condemned and what is held in honor. From Dr. Peale's viewpoint, the story of Fanny Hill is a tragedy because she did not demonstrate self-control. She refused to internalize the values inherent in the Judeo-Christian tradition and the catalog of sexual scenes in the book, fifty-two in all, are a symbol of the debased individual and the society in which he lives.

Dr. Peale and others, would be correct in saying that Fanny Hill did not demonstrate self-control. She did, however, come to appreciate the value of self-expression. At no time were her "clients" looked upon as a means to an end. She tried and did understand them and she was concerned about them as persons. When her lover, Charles, returned she was not filled with guilt and remorse. She accepted herself as she was and was able to offer him her love and devotion.

I have a feeling that many people fear the book *Fanny Hill,* not because of its sexual scenes, but because the author raises serious question with the issue of what is moral and what is immoral. He takes exception to the idea that repression and restraint create moral individuals. He develops the thought that self-expression is more human than self-control. And he dares to suggest that, in a situation which society calls immoral and debased, a genuine love and respect for life and for people, as human beings, can develop. Far from glorifying vice, John Cleland points an accusing finger at the individual who is so certain as to what it means to be a moral man.

There are those who will quickly say that this "message" will be missed by the average person who reads *Fanny Hill.* But this is precisely the point. We become so accustomed to pre-judging what is ethical and what is immoral that we are unable to recognize that what we accept as good may be nothing less than evil because it harms people.

I know of no book which more beautifully describes meaningful relationships between a man and a woman than does *Fanny Hill.* In many marriages, men use a woman for sexual gratification and otherwise, as well as vice versa. But this is not the case in the story of Fanny Hill. The point is simply that there are many, many ways in which we hurt, injure and degrade people that are far worse than either being or visiting a prostitute. We do this all in the name of morality.

At the same time that Dr. Peale is concerned with sick people, John Cleland attempts to describe healthy ones. *Fanny Hill* is a more modern and certainly more valuable book than *Sin, Sex and Self-Control* because the author does not tell us how to behave, but attempts to help us understand ourselves and the nature of love and understanding in being related to other persons. Dr. Peale's writing emphasizes the most useful commodities available to man—self-centeredness and self-control. John Cleland suggests that self-understanding and self-expression may not be as popular, but they are more humane.

The "Peale approach" to life breeds contentment, for it suggests that each one of us can be certain as to what is good and true. Standards for thinking and behavior are available and all we need to do is appropriate them for our use. In a day when life is marked by chaos and confusion, this viewpoint offers much in the way of comfort and satisfaction. There is only one trouble with it, however, and that is that it results in conformity, rigid behavior and a lack of understanding. It results in personality configurations that are marked with an intense interest in propositions about Truth and Right but, at the same time, build a wall against people. Such an attitude creates certainty, but there is little warmth. The idea develops that there are "my kind of people" and they are "right." It forces us to degrade, dismiss and ultimately attempt to destroy anyone who does not agree with us.

To be alive and sensitive to life means that we have to choose what we want. There is no possible way for a person to be a slave and free at the same time. Self-control and self-expression are at opposite ends of the continuum. As much as some persons would like to have both, it is necessary to make a choice, since restraint and openness are contradictory qualities. To internalize external values denies the possibility of self-expression. We must decide what we want, when it comes to confofmity and creativity. If we want people to behave in a structured and predictable manner, then the ideal of creativity cannot have meaning.

.   .   .   .   .

Long ago Plato said, "What is honored in a country will be cultivated there." More and more, we reward people for thinking alike and as a result, we become frightened, beyond belief, of those who take exception to the current consensus. If our society collapses, it will not be because people read a book such as *Fanny Hill.* It will fall, because we will have refused to understand it. Decadence, in a nation or an individual, arises not because there is a lack of ability to distingush between morality and immorality, but because the opportunity for self-expression has been so controlled or strangled that the society or the person becomes a robot.

The issue which a Dr. Peale will never understand, because he is a victim of it himself and which John Cleland describes with brilliant clarity and sensitive persuasion is that until we learn to respect ourselves enough that we leave each other alone, we cannot discover the meaning of morality.

Dr. Peale and Fanny Hill offer the two basic choices open to man. Man is free to choose an autocentric existence which is marked by freedom from ambiguity and responsibility. Autocentricity presupposes a "closed world" where life is predetermined and animal-like. In contrast to this view, there is the allocentric outlook which is marked by an "open encounter of the total person with the world." Growth, spontaneity and expression are the goals of such an existence.

Dr. Peale epitomizes the autocentric approach. He offers "warm blankets" and comfortable "cocoons" for those who want to lose their humanity. On the other hand, *Fanny Hill* represents the allocentric viewpoint which posits the possibility for man to raise his sights, stretch his imagination, cultivate his sensitiveness as well as deepen and broaden his perspectives. In discussing the autocentric idea. Floyd W. Matson writes,

> "Human beings conditioned to apathy and afflu-
> ence may well prefer this regressive path of least
> resistance, with its promise of escape from freedom
> and an end to striving. But we know at least that
> it is open to them to choose otherwise: in a word,
> to *choose themselves.*" (*The Broken Image*, page
> 193.)

In a day when people are overly sensitive in drawing lines between the good and the bad, the right and the wrong, as well as the true and the false, it seems to me that there is great irony in the availability of a book such as *Fanny Hill*. Prostitution may be the oldest profession in the world, but we are ever faced with a question which is becoming more and more disturbing: "What does a prostitute look like?"

Mr. Justice Clark, dissenting.

It is with regret that I write this dissenting opinion. However, the public should know of the continuous flow of pornographic material reaching this Court and the increasing problem States have in controlling it. *Memoirs of a Woman of Pleasure*, the book involved here, is typical. I have "stomached" past cases for almost 10 years without much outcry. Though I am not known to be a purist—or a shrinking violet—this book is too much even for me. It is important that the Court has refused to declare it obscene and thus affords it further circulation. In order to give my remarks the proper setting I have been obliged to portray the book's contents, which causes me embarrassment. However, quotations from typical episodes would so debase our Reports that I will not follow that course.

I.

Let me first pinpoint the effect of today's holding in the obscenity field. While there is no majority opinion in this case, there are three Justices who import a new test into that laid down in *Roth* v. *United States*, 354 U. S. 476 (1957), namely, that "[a] book cannot be pro-scribed unless it is found to be *utterly* without redeem-ing social value." I agree with my Brother White that such a condition rejects the basic holding of *Roth* and gives the smut artist free rein to carry on his dirty busi-ness. My vote in that case—which was the deciding one for the majority opinion—was cast solely because the Court declared the test of obscenity to be: "whether to the average person, applying contemporary community standards, the dominant theme of the material taken as a whole appeals to prurient interest." I understood that test to include only two constitutional requirements: (1) the book must be judged as a whole, not by its parts; and (2) it must be judged in terms of its appeal to the prurient interest of the average person, applying con-temporary community standards.[1] Indeed, obscenity was denoted in *Roth* as having "*such slight social value as a step to truth that any benefit that may be derived . . . is clearly outweighed by the social interest in order and morality. . . .*" At 485 (quoting *Chaplinsky* v. *New Hampshire*, 315 U. S. 568, 572 (1942)). Moreover, in no subsequent decision of this Court has any "utterly without redeeming social value" test been suggested, much less expounded. My Brother Harlan in *Manual*

Enterprises, Inc. v. *Day*, 370 U. S. 478 (1962), made no reference whatever to such a requirement in *Roth*. Rather he interpreted *Roth* as including a test of "patent offensiveness" besides "prurient appeal." Nor did my Brother Brennan in his concurring opinion in *Manual Enterprises* mention any "utterly without redeeming social value" test. The first reference to such a test was made by my Brother Brennan in *Jacobellis* v. *Ohio*, 378 U. S. 184, 191 (1964), seven years after *Roth*. In an opinion joined only by Justice Goldberg, he there wrote: "Recognizing that the test for obscenity enunciated [in *Roth*] . . . is not perfect, we think any substitute would raise equally difficult problems, and we therefore adhere to that standard." Nevertheless, he proceeded to add:

> "We would reiterate, however, our recognition in
> *Roth* that obscenity is excluded from the constitu-
> tional protection only because it is 'utterly without
> redeeming social importance,' . . . ."

This language was then repeated in the converse to announce this *non sequitur:*

> "It follows that material dealing with sex in a man-
> ner that advocates ideas . . . or that has literary or
> scientific or artistic value or any other form of social
> importance, may not be branded as obscenity and
> denied the constitutional protection." At 191.

Significantly no opinion in *Jacobellis*, other than that of my Brother Brennan, mentioned the "utterly without redeeming social importance" test which he there intro-duced into our many and varied previous opinions in obscenity cases. Indeed, rather than recognizing the "utterly without social importance" test, The Chief Justice in his dissent in *Jacobellis*, which I joined, spe-cifically stated:

> "In light of the foregoing, I would reiterate my
> acceptance of the rule of the *Roth* case: *Material is
> obscene and not constitutionally protected against
> regulation and proscription if* 'to the average per-
> son, applying contemporary community standards,
> the dominant theme of the material taken as a whole
> appeals to prurient interest.'" (Emphasis added.)
> At 202.

The Chief Justice and I further asserted that the enforcement of this rule should be committed to the state and federal courts whose judgments made pursuant to the *Roth* rule we would accept, limiting our review to a consideration of whether there is "sufficient evidence" in the record to support a finding of obscenity. At 202.

II.

Three members of the majority hold that reversal here is necessary solely because their novel "utterly without redeeming social value" test was not properly interpreted or applied by the Supreme Judicial Court of Massachu-setts. Massachusetts now has to retry the case although the "Findings of Fact, Rulings of Law and Order for Final Decree" of the trial court specifically held that "this book is 'utterly without redeeming social impor-tance' in the fields of art, literature, science, news or ideas of any social importance and that it is obscene, indecent and impure." I quote portions of the findings:

> "Opinions of experts are admitted in evidence to aid

the Court in its understanding and comprehension of the facts, but, of course, an expert cannot usurp the function of the Court. Highly artificial, stylistic writing and an abundance of metaphorical descriptions are contained in the book but the conclusions of some experts were pretty well strained in attempting to justify its claimed literary value: such as the book preached a moral that sex with love is better than sex without love, when Fanny's description of her sexual acts, particularly with the young boy she seduced, in Fanny's judgment at least, was to the contrary. *Careful review of all the expert testimony has been made,* but, the best evidence of all, is the book itself and it plainly has no value because of ideas, news or artistic, literary or scientific attributes. . . . Nor does it have any other merit. 'This Court will not adopt a rule of law which states obscenity is suppressible but well written obscenity is not.' Mr. Justice Scileppi in *People v. Fritch,* 13 N. Y. 2d 119." (Emphasis added.) Finding 20.

None of these findings of the trial court were overturned on appeal, although the Supreme Judicial Court of Massachusetts observed in addition that "the fact that the testimony may indicate this book has some minimal literary value does not mean it is of any social importance. We do not interpret the 'social importance' test as requiring that a book which appeals to prurient interest and is patently offensive must be unqualifiedly worthless before it can be deemed obscene." My Brother BRENNAN reverses on the basis of this casual statement, despite the specific findings of the trial court. Why, if the statement is erroneous, Brother BRENNAN does not affirm the holding of the trial court which beyond question is correct, one cannot tell. This course has often been followed in other cases.

In my view evidence of social importance is relevant to the determination of the ultimate question of obscenity. But social importance does not constitute a separate and distinct constitutional test. Such evidence must be considered together with evidence that the material in question appeals to prurient interest and is patently offensive. Accordingly, we must first turn to the book here under attack. I repeat that I regret having to depict the sordid episodes of this book.

III.

Memoirs is nothing more than a series of minutely and vividly described sexual episodes. The book starts with Fanny Hill, a young 15-year-old girl, arriving in London to seek household work. She goes to an employment office where through happenstance she meets the mistress of a bawdy house. This takes 10 pages. The remaining 200 pages of the book detail her initiation into various sexual experiences, from a lesbian encounter with a sister prostitute to all sorts and types of sexual debauchery in bawdy houses and as the mistress of a variety of men. This is presented to the reader through an uninterrupted succession of descriptions by Fanny, either as an observer or participant, of sexual adventures so vile that one of the male expert witnesses in the case was hesitant to repeat any one of them in the courtroom.

These scenes run the gamut of possible sexual experience such as lesbianism, female masturbation, homosexuality between young boys, the destruction of a maidenhead with consequent gory descriptions, the seduction of a young virgin boy, the flagellation of male by female, and vice versa, followed by fervid sexual engagement, and other abhorrent acts, including over two dozen separate bizarre descriptions of different sexual intercourses between male and female characters. In one sequence four girls in a bawdy house are required in the presence of one another to relate the lurid details of their loss of virginity and their glorification of it. This is followed the same evening by "publick trials" in which each of the four girls engages in sexual intercourse with a different man while the others witness, with Fanny giving a detailed description of the movement and reaction of each couple.

In each of the sexual scenes the exposed bodies of the participants are described in minute and individual detail. The pubic hair is often used for a background to the most vivid and precise descriptions of the response, condition, size, shape, and color of the sexual organs before, during and after orgasms. There are some short transitory passages between the various sexual episodes, but for the most part they only set the scene and identify the participants for the next orgy, or make smutty reference and comparison to past episodes.

There can be no doubt that the whole purpose of the book is to arouse the prurient interest. Likewise the repetition of sexual episode after episode and the candor with which they are described renders the book "patently offensive." These facts weigh heavily in any appraisal of the book's claims to "redeeming social importance."

Let us now turn to evidence of the book's alleged social value. While unfortunately the State offered little testimony,[2] the defense called several experts to attest that the book has literary merit and historical value. A careful reading of testimony, however, reveals that it has no substance. For example, the first witness testified:

"I think it is a work of art . . . it asks for and receives a literary response . . . presented in an orderly and organized fashion, with a fictional central character, and with a literary style . . . . I think the central character is . . . what I call an intellectual . . . someone who is extremely curious about life and who seeks . . . to record with accuracy the details of the external world, physical sensations, psychological responses . . . an empiricist . . . . I find that this tells me things . . . about the 18th century that I might not otherwise know."

If a book of art is one that asks for and receives a literary response, *Memoirs* is no work of art. The sole response evoked by the book is sensual. Nor does the orderly presentation of *Memoirs* make a difference; it presents nothing but lascivious scenes organized solely to arouse prurient interest and produce sustained erotic tension.[3] Certainly the book's baroque style cannot vitiate the determination of obscenity. From a legal standpoint, we must remember that obscenity is no less obscene though it be expressed in "elaborate language." Indeed, the more meticulous its presentation, the more it appeals to the prurient interest. To say that Fanny is an "intellectual" is an insult to those who travel under that tag. She was nothing but a harlot—a sensualist—exploiting her sexual attractions which she sold for fun, for money, for lodging and keep, for an inheritance, and finally for a husband. If she was curious about life, her curiosity extended only to the pursuit of sexual delight wherever she found it. The book describes nothing in the "external world" except bawdy houses and debaucheries. As an empiricist, Fanny confines her observations and "experiments" to sex, with primary attention to depraved, lewd, and deviant practices.

Other experts produced by the defense testified that the book emphasizes the profound "idea that a sensual passion is only truly experienced when it is associated with the emotion of love" and that the sexual relationship "can be a wholesome, healthy, experience itself," whereas in certain modern novels "the relationship between the sexes is seen as another manifestation of modern decadence, insterility or perversion." In my view this proves nothing as to social value. The state court properly gave such testimony no probative weight. A review offered by the defense noted that "where 'pornography' does not brutalize, it idealizes. The book is, in this sense, an erotic fantasy—and a male fantasy, at that, put into the mind of a woman. The male organ is phenomenal to the point of absurdity." Finally, it saw the book as "a minor fantasy, deluding as a guide to conduct, but respectful of our delight in the body . . . an interesting footnote in the history of the English novel." These unrelated assertions reveal to me nothing whatever of literary, historical, or social value. Another review called the book "a great novel . . . one which turns its convention upside down . . . ." Admittedly Cleland did not attempt "high art" because he was writing "an erotic novel. He can skip the elevation and get on with the erections." Fanny's "downfall" is seen as "one long delightful swoon into the depths of pleasurable sensation." Rather than indicating social value in the book, this evidence reveals just the contrary. Another item offered by the defense described Memoirs as being "widely accredited as the first deliberately dirty novel in English." However, the reviewer found Fanny to be "no common harlot. Her 'Memoirs' combine literary grace with a disarming enthusiasm for an activity which is, after all, only human. What is more, she never uses a dirty word." The short answer to such "expertise" is that none of these so-called attributes have any value to society. On the contrary, they accentuate the prurient appeal.

Another expert described the book as having "detectable literary merit" since it reflects "an effort to interpret a rather complex character . . . going through a number of very different adventures." To illustrate his assertion that the "writing is very skillfully done" this expert pointed to the description of a whore, "Phoebe, who is 'red-faced, fat and in her early 50's, who waddles into a room.' She doesn't walk in, she waddles in." Given this standard for "skillful writing," it is not suprising that he found the book to have merit.

The remaining experts testified in the same manner, claiming the book to be a "record of the historical, psychological, [and] social events of the period." One has but to read the history of the 18th century to disprove this assertion. The story depicts nothing besides the brothels that are present in metropolitan cities in every period of history. One expert noticed "in this book a tendency away from nakedness during the sexual act which I find an interesting sort of sociological observation" on tastes different from contemporary ones. As additional proof, he marvels that Fanny "refers constantly to the male sexual organ as an engine . . . which is pulling you away from the way these events would be described in the 19th or 20th century." How this adds social value to the book is beyond my comprehension. It only indicates the lengths to which these experts go in their effort to give the book some semblance of value. For example, the ubiquitous descriptions of sexual acts are excused as being necessary in tracing the "moral progress" of the heroine, and the giving of a silver watch to a servant is found to be "an odd and interesting custom that I would like to know more about." This only points up the bankruptcy of Memoirs in both purpose and content, adequately justifying the trial court's finding that it had absolutely no social value.

It is, of course, the duty of the judge or the jury to determine the question of obscenity, viewing the book by contemporary community standards. It can accept the appraisal of experts or discount their testimony in the light of the material itself or other relevant testimony. So-called "literary obscenity," i. e., the use of erotic fantasies of the hard-core type clothed in an engaging literary style has no constitutional protection. If a book deals solely with erotic material in a manner calculated to appeal to the prurient interest, it matters not that it may be expressed in beautiful prose. There are obviously dynamic connections between art and sex—the emotional, intellectual, and physical—but where the former is used solely to promote prurient appeal, it cannot claim constitutional immunity. Cleland uses this technique to promote the prurient appeal of Memoirs. It is true that Fanny's perverse experiences finally bring from her the observation that "the heights of [sexual] enjoyment cannot be achieved until true affection prepares the bed of passion." But this merely emphasizes that sex, wherever and however found, remains the sole theme of Memoirs. In my view, the book's repeated and unrelieved appeals to the prurient interest of the average person leave it utterly without redeeming social importance.

IV.

In his separate concurrence, my Brother DOUGLAS asserts there is no proof that obscenity produces antisocial conduct. I had thought that this question was foreclosed by the determination in Roth that obscenity was not protected by the First Amendment. I find it necessary to comment upon Brother DOUGLAS' views, however, because of the new requirement engrafted upon Roth by Brother BRENNAN, i. e., that material which "appeals to a prurient interest" and which is "patently offensive" may still not be suppressed unless it is "utterly without redeeming social value." The question of antisocial effect thus becomes relevant to the more limited question of social value. Brother BRENNAN indicates that the social importance criterion encompasses only such things as the artistic, literary, and historical qualities of the material. But the phrasing of the "utterly without redeeming social value" test suggests that other evidence must be considered. To say that social value may "redeem" implies that courts must balance alleged esthetic merit against the harmful consequences that may flow from pornography. Whatever the scope of the social value criterion—which need not be defined with precision here—it at least anticipates that the trier of fact will weigh evidence of the material's influence in causing deviant or criminal conduct, particularly sex crimes, as well as its effect upon the mental, moral, and physical health of the average person. Brother DOUGLAS' view as to the lack of proof in this area is not so firmly held among behavioral scientists as he would lead us to believe. For this reason, I should mention that there is a division of thought on the correlation between obscenity and socially deleterious behavior.

Psychological and physiological studies clearly indicate that many persons become sexually aroused from reading obscene material.[4] While erotic stimulation caused by pornography may be legally insignificant in itself, there are medical experts who believe that such stimulation frequently manifests itself in criminal sexual behavior or other antisocial conduct.[5] For example, Dr. George W. Henry of Cornell University has expressed the opinion that obscenity, with its exaggerated and morbid emphasis on sex, particularly abnormal and perverted practices, and its unrealistic presentation of sexual behavior and attitudes, may induce antisocial conduct by the average person.[6] A number of sociologists think that this material may have adverse effects upon individual mental health, with potentially disruptive consequences for the community.[7]

In addition, there is persuasive evidence from criminologists and police officials. Inspector Herbert Case of the Detroit Police Department contends that sex murder cases are invariably tied to some form of obscene literature.[8] And the Director of the Federal Bureau of Investigation, J. Edgar Hoover, has repeatedly emphasized that pornography is associated with an overwhelmingly large number of sex crimes. Again, while the correlation between possession of obscenity and deviant behavior has not been conclusively established, the files of our law enforcement agencies contain many reports of persons who patterned their criminal conduct after behavior depicted in obscene material.[9]

The clergy are also outspoken in their belief that pornography encourages violence, degeneracy and sexual misconduct. In a speech reported by the New York Journal-American August 7, 1964, Cardinal Spellman particularly stressed the direct influence obscenity has on immature persons. These and related views have been confirmed by practical experience. After years of service with the West London Mission, Rev. Donald Soper found that pornography was a primary cause of prostitution. Rolph, Does Pornography Matter? (1961), pp. 47–48.[10]

Congress and the legislatures of every State have enacted measures to restrict the distribution of erotic and pornographic material,[11] justifying these controls by reference to evidence that antisocial behavior may result in part from reading obscenity.[12] Likewise, upon another trial, the parties may offer this sort of evidence along with other "social value" characteristics that they attribute to the book.

But this is not all that Massachusetts courts might consider. I believe it can be established that the book "was commercially exploited for the sake of prurient appeal, to the exclusion of all other values" and should therefore be declared obscene under the test of commercial exploitation announced today in *Ginzburg* and *Mishkin*.

As I have stated, my study of *Memoirs* leads me to think that it has no conceivable "social importance." The author's obsession with sex, his minute descriptions of phalli, and his repetitious accounts of bawdy sexual experiences and deviant sexual behavior indicate the book was designed solely to appeal to prurient interests. In addition, the record before the Court contains extrinsic evidence tending to show that the publisher was fully aware that the book attracted readers desirous of vicarious sexual pleasure, and sought to profit solely from its prurient appeal. The publisher's "Introduction" recites that Cleland, a "never-do-well bohemian," wrote the book in 1749 to make a quick 20 guineas. Thereafter, various publications of the book, often "embellished with fresh inflammatory details" and "highly exaggerated illustrations," appeared in "surreptitious circulation." Indeed, the cover of *Memoirs* tempts the reader with the announcement that the sale of the book has finally been permitted "after 214 years of suppression." Although written in a sophisticated tone, the "Introduction" repeatedly informs the reader that he may expect graphic descriptions of genitals and sexual exploits. For instance, it states:

> "Here and there, Cleland's descriptions of lovemaking are marred by what perhaps could be best described as his adherence to the 'longitudinal fallacy'—the formidable bodily equipment of his most accomplished lovers is apt to be described with quite unnecessary relish . . . ."

Many other passages in the "Introduction" similarly reflect the publisher's "own evaluation" of the book's nature. The excerpt printed on the jacket of the hardcover edition is typical:

> "*Memoirs of a Woman of Pleasure* is the product of a luxurious and licentious, but not a commercially degraded, era. . . . For all its abounding improprieties, his priapic novel is not a vulgar book. It treats of pleasure as the aim and end of existence, and of sexual satisfaction as the epitome of pleasure, but does so in a style that, despite its inflammatory subject, never stoops to a gross or unbecoming word."

Cleland apparently wrote only one other book, a sequel called *Memoirs of a Coxcomb*, published by Lancer Books, Inc. The "Introduction" to that book labels *Memoirs of a Woman of Pleasure* as "the most sensational piece of erotica in English literature." I daresay that this fact alone explains why G. P. Putnam's Sons published this obscenity—preying upon prurient and carnal proclivities for its own pecuniary advantage. I would affirm the judgment.

Mr. Justice Harlan, dissenting.

The central development that emerges from the aftermath of *Roth* v. *United States*, 354 U. S. 476, is that no stable approach to the obscenity problem has yet been devised by this Court. Two Justices believe that the First and Fourteenth Amendments absolutely protect obscene and nonobscene material alike. Another Justice believes that neither the States nor the Federal Government may suppress any material save for "hard-core pornography." *Roth* in 1957 stressed prurience and utter lack of redeeming social importance;[1] as *Roth* has been expounded in this case, in *Ginzburg* v. *United States, post,* p. 463, and in *Mishkin* v. *New York, post,* p. 502, it has undergone significant transformation. The concept of "pandering," emphasized by the separate opinion of The Chief Justice in *Roth,* now emerges as an uncertain gloss or interpretive aid, and the further requisite of "patent offensiveness" has been made explicit as a result of intervening decisions. Given this tangled state of affairs, I feel free to adhere to the principles first set forth in my separate opinion in *Roth,* 354 U. S., at 496, which I continue to believe represent the soundest constitutional solution to this intractable problem.

My premise is that in the area of obscenity the Constitution does not bind the States and the Federal Government in precisely the same fashion. This approach is plainly consistent with the language of the First and Fourteenth Amendments and, in my opinion, more responsive to the proper functioning of a federal system of government in this area. See my opinion in *Roth,* 354 U. S., at 505–506. I believe it is also consistent with past decisions of this Court. Although some 40 years have passed since the Court first indicated that the Fourteenth Amendment protects "free speech," see *Gitlow* v. *New York,* 268 U. S. 652; *Fiske* v. *Kansas,* 274 U. S. 380, the decisions have never declared that every utterance the Federal Government may not reach or every regulatory scheme it may not enact is also beyond the power of the State. The very criteria used in opinions to delimit the protection of free speech—the gravity of the evil being regulated, see *Schneider* v. *State,* 308 U. S. 147; how "clear and present" is the danger, *Schenck* v. *United States,* 249 U. S. 47, 52 (Holmes, J.); the magnitude of "such invasion of free speech as is necessary to avoid the danger," *United States* v. *Dennis,* 183 F. 2d 201, 212 (L. Hand, J.)—may and do depend on the particular context in which power is exercised. When, for example, the Court in *Beauharnais* v. *Illinois,* 343 U. S. 250, upheld a criminal group-libel law because of the "social interest in order and morality," 343 U. S., at 257, it was acknowledging the responsibility and capacity of the States in such public-welfare matters and not committing itself to uphold any similar federal statute applying to such communications as Congress might otherwise regulate under the commerce power. See also *Kovacs* v. *Cooper,* 336 U. S. 77.

Federal suppression of allegedly obscene matter should, in my view, be constitutionally limited to that often described as "hard-core pornography." To be sure, that rubric is not a self-executing standard, but it does describe something that most judges and others will "know . . . when [they] see it" (Stewart, J., in *Jacobellis* v. *Ohio,* 378 U. S. 184, 197) and that leaves the smallest room for disagreement between those of varying tastes. To me it is plain, for instance, that *Fanny Hill* does not fall within this class and could not be barred from the federal mails. If further articulation is meaningful, I would characterize as "hard-core" that prurient material that is patently offensive or whose indecency is self-demonstrating and I would describe it substantially as does Mr. Justice Stewart's opinion in *Ginzburg, post,* p. 499. The Federal Government may be conceded a limited interest in excluding from the mails such gross pornography, almost universally condemned in this country.[2] But I believe the dangers of national censorship and the existence of primary responsibility at the state level amply justify drawing the line at this point.

State obscenity laws present problems of quite a different order. The varying conditions across the country, the range of views on the need and reasons for curbing obscenity, and the traditions of local self-government in matters of public welfare all favor a far more flexible attitude in defining the bounds for the States. From my standpoint, the Fourteenth Amendment requires of a State only that it apply criteria rationally related to the accepted notion of obscenity and that it reach results not wholly out of step with current American standards. As to criteria, it should be adequate if the court or jury considers such elements as offensiveness, pruriency, social value, and the like. The latitude which I believe the States deserve cautions against any federally imposed formula listing the exclusive ingredients of obscenity and fixing their proportions. This approach concededly lacks precision, but imprecision is characteristic of mediating constitutional standards;[3] voluntariness of a confession, clear and present danger, and probable cause are only the most ready illustrations. In time and with more litigated examples, predictability increases, but there is no shortcut to satisfactory solutions in this field, and there is no advantage in supposing otherwise.

I believe the tests set out in the prevailing opinion, judged by their application in this case, offer only an illusion of certainty and risk confusion and prejudice. The opinion declares that a book cannot be banned unless it is "utterly without redeeming social value" (*ante,* p. 418). To establish social value in the present case, a number of acknowledged experts in the field of literature testified that *Fanny Hill* held a respectable place in serious writing, and unless such largely uncontradicted testimony is accepted as decisive it is very hard to see that the "utterly without redeeming social value" test has any meaning at all. Yet the prevailing opinion, while denying that social value may be "weighed against" or "canceled by" prurience or offensiveness (*ante,* p. 419), terminates this case unwilling to give a conclusive decision on the status of *Fanny Hill* under the Constitution.[4] Apparently, the Court believes that the social value of the book may be negated if proof of pandering is present. Using this inherently vague "pandering" notion to offset "social value" wipes out any certainty the latter term might be given by reliance on experts, and admits into the case highly prejudicial evidence without appropriate restrictions. See my dissenting opinion in *Ginzburg, post,* p. 493. I think it more satisfactory to acknowledge that on this record the book has been shown to have some quantum of social value, that it may at the same time be deemed offensive and salacious, and that the State's decision to weigh these elements and to ban this particular work does not exceed constitutional limits.

A final aspect of the obscenity problem is the role this Court is to play in administering its standards, a matter that engendered justified concern at the oral argument of the cases now decided. Short of saying that no material relating to sex may be banned, or that all of it may be, I do not see how this Court can escape the task of reviewing obscenity decisions on a case-by-case basis. The views of literary or other experts could be made controlling, but those experts had their say in *Fanny Hill* and apparently the majority is no more willing than I to say that Massachusetts must abide by their verdict. Yet I venture to say that the Court's burden of decision would be ameliorated under the constitutional principles that I have advocated. "Hard-core pornography" for judging federal cases is one of the more tangible concepts in the field. As to the States, the due latitude my approach would leave them ensures that only the unusual case would require plenary review and correction by this Court.

There is plenty of room, I know, for disagreement in this area of constitutional law. Some will think that what I propose may encourage States to go too far in this field. Others will consider that the Court's present course unduly restricts state experimentation with the still elusive problem of obscenity. For myself, I believe it is the part of wisdom for those of us who happen currently to possess the "final word" to leave room for such experimentation, which indeed is the underlying genius of our federal system.

On the premises set forth in this opinion, supplementing what I have earlier said in my opinions in *Roth, supra, Manual Enterprises, Inc.* v. *Day,* 370 U. S. 478, and *Jacobellis* v. *Ohio,* 378 U. S., at 203, I would affirm the judgment of the Massachusetts Supreme Judicial Court.

MR. JUSTICE WHITE, dissenting.

In *Roth* v. *United States,* 354 U. S. 476, the Court held a publication to be obscene if its predominant theme appeals to the prurient interest in a manner exceeding customary limits of candor. Material of this kind, the Court said, is "utterly without redeeming social importance" and is therefore unprotected by the First Amendment.

To say that material within the *Roth* definition of obscenity is nevertheless not obscene if it has some redeeming social value is to reject one of the basic propositions of the *Roth* case—that such material is not protected *because* it is inherently and utterly without social value.

If "social importance" is to be used as the prevailing opinion uses it today, obscene material, however far beyond customary limits of candor, is immune if it has any literary style, if it contains any historical references or language characteristic of a bygone day, or even if it is printed or bound in an interesting way. Well written, especially effective obscenity is protected; the poorly written is vulnerable. And why shouldn't the fact that some people buy and read such material prove its "social value"?

A fortiori, if the predominant theme of the book appeals to the prurient interest as stated in *Roth* but the book nevertheless contains here and there a passage descriptive of character, geography or architecture, the book would not be "obscene" under the social importance test. I had thought that *Roth* counseled the contrary: that the character of the book is fixed by its predominant theme and is not altered by the presence of minor themes of a different nature. The *Roth* Court's emphatic reliance on the quotation from *Chaplinsky* v. *New Hampshire,* 315 U. S. 568, means nothing less:

> " '. . . There are certain well-defined and narrowly limited classes of speech, the prevention and punishment of which have never been thought to raise any Constitutional problem. *These include the lewd and obscene . . . . It has been well observed that such utterances are no essential part of any exposition of ideas, and are of such slight social value as a step to truth that any benefit that may be derived from them is clearly outweighed by the social interest in order and morality. . . .*' (Emphasis added.)" 354 U. S., at 485.

In my view, "social importance" is not an independent test of obscenity but is relevant only to determining the predominant prurient interest of the material, a determination which the court or the jury will make based on the material itself and all the evidence in the case, expert or otherwise.

Application of the *Roth* test, as I understand it, necessarily involves the exercise of judgment by legislatures, courts and juries. But this does not mean that there are no limits to what may be done in the name of *Roth.* Cf. *Jacobellis* v. *Ohio,* 378 U. S. 184. *Roth* does not mean that a legislature is free to ban books simply because they deal with sex or because they appeal to the prurient interest. Nor does it mean that if books like *Fanny Hill* are unprotected, their nonprurient appeal is necessarily lost to the world. Literary style, history, teachings about sex, character description (even of a prostitute) or moral lessons need not come wrapped in such packages. The fact that they do impeaches their claims to immunity from legislative censure.

Finally, it should be remembered that if the publication and sale of *Fanny Hill* and like books are proscribed, it is not the Constitution that imposes the ban. Censure stems from a legislative act, and legislatures are constitutionally free to embrace such books whenever they wish to do so. But if a State insists on treating *Fanny Hill* as obscene and forbidding its sale, the First Amendment does not prevent it from doing so.

I would affirm the judgment below.

JUSTICE BRENNAN'S OPINION NOTES

[1] The text of the statute appears in the Appendix.

[2] In dissenting from the Supreme Judicial Court's disposition in this case, 349 Mass. 69, 74–75, 206 N. E. 2d 403, 406–407 (1965), Justice Whittemore summarized this testimony:

"In the view of one or another or all of the following viz., the chairman of the English department at Williams College, a professor of English at Harvard College, an associate professor of English literature at Boston University, an associate professor of

English at Massachusetts Institute of Technology, and an assistant professor of English and American literature at Brandeis University, the book is a minor 'work of art' having 'literary merit' and 'historical value' and containing a good deal of 'deliberate, calculated comedy.' It is a piece of 'social history of interest to anyone who is interested in fiction as a way of understanding society in the past.' [1] A saving grace is that although many scenes, if translated

"[1] One of the witnesses testified in part as follows: 'Cleland is part of what I should call this cultural battle that is going on in the 18th century, a battle between a restricted Puritan, moralistic ethic that attempts to suppress freedom of the spirit, freedom of the flesh, and this element is competing with a freer attitude towards life, a more generous attitude towards life, a more wholesome attitude towards life, and this very attitude that is manifested in Fielding's great novel "Tom Jones" is also evident in Cleland's novel. . . . [Richardson's] "Pamela" is the story of a young country girl; [his] "Clarissa" is the story of a woman trapped in a house of prostitution. Obviously, then Cleland takes both these themes, the country girl, her initiation into life and into experience, and the story of a woman in a house of prostitution, and what he simply does is to take the situation and reverse the moral standards. Richardson believed that chastity was the most important thing in the world; Cleland and Fielding obviously did not and thought there were more important significant moral values.' "

into the present day language of 'the realistic, naturalistic novel, could be quite offensive' these scenes are not described in such language. The book contains no dirty words and its language 'functions . . . to create a distance, even when the sexual experiences are portrayed.' The response, therefore, is a literary response. The descriptions of depravity are not obscene because 'they are subordinate to an interest which is primarily literary'; Fanny's reaction to the scenes of depravity was 'anger,' 'disgust, horror, [and] indignation.' The book 'belongs to the history of English literature rather than the history of smut.' [2] "

"[2] In the opinion of the other academic witness, the headmaster of a private school, whose field is English literature, the book is without literary merit and is obscene, impure, hard core pornography, and is patently offensive."

[3] The record in this case is thus significantly different from the records in *Ginzburg v. United States, post,* p. 463, and *Mishkin v. New York, post,* p. 502. See pp. 420–421, *infra.*

[4] Section 28B makes it a criminal offense, *inter alia,* to import, print, publish, sell, loan, distribute, buy, procure, receive, or possess for the purpose of sale, loan, or distribution, "a book, knowing it to be obscene." Section 28H provides that in any prosecution under § 28B the decree obtained in a proceeding against the book "shall be admissible in evidence" and further that "[i]f prior to the said offence a final decree had been entered against the book, the defendant, if the book be obscene . . . shall be conclusively presumed to have known said book to be obscene . . . ." Thus a declaration of obscenity such as that obtained in this proceeding is likely to result in the total suppression of the book in the Commonwealth.

The constitutionality of § 28H has not been challenged in this appeal.

[5] Although the final decree provides no coercive relief but only a declaration of the book's obscenity, our adjudication of the merits of the issue tendered, viz., whether the state courts erred in declaring the book obscene, is not premature. There is no uncertainty as to the content of the material challenged, and the Attorney General's petition commencing this suit states that the book "is being imported, sold, loaned, or distributed in the Commonwealth." The declaration of obscenity is likely to have a serious inhibitory effect on the distribution of the book, and this probable impact is to no small measure derived from possible collateral uses of the declaration in subsequent prosecutions under the Massachusetts criminal obscenity statute. See n. 4, *supra.*

[6] We infer from the opinions below that the other adjectives describing the proscribed books in §§ 28C–28H, "indecent" and "impure," have either been read out of the statute or deemed synonymous with "obscene."

[7] "[M]aterial dealing with sex in a manner that advocates ideas . . . or that has literary or scientific or artistic value or any other form of social importance, may not be branded as obscenity

and denied the constitutional protection. Nor may the constitutional status of the material be made to turn on a 'weighing' of its social importance against its prurient appeal, for a work cannot be proscribed unless it is 'utterly' without social importance. See *Zeitlin v. Arnebergh,* 59 Cal. 2d 901, 920, 383 P. 2d 152, 165, 31 Cal. Rptr. 800, 813 (1963)." *Jacobellis v. Ohio,* 378 U. S. 184, 191 (opinion of BRENNAN, J.). Followed in, *e. g., People v. Bruce,* 31 Ill. 2d 459, 461, 202 N. E. 2d 497, 498 (1964); *Trans-Lux Distributing Corp. v. Maryland Bd. of Censors,* 240 Md. 98, 104–105, 213 A. 2d 235, 238–239 (1965).

[8] In his dissenting opinion, 349 Mass., at 76–78, 206 N. E. 2d, at 408–409, Justice Cutter stated that, although in his view the book was not "obscene" within the meaning of *Roth,* "it could reasonably be found that distribution of the book to persons under the age of eighteen would be a violation of G. L. c. 272, § 28, as tending to corrupt the morals of youth." (Section 28 makes it a crime to sell to "a person under the age of eighteen years a book . . . which is obscene . . . or manifestly tends to corrupt the morals of youth.") He concluded that the court should "limit the relief granted to a declaration that distribution of this book to persons under the age of eighteen may be found to constitute a violation of [G. L.] c. 272, § 28, if that section is reasonably applied . . . ." However, the decree was not so limited and we intimate no view concerning the constitutionality of such a limited declaration regarding *Memoirs.* Cf. *Jacobellis v. Ohio,* 378 U. S., at 195.

JUSTICE DOUGLAS'S OPINION NOTES

[1] *Memoirs* was the subject of what is generally regarded as the first recorded suppression of a literary work in this country on grounds of obscenity. See *Commonwealth v. Holmes,* 17 Mass. 336 (1821). The edition there condemned differed from the present volume in that it contained apparently erotic illustrations.

[2] *Memoirs,* at 213–214 (Putnam ed. 1963).

[3] The defense drew its witnesses from the various colleges located within the Commonwealth of Massachusetts. These included: Fred Holly Stocking, Professor of English and Chairman of the English Department, Williams College; John M. Bullitt, Professor of English and Master of Quincy House, Harvard College; Robert H. Sproat, Associate Professor of English Literature, Boston University; Norman N. Holland, Associate Professor of English, Massachusetts Institute of Technology; and Ira Konigsberg, Assistant Professor of English and American Literature, Brandeis University.

In addition, the defense introduced into evidence reviews of impartial literary critics. These are, in my opinion, of particular significance since their publication indicates that the book is of sufficient significance as to warrant serious critical comment. The reviews were by V. S. Pritchett, New York Review of Books, p. 1 (Oct. 31, 1963); Brigid Brophy, New Statesman, p. 710 (Nov. 15, 1963); and J. Donald Adams, New York Times Book Review, p. 2 (July 28, 1963). And the Appendix to this opinion contains another contemporary view.

[4] There are two reports of the case. The first is captioned *Le Roy v. Sr. Charles Sidney,* 1 Sid. 168, pl. 29 (K. B. 1663); the second is titled *Sir Charles Sydlyes Case,* 1 Keble 620 (K. B. 1663). Sir Charles had made a public appearance on a London balcony while nude, intoxicated, and talkative. He delivered a lengthy speech to the assembled crowd, uttered profanity, and hurled bottles containing what was later described as an "offensive liquor" upon the crowd. The proximate source of the "offensive liquor" appears to have been Sir Charles. Alpert, Judicial Censorship of Obscene Literature, 52 Harv. L. Rev. 40–43 (1938).

[5] *The Queen v. Read,* 11 Mod. 142 (Q. B. 1707).

[6] *Dominus Rex v. Curl,* 2 Strange 789 (K. B. 1727). See Straus, The Unspeakable Curll (1927).

[7] *Rex v. Wilkes,* 4 Burr. 2527 (K. B. 1770). The prosecution of Wilkes was a highly political action, for Wilkes was an outspoken critic of the government. See R. W. Postgate, That Devil Wilkes (1929). It has been suggested that the prosecution in this case was a convenient substitute for the less attractive charge of seditious libel. See Alpert, *supra,* at 45.

[8] See 354 U. S., at 483 and n. 13. For the most part, however, the early legislation was aimed at blasphemy and profanity. See 354 U. S., at 482–483 and n. 12. The first reported decision involv-

ing the publication of obscene literature does not come until 1821. See *Commonwealth v. Holmes*, 17 Mass. 336. It was not until after the Civil War that state prosecutions of this sort became commonplace. See Lockhart & McClure, Literature, The Law of Obscenity, and the Constitution, 38 Minn. L. Rev. 295, 324–325 (1954).

⁹ Tariff Act of 1842, c. 270, § 28, 5 Stat. 566 (prohibiting importation of obscene "prints"). Other federal legislation followed: the development of federal law is traced in Cairns, Paul, & Wishner, Sex Censorship: The Assumptions of Anti-Obscenity Laws and the Empirical Evidence, 46 Minn. L. Rev. 1009, 1010 n. 2 (1962).

¹⁰ See Cairns, Paul & Wishner, *supra*, 1034–1041; Lockhart & McClure, *supra*, at 382–387. And see the summary of Dr. Jahoda's studies prepared by her for Judge Frank, reprinted in *United States v. Roth*, 237 F. 2d 796, 815–816 (concurring opinion). Those who are concerned about children and erotic literature would do well to consider the counsel of Judge Bok:

"It will be asked whether one would care to have one's young daughter read these books. I suppose that by the time she is old enough to wish to read them she will have learned the biologic facts of life and the words that go with them. There is something seriously wrong at home if those facts have not been met and faced and sorted by then; it is not children so much as parents that should receive our concern about this. I should prefer that my own three daughters meet the facts of life and the literature of the world in my library than behind a neighbor's barn, for I can face the adversary there directly. If the young ladies are appalled by what they read, they can close the book at the bottom of page one; if they read further, they will learn what is in the world and in its people, and no parents who have been discerning with their children need fear the outcome. Nor can they hold it back, for life is a series of little battles and minor issues, and the burden of choice is on us all, every day, young and old." *Commonwealth v. Gordon*, 66 Pa. D. & C. 101, 110.

¹¹ It would be a futile effort even for a censor to attempt to remove all that might possibly stimulate antisocial sexual conduct:

"The majority [of individuals], needless to say, are somewhere between the over-scrupulous extremes of excitement and frigidity . . . . Within this variety, it is impossible to define 'hard-core' pornography, as if there were some singly lewd concept from which all profane ideas passed by imperceptible degrees into that sexuality called holy. But there is no 'hard-core.' Everything, every idea, is capable of being obscene if the personality perceiving it so apprehends it.

"It is for this reason that books, pictures, charades, ritual, the spoken word, *can* and *do* lead directly to conduct harmful to the self indulging in it and to others. Heinrich Pommerenke, who was a rapist, abuser, and mass slayer of women in Germany, was prompted to his series of ghastly deeds by Cecil B. DeMille's *The Ten Commandments*. During the scene of the Jewish women dancing about the Golden Calf, all the doubts of his life came clear: Women were the source of the world's trouble and it was his mission to both punish them for this and to execute them. Leaving the theater, he slew his first victim in a park nearby. John George Haigh, the British vampire who sucked his victims' blood through soda straws and dissolved their drained bodies in acid baths, first had his murder-inciting dreams and vampire-longings from watching the 'voluptuous' procedure of—an Anglican High Church Service!" Murphy, *supra*, at 668.

JUSTICE CLARK'S OPINION NOTES

¹ See Lockhart & McClure, Censorship of Obscenity: The Developing Constitutional Standards, 45 Minn. L. Rev. 5, 53–55 (1960).

² In a preface to the paperbook edition, "A Note on the American History of *Memoirs of a Woman of Pleasure*," the publisher itself mentions several critics who denied the book had any literary merit and found it totally undistinguished. These critics included Ralph Thompson and Clifton Fadiman. P. xviii.

³ As one review stated: "Yet all these pangs of defloration are in the service of erotic pleasure—Fanny's and the reader's. Postponing the culmination of Fanny's deflowering is equivalent to postponing the point where the reader has a mental orgasm."

⁴ For a summary of experiments with various sexual stimuli see Cairns, Paul & Wishner, Sex Censorship: The Assumptions of Anti-

Obscenity Laws and the Empirical Evidence, 46 Minn. L. Rev. 1009 (1962). The authors cite research by Kinsey disclosing that obscene literature stimulated a definite sexual response in a majority of the male and female subjects tested.

⁵ *E. g.*, Wertham, Seduction of the Innocent (1954), p. 164.

⁶ Testimony before the Subcommittee of the Judiciary Committee to Investigate Juvenile Delinquency, S. Rep. No. 2381, 84th Cong., 2d Sess., pp. 8–12 (1956).

⁷ Sorokin, The American Sex Revolution (1956).

⁸ Testimony before the House Select Committee on Current Pornographic Materials, H. R. Rep. No. 2510, 82d Cong., 2d Sess., p. 62 (1952).

⁹ See, *e. g.*, Hoover, Combating Merchants of Filth: The Role of the FBI, 25 U. Pitt. L. Rev. 469 (1964); Hoover, The Fight Against Filth, The American Legion Magazine (May 1961).

¹⁰ For a general discussion see Murphy, Censorship: Government and Obscenity (1963), pp. 131–151.

¹¹ The statutes are compiled in S. Rep. No. 2381, 84th Cong., 2d Sess., pp. 17–23 (1956). While New Mexico itself does not prohibit the distribution of obscenity, it has a statute giving municipalities the right to suppress "obscene" publications. N. M. Stat. § 14-17-14 (1965 Supp.).

¹² See Report of the New York State Joint Legislative Committee Studying the Publication and Dissemination of Offensive and Obscene Material (1958), pp. 141–166.

JUSTICE HARLAN'S OPINION NOTES

¹ Given my view of the applicable constitutional standards, I find no occasion to consider the place of "redeeming social importance" in the majority opinion in *Roth*, an issue which further divides the present Court.

² This interest may be viewed from different angles. Compelling the Post Office to aid actively in disseminating this most obnoxious material may simply appear too offensive in itself. Or, more concretely, use of the mails may facilitate or insulate distribution so greatly that federal inaction amounts to thwarting state regulation.

³ The deterrent effect of vagueness for that critical class of books near the law's borderline could in the past be ameliorated by devices like the Massachusetts *in rem* procedure used in this case. Of course, the Court's newly adopted "panderer" test, turning as it does on the motives and actions of the particular defendant, seriously undercuts the effort to give any seller a yes or no answer on a book in advance of his own criminal prosecution.

⁴ As I understand the prevailing opinion, its rationale is that the state court may not condemn *Fanny Hill* as obscene after finding the book to have a modicum of social value; the opinion does note that proof of pandering "might justify the conclusion" that the book wholly lacks social value (*ante*, p. 420). Given its premise for reversal, the opinion has "no occasion to assess" for itself the pruriency, offensiveness, or lack of social value of the book (*ante*, p. 420).

THE "PANDERING TEST" SENDS RALPH GINZBURG TO JAIL. "WHERE THE PURVEYOR'S SOLE EMPHASIS IS ON THE SEXUALLY PROVOCATIVE ASPECTS OF HIS PUBLICATIONS, THAT FACT MAY BE DECISIVE IN THE DETERMINATION OF OBSCENITY."

Ginzburg v. United States, 383 U.S. 463 (1966)

MR. JUSTICE BRENNAN delivered the opinion of the Court.

A judge sitting without a jury in the District Court

for the Eastern District of Pennsylvania [1] convicted petitioner Ginzburg and three corporations controlled by him upon all 28 counts of an indictment charging violation of the federal obscenity statute, 18 U. S. C. § 1461 (1964 ed.).[2] 224 F. Supp. 129. Each count alleged that a resident of the Eastern District received mailed matter, either one of three publications challenged as obscene, or advertising telling how and where the publications might be obtained. The Court of Appeals for the Third Circuit affirmed, 338 F. 2d 12. We granted certiorari, 380 U. S. 961. We affirm. Since petitioners do not argue that the trial judge misconceived or failed to apply the standards we first enunciated in *Roth* v. *United States*, 354 U. S. 476,[3] the only serious question is whether those standards were correctly applied.[4]

In the cases in which this Court has decided obscenity questions since *Roth*, it has regarded the materials as sufficient in themselves for the determination of the question. In the present case, however, the prosecution charged the offense in the context of the circumstances of production, sale, and publicity and assumed that, standing alone, the publications themselves might not be obscene. We agree that the question of obscenity may include consideration of the setting in which the publications were presented as an aid to determining the question of obscenity, and assume without deciding that the prosecution could not have succeeded otherwise. As in *Mishkin* v. *New York*, *post*, p. 502, and as did the courts below, 224 F. Supp., at 134, 338 F. 2d, at 14–15, we view the publications against a background of commercial exploitation of erotica solely for the sake of their prurient appeal.[5] The record in that regard amply supports the decision of the trial judge that the mailing of all three publications offended the statute.[6]

The three publications were EROS, a hard-cover magazine of expensive format; Liaison, a bi-weekly newsletter; and *The Housewife's Handbook on Selective Promiscuity* (hereinafter the *Handbook*), a short book. The issue of EROS specified in the indictment, Vol. 1, No. 4, contains 15 articles and photo-essays on the subject of love, sex, and sexual relations. The specified issue of Liaison, Vol. 1, No. 1, contains a prefatory "Letter from the Editors" announcing its dedication to "keeping sex an art and preventing it from becoming a science." The remainder of the issue consists of digests of two articles concerning sex and sexual relations which had earlier appeared in professional journals and a report of an interview with a psychotherapist who favors the broadest license in sexual relationships. As the trial judge noted, "[w]hile the treatment is largely superficial, it is presented entirely without restraint of any kind. According to defendants' own expert, it is entirely without literary merit." 224 F. Supp., at 134. The *Handbook* purports to be a sexual autobiography detailing with complete candor the author's sexual experiences from age 3 to age 36. The text includes, and prefatory and concluding sections of the book elaborate, her views on such subjects as sex education of children, laws regulating private consensual adult sexual practices, and the equality of women in sexual relationships. It was claimed at trial that women would find the book valuable, for example as a marriage manual or as an aid to the sex education of their children.

Besides testimony as to the merit of the material, there was abundant evidence to show that each of the accused publications was originated or sold as stock in trade of the sordid business of pandering—"the business of purveying textual or graphic matter openly advertised to appeal to the erotic interest of their customers."[7] EROS early sought mailing privileges from the postmasters of Intercourse and Blue Ball, Pennsylvania. The trial court found the obvious, that these hamlets were chosen only for the value their names would have in furthering petitioners' efforts to sell their publications on the basis of salacious appeal;[8] the facilities of the post offices were inadequate to handle the anticipated volume of mail, and the privileges were denied. Mailing privileges were then obtained from the postmaster of Middlesex, New Jersey. EROS and Liaison thereafter mailed several million circulars soliciting subscriptions from that post office; over 5,500 copies of the *Handbook* were mailed.

The "leer of the sensualist" also permeates the advertising for the three publications. The circulars sent for EROS and Liaison stressed the sexual candor of the respective publications, and openly boasted that the publishers would take full advantage of what they regarded as an unrestricted license allowed by law in the expression of sex and sexual matters.[9] The advertising for the *Handbook*, apparently mailed from New York, consisted almost entirely of a reproduction of the introduction of the book, written by one Dr. Albert Ellis. Although he alludes to the book's informational value and its putative therapeutic usefulness, his remarks are preoccupied with the book's sexual imagery. The solicitation was indiscriminate, not limited to those, such as physicians or psychiatrists, who might independently discern the book's therapeutic worth.[10] Inserted in each advertisement was a slip labeled "GUARANTEE" and reading, "Documentary Books, Inc. unconditionally guarantees full refund of the price of THE HOUSEWIFE'S HANDBOOK ON SELECTIVE PROMISCUITY if the book fails to reach you because of U. S. Post Office censorship interference." Similar slips appeared in the advertising for EROS and Liaison; they highlighted the gloss petitioners put on the publications, eliminating any doubt what the purchaser was being asked to buy.[11]

This evidence, in our view, was relevant in determining the ultimate question of obscenity and, in the context of this record, serves to resolve all ambiguity and doubt. The deliberate representation of petitioners' publications as erotically arousing, for example, stimulated the reader to accept them as prurient; he looks for titillation, not for saving intellectual content. Similarly, such representation would tend to force public confrontation with the potentially offensive aspects of the work; the brazenness of such an appeal heightens the offensiveness of the publications to those who are offended by such material. And the circumstances of presentation and dissemination of material are equally relevant to determining whether social importance claimed for material in the courtroom was, in the circumstances, pretense or reality—whether it was the basis upon which it was traded in the marketplace or a spurious claim for litigation purposes. Where the purveyor's sole emphasis is on the sexually provocative aspects of his publications, that fact may be decisive in the determination of obscenity. Certainly in a prosecution which, as here, does not necessarily imply suppression of the materials involved, the fact that they originate or are used as a subject of pandering is relevant to the application of the *Roth* test.

A proposition argued as to EROS, for example, is that the trial judge improperly found the magazine to be obscene as a whole, since he concluded that only four of the 15 articles predominantly appealed to prurient interest and substantially exceeded community standards of candor, while the other articles were admittedly nonoffensive. But the trial judge found that "[t]he deliberate and studied arrangement of EROS is editorialized for the purpose of appealing predominantly to prurient interest and to insulate through the inclusion of nonoffensive material." 224 F. Supp., at 131. However erroneous such a conclusion might be if unsupported by the evidence of pandering, the record here supports it. EROS was created, represented and sold solely as a claimed instrument of the sexual stimulation it would bring. Like the other publications, its pervasive treatment of sex and sexual matters rendered it available to exploitation by those who would make a business of pandering to "the widespread weakness for titillation by pornography."[12] Petitioners' own expert agreed, correctly we think, that "[i]f the object [of a work] is material gain for the creator through an appeal to the sexual curiosity and appetite," the work is pornographic. In other words, by animating sensual detail to give the publication a salacious cast, petitioners reinforced what is conceded by the Government to be an otherwise debatable conclusion.

A similar analysis applies to the judgment regarding the *Handbook*. The bulk of the proofs directed to social importance concerned this publication. Before selling publication rights to petitioners, its author had printed it privately; she sent circulars to persons whose names appeared on membership lists of medical and psychiatric associations, asserting its value as an adjunct to therapy. Over 12,000 sales resulted from this solicitation, and a number of witnesses testified that they found the work useful in their professional practice. The Government does not seriously contest the claim that the book has worth in such a controlled, or even neutral, environment. Petitioners, however, did not sell the book to such a limited audience, or focus their claims for it on its supposed therapeutic or educational value; rather, they deliberately emphasized the sexually provocative aspects of the work, in order to catch the salaciously disposed. They proclaimed its obscenity; and we cannot conclude that the court below erred in taking their own evaluation at its face value and declaring the book as a whole obscene despite the other evidence.[13]

The decision in *United States* v. *Rebhuhn*, 109 F. 2d 512, is persuasive authority for our conclusion.[14] That was a prosecution under the predecessor to § 1461, brought in the context of pandering of publications assumed useful to scholars and members of learned professions. The books involved were written by authors proved in many instances to have been men of scientific standing, as anthropologists or psychiatrists. The Court of Appeals for the Second Circuit therefore assumed that many of the books were entitled to the protection of the First Amendment, and "could lawfully have passed through the mails, if directed to those who would be likely to use them for the purposes for which they were written . . . ." 109 F. 2d, at 514. But the evidence, as here, was that the defendants had not disseminated them for their "proper use, but . . . woefully misused them, and it was that misuse which constituted the gravamen of the crime." *Id.*, at 515. Speaking for the Court in affirming the conviction, Judge Learned Hand said:

". . . [T]he works themselves had a place, though a limited one, in anthropology and in psychotherapy. They might also have been lawfully sold to laymen who wished seriously to study the sexual practices of savage or barbarous peoples, or sexual aberrations; in other words, most of them were not obscene per se. In several decisions we have held that the statute does not in all circumstances forbid the dissemination of such publications . . . . However, in the case at bar, the prosecution succeeded . . . when it showed that the defendants had indiscriminately flooded the mails with advertisements, plainly designed merely to catch the prurient, though under the guise of distributing works of scientific or literary merit. We do not mean that the distributor of such works is charged with a duty to insure that they shall reach only proper hands, nor need we say what care he must use, for these defendants exceeded any possible limit; the circulars were no more than appeals to the salaciously disposed, and no [fact finder] could have failed to pierce the fragile screen, set up to cover that purpose." 109 F. 2d, at 514–515.

We perceive no threat to First Amendment guarantees in thus holding that in close cases evidence of pandering may be probative with respect to the nature of the material in question and thus satisfy the *Roth* test.[15] No weight is ascribed to the fact that petitioners have profited from the sale of publications which we have assumed but do not hold cannot themselves be adjudged obscene in the abstract; to sanction consideration of this fact might indeed induce self-censorship, and offend the frequently stated principle that commercial activity, in itself, is no justification for narrowing the protection of expression secured by the First Amendment.[16] Rather, the fact that each of these publications was created or exploited entirely on the basis of its appeal to prurient interests[17] strengthens the conclusion that the transactions here were sales of illicit merchandise, not sales of constitutionally protected matter.[18] A conviction for mailing obscene publications, but explained in part by the presence of this element, does not necessarily suppress the materials in question, nor chill their proper distribution for a proper use. Nor should it inhibit the enterprise of others seeking through serious endeavor to advance human knowledge or understanding in science, literature, or art. All that will have been determined is that questionable publications are obscene in a context which brands them as obscene as that term is defined in *Roth*—a use inconsistent with any claim to the shelter of the First Amendment.[19] "The nature of the materials is, of course, relevant as an attribute of the defendant's conduct, but the materials are thus placed in context from which they draw color and character. A wholly

different result might be reached in a different setting."
Roth v. *United States*, 354 U. S., at 495 (WARREN, C. J.,
concurring).

It is important to stress that this analysis simply elabo-
rates the test by which the obscenity vel non of the
material must be judged. Where an exploitation of
interests in titillation by pornography is shown with
respect to material lending itself to such exploitation
through pervasive treatment or description of sexual
matters, such evidence may support the determination
that the material is obscene even though in other contexts the material would escape such condemnation.

Petitioners raise several procedural objections, principally directed to the findings which accompanied the
trial court's memorandum opinion, Fed. Rules Crim.
Proc. 23. Even on the assumption that petitioners' objections are well taken, we perceive no error affecting
their substantial rights.

Affirmed.

MR. JUSTICE BLACK, dissenting.

Only one stark fact emerges with clarity out of the
confusing welter of opinions and thousands of words
written in this and two other cases today.[1] That fact is
that Ginzburg, petitioner here, is now finally and authoritatively condemned to serve five years in prison .for
distributing printed matter about sex which neither
Ginzburg nor anyone else could possibly have known to
be criminal. Since, as I have said many times, I believe
the Federal Government is without any power whatever
under the Constitution to put any type of burden on
speech and expression of ideas of any kind (as distinguished from conduct), I agree with Part II of the dissent of my Brother DOUGLAS in this case, and I would
reverse Ginzburg's conviction on this ground alone.
Even assuming, however, that the Court is correct in
holding today that Congress does have power to clamp
official censorship on some subjects selected by the Court,
in some ways approved by it, I believe that the federal
obscenity statute as enacted by Congress and as enforced
by the Court against Ginzburg in this case should be
held invalid on two other grounds.

I.

Criminal punishment by government, although universally recognized as a necessity in limited areas of
conduct, is an exercise of one of government's most
awesome and dangerous powers. Consequently, wise and
good governments make all possible efforts to hedge this
dangerous power by restricting it within easily identifiable boundaries. Experience, and wisdom flowing out
of that experience, long ago led to the belief that agents
of government should not be vested with power and discretion to define and punish as criminal past conduct
which had not been clearly defined as a crime in advance.
To this end, at least in part, written laws came into being, marking the boundaries of conduct for which public
agents could thereafter impose punishment upon people.
In contrast, bad governments either wrote no general
rules of conduct at all, leaving that highly important task
to the unbridled discretion of government agents at the
moment of trial, or sometimes, history tells us, wrote
their laws in an unknown tongue so that people could not
understand them or else placed their written laws at such
inaccessible spots that people could not read them. It
seems to me that these harsh expedients used by bad
governments to punish people for conduct not previously
clearly marked as criminal are being used here to put
Mr. Ginzburg in prison for five years.

I agree with my Brother HARLAN that the Court has
in effect rewritten the federal obscenity statute and
thereby imposed on Ginzburg standards and criteria that
Congress never thought about; or if it did think about
them, certainly it did not adopt them. Consequently,
Ginzburg is, as I see it, having his conviction and sentence affirmed upon the basis of a statute amended by
this Court for violation of which amended statute he was
not charged in the courts below. Such an affirmance we
have said violates due process. *Cole* v. *Arkansas*, 333
U. S. 196. Compare *Shuttlesworth* v. *Birmingham*, 382
U. S. 87. Quite apart from this vice in the affirmance,
however, I think that the criteria declared by a majority
of the Court today as guidelines for a court or jury to determine whether Ginzburg or anyone else can be punished
as a common criminal for publishing or circulating obscene material are so vague and meaningless that they
practically leave the fate of a person charged with violating censorship statutes to the unbridled discretion, whim
and caprice of the judge or jury which tries him. I
shall separately discuss the three elements which a majority of the Court seems to consider material in proving
obscenity.[2]

(a) The first element considered necessary for determining obscenity is that the dominant theme of the
material taken as a whole must appeal to the prurient
interest in sex. It seems quite apparent to me that
human beings, serving either as judges or jurors, could
not be expected to give any sort of decision on this
element which would even remotely promise any kind of
uniformity in the enforcement of this law. What conclusion an individual, be he judge or juror, would reach
about whether the material appeals to "prurient interest
in sex" would depend largely in the long run not upon
testimony of witnesses such as can be given in ordinary
criminal cases where conduct is under scrutiny, but would
depend to a large extent upon the judge's or juror's personality, habits, inclinations, attitudes and other individual characteristics. In one community or in one courthouse a matter would be condemned as obscene under this
so-called criterion but in another community, maybe only
a few miles away, or in another courthouse in the same
community, the material could be given a clean bill of
health. In the final analysis the submission of such an
issue as this to a judge or jury amounts to practically
nothing more than a request for the judge or juror to
assert his own personal beliefs about whether the matter
should be allowed to be legally distributed. Upon this
subjective determination the law becomes certain for the
first and last time.

(b) The second element for determining obscenity as
it is described by my Brother BRENNAN is that the material must be "patently offensive because it affronts contemporary community standards relating to the description or representation of sexual matters . . . ." Nothing
that I see in any position adopted by a majority of the
Court today and nothing that has been said in previous
opinions for the Court leaves me with any kind of cer-

tainty as to whether the "community standards" [3] referred to are world-wide, nation-wide, section-wide, state-wide, country-wide, precinct-wide or township-wide. But even if some definite areas were mentioned, who is capable of assessing "community standards" on such a subject? Could one expect the same application of standards by jurors in Mississippi as in New York City, in Vermont as in California? So here again the guilt or innocence of a defendant charged with obscenity must depend in the final analysis upon the personal judgment and attitudes of particular individuals and the place where the trial is held. And one must remember that the Federal Government has the power to try a man for mailing obscene matter in a court 3,000 miles from his home.

(c) A third element which three of my Brethren think is required to establish obscenity is that the material must be "utterly without redeeming social value." This element seems to me to be as uncertain, if not even more uncertain, than is the unknown substance of the Milky Way. If we are to have a free society as contemplated by the Bill of Rights, then I can find little defense for leaving the liberty of American individuals subject to the judgment of a judge or jury as to whether material that provokes thought or stimulates desire is "utterly without redeeming social value . . . ." Whether a particular treatment of a particular subject is with or without social value in this evolving, dynamic society of ours is a question upon which no uniform agreement could possibly be reached among politicians, statesmen, professors, philosophers, scientists, religious groups or any other type of group. A case-by-case assessment of social values by individual judges and jurors is, I think, a dangerous technique for government to utilize in determining whether a man stays in or out of the penitentiary.

My conclusion is that certainly after the fourteen separate opinions handed down in these three cases today no person, not even the most learned judge much less a layman, is capable of knowing in advance of an ultimate decision in his particular case by this Court whether certain material comes within the area of "obscenity" as that term is confused by the Court today. For this reason even if, as appears from the result of the three cases today, this country is far along the way to a censorship of the subjects about which the people can talk or write, we need not commit further constitutional transgressions by leaving people in the dark as to what literature or what words or what symbols if distributed through the mails make a man a criminal. As bad and obnoxious as I believe governmental censorship is in a Nation that has accepted the First Amendment as its basic ideal for freedom, I am compelled to say that censorship that would stamp certain books and literature as illegal in advance of publication or conviction would in some ways be preferable to the unpredictable book-by-book censorship into which we have now drifted.

I close this part of my dissent by saying once again that I think the First Amendment forbids any kind or type or nature of governmental censorship over views as distinguished from conduct.

II.

It is obvious that the effect of the Court's decisions in the three obscenity cases handed down today is to make it exceedingly dangerous for people to discuss either orally or in writing anything about sex. Sex is a fact of life. Its pervasive influence is felt throughout the world and it cannot be ignored. Like all other facts of life it can lead to difficulty and trouble and sorrow and pain. But while it may lead to abuses, and has in many instances, no words need be spoken in order for people to know that the subject is one pleasantly interwoven in all human activities and involves the very substance of the creation of life itself. It is a subject which people are bound to consider and discuss whatever laws are passed by any government to try to suppress it. Though I do not suggest any way to solve the problems that may arise from sex or discussions about sex, of one thing I am confident, and that is that federal censorship is not the answer to these problems. I find it difficult to see how talk about sex can be placed under the kind of censorship the Court here approves without subjecting our society to more dangers than we can anticipate at the moment. It was to avoid exactly such dangers that the First Amendment was written and adopted. For myself I would follow the course which I believe is required by the First Amendment, that is, recognize that sex at least as much as any other aspect of life is so much a part of our society that its discussion should not be made a crime.

I would reverse this case.

Mr. Justice Douglas, dissenting.

Today's condemnation of the use of sex symbols to sell literature engrafts another exception on First Amendment rights that is as unwarranted as the judge-made exception concerning obscenity. This new exception condemns an advertising technique as old as history. The advertisements of our best magazines are chock-full of thighs, ankles, calves, bosoms, eyes, and hair, to draw the potential buyer's attention to lotions, tires, food, liquor, clothing, autos, and even insurance policies. The sexy advertisement neither adds to nor detracts from the quality of the merchandise being offered for sale. And I do not see how it adds to or detracts one whit from the legality of the book being distributed. A book should stand on its own, irrespective of the reasons why it was written or the wiles used in selling it. I cannot imagine any promotional effort that would make chapters 7 and 8 of the Song of Solomon any the less or any more worthy of First Amendment protection than does their unostentatious inclusion in the average edition of the Bible.

I.

The Court has, in a variety of contexts, insisted that preservation of rights safeguarded by the First Amendment requires vigilance. We have recognized that a "criminal prosecution under a statute regulating expression usually involves imponderables and contingencies that themselves may inhibit the full exercise of First Amendment freedoms." *Dombrowski* v. *Pfister*, 380 U. S. 479, 486. Where uncertainty is the distinguishing characteristic of a legal principle—in this case the Court's "pandering" theory—"the free dissemination of ideas may be the loser." *Smith* v. *California*, 361 U. S. 147, 151. The Court today, however, takes the other course, despite the admonition in *Speiser* v. *Randall*, 357 U. S.

513, 525, that "[t]he separation of legitimate from illegitimate speech calls for . . . sensitive tools." Before today, due regard for the frailties of free expression led us to reject insensitive procedures [1] and clumsy, vague, or overbroad substantive rules even in the realm of obscenity.[2] For as the Court emphasized in *Roth* v. *United States*, 354 U. S. 476, 488, "[t]he door barring federal and state intrusion into this area cannot be left ajar; it must be kept tightly closed and opened only the slightest crack necessary to prevent encroachment upon more important interests."

Certainly without the aura of sex in the promotion of these publications their contents cannot be said to be "utterly without redeeming social importance." *Roth* v. *United States, supra,* at 484.[3] One of the publications condemned today is the Housewife's Handbook on Selective Promiscuity, which a number of doctors and psychiatrists thought had clinical value. One clinical psychologist said: "I should like to recommend it, for example, to the people in my church to read, especially those who are having marital difficulties, in order to increase their tolerance and understanding for one another. Much of the book, I should think, would be very suitable reading for teen age people, especially teen age young women who could empathize strongly with the growing up period that Mrs. Rey [Anthony] relates, and could read on and be disabused of some of the unrealistic notions about marriage and sexual experiences. I should think this would make very good reading for the average man to help him gain a better appreciation of female sexuality."

The Rev. George Von Hilsheimer III, a Baptist minister,[4] testified that he has used the book "insistently in my pastoral counseling and in my formal psychological counseling":

> "The book is a history, a very unhappy history, of a series of sexual and psychological misadventures and the encounter of a quite typical and average American woman with quite typical and average American men. The fact that the book itself is the history of a woman who has had sexual adventures outside the normally accepted bounds of marriage which, of course for most Americans today, is a sort of serial polygamy, it does not teach or advocate this, but gives the women to whom I give the book at least a sense that their own experiences are not unusual, that their sexual failures are not unusual, and that they themselves should not be guilty because they are, what they say, sexual failures."

I would think the Baptist minister's evaluation would be enough to satisfy the Court's test, unless the censor's word is to be final or unless the experts are to be weighed in the censor's scales, in which event one Anthony Comstock would too often prove more weighty than a dozen more detached scholars, or unless we, the ultimate Board of Censors, are to lay down standards for review that give the censor the benefit of the "any evidence" rule or the "substantial evidence" rule as in the administrative law field. Cf. *Universal Camera Corp.* v. *Labor Board*, 340 U. S. 474. Or perhaps we mean to let the courts sift and choose among conflicting versions of the "redeeming social importance" of a particular book, making sure that they keep their findings clear of doubt lest we reverse, as we do today in *Memoirs* v. *Massachusetts, ante,* p. 413, because the lower court in an effort to be fair showed how two-sided the argument was. Since the test is whether the publication is "utterly without redeeming social importance," then I think we should honor the opinion of the Baptist minister who testified as an expert in the field of counseling.

Then there is the newsletter *Liaison*. One of the defendants' own witnesses, critic Dwight Macdonald, testified that while, in his opinion, it did not go beyond the customary limits of candor tolerated by the community, it was "an extremely tasteless, vulgar and repulsive issue." This may, perhaps, overstate the case, but *Liaison* is admittedly little more than a collection of "dirty" jokes and poems, with the possible exception of an interview with Dr. Albert Ellis. As to this material, I find wisdom in the words of the late Judge Jerome Frank:

> "Those whose views most judges know best are other lawyers. Judges can and should take judicial notice that, at many gatherings of lawyers at Bar Association or of alumni of our leading law schools, tales are told fully as 'obscene' as many of those distributed by men . . . convicted for violation of the obscenity statute. . . . 'One thinks of the lyrics sung . . . by a certain respected and conservative member of the faculty of a great law-school which considers itself the most distinguished and which is the Alma Mater of many judges sitting on upper courts.' "[5]

Liaison's appeal is neither literary nor spiritual. But neither is its appeal to a "shameful or morbid interest in nudity, sex, or excretion." The appeal is to the ribald sense of humor which is—for better or worse—a part of our culture. A mature society would not suppress this newsletter as obscene but would simply ignore it.

Then there is EROS. The Court affirms the judgment of the lower court, which found only four of the many articles and essays to be obscene. One of the four articles consisted of numerous ribald limericks, to which the views expressed as to *Liaison* would apply with equal force. Another was a photo essay entitled "Black and White in Color" which dealt with interracial love: a subject undoubtedly offensive to some members of our society. Critic Dwight Macdonald testified:

> "I suppose if you object to the idea of a Negro and a white person having sex together, then, of course, you would be horrified by it. I don't. From the artistic point of view I thought it was very good. In fact, I thought it was done with great taste, and I don't know how to say it—I never heard of him before, but he is obviously an extremely competent and accomplished photographer."

Another defense witness, Professor Horst W. Janson, presently the Chairman of the Fine Arts Department at New York University, testified:

> "I think they are outstandingly beautiful and artistic photographs. I can not imagine the theme being treated in a more lyrical and delicate manner than it has been done here.
>
> .   .   .   .   .
>
> "I might add here that of course photography in

appropriate hands is an artistic instrument and this particular photographer has shown a very great awareness of compositional devices and patterns that have a long and well-established history in western art.

. . . . .

"The very contrast in the color of the two bodies of course has presented him with certain opportunities that he would not have had with two models of the same color, and he has taken rather extraordinary and very delicate advantage of these contrasts."

The third article found specifically by the trial judge to be obscene was a discussion by Drs. Eberhard W. and Phyllis C. Kronhausen of erotic writing by women, with illustrative quotations.[6] The worth of the article was discussed by Dwight Macdonald, who stated:

"I thought [this was] an extremely interesting and important study with some remarkable quotations from the woman who had put down her sense of love-making, of sexual intercourse . . . in an extremely eloquent way. I have never seen this from the woman's point of view. I thought the point they made, the difference between the man's and the woman's approach to sexual intercourse was very well made and very important."

Still another article found obscene was a short introduction to and a lengthy excerpt from My Life and Loves by Frank Harris, about which there is little in the record. Suffice it to say that this seems to be a book of some literary stature. At least I find it difficult on this record to say that it is "utterly without redeeming social importance."[7]

Some of the tracts for which these publishers go to prison concern normal sex, some homosexuality, some the masochistic yearning that is probably present in everyone and dominant in some. Masochism is a desire to be punished or subdued. In the broad frame of reference the desire may be expressed in the longing to be whipped and lashed, bound and gagged, and cruelly treated.[8] Why is it unlawful to cater to the needs of this group? They are, to be sure, somewhat offbeat, nonconformist, and odd. But we are not in the realm of criminal conduct, only ideas and tastes. Some like Chopin, others like "rock and roll." Some are "normal," some are masochistic, some deviant in other respects, such as the homosexual. Another group also represented here translates mundane articles into sexual symbols. This group, like those embracing masochism, are anathema to the so-called stable majority. But why is freedom of the press and expression denied them? Are they to be barred from communicating in symbolisms important to them? When the Court today speaks of "social value," does it mean a "value" to the majority? Why is not a minority "value" cognizable? The masochistic group is one; the deviant group is another. Is it not important that members of those groups communicate with each other? Why is communication by the "written word" forbidden? If we were wise enough, we might know that communication may have greater therapeutical value than any sermon that those of the "normal" community can ever offer. But if the communication is of value to the masochistic community or to others of

the deviant community, how can it be said to be "utterly without redeeming social importance"? "Redeeming" to whom? "Importance" to whom?

We took quite a different stance in One, Inc. v. Olesen, 355 U. S. 371, where we unanimously reversed the decision of the Court of Appeals in 241 F. 2d 772 without opinion. Our holding was accurately described by Lockhart and McClure, Obscenity Censorship: The Core Constitutional Issue—What Is Obscene? 7 Utah L. Rev. 289, 293 (1961):

"[This] was a magazine for homosexuals entitled One—The Homosexual Magazine, which was definitely not a scientific or critical magazine, but appears to have been written to appeal to the tastes and interests of homosexuals."[9]

Man was not made in a fixed mould. If a publication caters to the idiosyncrasies of a minority, why does it not have some "social importance"? Each of us is a very temporary transient with likes and dislikes that cover the spectrum. However plebian my tastes may be, who am I to say that others' tastes must be so limited and that other tastes have no "social importance"? How can we know enough to probe the mysteries of the subconscious of our people and say that this is good for them and that is not? Catering to the most eccentric taste may have "social importance" in giving that minority an opportunity to express itself rather than to repress its inner desires, as I suggest in my separate opinion in Memoirs v. Massachusetts, ante, at 431–432. How can we know that this expression may not prevent antisocial conduct?

I find it difficult to say that a publication has no "social importance" because it caters to the taste of the most unorthodox amongst us. We members of this Court should be among the last to say what should be orthodox in literature. An omniscience would be required which few in our whole society possess.

II.

This leads me to the conclusion, previously noted, that the First Amendment allows all ideas to be expressed—whether orthodox, popular, offbeat, or repulsive. I do not think it permissible to draw lines between the "good" and the "bad" and be true to the constitutional mandate to let all ideas alone. If our Constitution permitted "reasonable" regulation of freedom of expression, as do the constitutions of some nations,[10] we would be in a field where the legislative and the judiciary would have much leeway. But under our charter all regulation or control of expression is barred. Government does not sit to reveal where the "truth" is. People are left to pick and choose between competing offerings. There is no compulsion to take and read what is repulsive any more than there is to spend one's time poring over government bulletins, political tracts, or theological treatises. The theory is that people are mature enough to pick and choose, to recognize trash when they see it, to be attracted to the literature that satisfies their deepest need, and, hopefully, to move from plateau to plateau and finally reach the world of enduring ideas.

I think this is the ideal of the Free Society written into our Constitution. We have no business acting as censors or endowing any group with censorship powers. It is shocking to me for us to send to prison anyone for publishing anything, especially tracts so distant from any incitement to action as the ones before us.

[This opinion applies also to *Mishkin* v. *New York, post,* p. 502.]

MR. JUSTICE HARLAN, dissenting.

I would reverse the convictions of Ginzburg and his three corporate co-defendants. The federal obscenity statute under which they were convicted, 18 U. S. C. § 1461 (1964 ed.), is concerned with unlawful shipment of "nonmailable" matter. In my opinion announcing the judgment of the Court in *Manual Enterprises, Inc.* v. *Day,* 370 U. S. 478, the background of the statute was assessed, and its focus was seen to be solely on the character of the material in question. That too has been the premise on which past cases in this Court arising under this statute, or its predecessors, have been decided. See, *e. g., Roth* v. *United States,* 354 U. S. 476. I believe that under this statute the Federal Government is constitutionally restricted to banning from the mails only "hardcore pornography," see my separate opinion in *Roth, supra,* at 507, and my dissenting opinion in *A Book Named "John Cleland's Memoirs"* v. *Attorney General of Massachusetts, ante,* p. 455. Because I do not think it can be maintained that the material in question here falls within that narrow class, I do not believe it can be excluded from the mails.

The Court recognizes the difficulty of justifying these convictions; the majority refuses to approve the trial judge's "exegesis of *Roth*" (note 3, *ante,* p. 465); it declines to approve the trial court's "characterizations" of the Handbook "outside" the "setting" which the majority for the first time announces to be crucial to this conviction (note 5, *ante,* p. 466). Moreover, the Court accepts the Government's concession that the Handbook has a certain "worth" when seen in something labeled a "controlled, or even neutral, environment" (*ante,* p. 472); the majority notes that these are "publications which we have assumed . . . cannot themselves be adjudged obscene in the abstract" (*ante,* p. 474). In fact, the Court in the last analysis sustains the convictions on the express assumption that the items held to be obscene are not, viewing them strictly, obscene at all (*ante,* p. 466).

This curious result is reached through the elaboration of a theory of obscenity entirely unrelated to the language, purposes, or history of the federal statute now being applied, and certainly different from the test used by the trial court to convict the defendants. While the precise holding of the Court is obscure, I take it that the objective test of *Roth,* which ultimately focuses on the material in question, is to be supplemented by another test that goes to the question whether the mailer's aim is to "pander" to or "titillate" those to whom he mails questionable matter.

Although it is not clear whether the majority views the panderer test as a statutory gloss or as constitutional doctrine, I read the opinion to be in the latter category.[1] The First Amendment, in the obscenity area, no longer fully protects material on its face nonobscene, for such material must now also be examined in the light of the defendant's conduct, attitude, motives. This seems to me a mere euphemism for allowing punishment of a person who mails otherwise constitutionally protected material just because a jury or a judge may not find him or his business agreeable. Were a State to enact a "panderer" statute under its police power, I have little doubt that—subject to clear drafting to avoid attacks on vagueness and equal protection grounds—such a statute would be constitutional. Possibly the same might be true of the Federal Government acting under its postal or commerce powers. What I fear the Court has done today is in effect to write a new statute, but without the sharply focused definitions and standards necessary in such a sensitive area. Casting such a dubious gloss over a straightforward 101-year-old statute (see 13 Stat. 507) is for me an astonishing piece of judicial improvisation.

It seems perfectly clear that the theory on which these convictions are now sustained is quite different from the basis on which the case was tried and decided by the District Court and affirmed by the Court of Appeals.[2] The District Court found the Handbook "patently offensive on its face" and without "the slightest redeeming social, artistic or literary importance or value"; it held that there was "no credible evidence that The Handbook has the slightest valid scientific importance for treatment of individuals in clinical psychiatry, psychology, or any field of medicine." 224 F. Supp. 129, 131. The trial court made similar findings as to Eros and Liaison. The majority's opinion, as I read it, casts doubts upon these explicit findings. As to the Handbook, the Court interprets an offhand remark by the government prosecutor at the sentencing hearing as a "concession," which the majority accepts, that the prosecution rested upon the conduct of the petitioner, and the Court explicitly refuses to accept the trial judge's "characterizations" of the book, which I take to be an implied rejection of the findings of fact upon which the conviction was in fact based (note 5, *ante,* p. 466). Similarly as to Eros, the Court implies that the finding of obscenity might be "erroneous" were it not supported "by the evidence of pandering" (*ante,* p. 471). The Court further characterizes the Eros decision, aside from pandering, as "an otherwise debatable conclusion" (*ante,* p. 471).

If there is anything to this new pandering dimension to the mailing statute, the Court should return the case for a new trial, for petitioners are at least entitled to a day in court on the question on which their guilt has ultimately come to depend. Compare the action of the Court in *Memoirs* v. *Massachusetts, ante,* p. 413, also decided today, where the Court affords the State an opportunity to prove in a subsequent prosecution that an accused purveyor of *Fanny Hill* in fact used pandering methods to secure distribution of the book.

If a new trial were given in the present case, as I read the Court's opinion, the burden would be on the Government to show that the motives of the defendants were to pander to "the widespread weakness for titillation by pornography" (*ante,* p. 471). I suppose that an analysis of the type of individuals receiving Eros and the Handbook would be relevant. If they were ordinary people, interested in purchasing Eros or the Handbook for one of a dozen personal reasons, this might be some evidence of pandering to the general public. On the other hand, as the Court suggests, the defendants could exonerate themselves by showing that they sent these works only or perhaps primarily (no standards are set) to psychiatrists and other serious-minded professional people. Also relevant would apparently be the nature of the mailer's advertisements or representations. Conceivably someone mailing to the public selective portions of a recognized classic with the avowed purpose of titillation would run the risk of conviction for mailing nonmailable matter. Presumably the Post Office under this theory might once again attempt to ban Lady Chatterley's Lover, which a lower court found not bannable in 1960 by an abstract application of *Roth*. *Grove Press, Inc.* v. *Christenberry*, 276 F. 2d 433. I would suppose that if the Government could show that Grove Press is pandering to people who are interested in the book's sexual passages and not in D. H. Lawrence's social theories or literary technique § 1461 could properly be invoked. Even the well-known opinions of Judge A. N. Hand in *United States* v. *One Book Entitled Ulysses*, 72 F. 2d 705, and of Judge Woolsey in the District Court, 5 F. Supp. 182, might be rendered nugatory if a mailer of Ulysses is found to be titillating readers with its "coarse, blasphemous, and obscene" portions, 72 F. 2d, at 707, rather than piloting them through the intricacies of Joyce's stream of consciousness.

In the past, as in the trial of these petitioners, evidence as to a defendant's conduct was admissible only to show relevant intent.[3] Now evidence not only as to conduct, but also as to attitude and motive, is admissible on the primary question of whether the material mailed is obscene. I have difficulty seeing how these inquiries are logically related to the question whether a particular work is obscene. In addition, I think such a test for obscenity is impermissibly vague, and unwarranted by anything in the First Amendment or in 18 U. S. C. § 1461.

I would reverse the judgments below.

MR. JUSTICE STEWART, dissenting.

Ralph Ginzburg has been sentenced to five years in prison for sending through the mail copies of a magazine, a pamphlet, and a book. There was testimony at his trial that these publications possess artistic and social merit. Personally, I have a hard time discerning any. Most of the material strikes me as both vulgar and unedifying. But if the First Amendment means anything, it means that a man cannot be sent to prison merely for distributing publications which offend a judge's esthetic sensibilities, mine or any other's.

Censorship reflects a society's lack of confidence in itself. It is a hallmark of an authoritarian regime. Long ago those who wrote our First Amendment charted a different course. They believed a society can be truly strong only when it is truly free. In the realm of expression they put their faith, for better or for worse, in the enlightened choice of the people, free from the interference of a policeman's intrusive thumb or a judge's heavy hand. So it is that the Constitution protects coarse expression as well as refined, and vulgarity no less than elegance. A book worthless to me may convey something of value to my neighbor. In the free society to which our Constitution has committed us, it is for each to choose for himself.[1]

Because such is the mandate of our Constitution, there is room for only the most restricted view of this Court's decision in *Roth* v. *United States*, 354 U. S. 476. In that case the Court held that "obscenity is not within the area of constitutionally protected speech or press." *Id.*, at 485. The Court there characterized obscenity as that which is "utterly without redeeming social importance," *id.*, at 484, "deals with sex in a manner appealing to prurient interest," *id.*, at 487, and "goes substantially beyond customary limits of candor in description or representation of such matters." *Id.*, at 487, n. 20.[2] In *Manual Enterprises* v. *Day*, 370 U. S. 478, I joined MR. JUSTICE HARLAN's opinion adding "patent indecency" as a further essential element of that which is not constitutionally protected.

There does exist a distinct and easily identifiable class of material in which all of these elements coalesce. It is that, and that alone, which I think government may constitutionally suppress, whether by criminal or civil sanctions. I have referred to such material before as hardcore pornography, without trying further to define it. *Jacobellis* v. *Ohio*, 378 U. S. 184, at 197 (concurring opinion). In order to prevent any possible misunderstanding, I have set out in the margin a description, borrowed from the Solicitor General's brief, of the kind of thing to which I have reference.[3] See also Lockhart and McClure, Censorship of Obscenity: The Developing Constitutional Standards, 45 Minn. L. Rev. 5, 63–64.

Although arguments can be made to the contrary, I accept the proposition that the general dissemination of matter of this description may be suppressed under valid laws.[4] That has long been the almost universal judgment of our society. See *Roth* v. *United States*, 354 U. S., at 485. But material of this sort is wholly different from the publications mailed by Ginzburg in the present case, and different not in degree but in kind.

The Court today appears to concede that the materials Ginzburg mailed were themselves protected by the First Amendment. But, the Court says, Ginzburg can still be sentenced to five years in prison for mailing them. Why? Because, says the Court, he was guilty of "commercial exploitation," of "pandering," and of "titillation." But Ginzburg was not charged with "commercial exploitation"; he was not charged with "pandering"; he was not charged with "titillation." Therefore, to affirm his conviction now on any of those grounds, even if otherwise valid, is to deny him due process of law. *Cole* v. *Arkansas*, 333 U. S. 196. But those grounds are *not*, of course, otherwise valid. Neither the statute under which Ginzburg was convicted nor any other federal statute I know of makes "commercial exploitation" or "pandering" or "titillation" a criminal offense. And any criminal law that sought to do so in the terms so elusively defined by the Court would, of course, be unconstitutionally vague and therefore void. All of these matters are developed in the dissenting opinions of my Brethren, and I simply note here that I fully agree with them.

For me, however, there is another aspect of the Court's opinion in this case that is even more regrettable. Today the Court assumes the power to deny Ralph Ginzburg the protection of the First Amendment because it disapproves of his "sordid business." That is a power the Court does not possess. For the First Amendment protects us all with an even hand. It applies to Ralph

Ginzburg with no less completeness and force than to G. P. Putnam's Sons.[5] In upholding and enforcing the Bill of Rights, this Court has no power to pick or to choose. When we lose sight of that fixed star of constitutional adjudication, we lose our way. For then we forsake a government of law and are left with government by Big Brother.

I dissent.

COURT'S OPINION NOTES

[1] No challenge was or is made to venue under 18 U. S. C. § 3237 (1964 ed.).

[2] The federal obscenity statute, 18 U. S. C. § 1461, provides in pertinent part:

"Every obscene, lewd, lascivious, indecent, filthy or vile article, matter, thing, device, cr substance; and—

. . . .

"Every written or printed card, letter, circular, book, pamphlet, advertisement, or notice of any kind giving information, directly or indirectly, where, or how, or from whom, or by what means any of such mentioned matters . . . may be obtained . . . .

. . . .

"Is declared to be nonmailable matter and shall not be conveyed in the mails or delivered from any post office or by any letter carrier.

"Whoever knowingly uses the mails for the mailing, carriage in the mails, or delivery of anything declared by this section to be nonmailable . . . shall be fined not more than $5,000 or imprisoned not more than five years, or both, for the first such offense . . . ."

[3] We are not, however, to be understood as approving all aspects of the trial judge's exegesis of *Roth*, for example his remarks that "the community as a whole is the proper consideration. In this community, our society, we have children of all ages, psychotics, feeble-minded and other susceptible elements. Just as they cannot set the pace for the average adult reader's taste, they cannot be overlooked as part of the community." 224 F. Supp., at 137. Compare *Butler* v. *Michigan*, 352 U. S. 380.

[4] The Government stipulated at trial that the circulars advertising the publications were not themselves obscene; therefore the convictions on the counts for mailing the advertising stand only if the mailing of the publications offended the statute.

[5] Our affirmance of the convictions for mailing EROS and Liaison is based upon their characteristics as a whole, including their editorial formats, and not upon particular articles contained, digested, or excerpted in them. Thus we do not decide whether particular articles, for example, in EROS, although identified by the trial judge as offensive, should be condemned as obscene whatever their setting. Similarly, we accept the Government's concession, note 13, *infra*, that the prosecution rested upon the manner in which the petitioners sold the *Handbook*; thus our affirmance implies no agreement with the trial judge's characterizations of the book outside that setting.

[6] It is suggested in dissent that petitioners were unaware that the record being established could be used in support of such an approach, and that petitioners should be afforded the opportunity of a new trial. However, the trial transcript clearly reveals that at several points the Government announced its theory that made the mode of distribution relevant to the determination of obscenity, and the trial court admitted evidence, otherwise irrelevant, toward that end.

[7] *Roth* v. *United States, supra*, 354 U. S., at 495–496 (WARREN, C. J., concurring).

[8] Evidence relating to petitioners' efforts to secure mailing privileges from these post offices was, contrary to the suggestion of MR. JUSTICE HARLAN in dissent, introduced for the purpose of supporting such a finding. Scienter had been stipulated prior to trial. The Government's position was revealed in the following colloquy, which occurred when it sought to introduce a letter to the postmaster of Blue Ball, Pennsylvania:

"The COURT. Who signed the letter?

"Mr. CREAMER. It is signed by Frank R. Brady, Associate Publisher of Mr. Ginzburg. It is on Eros Magazine, Incorporated's stationery.

"The COURT. And your objection is——

"Mr. SHAPIRO. It is in no way relevant to the particular issue or publication upon which the defendant has been indicted and in my view, even if there was an identification with respect to a particular issue, it would be of doubtful relevance in that event.

"The COURT. Anything else to say?

"Mr. CREAMER. If Your Honor pleases, there is a statement in this letter indicating that it would be advantageous to this publication to have it disseminated through Blue Ball, Pennsylvania, post office. I think this clearly goes to intent, as to what the purpose of publishing these magazines was. At least, it clearly establishes one of the reasons why they were disseminating this material.

"The COURT. Admitted."

[9] Thus, one EROS advertisement claimed:

"Eros is a child of its times. . . . [It] is the result of recent court decisions that have realistically interpreted America's obscenity laws and that have given to this country a new breadth of freedom of expression. . . . EROS takes full advantage of this new freedom of expression. It is *the* magazine of sexual candor."

In another, more lavish spread:

"EROS is a new quarterly devoted to the subjects of Love and Sex. In the few short weeks since its birth, EROS has established itself as the rave of the American intellectual community—and the rage of prudes everywhere! And it's no wonder: EROS handles the subjects of Love and Sex with complete candor. The publication of this magazine—which is frankly and avowedly concerned with erotica—has been enabled by recent court decisions ruling that a literary piece or painting, though explicitly sexual in content, has a right to be published if it is a genuine work of art.

"EROS is a genuine work of art. . . ."

An undisclosed number of advertisements for Liaison were mailed. The outer envelopes of these ads ask, "Are you among the chosen few?" The first line of the advertisement eliminates the ambiguity: "Are you a member of the sexual elite?" It continues:

"That is, are you among the few happy and enlightened individuals who believe that a man and woman can make love without feeling pangs of conscience? Can you read about love and sex and discuss them without blushing and stammering?

"If so, you ought to know about an important new periodical called *Liaison.*

. . . .

"In short, *Liaison* is Cupid's Chronicle. . . .

"Though *Liaison* handles the subjects of love and sex with complete candor, I wish to make it clear that it is not a scandal sheet and it is not written for the man in the street. *Liaison* is aimed at intelligent, educated adults who can accept love and sex as part of life.

". . . I'll venture to say that after you've read your first biweekly issue, *Liaison* will be your most eagerly awaited piece of mail."

[10] Note 13, *infra.*

[11] There is much additional evidence supporting the conclusion of petitioners' pandering. One of petitioners' former writers for Liaison, for example, testified about the editorial goals and practices of that publication.

[12] Schwartz, Morals Offenses and the Model Penal Code, 63 Col. L. Rev. 669, 677 (1963).

[13] The Government drew a distinction between the author's and petitioners' solicitation. At the sentencing proceeding the United States Attorney stated:

". . . [the author] was distributing . . . only to physicians; she never had widespread, indiscriminate distribution of the Handbook, and, consequently, the Post Office Department did not interfere . . . . If Mr. Ginzburg had distributed and sold and advertised these books solely to . . . physicians . . . we, of course, would not be here this morning with regard to The Housewife's Handbook . . . ."

[14] The Proposed Official Draft of the ALI Model Penal Code likewise recognizes the question of pandering as relevant to the obscenity issue, § 251.4 (4); Tentative Draft No. 6 (May 6, 1957), pp. 1–3, 13–17, 45–46, 53; Schwartz, *supra*, n. 12; see Craig, Suppressed Books, 195–206 (1963). Compare *Grove Press, Inc.* v. *Christenberry*, 175 F. Supp. 488, 496–497 (D. C. S. D. N. Y. 1959), aff'd 276 F. 2d 433 (C. A. 2d Cir. 1960); *United States* v. *One Book Entitled Ulysses*, 72 F. 2d 705, 707 (C. A. 2d Cir. 1934), affirming 5 F. Supp. 182 (D. C. S. D. N. Y. 1933). See also The Trial of Lady Chat-

terly—*Regina v. Penguin Books, Ltd.* (Rolph. ed. 1961).

15 Our conclusion is consistent with the statutory scheme. Although § 1461, in referring to "obscene . . . matter" may appear to deal with the qualities of material in the abstract, it is settled that the mode of distribution may be a significant part in the determination of the obscenity of the material involved. *United States v. Rebhuhn, supra.* Because the statute creates a criminal remedy, cf. *Manual Enterprises v. Day,* 370 U. S. 478, 495 (opinion of BRENNAN, J.), it readily admits such an interpretation, compare *United States v. 31 Photographs, etc.,* 156 F. Supp. 350 (D. C. S. D. N. Y. 1957).

16 See *New York Times v. Sullivan,* 376 U. S. 254, 265–266; *Smith v. California,* 361 U. S. 147, 150.

17 See *Valentine v. Chrestensen,* 316 U. S. 52, where the Court viewed handbills purporting to contain protected expression as merely commercial advertising. Compare that decision with *Jamison v. Texas,* 318 U. S. 413, and *Murdock v. Pennsylvania,* 319 U. S. 105, where speech having the characteristics of advertising was held to be an integral part of religious discussions and hence protected. Material sold solely to produce sexual arousal, like commercial advertising, does not escape regulation because it has been dressed up as speech, or in other contexts might be recognized as speech.

18 Compare *Breard v. Alexandria,* 341 U. S. 622, with *Martin v. Struthers,* 319 U. S. 141. Cf. *Kovacs v. Cooper,* 336 U. S. 77; *Giboney v. Empire Storage Co.,* 336 U. S. 490; *Cox v. Louisiana,* 379 U. S. 536, 559.

19 One who advertises and sells a work on the basis of its prurient appeal is not threatened by the perhaps inherent residual vagueness of the *Roth* test, cf. *Dombrowski v. Pfister,* 380 U. S. 479, 486–487, 491–492; such behavior is central to the objectives of criminal obscenity laws. ALI Model Penal Code, Tentative Draft No. 6 (May 6, 1957), pp. 1–3, 13–17; Comments to the Proposed Official Draft § 251.4, *supra*; Schwartz, Morals Offenses and the Model Penal Code, 63 Col. L. Rev. 669, 677–681 (1963); Paul & Schwartz, Federal Censorship—Obscenity in the Mail, 212–219 (1961); see *Mishkin v. New York, post,* p. 502, at 507, n. 5.

JUSTICE BLACK'S OPINION NOTES

1 See No. 49, *Mishkin v. New York, post,* p. 502, and No. 368, *Memoirs v. Massachusetts, ante,* p. 413.

2 As I understand all of the opinions in this case and the two related cases decided today, three things must be proven to establish material as obscene. In brief these are (1) the material must appeal to the prurient interest, (2) it must be patently offensive, and (3) it must have no redeeming social value. MR. JUSTICE BRENNAN in his opinion in *Memoirs v. Massachusetts, ante,* p. 413, which is joined by THE CHIEF JUSTICE and MR. JUSTICE FORTAS, is of the opinion that all three of these elements must coalesce before material can be labeled obscene. MR. JUSTICE CLARK in a dissenting opinion in *Memoirs* indicates, however, that proof of the first two elements alone is enough to show obscenity and that proof of the third—the material must be utterly without redeeming social value— is only an aid in proving the first two. In his dissenting opinion in *Memoirs* MR. JUSTICE WHITE states that material is obscene "if its predominant theme appeals to the prurient interest in a manner exceeding customary limits of candor." In the same opinion MR. JUSTICE WHITE states that the social importance test "is relevant only to determining the predominant prurient interest of the material."

3 See the opinion of MR. JUSTICE BRENNAN, concurred in by MR. Justice Goldberg in *Jacobellis v. Ohio,* 378 U. S. 184, but compare the dissent in that case of THE CHIEF JUSTICE, joined by MR. JUSTICE CLARK, at 199.

JUSTICE DOUGLAS'S OPINION NOTES

1 *Marcus v. Search Warrant,* 367 U. S. 717; *A Quantity of Books v. Kansas,* 378 U. S. 205; *Freedman v. Maryland,* 380 U. S. 51.

2 *Butler v. Michigan,* 352 U. S. 380; *Smith v. California,* 361 U. S. 147; *Manual Enterprises, Inc. v. Day,* 370 U. S. 478 (opinion of HARLAN, J.).

3 The Court's premise is that Ginzburg represented that his pub-

lications would be sexually arousing. The Court, however, recognized in *Roth:* "[S]ex and obscenity are not synonymous. Obscene material is material which deals with sex in a manner appealing to *prurient* interest . . . i. e., a shameful or morbid interest in nudity, sex, or excretion . . . ." *Id.,* 487 and n. 20 (emphasis added). The advertisements for these publications, which the majority quotes (*ante,* at 468–469, n. 9), promised candor in the treatment of matters pertaining to sex, and at the same time proclaimed that they were artistic or otherwise socially valuable. In effect, then, these advertisements represented that the publications are *not* obscene.

4 Rev. Von Hilsheimer obtained an A. B. at the University of Miami in 1951. He did graduate work in psychology and studied analysis and training therapy. Thereafter, he did graduate work as a theological student, and received a degree as a Doctor of Divinity from the University of Chicago in 1957. He had extensive experience as a group counselor, lecturer, and family counselor. He was a consultant to President Kennedy's Study Group on National Voluntary Services, and a member of the board of directors of Mobilization for Youth.

5 *United States v. Roth,* 237 F. 2d 796, 822 and n. 58 (concurring opinion).

6 The Kronhausens wrote Pornography and the Law (1959).

7 The extensive literary comment which the book's publication generated demonstrates that it is not "utterly without redeeming social importance." See, e. g., New York Review of Books, p. 6 (Jan. 9, 1964); New Yorker, pp. 79–80 (Jan. 4, 1964); Library Journal, pp. 4743–4744 (Dec. 15, 1963); New York Times Book Review, p. 10 (Nov. 10, 1963); Time, pp. 102–104 (Nov. 8, 1963); Newsweek, pp. 98–100 (Oct. 28, 1963); New Republic, pp. 23–27 (Dec. 28, 1963).

8 See Krafft-Ebing, Psychopathia Sexualis, p. 89 *et seq.* (1893); Eisler, Man Into Wolf, p. 23 *et seq.* (1951); Stekel, Sadism and Masochism (1929) *passim;* Bergler, Principles of Self-Damage (1959) *passim;* Reik, Masochism in Modern Man (1941) *passim.*

9 The Court of Appeals summarized the contents as follows:
"The article 'Sappho Remembered' is the story of a lesbian's influence on a young girl only twenty years of age but 'actually nearer sixteen in many essential ways of maturity,' in her struggle to choose between a life with the lesbian, or a normal married life with her childhood sweetheart. The lesbian's affair with her roommate while in college, resulting in the lesbian's expulsion from college, is recounted to bring in the jealousy angle. The climax is reached when the young girl gives up her chance for a normal married life to live with the lesbian. This article is nothing more than cheap pornography calculated to promote lesbianism. It falls far short of dealing with homosexuality from the scientific, historical and critical point of view.
"The poem 'Lord Samuel and Lord Montagu' is about the alleged homosexual activities of Lord Montagu and other British Peers and contains a warning to all males to avoid the public toilets while Lord Samuel is 'sniffing round the drains' of Piccadilly (London). . . .

.   .   .   .   .

"The stories 'All This and Heaven Too,' and 'Not Til the End,' pages 32–36, are similar to the story 'Sappho Remembered,' except that they relate to the activities of the homosexuals rather than lesbians." 241 F. 2d 772, 777, 778.

There are other decisions of ours which also reversed judgments condemning publications catering to a wider range of literary tastes than we seem to tolerate today. See, e. g., *Mounce v. United States,* 355 U. S. 180, vacating and remanding 247 F. 2d 148 (nudist magazines); *Sunshine Book Co. v. Summerfield,* 355 U. S. 372, reversing 101 U. S. App. D. C. 358, 249 F. 2d 114 (nudist magazine); *Tralins v. Gerstein,* 378 U. S. 576, reversing 151 So. 2d 19 (book titled "Pleasure Was My Business" depicting the happenings in a house of prostitution); *Grove Press v. Gerstein,* 378 U. S. 577, reversing 156 So. 2d 537 (book titled "Tropic of Cancer" by Henry Miller).

10 See, e. g., Constitution of the Union of Burma, Art. 17 (i), reprinted in I Peaslee, Constitutions of Nations, p. 281 (2d ed. 1956); Constitution of India, Art. 19 (2), II Peaslee, *op. cit. supra,* p. 227; Constitution of Ireland, Art. 40 (6)(1)(i), II Peaslee, *op. cit. supra,* p. 458; Federal Constitution of the Swiss Confederation, Art. 55, III Peaslee, *op. cit. supra,* p. 344; Constitution of Libya, Art. 22, I Peaslee, Constitutions of Nations, p. 438 (3d ed. 1965); Constitution of Nigeria, Art. 25 (2), *id.,* p. 605; Constitution of Zambia, Art. 22 (2), *id.,* pp. 1040–1041.

JUSTICE HARLAN'S OPINION NOTES

[1] The prevailing opinion in *Memoirs v. Massachusetts, ante*, p. 413, makes clearer the constitutional ramifications of this new doctrine.

[2] Although at one point in its opinion the Court of Appeals referred to "the shoddy business of pandering," 338 F. 2d 12, 15, a reading of the opinion as a whole plainly indicates that the Court of Appeals did not affirm these convictions on the basis on which this Court now sustains them.

[3] To show pandering, the Court relies heavily on the fact that the defendants sought mailing privileges from the postmasters of Intercourse and Blue Ball, Pennsylvania, before settling upon Middlesex, New Jersey, as a mailing point (*ante*. pp. 467–468). This evidence was admitted, however, only to show required scienter, see 338 F. 2d 12, 16. On appeal to the Court of Appeals and to this Court, petitioner Ginzburg asserted that at most the evidence shows the intent of petitioner Eros Magazine, Inc., and was erroneously used against him. The Court of Appeals held the point *de minimis*. 338 F. 2d, at 16–17, on the ground that the parties had stipulated the necessary intent. The United States, in its brief in this Court, likewise viewed this evidence as relating solely to *scienter*; nowhere did the United States attempt to sustain these convictions on anything like a pandering theory.

JUSTICE STEWART'S OPINION NOTES

[1] Different constitutional questions would arise in a case involving an assault upon individual privacy by publication in a manner so blatant or obtrusive as to make it difficult or impossible for an unwilling individual to avoid exposure to it. Cf. *e. g., Breard v. Alexandria*, 341 U. S. 622; *Public Utilities Commission of the District of Columbia v. Pollak*, 343 U. S. 451; *Griswold v. Connecticut*, 381 U. S. 479. Still other considerations might come into play with respect to laws limited in their effect to those deemed insufficiently adult to make an informed choice. No such issues were tendered in this case.

[2] It is not accurate to say that the *Roth* opinion "fashioned standards" for obscenity, because, as the Court explicitly stated, no issue was there presented as to the obscenity of the material involved. 354 U. S., at 481, n. 8. And in no subsequent case has a majority of the Court been able to agree on any such "standards."

[3] ". . . Such materials include photographs, both still and motion picture, with no pretense of artistic value, graphically depicting acts of sexual intercourse, including various acts of sodomy and sadism, and sometimes involving several participants in scenes of orgy-like character. They also include strips of 'drawings in comic-book format grossly depicting similar activities in an exaggerated fashion. There are, in addition, pamphlets and booklets, sometimes with photographic illustrations, verbally describing such activities in a bizarre manner with no attempt whatsoever to afford portrayals of character or situation and with no pretense to literary value. All of this material . . . cannot conceivably be characterized as embodying communication of ideas or artistic values inviolate under the First Amendment. . . ."

[4] During oral argument we were advised by government counsel that the vast majority of prosecutions under this statute involve material of this nature. Such prosecutions usually result in guilty pleas and never come to this Court.

[5] See *Memoirs v. Massachusetts. ante*, p. 413.

"WHERE THE MATERIAL IS DESIGNED FOR AND PRIMARILY DISEMINATED TO A CLEARLY DEFINED DEVIANT SEXUAL GROUP, RATHER THAN THE PUBLIC AT LARGE, THE PRURIENT-APPEAL REQUIREMENT OF THE *ROTH* TEST IS SATISFIED IF THE DOMINANT THEME OF THE MATERIAL TAKEN AS A WHOLE APPEALS TO THE PRURIENT INTEREST IN SEX OF THE MEMBERS OF THAT GROUP."

Mishkin v. New York, 383 U.S. 502 (1966)

MR. JUSTICE BRENNAN delivered the opinion of the Court.

This case. like *Ginzburg v. United States, ante*, p. 463. also decided today, involves convictions under a criminal obscenity statute. A panel of three judges of the Court of Special Sessions of the City of New York found appellant guilty of violating § 1141 of the New York Penal Law [1] by hiring others to prepare obscene books, publishing obscene books, and possessing obscene books with intent to sell them.[2] 26 Misc. 2d 152, 207 N. Y. S. 2d 390 (1960). He was sentenced to prison terms aggregating three years and ordered to pay $12,000 in fines for these crimes.[3] The Appellate Division, First Department, affirmed those convictions. 17 App. Div. 2d 243. 234 N. Y. S. 2d 342 (1962). The Court of Appeals affirmed without opinion. 15 N. Y. 2d 671, 204 N. E. 2d 209 (1964), remittitur amended. 15 N. Y. 2d 724, 205 N. E. 2d 201 (1965). We noted probable jurisdiction. 380 U. S. 960. We affirm.

Appellant was not prosecuted for anything he said or believed, but for what he did. for his dominant role in several enterprises engaged in producing and selling allegedly obscene books. Fifty books are involved in this case. They portray sexuality in many guises. Some depict relatively normal heterosexual relations, but more depict such deviations as sado-masochism, fetishism, and homosexuality. Many have covers with drawings of scantily clad women being whipped, beaten, tortured. or abused. Many, if not most, are photo-offsets of typewritten books written and illustrated by authors and artists according to detailed instructions given by the appellant. Typical of appellant's instructions was that related by one author who testified that appellant insisted that the books be "full of sex scenes and lesbian scenes . . . . [T]he sex had to be very strong, it had to be rough, it had to be clearly spelled out. . . . I had to write sex very bluntly, make the sex scenes very strong. . . . [T]he sex scenes had to be unusual sex scenes between men and women. and women and women, and men and men. . . . [H]e wanted scenes in which women were making love with women . . . . [H]e wanted sex scenes . . . in which there were lesbian scenes. He didn't call it lesbian. but he described women making love to women and men . . . making love to men, and there were spankings and scenes—sex in an abnormal and irregular fashion." Another author testified that appellant instructed him "to deal very graphically with . . . the darkening of the flesh under flagellation . . . ." Artists testified in similar vein as to appellant's instructions regarding illustrations and covers for the books.

All the books are cheaply prepared paperbound "pulps" with imprinted sales prices that are several thousand percent above costs. All but three were printed by a photo-offset printer who was paid 40¢ or 15¢ per copy, depending on whether it was a "thick" or "thin" book. The printer was instructed by appellant not to use appellant's name as publisher but to print some fictitious name on each book, to "make up any name and address." Appellant stored books on the printer's premises and paid part of the printer's rent for the storage space. The printer filled orders for the books, at appellant's direction, delivering them to appellant's retail store, Publishers' Outlet, and, on occasion, shipping books to other places. Appellant paid the authors, artists, and printer cash for their services, usually at his bookstore.

I.

Appellant attacks § 1141 as invalid on its face, contending that it exceeds First Amendment limitations by proscribing publications that are merely sadistic or masochistic, that the terms "sadistic" and "masochistic" are impermissibly vague, and that the term "obscene" is also impermissibly vague. We need not decide the merits of the first two contentions, for the New York courts held in this case that the terms "sadistic" and "masochistic," as well as the other adjectives used in § 1141 to describe proscribed books, are "synonymous with 'obscene.'" 26 Misc. 2d. at 154, 207 N. Y. S. 2d. at 393. The contention that the term "obscene" is also impermissibly vague fails under our holding in *Roth* v. *United States*, 354 U. S. 476, 491–492. Indeed, the definition of "obscene" adopted by the New York courts in interpreting § 1141 delimits a narrower class of conduct than that delimited under the *Roth* definition, *People* v. *Richmond County News, Inc.*, 9 N. Y. 2d 578, 586–587, 175 N. E. 2d 681, 685–686 (1961),[4] and thus § 1141, like the statutes in *Roth*, provides reasonably ascertainable standards of guilt.[5]

Appellant also objects that § 1141 is invalid as applied, *first*, because the books he was convicted of publishing, hiring others to prepare, and possessing for sale are not obscene, and *second*, because the proof of scienter is inadequate.

1. *The Nature of the Material.*—The First Amendment prohibits criminal prosecution for the publication and dissemination of allegedly obscene books that do not satisfy the *Roth* definition of obscenity. States are free to adopt other definitions of obscenity only to the extent that those adopted stay within the bounds set by the constitutional criteria of the *Roth* definition, which restrict the regulation of the publication and sale of books to that traditionally and universally tolerated in our society.

The New York courts have interpreted obscenity in § 1141 to cover only so-called "hard-core pornography," see *People* v. *Richmond County News, Inc.*, 9 N. Y. 2d 578, 586–587, 175 N. E. 2d 681, 685–686 (1961), quoted in note 4, *supra*. Since that definition of obscenity is more stringent than the *Roth* definition, the judgment that the constitutional criteria are satisfied is implicit in the application of § 1141 below. Indeed,

appellant's sole contention regarding the nature of the material is that some of the books involved in this prosecution,[6] those depicting various deviant sexual practices, such as flagellation, fetishism, and lesbianism, do not satisfy the prurient-appeal requirement because they do not appeal to a prurient interest of the "average person" in sex, that "instead of stimulating the erotic, they disgust and sicken." We reject this argument as being founded on an unrealistic interpretation of the prurient-appeal requirement.

Where the material is designed for and primarily disseminated to a clearly defined deviant sexual group, rather than the public at large, the prurient-appeal requirement of the *Roth* test is satisfied if the dominant theme of the material taken as a whole appeals to the prurient interest in sex of the members of that group. The reference to the "average" or "normal" person in *Roth*, 354 U. S., at 489–490, does not foreclose this holding.[7] In regard to the prurient-appeal requirement, the concept of the "average" or "normal" person was employed in *Roth* to serve the essentially negative purpose of expressing our rejection of that aspect of the *Hicklin* test, *Regina* v. *Hicklin*, [1868] L. R. 3 Q. B. 360, that made the impact on the most susceptible person determinative. We adjust the prurient-appeal requirement to social realities by permitting the appeal of this type of material to be assessed in terms of the sexual interests of its intended and probable recipient group; and since our holding requires that the recipient group be defined with more specificity than in terms of sexually immature persons,[8] it also avoids the inadequacy of the most-susceptible-person facet of the *Hicklin* test.

No substantial claim is made that the books depicting sexually deviant practices are devoid of prurient appeal to sexually deviant groups. The evidence fully establishes that these books were specifically conceived and marketed for such groups. Appellant instructed his authors and artists to prepare the books expressly to induce their purchase by persons who would probably be sexually stimulated by them. It was for this reason that appellant "wanted an emphasis on beatings and fetishism and clothing—irregular clothing, and that sort of thing, and again sex scenes between women; always sex scenes had to be very strong." And to be certain that authors fulfilled his purpose, appellant furnished them with such source materials as Caprio, Variations in Sexual Behavior, and Krafft-Ebing, Psychopathia Sexualis. Not only was there proof of the books' prurient appeal, compare *United States* v. *Klaw*, 350 F. 2d 155 (C. A. 2d Cir. 1965), but the proof was compelling; in addition appellant's own evaluation of his material confirms such a finding. See *Ginzburg* v. *United States*, ante, p. 463.

2. *Scienter.*—In *People* v. *Finkelstein*, 9 N. Y. 2d 342, 344–345, 174 N. E. 2d 470, 471 (1961), the New York Court of Appeals authoritatively interpreted § 1141 to require the "vital element of scienter," and it defined the required mental element in these terms:

"A reading of the statute [§ 1141] as a whole clearly indicates that only those who are in some manner aware of the *character* of the material they attempt to distribute should be punished. It is not innocent but *calculated purveyance* of filth which is exorcised . . . ."[9] (Emphasis added.)

Appellant's challenge to the validity of § 1141 founded on *Smith* v. *California*, 361 U. S. 147, is thus foreclosed,[10] and this construction of § 1141 makes it unnecessary for us to define today "what sort of mental element is requisite to a constitutionally permissible prosecution." *Id.,* at 154. The Constitution requires proof of scienter to avoid the hazard of self-censorship of constitutionally protected material and to compensate for the ambiguities inherent in the definition of obscenity. The New York definition of the scienter required by § 1141 amply serves those ends, and therefore fully meets the demands of the Constitution.[11] Cf. *Roth* v. *United States*, 354 U. S., at 495–496 (WARREN, C. J., concurring).

Appellant's principal argument is that there was insufficient proof of scienter. This argument is without merit. The evidence of scienter in this record consists, in part, of appellant's instructions to his artists and writers; his efforts to disguise his role in the enterprise that published and sold the books; the transparency of the character of the material in question, highlighted by the titles, covers, and illustrations; the massive number of obscene books appellant published, hired others to prepare, and possessed for sale; the repetitive quality of the sequences and formats of the books; and the exorbitant prices marked on the books. This evidence amply shows that appellant was "aware of the character of the material" and that his activity was "not innocent but calculated purveyance of filth."

II.

Appellant claims that all but one of the books were improperly admitted in evidence because they were fruits of illegal searches and seizures. This claim is not capable in itself of being brought here by appeal, but only by a petition for a writ of certiorari under 28 U. S. C. § 1257 (3) (1964 ed.) as specifically setting up a federal constitutional right.[12] Nevertheless, since appellant challenged the constitutionality of § 1141 in this prosecution, and the New York courts sustained the statute, the case is properly here on appeal, and our unrestricted notation of probable jurisdiction justified appellant's briefing of the search and seizure issue. *Flournoy* v. *Weiner*, 321 U. S. 253, 263; *Prudential Ins. Co.* v. *Cheek*, 259 U. S. 530, 547. The nonappealable issue is treated, however, as if contained in a petition for a writ of certiorari, see 28 U. S. C. § 2103 (1964 ed.), and the unrestricted notation of probable jurisdiction of the appeal is to be understood as a grant of the writ on that issue. The issue thus remains within our certiorari jurisdiction, and we may, for good reason, even at this stage, decline to decide the merits of the issue, much as we would dismiss a writ of certiorari as improvidently granted. We think that this is a case for such an exercise of our discretion.

The far-reaching and important questions tendered by this claim are not presented by the record with sufficient clarity to require or justify their decision. Appellant's standing to assert the claim in regard to all the seizures is not entirely clear; there is no finding on the extent or nature of his interest in two book stores, the Main Stem Book Shop and Midget Book Shop, in which some of the books were seized. The State seeks to justify the basement storeroom seizure, in part, on the basis of the consent of the printer-accomplice; but there were no

findings as to the authority of the printer over the access to the storeroom, or as to the voluntariness of his alleged consent. It is also maintained that the seizure in the storeroom was made on the authority of a search warrant; yet neither the affidavit upon which the warrant issued nor the warrant itself is in the record. Finally, while the search and seizure issue has a First Amendment aspect because of the alleged massive quality of the seizures, see *A Quantity of Copies of Books* v. *Kansas*, 378 U. S. 205, 206 (opinion of BRENNAN, J.); *Marcus* v. *Search Warrant*, 367 U. S. 717, the record in this regard is inadequate. There is neither evidence nor findings as to how many of the total available copies of the books in the various bookstores were seized and it is impossible to determine whether the books seized in the basement storeroom were on the threshold of dissemination. Indeed, this First Amendment aspect apparently was not presented or considered by the state courts, nor was it raised in appellant's jurisdictional statement; it appeared for the first time in his brief on the merits.

In light of these circumstances, which were not fully apprehended at the time we took the case, we decline to reach the merits of the search and seizure claim; insofar as notation of probable jurisdiction may be regarded as a grant of the certiorari writ on the search and seizure issue, that writ is dismissed as improvidently granted. "Examination of a case on the merits . . . may bring into 'proper focus' a consideration which . . . later indicates that the grant was improvident." *The Monrosa* v. *Carbon Black*, 359 U. S. 180, 184.

Affirmed.

[For dissenting opinion of MR. JUSTICE DOUGLAS, see *ante*, p. 482.]

APPENDIX TO OPINION OF THE COURT.
THE CONVICTIONS BEING REVIEWED.

| Exhibit No. | Title of Book | § 1141 Counts Naming the Book | | |
		Possession	Publishing	Hiring Others
1	Chances Go Around	1	63	111
2	Impact	2	64	112
3	Female Sultan	3	65	113
4	Satin Satellite	4		
5	Her Highness	5	67	115
6	Mistress of Leather	6	68	116
7	Educating Edna	7	69	117
8	Strange Passions	8	70	118
9	The Whipping Chorus Girls	9	71	119
10	Order Of The Day and Bound Maritally	10	72	120
11	Dance With the Dominant Whip	11	73	121
12	Cult Of The Spankers	12	74	122
13	Confessions	13	75	123
14 & 46	The Hours Of Torture	14 & 40	76	124
15 & 47	Bound In Rubber	15 & 41	77	125
16 & 48	Arduous Figure Training at Bondhaven	16 & 42	78	126
17 & 49	Return Visit To Fetterland	17 & 43	79	127
18	Fearful Ordeal In Restraintland	18	80	128
19 & 50	Women In Distress	19 & 44	81	129
20 & 54	Pleasure Parade No. 1	20 & 48	82	130
21 & 57	Screaming Flesh	21 & 51	86	134
22 & 58	Fury	22 & 52		
23	So Firm So Fully Packed	23	87	135
24	I'll Try Anything Twice	24		
25 & 59	Masque	25 & 53		
26	Catanis	26		

Exhibit No.	Title of Book	§ 1141 Counts Naming the Book Possession	Publishing	Hiring Others
27	The Violated Wrestler	27	89	137
28	Betrayal	28		
29	Swish Bottom	29	90	138
30	Raw Dames	30	91	139
31	The Strap Returns	31	92	140
32	Dangerous Years	32	93	141
43	Columns of Agony	37	95	144
44	The Tainted Pleasure	38	96	145
45	Intense Desire	39	97	146
51	Pleasure Parade No. 4	45	85	133
52	Pleasure Parade No. 3	46	84	132
53	Pleasure Parade No. 2	47	83	131
55	Sorority Girls Stringent Initiation	49	98	147
56	Terror At The Bizarre Museum	50	99	148
60	Temptation	57		
61	Peggy's Distress On Planet Venus	58	101	150
62	Ways of Discipline	59	102	151
63	Mrs. Tyrant's Finishing School	60	103	152
64	Perilous Assignment	61	104	153
68	Bondage Correspondence		107	156
69	Woman Impelled		106	155
70	Eye Witness		108	157
71	Stud Broad		109	158
72	Queen Bee		110	159

Mr. Justice Harlan, concurring.

On the issue of obscenity I concur in the judgment of affirmance on premises stated in my dissenting opinion in *A Book Named "John Cleland's Memoirs of a Woman of Pleasure"* v. *Attorney General of Massachusetts, ante,* p. 455. In all other respects I agree with and join the Court's opinion.

Mr. Justice Black, dissenting.

The Court here affirms convictions and prison sentences aggregating three years plus fines totaling $12,000 imposed on appellant Mishkin based on state charges that he hired others to prepare and publish obscene books and that Mishkin himself possessed such books. This Court has held in many cases that the Fourteenth Amendment makes the First applicable to the States. See for illustration cases collected in my concurring opinion in *Speiser* v. *Randall,* 357 U. S. 513, 530. Consequently upon the same grounds that I dissented from a five-year federal sentence imposed upon Ginzburg in No. 42, *ante,* p. 476, for sending "obscene" printed matter through the United States mails I dissent from affirmance of this three-year state sentence imposed on Mishkin. Neither in this case nor in *Ginzburg* have I read the alleged obscene matter. This is because I believe for reasons stated in my dissent in *Ginzburg* and in many other prior cases that this Court is without constitutional power to censor speech or press regardless of the particular subject discussed. I think the federal judiciary because it is appointed for life is the most appropriate tribunal that could be selected to interpret the Constitution and thereby mark the boundaries of what government agencies can and cannot do. But because of life tenure, as well as other reasons, the federal judiciary is the least appropriate branch of government to take over censorship responsibilities by deciding what pictures and writings people throughout the land can be permitted to see and read. When this Court makes particularized rules on what people can see and read, it determines which policies are reasonable and right, thereby performing the classical function of legislative bodies directly responsible to the people. Accordingly, I wish once more to express my objections to saddling this Court with the irksome and inevitably unpopular and unwholesome task of finally deciding by a case-by-case, sight-by-sight personal judgment of the members of this Court what pornography (whatever that means) is too hard core for people to see or read. If censorship of views about sex or any other subject is constitutional then I am reluctantly compelled to say that I believe the tedious, time-consuming and unwelcome responsibility for finally deciding what particular discussions or opinions must be suppressed in this country, should, for the good of this Court and of the Nation, be vested in some governmental institution or institutions other than this Court.

I would reverse these convictions. The three-year sentence imposed on Mishkin and the five-year sentence imposed on Ginzburg for expressing views about sex are minor in comparison with those more lengthy sentences that are inexorably bound to follow in state and federal courts as pressures and prejudices increase and grow more powerful, which of course they will. Nor is it a sufficient answer to these assuredly ever-increasing punishments to rely on this Court's power to strike down "cruel and unusual punishments" under the Eighth Amendment. Distorting or stretching that Amendment by reading it as granting unreviewable power to this Court to perform the legislative function of fixing punishments for all state and national offenses offers a sadly inadequate solution to the multitudinous problems generated by what I consider to be the un-American policy of censoring the thoughts and opinions of people. The only practical answer to these concededly almost unanswerable problems is, I think, for this Court to decline to act as a national board of censors over speech and press but instead to stick to its clearly authorized constitutional duty to adjudicate cases over things and conduct. Halfway censorship methods, no matter how laudably motivated, cannot in my judgment protect our cherished First Amendment freedoms from the destructive aggressions of both state and national government. I would reverse this case and announce that the First and Fourteenth Amendments taken together command that neither Congress nor the States shall pass laws which in any manner abridge freedom of speech and press—whatever the subjects discussed. I think the Founders of our Nation in adopting the First Amendment meant precisely that the Federal Government should pass "no law" regulating speech and press but should confine its legislation to the regulation of conduct. So too, that policy of the First Amendment made applicable to the States by the Fourteenth, leaves the States vast power to regulate conduct but no power at all, in my judgment, to make the expression of views a crime.

Mr. Justice Stewart, dissenting.

The appellant was sentenced to three years in prison for publishing numerous books. However tawdry those books may be, they are not hard-core pornography, and their publication is, therefore, protected by the First and Fourteenth Amendments. *Ginzburg* v. *United States, ante,* p. 497 (dissenting opinion). The judgment should be reversed.*

COURT'S OPINION NOTES

[1] Section 1141 of the Penal Law, in pertinent part, reads as follows:

"1. A person who . . . has in his possession with intent to sell, lend, distribute . . . any obscene, lewd, lascivious, filthy, indecent, sadistic, masochistic or disgusting book . . . or who . . . prints, utters, publishes, or in any manner manufactures, or prepares any such book . . . or who

"2. In any manner, hires, employs, uses or permits any person to do or assist in doing any act or thing mentioned in this section, or any of them,

"Is guilty of a misdemeanor . . . .

.   .   .   .   .

"4. The possession by any person of six or more identical or similar articles coming within the provisions of subdivision one of this section is presumptive evidence of a violation of this section.

"5. The publication for sale of any book, magazine or pamphlet designed, composed or illustrated as a whole to appeal to and commercially exploit prurient interest by combining covers, pictures, drawings, illustrations, caricatures, cartoons, words, stories and advertisements or any combination or combinations thereof devoted to the description, portrayal or deliberate suggestion of illicit sex, including adultery, prostitution, fornication, sexual crime and sexual perversion or to the exploitation of sex and nudity by the presentation of nude or partially nude female figures, posed, photographed or otherwise presented in a manner calculated to provoke or incite prurient interest, or any combination or combinations thereof, shall be a violation of this section."

[2] The information charged 159 counts of violating § 1141; in each instance a single count named a single book, although often the same book was the basis of three counts, each alleging one of the three types of § 1141 offenses. Of these, 11 counts were dismissed on motion of the prosecutor at the outset of the trial and verdicts of acquittal were entered on seven counts at the end of trial. The remaining § 1141 counts on which appellant was convicted are listed in the Appendix to this opinion.

Appellant was also convicted on 33 counts charging violations of § 330 of the General Business Law for failing to print the publisher's and printer's names and addresses on the books. The Appellate Division reversed the convictions under these counts, and the Court of Appeals affirmed. The State has not sought review of that decision in this Court.

[3] The trial court divided the counts into five groups for purposes of sentencing. One group consisted of the possession counts concerning books seized from a basement storeroom in a warehouse; a second group of possession counts concerned books seized from appellant's retail bookstore, Publishers' Outlet; the third consisted of the publishing counts; the fourth consisted of the counts charging him with hiring others to prepare the books, and the fifth consisted of the counts charging violations of the General Business Law. Sentences of one year and a $3,000 fine were imposed on one count of each of the first four groups; the prison sentences on the first three were made consecutive and that on the count in the fourth group was made concurrent with that in the third group. A $500 fine was imposed on one count in the fifth group. Sentence was suspended on the convictions on all other counts. The suspension of sentence does not render moot the claims as to invalidity of the convictions on those counts.

[4] "It [obscene material covered by § 1141] focuses predominantly upon what is sexually morbid, grossly perverse and bizarre, without any artistic or scientific purpose or justification. Recognizable 'by the insult it offers, invariably, to sex, and to the human spirit' (D. H. Lawrence, Pornography and Obscenity [1930], p. 12), it is to be differentiated from the bawdy and the ribald. Depicting dirt for dirt's sake, the obscene is the vile, rather than the coarse, the blow to sense, not merely to sensibility. It smacks, at times, of fantasy and unreality, of sexual perversion and sickness and represents, according to one thoughtful scholar, 'a debauchery of the sexual faculty.' (Murray, Literature and Censorship, 14 Books on Trial 393, 394; see, also, Lockhart and McClure, Censorship of Obscenity: The Developing Constitutional Standards, 45 Minn. L. Rev. 5, 65.)" 9 N. Y. 2d, at 587, 175 N. E. 2d, at 686.

See also People v. Fritch, 13 N. Y. 2d 119, 123, 192 N. E. 2d 713, 716 (1963):

"In addition to the foregoing tests imposed by the decisions of the [United States] Supreme Court, this court interpreted section 1141 of the Penal Law in People v. Richmond County News . . . as applicable only to material which may properly be termed 'hard-core pornography.'"

[5] The stringent scienter requirement of § 1141, as interpreted in People v. Finkelstein, 9 N. Y. 2d 342, 345, 174 N. E. 2d 470, 472 (1961), also eviscerates much of appellant's vagueness claim. See, infra, pp. 510–512. See generally, Boyce Motor Lines, Inc. v. United States, 342 U. S. 337, 342; American Communications Assn. v. Douds, 339 U. S. 382, 412–413; Screws v. United States, 325 U. S. 91, 101–104 (opinion of Mr. Justice Douglas); United States v. Ragen, 314 U. S. 513, 524; Gorin v. United States, 312 U. S. 19, 27–28; Hygrade Provision Co. v. Sherman, 266 U. S. 497, 501–503; Omaechevarria v. Idaho, 246 U. S. 343, 348.

[6] It could not be plausibly maintained that all of the appellant's books, including those dominated by descriptions of relatively normal heterosexual relationships, are devoid of the requisite prurient appeal.

[7] See Manual Enterprises, Inc. v. Day, 370 U. S. 478, 482 (opinion of Harlan, J.); Lockhart and McClure, Censorship of Obscenity: The Developing Constitutional Standards, 45 Minn. L. Rev. 5, 72–73 (1960).

It is true that some of the material in Alberts v. California, decided with Roth, resembled the deviant material involved here. But no issue involving the obscenity of the material was before us in either case. 354 U. S., at 481, n. 8. The basic question for decision there was whether the publication and sale of obscenity, however defined, could be criminally punished in light of First Amendment guarantees. Our discussion of definition was not intended to develop all the nuances of a definition required by the constitutional guarantees.

[8] See generally, 1 American Handbook of Psychiatry 593–604 (Arieti ed. 1959), for a description of the pertinent types of deviant sexual groups.

[9] For a similar scienter requirement see Model Penal Code § 251.4 (2); Commentary, Model Penal Code (Tentative Draft No. 6, 1957), 14, 49–51; cf. Schwartz, Morals Offenses and the Model Penal Code, 63 Col. L. Rev. 669, 677 (1963).

We do not read Judge Froessel's parenthetical reference to knowledge of the contents of the books in his opinion in People v. Finkelstein, 11 N. Y. 2d 300, 304, 183 N. E. 2d 661, 663 (1962), as a modification of this definition of scienter. Cf. People v. Fritch, 13 N. Y. 2d 119, 126, 192 N. E. 2d 713, 717–718 (1963).

[10] The scienter requirement set out in the text would seem to be, as a matter of state law, as applicable to publishers as it is to booksellers; both types of activities are encompassed within subdivision 1 of § 1141. Moreover, there is no need for us to speculate as to whether this scienter requirement is also present in subdivision 2 of § 1141 (making it a crime to hire others to prepare obscene books), for appellant's convictions for that offense involved books for the publication of which he was also convicted.

No constitutional claim was asserted below or in this Court as to the possible duplicative character of the hiring and publishing counts.

[11] The first appeal in Finkelstein defining the scienter required by § 1141 was decided after this case was tried, but before the Appellate Division and Court of Appeals affirmed these convictions. We therefore conclude that the state appellate courts were satisfied that the § 1141 scienter requirement was correctly applied at trial.

The § 1141 counts did not allege appellant's knowledge of the character of the books, but appellant has not argued, below or here, that this omission renders the information constitutionally inadequate.

[12] Unlike the claim here, the challenges decided in the appeals in Marcus v. Search Warrant, 367 U. S. 717, and A Quantity of Copies of Books v. Kansas, 378 U. S. 205, implicated the constitutional validity of statutory schemes establishing procedures for seizing the books.

JUSTICE STEWART'S OPINION NOTE

*See Ginzburg v. United States, ante. p. 497, at 499, note 3 (dissenting opinion). Moreover, there was no evidence at all that any of the books are the equivalent of hard-core pornography in the

eyes of any particularized group of readers. Cf. *United States* v. *Klaw,* 350 F. 2d 155 (C. A. 2d Cir.).

Although the New York Court of Appeals has purported to interpret § 1141 to cover only what it calls "hard-core pornography," this case makes abundantly clear that that phrase has by no means been limited in New York to the clearly identifiable and distinct class of material I have described in *Ginzburg* v. *United States, ante,* p. 497, at 499, note 3 (dissenting opinion).

PAPERBACKS *LUST POOL* AND *SHAME AGENT*, PLUS MAGAZINES *HIGH HEELS, SPREE, SWANK, GENT,* AND OTHERS, RECEIVE FIRST AMENDMENT PROTECTION FROM THE UNITED STATES SUPREME COURT: "IN NONE OF THE CASES WAS THERE A CLAIM THAT THE STATUTE IN QUESTION REFLECTED A SPECIFIC AND LIMITED STATE CONCERN FOR JUVENILES.... IN NONE WAS THERE ANY SUGGESTION OF AN ASSAULT UPON INDIVIDUAL PRIVACY BY PUBLICATION IN A MANNER SO OBTRUSIVE AS TO MAKE IT IMPOSSIBLE FOR AN UNWILLING INDIVIDUAL TO AVOID EXPOSURE TO IT.... AND IN NONE WAS THERE EVIDENCE OF THE SORT OF 'PANDERING' WHICH THE COURT FOUND SIGNIFICANT IN *GINZBURG* ...."

Redrup v. New York, 386 U.S. 767 (1967)

PER CURIAM.

These three cases arise from a recurring conflict—the conflict between asserted state power to suppress the distribution of books and magazines through criminal or civil proceedings, and the guarantees of the First and Fourteenth Amendments of the United States Constitution.

I.

In No. 3, *Redrup* v. *New York,* the petitioner was a clerk at a New York City newsstand. A plainclothes patrolman approached the newsstand, saw two paperback books on a rack—Lust Pool, and Shame Agent—and asked for them by name. The petitioner handed him the books and collected the price of $1.65. As a result of this transaction, the petitioner was charged in the New York City Criminal Court with violating a state criminal law.[1] He was convicted, and the conviction was affirmed on appeal.

In No. 16, *Austin* v. *Kentucky,* the petitioner owned and operated a retail bookstore and newsstand in Paducah, Kentucky. A woman resident of Paducah purchased two magazines from a salesgirl in the petitioner's store, after asking for them by name—High Heels, and Spree. As a result of this transaction the petitioner stands convicted in the Kentucky courts for violating a criminal law of that State.[2]

In No. 50, *Gent* v. *Arkansas,* the prosecuting attorney of the Eleventh Judicial District of Arkansas brought a civil proceeding under a state statute,[3] to have certain issues of various magazines declared obscene, to enjoin their distribution and to obtain a judgment ordering their surrender and destruction. The magazines proceeded

against were: Gent, Swank, Bachelor, Modern Man, Cavalcade, Gentleman, Ace, and Sir. The County Chancery Court entered the requested judgment after a trial with an advisory jury, and the Supreme Court of Arkansas affirmed, with minor modifications.[4]

In none of the cases was there a claim that the statute in question reflected a specific and limited state concern for juveniles. See *Prince* v. *Massachusetts,* 321 U. S. 158; cf. *Butler* v. *Michigan,* 352 U. S. 380. In none was there any suggestion of an assault upon individual privacy by publication in a manner so obtrusive as to make it impossible for an unwilling individual to avoid exposure to it. Cf. *Breard* v. *Alexandria,* 341 U. S. 622; *Public Utilities Comm'n* v. *Pollak,* 343 U. S. 451. And in none was there evidence of the sort of "pandering" which the Court found significant in *Ginzburg* v. *United States,* 383 U. S. 463.

II.

The Court originally limited review in these cases to certain particularized questions, upon the hypothesis that the material involved in each case was of a character described as "obscene in the constitutional sense" in *Memoirs* v. *Massachusetts,* 383 U. S. 413, 418.[5] But we have concluded that the hypothesis upon which the Court originally proceeded was invalid, and accordingly that the cases can and should be decided upon a common and controlling fundamental constitutional basis, without prejudice to the questions upon which review was originally granted. We have concluded, in short, that the distribution of the publications in each of these cases is protected by the First and Fourteenth Amendments from governmental suppression, whether criminal or civil, *in personam* or *in rem.*[6]

Two members of the Court have consistently adhered to the view that a State is utterly without power to suppress, control, or punish the distribution of any writings or pictures upon the ground of their "obscenity."[7] A third has held to the opinion that a State's power in this area is narrowly limited to a distinct and clearly identifiable class of material.[8] Others have subscribed to a not dissimilar standard, holding that a State may not constitutionally inhibit the distribution of literary material as obscene unless "(a) the dominant theme of the material taken as a whole appeals to a prurient interest in sex; (b) the material is patently offensive because it affronts contemporary community standards relating to the description or representation of sexual matters; and (c) the material is utterly without redeeming social value," emphasizing that the "three elements must coalesce," and that no such material can "be proscribed unless it is found to be *utterly* without redeeming social value." *Memoirs* v. *Massachusetts,* 383 U. S. 413, 418–419. Another Justice has not viewed the "social value" element as an independent factor in the judgment of obscenity. *Id.,* at 460–462 (dissenting opinion).

Whichever of these constitutional views is brought to bear upon the cases before us, it is clear that the judgments cannot stand. Accordingly, the judgment in each case is reversed.

It is so ordered.

MR. JUSTICE HARLAN, whom MR. JUSTICE CLARK joins, dissenting.

Two of these cases, *Redrup* v. *New York* and *Austin* v.

Kentucky, were taken to consider the standards governing the application of the *scienter* requirement announced in *Smith* v. *California*, 361 U. S. 147. for obscenity prosecutions. There it was held that a defendant criminally charged with purveying obscene material must be shown to have had some kind of knowledge of the character of such material; the quality of that knowledge, however, was not defined. The third case, *Gent* v. *Arkansas*, was taken to consider the validity of a comprehensive Arkansas anti-obscenity statute, in light of the doctrines of "vagueness" and "prior restraint." The writs of certiorari in *Redrup* and *Austin*, and the notation of probable jurisdiction in *Gent*, were respectively limited to these issues, thus laying aside, for the purposes of these cases, the permissibility of the state determinations as to the obscenity of the challenged publications. Accordingly, the obscenity *vel non* of these publications was not discussed in the briefs or oral arguments of any of the parties.

The three cases were argued together at the beginning of this Term. Today, the Court rules that the materials could not constitutionally be adjudged obscene by the States, thus rendering adjudication of the other issues unnecessary. In short, the Court disposes of the cases on the issue that was deliberately excluded from review, and refuses to pass on the questions that brought the cases here.

In my opinion these dispositions do not reflect well on the processes of the Court, and I think the issues for which the cases were taken should be decided. Failing that, I prefer to cast my vote to dismiss the writs in *Redrup* and *Austin* as improvidently granted and, in the circumstances, to dismiss the appeal in *Gent* for lack of a substantial federal question. I deem it more appropriate to defer an expression of my own views on the questions brought here until an occasion when the Court is prepared to come to grips with such issues.

NOTES

[1] N. Y. Pen. Law § 1141 (1).

[2] Ky. Rev. Stat. § 436.100. The Kentucky Court of Appeals denied plenary review of the petitioner's conviction, the Chief Justice dissenting. 386 S. W. 2d 270.

[3] Ark. Stat. Ann. §§ 41–2713 to 41–2728.

[4] 239 Ark. 474, 393 S. W. 2d 219.

[5] *Redrup* v. *New York*, 384 U. S. 916; *Austin* v. *Kentucky*, 384 U. S. 916; *Gent* v. *Arkansas*, 384 U. S. 937.

[6] In each of the cases before us, the contention that the publications involved were basically protected by the First and Fourteenth Amendments was timely but unsuccessfully asserted in the state proceedings. In each of these cases, this contention was properly and explicitly presented for review here.

[7] See *Ginzburg* v. *United States*, 383 U. S. 463, 476, 482 (dissenting opinions); *Jacobellis* v. *Ohio*, 378 U. S. 184, 196 (concurring opinion); *Roth* v. *United States*, 354 U. S. 476, 508 (dissenting opinion).

[8] See *Ginzburg* v. *United States*, 383 U. S. 463, 499, and n. 3 (dissenting opinion). See also Magrath, The Obscenity Cases: Grapes of Roth, 1966 Supreme Court Review 7, 69–77.

"IT IS ENOUGH FOR THE PURPOSES OF THIS CASE THAT WE INQUIRE WHETHER IT WAS CONSTITUTIONALLY IMPERMISSIBLE FOR NEW YORK . . . TO ACCORD MINORS UNDER 17 A MORE RESTRICTED RIGHT THAN THAT ASSURED TO ADULTS TO JUDGE AND DETERMINE FOR THEMSELVES WHAT SEX MATERIAL THEY MAY READ OR SEE. WE CONCLUDE THAT WE CANNOT SAY THAT THE STATUTE INVADES THE AREA OF FREEDOM OF EXPRESSION CONSTITUTIONALLY SECURED TO MINORS."

Ginsberg v. New York, 390 U.S. 629 (1968)

Mr. Justice Brennan delivered the opinion of the Court.

This case presents the question of the constitutionality on its face of a New York criminal obscenity statute which prohibits the sale to minors under 17 years of age of material defined to be obscene on the basis of its appeal to them whether or not it would be obscene to adults.

Appellant and his wife operate "Sam's Stationery and Luncheonette" in Bellmore, Long Island. They have a lunch counter, and, among other things, also sell magazines including some so-called "girlie" magazines. Appellant was prosecuted under two informations, each in two counts, which charged that he personally sold a 16-year-old boy two "girlie" magazines on each of two dates in October 1965, in violation of § 484–h of the New York Penal Law. He was tried before a judge without a jury in Nassau County District Court and was found guilty on both counts.[1] The judge found (1) that the magazines contained pictures which depicted female "nudity" in a manner defined in subsection 1 (b), that is "the showing of . . . female . . . buttocks with less than a full opaque covering, or the showing of the female breast with less than a fully opaque covering of any portion thereof below the top of the nipple . . . ," and (2) that the pictures were "harmful to minors" in that they had, within the meaning of subsection 1 (f) "that quality of . . . representation . . . of nudity . . . [which] . . . (i) predominantly appeals to the prurient, shameful or morbid interest of minors, and (ii) is patently offensive to prevailing standards in the adult community as a whole with respect to what is suitable material for minors, and (iii) is utterly without redeeming social importance for minors." He held that both sales to the 16-year-old boy therefore constituted the violation under § 484–h of "knowingly to sell . . . to a minor" under 17 of "(a) any picture . . . which depicts nudity . . . and which is harmful to minors," and "(b) any . . . magazine . . . which contains . . . [such pictures] . . . and which, taken as a whole, is harmful to minors." The conviction was affirmed without opinion by the Appellate Term, Second Department, of the Supreme Court. Appellant was denied leave to appeal to the New York Court of Appeals and then appealed to this Court. We noted probable jurisdiction. 388 U. S. 904. We affirm.[2]

I.

The "girlie" picture magazines involved in the sales here are not obscene for adults, *Redrup* v. *New York*, 386 U. S. 767.[3] But § 484-h does not bar the appellant from stocking the magazines and selling them to persons 17 years of age or older, and therefore the conviction is not invalid under our decision in *Butler* v. *Michigan*, 352 U. S. 380.

Obscenity is not within the area of protected speech or press. *Roth* v. *United States*, 354 U. S. 476, 485. The three-pronged test of subsection 1 (f) for judging the obscenity of material sold to minors under 17 is a variable from the formulation for determining obscenity under *Roth* stated in the plurality opinion in *Memoirs* v. *Massachusetts*, 383 U. S. 413, 418. Appellant's primary attack upon § 484-h is leveled at the power of the State to adapt this *Memoirs* formulation to define the material's obscenity on the basis of its appeal to minors, and thus exclude material so defined from the area of protected expression. He makes no argument that the magazines are not "harmful to minors" within the definition in subsection 1 (f). Thus "[n]o issue is presented . . . concerning the obscenity of the material involved." *Roth, supra*, at 481, n. 8.

The New York Court of Appeals "upheld the Legislature's power to employ variable concepts of obscenity"[4] in a case in which the same challenge to state power to enact such a law was also addressed to § 484-h. *Bookcase, Inc.* v. *Broderick*, 18 N. Y. 2d 71, 218 N. E. 2d 668, appeal dismissed for want of a properly presented federal question, *sub nom. Bookcase, Inc.* v. *Leary*, 385 U. S. 12. In sustaining state power to enact the law, the Court of Appeals said, *Bookcase, Inc.* v. *Broderick*, at 75, 218 N. E. 2d, at 671:

"[M]aterial which is protected for distribution to adults is not necessarily constitutionally protected from restriction upon its dissemination to children. In other words, the concept of obscenity or of unprotected matter may vary according to the group to whom the questionable material is directed or from whom it is quarantined. Because of the State's exigent interest in preventing distribution to children of objectionable material, it can exercise its power to protect the health, safety, welfare and morals of its community by barring the distribution to children of books recognized to be suitable for adults."

Appellant's attack is not that New York was without power to draw the line at age 17. Rather, his contention is the broad proposition that the scope of the constitutional freedom of expression secured to a citizen to read or see material concerned with sex cannot be made to depend upon whether the citizen is an adult or a minor. He accordingly insists that the denial to minors under 17 of access to material condemned by § 484-h, insofar as that material is not obscene for persons 17 years of age or older, constitutes an unconstitutional deprivation of protected liberty.

We have no occasion in this case to consider the impact of the guarantees of freedom of expression upon the totality of the relationship of the minor and the State, cf. *In re Gault*, 387 U. S. 1, 13. It is enough for the purposes of this case that we inquire whether it was constitutionally impermissible for New York, insofar as

§ 484-h does so, to accord minors under 17 a more restricted right than that assured to adults to judge and determine for themselves what sex material they may read or see. We conclude that we cannot say that the statute invades the area of freedom of expression constitutionally secured to minors.[5]

Appellant argues that there is an invasion of protected rights under § 484-h constitutionally indistinguishable from the invasions under the Nebraska statute forbidding children to study German, which was struck down in *Meyer* v. *Nebraska*, 262 U. S. 390; the Oregon statute interfering with children's attendance at private and parochial schools, which was struck down in *Pierce* v. *Society of Sisters*, 268 U. S. 510; and the statute compelling children against their religious scruples to give the flag salute, which was struck down in *West Virginia State Board of Education* v. *Barnette*, 319 U. S. 624. We reject that argument. We do not regard New York's regulation in defining obscenity on the basis of its appeal to minors under 17 as involving an invasion of such minors' constitutionally protected freedoms. Rather § 484-h simply adjusts the definition of obscenity "to social realities by permitting the appeal of this type of material to be assessed in terms of the sexual interests . . ." of such minors. *Mishkin* v. *New York*, 383 U. S. 502, 509; *Bookcase, Inc.* v. *Broderick, supra*, at 75, 218 N. E. 2d, at 671. That the State has power to make that adjustment seems clear, for we have recognized that even where there is an invasion of protected freedoms "the power of the state to control the conduct of children reaches beyond the scope of its authority over adults . . . ." *Prince* v. *Massachusetts*, 321 U. S. 158, 170.[6] In *Prince* we sustained the conviction of the guardian of a nine-year-old girl, both members of the sect of Jehovah's Witnesses, for violating the Massachusetts Child Labor Law by permitting the girl to sell the sect's religious tracts on the streets of Boston.

The well-being of its children is of course a subject within the State's constitutional power to regulate, and, in our view, two interests justify the limitations in § 484-h upon the availability of sex material to minors under 17, at least if it was rational for the legislature to find that the minors' exposure to such material might be harmful. First of all, constitutional interpretation has consistently recognized that the parents' claim to authority in their own household to direct the rearing of their children is basic in the structure of our society. "It is cardinal with us that the custody, care and nurture of the child reside first in the parents, whose primary function and freedom include preparation for obligations the state can neither supply nor hinder." *Prince* v. *Massachusetts, supra*, at 166. The legislature could properly conclude that parents and others, teachers for example, who have this primary responsibility for children's well-being are entitled to the support of laws designed to aid discharge of that responsibility. Indeed, subsection 1 (f)(ii) of § 484-h expressly recognizes the parental role in assessing sex-related material harmful to minors according "to prevailing standards in the adult community as a whole with respect to what is suitable material for minors." Moreover, the prohibition against sales to minors does not bar parents who so desire from purchasing the magazines for their children.[7]

The State also has an independent interest in the well-being of its youth. The New York Court of Appeals squarely bottomed its decision on that interest in *Bookcase, Inc. v. Broderick, supra,* at 75, 218 N. E. 2d, at 671. Judge Fuld, now Chief Judge Fuld, also emphasized its significance in the earlier case of *People v. Kahan,* 15 N. Y. 2d 311, 206 N. E. 2d 333, which had struck down the first version of § 484–h on grounds of vagueness. In his concurring opinion, *id.,* at 312, 206 N. E. 2d, at 334, he said:

> "While the supervision of children's reading may best be left to their parents, the knowledge that parental control or guidance cannot always be provided and society's transcendent interest in protecting the welfare of children justify reasonable regulation of the sale of material to them. It is, therefore, altogether fitting and proper for a state to include in a statute designed to regulate the sale of pornography to children special standards, broader than those embodied in legislation aimed at controlling dissemination of such material to adults."

In *Prince v. Massachusetts, supra,* at 165, this Court, too, recognized that the State has an interest "to protect the welfare of children" and to see that they are "safeguarded from abuses" which might prevent their "growth into free and independent well-developed men and citizens." The only question remaining, therefore, is whether the New York Legislature might rationally conclude, as it has, that exposure to the materials proscribed by § 484–h constitutes such an "abuse."

Section 484–e of the law states a legislative finding that the material condemned by § 484–h is "a basic factor in impairing the ethical and moral development of our youth and a clear and present danger to the people of the state." It is very doubtful that this finding expresses an accepted scientific fact.[8] But obscenity is not protected expression and may be suppressed without a showing of the circumstances which lie behind the phrase "clear and present danger" in its application to protected speech. *Roth v. United States, supra,* at 486–487.[9] To sustain state power to exclude material defined as obscenity by § 484–h requires only that we be able to say that it was not irrational for the legislature to find that exposure to material condemned by the statute is harmful to minors. In *Meyer v. Nebraska, supra,* at 400, we were able to say that children's knowledge of the German language "cannot reasonably be regarded as harmful." That cannot be said by us of minors' reading and seeing sex material. To be sure, there is no lack of "studies" which purport to demonstrate that obscenity is or is not "a basic factor in impairing the ethical and moral development of . . . youth and a clear and present danger to the people of the state." But the growing consensus of commentators is that "while these studies all agree that a causal link has not been demonstrated, they are equally agreed that a causal link has not been disproved either."[10] We do not demand of legislatures "scientifically certain criteria of legislation." *Noble State Bank v. Haskell,* 219 U. S. 104, 110. We therefore cannot say that § 484–h, in defining the obscenity of material on the basis of its appeal to minors under 17, has no rational relation to the objective of safeguard-

ing such minors from harm.

II.

Appellant challenges subsections (f) and (g) of § 484–h as in any event void for vagueness. The attack on subsection (f) is that the definition of obscenity "harmful to minors" is so vague that an honest distributor of publications cannot know when he might be held to have violated § 484–h. But the New York Court of Appeals construed this definition to be "virtually identical to the Supreme Court's most recent statement of the elements of obscenity. [*Memoirs v. Massachusetts,* 383 U. S. 413, 418]," *Bookcase, Inc. v. Broderick, supra,* at 76, 218 N. E. 2d, at 672. The definition therefore gives "men in acting adequate notice of what is prohibited" and does not offend the requirements of due process. *Roth v. United States, supra,* at 492; see also *Winters v. New York,* 333 U. S. 507, 520.

As is required by *Smith v. California,* 361 U. S. 147, § 484–h prohibits only those sales made "knowingly." The challenge to the *scienter* requirement of subsection (g) centers on the definition of "knowingly" insofar as it includes "reason to know" or "a belief or ground for belief which warrants further inspection or inquiry of both: (i) the character and content of any material described herein which is reasonably susceptible of examination by the defendant, and (ii) the age of the minor, provided however, that an honest mistake shall constitute an excuse from liability hereunder if the defendant made a reasonable bona fide attempt to ascertain the true age of such minor."

As to (i). § 484–h was passed after the New York Court of Appeals decided *People v. Finkelstein,* 9 N. Y. 2d 342, 174 N. E. 2d 470, which read the requirement of *scienter* into New York's general obscenity statute, § 1141 of the Penal Law. The constitutional requirement of *scienter,* in the sense of knowledge of the contents of material, rests on the necessity "to avoid the hazard of self-censorship of constitutionally protected material and to compensate for the ambiguities inherent in the definition of obscenity," *Mishkin v. New York, supra,* at 511. The Court of Appeals in *Finkelstein* interpreted § 1141 to require "the vital element of scienter" and defined that requirement in these terms: "A reading of the statute [§ 1141] as a whole clearly indicates that only those who are *in some manner aware of the character of the material* they attempt to distribute should be punished. It is not innocent but *calculated* purveyance of filth which is exorcised . . . ." 9 N. Y. 2d, at 344–345, 174 N. E. 2d, at 471. (Emphasis supplied.) In *Mishkin v. New York, supra,* at 510–511, we held that a challenge to the validity of § 1141 founded on *Smith v. California, supra,* was foreclosed in light of this construction. When § 484–h was before the New York Legislature its attention was directed to *People v. Finkelstein,* as defining the nature of *scienter* required to sustain the statute. 1965 N. Y. S. Leg. Ann. 54–56. We may therefore infer that the reference in provision (i) to knowledge of "the *character* and content of any material described herein" incorporates the gloss given the term "character" in *People v. Finkelstein.* In that circumstance *Mishkin* requires rejection of appellant's challenge to provision (i) and makes it unnecessary for us to define further today "what sort of mental element is requisite to a constitutionally permissible prosecution," *Smith* v. *California, supra,* at 154.

Appellant also attacks provision (ii) as impermissibly vague. This attack however is leveled only at the proviso according the defendant a defense of "honest mistake" as to the age of the minor. Appellant argues that "the statute does not tell the bookseller what effort he must make before he can be excused." The argument is wholly without merit. The proviso states expressly that the defendant must be acquitted on the ground of "honest mistake" if the defendant proves that he made "a reasonable bona fide attempt to ascertain the true age of such minor." Cf. 1967 Penal Law § 235.22 (2), n. 1, *supra.*

Affirmed.

[For concurring opinion of Mr. Justice Harlan see *post*, p. 704.]

APPENDIX A TO OPINION OF THE COURT.

New York Penal Law § 484–h as enacted by L. 1965, c. 327, provides:

§ 484–h. Exposing minors to harmful materials

1. Definitions. As used in this section:

(a) "Minor" means any person under the age of seventeen years.

(b) "Nudity" means the showing of the human male or female genitals, pubic area or buttocks with less than a full opaque covering, or the showing of the female breast with less than a fully opaque covering of any portion thereof below the top of the nipple, or the depiction of covered male genitals in a discernibly turgid state.

(c) "Sexual conduct" means acts of masturbation, homosexuality, sexual intercourse, or physical contact with a person's clothed or unclothed genitals, pubic area, buttocks or, if such person be a female, breast.

(d) "Sexual excitement" means the condition of human male or female genitals when in a state of sexual stimulation or arousal.

(e) "Sado-masochistic abuse" means flagellation or torture by or upon a person clad in undergarments, a mask or bizarre costume, or the condition of being fettered, bound or otherwise physically restrained on the part of one so clothed.

(f) "Harmful to minors" means that quality of any description or representation, in whatever form, of nudity, sexual conduct, sexual excitement, or sado-masochistic abuse, when it:

(i) predominantly appeals to the prurient, shameful or morbid interest of minors, and

(ii) is patently offensive to prevailing standards in the adult community as a whole with respect to what is suitable material for minors, and

(iii) is utterly without redeeming social importance for minors.

(g) "Knowingly" means having general knowledge of, or reason to know, or a belief or ground for belief which warrants further inspection or inquiry of both:

(i) the character and content of any material described herein which is reasonably susceptible of examination by the defendant, and

(ii) the age of the minor, provided however, that an honest mistake shall constitute an excuse from liability hereunder if the defendant made a reasonable bona fide attempt to ascertain the true age of such minor.

2. It shall be unlawful for any person knowingly to sell or loan for monetary consideration to a minor:

(a) any picture, photograph, drawing, sculpture, motion picture film, or similar visual representation or image of a person or portion of the human body which depicts nudity, sexual conduct or sado-masochistic abuse and which is harmful to minors, or

(b) any book, pamphlet, magazine, printed matter however reproduced, or sound recording which contains any matter enumerated in paragraph (a) of subdivision two hereof, or explicit and detailed verbal descriptions or narrative accounts of sexual excitement, sexual conduct or sado-masochistic abuse and which, taken as a whole, is harmful to minors.

3. It shall be unlawful for any person knowingly to exhibit for a monetary consideration to a minor or knowingly to sell to a minor an admission ticket or pass or knowingly to admit a minor for a monetary consideration to premises whereon there is exhibited, a motion picture, show or other presentation which, in whole or in part, depicts nudity, sexual conduct or sado-masochistic abuse and which is harmful to minors.

4. A violation of any provision hereof shall constitute a misdemeanor.

APPENDIX B TO OPINION OF THE COURT.

State obscenity statutes having some provision referring to distribution to minors are:
Cal. Pen. Code §§ 311–312 (Supp. 1966); Colo. Rev. Stat. Ann. §§ 40–9–16 to 40–9–27 (1963); Conn. Gen. Stat. Rev. §§ 53–243 to 53–245 (Supp. 1965); Del. Code Ann., Tit. 11, §§ 435, 711–713 (1953); Fla. Stat. Ann. §§ 847.011–847.06 (1965 and Supp. 1968); Ga. Code Ann. §§ 26–6301 to 26–6309a (Supp. 1967); Hawaii Rev. Laws § 267–8 (1955); Idaho Code Ann. §§ 18–1506 to 18–1510 (Supp. 1967); Ill. Ann. Stat., c. 38, §§ 11–20 to 11–21 (Supp. 1967); Iowa Code Ann. §§ 725.4–725.12 (1950); Ky. Rev. Stat. §§ 436.100–436.130, 436.540–436.580 (1963 and Supp. 1966); La. Rev. Stat. §§ 14:91.11, 14:92, 14:106 (Supp. 1967); Me. Rev. Stat. Ann., Tit. 17, §§ 2901–2905 (1964); Md. Ann. Code, Art. 27, §§ 417–425 (1957 and Supp. 1967); Mass. Gen. Laws Ann., c. 272, §§ 28–33 (1959 and Supp. 1968); Mich. Stat. Ann. §§ 28.575–28.579 (1954 and Supp. 1968); Mo. Ann. Stat. §§ 563.270–563.310 (1953 and Supp. 1967); Mont. Rev. Codes Ann. §§ 94–3601 to 94–3606 (1947 and Supp. 1967); Neb. Rev. Stat. §§ 28–926.09 to 28–926.10 (1965 Cum. Supp.); Nev. Rev. Stat. §§ 201.250, 207.180 (1965); N. H. Rev. Stat. Ann. §§ 571–A:1 to 571–A:5 (Supp. 1967); N. J. Stat. Ann. §§ 2A:115–1.1 to 2A:115–4 (Supp. 1967); N. C. Gen. Stat. § 14–189 (Supp. 1967); N. D. Cent. Code §§ 12–21–07 to 12–21–09 (1960); Ohio Rev. Code Ann. §§ 2903.10–2903.11, 2905.34–2905.39 (1954 and Supp.

1966); Okla. Stat. Ann., Tit. 21, §§ 1021–1024, 1032–1039 (1958 and Supp. 1967); Pa. Stat. Ann., Tit. 18, §§ 3831–3833, 4524 (1963 and Supp. 1967); R. I. Gen. Laws Ann. §§ 11–31–1 to 11–31–10 (1956 and Supp. 1967); S. C. Code Ann. §§ 16–414.1 to 16–421 (1962 and Supp. 1967); Tex. Pen. Code, Arts. 526, 527b (1952 and Supp. 1967); Utah Code Ann. §§ 76–39–5, 76–39–17 (Supp. 1967); Vt. Stat. Ann., Tit. 13, §§ 2801–2805 (1959); Va. Code Ann. §§ 18.1–227 to 18.1–236.3 (1960 and Supp. 1966); W. Va. Code Ann. § 61–8–11 (1966); Wyo. Stat. Ann. §§ 6–103, 7–148 (1957).

MR. JUSTICE STEWART, concurring in the result.

A doctrinaire, knee-jerk application of the First Amendment would, of course, dictate the nullification of this New York statute.[1] But that result is not required, I think, if we bear in mind what it is that the First Amendment protects.

The First Amendment guarantees liberty of human expression in order to preserve in our Nation what Mr. Justice Holmes called a "free trade in ideas."[2] To that end, the Constitution protects more than just a man's freedom to say or write or publish what he wants. It secures as well the liberty of each man to decide for himself what he will read and to what he will listen. The Constitution guarantees, in short, a society of free choice. Such a society presupposes the capacity of its members to choose.

When expression occurs in a setting where the capacity to make a choice is absent, government regulation of that expression may co-exist with and even implement First Amendment guarantees. So it was that this Court sustained a city ordinance prohibiting people from imposing their opinions on others "by way of sound trucks with loud and raucous noises on city streets."[3] And so it was that my Brothers BLACK and DOUGLAS thought that the First Amendment itself prohibits a person from foisting his uninvited views upon the members of a captive audience.[4]

I think a State may permissibly determine that, at least in some precisely delineated areas, a child[5]—like someone in a captive audience—is not possessed of that full capacity for individual choice which is the presupposition of First Amendment guarantees. It is only upon such a premise, I should suppose, that a State may deprive children of other rights—the right to marry, for example, or the right to vote—deprivations that would be constitutionally intolerable for adults.[6]

I cannot hold that this state law, on its face,[7] violates the First and Fourteenth Amendments.

MR. JUSTICE DOUGLAS, with whom MR. JUSTICE BLACK concurs, dissenting.

While I would be willing to reverse the judgment on the basis of Redrup v. New York, 386 U. S. 767, for the reasons stated by my Brother FORTAS, my objections strike deeper.

If we were in the field of substantive due process and seeking to measure the propriety of state law by the standards of the Fourteenth Amendment, I suppose there would be no difficulty under our decisions in sustaining this act. For there is a view held by many that the so-called "obscene" book or tract or magazine has a deleterious effect upon the young, although I seriously doubt the wisdom of trying by law to put the fresh, evanescent, natural blossoming of sex in the category of "sin."

That, however, was the view of our preceptor in this field, Anthony Comstock, who waged his war against "obscenity" from the year 1872 until his death in 1915. Some of his views are set forth in his book Traps for the Young, first published in 1883, excerpts from which I set out in Appendix I to this opinion.

The title of the book refers to "traps" created by Satan "for boys and girls especially." Comstock, of course, operated on the theory that every human has an "inborn tendency toward wrongdoing which is restrained mainly by fear of the final judgment." In his view any book which tended to remove that fear is a part of the "trap" which Satan created. Hence, Comstock would have condemned a much wider range of literature than the present Court is apparently inclined to do.[1]

It was Comstock who was responsible for the Federal Anti-Obscenity Act of March 3, 1873. 17 Stat. 598. It was he who was also responsible for the New York Act which soon followed. He was responsible for the organization of the New York Society for the Suppression of Vice, which by its act of incorporation was granted one-half of the fines levied on people successfully prosecuted by the Society or its agents.

I would conclude from Comstock and his Traps for the Young and from other authorities that a legislature could not be said to be wholly irrational[2] (Ferguson v. Skrupa, 372 U. S. 726; and see Williamson v. Lee Optical Co., 348 U. S. 483; Daniel v. Family Ins. Co., 336 U. S. 220; Olsen v. Nebraska, 313 U. S. 236) if it decided that sale of "obscene" material to the young should be banned.[3]

The problem under the First Amendment, however, has always seemed to me to be quite different. For its mandate (originally applicable only to the Federal Government but now applicable to the States as well by reason of the Fourteenth Amendment) is directed to any law "abridging the freedom of speech, or of the press." I appreciate that there are those who think that "obscenity" is impliedly excluded; but I have indicated on prior occasions why I have been unable to reach that conclusion.[4] See Ginzburg v. United States, 383 U. S. 463, 482 (dissenting opinion); Jacobellis v. Ohio, 378 U. S. 184, 196 (concurring opinion of MR. JUSTICE BLACK); Roth v. United States, 354 U. S. 476, 508 (dissenting opinion). And the corollary of that view, as I expressed it in Public Utilities Comm'n v. Pollak, 343 U. S. 451, 467, 468 (dissenting opinion), is that Big Brother can no more say what a person shall listen to or read than he can say what shall be published.

This is not to say that the Court and Anthony Comstock are wrong in concluding that the kind of literature New York condemns does harm. As a matter of fact, the notion of censorship is founded on the belief that speech and press sometimes do harm and therefore can be regulated. I once visited a foreign nation where the regime of censorship was so strict that all I could find in the bookstalls were tracts on religion and tracts on mathematics. Today the Court determines the constitutionality of New York's law regulating the sale of literature to children on the basis of the reasonableness of the law in light of the welfare of the child. If the problem of state and federal regulation of "obscenity" is in the field of substantive due process, I see no reason to limit the legislatures to protecting children alone. The "juvenile delinquents" I have known are mostly over 50 years of age. If rationality is the measure of the validity of this law, then I can see how modern Anthony Comstocks could make out a case for "protecting" many groups in our society, not merely children.

While I find the literature and movies which come to us for clearance exceedingly dull and boring, I understand how some can and do become very excited and alarmed and think that something should be done to stop the flow. It is one thing for parents [5] and the religious organizations to be active and involved. It is quite a different matter for the state to become implicated as a censor. As I read the First Amendment, it was designed to keep the state and the hands of all state officials off the printing presses of America and off the distribution systems for all printed literature. Anthony Comstock wanted it the other way; he indeed put the police and prosecutor in the middle of this publishing business.

I think it would require a constitutional amendment to achieve that result. If there were a constitutional amendment, perhaps the people of the country would come up with some national board of censorship. Censors are, of course, propelled by their own neuroses.[6] That is why a universally accepted definition of obscenity is impossible. Any definition is indeed highly subjective, turning on the neurosis of the censor. Those who have a deep-seated, subconscious conflict may well become either great crusaders against a particular kind of literature or avid customers of it.[7] That, of course, is the danger of letting any group of citizens be the judges of what other people, young or old, should read. Those would be issues to be canvassed and debated in case of a constitutional amendment creating a regime of censorship in the country. And if the people, in their wisdom, launched us on that course, it would be a considered choice.

Today this Court sits as the Nation's board of censors. With all respect, I do not know of any group in the country less qualified first, to know what obscenity is when they see it, and second, to have any considered judgment as to what the deleterious or beneficial impact of a particular publication may be on minds either young or old.

I would await a constitutional amendment that authorized the modern Anthony Comstocks to censor literature before publishers, authors, or distributors can be fined or jailed for what they print or sell.

APPENDIX I TO OPINION OF MR. JUSTICE DOUGLAS, DISSENTING.

A. COMSTOCK, TRAPS FOR THE YOUNG 20–22 (1883).

And it came to pass that as Satan went to and fro upon the earth, watching his traps and rejoicing over his numerous victims, he found room for improvement in some of his schemes. The daily press did not meet all his requirements. The *weekly* illustrated papers of crime would do for young men and sports, for brothels, gin-mills, and thieves' resorts, but were found to be so gross, so libidinous, so monstrous, that every decent person spurned them. They were excluded from the home on sight. They were too high-priced for children, and too cumbersome to be conveniently hid from the parent's eye or carried in the boy's pocket. So he resolved to make another trap for boys and girls especially.

He also resolved to make the most of these vile illustrated weekly papers, by lining the news-stands and shop-windows along the pathway of the children from home to school and church, so that they could not go to and from these places of instruction without giving him opportunity to defile their pure minds by flaunting these atrocities before their eyes.

And Satan rejoiced greatly that professing Christians were silent and apparently acquiesced in his plans. He found that our most refined men and women went freely to trade with persons who displayed these traps for sale; that few, if any, had moral courage to enter a protest against this public display of indecencies, and scarcely one in all the land had the boldness to say to the dealer in filth, "I will not give you one cent of my patronage so long as you sell these devil-traps to ruin the young." And he was proud of professing Christians and respectable citizens on this account, and caused honorable mention to be made of them in general order to his imps, because of the quiet and orderly assistance thus rendered him.

Satan stirred up certain of his willing tools on earth by the promise of a few paltry dollars to improve greatly on the death-dealing quality of the weekly death-traps, and forthwith came a series of new snares of fascinating construction, small and tempting in price, and baited with high-sounding names. These sure-ruin traps comprise a large variety of half-dime novels, five and ten cent story papers, and low-priced pamphlets for boys and girls.

This class includes the silly, insipid tale, the coarse, slangy story in the dialect of the barroom, the blood-and-thunder romance of border life, and the exaggerated details of crimes, real and imaginary. Some have highly colored sensational reports of real crimes, while others, and by far the larger number, deal with most improbable creations of fiction. The unreal far outstrips the real. Crimes are gilded, and lawlessness is painted to resemble valor, making a bid for bandits, brigands, murderers, thieves, and criminals in general. Who would go to the State prison, the gambling saloon, or the brothel to find a suitable companion for the child? Yet a more insidious foe is selected when these stories are allowed to become associates for the child's mind and to shape and direct the thoughts.

The finest fruits of civilization are consumed by these vermin. Nay, these products of corrupt minds are the eggs from which all kinds of villainies are hatched. Put the entire batch of these stories together, and I challenge the publishers and vendors to show a single instance where any boy or girl has been elevated in morals, or where any noble or refined instinct has been developed by them.

The leading character in many, if not in the vast majority of these stories, is some boy or girl who possesses usually extraordinary beauty of countenance, the most superb clothing, abundant wealth, the strength of a giant, the agility of a squirrel, the cunning of a fox, the brazen effrontery of the most daring villain, and who is utterly destitute of any regard for the laws of God or man. Such a one is foremost among desperadoes, the companion and beau-ideal of maidens, and the high favorite of some rich person, who by his patronage and indorsement lifts the young villain into lofty positions in society, and provides liberally of his wealth to secure him immunity for his crimes. These stories link the pure maiden with the most foul and loathsome criminals. Many of them favor violation of marriage laws and cheapen female virtue.

APPENDIX II TO OPINION OF MR. JUSTICE DOUGLAS, DISSENTING.

A SPECIAL TO THE WASHINGTON POST
[March 3, 1968]
by
AUSTIN C. WEHRWEIN

White Bear Lake, Minn., March 2.—Faced with the threat of a law suit, the school board in this community of 12,000 north of St. Paul is reviewing its mandatory sex education courses, but officials expressed fear that they couldn't please everybody.

Mothers threatened to picket and keep their children home when sex education films are scheduled. Mrs. Robert Murphy, the mother of five who led the protests, charged that the elementary school "took the privacy out of marriage."

"Now," she said, "our kids know what a shut bedroom door means. The program is taking their childhood away. The third graders went in to see a movie on birth and came out adults."

She said second-grade girls have taken to walking around with "apples and oranges under their blouses." Her seventh-grade son was given a study sheet on menstruation, she said, demanding "why should a seventh-grade boy have to know about menstruation?"

Mrs. Murphy, who fears the program will lead to experimentation, said that it was "pagan" and argued that even animals don't teach their young those things "before they're ready."

"One boy in our block told his mother, 'Guess what, next week our teacher's gonna tell us how daddy fertilized you,'" reported Mrs. Martin Capeder. "They don't need to know all that."

But Norman Jensen, principal of Lincoln School, said that the program, which runs from kindergarten through the 12th grade, was approved by the school district's PTA council, the White Bear Lake Ministerial Association and the district school board. It was based, he said, on polls that showed 80 per cent of the children got no home sex education, and the curriculum was designed to be "matter-of-fact."

The protesting parents insisted they had no objection to sex education as such, but some said girls should not get it until age 12, and boys only at age 15—"or when they start shaving."

(In nearby St. Paul Park, 71 parents have formed a group called "Concerned Parents Against Sex Education" and are planning legal action to prevent sex education from kindergarten through seventh grade. They have

also asked equal time with the PTAs of eight schools in the district "to discuss topics such as masturbation, contraceptives, unqualified instructors, religious belief, morality and attitudes.")

The White Bear protesters have presented the school board with a list of terms and definitions deemed objectionable. Designed for the seventh grade, it included vagina, clitoris, erection, intercourse and copulation. A film, called "Fertilization and Birth" depicts a woman giving birth. It has been made optional after being shown to all classes.

Mrs. Ginny McKay, a president of one of the local PTAs defended the program, saying "Sex is a natural and beautiful thing. We (the PTA) realized that the parents had to get around to where the kids have been for a long time."

But Mrs. Murphy predicted this result: "Instead of 15 [*sic*] and 15-year-old pregnant girls, they'll have 12 and 13-year-old pregnant girls."

APPENDIX III TO OPINION OF MR. JUSTICE DOUGLAS, DISSENTING.

(A). T. SCHROEDER, OBSCENE LITERATURE AND CONSTITUTIONAL LAW 277–278 (1911).

It thus appears that the only unifying element generalized in the word "obscene," (that is, the only thing common to every conception of obscenity and indecency), is subjective, is an affiliated emotion of disapproval. This emotion under varying circumstances of temperament and education in different persons, and in the same person in different stages of development, is aroused by entirely different stimuli, and by fear of the judgment of others, and so has become associated with an infinite variety of ever-changing objectives, with not even one common characteristic in objective nature; that is, in literature or art.

Since few men have identical experiences, and fewer still evolve to an agreement in their conceptional and emotional associations, it must follow that practically none have the same standards for judging the "obscene," even when their conclusions agree. The word "obscene," like such words as delicate, ugly, lovable, hateful, etc., is an abstraction not based upon a reasoned, nor sense-perceived, likeness between objectives, but the selection or classification under it is made, on the basis of similarity in the emotions aroused, by an infinite variety of images; and every classification thus made, in turn, depends in each person upon his fears, his hopes, his prior experience, suggestions, education, and the degree of neuro-sexual or psycho-sexual health. Because it is a matter wholly of emotions, it has come to be that "men think they know because they feel, and are firmly convinced because strongly agitated."

This, then, is a demonstration that obscenity exists only in the minds and emotions of those who believe in it, and is not a quality of a book or picture. Since, then, the general conception "obscene" is devoid of every objective element of unification; and since the subjective element, the associated emotion, is indefinable from its very nature, and inconstant as to the character of the stimulus capable of arousing it, and variable and immeasurable as to its relative degrees of intensity, it follows that the "obscene" is incapable of accurate definition or a general test adequate to secure uniformity of result, in its application by every person, to each book of doubtful "purity."

Being so essentially and inextricably involved with human emotions that no man can frame such a definition of the word "obscene," either in terms of the qualities of a book, or such that, *by it alone,* any judgment whatever is possible, much less is it possible that by any such alleged "test" every other man must reach the same conclusion about the obscenity of every conceivable book. Therefore, the so-called judicial "tests" of obscenity are not standards of judgment, but, on the contrary, by every such "test" the rule of decision is itself uncertain, and in terms invokes the varying experiences of the test[e]rs within the foggy realm of problematical speculation about psychic tendencies, without the help of which the "test" itself is meaningless and useless. It follows that to each person the "test," of criminality, which should be a general standard of judgment, unavoidably becomes a personal and particular standard, differing in all persons according to those varying experiences which they read into the judicial "test." It is this which makes uncertain, and, therefore, all the more objectionable, all the present laws against obscenity. Later it will be shown that this uncertainty in the criteria of guilt renders these laws unconstitutional.

(B). KALLEN, THE ETHICAL ASPECTS OF CENSORSHIP, IN 5 SOCIAL MEANING OF LEGAL CONCEPTS 34, 50–51 (N. Y. U. 1953).

To this authoritarian's will, difference is the same thing as inferiority, wickedness and corruption · he can apprehend it only as a devotion to error and a commitment to sin. He can acknowledge it only if he attributes to it moral turpitude and intellectual vice. Above all, difference must be for him, by its simple existence, an aggression against the good, the true, the beautiful and the right. His imperative is to destroy it; if he cannot destroy it, to contain it; if he cannot contain it, to hunt it down, cut it off and shut it out.

Certain schools of psychology suggest that this aggression is neither simple nor wholly aggression. They suggest that it expresses a compulsive need to bring to open contemplation the secret parts of the censor's psychosomatic personality, and a not less potent need to keep the secret and not suffer the shamefaced dishonor of their naked exposures. The censor's activities, in that they call for a constant public preoccupation with such secret parts, free his psyche from the penalties of such concern while transvaluing at the same time his pursuit and inspection of the obscene, the indecent, the pornographic, the blasphemous and the otherwise shameful into an honorable defense of the public morals. The censor, by purporting, quite unconscious of his actual dynamic, to protect the young from corruption, frees his consciousness to dwell upon corruption without shame or dishonor. Thus, Anthony Comstock could say with overt sincerity: "When the genius of the arts produces obscene, lewd and lascivious ideas, the deadly effect upon the young is just as perceptible as when the same ideas are represented by gross experience in prose and poetry. . . . If through the eye and ear the sensuous book, picture or story is

allowed to enter, the thoughts will be corrupted, the conscience seared, so such things reproduced by fancy in the thoughts awaken forces for evil which will explode with irresistible force carrying to destruction every human safeguard to virtue and honor." Did not evil Bernard Shaw, who gave the English language the word *comstockery,* declare himself, in his preface to *The Shewing-Up of Blanco Posnet,* "a specialist in immoral, heretical plays . . . to force the public to reconsider its morals"? So the brave Comstock passionately explored and fought the outer expressions of the inner forces of evil and thus saved virtue and honor from destruction.

But could this observation of his be made, save on the basis of introspection and not the scientific study of others? For such a study would reveal, for each single instance of which it was true, hundreds of thousands of others of which it was false. Like the correlation of misfortune with the sixth day of the week or the number 13, this basic comstockery signalizes a fear-projected superstition. It is an externalization of anxiety and fear, not a fact objectively studied and appraised. And the anxiety and fear are reaction-formations of the censor's inner self.

Of course, this is an incomplete description of the motivation and logic of censorship. In the great censorial establishments of the tradition, these more or less unconscious drives are usually items of a syndrome whose dominants are either greed for pelf, power, and prestige, reinforced by anxiety that they might be lost, or anxiety that they might be lost reinforced by insatiable demands for more.

Authoritarian societies usually insure these goods by means of a prescriptive creed and code for which their rulers claim supernatural origins and supernatural sanctions. The enforcement of the prescriptions is not entrusted to a censor alone. The ultimate police-power is held by the central hierarchy, and the censorship of the arts is only one department of the thought-policing.

(C). CRAWFORD, LITERATURE AND THE PSYCHOPATHIC, 10 PSYCHOANALYTIC REVIEW 440, 445–446 (1923).

Objection, then, to modern works on the ground that they are, in the words of the objectors, "immoral," is made principally on the basis of an actual desire to keep sexual psychopathies intact, or to keep the general scheme of repression, which inevitably involves psychopathic conditions, intact. The activities of persons professionally or otherwise definitely concerned with censorship furnish proof evident enough to the student of such matters that they themselves are highly abnormal. It is safe to say that every censorship has a psychopath back of it.

Carried to a logical end, censorship would inevitably destroy all literary art. Every sexual act is an instinctive feeling out for an understanding of life. Literary art, like every other type of creative effort, is a form of sublimation. It is a more conscious seeking for the same understanding that the common man instinctively seeks. The literary artist, having attained understanding, communicates that understanding to his readers. That understanding, whether of sexual or other matters, is certain to come into conflict with popular beliefs, fears, and taboos because these are, for the most part, based on error. . . . [T]he presence of an opinion concerning which one thinks it would be unprofitable, immoral, or unwise to inquire is, of itself, strong evidence that that opinion is nonrational. Most of the more deep-seated convictions of the human race belong to this category. Anyone who is seeking for understanding is certain to encounter this nonrational attitude.

The act of sublimation on the part of the writer necessarily involves an act of sublimation on the part of the reader. The typical psychopathic patient and the typical public have alike a deep-rooted unconscious aversion to sublimation. Inferiority and other complexes enter in to make the individual feel that acts of sublimation would destroy his comfortable, though illusory, sense of superiority. Again, there is the realization on the part of the mass of people that they are unable to sublimate as the artist does, and to admit his power and right to do so involves destruction of the specious sense of superiority to him. It is these two forms of aversion to sublimation which account for a considerable part of public objection to the arts. The common man and his leader, the psychopathic reformer, are aiming unconsciously at leveling humanity to a plane of pathological mediocrity.

To the student of abnormal psychology the legend, popular literature, and literature revelatory of actual life, are all significant. In the legend he finds race taboos, in the popular literature of the day he discovers this reinforced by the mass of contemporary and local taboos, in literature that aims to be realistically revelatory of life he finds material for study such as he can hardly obtain from any group of patients. The frankness which he seeks in vain from the persons with whom he comes into personal contact, he can find in literature. It is a field in which advances may be made comparable to the advances of actual scientific research.

Moreover, the student of abnormal psychology will commend realistic, revelatory literature not only to his patients, who are suffering from specific psychopathic difficulties, but to the public generally. He will realize that it is one of the most important factors in the development of human freedom. No one is less free than primitive man. The farther we can get from the attitude of the legend and its slightly more civilized successor, popular literature, the nearer we shall be to a significant way of life.

(D). J. RINALDO, PSYCHOANALYSIS OF THE "REFORMER" 56–60 (1921).

The other aspect of the humanist movement is a very sour and disgruntled puritanism, which seems at first glance to protest and contradict every step in the libidinous development. As a matter of fact it is just as much an hysterical outburst as the most sensuous flesh masses of Rubens, or the sinuous squirming lines of Louis XV decoration. Both are reactions to the same morbid past experience.

The Puritan like the sensualist rebels at the very beginning against the restraint of celibacy. Unfortunately, however, he finds himself unable to satisfy the libido in either normal gratification or healthy converted activities. His condition is as much one of super-excitement as that of the libertine. Unable to find satisfaction in other ways, from which for one reason or another he is inhibited, he develops a morbid irritation, contradicting, breaking, prohibiting and thwarting the manifestations of the very exciting causes.

Not being able to produce beautiful things he mars them, smashing stained glass windows, destroying sculptures, cutting down May-poles, forbidding dances, clipping the hair, covering the body with hideous misshapen garments and silencing laughter and song. He cannot build so he must destroy. He cannot create so he hinders creation. He is a sort of social abortionist and like an abortionist only comes into his own when there is an illegitimate brat to be torn from the womb. He cries against sin, but it is the pleasure of sin rather than the sin he fights. It is the enjoyment he is denied that he hates.

From no age or clime or condition is he absent; but never is he a dominant and deciding factor in society till that society has passed the bounds of sanity. Those who wait the midwife never call in the abortionist, nor does he ever cure the real sickness of his age. That he does survive abnormal periods to put his impress on the repressions of later days is due to the peculiar economy of his behavior. The libertine destroys himself, devouring his substance in self-satisfaction. The reformer devours others, being somewhat in the nature of a tax on vice, living by the very hysteria that destroys his homologous opposite.

In our own day we have reached another of those critical periods strikingly similar in its psychological symptoms and reactions, at least, to decadent Rome. We have the same development of extravagant religious cults, Spiritism, Dowieism, "The Purple Mother," all eagerly seized upon, filling the world with clamor and frenzy; the same mad seeking for pleasure, the same breaking and scattering of forms, the same orgy of gluttony and extravagance, the same crude emotionalism in art, letter and the theater, the same deformed and inverted sexual life.

Homo-sexualism may not be openly admitted, but the "sissy" and his red necktie are a familiar and easily understood property of popular jest and pantomime. It is all a mad jazz jumble of hysterical incongruities, dog dinners, monkey marriages, cubism, birth control, feminism, free-love, verse libre, and moving pictures. Through it all runs the strident note of puritanism. As one grows so does the other. Neither seems to precede or follow.

It would be a rash man indeed who would attempt to give later beginnings to the reform movements than to the license they seem so strongly to contradict. Significant indeed is the fact that their very license is the strongest appeal of the reformer. Every movie must preach a sermon and have a proper ending, but the attempted rape is as seldom missing as the telephone; and it is this that thrills and is expected to thrill.

The same sexual paradox we saw in the eunuch priests and harlot priestesses of Isis we see in the vice-crusading, vice-pandering reformers. Back of it all lies a morbid sexual condition, which is as much behind the anti-alcoholism of the prohibitionist, as behind the cropped head of his puritan father, and as much behind the birth-control, vice-crusading virgins as behind their more amiable sisters of Aphrodite.

Interpreted then in the light of their history, libertinism and reformism cannot be differentiated as cause and effect, action and reaction, but must be associated as a two-fold manifestation of the same thing, an hysterical condition. They differ in externals, only insofar as one operates in license and the other in repression, but both have the same genesis and their development is simultaneous.

(E). H. LASSWELL, PSYCHOPATHOLOGY AND POLITICS 94–96 (1930).

Another significant private motive, whose organization dates from early family days, but whose influence was prominent in adult behavior, was A's struggle to maintain his sexual repressions. ["A" is an unidentified, non-fictional person whose life history was studied by the author.] He erected his very elaborate personal prohibitions into generalized prohibitions for all society, and just as he laid down the law against brother-hatred, he condemned "irregular" sexuality and gambling and drinking, its associated indulgences. He was driven to protect himself from himself by so modifying the environment that his sexual impulses were least often aroused, but it is significant that he granted partial indulgence to his repressed sexuality by engaging in various activities closely associated with sexual operations. Thus his sermons against vice enabled him to let his mind dwell upon rich fantasies of seduction. His crusading ventures brought him to houses of ill fame, where partly clad women were discoverable in the back rooms. These activities were rationalized by arguing that it was up to him as a leader of the moral forces of the community to remove temptation from the path of youth. At no time did he make an objective inquiry into the many factors in society which increase or diminish prostitution. His motives were of such an order that he was prevented from self-discipline by prolonged inspection of social experience.

That A was never able to abolish his sexuality is sufficiently evident in his night dreams and day dreams. In spite of his efforts to "fight" these manifestations of his "antisocial impulses," they continued to appear. Among the direct and important consequences which they produced was a sense of sin, not only a sense of sexual sin, but a growing conviction of hypocrisy. His "battle" against "evil" impulses was only partially successful, and this produced a profound feeling of insecurity.

This self-punishing strain of insecurity might be alleviated, he found, by publicly reaffirming the creed of repression, and by distracting attention to other matters. A's rapid movements, dogmatic assertions, and diversified activities were means of escape from this gnawing sense of incapacity to cope with his own desires and to master himself. Uncertain of his power to control himself, he was very busy about controlling others, and engaged in endless committee sessions, personal conferences, and public meetings for the purpose. He always managed to submerge himself in a buzzing life of ceaseless activity; he could never stand privacy and solitude, since it drove him to a sense of futility; and he couldn't undertake prolonged and laborious study, since his feeling of insecurity demanded daily evidence of his importance in the world.

A's sexual drives continued to manifest themselves, and to challenge his resistances. He was continually alarmed by the luring fear that he might be impotent. Although he proposed marriage to two girls when he was a theology student, it is significant that he chose girls from his immediate entourage, and effected an almost instantaneous recovery from his disappointments. This warrants the inference that he was considerably relieved to postpone the test of his potency, and this inference is strengthened by the long years during which he cheerfully acquiesced in the postponement of his marriage to the woman who finally became his wife. He lived with people who valued sexual potency, particularly in its conventional and biological demonstration in marriage and children, and his unmarried state was the object of good-natured comment. His pastoral duties required him to "make calls" on the sisters of the church, and in spite of the cheer which he was sometimes able to bring to the bedridden, there was the faint whisper of a doubt that this was really a man's job. And though preaching was a socially respectable occupation, there was something of the ridiculous in the fact that one who had experienced very little of life should pass for a privileged censor of all mankind.

MR. JUSTICE FORTAS, dissenting.

This is a criminal prosecution. Sam Ginsberg and his wife operate a luncheonette at which magazines are offered for sale. A 16-year-old boy was enlisted by his mother to go to the luncheonette and buy some "girlie" magazines so that Ginsberg could be prosecuted. He went there, picked two magazines from a display case, paid for them, and walked out. Ginsberg's offense was duly reported to the authorities. The power of the State of New York was invoked. Ginsberg was prosecuted and convicted. The court imposed only a suspended sentence. But as the majority here points out, under New York law this conviction may mean that Ginsberg will lose the license necessary to operate his luncheonette.

The two magazines that the 16-year-old boy selected are vulgar "girlie" periodicals. However tasteless and tawdry they may be, we have ruled (as the Court acknowledges) that magazines indistinguishable from them in content and offensiveness are not "obscene" within the constitutional standards heretofore applied. See, e. g., Gent v. Arkansas, 386 U. S. 767 (1967). These rulings have been in cases involving adults.

The Court avoids facing the problem whether the magazines in the present case are "obscene" when viewed by a 16-year-old boy, although not "obscene" when viewed by someone 17 years of age or older. It says that Ginsberg's lawyer did not choose to challenge the conviction on the ground that the magazines are not "obscene." He chose only to attack the statute on its face. Therefore, the Court reasons, we need not look at the magazines and determine whether they may be excluded from the ambit of the First Amendment as "obscene" for purposes of this case. But this Court has made strong and comprehensive statements about its duty in First Amendment cases—statements with which I agree. See, e. g., Jacobellis v. Ohio, 378 U. S. 184, 187–190 (1964) (opinion of BRENNAN, J.).*

In my judgment, the Court cannot properly avoid its

fundamental duty to define "obscenity" for purposes of censorship of material sold to youths, merely because of counsel's position. By so doing the Court avoids the essence of the problem; for if the State's power to censor freed from the prohibitions of the First Amendment depends upon obscenity, and if obscenity turns on the specific content of the publication, how can we sustain the conviction here without deciding whether the particular magazines in question are obscene?

The Court certainly cannot mean that the States and cities and counties and villages have unlimited power to withhold anything and everything that is written or pictorial from younger people. But it here justifies the conviction of Sam Ginsberg because the impact of the Constitution, it says, is variable, and what is not obscene for an adult may be obscene for a child. This it calls "variable obscenity." I do not disagree with this, but I insist that to assess the principle—certainly to apply it—the Court must define it. We must know the extent to which literature or pictures may be less offensive than *Roth* requires in order to be "obscene" for purposes of a statute confined to youth. See *Roth* v. *United States*, 354 U. S. 476 (1957).

I agree that the State in the exercise of its police power—even in the First Amendment domain—may make proper and careful differentiation between adults and children. But I do not agree that this power may be used on an arbitrary, free-wheeling basis. This is not a case where, on any standard enunciated by the Court, the magazines are obscene, nor one where the seller is at fault. Petitioner is being prosecuted for the sale of magazines which he had a right under the decisions of this Court to offer for sale, and he is being prosecuted without proof of "fault"—without even a claim that he deliberately, calculatedly sought to induce children to buy "obscene" material. Bookselling should not be a hazardous profession.

The conviction of Ginsberg on the present facts is a serious invasion of freedom. To sustain the conviction without inquiry as to whether the material is "obscene" and without any evidence of pushing or pandering, in face of this Court's asserted solicitude for First Amendment values, is to give the State a role in the rearing of children which is contrary to our traditions and to our conception of family responsibility. Cf. *In re Gault*, 387 U. S. 1 (1967). It begs the question to present this undefined, unlimited censorship as an aid to parents in the rearing of their children. This decision does not merely protect children from activities which all sensible parents would condemn. Rather, its undefined and unlimited approval of state censorship in this area denies to children free access to books and works of art to which many parents may wish their children to have uninhibited access. For denial of access to these magazines, without any standard or definition of their allegedly distinguishing characteristics, is also denial of access to great works of art and literature.

If this statute were confined to the punishment of pushers or panderers of vulgar literature I would not be so concerned by the Court's failure to circumscribe state power by defining its limits in terms of the meaning of "obscenity" in this field. The State's police power may, within very broad limits, protect the parents and their children from public aggression of panderers and pushers. This is defensible on the theory that they cannot protect themselves from such assaults. But it does not follow that the State may convict a passive luncheonette operator of a crime because a 16-year-old boy maliciously and designedly picks up and pays for two girlie magazines which are presumably *not* obscene.

I would therefore reverse the conviction on the basis of *Redrup* v. *New York*, 386 U. S. 767 (1967) and *Ginzburg* v. *United States*, 383 U. S. 463 (1966).

COURT'S OPINION NOTES

[1] Appellant makes no attack upon § 484-h as applied. We therefore have no occasion to consider the sufficiency of the evidence, or such issues as burden of proof, whether expert evidence is either required or permissible, or any other questions which might be pertinent to the application of the statute. Appellant does argue that because the trial judge included a finding that two of the magazines "contained verbal descriptions and narrative accounts of sexual excitement and sexual conduct," an offense not charged in the informations, the conviction must be set aside under *Cole* v. *Arkansas*, 333 U. S. 196. But this case was tried and the appellant was found guilty only on the charges of selling magazines containing pictures depicting female nudity. It is therefore not a case where defendant was tried and convicted of a violation of one offense when he was charged with a distinctly and substantially different offense.

The full text of § 484-h is attached as Appendix A. It was enacted in L. 1965, c. 327, to replace an earlier version held invalid by the New York Court of Appeals in *People* v. *Kahan*, 15 N. Y. 2d 311, 206 N. E. 2d 333, and *People* v. *Bookcase, Inc.*, 14 N. Y. 2d 409, 201 N. E. 2d 14. Section 484-h in turn was replaced by L. 1967, c. 791, now §§ 235.20–235.22 of the Penal Law. The major changes under the 1967 law added a provision that the one charged with a violation "is presumed to [sell] with knowledge of the character and content of the material sold . . . ," and the provision that "it is an affirmative defense that: (a) The defendant had reasonable cause to believe that the minor involved was seventeen years old or more; and (b) Such minor exhibited to the defendant a draft card, driver's license, birth certificate or other official or apparently official document purporting to establish that such minor was seventeen years old or more." Neither addition is involved in this case. We intimate no view whatever upon the constitutional validity of the presumption. See in general *Smith* v. *California*, 361 U. S. 147; *Speiser* v. *Randall*, 357 U. S. 513; 41 N. Y. U. L. Rev. 791 (1966); 30 Albany L. Rev. 133 (1966).

The 1967 law also repealed outright § 484-i which had been enacted one week after § 484-h. L. 1965, c. 327. It forbade sales to minors under the age of 18. The New York Court of Appeals sustained its validity against a challenge that it was void for vagueness. *People* v. *Tannenbaum*, 18 N. Y. 2d 268, 220 N. E. 2d 783. For an analysis of § 484-i and a comparison with § 484-h see 33 Brooklyn L. Rev. 329 (1967).

[2] The case is not moot. The appellant might have been sentenced to one year's imprisonment, or a $500 fine or both. N. Y. Penal Law § 1937. The trial judge however exercised authority under N. Y. Penal Law § 2188 and on May 17, 1966, suspended sentence on all counts. Under § 470-a of the New York Code of Criminal Procedure, the judge could thereafter recall appellant and impose sentence only within one year, or before May 17, 1967. The judge did not do so. Although *St. Pierre* v. *United States*, 319 U. S. 41, held that a criminal case had become moot when the petitioner finished serving his sentence before direct review in this Court, *St. Pierre* also recognized that the case would not have been moot had "petitioner shown that under either state or federal law further penalties or disabilities can be imposed on him as result of the judgment which has now been satisfied." *Id.*, at 43. The State of New York concedes in its brief in this Court addressed to mootness "that certain disabilities do flow from the conviction." The brief states that among these is "the possibility of ineligibility for licensing under

state and municipal license laws regulating various lawful occupations . . . ." Since the argument, the parties advised the Court that, although this is the first time appellant has been convicted of any crime, this conviction might result in the revocation of the license required by municipal law as a prerequisite to engaging in the luncheonette business he carries on in Bellmore, New York. Bellmore is an "unincorporated village" within the Town of Hempstead, Long Island, 1967 N. Y. S. Leg. Man. 1154. The town has a licensing ordinance which provides that the "Commissioner of Buildings . . . may suspend or revoke any license issued, in his discretion, for . . . (e) conviction of any crime." LL 21, Town of Hempstead, eff. December 1, 1966, § 8.1 (e). In these circumstances the case is not moot since the conviction may entail collateral consequences sufficient to bring the case within the *St. Pierre* exception. See *Fiswick* v. *United States*, 329 U. S. 211, 220–222. We were not able to reach that conclusion in *Tannenbaum* v. *New York*, 388 U. S. 439, or *Jacobs* v. *New York*, 388 U. S. 431, in which the appeals were dismissed as moot. In *Tannenbaum* there was no contention that the convictions under the now repealed § 484–i entailed any collateral consequences. In *Jacobs* the appeal was dismissed on motion of the State which alleged, *inter alia*, that New York law did not impose "any further penalty upon conviction of the misdemeanor here in issue." Appellant did not there show, or contend, that his license might be revoked for "conviction of any crime"; he asserted only that the conviction might be the basis of a suspension under a provision of the Administrative Code of the City of New York requiring the Department of Licenses to assure that motion picture theatres are not conducted in a manner offensive to "public morals."

[3] One of the magazines was an issue of the magazine "Sir." We held in *Gent* v. *Arkansas*, decided with *Redrup* v. *New York*, 386 U. S. 767, 769, that an Arkansas statute which did not reflect a specific and limited state concern for juveniles was unconstitutional insofar as it was applied to suppress distribution of another issue of that magazine. Other cases which turned on findings of nonobscenity of this type of magazine include: *Central Magazine Sales, Ltd.* v. *United States*, 389 U. S. 50; *Conner* v. *City of Hammond*, 389 U. S. 48; *Potomac News Co.* v. *United States*, 389 U. S. 47; *Mazes* v. *Ohio*, 388 U. S. 453; *A Quantity of Books* v. *Kansas*, 388 U. S. 452; *Books, Inc.* v. *United States*, 388 U. S. 449; *Aday* v. *United States*, 388 U. S. 447; *Avansino* v. *New York*, 388 U. S. 446; *Sheperd* v. *New York*, 388 U. S. 444; *Friedman* v. *New York*, 388 U. S. 441; *Keney* v. *New York*, 388 U. S. 440; see also *Rosenbloom* v. *Virginia*, 388 U. S. 450; *Sunshine Book Co.* v. *Summerfield*, 355 U. S. 372.

[4] *People* v. *Tannenbaum*, 18 N. Y. 2d 268, 270, 220 N. E. 2d 783, 785, dismissed as moot, 388 U. S. 439. The concept of variable obscenity is developed in Lockhart & McClure, Censorship of Obscenity: The Developing Constitutional Standards, 45 Minn. L. Rev. 5 (1960). At 85 the authors state:

"Variable obscenity . . . furnishes a useful analytical tool for dealing with the problem of denying adolescents access to material aimed at a primary audience of sexually mature adults. For variable obscenity focuses attention upon the make-up of primary and peripheral audiences in varying circumstances, and provides a reasonably satisfactory means for delineating the obscene in each circumstance."

[5] Suggestions that legislatures might give attention to laws dealing specifically with safeguarding children against pornographic material have been made by many judges and commentators. See, *e. g.*, *Jacobellis* v. *Ohio*, 378 U. S. 184, 195 (opinion of JUSTICES BRENNAN and Goldberg); *id.*, at 201 (dissenting opinion of THE CHIEF JUSTICE); *Ginzburg* v. *United States*, 383 U. S. 463, 498, n. 1 (dissenting opinion of MR. JUSTICE STEWART); *Interstate Circuit, Inc.* v. *City of Dallas*, 366 F. 2d 590, 593; *In re Louisiana News Co.*, 187 F. Supp. 241, 247; *United States* v. *Levine*, 83 F. 2d 156; *United States* v. *Dennett*, 39 F. 2d 564; R. Kuh, Foolish Figleaves? 258–260 (1967); Emerson, Toward a General Theory of the First Amendment, 72 Yale L. J. 877, 939 (1963); Gerber, A Suggested Solution to the Riddle of Obscenity, 112 U. Pa. L. Rev. 834, 848 (1964); Henkin, Morals and the Constitution: The Sin of Obscenity, 63 Col. L. Rev. 391, 413, n. 68 (1963); Kalven, The Metaphysics of the Law of Obscenity, 1960 Sup. Ct. Rev. 1, 7; Magrath, The Obscenity Cases: Grapes of Roth, 1966 Sup. Ct. Rev. 7, 75.

The obscenity laws of 35 other States include provisions referring to minors. The laws are listed in Appendix B to this opinion.

None is a precise counterpart of New York's § 484–h and we imply no view whatever on questions of their constitutionality.

[6] Many commentators, including many committed to the proposition that "[n]o general restriction on expression in terms of 'obscenity' can . . . be reconciled with the first amendment," recognize that "the power of the state to control the conduct of children reaches beyond the scope of its authority over adults," and accordingly acknowledge a supervening state interest in the regulation of literature sold to children, Emerson, Toward a General Theory of the First Amendment, 72 Yale L. J. 877, 938, 939 (1963):

"Different factors come into play, also, where the interest at stake is the effect of erotic expression upon children. The world of children is not strictly part of the adult realm of free expression. The factor of immaturity, and perhaps other considerations, impose different rules. Without attempting here to formulate the principles relevant to freedom of expression for children, it suffices to say that regulations of communication addressed to them need not conform to the requirements of the first amendment in the same way as those applicable to adults."

See also Gerber, *supra*, at 848; Kalven, *supra*, at 7; Magrath, *supra*, at 75. *Prince* v. *Massachusetts* is urged to be constitutional authority for such regulation. See, *e. g.*, Kuh, *supra*, at 258–260; Comment, Exclusion of Children from Violent Movies, 67 Col. L. Rev. 1149, 1159–1160 (1967); Note, Constitutional Problems in Obscenity Legislation Protecting Children, 54 Geo. L. J. 1379 (1966).

[7] One commentator who argues that obscenity legislation might be constitutionally defective as an imposition of a single standard of public morality would give effect to the parental role and accept laws relating only to minors. Henkin, Morals and the Constitution: The Sin of Obscenity, 63 Col. L. Rev. 391, 413, n. 68 (1963):

"One must consider also how much difference it makes if laws are designed to protect only the morals of a child. While many of the constitutional arguments against morals legislation apply equally to legislation protecting the morals of children, one can well distinguish laws which do not impose a morality on children, but which support the right of parents to deal with the morals of their children as they see fit."

See also Elias, Sex Publications and Moral Corruption: The Supreme Court Dilemma, 9 Wm. & Mary L. Rev. 302, 320–321 (1967)

[8] Compare *Memoirs* v. *Massachusetts*, 383 U. S., at 424 (opinion of DOUGLAS, J.) with *id.*, at 441 (opinion of Clark, J.). See Kuh, *supra*, cc. 18–19; Gaylin, Book Review, 77 Yale L. J. 579, 591–595 (1968); Magrath, *supra*, at 52.

[9] Our conclusion in *Roth*, at 486–487, that the clear and present danger test was irrelevant to the determination of obscenity made it unnecessary in that case to consider the debate among the authorities whether exposure to pornography caused antisocial consequences. See also *Mishkin* v. *New York*, *supra*; *Ginzburg* v. *United States*, *supra*; *Memoirs* v. *Massachusetts*, *supra*.

[10] Magrath, *supra*, at 52. See, *e. g.*, *id.*, at 49–56; Dibble, Obscenity: A State Quarantine to Protect Children, 39 So. Cal. L. Rev. 345 (1966); Wall, Obscenity and Youth: The Problem and a Possible Solution, Crim. L. Bull., Vol. 1, No. 8, pp. 28, 30 (1965); Note, 55 Cal. L. Rev. 926, 934 (1967); Comment, 34 Ford. L. Rev. 692, 694 (1966). See also J. Paul & M. Schwartz, Federal Censorship: Obscenity in the Mail, 191–192; Blakey, Book Review, 41 Notre Dame Law. 1055, 1060, n. 46 (1966); Green, Obscenity, Censorship, and Juvenile Delinquency, 14 U. Toronto L. Rev. 229, 249 (1962); Lockhart & McClure, Literature, The Law of Obscenity, and the Constitution, 38 Minn. L. Rev. 295, 373–385 (1954); Note, 52 Ky. L. J. 429, 447 (1964). But despite the vigor of the ongoing controversy whether obscene material will perceptibly create a danger of antisocial conduct, or will probably induce its recipients to such conduct, a medical practitioner recently suggested that the possibility of harmful effects to youth cannot be dismissed as frivolous. Dr. Gaylin of the Columbia University Psychoanalytic Clinic, reporting on the views of some psychiatrists in 77 Yale L. J., at 592–593, said:

"It is in the period of growth [of youth] when these patterns of behavior are laid down, when environmental stimuli of all sorts must be integrated into a workable sense of self, when sensuality is being defined and fears elaborated, when pleasure confronts security and impulse encounters control—it is in this period, undramatically and with time, that legalized pornography may conceivably be damaging."

Dr. Gaylin emphasizes that a child might not be as well prepared as an adult to make an intelligent choice as to the material he chooses to read:

"[P]sychiatrists . . . made a distinction between the reading of pornography, as unlikely to be per se harmful, and the permitting of the reading of pornography, which was conceived as potentially destructive. The child is protected in his reading of pornography by the knowledge that it is pornographic, i. e., disapproved. It is outside of parental standards and not a part of his identification processes. To openly permit implies parental approval and even suggests seductive encouragement. If this is so of parental approval, it is equally so of societal approval—another potent influence on the developing ego." Id., at 594.

JUSTICE STEWART'S OPINION NOTES

[1] The First Amendment is made applicable to the States through the Fourteenth Amendment. Stromberg v. California, 283 U. S. 359.

[2] Abrams v. United States, 250 U. S. 616, 630 (dissenting opinion).

[3] Kovacs v. Cooper, 336 U. S. 77, 86.

[4] Public Utilities Comm'n v. Pollak, 343 U. S. 451, 466 (dissenting opinion of Mr. Justice Black), 467 (dissenting opinion of Mr. Justice Douglas).

[5] The appellant does not challenge New York's power to draw the line at age 17, and I intimate no view upon that question.

[6] Compare Loving v. Virginia, 388 U. S. 1, 12; Carrington v. Rash, 380 U. S. 89, 96.

[7] As the Court notes, the appellant makes no argument that the material in this case was not "harmful to minors" within the statutory definition, or that the statute was unconstitutionally applied.

JUSTICE DOUGLAS'S OPINION NOTES

[1] Two writers have explained Comstock as follows:

"He must have known that he could not wall out from his own mind all erotic fancies, and so he turned all the more fiercely upon the ribaldry of others." H. Broun & M. Leech, Anthony Comstock 27 (1927).

A notable forerunner of Comstock was an Englishman, Thomas Bowdler. Armed with a talent for discovering the "offensive," Bowdler expurgated Shakespeare's plays and Gibbon's History of the Decline and Fall of the Roman Empire. The result was "The Family Shakespeare," first published in 10 volumes in 1818, and a version of Gibbon's famous history "omitting everything of an immoral or irreligious nature, and incidentally rearranging the order of chapters to be in the strict chronology so dear to the obsessional heart." M. Wilson, The Obsessional Compromise, A Note on Thomas Bowdler (1965) (paper in Library of the American Psychiatric Association, Washington, D. C.).

[2] "The effectiveness of more subtle forms of censorship as an instrument of social control can be very great. They are effective over a wider field of behavior than is propaganda in that they affect convivial and 'purely personal' behavior.

"The principle is that certain verbal formulae shall not be stated, in print or in conversation; from this the restriction extends to the discussion of certain topics. A perhaps quite rationally formulated taboo is imposed; it becomes a quasi-religious factor for the members of the group who subscribe to it. If they are a majority, and the taboo does not affect some master-symbol of an influential minority, it is apt to become quite universal in its effect. A great number of taboos—to expressive and to other acts—are embodied in the mores of any people. The sanction behind each taboo largely determines its durability—in the sense of resistance opposed to the development of contradictory counter-mores, or of simple disintegration from failure to give returns in personal security. If it is to succeed for a long time, there must be recurrent reaffirmations of the taboo in connection with the sanctioning power.

"The occasional circulation of stories about a breach of the taboo and the evil consequences that flowed from this to the offender and to the public cause (the sanctioning power) well serves this purpose. Censorship of this sort has the color of voluntary acceptance of a ritualistic avoidance, in behalf of oneself and the higher power. A violation, after the primitive patterns to which we

have all been exposed, strikes at both the sinner and his god." The William Alanson White Psychiatric Foundation Memorandum: Propaganda & Censorship, 3 Psychiatry 628, 631 (1940).

[3] And see Gaylin, Book Review: The Prickly Problems of Pornography, 77 Yale L. J. 579, 594.

[4] My Brother Harlan says that no other Justice of this Court, past or present, has ever "stated his acceptance" of the view that "obscenity" is within the protection of the First and Fourteenth Amendments. Post, at 705. That observation, however, should not be understood as demonstrating that no other members of this Court, since its first Term in 1790, have adhered to the view of my Brother Black and myself. For the issue "whether obscenity is utterance within the area of protected speech and press" was only "squarely presented" to this Court for the first time in 1957. Roth v. United States, 354 U. S. 476, 481. This is indeed understandable, for the state legislatures have borne the main burden in enacting laws dealing with "obscenity"; and the strictures of the First Amendment were not applied to them through the Fourteenth until comparatively late in our history. In Gitlow v. New York, 268 U. S. 652, decided in 1925, the Court assumed that the right of free speech was among the freedoms protected against state infringement by the Due Process Clause of the Fourteenth Amendment. See also Whitney v. California, 274 U. S. 357, 371, 373; Fiske v. Kansas, 274 U. S. 380. In 1931, Stromberg v. California, 283 U. S. 359, held that the right of free speech was guaranteed in full measure by the Fourteenth Amendment. But even after these events "obscenity" cases were not inundating this Court; and even as late as 1948, the Court could say that many state obscenity statutes had "lain dormant for decades." Winters v. New York, 333 U. S. 507, 511. In several cases prior to Roth, the Court reviewed convictions under federal statutes forbidding the sending of "obscene" materials through the mails. But in none of these cases was the question squarely presented or decided whether "obscenity" was protected speech under the First Amendment; rather, the issues were limited to matters of statutory construction, or questions of procedure, such as the sufficiency of the indictment. See United States v. Chase, 135 U. S. 255; Grimm v. United States, 156 U. S. 604; Rosen v. United States, 161 U. S. 29; Swearingen v. United States, 161 U. S. 446; Andrews v. United States, 162 U. S. 420; Price v. United States, 165 U. S. 311; Dunlop v. United States, 165 U. S. 486; Bartell v. United States, 227 U. S. 427; Dysart v. United States, 272 U. S. 655; United States v. Limehouse, 285 U. S. 424. Thus, Roth v. United States, supra, which involved both a challenge to 18 U. S. C. §1461 (punishing the mailing of "obscene" material) and, in a consolidated case (Alberts v. California), an attack upon Cal. Pen. Code § 311 (prohibiting, inter alia, the keeping for sale or advertising of "obscene" material), was the first case authoritatively to measure federal and state obscenity statutes against the prohibitions of the First and Fourteenth Amendments. I cannot speak for those who preceded us in time; but neither can I interpret occasional utterances suggesting that "obscenity" was not protected by the First Amendment as considered expressions of the views of any particular Justices of the Court. See, e. g., Chaplinsky v. New Hampshire, 315 U. S. 568, 571–572; Beauharnais v. Illinois, 343 U. S. 250, 266. The most that can be said, then, is that no other members of this Court since 1957 have adhered to the view of my Brother Black and myself.

[5] See Appendix II to this opinion.

[6] Reverend Fr. Juan de Castaniza of the 16th century explained those who denounced obscenity as expressing only their own feelings. In his view they had too much reason to suspect themselves of being "obscene," since "vicious men are always prone to think others like themselves." T. Schroeder, A Challenge to Sex Censors 44–45 (1938).

"Obscenity, like witchcraft . . . consists, broadly speaking, of a [delusional] projection of certain emotions (which, as the very word implies, emanate from within) to external things and an endowment of such things (or in the case of witchcraft, of such persons) with the moral qualities corresponding to these inward states. . . .

"Thus persons responsible for the persistent attempts to suppress the dissemination of popular knowledge concerning sex matters betray themselves unwittingly as the bearers of the very impulses they would so ostentatiously help others to avoid. Such persons should know through their own experience that ignorance of a subject does not insure immunity against the evils of which it treats, nor does the propitiatory act of noisy public disapproval of certain evils signify innocence or personal purity." Van Teslaar, Book Review, 8 J. Abnormal Psychology 282, 286 (1913).

[7] See Appendix III to this opinion.

JUSTICE FORTAS'S OPINION NOTE

[*] "[W]e reaffirm the principle that, in 'obscenity' cases as in all others involving rights derived from the First Amendment guarantees of free expression, this Court cannot avoid making an independent constitutional judgment on the facts of the case as to whether the material involved is constitutionally protected." 378 U. S., at 190. See *Cox* v. *Louisiana*, 379 U. S. 536, 545, n. 8 (1965).

"IF THE GOVERNMENT HAS NO SUBSTANTIAL INTEREST IN PREVENTING A CITIZEN FROM READING BOOKS AND WATCHING FILMS IN THE PRIVACY OF HIS HOME, THEN CLEARLY IT CAN HAVE NO GREATER INTEREST IN PREVENTING OR PROHIBITING HIM FROM ACQUIRING THEM."

United States v. Lethe, 312 F.Supp. 421 (1970)

MacBRIDE, Chief Judge.

Defendant has been indicted for violations of 18 U.S.C. § 1461 (Mailing Obscene Matter). The indictment is in ten counts. Six counts allege that defendant mailed advertisements for obscene matter which were "nonmailable". Four counts allege that defendant mailed obscene books or films which were "nonmailable." Defendant moves to dismiss the indictment on several grounds. He also moves to inspect the grand jury minutes.

The United States Attorney indicates that the grand jury proceedings were not transcribed. The only records of the grand jury's action in this case have been turned over to defendant. There is no impropriety in this, as the Court of Appeals for the Ninth Circuit has repeatedly held. *See* Jack v. United States, 409 F.2d 522 (9th Cir. 1969); Loux v. United States, 389 F.2d 911 (9th Cir. 1968), cert. denied, 393 U.S. 867, 89 S.Ct. 151, 21 L.Ed.2d 135. I do not find any merit in defendant's contention that because this case involves the First Amendment, the rule must be different. He has advanced no persuasive authority or reasoning for his contention. Defendant's contention that there must be a pre-indictment adversary hearing on the issue of obscenity is similarly without support and is rejected.

Defendant also argues that the material in question, including the advertisements, is constitutionally protected and that the court must view it prior to trial and determine if it is constitutionally protected. It is of course true that the question of obscenity is a constitutional one which must be passed upon by the court,[1] but it does not follow from this that the decision must be made prior to trial.[2] Defendant's suggested procedure would require in effect two trials. The only purpose to be served would be to give defendant a preview of the government's case.

I have recently held that after the seizure of an obscene film pursuant to a warrant issued on probable cause, the issuing magistrate must, as soon as is practicable, view the film and determine whether or not it is constitutionally protected.[3] But the search and seizure situation is distinguishable from the present case. Whenever there is a forcible seizure there is a danger of governmental suppression of all copies before a judicial determination of the constitutional status of the material seized. This is especially true in the case of commercial films because the exhibitor will not generally have more than one print. However, where a defendant has voluntarily parted with literature or films, as in the instant case, he cannot complain of a suppression when he is later prosecuted.[4] I conclude that no judicial determination is required prior to trial.

I turn now to defendant's substantive attack on the indictment. He asserts that the government cannot constitutionally make it a crime to send obscene materials through the mails to an adult who requests them. His argument is based primarily upon Stanley v. Georgia, 394 U.S. 557, 89 S.Ct. 1243, 22 L.Ed.2d 542 (1969), which held that "the First and Fourteenth Amendments prohibit making mere private possession of obscene material a crime." 394 U.S. at 568, 89 S.Ct. at 1249. The right to possess, he argues, implies the right to buy or receive, and the right to buy or receive is meaningless unless someone has the right to sell or send.

Before *Stanley*, the quick answer to defendant's argument would have been that Roth v. United States, 354 U.S. 476, 77 S.Ct. 1304 (1957), held that obscenity was outside the protection of the First Amendment, and the government could regulate its possession and distribution at will, like any other contraband. However, *Stanley* clearly indicates that *Roth* does not go that far:

Roth and its progeny certainly do mean that the First and Fourteenth Amendments recognize a valid governmental interest in dealing with the problem of obscenity. But the assertion of that interest cannot, in every context, be insulated from all constitutional protections. Neither *Roth* or any other decision of this Court reaches that far. (394 U.S. at 563, 89 S.Ct. at 1246, 1247)

The Court then proceeded to examine the constitutional implications and the governmental interests involved in the Georgia statute forbidding mere private possession of obscene material.

It is true that in *Stanley* the Court recognized the important governmental interest in regulating commercial distribution of obscene matter:

" 'The door barring federal and state intrusion into [the area of First Amendment rights] cannot be left ajar; it must be kept tightly closed and opened only the slightest crack necessary to prevent encroachment upon more important interests.' [citing Roth] *Roth* and the cases following it discerned such an 'important interest' in the regulation of commercial distribution of obscene material. (394 U.S. at 563–564, 89 S.Ct. at 1247)"

But to say that the government has an "important interest" in the regulation of commercial distribution is not to immunize all statutes touching commercial distribution from further judicial scrutiny.[5] In *Stanley* itself the State sought to justify its statute on the ground that it was a necessary incident to its statutory scheme prohibiting distribution. This did not prevent the Court from weighing the governmental interests against the protections of the Constitution.

Thus, while recognizing the government's legitimate interest in regulating distribution, I proceed to examine the constitutional implications of prohibiting use of the mails for distribution of obscene materials to one who has requested them.[6] I start with the proposition that the government may not legislate to control what books or films a person may possess in his house regardless of their content.

"If the First Amendment means anything, it means that a State has no business telling a man, sitting alone in his own house, what books he may read or what films he may watch. Our whole constitutional heritage rebels at the thought of giving government the power to control men's minds. Stanley v. Georgia, 394 U.S. 557, 565, 89 S.Ct. 1243, 1248 (1969)."

If the government has no substantial interest in preventing a citizen from reading books and watching films in the privacy of his home, then clearly it can have no greater interest in preventing or prohibiting him from acquiring them. The only possible purpose in preventing him from acquiring them is to prevent him from enjoying them.

"It is now well established that the Constitution protects the right to receive information and ideas. 'This freedom [of speech and press] * * * necessarily protects the right to receive * * *.' [Citations] This right to receive information and ideas, regardless of their social worth, * * * is fundamental to our free society. Stanley v. Georgia, 394 U.S. 557, 564, 89 S.Ct. 1243 (1969)."

The governmental interest is not augmented because a person *buys* the material instead of receiving it some other way.[7] Thus, I conclude that a person has a constitutional right to buy or receive obscene material.

The final step is not difficult. Can it be reasonably argued that although the government may not directly prevent someone from buying a book, it may achieve the same result indirectly by making it a crime to sell the book to him? I think not, unless the government can demonstrate it has some substantial interest in preventing the sale other than keeping the purchaser from buying.

There are basically only four goals which have been used to justify restrictions on dissemination of obscene material: (1) preventing crimes of sexual violence, (2) protecting the society's moral fabric, (3) protecting children from exposure to obscenity, and (4) preventing "assaults" on the sensibilities of an unwilling public.[8] It is clear from *Stanley* that the Supreme Court does not consider either of the first two legitimate justifications for obscenity legislation:

"[I]n the face of * * * traditional notions of individual liberty, Georgia asserts the right to protect the individual's mind from the effects of obscenity. We are not certain that this argument amounts to anything more than the assertion that the State has the right to control the moral content of a person's thoughts. To some, this may be a noble purpose, but it is wholly inconsistent with the philosophy of the First Amendment * * * '[The Constitution's] guarantee is not confined to the expression of ideas that are conventional or shared by a majority * * *. And in the realm of ideas it protects expression which is eloquent no less than that which is unconvincing.' Cf. Joseph Burstyn, Inc. v. Wilson, 345 U.S. 495, 72 S.Ct. 777, 96 L.Ed. 1098 * * * (1952). Nor is it relevant that obscene materials in general, or the particular films before the Court, are arguably devoid of any ideological content. The line between the transmission of ideas and mere entertainment is much too elusive for a Court to draw, if indeed such a line can be drawn at all. * * * Whatever the power of the state to control public dissemination of ideas inimical to the public morality, it cannot constitutionally premise legislation on the desirability of controlling a person's private thoughts.

"Perhaps recognizing this, Georgia asserts that exposure to obscene materials may lead to deviant sexual behavior or crimes of sexual violence. There appears to be little empirical basis for that assertion. But more important, if the State is only concerned about printed or filmed materials inducing antisocial conduct, we believe that in the context of private consumption of ideas and information we should adhere to the view that '[a]mong free men, the deterrents ordinarily to be applied to prevent crime are education and punishment for violations of the law * * *.' Whitney v. California, 274 U.S. 357, 378, 47 S.Ct. 641, 649, 71 L.Ed. 1095, * * * (1927) (Brandeis, J., concurring). * * * Given the present state of knowledge, the State may no more prohibit mere possession of obscene matter on the ground that it may lead to antisocial conduct than it may prohibit possession of chemistry books on the ground that they may lead to the manufacture of homemade spirits. [footnotes omitted] (394 U.S. at 565–567, 89 S.Ct. at 1248–1249)"

See also Redrup v. New York, 386 U.S. 767, 87 S.Ct. 1414 (1967). The Supreme Court has recognized the protection of children[9] and the protection of an unwilling public from obtrusive invasions of privacy[10] as proper governmental interests justifying obscenity laws. But neither of these can be used to justify prohibiting mailings to a requesting adult. There is no public display, and children are not involved.[11] No valid governmental interest remains, and the conclusion is inescapable that the government cannot constitutionally bring such a prosecution.[12]

This case is strikingly similar to Griswold v. Connecticut, 381 U.S. 479, 85 S.Ct. 1678 (1965). In *Griswold* the Court reversed the convictions of people who had given information, instruction and medical advice to married persons as to the means of preventing conception. The Court reasoned that the Constitution guarantees married couples the right to be free to choose whether or not to employ contraception. This includes the right to receive information and devices from a birth control clinic. The right to practice birth control would be meaningless if the State were permitted to prevent people from receiving information and devices. In *Stanley* the Court recognized the right of a person to choose what he will read and observe.[13] The distributor must similarly be allowed to provide what the person is entitled to see.

It remains to consider the argument that the government has plenary power to regulate the content of the mails. This doctrine originated in Ex parte Jackson, 96 U.S. 727, 24 L.Ed. 877 (1878), and Public Clearing House v. Coyne, 194 U.S. 497, 24 S.Ct. 789, 48 L.Ed. 1092 (1904), and has never been expressly overruled. Whatever its continued vitality in other situations,[14] it is clear that it no longer applies in a First Amendment context.[15]

I am aware of the groundswell of support in the country for laws cracking down on smut peddlers. Numerous laws in this area are being considered in Congress. My decision today will certainly not comfort those who are concerned about this problem. But this decision is narrowly circumscribed. It will interfere only with those laws which seek to tell an adult what literature or films he may acquire for his own enjoyment. We may not always agree with the literary tastes of our fellow citizens, but we may not impose our tastes upon others by censorship or other means unless some greater interest of society is at stake. That is the price we pay for a free society. As I have attempted to show, there is no governmental interest other than "thought control" to sustain this attempted prosecution; therefore, four counts of this indictment must be dismissed.

The counts in the indictment involving the mailing of obscene matter to an adult requesting it are Three, Six, Eight and Ten. Defendant's motion to dismiss these counts is granted. The remaining counts involve unsolicited material. The rest of defendant's motions are denied.

It is so ordered.

NOTES

1. *See e. g.*, Roth v. United States, 354 U.S. 476, 77 S.Ct. 1304, 1 L.Ed.2d 1498 (1957).

2. *Cf.* United States v. Fruchauf, 365 U.S. 146, 81 S.Ct. 547, 5 L.Ed.2d 476 (1961).

3. *See* Merritt v. Lewis, 309 F.Supp. 1249, 1254 (E.D.Cal. January 19, 1970 and January 28, 1970).

4. An obscenity prosecution may have a chilling effect on the further distribution of the material being prosecuted, but this is not sufficient reason to alter the normal procedures. I know of no authority which suggests otherwise.

5. *See* Redrup v. New York, 386 U.S. 767, 87 S.Ct. 1414, 18 L.Ed.2d 515 (1967); Karalexis v. Byrne, 306 F.Supp. 1363 (D.Mass.1969), (three-judge court).

6. To the extent that defendant's argument depends on asserting the constitutional rights of those to whom he distributes, defendant has standing to do so. *See* Griswold v. Connecticut, 381 U.S. 479, 85 S.Ct. 1678, 14 L.Ed.2d 510 (1965).

7. Commercial activity per se is no grounds for regulation. Ginzburg v. United States, 383 U.S. 463, 474, 86 S.Ct. 942, 16 L.Ed.2d 31 (1966); New York Times Co. v. Sullivan, 376 U.S. 254, 265–266, 84 S.Ct. 710, 11 L.Ed.2d 686 (1964); Smith v. California, 361 U.S. 147, 150, 80 S.Ct. 215, 4 L.Ed.2d 205 (1959).

8. Note, The New Metaphysics of the Law of Obscenity, 57 California Law Review 1257, 1276 (1969).

9. *See* Stanley v. Georgia, 394 U.S. 557, 567, 89 S.Ct. 1243 (1969); Ginsberg v. New York, 390 U.S. 629, 88 S.Ct. 1274, 20 L.Ed.2d 195 (1968); Butler v. Michigan, 352 U.S. 380, 77 S.Ct. 524, 1 L.Ed.2d 412 (1956).

10. *See* Stanley v. Georgia, *supra*, 394 U.S. at 567, 89 S.Ct. 1243; Redrup v. New York, 386 U.S. 767, 769, 87 S.Ct. 1414 (1967).

11. The argument that the government may restrict distribution to adults as necessary to insure protection of children is foreclosed by Butler v. Michigan, 352 U.S. 380, 77 S.Ct. 524 (1956).

12. *See* Note, The New Metaphysics of the Law of Obscenity, 57 California Law Review 1257, 1278–79 (1969). The commentators are apparently unanimous in concluding that *Stanley* cannot logically be restricted to its facts. *See* D. Engdahl, Requiem for Roth: Obscenity Doctrine is Changing, 68 Michigan Law Review 185, 229 (1969); 83 Harvard Law Review, 147 (1969); 21 Baylor Law Review 502, 511 (1969); 11 William and Mary Law

Review 261 (1969).

13. 394 U.S. at 505, 89 S.Ct. 1243.

14. "The hoary dogma of Ex parte Jackson * * * and Public Clearing House v. Coyne * * * that the use of the mails is a privilege on which the Government may impose such conditions as it chooses, has long since evaporated. [Citations] " Roth v. United States, 354 U.S. 476, 505, 77 S.Ct. 1304, 1319 (1957) (Justice Harlan dissenting).

15. *See* Lamont v. Postmaster General, 381 U.S. 301, 85 S.Ct. 1493, 14 L.Ed.2d 398 (1965); Hannegan v. Esquire, Inc., 327 U.S. 146, 66 S.Ct. 456, 90 L.Ed. 586 (1946); United States v. Van Leeuwen, 397 U.S. 249, 90 S.Ct. 1029, 25 L.Ed.2d 282 (March 23, 1970): " '[T]he use of the mails is almost as much a part of free speech as the right to use our tongues.' " (397 U.S. at 251, 90 S.Ct. at 1032) [quoting Mr. Justice Holmes in Milwaukee Social Democratic Pub. Co. v. Burleson, 255 U.S. 407, 437, 41 S.Ct. 352, 65 L.Ed. 704 (1921) (dissenting opinion)].

REIDEL HAS NO CONSTITUTIONAL RIGHT TO MAIL "THE TRUE FACTS ABOUT IMPORTED PORNOGRAPHY" TO CONSENTING ADULTS

United States v. Reidel, 402 U.S. 351 (1971)

MR. JUSTICE WHITE delivered the opinion of the Court.

Section 1461 of Title 18, U. S. C., prohibits the knowing use of the mails for the delivery of obscene matter.[1] The issue presented by the jurisdictional statement in this case is whether § 1461 is constitutional as applied to the distribution of obscene materials to willing recipients who state that they are adults. The District Court held that it was not.[2] We disagree and reverse the judgment.

I

On April 15, 1970, the appellee, Norman Reidel, was indicted on three counts, each count charging him with having mailed a single copy of an illustrated booklet entitled The True Facts About Imported Pornography. One of the copies had been mailed to a postal inspector stipulated to be over the age of 21, who had responded to a newspaper advertisement.[3] The other two copies had been seized during a search of appellee's business premises; both of them had been deposited in the mail by Reidel but had been returned to him in their original mailing envelopes bearing the mark "undelivered." As to these two booklets, the Government conceded that it had no evidence as to the identity or age of the addressees or as to their willingness to receive the booklets. Nor does the record indicate why the booklets were returned undelivered.

Reidel moved in the District Court before trial to dismiss the indictment, contending, among other things, that § 1461 was unconstitutional. Assuming for the purpose of the motion that the booklets were obscene, the trial judge granted the motion to dismiss on the ground that Reidel had made a constitutionally protected delivery and hence that § 1461 was unconstitutional as applied to him. The Government's direct appeal is here under 18 U. S. C. § 3731.

II

In *Roth* v. *United States,* 354 U. S. 476 (1957), Roth was convicted under § 1461 for mailing obscene circulars and advertising.[4] The Court affirmed the conviction, holding that "obscenity is not within the area of constitutionally protected speech or press," *id.,* at 485, and that § 1461, "applied according to the proper standard for judging obscenity, do[es] not offend constitutional safeguards against convictions based upon protected material, or fail to give men in acting adequate notice of what is prohibited." *Id.,* at 492. *Roth* has not been overruled. It remains the law in this Court and governs this case. Reidel, like Roth, was charged with using the mails for the distribution of obscene material. His conviction, if it occurs and the materials are found in fact to be obscene, would be no more vulnerable than was Roth's.

Stanley v. *Georgia,* 394 U. S. 557 (1969), compels no different result. There, pornographic films were found in Stanley's home and he was convicted under Georgia statutes for possessing obscene material. This Court reversed the conviction, holding that the mere private possession of obscene matter cannot constitutionally be made a crime. But it neither overruled nor disturbed the holding in *Roth.* Indeed, in the Court's view, the constitutionality of proscribing private possession of obscenity was a matter of first impression in this Court, a question neither involved nor decided in *Roth.* The Court made its point expressly: "*Roth* and the cases following that decision are not impaired by today's holding. As we have said, the States retain broad power to regulate obscenity; that power simply does not extend to mere possession by the individual in the privacy of his own home." *Id.,* at 568. Nothing in *Stanley* questioned the validity of *Roth* insofar as the distribution of obscene material was concerned. Clearly the Court had no thought of questioning the validity of § 1461 as applied to those who, like Reidel, are routinely disseminating obscenity through the mails and who have no claim, and could make none, about unwanted governmental intrusions into the privacy of their home. The Court considered this sufficiently clear to warrant summary affirmance of the judgment of the United States District Court for the Northern District of Georgia rejecting claims that under *Stanley* v. *Georgia,* Georgia's obscenity statute could not be applied to book sellers. *Gable* v. *Jenkins,* 397 U. S. 592 (1970).

The District Court ignored both *Roth* and the express limitations on the reach of the *Stanley* decision. Relying on the statement in *Stanley* that "the Constitution protects the right to receive information and ideas . . . regardless of their social worth," 394 U. S., at 564, the trial judge reasoned that "if a person has the right to receive and possess this material, then someone must have the right to deliver it to him." He concluded that § 1461 could not be validly applied "where obscene material is not directed at children, or it is not directed at an unwilling public, where the material such as in this case is solicited by adults . . . ."

The District Court gave *Stanley* too wide a sweep. To extrapolate from Stanley's right to have and peruse obscene material in the privacy of his own home a First Amendment right in Reidel to sell it to him would effectively scuttle *Roth,* the precise result that the *Stanley* opinion abjured. Whatever the scope of the "right to receive" referred to in *Stanley,* it is not so broad as to immunize the dealings in obscenity in which Reidel engaged here—dealings that *Roth* held unprotected by the First Amendment.

The right Stanley asserted was "the right to read or observe what he pleases—the right to satisfy his intellectual and emotional needs in the privacy of his own home." 394 U. S., at 565. The Court's response was that "a State has no business telling a man, sitting alone in his own house, what books he may read or what films he may watch. Our whole constitutional heritage rebels at the thought of giving government the power to control men's minds." *Ibid.* The focus of this language was on freedom of mind and thought and on the privacy of one's home. It does not require that we fashion or recognize a constitutional right in people like Reidel to distribute or sell obscene materials. The personal constitutional rights of those like Stanley to possess and read obscenity in their homes and their freedom of mind and thought do not depend on whether the materials are obscene or whether obscenity is constitutionally protected. Their rights to have and view that material in private are independently saved by the Constitution.

Reidel is in a wholly different position. He has no complaints about governmental violations of his private thoughts or fantasies, but stands squarely on a claimed First Amendment right to do business in obscenity and use the mails in the process. But *Roth* has squarely placed obscenity and its distribution outside the reach of the First Amendment and they remain there today. *Stanley* did not overrule *Roth* and we decline to do so now.

III

A postscript is appropriate. *Roth* and like cases have interpreted the First Amendment not to insulate obscenity from statutory regulation. But the Amendment itself neither proscribes dealings in obscenity nor directs or suggests legislative oversight in this area. The relevant constitutional issues have arisen in the courts only because lawmakers having the exclusive legislative power have consistently insisted on making the distribution of obscenity a crime or otherwise regulating such materials and because the laws they pass are challenged as unconstitutional invasions of free speech and press.

It is urged that there is developing sentiment that adults should have complete freedom to produce, deal in, possess, and consume whatever communicative materials may appeal to them and that the law's involvement with obscenity should be limited to those situations where children are involved or where it is necessary to prevent imposition on unwilling recipients of whatever age. The concepts involved are said to be so elusive and the laws so inherently unenforceable without extravagant expend-itures of time and effort by enforcement officers and the courts that basic reassessment is not only wise but essential. This may prove to be the desirable and even-tual legislative course. But if it is, the task of restruc-turing the obscenity laws lies with those who pass, repeal, and amend statutes and ordinances. *Roth* and like cases pose no obstacle to such developments.

The judgment of the District Court is reversed.

So ordered.

[For dissenting opinion of MR. JUSTICE BLACK, see *post*, p. 379.]

MR. JUSTICE HARLAN, concurring.

I join the opinion of the Court which, as I understand it, holds that the Federal Government may prohibit the use of the mails for commercial distribution of materials properly classifiable as obscene.* The Court today cor-rectly rejects the contention that the recognition in *Stan-ley* v. *Georgia,* 394 U. S. 557 (1969), that private posses-sion of obscene materials is constitutionally privileged under the First Amendment carries with it a "right to receive" such materials through any modes of distribution as long as adequate precautions are taken to prevent the dissemination to unconsenting adults and children. Ap-pellee here contends, in effect, that the *Stanley* "right to receive" language, 394 U. S., at 564–565, constituted recognition that obscenity was constitutionally protected for its content. Governmental efforts to proscribe ob-scenity as such would, on this interpretation, not be constitutional; rather, the power of both the State and Federal Governments would now be restricted to the reg-ulation of the constitutionally protected right to engage in this category of "speech" in light of otherwise permis-sible state interests, such as the protection of privacy or the protection of children.

That interpretation of *Stanley,* however, is flatly incon-sistent with the square holding of *Roth* v. *United States,* 354 U. S. 476, 485 (1957):

"We hold that obscenity is not within the area of constitutionally protected speech or press."

Either *Roth* means that government may proscribe ob-scenity as such rather than merely regulate it with refer-ence to other state interests, or *Roth* means nothing at all. And *Stanley,* far from overruling *Roth,* did not even purport to limit that case to its facts:

"We hold that the First and Fourteenth Amend-ments prohibit making mere private possession of obscene material a crime. *Roth* and the cases fol-lowing that decision are not impaired by today's holding. . . ." 394 U. S., at 568.

In view of *Stanley's* explicit reaffirmance of *Roth,* I do not read the former case as limiting governmental power to deal with obscenity to modes of regulation geared to public interests to be judicially assessed as legitimate or illegitimate in light of the nature of obscenity as a special

---

*Of course, the obscenity *vel non* of the materials is not presented at this juncture of the case.

category of constitutionally protected speech. Rather, I understand *Stanley* to rest in relevant part on the prop-osition that the power which *Roth* recognized in both State and Federal Governments to proscribe obscenity as constitutionally unprotected cannot be exercised to the exclusion of other constitutionally protected interests of the individual. That treatment of *Stanley* is consistent with the Court's approach to the problem of prior re-straints in the obscenity area; if government chooses a system of prior restraints as an aid to its goal of pro-scribing obscenity, the system must be designed to mini-mize impact on speech which is constitutionally pro-tected. *Blount* v. *Rizzi,* 400 U. S. 410, 416 (1971); *Marcus* v. *Search Warrant,* 367 U. S. 717, 731 (1961). See *Freedman* v. *Maryland,* 380 U. S. 51 (1965).

The analogous constitutionally protected interest in the *Stanley* situation which restricts governmental efforts to proscribe obscenity is the First Amendment right of the individual to be free from governmental programs of thought control, however such programs might be justi-fied in terms of permissible state objectives. For me, at least, *Stanley* rests on the proposition that freedom from governmental manipulation of the content of a man's mind necessitates a ban on punishment for the mere pos-session of the memorabilia of a man's thoughts and dreams, unless that punishment can be related to a state interest of a stronger nature than the simple desire to proscribe obscenity as such. In other words, the "right to receive" recognized in *Stanley* is not a right to the existence of modes of distribution of obscenity which the State could destroy without serious risk of infringing on the privacy of a man's thoughts; rather, it is a right to a protective zone ensuring the freedom of a man's inner life, be it rich or sordid. Cf. *West Virginia State Board of Education* v. *Barnette,* 319 U. S. 624, 642 (1943).

MR. JUSTICE MARSHALL, dissenting in No. 133, *post*, p. 363, and concurring in the judgment in No. 534.

Only two years ago in *Stanley* v. *Georgia,* 394 U. S. 557 (1969), the Court fully canvassed the range of state interests that might possibly justify regulation of ob-scenity. That decision refused to legitimize the argu-ment that obscene materials could be outlawed because the materials might somehow encourage antisocial con-duct, and unequivocally rejected the outlandish notion that the State may police the thoughts of its citizenry. The Court did, however, approve the validity of regu-latory action taken to protect children and unwilling adults from exposure to materials deemed to be obscene. The need for such protection of course arises when ob-scenity is distributed or displayed publicly; and the Court reaffirmed the principles of *Roth* v. *United States,* 354 U. S. 476 (1957), *Redrup* v. *New York,* 386 U. S. 767 (1967), and other decisions that involved the com-mercial distribution of obscene materials. Thus, *Stanley* turned on an assessment of which state interests may legitimately underpin governmental action, and it is disingenuous to contend that Stanley's conviction was reversed because his home, rather than his person or luggage, was the locus of a search.

I would employ a similar adjudicative approach in deciding the cases presently before the Court. In No. 133 the material in question was seized from claimant's luggage upon his return to the United States from a European trip. Although claimant stipulated that he intended to use some of the photographs to illustrate a book which would be later distributed commercially, the seized items were then in his purely private possession and threatened neither children nor anyone else. In my view, the Government has ample opportunity to protect its valid interests if and when commercial distribution should take place. Since threats to these interests arise in the context of public or commercial distribution, the magnitude of the threats can best be assessed when distribution actually occurs; and it is always possible that claimant might include only some of the photographs in the final commercial product or might later abandon his intention to use any of them.* I find particularly troubling the plurality's suggestion that there is no need to scrutinize the Government's behavior because a "border search" is involved. While necessity may dictate some diminution of traditional constitutional safeguards at our Nation's borders, I should have thought that any such reduction would heighten the need jealously to protect those liberties that remain rather than justify the suspension of any and all safeguards.

No. 534 presents a different situation in which allegedly obscene materials were distributed through the mails. Plainly, any such mail order distribution poses the danger that obscenity will be sent to children, and although the appellee in No. 534 indicated his intent to sell only to adults who requested his wares, the sole safeguard designed to prevent the receipt of his merchandise by minors was his requirement that buyers declare their age. While the record does not reveal that any children actually received appellee's materials, I believe that distributors of purportedly obscene merchandise may be required to take more stringent steps to guard against possible receipt by minors. This case comes to us without the benefit of a full trial, and, on this sparse record, I am not prepared to find that appellee's conduct was not within a constitutionally valid construction of the federal statute.

Accordingly, I dissent in No. 133 and concur in the judgment in No. 534.

NOTES

[1] The statute in pertinent part provides:

"Every obscene, lewd, lascivious, indecent, filthy or vile article, matter, thing, device, or substance; and—

.   .   .   .   .

"Every written or printed card, letter, circular, book, pamphlet, advertisement, or notice of any kind giving information, directly or indirectly, where, or how, or from whom, or by what means any of such mentioned matters, articles, or things may be obtained or made, or where or by whom any act or operation of any kind for the procuring or producing of abortion will be done or performed, or how

or by what means conception may be prevented or abortion produced, whether sealed or unsealed . . . .

.   .   .   .   .

"Is declared to be nonmailable matter and shall not be conveyed in the mails or delivered from any post office or by any letter carrier.

"Whoever knowingly uses the mails for the mailing, carriage in the mails, or delivery of anything declared by this section to be nonmailable, or knowingly causes to be delivered by mail according to the direction thereon, or at the place at which it is directed to be delivered by the person to whom it is addressed, or knowingly takes any such thing from the mails for the purpose of circulating or disposing thereof, or of aiding in the circulation or disposition thereof, shall be fined not more than $5,000 or imprisoned not more than five years, or both, for the first such offense, and shall be fined not more than $10,000 or imprisoned not more than ten years, or both, for each such offense thereafter."

[2] The trial judge did not issue a written opinion but ruled orally from the bench.

[3] The advertisement was as follows:

"IMPORTED PORNOGRAPHY—learn the true facts before sending money abroad. Send $1.00 for our fully illustrated booklet. You must be 21 years of age and so state. Normax Press, P. O. Box 989, Fontana, California, 92335."

[4] Roth v. United States was heard and decided with Alberts v. California, in which the Court upheld the obscenity provisions of the California Penal Code.

JUSTICES BURGER, BLACKMUN, POWELL, REHNQUIST, AND WHITE REJECT THE "UTTERLY WITHOUT REDEEMING SOCIAL VALUE" TEST, INTERPRET "COMMUNITY STANDARDS" TO MEAN LOCAL AND NOT NATIONAL COMMUNITY STANDARDS, AND DENY FIRST AMENDMENT PROTECTION TO SEVERAL SEXUALLY EXPLICIT BROCHURES MAILED TO "UNWILLING RECIPIENTS"

Miller v. California, 413 U.S. 15 (1973)

MR. CHIEF JUSTICE BURGER delivered the opinion of the Court.

This is one of a group of "obscenity-pornography" cases being reviewed by the Court in a re-examination of standards enunciated in earlier cases involving what Mr. Justice Harlan called "the intractable obscenity problem." *Interstate Circuit, Inc.* v. *Dallas*, 390 U. S. 676, 704 (1968) (concurring and dissenting).

Appellant conducted a mass mailing campaign to advertise the sale of illustrated books, euphemistically called "adult" material. After a jury trial, he was convicted of violating California Penal Code § 311.2 (a), a misdemeanor, by knowingly distributing obscene matter,[1] and the Appellate Department, Superior Court of California, County of Orange, summarily affirmed the judgment without opinion. Appellant's conviction was specifically based on his conduct in causing five unsolicited advertising brochures to be sent through the mail in an envelope addressed to a restaurant in Newport Beach, California. The envelope was opened by the

---

*Moreover, the items seized in this case were only a component of a product which might ultimately be distributed, and viewing them in isolation is inconsistent with the principle that determinations of obscenity should focus on an entire work, see, e. g., *Roth* v. *United States*, 354 U. S. 476, 489 (1957).

manager of the restaurant and his mother. They had not requested the brochures; they complained to the police.

The brochures advertise four books entitled "Intercourse," "Man-Woman," "Sex Orgies Illustrated," and "An Illustrated History of Pornography," and a film entitled "Marital Intercourse." While the brochures contain some descriptive printed material, primarily they consist of pictures and drawings very explicitly depicting men and women in groups of two or more engaging in a variety of sexual activities, with genitals often prominently displayed.

I

This case involves the application of a State's criminal obscenity statute to a situation in which sexually explicit materials have been thrust by aggressive sales action upon unwilling recipients who had in no way indicated any desire to receive such materials. This Court has recognized that the States have a legitimate interest in prohibiting dissemination or exhibition of obscene material [2] when the mode of dissemination carries with it a significant danger of offending the sensibilities of unwilling recipients or of exposure to juveniles. *Stanley v. Georgia*, 394 U. S. 557, 567 (1969); *Ginsberg v. New York*, 390 U. S. 629, 637–643 (1968); *Interstate Circuit, Inc. v. Dallas, supra,* at 690; *Redrup v. New York*, 386 U. S. 767, 769 (1967); *Jacobellis v. Ohio*, 378 U. S. 184, 195 (1964). See *Rabe v. Washington*, 405 U. S. 313, 317 (1972) (BURGER, C. J., concurring); *United States v. Reidel*, 402 U. S. 351, 360–362 (1971) (opinion of MARSHALL, J.); *Joseph Burstyn, Inc. v. Wilson*, 343 U. S. 495, 502 (1952); *Breard v. Alexandria*, 341 U. S. 622, 644–645 (1951); *Kovacs v. Cooper*, 336 U. S. 77, 88–89 (1949); *Prince v. Massachusetts*, 321 U. S. 158, 169–170 (1944). Cf. *Butler v. Michigan*, 352 U. S. 380, 382–383 (1957); *Public Utilities Comm'n v. Pollak*, 343 U. S. 451, 464–465 (1952). It is in this context that we are called on to define the standards which must be used to identify obscene material that a State may regulate without infringing on the First Amendment as applicable to the States through the Fourteenth Amendment.

The dissent of MR. JUSTICE BRENNAN reviews the background of the obscenity problem, but since the Court now undertakes to formulate standards more concrete than those in the past, it is useful for us to focus on two of the landmark cases in the somewhat tortured history of the Court's obscenity decisions. In *Roth v. United States*, 354 U. S. 476 (1957), the Court sustained a conviction under a federal statute punishing the mailing of "obscene, lewd, lascivious or filthy . . ." materials. The key to that holding was the Court's rejection of the claim that obscene materials were protected by the First Amendment. Five Justices joined in the opinion stating:

"All ideas having even the slightest redeeming social importance—unorthodox ideas, controversial ideas, even ideas hateful to the prevailing climate of opinion—have the full protection of the [First Amendment] guaranties, unless excludable because they encroach upon the limited area of more important interests. But implicit in the history of the First Amendment is the rejection of obscenity as utterly without redeeming social importance. . . .

This is the same judgment expressed by this Court in *Chaplinsky v. New Hampshire*, 315 U. S. 568, 571–572:

"'. . . There are certain well-defined and narrowly limited classes of speech, the prevention and punishment of which have never been thought to raise any Constitutional problem. *These include the lewd and obscene . . . . It has been well observed that such utterances are no essential part of any exposition of ideas, and are of such slight social value as a step to truth that any benefit that may be derived from them is clearly outweighed by the social interest in order and morality. . . .'* [Emphasis by Court in *Roth* opinion.]

"We hold that obscenity is not within the area of constitutionally protected speech or press." 354 U. S., at 484–485 (footnotes omitted).

Nine years later, in *Memoirs v. Massachusetts*, 383 U. S. 413 (1966), the Court veered sharply away from the *Roth* concept and, with only three Justices in the plurality opinion, articulated a new test of obscenity. The plurality held that under the *Roth* definition

"as elaborated in subsequent cases, three elements must coalesce: it must be established that (a) the dominant theme of the material taken as a whole appeals to a prurient interest in sex; (b) the material is patently offensive because it affronts contemporary community standards relating to the description or representation of sexual matters; and (c) the material is utterly without redeeming social value." *Id.*, at 418.

The sharpness of the break with *Roth*, represented by the third element of the *Memoirs* test and emphasized by MR. JUSTICE WHITE's dissent, *id.*, at 460–462, was further underscored when the *Memoirs* plurality went on to state:

"The Supreme Judicial Court erred in holding that a book need not be 'unqualifiedly worthless before it can be deemed obscene.' A book cannot be proscribed unless it is found to be *utterly* without redeeming social value." *Id.*, at 419 (emphasis in original).

While *Roth* presumed "obscenity" to be "utterly without redeeming social importance." *Memoirs* required that to prove obscenity it must be affirmatively established that the material is "*utterly* without redeeming social value." Thus, even as they repeated the words of *Roth*, the *Memoirs* plurality produced a drastically altered test that called on the prosecution to prove a negative, *i. e.*, that the material was "*utterly* without redeeming social value"—a burden virtually impossible to discharge under our criminal standards of proof. Such considerations caused Mr. Justice Harlan to wonder if the "*utterly* without redeeming social value" test had any meaning at all. See *Memoirs v. Massachusetts, id.*, at 459 (Harlan, J., dissenting). See also *id.*, at 461 (WHITE, J., dissenting); *United States v. Groner*, 479 F. 2d 577, 579–581 (CA5 1973).

Apart from the initial formulation in the *Roth* case, no majority of the Court has at any given time been able to agree on a standard to determine what constitutes obscene, pornographic material subject to regulation under the States' police power. See, *e. g., Redrup* v. *New York*, 386 U. S., at 770–771. We have seen "a variety of views among the members of the Court unmatched in any other course of constitutional adjudication." *Interstate Circuit, Inc.* v. *Dallas*, 390 U. S., at 704–705 (Harlan, J., concurring and dissenting) (footnote omitted).[3] This is not remarkable, for in the area of freedom of speech and press the courts must always remain sensitive to any infringement on genuinely serious literary, artistic, political, or scientific expression. This is an area in which there are few eternal verities.

The case we now review was tried on the theory that the California Penal Code § 311 approximately incorporates the three-stage *Memoirs* test, *supra*. But now the *Memoirs* test has been abandoned as unworkable by its author,[4] and no Member of the Court today supports the *Memoirs* formulation.

II

This much has been categorically settled by the Court, that obscene material is unprotected by the First Amendment. *Kois* v. *Wisconsin*, 408 U. S. 229 (1972); *United States* v. *Reidel*, 402 U. S., at 354; *Roth* v. *United States*, *supra*, at 485.[5] "The First and Fourteenth Amendments have never been treated as absolutes [footnote omitted]." *Breard* v. *Alexandria*, 341 U. S., at 642, and cases cited. See *Times Film Corp.* v. *Chicago*, 365 U. S. 43, 47–50 (1961); *Joseph Burstyn, Inc.* v. *Wilson*, 343 U. S., at 502. We acknowledge, however, the inherent dangers of undertaking to regulate any form of expression. State statutes designed to regulate obscene materials must be carefully limited. See *Interstate Circuit, Inc.* v. *Dallas*, *supra*, at 682–685. As a result, we now confine the permissible scope of such regulation to works which depict or describe sexual conduct. That conduct must be specifically defined by the applicable state law, as written or authoritatively construed.[6] A state offense must also be limited to works which, taken as a whole, appeal to the prurient interest in sex, which portray sexual conduct in a patently offensive way, and which, taken as a whole, do not have serious literary, artistic, political, or scientific value.

The basic guidelines for the trier of fact must be: (a) whether "the average person, applying contemporary community standards" would find that the work, taken as a whole, appeals to the prurient interest, *Kois* v. *Wisconsin*, *supra*, at 230, quoting *Roth* v. *United States*, *supra*, at 489; (b) whether the work depicts or describes, in a patently offensive way, sexual conduct specifically defined by the applicable state law; and (c) whether the work, taken as a whole, lacks serious literary, artistic, political, or scientific value. We do not adopt as a constitutional standard the "*utterly* without redeeming social value" test of *Memoirs* v. *Massachusetts*, 383 U. S., at 419; that concept has never commanded the adherence of more than three Justices at one time.[7] See *supra*, at 21. If a state law that regulates obscene material is thus limited, as written or construed, the First Amendment values applicable to the States through the Fourteenth Amendment are adequately protected by the ultimate power of appellate courts to conduct an

independent review of constitutional claims when necessary. See *Kois* v. *Wisconsin*, *supra*, at 232; *Memoirs* v. *Massachusetts*, *supra*, at 459–460 (Harlan, J., dissenting); *Jacobellis* v. *Ohio*, 378 U. S., at 204 (Harlan, J., dissenting); *New York Times Co.* v. *Sullivan*, 376 U. S. 254, 284–285 (1964); *Roth* v. *United States*, *supra*, at 497–498 (Harlan, J., concurring and dissenting).

We emphasize that it is not our function to propose regulatory schemes for the States. That must await their concrete legislative efforts. It is possible, however, to give a few plain examples of what a state statute could define for regulation under part (b) of the standard announced in this opinion, *supra:*

(a) Patently offensive representations or descriptions of ultimate sexual acts, normal or perverted, actual or simulated.

(b) Patently offensive representations or descriptions of masturbation, excretory functions, and lewd exhibition of the genitals.

Sex and nudity may not be exploited without limit by films or pictures exhibited or sold in places of public accommodation any more than live sex and nudity can be exhibited or sold without limit in such public places.[8] At a minimum, prurient, patently offensive depiction or description of sexual conduct must have serious literary, artistic, political, or scientific value to merit First Amendment protection. See *Kois* v. *Wisconsin*, *supra*, at 230–232; *Roth* v. *United States*, *supra*, at 487; *Thornhill* v. *Alabama*, 310 U. S. 88, 101–102 (1940). For example, medical books for the education of physicians and related personnel necessarily use graphic illustrations and descriptions of human anatomy. In resolving the inevitably sensitive questions of fact and law, we must continue to rely on the jury system, accompanied by the safeguards that judges, rules of evidence, presumption of innocence, and other protective features provide, as we do with rape, murder, and a host of other offenses against society and its individual members.[9]

MR. JUSTICE BRENNAN, author of the opinions of the Court, or the plurality opinions, in *Roth* v. *United States*, *supra; Jacobellis* v. *Ohio*, *supra; Ginzburg* v. *United States*, 383 U. S. 463 (1966), *Mishkin* v. *New York*, 383 U. S. 502 (1966); and *Memoirs* v. *Massachusetts*, *supra*, has abandoned his former position and now maintains that no formulation of this Court, the Congress, or the States can adequately distinguish obscene material unprotected by the First Amendment from protected expression, *Paris Adult Theatre I* v. *Slaton*, *post*, p. 73 (BRENNAN, J., dissenting). Paradoxically, MR. JUSTICE BRENNAN indicates that suppression of unprotected obscene material is permissible to avoid exposure to unconsenting adults, as in this case, and to juveniles, although he gives no indication of how the division between protected and nonprotected materials may be drawn with greater precision for these purposes than for regulation of commercial exposure to consenting adults only. Nor does he indicate where in the Constitution he finds the authority to distinguish between a willing "adult" one month past the state law age of majority and a willing "juvenile" one month younger.

Under the holdings announced today, no one will be subject to prosecution for the sale or exposure of obscene materials unless these materials depict or describe patently offensive "hard core" sexual conduct specifically defined by the regulating state law, as written or construed. We are satisfied that these specific prerequisites will provide fair notice to a dealer in such materials that his public and commercial activities may bring prosecution. See *Roth* v. *United States, supra,* at 491–492. Cf. *Ginsberg* v. *New York,* 390 U. S., at 643.[10] If the inability to define regulated materials with ultimate, god-like precision altogether removes the power of the States or the Congress to regulate, then "hard core" pornography may be exposed without limit to the juvenile, the passerby, and the consenting adult alike, as, indeed, MR. JUSTICE DOUGLAS contends. As to MR. JUSTICE DOUGLAS' position, see *United States* v. *Thirty-seven Photographs,* 402 U. S. 363, 379–380 (1971) (Black, J., joined by DOUGLAS, J., dissenting); *Ginzburg* v. *United States, supra,* at 476, 491–492 (Black, J., and DOUGLAS, J., dissenting); *Jacobellis* v. *Ohio, supra,* at 196 (Black, J., joined by DOUGLAS, J., concurring); *Roth, supra,* at 508–514 (DOUGLAS, J., dissenting). In this belief, however, MR. JUSTICE DOUGLAS now stands alone.

MR. JUSTICE BRENNAN also emphasizes "institutional stress" in justification of his change of view. Noting that "[t]he number of obscenity cases on our docket gives ample testimony to the burden that has been placed upon this Court," he quite rightly remarks that the examination of contested materials "is hardly a source of edification to the members of this Court." *Paris Adult Theatre I* v. *Slaton, post,* at 92, 93. He also notes, and we agree, that "uncertainty of the standards creates a continuing source of tension between state and federal courts . . . ." "The problem is . . . that one cannot say with certainty that material is obscene until at least five members of this Court, applying inevitably obscure standards, have pronounced it so." *Id.,* at 93, 92.

It is certainly true that the absence, since *Roth,* of a single majority view of this Court as to proper standards for testing obscenity has placed a strain on both state and federal courts. But today, for the first time since *Roth* was decided in 1957, a majority of this Court has agreed on concrete guidelines to isolate "hard core" pornography from expression protected by the First Amendment. Now we may abandon the casual practice of *Redrup* v. *New York,* 386 U. S. 767 (1967), and attempt to provide positive guidance to federal and state courts alike.

This may not be an easy road, free from difficulty. But no amount of "fatigue" should lead us to adopt a convenient "institutional" rationale—an absolutist, "anything goes" view of the First Amendment—because it will lighten our burdens.[11] "Such an abnegation of judicial supervision in this field would be inconsistent with our duty to uphold the constitutional guarantees." *Jacobellis* v. *Ohio, supra,* at 187–188 (opinion of BRENNAN, J.). Nor should we remedy "tension between state and federal courts" by arbitrarily depriving the States of a power reserved to them under the Constitution, a power which they have enjoyed and exercised continuously from before the adoption of the First Amendment to this day. See *Roth* v. *United States, supra,* at 482–485. "Our duty admits of no 'substitute for facing up to the tough individual problems of constitutional judg-

ment involved in every obscenity case.' [*Roth* v. *United States, supra,* at 498]; see *Manual Enterprises, Inc.* v. *Day,* 370 U. S. 478, 488 (opinion of Harlan, J.) [footnote omitted]." *Jacobellis* v. *Ohio, supra,* at 188 (opinion of BRENNAN, J.).

III

Under a national Constitution, fundamental First Amendment limitations on the powers of the States do not vary from community to community, but this does not mean that there are, or should or can be, fixed, uniform national standards of precisely what appeals to the "prurient interest" or is "patently offensive." These are essentially questions of fact, and our nation is simply too big and too diverse for this Court to reasonably expect that such standards could be articulated for all 50 States in a single formulation, even assuming the prerequisite consensus exists. When triers of fact are asked to decide whether "the average person, applying contemporary community standards" would consider certain materials "prurient," it would be unrealistic to require that the answer be based on some abstract formulation. The adversary system, with lay jurors as the usual ultimate factfinders in criminal prosecutions, has historically permitted triers of fact to draw on the standards of their community, guided always by limiting instructions on the law. To require a State to structure obscenity proceedings around evidence of a *national* "community standard" would be an exercise in futility.

As noted before, this case was tried on the theory that the California obscenity statute sought to incorporate the tripartite test of *Memoirs.* This, a "national" standard of First Amendment protection enumerated by a plurality of this Court, was correctly regarded at the time of trial as limiting state prosecution under the controlling case law. The jury, however, was explicitly instructed that, in determining whether the "dominant theme of the material as a whole . . . appeals to the prurient interest" and in determining whether the material "goes substantially beyond customary limits of candor and affronts contemporary community standards of decency," it was to apply "contemporary community standards of the State of California."

During the trial, both the prosecution and the defense assumed that the relevant "community standards" in making the factual determination of obscenity were those of the State of California, not some hypothetical standard of the entire United States of America. Defense counsel at trial never objected to the testimony of the State's expert on community standards [12] or to the instructions of the trial judge on "statewide" standards. On appeal to the Appellate Department, Superior Court of California, County of Orange, appellant for the first time contended that application of state, rather than national, standards violated the First and Fourteenth Amendments.

We conclude that neither the State's alleged failure to offer evidence of "national standards," nor the trial court's charge that the jury consider state community standards, were constitutional errors. Nothing in the First Amendment requires that a jury must consider hypothetical and unascertainable "national standards" when attempting to determine whether certain materials are obscene as a matter of fact. Mr. Chief Justice Warren pointedly commented in his dissent in *Jacobellis* v. *Ohio, supra,* at 200:

> "It is my belief that when the Court said in *Roth* that obscenity is to be defined by reference to 'community standards,' it meant community standards—not a national standard, as is sometimes argued. I believe that there is no provable 'national standard' . . . . At all events, this Court has not been able to enunciate one, and it would be unreasonable to expect local courts to divine one."

It is neither realistic nor constitutionally sound to read the First Amendment as requiring that the people of Maine or Mississippi accept public depiction of conduct found tolerable in Las Vegas, or New York City.[13] See *Hoyt* v. *Minnesota,* 399 U. S. 524–525 (1970) (BLACKMUN, J., dissenting); *Walker* v. *Ohio,* 398 U. S. 434 (1970) (BURGER, C. J., dissenting); *id.,* at 434–435 (Harlan, J., dissenting); *Cain* v. *Kentucky,* 397 U. S. 319 (1970) (BURGER, C. J., dissenting); *id.,* at 319–320 (Harlan, J., dissenting); *United States* v. *Groner,* 479 F. 2d, at 581–583; O'Meara, Shaffer, Obscenity in The Supreme Court: A note on *Jacobellis* v. *Ohio,* 40 Notre Dame Law. 1, 6–7. See also *Memoirs* v. *Massachusetts,* 383 U. S., at 458 (Harlan, J., dissenting); *Jacobellis* v. *Ohio, supra,* at 203–204 (Harlan, J., dissenting). *Roth* v. *United States, supra,* at 505–506 (Harlan, J., concurring and dissenting). People in different States vary in their tastes and attitudes, and this diversity is not to be strangled by the absolutism of imposed uniformity. As the Court made clear in *Mishkin* v. *New York,* 383 U. S., at 508–509, the primary concern with requiring a jury to apply the standard of "the average person, applying contemporary community standards" is to be certain that, so far as material is not aimed at a deviant group, it will be judged by its impact on an average person, rather than a particularly susceptible or sensitive person—or indeed a totally insensitive one. See *Roth* v. *United States, supra,* at 489. Cf. the now discredited test in *Regina* v. *Hicklin,* [1868] L. R. 3 Q. B. 360. We hold that the requirement that the jury evaluate the materials with reference to "contemporary standards of the State of California" serves this protective purpose and is constitutionally adequate.[14]

IV

The dissenting Justices sound the alarm of repression. But, in our view, to equate the free and robust exchange of ideas and political debate with commercial exploitation of obscene material demeans the grand conception of the First Amendment and its high purposes in the historic struggle for freedom. It is a "misuse of the great guarantees of free speech and free press . . . ." *Breard* v. *Alexandria,* 341 U. S., at 645. The First Amendment protects works which, taken as a whole, have serious literary, artistic, political, or scientific value, regardless of whether the government or a majority of the people approve of the ideas these works represent. "The protection given speech and press was fashioned to assure unfettered interchange of *ideas* for the bringing about of political and social changes desired by the people," *Roth* v. *United States, supra,* at 484 (emphasis added). See *Kois* v. *Wisconsin,* 408 U. S., at 230–232; *Thornhill* v.

Alabama, 310 U. S., at 101–102. But the public portrayal of hard core sexual conduct for its own sake, and for the ensuing commercial gain, is a different matter.[15]

There is no evidence, empirical or historical, that the stern 19th century American censorship of public distribution and display of material relating to sex, see *Roth* v. *United States, supra,* at 482–485, in any way limited or affected expression of serious literary, artistic, political, or scientific ideas. On the contrary, it is beyond any question that the era following Thomas Jefferson to Theodore Roosevelt was an "extraordinarily vigorous period," not just in economics and politics, but in *belles lettres* and in "the outlying fields of social and political philosophies."[16] We do not see the harsh hand of censorship of ideas—good or bad, sound or unsound—and "repression" of political liberty lurking in every state regulation of commercial exploitation of human interest in sex.

MR. JUSTICE BRENNAN finds "it is hard to see how state-ordered regimentation of our minds can ever be forestalled." *Paris Adult Theatre I* v. *Slaton, post,* at 110 (BRENNAN, J., dissenting). These doleful anticipations assume that courts cannot distinguish commerce in ideas, protected by the First Amendment, from commercial exploitation of obscene material. Moreover, state regulation of hard core pornography so as to make it unavailable to nonadults, a regulation which MR. JUSTICE BRENNAN finds constitutionally permissible, has all the elements of "censorship" for adults; indeed even more rigid enforcement techniques may be called for with such dichotomy of regulation. See *Interstate Circuit, Inc.* v. *Dallas,* 390 U. S., at 690.[17] One can concede that the "sexual revolution" of recent years may have had useful byproducts in striking layers of prudery from a subject long irrationally kept from needed ventilation. But it does not follow that no regulation of patently offensive "hard core" materials is needed or permissible; civilized people do not allow unregulated access to heroin because it is a derivative of medicinal morphine.

In sum, we (a) reaffirm the *Roth* holding that obscene material is not protected by the First Amendment; (b) hold that such material can be regulated by the States, subject to the specific safeguards enunciated above, without a showing that the material is "*utterly* without redeeming social value"; and (c) hold that obscenity is to be determined by applying "contemporary community standards," see *Kois* v. *Wisconsin, supra,* at 230, and *Roth* v. *United States, supra,* at 489, not "national standards." The judgment of the Appellate Department of the Superior Court, Orange County, California, is vacated and the case remanded to that court for further proceedings not inconsistent with the First Amendment standards established by this opinion. See *United States* v. *12 200-ft. Reels of Film, post,* at 130 n. 7.

Vacated and remanded.

MR. JUSTICE DOUGLAS, dissenting.

I

Today we leave open the way for California[1] to send

a man to prison for distributing brochures that advertise books and a movie under freshly written standards defining obscenity which until today's decision were never the part of any law.

The Court has worked hard to define obscenity and concededly has failed. In *Roth* v. *United States*, 354 U. S. 476, it ruled that "[o]bscene material is material which deals with sex in a manner appealing to prurient interest." *Id.*, at 487. Obscenity, it was said, was rejected by the First Amendment because it is "utterly without redeeming social importance." *Id.*, at 484. The presence of a "prurient interest" was to be determined by "contemporary community standards." *Id.*, at 489. That test, it has been said, could not be determined by one standard here and another standard there, *Jacobellis* v. *Ohio*, 378 U. S. 184, 194, but "on the basis of a national standard." *Id.*, at 195. My Brother Stewart in *Jacobellis* commented that the difficulty of the Court in giving content to obscenity was that it was "faced with the task of trying to define what may be indefinable." *Id.*, at 197.

In *Memoirs* v. *Massachusetts*, 383 U. S. 413, 418, the *Roth* test was elaborated to read as follows: "[T]hree elements must coalesce: it must be established that (a) the dominant theme of the material taken as a whole appeals to a prurient interest in sex; (b) the material is patently offensive because it affronts contemporary community standards relating to the description or representation of sexual matters; and (c) the material is utterly without redeeming social value."

In *Ginzburg* v. *United States*, 383 U. S. 463, a publisher was sent to prison, not for the kind of books and periodicals he sold, but for the manner in which the publications were advertised. The "leer of the sensualist" was said to permeate the advertisements. *Id.*, at 468. The Court said, "Where the purveyor's sole emphasis is on the sexually provocative aspects of his publications, that fact may be decisive in the determination of obscenity." *Id.*, at 470. As Mr. Justice Black said in dissent, ". . . Ginzburg . . . is now finally and authoritatively condemned to serve five years in prison for distributing printed matter about sex which neither Ginzburg nor anyone else could possibly have known to be criminal." *Id.*, at 476. That observation by Mr. Justice Black is underlined by the fact that the *Ginzburg* decision was five to four.

A further refinement was added by *Ginsberg* v. *New York*, 390 U. S. 629, 641, where the Court held that "it was not irrational for the legislature to find that exposure to material condemned by the statute is harmful to minors."

But even those members of this Court who had created the new and changing standards of "obscenity" could not agree on their application. And so we adopted a *per curiam* treatment of so-called obscene publications that seemed to pass constitutional muster under the several constitutional tests which had been formulated. See *Redrup* v. *New York*, 386 U. S. 767. Some condemn it if its "dominant tendency might be to 'deprave or corrupt' a reader."[2] Others look not to the content of the book but to whether it is advertised " 'to appeal to the erotic interests of customers.' "[3] Some condemn only "hard-

core pornography"; but even then a true definition is lacking. It has indeed been said of that definition, "I could never succeed in [defining it] intelligibly," but "I know it when I see it."[4]

Today we would add a new three-pronged test: "(a) whether 'the average person, applying contemporary community standards' would find that the work, taken as a whole, appeals to the prurient interest, . . . (b) whether the work depicts or describes, in a patently offensive way, sexual conduct specifically defined by the applicable state law, and (c) whether the work, taken as a whole, lacks serious literary, artistic, political, or scientific value."

Those are the standards we ourselves have written into the Constitution.[5] Yet how under these vague tests can we sustain convictions for the sale of an article prior to the time when some court has declared it to be obscene?

Today the Court retreats from the earlier formulations of the constitutional test and undertakes to make new definitions. This effort, like the earlier ones, is earnest and well intentioned. The difficulty is that we do not deal with constitutional terms, since "obscenity" is not mentioned in the Constitution or Bill of Rights. And the First Amendment makes no such exception from "the press" which it undertakes to protect nor, as I have said on other occasions, is an exception necessarily implied, for there was no recognized exception to the free press at the time the Bill of Rights was adopted which treated "obscene" publications differently from other types of papers, magazines, and books. So there are no constitutional guidelines for deciding what is and what is not "obscene." The Court is at large because we deal with tastes and standards of literature. What shocks me may be sustenance for my neighbor. What causes one person to boil up in rage over one pamphlet or movie may reflect only his neurosis, not shared by others. We deal here with a regime of censorship which, if adopted, should be done by constitutional amendment after full debate by the people.

Obscenity cases usually generate tremendous emotional outbursts. They have no business being in the courts. If a constitutional amendment authorized censorship, the censor would probably be an administrative agency. Then criminal prosecutions could follow as, if, and when publishers defied the censor and sold their literature. Under that regime a publisher would know when he was on dangerous ground. Under the present regime— whether the old standards or the new ones are used—the criminal law becomes a trap. A brand new test would put a publisher behind bars under a new law improvised by the courts after the publication. That was done in *Ginzburg* and has all the evils of an *ex post facto* law.

My contention is that until a civil proceeding has placed a tract beyond the pale, no criminal prosecution should be sustained. For no more vivid illustration of vague and uncertain laws could be designed than those we have fashioned. As Mr. Justice Harlan has said:

"The upshot of all this divergence in viewpoint is that anyone who undertakes to examine the Court's decisions since *Roth* which have held particular material obscene or not obscene would find himself in utter bewilderment." *Interstate Circuit, Inc.* v. *Dallas*, 390 U. S. 676, 707.

In *Bouie* v. *City of Columbia*, 378 U. S. 347, we upset a conviction for remaining on property after being asked to leave, while the only unlawful act charged by the statute was entering. We held that the defendants had received no "fair warning, at the time of their conduct" while on the property "that the act for which they now stand convicted was rendered criminal" by the state statute. *Id.*, at 355. The same requirement of "fair warning" is due here, as much as in *Bouie*. The latter involved racial discrimination; the present case involves rights earnestly urged as being protected by the First Amendment. In any case—certainly when constitutional rights are concerned—we should not allow men to go to prison or be fined when they had no "fair warning" that what they did was criminal conduct.

II

If a specific book, play, paper, or motion picture has in a civil proceeding been condemned as obscene and review of that finding has been completed, and thereafter a person publishes, shows, or displays that particular book or film, then a vague law has been made specific. There would remain the underlying question whether the First Amendment allows an implied exception in the case of obscenity. I do not think it does [6] and my views on the issue have been stated over and over again.[7] But at least a criminal prosecution brought at that juncture would not violate the time-honored void-for-vagueness test.[8]

No such protective procedure has been designed by California in this case. Obscenity—which even we cannot define with precision—is a hodge-podge. To send men to jail for violating standards they cannot understand, construe, and apply is a monstrous thing to do in a Nation dedicated to fair trials and due process.

III

While the right to know is the corollary of the right to speak or publish, no one can be forced by government to listen to disclosure that he finds offensive. That was the basis of my dissent in *Public Utilities Comm'n* v. *Pollak*, 343 U. S. 451, 467 (1952), where I protested against making a streetcar audience a "captive" audience. There is no "captive audience" problem in these obscenity cases. No one is being compelled to look or to listen. Those who enter news stands or bookstalls may be offended by what they see. But they are not compelled by the State to frequent those places; and it is only state or governmental action against which the First Amendment, applicable to the States by virtue of the Fourteenth, raises a ban.

The idea that the First Amendment permits government to ban publications that are "offensive" to some people puts an ominous gloss on freedom of the press. That test would make it possible to ban any paper or any journal or magazine in some benighted place. The First Amendment was designed "to invite dispute," to induce "a condition of unrest," to "create dissatisfaction with conditions as they are," and even to stir "people to anger." *Terminiello* v.

Chicago, 337 U. S. 1, 4. The idea that the First Amendment permits punishment for ideas that are "offensive" to the particular judge or jury sitting in judgment is astounding. No greater leveler of speech or literature has ever been designed. To give the power to the censor, as we do today, is to make a sharp and radical break with the traditions of a free society. The First Amendment was not fashioned as a vehicle for dispensing tranquilizers to the people. Its prime function was to keep debate open to "offensive" as well as to "staid" people. The tendency throughout history has been to subdue the individual and to exalt the power of government. The use of the standard "offensive" gives authority to government that cuts the very vitals out of the First Amendment.[9] As is intimated by the Court's opinion, the materials before us may be garbage. But so is much of what is said in political campaigns, in the daily press, on TV, or over the radio. By reason of the First Amendment—and solely because of it—speakers and publishers have not been threatened or subdued because their thoughts and ideas may be "offensive" to some.

The standard "offensive" is unconstitutional in yet another way. In *Coates* v. *City of Cincinnati*, 402 U. S. 611, we had before us a municipal ordinance that made it a crime for three or more persons to assemble on a street and conduct themselves "in a manner annoying to persons passing by." We struck it down, saying: "If three or more people meet together on a sidewalk or street corner, they must conduct themselves so as not to annoy any police officer or other person who should happen to pass by. In our opinion this ordinance is unconstitutionally vague because it subjects the exercise of the right of assembly to an unascertainable standard, and unconstitutionally broad because it authorizes the punishment of constitutionally protected conduct.

"Conduct that annoys some people does not annoy others. Thus, the ordinance is vague, not in the sense that it requires a person to conform his conduct to an imprecise but comprehensive normative standard, but rather in the sense that no standard of conduct is specified at all." *Id.*, at 614.

How we can deny Ohio the convenience of punishing people who "annoy" others and allow California power to punish people who publish materials "offensive" to some people is difficult to square with constitutional requirements.

If there are to be restraints on what is obscene, then a constitutional amendment should be the way of achieving the end. There are societies where religion and mathematics are the only free segments. It would be a dark day for America if that were our destiny. But the people can make it such if they choose to write obscenity into the Constitution and define it.

We deal with highly emotional, not rational, questions. To many the Song of Solomon is obscene. I do not think we, the judges, were ever given the constitutional power to make definitions of obscenity. If it is to be defined, let the people debate and decide by a constitutional amendment what they want to ban as obscene and what standards they want the legislatures and the courts to apply. Perhaps the people will decide that the path towards a mature, integrated society requires that all ideas competing for acceptance must have no censor. Perhaps they will decide otherwise. Whatever the choice, the courts will have some guidelines. Now we have none except our own predilections.

MR. JUSTICE BRENNAN, with whom MR. JUSTICE STEWART and MR. JUSTICE MARSHALL join, dissenting.

In my dissent in *Paris Adult Theatre I* v. *Slaton, post,* p. 73, decided this date, I noted that I had no occasion to consider the extent of state power to regulate the distribution of sexually oriented material to juveniles or the offensive exposure of such material to unconsenting adults. In the case before us, appellant was convicted of distributing obscene matter in violation of California Penal Code § 311.2, on the basis of evidence that he had caused to be mailed unsolicited brochures advertising various books and a movie. I need not now decide whether a statute might be drawn to impose, within the requirements of the First Amendment, criminal penalties for the precise conduct at issue here. For it is clear that under my dissent in *Paris Adult Theatre I*, the statute under which the prosecution was brought is unconstitutionally overbroad, and therefore invalid on its face.* "[T]he transcendent value to all society of constitutionally protected expression is deemed to justify allowing 'attacks on overly broad statutes with no requirement that the person making the attack demonstrate that his own conduct could not be regulated by a statute drawn with the requisite narrow specificity.' " *Gooding* v. *Wilson*, 405 U. S. 518, 521 (1972), quoting from *Dombrowski* v. *Pfister*, 380 U. S. 479, 486 (1965). See also *Baggett* v. *Bullitt*, 377 U. S. 360, 366 (1964); *Coates* v. *City of Cincinnati*, 402 U. S. 611, 616 (1971); *id.,* at 619–620 (WHITE, J., dissenting); *United States* v. *Raines*, 362 U. S. 17, 21–22 (1960); *NAACP* v. *Button*, 371 U. S. 415, 433 (1963). Since my view in *Paris Adult Theatre I* represents a substantial departure from the course of our prior decisions, and since the state courts have as yet had no opportunity to consider whether a "readily apparent construction suggests itself as a vehicle for rehabilitating the [statute] in a single prosecution," *Dombrowski* v. *Pfister, supra,* at 491, I would reverse the judgment of the Appellate Department of the Superior Court and remand the case for proceedings not inconsistent with this opinion. See *Coates* v. *City of Cincinnati, supra,* at 616.

COURT'S OPINION NOTES

¹ At the time of the commission of the alleged offense, which was prior to June 25, 1969, § 311.2 (a) and § 311 of the California Penal Code read in relevant part:

"§ 311.2 Sending or bringing into state for sale or distribution; printing, exhibiting, distributing or possessing within state

"(a) Every person who knowingly: sends or causes to be sent, or brings or causes to be brought, into this state for sale or distribution, or in this state prepares, publishes, prints, exhibits, distributes, or offers to distribute, or has in his possession with intent to distribute or to exhibit or offer to distribute, any obscene matter is guilty of a misdemeanor. . . ."

"§ 311. Definitions

"As used in this chapter:

"(a) 'Obscene' means that to the average person, applying con-

temporary standards, the predominant appeal of the matter, taken as a whole, is to prurient interest, i. e., a shameful or morbid interest in nudity, sex, or excretion, which goes substantially beyond customary limits of candor in description or representation of such matters and is matter which is utterly without redeeming social importance.

"(b) 'Matter' means any book, magazine, newspaper, or other printed or written material or any picture, drawing, photograph, motion picture, or other pictorial representation or any statue or other figure, or any recording, transcription or mechanical, chemical or electrical reproduction or any other articles, equipment, machines or materials.

"(c) 'Person' means any individual, partnership, firm, association, corporation, or other legal entity.

"(d) 'Distribute' means to transfer possession of, whether with or without consideration.

"(e) 'Knowingly' means having knowledge that the matter is obscene."

Section 311 (e) of the California Penal Code, *supra,* was amended on June 25, 1969, to read as follows:

"(e) 'Knowingly' means being aware of the character of the matter."

Cal. Amended Stats. 1969, c. 249, § 1, p. 598. Despite appellant's contentions to the contrary, the record indicates that the new § 311 (e) was not applied *ex post facto* to his case, but only the old § 311 (e) as construed by state decisions prior to the commission of the alleged offense. See *People* v. *Pinkus*, 256 Cal. App. 2d 941, 948–950, 63 Cal. Rptr. 680, 685–686 (App. Dept., Superior Ct., Los Angeles, 1967); *People* v. *Campise*, 242 Cal. App. 2d 905, 914, 51 Cal. Rptr. 815, 821 (App. Dept., Superior Ct., San Diego, 1966). Cf. *Bouie* v. *City of Columbia*, 378 U. S. 347 (1964). Nor did § 311.2, *supra,* as applied, create any "direct, immediate burden on the performance of the postal functions," or infringe on congressional commerce powers under Art. I, § 8, cl. 3. *Roth* v. *United States*, 354 U. S. 476, 494 (1957), quoting *Railway Mail Assn.* v. *Corsi*, 326 U. S. 88, 96 (1945). See also *Mishkin* v. *New York*, 383 U. S. 502, 506 (1966); *Smith* v. *California*, 361 U. S. 147, 150–152 (1959).

² This Court has defined "obscene material" as "material which deals with sex in a manner appealing to prurient interest," *Roth* v. *United States, supra,* at 487, but the *Roth* definition does not reflect the precise meaning of "obscene" as traditionally used in the English language. Derived from the Latin *obscaenus, ob,* to, plus *caenum,* filth, "obscene" is defined in the Webster's Third New International Dictionary (Unabridged 1969) as "1a: disgusting to the senses . . . b: grossly repugnant to the generally accepted notions of what is appropriate . . . 2: offensive or revolting as countering or violating some ideal or principle." The Oxford English Dictionary (1933 ed.) gives a similar definition, "[o]ffensive to the senses, or to taste or refinement; disgusting, repulsive, filthy, foul, abominable, loathsome."

The material we are discussing in this case is more accurately defined as "pornography" or "pornographic material." "Pornography" derives from the Greek (*pornē,* harlot, and *graphos,* writing). The word now means "1: a description of prostitutes or prostitution 2: a depiction (as in writing or painting) of licentiousness or lewdness: a portrayal of erotic behavior designed to cause sexual excitement." Webster's Third New International Dictionary, *supra.* Pornographic material which is obscene forms a sub-group of all "obscene" expression, but not the whole, at least as the word "obscene" is now used in our language. We note, therefore, that the words "obscene material," as used in this case, have a specific judicial meaning which derives from the *Roth* case, i. e., obscene material "which deals with sex." *Roth, supra,* at 487. See also ALI Model Penal Code § 251.4 (1) "Obscene Defined." (Official Draft 1962.)

³ In the absence of a majority view, this Court was compelled to embark on the practice of summarily reversing convictions for the dissemination of materials that at least five members of the Court, applying their separate tests, found to be protected by the First Amendment. *Redrup* v. *New York*, 386 U. S. 767 (1967). Thirty-one cases have been decided in this manner. Beyond the necessity of circumstances, however, no justification has ever been offered in support of the *Redrup* "policy." See *Walker* v.

Ohio, 398 U. S. 434–435 (1970) (dissenting opinions of BURGER, C. J., and Harlan, J.). The *Redrup* procedure has cast us in the role of an unreviewable board of censorship for the 50 States, subjectively judging each piece of material brought before us.

[4] See the dissenting opinion of MR. JUSTICE BRENNAN in *Paris Adult Theatre I* v. *Slaton, post*, p. 73.

[5] As Mr. Chief Justice Warren stated, dissenting, in *Jacobellis* v. *Ohio*, 378 U. S. 184, 200 (1964):

"For all the sound and fury that the *Roth* test has generated, it has not been proved unsound, and I believe that we should try to live with it—at least until a more satisfactory definition is evolved. No government—be it federal, state, or local—should be forced to choose between repressing all material, including that within the realm of decency, and allowing unrestrained license to publish any material, no matter how vile. There must be a rule of reason in this as in other areas of the law, and we have attempted in the *Roth* case to provide such a rule."

[6] See, *e. g.*, Oregon Laws 1971, c. 743, Art. 29, §§ 255–262, and Hawaii Penal Code, Tit. 37, §§ 1210–1216, 1972 Hawaii Session Laws, Act 9, c. 12, pt. II, pp. 126–129, as examples of state laws directed at depiction of defined physical conduct, as opposed to expression. Other state formulations could be equally valid in this respect. In giving the Oregon and Hawaii statutes as examples, we do not wish to be understood as approving of them in all other respects nor as establishing their limits as the extent of state power.

We do not hold, as MR. JUSTICE BRENNAN intimates, that all States other than Oregon must now enact new obscenity statutes. Other existing state statutes, as construed heretofore or hereafter, may well be adequate. See *United States* v. *12 200-ft. Reels of Film, post*, at 130 n. 7.

[7] "A quotation from Voltaire in the flyleaf of a book will not constitutionally redeem an otherwise obscene publication . . . ." *Kois* v. *Wisconsin*, 408 U. S. 229, 231 (1972). See *Memoirs* v. *Massachusetts*, 383 U. S. 413, 461 (1966) (WHITE, J., dissenting). We also reject, as a constitutional standard, the ambiguous concept of "social importance." See *id.*, at 462 (WHITE, J., dissenting).

[8] Although we are not presented here with the problem of regulating lewd public conduct itself, the States have greater power to regulate nonverbal, physical conduct than to suppress depictions or descriptions of the same behavior. In *United States* v. *O'Brien*, 391 U. S. 367, 377 (1968), a case not dealing with obscenity, the Court held a State regulation of conduct which itself embodied both speech and nonspeech elements to be "sufficiently justified if . . . it furthers an important or substantial governmental interest; if the governmental interest is unrelated to the suppression of free expression; and if the incidental restriction on alleged First Amendment freedoms is no greater than is essential to the furtherance of that interest." See *California* v. *LaRue*, 409 U. S. 109, 117–118 (1972).

[9] The mere fact juries may reach different conclusions as to the same material does not mean that constitutional rights are abridged. As this Court observed in *Roth* v. *United States*, 354 U. S., at 492 n. 30, "it is common experience that different juries may reach different results under any criminal statute. That is one of the consequences we accept under our jury system. Cf. *Dunlop* v. *United States,* 165 U. S. 486, 499–500."

[10] As MR. JUSTICE BRENNAN stated for the Court in *Roth* v. *United States, supra*, at 491–492:

"Many decisions have recognized that these terms of obscenity statutes are not precise. [Footnote omitted.] This Court, however, has consistently held that lack of precision is not itself offensive to the requirements of due process. '. . . [T]he Constitution does not require impossible standards'; all that is required is that the language 'conveys sufficiently definite warning as to the proscribed conduct when measured by common understanding and practices. . . .' *United States* v. *Petrillo*, 332 U. S. 1, 7–8. These words, applied according to the proper standard for judging obscenity, already discussed, give adequate warning of the conduct proscribed and mark '. . . boundaries sufficiently distinct for judges and juries fairly to administer the law . . . . That there may be marginal cases in which it is difficult to determine the side of the line on which a particular fact situation falls is no sufficient reason to hold the language too ambiguous to define a criminal offense. . . .' *Id.*, at 7. See also *United States* v. *Harriss*, 347 U. S. 612, 624,

n. 15; *Boyce Motor Lines, Inc.* v. *United States*, 342 U. S. 337, 340; *United States* v. *Ragen*, 314 U. S. 513, 523–524; *United States* v. *Wurzbach*, 280 U. S. 396; *Hygrade Provision Co.* v. *Sherman*, 266 U. S. 497; *Fox* v. *Washington*, 236 U. S. 273; *Nash* v. *United States*, 229 U. S. 373."

[11] We must note, in addition, that any assumption concerning the relative burdens of the past and the probable burden under the standards now adopted is pure speculation.

[12] The record simply does not support appellant's contention, belatedly raised on appeal, that the State's expert was unqualified to give evidence on California "community standards." The expert, a police officer with many years of specialization in obscenity offenses, had conducted an extensive statewide survey and had given expert evidence on 26 occasions in the year prior to this trial. Allowing such expert testimony was certainly not constitutional error. Cf. *United States* v. *Augenblick*, 393 U. S. 348, 356 (1969).

[13] In *Jacobellis* v. *Ohio*, 378 U. S. 184 (1964), two Justices argued that application of "local" community standards would run the risk of preventing dissemination of materials in some places because sellers would be unwilling to risk criminal conviction by testing variations in standards from place to place. *Id.*, at 193–195 (opinion of BRENNAN, J., joined by Goldberg, J.). The use of "national" standards, however, necessarily implies that materials found tolerable in some places, but not under the "national" criteria, will nevertheless be unavailable where they are acceptable. Thus, in terms of danger to free expression, the potential for suppression seems at least as great in the application of a single nationwide standard as in allowing distribution in accordance with local tastes, a point which Mr. Justice Harlan often emphasized. See *Roth* v. *United States*, 354 U. S., at 506.

Appellant also argues that adherence to a "national standard" is necessary "in order to avoid unconscionable burdens on the free flow of interstate commerce." As noted *supra*, at 18 n. 1, the application of domestic state police powers in this case did not intrude on any congressional powers under Art. I, § 8, cl. 3, for there is no indication that appellant's materials were ever distributed interstate. Appellant's argument would appear without substance in any event. Obscene material may be validly regulated by a State in the exercise of its traditional local power to protect the general welfare of its population despite some possible incidental effect on the flow of such materials across state lines. See, *e. g.*, *Head* v. *New Mexico Board*, 374 U. S. 424 (1963); *Huron Portland Cement Co.* v. *Detroit*, 362 U. S. 440 (1960); *Breard* v. *Alexandria*, 341 U. S. 622 (1951); *H. P. Hood & Sons* v. *Du Mond*, 336 U. S. 525 (1949); *Southern Pacific Co.* v. *Arizona*, 325 U. S. 761 (1945); *Baldwin* v. *G. A. F. Seelig, Inc.*, 294 U. S. 511 (1935); *Sligh* v. *Kirkwood*, 237 U. S. 52 (1915).

[14] Appellant's jurisdictional statement contends that he was subjected to "double jeopardy" because a Los Angeles County trial judge dismissed, before trial, a prior prosecution based on the same brochures, but apparently alleging exposures at a different time in a different setting. Appellant argues that once material has been found not to be obscene in one proceeding, the State is "collaterally estopped" from ever alleging it to be obscene in a different proceeding. It is not clear from the record that appellant properly raised this issue, better regarded as a question of procedural due process than a "double jeopardy" claim, in the state courts below. Appellant failed to address any portion of his brief on the merits to this issue, and appellee contends that the question was waived under California law because it was improperly pleaded at trial. Nor is it totally clear from the record before us what collateral effect the pretrial dismissal might have under state law. The dismissal was based, at least in part, on a failure of the prosecution to present affirmative evidence required by state law, evidence which was apparently presented in this case. Appellant's contention, therefore, is best left to the California courts for further consideration on remand. The issue is not, in any event, a proper subject for appeal. See *Mishkin* v. *New York*, 383 U. S. 502, 512–514 (1966).

[15] In the apt words of Mr. Chief Justice Warren, appellant in this case was "plainly engaged in the commercial exploitation of the morbid and shameful craving for materials with prurient effect. I believe that the State and Federal Governments can constitutionally punish such conduct. That is all that these cases present to us,

and that is all we need to decide." *Roth* v. *United States, supra,* at 496 (concurring opinion).

[16] See 2 V. Parrington, Main Currents in American Thought *ix et seq.* (1930). As to the latter part of the 19th century, Parrington observed "A new age had come and other dreams—the age and the dreams of a middle-class sovereignty . . . . From the crude and vast romanticisms of that vigorous sovereignty emerged eventually a spirit of realistic criticism, seeking to evaluate the worth of this new America, and discover if possible other philosophies to take the place of those which had gone down in the fierce battles of the Civil War." *Id.,* at 474. Cf. 2 S. Morison, H. Commager & W. Leuchtenburg, The Growth of the American Republic 197–233 (6th ed. 1969); Paths of American Thought 123–166, 203–290 (A. Schlesinger & M. White ed. 1963) (articles of Fleming, Lerner, Morton & Lucia White, E. Rostow, Samuelson, Kazin, Hofstadter); and H. Wish, Society and Thought in Modern America 337–386 (1952).

[17] "[W]e have indicated . . . that because of its strong and abiding interest in youth, a State may regulate the dissemination to juveniles of, and their access to, material objectionable as to them, but which a State clearly could not regulate as to adults. *Ginsberg* v. *New York, . . .* [390 U. S. 629 (1968)]." *Interstate Circuit, Inc.* v. *Dallas,* 390 U. S. 676, 690 (1968) (footnote omitted).

JUSTICE DOUGLAS'S OPINION NOTES

[1] California defines "obscene matter" as "matter, taken as a whole, the predominant appeal of which to the average person, applying contemporary standards, is to prurient interest, i. e., a shameful or morbid interest in nudity, sex, or excretion; and is matter which taken as a whole goes substantially beyond customary limits of candor in description or representation of such matters; and is matter which taken as a whole is utterly without redeeming social importance." Calif. Penal Code § 311 (a).

[2] *Roth* v. *United States,* 354 U. S. 476, 502 (opinion of Harlan, J.).

[3] *Ginzburg* v. *United States,* 383 U. S. 463, 467.

[4] *Jacobellis* v. *Ohio,* 378 U. S. 184, 197 (STEWART, J., concurring).

[5] At the conclusion of a two-year study, the U. S. Commission on Obscenity and Pornography determined that the standards we have written interfere with constitutionally protected materials:

"Society's attempts to legislate for adults in the area of obscenity have not been successful. Present laws prohibiting the consensual sale or distribution of explicit sexual materials to adults are extremely unsatisfactory in their practical application. The Constitution permits material to be deemed 'obscene' for adults only if, as a whole, it appeals to the 'prurient' interest of the average person, is 'patently offensive' in light of 'community standards,' and lacks 'redeeming social value.' These vague and highly subjective aesthetic, psychological and moral tests do not provide meaningful guidance for law enforcement officials, juries or courts. As a result, law is inconsistently and sometimes erroneously applied and the distinctions made by courts between prohibited and permissible materials often appear indefensible. Errors in the application of the law and uncertainty about its scope also cause interference with the communication of constitutionally protected materials." Report of the Commission on Obscenity and Pornography 53 (1970).

[6] It is said that "obscene" publications can be banned on authority of restraints on communications incident to decrees restraining unlawful business monopolies or unlawful restraints of trade, *Sugar Institute* v. *United States,* 297 U. S. 553, 597, or communications respecting the sale of spurious or fraudulent securities. *Hall* v. *Geiger-Jones Co.,* 242 U. S. 539, 549; *Caldwell* v. *Sioux Falls Stock Yards Co.,* 242 U. S. 559, 567; *Merrick* v. *Halsey & Co.,* 242 U. S. 568, 584. The First Amendment answer is that whenever speech and conduct are brigaded—as they are when one shouts "Fire" in a crowded theater—speech can be outlawed. Mr. Justice Black, writing for a unanimous Court in *Giboney* v. *Empire Storage Co.,* 336 U. S. 490, stated that labor unions could be restrained from picketing a firm in support of a secondary boycott which a State had validly outlawed. Mr. Justice Black said: "It rarely has been suggested that the constitutional freedom for speech and press extends its immunity to speech or writing used as an integral part of conduct

in violation of a valid criminal statute. We reject the contention now." *Id.,* at 498.

[7] See *United States* v. *12 200-ft. Reels of Film, post,* p. 123; *United States* v. *Orito, post,* p. 139; *Kois* v. *Wisconsin,* 408 U. S. 229; *Byrne* v. *Karalexis,* 396 U. S. 976, 977; *Ginsberg* v. *New York,* 390 U. S. 629, 650; *Jacobs* v. *New York,* 388 U. S. 431, 436; *Ginzburg* v. *United States,* 383 U. S. 463, 482; *Memoirs* v. *Massachusetts,* 383 U. S. 413, 424; *Bantam Books, Inc.* v. *Sullivan,* 372 U. S. 58, 72; *Times Film Corp.* v. *Chicago,* 365 U. S. 43, 78; *Smith* v. *California,* 361 U. S. 147, 167; *Kingsley Pictures Corp.* v. *Regents,* 360 U. S. 684, 697; *Roth* v. *United States,* 354 U. S. 476, 508; *Kingsley Books, Inc.* v. *Brown,* 354 U. S. 436, 446; *Superior Films, Inc.* v. *Department of Education,* 346 U. S. 587, 588; *Gelling* v. *Texas,* 343 U. S. 960.

[8] The Commission on Obscenity and Pornography has advocated such a procedure:

"The Commission recommends the enactment, in all jurisdictions which enact or retain provisions prohibiting the dissemination of sexual materials to adults or young persons, of legislation authorizing prosecutors to obtain declaratory judgments as to whether particular materials fall within existing legal prohibitions . . . .

"A declaratory judgment procedure . . . would permit prosecutors to proceed civilly, rather than through the criminal process, against suspected violations of obscenity prohibition. If such civil procedures are utilized, penalties would be imposed for violation of the law only with respect to conduct occurring after a civil declaration is obtained. The Commission believes this course of action to be appropriate whenever there is any existing doubt regarding the legal status of materials; where other alternatives are available, the criminal process should not ordinarily be invoked against persons who might have reasonably believed, in good faith, that the books or films they distributed were entitled to constitutional protection, for the threat of criminal sanctions might otherwise deter the free distribution of constitutionally protected material." Report of the Commission on Obscenity and Pornography 63 (1970).

[9] Obscenity law has had a capricious history:

"The white slave traffic was first exposed by W. T. Stead in a magazine article, 'The Maiden Tribute.' The English law did absolutely nothing to the profiteers in vice, but put Stead in prison for a year for writing about an indecent subject. When the law supplies no definite standard of criminality, a judge in deciding what is indecent or profane may consciously disregard the sound test of present injury, and proceeding upon an entirely different theory may condemn the defendant because his words express ideas which are thought liable to cause bad future consequences. Thus musical comedies enjoy almost unbridled license, while a problem play is often forbidden because opposed to our views of marriage. In the same way, the law of blasphemy has been used against Shelley's *Queen Mab* and the decorous promulgation of pantheistic ideas, on the ground that to attack religion is to loosen the bonds of society and endanger the state. This is simply a roundabout modern method to make heterodoxy in sex matters and even in religion a crime." Z. Chafee, Free Speech in the United States 151 (1942).

JUSTICE BRENNAN'S OPINION NOTE

*Cal. Penal Code § 311.2(a) provides that "Every person who knowingly: sends or causes to be sent, or brings or causes to be brought, into the state for sale or distribution, or in this state prepares, publishes, prints, exhibits, distributes, or offers to distribute, or has in his possession with intent to distribute or to exhibit or offer to distribute, any obscene matter is guilty of a misdemeanor."

JUSTICES BURGER, BLACKMUN, POWELL, REHN-
QUIST, AND WHITE DECLARE *SUITE 69* OBSCENE
AND NOT PROTECTED BY THE FIRST AMENDMENT;
"FOR GOOD OR ILL, A BOOK HAS A CONTINUING
LIFE. IT IS PASSED HAND TO HAND, AND WE CAN
TAKE NOTE OF THE TENDENCY OF WIDELY CIRCU-
LATED BOOKS OF THIS CATEGORY TO REACH THE
IMPRESSIONABLE YOUNG AND HAVE A CON-
TINUING IMPACT. A STATE COULD REASONABLY
REGARD THE 'HARD CORE' CONDUCT DESCRIBED
BY SUITE 69 AS CAPABLE OF ENCOURAGING OR
CAUSING ANTISOCIAL BEHAVIOR, ESPECIALLY IN
ITS IMPACT ON YOUNG PEOPLE."

Kaplan v. California, 413 U.S. 115 (1973)

MR. CHIEF JUSTICE BURGER delivered the opinion of
the Court.

We granted certiorari to the Appellate Department of
the Superior Court of California for the County of Los
Angeles to review the petitioner's conviction for violation
of California statutes regarding obscenity.

Petitioner was the proprietor of the Peek-A-Boo Bookstore, one of the approximately 250 "adult" bookstores
in the city of Los Angeles, California.[1] On May 14,
1969, in response to citizen complaints, an undercover
police officer entered the store and began to peruse several
books and magazines. Petitioner advised the officer that
the store "was not a library." The officer then asked
petitioner if he had "any good sexy books." Petitioner
replied that "all of our books are sexy" and exhibited a
lewd photograph. At petitioner's recommendation, and
after petitioner had read aloud a sample paragraph, the
officer purchased the book Suite 69. On the basis of this
sale, petitioner was convicted by a jury of violating California Penal Code § 311.2,[2] a misdemeanor.

The book, Suite 69, has a plain cover and contains no
pictures. It is made up entirely of repetitive descriptions of physical, sexual conduct, "clinically" explicit
and offensive to the point of being nauseous; there is
only the most tenuous "plot." Almost every conceivable
variety of sexual contact, homosexual and heterosexual, is
described. Whether one samples every 5th, 10th, or
20th page, beginning at any point or page at random, the
content is unvarying.

At trial both sides presented testimony, by persons
accepted to be "experts," as to the content and nature
of the book. The book itself was received in evidence,
and read, in its entirety, to the jury. Each juror in-
spected the book. But the State offered no "expert"
evidence that the book was "utterly without socially redeeming value," or any evidence of "national standards."

On appeal, the Appellate Department of the Superior
Court of California for the County of Los Angeles affirmed petitioner's conviction. Relying on the dissenting
opinions in *Jacobellis* v. *Ohio*, 378 U. S. 184, 199, 203
(1964), and MR. JUSTICE WHITE's dissent in *Memoirs* v.
Massachusetts, 383 U. S. 413, 462 (1966), it concluded
that evidence of a "national" standard of obscenity was
not required. It also decided that the State did not
always have to present "expert" evidence that the book
lacked "socially redeeming value," and that "[i]n light . . .
of the circumstances surrounding the sale" and the nature
of the book itself, there was sufficient evidence to sustain
petitioner's conviction. Finally, the state court considered petitioner's argument that the book was not
"obscene" as a matter of constitutional law. Pointing
out that petitioner was arguing, in part, that all books
were constitutionally protected in an absolute sense, it
rejected that thesis. On "independent review," it concluded "Suite 69 appeals to a prurient interest in sex
and is beyond the customary limits of candor within the
State of California." It held that the book was not protected by the First Amendment. We agree.

This case squarely presents the issue of whether expression by words alone can be legally "obscene" in the sense
of being unprotected by the First Amendment.[3] When
the Court declared that obscenity is not a form of expression protected by the First Amendment, no distinction was made as to the medium of the expression. See
Roth v. *United States*, 354 U. S. 476, 481–485 (1957).
Obscenity can, of course, manifest itself in conduct, in
the pictorial representation of conduct, or in the written
and oral description of conduct. The Court has applied
similarly conceived First Amendment standards to moving pictures, to photographs, and to words in books. See
Freedman v. *Maryland*, 380 U. S. 51, 57 (1965); *Jacobellis*
v. *Ohio, supra*, at 187–188; *Times Film Corp.* v. *Chicago*,
365 U. S. 43, 46 (1961); *id.*, at 51 (Warren, C. J., dissenting); *Kingsley Pictures Corp.* v. *Regents*, 360 U. S.
684, 689–690 (1959); *Superior Films, Inc.* v. *Dept. of Education*, 346 U. S. 587, 589 (1954) (DOUGLAS, J., concurring); *Joseph Burstyn, Inc.* v. *Wilson*, 343 U. S. 495, 503
(1952).

Because of a profound commitment to protecting communication of ideas, any restraint on expression by way
of the printed word or in speech stimulates a traditional
and emotional response, unlike the response to obscene
pictures of flagrant human conduct. A book seems to
have a different and preferred place in our hierarchy of
values, and so it should be. But this generalization, like
so many, is qualified by the book's content. As with
pictures, films, paintings, drawings, and engravings, both
oral utterance and the printed word have First Amendment protection until they collide with the long-settled
position of this Court that obscenity is not protected by
the Constitution. *Miller* v. *California, ante*, at 23–25;
Roth v. *United States, supra*, at 483–485.

For good or ill, a book has a continuing life. It is
passed hand to hand, and we can take note of the tendency of widely circulated books of this category to reach
the impressionable young and have a continuing impact.[4]
A State could reasonably regard the "hard core" conduct
described by Suite 69 as capable of encouraging or causing
antisocial behavior, especially in its impact on young
people. States need not wait until behavioral experts
or educators can provide empirical data before enacting
controls of commerce in obscene materials unprotected by
the First Amendment or by a constitutional right to privacy. We have noted the power of a legislative body to
enact such regulatory laws on the basis of unprovable
assumptions. See *Paris Adult Theatre I* v. *Slaton, ante*,
at 60–63.

Prior to trial, petitioner moved to dismiss the complaint on the basis that sale of sexually oriented material to consenting adults is constitutionally protected. In connection with this motion only, the prosecution stipulated that it did not claim that petitioner either disseminated any material to minors or thrust it upon the general public. The trial court denied the motion. Today, this Court, in *Paris Adult Theatre I v. Slaton, ante,* at 68–69, reaffirms that commercial exposure and sale of obscene materials to anyone, including consenting adults, is subject to state regulation. See also *United States v. Orito, post,* at 141–144; *United States v. 12 200-ft. Reels of Film, post,* at 128; *United States v. Thirty-seven Photographs,* 402 U. S. 363, 376 (1971) (opinion of WHITE, J.); *United States v. Reidel,* 402 U. S. 351, 355 356 (1971). The denial of petitioner's motion was, therefore, not error.

At trial the prosecution tendered the book itself into evidence and also tendered, as an expert witness, a police officer in the vice squad. The officer testified to extensive experience with pornographic materials and gave his opinion that Suite 69, taken as a whole, predominantly appealed to the prurient interest of the average person in the State of California, "applying contemporary standards," and that the book went "substantially beyond the customary limits of candor" in the State of California. The witness explained specifically how the book did so, that it was a purveyor of perverted sex for its own sake. No "expert" state testimony was offered that the book was obscene under "national standards," or that the book was "utterly without redeeming social importance," despite "expert" defense testimony to the contrary.

In *Miller v. California, ante,* p. 15, the Court today holds that the " 'contemporary community standards of the State of California,' " as opposed to "national standards," are constitutionally adequate to establish whether a work is obscene. We also reject in *Paris Adult Theatre I v. Slaton, ante,* p. 49, any constitutional need for "expert" testimony on behalf of the prosecution, or for any other ancillary evidence of obscenity, once the allegedly obscene material itself is placed in evidence. *Paris Adult Theatre I, ante,* at 56. The defense should be free to introduce appropriate expert testimony, see *Smith v. California,* 361 U. S. 147, 164–165 (1959) (Frankfurter, J., concurring), but in "the cases in which this Court has decided obscenity questions since *Roth,* it has regarded the materials as sufficient in themselves for the determination of the question." *Ginzburg v. United States,* 383 U. S. 463, 465 (1966). See *United States v. Groner,* 479 F. 2d 577, 579–586 (CA5 1973). On the record in this case, the prosecution's evidence was sufficient, as a matter of federal constitutional law, to support petitioner's conviction.[5]

Both *Miller v. California, supra,* and this case involve California obscenity statutes. The judgment of the Appellate Department of the Superior Court of California for the County of Los Angeles is vacated, and the case remanded to that court for further proceedings not inconsistent with this opinion, *Miller v. California, supra,* and *Paris Adult Theatre I v. Slaton, supra.* See *United States v. 12 200-ft. Reels of Film, post,* at 130 n. 7, decided today.

Vacated and remanded.

MR. JUSTICE DOUGLAS would vacate and remand for dismissal of the criminal complaint under which petitioner was found guilty because "obscenity" as defined by the California courts and by this Court is too vague to satisfy the requirements of due process. See *Miller v. California, ante,* p. 37 (DOUGLAS, J., dissenting).

MR. JUSTICE BRENNAN, with whom MR. JUSTICE STEWART and MR. JUSTICE MARSHALL join, dissenting.

I would reverse the judgment of the Appellate Department of the Superior Court of California and remand the case for further proceedings not inconsistent with my dissenting opinion in *Paris Adult Theatre I v. Slaton, ante,* p. 73. See my dissent in *Miller v. California, ante,* p. 47.

NOTES

[1] The number of these stores was so estimated by both parties at oral argument. These stores purport to bar minors from the premises. In this case there is no evidence that petitioner sold materials to juveniles. Cf. *Miller v. California, ante,* at 18–20.

[2] The California Penal Code § 311.2, at the time of the commission of the alleged offense, read in relevant part:

"(a) Every person who knowingly: sends or causes to be sent, or brings or causes to be brought, into this state for sale or distribution, or in this state prepares, publishes, prints, exhibits, distributes, or offers to distribute, or has in his possession with intent to distribute or to exhibit or offer to distribute, any obscene matter is guilty of a misdemeanor. . . ."

California Penal Code § 311, at the time of the commission of the alleged offense, provided as follows:

"As used in this chapter:

"(a) 'Obscene' means that to the average person, applying contemporary standards, the predominant appeal of the matter, taken as a whole, is to prurient interest, *i. e.,* a shameful or morbid interest in nudity, sex, or excretion, which goes substantially beyond customary limits of candor in description or representation of such matters and is matter which is utterly without redeeming social importance.

"(b) 'Matter' means any book, magazine, newspaper, or other printed or written material or any picture, drawing, photograph, motion picture, or other pictorial representation or any statue or other figure, or any recording, transcription or mechanical, chemical or electrical reproduction or any other articles, equipment, machines or materials.

"(c) 'Person' means any individual, partnership, firm, association, corporation, or other legal entity.

"(d) 'Distribute' means to transfer possession of, whether with or without consideration.

"(e) 'Knowingly' means having knowledge that the matter is obscene."

[3] This Court, since *Roth v. United States,* 354 U. S. 476 (1957), has only once held books to be obscene. That case was *Mishkin v. New York,* 383 U. S. 502 (1966), and the books involved were very similar in content to Suite 69. But most of the *Mishkin* books, if not all, were illustrated. See *id.,* at 505, 514–515. Prior to *Roth,* this Court affirmed, by an equally divided Court, a conviction for sale of an unillustrated book. *Doubleday & Co., Inc. v. New York,* 335 U. S. 848 (1948). This Court has always rigorously scrutinized judgments involving books for possible violation of First Amendment rights, and has regularly reversed convictions on that basis. See *Childs v. Oregon,* 401 U. S. 1006 (1971); *Walker v. Ohio,* 398 U. S. 434 (1970); *Keney v. New York,* 388 U. S. 440 (1967); *Friedman v. New York,* 388 U. S. 441 (1967); *Sheperd v. New York,* 388 U. S. 444 (1967); *Avansino v. New York,* 388 U. S. 446 (1967); *Corinth Publications, Inc. v. Wesberry,* 388 U. S. 448 (1967); *Books, Inc. v. United States,* 388 U. S. 449 (1967); *A Quantity of Books v. Kansas,* 388 U. S. 452 (1967); *Redrup v. New York,* 386 U. S. 767 (1967); *Memoirs v. Massachusetts,* 383 U. S. 413 (1966); *Tralins v. Gerstein,* 378 U. S. 576 (1964); *Grove Press, Inc. v. Gerstein,* 378 U. S. 577 (1964); *A*

Quantity of Books v. *Kansas*, 378 U. S. 205 (1964); *Marcus* v. *Search Warrant*, 367 U. S. 717 (1961); *Smith* v. *California*, 361 U. S. 147 (1959); *Kingsley Books, Inc.* v. *Brown*, 354 U. S. 436 (1957).

[4] See *Paris Adult Theatre I* v. *Slaton, ante*, at 58 n. 7; Report of the Commission on Obscenity and Pornography 401 (1970) (Hill-Link Minority Report).

[5] As the prosecution's introduction of the book itself into evidence was adequate, as a matter of federal constitutional law, to establish the book's obscenity, we need not consider petitioner's claim that evidence of pandering was wrongly considered on appeal to support the jury finding of obscenity. Petitioner's additional claims that his conviction was affirmed on the basis of a "theory" of "pandering" not considered at trial and that he was subjected to retroactive application of a state statute are meritless on the record.

FILMS, PHOTOGRAPHS, AND OBSCENITY

FILMS, PHOTOGRAPHS,
AND OBSCENITY

MOTION PICTURES ARE NOT ORGANS OF PUBLIC OPINION AND ARE NOT PROTECTED BY THE FIRST AMENDMENT

Mutual Film Corp. v. Ohio Indus'l. Comm., 236 U.S. 230 (1915)

MR. JUSTICE MCKENNA, after stating the case as above, delivered the opinion of the court.

Complainant directs its argument to three propositions: (1) The statute in controversy imposes an unlawful burden on interstate commerce; (2) it violates the freedom of speech and publication guaranteed by § 11, art. 1, of the constitution of the State of Ohio; [1] and (3) it attempts to delegate legislative power to censors and to other boards to determine whether the statute offends in the particulars designated.

It is necessary to consider only §§ 3, 4 and 5. Section 3 makes it the duty of the board to examine and censor motion picture films to be publicly exhibited and displayed in the State of Ohio. The films are required to be exhibited to the board before they are delivered to the exhibitor for exhibition, for which a fee is charged.

Section 4. "Only such films as are in the judgment and discretion of the board of censors of a moral, educational or amusing and harmless character shall be passed and approved by such board." The films are required to be stamped or designated in a proper manner.

Section 5. The board may work in conjunction with censor boards of other States as a censor congress, and the action of such congress in approving or rejecting films shall be considered as the action of the state board, and all films passed, approved, stamped and numbered by such congress, when the fees therefor are paid shall be considered approved by the board.

By § 7 a penalty is imposed for each exhibition of films without the approval of the board, and by § 8 any person dissatisfied with the order of the board is given the same rights and remedies for hearing and reviewing, amendment or vacation of the order "as is provided in the case of persons dissatisfied with the orders of the industrial commission."

The censorship, therefore, is only of films intended for exhibition in Ohio, and we can immediately put to one side the contention that it imposes a burden on interstate commerce. It is true that according to the allegations of the bill some of the films of complainant are shipped from Detroit, Michigan, but they are distributed to exhibitors, purchasers, renters and lessors in Ohio, for exhibition in Ohio, and this determines the application of the statute. In other words, it is only films which are "to be publicly exhibited and displayed in the State of Ohio" which are required to be examined and censored. It would be straining the doctrine of original packages to say that the films retain that form and composition even when unrolling and exhibiting to audiences, or, being ready for renting for the purpose of exhibition within the State, could not be disclosed to the state officers. If this be so, whatever the power of the State to prevent the exhibition of films not approved—and for the purpose of this contention we must assume the power is otherwise plenary—films brought from another State, and only because so brought, would be exempt from the power, and films made in the State would be subject to it. There must be some time when the films are subject to the law of the State, and necessarily when they are in the hands of the exchanges ready to be rented to exhibitors or have passed to the latter, they are in consumption, and mingled as much as from their nature they can be with other property of the State.

It is true that the statute requires them to be submitted to the board before they are delivered to the exhibitor, but we have seen that the films are shipped to "exchanges" and by them rented to exhibitors, and the "exchanges" are described as "nothing more or less than circulating libraries or clearing houses." And one film "serves in many theatres from day to day until it is worn out."

The next contention is that the statute violates the freedom of speech and publication guaranteed by the Ohio constitution. In its discussion counsel have gone into a very elaborate description of moving picture exhibitions and their many useful purposes as graphic expressions of opinion and sentiments, as exponents of policies, as teachers of science and history, as useful, interesting, amusing, educational and moral. And a list of the "campaigns," as counsel call them, which may be carried on is given. We may concede the praise. It is not questioned by the Ohio statute and under its comprehensive description, "campaigns" of an infinite variety may be conducted. Films of a "moral, educational or amusing and harmless character shall be passed and approved" are the words of the statute. No exhibition, therefore, or "campaign" of complainant will be prevented if its pictures have those qualities. Therefore, however missionary of opinion films are or may become, however educational or entertaining, there is no impediment to their value or effect in the Ohio statute. But they may be used for evil, and against that possibility the statute was enacted. Their power of amusement and, it may be, education, the audiences they assemble, not of women alone nor of men alone, but together, not of adults only, but of children, make them the more insidious in corruption by a pretense of worthy purpose or if they should degenerate from worthy purpose. Indeed, we may go beyond that possibility. They take their attraction from the general interest, eager and wholesome it may be, in their subjects, but a prurient interest may be excited and appealed to. Besides, there are some things which should not have pictorial representation in public places and to all audiences. And not only the State of Ohio but other States have considered it to be in the interest of the public morals and welfare to supervise moving picture exhibitions. We would have to shut our eyes to the facts of the world to regard the precaution unreasonable or the legislation to effect it a mere wanton interference with personal liberty.

We do not understand that a possibility of an evil employment of films is denied, but a freedom from the censorship of the law and a precedent right of exhibition are asserted, subsequent responsibility only, it is contended, being incurred for abuse. In other words, as we have seen, the constitution of Ohio is invoked and an exhibition of films is assimilated to the freedom of speech, writing and publication assured by that instrument and for the abuse of which only is there responsibility, and, it is insisted, that as no law may be passed "to restrain the liberty of speech or of the press," no law may be passed to subject moving pictures to censorship before their exhibition.

We need not pause to dilate upon the freedom of opinion and its expression, and whether by speech, writing or printing. They are too certain to need discussion—of such conceded value as to need no supporting praise. Nor can there be any doubt of their breadth nor that their underlying safeguard is, to use the words of another, "that opinion is free and that conduct alone is amenable to the law."

Are moving pictures within the principle, as it is contended they are? They, indeed, may be mediums of thought, but so are many things. So is the theatre, the circus, and all other shows and spectacles, and their performances may be thus brought by the like reasoning under the same immunity from repression or supervision as the public press,—made the same agencies of civil liberty.

Counsel have not shrunk from this extension of their contention and cite a case in this court where the title of drama was accorded to pantomime;[2] and such and other spectacles are said by counsel to be publications of ideas, satisfying the definition of the dictionaries,—that is, and we quote counsel, a means of making or announcing publicly something that otherwise might have remained private or unknown,—and this being peculiarly the purpose and effect of moving pictures they come directly, it is contended, under the protection of the Ohio constitution.

The first impulse of the mind is to reject the contention. We immediately feel that the argument is wrong or strained which extends the guaranties of free opinion and speech to the multitudinous shows which are advertised on the bill-boards of our cities and towns and which regards them as emblems of public safety, to use the words of Lord Camden, quoted by counsel, and which seeks to bring motion pictures and other spectacles into practical and legal similitude to a free press and liberty of opinion.

The judicial sense supporting the common sense of the country is against the contention. As pointed out by the District Court, the police power is familiarly exercised in granting or withholding licenses for theatrical performances as a means of their regulation. The court cited the following cases: *Marmet* v. *State*, 45 Ohio, 63, 72, 73; *Baker* v. *Cincinnati*, 11 Ohio St. 534; *Commonwealth* v. *McGann*, 213 Massachusetts, 213, 215; *People* v. *Steele*, 231 Illinois, 340, 344, 345.

The exercise of the power upon moving picture exhibitions has been sustained. *Greenberg* v. *Western Turf Ass'n*, 148 California, 126; *Laurelle* v. *Bush*, 17 Cal. App. 409; *State* v. *Loden*, 117 Maryland, 373; *Block* v. *Chicago*, 239 Illinois, 251; *Higgins* v. *Lacroix*, 119 Minnesota, 145. See also *State* v. *Morris*, 76 Atl. Rep. 479; *People* v. *Gaynor*, 137 N. Y. S. 196, 199; *McKenzie* v. *McClellan*, 116 N. Y. S. 645, 646.

It seems not to have occurred to anybody in the cited cases that freedom of opinion was repressed in the exertion of the power which was illustrated. The rights of property were only considered as involved. It cannot be put out of view that the exhibition of moving pictures is a business pure and simple, originated and conducted for profit, like other spectacles, not to be regarded, nor intended to be regarded by the Ohio constitution, we think, as part of the press of the country or as organs of public opinion. They are mere representations of events, of ideas and sentiments published and known, vivid, useful and entertaining no doubt, but, as we have said, capable of evil, having power for it, the greater because of their attractiveness and manner of exhibition. It was this capability and power, and it may be in experience of them, that induced the State of Ohio, in addition to prescribing penalties for immoral exhibitions, as it does in its Criminal Code, to require censorship before exhibition, as it does by the act under review. We cannot regard this as beyond the power of government.

It does not militate against the strength of these considerations that motion pictures may be used to amuse and instruct in other places than theatres—in churches, for instance, and in Sunday schools and public schools. Nor are we called upon to say on this record whether such exceptions would be within the provisions of the statute nor to anticipate that it will be so declared by the state courts or so enforced by the state officers.

The next contention of complainant is that the Ohio statute is a delegation of legislative power and void for that if not for the other reasons charged against it, which we have discussed. While administration and legislation are quite distinct powers, the line which separates exactly their exercise is not easy to define in words. It is best recognized in illustrations. Undoubtedly the legislature must declare the policy of the law and fix the legal principles which are to control in given cases; but an administrative body may be invested with the power to ascertain the facts and conditions to which the policy and principles apply. If this could not be done there would be infinite confusion in the laws, and in an effort to detail and to particularize, they would miss sufficiency both in provision and execution.

The objection to the statute is that it furnishes no standard of what is educational, moral, amusing or harmless, and hence leaves decision to arbitrary judgment, whim and caprice; or, aside from those extremes, leaving it to the different views which might be entertained of the effect of the pictures, permitting the "personal equation" to enter, resulting "in unjust discrimination against some propagandist film," while others might be approved without question. But the statute by its provisions guards against such variant judgments, and its terms, like other general terms, get precision from the sense and experience of men and become certain and useful guides in reasoning and conduct. The exact specification of the instances of their application would be as impossible as the attempt would be futile. Upon such sense and experience, therefore, the law properly relies. This has many analogies and direct examples in cases, and we may cite *Gundling* v. *Chicago*, 177 U. S. 183; *Red "C" Oil Manufacturing Co.* v. *North Carolina*, 222 U. S. 380; *Bridge Co.* v. *United States*, 216 U. S. 177; *Buttfield* v. *Stranahan*, 192 U. S. 470. See also *Waters-Pierce Oil Co.* v. *Texas*, 212 U. S. 86. If this were not so, the many administrative agencies created by the state and National governments would be denuded of their utility and government in some of its most important exercises become impossible.

To sustain the attack upon the statute as a delegation of legislative power, complainant cites *Harmon* v. *State*, 66 Ohio St. 249. In that case a statute of the State committing to a certain officer the duty of issuing a license to one desiring to act as an engineer if "found trustworthy and competent," was declared invalid because, as the court said, no standard was furnished by the General Assembly as to qualification, and no specification as to wherein the applicant should be trustworthy and competent, but all was "left to the opinion, finding and caprice of the examiner." The case can be distinguished. Besides, later cases have recognized the difficulty of exact separation of the powers of government, and announced the principle that legislative power is completely exercised where the law "is perfect, final and decisive in all of its parts, and the discretion given only relates to its execution." Cases are cited in illustration. And the principle finds further illustration in the decisions of the courts of lesser authority but which exhibit the juridical sense of the State as to the delegation of powers.

Section 5 of the statute, which provides for a censor congress of the censor board and the boards of other States, is referred to in emphasis of complainant's objection that the statute delegates legislative power. But, as complainant says, such congress is "at present nonexistent and nebulous," and we are, therefore, not called upon to anticipate its action or pass upon the validity of § 5.

We may close this topic with a quotation of the very apt comment of the District Court upon the statute. After remarking that the language of the statute "might have been extended by descriptive and illustrative words," but doubting that it would have been the more intelligible and that probably by being more restrictive might be more easily thwarted, the court said: "In view of the range of subjects which complainants claim to have already compassed, not to speak of the natural development that will ensue, it would be next to impossible to devise language that would be at once comprehensive and automatic."

In conclusion we may observe that the Ohio statute gives a review by the courts of the State of the decision of the board of censors.

Decree affirmed.

NOTES

[1] "Section 11. Every citizen may freely speak, write, and publish his sentiments on all subjects, being responsible for the abuse of the right; and no law shall be passed to restrain or abridge the liberty of speech, or of the press. In all criminal prosecutions for libel, the truth may be given in evidence to the jury, and if it shall appear to the jury that the matter charged as libelous is true, and was published with good motives, and for justifiable ends, the party shall be acquitted."

[2] *Kalem* v. *Harper Bros.*, 222 U. S. 55.

THE FILMS "LA RONDE" AND "M" GET FIRST AMENDMENT PROTECTION FROM THE UNITED STATES SUPREME COURT

Superior Films, Inc. v. *Department of Education*, 346 U.S. 587 (1953)

PER CURIAM.

The judgments are reversed. *Joseph Burstyn, Inc.* v. *Wilson*, 343 U. S. 495.

MR. JUSTICE DOUGLAS, with whom MR. JUSTICE BLACK agrees, concurring.

The argument of Ohio and New York that the government may establish censorship over moving pictures is one I cannot accept. In 1925 Minnesota passed a law aimed at suppressing before publication any "malicious, scandalous and defamatory newspaper." The Court, speaking through Chief Justice Hughes, struck down that law as violating the Fourteenth Amendment, which has made the First Amendment applicable to the States. *Near* v. *Minnesota*, 283 U. S. 697. The "chief purpose" of the constitutional guaranty of liberty of the press, said the Court, was "to prevent previous restraints upon publication." *Id.*, p. 713.

The history of censorship is so well known it need not be summarized here. Certainly a system, still in force in some nations, which required a newspaper to submit to a board its news items, editorials, and cartoons before it published them could not be sustained. Nor could book publishers be required to submit their novels, poems, and tracts to censors for clearance before publication. Any such scheme of censorship would be in irreconcilable conflict with the language and purpose of the First Amendment.

Nor is it conceivable to me that producers of plays for the legitimate theatre or for television could be required to submit their manuscripts to censors on pain of penalty for producing them without approval. Certainly the spoken word is as freely protected against prior restraints as that which is written. Such indeed is the force of our decision in *Thomas* v. *Collins*, 323 U. S. 516, 540. The freedom of the platform which it espouses carries with it freedom of the stage.

The same result in the case of motion pictures necessarily follows as a consequence of our holding in *Joseph Burstyn, Inc.* v. *Wilson*, 343 U. S. 495, 502, that motion pictures are "within the free speech and free press guaranty of the First and Fourteenth Amendments."

Motion pictures are of course a different medium of expression than the public speech, the radio, the stage, the novel, or the magazine. But the First Amendment draws no distinction between the various methods of communicating ideas. On occasion one may be more powerful or effective than another. The movie, like the public speech, radio, or television, is transitory—here now and gone in an instant. The novel, the short story, the poem in printed form are permanently at hand to reenact the drama or to retell the story over and again. Which medium will give the most excitement and have the most enduring effect will vary with the theme and the actors. It is not for the censor to determine in any case. The First and the Fourteenth Amendments say that Congress and the States shall make "no law" which abridges freedom of speech or of the press. In order to sanction a system of censorship I would have to say that "no law" does not mean what it says, that "no law" is qualified to mean "some" laws. I cannot take that step.

In this Nation every writer, actor, or producer, no matter what medium of expression he may use, should be freed from the censor.

"THAT A MOTION PICTURE WHICH PANDERS TO BASE HUMAN EMOTIONS IS A BREEDING GROUND FOR SENSUALTY, DEPRAVITY, LICENTIOUSNESS AND SEXUAL IMMORALITY CAN HARDLY BE DOUBTED. THAT THESE VICES REPRESENT A 'CLEAR AND PRESENT DANGER' TO THE BODY SOCIAL SEEMS MANIFESTLY CLEAR. THE DANGER TO YOUTH IS SELF EVIDENT." THE FILM "LA RONDE" IS CENSORED ON THE GROUNDS THAT IT IS "IMMORAL" AND THAT ITS EXHIBITION WOULD TEND TO CORRUPT MORALS.

Commercial Pictures Corp. v. Board of Regents, Inc., 113 N.E.2d 502 (1953)

FROESSEL, Judge.

The Motion Picture Division of the State Education Department and the Regents of the University of the State of New York have determined that the motion picture "La Ronde" (revised), produced in France, is not entitled to be licensed for public exhibition, upon the ground that it is "immoral" and "would tend to corrupt morals" within the meaning of section 122 of the Education Law of this State, McK.Consol.Laws, c. 16. The Appellate Division has confirmed the determination.

The film from beginning to end deals with promiscuity, adultery, fornication and seduction. It portrays ten episodes, with a narrator. Except for the husband and wife episode, each deals with an illicit amorous adventure between two persons, one of the two partners becoming the principal in the next. The first episode begins with a prostitute and a soldier. Since the former's room is ten minutes walk from their meeting place on the street, and the soldier must hurry back to his barracks, they take advantage of the local environment. She informs him that "civilians" pay, but for "boys like you it's nothing". The cycle continues with the soldier and a parlormaid; the parlormaid and her employer's son; the latter and a young married woman; the married woman and her husband; the husband and a young girl; the girl and a poet; the poet and an actress; the actress and a count, and finally the count and the prostitute. At the very end, the narrator reminds the audience of the author's thesis: "It is the story of everyone".

Petitioner contends that the statute is invalid, in that it imposes a prior restraint upon the exercise of freedom of speech and press, relying principally upon Joseph Burstyn, Inc., v. Wilson, 1952, 343 U.S. 495, 72 S.Ct. 777, 96 L.Ed. 1098, which overruled Mutual Film Corp. v. Industrial Comm. of Ohio, 1915, 236 U.S. 230, 35 S.Ct. 387, 59 L.Ed. 552. In addition, it is contended that the standard here applied is too vague and indefinite to satisfy the requirements of due process. Respondent maintains that the Burstyn case, supra, is not controlling here, and that the standard in question is sufficiently clear and definite. The issues so presented may be posed thus:

(1) Are motion pictures, as part of the press, altogether exempt from prior restraint or censorship?

(2) Do the words "immoral" and "tend to corrupt morals", in section 122 of the Education Law, viewed in the perspective of their legislative setting, fail to provide a standard adequate to satisfy the requirements of due process?

(3) Has the statute been properly applied herein?

1. Our answer to the first question must be in the negative, as it was in the Burstyn case in this court, Joseph Burstyn, Inc., v. Wilson, 303 N.Y. 242, 262, 101 N.E. 2d 665, 674; see, also, concurring opinion of Desmond, J., 303 N.Y. at pages 263–264, 101 N.E.2d 675. That question was not reached by the Supreme Court of the United States in Joseph Burstyn, Inc., v. Wilson, supra, 343 U.S. 495, at pages 502–503, 505–506, 72 S.Ct. 777, at page 781, and the language employed therein aptly refutes the notion that all media of communication may be grouped under a precise and absolute rule: "To hold that liberty of expression by means of motion pictures is guaranteed by the First and Fourteenth Amendments, however, is not the end of our problem. It does not follow that the Constitution requires absolute freedom to exhibit every motion picture of every kind at all times and all places. That much is evident from the series of decisions of this Court with respect to other media of communication of ideas. Nor does it follow that motion pictures are necessarily subject to the precise rules governing any other particular method of expression. Each method tends to present its own peculiar problems." Nor did Gelling v. Texas, 343 U.S. 960, 72 S.Ct. 1002, 96 L.Ed. 1359, decided the week following on the authority of the Burstyn case, supra, 343 U.S. 495, 72 S.Ct. 777, resolve the issue left open therein.

Insofar, then, as motion pictures tend to present their "own peculiar problems", we think they may properly become the subject of special measures of control. If, as we believe, motion pictures may present a "clear and present danger" of substantive evil to the community, Schenck v. United States, 249 U.S. 47, 52, 39 S.Ct. 247, 63 L.Ed. 470, then the Legislature may act to guard against such evil, though in so doing it overrides to a degree the right to free expression. Poulos v. State of New Hampshire, 345 U.S. 395, 73 S.Ct. 760; Beauharnais v. People of State of Illinois, 343 U.S. 250, 72 S.Ct. 725, 96 L.Ed. 919; Dennis v. United States, 341 U.S. 494, 71 S.Ct. 857, 95 L.Ed. 1137; American Communications Ass'n v. Douds, 339 U.S. 382, 70 S.Ct. 674, 94 L.Ed. 925; Kovacs v. Cooper, 336 U.S. 77, 89 S.Ct. 448, 93 L.Ed. 513; Chaplinsky v. State of New Hampshire, 315 U.S. 568, 62 S.Ct. 766, 86 L.Ed. 1031; Schenck v. United States, supra; Fox v. Washington, 236 U.S. 273, 35 S.Ct. 383, 59 L.Ed. 573. As was said in Crowley v. Christensen, 137 U.S. 86, 89, 11 S.Ct. 13, 15, 34 L.Ed. 620: "the possession and enjoyment of all rights are subject to such reasonable conditions as may be deemed by the governing authority of the country essential to the safety, health, peace, good order, and morals of the community. Even liberty itself, the greatest of all rights, is not unrestricted license to act according to one's own will."

The highest court in the land has recognized the right of the State to act to protect its citizens, even to the extreme of interfering with personal liberty, against the threat of disease. Jacobson v. Com. of Massachusetts, 197 U.S. 11, 25 S.Ct. 358, 49 L.Ed. 643. In that case, the court declared, 197 U.S. at page 27, 25 S.Ct. at page 362: "Upon the principle of self-defense, of paramount necessity, a community has the right to protect itself against an epidemic of disease which threatens the safety of its members." The same court later held that principle broad enough to permit the State to protect itself against the perpetuation of hereditary strains of imbecility through sterilization. Buch v. Bell, 274 U.S. 200, 207, 47 S.Ct. 584, 71 L.Ed. 1000. If it may so act to prevent physical disease, or the birth of the "manifestly unfit," may it not likewise act to prevent moral corruption, when the consequences thereof affect not only family life, as we know it in this State and country, but the health and welfare of our people as well?

The problem of preserving individual rights under the Constitution and still securing to the State the right to protect itself is not always an easy one, and it is sometimes difficult to find the proper balance between them. There is no mathematical formula for accommodating the rights of the individual to the good of the community, and we fully recognize that care must be exercised when preserving one not to suppress the other. But there "is no basis for saying that freedom and order are not compatible. That would be a decision of desperation. Regulation and suppression are not the same, either in purpose or result, and courts of justice can tell the difference." Poulos v. State of New Hampshire, supra, 345 U.S. at page 488, 73 S.Ct. at page 768.

Of course it is true that the State may not impose upon its inhabitants the moral code of saints, but, if it is to survive, it must be free to take such reasonable and appropriate measures as may be deemed necessary to preserve the institution of marriage and the home, and the health and welfare of its inhabitants. History bears witness to the fate of peoples who have become indifferent to the vice of indiscriminate sexual immorality — a most serious threat to the family, the home and the State. An attempt to combat such threat is embodied in the sections of the Education Law here challenged. It should not be thwarted by any doctrinaire approach to the problems of free speech raised thereby.

That a motion picture which panders to base human emotions is a breeding ground for sensuality, depravity, licentiousness and sexual immorality can hardly be doubted. That these vices represent a "clear and present danger" to the body social seems manifestly clear. The danger to youth is self-evident. And so adults, who may react with limited concern to a portrayal of larceny, will tend to react quite differently to a presentation wholly devoted to promiscuity, seductively portrayed in such manner as to invite concupiscence and condone its promiscuous satisfaction, with its evil social consequences. A single motion picture may be seen simultaneously in theatres throughout the State. May nothing be done to prevent countless individuals from being exposed to its vicious effects? To us the answer seems obvious, especially in the light of recent technical developments which render the problem more acute than ever. Now we have commercially feasible three dimensional projection, some forms of which are said to bring the audience "right into the picture". There can be no doubt that attempts will be made to bring the audience right into the bedchamber if it be held that the State is impotent to apply preventive measures.

Such preventive measures necessarily embrace some form of censorship. It is significant that the American motion picture industry has adopted that very method of self-discipline as the effective remedy for immoral motion pictures through its well-known Code of Production Standards. The people of this State should not be compelled to rely upon the motion picture industry's own standards of review; nor, in the case of a foreign film, solely upon the customs officials, U.S.C.A., tit. 19, § 1305, for their judgment "in admitting the film did not prevent the state officers from arriving at a different judgment when it came to the exhibition of the film and the granting of a license therefor." Eureka Productions v. Lehman, D.C., 17 F.Supp. 259, 261, affirmed 302 U.S. 634, 58 S.Ct. 15, 82 L.Ed. 494, Id., 304 U.S. 541, 58 S.Ct. 944, 82 L.Ed. 1517. They have the right to exercise their own sovereign powers to determine for themselves what motion pictures transgress the bounds of decency and sexual morality laid down by common consent.

As we see it, a statute which operates within limits suited to the attainment of such objectives, as does the enactment here challenged, is a reasonable and valid exercise of the police power. No other method will afford reasonably adequate protection to the public. Moreover, our statute places its administration in the hands of a responsible State agency, rather than with local officers who may at times be subject to petty prejudices or varying provincial views. Neither is it entirely out of place to point out that experience has demonstrated over the years that such censorship has been and can be carried out without undue hardship or even inconvenience as to motion pictures which meet the standards for public exhibition. We conclude, therefore, that censorship, as such, is not in every case inimical to the rights of free speech and press guaranteed by the Constitution, so far as motion pictures are concerned.

2. We now turn to a consideration of the standard applied herein. Section 212 of the Education Law provides that a motion picture shall not be licensed if it is "obscene, indecent, *immoral,* inhuman, sacrilegious, or is of *such a character that its exhibition would tend to corrupt morals or incite to crime*". We are concerned here only with the

words we have italicized. Appellant would have us read them as though they stood alone, without other guide than their dictionary meanings, and thereby find them too broad and vague to serve as a valid standard for the limitation of constitutional rights. The Legislature has not used them in a vacuum, however, but in context with other words and in a setting with other statutes *in pari materia,* as e.g., sections 1140-a and 1141 of the Penal Law, McK.Consol.Laws, c. 40. Moreover, the "use of common experience as a glossary is necessary to meet the practical demands of legislation", and the "requirement of reasonable certainty does not preclude the use of ordinary terms to express ideas which find adequate interpretation in common usage and understanding", Sproles v. Binford, 286 U.S. 374, 393, 52 S.Ct. 581, 587, 76 L.Ed. 1167. Even in criminal law, "The test is whether the language conveys sufficiently definite warning as to the proscribed conduct when measured by common understanding and practices." Jordan v. De George, 341 U.S. 223, 231-232, 71 S.Ct. 703, 708, 95 L.Ed. 886.

Our Legislature has used the word "immoral", or its variants, in numerous other statutes, see Penal Law, §§ 483, 483–a, 483–b, 485, subd. 5; § 485–a, subd. 5; §§ 486, 494, 1140–a, 1141, 1141–a, 1147, 1290, subd. 4; §§ 1944–a, 2460; Education Law, §§ 2212, 3012, subd. 2; § 3013, subd. 2; §§ 3020, 6804; General Business Law, McK. Consol.Laws, c. 20, §§ 190, 191, subd. 3. Upon the basis of that standard, liberty, civil service tenure, and business licenses have been lost. To adopt the approach urged by petitioner would certainly throw doubt upon many of these enactments.

Accordingly to common understanding, the terms "immoral" and "morals" must be taken to refer to the moral standards of the community, the "norm or standard of behavior which struggles to make itself articulate in law." Cardozo, Paradoxes of Legal Science, pp. 17, 41–42. Thus the standards of any special and particular segment of the whole population are not to control, but those held by the community at large. As was said in Block v. City of Chicago, 239 Ill. 251, 263–264, 87 N.E. 1011, 1015; "There are the shameless and unclean, to whom nothing is defilement, and from whose point of view no picture would be considered immoral or obscene. Perhaps others could be found, with no laxity of morals, who pay homage to art and would not regard anything as indelicate or indecent which had artistic merit, and would look upon any person entertaining different sentiments as of inferior intelligence, without proper training on the subject, and blinded with bigotry. Both classes are exceptional, and the average person of healthy and wholesome mind knows well enough what the words 'immoral' and 'obscene' mean and can intelligently apply the test to any picture presented to him."

As applied to the general moral standards of the community, it is urged that such a standard may be too broad, although standards equally broad have been successfully applied. The term "moral turpitude" has been held adequate to satisfy even the strict rule applicable to criminal statutes, with the comment that "doubt as to the adequacy of a standard in less obvious cases does not render that standard unconstitutional". Jordan v. De George, 341 U.S. 223, 232, 71 S.Ct. 703, 708, supra. So, too, the term "good moral character", as used in the immigration and nationality laws, must frequently be applied by the courts. In so doing, their measure is the "common standards of morality" prevalent in the community, Estrin v. United States, 2 Cir., 80 F.2d 105, or the "common conscience" of the community. Johnson v. United States, 2 Cir., 186 F.2d 588, 590.

It is not a valid criticism that such general moral standards may vary slightly from generation to generation. Such variations are inevitable and do not affect the application of the principle at a particular period in time. See Parmelee v. United States, 72 App.D.C. 203, 113 F.2d 729. Neither may a standard be criticized on the ground that individual opinions may differ as to a particular application thereof. There is no principle or standard not subject to that infirmity, including the most specific provisions of the First Amendment. Rochin v. California, 342 U.S. 165, 170, 72 S.Ct. 205, 96 L.Ed. 183. particular application thereof. There is no principle or standard not subject to that infirmity, including the most specific provisions of the First Amendment. Rochin v. California, 342 U.S. 165, 170, 72 S.Ct. 205, 96 L.Ed. 183.

We are not unmindful of the fact that the provisions here in question, considered in the abstract, may be deemed broad, even as limited by common usage. Even in such case, however, it has been said that language "does not stand by itself * * * but is part of the whole body of common and statute law * * * and is to be judged in that context." Musser v. Utah, 333 U.S. 95, 97, 68 S.Ct. 397, 398, 92 L.Ed. 562. In the case now before us, we should not "parse the statute as grammarians or treat it as an abstract exercise in lexicography", Beauharnais v. People of State of Illinois, 343 U.S. 250, 253, 72 S.Ct. 725, 729, supra, but should read it as it was meant to be read by the Legislature that enacted it. In many of the statutes in which our Legislature has used the word "immoral" it obviously refers to sexual immorality. It is our view that it is used similarly in section 122 of the Education Law, as can be perceived in the statute itself, and in the construction put upon it, not only by the Regents herein, but by this court as well.

Turning to the statute, it will be noted that there is a related usage—a gradation of language, proceeding from "obscene" to "indecent" to "immoral", words frequently used together in statutory enactments, and thence to generically different categories: "inhuman" and "sacrilegious". That juxtaposition colors the word "immoral" and justifies the application of the rule *ejusdem generis,* particularly when coupled with the subsequent expression "tend to corrupt morals", as was done here. See McKinney's Consol.Laws of N.Y., Book 1, Statutes, 1942 ed., § 239; Penal Law, §§ 1140–a, 1141, where "obscene, indecent, immoral" are likewise grouped together; People v. Wendling, 258 N.Y. 451, 180 N.E. 169, 81 A.L.R. 799; People v. Muller, 96 N.Y. 408; Regina v. Hicklin, L.R. 3 Q.B. 360, 369–370; see, also, Eureka Productions v. Lehman, D.C., 17 F.Supp. 259, affirmed 302 U.S. 634, 58 S.Ct. 15, 82 L.Ed. 494, Id., 304 U.S. 541, 58 S.Ct. 944, 82 L.Ed. 1517, supra; Swearingen v. United States, 161 U.S. 446, 451, 16 S.Ct. 562, 40 L.Ed. 765.

Apart from these considerations, it would appear that we have already construed the statute in precisely this manner. Section 1140-a of the Penal Law, and related sections, have been held to apply to motion pictures even prior to their express inclusion therein. Hughes Tool Co. v. Fielding, 297 N.Y. 1024, 80 N.E.2d 540. The theory of that decision was that the Education Law and the Penal Law constitute complementary parts of a related whole.

As used in the said Penal Law sections, the word "immoral" clearly relates to sexual immorality. Accordingly, its meaning in the Education Law should be the same, and the unpublished minutes of the proceedings of this court indicate that it was so treated in that case.[1]

Viewing the statute under consideration in its proper setting, then, the words "immoral" and "tend to corrupt morals" as used therein relate to standards of sexual morality. As such they are not vague or indefinite. In this sense they are kindred to "obscene" and "indecent", of which we have said: "They are words in common use, and every person of ordinary intelligence understands their meaning, and readily and in most cases accurately applies them to any object or thing brought to his attention which involves a judgment as to the quality indicated. It does not require an expert in art or literature to determine whether a picture is obscene or whether printed words are offensive to decency and good morals." People v. Muller, supra, 96 N.Y. at page 410–411. See, also Chaplinsky v. State of New Hampshire, 315 U.S. 568, 571–572, 62 S.Ct. 766, 86 L.Ed. 1031, supra. It should be remembered that we are not here dealing with a moral concept about which our people widely differ; sexual immorality is condemned throughout our land.

3. The remaining question is whether the statute has been properly invoked against the motion picture "La Ronde". We have already noted that it is concerned solely with promiscuous sex relations and are told: "It is the story of everyone". Although vulgar pornography is avoided, suggestive dialogue and action are present throughout and not merely incidentally, depicting promiscuity as the natural and normal relation between the sexes, whether married or unmarried. Can we disagree with the judgment that such a picture will tend to corrupt morals? To do so would close our eyes to the obvious facts of life. The story is patterned after the book which was condemned for obscenity in People v. Pesky, 230 App. Div. 200, 202, 243 N.Y.S. 193, 196, affirmed 254 N.Y. 373, 173 N.E.227. There the Appellate Division stated "there was nothing to it except a description of the licentious * * * without a single redeeming feature." The author of the original work himself felt that it "might very well be misunderstood and misinterpreted", and so it was privately published. Even among the favorable reviews submitted by petitioner were such comments as:

"The details are concrete enough to make one blush unseen * * * .

"With something less than tremulous delicacy, he [the director] and his associate artists, speak quite freely upon the joys and woes of amorous adventure."

It may also be noted that among the industry's self-imposed limitations pertaining to sex are the following: "The sanctity of the institution of marriage and the home shall be upheld. Pictures shall not infer that low forms of sex relationship are the accepted or common thing." Code of Production Standards, "Particular Applications" II, 1950 Year Book of Motion Pictures, pp. 920–922. "La Ronde" infers just that. In the minds of American motion picture producers, then, such a picture as is now before us would tend to "lower the moral standards of those who see it." Code of Production Standards, "General Principles"[1].

We think it plain that we cannot say that the Regents were wrong in refusing the license herein. It has been suggested that we should form an independent judgment as to each picture which might become the subject of controversy between the distributor and the Regents, but that would simply mean that the powers granted to the Regents by statute could be arrogated to this court by judicial action. In the scheme of things, there must be some agency to which is entrusted the fact-finding power. In criminal cases it is the jury; in matters of administration generally, it is the administrative agency; in motion picture review, it is the Regents. No constitutional argument can be presented for having it otherwise. If the Regents err in law, we sit to correct them. If they must exercise their fact-finding powers in a close case and do so honestly and fairly, then due process has been observed. See Nash v. United States, 229 U.S. 373, 377, 33 S.Ct. 780, 57 L.Ed. 1232.

It is not for us to question the wisdom of placing that fact-finding power in the hands of the Regents rather than the courts. Neither do we think any such debate could be very productive, for strong and persuasive arguments can be made to the effect that an experienced administrative body is better qualified than a court to judge the effect of a particular motion picture, and that we of the judicial branch should not be left "at liberty to substitute our judgment for theirs, or to supersede their function as the spokesmen of the thought and sentiment of the community in applying to the [motion picture] * * * the standard of propriety established by the statute", People v. Pesky, supra, 254 N.Y. at pages 373–374, 173 N.E. at page 227.

In summary, we conclude that motion pictures may be censored, upon proper grounds, and that sexual immorality is one such ground. The standard "immoral" and "tend to corrupt morals" embodied in the statute and here applied relates to sexual immorality, and the Regents had the right to find that the motion picture in question falls within the prohibited category.

The order appealed from should be affirmed, with costs.

DESMOND, Judge (concurring).

I concur for affirmance.

We review the refusal by the Board of Regents of the State of New York, acting under sections 120 and 122 of the State Education Law, to license the exhibition in New York State of the motion picture "La Ronde". Section 122 directs that every submitted motion picture film be licensed "unless such film or a part thereof is obscene, indecent, immoral, inhuman, sacrilegious, or is of such a character that its exhibition would tend to corrupt morals or incite to crime". The stated ground for the Regents' refusal here was that "La Ronde" was "immoral and tended to corrupt morals". The film depicts a series of illicit sexual adventures, nothing more, and is a close adaptation, for the screen, from Schnitzler's novel "Reigen" which translated into English as "Hands Around", was held to be criminally obscene in People v. Pesky, 230 App.Div. 200, 243 N.Y.S. 193, affirmed 254 N.Y. 373, 173 N.E. 227. We have seen this motion picture, and while we agree with appellant's counsel that it "has a distinguished cast and a brilliant production", we find, too, that its only discoverable theme is this: that everyone is sexually promiscuous, and that life is just a "round" of sexual promiscuity. It would be understatement to apply to this photoplay the characterization given another film in Eureka Productions v. Byrne, 252 App. Div. 355, 357, 300 N.Y.S. 218, 221, that it "unduly emphasizes the carnal side of the sex relationship". This picture has no other content.

On this appeal, it seems to us, these three questions of law are to be answered, and in this order:

1. Is all pre-censorship of motion pictures violative of the First Amendment to the Federal Constitution?

2. If not, is the New York statute unconstitutional, for lack of precise standards, at the point where it permits the banning of a picture on a charge that it is "immoral" or "tends to corrupt morals"?

3. If questions 1 and 2 are both answered in the negative, was there reasonable basis here for the Regents' finding that "La Ronde" is immoral and tends to corrupt morals?

Our answers are these:

1. The New York State's motion picture censorship statute was enacted in 1921, L. 1921, ch. 715, was held constitutional by this court in 1923, Pathe Exch. v. Cobb, 236 N.Y. 539, 142 N.E. 274, and, except as to its use of "sacrilegious" as one of its standards, has never been held invalid. Our law, under which thousands of pictures have been licensed or denied licenses, is typical of the eight State statutes and perhaps seventy-five municipal ordinances that have made their appearance since the first such enactment: the Chicago ordinance of 1907, Block v. City of Chicago, 239 Ill. 251, 87 N.E. 1011. In the Federal courts, such censorship statutes were, beginning about 1915, held not to contravene the First Amendment, which, it was at that time held, did not apply to motion pictures, since the exhibition thereof was then regarded as a mere part of the business of providing entertainment in theatres, see Mutual Film Corp. v. Ohio Ind. Comm., 236 U.S. 230, 35 S.Ct. 387, 59 L.Ed. 552; Mutual Film Co. v. Ohio Ind. Comm., 236 U.S. 247, 35 S.Ct. 393, 59 L.Ed. 561; Mutual Film Corp. of Missouri v. Hodges, 236 U.S. 248, 35 S.Ct. 393, 59 L.Ed. 561. There were numerous similar holdings in various Federal and State courts. Appreciating the delicacy of the questions inherent in all censorship, but realizing, too, the danger, especially to the immature, of the free showing of demoralizing films (New York since 1909 has, for instance, limited attendance of children at motion picture theatres—see Penal Law, § 484, subd. 1), this sovereign State put the licensing power in one of its most powerful and most respected governmental bodies, the Board of Regents, a "citizens' board" which is at the head of the State's educational system. Censorship in New York is, therefore, carried on at the highest levels of responsible State Government.

In 1951, this court re-examined, in Matter of Joseph Burstyn, Inc. v. Wilson, 303 N.Y. 242, 101 N.E.2d 665, the question of the constitutionality of pre-censorship of films, and found no reason to change our earlier decision. Later, the Supreme Court of the United States, in the same Burstyn case, 343 U.S. 495, 72 S.Ct. 777, 96 L.Ed. 1098, decided for the first time (it has intimated this result in 1948 in United States v. Paramount Pictures, 334 U.S. 131, 166, 68 S.Ct. 915, 92 L.Ed. 1260), that expression by means of motion pictures is included within the free speech and free press guarantee of the First and Fourteenth Amendments. Going further, the highest court held that the word "sacrilegious" provided no valid test or standard, since it subjected films to "conflicting currents of religious views" supra, 343 U.S. at page 504, 72 S.Ct. at page 782. But the Supreme Court found it unnecessary, in Burstyn, to decide whether a State may censor motion pictures under a clearly drawn statute designed and applied to prevent, for instance, the showing of obscene films. 343

U.S. at pages 505–506, 72 S.Ct. 777. Thus the Burstyn decision, while it ruled out "sacrilegious" as a permissible censoring standard, certainly did not strike down, completely, the police power of the States to pre-censor motion pictures. "It does not follow" said the court, supra, 343 U.S. at page 502, 72 S.Ct. at page 781, "that the Constitution requires absolute freedom to exhibit every motion picture of every kind at all times and all places." Historically, of course, the First Amendment has never provided immunity for every possible use of language. Robertson v. Baldwin, 165 U.S. 275, 281, 17 S.Ct. 326, 41 L.Ed. 715; Frohwerk v. United States, 249 U.S. 204, 206, 39 S.Ct. 249, 63 L.Ed. 561.

The constitutional doctrine which forbids pre-censorship of the press, Near v. State of Minnesota ex rel. Olson, 283 U.S. 697, 51 S.Ct. 625, 75 L.Ed. 1357, expresses, primarily, the insistence of the American people that the publication of ideas and opinions, expecially as to governments, public officers, and public questions should not be restrained here, as they had been elsewhere. See Patterson v. State of Colorado, 205 U.S. 454, 464, 465, 27 S.Ct. 556, 51 L.Ed. 879. And the doctrine itself has been subject always to an exception, as to publications which tend to corrupt morals or incite to crime or vice. See People v. Gitlow, 234 N.Y. 132, 136 N.E. 317; People v. Most, 171 N.Y. 423, 431, 64 N.E. 175, 178; Pathe Exch. v. Cobb, 202 App.Div. 450, 195 N.Y.S. 661, affirmed 236 N.Y. 539, 142 N.E. 274, supra; Patterson v. State of Colorado, 205 U.S. 454, 27 S.Ct. 556, 51 L.Ed. 879, supra; Schenck v. United States, 249 U.S. 47, 39 S.Ct. 247, 63 L.Ed. 470; Gitlow v. New York, 268 U.S. 652, 666, 45 S.Ct. 625, 69 L.Ed. 1138; People v. Croswell, 1804, 3 Johns.Cas. 337, 392; Cooley on Constitutional Limitations [7th ed.], pp. 604–605. That exception usually finds application in postpunishment rather than precensorship, but the system of distribution and showing of motion pictures makes it feasible, if not necessary, to examine and license or refuse to license them before exhibition to audiences. We realize, as does everyone else, and as did the Supreme Court in 1915 in Mutual Film Corp. v. Ohio Ind. Comm., supra, and in 1952 in Joseph Burstyn, Inc., v. Wilson, supra, that motion pictures have vast potentialities for evil, and we know, as practical people, that there is no effective way to suppress the damaging ones except by a system of censorship, see Superior Films v. Department of Educ., 1953, 159 Ohio St. 315, 112 N.E.2d 311. "Justification for upholding a censorship statute couched in indefinite terms may lie in the interest to be protected and not in semantics" 37 Minn.L.Rev., p. 211. So, unless and until so constrained by higher judicial authority, we will not say that the police power of our State cannot be used to keep such evil from our people.

2. Next, we answer the question as to the sufficiency, as a standard for licensing, of the statutory language: "immoral" and "tend to corrupt morals". We know that "immoral" is rather a sweeping term, of large and perhaps not mathematically delimited meaning, but we know, too, that if statutes could use only scientifically exact terminology, much of our statute law would be invalid. Words and phrases like "moral", "immoral", "good moral character", "impairing morals", etc., abound in New York statutes. See, for instance, Social Welfare Law, McK.Consol. Laws, c. 55 § 448; Penal Law, §§ 483, 485–a, 486, 494, 580, subd. 6; §§ 1140–a, 1141, 1141–a, 1145, 1147, 1148, 1933; Education Law, §§ 2212, 3012, 3013, 3020, 6804;

General Business Law, §§ 190, 191; Agriculture and Markets Law, McK.Consol. Laws, c. 69, §§ 57, 57—a, and zoning statutes such as Village Law, McK.Consol. Laws, c. 64, § 175, and Town Law, McK.Consol. Laws, c. 62, § 261. In some of those statutes, the verbiage, because of context, limits itself to sexual morals—not so here, we think. Sexual impurity is only one form of immorality. See Swearingen v. United States, 161 U.S. 446, 451, 16 S.Ct. 562, 40 L.Ed. 765. This picture "La Ronde" could be classed as "immoral" in the narrower sense, too, but the statutory meaning here is the usual or dictionary one (including the law dictionaries), and its reference is to the generally accepted civilized code of morals—its prohibition is of material *"contra bonos mores"*. That, too, is the clearly intended meaning in several other censorship statutes. Block v. City of Chicago, 239 Ill. 251, 264, 87 N.E. 1011, supra; People ex rel. First Nat. Pictures v. Dever, 242 Ill. App. 1; Schuman v. Pickert, 277 Mich. 225, 229, 269 N.W. 152; see United States v. One Obscene Book Entitled "Married Love", D.C., 48 F.2d 821, 823. If it meant, in our statute, sexually vicious only, the word "immoral" would be tautological and repetitious, since it is there coupled with "obscene" and "indecent". And why should our Legislature have placed a ban on one kind, only, of immorality? "Immoral" (or its antonym "moral") is a listed standard in at least five (besides New York) State motion picture censorship laws (those of Pennsylvania, Ohio, Virginia, Kansas, Maryland). Indeed, the very word "moral" in the Ohio law was taken in its usual broad sense and held to be sufficiently definite for these purposes, in Mutual Film Corp. v. Ohio Ind. Comm. in these words, 236 U.S. 230, 245—246, 35 S.Ct. 392, supra: "The objection to the statute is that it furnishes no standard of what is educational, moral, amusing, or harmless, and hence leaves decision to arbitrary judgment, whim, and caprice * * * . But the statute by its provisions guards against such variant judgments, and its terms, like other general terms, get precision from the sense and experience of men, and become certain and useful guides in reasoning and conduct. The exact specification of the instances of their application would be as impossible as the attempt would be futile. Upon such sense and experience, therefore, the law properly relies." We think the Supreme Court there must have read "moral" in the meaning we give it here, and the Supreme Court there pointed out that, unless words of such seeming generality were valid in statutes, government itself would become impossible. There can be no objection to the use, in a statute, of a word like "immoral" which includes many things, all of which are intended by the Legislature to be covered; otherwise, there would be barred from statutory use such customary verbiage as "fraudulent", "due", "negligent", "arbitrary", "reasonable", etc. Legislatures use such words, not "vaguely" but inclusively. That a word has many meanings, one or more of which are definitely pointed up by the surrounding verbiage, is no more reason for barring its use than if the word had one meaning only. It is too late to change the common usage of the word "immoral", or to ascribe absurdity to it, so as to invalidate a statute. Although the Supreme Court, in Burstyn, supra, reversed that part of the Mutual Film Corp, holding which deals with the free speech question, Mutual's rule as to the propriety of "moral" or "immoral", as a motion picture censorship standard in Ohio remains undisturbed, so far as we know. So the Ohio Supreme Court pointed out, on April 29, 1953, in Superior Films v. Department of Educ. (159 Ohio St. 315, 112 N.E.2d 311, supra).

Long ago our court, Lyon v. Mitchell, 36 N.Y. 235, 238, approved definitions of "morality" as " 'that science which teaches men their duty, and the reason of it' " and as " 'the rule which teaches us to live soberly and honestly. It hath four chief virtues, justice, prudence, temperance and fortitude' ". In that opinion, in 1867, our great predecessors on this bench wrote that: "Sound morals, as taught by the wise men of antiquity, as confirmed by the precepts of the gospel * * * are unchangeable. They are the same yesterday and today." We see no reason to retreat from those ideas. "We are a religious people whose institutions presuppose a Supreme Being", Zorach v. Clauson, 343 U.S. 306, 313, 72 S.Ct. 679, 684, 96 L.Ed. 954. Our Federal and State Constitutions assume that the moral code, which is part of God's order in this world, exists as the substance of society. The people of this State have acted through their Legislature, on that assumption. We have not so cast ourselves adrift from that code, nor are we so far gone in cynicism, that the word "immoral" has no meaning for us. Our duty, as a court, is to uphold and enforce the laws, not seek reasons for destroying them.

3. If there be validity, to our answers above numbered 1 and 2, we will have no difficulty with the third question, that is, as to whether the Regents were justified in finding that "La Ronde" is immoral, and tends to corrupt morals. It is of no pertinence here that great literature of all ages, including the Sacred Scriptures, abounds with descriptions of rapes, fornications and adulteries. The difference here is that the whole theme, motif and subject matter of this film, its dominant and sole effect, is sexual immorality. The totality of it, and every part of it, is sexual immorality. The point is not that it depicts immoral conduct—it glorifies and romanticizes it, and conveys the idea that it is universal and inevitable. Are we as a court to say as matter of law that it does not thus "tend to corrupt morals"? This court should hold that the State of New York may prevent the publication of such matter, the obvious tendency of which is "to deprave or corrupt those whose minds are open to such immoral influences, and who might come into contact with it." People v. Muller, 96 N.Y. 408, 411, following Regina v. Hicklin, L.R. 3 Q.B. 360, 369—370; See People v. Doubleday & Co., 297 N.Y. 687, 77 N.E.2d 6, affirmed 335 U.S. 848, 69 S.Ct. 79, 93 L.Ed. 398; United States v. Dennett, 2 Cir., 39 F.2d 564, 76 A.L.R. 1092; United States v. Levine, 2 Cir., 83 F.2d 156. Such is the valid State policy and purpose, and we enforce it by affirming the Regents' determination.

The order should be affirmed, with costs.

CONWAY, Judge (concurring).

I am in entire accord with the opinion of Judge FROESSEL but believe that we may properly go further and therefore I fully agree also with the view stated by Judge DESMOND in his concurring opinion.

DYE, Judge (dissenting).

By the decision about to be made a majority of this court approves as a valid enactment, the New York motion picture licensing statute, notwithstanding that it provides for censorship in advance, which as we read it, constitutes an infringement of the basic civil right of freedom of speech and publication contrary to due process. U.S.Const. 1st, 5th, 14th Amends.; N.Y.Const. art. I, §§ 6, 8; Education Law, § 122. I must therefore record my dissent.

The question arises out of the refusal of the State Board of Regents to approve the issuance of a license to permit the showing of the motion picture film "La Ronde" for the reason, couched in the language of the statute, "that the said film is 'immoral' and that its exhibition 'would tend to corrupt morals' within the meaning of Section 122 of the Education Law."

The case is before us in an appeal as of right from an order of the Appellate Division, Third Judicial Department, entered in a proceeding under article 78 of the Civil Practice Act, at the instance of this appellant, Education Law, § 124, and heard by the Appellate Division in the first instance. Civil Practice Act, § 1296. When the petitioner, a California corporation and sole owner of the distribution rights of the said picture in the United States, first applied for an exhibitor's license, Education Law, §§ 120–122, the director of the motion picture division refused it on the ground that the picture was "immoral" and "would tend to corrupt morals". Following established practice in such circumstances, the petitioner re-edited the film and re-submitted its application, but even so the director again refused to issue a license. A review of his determination was then had before a three-man committee of the State Board of Regents, Education Law, § 124, which, after viewing the picture, as we have said, confirmed the director's determination. In the court below the confirmation of the determination and the dismissal of the proceedings was on the ground that the applicable statute was a valid enactment and that confirmation was required under familiar doctrine limiting the function of a reviewing court whenever there is "warrant in the record and a reasonable basis in law" for the board's determination. In other words if the issue is debatable, the action of the administrative body is to be upheld. Mounting & Finishing Co. v. McGoldrick, 294 N.Y. 104, 60 N.E.2d 825. However correct that may be as a rule of thumb in the review of administrative cases turning on a controverted issue of fact, it is inapplicable in a case involving fundamental civil rights secured by the State and Federal Constitutions for then a determination must be so clear, as the dissenting Judges in the court below observed, "that any conclusion to the contrary would not be entertained by any reasonable mind. It is wholly inconsistent with a constitutional guarantee to leave any debatable issue of morals, involved in any form of protected expression, to the final decision of an administrative agency." Commercial Pictures Corp. v. Board of Regents, 280 App.Div. 260, 265, 114 N.Y.S.2d 561, 566. In such a situation "the reviewing court is bound to re-examine the whole record" in the light of the challenge made, Joseph Burstyn, Inc., v. Wilson, 343 U.S. 495, 72 S.Ct. 777, 96 L.Ed. 1098; Universal Camera Corp. v. National Labor Relations Bd., 340 U.S. 474, 71 S.Ct. 456, 95 L.Ed. 456; Niemotko v. Maryland, 340 U.S. 268, 71 S.Ct. 325, 328, 95 L.Ed. 267, 280; Norris v. Alabama, 294 U.S. 587, 55 S.Ct. 579, 79 L.Ed. 1074.

Since the decision in Joseph Burstyn, Inc., v. Wilson, 343 U.S. 495, 72 S.Ct. 777, 96 L.Ed. 1098, supra, reversing 303 N.Y. 242, 101 N.E.2d 665, there is no longer any doubt but that motion picture films enjoy the same constitutional freedom and protection accorded other media of human expression, cf. United States v. Paramount Pictures, 334 U.S. 131, 68 S.Ct. 915, 92 L.Ed. 1260; Stromberg v. California, 283 U.S. 359, 51 S.Ct. 532, 75 L.Ed. 117, and this is so even though motion pictures as such are primarily designed to entertain at exhibitions conducted for private profit and even though motion picture films as such possess "a greater capacity for evil, particularly among the youth of a community, than other modes of expression", Burstyn, supra, 343 U.S. at page 502, 72 S.Ct. at page 780.

In the Burstyn case, supra, the Board of Regents had refused a license to show the motion picture entitled "The Miracle" on the ground that it was "sacrilegious" within the meaning of section 122 of the Education Law. When the case was in this court we approved such determination in reliance on the validity of regulation by prior censorship in accordance with our decision in Pathe Exch. v. Cobb, 236 N.Y. 539, 142 N.E. 274, affirming 202 App. Div. 450, 195 N.Y.S. 661. That decision, in turn, had followed Mutual Film Corp. v. Ohio Ind. Comm., 236 U.S. 230, 35 S.Ct. 387, 59 L.Ed. 552, Mutual Film Co. v. Ohio Ind. Comm., 236 U.S. 247, 35 S.Ct. 393, 59 L.Ed. 561, and Mutual Film Corp. v. Hodges, 236 U.S. 248, 35 S.Ct. 393, 59 L.Ed. 561, in which the United States Supreme Court had approved as a valid enactment in Ohio, a pre-censorship statute.

We note that in deciding the Burstyn case supra, 343 U.S. at page 505–506, 72 S.Ct. 777, 783, the United States Supreme Court found it unnecessary to pass on the issue of prior censorship preferring to leave such question until presented "under a clearly drawn statute designed and applied to prevent the showing of obscene films" since the term "sacrilegious", the sole standard under attack, afforded an adequate basis for reversal. Nonetheless, that is not to say the learned court was unmindful of the iniquity of prior restraint which (in the field of publication) they long before had ruled, 343 U.S. at page 503, 72 S.Ct. 781, was an "infringement upon freedom of expression to be especially condemned." Thomas v. Collins, 323 U.S. 516, 65 S.Ct. 315, 89 L.Ed. 430; Lovell v. City of Griffin, 303 U.S. 444, 58 S.Ct. 666, 82 L.Ed. 949; Grosjean v. American Press Co., 297 U.S. 233, 56 S.Ct. 444, 80 L.Ed. 660; Near v. State of Minnesota, 283 U.S. 697, 51 S.Ct. 625, 75 L.Ed. 1357; Patterson v. State of Colorado, 205 U.S. 454, 27 S.Ct. 556, 51 L.Ed. 879.

Since the courts no longer see any distinction separating motion picture film from the protection accorded other media of communication, it follows as a matter of reason and logic that prior censorship of motion pictures is as to them as it is in other fields of expression, a denial of due process. In saying this we are, of course, mindful of the correlative obligation that in its exercise and enjoyment such right is not unlimited and absolute at all times and under all circumstances, Chaplinsky v. New Hampshire, 315 U.S. 568, 62 S.Ct. 766, 86 L.Ed. 1031; Cox v. New Hampshire, 312 U.S. 569, 61 S.Ct. 762, 85 L.Ed. 1049, but that such freedom may properly be restrained when inimical to the public welfare, Gitlow v. New York, 268 U.S. 652, 45 S.Ct. 625, 69 L.Ed. 1138, and the State may punish its abuse, Near v. Minnesota, supra. It is equally well established that before such limitation may be imposed the abuse complained of is to be examined in all cases to determine whether it is of such a nature "as to create a clear and present danger [and] will bring about the substantive evils that Congress has a right to prevent", Schenck v. United States, 249 U.S. 47, 52, 39 S.Ct. 247, 249, 63 L.Ed. 470, which danger should be "apparent and imminent" Thornhill v. Alabama, 310 U.S. 88, 60 S.Ct. 736, 84 L.Ed. 1093, such, for example, as a threat to overthrow the government by unconstitutional means, Dennis v. United States, 341 U.S. 494, 71 S.Ct. 857, 95

L.Ed. 1137. By the same token, when public safety is involved, its restraint will be approved as a proper exercise of the police power, Feiner v. People of State of New York, 340 U.S. 315, 71 S.Ct. 303, 95 L.Ed. 267, affirming 300 N.Y. 391, 91 N.E.2d 316; Kovacs v. Cooper, 336 U.S. 77, 69 S.Ct. 448, 93 L.Ed. 513, or, to state it differently, there must be present some "overriding public interest" (see dissenting opinion per Fuld, J., in Joseph Burstyn, Inc., v. Wilson, supra, 303 N.Y. at page 269, 101 N.E.2d at page 679; Thornhill v. Alabama, supra), mere fear of possible injury is not enough. Terminiello v. Chicago, 337 U.S. 1, 69 S.Ct. 894, 93 L.Ed. 1131.

Having in mind these well-recognized principles, it is pertinent to inquire what if anything there is about "La Ronde" that requires denial of constitutional safeguards and the imposition of the sanction of prior restraint. Is it because a showing would offend against some overriding need—would constitute a danger clear and present? We think not.

According to the record, the picture "La Ronde" since its admission through Customs without objection. U.S.Code, tit. 18, § 1462; U.S.C.A. tit. 19, § 1305, has been exhibited throughout the United States in cities and towns in the States of Arizona, California, Colorado, Connecticut, Delaware, Florida, Kentucky, Louisiana, Maine, Massachusetts, Michigan, Missouri, New Jersey, Oklahoma, Oregon, Texas and Washington, D.C. Nowhere had the showing of "La Ronde" been banned except in New York. While experience elsewhere is not binding on the courts in New York, the opinions of qualified critics may be considered. United States v. One Book Entitled Ulysses, 2 Cir., 72 F.2d 705. We deem it significant that in the States of Louisiana, LSA–R.S. tit. 4, §§ 301–307, and Massachusetts, Mass.Ann.Law, ch. 136 §§ 2–4, having censorship laws, though to be sure, not as comprehensive as that in New York, the picture has had an unhampered showing as well as in places where municipal codes are in effect such as Detroit, Michigan; Salem, Oregon and Houston, Texas, to mention a few, a circumstance indicating that in a large segment of society the picture is not offensive per se. Such a showing in other States and cities of this country, where prior restraint was available and not invoked, and elsewhere having no such statutes, all without untoward incident or complaint is a convincing testimonial that it is not inimical to the public peace, welfare and safety. On the contrary, we are told that the showing elsewhere has been well received and has elicited favorable acclaim by the premier dramatic critics of eminent publications in which we may read:

"La Ronde is all of a piece, as any round should be, setting up a mocking harmony of desire and disillusion, vanity, pleasure and deceit. It is never prurient, smirking or pornographic. For all the intimacy of its nuances, the film's approach is dryly detached and completely charming; it spoofs sex rather than exploits it, much as Britain's satiric Kind Hearts and Coronets makes sport of murder." Time Magaine, Oct. 22, 1951.

"Here is a lovely motion picture, a gay, a glad, a sad, a sentimental movie * * about Vienna at the turn of the century, the Vienna of candlelight and carriages, of wine, women and waltzes. * * * All this is told with a combination of irony, candor and gentleness that makes of the whole a total gem of a motion picture. * * * a picture about illicit love, but it is told without prudishness and with a deftness, discretion and understanding that make it more moral than most censor-shackled pictures on the subject." Daily News, Los Angeles, Sept. 21, 1951.

"The players * * * are among the cream of French talent and virtually flawless here." Los Angeles Times, Sept. 21, 1951.

"The * * * players * * * represent the cream of France's romantic actors." The Evening Star, Washington, D.C., July 28, 1951.

" * * * a splendid and glittering cast that includes Anton Walbrook, Gerard Philipe, Isa Miranda, Dannielle Darrieux, Daniel Gelin, Simone Simon, Jean-Louis Barrault, Fernand Gravet, and Odette Joveux. * * * their portrayals have that quality of nuance that makes a second viewing almost obligatory. * * * Through the strata of a world-weary Viennese society the story spirals, until we find we have arrived at much the same point from which we have begun. It's more sad than bitter, more ironic than funny, and there's some haunting little message underneath it all, though, to be sure, you are never quite told what it is. * * * delicately done and in excellent taste." Saturday Review of Literature, Nov. 10, 1951.

In addition, it has been shown in the principal cities of most foreign countries and has received special recognition for merit from several motion picture academies as, for instance, in Cuba as the best film of 1951, by the British Film Academy in London as the best film from any source, British or foreign, and in 1952, a nomination for an award at the Hollywood Academy.

Nonetheless if it may be said that prior censorship serves a necessary and needful public purpose warranting the abridgement of the right of free speech and press, it remains for the statute under review to meet the test of definiteness required to constitute a valid delegation of legislative power to an administrative agency. Unless it does so, it cannot be regarded as the "clearly drawn statute" envisioned by the Supreme Court, Burstyn, supra, 343 U.S. at page 506, 72 S.Ct. at page 783; Kunz v. New York, 340 U.S. 290, 71 S.Ct. 312, 95 L.Ed. 280; Winters v. New York, 333 U.S. 507, 68 S.Ct. 665, 92 L.Ed. 840; Connally v. General Constr. Co., 269 U.S. 385, 46 S.Ct. 126, 70 L.Ed. 322; Small Co. v. American Sugar Ref. Co., 267 U.S. 233, 45 S.Ct. 295, 69 L.Ed. 589; United States v. L. Cohen Grocery Co., 255 U.S. 81, 41 S.Ct. 298, 65 L.Ed. 516, and we too apply such principle whenever needed. Packer Collegiate Inst. v. University of State of N.Y., 298 N.Y. 184, 81 N.E.2d 80; Fink v. Cole, 302 N.Y. 216, 97 N.E.2d 873; Small v. Moss, 279 N.Y. 288, 18 N.E.2d 281.

It is indeed significant that when the Legislature enacted the censorship statute under review it omitted to provide any criteria or standards to guide the Board of Regents in performing the administrative functions required of it, but was content to use language of broad and general import leaving its meaning and application to the individual judgment of its director of the motion picture division in the first instance, § 122, or if denied, to a committee of three members of the board, § 124.

Indefiniteness affords opportunity for arbitrariness, the tendency to which is nowhere better illustrated than in the field of administrative law. It is for this reason that delegation of legislative power is carefully scrutinized, whether to a private agency, Fink v. Cole, supra, or to a governmental agency, Packer Collegiate Inst. v. University of State of N.Y., supra; Small v. Moss, supra. If this is not enough, then the board itself has been equally delinquent in failing to adopt rules and regulations for the guidance of its motion picture division in the exercise of censorship powers, but has left the generality of the statutory language to gain precision "from sense and experience" Mutual Film cases, supra, a method no longer approved, Burstyn, and is particularly objectionable here as it vests unlimited restraining control over motion pictures in a censor limited only by what an individual director of the motion picture division or, upon review, by what three members of the board itself happen to think about a particular picture at a given time, cf. Winters v. New York, supra; Gelling v. Texas, 343 U.S. 960, 72 S.Ct. 1002, 96 L.Ed. 1359. Such lack, it goes without saying, leaves an appellate court at a very great disadvantage. We do not know what standards guided the agency in making its determination. To supply such legislative omission by judicial fiat is not permissible under the division of governmental powers as fixed by the Constitution. It has long been recognized that courts may not usurp the legislative function under the guise of adjudication. The evils of allowing an administrative agency, however worthy its purpose, to function without proper legislative guidance is well illustrated by this very case. The lack of proper standards and guidance has led the State Board of Regents into a most surprising record of inconsistency and illustrates at first hand the evils of slap-dash censorship. For instance, we do not know whether they apply the terms "immoral" and "tend to corrupt morals" to pictures dealing with sex impurity or to pictures dealing with any matter which could be deemed *contra bonos mores*. Here we have a picture which, concededly, is not obscene or indecent but which nonetheless is banned from a New York showing because deemed "immoral" and its exhibition "would tend to corrupt morals" which is difficult to reconcile with the issuance of permits to show other pictures dealing not only with illicit love but also crime, such as Dreiser's "American Tragedy" (based on People v. Gillette, 191 N.Y. 107, 83 N.E. 680), "A Street Car Named Desire" and "The Outlaw", and those of a lurid type whose blow-up posters call attention to "Outcast Girls", "Female Sex", "Naked Realism". The case at hand is the only instance brought to our attention where denial has been based solely on the term "immoral" which the Regents applied because "promiscuity" is the central theme. True, the term "immoral" has been used in numerous other instances but always, we note, in juxtaposition with the word "obscene" or "indecent". The term "obscene" as used in the criminal statutes, has been interpreted in the United States Supreme Court as meaning the subject matter must be of a "lewd, lascivious, and obscene tendency, calculated to corrupt and debauch the minds and morals of those into whose hands it might fall", Swearingen v. United States, 161 U.S. 446, 451, 16 S.Ct. 562, 564, 40 L.Ed. 765, and in our own court we have said that the test of an obscene book is whether "the tendency of the matter charged as obscenity is to deprave or corrupt those whose minds are open to such immoral influences, and who might come into contact with it", People v. Muller, 96 N.Y. 408, 411, following Regina v. Hicklin, L.R. 3 Q.B. 360, 369–370; People v. Doubleday & Co., 297 N.Y. 687, 77 N.E.2d 6, affirmed 335 U.S. 848, 69 S.Ct. 79, 93 L.Ed. 398.

The term "immoral" when not connected with "obscene"—and here it is not—for indeed the motion picture "La Ronde" was not banned upon the ground of obscenity—has a variety of meanings varying according to time, geography and to some extent, subjective judgment. Cardozo, Paradoxes of Legal Science; Foy Productions v. Graves, 253 App.Div. 475, 3 N.Y.S.2d 573; Parmelee v. United States, 72 App.D.C. 203, 113 F.2d 729; United States v. Kennerley, D.C., 209 F. 119. The lexicographers have defined "immoral" as the opposite of moral (Oxford Dictionary) which term may and does include illicit sexual behavior (Funk & Wagnalls) but the meaning is not limited to sex impurity but includes in addition offenses hostile "to public welfare," Black's Law Dictionary, "inimical to rights or * * * interests of others", "corrupt", "depraved" and sometimes "unprofessional" conduct or, 42 C.J.S., pp. 395–396, to state it broadly, anything *contra bonos mores*.

Resort to the criminal statutes dealing with obscenity and the cases construing such statutes are of little help in solving our present problem for here we deal with a licensing statute authorizing restraint in advance. In the one we deal with evidentiary requirements sufficient to support the conviction beyond "reasonable doubt" while in the other when the issue is debatable "some" evidence is sufficient. In the one the proof must meet the standards of the hearsay rule to assure competency, relevance and materiality while in the other formal rules of evidence may be dispensed with entirely. Criminal statutes are designed to apprise the citizen of what constitutes an offense against society in advance of the fact. The term "immoral" as used in this pre-censorship statute, without more, affords little help in advising the citizen of what constitutes a violating offense. All that the petitioner has to guide him here is the circumstance that wherever shown in the United States, except New York, the picture "La Ronde" does not offend.

To strike the term "immoral" and the words "tend to corrupt morals" from the statute as indefinite and undefinable will work no serious result. For years New York State has had statutes dealing with obscenity and indecency broad enough to sanction "after the fact" criminal prosecution and punishment, application of which has successfully regulated the publication and sale of books and periodicals without prior censorship, Penal Law, §§ 1141; cf. Winters v. New York, supra, as well as statutes sanctioning the punishment of persons presenting obscene, indecent, immoral or impure drama, plays or exhibition shows or entertainment. Penal Law, § 1140–a.

In addition, the word "obscene", when compared with the word "immoral" has a clear and authoritative judicial definition. The Federal standard is whether the book taken as a whole has a "libidinous effect", Hannegan v. Esquire, Inc., 327 U.S. 146, 66 S.Ct. 456, 90 L.Ed. 586; United States v. One Book Entitled Ulysses, 2 Cir., 72 F.2d 705, supra. In New York the test is "whether the tendency of the [work] is to excite lustful and lecherous desire." People v. Wendling, 258 N.Y. 451, 453, 180 N.E. 169, 81 A.L.R. 799; People v. Eastman, 188 N.Y. 478, 480, 81 N.E. 459, 460; People v. Muller, supra. Under this definition "La Ronde" is certainly not "obscene". It has been condemned only on the ground that it is "immoral" and that its presentation "would tend to corrupt morals". The statute sets up no standard defining the term "immoral" and, unlike the word "obscenity" in the criminal statutes, there are no judicial opinions which set forth a workable guide for the censor. As the dissenting opinion in the Appellate Division noted 280 App.Div. at page 266, 114 N.Y.S.2d at page 566, "La Ronde", according to the Regents, "deals with illicit love, usually regarded as immoral. But so is murder. The theme alone does not furnish a valid ground for previous restraint. As to its presentation corrupting the morals of the public, this issue is highly debatable. The record indicates a vast body of informed opinion to the contrary. Under such circumstances the action of the Regents impinges on petitioner's constitutional right of free expression." Since reasonable men may differ on the import and effect of "La Ronde", it follows that there is not a "clear and present danger" sufficiently imminent to override the protection of the United States Constitution, Thornhill v. Alabama, supra, 310 U.S. at page 105, 60 S.Ct. 736.

Under all the circumstances, and this includes the inconsistency between the varying views expressed in the opinions for affirmance herein, we deem the terms "immoral" and "tend to corrupt morals" as used in the statute to be so indefinite as to require reversal here. Indefiniteness in motion picture censorship statutes was condemned in Burstyn, supra, and later in Gelling v. Texas, 343 U.S. 960, 72 S.Ct. 1002, 96 L.Ed. 1359, supra. There the United States Supreme Court dealt with an ordinance of the city of Marshall, Texas, which authorized a local board of censors to deny permission to the showing of a motion picture when, in the opinion of the board, it was "of such character as to be prejudicial to the best interests of the people of said City"—inartistic language to be sure, but nonetheless having an intent to restrain the showing of motion pictures inimical to the public interest. Two Justices wrote concurring opinions that elucidate the bare Per Curiam for reversal, Mr. Justice Frankfurter seeing offense to the Fourteenth Amendment on the score of indefiniteness, citing Burstyn and Winters, while Mr. Justice Douglas said, 343 U.S. at page 961, 72 S.Ct. at page 1002: "The evil of prior restraint, condemned by Near v. [State of] Minnesota, 283 U.S. 697, 51 S.Ct. 625, 75 L.Ed. 1357, in the case of newspapers and by [Joseph] Burstyn, Inc., v. Wilson, 343 U.S. 495, 72 S.Ct. 777 [96 L.Ed. 1098], in the case of motion pictures, is present here in flagrant form. If a board of censors can tell the American people what it is in their best interests to see or to read or to hear (cf. Public Utilities Comm. [of District of Columbia] v. Pollak, 343 U.S. 451, 72 S.Ct. 816 [96 L.Ed. 1068]), then thought is regimented, authority substituted for liberty, and the great purpose of the First Amendment to keep uncontrolled the freedom of expression defeated."

This thought is not new for indeed thirty years ago a distinguished Governor of this State in his message to the Legislature recommending repeal of an almost identical censorship statute, L.1921, ch. 715, § 5, had this to say: "Censorship is not in keeping with our ideas of liberty and of freedom of worship or freedom of speech. The people of the State themselves have declared that every citizen may freely speak, write and publish his sentiments on all subjects, being responsible for the abuse of that right, and no law shall be passed to restrain or abridge liberty of speech or of the press. This fundamental principle has equal application to all methods of expression." Public Papers of Alfred E. Smith [1923], pp. 60, 61.

As has been said in a great variety of ways, we deem the evil complained of here is far less dangerous to the community than the danger flowing from the suppression of clear constitutional protection. In our zeal to regulate by requiring licenses in advance we are prone to forget the struggle behind our free institutions. We must keep in mind on all occasions that beneficent aims however laudable and well directed can never serve in lieu of constitutional powers, Carter v. Carter Coal Co., 298 U.S. 238, 56 S.Ct. 855, 80 L.Ed. 1160, for as was said in Lovell v. City of Griffin, 303 U.S. 444, 451, 58 S.Ct. 666, 669, 82 L.Ed. 949, supra, "The struggle for the freedom of the press was primarily directed against the power of the licensor."

It is no answer to say that the exhibition of motion pictures has a potential for evil which can not be successfully dealt with except by censorship in advance. Such a conclusion overlooks the very significant circumstance that other media of expression are not so censored, for they may not be, but are nonetheless successfully controlled by our penal laws, Penal Law, § 1140–a, which have been resorted to whenever necessary. One of the most recent occasions was the banning of "The Outlaw", a motion picture, by the commissioners of license and the police in New York City, because deemed obscene, indecent and immoral, notwithstanding that the Board of Regents had theretofore issued it a license. Hughes Tool Co. v. Fielding, 297 N.Y. 1024, 80 N.E.2d 540, affirming 272 App.Div. 1048, 76 N.Y.S.2d 287. Reported instances of resort to criminal sanctions as a method of control are relatively infrequent but this is not at all surprising as the industry itself has its own Production Code in which it recognizes its responsibility to the public to provide approved entertainment in connection with which the potential power of the public boycott is not overlooked, exerting as it does, a direct influence in the box office, on the profitable operation of which the producers must depend (cf. Motion Pictures and the First Amendment, 60 Yale L.J. 696).

In conclusion then, it must be said that the New York censorship statute as applied in advance to the exhibition of motion pictures infringes constitutional freedom of speech and press, that the within case is not so exceptional as to require banning under a valid exercise of the police power and that the statute is invalid in any event for lack of definitive administrative criteria.

The order appealed from should be reversed and the matter remitted to the Board of Regents with direction to issue a license.

FULD, Judge (dissenting).

I agree with Judge DYE and, for myself, would add these words only to underscore what he has written.

That the freedom of expression assured by the First Amendment is not limited to "the air-borne voice, the pen, and the printing press," Chafee, Free Speech in the United States (1941), p. 545, but extends as well to motion pictures, is now beyond dispute. See Gelling v. Texas, 343 U.S. 960, 72 S.Ct. 1002, 96 L.Ed. 1359; Joseph Burstyn, Inc., v. Wilson, 343 U.S. 495, 72 S.Ct. 777, 96 L.Ed. 1098. While I conceive that any legislation imposing a previous restraint on the exhibition of moving pictures is condemned by the Constitution, I do not believe it necessary to invoke the broad principle to reach a decision in this case. Here again, as in Burstyn, the censorship statute must fall because of the lack of a sufficiently definite standard or guide for administrative action.

The Education Law provision under review authorizes the Regents to prohibit, in advance, the exhibition of any picture which they deem "immoral" or which they conclude may "tend to corrupt morals". Terms of such vague and undefined limits, however, fail to furnish the objective criterion necessary to insure that there shall be no interference with the exercise of rights secured by the First

Amendment. By attempting to cover so much, the catch-all provision barring motion pictures which the censors believe "immoral" effectively covers nothing. The ephemeral and ambiguous character of the term is highlighted by the variant views of the very judges who now write to uphold the statute. Words as subjective as those under consideration find meaning only in the mind of the viewer and observer, render impossible administration of the statute and offend against due process. "Prohibition through words that fail to convey what is permitted and what is prohibited for want of appropriate objective standards, offends Due Process in two ways. First, it does not sufficiently apprise those bent on obedience of law of what may reasonably be foreseen to be found illicit by the law-enforcing authority, whether court or jury or administrative agency. Secondly, where licensing is rested, in the first instance, in an administrative agency, the available judicial review is in effect rendered inoperative." Joseph Burstyn, Inc., v. Wilson, supra, 343 U.S., at page 532, 72 S.Ct. at page 796, per Frankfurter, J., concurring; see, also, Gelling v. Texas, supra, 343 U.S. 960, 72 S.Ct. 1002, 96 L.Ed. 1359; Musser v. Utah, 333 U.S. 95, 68 S.Ct. 397, 92 L.Ed. 562.

I would reverse and annul the determination of the Board of Regents.

LEWIS, J., concurs with FROESSEL, J.

DESMOND, J., votes for affirmance in a separate opinion.

CONWAY, J., in a memorandum, concurs in the opinions of FROESSEL and DESMOND, JJ.

DYE, J., dissents in an opinion in which FULD, J., concurs, and votes for reversal in a separate opinion.

LOUGHRAN, C.J., deceased.

Order affirmed.

NOTE

1. After our decision therein, section 1141 of the Penal Law was amended to exempt from its provisions moving picture films licensed by the State Department of Education. L.1950, ch. 624. If, therefore, the State be required to grant a license here, petitioner will be immune from criminal prosecution.

NEW YORK'S SUPPRESSION OF THE FILM "LADY CHATTERLEY'S LOVER" IS DECLARED A VIOLATION OF FIRST AMENDMENT RIGHTS

Kingsley Pictures v. Regents, 360 U.S. 684 (1959)

MR. JUSTICE STEWART delivered the opinion of the Court.

Once again the Court is required to consider the impact of New York's motion picture licensing law upon First Amendment liberties, protected by the Fourteenth Amendment from infringement by the States. Cf. *Joseph Burstyn, Inc.* v. *Wilson*, 343 U.S. 495.

The New York statute makes it unlawful "to exhibit, or to sell, lease or lend for exhibition at any place of amusement for pay or in connection with any business in the state of New York, any motion picture film or reel [with certain exceptions not relevant here], unless there is at the time in full force and effect a valid license or permit therefor of the education department. . . ."[1] The law provides that a license shall issue "unless such film or a part thereof is obscene, indecent, immoral, inhuman, sacrilegious, or is of such a character that its exhibition would tend to corrupt morals or incite to crime. . . ."[2] A recent statutory amendment provides that, "the term 'immoral' and the phrase 'of such a character that its exhibition would tend to corrupt morals' shall denote a motion picture film or part thereof, the dominant purpose or effect of which is erotic or pornographic; or which portrays acts of sexual immorality, perversion, or lewdness, or which expressly or impliedly presents such acts as desirable, acceptable or proper patterns of behavior."[3]

As the distributor of a motion picture entitled "Lady Chatterley's Lover," the appellant Kingsley submitted that film to the Motion Picture Division of the New York Education Department for a license. Finding three isolated scenes in the film " 'immoral' within the intent of our Law," the Division refused to issue a license until the scenes in question were deleted. The distributor petitioned the Regents of the University of the State of New York for a review of that ruling.[4] The Regents upheld the denial of a license, but on the broader ground that "the whole theme of this motion picture is immoral under said law, for that theme is the presentation of adultery as a desirable, acceptable and proper pattern of behavior."

Kingsley sought judicial review of the Regents' determination.[5] The Appellate Division unanimously annulled the action of the Regents and directed that a license be issued. 4 App. Div. 2d 348, 165 N. Y. S. 2d 681. A sharply divided Court of Appeals, however, reversed the Appellate Division and upheld the Regents' refusal to license the film for exhibition. 4 N. Y. 2d 349, 151 N. E. 2d 197, 175 N. Y. S. 2d 39.[6]

The Court of Appeals unanimously and explicitly rejected any notion that the film is obscene.[7] See *Roth* v. *United States*, 354 U. S. 476. Rather, the court found that the picture as a whole "alluringly portrays adultery as proper behavior." As Chief Judge Conway's prevailing opinion emphasized, therefore, the only portion of the statute involved in this case is that part of §§ 122 and 122-a of the Education Law requiring the denial of a license to motion pictures "which are immoral in that they *portray* 'acts of sexual immorality . . . as desirable, acceptable or proper patterns of behavior.' "[8] 4 N. Y. 2d, at 351, 151 N. E. 2d, at 197, 175 N. Y. S. 2d, at 40. A majority of the Court of Appeals ascribed to that language a precise purpose of the New York Legislature to require the denial of a license to a motion picture "because its subject matter is adultery presented as being right and desirable for certain people under certain circumstances."[9] 4 N. Y. 2d, at 369, 151 N. E. 2d, at 208, 175 N. Y. S. 2d, at 55 (concurring opinion). We accept the premise that the motion picture here in question can be so characterized. We accept too, as we must, the construction of the New York Legislature's language which the Court of Appeals has put upon it. *Albertson* v. *Millard*, 345 U. S. 242; *United States* v. *Burnison*, 339 U. S. 87; *Aero Mayflower Transit Co.* v. *Board of R. R. Comm'rs*, 332 U. S. 495. That construction, we emphasize, gives to the term "sexual immorality" a concept entirely different from the concept embraced in words like "obscenity" or "pornography." [10] Moreover, it is not suggested that the film would itself operate as an incitement to illegal action. Rather, the New York Court of Appeals tells us that the relevant portion of the New York Education Law requires the denial of a license to any motion picture which approvingly portrays an adulterous relationship, quite without reference to the manner of its portrayal.

What New York has done, therefore, is to prevent the exhibition of a motion picture because that picture advocates an idea—that adultery under certain circumstances may be proper behavior. Yet the First Amendment's basic guarantee is of freedom to advocate ideas. The State, quite simply, has thus struck at the very heart of constitutionally protected liberty.

It is contended that the State's action was justified because the motion picture attractively portrays a relationship which is contrary to the moral standards, the religious precepts, and the legal code of its citizenry. This argument misconceives what it is that the Constitution protects. Its guarantee is not confined to the expression of ideas that are conventional or shared by a majority. It protects advocacy of the opinion that adultery may sometimes be proper, no less than advocacy of socialism or the single tax. And in the realm of ideas it protects expression which is eloquent no less than that which is unconvincing.

Advocacy of conduct proscribed by law is not, as Mr. Justice Brandeis long ago pointed out, "a justification for denying free speech where the advocacy falls short of incitement and there is nothing to indicate that the advocacy would be immediately acted on." *Whitney* v. *California*, 274 U. S. 357, at 376 (concurring opinion). "Among free men, the deterrents ordinarily to be applied to prevent crime are education and punishment for violations of the law, not abridgment of the rights of free speech. . . ." *Id.*, at 378.[11]

The inflexible command which the New York Court of Appeals has attributed to the State Legislature thus cuts so close to the core of constitutional freedom as to make it quite needless in this case to examine the periphery. Specifically, there is no occasion to consider the appellant's contention that the State is entirely without power to require films of any kind to be licensed prior to their exhibition. Nor need we here determine whether, despite problems peculiar to motion pictures, the controls which a State may impose upon this medium of expression are precisely coextensive with those allowable for newspapers,[12] books,[13] or individual speech.[14] It is enough for the present case to reaffirm that motion pictures are within the First and Fourteenth Amendments' basic protection. *Joseph Burstyn, Inc.* v. *Wilson*, 343 U. S. 495.

Reversed.

MR. JUSTICE BLACK, concurring.

I concur in the Court's opinion and judgment but add a few words because of concurring opinions by several Justices who rely on their appraisal of the movie Lady Chatterley's Lover for holding that New York cannot constitutionally bar it. Unlike them, I have not seen the picture. My view is that stated by MR. JUSTICE DOUGLAS, that prior censorship of moving pictures like prior censorship of newspapers and books violates the First and Fourteenth Amendments. If despite the Constitution, however, this Nation is to embark on the dangerous road of censorship, my belief is that this Court is about the most inappropriate Supreme Board of Censors that could be found. So far as I know, judges possess no special expertise providing exceptional competency to set standards and to supervise the private morals of the Nation. In addition, the Justices of this Court seem especially unsuited to make the kind of value judgments—as to what movies are good or bad for local communities—which the concurring opinions appear to require. We are told that the only way we can decide whether a State or municipality can constitutionally bar movies is for this Court to view and appraise each movie on a case-by-case basis. Under these circumstances, every member of the Court must exercise his own judgment as to how bad a picture is, a judgment which is ultimately based at least in large part on his own standard of what is immoral. The end result of such decisions seems to me to be a purely personal determination by individual Justices as to whether a particular picture viewed is too bad to allow it to be seen by the public. Such an individualized determination cannot be guided by reasonably fixed and certain standards. Accordingly, neither States nor moving picture makers can possibly know in advance, with any fair degree of certainty, what can or cannot be done in the field of movie making and exhibiting. This uncertainty cannot easily be reconciled with the rule of law which our Constitution envisages.

The different standards which different people may use to decide about the badness of pictures are well illustrated by the contrasting standards mentioned in the opinion of the New York Court of Appeals and the concurring opinion of MR. JUSTICE FRANKFURTER here. As I read the New York court's opinion this movie was held immoral and banned because it makes adultery too alluring. MR. JUSTICE FRANKFURTER quotes Mr. Lawrence, author of the book from which the movie was made, as believing censorship should be applied only to publications that make sex look ugly, that is, as I understand it, less alluring.

In my judgment, this Court should not permit itself to get into the very center of such policy controversies, which have so little in common with lawsuits.

MR. JUSTICE FRANKFURTER, concurring in the result.

As one whose taste in art and literature hardly qualifies him for the *avant-garde*, I am more than surprised, after viewing the picture, that the New York authorities should have banned "Lady Chatterley's Lover." To assume that this motion picture would have offended Victorian moral sensibilities is to rely only on the stuffiest of Victorian conventions. Whatever one's personal preferences may be about such matters, the refusal to license the exhibition of this picture, on the basis of the 1954 amendment to the New York State Education Law, can only mean that that enactment forbids the public showing of any film that deals with adultery except by way of sermonizing condemnation or depicts any physical manifestation of an illicit amorous relation. Since the denial of a license by the Board of Regents was confirmed by the highest court of the State, I have no choice but to agree with this Court's judgment in holding that the State exceeded the bounds of free expression protected by the "liberty" of the Fourteenth Amendment. But I also believe that the Court's opinion takes ground that exceeds the appropriate limits for decision. By way of reinforcing my brother HARLAN's objections to the scope of the Court's opinion, I add the following.

Even the author of "Lady Chatterley's Lover" did not altogether rule out censorship, nor was his passionate zeal on behalf of society's profound interest in the endeavors of true artists so doctrinaire as to be unmindful of the facts of life regarding the sordid exploitation of man's nature and impulses. He knew there was such a thing as pornography, dirt for dirt's sake, or, to be more accurate, dirt for money's sake. This is what D. H. Lawrence wrote:

> "But even I would censor genuine pornography, rigorously. It would not be very difficult. In the first place, genuine pornography is almost always underworld, it doesn't come into the open. In the second, you can recognize it by the insult it offers invariably, to sex, and to the human spirit.
>
> "Pornography is the attempt to insult sex, to do dirt on it. This is unpardonable. Take the very lowest instance, the picture post-card sold underhand, by the underworld, in most cities. What I have seen of them have been of an ugliness to make you cry. The insult to the human body, the insult to a vital human relationship! Ugly and cheap they make the human nudity, ugly and degraded they make the sexual act, trivial and cheap and nasty." (D. H. Lawrence, Pornography and Obscenity, pp. 12–13.)

This traffic has not lessened since Lawrence wrote. Apparently it is on the increase. In the course of the recent debate in both Houses of Parliament on the Obscene Publications Bill, now on its way to passage, designed to free British authors from the hazards of too rigorous application in our day of Lord Cockburn's ruling, in 1868, in *Regina* v. *Hicklin*, L. R. 3 Q. B. 360, weighty experience was adduced regarding the extensive dissemination of pornographic materials.[1] See 597 Parliamentary Debates, H. C., No. 36 (Tuesday, December 16, 1958), cols. 992 *et seq.*, and 216 Parliamentary Debates H. L., No. 77 (Tuesday, June 2, 1959), cols. 489 *et seq.* Nor is there any reason to believe that on this side of the ocean there has been a diminution in the pornographic business which years ago sought a flourishing market in some of the leading secondary schools for boys, who presumably had more means than boys in the public high schools.

It is not surprising, therefore, that the pertinacious, eloquent and free-spirited promoters of the liberalizing legislation in Great Britain did not conceive the needs of a civilized society, in assuring the utmost freedom to those who make literature and art possible—authors, artists, publishers, producers, book sellers—easily attainable by sounding abstract and unqualified dogmas about freedom.

They had a keen awareness that freedom of expression is no more an absolute than any other freedom, an awareness that is reflected in the opinions of Mr. Justice Holmes and Mr. Justice Brandeis, to whom we predominantly owe the present constitutional safeguards on behalf of freedom of expression. And see *Near* v. *Minnesota*, 283 U. S. 697, 715–716, for limitations on constitutionally protected freedom of speech.[2]

In short, there is an evil against which a State may constitutionally protect itself, whatever we may think about the questions of policy involved. The real problem is the formulation of constitutionally allowable safeguards which society may take against evil without impinging upon the necessary dependence of a free society upon the fullest scope of free expression. One cannot read the debates in the House of Commons and the House of Lords and not realize the difficulty of reconciling these conflicting interests, in the framing of legislation on the ends of which there was agreement, even for those who most generously espouse that freedom of expression without which all freedom gradually withers.

It is not our province to meet these recalcitrant problems of legislative drafting. Ours is the vital but very limited task of scrutinizing the work of the draftsmen in order to determine whether they have kept within the narrow limits of the kind of censorship which even D. H. Lawrence deemed necessary. The legislation must not be so vague, the language so loose, as to leave to those who have to apply it too wide a discretion for sweeping within its condemnation what is permissible expression as well as what society may permissibly prohibit. Always remembering that the widest scope of freedom is to be given to the adventurous and imaginative exercise of the human spirit, we have struck down legislation phrased in language intrinsically vague, unless it be responsive to the common understanding of men even though not susceptible of explicit definition. The ultimate reason for invalidating such laws is that they lead to timidity and inertia and thereby discourage the boldness of expression indispensable for a progressive society.

The New York legislation of 1954 was the product of careful lawyers who sought to meet decisions of this Court which had left no doubt that a motion-picture licensing law is not inherently outside the scope of the regulatory powers of a State under the Fourteenth Amendment. The Court does not strike the law down because of vagueness, as we struck down prior New York legislation. Nor does it reverse the judgment of the New York Court of Appeals, as I would, because in applying the New York law to "Lady Chatterley's Lover" it applied it to a picture to which it cannot be applied without invading the area of constitutionally free expression. The difficulty which the Court finds seems to derive from some expressions culled here and there from the opinion of the Chief Judge of the New York Court of Appeals. This leads the Court to give the phrase "acts of sexual immorality . . as desirable, acceptable or proper patterns of behavior" an innocent content, meaning, in effect, an allowable subject matter for discussion. But, surely, to attribute that result to the decision of the Court of Appeals, on the basis of a few detached phrases of Chief Judge Conway, is to break a faggot into pieces, is to forget that the meaning of language is to be felt and its phrases not to be treated disjointedly. "Sexual immorality" is not a new phrase in this branch of law and its implications dominate the context. I hardly conceive it possible that the Court would strike down as unconstitutional the federal statute against mailing lewd, obscene and lascivious matter, which has been the law of the land for nearly a hundred years, see the Act of March 3, 1865, 13 Stat. 507, and March 3, 1873, 17 Stat. 599, whatever specific instances may be found not within its allowable prohibition. In sustaining this legislation this Court gave the words "lewd, obscene and lascivious" concreteness by saying that they concern "sexual immorality." And only very recently the Court sustained the constitutionality of the statute. *Roth* v. *United States*, 354 U. S. 476.

Unless I misread the opinion of the Court, it strikes down the New York legislation in order to escape the task of deciding whether a particular picture is entitled to the protection of expression under the Fourteenth Amendment. Such an exercise of the judicial function, however onerous or ungrateful, inheres in the very nature of the judicial enforcement of the Due Process Clause. We cannot escape such instance-by-instance, case-by-case application of that clause in all the varieties of situations that come before this Court. It would be comfortable if, by a comprehensive formula, we could decide when a confession is coerced so as to vitiate a state conviction. There is no such talismanic formula. Every Term we have to examine the particular circumstances of a particular case in order to apply generalities which no one disputes. It would be equally comfortable if a general formula could determine the unfairness of a state trial for want of counsel. But, except in capital cases, we have to thread our way, Term after Term, through the particular circumstances of a particular case in relation to a particular defendant in order to ascertain whether due process was denied in the unique situation before us. We are constantly called upon to consider the alleged misconduct of a prosecutor as vitiating the fairness of a particular trial or the inflamed state of public opinion in a particular case as undermining the constitutional right to due process. Again, in the series of cases coming here from the state courts, in which due process was invoked to enforce separation of church and state, decision certainly turned on the particularities of the specific situations before the Court. It is needless to multiply instances. It is the nature of the concept of due process, and, I venture to believe, its high serviceability in our constitutional system, that the judicial enforcement of the Due Process Clause is the very antithesis of a Procrustean rule. This was recognized in the first full-dress discussion of the Due Process Clause of the Fourteenth Amendment, when the Court defined the nature of the problem as a "gradual process of judicial inclusion and exclusion, as the cases presented for decision shall require, with the reasons on which such decision may be founded." *Davidson* v. *New Orleans*, 96 U. S. 97, 104. The task is onerous and exacting, demanding as it does the utmost discipline in objectivity, the severest control of personal predilections. But it cannot be escaped, not even by disavowing that such is the nature of our task.

MR. JUSTICE DOUGLAS, with whom MR. JUSTICE BLACK joins, concurring.

While I join in the opinion of the Court, I adhere to the views I expressed in *Superior Films* v. *Department of Education*, 346 U. S. 587, 588–589, that censorship of movies is unconstitutional, since it is a form of "previous restraint" that is as much at war with the First Amendment, made applicable to the States through the Fourteenth, as the censorship struck down in *Near* v. *Minnesota*, 283 U. S. 697. If a particular movie violates a valid law, the exhibitor can be prosecuted in the usual way. I can find in the First Amendment no room for any censor whether he is scanning an editorial, reading a news broadcast, editing a novel or a play, or previewing a movie.

Reference is made to British law and British practice. But they have little relevance to our problem, since we live under a written Constitution. What is entrusted to the keeping of the legislature in England is protected from legislative interference or regulation here. As we stated in *Bridges* v. *California*, 314 U. S. 252, 265, "No purpose in ratifying the Bill of Rights was clearer than that of securing for the people of the United States much greater freedom of religion, expression, assembly, and petition than the people of Great Britain had ever enjoyed." If we had a provision in our Constitution for "reasonable" regulation of the press such as India has included in hers,[1] there would be room for argument that censorship in the interests of morality would be permissible. Judges sometimes try to read the word "reasonable" into the First Amendment or make the rights it grants subject to reasonable regulation (see *Beauharnais* v. *Illinois*, 343 U. S. 250, 262; *Dennis* v. *United States*, 341 U. S. 494, 523–525), or apply to the States a watered-down version of the First Amendment. See *Roth* v. *United States*, 354 U. S. 476, 505–506. But its language, in terms that are absolute, is utterly at war with censorship. Different questions may arise as to censorship of some news when the Nation is actually at war. But any possible exceptions are extremely limited. That is why the tradition represented by *Near* v. *Minnesota, supra,* represents our constitutional ideal.

Happily government censorship has put down few roots in this country. The American tradition is represented by *Near* v. *Minnesota, supra.* See Lockhart and McClure, Literature, The Law of Obscenity, and the Constitution, 38 Minn. L. Rev. 295, 324–325; Alpert, Judicial Censorship of Obscene Literature, 52 Harv. L. Rev. 40, 53 *et seq.* We have in the United States no counterpart of the Lord Chamberlain who is censor over England's stage. As late as 1941 only six States had systems of censorship for movies. Chafee, Free Speech in the United States (1941), p. 540. That number has now been reduced to four [2]—Kansas, Maryland, New York, and Virginia—plus a few cities. Even in these areas, censorship of movies shown on television gives way by reason of the Federal Communications Act. See *Allen B. Dumont Laboratories* v. *Carroll*, 184 F. 2d 153. And from what information is available, movie censors do not seem to be very active.[3] Deletion of the residual part of censorship that remains would constitute the elimination of an institution that intrudes on First Amendment rights.

Mr. Justice Clark, concurring in the result.

I can take the words of the majority of the New York Court of Appeals only in their clear, unsophisticated and common meaning. They say that §§ 122 and 122-a of New York's Education Law "require the denial of a license to motion pictures which are immoral in that they portray 'acts of sexual immorality . . . as desirable, acceptable or proper patterns of behavior.'" That court states the issue in the case in this language:

"Moving pictures are our only concern and, what is more to the point, only those motion pictures which alluringly present acts of sexual immorality as proper behavior." 4 N. Y. 2d 349, 361, 151 N. E. 2d 197, 203, 175 N. Y. S. 2d 39, 48.

Moreover, it is significant to note that in its 14-page opinion that court says again and again, in fact 15 times, that the picture "Lady Chatterley's Lover" is proscribed because of its "espousal" of sexual immorality as "desirable" or as "proper conduct for the people of our State."*

The minority of my brothers here, however, twist this holding into one that New York's Act requires "obscenity or incitement, not just abstract expressions of opinion." But I cannot so obliterate the repeated declarations above-mentioned that were made not only 15 times by the Court of Appeals but which were the basis of the Board of Regents' decision as well. Such a construction would raise many problems, not the least of which would be our failure to accept New York's interpretation of the scope of its own Act. I feel, as does the majority here, bound by their holding.

In this context, the Act comes within the ban of *Joseph Burstyn, Inc.*, v. *Wilson,* 343 U. S. 495 (1952). We held there that "expression by means of motion pictures is included within the free speech and free press guaranty of the First and Fourteenth Amendments." *Id.,* at 502. Referring to *Near* v. *Minnesota,* 283 U. S. 697 (1931), we said that while "a major purpose of the First Amendment guaranty of a free press was to prevent prior restraints upon publication" such protection was not unlimited but did place on the State "a heavy burden to demonstrate that the limitation challenged" was exceptional. *Id.,* at 503–504. The standard applied there was the word "sacrilegious" and we found it set the censor "adrift upon a boundless sea amid a myriad of conflicting currents of religious views . . . ." *Id.,* at 504. We struck it down.

Here the standard is the portrayal of "acts of sexual

immorality . . . as desirable, acceptable or proper patterns of behavior." Motion picture plays invariably have a hero, a villain, supporting characters, a location, a plot, a diversion from the main theme and usually a moral. As we said in *Burstyn:* "They may affect public attitudes and behavior in a variety of ways, ranging from direct espousal of a political or social doctrine to the subtle shaping of thought which characterizes all artistic expression." 343 U. S., at 501. What may be to one viewer the glorification of an idea as being "desirable, acceptable or proper" may to the notions of another be entirely devoid of such a teaching. The only limits on the censor's discretion is his understanding of what is included within the term "desirable, acceptable or proper." This is nothing less than a roving commission in which individual impressions become the yardstick of action, and result in regulation in accordance with the beliefs of the individual censor rather than regulation by law. Even here three of my brothers "cannot regard this film as depicting anything more than a somewhat unusual, and rather pathetic, 'love triangle.'" At least three—perhaps four—of the members of New York's highest court thought otherwise. I need only say that the obscurity of the standard presents such a choice of difficulties that even the most experienced find themselves at dagger's point.

It may be, as Chief Judge Conway said, "that our public morality, possibly more than ever before, needs every protection government can give." 4 N. Y. 2d, at 363, 151 N. E. 2d, at 204–205, 175 N. Y. S. 2d, at 50. And, as my Brother Harlan points out, "each time such a statute is struck down, the State is left in more confusion." This is true where broad grounds are employed leaving no indication as to what may be necessary to meet the requirements of due process. I see no grounds for confusion, however, were a statute to ban "pornographic" films, or those that "portray *acts* of sexual immorality, perversion or lewdness." If New York's statute had been so construed by its highest court I believe it would have met the requirements of due process. Instead, it placed more emphasis on what the film teaches than on what it depicts. There is where the confusion enters. For this reason, I would reverse on the authority of *Burstyn.*

Mr. Justice Harlan, whom Mr. Justice Frankfurter and Mr. Justice Whittaker join, concurring in the result.

I think the Court has moved too swiftly in striking down a statute which is the product of a deliberate and conscientious effort on the part of New York to meet constitutional objections raised by this Court's decisions respecting predecessor statutes in this field. But although I disagree with the Court that the parts of §§ 122 and 122-a of the New York Education Law, 16 N. Y. Laws Ann. § 122 (McKinney 1953), 16 N. Y. Laws Ann. § 122-a (McKinney Supp. 1958), here particularly involved are unconstitutional on their face, I believe that in their application to this film constitutional bounds were exceeded.

I.

Section 122-a of the State Education Law was passed in 1954 to meet this Court's decision in *Commercial Pictures Corp.* v. *Regents,* 346 U. S. 587, which overturned

---

*The phrase is not always identical but varies from the words of the statute, "acts of sexual immorality . . . as desirable, acceptable or proper patterns of behavior," to such terms "as proper conduct for the people of our State"; "exaltation of illicit sexual love in derogation of the restraints of marriage"; as "a proper pattern of behavior"; "the espousal of sexually immoral acts"; "which debase fundamental sexual morality by portraying its converse to the people as alluring and desirable"; "which alluringly portrays sexually immoral acts as proper behavior"; "by presenting . . . [adultery] in a clearly approbatory manner"; "which alluringly portrays adultery as proper behavior"; "which alluringly portray acts of sexual immorality (here adultery) and recommend them as a proper way of life"; "which alluringly portray adultery as proper and desirable"; and "which alluringly portray acts of sexual immorality by adultery as proper behavior."

the New York Court of Appeals' holding in *In re Commercial Pictures Corp. v. Board of Regents*, 305 N. Y. 336, 113 N. E. 2d 502, that the film *La Ronde* could be banned as "immoral" and as "tend[ing] to corrupt morals" under § 122.[1] The Court's decision in *Commercial Pictures* was but a one line *per curiam* with a citation to *Joseph Burstyn, Inc. v. Wilson*, 343 U. S. 495, which in turn had held for naught not the word "immoral" but the term "sacrilegious" in the statute.

New York, nevertheless, set about repairing its statute. This it did by enacting § 122-a which in the respects emphasized in the present opinion of Chief Judge Conway as pertinent here defines an "immoral" motion picture film as one which portrays " 'acts of sexual immorality . . . as desirable, acceptable or proper patterns of behavior.' " 4 N. Y. 2d 349, 351, 151 N. E. 2d 197, 175 N. Y. S. 2d 39.[2] The Court now holds this part of New York's effort unconstitutional on its face under the Fourteenth Amendment. I cannot agree.

The Court does not suggest that these provisions are bad for vagueness.[3] Any such suggestion appears to me untenable in view of the long-standing usage in this Court of the concept "sexual immorality" to explain in part the meaning of "obscenity." See, *e. g.*, *Swearingen* v. *United States*, 161 U. S. 446, 451.[4] Instead, the Court finds a constitutional vice in these provisions in that they require, so it is said, neither "obscenity" nor incitement to "sexual immorality," but strike of their own force at the mere advocacy of "an idea—that adultery under certain circumstances may be proper behavior"; expressions of "opinion that adultery may sometimes be proper . . . ." I think this characterization of these provisions misconceives the construction put upon them by the prevailing opinions in the Court of Appeals. Granting that the abstract public discussion or advocacy of adultery, unaccompanied by obscene portrayal or actual incitement to such behavior, may not constitutionally be proscribed by the State, I do not read those opinions to hold that the statute on its face undertakes any such proscription. Chief Judge Conway's opinion, which was joined by two others of the seven judges of the Court of Appeals, and in the thrust of which one more concurred, to be sure with some doubt, states (4 N. Y. 2d, at 356, 151 N. E. 2d, at 200, 175 N. Y. S. 2d, at 44):

> "It should first be emphasized that the scope of section 122-a is not mere expression of opinion in the form, for example, of a filmed lecture whose subject matter is the espousal of adultery. We reiterate that this case involves the espousal of sexually immoral acts (here adultery) *plus* actual scenes of a suggestive and obscene nature." [·] (Emphasis in original.)

The opinion elsewhere, as indeed is also the case with §§ 122 and 122-a themselves when independently read in their entirety, is instinct with the notion that mere abstract expressions of opinion regarding the desirability of sexual immorality, unaccompanied by obscenity[5] or incitement, are not proscribed. See 4 N. Y. 2d 349, especially at 351–352, 354, 356–358, 361, 363–364; 151 N. E. 2d 197, at 197, 199, 200–201, 203, 204–205; 175 N. Y. S. 2d 39, at 40, 42, 44–46, 48, 50–51; and Notes 1 and 2, *supra*. It is the corruption of public morals,

occasioned by the inciting effect of a particular portrayal or by what New York has deemed the necessary effect of obscenity, at which the statute is aimed. In the words of Chief Judge Conway, "There is no difference in substance between motion pictures which are corruptive of the public morals, and sexually suggestive, because of a predominance of suggestive scenes, and those which achieve precisely the same effect by presenting only several such scenes in a clearly approbatory manner throughout the course of the film. *The law is concerned with effect, not merely with but one means of producing it . . . the objection lies in the corrosive effect upon the public sense of sexual morality.*" 4 N. Y. 2d, at 358, 151 N. E. 2d, at 201, 175 N. Y. S. 2d, at 46. (Emphasis in original.)

I do not understand that the Court would question the constitutionality of the particular portions of the statute with which we are here concerned if the Court read, as I do, the majority opinions in the Court of Appeals as construing these provisions to require obscenity or incitement, not just mere abstract expressions of opinion. It is difficult to understand why the Court should strain to read those opinions as it has. Our usual course in constitutional adjudication is precisely the opposite.

II.

The application of the statute to this film is quite a different matter. I have heretofore ventured the view that in this field the States have wider constitutional latitude than the Federal Government. See the writer's separate opinion in *Roth* v. *United States* and *Alberts* v. *California*, 354 U. S. 476, 496. With that approach, I have viewed this film.

Giving descriptive expression to what in matters of this kind are in the last analysis bound to be but individual subjective impressions, objectively as one may try to discharge his duty as a judge, is not apt to be repaying. I shall therefore content myself with saying that, according full respect to, and with, I hope, sympathetic consideration for, the views and characterizations expressed by others, I cannot regard this film as depicting anything more than a somewhat unusual, and rather pathetic, "love triangle," lacking in anything that could properly be termed obscene or corruptive of the public morals by inciting the commission of adultery. I therefore think that in banning this film New York has exceeded constitutional limits.

I conclude with one further observation. It is sometimes said that this Court should shun considering the particularities of individual cases in this difficult field lest the Court become a final "board of censorship." But I cannot understand why it should be thought that the process of constitutional judgment in this realm somehow stands apart from that involved in other fields, particularly those presenting questions of due process. Nor can I see, short of holding that all state "censorship" laws are constitutionally impermissible, a course from which the Court is carefully abstaining, how the Court can hope ultimately to spare itself the necessity for individualized adjudication. In the very nature of things the problems in this area are ones of individual cases, see *Roth* v. *United States* and *Alberts* v. *California, supra*, at 496–498, for a "censorship" statute can hardly be contrived that would in effect be self-executing. And, lastly, each time such a statute is struck down, the State is left in more confusion, as witness New York's experience with its statute.

Because I believe the New York statute was unconstitutionally applied in this instance I concur in the judgment of the Court.

COURT'S OPINION NOTES

[1] McKinney's N. Y. Laws, 1953, Education Law, § 129.

[2] McKinney's N. Y. Laws, 1953, Education Law, § 122.

[3] McKinney's N. Y. Laws, 1953 (Cum. Supp. 1958), Education Law, § 122-a.

[4] "An applicant for a license or permit, in case his application be denied by the director of the division or by the officer authorized to issue the same, shall have the right of review by the regents." McKinney's N. Y. Laws, 1953, Education Law, § 124.

[5] The proceeding was brought under Art. 78 of the New York Civil Practice Act, Gilbert-Bliss' N. Y. Civ. Prac., Vol. 6B, 1944, 1949 Supp., § 1283 et seq. See also, McKinney's N. Y. Laws, 1953, Education Law, § 124.

[6] Although four of the seven judges of the Court of Appeals voted to reverse the order of the Appellate Division, only three of them were of the clear opinion that denial of a license was permissible under the Constitution. Chief Judge Conway wrote an opinion in which Judges Froessel and Burke concurred, concluding that denial of the license was constitutionally permissible. Judge Desmond wrote a separate concurring opinion in which he stated: "I confess doubt as to the validity of such a statute but I do not know how that doubt can be resolved unless we reverse here and let the Supreme Court have the final say." 4 N. Y. 2d, at 369, 151 N. E. 2d, at 208, 175 N. Y. S. 2d, at 55. Judge Dye, Judge Fuld, and Judge Van Voorhis wrote separate dissenting opinions.

[7] The opinion written by Chief Judge Conway stated: "[I]t is curious indeed to say in one breath, as some do, that obscene motion pictures may be censored, and then in another breath that motion pictures which alluringly portray adultery as proper and desirable may not be censored. As stated above, 'The law is concerned with effect, not merely with but one means of producing it.' It must be firmly borne in mind that to give obscenity, as defined, the stature of the only constitutional limitation is to extend an invitation to corrupt the public morals by methods of presentation which craft will insure do not fall squarely within the definition of that term. Precedent, just as sound principle, will not support a statement that motion pictures must be 'out and out' obscene before they may be censored." 4 N. Y. 2d, at 364, 151 N. E. 2d, at 205, 175 N. Y. S. 2d, at 51.

Judge Desmond's concurring opinion stated: "[It is not] necessarily determinative that this film is not obscene in the dictionary sense. . . ." 4 N. Y. 2d, at 369, 151 N. E. 2d, at 208, 175 N. Y. S. 2d, at 55. Judge Dye's dissenting opinion stated: "No one contends that the film in question is obscene within the narrow legal limits of obscenity as recently defined by the Supreme Court. . . ." 4 N. Y. 2d, at 371, 151 N. E. 2d, at 210, 175 N. Y. S. 2d, at 57. Judge Van Voorhis' dissenting opinion stated: "[I]t is impossible to write off this entire drama as 'mere pornography' . . . ." Judge Van Voorhis, however, would have remitted the case to the Board of Regents to consider whether certain "passages" in the film "might have been eliminated as 'obscene' without doing violence to constitutional liberties." 4 N. Y. 2d, at 375, 151 N. E. 2d, at 212, 175 N. Y. S. 2d, at 60.

[8] This is also emphasized in the brief of counsel for the Regents, which states, "The full definition is not before this Court—only these parts of the definition as cited—and any debate as to whether other parts of the definition are a proper standard has no bearing in this case."

[9] In concurring, Judge Desmond agreed that this was the meaning of the statutory language in question, and that "the theme and content of this film fairly deserve that characterization. . . ." 4 N. Y. 2d, at 366, 151 N. E. 2d, at 206, 175 N. Y. S. 2d, at 52.

[10] See by way of contrast, Swearingen v. United States, 161 U. S. 446; United States v. Limehouse, 285 U. S. 424.

[11] Thomas Jefferson wrote more than a hundred and fifty years ago, "But we have nothing to fear from the demoralizing reasonings of some, if others are left free to demonstrate their errors. And especially when the law stands ready to punish the first criminal act produced by the false reasoning. These are safer correctives than the conscience of a judge." Letter of Thomas Jefferson to Elijah Boardman, July 3, 1801, Jefferson Papers, Library of Congress, Vol. 115, folio 19761.

[12] Cf. Near v. Minnesota, 283 U. S. 697.

[13] Cf. Kingsley Books, Inc. v. Brown, 354 U. S. 436; Alberts v. California, 354 U. S. 476.

[14] Cf. Thomas v. Collins, 323 U. S. 516; Thornhill v. Alabama, 310 U. S. 88.

JUSTICE FRANKFURTER'S CONCURRING OPINION NOTES

[1] "In the course of our enquiries, we have been impressed with the existence of a considerable and lucrative trade in pornography . . . ." Report of the Select Committee on Obscene Publications to the House of Commons, March 20, 1958, p. IV.

[2] "The objection has also been made that the principle as to immunity from previous restraint is stated too broadly, if every such restraint is deemed to be prohibited. That is undoubtedly true; the protection even as to previous restraint is not absolutely unlimited. But the limitation has been recognized only in exceptional cases . . . ." 283 U. S., at 715–716.

JUSTICE DOUGLAS'S CONCURRING OPINION NOTES

[1] Section 19 (2) of the Indian Constitution permits "reasonable restrictions" on the exercise of the right of freedom of speech and expression in the interests, inter alia, of "decency or morality . . . defamation or incitement to an offence." This limitation is strictly construed; any restriction amounting to an "imposition" which will "operate harshly" on speech or the press will be held invalid. See Seshadri v. District Magistrate, Tangore, 41 A. I. R. (Sup. Ct.) 747, 749.

[2] See Note, 71 Harv. L. Rev. 326, 328, n. 14.

[3] Id., p. 332.

JUSTICE HARLAN'S CONCURRING OPINION NOTES

[1] Section 122 provides: "The director of the [motion picture] division or, when authorized by the regents, the officers of a local office or bureau shall cause to be promptly examined every motion picture film submitted to them as herein required, and unless such film or a part thereof is obscene, indecent, immoral, inhuman, sacrilegious, or is of such a character that its exhibition would tend to corrupt morals or incite to crime, shall issue a license therefor. If such director or, when so authorized, such officer shall not license any film submitted, he shall furnish to the applicant therefor a written report of the reasons for his refusal and a description of each rejected part of a film not rejected in toto."

[2] Section 122-a provides:

"1. For the purpose of section one hundred twenty-two of this chapter, the term 'immoral' and the phrase 'of such a character that its exhibition would tend to corrupt morals' shall denote a motion picture film or part thereof, the dominant purpose or effect of which is erotic or pornographic; or which portrays acts of sexual immorality, perversion, or lewdness, or which expressly or impliedly presents such acts as desirable, acceptable or proper patterns of behavior.

"2. For the purpose of section one hundred twenty-two of this chapter, the term 'incite to crime' shall denote a motion picture the dominant purpose or effect of which is to suggest that the commission of criminal acts or contempt for law is profitable, desirable, acceptable, or respectable behavior; or which advocates or teaches the use of, or the methods of use of, narcotics or habit-forming drugs."

[3] The bill that became § 122-a was introduced at the request of the State Education Department, which noted in a memorandum that "the issue of censorship, as such, is not involved in this bill. This bill merely attempts to follow out the criticism of the United

States Supreme Court by defining the words 'immoral' and 'incite to crime.'" N. Y. S. Legis. Ann., 1954, 36. In a memorandum accompanying his approval of the measure, the then Governor of New York, himself a lawyer, wrote:

"Since 1921, the Education Law of this State has required the licensing of motion pictures and authorized refusal of a license for a motion picture which is 'obscene, indecent, immoral' or which would 'tend to corrupt morals or incite to crime.'

"Recent Supreme Court decisions have indicated that the term 'immoral' may not be sufficiently definite for constitutional purposes. The primary purpose of this bill is to define 'immoral' and 'tend to corrupt morals' in conformance with the apparent requirements of these cases. It does so by defining them in terms of 'sexual immorality.' The words selected for this definition are based on judicial opinions which have given exhaustive and reasoned treatment to the subject.

"The bill does not create any new licensing system, expand the scope of motion picture censorship, or enlarge the area of permissible prior restraint. Its sole purpose is to give to the section more precision to make it conform to the tenor of recent court decisions and proscribe the exploitation of 'filth for the sake of filth.' It does so as accurately as language permits in 'words well understood through long use.' [*People v. Winters*, 333 U. S. 507, 518 (1948)].

.   .   .   .   .

"The language of the Supreme Court of the United States, in a recent opinion of this precise problem, should be noted:

"'To hold that liberty and expression by means of motion pictures is guaranteed by the First and Fourteenth Amendments, however, is not the end of our problem. It does not follow that the Constitution requires absolute freedom to exhibit every motion picture of every kind at all times and all places.' [*Burstyn v. Wilson*, 343 U. S. 495, at 502].

"So long as the State has the responsibility for interdicting motion pictures which transgress the bounds of decency, we have the responsibility for furnishing guide lines to the agency charged with enforcing the law." *Id.*, at 408.

[4] Certainly it cannot be claimed that adultery is not a form of "sexual immorality"; indeed adultery is made a crime in New York. N. Y. Penal Law §§ 100–103, 39 N. Y. Laws Ann. §§ 100–103 (McKinney 1944).

[5] Nothing in Judge Dye's dissenting opinion, to which the Court refers in Note 7 of its opinion, can be taken as militating against this view of the prevailing opinions in the Court of Appeals. Judge Dye simply disagreed with the majority of the Court of Appeals as to the adequacy of the § 122-a definition of "immoral" to overcome prior constitutional objections to that term. See 4 N. Y. 2d, at 371, 151 N. E. 2d, at 209–210, 175 N. Y. S. 2d, at 57; see also the dissenting opinion of Judge Van Voorhis, 4 N. Y. 2d, at 374, 151 N. E. 2d, at 212, 175 N. Y. S. 2d, at 60.

THE FILM "LES AMANTS" ("THE LOVERS") IS NOT OBSCENE

Jacobellis v. Ohio, 378 U.S. 184 (1964)

MR. JUSTICE BRENNAN announced the judgment of the Court and delivered an opinion in which MR. JUSTICE GOLDBERG joins.

Appellant, Nico Jacobellis, manager of a motion picture theater in Cleveland Heights, Ohio, was convicted on two counts of possessing and exhibiting an obscene film in violation of Ohio Revised Code (1963 Supp.), § 2905.34.[1] He was fined $500 on the first count and $2,000 on the

second, and was sentenced to the workhouse if the fines were not paid. His conviction, by a court of three judges upon waiver of trial by jury, was affirmed by an intermediate appellate court, 115 Ohio App. 226, 175 N. E. 2d 123, and by the Supreme Court of Ohio, 173 Ohio St. 22, 179 N. E. 2d 777. We noted probable jurisdiction of the appeal, 371 U. S. 808, and subsequently restored the case to the calendar for reargument, 373 U. S. 901. The dispositive question is whether the state courts properly found that the motion picture involved, a French film called *"Les Amants"* ("The Lovers"), was obscene and hence not entitled to the protection for free expression that is guaranteed by the First and Fourteenth Amendments. We conclude that the film is not obscene and that the judgment must accordingly be reversed.

Motion pictures are within the ambit of the constitutional guarantees of freedom of speech and of the press. *Joseph Burstyn, Inc.*, v. *Wilson*, 343 U. S. 495. But in *Roth* v. *United States* and *Alberts* v. *California*, 354 U. S. 476, we held that obscenity is not subject to those guarantees. Application of an obscenity law to suppress a motion picture thus requires ascertainment of the "dim and uncertain line" that often separates obscenity from constitutionally protected expression. *Bantam Books, Inc.*, v. *Sullivan*, 372 U. S. 58, 66; see *Speiser* v. *Randall*, 357 U. S. 513, 525.[2] It has been suggested that this is a task in which our Court need not involve itself. We are told that the determination whether a particular motion picture, book, or other work of expression is obscene can be treated as a purely factual judgment on which a jury's verdict is all but conclusive, or that in any event the decision can be left essentially to state and lower federal courts, with this Court exercising only a limited review such as that needed to determine whether the ruling below is supported by "sufficient evidence." The suggestion is appealing, since it would lift from our shoulders a difficult, recurring, and unpleasant task. But we cannot accept it. Such an abnegation of judicial supervision in this field would be inconsistent with our duty to uphold the constitutional guarantees. Since it is only "obscenity" that is excluded from the constitutional protection, the question whether a particular work is obscene necessarily implicates an issue of constitutional law. See *Roth* v. *United States, supra*, 354 U. S., at 497–498 (separate opinion). Such an issue, we think, must ultimately be decided by this Court. Our duty admits of no "substitute for facing up to the tough individual problems of constitutional judgment involved in every obscenity case." *Id.*, at 498; see *Manual Enterprises, Inc.*, v. *Day*, 370 U. S. 478, 488 (opinion of HARLAN, J.).[3]

In other areas involving constitutional rights under the Due Process Clause, the Court has consistently recognized its duty to apply the applicable rules of law upon the basis of an independent review of the facts of each case. *E. g.*, *Watts* v. *Indiana*, 338 U. S. 49, 51; *Norris* v. *Alabama*, 294 U. S. 587, 590.[4] And this has been particularly true where rights have been asserted under the First Amendment guarantees of free expression. Thus in *Pennekamp* v. *Florida*, 328 U. S. 331, 335, the Court stated:

"The Constitution has imposed upon this Court

final authority to determine the meaning and application of those words of that instrument which require interpretation to resolve judicial issues. With that responsibility, we are compelled to examine for ourselves the statements in issue and the circumstances under which they were made to see whether or not they . . . are of a character which the principles of the First Amendment, as adopted by the Due Process Clause of the Fourteenth Amendment, protect." [5]

We cannot understand why the Court's duty should be any different in the present case, where Jacobellis has been subjected to a criminal conviction for disseminating a work of expression and is challenging that conviction as a deprivation of rights guaranteed by the First and Fourteenth Amendments. Nor can we understand why the Court's performance of its constitutional and judicial function in this sort of case should be denigrated by such epithets as "censor" or "super-censor." In judging alleged obscenity the Court is no more "censoring" expression than it has in other cases "censored" criticism of judges and public officials, advocacy of governmental overthrow, or speech alleged to constitute a breach of the peace. Use of an opprobrious label can neither obscure nor impugn the Court's performance of its obligation to test challenged judgments against the guarantees of the First and Fourteenth Amendments and, in doing so, to delineate the scope of constitutionally protected speech. Hence we reaffirm the principle that, in "obscenity" cases as in all others involving rights derived from the First Amendment guarantees of free expression, this Court cannot avoid making an independent constitutional judgment on the facts of the case as to whether the material involved is constitutionally protected. [6]

The question of the proper standard for making this determination has been the subject· of much discussion and controversy since our decision in *Roth* seven years ago. Recognizing that the test for obscenity enunciated there—"whether to the average person, applying contemporary community standards, the dominant theme of the material taken as a whole appeals to prurient interest," 354 U. S., at 489—is not perfect, we think any substitute would raise equally difficult problems, and we therefore adhere to that standard. We would reiterate, however, our recognition in *Roth* that obscenity is excluded from the constitutional protection only because it is "utterly without redeeming social importance," and that "the portrayal of sex, *e. g.*, in art, literature and scientific works, is not itself sufficient reason to deny material the constitutional protection of freedom of speech and press." *Id.*, at 484, 487. It follows that material dealing with sex in a manner that advocates ideas, *Kingsley Int'l Pictures Corp.* v. *Regents*, 360 U. S. 684, or that has literary or scientific or artistic value or any other form of social importance, may not be branded as obscenity and denied the constitutional protection. [7] Nor may the constitutional status of the material be made to turn on a "weighing" of its social importance against its prurient appeal, for a work cannot be proscribed unless it is "utterly" without social importance. See *Zeitlin* v. *Arnebergh*, 59 Cal. 2d 901, 920, 383 P. 2d 152, 165, 31 Cal. Rptr. 800, 813 (1963). It should also be recognized that the *Roth* standard requires in the first instance

a finding that the material "goes substantially beyond customary limits of candor in description or representation of such matters." This was a requirement of the Model Penal Code test that we approved in *Roth*, 354 U. S., at 487, n. 20, and it is explicitly reaffirmed in the more recent Proposed Official Draft of the Code. [8] In the absence of such a deviation from society's standards of decency, we do not see how any official inquiry into the allegedly prurient appeal of a work of expression can be squared with the guarantees of the First and Fourteenth Amendments. See *Manual Enterprises, Inc.*, v. *Day*, 370 U. S. 478, 482–488 (opinion of HARLAN, J.).

It has been suggested that the "contemporary community standards" aspect of the *Roth* test implies a determination of the constitutional question of obscenity in each case by the standards of the particular local community from which the case arises. This is an incorrect reading of *Roth*. The concept of "contemporary community standards" was first expressed by Judge Learned Hand in *United States* v. *Kennerley*, 209 F. 119, 121 (D. C. S. D. N. Y. 1913), where he said:

"Yet, if the time is not yet when men think innocent all that which is honestly germane to a pure subject, however little it may mince its words, still I scarcely think that they would forbid all which might corrupt the most corruptible, or that society is prepared to accept for its own limitations those which may perhaps be necessary to the weakest of its members. If there be no abstract definition, such as I have suggested, should not the word 'obscene' be allowed to indicate the present critical point in the compromise between candor and shame at which *the community may have arrived here and now?* . . . To put thought in leash to the *average conscience of the time* is perhaps tolerable, but to fetter it by the necessities of the lowest and least capable seems a fatal policy.

"Nor is it an objection, I think, that such an interpretation gives to the words of the statute a varying meaning from time to time. Such words as these do not embalm the precise morals of an age or place; while they presuppose that some things will always be shocking to the public taste, the vague subject-matter is left to the gradual development of general notions about what is decent. . . ." (Italics added.)

It seems clear that in this passage Judge Hand was referring not to state and local "communities," but rather to "the community" in the sense of "society at large; . . . the public, or people in general." [9] Thus, he recognized that under his standard the concept of obscenity would have "a varying meaning from time to time"—not from county to county, or town to town.

We do not see how any "local" definition of the "community" could properly be employed in delineating the area of expression that is protected by the Federal Constitution. MR. JUSTICE HARLAN pointed out in *Manual Enterprises, Inc.*, v. *Day, supra*, 370 U. S., at 488, that a standard based on a particular local community would have "the intolerable consequence of denying some sections of the country access to material, there deemed acceptable, which in others might be considered offensive to prevailing community standards of decency. Cf. *But-*

ler v. *Michigan*, 352 U. S. 380." It is true that *Manual Enterprises* dealt with the federal statute banning obscenity from the mails. But the mails are not the only means by which works of expression cross local-community lines in this country. It can hardly be assumed that all the patrons of a particular library, bookstand, or motion picture theater are residents of the smallest local "community" that can be drawn around that establishment. Furthermore, to sustain the suppression of a particular book or film in one locality would deter its dissemination in other localities where it might be held not obscene, since sellers and exhibitors would be reluctant to risk criminal conviction in testing the variation between the two places. It would be a hardy person who would sell a book or exhibit a film anywhere in the land after this Court had sustained the judgment of one "community" holding it to be outside the constitutional protection. The result would thus be "to restrict the public's access to forms of the printed word which the State could not constitutionally suppress directly." *Smith* v. *California*, 361 U. S. 147, 154.

It is true that local communities throughout the land are in fact diverse, and that in cases such as this one the Court is confronted with the task of reconciling the rights of such communities with the rights of individuals. Communities vary, however, in many respects other than their toleration of alleged obscenity, and such variances have never been considered to require or justify a varying standard for application of the Federal Constitution. The Court has regularly been compelled, in reviewing criminal convictions challenged under the Due Process Clause of the Fourteenth Amendment, to reconcile the conflicting rights of the local community which brought the prosecution and of the individual defendant. Such a task is admittedly difficult and delicate, but it is inherent in the Court's duty of determining whether a particular conviction worked a deprivation of rights guaranteed by the Federal Constitution. The Court has not shrunk from discharging that duty in other areas, and we see no reason why it should do so here. The Court has explicitly refused to tolerate a result whereby "the constitutional limits of free expression in the Nation would vary with state lines," *Pennekamp* v. *Florida, supra*, 328 U. S., at 335; we see even less justification for allowing such limits to vary with town or county lines. We thus reaffirm the position taken in *Roth* to the effect that the constitutional status of an allegedly obscene work must be determined on the basis of a national standard.[10] It is, after all, a national Constitution we are expounding.

We recognize the legitimate and indeed exigent interest of States and localities throughout the Nation in preventing the dissemination of material deemed harmful to children. But that interest does not justify a total suppression of such material, the effect of which would be to "reduce the adult population . . . to reading only what is fit for children." *Butler* v. *Michigan*, 352 U. S. 380, 383. State and local authorities might well consider whether their objectives in this area would be better served by laws aimed specifically at preventing distribution of objectionable material to children, rather than at totally prohibiting its dissemination.[11] Since the present conviction is based upon exhibition of the film to the public at large and not upon its exhibition to children, the judgment must be reviewed under the strict standard applicable in determining the scope of the expression that is protected by the Constitution.

We have applied that standard to the motion picture in question. "The Lovers" involves a woman bored with her life and marriage who abandons her husband and family for a young archaeologist with whom she has suddenly fallen in love. There is an explicit love scene in the last reel of the film, and the State's objections are based almost entirely upon that scene. The film was favorably reviewed in a number of national publications, although disparaged in others, and was rated by at least two critics of national stature among the best films of the year in which it was produced. It was shown in approximately 100 of the larger cities in the United States, including Columbus and Toledo, Ohio. We have viewed the film, in the light of the record made in the trial court, and we conclude that it is not obscene within the standards enunciated in *Roth* v. *United States* and *Alberts* v. *California*, which we reaffirm here.

Reversed.

Mr. Justice White concurs in the judgment.

Opinion of Mr. Justice Black, with whom Mr. Justice Douglas joins.

I concur in the reversal of this judgment. My belief, as stated in *Kingsley International Pictures Corp.* v. *Regents*, 360 U. S. 684, 690, is that "If despite the Constitution . . . this Nation is to embark on the dangerous road of censorship, . . . this Court is about the most inappropriate Supreme Board of Censors that could be found." My reason for reversing is that I think the conviction of appellant or anyone else for exhibiting a motion picture abridges freedom of the press as safeguarded by the First Amendment, which is made obligatory on the States by the Fourteenth. See my concurring opinions in *Quantity of Copies of Books* v. *Kansas, post*, p. 213; *Smith* v. *California*, 361 U. S. 147, 155; *Kingsley International Pictures Corp.* v. *Regents, supra*. See also the dissenting opinion of Mr. Justice Douglas in *Roth* v. *United States*, 354 U. S. 476, 508, and his concurring opinion in *Superior Films, Inc.*, v. *Department of Education*, 346 U. S. 587, 588, in both of which I joined.

Mr. Justice Stewart, concurring.

It is possible to read the Court's opinion in *Roth* v. *United States* and *Alberts* v. *California*, 354 U. S. 476, in a variety of ways. In saying this, I imply no criticism of the Court, which in those cases was faced with the task of trying to define what may be indefinable. I have reached the conclusion, which I think is confirmed at least by negative implication in the Court's decisions since *Roth* and *Alberts*,[1] that under the First and Fourteenth Amendments criminal laws in this area are constitutionally limited to hard-core pornography.[2] I shall not today attempt further to define the kinds of material I understand to be embraced within that shorthand description; and perhaps I could never succeed in intelligibly doing so. But I know it when I see it, and the motion picture involved in this case is not that.

MR. JUSTICE GOLDBERG, concurring.

The question presented is whether the First and Fourteenth Amendments permit the imposition of criminal punishment for exhibiting the motion picture entitled "The Lovers." I have viewed the film and I wish merely to add to my Brother BRENNAN's description that the love scene deemed objectionable is so fragmentary and fleeting that only a censor's alert would make an audience conscious that something "questionable" is being portrayed. Except for this rapid sequence, the film concerns itself with the history of an ill-matched and unhappy marriage—a familiar subject in old and new novels and in current television soap operas.

Although I fully agree with what my Brother BRENNAN has written, I am also of the view that adherence to the principles stated in *Joseph Burstyn, Inc.*, v. *Wilson*, 343 U. S. 495, requires reversal. In *Burstyn* MR. JUSTICE CLARK, delivering the unanimous judgment of the Court, said:

> "[E]xpression by means of motion pictures is included within the free speech and free press guaranty of the First and Fourteenth Amendments. . . .
>
> "To hold that liberty of expression by means of motion pictures is guaranteed by the First and Fourteenth Amendments, however, is not the end of our problem. It does not follow that the Constitution requires absolute freedom to exhibit every motion picture of every kind at all times and all places. . . . Nor does it follow that motion pictures are necessarily subject to the precise rules governing any other particular method of expression. Each method tends to present its own peculiar problems. But the basic principles of freedom of speech and the press, like the First Amendment's command, do not vary. Those principles, as they have frequently been enunciated by this Court, make freedom of expression the rule." *Id.*, at 502–503.

As in *Burstyn* "[t]here is no justification in this case for making an exception to that rule," *id.*, at 503, for by any arguable standard the exhibitors of this motion picture may not be criminally prosecuted unless the exaggerated character of the advertising rather than the obscenity of the film is to be the constitutional criterion.

THE CHIEF JUSTICE, with whom MR. JUSTICE CLARK joins, dissenting.

In this and other cases in this area of the law, which are coming to us in ever-increasing numbers, we are faced with the resolution of rights basic both to individuals and to society as a whole. Specifically, we are called upon to reconcile the right of the Nation and of the States to maintain a decent society and, on the other hand, the right of individuals to express themselves freely in accordance with the guarantees of the First and Fourteenth Amendments. Although the Federal Government and virtually every State has had laws proscribing obscenity since the Union was formed, and although this Court has recently decided that obscenity is not within the protection of the First Amendment,[1] neither courts nor legislatures have been able to evolve a truly satisfactory definition of obscenity. In other areas of the law, terms like "negligence," although in common use for centuries, have been difficult to define except in the most general manner. Yet the courts have been able to function in such areas with a reasonable degree of efficiency. The obscenity problem, however, is aggravated by the fact that it involves the area of public expression, an area in which a broad range of freedom is vital to our society and is constitutionally protected.

Recently this Court put its hand to the task of defining the term "obscenity" in *Roth* v. *United States*, 354 U. S. 476. The definition enunciated in that case has generated much legal speculation as well as further judicial interpretation by state and federal courts. It has also been relied upon by legislatures. Yet obscenity cases continue to come to this Court, and it becomes increasingly apparent that we must settle as well as we can the question of what constitutes "obscenity" and the question of what standards are permissible in enforcing proscriptions against obscene matter. This Court hears cases such as the instant one not merely to rule upon the alleged obscenity of a specific film or book but to establish principles for the guidance of lower courts and legislatures. Yet most of our decisions since *Roth* have been given without opinion and have thus failed to furnish such guidance. Nor does the Court in the instant case—which has now been twice argued before us—shed any greater light on the problem. Therefore, I consider it appropriate to state my views at this time.

For all the sound and fury that the *Roth* test has generated, it has not been proved unsound, and I believe that we should try to live with it—at least until a more satisfactory definition is evolved. No government—be it federal, state, or local—should be forced to choose between repressing all material, including that within the realm of decency, and allowing unrestrained license to publish any material, no matter how vile. There must be a rule of reason in this as in other areas of the law, and we have attempted in the *Roth* case to provide such a rule.

It is my belief that when the Court said in *Roth* that obscenity is to be defined by reference to "community standards," it meant community standards—not a national standard, as is sometimes argued. I believe that there is no provable "national standard," and perhaps there should be none. At all events, this Court has not been able to enunciate one, and it would be unreasonable to expect local courts to divine one. It is said that such a "community" approach may well result in material being proscribed as obscene in one community but not in another, and, in all probability, that is true. But communities throughout the Nation are in fact diverse, and it must be remembered that, in cases such as this one, the Court is confronted with the task of reconciling conflicting rights of the diverse communities within our society and of individuals.

We are told that only "hard core pornography" should be denied the protection of the First Amendment. But who can define "hard core pornography" with any greater clarity than "obscenity"? And even if we were to retreat to that position, we would soon be faced with the need to define that term just as we now are faced with the need to define "obscenity." Meanwhile, those who profit from the commercial exploitation of obscenity would continue to ply their trade unmolested.

In my opinion, the use to which various materials are put—not just the words and pictures themselves—must be considered in determining whether or not the materials are obscene. A technical or legal treatise on pornography may well be inoffensive under most circumstances but, at the same time, "obscene" in the extreme when sold or displayed to children.[2]

Finally, material which is in fact obscene under the *Roth* test may be proscribed in a number of ways—for instance, by confiscation of the material or by prosecution of those who disseminate it—provided always that the proscription, whatever it may be, is imposed in accordance with constitutional standards. If the proceeding involved is criminal, there must be a right to a jury trial, a right to counsel, and all the other safeguards necessary to assure due process of law. If the proceeding is civil in nature, the constitutional requirements applicable in such a case must also be observed. There has been some tendency in dealing with this area of the law for enforcement agencies to do only that which is easy to do—for instance, to seize and destroy books with only a minimum of protection. As a result, courts are often presented with procedurally bad cases and, in dealing with them, appear to be acquiescing in the dissemination of obscenity. But if cases were well prepared and were conducted with the appropriate concern for constitutional safeguards, courts would not hesitate to enforce the laws against obscenity. Thus, enforcement agencies must realize that there is no royal road to enforcement; hard and conscientious work is required.

In light of the foregoing, I would reiterate my acceptance of the rule of the *Roth* case: Material is obscene and not constitutionally protected against regulation and proscription if "to the average person, applying contemporary community standards, the dominant theme of the material taken as a whole appeals to prurient interest." 354 U. S., at 489. I would commit the enforcement of this rule to the appropriate state and federal courts, and I would accept their judgments made pursuant to the *Roth* rule, limiting myself to a consideration only of whether there is sufficient evidence in the record upon which a finding of obscenity could be made. If there is no evidence in the record upon which such a finding could be made, obviously the material involved cannot be held obscene. Cf. *Thompson* v. *City of Louisville*, 362 U. S. 199. But since a mere modicum of evidence may satisfy a "no evidence" standard, I am unwilling to give the important constitutional right of free expression such limited protection. However, protection of society's right to maintain its moral fiber and the effective administration of justice require that this Court not establish itself as an ultimate censor, in each case reading the entire record, viewing the accused material, and making an independent *de novo* judgment on the question of obscenity. Therefore, once a finding of obscenity has been made below under a proper application of the *Roth* test, I would apply a "sufficient evidence" standard of review—requiring something more than merely any evidence but something less than "substantial evidence on the record [including the allegedly obscene material] as a whole." Cf. *Universal Camera Corp.* v. *Labor Board*, 340 U. S. 474. This is the only reasonable way I can see to obviate the necessity of this Court's sitting as the Super Censor of all the obscenity purveyed throughout the Nation.

While in this case, I do not subscribe to some of the State's extravagant contentions, neither can I say that the courts below acted with intemperance or without sufficient evidence in finding the moving picture obscene within the meaning of the *Roth* test. Therefore, I would affirm the judgment.

Mr. Justice Harlan, dissenting.

While agreeing with my Brother Brennan's opinion that the responsibilities of the Court in this area are no different from those which attend the adjudication of kindred constitutional questions, I have heretofore expressed the view that the States are constitutionally permitted greater latitude in determining what is bannable on the score of obscenity than is so with the Federal Government. See my opinion in *Roth* v. *United States*, 354 U. S. 476, 496; cf. my opinion in *Manual Enterprises, Inc.*, v. *Day*, 370 U. S. 478. While, as correctly said in Mr. Justice Brennan's opinion, the Court has not accepted that view, I nonetheless feel free to adhere to it in this still developing aspect of constitutional law.

The more I see of these obscenity cases the more convinced I become that in permitting the States wide, but not federally unrestricted, scope in this field, while holding the Federal Government with a tight rein, lies the best promise for achieving a sensible accommodation between the public interest sought to be served by obscenity laws (cf. my dissenting opinion in *Bantam Books, Inc.*, v. *Sullivan*, 372 U. S. 58, 76, 77) and protection of genuine rights of free expression.

I experience no greater ease than do other members of the Court in attempting to verbalize generally the respective constitutional tests, for in truth the matter in the last analysis depends on how particular challenged material happens to strike the minds of jurors or judges and ultimately those of a majority of the members of this Court. The application of any general constitutional tests must thus necessarily be pricked out on a case-by-case basis, but as a point of departure I would apply to the Federal Government the *Roth* standards as amplified in my opinion in *Manual Enterprises, supra*. As to the States, I would make the federal test one of rationality. I would not prohibit them from banning any material which, taken as a whole, has been reasonably found in state judicial proceedings to treat with sex in a fundamentally offensive manner, under rationally established criteria for judging such material.

On this basis, having viewed the motion picture in question, I think the State acted within permissible limits in condemning the film and would affirm the judgment of the Ohio Supreme Court.

JUSTICE BRENNAN'S OPINION NOTES

[1] *"Selling, exhibiting, and possessing obscene literature or drugs, for criminal purposes.*

"No person shall knowingly sell, lend, give away, exhibit, or offer to sell, lend, give away, or exhibit, or publish or offer to publish or have in his possession or under his control an obscene, lewd, or lascivious book, magazine, pamphlet, paper, writing, advertisement, circular, print, picture, photograph, motion picture film, or book, pamphlet, paper, magazine not wholly obscene but containing lewd or lascivious articles, advertisements, photographs, or drawing, representation, figure, image, cast, instrument, or article of an indecent or immoral nature, or a drug, medicine, article, or thing intended for the prevention of conception or for causing an abortion, or advertise any of them for sale, or write, print, or cause to be written or printed a card, book, pamphlet, advertisement, or notice giving information when, where, how, of whom, or by what means any of such articles or things can be purchased or obtained, or manufacture, draw, print, or make such articles or things, or sell, give away, or show to a minor, a book, pamphlet, magazine, newspaper, story paper, or other paper devoted to the publication, or principally made up, of criminal news, police reports, or accounts of criminal deeds, or pictures and stories of immoral deeds, lust, or crime, or exhibit upon a street or highway or in a place which may be within the view of a minor, any of such books, papers, magazines, or pictures.

"Whoever violates this section shall be fined not less than two hundred nor more than two thousand dollars or imprisoned not less than one nor more than seven years, or both."

² It is too late in the day to argue that the location of the line is different, and the task of ascertaining it easier, when a state rather than a federal obscenity law is involved. The view that the constitutional guarantees of free expression do not apply as fully to the States as they do to the Federal Government was rejected in *Roth-Alberts, supra,* where the Court's single opinion applied the same standards to both a state and a federal conviction. Cf. *Ker* v. *California,* 374 U. S. 23, 33; *Malloy* v. *Hogan, ante,* pp. 1, 10–11.

³ See *Kingsley Int'l Pictures Corp.* v. *Regents,* 360 U. S. 684, 708 (separate opinion):
"It is sometimes said that this Court should shun considering the particularities of individual cases in this difficult field lest the Court become a final 'board of censorship.' But I cannot understand why it should be thought that the process of constitutional judgment in this realm somehow stands apart from that involved in other fields, particularly those presenting questions of due process. . . ."
See also Lockhart and McClure, Censorship of Obscenity: The Developing Constitutional Standards, 45 Minn. L. Rev. 5, 116 (1960): "This obligation—to reach an independent judgment in applying constitutional standards and criteria to constitutional issues that may be cast by lower courts 'in the form of determinations of fact'— appears fully applicable to findings of obscenity by juries, trial courts, and administrative agencies. The Supreme Court is subject to that obligation, as is every court before which the constitutional issue is raised."
And see *id.,* at 119:
"It may be true . . . that judges 'possess no special expertise' qualifying them 'to supervise the private morals of the Nation' or to decide 'what movies are good or bad for local communities.' But they do have a far keener understanding of the importance of free expression than do most government administrators or jurors, and they have had considerable experience in making value judgments of the type required by the constitutional standards for obscenity. If freedom is to be preserved, neither government censorship experts nor juries can be left to make the final effective decisions restraining free expression. Their decisions must be subject to effective, independent review, and we know of no group better qualified for that review than the appellate judges of this country under the guidance of the Supreme Court."

⁴ See also *Fiske* v. *Kansas,* 274 U. S. 380, 385–386; *Haynes* v. *Washington,* 373 U. S. 503, 515–516; *Chambers* v. *Florida,* 309 U. S. 227, 229; *Hooven & Allison Co.* v. *Evatt,* 324 U. S. 652, 659; *Lisenba* v. *California,* 314 U. S. 219, 237–238; *Ashcraft* v. *Tennessee,* 322 U. S. 143, 147–148; *Napue* v. *Illinois,* 360 U. S. 264, 271.

⁵ See also *Niemotko* v. *Maryland,* 340 U. S. 268, 271; *Craig* v. *Harney,* 331 U. S. 367, 373–374; *Bridges* v. *California,* 314 U. S. 252, 271; *Edwards* v. *South Carolina,* 372 U. S. 229, 235; *New York Times Co.* v. *Sullivan,* 376 U. S. 254, 285.

⁶ This is precisely what the Court did in *Times Film Corp.* v. *City of Chicago,* 355 U. S. 35; *One, Inc.,* v. *Olesen,* 355 U. S. 371; and *Sunshine Book Co.* v. *Summerfield,* 355 U. S. 372. The obligation has been recognized by state courts as well. See, *e. g.,* *State* v. *Hudson County News Co.,* 41 N. J. 247, 256–257, 196 A. 2d 225, 230 (1963); *Zeitlin* v. *Arnebergh,* 59 Cal. 2d 901, 909–911, 383 P. 2d 152, 157–158, 31 Cal. Rptr. 800, 805–806 (1963); *People* v. *Richmond County News, Inc.,* 9 N. Y. 2d 578, 580–581, 175 N. E. 2d 681, 681–682, 216 N. Y. S. 2d 369, 370 (1961). See also American Law

Institute, Model Penal Code, Proposed Official Draft (May 4, 1962), § 251.4 (4).

Nor do we think our duty of constitutional adjudication in this area can properly be relaxed by reliance on a "sufficient evidence" standard of review. Even in judicial review of administrative agency determinations, questions of "constitutional fact" have been held to require *de novo* review. *Ng Fung Ho* v. *White,* 259 U. S. 276, 284–285; *Crowell* v. *Benson,* 285 U. S. 22, 54–65.

⁷ See, *e. g., Attorney General* v. *Book Named "Tropic of Cancer,"* 345 Mass. 11, 184 N. E. 2d 328 (Mass. 1962); *Zeitlin* v. *Arnebergh,* 59 Cal. 2d 901, 383 P. 2d 152, 31 Cal. Rptr. 800 (1963).

⁸ American Law Institute, Model Penal Code, Proposed Official Draft (May 4, 1962), § 251.4 (1):
"Material is obscene if, considered as a whole, its predominant appeal is to prurient interest . . . and if *in addition* it goes substantially beyond customary limits of candor in describing or representing such matters." (Italics added.)

⁹ Webster's New International Dictionary (2d ed. 1949), at 542.

¹⁰ See *State* v. *Hudson County News Co.,* 41 N. J. 247, 266, 196 A. 2d 225, 235 (1963). Lockhart and McClure, note 3, *supra,* 45 Minn. L. Rev., at 108–112; American Law Institute, Model Penal Code, Tentative Draft No. 6 (May 6, 1957), at 45; Proposed Official Draft (May 4, 1962), § 251.4 (4) (d).

¹¹ See *State* v. *Settle,* 90 R. I. 195, 156 A. 2d 921 (1959).

JUSTICE STEWART'S OPINION NOTES

¹ *Times Film Corp.* v. *City of Chicago,* 355 U. S. 35, reversing 244 F. 2d 432; *One, Incorporated,* v. *Olesen,* 355 U. S. 371, reversing 241 F. 2d 772; *Sunshine Book Co.* v. *Summerfield,* 355 U. S. 372, reversing 101 U. S. App. D. C. 358, 249 F. 2d 114; *Manual Enterprises* v. *Day,* 370 U. S. 478 (opinion of HARLAN, J.).

² Cf. *People* v. *Richmond County News,* 9 N. Y. 2d 578, 175 N. E. 2d 681, 216 N. Y. S. 2d 369.

CHIEF JUSTICE'S OPINION NOTES

¹ *Roth* v. *United States.* 354 U. S. 476.

² In the instant case, for example, the advertisements published to induce the public to view the motion picture provide some evidence of the film's dominant theme: "When all conventions explode . . . in the most daring love story ever filmed!" "As close to authentic amour as is possible on the screen." "The frankest love scenes yet seen on film." "Contains one of the longest and most sensuous love scenes to be seen in this country."

THE FILM "I AM CURIOUS-YELLOW" IS NOT OBSCENE FOR THE DOMINANT THEME OF THE FILM "IS CERTAINLY NOT SEX" AND "IT IS EVEN MORE CLEAR THAT 'I AM CURIOUS' IS NOT UTTERLY WITHOUT REDEEMING SOCIAL VALUE."

United States v. *A Motion Picture Film Entitled "I Am Curious-Yellow,"* 404 F.2d 196 (1968)

HAYS, Circuit Judge:
This is an appeal from a judgment of the district court, after a jury trial, ordering the forfeiture and confiscation under Section 305 of the Tariff Act of 1930, 19 U.S.C. § 1305 (1964)¹ of the motion picture entitled "I Am Curious-Yellow." We reverse the judgment on the ground that under standards established by the Supreme Court the showing of the picture cannot be inhibited.

"I Am Curious-Yellow" was produced in Sweden and the dialogue is in Swedish; English subtitles have been added. As with many other contemporary artistic productions there can be a difference of opinion as to what the picture is "about."[2] It would perhaps not be demonstrably wrong to say that it is concerned with that subject which has become such a commonplace in contemporary fiction and drama, the search for identity. It is the story of a young girl who is trying to work out her relationship to such political, social, and economic problems as the possibility of a classless society, the acceptance of the Franco regime, and the policy and practice of nonviolence. At one point the girl experiments with oriental religious ritual and meditation. The girl's inter-personal relationships are also pictured, including particularly her relation to her father, presented as an idealist who has become disillusioned and has given up meaningful activity. A fairly large portion of the film is devoted to the relations between the girl and her young lover.

A number of different techniques are employed in the production of the film. For example much of the early part is in terms of "cinema verité," showing the girl asking questions on subjects of public importance of the ordinary man or woman in the street. The problem of the nature of reality is suggested by passages representing the girl's fantasies and by the injection into the story of material concerning the making of the picture itself, such as the director's relations with the leading actress.

There are a number of scenes which show the young girl and her lover nude. Several scenes depict sexual intercourse under varying circumstances, some of them quite unusual. There are scenes of oral-genital activity.

It seems to be conceded that the sexual content of the film is presented with greater explicitness than has been seen in any other film produced for general viewing. The question for decision is whether, going farther in this direction than any previous production, the film exceeds the limits established by the courts.

The government argues with considerable cogency that the standards by which motion pictures are to be judged may be different from those that are used in the case of books. It points out that a motion picture reproduces actual conduct so that it can be seen and heard. Books are read by individuals in private, whereas motion pictures are viewed in public. Nudity and sexual activity in motion pictures, it is argued, bear a close resemblance to nudity and sexual activity in a public place. Obviously conduct of this type may be forbidden.

No doubt the standards by which motion pictures are to be judged differ in some particulars from those to be applied to books, see Freedman v. Maryland, 380 U.S. 51, 60–61, 85 S.Ct. 734, 13 L.Ed.2d 649 (1965); Joseph Burstyn, Inc. v. Wilson, 343 U.S. 495, 503, 72 S.Ct. 777, 96 L.Ed. 1098 (1952); United States v. One Carton Positive Motion Picture Film Entitled "491," 367 F.2d 889, 907 (2d Cir.1966) (Lumbard, Ch. J., dissenting); but see Jacobellis v. Ohio, 378 U.S. 184, 84 S.Ct. 1676, 12 L.Ed.2d 793 (1964), Nevertheless the comparison urged by the government between nudity and sexual activity in a public place and the same matters as portrayed in a motion picture such as "I Am Curious" is far fetched. In the motion picture the material is a part of an artistic whole and is united with and related to the story and the characters which are presented. This is vastly different from a sudden unrelated episode taking place in public. The exhibition in

a motion picture of an isolated instance of sexual intercourse or of irrelevant nudity, which would indeed be equivalent to public display, could be halted under the established standards, just as could similar material if it appeared in print.

Whatever differences there may be in the application of obscenity standards, a motion picture, like a book, is clearly entitled to the protection of the first amendment. Joseph Burstyn, Inc. v. Wilson, supra; Interstate Circuit, Inc. v. City of Dallas, 390 U.S. 676, 88 S.Ct. 1298, 20 L.Ed.2d 225 (1968). And the test of whether a motion picture is to be condemned is the three-fold test stated in A Book Named "John Cleland's Memoirs of a Woman of Pleasure" v. Atty. Gen. of Com. of Massachusetts, 383 U.S. 413, 418, 86 S.Ct. 975, 977, 16 L.Ed.2d 1 (1966):

"[T]hree elements must coalesce: it must be established that (a) the dominant theme of the material taken as a whole appeals to a prurient interest in sex; (b) the material is patently offensive because it affronts contemporary community standards relating to the description or representation of sexual matters; and (c) the material is utterly without redeeming social value."

The issue of the obscenity of "I Am Curious" was submitted to the jury under this three-fold test and the jury found the picture obscene. However, in our view obscenity *vel non* is not an issue of fact with respect to which the jury's finding has its usual conclusive effect. It is rather an issue of constitutional law that must eventually be decided by the court. As Mr. Justice Harlan said in Roth v. United States, 354 U.S. 476, 497–98, 77 S.Ct. 1304, 1316, 1 L.Ed.2d 1498 (1957) (concurring and dissenting):

"[I]f 'obscenity' is to be suppressed, the question whether a particular work is of that character involves not really an issue of fact but a question of constitutional *judgment* of the most sensitive and delicate kind. Many juries might find that Joyce's 'Ulysses' or Boccaccio's 'Decameron' was obscene, and yet the conviction of a defendant for selling either book would raise, for me, the gravest constitutional problems, for no such verdict could convince me, without more, that these books are 'utterly without redeeming social importance.' " (Emphasis in original.)

See also the remarks of Mr. Justice Brennan in Jacobellis v. Ohio, supra, 378 U.S. at 187–90, 84 S.Ct. 1676.

Applying the *Memoirs* standards we find that the picture cannot be classified as obscene on at least two of the three grounds comprising the test.

Although sexual conduct is undeniably an important aspect of the picture and may be thought of as constituting one of its principal themes, it cannot be said that "the dominant theme of the material taken as a whole appeals to a prurient interest in sex." Whatever the dominant theme may be said to be (see footnote 2 supra) it is certainly not sex. Moreover, not only is the sexual theme subordinate, but it is handled in such a way as to make it at least extremely doubtful that interest in it should be characterized as "prurient."

It is even more clear that "I Am Curious" is not utterly without redeeming social value. Whatever weight we may attach to the opinions of the "experts" who testified to the picture's social importance, and whether or not we ourselves consider the ideas of the picture particularly interesting or the production artistically successful, it is quite certain that "I Am Curious" does present ideas and does strive to present these ideas artistically. It falls within the ambit of intellectual effort that the first amendment was designed to protect.

On the issue of whether the picture is "patently offensive because it affronts contemporary community standards relating to the description or representation of sexual matters," the jury's verdict may carry more weight. (But see Jacobellis v. Ohio, supra, 378 U.S. at 192–95, 84 S.Ct. at 1680; cf. United States v. Klaw, 350 F.2d 155 (2d Cir. 1965); see also Ginzburg v. United States, 383 U.S. 463, 479–80, 86 S.Ct. 942, 16 L.Ed.2d 31 (1966) (Black, J., dissenting)). However, it is unnecessary for us to pass upon this third test, since the picture is not obscene under the other two of the Supreme Court's standards.

We hold, therefore, that the picture cannot be condemned under Section 305.

FRIENDLY, Circuit Judge (concurring):

This court's responsibility here is limited. We are not, as Chief Judge Lumbard's dissent seems to assume, writing on what is largely a clean slate, but rather on one already well covered by our superiors. Our duty as an inferior federal court is to apply, as best we can, the standards the Supreme Court has decreed with regard to obscenity. That task, to be sure, is not altogether easy in light of the divergence of views within the Court and the consequent multiplicity of opinions; a scholarly article has deduced from the spate of decisions in 1966 no less than "five separate and contradictory tests." Magrath, The Obscenity Cases: Grapes of Roth, 1966 Sup. Court Rev. 7, 56–57.[1]

If the governing rule were still what Mr. Justice Brennan stated in Roth v. United States, 354 U.S. 476, 489, 77 S.Ct. 1304, 1 L.Ed.2d 1498 (1957), namely, "whether to the average person, applying contemporary community standards, the dominant theme of the material taken as a whole appeals to prurient interest," I might well join Chief Judge Lumbard for affirmance. But, quite clearly, it is not. The modification began with the opinion of Mr. Justice Brennan, writing also for Mr. Justice Goldberg, in Jacobellis v. Ohio, 378 U.S. 184, 191–192, 84 S.Ct. 1676 (1964), and the transformation was completed in A Book Named "John Cleland's Memoirs of a Woman of Pleasure" v. Massachusetts, 383 U.S. 413, 86 S.Ct. 975 (1966). There Mr. Justice Brennan, in an opinion joined by the Chief Justice and Mr. Justice Fortas, while professing adherence to *Roth*, emerged with a much more permissive standard. Under *Memoirs* a publication cannot be condemned simply because "the dominant theme of the material taken as a whole appeals to a prurient interest in sex" and "the material is patently offensive because it affronts contemporary community standards relating to the description or representation of sexual matters." Although these criteria are met, "a book cannot be proscribed unless it is found to be *utterly* without redeeming social value. This is so even though the book is found to possess the requisite prurient appeal and to be patently offensive. Each of the three federal constitutional criteria is to be applied independently: the social value of the book can neither be weighed against nor canceled by its prurient appeal or patent offensiveness." 383 U.S. at 418–420, 86 S.Ct. at 978. The deliberate character of this change was highlighted in the dissents of Mr. Justice Clark, 383 U.S. at 451, 86 S.Ct. 975, and Mr. Justice White, 383 U.S. at 460–462, 86 S.Ct. 975. Judge Hays' opinion sufficiently demonstrates the existence of the required modicum of social value here.

It is true that in *Memoirs* Mr. Justice Brennan wrote only for three Justices. But it is plain that three other members of that bench would have opted for an even more permissive standard and a fourth would have done so for federal action. Justices Black and Douglas have consistently considered all obscene matter to be "constitutionally protected, except where it can be shown to be so brigaded with illegal action that it constitutes a clear and present danger to significant social interests," Magrath, supra, 1966 Sup. Court Rev. at 56. Mr. Justice Stewart believes that the First Amendment permits the outlawing only of hard-core pornography, Jacobellis v. Ohio, supra, 378 U.S. at 197, 84 S.Ct. 1676 (concurring), and Ginzburg v. United States, 383 U.S. 463, 499–500, 86 S.Ct. 942 (1966) (dissenting). Mr. Justice Harlan initiated the hard-core pornography limitation with respect to federal action although he would allow greater leeway to the states, Roth v. United States, supra, 354 U.S. at 496, 77 S.Ct. 1304 (concurring and dissenting), and he continues to hold this view, Ginzburg v. United States, supra, 383 U.S. at 493, 86 S.Ct. 942 (dissenting).

While I do not challenge Chief Judge Lumbard's views about the offensive character of the extensive displays of nudity and sexual activity in "I Am Curious-Yellow,"[2] the latter falls short of Mr. Justice Clark's description of those which apparently comprise almost all of "Memoirs of a Woman of Pleasure," 383 U.S. at 445–446, 86 S.Ct. at 989. Not truly disputing that, the Government makes two arguments for a different result here. The first is that a stricter standard should apply to motion pictures and plays than to books. Although, for reasons indicated in the opinions of both of my brothers, there might be merit to this as an original question, I find nothing in the Supreme Court's opinions that would justify a lower court in embarking on such a doctrinal innovation, which might import further confusion into a subject already sufficiently confounded. *Jacobellis* related to a film and neither the majority nor the dissenting opinions suggested that any stricter standard would apply. The 5-to-4 *per curiam* affirmance in Landau v. Fording, 388 U.S. 456, 87 S.Ct. 2109, 18 L.Ed.2d 1317 (1967), affords too frail a foundation to support a construction of this sort.[3] The other is that there is no sufficient nexus in this film between the scenes of nudity and sexual activity and the problems of the girl—one could hardly call her the heroine—in trying to work out her relationship with life. Although *Memoirs* did not in terms require such a nexus, I would agree that the presence of "redeeming social value" should not save the day if the sexual episodes were simply lugged in and bore no relationship whatever to the theme; a truly pornographic film would not be rescued by inclusion of a few verses from the Psalms. While this case may come somewhat close to the line, I cannot conscientiously say that a connection between the serious purpose and the sexual episodes and displays of nudity is wholly wanting.

The only point requiring further discussion is Chief Judge Lumbard's elevation of the role of the jury. This has its attractiveness, if only in relieving busy appellate courts from having to spend so much time on cases like this. See O'Meara & Shaffer, Obscenity in the Supreme Court: A Note on Jacobellis v. Ohio, 40 Notre Dame Lawyer 1 (1964). But I find little support for his thesis in the many opinions of members of the Supreme Court during the last decade. Even Chief Justice Warren's more moderate statement in dissent in Jacobellis v. Ohio, supra, 378 U.S. at 202–203, 84 S.Ct. at 1686, that he would subject the judgments of lower courts "to a consideration only of whether there is sufficient evidence in the record upon which a finding of obscenity could be made," was concurred in solely by Mr. Justice Clark. Squarely to the contrary are Mr. Justice Harlan's observations in dissent in Roth v. United States, supra, 354 U.S. at 497–498, 77 S.Ct. 1304, and in speaking for himself and Mr. Justice Stewart in Manual Enterprises, Inc. v. Day, 370 U.S. 478, 488, 82 S.Ct. 1432, 8 L.Ed.2d 639 (1962), and Mr. Justice Brennan's expressions for himself and Mr. Justice Goldberg, joined in this respect by Mr. Justice Harlan, in Jacobellis v. Ohio, supra, 378 U.S. at 189–190, 203, 84 S.Ct. 1676. Placing the decisional task upon judges is a natural consequence of the emphasis on "a national standard of decency," Manual Enterprises v. Day, supra, 370 U.S. at 488, 82 S.Ct. 1432 (Harlan, J.), and Jacobellis v. Ohio, supra, 378 U.S. at 194–195, 84 S.Ct. 1676 (Brennan, J.), a principle peculiarly applicable to a federal statute governing the exclusion of a film from the entire United States.[4] Likewise the jury has no special competence on the issue of "redeeming social value." Finally, the Director of the Imports Compliance Division of the Bureau of Customs here conceded that the film had social value; the contrary verdict cannot be supported, for reasons outlined in Judge Hays' opinion; and the issue of a sufficient nexus is peculiarly unsusceptible for jury determination and never was submitted to it.

When all this has been said, I am no happier than Chief Judge Lumbard about allowing Grove Press to bring this film into the United States. But our individual happiness or unhappiness is unimportant, and that result is dictated by Supreme Court decisions. If we could depart from the plurality opinions in favor of the hard-core pornography test advocated by Mr. Justice Stewart and, for federal action, by Mr. Justice Harlan—which, we are told, would at least have the merit of manageability, see Magrath, supra, 1966 Sup. Court Rev. at 69–77—reversal would be still more clearly dictated. What we ought to make plain, however, and not at all in a "tongue-in-cheek" fashion, is that our ruling is limited in two respects. The importer has represented that it intends to require exhibitors to exclude minors from the audience; it must realize that if this representation should be violated, the film and its distributors and exhibitors will be subject to attack under the principal of Ginsberg v. New York, 390 U.S. 629, 88 S.Ct. 1274, 20 L.Ed.2d 195 (1968). The importer, distributors and exhibitors should also realize that if they advertise the film in a manner calculated to capitalize on its extensive portrayals of nudity and sexual activity rather than its supposed serious message, Ginzburg v. United States, 383 U.S. 463, 86 S.Ct. 942, 16 L.Ed.2d 31 (1966), will be applicable.

With these reservations and with no little distaste, I concur for reversal.

LUMBARD, Chief Judge (dissenting):

I dissent and vote to affirm the judgment of the district court which held that the film I Am Curious-Yellow should be barred from importation into the United States. That judgment was entered upon the verdict of a jury which, after seeing the motion picture and hearing the "experts" regarding its significance, unanimously found that its dominant theme appeals to a prurient interest in sex, that it is patently offensive because it affronts contemporary community standards, and that it is utterly without redeeming social value. All are agreed that Judge Murphy's charge correctly stated the law and instructed the jury. Indeed, counsel for the appellant took no excep-

tion whatever to the charge. I see no good reason why that jury verdict should be disturbed.

My colleagues give no satisfactory explanation why jurors are not as qualified as they to pass upon such questions. The conclusion is inescapable that they really think that the issue of obscenity can be entrusted to juries only if the judges themselves (or, as here, a majority of them) think the matters in question go beyond the limits allowed by law. I had not supposed that only those who wear federal judicial robes are qualified to decide whether a motion picture has any redeeming social value.

It is admitted that in its explicitness this picture goes beyond anything thus far exhibited in this country. As my brother Hays says, "It seems to be conceded that the sexual content of the film is presented with greater explicitness than has been seen in any other film produced for general viewing." The sexual aspect of the film does not arise from the plot, as that is non-existent; it arises from a decision by the director, Vilgot Sjornan, to produce a film which would shock the audience. He testified that in making the film he deliberately broke sexual taboos or cliches knowing that this would be shocking to the public.

The excerpts from the director's diary which were published in Sweden emphasize sex and the breaking away from old cliches about sex. The diary makes no mention whatever of any of the aspects of the film which it is claimed give it redeeming social value—the class structure in Sweden, ideas of non-violence, and the like.

Whatever one can say about the alleged significance of the film, which to this captive onlooker was a continuous and unrelieved boredom except for the sexual scenes, it is almost impossible to remember anything about it. The only impact the picture has and the only impact it was designed to have are the sexual scenes; its only interest to the viewer arises from the uncertainty of the method of mutual sexual gratification in which hero and heroine will next indulge.

While the sex is heterosexual, the participants indulge in acts of fellatio and cunnilingus. Needless to say these acts bear no conceivable relevance to any social value, except that of box-office appeal. Moreover, the sexual scenes have nothing whatever to do with the remainder of the picture. Obviously the only interest aroused for the average person is a prurient interest. Nor is it persuasive that the explicit sex scenes take only about 10 minutes out of 120. The enormous visual impact of a motion picture as distinguished from other media cannot be disregarded. Cf. Freedman v. Maryland, 380 U.S. 51, 61, 85 S.Ct. 734. 13 L.Ed.2d 649 (1965). The combination of sight and sound, in the darkness of the movie theater, result in a uniquely forceful impact on the audience. Because of the nature of this medium, sexual scenes in a motion picture may transcend the bounds of constitutional protection long before a frank description of the same scenes in a book or magazine. Cf. Landau v. Fording, 245 Cal.App.2d 820, 54 Cal.Rptr. 177 (1966), aff'd per curiam, 388 U.S. 456, 87 S.Ct. 2109, 18 L.Ed.2d 1317 (1967). Undoubtedly, the jury was aware of the difference between movies and other media when it found this film to be obscene.

But the majority would take away from the jury the power to pass on these not too difficult and complicated questions by saying that obscenity is "an issue of constitutional law" rather than an issue of fact with respect to which the jury's finding has its usual conclusive effect. To me this simply means that juries are not to be trusted where a majority of the judges disagree with them.

The action of the majority in nullifying the findings of the jury here goes beyond any case thus far decided in the obscenity area. No case is cited and I can find no case where the Supreme Court has set aside the verdict of a jury which has, under proper instructions, found present the three elements of obscenity as established by Roth v. United States, 354 U.S. 476, 77 S.Ct. 1304, 1 L.Ed.2d 1498 (1957) and Jacobellis v. Ohio, 378 U.S. 184, 84 S.Ct. 1676, 12 L.Ed.2d 793 (1964). There is no reason to suspect that judges are in any better position to pass judgment on these matters than are jurors. Compare Mr. Justice Brennan's remarks in Kingsley Books, Inc. v. Brown, 354 U.S. 436, 448, 77 S.Ct. 1325, 1331, 1 L.Ed.2d 1469 (dissenting opinion):

"The jury represents a cross-section of the community and has a special aptitude for reflecting the view of the average person. Jury trial of obscenity therefore provides a peculiarly competent application of the standard for judging obscenity which, by its definition, calls for an appraisal of material according to the average person's application of contemporary community standards."[1]

With due deference to the very considerable intellectual attainments of my colleagues, I submit that when it comes to a question of what goes beyond the permissible in arousing prurient interest in sex, the verdict of a jury of twelve men and women is a far better and more accurate reflection of community standards and social value.[2] The jurors are drawn from all walks of life[3] and their less pretentious positions in the community qualify them to answer the questions put to them by Judge Murphy at least as well as circuit judges in their middle sixties who cerebrate in the ivory towers of the judiciary.[4]

It remains only to comment on Judge Friendly's tongue-in-cheek admonition to the exhibitors. They are cautioned that state authorities may still intervene if minors are admitted to see the picture or if the film is advertised to capitalize on nudity and sexual activity. All of which seems to me to amount to a concession that the entire public ought to be protected against the exploitation for profit of a film which a jury has outlawed for obscenity in violation of the federal statute. However, as the contrary view of my brothers has prevailed here, I join Judge Friendly in pointing out that state and local authorities may intervene if minors are admitted to the audience or if those who promote the exhibition of the film do so in ways which capitalize on the film's "extensive portrayals of nudity and sexual activity."

I would affirm the judgment of the district court which barred this film from importation.

COURT'S OPINION NOTES

1. § 1305. Immoral Articles; Prohibition of Importation
(a) All persons are prohibited from importing into the United States from any foreign country any book, pamphlet, paper, writing, advertisement, circular, print, picture, or drawing containing any matter advocating or urging treason or insurrection against the United States, or forcible resistance to any law of the United States, or containing any threat to take the life of or inflict bodily harm upon any person in the United States, or any obscene book, pamphlet, paper, writing, advertisement, circular, print, picture, drawing, or other representation, figure, or image on or of paper or other material, or any cast, instru-

ment, or other article which is obscene or immoral, or any drug or medicine or any article whatever for the prevention of conception or for causing unlawful abortion, or any lottery ticket, or any printed paper that may be used as a lottery ticket, or any advertisement of any lottery. No such articles whether imported separately or contained in packages with other goods entitled to entry, shall be admitted to entry; and all such articles and, unless it appears to the satisfaction of the collector that the obscene or other prohibited articles contained in the package were enclosed therein without the knowledge or consent of the importer, owner, agent, or consignee, the entire contents of the package in which such articles are contained, shall be subject to seizure and forfeiture as hereinafter provided: *Provided*, That the drugs hereinbefore mentioned, when imported in bulk and not put up for any of the purposes hereinbefore specified, are excepted from the operation of this subdivision: *Provided further*, That the Secretary of the Treasury may, in his discretion, admit the so-called classics or books of recognized and established literary or scientific merit, but may, in his discretion, admit such classics or books only when imported for non-commercial purposes.

Upon the appearance of any such book or matter at any customs office, the same shall be seized and held by the collector to await the judgment of the district court as hereinafter provided; and no protest shall be taken to the United States Customs Court from the decision of the collector. Upon the seizure of such book or matter the collector shall transmit information thereof to the district attorney of the district in which is situated the office at which such seizure has taken place, who shall institute proceedings in the district court for the forfeiture, confiscation, and destruction of the book or matter seized. Upon the adjudication that such book or matter thus seized is of the character the entry of which is by this section prohibited, it shall be ordered destroyed and shall be destroyed. Upon adjudication that such book or matter thus seized is not of the character the entry of which is by this section prohibited, it shall not be excluded from entry under the provisions of this section.

In any such proceeding any party in interest may upon demand have the facts at issue determined by a jury and any party may have an appeal or the right of review as in the case of ordinary actions or suits.

2. Thirteen "experts" (professional critics, English professors, a minister, sociology professors, a "professor of film," psychiatrists, a novelist) gave testimony as to their views of the social value of the film. Some of their answers to questions as to the dominant theme of the film were: change, transition; the nature of reality or of "modern" reality; the New Left; the interrelationship of various aspects of human activity; the quest for values; the beliefs and commitments of the young; the younger generation; the generation gap; the relationship between fantasy and reality; young people's search for identity and self-recognition; political, social and sexual maturity; political responsibility; the use of ritual to establish fundamental truth; the nature of politics; the complexity of modern reality.

JUDGE FRIENDLY'S OPINION NOTES

1. The author notes that these three decisions, Memoirs v. Massachusetts, 383 U.S. 413, 86 S.Ct. 975 (1966); Ginzburg v. United States. 383 U.S. 463, 86 S.Ct. 942 (1966);

and Mishkin v. New York, 383 U.S. 502, 86 S.Ct. 958, 16 L.Ed.2d 56 (1966), gave rise to fourteen opinions, which spread over more than a hundred pages of the United States Reports. Id. at 7–8.

2. Some but by no means all of the latter would fit Mr. Justice Goldberg's description of "fragmentary and fleeting." Jacobellis v. Ohio, supra, 378 U.S. at 197–198, 84 S.Ct. 1676.

3. At the argument appellant's counsel pointed to a number of factors present in *Landau* but not here that could have provided the basis for that decision.

4. Mr. Justice Brennan's dissent in Kingsley Books, Inc. v. Brown, 354 U.S. 436, 447, 77 S.Ct. 1325, 1 L.Ed.2d 1469 (1957), quoted in the dissent here, antedated development of the "national standard" concept. While the jury is well adapted to reflect "the voice of the countryside," see 2 Pollock & Maitland, History of English Law 624 (2d ed. 1952), it would have even more difficulty than judges in determining what would be offensive nationally. See O'Meara & Shaffer, supra, at 8.

JUDGE LUMBARD'S OPINION NOTES

1. See also Chief Justice Warren, dissenting in Jacobellis, 378 U.S. at 199, 84 S.Ct. at 1686:

"[P]rotection of society's right to maintain its moral fibre and the effective administration of justice require that this Court not establish itself as an ultimate censor, in each case reading the entire record, viewing the accused material, and making an independent de novo judgment on the question of obscenity. Therefore, once a finding of obscenity has been made below under a proper application of the Roth test, I would apply a 'sufficient evidence' standard of review * * *."

2. It is no answer that so-called "experts" testified to social value of the film. Neither juries nor appellate courts are bound by expert testimony. Compare Landau v. Fording, 245 Cal.App.2d 280, 54 Cal.Rptr. 177 (1966), aff'd per curiam, 388 U.S. 456, 87 S.Ct. 2109, 18 L.Ed.2d 1317 (1967), where the film Un Chant D'Amour was held to be obscene notwithstanding testimony in support of the film by seven expert witnesses.

When "expert" witnesses testify, as one did here, that a film such as I Am Curious has religious and moral significance, it is understandable that the jury pays little attention to their testimony. Cf. Transcript at 148–51.

3. The records of the district court show that the jury in this case was made up of 7 men and 5 women who resided in New York City and its suburbs. They ranged in age from 32 to 68 years and engaged in widely varying occupations.

4. Compare Mr. Justice Black, dissenting in Mishkin v. New York, 383 U.S. 502, 515, 516, 86 S.Ct. 958, 968, 16 L.Ed.2d 56 (1966):

"But because of life tenure, as well as other reasons, the federal judiciary is the least appropriate branch of government to take over censorship responsibilities by deciding what pictures and writings people throughout the land can be permitted to see and read."

MERE PRIVATE POSSESSION OF OBSCENE MATERIALS IN ONE'S HOME IS HELD CONSTITUTIONAL

Stanley v. Georgia, 394 U.S. 557 (1969)

MR. JUSTICE MARSHALL delivered the opinion of the Court.

An investigation of appellant's alleged bookmaking activities led to the issuance of a search warrant for appellant's home. Under authority of this warrant, federal and state agents secured entrance. They found very little evidence of bookmaking activity, but while looking through a desk drawer in an upstairs bedroom, one of the federal agents, accompanied by a state officer, found three reels of eight-millimeter film. Using a projector and screen found in an upstairs living room, they viewed the films. The state officer concluded that they were obscene and seized them. Since a further examination of the bedroom indicated that appellant occupied it, he was charged with possession of obscene matter and placed under arrest. He was later indicted for "knowingly hav[ing] possession of . . . obscene matter" in violation of Georgia law.[1] Appellant was tried before a jury and convicted. The Supreme Court of Georgia affirmed. *Stanley v. State*, 224 Ga. 259, 161 S. E. 2d 309 (1968). We noted probable jurisdiction of an appeal brought under 28 U. S. C. § 1257 (2). 393 U. S. 819 (1968).

Appellant raises several challenges to the validity of his conviction.[2] We find it necessary to consider only one. Appellant argues here, and argued below, that the Georgia obscenity statute, insofar as it punishes mere private possession of obscene matter, violates the First Amendment, as made applicable to the States by the Fourteenth Amendment. For reasons set forth below, we agree that the mere private possession of obscene matter cannot constitutionally be made a crime.

The court below saw no valid constitutional objection to the Georgia statute, even though it extends further than the typical statute forbidding commercial sales of obscene material. It held that "[i]t is not essential to an indictment charging one with possession of obscene matter that it be alleged that such possession was 'with intent to sell, expose or circulate the same.' " *Stanley v. State, supra,* at 261, 161 S. E. 2d, at 311. The State and appellant both agree that the question here before us is whether "a statute imposing criminal sanctions upon the mere [knowing] possession of obscene matter" is constitutional. In this context, Georgia concedes that the present case appears to be one of "first impression . . . on this exact point,"[3] but contends that since "obscenity is not within the area of constitutionally protected speech or press," *Roth* v. *United States*, 354 U. S. 476, 485 (1957), the States are free, subject to the limits of other provisions of the Constitution, see, *e. g.*, *Ginsberg* v. *New York*, 390 U. S. 629, 637–645 (1968), to deal with it any way deemed necessary, just as they may deal with possession of other things thought to be detrimental to the welfare of their citizens. If the State can protect the body of a citizen, may it not, argues Georgia, protect his mind?

It is true that *Roth* does declare, seemingly without qualification, that obscenity is not protected by the First Amendment. That statement has been repeated in various forms in subsequent cases. See, *e. g., Smith* v. *California*, 361 U. S. 147, 152 (1959); *Jacobellis* v. *Ohio*, 378 U. S. 184, 186–187 (1964) (opinion of BRENNAN, J.); *Ginsberg* v. *New York, supra*, at 635. However, neither *Roth* nor any subsequent decision of this Court dealt with the precise problem involved in the present case. Roth was convicted of mailing obscene circulars and advertising, and an obscene book, in violation of a federal obscenity statute.[4] The defendant in a companion case, *Alberts* v. *California*, 354 U. S. 476 (1957), was convicted of "lewdly keeping for sale obscene and indecent books, and [of] writing, composing and publishing an obscene advertisement of them . . . ." *Id.,* at 481. None of the statements cited by the Court in *Roth* for the proposition that "this Court has always assumed that obscenity is not protected by the freedoms of speech and press" were made in the context of a statute punishing mere private possession of obscene material; the cases cited deal for the most part with use of the mails to distribute objectionable material or with some form of public distribution or dissemination.[5] Moreover, none of this Court's decisions subsequent to *Roth* involved prosecution for private possession of obscene materials. Those cases dealt with the power of the State and Federal Governments to prohibit or regulate certain public actions taken or intended to be taken with respect to obscene matter.[6] Indeed, with one exception, we have been unable to discover any case in which the issue in the present case has been fully considered.[7]

In this context, we do not believe that this case can be decided simply by citing *Roth*. *Roth* and its progeny certainly do mean that the First and Fourteenth Amendments recognize a valid governmental interest in dealing with the problem of obscenity. But the assertion of that interest cannot, in every context, be insulated from all constitutional protections. Neither *Roth* nor any other decision of this Court reaches that far. As the Court said in *Roth* itself, "[c]easeless vigilance is the watchword to prevent . . . erosion [of First Amendment rights] by Congress or by the States. The door barring federal and state intrusion into this area cannot be left ajar; it must be kept tightly closed and opened only the slightest crack necessary to prevent encroachment upon more important interests." 354 U. S., at 488. *Roth* and the cases following it discerned such an "important interest" in the regulation of commercial distribution of obscene material. That holding cannot foreclose an examination of the constitutional implications of a statute forbidding mere private possession of such material.

It is now well established that the Constitution protects the right to receive information and ideas. "This freedom [of speech and press] . . . necessarily protects the right to receive . . . ." *Martin* v. *City of Struthers*, 319 U. S. 141, 143 (1943); see *Griswold* v. *Connecticut*, 381 U. S. 479, 482 (1965); *Lamont* v. *Postmaster General*, 381 U. S. 301, 307–308 (1965) (BRENNAN, J., concurring); cf. *Pierce* v. *Society of Sisters*, 268 U. S. 510 (1925). This right to receive information and ideas, regardless of their social worth, see *Winters* v. *New York*, 333 U. S. 507, 510 (1948), is fundamental to our free society. Moreover, in the context of this case—a prosecution for mere possession of printed or filmed matter in the privacy of a person's own home—that right takes on an added dimension. For also fundamental is the right to be free, except in very limited circumstances, from unwanted governmental intrusions into one's privacy.

> "The makers of our Constitution undertook to secure conditions favorable to the pursuit of happiness. They recognized the significance of man's spiritual nature, of his feelings and of his intellect. They knew that only a part of the pain, pleasure and satisfactions of life are to be found in material things. They sought to protect Americans in their beliefs, their thoughts, their emotions and their sensations. They conferred, as against the Government, the right to be let alone—the most comprehensive of rights and the right most valued by civilized man." *Olmstead* v. *United States*, 277 U. S. 438, 478 (1928) (Brandeis, J., dissenting).

See *Griswold* v. *Connecticut, supra;* cf. *NAACP* v. *Alabama*, 357 U. S. 449, 462 (1958).

These are the rights that appellant is asserting in the case before us. He is asserting the right to read or observe what he pleases—the right to satisfy his intellectual and emotional needs in the privacy of his own home. He is asserting the right to be free from state inquiry into the contents of his library. Georgia contends that appellant does not have these rights, that there are certain types of materials that the individual may not read or even possess. Georgia justifies this assertion by arguing that the films in the present case are obscene. But we think that mere categorization of these films as "obscene" is insufficient justification for such a drastic invasion of personal liberties guaranteed by the First and Fourteenth Amendments. Whatever may be the justifications for other statutes regulating obscenity, we do not think they reach into the privacy of one's own home. If the First Amendment means anything, it means that a State has no business telling a man, sitting alone in his own house, what books he may read or what films he may watch. Our whole constitutional heritage rebels at the thought of giving government the power to control men's minds.

And yet, in the face of these traditional notions of individual liberty, Georgia asserts the right to protect the individual's mind from the effects of obscenity. We are not certain that this argument amounts to anything more than the assertion that the State has the right to control the moral content of a person's thoughts.[8] To some, this may be a noble purpose, but it is wholly inconsistent with the philosophy of the First Amendment. As the Court said in *Kingsley International Pictures Corp.* v. *Regents*, 360 U. S. 684, 688–689 (1959), "[t]his argument misconceives what it is that the Constitution protects. Its guarantee is not confined to the expression of ideas that are conventional or shared by a majority. . . . And in the realm of ideas it protects expression which is eloquent no less than that which is unconvincing." Cf. *Joseph Burstyn, Inc.* v. *Wilson*, 343 U. S. 495 (1952).

Nor is it relevant that obscene materials in general, or the particular films before the Court, are arguably devoid of any ideological content. The line between the transmission of ideas and mere entertainment is much too elusive for this Court to draw, if indeed such a line can be drawn at all. See *Winters* v. *New York, supra,* at 510. Whatever the power of the state to control public dissemination of ideas inimical to the public morality, it cannot constitutionally premise legislation on the desirability of controlling a person's private thoughts.

Perhaps recognizing this, Georgia asserts that exposure to obscene materials may lead to deviant sexual behavior or crimes of sexual violence. There appears to be little empirical basis for that assertion.[9] But more-important, if the State is only concerned about printed or filmed materials inducing antisocial conduct, we believe that in the context of private consumption of ideas and information we should adhere to the view that "[a]mong free men, the deterrents ordinarily to be applied to prevent crime are education and punishment for violations of the law . . . ." *Whitney* v. *California,* 274 U. S. 357, 378 (1927) (Brandeis, J., concurring). See Emerson, Toward a General Theory of the First Amendment, 72 Yale L. J. 877, 938 (1963). Given the present state of knowledge, the State may no more prohibit mere possession of obscene matter on the ground that it may lead to antisocial conduct than it may prohibit possession of chemistry books on the ground that they may lead to the manufacture of homemade spirits.

It is true that in *Roth* this Court rejected the necessity of proving that exposure to obscene material would create a clear and present danger of antisocial conduct or would probably induce its recipients to such conduct. 354 U. S., at 486–487. But that case dealt with public distribution of obscene materials and such distribution is subject to different objections. For example, there is always the danger that obscene material might fall into the hands of children, see *Ginsberg* v. *New York, supra,* or that it might intrude upon the sensibilities or privacy of the general public.[10] See *Redrup* v. *New York,* 386 U. S. 767, 769 (1967). No such dangers are present in this case.

Finally, we are faced with the argument that prohibition of possession of obscene materials is a necessary incident to statutory schemes prohibiting distribution. That argument is based on alleged difficulties of proving an intent to distribute or in producing evidence of actual distribution. We are not convinced that such difficulties exist, but even if they did we do not think that they would justify infringement of the individual's right to read or observe what he pleases. Because that right is so fundamental to our scheme of individual liberty, its restriction may not be justified by the need to ease the administration of otherwise valid criminal laws. See *Smith* v. *California,* 361 U. S. 147 (1959).

We hold that the First and Fourteenth Amendments prohibit making mere private possession of obscene material a crime.[11] *Roth* and the cases following that decision are not impaired by today's holding. As we have said, the States retain broad power to regulate obscenity; that power simply does not extend to mere

possession by the individual in the privacy of his own home. Accordingly, the judgment of the court below is reversed and the case is remanded for proceedings not inconsistent with this opinion.

It is so ordered.

MR. JUSTICE BLACK, concurring.

I agree with the Court that the mere possession of reading matter or movie films, whether labeled obscene or not, cannot be made a crime by a State without violating the First Amendment, made applicable to the States by the Fourteenth. My reasons for this belief have been set out in many of my prior opinions, as for example, *Smith* v. *California,* 361 U. S. 147, 155 (concurring opinion), and *Ginzburg* v. *United States,* 383 U. S. 463, 476 (dissenting opinion).

MR. JUSTICE STEWART, with whom MR. JUSTICE BRENNAN and MR. JUSTICE WHITE join, concurring in the result.

Before the commencement of the trial in this case, the appellant filed a motion to suppress the films as evidence upon the ground that they had been seized in violation of the Fourth and Fourteenth Amendments. The motion was denied, and the films were admitted in evidence at the trial. In affirming the appellant's conviction, the Georgia Supreme Court specifically determined that the films had been lawfully seized. The appellant correctly contends that this determination was clearly wrong under established principles of constitutional law. But the Court today disregards this preliminary issue in its hurry to move on to newer constitutional frontiers. I cannot so readily overlook the serious inroads upon Fourth Amendment guarantees countenanced in this case by the Georgia courts.

The Fourth Amendment provides that "no Warrants shall issue, but upon probable cause, supported by Oath or affirmation, and particularly describing the place to be searched, and the persons or things to be seized." The purpose of these clear and precise words was to guarantee to the people of this Nation that they should forever be secure from the general searches and unrestrained seizures that had been a hated hallmark of colonial rule under the notorious writs of assistance of the British Crown. See *Stanford* v. *Texas,* 379 U. S. 476, 481. This most basic of Fourth Amendment guarantees was frustrated in the present case, I think, in a manner made the more pernicious by its very subtlety. For what happened here was that a search that began as perfectly lawful became the occasion for an unwarranted and unconstitutional seizure of the films.

The state and federal officers gained admission to the appellant's house under the authority of a search warrant issued by a United States Commissioner. The warrant described "the place to be searched" with particularity.[1] With like particularity, it described the "things to be seized"—equipment, records, and other material used in or derived from an illegal wagering business.[2] And the warrant was issued only after the Commissioner had been apprised of more than adequate probable cause to issue it.[3]

There can be no doubt, therefore, that the agents were

lawfully present in the appellant's house, lawfully authorized to search for any and all of the items specified in the warrant, and lawfully empowered to seize any such items they might find.[4] It follows, therefore, that the agents were acting within the authority of the warrant when they proceeded to the appellant's upstairs bedroom and pulled open the drawers of his desk. But when they found in one of those drawers not gambling material but moving picture films, the warrant gave them no authority to seize the films.

The controlling constitutional principle was stated in two sentences by this Court more than 40 years ago:

> "The requirement that warrants shall particularly describe the things to be seized makes general searches under them impossible and prevents the seizure of one thing under a warrant describing another. As to what is to be taken, nothing is left to the discretion of the officer executing the warrant." *Marron* v. *United States*, 275 U. S. 192, 196.

This is not a case where agents in the course of a lawful search came upon contraband, criminal activity, or criminal evidence[5] in plain view. For the record makes clear that the contents of the films could not be determined by mere inspection. And this is not a case that presents any questions as to the permissible scope of a search made incident to a lawful arrest. For the appellant had not been arrested when the agents found the films. After finding them, the agents spent some 50 minutes exhibiting them by means of the appellant's projector in another upstairs room. Only then did the agents return downstairs and arrest the appellant.

Even in the much-criticized case of *United States* v. *Rabinowitz*, 339 U. S. 56, the Court emphasized that "exploratory searches . . . cannot be undertaken by officers with or without a warrant." *Id.*, at 62. This record presents a bald violation of that basic constitutional rule. To condone what happened here is to invite a government official to use a seemingly precise and legal warrant only as a ticket to get into a man's home, and, once inside, to launch forth upon unconfined searches and indiscriminate seizures as if armed with all the unbridled and illegal power of a general warrant.

Because the films were seized in violation of the Fourth and Fourteenth Amendments, they were inadmissible in evidence at the appellant's trial. *Mapp* v. *Ohio*, 367 U. S. 643. Accordingly, the judgment of conviction must be reversed.

COURT'S OPINION NOTES

[1] "Any person who shall knowingly bring or cause to be brought into this State for sale or exhibition, or who shall knowingly sell or offer to sell, or who shall knowingly lend or give away or offer to lend or give away, or who shall knowingly have possession of, or who shall knowingly exhibit or transmit to another, any obscene matter, or who shall knowingly advertise for sale by any form of notice, printed, written, or verbal, any obscene matter, or who shall knowingly manufacture, draw, duplicate or print any obscene matter with intent to sell, expose or circulate the same, shall, if such person has knowledge or reasonably should know of the obscene nature of such matter, be guilty of a felony, and, upon conviction thereof, shall be punished by confinement in the penitentiary for not less than one year nor more than five years: Provided, however, in the event the jury so recommends, such person may be punished as for a misdemeanor. As used herein, a matter is obscene if, considered as a whole, applying contemporary community standards, its predominant appeal is to prurient interest, i. e., a shameful or morbid interest in nudity, sex or excretion." Ga. Code Ann. § 26–6301 (Supp. 1968).

[2] Appellant does not argue that the films are not obscene. For the purpose of this opinion, we assume that they are obscene under any of the tests advanced by members of this Court. See *Redrup* v. *New York*, 386 U. S. 767 (1967).

[3] The issue was before the Court in *Mapp* v. *Ohio*, 367 U. S. 643 (1961), but that case was decided on other grounds. MR. JUSTICE STEWART, although disagreeing with the majority opinion in *Mapp*, would have reversed the judgment in that case on the ground that the Ohio statute proscribing mere possession of obscene material was "not 'consistent with the rights of free thought and expression assured against state action by the Fourteenth Amendment.'" *Id.*, at 672.

[4] 18 U. S. C. § 1461.

[5] *Ex parte Jackson*, 96 U. S. 727, 736–737 (1878) (use of the mails); *United States* v. *Chase*, 135 U. S. 255, 261 (1890) (use of the mails); *Robertson* v. *Baldwin*, 165 U. S. 275, 281 (1897) (publication); *Public Clearing House* v. *Coyne*, 194 U. S. 497, 508 (1904) (use of the mails); *Hoke* v. *United States*, 227 U. S. 308, 322 (1913) (use of interstate facilities); *Near* v. *Minnesota*, 283 U. S. 697, 716 (1931) (publication); *Chaplinsky* v. *New Hampshire*, 315 U. S. 568, 571–572 (1942) (utterances); *Hannegan* v. *Esquire, Inc.*, 327 U. S. 146, 158 (1946) (use of the mails); *Winters* v. *New York*, 333 U. S. 507, 510 (1948) (possession with intent to sell); *Beauharnais* v. *Illinois*, 343 U. S. 250, 266 (1952) (libel).

[6] Many of the cases involved prosecutions for sale or distribution of obscene materials or possession with intent to sell or distribute. See *Redrup* v. *New York*, 386 U. S. 767 (1967); *Mishkin* v. *New York*, 383 U. S. 502 (1966); *Ginzburg* v. *United States*, 383 U. S. 463 (1966); *Jacobellis* v. *Ohio*, 378 U. S. 184 (1964); *Smith* v. *California*, 361 U. S. 147 (1959). Our most recent decision involved a prosecution for sale of obscene material to children. *Ginsberg* v. *New York*, 390 U. S. 629 (1968); cf. *Interstate Circuit, Inc.* v. *City of Dallas*, 390 U. S. 676 (1968). Other cases involved federal or state statutory procedures for preventing the distribution or mailing of obscene material, or procedures for predistribution approval. See *Freedman* v. *Maryland*, 380 U. S. 51 (1965); *Bantam Books, Inc.* v. *Sullivan*, 372 U. S. 58 (1963); *Manual Enterprises, Inc.* v. *Day*, 370 U. S. 478 (1962). Still another case dealt with an attempt to seize obscene material "kept for the purpose of being sold, published, exhibited . . . or otherwise distributed or circulated . . . ." *Marcus* v. *Search Warrant*, 367 U. S. 717, 719 (1961); see also *A Quantity of Books* v. *Kansas*, 378 U. S. 205 (1964). *Memoirs* v. *Massachusetts*, 383 U. S. 413 (1966), was a proceeding in equity against a book. However, possession of a book determined to be obscene in such a proceeding was made criminal only when "for the purpose of sale, loan or distribution." *Id.*, at 422.

[7] The Supreme Court of Ohio considered the issue in *State* v. *Mapp*, 170 Ohio St. 427, 166 N. E. 2d 387 (1960). Four of the seven judges of that court felt that criminal prosecution for mere private possession of obscene materials was prohibited by the Constitution. However, Ohio law required the concurrence of "all but one of the judges" to declare a state law unconstitutional. The view of the "dissenting" judges was expressed by Judge Herbert:

"I cannot agree that mere private possession of . . . [obscene] literature by an adult should constitute a crime. The right of the individual to read, to believe or disbelieve, and to think without governmental supervision is one of our basic liberties, but to dictate to the mature adult what books he may have in his own private library seems to the writer to be a clear infringement of his constitutional rights as an individual." 170 Ohio St., at 437, 166 N. E. 2d, at 393.

Shortly thereafter, the Supreme Court of Ohio interpreted the Ohio statute to require proof of "possession and control for the purpose of circulation or exhibition." *State* v. *Jacobellis*, 173 Ohio St. 22, 27–28, 179 N. E. 2d 777, 781 (1962), rev'd on other grounds, 378 U. S. 184 (1964). The interpretation was designed to avoid the constitutional problem posed by the "dissenters" in *Mapp*. See *State* v. *Ross*, 12 Ohio St. 2d 37, 231 N. E. 2d 299 (1967).

Other cases dealing with nonpublic distribution of obscene material or with legitimate uses of obscene material have expressed similar reluctance to make such activity criminal, albeit largely on statutory grounds. In *United States* v. *Chase*, 135 U. S. 255 (1890), the Court held that federal law did not make criminal the mailing of a private sealed obscene letter on the ground that the law's purpose was to purge the mails of obscene matter "as far as was consistent with the rights reserved to the people, and with a due regard to the security of private correspondence . . . ." 135 U. S., at 261. The law was later amended to include letters and was sustained in that form. *Andrews* v. *United States*, 162 U. S. 420 (1896). In *United States* v. *31 Photographs*, 156 F. Supp. 350 (D. C. S. D. N. Y. 1957), the court denied an attempt by the Government to confiscate certain materials sought to be imported into the United States by the Institute for Sex Research, Inc., at Indiana University. The court found, applying the *Roth* formulation, that the materials would not appeal to the "prurient interest" of those seeking to import and utilize the materials. Thus, the statute permitting seizure of "obscene" materials was not applicable. The court found it unnecessary to reach the constitutional questions presented by the claimant, but did note its belief that "the statement . . . [in *Roth*] concerning the rejection of obscenity must be interpreted in the light of the widespread distribution of the material in Roth." 156 F. Supp., at 360, n. 40. See also *Redmond* v. *United States*, 384 U. S. 264 (1966), where this Court granted the Solicitor General's motion to vacate and remand with instructions to dismiss an information charging a violation of a federal obscenity statute in a case where a husband and wife mailed undeveloped films of each other posing in the nude to an out-of-state firm for developing. But see *Ackerman* v. *United States*, 293 F. 2d 449 (C. A. 9th Cir. 1961).

8 "Communities believe, and act on the belief, that obscenity is immoral, is wrong for the individual, and has no place in a decent society. They believe, too, that adults as well as children are corruptible in morals and character, and that obscenity is a source of corruption that should be eliminated. Obscenity is not suppressed primarily for the protection of others. Much of it is suppressed for the purity of the community and for the salvation and welfare of the 'consumer.' Obscenity, at bottom, is not crime. Obscenity is sin." Henkin, Morals and the Constitution: The Sin of Obscenity. 63 Col. L. Rev. 391, 395 (1963).

9 See, *e. g.*, Cairns, Paul, & Wishner, Sex Censorship: The Assumptions of Anti-Obscenity Laws and the Empirical Evidence, 46 Minn. L. Rev. 1009 (1962): see also M. Jahoda, The Impact of Literature: A Psychological Discussion of Some Assumptions in the Censorship Debate (1954), summarized in the concurring opinion of Judge Frank in *United States* v. *Roth*, 237 F. 2d 796, 814–816 (C. A. 2d Cir. 1956).

10 The Model Penal Code provisions dealing with obscene materials are limited to cases of commercial dissemination. Model Penal Code § 251.4 (Prop. Official Draft 1962); see also Model Penal Code § 207.10 and comment 4 (Tent. Draft No. 6, 1957); H. Packer, The Limits of the Criminal Sanction 316–328 (1968); Schwartz, Morals Offenses and the Model Penal Code, 63 Col. L. Rev. 669 (1963).

11 What we have said in no way infringes upon the power of the State or Federal Government to make possession of other items, such as narcotics, firearms, or stolen goods, a crime. Our holding in the present case turns upon the Georgia statute's infringement of fundamental liberties protected by the First and Fourteenth Amendments. No First Amendment rights are involved in most statutes making mere possession criminal.

Nor do we mean to express any opinion on statutes making criminal possession of other types of printed, filmed, or recorded materials. See, *e. g.*, 18 U. S. C. § 793 (d), which makes criminal the otherwise lawful possession of materials which "the possessor has reason to believe could be used to the injury of the United States or to the advantage of any foreign nation . . . ." In such cases, compelling reasons may exist for overriding the right of the individual to possess those materials.

JUSTICE BLACK'S CONCURRING OPINION NOTES

1 "[T]he premises known as 280 Springside Drive, S. E., two story residence with an annex on the main floor constructed of brick and frame, in Atlanta, Fulton County, Georgia, in the Northern District of Georgia . . . ."

2 "[B]ookmaking records, wagering paraphernalia consisting of bet slips, account sheets, recap sheets, collection sheets, adding machines,

money used in or derived from the wagering business, records of purchases, records of real estate and bank transactions, the money for which was derived from the wagering business, and any other property used in the wagering business, which are being used and/or have been used in the operation of a bookmaking business or represent the fruits of a bookmaking business being operated in violation of Sections 4411, 4412 and 7203 IRC of 1954."

3 Before the Commissioner were no less than four lengthy and detailed affidavits, setting out the grounds for the affiants' reasonable belief that the appellant was engaged in an illegal gambling enterprise, and that the paraphernalia of his trade were concealed in his house.

4 The fact that almost no gambling material was actually found has no bearing, of course, upon the validity of the search. The constitutionality of a search depends in no measure upon what it brings to light. *Byars* v. *United States*, 273 U. S. 28, 29.

5 See *Warden* v. *Hayden*, 387 U. S. 294.

FILM "THERESE AND ISABELLE" IS NOT OBSCENE

Duggan v. *Guild Theatre, Inc.*, 258 A.2d 858 (1969)

ROBERTS, Justice.

In Commonwealth v. Guild Theatre, Inc., 432 Pa. 378, 248 A.2d 45 (1968), we vacated a preliminary injunction which had barred the showing of the film "Therese and Isabelle" in Allegheny County. The case then went to trial and the chancellor, aided by an "advisory jury," held the movie obscene and issued a permanent injunction. This appeal followed. Appellants assign two principal grounds for reversal: that the district attorney could not proceed in this case by means of an injunction; and that "Therese and Isabelle" is not constitutionally obscene. We hold that while the district attorney may seek to enjoin the showing of an obscene movie, "Therese and Isabelle" is not obscene. Accordingly, we reverse and vacate the decree granting the injunction.

Appellants' first contention, that the district attorney has no standing[1] to seek an injunction here, is based on the Act of July 31, 1968, P.L.——, 18 P.S. § 4524 (Supp. 1969). Section 4 of that act repealed Act of September 17, 1959, P.L. 902, 4 P.S. § 70.10, which had given the Board of Censors standing to seek an injunction against obscene movies. The 1968 act did not, however, repeal the statute which makes criminal the showing of an obscene movie. See Act of June 24, 1939, P.L. 872, § 528, as amended, 18 P.S. § 4528. The act did consolidate various statutes dealing with sale and distribution of obscene works to adults and minors. In section 1(b), which sets out separate provisions relating only to minors, the act specifically mentions sound recordings, sculpture, and motion pictures, none of which media are mentioned in section 1(a) which deals with adults. Section 1(g), which gives the district attorney standing to seek an injunction, only enumerates the media mentioned in section 1(a). Thus appellants argue, quite persuasively, that since the Legislature failed to use the term "motion pictures" in 1(g), a term used elsewhere in the statute, the district attorney has no power to seek an injunction under the statute.[2]

We agree that his authority cannot be derived from that

statute. But that does not mean he lacks standing to institute an equitable proceeding here, for we cannot say that the Legislature was required to statutorily create standing to enable the district attorney to seek an injunction against an obscene movie. Obscenity is a public evil, long recognized in this Commonwealth to result in a particular type of public harm. See Commonwealth v. Sharpless, 2 Sergeant & Rawle (Pa.) 91 (1815). Where, as here, the district attorney is seeking to protect the public from a continuing dissemination of an allegedly obscene work, we cannot say that he lacks standing to vindicate this public right in a court of equity.[3]

Since the district attorney does have standing to initiate an injunctive proceeding against an allegedly obscene movie, we must now consider the question of whether "Therese and Isabelle" is obscene. The last opinion in which we dealt at length with the problem of what constitutes obscenity in the constitutional sense is Commonwealth v. Dell Publications, Inc., 427 Pa. 189, 233 A.2d 840 (1967), cert. denied, 390 U.S. 948, 88 S.Ct. 1038, 19 L.Ed.2d 1140 (1968). Although it is not now necessary to repeat all we said in that opinion, three propositions stand out.

The first is that this Court must make "an independent constitutional judgment on the facts of the case as to whether the material involved is constitutionally protected." Jacobellis v. Ohio, 378 U.S. 184, 190, 84 S.Ct. 1676, 1679, 12 L.Ed.2d 793 (1964). The second proposition is that "the evidence must be viewed in a light favorable to the * * * [work's] circulation." Dell Publications, 427 Pa. at 196, 233 A.2d at 844 (citing Roth v. United States, 354 U.S. 476, 77 S.Ct. 1304, 1 L.Ed. 2d 1498 (1957), and A Book Named "John Cleland's Memoirs of a Woman of Pleasure" v. Attorney General of Com. of Massachusetts, 383 U.S. 413, 86 S.Ct. 975, 16 L.Ed.2d 1 (1966)). The third proposition is that to find obscenity, "three elements must coalesce: it must be established that (a) the dominant theme of the material taken as a whole appeals to a prurient interest in sex; (b) the material is patently offensive because it affronts contemporary community standards relating to the description or representation of sexual matters; and (c) the material is utterly without redeeming social value." Memoirs v. Massachusetts, 383 U.S. at 418, 86 S.Ct. at 977.

There are no United States Supreme Court decisions since Dell Publications which would lead us to a different view of what constitutes obscenity. The district attorney, however, argues that for two reasons we should depart from the proposition set out in Jacobellis and Memoirs, and relied on in Dell Publications. For one, the instant case is a proceeding in equity, rather than a criminal proceeding as in Jacobellis, supra. Therefore, it is argued, our standard of review should, for some reason, be different. This argument overlooks the fact that the Jacobellis standard of review was adopted because First Amendment guarantees were involved, and not because the proceedings were criminal. See Jacobellis, 378 U.S. at 189, 84 S.Ct. at 1679. This being a federal constitutional standard, we may not depart from it. We thus may not constitutionally overrule this part of our decision in Dell Publications, a case which involved an equity proceeding.

The district attorney next urges that a different standard for determining obscenity should be used when dealing with motion pictures. He argues that a motion picture reproduces actual conduct through sight and sound and

therefore, the impact on the viewer is far more vivid. Presumably the district attorney is arguing that if the medium can portray what is alleged to be obscene with greater impact, the medium itself is deserving of less constitutional protection. We cannot accept this argument, for the First Amendment permits no such limitation on its protection of free expression.

This is so for at least two reasons. First, as a factual matter, we cannot say that the impact of an obscene work will always be greater when put on film. Each medium has a different type of impact, one which is difficult to quantify on any sort of obscenity scale. A nude figure seen on the screen for a short time may very well have less impact than a nude figure in a magazine, which can be leered at leisurely. Since we cannot say that the medium of motion pictures will inevitably render a work more obscene, we are constitutionally precluded from adopting a less protective constitutional standard.

Second, we find no indication in any United States Supreme Court decision that movies are to be treated differently than any other medium. As Judge Friendly has recently pointed out, "Jacobellis related to a film and neither the majority nor the dissenting opinions suggested that any stricter standard would apply." United States v. A Motion Picture Film Entitled "I Am Curious—Yellow", 404 F.2d 196, 201 (2d Cir. 1968) (concurring opinion). Landau v. Fording, 54 Cal. Rptr. 177, 245 Cal.App.2d 820 (Ct.App. 1966), aff'd, 388 U.S. 456, 87 S.Ct. 2109, 18 L.Ed.2d 1317 (1967), does not support the district attorney's position. Although the lower court's opinion in that case does indicate the possibility of a different test for movies, and the United States Supreme Court did affirm five to four, the affirmance was without opinion. The conclusion that the Supreme Court approved this different test cannot be drawn from such silence, particularly since there was evidence of pandering and because the movie itself was classified by the lower court as being "hard-core pornography."[4] We agree with Judge Friendly that the per curiam affirmance "affords too frail a foundation" to support a different test for movies. I Am Curious—Yellow, 404 F.2d at 201.

Since our decision in Dell Publications is still constitutionally controlling, we must now apply it to the facts of this case.

The chancellor found that the dominant theme of the material taken as a whole appeals to a prurient interest in sex. The district attorney urges that no evidence other than the film need be introduced to prove violation of this standard, since "[t]his area is one where a judge's subjective reaction is most relevant." Dell Publications, 427 Pa. at 201, 233 A.2d at 847. That may be so where all agree that the "dominant theme of the work as whole" is sex, leaving only the question of whether this theme appeals to a prurient interest in sex. But we could obviously not rely on a trial judge's "subjective reaction" to "King Lear," for example, since its dominant theme has nothing to do with sex. Compare I Am Curious—Yellow, 404 F.2d at 199 (holding picture not obscene; whatever the dominant theme may be, "it is certainly not sex"). Here there was considerable testimony that the dominant theme was not sexual. Thus, unlike our task in "Candy" where the theme was quite clear, we must make our own "independent constitutional judgment" as to whether the dominant theme is sexual.

It would appear from testimony given by witnesses for

both sides that the dominant theme of the work is that of loneliness, the loneliness of a young girl, not wanted by her mother, who turns to another young girl for affection.[5] As a result of this lack of maternal affection, the movie tells us, the girl becomes entwined in a homosexual relationship. Does this then make the dominant theme of the work as a whole a sexual one? Taking the evidence in a light favorable to the movie's dissemination, as we must, we cannot say that it does.[6]

Even if the dominant theme were one of homosexual love, we would still be unable to say that its appeal was to a prurient interest in sex. As the United States Supreme Court has stated, even when a motion picture "portrays a relationship which is contrary to the moral standards, the religious precepts, and the legal code of its citizenry," the constitution nevertheless protects such ideas. Kingsley International Pictures Corp. v. Regents, 360 U.S. 684, 688, 79 S.Ct. 1362, 1365, 3 L.Ed.2d 1512 (1959) (holding not obscene the motion picture version of "Lady Chatterly's Lover"). A movie which tells a story of homosexual love is one which, some years ago, may have appealed to a viewer's prurient interest in sex. But we cannot say today, in an era of "Myra Breckenridge" and "The Fox," that this theme has such an appeal. Compare I. M. Amusement Corp. v. Ohio, 389 U.S. 573, 88 S.Ct. 690, 19 L.Ed.2d 776 (1968) (holding not obscene a movie involving "movie pin-ups" and a nude lesbian love scene). Clearly, it is the standard of today by which we must judge. See Dell Publications, 427 Pa. at 202, 233 A.2d at 847 (citing Jacobellis, supra, and Smith v. California, 361 U.S. 147, 160, 169, 80 S.Ct. 215, 222, 227, 4 L.Ed.2d 205 (1959)).

Nor has the district attorney proved that this movie "affronts contemporary community standards" relating to the representation of sexual matters. Each one of his witnesses called to testify as to contemporary community standards admitted that they had no idea what these standards were. The district attorney in his brief admits that he produced no expert testimony on this issue, yet urges us to find that the movie affronts contemporary standards. This we cannot do. Courts of law are not capable of deciding what contemporary standards are, without the benefit of any evidence whatsoever.[7] Cf. Dell Publications, 427 Pa. at 193, 233 A.2d.

As for the third independent test, the district attorney has not proved "Therese and Isabelle" to be utterly without redeeming social value. One of his witnesses, after stating that the movie was "practically devoid" of social value, admitted he did not even know what the term means. Another one of his witnesses felt that works declared not obscene in twenty-two recent United States Supreme Court decisions were utterly without redeeming social value. As for "Therese and Isabelle," he believed only that a jury *could* find it utterly without social value.

The defense witnesses, on the other hand, were able to demonstrate that the film did have redeeming social value. For example, one witness, a former New York State film censor, testified that the movie "points up the destructive effect that the lack of parental love has on a young person. It shows how young people caught in this kind of situation can very easily, in their search for affection or love, become involved in this kind of exploratory or transitory homosexual relationship." Another witness, who was chairman of this Commonwealth's Board of Censors before it was disbanded, felt that the effects of maternal rejection shown in the movie were a lesson for parents. Compare

Robert-Arthur Management Corp. v. Tennessee, 389 U.S. 578, 88 S.Ct. 691, 19 L.Ed.2d 777 (1968) (holding not obscene a movie which informs people that "sexual filth" exists in the world). We can hardly say that such testimony is merely a "spurious claim for litigation purposes," as the district attorney urges, particularly since it conforms to the plot of the movie. There is obviously some social value in presenting these ideas, even if we dislike the message, or think it is incorrect, or even think it is not presented as convincingly as possible.

Thus the Commonwealth has not shown, under any one of the three independent standards set forth in *Memoirs* and *Dell Publications*, that "Therese and Isabelle" is constitutionally obscene. We also note that none of the circumstances identified in Redrup v. New York, 386 U.S. 767, 768, 87 S.Ct. 1414, 1415, 18 L.Ed.2d 515 (1967), are present in this case. The injunction does not reflect "a specific and limited state concern for juveniles," there was no evidence of an assault upon individual privacy in a manner so obtrusive as to make it impossible to avoid exposure, and there was no evidence of "pandering."

We must, therefore, hold that "Therese and Isabelle" may not constitutionally be banned. Accordingly, the decree restraining the exhibition of the movie is vacated and the case is dismissed.

COHEN, J., filed a concurring opinion in which JONES, J., joined.

EAGEN and POMEROY, JJ., concur in the result.

BELL, C. J., filed a dissenting opinion.

COHEN, Justice (concurring).

The majority opinion makes no mention of the unusual procedure employed by appellee. He originally filed a complaint in equity at No. 888 October Term, 1968D, on July 19, 1968. That action was the subject of this Court's opinion in Commonwealth v. Guild Theatre, Inc., 432 Pa. 378, 248 A.2d 45 (1968) in which we vacated the injunction for two reasons: (a) a hearing without notice and (b) censorship without provision for a prompt judicial decision. That decision was filed on November 12, 1968.

Instead of proceeding further with that action, appellee, on November 25, 1968, filed another complaint in equity at No. 2692 January Term, 1969. Apparently he did this because he did not want to continue with an action once tainted by unconstitutional procedures. In preliminary objections to the second complaint, appellant argued that there was pending a prior action, 12 P.S.App.R.C.P. 1509, 1017(b) (5), and that the second action should be stayed or dismissed because the relief sought and the parties involved in both actions were identical. Dickerson v. Dickerson Overseas Company, 369 Pa. 244, 85 A.2d 102 (1952); Tamburrino v. The Pennsylvania Railroad Co., 17 Pa.Dist. & Co.R.2d 156 (1958); 4 Standard Pennsylvania Practice, Ch. 13, § 26.

In its opinion, the lower court "overruled the objection based on the pendency of a prior action because the District Attorney stated for the record that the prior action was abandoned and discontinued." Any abandonment and discontinuance was without notice to or the consent of appellant. In view of this unusual method of proceeding, I would vacate the decree on the ground of *lis pendens* and not reach the other issues raised here.

JONES, J., joins in this concurring opinion.

BELL, Chief Justice (dissenting).

For the reasons set forth in my dissenting Opinion in Commonwealth v. Dell Publications, Inc., 427 Pa. 189

(pages 221–223), 233 A.2d 840, and my dissenting Opinion in Commonwealth v. Baer, Pa., 257 A.2d 254, filed October 9, 1969, this is an obscene movie, and I dissent.

NOTES

1. We are not here involved with the question of whether equity has jurisdiction to entertain this proceeding. Jurisdiction is conferred by the Act of June 16, 1836, P.L. 784, § 13, 17 P.S. § 282, and the Act of February 14, 1857, P.L. 39, § 1, 17 P.S. § 283. They provide that common pleas has jurisdiction relating to "[t]he prevention or restraint of the commission or continuance of acts contrary to law and prejudicial to the interests of the community or the rights of individuals." Although Section 1(g) of the Act of July 31, 1968, 18 P.S. § 4524 (Supp.1969) does specifically confer jurisdiction for injunctions against designated media other than movies, there is no reason to assume that the Legislature is required to specifically enumerate each type of case in which equity may act. The Legislature did not specifically confer equity jurisdiction in the now repealed statute giving the Board of Censors standing to seek injunctions against obscene movies. See Act of September 17, 1959, P.L. 902, 4 P.S. § 70.10. It is enough that the Legislature has passed the general statute, supra.

2. The district attorney concedes in his brief that motion pictures, generally, are not covered by 1(g). He argues that since "printed matter" and "photographs" are mentioned, and since this movie has subtitles, "Therese and Isabelle" may be reached under the statute. Such a construction would, of course, lead to the absurd conclusion that the Legislature intended that only foreign-language, non-dubbed, movies are enjoinable.

3. We do not pass on any procedural problems which may arise when a district attorney seeks an injunction, since such problems are no longer involved in this litigation. See Commonwealth v. Guild Theatre, 432 Pa. 378, 248 A.2d 45 (1968). Compare Grove Press, Inc. v. City of Philadelphia, 418 F.2d 82 (3d Cir.) (filed November 3, 1969) (holding unconstitutional the use of Pennsylvania's *preliminary* injunctive process against an allegedly obscene movie, since the preliminary process " 'fails to provide adequate safeguards against undue inhibition of protected expression' "). Nor do we pass on the propriety of empaneling an "advisory" jury, or on the propriety of submitting to that jury difficult questions of constitutional law.

4. The movie was thirty minutes long and depicted "acts of male masturbation, fellatio, oral copulation, voyeurism, nudity, sadism and sodomy without any clear reference or relation to a dominant theme." *Landau*, supra. 54 Cal.Rptr. at 181, 245 Cal.App.2d at 827.

5. Marie Torre, a witness for the district attorney who is a reporter for a Pittsburgh television station, testified: "Well, the plot is really a very simple one and it didn't require a good deal of imagination to come up with a plot of this kind. It's two girls, two Lesbians. * * * Lesbianism being an abnormal thing, you would have to, of course, give a little bit of background as to why the girl turned out this way. So in this case, she was not wanted by her mother—at least this was the theme they tried to project—that she was hungry for love and turned to someone who would give it, and it happened to be another girl."

Dr. Otto Von Mering, a witness for the defense who is a Professor of Anthropology, School of Medicine, Department of Psychiatry at the University of Pittsburgh, put it perhaps a bit more elegantly: "[T]he basic theme is the classic one of the adolescent, namely, of loneliness and not knowing sometime to whom you should turn, and even deeper than that. Perhaps the problem is dealing with the theme of mistrust: how do I come to trust another person? And, in a way, the experience of this person was an episode in the search for trust in other people."

6. Mr. Clancy, an attorney for Citizens for Decent Literature, testified for the district attorney that about a total of sixteen minutes out of the two-hour film, and five scenes out of thirty, dealt with sexual activity. This further reinforces our view that the dominant theme of the film is not sexual. Compare Landau v. Fording, supra note 4.

7. The appellants offered to introduce evidence at trial that "Therese and Isabelle" had played at 386, out of 800, first-run movie theatres in the country. The chancellor, although realizing that community standards must be judged nationally, refused to admit this evidence. Such a ruling is clear error.

UNITED STATES CUSTOMS CONFISCATES THIRTY SEVEN "OBSCENE" PHOTOGRAPHS FOUND IN A TRAVELER'S LUGGAGE AND THE CONFISCATION IS HELD CONSTITUTIONAL

United States v. Thirty Seven Photographs, 402 U.S. 363 (1971)

MR. JUSTICE WHITE announced the judgment of the Court and an opinion in which THE CHIEF JUSTICE, MR. JUSTICE BRENNAN, and MR. JUSTICE BLACKMUN join.*

When Milton Luros returned to the United States from Europe on October 24, 1969, he brought with him in his luggage the 37 photographs here involved. United States customs agents, acting pursuant to § 305 of the Tariff Act of 1930, as amended, 46 Stat. 688, 19 U. S. C. § 1305 (a),[1] seized the photographs as obscene. They referred the matter to the United States Attorney, who on November 6 instituted proceedings in the United States District Court for forfeiture of the material. Luros, as claimant, answered, denying the photographs were obscene and setting up a counterclaim alleging the unconstitutionality of § 1305 (a) on its face and as applied to him. He demanded that a three-judge court be convened to issue an injunction prayed for in the counterclaim. The parties stipulated a time for hearing the three-judge court motion. A formal order convening the court was entered on November 20. The parties then stipulated a briefing schedule expiring on December 16. The court ordered a hearing for January 9, 1970, also suggesting the parties stipulate facts, which they did. The stipulation revealed, among other things, that some or all of the 37 photographs were intended to be incorporated in a hard cover edition of The Kama Sutra of Vatsyayana, a widely distributed book candidly describing a large number of sexual positions. Hearing was held as scheduled on January 9, and on January 27 the three-judge court filed its judgment and opinion declaring § 1305 (a) unconstitutional and enjoining its enforcement against the 37 photographs, which were ordered returned to Luros. 309 F. Supp. 36 (CD Cal. 1970). The judgment of invalidity rested on two grounds: first, that the section failed to comply with the procedural requirements of *Freedman* v. *Maryland*, 380 U. S. 51 (1965), and second, that under *Stanley* v. *Georgia*, 394 U. S. 557 (1969), § 1305 (a) could not validly be applied to the seized material. We shall deal with each of these grounds separately.

I

In *Freedman* v. *Maryland, supra,* we struck down a state scheme for administrative licensing of motion pictures, holding "that, because only a judicial determination in an adversary proceeding ensures the necessary sensitivity to freedom of expression, only a procedure requiring a judicial determination suffices to impose a valid final restraint." 380 U. S., at 58. To insure that a judicial determination occurs promptly so that administrative delay does not in itself become a form of censorship, we further held, (1) there must be assurance, "by statute or authoritative judicial construction, that the censor will, within a specified brief period, either issue a license or go to court to restrain showing the film"; (2) "[a]ny restraint imposed in advance of a final judicial determination on the merits must similarly be limited to preservation of the status quo for the shortest fixed period compatible with sound judicial resolution"; and (3) "the procedure must also assure a prompt final judicial decision" to minimize the impact of possibly erroneous administrative action. *Id.,* at 58–59.

Subsequently, we invalidated Chicago's motion picture censorship ordinance because it permitted an unduly long administrative procedure before the invocation of judicial action and also because the ordinance, although requiring prompt resort to the courts after administrative decision and an early hearing, did not assure "a prompt judicial decision of the question of the alleged obscenity of the film." *Teitel Film Corp.* v. *Cusack,* 390 U. S. 139, 141 (1968). So, too, in *Blount* v. *Rizzi,* 400 U. S. 410 (1971), we held unconstitutional certain provisions of the postal laws designed to control use of the mails for commerce in obscene materials. Under those laws an administrative order restricting use of the mails could become effective without judicial approval, the burden of obtaining prompt judicial review was placed upon the user of the mails rather than the Government, and the interim judicial order, which the Government was permitted, though not required, to obtain pending completion of administrative action, was not limited to preserving the status quo for the shortest fixed period compatible with sound judicial administration.

As enacted by Congress, § 1305 (a) does not contain explicit time limits of the sort required by *Freedman, Teitel,* and *Blount.*[2] These cases do not, however, require that we pass upon the constitutionality of § 1305 (a), for it is possible to construe the section to bring it in harmony with constitutional requirements. It is true that we noted in *Blount* that "it is for Congress, not this Court, to rewrite the statute," 400 U. S., at 419, and that we similarly refused to rewrite Maryland's statute and Chicago's ordinance in *Freedman* and *Teitel.* On the other hand, we must remember that, "[w]hen the validity of an act of the Congress is drawn in question, and . . . a serious doubt of constitutionality is raised, it is a cardinal principle that this Court will first ascertain whether a construction of the statute is fairly possible by which the question may be avoided." *Crowell* v. *Benson,* 285 U. S. 22, 62 (1932). Accord, e. g., *Haynes* v. *United States,* 390 U. S. 85, 92 (1968) (dictum); *Schneider* v. *Smith,* 390 U. S. 17, 27 (1968); *United States* v. *Rumely,* 345 U. S. 41, 45 (1953); *Ashwander* v. *Tennessee Valley Authority,* 297 U. S. 288, 348 (1936) (Brandeis, J., concurring). This cardinal principle did not govern *Freedman, Teitel,* and *Blount* only because the statutes there involved could not be construed so as to avoid all constitutional difficulties.

The obstacle in *Freedman* and *Teitel* was that the statutes were enacted pursuant to state rather than federal authority; while *Freedman* recognized that a statute failing to specify time limits could be saved by judicial construction, it held that such construction had to be "authoritative," 380 U. S., at 59, and we lack jurisdiction authoritatively to construe state legislation. Cf. *General Trading Co.* v. *State Tax Comm'n,* 322 U. S. 335, 337 (1944). In *Blount,* we were dealing with a federal statute and thus had power to give it an authoritative construction; salvation of that statute, however, would have required its complete rewriting in a manner inconsistent with the expressed intentions of some of its authors. For the statute at issue in *Blount* not only failed to specify time limits within which judicial proceedings must be instituted and completed; it also failed to give any authorization at all to the administrative agency, upon a determination that material was obscene, to seek judicial review. To have saved the statute we would thus have been required to give such authorization and to create mechanisms for carrying it into effect, and we would have had to do this in the face of legislative history indicating that the Postmaster General, when he had testified before Congress, had expressly sought to forestall judicial review pending completion of administrative proceedings. See 400 U. S., at 420 n. 8.

No such obstacles confront us in construing § 1305 (a). In fact, the reading into the section of the time limits required by *Freedman* is fully consistent with its legislative purpose. When the statute, which in its present form dates back to 1930, was first presented to the Senate, concern immediately arose that it did not provide for determinations of obscenity to be made by courts rather than administrative officers and that it did not require that judicial rulings be obtained promptly. In language strikingly parallel to that of the Court in *Freedman,* Senator Walsh protested against the "attempt to enact a law that would vest an administrative officer with power to take books and confiscate them and destroy them, because, in his judgment, they were obscene or indecent," and urged that the law "oblige him to go into court and file his information there . . . and have it determined in the usual way, the same as every other crime is determined." 72 Cong. Rec. 5419. Senator Wheeler likewise could not "conceive how any man" could "possibly object" to an amendment to the proposed legislation that required a customs officer, if he concluded material was obscene, to "tur[n] it over to the district attorney, and the district attorney prosecutes the man, and he has the right of trial by jury in that case." 71 Cong. Rec. 4466. Other Senators similarly indicated their aversion to censorship "by customs clerks and bureaucratic officials," *id.*, at 4437 (remarks of Sen. Dill), preferring that determinations of obscenity should be left to courts and juries. See, *e. g., id.*, at 4433–4439, 4448, 4452–4459; 72 Cong. Rec. 5417–5423, 5492, 5497. Senators also expressed the concern later expressed in *Freedman* that judicial proceedings be commenced and concluded promptly. Speaking in favor of another amendment, Senator Pittman noted that a customs officer seizing obscene matter "should *immediately* report to the nearest United States district attorney having authority under the law to proceed to confiscate . . . ." *Id.*, at 5420 (emphasis added). Commenting on an early draft of another amendment that was ultimately adopted, Senator Swanson noted that officers would be required to go to court "immediately." *Id.*, at 5422. Then he added:

> "The *minute* there is a suspicion on the part of a revenue or customs officer that a certain book is improper to be admitted into this country, he presents the matter to the district court, and there will be a *prompt* determination of the matter by a decision of that court." *Id.*, at 5424 (emphasis added).

Before it finally emerged from Congress, § 1305 (a) was amended in response to objections of the sort voiced above: it thus reflects the same policy considerations that induced this Court to hold in *Freedman* that censors must resort to the courts "within a specified brief period" and that such resort must be followed by "a prompt final judicial decision . . . ." 380 U. S., at 59. Congress' sole omission was its failure to specify exact time limits within which resort to the courts must be had and judicial proceedings be completed. No one during the congressional debates ever suggested inclusion of such limits, perhaps because experience had not yet demonstrated a need for them. Since 1930, however, the need has become clear. Our researches have disclosed cases sanctioning delays of as long as 40 days and even six months between seizure of obscene goods and commencement of judicial proceedings. See *United States* v. *77 Cartons of Magazines*, 300 F. Supp. 851 (ND Cal. 1969); *United States* v. *One Carton Positive Motion Picture Film Entitled "491,"* 247 F. Supp. 450 (SDNY 1965), rev'd on other grounds, 367 F. 2d 889 (CA2 1966). Similarly, we have found cases in which completion of judicial proceedings has taken as long as three, four, and even seven months. See *United States* v. *Ten Erotic Paintings*, 311 F. Supp. 884 (Md. 1970); *United States* v. *35 MM Color Motion Picture Film Entitled "Language of Love,"* 311 F. Supp. 108 (SDNY 1970); *United States* v. *One Carton Positive Motion Picture Film Entitled "491,"* supra. We conclude that to sanction such delays would be clearly inconsistent with the concern for promptness that was so frequently articulated during the course of the Senate's debates, and that fidelity to Congress' pur-

pose dictates that we read explicit time limits into the section. The only alternative would be to hold § 1305 (a) unconstitutional in its entirety, but Congress has explicitly directed that the section not be invalidated in its entirety merely because its application to some persons be adjudged unlawful. See 19 U. S. C. § 1652. Nor does the construction of § 1305 (a) to include specific time limits require us to decide issues of policy appropriately left to the Congress or raise other questions upon which Congress possesses special legislative expertise, for Congress has already set its course in favor of promptness and we possess as much expertise as Congress in determining the sole remaining question—that of the speed with which prosecutorial and judicial institutions can, as a practical matter, be expected to function in adjudicating § 1305 (a) matters. We accordingly see no reason for declining to specify the time limits which must be incorporated into § 1305 (a)—a specification that is fully consistent with congressional purpose and that will obviate the constitutional objections raised by claimant. Indeed, we conclude that the legislative history of the section and the policy of giving legislation a saving construction in order to avoid decision of constitutional questions require that we undertake this task of statutory construction.

We begin by examining cases in the lower federal courts in which proceedings have been brought under § 1305 (a). That examination indicates that in many of the cases that have come to our attention the Government in fact instituted forfeiture proceedings within 14 days of the date of seizure of the allegedly obscene goods, see *United States* v. *Reliable Sales Co.*, 376 F. 2d 803 (CA4 1967); *United States* v. *1,000 Copies of a Magazine Entitled "Solis,"* 254 F. Supp. 595 (Md. 1966); *United States* v. *56 Cartons Containing 19,500 Copies of a Magazine Entitled "Hellenic Sun,"* 253 F. Supp. 498 (Md. 1966), aff'd, 373 F. 2d 635 (CA4 1967); *United States* v. *392 Copies of a Magazine Entitled "Exclusive,"* 253 F. Supp. 485 (Md. 1966); and judicial proceedings were completed within 60 days of their commencement. See *United States* v. *Reliable Sales Co., supra; United States* v. *1,000 Copies of a Magazine Entitled "Solis," supra; United States* v. *56 Cartons Containing 19,500 Copies of a Magazine Entitled "Hellenic Sun," supra; United States* v. *392 Copies of a Magazine Entitled "Exclusive," supra; United States* v. *127,295 Copies of Magazines, More or Less*, 295 F. Supp. 1186 (Md. 1968). Given this record, it seems clear that no undue hardship will be imposed upon the Government and the lower federal courts by requiring that forfeiture proceedings be commenced within 14 days and completed within 60 days of their commencement; nor does a delay of as much as 74 days seem undue for importers engaged in the lengthy process of bringing goods into this country from abroad. Accordingly, we construe § 1305 (a) to require intervals of no more than 14 days from seizure of the goods to the institution of judicial proceedings for their forfeiture and no longer than 60 days from the filing of the action to final decision in the district court. No seizure or forfeiture will be invalidated for delay, however, where the claimant is responsible for extending either administrative action or judicial determination beyond the allowable time limits or where administrative or judicial proceedings are postponed pending the consideration of constitutional issues appropriate only for a three-judge court.

Of course, we do not now decide that these are the only constitutionally permissible time limits. We note, furthermore, that constitutionally permissible limits may vary in different contexts; in other contexts, such as a claim by a state censor that a movie is obscene, the Constitution may impose different requirements with respect to the time between the making of the claim and the institution of judicial proceedings or between their commencement and completion than in the context of a claim of obscenity made by customs officials at the border. We decide none of these questions today. We do nothing in this case but construe § 1305 (a) in its present form, fully cognizant that Congress may re-enact it in a new form specifying new time limits, upon whose constitutionality we may then be required to pass.

So construed, § 1305 (a) may constitutionally be applied to the case before us. Seizure in the present case took place on October 24 and forfeiture proceedings were instituted on November 6—a mere 13 days after seizure. Moreover, decision on the obscenity of Luros' materials might well have been forthcoming within 60 days had claimant not challenged the validity of the statute and caused a three-judge court to be convened. We hold that proceedings of such brevity fully meet the constitutional standards set out in *Freedman*, *Teitel*, and *Blount*. Section 1305 (a) accordingly may be applied to the 37 photographs, providing that on remand the obscenity issue is resolved in the District Court within 60 days, excluding any delays caused by Luros.

II

We next consider Luros' second claim, which is based upon *Stanley* v. *Georgia, supra*. On the authority of *Stanley*, Luros urged the trial court to construe the First Amendment as forbidding any restraints on obscenity except where necessary to protect children or where it intruded itself upon the sensitivity or privacy of an unwilling adult. Without rejecting this position, the trial court read *Stanley* as protecting, at the very least, the right to read obscene material in the privacy of one's own home and to receive it for that purpose. It therefore held that § 1305 (a), which bars the importation of obscenity for private use as well as for commercial distribution, is overbroad and hence unconstitutional.[3]

The trial court erred in reading *Stanley* as immunizing from seizure obscene materials possessed at a port of entry for the purpose of importation for private use. In *United States* v. *Reidel, ante*, p. 351, we have today held that Congress may constitutionally prevent the mails from being used for distributing pornography. In this case, neither Luros nor his putative buyers have rights that are infringed by the exclusion of obscenity from incoming foreign commerce. By the same token, obscene materials may be removed from the channels of commerce when discovered in the luggage of a returning foreign traveler even though intended solely for his private use. That the private user under *Stanley* may not be prosecuted for possession of obscenity in his home does not mean that he is entitled to import it from abroad free from the power of Congress to exclude noxious articles from commerce. *Stanley's* emphasis was on the freedom

of thought and mind in the privacy of the home. But a port of entry is not a traveler's home. His right to be let alone neither prevents the search of his luggage nor the seizure of unprotected, but illegal, materials when his possession of them is discovered during such a search. Customs officers characteristically inspect luggage and their power to do so is not questioned in this case; it is an old practice and is intimately associated with excluding illegal articles from the country. Whatever the scope of the right to receive obscenity adumbrated in *Stanley*, that right, as we said in *Reidel*, does not extend to one who is seeking, as was Luros here, to distribute obscene materials to the public, nor does it extend to one seeking to import obscene materials from abroad, whether for private use or public distribution. As we held in *Roth* v. *United States*, 354 U. S. 476 (1957), and reiterated today in *Reidel, supra*, obscenity is not within the scope of First Amendment protection. Hence Congress may declare it contraband and prohibit its importation, as it has elected in § 1305 (a) to do.

The judgment of the District Court is reversed and the case is remanded for further proceedings consistent with this opinion.

It is so ordered.

[For dissenting opinion of MR. JUSTICE MARSHALL, see *ante*, p. 360.]

MR. JUSTICE HARLAN, concurring in the judgment and in Part I of MR. JUSTICE WHITE's opinion.

I agree, for the reasons set forth in Part I of MR. JUSTICE WHITE's opinion, that this statute may and should be construed as requiring administrative and judicial action within specified time limits that will avoid the constitutional issue that would otherwise be presented by *Freedman* v. *Maryland*, 380 U. S. 51 (1965). Our decision today in *United States* v. *Reidel, ante*, p. 351, forecloses Luros' claim that the Government may not prohibit the importation of obscene materials for commercial distribution.

Luros also attacked the statute on its face as overbroad because of its apparent prohibition of importation for private use. A statutory scheme purporting to proscribe only importation for commercial purposes would certainly be sufficiently clear to withstand a facial attack on the statute based on the notion that the line between commercial and private importation is so unclear as to inhibit the alleged right to import for private use. Cf. *Breard* v. *Alexandria*, 341 U. S. 622 (1951). It is incontestable that 19 U. S. C. § 1305 (a) is intended to cover at the very least importation of obscene materials for commercial purposes. See n. 1 of MR. JUSTICE WHITE's opinion. Since the parties stipulated that the materials were imported for commercial purposes, Luros cannot claim that his primary conduct was not intended to be within the statute's sweep. Cf. *Dombrowski* v. *Pfister*, 380 U. S. 479, 491–492 (1965). Finally, the statute includes a severability clause. 19 U. S. C. § 1652.

Thus it is apparent that we could only narrow the statute's sweep to commercial importation, were we to determine that importation for private use is constitutionally privileged. In these circumstances, the argument that Luros should be allowed to raise the question of constitutional privilege to import for private use, in order to protect the alleged First Amendment rights of private importers of obscenity from the "chilling effects" of the statute's presence on the books, seems to me to be clearly outweighed by the policy that the resolution of constitutional questions should be avoided where not necessary to the decision of the case at hand.

I would hold that Luros lacked standing to raise the overbreadth claim. See Note, The First Amendment Overbreadth Doctrine, 83 Harv. L. Rev. 844, 910 (1970).

On the foregoing premises I join Part I of the Court's opinion and as to Part II, concur in the judgment.*

MR. JUSTICE STEWART, concurring in the judgment and in Part I of MR. JUSTICE WHITE's opinion.

I agree that the First Amendment does not prevent the border seizure of obscene materials sought to be imported for commercial dissemination. For the reasons expressed in Part I of MR. JUSTICE WHITE's opinion, I also agree that *Freedman* v. *Maryland,* 380 U. S. 51, requires that there be time limits for the initiation of forfeiture proceedings and for the completion of the judicial determination of obscenity.

But I would not in this case decide, even by way of dicta, that the Government may lawfully seize literary material intended for the purely private use of the importer.[1] The terms of the statute appear to apply to an American tourist who, after exercising his constitutionally protected liberty to travel abroad,[2] returns home with a single book in his luggage, with no intention of selling it or otherwise using it, except to read it. If the Government can constitutionally take the book away from him as he passes through customs, then I do not understand the meaning of *Stanley* v. *Georgia,* 394 U. S. 557.

MR. JUSTICE BLACK, with whom MR. JUSTICE DOUGLAS joins, dissenting.*

I

I dissent from the judgments of the Court for the reasons stated in many of my prior opinions. See, *e. g., Smith* v. *California,* 361 U. S. 147, 155 (1959) (BLACK, J., concurring); *Ginzburg* v. *United States,* 383 U. S. 463, 476 (1966) (BLACK, J., dissenting). In my view the First Amendment denies Congress the power to act as censor and determine what books our citizens may read and what pictures they may watch.

I particularly regret to see the Court revive the doctrine of *Roth* v. *United States,* 354 U. S. 476 (1957), that "obscenity" is speech for some reason unprotected by the First Amendment. As the Court's many decisions in this area demonstrate, it is extremely difficult for judges or any other citizens to agree on what is "obscene." Since the distinctions between protected speech and "obscenity" are so elusive and obscure, almost every "obscenity" case involves difficult constitutional issues. After *Roth* our docket and those of other courts have constantly been crowded with cases where judges are called upon to decide whether a particular book, magazine, or movie may be banned. I have expressed before my view that I can imagine no task for which this Court of lifetime judges is less equipped to deal. *Smith* v. *California, supra,* (BLACK, J., concurring).

In view of the difficulties with the *Roth* approach, it is not surprising that many recent decisions have at least implicitly suggested that it should be abandoned. See *Stanley* v. *Georgia,* 394 U. S. 557 (1969); *Redrup* v. *New York,* 386 U. S. 767 (1967). Despite the proved shortcomings of *Roth,* the majority in *Reidel* today reaffirms the validity of that dubious decision. Thus, for the foreseeable future this Court must sit as a Board of Supreme Censors, sifting through books and magazines and watching movies because some official fears they deal too explicitly with sex. I can imagine no more distasteful, useless, and time-consuming task for the members of this Court than perusing this material to determine whether it has "redeeming social value." This absurd spectacle could be avoided if we would adhere to the literal command of the First Amendment that "Congress shall make no law . . . abridging the freedom of speech, or of the press . . . ."

II

Wholly aside from my own views of what the First Amendment demands, I do not see how the reasoning of MR. JUSTICE WHITE's opinion today in *Thirty-Seven Photographs* can be reconciled with the holdings of earlier cases. That opinion insists that the trial court erred in reading *Stanley* v. *Georgia, supra,* "as immunizing from seizure obscene materials possessed at a port of entry for the purpose of importation for private use." *Ante,* at 376. But it is never satisfactorily explained just why the trial court's reading of *Stanley* was erroneous. It would seem to me that if a citizen had a right to possess "obscene" material in the privacy of his home he should have the right to receive it voluntarily through the mail. Certainly when a man legally purchases such material abroad he should be able to bring it with him through customs to read later in his home. The mere act of importation for private use can hardly be more offensive to others than is private perusal in one's home. The right to read and view any literature and pictures at home is hollow indeed if it does not include a right to carry that material privately in one's luggage when entering the country.

The plurality opinion seems to suggest that *Thirty-Seven Photographs* differs from *Stanley* because "Customs officers characteristically inspect luggage and their power to do so is not questioned in this case . . . ." *Ante,* at 376. But surely this observation does not distinguish *Stanley,* because police frequently search private homes as well, and their power to do so is unquestioned so long as the search is reasonable within the meaning of the Fourth Amendment.

Perhaps, however, the plurality reasons silently that a prohibition against importation of obscene materials for private use is constitutionally permissible because it is necessary to prevent ultimate commercial distribution of obscenity. It may feel that an importer's intent to distribute obscene materials commercially is so difficult to prove that all such importation may be outlawed without offending the First Amendment. A very similar argument was made by the State in *Stanley* when it urged that enforcement of a possession law was necessary because of the difficulties of proving intent to distribute or actual distribution. However, the Court unequivocally rejected that argument because an individual's right to "read or observe what he pleases" is so "fundamental to our scheme of individual liberty." 394 U. S., at 568.

Furthermore, any argument that all importation may be banned to stop possible commercial distribution simply ignores numerous holdings of this Court that legislation touching on First Amendment freedoms must be precisely and narrowly drawn to avoid stifling the expression the Amendment was designed to protect. Certainly the Court has repeatedly applied the rule against overbreadth in past censorship cases, as in *Butler* v. *Michigan*, 352 U. S. 380 (1957), where we held that the State could not quarantine "the general reading public against books not too rugged for grown men and women in order to shield juvenile innocence." *Id.*, at 383. Cf. *Thornhill* v. *Alabama*, 310 U. S. 88 (1940); *United States* v. *Robel*, 389 U. S. 258 (1967).

Since the plurality opinion offers no plausible reason to distinguish private possession of "obscenity" from importation for private use, I can only conclude that at least four members of the Court would overrule *Stanley*. Or perhaps in the future that case will be recognized as good law only when a man writes salacious books in his attic, prints them in his basement, and reads them in his living room.

The plurality opinion appears to concede that the customs obscenity statute is unconstitutional on its face after the Court's decision in *Freedman* v. *Maryland*, 380 U. S. 51 (1965), because this law specifies no time limits within which forfeiture proceedings must be started against seized books or pictures, and it does not require a prompt final judicial hearing on obscenity. *Ante*, at 368–369. Once the plurality has reached this determination, the proper course would be to affirm the lower court's decision. But the plurality goes on to rewrite the statute by adding specific time limits. The plurality then notes that the Government here has conveniently stayed within these judicially manufactured limits by one day, and on that premise it concludes the statute may be enforced in this case. In my view the plurality's action in rewriting this statute represents a seizure of legislative power that we simply do not possess under the Constitution.

Certainly claimant Luros has standing to raise the claim that the customs statute's failure to provide for prompt judicial decision renders it unconstitutional. Our previous decisions make clear that such censorship statutes may be challenged on their face as a violation of First Amendment rights "whether or not [a defendant's] conduct could be proscribed by a properly drawn statute." *Freedman* v. *Maryland*, *supra*, at 56. This is true because of the "danger of tolerating, in the area of First Amendment freedoms, the existence of a penal statute susceptible of sweeping and improper application." *NAACP* v. *Button*, 371 U. S. 415, 433 (1963). Since this censorship statute is unconstitutional on its face, and claimant has standing to challenge it as such, that should end the case without further ado. But the plurality nimbly avoids this result by writing a new censorship statute.

I simply cannot understand how the plurality determines it has the power to substitute the new statute for the one that the duly elected representatives of the people have enacted. The plurality betrays its uneasiness when it concedes that we specifically refused to undertake any such legislative task in *Freedman, supra*, and in *Blount* v. *Rizzi*, 400 U. S. 410 (1971). After holding the Maryland movie censorship law unconstitutional in *Freedman*, the Court stated:

> "How or whether Maryland is to incorporate the required procedural safeguards in the statutory scheme is, of course, for the State to decide." 380 U. S., at 60.

With all deference, I would suggest that the decision whether and how the customs obscenity law should be rewritten is a task for the Congress, not this Court. Congress might decide to write an entirely different law, or even decide that the Nation can well live without such a statute.

The plurality claims to find power to rewrite the customs obscenity law in the statute's legislative history and in the rule that statutes should be construed to avoid constitutional questions. *Ante*, at 373. I agree, of course, that statutes should be construed to uphold their constitutionality when this can be done without misusing the legislative history and substituting a new statute for the one that Congress has passed. But this rule of construction does not justify the plurality's acting like a legislature or one of its committees and redrafting the statute in a manner not supported by the deliberations of Congress or by our previous decisions in censorship cases.

The plurality relies principally on statements made by Senators Swanson and Pittman when the customs obscenity legislation was under discussion on the Senate floor. The defect in the Court's reliance is that the Senators' statements did not refer to the version of the law that was passed by Congress. Senator Pittman, objecting to one of the very first drafts of the law, said:

> "Why would it not protect the public entirely if we were to provide for the seizure as now provided and that the property should be held by the officer seizing, and that he should immediately report to the nearest United States district attorney having authority under the law to proceed to confiscate...." 72 Cong. Rec. 5240.

A few minutes later Senator Walsh of Montana announced he would propose an amendment "that would meet the suggestion made by the Senator from Nevada [Mr. Pittman] ...." *Id.*, at 5421. As Senator Walsh first presented his amendment it read:

> "Upon the appearance of any such book or other matter at any customs office the collector thereof shall *immediately* transmit information thereof to the district attorney of the district in which such port is situated, who shall *immediately* institute proceedings in the district court for the forfeiture and destruction of the same ...." *Ibid.* (Emphasis added.)

Senator Swanson was referring to this *first draft* of the Walsh amendment when he made the remarks cited by the plurality that officers would be required to go to court "immediately" and that there would be a "prompt" decision on the matter. *Id.*, at 5422, 5424. But just after Swanson's statement the Walsh amendment was changed on the Senate floor to read as follows:

"Upon the seizure of such book or matter the *collector shall transmit* information thereof to the district attorney of the district in which is situated the office at which such seizure has taken place, *who shall institute* proceedings in the district court for the forfeiture, confiscation, and destruction of the book or matter seized." *Id.,* at 5424. (Emphasis added.)

Thus the requirement that officers go to court "immediately" was dropped in the second draft of the Walsh amendment, and the language of this second draft was enacted into law. The comments quoted and relied upon by the plurality were made with reference to an amendment draft that was not adopted by the Senate and is not now the law. This legislative history just referred to provides no support that I can see for the Court's action today. To the extent that these debates tell us anything about the Senate's attitude toward prompt judicial review of censorship decisions they show simply that the issue was put before the Senate but that it did not choose to require prompt judicial review.

The plurality concedes that in previous censorship cases we have considered the validity of the statutes before us on their face, and we have refused to rewrite them. Although some of these cases did involve state statutes, in *Blount* v. *Rizzi,* 400 U. S. 410 (1971), we specifically declined to attempt to save a federal obscenity mail-blocking statute by redrafting it. The Court there plainly declared: "it is for Congress, not this Court, to rewrite the statute." *Id.,* at 419. The plurality in its opinion now seeks to distinguish *Blount* because saving the mail-blocking statute by requiring prompt judicial review "would have required its complete rewriting in a manner inconsistent with the expressed intentions of some of its authors." *Ante,* at 369. But the only "expressed intention" cited by the plurality to support this argument is testimony by the Postmaster General that he wanted to forestall judicial review pending completion of administrative mail-blocking proceedings. *Ante,* at 370. That insignificant piece of legislative history would have posed no obstacle to the Court's saving the mail-blocking statute by requiring prompt judicial review *after* prompt administrative proceedings. Yet the Court in *Blount* properly refused to undertake such a legislative task, just as it did in the cases involving state censorship statutes.

The plurality also purports to justify its judicial legislation by pointing to the severability provisions contained in 19 U. S. C. § 1652. It is difficult to see how this distinguishes earlier cases, since the statutes struck down in *Freedman* v. *Maryland, supra,* and *Teitel Film Corp.* v. *Cusack,* 390 U. S. 139 (1968), also contained severability provisions. See Md. Ann. Code, Art. 66A, § 24 (1957), Municipal Code of Chicago § 155–7.4 (1961).

The plurality is not entirely clear whether the time limits it imposes stem from the legislative history of the customs law or from the demands of the First Amendment. At one point we are told that 14 days and 60 days are not the "only constitutionally permissible time limits," and that if Congress imposes new rules this would present a new constitutional question. *Ante,* at 374. This strongly suggests the time limits stem from the Court's power to "interpret" or "construe" federal statutes, not from the Constitution. But since the Court's action today has no support in the legislative history or the wording of the statute, it appears much more likely that the time limits are derived from the First Amendment itself. If the plurality is really drawing its rules from the First Amendment, I find the process of derivation both peculiar and disturbing. The rules are not derived by considering what the First Amendment demands, but by surveying previously litigated cases and then guessing what limits would not pose an "undue hardship" on the Government and the lower federal courts. *Ante,* at 373. Scant attention is given to the First Amendment rights of persons entering the country. Certainly it gives little comfort to an American bringing a book home to Colorado or Alabama for personal reading to be informed without explanation that a 74-day delay at New York harbor is not "undue." Faced with such lengthy legal proceedings and the need to hire a lawyer far from home, he is likely to be coerced into giving up his First Amendment rights. Thus the whims of customs clerks or the congestion of their business will determine what Americans may read.

I would simply leave this statute as the Congress wrote it and affirm the judgment of the District Court.

I do not understand why the plurality feels so free to abandon previous precedents protecting the cherished freedoms of press and speech. I cannot, of course, believe it is bowing to popular passions and what it perceives to be the temper of the times. As I have said before, "Our Constitution was not written in the sands to be washed away by each wave of new judges blown in by each successive political wind that brings new political administrations into temporary power." *Turner* v. *United States,* 396 U. S. 398, 426 (1970) (BLACK, J., dissenting). In any society there come times when the public is seized with fear and the importance of basic freedoms is easily forgotten. I hope, however, "that in calmer times, when present pressures, passions and fears subside, this or some later Court will restore the First Amendment liberties to the high preferred place where they belong in a free society." *Dennis* v. *United States,* 341 U. S. 494, 581 (1951) (BLACK, J., dissenting).

COURT'S OPINION NOTES

**MR. JUSTICE HARLAN and MR. JUSTICE STEWART also join Part I of the opinion.
[1] 19 U. S. C. § 1305 (a) provides in pertinent part:
"All persons are prohibited from importing into the United States from any foreign country . . . any obscene book, pamphlet, paper, writing, advertisement, circular, print, picture, drawing, or other representation, figure, or image on or of paper or other material, or any cast, instrument, or other article which is obscene or immoral . . . . No such articles whether imported separately or contained in packages with other goods entitled to entry, shall be admitted to entry; and all such articles and, unless it appears to the satisfaction of the collector that the obscene or other prohibited articles contained in the package were inclosed therein without the knowledge or consent of the importer, owner, agent, or consignee, the entire contents of the package in which such articles are con-

tained, shall be subject to seizure and forfeiture as hereinafter provided . . . . *Provided, further,* That the Secretary of the Treasury may, in his discretion, admit the so-called classics or books of recognized and established literary or scientific merit, but may, in his discretion, admit such classics or books only when imported for noncommercial purposes.

"Upon the appearance of any such book or matter at any customs office, the same shall be seized and held by the collector to await the judgment of the district court as hereinafter provided; and no protest shall be taken to the United States Customs Court from the decision of the collector. Upon the seizure of such book or matter the collector shall transmit information thereof to the district attorney of the district in which is situated the office at which such seizure has taken place, who shall institute proceedings in the district court for the forfeiture, confiscation, and destruction of the book or matter seized. Upon the adjudication that such book or matter thus seized is of the character the entry of which is by this section prohibited, it shall be ordered destroyed and shall be destroyed. Upon adjudication that such book or matter thus seized is not of the character the entry of which is by this section prohibited, it shall not be excluded from entry under the provisions of this section.

"In any such proceeding any party in interest may upon demand have the facts at issue determined by a jury and any party may have an appeal or the right of review as in the case of ordinary actions or suits."

² The United States urges that we find time limits in 19 U. S. C. §§ 1602 and 1604. Section 1602 provides that customs agents who seize goods must "report every such seizure immediately" to the collector of the district, while § 1604 provides that, once a case has been turned over to a United States Attorney, it shall be his duty "immediately to inquire into the facts" and "forthwith to cause the proper proceedings to be commenced and prosecuted, without delay," if he concludes judicial proceedings are appropriate. We need not decide, however, whether §§ 1602 and 1604 can properly be applied to cure the invalidity of § 1305 (a), for even if they were applicable, they would not provide adequate time limits and would not cure its invalidity. The two sections contain no specific time limits, nor do they require the collector to act promptly in referring a matter to the United States Attorney for prosecution. Another flaw is that § 1604 requires that, if the United States Attorney declines to prosecute, he must report the facts to the Secretary of the Treasury for his direction, but the Secretary is under no duty to act with speed. The final flaw is that neither section requires the District Court in which a case is commenced to come promptly to a final decision.

³ The District Court's opinion is not entirely clear. The court may have reasoned that Luros had a right to import the 37 photographs in question for planned distribution to the general public, but our decision today in *United States* v. *Reidel, ante,* p. 351, makes it clear that such reasoning would have been in error. On the other hand, the District Court may have reasoned that, while Luros had no right to import the photographs for distribution, a person would have a right under *Stanley* to import them for his own private use and that § 1305 (a) was therefore void as overbroad because it prohibits both sorts of importation. If this was the court's reasoning, the proper approach, however, was not to invalidate the section in its entirety, but to construe it narrowly and hold it valid in its application to Luros. This was made clear in *Dombrowski* v. *Pfister,* 380 U. S. 479, 491–492 (1965), where the Court noted that, once the overbreadth of a statute has been sufficiently dealt with, it may be applied to prior conduct foreseeably within its valid sweep.

JUSTICE HARLAN'S CONCURRING OPINION NOTES

*Again, as in *United States* v. *Reidel, supra,* the obscenity *vel non* of the seized materials is not presented at this juncture of the case.

JUSTICE BLACK'S DISSENTING OPINION NOTES

¹ As Mr. Justice White's opinion correctly says, even if seizure of material for private use is unconstitutional, the statute can still stand in appropriately narrowed form, and the seizure in this case clearly

falls within the valid sweep of such a narrowed statute. *Ante,* at 375, n. 3.

² *Aptheker* v. *Secretary of State,* 378 U. S. 500.

*[This opinion applies also to No. 534, *United States* v. *Reidel, ante,* p. 351.]

JUSTICE BURGER STATES IN FOOTNOTE NO. 2 IN A DRIVE-IN MOVIE CASE THAT OBSCENITY IS LIKE LIBEL—THERE IS NO NEED TO LOOK AT THE MATERIAL AS A WHOLE AS REQUIRED BY *ROTH*

Rabe v. Washington, 405 U.S. 313 (1972)

PER CURIAM.

Petitioner was the manager of the Park Y Drive-In Theatre in Richland, Washington, where the motion picture Carmen Baby was shown. The motion picture is a loose adaptation of Bizet's opera Carmen, containing sexually frank scenes but no instances of sexual consummation are explicitly portrayed. After viewing the film from outside the theater fence on two successive evenings, a police officer obtained a warrant and arrested petitioner for violating Washington's obscenity statute. Wash. Rev. Code § 9.68.010. Petitioner was later convicted and, on appeal, the Supreme Court of Washington affirmed. 79 Wash. 2d 254, 484 P. 2d 917 (1971). We granted certiorari. 404 U. S. 909. We reverse petitioner's conviction.

The statute under which petitioner was convicted, Wash. Rev. Code § 9.68.010, made criminal the knowing display of "obscene" motion pictures:

"Every person who—

"(1) Having knowledge of the contents thereof shall exhibit, sell, distribute, display for sale or distribution, or having knowledge of the contents thereof shall have in his possession with the intent to sell or distribute any book, magazine, pamphlet, comic book, newspaper, writing, photograph, motion picture film, phonograph record, tape or wire recording, picture, drawing, figure, image, or any object or thing which is obscene; or

"(2) Having knowledge of the contents thereof shall cause to be performed or exhibited, or shall engage in the performance or exhibition of any show, act, play, dance or motion picture which is obscene;

"Shall be guilty of a gross misdemeanor."

In affirming petitioner's conviction, however, the Supreme Court of Washington did not hold that Carmen Baby was obscene under the test laid down by this Court's prior decisions. E. g., *Roth* v. *United States,* 354 U. S. 476; *Memoirs* v. *Massachusetts,* 383 U. S. 413. Uncertain "whether the movie was offensive to the standards relating to sexual matters in that area and whether the movie advocated ideas or was of artistic or literary value," the court concluded that if it "were to apply the strict rules of *Roth,* the film 'Carmen Baby' probably would pass the definitional obscenity test if the viewing audience consisted only of consenting adults." 79 Wash. 2d, at 263, 484 P. 2d, at 922. Respondent read the opinion of the Supreme Court of Washington more narrowly, but nonetheless implied that because the film had "redeeming social value" it was not, by itself, "obscene" under the *Roth* standard. The Supreme Court of Washington nonetheless upheld the conviction, reasoning that in "the *context* of its exhibition," Carmen Baby was obscene. *Ibid.*

To avoid the constitutional vice of vagueness, it is necessary, at a minimum, that a statute give fair notice that certain conduct is proscribed. The statute under which petitioner was prosecuted, however, made no mention that the "context" or location of the exhibition was an element of the offense somehow modifying the word "obscene." Petitioner's conviction was thus affirmed under a statute with a meaning quite different from the one he was charged with violating.

"It is as much a violation of due process to send an accused to prison following conviction of a charge on which he was never tried as it would be to convict him upon a charge that was never made." *Cole v. Arkansas*, 333 U. S. 196, 201. Petitioner's conviction cannot, therefore, be allowed to stand. *Gregory v. City of Chicago*, 394 U. S. 111; *Garner v. Louisiana*, 368 U. S. 157; *Cole v. Arkansas, supra.*

Under the interpretation given § 9.68.010 by the Supreme Court of Washington, petitioner is criminally punished for showing Carmen Baby in a drive-in but he may exhibit it to adults in an indoor theater with impunity. The statute, so construed, is impermissibly vague as applied to petitioner because of its failure to give him fair notice that criminal liability is dependent upon the place where the film is shown.

What we said last Term in *Cohen v. California*, 403 U. S. 15, 19, answers respondent's contention that the peculiar interest in prohibiting outdoor displays of sexually frank motion pictures justifies the application of this statute to petitioner:

> "Any attempt to support this conviction on the ground that the statute seeks to preserve an appropriately decorous atmosphere in the courthouse where Cohen was arrested must fail in the absence of any language in the statute that would have put appellant on notice that certain kinds of otherwise permissible speech or conduct would nevertheless, under California law, not be tolerated in certain places. . . . No fair reading of the phrase 'offensive conduct' can be said sufficiently to inform the ordinary person that distinctions between certain locations are thereby created."

We need not decide the broad constitutional questions tendered to us by the parties. We hold simply that a State may not criminally punish the exhibition at a drive-in theater of a motion picture where the statute, used to support the conviction, has not given fair notice that the location of the exhibition was a vital element of the offense.

The judgment of the Supreme Court of Washington is

Reversed.

MR. CHIEF JUSTICE BURGER, with whom MR. JUSTICE REHNQUIST joins, concurring.

I concur solely on the ground that petitioner's conviction under Washington's general obscenity statute cannot, under the circumstances of this case, be sustained consistent with the fundamental notice requirements of the Due Process Clause. The evidence in this case, however, revealed that the screen of petitioner's theater was clearly visible to motorists passing on a nearby public highway and to 12 to 15 nearby family residences. In addition, young teenage children were observed viewing the film from outside the chain link fence enclosing the theater grounds. I, for one, would be unwilling to hold that the First Amendment prevents a State from prohibiting such a public display of scenes depicting explicit sexual activities if the State undertook to do so under a statute narrowly drawn to protect the public from potential exposure to such offensive materials. See *Redrup* v. *New York*, 386 U. S. 767 (1967).[1]

Public displays of explicit materials such as are described in this record are not significantly different from any noxious public nuisance traditionally within the power of the States to regulate and prohibit, and, in my view, involve no significant countervailing First Amendment considerations.[2] That this record shows an offensive nuisance that could properly be prohibited, I have no doubt, but the state statute and charge did not give the notice constitutionally required.

NOTES

[1] For examples of recent statutes regulating public displays, see Ariz. Rev. Stat. Ann. § 13–537 (Supp. 1971–1972); N. Y. Penal Law §§ 245.10–245.11 (Supp. 1971–1972).

[2] Under such circumstances, where the very method of display may thrust isolated scenes on the public, the *Roth* v. *United States*, 354 U. S. 476, 489 (1957), requirement that the materials be "taken as a whole" has little relevance. For me, the First Amendment must be treated in this context as it would in a libel action: if there is some libel in a book, article, or speech we do not average the tone and tenor of the whole; the libelous part is not protected.

THE FILM "DEEP THROAT" IS DECLARED OBSCENE IN NEW YORK CITY

People v. Mature Enterprises, Inc., 343 N.Y.S.2d 911 (1973)

JOEL J. TYLER, Judge.

We are again thrust into the overexplored thicket of obscenity law. The defendant is charged with promotion, or possession with intent to promote, obscene material, knowing the contents and character thereof, all in violation of Penal Law § 235.05, Subd. 1, a class A misdemeanor.[1] It was tried before the Court without a jury.[2]

What is involved is the showing in a public theatre, at a $5.00 per admission charge, the film "Deep Throat." The case has engendered some public interest here and elsewhere. However, it is not unique. Many cases dealing with depiction of the same or similar deviate sexual behavior have been reported, but few have had such a full measure of directed publicity.

The Film

The film runs 62 minutes. It is in color and in sound, and boasts a musical score. Following the first innocuous scene ("heroine" driving a car), the film runs from one act of explicit sex into another, forthrightly demonstrating heterosexual intercourse and a variety of deviate sexual acts, not "fragmentary and fleeting" as to be de minimis as in Jacobellis v. Ohio, 378 U.S. 184, 197–198, 84 S.Ct. 1676, 12 L.Ed.2d 793 [1964], Goldberg, J., or 10 minutes out of a 120-minute movie as in I Am Curious Yellow (404 F.2d 196, 203, infra); but here it permeates and engulfs the film from beginning to end. The camera angle, emphasis and close-up zooms were directed, as in United States v. Kaehler, D.C., 353 F.Supp. 476, 477, "toward a maximum exposure in detail of the genitalia" during the gymnastics, gyrations, bobbing, trundling, surging, ebb and flowing, eddying, moaning, groaning and sighing, all with evullience and gusto.

There were so many and varied forms of sexual activity one would tend to lose count of them. However, the news reporters were more adept and counted seven separate acts of fellatio and four of cunnilingus (Newsweek, 1/15/73, p. 50; New York Times Mag. Sec. 1/31/73, p. 28). Such concentration upon the acts of fellatio and cunnilingus overlooked the numerous clear, clinical acts of sexual intercourse, anal sodomy, female masturbation, clear depiction of seminal fluid ejaculation and an orgy scene—a Sodom and Gomorrah gone wild before the fire—all of which is enlivened with the now famous "four letter words" and finally with bells ringing and rockets bursting in climactic ecstasy.

The performance of one sexual act runs almost headlong into the other. One defense witness thought 75 to 80% of the film involved depiction of explicit sexual activity and another viewed it at over 50%. A timekeeper may have clocked a higher percentage. Nothing was faked or simulated; it was as explicit as and as exquisite as life. One defense witness said he saw "realism and genuine sexual experience." No imagination was needed, since it was intended to appeal to the imbecile as well.

The defense expert witnesses testified that the film possessed entertainment value and humor. The court in People ex rel. Hicks v. "Sarong Gals", 27 Cal.App.3d 46, 52, 103 Cal.Rptr. 414, 417 (1972) appropriately answered that tedious and tenuous argument often, but conscientiously, made in obscenity cases which have nothing to redeem them:

"Presumably the Romans of the First Century derived entertainment from witnessing Christians being devoured by lions. Given the right audience, the spectacle of a man committing an act of sodomy on another man would provide entertainment value. However, neither this spectacle nor the activities described in the instant case are invested with constitutionally protected values merely because they entertain viewers. However chaotic the law may be in this field, no court has yet adopted such an extreme result."

In passing, it should be noted that the defense "expert" witnesses were unpersuasive in the main. For example, a defense psychologist testified that he would use films like Deep Throat as classroom sex educational material not only in colleges but for certain high school students as well.

The alleged "humor" of the film is sick, and designed on a level to appeal especially to those first learning that boys and girls are different. Drama critic, Vincent Canby, characterizes the jokes as "dumb gags,—[which] cannot disguise the straight porno intent."[3] This, the defense experts here maintain, helps redeem the film as worthwhile. As to plot, there is none, unless you exclude the sexual activity, which is the sole plot. And as to character development, a desirable and necessary concomitant of meaningful film, stage or book, again there is none, unless, of course, one means that the progression (or retrogression) of multiple and varied nymphomania to a singular form (fellatio) is evidence of this attribute.

Oh, yes! There is a gossamer of a story line—the heroine's all-engrossing search for sexual gratification, and when all sexual endeavors fail to gratify, her unique problem is successfully diagnosed to exist in her throat. She then seeks to fill the doctor's prescription by repeated episodes of fellatio, which Nora Ephron, euphemistically characterizes, as "compensatory behavior." (Esquire, Feb., 1973)

The defense experts testified that they see the film legitimatizing woman's need and "life right" (as one put it) for sexual gratification, equal with that of men. They also see in the film the thoughtful lesson that sex should not be unavailingly monolithic (usual face-to-face relationship),[4] but should take varied forms, with complete sexual gratification as the crowning goal, or as the film seems to advertise in its plebian fashion—"different strokes for different folks"; or as others, less articulate, might say, "there's more than one way to skin the cat." These unusual and startling revelations are of social value, they say, not only for the bedroom, but necessary as an object lesson for a public forum.

The alleged story lines are the facade, the sheer negligee through which clearly shines the producer's and the defendant's true and only purpose, that is, the presentation of unmistakably hard-core pornography, where "imagination has gone to work in the porno-vineyards"—a quotation by a newsman, and adopted by the defendant in its newspaper advertisements (Exhibits 2 and 4 in evidence). One defense expert actually, but unwittingly, confirms the charade when he says that the "plot" of the film "provides a thread on which the various sequence of sexual acts would be hung."

Movie critic Judith Crist characterizes the production "idiot moviemaking" and the actors "awful" (New York Magazine, 2/5/73, p. 64). I agree, except to add that a female, who would readily and with apparent, anxious abandon, submit to the insertion of a glass dildoe container into her vagina, have liquid poured therein and then drink it by means of a tube, as was done here to and by the "superstar", is not a reflection merely upon her thespian ability, but a clinical example of extraordinary perversion, degeneracy and possible amentia.[5] Whatever talent superstar has seems confined to her magnificant appetite and sword-swallowing faculty for fellatio.

In this Court's view, the film and its genre have a significant meaning and impact, transcending this case, for all society (including for those who have seen the movie), as noted in the Appendix, attached hereto.

The Law

Penal Law § 235.05, and particularly the definition of "obscene" in § 235.00, subd. 1, represents the New York Legislature's attempt to codify the federal rules first enunciated in Roth v. United States, 354 U.S. 476, 489, 77 S.Ct. 1304, 1 L.Ed.2d 1498 (1957); reiterated in Jacobellis v. Ohio, 378 U.S. 184, 84 S.Ct. 1676, 12 L.Ed.2d 793 (1964), which also equated "contemporary community standards" with "national" rather than any local standards; and elaborated and summarized in A Book Named "John Cleland's Memoirs of a Woman of Pleasure" v. Attorney General of Massachusetts, 383 U.S. 413, 418–419, 86 S.Ct. 975, 16 L.Ed.2d 1 (1967) (involving the famous "Fanny Hill" book; and, hereinafter, referred to merely as "Memoirs"); and further elaborated by Redrup v. New York, 386 U.S. 767, 87 S.Ct. 1414, 18 L.Ed.2d 515 (1967). (See: McKinney's Practice Commentary, Book 39, p. 69).

The determination of obscenity involves the "independent" application of three separate tests, all of which must "coalesce" and be directed to the "average person." According to the Roth-Memoirs test, material may be deemed obscene if: (a) the dominant theme of the material taken as a whole appeals to prurient interest in sex; (b) it is patently offensive because it affronts contemporary community standards relating to the description or representation of sexual matters, and (c) the material is utterly without redeeming social value.[6]

The tests were adjusted as they apply to sexual deviants by Mishkin v. New York, 383 U.S. 502, 86 S.Ct. 958, 16 L.Ed.2d 56 (1966), and given a different dimension in "close" cases, where "pandering", if found, will move such a case over the brink into the pool of obscenity, Ginzburg v. United States, 383 U.S. 463, 86 S.Ct. 942, 16 L.Ed.2d 31 (1966), as would the finding of any one of the three added tests in Redrup, supra. [People v. Stabile, 58 Misc.2d 905, 296 N.Y.S.2d 815 (1969); Shinall v. Worrell, D.C., 319 F.Supp. 485 (1970).]

Clearly, this case does not involve admission to the theatre of minors (P.L. §§ 235.20, 235.21; Jacobellis v. Ohio, 378 U.S. 184, 195, 84 S.Ct. 1676, 12 L.Ed.2d 793; supra). Nor is there evidence that the film, in some manner, has been foisted upon an unwilling public or individual, in violation of his right to privacy (Redrup, supra). Nor is there, nor could there be a claim by defendant of lack of scienter. (Smith v. California, 361 U.S. 147, 80 S.Ct. 215, 4 L.Ed.2d 205 (1959)).

There is a claim, however, that the film here was pandered in violation of the criterion of Ginzburg, supra, in that the newspaper ads evidenced an intent to commercially exploit the film for the sake of its prurient appeal, and should be condemned for this among other reasons. There is evidence of pandering here. However, Ginzburg is applicable only in "close" cases; and Deep Throat is far from a close case; it is a classic case; and, therefore, we need not rely on this prohibition to legally sanction it. Furthermore, although the advertisements placed in evidence, speak of the film as "The very best porn film ever made" and "Imagination has gone to work in the porno-vineyards"; and courts should "accept [the purveyor's] evaluation at its face value" (*Memoirs*, supra, 383 U.S. p. 420, 86 S.Ct. p. 978), we do not equate that chest thumping with the circumstances of presentation and dissemination condemned in *Ginzburg*. There is no reason to dwell on this comparatively tenuous element, when there is so much more in the "vineyards" of this film, offering a direct and clear basis for legal sanction. Accordingly, let us consider: Is the film obscene under the law?

Admittedly, the "guidelines" of *Roth-Memoirs* are distressingly ambiguous. But some would maintain there is merit in ambiguity, to meet the shifts of society's national values and moral imperatives. ". . . the criminal law which deals with imperfect humanity cannot await the perfect definition—nor the perfect society in which, perhaps, no definitions would be necessary." (Hofstadter and Levittan, No Glory, No Beauty, No Stars—Just Mud, N.Y.S. Bar Jour., Feb. 1965, p. 38). We embark to apply the tests to the film, with no trepidations or uncertainty in this particular case.

We begin with the premise, well-established, that motion pictures, as other forms of communication, are equally entitled to constitutional protection under the First Amendment. Joseph Burstyn, Inc. v. Wilson, 343 U.S. 495, 72 S.Ct. 777, 96 L.Ed. 1098 (1952), Kupferman and O'Brien, Motion Picture Censorship—The Memphis Blues, 36 Cornell Law Rev. 273, 288 (1951). And they are protected against State abridgement by the 14th Amendment. Gitlow v. New York, 268 U.S. 652, 45 S.Ct. 625, 69 L.Ed. 1138 (1952); Thomas v. Collins, 323 U.S. 516, 65 S.Ct. 315, 89 L.Ed. 430 (1945).

Motion pictures are understood to encompass problems peculiar to that form of expression, not subject to the precise rules governing other communication media. Accordingly, the Constitution does not require "absolute freedom to exhibit every motion picture of every kind at all times and places. . . ." Joseph Burstyn, Inc. v. Wilson, supra, 343 U.S. p. 502, 72 S.Ct. p. 781; Mtr. of Trans-Lux Distr. v. Bd. of Regents, 14 N.Y.2d 88, 92, 248 N.Y.S.2d 857, 860, 198 N.E.2d 242, 244 (1964), rev'd on other grounds, 380 U.S. 259, 85 S.Ct. 952, 13 L.Ed.2d 959.

We have here a film and not a novel, book or magazine, and this, we believe, adds a different and significant dimension to the question. Stanley Kaufman notes (22 The Public Interest, p. 31, Winter 1971) a discernible difference in the one-to-one relationship of writer and reader "in psychic and social senses," from the employment of people to enact sexual fantasies on stage and screen before an audience. The stark reality and impact of a movie is undeniably as impressive as the viewing of a true-life situation on the open street. Certainly, to read descriptions of explicit sexual activity as shown in Deep Throat, or merely to hear them discussed, can never have that same poignancy and cannot create that same lasting impression upon the human mind or appeal to the prurient as does the observation of the acts in a true life situation or on the screen. Freedman v. State of Maryland, 380 U.S. 51, 61, 85 S.Ct. 734, 13 L.Ed.2d 649 (1965); United States v. A Motion Picture Film (I Am Curious Yellow), 2 Cir., 404 F.2d 196, 203 (1966); United States v. A Motion Picture Entitled "Pattern of Evil," D.C., 304 F.Supp. 197, 202 (1969); People v. Bercowitz, 61 Misc.2d 974, 981–983, 308 N.Y.S.2d 1, 9–11 (1970).

Because of a film's unique, shocking quality, we cannot disregard its potent visual impact in depicting, as does Deep Throat, the fellatio, cunnilingus, masturbation, sexual intercourse, and other sexual activity. Such depiction of clearly discernible acts "transcend the bounds of the constitutional guarantee long before a frank description of the same scenes in the written word." Landau v. Fording, 245 Cal.App.2d 820, 54 Cal.Rptr. 177, 181, aff'd, 388 U.S. 456, 87 S.Ct. 2109, 18 L.Ed.2d 1317 (1967), rehg. den., 389 U.S. 889, 88 S.Ct. 16, 19 L.Ed.2d 199. Accordingly, the appeal to prurience, the recognition of patent offensiveness, the violation of community standards and absence of social value will be realized more readily and more assuredly with a film than in a writing.

This difference seems to have motivated the Supreme Court in its almost consistent refusal to reject as obscene the written word, such as those in Tropic of Cancer (Grove Press, Inc. v. Gerstein, 378 U.S. 577, 84 S.Ct. 1909, 12 L.Ed.2d 1035 [1964] and Fanny Hill (*Memoirs*, supra). Since Redrup v. New York, supra, the Supreme Court, in seven cases, overruled obscenity convictions involving the publication of novels.[7] As a result, the Court in State v. Carlson, Minn., 202 N.W.2d 640, 645 (1972), concludes—"Apparently the rulings demonstrate that the printed word, no matter how tawdry, is not obscene."

It is Hard-core Pornography

Hard-core pornography was the sole class of material declared impermissible, prior to the adoption of P.L. § 235.05. People v. Richmond County News, 9 N.Y.2d 578, 586, 216 N.Y.S.2d 369, 375, 175 N.E.2d 681, 685 (1961); People v. Weingarten, 25 N.Y.2d 639, 306 N.Y.S.2d 17, 254 N.E.2d 232 (1969). However, in Mishkin v. New York, 383 U.S. 502, 506, 86 S.Ct. 958, 16 L.Ed.2d 56, supra, the Court explained that *Roth-Memoirs* criteria expanded the test to include additional classes of material within legal restraint, and apparently, hard-core now remains but one of many conceivable illegalities. Redrup v. New York, supra.

This Court has previously indicated the substantial evidence pointing to the reality that the Supreme Court in *Roth*, supra, and since then, has equated obscenity with hard-core pornography, without expressly saying so, and that *Redrup* lends additional support to the view that that Court will limit its condemnations to hard-core only. People v. Kirkpatrick, 64 Misc.2d 1055, 1077–1079, 316 N.Y.S.2d 37, 59–62 (1970); aff'd, 69 Misc.2d 212, 329 N.Y.S.2d 769. In the light of the present position of our forever modulating social standards, it is not far-fetched to predict that our high Court will eventually and, in fact, expressly say so. It would make more sense than the manifold rules of *Roth-Memoirs*. In fact, at least one jurist apparently believes that the Court has already taken this position, when he concludes "that the definition of obscenity contained in Section 235.05 of the Penal Law and 'hard-core' pornography are synonymous, and it is only this 'clearly identifiable class of material . . .' which is proscribed in New York." People v. Druss, N.Y.L.J. 1/18/73, Col. 3.

What is hard-core pornography and its connection with Deep Throat?

We know sex is not obscene; *Roth, supra* tells us that when it says "Sex and obscenity are not synonymous" (354 U.S. p. 487, 77 S.Ct. p. 1310). Now, that we know what it is not, then what is obscenity? Admittedly, "obscenity" almost defies meaningful definition. Jacobellis v. Ohio, 378 U.S. 184, 199, 84 S.Ct. 1676, 12 L.Ed.2d 793, supra; Alpert, Judicial Censorship and Obscene Literature, 52 Harv.L.Rev. 40, 47 (1938). Is hard-core any more susceptible to exact delineation? Chief Justice Warren finds both tasks impossible, with the comment—"But who can define 'hard core pornography' with any greater clarity than 'obscenity' " (*Jacobellis*, supra, p. 201, 84 S.Ct. p. 1685).[8]

But yet others find it readily definable and certainly more readily identifiable as a reasonably precise concept, which "theoretically, could unite a strong majority of the Supreme Court", Magrath, The Obscenity Cases: Grapes of Roth, 99 Sup.Ct.Rev. 1, 69 (1966).[9] My learned brother Judge William J. Shea recently advised that "Hard core pornography is a specific type of obscenity, it is obscenity in its easiest recognizable form. It contains 'something more' than obscenity in its general or hard to recognize form and that 'something' is its depiction of *actual* sexual activity, including intercourse and deviate acts." People v. Wrench, Sup., 341 N.Y.S.2d 985. Also my brother, Judge Arthur Goldberg (and Yeargin) agree, that the decisions involving explicit sexual activity represent the distinction to "indicate palpable lines between obscenity and protected expression." People v. Bercowitz, 61 Misc.2d 974, 978, 308 N.Y.S.2d 1, 6 (1970).[10] The Report of the Commission on Obscenity and Pornography (New York Times Ed. 1970, pp. 22, 425) agrees that explicit sex is distinguishing feature of hard-core pornography from other obscenity in that it demonstrates "sexual intercourse, depicting vaginal, anal or oral penetration."

They are on good ground and have much support. For example: Ginzburg v. United States, 383 U.S. 463, 499, 86 S.Ct. 942, 16 L.Ed.2d 31, supra; People v. Noroff, 67 Cal.2d 791, 794, fn. 6, 63 Cal.Rptr. 575, 433 P.2d 479 (1967); Hunt v. Keriakos, 1 Cir., 428 F.2d 606 (1970), cert. den., 400 U.S. 929, 91 S.Ct. 185, 27 L.Ed.2d 189; Wagonheim v. Md. St. Bd. of Censors, 255 Md. 297, 258 A.2d 240 (1969), aff'd, 401 U.S. 480, 91 S.Ct. 966, 28 L.Ed.2d 205 (1971); State v. Amato, 49 Wis.2d 638, 645, 183 N.W.2d 29 (1971), cert. den., 404 U.S. 1063, 92 S.Ct. 735, 30 L.Ed.2d 751 (1972); State v. Carlson, Minn., 202 N.W.2d 640, 647, supra; People v. Clark, 60 Misc.2d 1073, 304 N.Y.S.2d 326 (1969); People v. Morgan, 68 Misc.2d 667, 326 N.Y.S.2d 976 (1971).

The explicit sexual activity represents the "hard-core" feature of the material, while the "pornography" and its prurient appeal is distinguished by its pervasive hallucinatory quality, its ability to produce physical concomitants of sexual excitement and emotion (Kronhausen, Pornography and The Law, pp. 285–86, 329–331 [1969]). Such material has "the character of the daydream—the product of sheer fantasy." (Margaret Mead, Sex and Censorship in Contemporary Society, New World Writings, p. 19 [1953]). As the Kronhausens noted, life, unlike hard-core, "seldom presents us with a succession of erotic experiences one more stimulating and exciting than the other" (at p. 328).

Because of hard-core's ready prurient appeal it is "patently offensive," and its "indecency speaks for itself." *Memoirs*, supra, 383 U.S. p. 457, 86 S.Ct. 975; Womack v. United States, 111 U.S.App.D.C. 8, 294 F.2d 204, 206 (1961), cert. den., 365 U.S. 859, 81 S.Ct. 826, 5 L.Ed.2d 822. It constitutes "obscenity per se". Donnenberg v. State, 1 Md.App. 591, 600, 232 A.2d 264 (1967); Morris v. United States, D.C.App., 259 A.2d 337, 341 (1969) and condemnable as if *res ipsa loquitur*, requiring no expert testimony to explain or justify it. United States v. Wild, 2 Cir., 422 F.2d 34, 36 (1969), cert. den., 402 U.S. 986, 91 S.Ct. 1644, 29 L.Ed.2d 152; Womack v. United States, supra, 294 F.2d p. 206; Hudson v. United States, D.C.App., 234 A.2d 903, 906 (1967); United States v. Young, 9 Cir., 465 F.2d 1096, 1099 (1972); People v. Tenga, N.Y.L.J. 12/21/72, p. 2 (App. Tm., 1st Dept.) [England permits expert testimony only to explain "public good" (i. e. social value) of the material, not "obscene or no" (i. e. prurient appeal, community standards, etc., Regina v. Anderson, 1 Q.B. 304, 313 (1972)].

Since its brazenness is a direct assault upon long held concepts of national morality and propriety, it is readily recognized throughout the nation by all those not beyond the pale. Apparently, the lay press had no trouble identifying Deep Throat as unmistakable hard-core pornography. ". . . it scarcely could be more hard-core," says Thomas Meehan in Saturday Review, p. 80, March, 1973. ". . . the film is solidly hard-core pornography." (The New York Times, 12/30/72, p. 22). It is a "hard-core" sex film (New York Post, 1/3/73, p. 10); and it is a "hard-core porno movie" (Time mag. 1/15/73, p. 46).

What is the purpose and effect of hard-core pornography? Its aim is "to shock, revolt or embarrass" and brutalize (Benjamin Spock, Decent and Indecent [1969], pp. 83–84); "to insult sex, to do dirt on it . . . to insult the human body" and "a vital human relationship" (D. H. Lawrence, Pornography and Obscenity in Sex, Literature and Censorship, pp. 74–79 [1953]); People v. Bercowitz, supra, 61 Misc.2d pp. 980–981, 308 N.Y.S.2d pp. 8–9. I believe Mr. Justice Theodore R. Kupferman of our Appellate Division would agree. As an attorney, he specialized in censorship and obscenity law. In an enlightening article to the theatrical trade on the law of obscenity (Variety, 1/5/72, pp. 12, 60) he points out that a more easily enforced standard ". is that while sex is accepted, pornography and obscenity will be recognized in brutalizing or insulting sex."

The United States Supreme Court has never dealt with material so brazenly explicit as the scenes of Deep Throat, but it has dealt with some cases involving explicit sex activity in films; most, however, dealt with other varieties of sexuality. For example, in Jacobellis v. Ohio, supra, the first film case since *Roth*, the Supreme Court considered the film *Les Amants* which it found legally permissible. But there the court found only one "explicit love scene in the last reel of the film" (378 U.S. p. 196, 84 S.Ct. p. 1682), and Justice Goldberg further found it "fragmentary and fleeting" as to be de minimis (pp. 197–198, 84 S.Ct. 1676). And certainly what may have been "explicit" then (1964) may very well be quite different from what we have today or in Deep Throat.

In Landau v. Fording, supra, the first case where the Supreme Court found obscenity in a film, the activity there was quite explicit, depicting two males engaged in "male masturbation, fellatio, oral copulation, voyeurism, nudity, sadism and sodomy" (54 Cal.Rptr. at p. 181). It is plain such activity approached, but did not equal, the explicitness of Deep Throat. But it had no music or sound, as in Deep Throat, to sharpen the prurient appeal with grunts, sighs and other sounds of orgasmic pleasure.

The majority of the Second Circuit Court of Appeals, gave its stamp of approval to the film, I Am Curious Yellow, in spite of its finding of "sexual intercourse under varying circumstances, some of them quite unusual. There were scenes of oral-genital activity." Judge Lumbard, in his dissent, explained that "unusual" sexual activity, as fellatio and cunnilingus. (United States v. A Motion Picture, etc., 404 F.2d 196, 198, 203, supra.) But, significantly, when this film finally went to the United States Supreme Court from another jurisdiction, it affirmed the conviction of obscenity. Wagonheim v. Md. St. Bd. of Censors, 255 Md. 297, 258 A.2d 240 (1969); aff'd, 401 U.S. 480, 91 S.Ct. 966, 28 L.Ed.2d 205 (1971). Convictions were also obtained in Georgia (Evans Theatre v. Slaton, 227 Ga. 377, 180 S.E.2d 712 [1971], cert. den., 404 U.S. 950, 92 S.Ct. 281, 30 L.Ed.2d 267); Missouri (Hoffman v. Dickinson Operating Co., 468 S.W.2d 26); Ohio (Grove Press, Inc. v. Flask, D.C., 326 F.Supp. 574, cert. filed, not perfected).

Since the pivotal decision of Redrup v. New York, supra, sex movies were the subject of nine per curiam reversals by the United States Supreme Court.[11] In those cases in which the sexual activity is reported below, we find much nudity and sexual activity but nowhere do we find actual copulation or oral-genital contact. Where sexual intercourse is depicted, it is usually suggested or simulated. None of the nine movies even approximate the sexual depictions in Deep Throat.

When hard-core pornography (and I have yet to see reported anything equal in sexual activity to Deep Throat) is clearly involved, the United States Supreme Court has affirmed a conviction, as it did in *Landau*, or denied certiorari, as it did in Wilhoit v. United States, D.C.App., 279 A.2d 505 (1971), cert. den., 404 U.S. 994, 92 S.Ct. 538, 30 L.Ed.2d 546; State v. Amato, 49 Wis.2d 638, 183 N.W.2d 29 (1971), cert. den., 404 U.S. 1063, 92 S.Ct. 735, 30 L.Ed.2d 751 (1972). Many other courts have followed suit. For example: People v. G. I. Distributors, Inc., 20 N.Y.2d 104, 281 N.Y.S.2d 795, 228 N.E.2d 787 (1967), cert. den., 389 U.S. 905, 88 S.Ct. 218, 19 L.Ed.2d 219; People v. Bercowitz, supra; United States v. Berger, D.C., 325 F.Supp. 249 (1970); United States v. Strand Art Theatre Corp., D.C., 325 F.Supp. 256 (1970); People v. Heller, 29 N.Y.2d 319, 327 N.Y.S.2d 628, 277 N.E.2d 651 (1971), cert. granted, 406 U.S. 916, 92 S.Ct. 1765, 32 L.Ed.2d 115 (pending); Slaton v. Paris Adult Theatre, 228 Ga. 343, 185 S.E.2d 768 (1971), cert. granted, 408 U.S. 921, 92 S.Ct. 2487, 33 L.Ed.2d 331 (pending); United States v. Young, 9 Cir., 465 F.2d 1096 (1972); State v. Lebewitz, Minn., 202 N.W.2d 648 (1972); United States v. Koehler (D.C. Iowa) 353 F.Supp. 476 (1973).

If defendant's counsel had submitted a post-trial brief, we are certain he would have mentioned in his support United States v. 35 mm. Motion Picture Film ("Language of Love"), 2 Cir., 432 F.2d 705 (1970).[12] However, a careful reading of that case will reveal substantive differences between it and the subject film, which the Court there found justified the ruling. In "Language of Love," the court noted, "The explicit scenes of sexual activity consist *almost exclusively* of normal hetero-sexual relations between adults in private. Female masturbation, cunnilingus (*but not fellatio* . . .) and *one fleeting instance* of actual insertion are shown . . ." (p. 707, fn. 2, emphasis supplied). Deep Throat not only has female masturbation, but numerous depictions of cunnilingus and fellatio, clear and stark, from almost its beginning to its bitter end (for the film's major theme is fellatio); and with one disgusting scene of seminal fluid ejaculation into and about the "superstar's" mouth. Deep Throat also boasts of scenes of anal sodomy, an orgy scene, and several scenes of normal hetero-sexual intercourse, but unlike the other film, it also shows actual insertion in each such scene with purposeful camera focusing close upon the genitals while so engaged.

But the differences are not merely to be found in the number and variety of such activity. Significantly, "Language of Love" was found obscene by a jury; but that was overturned on appeal. And on appeal the court found the described sexual acts with "seemingly interminable" psychological, medical and sociological discussions by doctors and other specialists recognized in their respective fields, making up almost all of the film (p. 707). Further, as indicative of its sex educational purposes, the film includes a demonstration of proper placement of contraceptive devices during the course of a gynecological examination by one of the doctors (p. 707). (Also: United States v. Stewart, D.C., 336 F.Supp. 299 (1971); Haldeman v. United States, 10 Cir., 340 F.2d 59 (1965)). To compare then Deep Throat with that film, is not to have seen Deep Throat, because in the one (Deep Throat) there lurks behind each elm "the leer of the sensualist" (Ginzburg v. United States, supra, 383 U.S. p. 468, 86 S.Ct. 942). We do not understand our condemnation of Deep Throat as running counter to Kingsley Pictures Corp. v. Regents, Etc., 360 U.S. 684, 79 S.Ct. 1362, 3 L.Ed.2d 1512 (1959), which distinguishes the communication of any idea, however deviant from orthodoxy with "the manner of portrayal" (p. 688, 79 S.Ct. 1362). Not only do we hold here that the manner of portrayal, in fact, appeals, and its sole purpose is to appeal, to prurient interest in sex, but we discern no "idea" worthy of protection. As we stated in People v. Buckley, 65 Misc.2d 917, 922, 320 N.Y.S.2d 91, 98 (1971) aff'd Sup., 340 N.Y.S.2d 191, ". . . the use of the word 'redeeming' in the social value test is a limiting factor—i. e. the social value of a publication *as a whole* must at least have a modicum of significance to release it from blame. . . ."

"In 'Memoirs' the Supreme Court held that the social value of Cleland's book, however small it may have been in terms of its literary merit and its depiction of the mores of a particular period, redeemed its prurient-candid sexual references. We find no such qualitative redemption . . . ," the Court held there as to the publication it was considering. And I find no such qualitative redemption in Deep Throat either.

Defendant asks us to be guided by the jury in Binghamton, New York, which acquitted another corporate defendant of the charge of obscenity, involving this film. Counsel appears to urge that surely a jury is far more receptive and attuned to what material does or does not affront community standards, than would a cloistered judge. An examination of the certified minutes, announcing the verdict in that case, gives reason to believe that the jury there had possibly a different view of the film than the verdict would imply.[13]

Of course, it is academic that a jury's role stops at the determination of the fact situation. But the determination of obscenity transcends merely fact finding; it is intimately admixed with the determination of constitutional law and that decision is solely for a court, which may not permit the usurpation of that function by a jury. Necessarily, in the determination of the constitutional imperatives, the Court must make assessments of the dominant theme, prurient interest, national community standards, redeeming social value and the like. Roth v. United States, supra, 354 U.S. pp. 497–498, 77 S.Ct. 1304; Jacobellis v. Ohio, supra, 378 U.S. pp. 188, 190, 84 S.Ct. 1676; *Memoirs*, supra, 383 U.S. pp. 450, 462, 86 S.Ct. 975; United States v. 35 mm. Motion Picture Film, Inc., supra, 432 F.2d pp. 709–711; People v. Kirkpatrick, 64 Misc.2d 1055, supra at p. 1072, 316 N.Y.S.2d 37, at p. 54. For this reason courts do, when justified, overturn jury verdicts in this area of law. United States v. 35 mm. Motion Picture Film, Inc., supra; United States v. A Motion Picture (I Am Curious Yellow), supra.

When All Is Said

Deep Throat—a nadir of decadence—is indisputably obscene by any legal measurement, and particularly violative of Penal Law § 235.05.

It goes substantially beyond "the present critical point in the compromise between candor and shame at which the [national] community may have arrived here and now." (United States v. Kennerley, D.C., 209 F. 119, 121 [1913], brackets added). It is another manifestation of the refusal to use words as emotional symbols unrelated to the purely physical. There is no effort, by word or conduct, to cut through the imponderable barriers of human understanding to the defense of human integrity. It, in fact, denigrates that integrity of man and particularly, woman, the expert witnesses, notwithstanding. It does this by objectifying and insulting woman, as Anthony Burgess, the author, puts it, by "making woman the sexual instrument come before woman the human being." (New York Times Book Review, 1/2/72, p. 1). Thus it supports the misogynist's view.

Its dominant theme, and in fact, its only theme is to appeal to prurience in sex. It is hard-core pornography with a vengeance. "It creates an abstract paradise in which the only emotion is lust and the only event orgasm and the only inhabitants animated phalluses and vulvae." (Anthony Burgess, supra, speaking of pornography generally, supra, and well applied here). It is neither redeemed nor redeemable, lest it be by the good camera work, editing, clarity, good color and lack of grain, which defense witness, a movie critic, was seemingly impressed with. But that is hardly enough to remove it from the pale of obscenity.[14]

It does, in fact, demean and pervert the sexual experience, and insults it shamelessly, without tenderness and without understanding of its role as a concomitant of the human condition. Therefore, it does dirt on it; it insults sex and the human body as D. H. Lawrence would describe condemnable obscenity (Sex, Literature and Censorship, pp. 69, 74–79 [1953]). It "focuses predominantly upon what is sexually morbid, grossly perverse and bizarre * * *. It smacks, at times, of fantasy and unreality, of sexual perversion and sickness." (People v. Richmond County News, 9 N.Y.2d 578, 587, 216 N.Y.S.2d 369, 376, 175 N.E.2d 681 [1961]). Justice Stewart says he knows hard core pornography when he merely sees it (Jacobellis v. Ohio, supra, 378 U.S. p. 197, 84 S.Ct. 1676). We have seen it in Deep Throat, and this is one throat that deserves to be cut. I readily perform the operation in finding the defendant guilty as charged, as to both cases.

APPENDIX

What Is It All About?

To accept the defense arguments, that this indisputably obscene film—this feast of carrion and squalor—is constitutionally protected and outside the ambit of prohibition of P.L. § 235.05, would deny, in my view, any validity or meaning to our and all anti-obscenity laws and to the volumes of precedents supporting them. And it would also support the position of those who say that the State has no legitimate

power or justification to legislate on matters of morality and particularly sexual morality. To this end, I believe, the defendant's arguments are essentially directed, without expressly saying so.[1]

It is, of course, a predicate of historical truth that the police power extends not only to the preservation of good order but similarly to the preservation of public morals. Such regulation has always been thought to satisfy certain important imperatives in a systematic manner, which is generally considered to be valuable. The state is said to have a legitimate right to legislate in the field of morality, and particularly sexual morality, and this right is deeply part of our law. Boston Beer Co. v. Massachusetts, 97 U.S. 25, 33, 24 L.Ed. 989 (1878); Lochner v. New York, 198 U.S. 45, 53, 25 S.Ct. 539, 49 L.Ed. 937 (1905); Roth v. United States, supra, 354 U.S. pp. 485, 502, 77 L.Ed. 1304; Stanley v. Georgia, 394 U.S. 557, 566, 89 S.Ct. 1243, 22 L.Ed.2d 542 (1969); Poe v. Ullman, 367 U.S. 497, 545–546, 81 S.Ct. 1752, 6 L.Ed.2d 989 (1961); Henkin, Morals and the Constitution: The Sin of Obscenity, 63 Col.L.Rev. 391.[2]

Recognizing then that, historically, the state had, and, the courts say, it still has, a legitimate social interest in this regard, should it continue to exercise the power with respect to all moral issues, particularly as to sexual morality; and if so, should it extend to the private as well as the public area. This debate has plagued and excited the ages, and today's liberality will not resolve it. And, of course, Deep Throat is vigorously part of that discussion.

Today's debate is somewhat circumscribed about public, rather than private, morality. Our understanding, cultured by the gentle pressures and experimentation of centuries, has, I believe, refined itself to the point where society will tolerate any conduct in private if non-injurious and not disruptive to others. For this reason many would recommend an end to the crime of consensual sodomy in private, leaving its public prohibition. The willing receipt and possession of obscene material, and the private thoughts generated by it, are now enshrined with the private bedroom, as safe from government encroachment, and now understood to be a basic constitutional right. That, of course, is the Court's meaning of Stanley v. Georgia, supra, and what it did, I believe, was merely to reflect the consensus of our People as well as good constitutional law.

But it also recognized a verity of the ages—that in all civilized societies, certain things which could be done in private should not, with impunity, be done in public. The Court said that in *Stanley*, did it not, when it confirmed the State's power and justification to control "dissemination of ideas inimical to the public morality" (394 U.S. p. 566, 89 S.Ct. p. 1249). And this basic and ancient postulate appears to represent the Will of the People, as reflected in the anti-obscenity laws in each of our 50 States and federal government. (Roth v. United States, supra, 354 U.S. p. 485, 77 S.Ct. 1304). This also appears to be the reason that large forward-thinking citizen organizations, such as the Alliance For A Safer New York (a conglomerate of about 80 New York City civic, religious and labor organizations) can recommend the repeal of almost all laws relating to "victimless crimes," including consensual sodomy, but "has not yet evolved a definite policy" as to "pornography" (Edwin Kiester, Jr., "Crimes With No Victims", 1972, p. 73). It would appear then that the United States Supreme Court (and lower courts accepting its leadership) and our People see a possible social effect of obscenity, but are unconcerned with its private manifestation, where society believes, social effect, if any, is *de minimis*.

However, there are thoughtful commentators, like Mr. Justice Douglas, who oppose anti-obscenity laws upon the main ground that they see no causal relationship between obscenity and illegal or anti-social conduct. They would go further and divorce the State from all moral concerns (both private and public) not demonstrated to be "brigaded with illegal action." (Memoirs v. Massachusetts, supra, 383 U.S. p. 426, 86 S.Ct. 975). Also: The Report of the Commission on Obscenity and Pornography, 1970. Since no unequivocally scientific relationship has been found, shall we abolish anti-obscenity laws (public morality) to await the behavioral sciences' proof of the connection? The United States Supreme Court has refused to decide the question or even concern itself with the argument. "That function," it says, "belongs to the state legislatures." Roth v. United States, supra, 354 U.S. pp. 486, 501, 77 S.Ct. 1304; Beauharnais v. Illinois, 343 U.S. 250, 266, 72 S.Ct. 725, 96 L.Ed. 919 (1952).

Without scientific proof, is there not a basis in logic and common experience that the sky-is-the-limit type of pornography, especially the Deep Throat kind, has an eroding and corrupting effect on society's moral fabric, which, as aforesaid, we always thought important to enshrine? Our laws are full of inferences and assumptions, requiring no support of "hard" proof, because we "know" by life's experiences, that abstract truth is no less valid, given the proper context, than scientific formulation.

And so, can we not agree with Justice Harlan when he says (*Roth, supra,* 354 U.S. p. 502, 77 S.Ct. p. 1318), that assuming there is no empirical evidence that obscenity causes, in an immediate sense, anti-social conduct, nevertheless—

"The State can reasonably draw the inference that over a long period of time the indiscriminate dissemination of materials, the essential character of which is to degrade sex, will have an eroding effect on moral standards."

Our armchair nihilists would have us abrogate the anti-obscenity laws with the argument that matters of sex and propriety are subjects best taught in the schools, and the liberty of the adult to see and read what he wishes should not be diminished for the supposed protection of the young. But may we not ask: Where there are no societal restraints, by law and language, will not the parent, the church, the synagogue and the school, being all alone, fall in their effort? Many see the schools, where wholesome disciplines and logical restraints are fast dissipating (and where challenge to authority often and quickly results in the school's surrender) soon joining the permissiveness and cynicism of its surrounding, polluting environment.[4]

Character is shaped by the sum total of the influences and incitations, which ply the sea of the mind. It admittedly begins with consciousness itself. The much respected, the late Justice Samuel H. Hofstadter of the New York State Supreme Court and my colleague, Judge Shirley R. Levittan agree, with so many others, that books, movies, magazines and all the social stimuli affect us, imperceptibly perhaps when taken singly, but measurably when accepted cumulatively. "It is a poor service to the cause of intellectual freedom and artistic feeling," they said "to pretend that art and literature have no effect on conduct."[5] Irving Kristol, Professor of Urban Values at New York University, cogently speaks of the matter in this fashion (New York Times Mag., 3/28/71, p. 24):

"After all, if you believe that no one was ever corrupted by a book, you have also to believe that no one was ever improved by a book (or a play or a movie). You have to believe, in other words, that all art is morally trivial and that, consequently, all education is morally irrelevant. No one, not even a university professor, really believes that."

What then is the resultant quality of character when influenced, over long periods of time, by a suffusion of obscenity? The sages and our common man have never viewed it as having a salutary but rather a negative effect (notwithstanding Justice Douglas and the majority report of the Commission on Obscenity and Pornography). They learned that cheapness breeds cheapness, and filth more filth. They understand that what it does, to again quote Professor Kristol, is "to deprive human beings of their specifically human dimension. That is what obscenity is all about." It relegates the "human dimension" to the debased level of the unfeeling, shameless and loveless beast. Our present-day nihilists fail to understand this connection and its validity in either practical or philosophical terms. What the absolutists seek is not temperance, the logicality of civilized conduct and which our present obscenity laws attempt to achieve, but rather self-indulgence, which is the historic touchstone for intellectual indolence and destruction.

Further, were we to remove indiscriminately, societal safeguards, and permit everyone "to do his thing," what disciplines remain to distinguish the worthy from the gross trash, the gross such as Deep Throat?[6] And would not this new liberty of total permissiveness become a "Magna Carta for the pornographer,"[7] to give license to ascend to greater and greater heights of degradation and violence, to depictions and perhaps the glorification of necrophilia and bestiality, and then, whatever? If we are to become inundated, as we are fast becoming, with trash in the arts, in language, in dress and so much more that makes for society's acceptable norms, what enlightened standards would remain to permit us to ascend "from plateau to plateau and finally reach the world of enduring ideas" (Ginzburg v. United States, 383 U.S. 463, 492, 86 S.Ct. 942, 969, 975 [1966], dissent, Douglas, J.). Can there be value in a society where everything has value?

Justice Harlan, in the aforesaid quote, raises a question which many find cogent and troubling in the light of our new "sexual liberty." What many see in the unrestrained depiction of explicit sexuality and in gross obscenity generally, is the serious and damaging inroads into the tone of society, the mode, the style and quality of life, now and in the future. It hangs as a pervasive malaise over our moral conscious-ness. Alexander Bickel (The Public Interest, No. 22, Winter, 1971, p. 26) speaks of it in this fashion:

"A man may be entitled to read an obscene book in his room, or expose himself indecently there, or masturbate, or flog himself, if that is possible, or what have you. We should protect his privacy. But if he demands a right to obtain books and pictures he wants in the market, and to foregather in public places—discreet, if you will, but accessible to all—with others who share his tastes, then to grant him his right is to affect the world about the rest of us, and to impinge on other privacies. Even supposing that each of us can, if he wishes, effectively avert the eye and stop the ear (which, in truth, we cannot), what is commonly read and seen and heard and done intrudes upon us all, want it or not."

There it is. Deep Throat and all its genre, *want it or not,* impinges unavoidably on the privacy of each of us, especially the multitudes upon multitudes who have not and will not pay the $5.00 admission fee or any price.

Further, it pollutes as noxious gas and helps deteriorate the fiber of great city places such as Times Square. It often attracts the unsavory to own, operate and maintain it. In a long investigatory article, dated December 10, 1972, reporters Ralph Blumenthal and Nicholas Gage (The New York Times, p. 1) stated—

"In less than four years, organized crime 'families' in New York have made pornography their fastest growing new racket . . . Racketeers have also discovered that pornography has a major advantage over traditional rackets. Confusing and sometimes contradictory court decisions make distributing pornographic material a lot safer than making book, selling heroin or loan-sharking. . . Other Mafiosi are known to be investing in film in which sexual acts are part of some kind of story line. The films are often shown in commercial theaters."

These important issues can cause famous liberals, such as Lord Devlin and Professor H. L. A. Hart to fervently and brilliantly differ in public debate.[8] They can also cause liberals like Drs. Phyllis and Eberhard Kronhausen, D. H. Lawrence, Dr. Benjamin Spock, Morris Ernst, and many others, to decry the brutalization of society, represented by the present proliferating hard-core pornography in films, books and magazines.[9] They can cause such representatives of the liberal press, as The New York Times, to editorialize, as it did on April 1, 1969, (p. 46), in this manner:

"The explicit portrayal on the stage of sexual intercourse is the final step in the erosion of taste and subtlety in the theater. It reduces actors to mere exhibitionists, turns audiences into voyeurs and debases sexual relationships almost to the level of prostitution.

It is difficult to see any great principle of civil liberties involved when persons indulging themselves on-stage in this kind of peep-show activity . . . in displaying sodomy and other sexual aberrations, reached the *reductio ad obscenum* of the theatrical art. While there may be no difference in principle between pornography on the stage, on the screen and on the printed page, there is a difference in immediacy and in direct visual impact when it is carried out by live actors before a (presumably) live audience.

The fact that the legally enforceable standards of public decency have been interpreted away by the courts almost to the point of no return does not absolve artists, producers or publishers from all responsibility or restraint in pandering to the lowest possible public taste in quest of the largest possible monetary reward. Nor does the fact that a play, film, article or book attacks the so-called 'establishment,' revels in gutter language or drools over every known or unknown form of erotica justify the suspension of sophisticated critical judgment.

Yet this does seem to be just what has been suspended in the case of many recent works, viz., one current best-seller hailed as a 'masterpiece,' which, wallowing in a self-indulgent public psychoanalysis, drowns its literary merits in revolting sex excesses.

The utter degradation of taste in pursuit of the dollar is perhaps best observed in films, both domestic and foreign, such as one of the more notorious Swedish imports, refreshingly described by one reviewer unafraid of being called a 'square' as 'pseudo-pornography at its ugliest and least titillating and pseudo-sociology at its lowest point of technical ineptitude.'

Far from providing a measure of cultural emancipation, such descents into degeneracy represent caricatures of art, deserving no exemption from the laws of common decency merely because they masquerade as drama or literature. It is preposterous to banish topless waitresses when there is no bottom to voyeurism on the stage or in the movie houses."

(Certainly, what the editors say of the stage is stark reality as well on the screen.)

These issues can also deeply disturb a thoughtful judge. And although his views may very well be the unwitting distillation of his social history, which Justice Cardozo characterized as "the empire of [these] subconscious loyalties,"[10] they cannot be dismissed merely as private notions; for they are imbedded into and built upon ancient and continuing vibrant constitutional verities. So armed, he must, and is expected to exhibit the courage to express and support common moral standards, no less than the courage to express innovation, when law and circumstance require.

As noted, these fundamental issues do not require nor have they resulted in the positioning of the civil libertarians on the one side and the alinement of the philosophical conservatives on the other. Basic here, is not merely the legality of one film, but essentially whether criminal sanctions against promoting (P.L. § 235.00, subd. 4) obscene material shall be fully lifted, as an acquittal here would certainly and affirmatively imply. On this issue citizens of both persuasions join hands.

As a society we have come upon the crossroads, but we have not as yet crossed the road. To find Deep Throat, and the rest of its genre, legally viable, will not only cross the road, but would help obliterate it as well. The law, common sense and the history of experience, tell us that this is not in society's best interest, nor do present community standards, whether national or state, demand it.

JUDGE TYLER'S OPINION NOTES

[1] The defendant was charged with two separate violations, in that, it presented the film involved on August 17, 1972 (Docket No. A54434) and on August 29, 1972 (Docket No. A63354).

[2] The defendant moved in the Supreme Court for a jury trial; the motion was denied, in that the defendant, as a corporation, had no right to a jury trial. Mature Enterprises v. Hogan, N.Y.L.J. Nov. 16, 1972.

[3] New York Times, Arts and Leisure Sect., p. 1, 1/21/73. Ellen Willis in The New York Review of Books, Jan. 25, 1973 (pp. 22, 23), characterizes the jokes as "moronic."

[4] One witness further identified it as "the missionary position," enlightening the court with his learned advice that missionaries also had something to do with sex education.

[5] Nora Ephron, in reporting a conversation she had with the female lead (Esquire, Feb. 1973), reports that this "actress" said—"I totally enjoyed myself making the movie and all of a sudden I'm what you call a superstar." Also, one defense witness thought this scene "had humor."

[6] Penal Law § 235.00, subd. 1 differs slightly in language but its meaning and intent are the same.

[7] Childs v. Oregon, 401 U.S. 1006, 91 S.Ct. 1248, 28 L.Ed.2d 542 (1971); Hoyt v. Minnesota, 399 U.S. 524, 90 S.Ct. 2241, 26 L.Ed.2d 782 (1970); Mazes v. Ohio, 388 U.S. 453, 87 S.Ct. 2105, 18 L.Ed.2d 1315 (1967); A Quantity of Copies of Books v. Kansas, 388 U.S. 452, 87 S.Ct. 2104, 18 L.Ed.2d 1314 (1967); Books, Inc. v. United States, 388 U.S. 449, 87 S.Ct. 2098, 18 L.Ed.2d 1311 (1967); Corinth Publications, Inc. v. Wesberry, 388 U.S. 448, 87 S.Ct. 2096, 18 L.Ed.2d 1310; Aday v. United States, 388 U.S. 447, 87 S.Ct. 2095, 18 L.Ed.2d 1309 (1967).

[8] "It is no easier to define hard-core pornography than obscenity. Experience, including that of judicial expertise, demonstrates that any attempt at such formal verbal expression is doomed to failure, * * *. Legal definitions reflecting earlier stimuli distort the present when dogmatically applied" Hofstadter and Levittan, "No Glory, No Beauty, No Stars—Just Mud," N.Y.S. Bar Jour., Feb., 1965, p. 40.

[9] Justice Stewart would limit proscription to hard-core, in which he sees "a distinct and easily identifiable class of material in which all of these elements [Roth-Memoirs criteria] coalesce." (Ginzburg v. U. S., 383 U.S. 463, 499, 86 S.Ct. 942, 957, supra). Justice Harlan agrees, when he says hard-core ". . . does describe something that most judges and others will 'know . . . when [they] see it' . . . and leaves the smallest room for disagreement between those of varying tastes" (*Memoirs*, supra, 383 U.S. p. 457, 86 S.Ct. p. 997.) He also expressed this view in Roth v. United States, supra, 354 U.S. pp. 507–508, 77 S.Ct. 1304.

Albert B. Gerber, Esq. specializes in obscenity and pornography litigation, and authored Sex, Pornography and Justice (1969). He consistently opposes anti-obscenity laws. However, he tells us that ". . . where sexual acts and perversions are imitated on stage, it is dubious whether any court for a long time to come will grant the protection of the Constitution." Wilson Library Bulletin, Feb. 1970 (p. 544). Of course, there is nothing simulated or imitated in Deep Throat; it is quite real.

[10] D. H. Lawrence, the author of Lady Chatterly's Lover, understands hard-core pornography "by the insult it offers, invariably, to sex and to the human spirit. Pornography is the attempt to insult sex, to do dirt on it . . . Such material is an . . . insult to the human body, the insult to a vital human relationship. Ugly and cheap they make the human nudity; ugly and degraded they make the sexual act trivial and cheap and nasty." And such material we would vigorously have censored. Pornography and Obscenity in Sex, Literature and Censorship (1953), pp. 74–79.

Mr. Justice Stewart describes it as material "with no pretense of artistic value, graphically depicting acts of sexual intercourse, including various acts of sodomy and sadism, and sometimes involving several participants in scenes of orgy-like character." Ginzburg v. United States, 383 U.S. 463, 499, fn. 3, 86 S.Ct. 942, 957, 16 L.Ed.2d 31 (1966).

People v. Richmond County News, 9 N.Y.2d 578, 587, 216 N.Y.S.2d 369, 376, 175 N.E.2d 681, tells us that hard-core "focuses predominantly upon what is sexually morbid, grossly perverse and bizarre . . . depicting dirt for dirt's sake, the obscene is the vile, rather than the coarse, the blow to the sense, not merely to sensibility, it smacks, at times, of fantasy and unreality of sexual perversion and sickness."

[11] Ratner v. California, 388 U.S. 442, 87 S.Ct. 2092, 18 L.Ed.2d 1304 (1967), sex acts not described; Cobert v. New York, 388 U.S. 443, 87 S.Ct. 2092, 18 L.Ed.2d 1305 (1967), stag film for private home use, sex acts not described; Schackman v. California, 388 U.S. 454, 87 S.Ct. 2107, 18 L.Ed.2d 1316 (1967), peep show movies for coin operated machines, sex simulated; I. M. Amusement Corp. v. Ohio, 389 U.S. 573, 88 S.Ct. 690, 19 L.Ed.2d 776 (1968), 2 nude women acting parts of lesbians, fondling themselves; Robert-Arthur Management Corp. v. Tennessee, 389 U.S. 578, 88 S.Ct. 691, 19 L.Ed.2d 777 (1968), nude women caressing each other in lesbian fashion; Cain v. Kentucky, 397 U.S. 319, 90 S.Ct. 1110, 25 L.Ed.2d 334 (1970), nude woman caressing herself, man kisses her stomach, then camera focuses on expression of satisfaction during intercourse, then other similar acts of intercourse; Bloss v. Michigan, 402 U.S. 938, 91 S.Ct. 1615, 29 L.Ed.2d 106 (1971), sex acts not described; Hartstein v. Missouri, 404 U.S. 988, 92 S.Ct. 531, 30 L.Ed.2d 539 (1971), nude women gyrating and scenes of physical violence; Pinkus v. Pitchess, 400 U.S. 922, 91 S.Ct. 185, 27 L.Ed.2d 183 (1971), stag movie for private home use; woman feigns self-induced sexual satisfaction.

[12] Certiorari was granted for United States v. Unicorn Enterprises, Inc. involving the same film (401 U.S. 907, 91 S.Ct. 881, 27 L.Ed.2d 804 [1971]), and covered this case as well. However, the writ of certiorari was later dismissed pursuant to agreement of the attorneys (403 U.S. 925, 91 S.Ct. 2241, 29 L.Ed.2d 704 [1971]).

[13] During the trial of this case, defense counsel represented to the Court that the Binghamton jury made a "special finding" (whatever that might conceivably mean) of obscenity. I requested counsel to secure a copy of the "special finding." He failed to do so. The Court, however, has secured a certified copy of that portion of the minutes announcing the verdict. This is what was said:

"The Court: Mr. Benson, has the jury arrived at a verdict?

The Foreman: Yes, we have, your Honor.

The Court: What is your verdict?

The Foreman: Not guilty. I would like to request that I be able to make a statement.

The Court: Just a minute. Is this verdict unanimous?

The Foreman: It is.

The Court: Do you wish the jury polled?

Mr. Coutant: No, your Honor.

The Court: What comment do you wish to make?

The Foreman: We wish to have in the record that this verdict does not reflect our personal opinions but rather it is the result of what we feel to be an extremely poorly and loosely written law.

The Court: Very well."

Now, we wonder, in the light of the foreman's statement, what was the real meaning of the verdict and what did it say of the community standards in Binghamton, New York. (People v. Binghamton Theatres, Inc., tried Dec. 12–16, 1972 before City Court Judge Walter T. Gorman).

[14] "This court will not adopt a rule of law which states that obscenity is suppressible but well-written [or a technically well produced] obscenity is not." (People v. Fritch, 13 N.Y.2d 119, 126, 243 N.Y.S.2d 1, 7, 192 N.E.2d 713 [matter in brackets added]).

"A Michelangelo could find no solace from legal restraint if his art be obscene." (People v. Kirkpatrick, 64 Misc.2d 1055, 1086, 316 N.Y.S.2d 37, 67, supra).

APPENDIX NOTES

[1] There is now before the United States Supreme Court three cases which raise basic questions as to all anti-obscenity laws, particularly whether obscene material may be disseminated to consenting adults. California v. Kaplan, 23 Cal.App.3d Supp. 9, 100 Cal.Rptr. 372, cert. granted 408 U.S. 921, 92 S.Ct. 2493, 33 L.Ed.2d 331; Slaton v. Paris Adult Theatre, 228 Ga. 343, 185 S.E.2d 768, cert. granted, 408 U.S. 921, 92 S.Ct. 2487, 33 L.Ed.2d 331; Alexander v. Virginia, 212 Va. 554, 186 S.E.2d 43, cert. granted, 408 U.S. 921, 92 S.Ct. 2490, 33 L.Ed.2d 332.

[2] In Poe v. Ullman, *supra*, Harlan, J., had this to say in his dissent:

"Yet the very inclusion of the category of morality among state concerns indicates that society is not limited in its objects only to the physical well-being of the community, but has traditionally concerned itself with the moral soundness of its people as well. Indeed to attempt a line between public behavior and that which is purely consensual or solitary would be to withdraw from community concern a range of subjects with which every society in civilized times has found it necessary to deal. The laws regarding marriage which provide both when the sexual powers may be used and the legal and societal context in which children are born and brought up, as well as laws forbidding adultery, fornication and homosexual practices which express the negative of the proposition, confining sexuality to lawful marriage, form a pattern so deeply pressed into the substance of our social life that any Constitutional doctrine in this area must build upon that basis. Compare McGowan v. Maryland, 366 U.S. 420, 81 S.Ct. 1101, 1153, 1218, 6 L.Ed.2d 393."

[3] The Report of the Commission on Obscenity and Pornography (The New York Times Ed. 1970) claims to prove the absence of this connection. However, the minority report illustrates several instances that the majority's research was inaccurate and the methods used unprofessional. Others refuse to accept the majority's report as convincing proof. Also President Nixon and a majority of the Senate by a vote of 60 to 5 rejected that report. N. Y. Times, 10/14/1970, p. 30, col. 3.

John Stuart Mill denied that the State may legislate on moral matters and could only do so "over any member of a civilized community against his will as to prevent harm to others"; and moral harm, he said, is not sufficient to warrant legal forbearance. (On Liberty, Chap. I). Our present day disciples often quote Mill with relish.

[4] In its course "Filmmakers" (for which it charges $60), New York University has as its guest lecturer the executive producer of Deep Throat, whose subject will be "sensuality, eroticism and the law, and excerpts from Deep Throat are screened" (Bulletin, School of Continuing Education, Spring 1973, p. 35). Is this to be a new art form, with bigger, better and deeper Deep Throats?

5 "No Glory, No Beauty, No Stars—Just Mud," N.Y.S. Bar Jour., Vol. 37 No. 2, Apr. 1965.

6 Vincent Canby in his discussion of the merits, or more exactly the demerits, of the film characterized it as "junk" and remained junk, even after seeing it a second time. N. Y. Times 1/21/73, Arts & Leisure Sect. p. 1.

7 Minority Report—Commission on Obscenity and Pornography, *supra*, p. 456.

8 Lord Patrick Devlin (The Enforcement of Morals, Oxford Univ. Press 1968 ed.) postulated that what makes a collection of citizens a society is a "shared morality," which acts as "the cement of society" and that any loosening of the cement contributes to its disintegration; that the State should use the law to preserve morality (including sexual morality) as it uses it to safeguard anything else essential to its existence; that there is no theoretical limits to the power of the State to legislate against immorality, and that changes in the moral code must come very slowly where the society sees a needed departure from and finds a substitute for established moral standards. He generally sees no basic difference between private and public morality, when he says—"The suppression of vice is as much the law's business as the suppression of subversive activities; it is no more possible to define a sphere of private morality than it is to define one of private subversive activity" (pp. 13–14).

Professor H. L. A. Hart (Law, Liberty and Morality; Vintage Books, 1963 ed.) agrees that society may use the law to preserve morality, but disagrees that sexual morality is a legitimate State concern, and its enforcement has no "utilitarian reason" or "universal value" as necessary to society's survival. Also: Louis Henkin; Morals and the Constitution: The Sin of Obscenity, 63 Col.L.Rev. 391 (1963); Basil Mitchell: Law, Morality and Religion in a Secular Society; Oxford Univ. Press, (1970).

9 Kronhausen, Pornography and the Law, 1959; D. H. Lawrence, Pornography and Obscenity in Sex, Literature and Censorship, 1953; Dr. Benjamin Spock, Decent and Indecent, 1969.

Morris Ernst, the defender of Joyce's "Ulysses," and other material, described as "the noted civil liberties lawyer and a long time opponent of censorship" in a news article appearing in the New York Times, 1/5/1970, p. 46, col. 2, is quoted as saying that he would not choose "to live in a society without limits to freedom." Further, "Whereas I defended the book and legitimatized a four-letter word, that doesn't mean that * * * sodomy on the stage or masturbation in the public arena here and the world over." Further, "I deeply resent the idea that the lowest common denominator, the most tawdry magazine, pandering for profit * * * should be able to compete in the marketplace with no restraints."

10 Benjamin Cardozo, The Nature of the Judicial Process, Yale Univ. Press, 1921, p. 175.

JUSTICES BURGER, BLACKMUN, POWELL, REHN-QUIST, AND WHITE DECLARE "OBSCENE FILMS DO NOT ACQUIRE CONSTITUTIONAL IMMUNITY FROM STATE REGULATION SIMPLY BECAUSE THEY ARE EXHIBITED FOR CONSENTING ADULTS ONLY"; "ALTHOUGH THERE IS NO CONCLUSIVE PROOF OF A CONNECTION BETWEEN ANTISOCIAL BEHAV-IOR AND OBSCENE MATERIALS, THE LEGISLATURE OF GEORGIA COULD QUITE REASONABLY DETER-MINE THAT SUCH A CONNECTION DOES OR MIGHT EXIST."

Paris Adult Theatre I v. Slaton, 413 U.S. 49 (1973)

MR. CHIEF JUSTICE BURGER delivered the opinion of the Court.

Petitioners are two Atlanta, Georgia, movie theaters and their owners and managers, operating in the style of "adult" theaters. On December 28, 1970, respondents, the local state district attorney and the solicitor for the local state trial court, filed civil complaints in that court alleging that petitioners were exhibiting to the public for paid admission two allegedly obscene films, contrary to Georgia Code Ann. § 26–2101.[1] The two films in question, "Magic Mirror" and "It All Comes Out in the End," depict sexual conduct characterized by the Georgia Supreme Court as "hard core pornography" leaving "little to the imagination."

Respondents' complaints, made on behalf of the State of Georgia, demanded that the two films be declared obscene and that petitioners be enjoined from exhibiting the films. The exhibition of the films was not enjoined, but a temporary injunction was granted *ex parte* by the local trial court, restraining petitioners from destroying the films or removing them from the jurisdiction. Petitioners were further ordered to have one print each of the films in court on January 13, 1971, together with the proper viewing equipment.

On January 13, 1971, 15 days after the proceedings began, the films were produced by petitioners at a jury-waived trial. Certain photographs, also produced at trial, were stipulated to portray the single entrance to both Paris Adult Theatre I and Paris Adult Theatre II as it appeared at the time of the complaints. These photographs show a conventional, inoffensive theater entrance, without any pictures, but with signs indicating that the theaters exhibit "Atlanta's Finest Mature Feature Films." On the door itself is a sign saying: "Adult Theatre—You must be 21 and able to prove it. If viewing the nude body offends you, Please Do Not Enter."

The two films were exhibited to the trial court. The only other state evidence was testimony by criminal investigators that they had paid admission to see the films and that nothing on the outside of the theater indicated the full nature of what was shown. In particular, nothing indicated that the films depicted—as they did—scenes of simulated fellatio, cunnilingus, and group sex intercourse. There was no evidence presented that minors had ever entered the theaters. Nor was there evidence presented that petitioners had a systematic policy of barring minors, apart from posting signs at the entrance. On April 12, 1971, the trial judge dismissed respondents' complaints. He assumed "that obscenity is established," but stated:

"It appears to the Court that the display of these films in a commercial theatre, when surrounded by requisite notice to the public of their nature and by reasonable protection against the exposure of these films to minors, is constitutionally permissible."

On appeal, the Georgia Supreme Court unanimously reversed. It assumed that the adult theaters in question barred minors and gave a full warning to the general public of the nature of the films shown, but held that the films were without protection under the First Amendment. Citing the opinion of this Court in *United States v. Reidel*, 402 U. S. 351 (1971), the Georgia court stated that "the sale and delivery of obscene material to willing adults is not protected under the first amendment." The Georgia court also held *Stanley* v. *Georgia*, 394 U. S. 557 (1969), to be inapposite since it did not deal with "the commercial distribution of pornography, but with the right of Stanley to possess, in the privacy of his home, pornographic films." 228 Ga. 343, 345, 185 S. E. 2d 768, 769 (1971). After viewing the films, the Georgia Supreme Court held that their exhibition should have been enjoined, stating:

"The films in this case leave little to the imagination. It is plain what they purport to depict, that is, conduct of the most salacious character. We hold that these films are also hard core pornography, and the showing of such films should have been enjoined since their exhibition is not protected by the first amendment." 228 Ga., at 347, 185 S. E. 2d, at 770.

I

It should be clear from the outset that we do not undertake to tell the States what they must do, but rather to define the area in which they may chart their own course in dealing with obscene material. This Court has consistently held that obscene material is not protected by the First Amendment as a limitation on the state police power by virtue of the Fourteenth Amendment. *Miller* v. *California, ante,* at 23–25; *Kois* v. *Wisconsin,* 408 U. S. 229, 230 (1972); *United States* v. *Reidel, supra,* at 354; *Roth* v. *United States,* 354 U. S. 476, 485 (1957).

Georgia case law permits a civil injunction of the exhibition of obscene materials. See *1024 Peachtree Corp.* v. *Slaton,* 228 Ga. 102, 184 S. E. 2d 144 (1971); *Walter* v. *Slaton,* 227 Ga. 676, 182 S. E. 2d 464 (1971); *Evans Theatre Corp.* v. *Slaton,* 227 Ga. 377, 180 S. E. 2d 712 (1971). While this procedure is civil in nature, and does not directly involve the state criminal statute proscribing exhibition of obscene material,[2] the Georgia case law permitting civil injunction does adopt the definition of "obscene materials" used by the criminal statute.[3] Today, in *Miller* v. *California, supra,* we have sought to clarify the constitutional definition of obscene material subject to regulation by the States, and we vacate and remand this case for reconsideration in light of *Miller.*

This is not to be read as disapproval of the Georgia civil procedure employed in this case, assuming the use of a constitutionally acceptable standard for determining what is unprotected by the First Amendment. On the contrary, such a procedure provides an exhibitor or purveyor of materials the best possible notice, prior to any criminal indictments, as to whether the materials are unprotected by the First Amendment and subject to state regulation.[4] See *Kingsley Books, Inc.* v. *Brown,* 354 U. S. 436, 441–444 (1957). Here, Georgia imposed no restraint on the exhibition of the films involved in this case until after a full adversary proceeding and a final judicial determination by the Georgia Supreme Court that the materials were constitutionally unprotected.[5] Thus the standards of *Blount* v. *Rizzi,* 400 U. S. 410, 417 (1971); *Teitel Film Corp.* v. *Cusack,* 390 U. S. 139, 141–142 (1968); *Freedman* v. *Maryland,* 380 U. S. 51, 58–59 (1965), and *Kingsley Books, Inc.* v. *Brown, supra,* at 443–445, were met. Cf. *United States* v. *Thirty-seven Photographs,* 402 U. S. 363, 367–369 (1971) (opinion of WHITE, J.).

Nor was it error to fail to require "expert" affirmative evidence that the materials were obscene when the materials themselves were actually placed in evidence. *United States* v. *Groner,* 479 F. 2d 577, 579–586 (CA5 1973); *id.,* at 586–588 (Ainsworth, J., concurring); *id.,* at 588–589 (Clark, J., concurring); *United States* v. *Wild,* 422 F. 2d 34, 35–36 (CA2 1969), cert. denied, 402 U. S. 986 (1971); *Kahm* v. *United States,* 300 F. 2d 78, 84 (CA5), cert. denied, 369 U. S. 859 (1962); *State* v. *Amato,* 49 Wis. 2d 638, 645, 183 N. W. 2d 29, 32 (1971), cert. denied *sub nom. Amato* v. *Wisconsin,* 404

U. S. 1063 (1972). See *Smith* v. *California,* 361 U. S. 147, 172 (1959) (Harlan, J., concurring and dissenting); *United States* v. *Brown,* 328 F. Supp. 196, 199 (ED Va. 1971). The films, obviously, are the best evidence of what they represent.[6] "In the cases in which this Court has decided obscenity questions since *Roth,* it has regarded the materials as sufficient in themselves for the determination of the question." *Ginzburg* v. *United States,* 383 U. S. 463, 465 (1966).

II

We categorically disapprove the theory, apparently adopted by the trial judge, that obscene, pornographic films acquire constitutional immunity from state regulation simply because they are exhibited for consenting adults only. This holding was properly rejected by the Georgia Supreme Court. Although we have often pointedly recognized the high importance of the state interest in regulating the exposure of obscene materials to juveniles and unconsenting adults, see *Miller* v. *California, ante,* at 18–20; *Stanley* v. *Georgia, supra,* at 567; *Redrup* v. *New York,* 386 U. S. 767, 769 (1967), this Court has never declared these to be the only legitimate state interests permitting regulation of obscene material. The States have a long-recognized legitimate interest in regulating the use of obscene material in local commerce and in all places of public accommodation, as long as these regulations do not run afoul of specific constitutional prohibitions. See *United States* v. *Thirty-seven Photographs, supra,* at 376–377 (opinion of WHITE, J.); *United States* v. *Reidel,* 402 U. S., at 354–356. Cf. *United States* v. *Thirty-seven Photographs, supra,* at 378 (STEWART, J., concurring). "In an unbroken series of cases extending over a long stretch of this Court's history, it has been accepted as a postulate that 'the primary requirements of decency may be enforced against obscene publications.' [*Near* v. *Minnesota,* 283 U. S. 697, 716 (1931)]." *Kingsley Books, Inc.* v. *Brown, supra,* at 440.

In particular, we hold that there are legitimate state interests at stake in stemming the tide of commercialized obscenity, even assuming it is feasible to enforce effective safeguards against exposure to juveniles and to passersby.[7] Rights and interests "other than those of the advocates are involved." *Breard* v. *Alexandria,* 341 U. S. 622, 642 (1951). These include the interest of the public in the quality of life and the total community environment, the tone of commerce in the great city centers, and, possibly, the public safety itself. The Hill-Link Minority Report of the Commission on Obscenity and Pornography indicates that there is at least an arguable correlation between obscene material and crime.[8] Quite apart from sex crimes, however, there remains one problem of large proportions aptly described by Professor Bickel:

"It concerns the tone of the society, the mode, or to use terms that have perhaps greater currency, the style and quality of life, now and in the future. A man may be entitled to read an obscene book in his room, or expose himself indecently there . . . . We should protect his privacy. But if he demands a right to obtain the books and pictures he wants in the market, and to foregather in public places—discreet, if you will, but accessible to all—with others who share his tastes, *then to grant him his right is to affect the world about the rest of us, and to impinge on other privacies.* Even supposing that each of us can, if he wishes, effectively avert the eye and stop the ear (which, in truth, we cannot), what is commonly read and seen and heard and done intrudes upon us all, want it or not." 22 The Public Interest 25–26 (Winter 1971).[9] (Emphasis added.)

As Mr. Chief Justice Warren stated, there is a "right of the Nation and of the States to maintain a decent society . . . ," *Jacobellis* v. *Ohio,* 378 U. S. 184, 199 (1964) (dissenting opinion).[10] See *Memoirs* v. *Massachusetts,* 383 U. S. 413, 457 (1966) (Harlan, J., dissenting); *Beauharnais* v. *Illinois,* 343 U. S. 250, 256–257 (1952); *Kovacs* v. *Cooper,* 336 U. S. 77, 86–88 (1949).

But, it is argued, there are no scientific data which conclusively demonstrate that exposure to obscene material adversely affects men and women or their society. It is urged on behalf of the petitioners that, absent such a demonstration, any kind of state regulation is "impermissible." We reject this argument. It is not for us to resolve empirical uncertainties underlying state legislation, save in the exceptional case where that legislation plainly impinges upon rights protected by the Constitution itself.[11] MR. JUSTICE BRENNAN, speaking for the Court in *Ginsberg* v. *New York,* 390 U. S. 629, 642–643 (1968), said: "We do not demand of legislatures 'scientifically certain criteria of legislation.' *Noble State Bank* v. *Haskell,* 219 U. S. 104, 110." Although there is no conclusive proof of a connection between antisocial behavior and obscene material, the legislature of Georgia could quite reasonably determine that such a connection does or might exist. In deciding *Roth,* this Court implicitly accepted that a legislature could legitimately act on such a conclusion to protect *"the social interest in order and morality."* *Roth* v. *United States,* 354 U. S., at 485, quoting *Chaplinsky* v. *New Hampshire,* 315 U. S. 568, 572 (1942) (emphasis added in *Roth*).[12]

From the beginning of civilized societies, legislators and judges have acted on various unprovable assumptions. Such assumptions underlie much lawful state regulation of commercial and business affairs. See *Ferguson* v. *Skrupa,* 372 U. S. 726, 730 (1963); *Breard* v. *Alexandria,* 341 U. S., at 632–633, 641–645; *Lincoln Federal Labor Union* v. *Northwestern Iron & Metal Co.,* 335 U. S. 525, 536–537 (1949). The same is true of the federal securities and antitrust laws and a host of federal regulations. See *SEC* v. *Capital Gains Research Bureau, Inc.,* 375 U. S. 180, 186–195 (1963); *American Power & Light Co.* v. *SEC,* 329 U. S. 90, 99–103 (1946); *North American Co.* v. *SEC,* 327 U. S. 686, 705–707 (1946), and cases cited. See also *Brooks* v. *United States,* 267 U. S. 432, 436–437 (1925), and *Hoke* v. *United States,* 227 U. S. 308, 322 (1913). On the basis of these assumptions both Congress and state legislatures have, for example, drastically restricted associational rights by adopting antitrust laws, and have strictly regulated public expression by issuers of and dealers in securities, profit sharing "coupons," and "trading stamps," commanding what they must and must not publish and announce. See *Sugar Institute, Inc.* v. *United States,* 297 U. S. 553, 597–602 (1936); *Merrick* v. *N. W. Halsey & Co.,* 242 U. S. 568, 584–589 (1917); *Caldwell* v. *Sioux Falls Stock Yards Co.,* 242 U. S. 559, 567–568 (1917); *Hall* v. *Geiger-Jones Co.,* 242 U. S. 539, 548–552 (1917); *Tanner* v. *Little,* 240 U. S. 369, 383–386 (1916); *Rast* v. *Van Deman & Lewis Co.,* 240 U. S. 342, 363–368 (1916). Understandably those who entertain an absolutist view of the First Amendment find it uncomfortable to explain why rights of association, speech, and press should be severely restrained in the marketplace of goods and money, but not in the marketplace of pornography.

Likewise, when legislatures and administrators act to protect the physical environment from pollution and to preserve our resources of forests, streams, and parks, they must act on such imponderables as the impact of a new highway near or through an existing park or wilderness area. See *Citizens to Preserve Overton Park* v. *Volpe,* 401 U. S. 402, 417–420 (1971). Thus, § 18 (a) of the Federal-Aid Highway Act of 1968, 23 U. S. C. § 138, and the Department of Transportation Act of 1966, as amended, 82 Stat. 824, 49 U. S. C. § 1653 (f), have been described by Mr. Justice Black as "a solemn determination of the highest law-making body of this Nation that the beauty and health-giving facilities of our parks are not to be taken away for public roads without hearings, factfindings, and policy determinations under the supervision of a Cabinet officer . . . ." *Citizens to Preserve Overton Park, supra,* at 421 (separate opinion joined by BRENNAN, J.). The fact that a congressional directive reflects unprovable assumptions about what is good for the people, including imponderable aesthetic assumptions, is not a sufficient reason to find that statute unconstitutional.

If we accept the unprovable assumption that a complete education requires certain books, see *Board of Education* v. *Allen,* 392 U. S. 236, 245 (1968), and *Johnson* v. *New York State Education Dept.,* 449 F. 2d 871, 882–883 (CA2 1971) (dissenting opinion), vacated and remanded to consider mootness, 409 U. S. 75 (1972), *id.,* at 76–77 (MARSHALL, J., concurring), and the well nigh universal belief that good books, plays, and art lift the spirit, improve the mind, enrich the human personality, and develop character, can we then say that a state legislature may not act on the corollary assumption that commerce in obscene books, or public exhibitions focused on obscene conduct, have a tendency to exert a corrupting and debasing impact leading to antisocial behavior? "Many of these effects may be intangible and indistinct, but they are nonetheless real." *American Power & Light Co., supra,* at 103. Mr. Justice Cardozo said that all laws in Western civilization are "guided by a robust common sense . . . ." *Steward Machine Co.* v. *Davis,* 301 U. S. 548, 590 (1937). The sum of experience, including that of the past two decades, affords an ample basis for legislatures to conclude that a sensitive, key relationship of human existence, central to family life, community welfare, and the development of human personality, can be debased and distorted by crass commercial exploitation of sex. Nothing in the Constitution prohibits a State from reaching such a conclusion and acting on it legislatively simply because there is no conclusive evidence or empirical data.

It is argued that individual "free will" must govern, even in activities beyond the protection of the First Amendment and other constitutional guarantees of privacy, and that government cannot legitimately impede an individual's desire to see or acquire obscene plays, movies, and books. We do indeed base our society on certain assumptions that people have the capacity for free choice. Most exercises of individual free choice—those in politics, religion, and expression of ideas—are explicitly protected by the Constitution. Totally unlimited play for free will, however, is not allowed in our or any other society. We have just noted, for example, that neither the First Amendment nor "free will" precludes States from having "blue sky" laws to regulate what sellers of securities may write or publish about their wares. See *supra*, at 61–62. Such laws are to protect the weak, the uninformed, the unsuspecting, and the gullible from the exercise of their own volition. Nor do modern societies leave disposal of garbage and sewage up to the individual "free will," but impose regulation to protect both public health and the appearance of public places. States are told by some that they must await a "laissez faire" market solution to the obscenity-pornography problem, paradoxically "by people who have never otherwise had a kind word to say for laissez-faire," particularly in solving urban, commercial, and environmental pollution problems. See I. Kristol, On the Democratic Idea in America 37 (1972).

The States, of course, may follow such a "laissez faire" policy and drop all controls on commercialized obscenity, if that is what they prefer, just as they can ignore consumer protection in the marketplace, but nothing in the Constitution *compels* the States to do so with regard to matters falling within state jurisdiction. See *United States* v. *Reidel*, 402 U. S., at 357; *Memoirs* v. *Massachusetts*, 383 U. S., at 462 (WHITE, J., dissenting). "We do not sit as a super-legislature to determine the wisdom, need, and propriety of laws that touch economic problems, business affairs, or social conditions." *Griswold* v. *Connecticut*, 381 U. S. 479, 482 (1965). See *Ferguson* v. *Skrupa*, 372 U. S., at 731; *Day-Brite Lighting, Inc.* v *Missouri*, 342 U. S. 421, 423 (1952).

It is asserted, however, that standards for evaluating state commercial regulations are inapposite in the present context, as state regulation of access by consenting adults to obscene material violates the constitutionally protected right to privacy enjoyed by petitioners' customers. Even assuming that petitioners have vicarious standing to assert potential customers' rights, it is unavailing to compare a theater open to the public for a fee, with the private home of *Stanley* v. *Georgia*, 394 U. S., at 568, and the marital bedroom of *Griswold* v. *Connecticut, supra*, at 485–486. This Court, has, on numerous occasions, refused to hold that commercial ventures such as a motion-picture house are "private" for the purpose of civil rights litigation and civil rights statutes. See *Sullivan* v. *Little Hunting Park, Inc.*, 396 U. S. 229, 236 (1969); *Daniel* v. *Paul*, 395 U. S. 298, 305–308 (1969); *Blow* v. *North Carolina*, 379 U. S. 684, 685–686 (1965); *Hamm* v. *Rock Hill*, 379 U. S. 306, 307–308 (1964); *Heart of Atlanta Motel, Inc.* v. *United States*, 379 U. S. 241, 247, 260–261 (1964). The Civil Rights Act of 1964 specifically defines motion-picture houses and theaters as places of "public accommodation" covered by the Act as operations affecting commerce. 78 Stat. 243, 42 U. S. C. §§ 2000a (b)(3), (c).

Our prior decisions recognizing a right to privacy guaranteed by the Fourteenth Amendment included "only personal rights that can be deemed 'fundamental' or 'implicit in the concept of ordered liberty.' *Palko* v. *Connecticut*, 302 U. S. 319, 325 (1937)." *Roe* v. *Wade*, 410 U. S. 113, 152 (1973). This privacy right encompasses and protects the personal intimacies of the home, the family, marriage, motherhood, procreation, and child rearing. Cf. *Eisenstadt* v. *Baird*, 405 U. S. 438, 453–454 (1972); *id.*, at 460, 463–465 (WHITE, J., concurring); *Stanley* v. *Georgia, supra*, at 568; *Loving* v. *Virginia*, 388 U. S. 1, 12 (1967); *Griswold* v. *Connecticut, supra*, at 486; *Prince* v. *Massachusetts*, 321 U. S. 158, 166 (1944); *Skinner* v. *Oklahoma*, 316 U. S. 535, 541 (1942); *Pierce* v. *Society of Sisters*, 268 U. S. 510, 535 (1925); *Meyer* v. *Nebraska*, 262 U. S. 390, 399 (1923). Nothing, however, in this Court's decisions intimates that there is any "fundamental" privacy right "implicit in the concept of ordered liberty" to watch obscene movies in places of public accommodation.

If obscene material unprotected by the First Amendment in itself carried with it a "penumbra" of constitutionally protected privacy, this Court would not have found it necessary to decide *Stanley* on the narrow basis of the "privacy of the home," which was hardly more than a reaffirmation that "a man's home is his castle." Cf. *Stanley* v. *Georgia, supra*, at 564.[13] Moreover, we have declined to equate the privacy of the home relied on in *Stanley* with a "zone" of "privacy" that follows a distributor or a consumer of obscene materials wherever he goes. See *United States* v. *Orito, post*, at 141–143; *United States* v. *12 200-ft. Reels of Film, post*, at 126–129; *United States* v. *Thirty-seven Photographs*, 402 U. S., at 376–377 (opinion of WHITE, J.); *United States* v. *Reidel, supra*, at 355. The idea of a "privacy" right and a place of public accommodation are, in this context, mutually exclusive. Conduct or depictions of conduct that the state police power can prohibit on a public street do not become automatically protected by the Constitution merely because the conduct is moved to a bar or a "live" theater stage, any more than a "live" performance of a man and woman locked in a sexual embrace at high noon in Times Square is protected by the Constitution because they simultaneously engage in a valid political dialogue.

It is also argued that the State has no legitimate interest in "control [of] the moral content of a person's thoughts," *Stanley* v. *Georgia, supra*, at 565, and we need not quarrel with this. But we reject the claim that the State of Georgia is here attempting to control the minds or thoughts of those who patronize theaters. Preventing unlimited display or distribution of obscene material, which by definition lacks any serious literary, artistic, political, or scientific value as communication, *Miller v. California, ante*, at 24, 34, is distinct from a control of reason and the intellect. Cf. *Kois v. Wisconsin*, 408 U. S. 229 (1972); *Roth v. United States, supra*, at 485–487; *Thornhill v. Alabama*, 310 U. S. 88, 101–102 (1940); Finnis, "Reason and Passion": The Constitutional Dialectic of Free Speech and Obscenity, 116 U. Pa. L. Rev. 222, 229–230, 241–243 (1967). Where communication of ideas, protected by the First Amendment, is not involved, or the particular privacy of the home protected by *Stanley*, or any of the other "areas or zones" of constitutionally protected privacy, the mere fact that, as a consequence, some human "utterances" or "thoughts" may be incidentally affected does not bar the State from acting to protect legitimate state interests. Cf. *Roth v. United States, supra*, at 483, 485–487; *Beauharnais v. Illinois*, 343 U. S., at 256–257. The fantasies of a drug addict are his own and beyond the reach of government, but government regulation of drug sales is not prohibited by the Constitution. Cf. *United States v. Reidel, supra*, at 359–360 (Harlan, J., concurring).

Finally, petitioners argue that conduct which directly involves "consenting adults" only has, for that sole reason, a special claim to constitutional protection. Our Constitution establishes a broad range of conditions on the exercise of power by the States, but for us to say that our Constitution incorporates the proposition that conduct involving consenting adults only is always beyond state regulation,[14] is a step we are unable to take.[15] Commercial exploitation of depictions, descriptions, or exhibitions of obscene conduct on commercial premises open to the adult public falls within a State's broad power to regulate commerce and protect the public environment. The issue in this context goes beyond whether someone, or even the majority, considers the conduct depicted as "wrong" or "sinful." The States have the power to make a morally neutral judgment that public exhibition of obscene material, or commerce in such material, has a tendency to injure the community as a whole, to endanger the public safety, or to jeopardize, in Mr. Chief Justice Warren's words, the States' "right . . . to maintain a decent society." *Jacobellis v. Ohio*, 378 U. S., at 199 (dissenting opinion).

To summarize, we have today reaffirmed the basic holding of *Roth v. United States, supra*, that obscene material has no protection under the First Amendment. See *Miller v. California, supra*, and *Kaplan v. California, post*, p. 115. We have directed our holdings, not at thoughts or speech, but at depiction and description of specifically defined sexual conduct that States may regulate within limits designed to prevent infringement of First Amendment rights. We have also reaffirmed the holdings of *United States v. Reidel, supra*, and *United States. v. Thirty-seven Photographs, supra*, that commerce in obscene material is unprotected by any constitutional doctrine of privacy. *United States v. Orito, post*, at 141–143; *United States v. 12 200-ft. Reels of Film, post*, at 126–129. In this case we hold that the States have a legitimate interest in regulating commerce in obscene material and in regulating exhibition of obscene material in places of public accommodation,

including so-called "adult" theaters from which minors are excluded. In light of these holdings, nothing precludes the State of Georgia from the regulation of the allegedly obscene material exhibited in Paris Adult Theatre I or II, provided that the applicable Georgia law, as written or authoritatively interpreted by the Georgia courts, meets the First Amendment standards set forth in *Miller v. California, ante*, at 23–25. The judgment is vacated and the case remanded to the Georgia Supreme Court for further proceedings not inconsistent with this opinion and *Miller v. California, supra*. See *United States v. 12 200-ft. Reels of Film, post*, at 130 n. 7.

Vacated and remanded.

Mr. Justice Douglas, dissenting.

My Brother Brennan is to be commended for seeking a new path through the thicket which the Court entered when it undertook to sustain the constitutionality of obscenity laws and to place limits on their application. I have expressed on numerous occasions my disagreement with the basic decision that held that "obscenity" was not protected by the First Amendment. I disagreed also with the definitions that evolved. Art and literature reflect tastes; and tastes, like musical appreciation, are hardly reducible to precise definitions. That is one reason I have always felt that "obscenity" was not an exception to the First Amendment. For matters of taste, like matters of belief, turn on the idiosyncrasies of individuals. They are too personal to define and too emotional and vague to apply, as witness the prison term for Ralph Ginzburg, *Ginzburg v. United States*, 383 U. S. 463, not for what he printed but for the sexy manner in which he advertised his creations.

The other reason I could not bring myself to conclude that "obscenity" was not covered by the First Amendment was that prior to the adoption of our Constitution and Bill of Rights the Colonies had no law excluding "obscenity" from the regime of freedom of expression and press that then existed. I could find no such laws; and more important, our leading colonial expert, Julius Goebel, could find none, J. Goebel, Development of Legal Institutions (1946); J. Goebel, Felony and Misdemeanor (1937). So I became convinced that the creation of the "obscenity" exception to the First Amendment was a legislative and judicial *tour de force;* that if we were to have such a regime of censorship and punishment, it should be done by constitutional amendment.

People are, of course, offended by many offerings made by merchants in this area. They are also offended by political pronouncements, sociological themes, and by stories of official misconduct. The list of activities and publications and pronouncements that offend someone is endless. Some of it goes on in private; some of it is inescapably public, as when a government official generates crime, becomes a blatant offender of the moral sensibilities of the people, engages in burglary, or breaches the privacy of the telephone, the conference room, or the home. Life in this crowded modern technological world creates many offensive statements and many offensive deeds. There is no protection against offensive ideas, only against offensive conduct.

"Obscenity" at most is the expression of offensive ideas. There are regimes in the world where ideas "offensive" to the majority (or at least to those who control the majority) are suppressed. There life proceeds at a monotonous pace. Most of us would find that world offensive. One of the most offensive experiences in my life was a visit to a nation where bookstalls were filled only with books on mathematics and books on religion.

I am sure I would find offensive most of the books and movies charged with being obscene. But in a life that has not been short, I have yet to be trapped into seeing or reading something that would offend me. I never read or see the materials coming to the Court under charges of "obscenity," because I have thought the First Amendment made it unconstitutional for me to act as a censor. I see ads in bookstores and neon lights over theaters that resemble bait for those who seek vicarious exhilaration. As a parent or a priest or as a teacher I would have no compunction in edging my children or wards away from the books and movies that did no more than excite man's base instincts. But I never supposed that government was permitted to sit in judgment on one's tastes or beliefs—save as they involved action within the reach of the police power of government.

I applaud the effort of my Brother BRENNAN to forsake the low road which the Court has followed in this field. The new regime he would inaugurate is much closer than the old to the policy of abstention which the First Amendment proclaims. But since we do not have here the unique series of problems raised by government-imposed or government-approved captive audiences, cf. *Public Utilities Comm'n v. Pollak,* 343 U. S. 451, I see no constitutional basis for fashioning a rule that makes a publisher, producer, bookseller, librarian, or movie house criminally responsible, when he fails to take affirmative steps to protect the consumer against literature or books offensive* to those who temporarily occupy the seats of the mighty.

When man was first in the jungle he took care of himself. When he entered a societal group, controls were necessarily imposed. But our society—unlike most in the world—presupposes that freedom and liberty are in a frame of reference that makes the individual, not government, the keeper of his tastes, beliefs, and ideas. That is the philosophy of the First Amendment; and it is the article of faith that sets us apart from most nations in the world.

MR. JUSTICE BRENNAN, with whom MR. JUSTICE STEWART and MR. JUSTICE MARSHALL join, dissenting.

This case requires the Court to confront once again the vexing problem of reconciling state efforts to suppress sexually oriented expression with the protections of the First Amendment, as applied to the States through the Fourteenth Amendment. No other aspect of the First Amendment has, in recent years, demanded so substantial a commitment of our time, generated such disharmony of views, and remained so resistant to the formulation of stable and manageable standards. I am convinced that the approach initiated 16 years ago in

Roth v. United States, 354 U. S. 476 (1957), and culminating in the Court's decision today, cannot bring stability to this area of the law without jeopardizing fundamental First Amendment values, and I have concluded that the time has come to make a significant departure from that approach.

In this civil action in the Superior Court of Fulton County, the State of Georgia sought to enjoin the showing of two motion pictures, It All Comes Out In The End, and Magic Mirror, at the Paris Adult Theatres (I and II) in Atlanta, Georgia. The State alleged that the films were obscene under the standards set forth in Georgia Code Ann. § 26–2101.[1] The trial court denied injunctive relief, holding that even though the films could be considered obscene, their commercial presentation could not constitutionally be barred in the absence of proof that they were shown to minors or unconsenting adults. Reversing, the Supreme Court of Georgia found the films obscene, and held that the care taken to avoid exposure to minors and unconsenting adults was without constitutional significance.

I

The Paris Adult Theatres are two commercial cinemas, linked by a common box office and lobby, on Peachtree Street in Atlanta, Georgia. On December 28, 1970, investigators employed by the Criminal Court of Fulton County entered the theaters as paying customers and viewed each of the films which are the subject of this action. Thereafter, two separate complaints, one for each of the two films, were filed in the Superior Court seeking a declaration that the films were obscene and an injunction against their continued presentation to the public. The complaints alleged that the films were "a flagrant violation of Georgia Code Section 26–2101 in that the sole and dominant theme[s] of the said motion picture film[s] considered as a whole and applying contemporary community standards [appeal] to the prurient interest in sex, nudity and excretion, and that the said motion picture film[s are] utterly and absolutely without any redeeming social value whatsoever, and [transgress] beyond the customary limits of candor in describing and discussing sexual matters." App. 20, 39.

Although the language of the complaints roughly tracked the language of § 26–2101, which imposes criminal penalties on persons who knowingly distribute obscene materials,[2] this proceeding was not brought pursuant to that statute. Instead, the State initiated a nonstatutory civil proceeding to determine the obscenity of the films and to enjoin their exhibition. While the parties waived jury trial and stipulated that the decision of the trial court would be final on the issue of obscenity, the State has not indicated whether it intends to bring a criminal action under the statute in the event that it succeeds in proving the films obscene.

Upon the filing of the complaints, the trial court scheduled a hearing for January 13, 1971, and entered an order temporarily restraining the defendants from concealing, destroying, altering, or removing the films from the jurisdiction, but not from exhibiting the films to the public *pendente lite.* In addition to viewing the films at the hearing, the trial court heard the testimony of witnesses and admitted into evidence photographs that were stipulated to depict accurately the facade of the theater. The witnesses testified that the exterior of the theater was adorned with prominent signs reading "Adults Only," "You Must Be 21 and Able to Prove It," and "If the Nude Body Offends You, Do Not Enter." Nothing on the outside of the theater described the films with specificity. Nor were pictures displayed on the outside of the theater to draw the attention of passersby to the contents of the films. The admission charge to the theaters was $3. The trial court heard no evidence that minors had ever entered the theater, but also heard no evidence that petitioners had enforced a systematic policy of screening out minors (apart from the posting of the notices referred to above).

On the basis of the evidence submitted, the trial court concluded that the films could fairly be considered obscene, "[a]ssuming that obscenity is established by a finding that the actors cavorted about in the nude indiscriminately," but held, nonetheless, that "the display of these films in a commercial theatre, when surrounded by requisite notice to the public of their nature and by reasonable protection against the exposure of these films to minors, is constitutionally permissible." [3] Since the issue did not arise in a statutory proceeding, the trial court was not required to pass upon the constitutionality of any state statute, on its face or as applied, in denying the injunction sought by the State.

The Supreme Court of Georgia unanimously reversed, reasoning that the lower court's reliance on *Stanley* v. *Georgia*, 394 U. S. 557 (1969), was misplaced in view of our subsequent decision in *United States* v. *Reidel*, 402 U. S. 351 (1971):

> "In [*Reidel*] the Supreme Court expressly held that the government could constitutionally prohibit the distribution of obscene materials through the mails, even though the distribution be limited to willing recipients who state that they are adults, and, further, that the constitutional right of a person to possess obscene material in the privacy of his own home, as expressed in the *Stanley* case, does not carry with it the right to sell and deliver such material. . . . Those who choose to pass through the front door of the defendant's theater and purchase a ticket to view the films and who certify thereby that they are more than 21 years of age are willing recipients of the material in the same legal sense as were those in the *Reidel* case, who, after reading the newspaper advertisements of the material, mailed an order to the defendant accepting his solicitation to sell them the obscene booklet there. That case clearly establishes once and for all that the sale and delivery of obscene material to willing adults is not protected under the first amendment." 228 Ga. 343, 346, 185 S. E. 2d 768, 769–770 (1971).

The decision of the Georgia Supreme Court rested squarely on its conclusion that the State could constitutionally suppress these films even if they were displayed only to persons over the age of 21 who were aware of the nature of their contents and who had consented to viewing them. For the reasons set forth in this opinion, I am convinced of the invalidity of that conclusion of law, and I would therefore vacate the judgment of the Georgia Supreme Court. I have no occasion to consider the extent of state power to regulate the distribution of sexually oriented materials to juveniles or to unconsenting adults. Nor am I required, for the purposes of this review, to consider whether or not these petitioners had, in fact, taken precautions to avoid exposure of films to minors or unconsenting adults.

II

In *Roth* v. *United States,* 354 U. S. 476 (1957), the Court held that obscenity, although expression, falls outside the area of speech or press constitutionally protected under the First and Fourteenth Amendments against state or federal infringement. But at the same time we emphasized in *Roth* that "sex and obscenity are not synonymous," *id.,* at 487, and that matter which is sexually oriented but not obscene is fully protected by the Constitution. For we recognized that "[s]ex, a great and mysterious motive force in human life, has indisputably been a subject of absorbing interest to mankind through the ages; it is one of the vital problems of human interest and public concern." *Ibid.*[4] *Roth* rested, in other words, on what has been termed a two-level approach to the question of obscenity.[5] While much criticized,[6] that approach has been endorsed by all but two members of this Court who have addressed the question since *Roth.* Yet our efforts to implement that approach demonstrate that agreement on the existence of something called "obscenity" is still a long and painful step from agreement on a workable definition of the term.

Recognizing that "the freedoms of expression . . . are vulnerable to gravely damaging yet barely visible encroachments," *Bantam Books, Inc.* v. *Sullivan,* 372 U. S. 58, 66 (1963), we have demanded that "sensitive tools" be used to carry out the "separation of legitimate from illegitimate speech." *Speiser* v. *Randall,* 357 U. S. 513, 525 (1958). The essence of our problem in the obscenity area is that we have been unable to provide "sensitive tools" to separate obscenity from other sexually oriented but constitutionally protected speech, so that efforts to suppress the former do not spill over into the suppression of the latter. The attempt, as the late Mr. Justice Harlan observed, has only "produced a variety of views among the members of the Court unmatched in any other course of constitutional adjudication." *Interstate Circuit, Inc.* v. *Dallas,* 390 U. S. 676, 704–705 (1968) (separate opinion).

To be sure, five members of the Court did agree in *Roth* that obscenity could be determined by asking "whether to the average person, applying contemporary community standards, the dominant theme of the material taken as a whole appeals to prurient interest." 354 U. S., at 489. But agreement on that test—achieved in the abstract and without reference to the particular material before the Court, see *id.,* at 481 n. 8—was, to say the least, short lived. By 1967 the following views had emerged: Mr. Justice Black and MR. JUSTICE DOUGLAS consistently maintained that government is wholly powerless to regulate any sexually oriented matter on the ground of its obscenity. See, *e. g., Ginzburg* v. *United States,* 383 U. S. 463, 476, 482 (1966) (dissenting opinions); *Jacobellis* v. *Ohio,* 378 U. S. 184, 196 (1964) (concurring opinion); *Roth* v. *United States, supra,* at 508 (dissenting opinion). Mr. Justice Harlan, on the other hand, believed that the Federal Government in the exercise of its enumerated powers could control the distribution of "hard core" pornography, while the States were afforded more latitude to "[ban] any material which, taken as a whole, has been reasonably found in state judicial proceedings to treat with sex in a fundamentally offensive manner, under rationally established criteria for judging such material." *Jacobellis* v. *Ohio, supra,* at 204 (dissenting opinion). See also, *e. g., Ginzburg* v. *United States, supra,* at 493 (dissenting opinion); *A Quantity of Books* v. *Kansas,* 378 U. S. 205, 215 (1964) (dissenting opinion joined by Clark, J.); *Roth, supra,* at 496 (separate opinion). MR. JUSTICE STEWART regarded "hard core" pornography as the limit of both federal and state power. See, *e. g., Ginzburg* v. *United States, supra,* at 497 (dissenting opinion); *Jacobellis* v. *Ohio, supra,* at 197 (concurring opinion).

The view that, until today, enjoyed the most, but not majority, support was an interpretation of *Roth* (and not, as the Court suggests, a veering "sharply away from the *Roth* concept" and the articulation of "a new test of obscenity," *Miller* v. *California, ante,* at 21) adopted by Mr. Chief Justice Warren, Mr. Justice Fortas, and the author of this opinion in *Memoirs* v. *Massachusetts,* 383 U. S. 413 (1966). We expressed the view that Federal or State Governments could control the distribution of material where "three elements . . . coalesce: it must be established that (a) the dominant theme of the material taken as a whole appeals to a prurient interest in sex; (b) the material is patently offensive because it affronts contemporary community standards relating to the description or representation of sexual matters; and (c) the material is utterly without redeeming social value." *Id.,* at 418. Even this formulation, however, concealed differences of opinion. Compare *Jacobellis* v. *Ohio, supra,* at 192–195 (BRENNAN, J., joined by Goldberg, J.) (community standards national), with *id.,* at 200–201 (Warren, C. J., joined by Clark, J., dissenting) (community standards local).[7] Moreover, it did not provide a definition covering all situations. See *Mishkin* v. *New York,* 383 U. S. 502 (1966) (prurient appeal defined in terms of a deviant sexual group); *Ginzburg* v. *United States, supra* ("pandering" probative evidence of obscenity in close cases). See also *Ginsberg* v. *New York,* 390 U. S. 629 (1968) (obscenity for juveniles). Nor, finally, did it ever command a majority of the Court. Aside from the other views described above, Mr. Justice Clark believed that "social importance" could only "be considered together with evidence that the material in question appeals to prurient interest and is patently offensive." *Memoirs* v. *Massachusetts, supra,* at 445 (dissenting opinion). Similarly, MR. JUSTICE WHITE regarded "a publication to be obscene if its predominant theme appeals to the prurient interest in a manner exceeding customary limits of candor," *id.,* at 460–461 (dissenting opinion), and regarded " 'social importance' . . . not [as] an independent test of obscenity but [as] relevant only to determining the predominant prurient interest of the material . . . ." *Id.,* at 462.

In the face of this divergence of opinion the Court began the practice in 1967 in *Redrup* v. *New York,* 386

U. S. 767 (1967), of *per curiam* reversals of convictions for the dissemination of materials that at least five members of the Court, applying their separate tests, deemed not to be obscene.[8] This approach capped the attempt in *Roth* to separate all forms of sexually oriented expression into two categories—the one subject to full governmental suppression and the other beyond the reach of governmental regulation to the same extent as any other protected form of speech or press. Today a majority of the Court offers a slightly altered formulation of the basic *Roth* test, while leaving entirely unchanged the underlying approach.

III

Our experience with the *Roth* approach has certainly taught us that the outright suppression of obscenity cannot be reconciled with the fundamental principles of the First and Fourteenth Amendments. For we have failed to formulate a standard that sharply distinguishes protected from unprotected speech, and out of necessity, we have resorted to the *Redrup* approach, which resolves cases as between the parties, but offers only the most obscure guidance to legislation, adjudication by other courts, and primary conduct. By disposing of cases through summary reversal or denial of certiorari we have deliberately and effectively obscured the rationale underlying the decisions. It comes as no surprise that judicial attempts to follow our lead conscientiously have often ended in hopeless confusion.

Of course, the vagueness problem would be largely of our own creation if it stemmed primarily from our failure to reach a consensus on any one standard. But after 16 years of experimentation and debate I am reluctantly forced to the conclusion that none of the available formulas, including the one announced today, can reduce the vagueness to a tolerable level while at the same time striking an acceptable balance between the protections of the First and Fourteenth Amendments, on the one hand, and on the other the asserted state interest in regulating the dissemination of certain sexually oriented materials. Any effort to draw a constitutionally acceptable boundary on state power must resort to such indefinite concepts as "prurient interest," "patent offensiveness," "serious literary value," and the like. The meaning of these concepts necessarily varies with the experience, outlook, and even idiosyncrasies of the person defining them. Although we have assumed that obscenity does exist and that we "know it when [we] see it," *Jacobellis* v. *Ohio, supra,* at 197 (STEWART, J., concurring), we are manifestly unable to describe it in advance except by reference to concepts so elusive that they fail to distinguish clearly between protected and unprotected speech.

We have more than once previously acknowledged that "constitutionally protected expression . . . is often separated from obscenity only by a dim and uncertain line." *Bantam Books, Inc.* v. *Sullivan,* 372 U. S., at 66. See also, *e. g., Mishkin* v. *New York, supra,* at 511. Added to the "perhaps inherent residual vagueness" of each of the current multitude of standards, *Ginzburg* v. *United States, supra,* at 475 n. 19, is the further complication that the obscenity of any particular item may depend upon nuances of presentation and the context of its dissemination. See *ibid*. *Redrup* itself suggested that obtrusive exposure to unwilling individuals, distribution to juveniles, and "pandering" may also bear upon the determination of obscenity. See *Redrup v. New York, supra*, at 769. As Mr. Chief Justice Warren stated in a related vein, obscenity is a function of the circumstances of its dissemination:

> "It is not the book that is on trial; it is a person. The conduct of the defendant is the central issue, not the obscenity of a book or picture. The nature of the materials is, of course, relevant as an attribute of the defendant's conduct, but the materials are thus placed in context from which they draw color and character." *Roth*, 354 U. S., at 495 (concurring opinion).

See also, *e. g., Jacobellis v. Ohio, supra*, at 201 (dissenting opinion); *Kingsley Books, Inc. v. Brown*, 354 U. S. 436, 445–446 (1957) (dissenting opinion). I need hardly point out that the factors which must be taken into account are judgmental and can only be applied on "a case-by-case, sight-by-sight" basis. *Mishkin v. New York, supra*, at 516 (Black, J., dissenting). These considerations suggest that no one definition, no matter how precisely or narrowly drawn, can possibly suffice for all situations, or carve out fully suppressible expression from all media without also creating a substantial risk of encroachment upon the guarantees of the Due Process Clause and the First Amendment.[9]

The vagueness of the standards in the obscenity area produces a number of separate problems, and any improvement must rest on an understanding that the problems are to some extent distinct. First, a vague statute fails to provide adequate notice to persons who are engaged in the type of conduct that the statute could be thought to proscribe. The Due Process Clause of the Fourteenth Amendment requires that all criminal laws provide fair notice of "what the State commands or forbids." *Lanzetta v. New Jersey*, 306 U. S. 451, 453 (1939); *Connally v. General Construction Co.*, 269 U. S. 385 (1926). In the service of this general principle we have repeatedly held that the definition of obscenity must provide adequate notice of exactly what is prohibited from dissemination. See, *e. g., Rabe v. Washington*, 405 U. S. 313 (1972); *Interstate Circuit, Inc. v. Dallas* 390 U. S. 676 (1968); *Winters v. New York*, 333 U. S. 507 (1948). While various tests have been upheld under the Due Process Clause, see *Ginsberg v. New York*, 390 U. S., at 643; *Mishkin v. New York, supra*, at 506–507; *Roth v. United States, supra*, at 491–492, I have grave doubts that any of those tests could be sustained today. For I know of no satisfactory answer to the assertion by Mr. Justice Black, "after the fourteen separate opinions handed down" in the trilogy of cases decided in 1966, that "no person, not even the most learned judge much less a layman, is capable of knowing in advance of an ultimate decision in his particular case by this Court whether certain material comes within the area of 'obscenity' . . . ." *Ginzburg v. United States, supra*, at 480–481 (dissenting opinion). See also the statement of Mr. Justice Harlan in *Interstate Circuit, Inc. v. Dallas, supra*, at 707 (separate

opinion). As Mr. Chief Justice Warren pointed out, "[t]he constitutional requirement of definiteness is violated by a criminal statute that fails to give a person of ordinary intelligence fair notice that his contemplated conduct is forbidden by the statute. The underlying principle is that no man shall be held criminally responsible for conduct which he could not reasonably understand to be proscribed." *United States v. Harriss*, 347 U. S. 612, 617 (1954). In this context, even the most painstaking efforts to determine in advance whether certain sexually oriented expression is obscene must inevitably prove unavailing. For the insufficiency of the notice compels persons to guess not only whether their conduct is covered by a criminal statute, but also whether their conduct falls within the constitutionally permissible reach of the statute. The resulting level of uncertainty is utterly intolerable, not alone because it makes "[b]ookselling . . . a hazardous profession," *Ginsberg v. New York, supra*, at 674 (Fortas, J., dissenting), but as well because it invites arbitrary and erratic enforcement of the law. See, *e. g., Papachristou v. City of Jacksonville*, 405 U. S. 156 (1972); *Gregory v. City of Chicago*, 394 U. S. 111, 120 (1969) (Black, J., concurring); *Niemotko v. Maryland*, 340 U. S. 268 (1951); *Cantwell v. Connecticut*, 310 U. S. 296, 308 (1940); *Thornhill v. Alabama*, 310 U. S. 88 (1940).

In addition to problems that arise when any criminal statute fails to afford fair notice of what it forbids, a vague statute in the areas of speech and press creates a second level of difficulty. We have indicated that "stricter standards of permissible statutory vagueness may be applied to a statute having a potentially inhibiting effect on speech; a man may the less be required to act at his peril here, because the free dissemination of ideas may be the loser." [10] *Smith v. California*, 361 U. S. 147, 151 (1959). That proposition draws its strength from our recognition that

> "[t]he fundamental freedoms of speech and press have contributed greatly to the development and well-being of our free society and are indispensable to its continued growth. Ceaseless vigilance is the watchword to prevent their erosion by Congress or by the States. The door barring federal and state intrusion into this area cannot be left ajar . . . ." *Roth, supra*, at 488.[11]

To implement this general principle, and recognizing the inherent vagueness of any definition of obscenity, we have held that the definition of obscenity must be drawn as narrowly as possible so as to minimize the interference with protected expression. Thus, in *Roth* we rejected the test of *Regina v. Hicklin*, [1868] L. R. 3 Q. B. 360, that "[judged] obscenity by the effect of isolated passages upon the most susceptible persons." 354 U. S., at 489. That test, we held in *Roth*, "might well encompass material legitimately treating with sex . . . ." *Ibid.* Cf. *Mishkin v. New York, supra*, at 509. And we have supplemented the *Roth* standard with additional tests in an effort to hold in check the corrosive effect of vagueness on the guarantees of the First Amendment.[12] We have held, for example, that "a State is not free to adopt whatever procedures it pleases for dealing with obscenity . . . ." *Marcus v. Search War-*

rant, 367 U. S. 717, 731 (1961). "Rather, the First Amendment requires that procedures be incorporated that 'ensure against the curtailment of constitutionally protected expression . . . .' " *Blount* v. *Rizzi,* 400 U. S. 410, 416 (1971), quoting from *Bantam Books, Inc.,* v. *Sullivan,* 372 U. S., at 66. See generally *Rizzi, supra,* at 417; *United States* v. *Thirty-seven Photographs,* 402 U. S. 363, 367–375 (1971); *Lee Art Theatre, Inc.* v. *Virginia,* 392 U. S. 636 (1968); *Freedman* v. *Maryland,* 380 U. S. 51, 58–60 (1965); *A Quantity of Books* v. *Kansas,* 378 U. S. 205 (1964) (plurality opinion).

Similarly, we have held that a State cannot impose criminal sanctions for the possession of obscene material absent proof that the possessor had knowledge of the contents of the material. *Smith* v. *California, supra.* "Proof of scienter" is necessary "to avoid the hazard of self-censorship of constitutionally protected material and to compensate for the ambiguities inherent in the definition of obscenity." *Mishkin* v. *New York, supra,* at 511; *Ginsberg* v. *New York, supra,* at 644–645. In short,

"[t]he objectionable quality of vagueness and overbreadth . . . [is] the danger of tolerating, in the area of First Amendment freedoms, the existence of a penal statute susceptible of sweeping and improper application. Cf. *Marcus* v. *Search Warrant,* 367 U. S. 717, 733. These freedoms are delicate and vulnerable, as well as supremely precious in our society. The threat of sanctions may deter their exercise almost as potently as the actual application of sanctions. Cf. *Smith* v. *California,* [361 U. S.], at 151–154; *Speiser* v. *Randall,* 357 U. S. 513, 526. Because First Amendment freedoms need breathing space to survive, government may regulate in the area only with narrow specificity. *Cantwell* v. *Connecticut,* 310 U. S. 296, 311." *NAACP* v. *Button,* 371 U. S. 415, 432–433 (1963).

The problems of fair notice and chilling protected speech are very grave standing alone. But it does not detract from their importance to recognize that a vague statute in this area creates a third, although admittedly more subtle, set of problems. These problems concern the institutional stress that inevitably results where the line separating protected from unprotected speech is excessively vague. In *Roth* we conceded that "there may be marginal cases in which it is difficult to determine the side of the line on which a particular fact situation falls . . . ." 354 U. S., at 491–492. Our subsequent experience demonstrates that almost every case is "marginal." And since the "margin" marks the point of separation between protected and unprotected speech, we are left with a system in which almost every obscenity case presents a constitutional question of exceptional difficulty. "The suppression of a particular writing or other tangible form of expression is . . . an *individual* matter, and in the nature of things every such suppression raises an individual constitutional problem, in which a reviewing court must determine for *itself* whether the attacked expression is suppressable within constitutional standards." *Roth, supra,* at 497 (separate opinion of Harlan, J.).

Examining the rationale, both explicit and implicit,

of our vagueness decisions, one commentator has viewed these decisions as an attempt by the Court to establish an "insulating buffer zone of added protection at the peripheries of several of the Bill of Rights freedoms." Note, The Void-for-Vagueness Doctrine in the Supreme Court, 109 U. Pa. L. Rev. 67, 75 (1960). The buffer zone enables the Court to fend off legislative attempts "to pass to the courts—and ultimately to the Supreme Court—the awesome task of making case by case at once the criminal and the constitutional law." *Id.,* at 81. Thus,

"[b]ecause of the Court's limited power to reexamine fact on a cold record, what appears to be going on in the administration of the law must be forced, by restrictive procedures, to reflect what is really going on; and because of the impossibility, through sheer volume of cases, of the Court's effectively policing law administration case by case, those procedures must be framed to assure, as well as procedures can assure, a certain overall *probability* of regularity. *Id.,* at 89 (emphasis in original).

As a result of our failure to define standards with predictable application to any given piece of material, there is no probability of regularity in obscenity decisions by state and lower federal courts. That is not to say that these courts have performed badly in this area or paid insufficient attention to the principles we have established. The problem is, rather, that one cannot say with certainty that material is obscene until at least five members of this Court, applying inevitably obscure standards, have pronounced it so. The number of obscenity cases on our docket gives ample testimony to the burden that has been placed upon this Court.

But the sheer number of the cases does not define the full extent of the institutional problem. For, quite apart from the number of cases involved and the need to make a fresh constitutional determination in each case, we are tied to the "absurd business of perusing and viewing the miserable stuff that pours into the Court . . . ." *Interstate Circuit, Inc.* v. *Dallas,* 390 U. S., at 707 (separate opinion of Harlan, J.). While the material may have varying degrees of social importance, it is hardly a source of edification to the members of this Court who are compelled to view it before passing on its obscenity. Cf. *Mishkin* v. *New York, supra,* at 516–517 (Black, J., dissenting).

Moreover, we have managed the burden of deciding scores of obscenity cases by relying on *per curiam* reversals or denials of certiorari—a practice which conceals the rationale of decision and gives at least the appearance of arbitrary action by this Court. See *Bloss* v. *Dykema,* 398 U. S. 278 (1970) (Harlan, J., dissenting). More important, no less than the procedural schemes struck down in such cases as *Blount* v. *Rizzi, supra,* and *Freedman* v. *Maryland, supra,* the practice effectively censors protected expression by leaving lower court determinations of obscenity intact even though the status of the allegedly obscene material is entirely unsettled until final review here. In addition, the uncertainty of the standards creates a continuing source of tension between state and federal courts, since the need for an independent determination by this Court seems to render superfluous even the most conscientious analysis by state tribunals. And our inability to justify our decisions with a persuasive rationale—or indeed, any rationale at all—necessarily creates the impression that we are merely second-guessing state court judges.

The severe problems arising from the lack of fair notice, from the chill on protected expression, and from the stress imposed on the state and federal judicial machinery persuade me that a significant change in direction is urgently required. I turn, therefore, to the alternatives that are now open.

IV

1. The approach requiring the smallest deviation from our present course would be to draw a new line between protected and unprotected speech, still permitting the States to suppress all material on the unprotected side of the line. In my view, clarity cannot be obtained pursuant to this approach except by drawing a line that resolves all doubt in favor of state power and against the guarantees of the First Amendment. We could hold, for example, that any depiction or description of human sexual organs, irrespective of the manner or purpose of the portrayal, is outside the protection of the First Amendment and therefore open to suppression by the States. That formula would, no doubt, offer much fairer notice of the reach of any state statute drawn at the boundary of the State's constitutional power. And it would also, in all likelihood, give rise to a substantial probability of regularity in most judicial determinations under the standard. But such a standard would be appallingly overbroad, permitting the suppression of a vast range of literary, scientific, and artistic masterpieces. Neither the First Amendment nor any free community could possibly tolerate such a standard. Yet short of that extreme it is hard to see how any choice of words could reduce the vagueness problem to tolerable proportions, so long as we remain committed to the view that some class of materials is subject to outright suppression by the State.

2. The alternative adopted by the Court today recognizes that a prohibition against any depiction or description of human sexual organs could not be reconciled with the guarantees of the First Amendment. But the Court does retain the view that certain sexually oriented material can be considered obscene and therefore unprotected by the First and Fourteenth Amendments. To describe that unprotected class of expression, the Court adopts a restatement of the *Roth-Memoirs* definition of obscenity: "The basic guidelines for the trier of fact must be: (a) whether 'the average person, applying contemporary community standards' would find that the work, taken as a whole, appeals to the prurient interest . . . (b) whether the work depicts or describes, in a patently offensive way, sexual conduct specifically defined by the applicable state law, and (c) whether the work, taken as a whole, lacks serious literary, artistic, political, or scientific value." *Miller* v. *California, ante,* at 24. In apparent illustration of "sexual conduct," as that term is used in the test's second element, the Court

identifies "(a) Patently offensive representations or descriptions of ultimate sexual acts, normal or perverted, actual or simulated," and "(b) Patently offensive representations or descriptions of masturbation, excretory functions, and lewd exhibition of the genitals." *Id.,* at 25.

The differences between this formulation and the three-pronged *Memoirs* test are, for the most part, academic.[13] The first element of the Court's test is virtually identical to the *Memoirs* requirement that "the dominant theme of the material taken as a whole [must appeal] to a prurient interest in sex." 383 U. S., at 418. Whereas the second prong of the *Memoirs* test demanded that the material be "patently offensive because it affronts contemporary community standards relating to the description or representation of sexual matters," *ibid.,* the test adopted today requires that the material describe, "in a patently offensive way, sexual conduct specifically defined by the applicable state law." *Miller* v. *California, ante,* at 24. The third component of the *Memoirs* test is that the material must be "utterly without redeeming social value." 383 U. S., at 418. The Court's rephrasing requires that the work, taken as a whole, must be proved to lack "serious literary, artistic, political, or scientific value." *Miller, ante,* at 24.

The Court evidently recognizes that difficulties with the *Roth* approach necessitate a significant change of direction. But the Court does not describe its understanding of those difficulties, nor does it indicate how the restatement of the *Memoirs* test is in any way responsive to the problems that have arisen. In my view, the restatement leaves unresolved the very difficulties that compel our rejection of the underlying *Roth* approach, while at the same time contributing substantial difficulties of its own. The modification of the *Memoirs* test may prove sufficient to jeopardize the analytic underpinnings of the entire scheme. And today's restatement will likely have the effect, whether or not intended, of permitting far more sweeping suppression of sexually oriented expression, including expression that would almost surely be held protected under our current formulation.

Although the Court's restatement substantially tracks the three-part test announced in *Memoirs* v. *Massachusetts, supra,* it does purport to modify the "social value" component of the test. Instead of requiring, as did *Roth* and *Memoirs,* that state suppression be limited to materials utterly lacking in social value, the Court today permits suppression if the government can prove that the materials lack "*serious* literary, artistic, political or scientific value." But the definition of "obscenity" as expression utterly lacking in social importance is the key to the conceptual basis of *Roth* and our subsequent opinions. In *Roth* we held that certain expression is obscene, and thus outside the protection of the First Amendment, precisely *because* it lacks even the slightest redeeming social value. See *Roth* v. *United States, supra,* at 484–485;[14] *Jacobellis* v. *Ohio,* 378 U. S., at 191; *Zeitlin* v. *Arnebergh,* 59 Cal. 2d 901, 920, 383 P. 2d 152, 165; cf. *New York Times Co.* v. *Sullivan,* 376 U. S. 254 (1964); *Garrison* v. *Louisiana,* 379 U. S. 64, 75 (1964); *Chaplinsky* v. *New Hampshire,* 315 U. S.

568, 572 (1942); Kalven, The Metaphysics of the Law of Obscenity, 1960 Sup. Ct. Rev. 1. The Court's approach necessarily assumes that some works will be deemed obscene—even though they clearly have *some* social value—because the State was able to prove that the value, measured by some unspecified standard, was not sufficiently "serious" to warrant constitutional protection. That result is not merely inconsistent with our holding in *Roth;* it is nothing less than a rejection of the fundamental First Amendment premises and rationale of the *Roth* opinion and an invitation to widespread suppression of sexually oriented speech. Before today, the protections of the First Amendment have never been thought limited to expressions of *serious* literary or political value. See *Gooding* v. *Wilson,* 405 U. S. 518 (1972); *Cohen* v. *California,* 403 U. S. 15, 25–26 (1971); *Terminiello* v. *Chicago,* 337 U. S. 1, 4–5 (1949).

Although the Court concedes that "*Roth* presumed 'obscenity' to be 'utterly without redeeming social importance,' " it argues that *Memoirs* produced "a drastically altered test that called on the prosecution to prove a negative, *i. e.,* that the material was 'utterly without redeeming social value'—a burden virtually impossible to discharge under our criminal standards of proof." [15] One should hardly need to point out that under the third component of the Court's test the prosecution is still required to "prove a negative"—*i. e.,* that the material lacks serious literary, artistic, political, or scientific value. Whether it will be easier to prove that material lacks "serious" value than to prove that it lacks any value at all remains, of course, to be seen.

In any case, even if the Court's approach left undamaged the conceptual framework of *Roth,* and even if it clearly barred the suppression of works with at least some social value, I would nevertheless be compelled to reject it. For it is beyond dispute that the approach can have no ameliorative impact on the cluster of problems that grow out of the vagueness of our current standards. Indeed, even the Court makes no argument that the reformulation will provide fairer notice to booksellers, theater owners, and the reading and viewing public. Nor does the Court contend that the approach will provide clearer guidance to law enforcement officials or reduce the chill on protected expression. Nor, finally, does the Court suggest that the approach will mitigate to the slightest degree the institutional problems that have plagued this Court and the state and federal judiciary as a direct result of the uncertainty inherent in any definition of obscenity.

Of course, the Court's restated *Roth* test does limit the definition of obscenity to depictions of physical conduct and explicit sexual acts. And that limitation may seem, at first glance, a welcome and clarifying addition to the *Roth-Memoirs* formula. But, just as the agreement in *Roth* on an abstract definition of obscenity gave little hint of the extreme difficulty that was to follow in attempting to apply that definition to specific material, the mere formulation of a "physical conduct" test is no assurance that it can be applied with any greater facility. The Court does not indicate how it would apply its test to the materials involved in *Miller* v. *California, supra,* and we can only speculate as to its application. But

even a confirmed optimist could find little realistic comfort in the adoption of such a test. Indeed, the valiant attempt of one lower federal court to draw the constitutional line at depictions of explicit sexual conduct seems to belie any suggestion that this approach marks the road to clarity. [16] The Court surely demonstrates little sensitivity to our own institutional problems, much less the other vagueness-related difficulties, in establishing a system that requires us to consider whether a description of human genitals is sufficiently "lewd" to deprive it of constitutional protection; whether a sexual act is "ultimate"; whether the conduct depicted in materials before us fits within one of the categories of conduct whose depiction the State and Federal Governments have attempted to suppress; and a host of equally pointless inquiries. In addition, adoption of such a test does not, presumably, obviate the need for consideration of the nuances of presentation of sexually oriented material, yet it hardly clarifies the application of those opaque but important factors.

If the application of the "physical conduct" test to pictorial material is fraught with difficulty, its application to textual material carries the potential for extraordinary abuse. Surely we have passed the point where the mere written description of sexual conduct is deprived of First Amendment protection. Yet the test offers no guidance to us, or anyone else, in determining which written descriptions of sexual conduct are protected, and which are not.

Ultimately, the reformulation must fail because it still leaves in this Court the responsibility of determining in each case whether the materials are protected by the First Amendment. The Court concedes that even under its restated formulation, the First Amendment interests at stake require "appellate courts to conduct an independent review of constitutional claims when necessary," *Miller* v. *California, ante,* at 25, citing Mr. Justice Harlan's opinion in *Roth,* where he stated, "I do not understand how the Court can resolve the constitutional problems now before it without making its own independent judgment upon the character of the material upon which these convictions were based." 354 U. S., at 498. Thus, the Court's new formulation will not relieve us of "the awesome task of making case by case at once the criminal and the constitutional law." [17] And the careful efforts of state and lower federal courts to apply the standard will remain an essentially pointless exercise, in view of the need for an ultimate decision by this Court. In addition, since the status of sexually oriented material will necessarily remain in doubt until final decision by this Court, the new approach will not diminish the chill on protected expression that derives from the uncertainty of the underlying standard. I am convinced that a definition of obscenity in terms of physical conduct cannot provide sufficient clarity to afford fair notice, to avoid a chill on protected expression, and to minimize the institutional stress, so long as that definition is used to justify the outright suppression of any material that is asserted to fall within its terms.

3. I have also considered the possibility of reducing our own role, and the role of appellate courts generally, in determining whether particular matter is obscene. Thus,

we might conclude that juries are best suited to determine obscenity *vel non* and that jury verdicts in this area should not be set aside except in cases of extreme departure from prevailing standards. Or, more generally, we might adopt the position that where a lower federal or state court has conscientiously applied the constitutional standard, its finding of obscenity will be no more vulnerable to reversal by this Court than any finding of fact. Cf. *Interstate Circuit, Inc. v. Dallas*, 390 U. S., at 706–707 (separate opinion of Harlan, J.). While the point was not clearly resolved prior to our decision in *Redrup v. New York*, 386 U. S. 767 (1967),[18] it is implicit in that decision that the First Amendment requires an independent review by appellate courts of the constitutional fact of obscenity.[19] That result is required by principles applicable to the obscenity issue no less than to any other area involving free expression, see, *e. g.*, *New York Times Co. v. Sullivan*, 376 U. S. 254, 284–285 (1964), or other constitutional right.[20] In any event, even if the Constitution would permit us to refrain from judging for ourselves the alleged obscenity of particular materials, that approach would solve at best only a small part of our problem. For while it would mitigate the institutional stress produced by the *Roth* approach, it would neither offer nor produce any cure for the other vices of vagueness. Far from providing a clearer guide to permissible primary conduct, the approach would inevitably lead to even greater uncertainty and the consequent due process problems of fair notice. And the approach would expose much protected, sexually oriented expression to the vagaries of jury determinations. Cf. *Herndon v. Lowry*, 301 U. S. 242, 263 (1937). Plainly, the institutional gain would be more than offset by the unprecedented infringement of First Amendment rights.

4. Finally, I have considered the view, urged so forcefully since 1957 by our Brothers Black and Douglas, that the First Amendment bars the suppression of any sexually oriented expression. That position would effect a sharp reduction, although perhaps not a total elimination, of the uncertainty that surrounds our current approach. Nevertheless, I am convinced that it would achieve that desirable goal only by stripping the States of power to an extent that cannot be justified by the commands of the Constitution, at least so long as there is available an alternative approach that strikes a better balance between the guarantee of free expression and the States' legitimate interests.

V

Our experience since *Roth* requires us not only to abandon the effort to pick out obscene materials on a case-by-case basis, but also to reconsider a fundamental postulate of *Roth:* that there exists a definable class of sexually oriented expression that may be totally suppressed by the Federal and State Governments. Assuming that such a class of expression does in fact exist,[21] I am forced to conclude that the concept of "obscenity" cannot be defined with sufficient specificity and clarity to provide fair notice to persons who create and distribute sexually oriented materials, to prevent substantial erosion of protected speech as a byproduct of the attempt to suppress unprotected speech, and to

avoid very costly institutional harms. Given these inevitable side effects of state efforts to suppress what is assumed to be *unprotected* speech, we must scrutinize with care the state interest that is asserted to justify the suppression. For in the absence of some very substantial interest in suppressing such speech, we can hardly condone the ill effects that seem to flow inevitably from the effort.[22]

Obscenity laws have a long history in this country. Most of the States that had ratified the Constitution by 1792 punished the related crime of blasphemy or profanity despite the guarantees of free expression in their constitutions, and Massachusetts expressly prohibited the "Composing, Writing, Printing or Publishing, of any Filthy Obscene or Prophane Song, Pamphlet, Libel or Mock-Sermon, in Imitation or in Mimicking of Preaching, or any other part of Divine Worship." Acts and Laws of Massachusetts Bay Colony (1726), Acts of 1711–1712, c. 1, p. 218. In 1815 the first reported obscenity conviction was obtained under the common law of Pennsylvania. See *Commonwealth v. Sharpless*, 2 S. & R. 91. A conviction in Massachusetts under its common law and colonial statute followed six years later. See *Commonwealth v. Holmes*, 17 Mass. 336 (1821). In 1821 Vermont passed the first state law proscribing the publication or sale of "lewd or obscene" material, Laws of Vermont, 1824, c. XXXII, No. 1, § 23, and federal legislation barring the importation of similar matter appeared in 1842. See Customs Law of 1842, § 28, 5 Stat. 566. Although the number of early obscenity laws was small and their enforcement exceedingly lax, the situation significantly changed after about 1870 when Federal and State Governments, mainly as a result of the efforts of Anthony Comstock, took an active interest in the suppression of obscenity. By the end of the 19th century at least 30 States had some type of general prohibition on the dissemination of obscene materials, and by the time of our decision in *Roth* no State was without some provision on the subject. The Federal Government meanwhile had enacted no fewer than 20 obscenity laws between 1842 and 1956. See *Roth v. United States*, 354 U. S., at 482–483, 485; Report of the Commission on Obscenity and Pornography 300–301 (1970).

This history caused us to conclude in *Roth* "that the unconditional phrasing of the First Amendment [that "Congress shall make no law . . . abridging the freedom of speech, or of the press . . ."] was not intended to protect every utterance." 354 U. S., at 483. It also caused us to hold, as numerous prior decisions of this Court had assumed, see *id.*, at 481, that obscenity could be denied the protection of the First Amendment and hence suppressed because it is a form of expression "utterly without redeeming social importance," *id.*, at 484, as "mirrored in the universal judgment that [it] should be restrained . . . ." *Id.*, at 485.

Because we assumed—incorrectly, as experience has proved—that obscenity could be separated from other sexually oriented expression without significant costs either to the First Amendment or to the judicial machinery charged with the task of safeguarding First Amendment freedoms, we had no occasion in *Roth* to probe the asserted state interest in curtailing unprotected, sexually oriented speech. Yet, as we have increasingly come to appreciate the vagueness of the concept of obscenity, we have begun to recognize and articulate the state interests at stake. Significantly, in *Redrup* v. *New York*, 386 U. S. 767 (1967), where we set aside findings of obscenity with regard to three sets of material, we pointed out that

> "[i]n none of the cases was there a claim that the statute in question reflected a specific and limited state concern for juveniles. See *Prince* v. *Massachusetts*, 321 U. S. 158; cf. *Butler* v. *Michigan*, 352 U. S. 380. In none was there any suggestion of an assault upon individual privacy by publication in a manner so obtrusive as to make it impossible for an unwilling individual to avoid exposure to it. Cf. *Breard* v. *Alexandria*, 341 U. S. 622; *Public Utilities Comm'n* v. *Pollak*, 343 U. S. 451. And in none was there evidence of the sort of 'pandering' which the Court found significant in *Ginzburg* v. *United States*, 383 U. S. 463." 386 U. S., at 769.

See *Rowan* v. *Post Office Dept.*, 397 U. S. 728 (1970), *Stanley* v. *Georgia*, 394 U. S., at 567.[23]

The opinions in *Redrup* and *Stanley* v. *Georgia* reflected our emerging view that the state interests in protecting children and in protecting unconsenting adults may stand on a different footing from the other asserted state interests. It may well be, as one commentator has argued, that "exposure to [erotic material] is for some persons an intense emotional experience. A communication of this nature, imposed upon a person contrary to his wishes, has all the characteristics of a physical assault. . . . [And it] constitutes an invasion of his privacy . . . ."[24] But cf. *Cohen* v. *California*, 403 U. S., at 21–22. Similarly, if children are "not possessed of that full capacity for individual choice which is the presupposition of the First Amendment guarantees," *Ginsberg* v. *New York*, 390 U. S., at 649–650 (STEWART, J., concurring), then the State may have a substantial interest in precluding the flow of obscene materials even to consenting juveniles.[25] But cf. *id.*, at 673–674 (Fortas, J., dissenting).

But, whatever the strength of the state interests in protecting juveniles and unconsenting adults from exposure to sexually oriented materials, those interests cannot be asserted in defense of the holding of the Georgia Supreme Court in this case. That court assumed for the purposes of its decision that the films in issue were exhibited only to persons over the age of 21 who viewed them willingly and with prior knowledge of the nature of their contents. And on that assumption the state court held that the films could still be suppressed. The justification for the suppression must be found, therefore, in some independent interest in regulating the reading and viewing habits of consenting adults.

At the outset it should be noted that virtually all of the interests that might be asserted in defense of suppression, laying aside the special interests associated with distribution to juveniles and unconsenting adults, were also posited in *Stanley* v. *Georgia, supra,* where we held that the State could not make the "mere private possession of obscene material a crime." *Id.,* at 568. That de-

cision presages the conclusions I reach here today.

In *Stanley* we pointed out that "[t]here appears to be little empirical basis for" the assertion that "exposure to obscene materials may lead to deviant sexual behavior or crimes of sexual violence." *Id.,* at 566 and n. 9.[26] In any event, we added that "if the State is only concerned about printed or filmed materials inducing antisocial conduct, we believe that in the context of private consumption of ideas and information we should adhere to the view that '[a]mong free men, the deterrents ordinarily to be applied to prevent crime are education and punishment for violations of the law . . . .' *Whitney* v. *California*, 274 U. S. 357, 378 (1927) (Brandeis, J., concurring)." *Id.,* at 566–567.

Moreover, in *Stanley* we rejected as "wholly inconsistent with the philosophy of the First Amendment," *id.,* at 566, the notion that there is a legitimate state concern in the "control [of] the moral content of a person's thoughts," *id.,* at 565, and we held that a State "cannot constitutionally premise legislation on the desirability of controlling a person's private thoughts." *Id.,* at 566. That is not to say, of course, that a State must remain utterly indifferent to—and take no action bearing on—the morality of the community. The traditional description of state police power does embrace the regulation of morals as well as the health, safety, and general welfare of the citizenry. See, *e. g., Village of Euclid* v. *Ambler Realty Co.*, 272 U. S. 365, 395 (1926). And much legislation—compulsory public education laws, civil rights laws, even the abolition of capital punishment—is grounded, at least in part, on a concern with the morality of the community. But the State's interest in regulating morality by suppressing obscenity, while often asserted, remains essentially unfocused and ill defined. And, since the attempt to curtail unprotected speech necessarily spills over into the area of protected speech, the effort to serve this speculative interest through the suppression of obscene material must tread heavily on rights protected by the First Amendment.

In *Roe* v. *Wade*, 410 U. S. 113 (1973), we held constitutionally invalid a state abortion law, even though we were aware of

> "the sensitive and emotional nature of the abortion controversy, of the vigorous opposing views, even among physicians, and of the deep and seemingly absolute convictions that the subject inspires. One's philosophy, one's experiences, one's exposure to the raw edges of human existence, one's religious training, one's attitudes toward life and family and their values, and the moral standards one establishes and seeks to observe, are all likely to influence and to color one's thinking and conclusions about abortion." *Id.,* at 116.

Like the proscription of abortions, the effort to suppress obscenity is predicated on unprovable, although strongly held, assumptions about human behavior, morality, sex, and religion.[27] The existence of these assumptions cannot validate a statute that substantially undermines the guarantees of the First Amendment, any more than the existence of similar assumptions on the issue of abortion can validate a statute that infringes the constitutionally protected privacy interests of a pregnant woman.

If, as the Court today assumes, "a state legislature may . . . act on the . . . assumption that commerce in obscene books, or public exhibitions focused on obscene conduct, have a tendency to exert a corrupting and debasing impact leading to antisocial behavior," *ante,* at 63, then it is hard to see how state-ordered regimentation of our minds can ever be forestalled. For if a State may, in an effort to maintain or create a particular moral tone, prescribe what its citizens cannot read or cannot see, then it would seem to follow that in pursuit of that same objective a State could decree that its citizens must read certain books or must view certain films. Cf. *United States* v. *Roth,* 237 F. 2d 796, 823 (CA2 1956) (Frank, J., concurring). However laudable its goal—and that is obviously a question on which reasonable minds may differ—the State cannot proceed by means that violate the Constitution. The precise point was established a half century ago in *Meyer* v. *Nebraska,* 262 U. S. 390 (1923).

"That the State may do much, go very far, indeed, in order to improve the quality of its citizens, physically, mentally and morally, is clear; but the individual has certain fundamental rights which must be respected. The protection of the Constitution extends to all, to those who speak other languages as well as to those born with English on the tongue. Perhaps it would be highly advantageous if all had ready understanding of our ordinary speech, but this cannot be coerced by methods which conflict with the Constitution—a desirable end cannot be promoted by prohibited means.

"For the welfare of his Ideal Commonwealth, Plato suggested a law which should provide: 'That the wives of our guardians are to be common, and their children are to be common, and no parent is to know his own child, nor any child his parent. . . . The proper officers will take the offspring of the good parents to the pen or fold, and there they will deposit them with certain nurses who dwell in a separate quarter; but the offspring of the inferior, or of the better when they chance to be deformed, will be put away in some mysterious, unknown place, as they should be.' In order to submerge the individual and develop ideal citizens, Sparta assembled the males at seven into barracks and intrusted their subsequent education and training to official guardians. Although such measures have been deliberately approved by men of great genius, their ideas touching the relation between individual and State were wholly different from those upon which our institutions rest; and it hardly will be affirmed that any legislature could impose such restrictions upon the people of a State without doing violence to both letter and spirit of the Constitution." *Id.,* at 401–402.

Recognizing these principles, we have held that so-called thematic obscenity—obscenity which might persuade the viewer or reader to engage in "obscene" conduct—is not outside the protection of the First Amendment:

"It is contended that the State's action was justified because the motion picture attractively portrays a relationship which is contrary to the moral standards, the religious precepts, and the legal code of its citizenry. This argument misconceives what it is that the Constitution protects. Its guarantee is not confined to the expression of ideas that are conventional or shared by a majority. It protects advocacy of the opinion that adultery may sometimes be proper, no less than advocacy of socialism or the single tax. And in the realm of ideas it protects expression which is eloquent no less than that which is unconvincing." *Kingsley Pictures Corp.* v. *Regents,* 360 U. S. 684, 688–689 (1959).

Even a legitimate, sharply focused state concern for the morality of the community cannot, in other words, justify an assault on the protections of the First Amendment. Cf. *Griswold* v. *Connecticut,* 381 U. S. 479 (1965); *Eisenstadt* v. *Baird,* 405 U. S. 438 (1972); *Loving* v. *Virginia,* 388 U. S. 1 (1967). Where the state interest in regulation of morality is vague and ill defined, interference with the guarantees of the First Amendment is even more difficult to justify.[28]

In short, while I cannot say that the interests of the State—apart from the question of juveniles and unconsenting adults—are trivial or nonexistent, I am compelled to conclude that these interests cannot justify the substantial damage to constitutional rights and to this Nation's judicial machinery that inevitably results from state efforts to bar the distribution even of unprotected material to consenting adults. *NAACP* v. *Alabama,* 377 U. S. 288, 307 (1964); *Cantwell* v. *Connecticut,* 310 U. S., at 304. I would hold, therefore, that at least in the absence of distribution to juveniles or obtrusive exposure to unconsenting adults, the First and Fourteenth Amendments prohibit the State and Federal Governments from attempting wholly to suppress sexually oriented materials on the basis of their allegedly "obscene" contents. Nothing in this approach precludes those governments from taking action to serve what may be strong and legitimate interests through regulation of the manner of distribution of sexually oriented material.

VI

Two Terms ago we noted that

"there is developing sentiment that adults should have complete freedom to produce, deal in, possess and consume whatever communicative materials may appeal to them and that the law's involvement with obscenity should be limited to those situations where children are involved or where it is necessary to prevent imposition on unwilling recipients of whatever age. The concepts involved are said to be so elusive and the laws so inherently unenforceable without extravagant expenditures of time and effort by enforcement officers and the courts that basic reassessment is not only wise but essential." *United States* v. *Reidel,* 402 U. S., at 357.

Nevertheless, we concluded that "the task of restructuring the obscenity laws lies with those who pass, repeal, and amend statutes and ordinances." *Ibid.* But the law of obscenity has been fashioned by this Court—and necessarily so under our duty to enforce the Constitution. It is surely the duty of this Court, as expounder of the Constitution, to provide a remedy for the present unsatisfactory state of affairs. I do not pretend to have found a complete and infallible answer to what Mr. Justice Harlan called "the intractable obscenity problem." *Interstate Circuit, Inc.* v. *Dallas*, 390 U. S., at 704 (separate opinion). See also *Memoirs* v. *Massachusetts*, 383 U. S., at 456 (dissenting opinion). Difficult questions must still be faced, notably in the areas of distribution to juveniles and offensive exposure to unconsenting adults. Whatever the extent of state power to regulate in those areas,[29] it should be clear that the view I espouse today would introduce a large measure of clarity to this troubled area, would reduce the institutional pressure on this Court and the rest of the State and Federal Judiciary, and would guarantee fuller freedom of expression while leaving room for the protection of legitimate governmental interests. Since the Supreme Court of Georgia erroneously concluded that the State has power to suppress sexually oriented material even in the absence of distribution to juveniles or exposure to unconsenting adults, I would reverse that judgment and remand the case to that court for further proceedings not inconsistent with this opinion.

COURT'S OPINION NOTES

[1] This is a civil proceeding. Georgia Code Ann. § 26–2101 defines a criminal offense, but the exhibition of materials found to be "obscene" as defined by that statute may be enjoined in a civil proceeding under Georgia case law. *1024 Peachtree Corp.* v. *Slaton*, 228 Ga. 102, 184 S. E. 2d 144 (1971); *Walter* v. *Slaton*, 227 Ga. 676, 182 S. E. 2d 464 (1971); *Evans Theatre Corp.* v. *Slaton*, 227 Ga. 377, 180 S. E. 2d 712 (1971). See *infra*, at 54. Georgia Code Ann. § 26–2101 reads in relevant part:

"Distributing obscene materials.

"(a) A person commits the offense of distributing obscene materials when he sells, lends, rents, leases, gives, advertises, publishes, exhibits or otherwise disseminates to any person any obscene material of any description, knowing the obscene nature thereof, or who offers to do so, or who possesses such material with the intent so to do . . . .

"(b) Material is obscene if considered as a whole, applying community standards, its predominant appeal is to prurient interest, that is, a shameful or morbid interest in nudity, sex or excretion, and utterly without redeeming social value and if, in addition, it goes substantially beyond customary limits of candor in describing or representing such matters. . . .

.   .   .   .   .

"(d) A person convicted of distributing obscene material shall for the first offense be punished as for a misdemeanor, and for any subsequent offense shall be punished by imprisonment for not less than one nor more than five years, or by a fine not to exceed $5,000, or both."

The constitutionality of Georgia Code Ann. § 26–2101 was upheld against First Amendment and due process challenges in *Gable* v. *Jenkins*, 309 F. Supp. 998 (ND Ga. 1969), aff'd *per curiam*, 397 U. S. 592 (1970).

[2] See Georgia Code Ann. § 26–2101, set out *supra*, at 51 n. 1.

[3] In *Walter* v. *Slaton*, 227 Ga. 676, 182 S. E. 2d 464 (1971), the Georgia Supreme Court described the cases before it as follows:

"Each case was commenced as a civil action by the District Attorney of the Superior Court of Fulton County jointly with the Solicitor of the Criminal Court of Fulton County. In each case the plaintiffs alleged that the defendants named therein were conducting a business of exhibiting motion picture films to members of the public; that they were in control and possession of the described motion picture film which they were exhibiting to the public on a fee basis; that said film 'constitutes a flagrant violation of Ga. Code § 26–2101 in that the sole and dominant theme of the motion picture film . . . considered as a whole, and applying contemporary standards, appeals to the prurient interest in sex and nudity, and that said motion picture film is utterly and absolutely without any redeeming social value whatsoever and transgresses beyond the customary limits of candor in describing and discussing sexual matters.'" *Id.*, at 676–677, 182 S. E. 2d, at 465.

[4] This procedure would have even more merit if the exhibitor or purveyor could also test the issue of obscenity in a similar civil action, prior to any exposure to criminal penalty. We are not here presented with the problem of whether a holding that materials were not obscene could be circumvented in a later proceeding by evidence of pandering. See *Memoirs* v. *Massachusetts*, 383 U. S. 413, 458 n. 3 (1966) (Harlan, J., dissenting); *Ginzburg* v. *United States*, 383 U. S. 463, 496 (1966) (Harlan, J., dissenting).

[5] At the specific request of petitioners' counsel, the copies of the films produced for the trial court were placed in the "administrative custody" of that court pending the outcome of this litigation.

[6] This is not a subject that lends itself to the traditional use of expert testimony. Such testimony is usually admitted for the purpose of explaining to lay jurors what they otherwise could not understand. Cf. 2 J. Wigmore, Evidence §§ 556, 559 (3d ed. 1940). No such assistance is needed by jurors in obscenity cases; indeed the "expert witness" practices employed in these cases have often made a mockery out of the otherwise sound concept of expert testimony. See *United States* v. *Groner*, 479 F. 2d 577, 585–586 (CA5 1973); *id.*, at 587–588 (Ainsworth, J., concurring). "Simply stated, hard core pornography . . . can and does speak for itself." *United States* v. *Wild*, 422 F. 2d 34, 36 (CA2 1970), cert. denied, 402 U. S. 986 (1971). We reserve judgment, however, on the extreme case, not presented here, where contested materials are directed at such a bizarre deviant group that the experience of the trier of fact would be plainly inadequate to judge whether the material appeals to the prurient interest. See *Mishkin* v. *New York*, 383 U. S. 502, 508–510 (1966); *United States* v. *Klaw*, 350 F. 2d 155, 167–168 (CA2 1965).

[7] It is conceivable that an "adult" theater can—if it really insists—prevent the exposure of its obscene wares to juveniles. An "adult" bookstore, dealing in obscene books, magazines, and pictures, cannot realistically make this claim. The Hill-Link Minority Report of the Commission on Obscenity and Pornography emphasizes evidence (the Abelson National Survey of Youth and Adults) that, although most pornography may be bought by elders, "the heavy users and most highly exposed people to pornography are adolescent females (among women) and adolescent and young adult males (among men)." The Report of the Commission on Obscenity and Pornography 401 (1970). The legitimate interest in preventing exposure of juveniles to obscene material cannot be fully served by simply barring juveniles from the immediate physical premises of "adult" bookstores, when there is a flourishing "outside business" in these materials.

[8] The Report of the Commission on Obscenity and Pornography 390–412 (1970) (Hill-Link Minority Report). For a discussion of earlier studies indicating "a division of thought [among behavioral scientists] on the correlation between obscenity and socially deleterious behavior," *Memoirs* v. *Massachusetts, supra*, at 451, and references to expert opinions that obscene material may induce crime and antisocial conduct, see *id.*, at 451–453 (Clark, J., dissenting). As Mr. Justice Clark emphasized:

"While erotic stimulation caused by pornography may be legally insignificant in itself, there are medical experts who believe that such stimulation frequently manifests itself in criminal sexual behavior or other antisocial conduct. For example, Dr. George W. Henry of Cornell University has expressed the opinion that obscenity, with its exaggerated and morbid emphasis on sex, particularly abnormal and perverted practices, and its unrealistic presentation of sexual behavior and attitudes, may induce antisocial conduct by the average person. A number of sociologists think that this material may have adverse effects upon individual mental health, with potentially disruptive consequences for the community.

.   .   .   .   .

"Congress and the legislatures of every State have enacted measures to restrict the distribution of erotic and pornographic material, justifying these controls by reference to evidence that antisocial behavior may result in part from reading obscenity." *Id.*, at 452–453 (footnotes omitted).

[9] See also Berns, Pornography vs. Democracy: The Case for Censorship, in 22 The Public Interest 3 (Winter 1971); van den Haag, in Censorship: For & Against 156–157 (H. Hart ed. 1971).

[10] "In this and other cases in this area of the law, which are coming to us in ever-increasing numbers, we are faced with the resolution of rights basic both to individuals and to society as a whole. Specifically, we are called upon to reconcile the right of the Nation and of the States to maintain a decent society and, on the other hand, the right of individuals to express themselves freely in accordance with the guarantees of the First and Fourteenth Amendments." *Jacobellis v. Ohio, supra*, at 199 (Warren, C. J., dissenting).

[11] Mr. Justice Holmes stated in another context, that:

"[T]he proper course is to recognize that a state legislature can do whatever it sees fit to do unless it is restrained by some express prohibition in the Constitution of the United States or of the State, and that Courts should be careful not to extend such prohibitions beyond their obvious meaning by reading into them conceptions of public policy that the particular Court may happen to entertain." *Tyson & Brother v. Banton*, 273 U. S. 418, 446 (1927) (dissenting opinion joined by Brandeis, J.).

[12] "It has been well observed that such [lewd and obscene] utterances are no essential part of any exposition of ideas, and are of such slight social value as a step to truth that any benefit that may be derived from them is clearly outweighed by the social interest in order and morality." *Roth v. United States*, 354 U. S. 476, 485 (1957), quoting *Chaplinsky v. New Hampshire*, 315 U. S. 568, 572 (1942) (emphasis added in *Roth*).

[13] The protection afforded by *Stanley v. Georgia*, 394 U. S. 557 (1969), is restricted to a place, the home. In contrast, the constitutionally protected privacy of family, marriage, motherhood, procreation, and child rearing is not just concerned with a particular place, but with a protected intimate relationship. Such protected privacy extends to the doctor's office, the hospital, the hotel room, or as otherwise required to safeguard the right to intimacy involved. Cf. *Roe v. Wade*, 410 U. S. 113, 152–154 (1973); *Griswold v. Connecticut*, 381 U. S. 479, 485–486 (1965). Obviously, there is no necessary or legitimate expectation of privacy which would extend to marital intercourse on a street corner or a theater stage.

[14] Cf. J. Mill, On Liberty 13 (1955 ed.).

[15] The state statute books are replete with constitutionally unchallenged laws against prostitution, suicide, voluntary self-mutilation, brutalizing "bare fist" prize fights, and duels, although these crimes may only directly involve "consenting adults." Statutes making bigamy a crime surely cut into an individual's freedom to associate, but few today seriously claim such statutes violate the First Amendment or any other constitutional provision. See *Davis v. Beason*, 133 U. S. 333, 344–345 (1890). Consider also the language of this Court in *McLaughlin v. Florida*, 379 U. S. 184, 196 (1964), as to adultery; *Southern Surety Co. v. Oklahoma*, 241 U. S. 582, 586 (1916), as to fornication; *Hoke v. United States*, 227 U. S. 308, 320–322 (1913), and *Caminetti v. United States*, 242 U. S. 470, 484–487, 491–492 (1917), as to "white slavery"; *Murphy v. California*, 225 U. S. 623, 629 (1912), as to billiard halls; and the *Lottery Case*, 188 U. S. 321, 355–356 (1903), as to gambling. See also the summary of state statutes prohibiting bear baiting, cockfighting, and other brutalizing animal "sports," in Stevens, Fighting and Baiting, in Animals and Their Legal Rights 112–127 (Leavitt ed. 1970). As Professor Irving Kristol has observed: "Bearbaiting and cockfighting are prohibited only in part out of compassion for the suffering animals; the main reason they were abolished was because it was felt that they debased and brutalized the citizenry who flocked to witness such spectacles." On the Democratic Idea in America 33 (1972).

JUSTICE DOUGLAS'S OPINION NOTE

*What we do today is rather ominous as respects librarians. The net now designed by the Court is so finely meshed that, taken literally, it could result in raids on libraries. Libraries, I had always assumed, were sacrosanct, representing every part of the spectrum. If what is offensive to the most influential person or group in a community can be purged from a library, the library system would be destroyed.

A few States exempt librarians from laws curbing distribution of "obscene" literature. California's law, however, provides: "Every person who, with knowledge that a person is a minor, or who fails to exercise reasonable care in ascertaining the true age of a minor, knowingly distributes to or sends or causes to be sent to, or exhibits to, or offers to distribute or exhibit any harmful matter to a minor, is guilty of a misdemeanor." Calif. Penal Code § 313.1.

A "minor" is one under 18 years of age; the word "distribute" means "to transfer possession"; "matter" includes "any book, magazine, newspaper, or other printed or written material." *Id.*, §§ 313 (b), (d), (g).

"Harmful matter" is defined in § 313 (a) to mean "matter, taken as a whole, the predominant appeal of which to the average person, applying contemporary standards, is to prurient interest, *i. e.*, a shameful or morbid interest in nudity, sex, or excretion; and is matter which taken as a whole goes substantially beyond customary limits of candor in description or representation of such matters; and is matter which taken as a whole is utterly without redeeming social importance for minors."

JUSTICE BRENNAN'S OPINION NOTES

[1] Ga. Code Ann. § 26–2101 provides in pertinent part that

"(b) Material is obscene if considered as a whole, applying community standards, its predominant appeal is to prurient interest, that is, a shameful or morbid interest in nudity, sex or excretion, and utterly without redeeming social value and if, in addition, it goes substantially beyond customary limits of candor in describing or representing such matters. Undeveloped photographs, molds, printing plates and the like shall be deemed obscene notwithstanding that processing or other acts may be required to make the obscenity patent or to disseminate it."

[2] Ga. Code § 26–2101 (a):

"A person commits the offense of distributing obscene materials [as described in subsection (b), n. 1, *supra*] when he sells, lends, rents, leases, gives, advertises, publishes, exhibits or otherwise disseminates to any person any obscene material of any description, knowing the obscene nature thereof, or who offers to do so, or who possesses such material with the intent so to do . . . ."

[3] The precise holding of the trial court is not free from ambiguity. After pointing out that the films could be considered obscene, and that they still could not be suppressed in the absence of exposure to juveniles or unconsenting adults, the trial court concluded that "[i]t is the judgment of this court that the films, even though they display the human body and the human personality in a most degrading fashion, are not obscene." It is not clear whether the trial court found that the films were not obscene in the sense that they were protected expression under the standards of *Roth v. United States*, 354 U. S. 476 (1957), and *Redrup v. New York*, 386 U. S. 767 (1967), or whether it used the expression "not obscene" as a term of art to indicate that the films could not be suppressed even though they were not protected under the *Roth-Redrup* standards. In any case, the Georgia Supreme Court viewed the trial court's opinion as holding that the films could not be suppressed, even if they were unprotected expression, provided that they were not exhibited to juveniles or unconsenting adults.

[4] "As to all such problems, this Court said in *Thornhill v. Alabama*, 310 U. S. 88, 101–102 (1940):

" 'The freedom of speech and of the press guaranteed by the Constitution embraces at the least the liberty to discuss publicly and truthfully *all matters of public concern* without previous restraint or fear of subsequent punishment. The exigencies of the colonial period and the efforts to secure freedom from oppressive administration developed a broadened conception of these liberties as adequate to supply the public need for *information and education with respect to the significant issues of the times*. . . . Freedom of discussion, if it would fulfill its historic function in this nation, must embrace *all issues about which information is needed or appropriate to enable the members of society to cope with the exigencies of their period.'* (Emphasis added.)" *Roth,* 354 U. S., at 487–488.

See also, *e. g., Thomas v. Collins,* 323 U. S. 516, 531 (1945) ("the rights of free speech and a free press are not confined to any field of human interest").

[5] See, *e. g.,* Kalven, The Metaphysics of the Law of Obscenity, 1960 Sup. Ct. Rev. 1, 10–11; cf. *Beauharnais v. Illinois,* 343 U. S. 250 (1952).

[6] See, *e. g.,* T. Emerson, The System of Freedom of Expression 487 (1970); Kalven, *supra,* n. 5; Comment, More Ado About Dirty Books, 75 Yale L. J. 1364 (1966).

[7] On the question of community standards see also *Hoyt v. Minnesota,* 399 U. S. 524 (1970) (BLACKMUN, J., joined by BURGER, C. J., and Harlan, J., dissenting) (flexibility for state standards); *Cain v. Kentucky,* 397 U. S. 319 (1970) (BURGER, C. J., dissenting) (same); *Manual Enterprises v. Day,* 370 U. S. 478, 488 (1962) (Harlan, J., joined by STEWART, J.) (national standards in context of federal prosecution).

[8] No fewer than 31 cases have been disposed of in this fashion. Aside from the three cases reversed in *Redrup,* they are: *Keney v. New York,* 388 U. S. 440 (1967); *Friedman v. New York,* 388 U. S. 441 (1967); *Ratner v. California,* 388 U. S. 442 (1967); *Cobert v. New York,* 388 U. S. 443 (1967); *Sheperd v. New York,* 388 U. S. 444 (1967); *Avansino v. New York,* 388 U. S. 446 (1967); *Aday v. New York,* 388 U. S. 447 (1967); *Books, Inc. v. United States,* 388 U. S. 449 (1967); *A Quantity of Books v. Kansas,* 388 U. S. 452 (1967); *Mazes v. Ohio,* 388 U. S. 453 (1967); *Schackman v. California,* 388 U. S. 454 (1967); *Potomac News Co. v. United States,* 389 U. S. 47 (1967); *Conner v. City of Hammond,* 389 U. S. 48 (1967); *Central Magazine Sales, Ltd. v. United States,* 389 U. S. 50 (1967); *Chance v. California,* 389 U. S. 89 (1967); *I. M. Amusement Corp. v. Ohio,* 389 U. S. 573 (1968); *Robert-Arthur Management Corp. v. Tennessee,* 389 U. S. 578 (1968); *Felton v. City of Pensacola,* 390 U. S. 340 (1968); *Henry v. Louisiana,* 392 U. S. 655 (1968); *Cain v. Kentucky, supra; Bloss v. Dykema,* 398 U. S. 278 (1970); *Walker v. Ohio,* 398 U. S. 434 (1970); *Hoyt v. Minnesota, supra; Childs v. Oregon,* 401 U. S. 1006 (1971); *Bloss v. Michigan,* 402 U. S. 938 (1971); *Burgin v. South Carolina,* 404 U. S. 809 (1971); *Hartstein v. Missouri,* 404 U. S. 988 (1971); *Wiener v. California,* 404 U. S. 988 (1971).

[9] Although I did not join the opinion of the Court in *Stanley v Georgia,* 394 U. S. 557 (1969), I am now inclined to agree that "the Constitution protects the right to receive information and ideas," and that "[t]his right to receive information and ideas, regardless of their social worth . . . is fundamental to our free society." *Id.,* at 564. See *Martin v. City of Struthers,* 319 U. S. 141, 143 (1943); *Winters v. New York,* 333 U. S. 507, 510 (1948); *Lamont v. Postmaster General,* 381 U. S. 301, 307–308 (1965) (concurring opinion). This right is closely tied, as *Stanley* recognized, to "the right to be free, except in very limited circumstances, from unwarranted governmental intrusions into one's privacy." 394 U. S., at 564. See *Griswold v. Connecticut,* 381 U. S. 479 (1965); *Olmstead v. United States,* 277 U. S. 438, 478 (1928) (Brandeis, J., dissenting). It is similarly related to "the right of the individual, married or single, to be free from unwarranted governmental intrusion into matters so fundamentally affecting a person as the decision whether to bear or beget a child," italics omitted) *Eisenstadt v. Baird,* 405 U. S. 438 453 (1972), and the right to exercise "autonomous control over the development and expression of one's intellect, interests, tastes, and personality." (Italics omitted.) *Doe v. Bolton,* 410 U. S. 179, 211 (1973) (DOUGLAS, J., concurring). It seems to me that the recognition of these intertwining rights calls in question the validity of the two-level approach recognized in *Roth.* After all, if a person has the right to receive information without regard to its social worth—that is, without regard to its obscenity— then it would seem to follow that a State could not constitutionally punish one who undertakes to provide this information to a *willing, adult* recipient. See *Eisenstadt v. Baird, supra,* at 443–446. In any event, I need not rely on this line of analysis or explore all of its possible ramifications, for there is available a narrower basis on which to rest this decision. Whether or not a class of "obscene" and thus entirely unprotected speech does exist, I am forced to conclude that the class is incapable of definition with sufficient clarity to withstand attack on vagueness grounds. Accordingly, it is on

principles of the void-for-vagueness doctrine that this opinion exclusively relies.

[10] In this regard, the problems of vagueness and overbreadth are, plainly, closely intertwined. See *NAACP v. Button,* 371 U. S. 415, 432–433 (1963); Note, The First Amendment Overbreadth Doctrine, 83 Harv. L. Rev. 844, 845 (1970). Cf. *infra,* at 93–94.

[11] See also *Speiser v. Randall,* 357 U. S. 513 (1958); cf. *Barenblatt v. United States,* 360 U. S. 109, 137–138 (1959) (Black, J., dissenting):

"This Court . . . has emphasized that the 'vice of vagueness' is especially pernicious where legislative power over an area involving speech, press, petition and assembly is involved. . . . For a statute broad enough to support infringement of speech, writings, thoughts and public assemblies, against the unequivocal command of the First Amendment necessarily leaves all persons to guess just what the law really means to cover, and fear of a wrong guess inevitably leads people to forego the very rights the Constitution sought to protect above all others. Vagueness becomes even more intolerable in this area if one accepts, as the Court today does, a balancing test to decide if First Amendment rights shall be protected. It is difficult at best to make a man guess—at the penalty of imprisonment—whether a court will consider the State's need for certain information superior to society's interest in unfettered freedom. It is unconscionable to make him choose between the right to keep silent and the need to speak when the statute supposedly establishing the 'state's interest' is too vague to give him guidance." (Citations omitted.)

[12] Note, The First Amendment Overbreadth Doctrine, 83 Harv. L. Rev. 844, 885–886 and n. 158 (1970) ("Thus in the area of obscenity the overbreadth doctrine operates interstitially, when no line of privilege is apposite or yet to be found, to control the impact of schemes designed to curb distribution of unprotected material").

[13] While the Court's modification of the *Memoirs* test is small, it should still prove sufficient to invalidate virtually every state law relating to the suppression of obscenity. For, under the Court's restatement, a statute must specifically enumerate certain forms of sexual conduct, the depiction of which is to be prohibited. It seems highly doubtful to me that state courts will be able to construe state statutes so as to incorporate a carefully itemized list of various forms of sexual conduct, and thus to bring them into conformity with the Court's requirements. Cf. *Blount v. Rizzi,* 400 U. S. 410, 419 (1971). The statutes of at least one State should, however, escape the wholesale invalidation. Oregon has recently revised its statute to prohibit only the distribution of obscene materials to juveniles or unconsenting adults. The enactment of this principle is, of course, a choice constitutionally open to every State, even under the Court's decision. See Oregon Laws 1971, c. 743, Art. 29, §§ 255–262.

[14] "All ideas having even the slightest redeeming social importance—unorthodox ideas, controversial ideas, even ideas hateful to the prevailing climate of opinion—have the full protection of the guaranties, unless excludable because they encroach upon the limited area of more important interests. But implicit in the history of the First Amendment is the rejection of obscenity as utterly without redeeming social importance." *Roth v. United States, supra,* at 484.

[15] *Miller v. California, ante,* at 22.

[16] *Huffman v. United States,* 152 U. S. App. D. C. 238, 470 F. 2d 386 (1971). The test apparently requires an effort to distinguish between "singles" and "duals," between "erect penises" and "semierect penises," and between "ongoing sexual activity" and "imminent sexual activity."

[17] Note, The Void-for-Vagueness Doctrine in the Supreme Court, 109 U. Pa. L. Rev. 67, 81 (1960).

[18] Compare *Ginsberg v. New York,* 390 U. S. 629, 672 (1968) (Fortas, J., dissenting), *Jacobellis v. Ohio,* 378 U. S. 184, 187–190 (1964) (BRENNAN, J., joined by Goldberg, J.), *Manual Enterprises v. Day,* 370 U. S., at 488 (Harlan, J., joined by STEWART, J.), and *Kingsley Pictures Corp. v. Regents,* 360 U. S. 684, 696–697 (1959) (Frankfurter, J., concurring), *id.,* at 708 (Harlan, J., joined by Frankfurter, J., and Whittaker, J., concurring), with *Jacobellis v. Ohio, supra,* at 202–203 (Warren, C. J., joined by Clark, J., dissenting), *Roth v. United States,* 354 U. S., at 492 n. 30, and *Kingsley Books, Inc. v. Brown,* 354 U. S. 436, 448 (1957) (BRENNAN, J., dissenting). See also *Walker v. Ohio,* 398 U. S. 434 (1970) (BURGER, C. J., dissenting).

[19] Mr. Justice Harlan, it bears noting, considered this requirement critical for review of not only federal but state convictions, despite his view that the States were accorded more latitude than the Federal Government in defining obscenity. See, *e. g., Roth, supra,* at 502–503 (separate opinion).

[20] See generally *Culombe v. Connecticut,* 367 U. S. 568, 603–606 (1961) (opinion of Frankfurter, J.); cf. *Crowell v. Benson,* 285 U. S. 22, 54–65 (1932); *Ng Fung Ho v. White,* 259 U. S. 276, 284–285 (1922).

[21] See n. 9, *supra.*

[22] Cf. *United States v. O'Brien,* 391 U. S. 367, 376–377 (1968): "This Court has held that when 'speech' and 'nonspeech' elements are combined in the same course of conduct, a sufficiently important governmental interest in regulating the nonspeech element can justify incidental limitations on First Amendment freedoms. To characterize the quality of the governmental interest which must appear, the Court has employed a variety of descriptive terms: compelling; substantial; subordinating; paramount; cogent; strong. Whatever imprecision inheres in these terms, we think it clear that a government regulation is sufficiently justified if it is within the constitutional power of the Government; if it furthers an important or substantial governmental interest; if the governmental interest is unrelated to the suppression of free expression; and if the incidental restriction on alleged First Amendment freedoms is no greater than is essential to the furtherance of that interest." (Footnotes omitted.) See also *Speiser v. Randall,* 357 U. S. 513 (1958).

[23] See also *Rabe v. Washington,* 405 U. S. 313, 317 (1972) (concurring opinion); *United States v. Reidel,* 402 U. S. 351, 360–362 (1971) (separate opinion); *Ginsberg v. New York,* 390 U. S. 629 (1968); *id.,* at 674–675 (dissenting opinion); *Redmond v. United States,* 384 U. S. 264, 265 (1966); *Ginzburg v. United States,* 383 U. S. 463 (1966); *id.,* at 498 n. 1 (dissenting opinion); *Memoirs v. Massachusetts,* 383 U. S. 413, 421 n. 8 (1966); *Jacobellis v. Ohio,* 378 U. S., at 195 (1964) (opinion of BRENNAN, J., joined by Goldberg, J.); *id.,* at 201 (dissenting opinion). See also Report of the Commission on Obscenity and Pornography 300–301 (1970) (focus of early obscenity laws on protection of youth).

[24] T. Emerson, The System of Freedom of Expression 496 (1970).

[25] See *ibid.*

[26] Indeed, since *Stanley* was decided, the President's Commission on Obscenity and Pornography has concluded:

"In sum, empirical research designed to clarify the question has found no evidence to date that exposure to explicit sexual materials plays a significant role in the causation of delinquent or criminal behavior among youth or adults. The Commission cannot conclude that exposure to erotic materials is a factor in the causation of sex crime or sex delinquency." Report of the Commission on Obscenity and Pornography 27 (1970) (footnote omitted).

To the contrary, the Commission found that "[o]n the positive side, explicit sexual materials are sought as a source of entertainment and information by substantial numbers of American adults. At times, these materials also appear to serve to increase and facilitate constructive communication about sexual matters within marriage." *Id.,* at 53.

[27] See Henkin, Morals and the Constitution: The Sin of Obscenity, 63 Col. L. Rev. 391, 395 (1963).

[28] "[I]n our system, undifferentiated fear or apprehension of disturbance is not enough to overcome the right to freedom of expression. Any departure from absolute regimentation may cause trouble. Any variation from the majority's opinion may inspire fear. Any word spoken, in class, in the lunchroom, or on the campus, that deviates from the views of another person may start an argument or cause a disturbance. But our Constitution says we must take this risk, *Terminiello v. Chicago,* 337 U. S. 1 (1949); and our history says that it is this sort of hazardous freedom—this kind of openness—that is the basis of our national strength and of the independence and vigor of Americans who grow up and live in this relatively permissive, often disputatious, society." *Tinker v. Des Moines School District,* 393 U. S. 503, 508–509 (1969). See also *Cohen v. California,* 403 U. S. 15, 23 (1971).

[29] The Court erroneously states, *Miller v. California, ante,* at 27, that the author of this opinion "indicates that suppression of unprotected obscene material is permissible to avoid exposure to unconsenting adults . . . and to juveniles . . . ." I defer expression of my views as to the scope of state power in these areas until cases squarely presenting these questions are before the Court. See n. 9, *supra; Miller v. California, supra* (dissenting opinion).

INTERSTATE TRANSPORTATION OF "OBSCENE" FILMS IS PROHIBITED: ". . . WE CANNOT SAY THAT THE CONSTITUTION FORBIDS COMPREHENSIVE FEDERAL REGULATION OF INTERSTATE TRANSPORTATION OF OBSCENE MATERIAL MERELY BECAUSE SUCH TRANSPORT MAY BE BY PRIVATE CARRIAGE, OR BECAUSE THE MATERIAL IS INTENDED FOR PRIVATE USE OF THE TRANSPORTER."

United States v. Orito, 413 U.S. 139 (1973)

MR. CHIEF JUSTICE BURGER delivered the opinion of the Court.

Appellee Orito was charged in the United States District Court for the Eastern District of Wisconsin with a violation of 18 U. S. C. § 1462 [1] in that he did "knowingly transport and carry in interstate commerce from San Francisco . . . to Milwaukee . . . by means of a common carrier, that is, Trans-World Airlines and North Central Airlines, copies of [specified] obscene, lewd, lascivious, and filthy materials . . . ." The materials specified included some 83 reels of film, with as many as eight to 10 copies of some of the films. Appellee moved to dismiss the indictment on the ground that the statute violated his First and Ninth Amendment rights.[2] The District Court granted his motion, holding that the statute was unconstitutionally overbroad since it failed to distinguish between "public" and "non-public" transportation of obscene material. The District Court interpreted this Court's decisions in *Griswold v. Connecticut,* 381 U. S. 479 (1965); *Redrup v. New York,* 386 U. S. 767 (1967); and *Stanley v. Georgia,* 394 U. S. 557 (1969), to establish the proposition that "non-public transportation" of obscene material was constitutionally protected.[3]

Although the District Court held the statute void on its face for overbreadth, it is not clear whether the statute was held to be overbroad because it covered transportation intended solely for the private use of the transporter, or because, regardless of the intended use of the material, the statute extended to "private carriage" or "nonpublic" transportation which in itself involved no risk of exposure to children or unwilling adults. The United States brought this direct appeal under the former 18 U. S. C. § 3731 (1964 ed.) now amended, Pub. L. 91–644, § 14 (a), 84 Stat. 1890. See *United States v. Spector,* 343 U. S. 169, 171 (1952).

The District Court erred in striking down 18 U. S. C. § 1462 and dismissing appellee's indictment on these "privacy" grounds. The essence of appellee's contentions is that *Stanley* has firmly established the right to possess obscene material in the privacy of the home and that this creates a correlative right to receive it, transport it, or distribute it. We have rejected that reasoning. This case was decided by the District Court before our decisions in *United States* v. *Thirty-seven Photographs*, 402 U. S. 363 (1971), and *United States* v. *Reidel*, 402 U. S. 351 (1971). Those holdings negate the idea that some zone of constitutionally protected privacy follows such material when it is moved outside the home area protected by *Stanley*.[4] *United States* v. *Thirty-seven Photographs, supra*, at 376 (opinion of WHITE, J.). *United States* v. *Reidel, supra*, at 354-356. See *United States* v. *Zacher*, 332 F. Supp. 883, 885-886 (ED Wis. 1971). But cf. *United States* v. *Thirty-seven Photographs, supra*, at 379 (STEWART, J., concurring).

The Constitution extends special safeguards to the privacy of the home, just as it protects other special privacy rights such as those of marriage, procreation, motherhood, child rearing, and education. See *Eisenstadt* v. *Baird*, 405 U. S. 438, 453-454 (1972); *Loving* v. *Virginia*, 388 U. S. 1, 12 (1967); *Griswold* v. *Connecticut, supra*, at 486; *Prince* v. *Massachusetts*, 321 U. S. 158, 166 (1944); *Skinner* v. *Oklahoma*, 316 U. S. 535, 541 (1942); *Pierce* v. *Society of Sisters*, 268 U. S. 510, 535 (1925). But viewing obscene films in a commercial theater open to the adult public, see *Paris Adult Theatre I* v. *Slaton, ante*, at 65-67, or transporting such films in common carriers in interstate commerce, has no claim to such special consideration.[5] It is hardly necessary to catalog the myriad activities that may be lawfully conducted within the privacy and confines of the home, but may be prohibited in public. The Court has consistently rejected constitutional protection for obscene material outside the home. See *United States* v. *12 200-ft. Reels of Film, ante*, at 126-129; *Miller* v. *California, ante*, at 23; *United States* v. *Reidel, supra*, at 354-356 (opinion of WHITE, J.); *id.*, at 357-360 (Harlan, J., concurring); *Roth* v. *United States*, 354 U. S. 476, 484-485 (1957).

Given (a) that obscene material is not protected under the First Amendment, *Miller* v. *California, supra*, *Roth* v. *United States, supra*. (b) that the Government has a legitimate interest in protecting the public commercial environment by preventing such material from entering the stream of commerce, see *Paris Adult Theatre I, ante*, at 57-64, and (c) that no constitutionally protected privacy is involved, *United States* v. *Thirty-seven Photographs, supra*, at 376 (opinion of WHITE, J.), we cannot say that the Constitution forbids comprehensive federal regulation of interstate transportation of obscene material merely because such transport may be by private carriage, or because the material is intended for the private use of the transporter. That the transporter has an abstract proprietary power to shield the obscene material from all others and to guard the material with the same privacy as in the home is not controlling. Congress may regulate on the basis of the natural tendency of material in the home being kept private and the contrary tendency once material leaves that area, regardless of a transporter's professed intent. Congress could reasonably determine such regulation to be necessary to effect per-

missible federal control of interstate commerce in obscene material, based as that regulation is on a legislatively determined risk of ultimate exposure to juveniles or to the public and the harm that exposure could cause. See *Paris Adult Theatre I* v. *Slaton, ante*, at 57-63. See also *United States* v. *Alpers*, 338 U. S. 680, 681-685 (1950); *Brooks* v. *United States*, 267 U. S. 432, 436-437 (1925); *Weber* v. *Freed*, 239 U. S. 325, 329-330 (1915). "The motive and purpose of a regulation of interstate commerce are matters for the legislative judgment upon the exercise of which the Constitution places no restriction and over which the courts are given no control. *McCray* v. *United States*, 195 U. S. 27; *Sonzinsky* v. *United States*, 300 U. S. 506, 513 and cases cited." *United States* v. *Darby*, 312 U. S. 100, 115 (1941). "It is sufficient to reiterate the well-settled principle that Congress may impose relevant conditions and requirements on those who use the channels of interstate commerce in order that those channels will not become the means of promoting or spreading evil, whether of a physical, moral or economic nature." *North American Co.* v. *SEC*, 327 U. S. 686, 705 (1946).[6]

As this case came to us on the District Court's summary dismissal of the indictment, no determination of the obscenity of the material involved has been made. Today, for the first time since *Roth* v. *United States, supra*, we have arrived at standards accepted by a majority of this Court for distinguishing obscene material, unprotected by the First Amendment, from protected free speech. See *Miller* v. *California, ante*, at 23-25, *United States* v. *12 200-ft. Reels of Film, ante*, at 130 n. 7. The decision of the District Court is therefore vacated and the case is remanded for reconsideration of the sufficiency of the indictment in light of *Miller* v. *California, supra*; *United States* v. *12 200-ft. Reels, supra*; and this opinion.

Vacated and remanded.

MR. JUSTICE DOUGLAS, dissenting.

We held in *Stanley* v. *Georgia*, 394 U. S. 557, that an individual reading or examining "obscene" materials in the privacy of his home is protected against state prosecution by reason of the First Amendment made applicable to the States by reason of the Fourteenth. We said:

"These are the rights that appellant is asserting in the case before us. He is asserting the right to read or observe what he pleases—the right to satisfy his intellectual and emotional needs in the privacy of his own home. He is asserting the right to be free from state inquiry into the contents of his library. Georgia contends that appellant does not have these rights, that there are certain types of materials that the individual may not read or even possess. Georgia justifies this assertion by arguing that the films in the present case are obscene. But we think that mere categorization of these films as 'obscene' is insufficient justification for such a drastic invasion of personal liberties guaranteed by the First and Fourteenth Amendments. Whatever may be the justifications for other statutes regulating obscenity, we do not think they reach into the privacy of one's

own home. If the First Amendment means anything, it means that a State has no business telling a man, sitting alone in his own house, what books he may read or what films he may watch. Our whole constitutional heritage rebels at the thought of giving government the power to control men's minds."
Id., at 565.

By that reasoning a person who reads an "obscene" book on an airline or bus or train is protected. So is he who carries an "obscene" book in his pocket during a journey for his intended personal enjoyment. So is he who carries the book in his baggage or has a trucking company move his household effects to a new residence. Yet 18 U. S. C. § 1462* makes such interstate carriage unlawful. Appellee therefore moved to dismiss the indictment on the ground that § 1462 is so broad as to cover "obscene" material designed for personal use.

The District Court granted the motion, holding that § 1462 was overbroad and in violation of the First Amendment.

The conclusion is too obvious for argument, unless we are to overrule *Stanley.* I would abide by *Stanley* and affirm the judgment dismissing the indictment.

Mr. Justice Brennan, with whom Mr. Justice Stewart and Mr. Justice Marshall join, dissenting.

We noted probable jurisdiction to consider the constitutionality of 18 U. S. C. § 1462, which makes it a federal offense to "[bring] into the United States, or any place subject to the jurisdiction thereof, or knowingly [use] any express company or other common carrier, for carriage in interstate or foreign commerce—(a) any obscene, lewd, lascivious, or filthy book, pamphlet, picture, motion-picture film, paper, letter, writing, print, or other matter of indecent character." Appellee was charged in a one-count indictment with having knowingly transported in interstate commerce over 80 reels of allegedly obscene motion picture film. Relying primarily on our decision in *Stanley* v. *Georgia,* 394 U. S. 557 (1969), the United States District Court for the Eastern District of Wisconsin dismissed the indictment, holding the statute unconstitutional on its face:

"To prevent the pandering of obscene materials or its exposure to children or to unwilling adults, the government has a substantial and valid interest to bar the non-private transportation of such materials. However, the statute which is now before the court does not so delimit the government's prerogatives; on its face, it forbids the transportation of obscene materials. Thus, it applies to non-public transportation in the absence of a special governmental interest. The statute is thus overbroad, in violation of the first and ninth amendments, and is therefore unconstitutional." 338 F. Supp. 308, 311 (ED Wis. 1970).

Under the view expressed in my dissent today in *Paris Adult Theatre I* v. *Slaton, ante,* p. 73, it is clear that the statute before us cannot stand. Whatever the extent of the Federal Government's power to bar the distribution of allegedly obscene material to juveniles or the offensive exposure of such material to unconsenting adults, the statute before us is clearly overbroad and unconstitutional on its face. See my dissent in *Miller* v. *California, ante,* p. 47. I would therefore affirm the judgment of the District Court.

COURT'S OPINION NOTES

[1] Title 18 U. S. C. § 1462 provides in pertinent part:
"Whoever brings into the United States, or any place subject to the jurisdiction thereof, or knowingly uses any express company or other common carrier, for carriage in interstate or foreign commerce—
"(a) any obscene, lewd, lascivious, or filthy book, pamphlet, picture, motion-picture film, paper, letter, writing, print, or other matter of indecent character; . . .

.   .   .   .

"Shall be fined not more than $5,000 or imprisoned not more than five years, or both, for the first such offense and shall be fined not more than $10,000 or imprisoned not more than ten years, or both, for each such offense thereafter."
[2] Appellee also moved to dismiss the indictment on the grounds that 18 U. S. C. § 1462 does not require proof of *scienter.* That issue was not reached by the District Court and is not before us now.
[3] The District Court stated:
"By analogy, it follows that with the right to read obscene matters comes the right to transport or to receive such material when done in a fashion that does not pander it or impose it upon unwilling adults or upon minors.

.   .   .   .

"I find no meaningful distinction between the private possession which was held to be protected in *Stanley* and the non-public transportation which the statute at bar proscribes." 338 F. Supp. 308, 310 (1970).
[4] "These are the rights that appellant is asserting in the case before us. He is asserting the right to read or observe what he pleases—the right to satisfy his intellectual and emotional needs *in the privacy of his own home.*" *Stanley* v. *Georgia,* 394 U. S. 557, 565 (1969). (Emphasis added.)
[5] The Solicitor General indicates that the tariffs of most, if not all, common carriers include a right of inspection. Resorting to common carriers, like entering a place of public accommodation, does not involve the privacies associated with the home. See *United States* v. *Thirty-seven Photographs,* 402 U. S. 363, 376 (1971) (opinion of White, J.); *United States* v. *Reidel,* 402 U. S. 351, 359–360 (1971) (Harlan, J., concurring); *Poe* v. *Ullman,* 367 U. S. 497, 551–552 (1961) (Harlan, J., dissenting); *Miller* v. *United States,* 431 F. 2d 655, 657 (CA9 1970); *United States* v. *Melvin,* 419 F. 2d 136, 139 (CA4 1969).
[6] "Congress can certainly regulate interstate commerce to the extent of forbidding and punishing the use of such commerce as an agency to promote immorality, dishonesty or the spread of any evil or harm to the people of other States from the State of origin. In doing this it is merely exercising the police power, for the benefit of the public, within the field of interstate commerce. . . . In the *Lottery Case,* 188 U. S. 321, it was held that Congress might pass a law punishing the transmission of lottery tickets from one State to another, in order to prevent the carriage of those tickets to be sold in other States and thus demoralize, through a spread of the gambling habit, individuals who were likely to purchase. . . . In *Hoke* v. *United States,* 227 U. S. 308 and *Caminetti* v. *United States,* 242 U. S. 470, the so-called White Slave Traffic Act, which was construed to punish any person engaged in enticing a woman from one State to another for immoral ends, whether for commercial purposes or otherwise, was valid because it was intended to prevent the use of interstate commerce to facilitate prostitution or concubinage, and other forms of immorality. . . . In *Weber* v. *Freed,* 239 U. S. 325, it was held that Congress had power to prohibit the importation of pictorial representations of prize fights designed for public exhibition, because of the demoralizing effect of such exhibitions in the State of destination." *Brooks* v. *United States,* 267 U. S. 432, 436–437 (1925).

JUSTICE DOUGLAS'S OPINION NOTES

*"Whoever brings into the United States, or any place subject to the jurisdiction thereof, or knowingly uses any express company or other common carrier, for carriage in interstate or foreign commerce—

"(a) any obscene, lewd, lascivious, or filthy book, pamphlet, picture, motion-picture film, paper, letter, writing, print, or other matter of indecent character."

JUSTICES BURGER, BLACKMUN, POWELL, REHNQUIST, AND WHITE DECLARE FEDERAL STATUTE PROHIBITING IMPORTATION OF OBSCENE MATERIALS CONSTITUTIONAL; "WE ARE NOT DISPOSED TO EXTEND THE PRECISE, CAREFULLY LIMITED HOLDING OF *STANLEY* TO PERMIT IMPORTATION OF ADMITTEDLY OBSCENE MATERIAL SIMPLY BECAUSE THEY ARE IMPORTED FOR PRIVATE USE ONLY. TO ALLOW SUCH A CLAIM WOULD BE NOT UNLIKE COMPELLING THE GOVERNMENT TO PERMIT IMPORTATION OF PROHIBITED OR CONTROLLED DRUGS FOR PRIVATE CONSUMPTION AS LONG AS SUCH DRUGS ARE NOT FOR PUBLIC DISTRIBUTION OR SALE."

United States v. 12 200-Ft. Reels of Film, 413 U.S. 123 (1973)

MR. CHIEF JUSTICE BURGER delivered the opinion of the Court.

We noted probable jurisdiction to review a summary decision of the United States District Court for the Central District of California holding that § 305(a) of the Tariff Act of 1930, 46 Stat. 688, as amended, 19 U. S. C. § 1305 (a) was "unconstitutional on its face" and dismissing a forfeiture action brought under that statute.[1] The statute provides in pertinent part:

"All persons are prohibited from importing into the United States from any foreign country . . . any obscene book, pamphlet, paper, writing, advertisement, circular, print, picture, drawing, or other representation, figure, or image on or of paper or other material, or any cast, instrument, or other article which is obscene or immoral . . . . No such articles whether imported separately or contained in packages with other goods entitled to entry, shall be admitted to entry; and all such articles and, unless it appears to the satisfaction of the appropriate customs officer that the obscene or other prohibited articles contained in the package were inclosed therein without the knowledge or consent of the importer, owner, agent, or consignee, the entire contents of the package in which such articles are contained, shall be subject to seizure and forfeiture as hereinafter provided . . . . *Provided further*, That the Secretary of the Treasury may, in his discretion, admit the so-called classics or books of recognized and established literary or scientific merit, but may,

in his discretion, admit such classics or books only when imported for noncommercial purposes."

On April 2, 1970, the claimant Paladini sought to carry movie films, color slides, photographs and other printed and graphic material into the United States from Mexico. The materials were seized as being obscene by customs officers at a port of entry, Los Angeles Airport, and made the subject of a forfeiture action under 19 U. S. C. § 1305 (a). The District Court dismissed the Government's complaint, relying on the decision of a three-judge district court in *United States v. Thirty-seven Photographs*, 309 F. Supp. 36 (CD Cal. 1970), which we later reversed, 402 U. S. 363 (1971). That case concerned photographs concededly imported for commercial purposes. The narrow issue directly presented in this case, and not in *Thirty-seven Photographs*, is whether the United States may constitutionally prohibit importation of obscene material which the importer claims is for private, personal use and possession only.[2]

Import restrictions and searches of persons or packages at the national borders rest on different considerations and different rules of constitutional law from domestic regulations. The Constitution gives Congress broad, comprehensive powers "[t]o regulate Commerce with foreign Nations." Art. I, § 8, cl. 3. Historically such broad powers have been necessary to prevent smuggling and to prevent prohibited articles from entry. See *United States v. Thirty-seven Photographs*, 402 U. S., at 376–377 (opinion of WHITE, J.); *Carroll v. United States*, 267 U. S. 132, 154 (1925); *Brolan v. United States*, 236 U. S. 216, 218 (1915); *Boyd v. United States*, 116 U. S. 616, 623–624 (1886); *Alexander v. United States*, 362 F. 2d 379, 382 (CA9), cert. denied, 385 U. S. 977 (1966). The plenary power of Congress to regulate imports is illustrated in a holding of this Court which sustained the validity of an Act of Congress prohibiting the importation of "any film or other pictorial representation of any prize fight . . . designed to be used or [that] may be used for purposes of public exhibition"[3] in view of "the complete power of Congress over foreign commerce and its authority to prohibit the introduction of foreign articles . . . . *Buttfield* v. *Stranahan*, 192 U. S. 470; *The Abby Dodge*, 223 U. S. 166, 176; *Brolan* v. *United States*, 236 U. S. 216." *Weber* v. *Freed*, 239 U. S. 325, 329 (1915).

Claimant relies on the First Amendment and our decision in *Stanley v. Georgia*, 394 U. S. 557 (1969). But it is now well established that obscene material is not protected by the First Amendment. *Roth v. United States*, 354 U. S. 476, 485 (1957), reaffirmed today in *Miller v. California, ante*, at 23. As we have noted in *United States v. Orito, post*, at 141–143, also decided today, *Stanley* depended, not on any First Amendment right to purchase or possess obscene materials, but on the right to privacy in the home. Three concurring Justices indicated that the case could have been disposed of on Fourth Amendment grounds without reference to the nature of the materials. *Stanley v. Georgia, supra*, at 569 (STEWART, J., joined by BRENNAN and WHITE, JJ., concurring).

In particular, claimant contends that, under *Stanley*, the right to possess obscene material in the privacy of the home creates a right to acquire it or import it from another country. This overlooks the explicitly narrow and precisely delineated privacy right on which *Stanley* rests. That holding reflects no more than what Mr. Justice Harlan characterized as the law's "solicitude to protect the privacies of the life within [the home]." *Poe* v. *Ullman,* 367 U. S. 497, 551 (1961) (dissenting opinion).[4] The seductive plausibility of single steps in a chain of evolutionary development of a legal rule is often not perceived until a third, fourth, or fifth "logical" extension occurs. Each step, when taken, appeared a reasonable step in relation to that which preceded it, although the aggregate or end result is one that would never have been seriously considered in the first instance.[5] This kind of gestative propensity calls for the "line drawing" familiar in the judicial, as in the legislative process: "thus far but not beyond." Perspectives may change, but our conclusion is that *Stanley* represents such a line of demarcation; and it is not unreasonable to assume that had it not been so delineated, *Stanley* would not be the law today. See *United States* v. *Reidel,* 402 U. S. 351, 354–356 (1971); *id.,* at 357–360 (Harlan, J., concurring). See also *Miller* v. *United States,* 431 F. 2d 655, 657 (CA9 1970); *United States* v. *Fragus,* 428 F. 2d 1211, 1213 (CA5 1970); *United States* v. *Melvin,* 419 F. 2d 136, 139 (CA4 1969); *Gable* v. *Jenkins,* 309 F. Supp. 998, 1000–1001 (ND Ga. 1969), aff'd, 397 U. S. 592 (1970). Cf. *Karalexis* v. *Byrne,* 306 F. Supp. 1363, 1366 (Mass. 1969), vacated on other grounds *sub nom. Byrne* v. *Karalexis,* 401 U. S. 216 (1971).

We are not disposed to extend the precise, carefully limited holding of *Stanley* to permit importation of admittedly obscene material simply because they are imported for private use only. To allow such a claim would be not unlike compelling the Government to permit importation of prohibited or controlled drugs for private consumption as long as such drugs are not for public distribution or sale. We have already indicated that the protected right to possess obscene material in the privacy of one's home does not give rise to a correlative right to have someone sell or give it to others. *United States* v. *Thirty-seven Photographs, supra,* at 376 (opinion of WHITE, J.), and *United States* v. *Reidel, supra,* at 355. Nor is there any correlative right to transport obscene material in interstate commerce. *United States* v. *Orito, post,* at 142–144.[6] It follows that *Stanley* does not permit one to go abroad and bring such material into the country for private purposes. "*Stanley's* emphasis was on the freedom of thought and mind in the privacy of the home. But a port of entry is not a traveler's home." *United States* v. *Thirty-seven Photographs, supra,* at 376 (opinion of WHITE, J.).

This is not to say that Congress could not allow an exemption for private use, with or without appropriate guarantees such as bonding, or permit the transportation of obscene material under conditions insuring privacy. But Congress has not seen fit to do so, and the holding in *Roth* v. *United States, supra,* read with the narrow holding of *Stanley* v. *Georgia, supra,* does not afford a basis for claimant's arguments. The Constitution does not compel, and Congress has not authorized, an exception for private use of obscene material. See *Paris Adult Theatre I* v. *Slaton, ante,* at 64–69; *United States* v. *Reidel, supra,* at 357; *Memoirs* v. *Massachusetts,* 383 U. S. 413, 462 (1966) (WHITE, J., dissenting).

The attack on the overbreadth of the statute is thus foreclosed, but, independently, we should note that it is extremely difficult to control the uses to which obscene material is put once it enters this country. Even single copies, represented to be for personal use, can be quickly and cheaply duplicated by modern technology thus facilitating wide-scale distribution. While it is true that a large volume of obscene material on microfilm could rather easily be smuggled into the United States by mail, or otherwise, and could be enlarged or reproduced for commercial purposes, Congress is not precluded from barring some avenues of illegal importation because avenues exist that are more difficult to regulate. See *American Power & Light Co.* v. *SEC,* 329 U. S. 90, 99–100 (1946).

As this case came to us on the District Court's summary dismissal of the forfeiture action, no determination of the obscenity of the materials involved has been made. We have today arrived at standards for testing the constitutionality of state legislation regulating obscenity. See *Miller* v. *California, ante,* at 23–25. These standards are applicable to federal legislation.[7] The judgment of the District Court is vacated and the case is remanded for further proceedings consistent with this opinion, *Miller* v. *California, supra,* and *United States* v. *Orito, supra,* both decided today.

Vacated and remanded.

MR. JUSTICE DOUGLAS, dissenting.

I know of no constitutional way by which a book, tract, paper, postcard, or film may be made contraband because of its contents. The Constitution never purported to give the Federal Government censorship or oversight over literature or artistic productions, save as they might be governed by the Patent and Copyright Clause of Art. I, § 8, cl. 8, of the Constitution.[1] To be sure the Colonies had enacted statutes which limited the freedom of speech, see *Roth* v. *United States,* 354 U. S. 476, 482–484, nn. 10–13, and in the early 19th century the States punished obscene libel as a common-law crime. *Knowles* v. *State,* 3 Day 103 (Conn. 1808) (signs depicting "monster"); *Commonwealth* v. *Holmes,* 17 Mass. 336 (1821) (John Cleland's Memoirs of a Woman of Pleasure); *State* v. *Appling,* 25 Mo. 315, 316 (1857) (utterance of words "too vulgar to be inserted in this opinion"); *Commonwealth* v. *Sharpless,* 2 S. & R. 91, 92 (1815) ("lewd, wicked, scandalous, infamous, . . . and indecent posture with a woman").

To construe this history, as this Court does today in *Miller* v. *California, ante,* p. 15, as qualifying the plain import of the First Amendment is both a *non sequitur* and a disregard of the Tenth Amendment.

"[W]hatever may [have been] the form which the several States . . . adopted in making declarations in favor of particular rights," James Madison, the author of the First Amendment, tells us, "the great object in view [was] to limit and qualify the powers of [the Federal] Government, by excepting out of the grant of power those cases in which the Government ought not to act, or to act only in a particular mode." 1

Annals of Cong. 437. Surely no one should argue that the retention by the States of vestiges of established religions after the enactment of the Establishment and Free Exercise Clauses saps these clauses of their meaning.[2] Yet it was precisely upon such reasoning that this Court, in *Roth,* exempted the bawdry from the protection of the First Amendment.

When it was enacted, the Bill of Rights applied only to the Federal Government, *Barron* v. *Mayor of Baltimore,* 7 Pet. 243, and the Tenth Amendment reserved the residuum of power to the States and the people. That the States, at some later date, may have exercised this reserved power in the form of laws restricting expression in no wise detracts from the express prohibition of the First Amendment. Only when the Fourteenth Amendment was passed did it become even possible to argue that through it the First Amendment became applicable to the States. But that goal was not attained until the ruling of this Court in 1931 that the reach of the Fourteenth Amendment included the First Amendment. See *Stromberg* v. *California,* 283 U. S. 359, 368.

At the very beginning, however, the First Amendment applied only to the Federal Government and there is not the slightest evidence that the Framers intended to put the newly created federal regime into the role of ombudsman over literature. Tying censorship to the movement of literature or films in interstate commerce or into foreign commerce would have been an easy way for a government of delegated powers to impair the liberty of expression. It was to bar such suppression that we have the First Amendment. I dare say Jefferson and Madison would be appalled at what the Court espouses today.

The First Amendment was the product of a robust, not a prudish, age. The four decades prior to its enactment "saw the publication, virtually without molestation from any authority, of two classics of pornographic literature." D. Loth, The Erotic in Literature 108 (1961). In addition to William King's The Toast, there was John Cleland's Memoirs of a Woman of Pleasure which has been described as the "most important work of genuine pornography that has been published in English . . . ." L. Markun, Mrs. Grundy 191 (1930). In England, Harris' List of Covent Garden Ladies, a catalog used by prostitutes to advertise their trade, enjoyed open circulation. N. St. John-Stevas, Obscenity and the Law 25 (1956). Bibliographies of pornographic literature list countless erotic works which were published in this time. See, *e. g.,* A. Craig, Suppressed Books (1963); P. Fraxi, Catena Librorum Tacendorum (1885); W. Gallichan, The Poison of Prudery (1929); D. Loth, *supra;* L. Markun, *supra.* This was the age when Benjamin Franklin wrote his "Advice to a Young Man on Choosing a Mistress" and "A Letter to the Royal Academy at Brussels." "When the United States became a nation, none of the fathers of the country were any more concerned than Franklin with the question of pornography. John Quincy Adams had a strongly puritanical bent for a man of his literary interests, and even he wrote of Tom Jones that it was 'one of the best novels in the language.'" Loth, *supra,* at 120. It was in this milieu that Madison admonished against any "distinction between the freedom and licentiousness of the press."

S. Padover, The Complete Madison 295 (1953). The Anthony Comstocks, the Thomas Bowdlers and Victorian hypocrisy—the predecessors of our present obscenity laws—had yet to come upon the stage.[3]

Julius Goebel, our leading expert on colonial law, does not so much as allude to punishment of obscenity.[4] J. Goebel, Development of Legal Institutions (1946); J. Goebel, Felony and Misdemeanor (1937); J. Goebel & T. Naughton, Law Enforcement in Colonial New York (1944).

Nor is there any basis in the legal history antedating the First Amendment for the creation of an obscenity exception. *Memoirs* v. *Massachusetts,* 383 U. S. 413, 424 (DOUGLAS, J., concurring). The first reported case involving obscene conduct was not until 1663. There, the defendant was fined for "shewing himself naked in a balkony, and throwing down bottles (pist in) vi & armis among the people in Convent Garden, contra pacem, and to the scandal of the Government." *Sir Charles Sydlyes Case,* 83 Eng. Rep. 1146–1147 (K. B. 1663). Rather than being a fountainhead for a body of law proscribing obscene literature, later courts viewed this case simply as an instance of assault, criminal breach of the peace, or indecent exposure. *E. g., Bradlaugh* v. *Queen,* L. R. 3 Q. B. 569, 634 (1878); *Rex* v. *Curl,* 93 Eng. Rep. 849, 851 (K. B. 1727) (Fortescue, J., dissenting).

The advent of the printing press spurred censorship in England, but the ribald and the obscene were not, at first, within the scope of that which was officially banned. The censorship of the Star Chamber and the licensing of books under the Tudors and Stuarts was aimed at the blasphemous or heretical, the seditious or treasonous. At that date, the government made no effort to prohibit the dissemination of obscenity. Rather, obscene literature was considered to raise a moral question properly cognizable only by ecclesiastical, and not the common-law, courts.[5] "A crime that shakes religion (a), as profaneness on the stage, &c. is indictable (b); but writing an obscene book, as that intitled, 'The Fifteen Plagues of a Maidenhead,' is not indictable, but punishable only in the Spiritual Court (c)." *Queen* v. *Read,* 88 Eng. Rep. 953 (K. B. 1707). To be sure, *Read* was ultimately overruled and the crime of obscene libel established. *Rex* v. *Curl, supra.* It is noteworthy, however, that the only reported cases of obscene libel involved politically unpopular defendants. *Ibid.; Rex* v. *Wilkes,* 98 Eng. Rep. 327 (K. B. 1770).

In any event, what we said in *Bridges* v. *California,* 314 U. S. 252, 264–265 (1941), would dispose of any argument that earlier restrictions on free expression should be read into the First Amendment:

"[T]o assume that English common law in this field became ours is to deny the generally accepted historical belief that 'one of the objects of the Revolution was to get rid of the English common law on liberty of speech and of the press.' . . .

"More specifically, it is to forget the environment in which the First Amendment was ratified. In presenting the proposals which were later embodied in the Bill of Rights, James Madison, the leader in the preparation of the First Amendment, said: 'Although I know whenever the great rights, the trial by jury, freedom of the press, or liberty of conscience, come in question in that body [Parliament], the invasion of them is resisted by able advocates, yet their Magna Charta does not contain any one provision for the security of those rights, respecting which the people of America are most alarmed. The freedom of the press and rights of conscience, those choicest privileges of the people, are unguarded in the British Constitution.' "

This Court has nonetheless engrafted an exception upon the clear meaning of words written in the 18th century. But see *id.*, at 264–265; *Grosjean* v. *American Press Co.*, 297 U. S. 233, 249.

Our efforts to define obscenity have not been productive of meaningful standards. What is "obscene" is highly subjective, varying from judge to judge, from juryman to juryman.

"The fireside banter of Chaucer's Canterbury Pilgrims was disgusting obscenity to Victorian-type moralists whose co-ed granddaughters shock the Victorian-type moralists of today. Words that are obscene in England have not a hint of impropriety in the United States, and *vice versa.* The English language is full of innocent words and phrases with obscene ancestry." I. Brant, The Bill of Rights 490 (1965).

So speaks our leading First Amendment historian; and he went on to say that this Court's decisions "seemed to multiply standards instead of creating one." *Id.*, at 491. The reason is not the inability or mediocrity of judges.

"What is the reason for this multiple sclerosis of the judicial faculty? It is due to the fact stated above, that obscenity is a matter of taste and social custom, not of fact." *Id.*, at 491–492.

Taste and custom are part of it; but, as I have said on other occasions,[6] the neuroses of judges, lawmakers, and of the so-called "experts" who have taken the place of Anthony Comstock, also play a major role.

Finally, it is ironic to me that in this Nation many pages must be written and many hours spent to explain why a person who can read whatever he desires, *Stanley* v. *Georgia*, 394 U. S. 557, may not without violating a law carry that literature in his briefcase or bring it home from abroad. Unless there is that ancillary right, one's *Stanley* rights could be realized, as has been suggested, only if one wrote or designed a tract in his attic and printed or processed it in his basement, so as to be able to read it in his study. *United States* v. *Thirty-seven Photographs*, 402 U. S. 363, 382 (Black, J., dissenting).

Most of the items that come this way denounced as "obscene" are in my view trash. I would find few, if any, that had by my standards any redeeming social value. But what may be trash to me may be prized by others.[7] Moreover, by what right under the Constitution do five of us have to impose our set of values on the literature of the day? There is danger in that course, the danger of bending the popular mind to new norms of conformity. There is, of course, also danger in tolerance, for tolerance often leads to robust or even ribald productions. Yet that is part of the risk of the First Amendment.

Irving Brant summed the matter up:

"Blessed with a form of government that requires universal liberty of thought and expression, blessed with a social and economic system built on that same foundation, the American people have created the danger they fear by denying to themselves the liberties they cherish." Brant, *supra*, at 493.

MR. JUSTICE BRENNAN, with whom MR. JUSTICE STEWART and MR. JUSTICE MARSHALL join, dissenting.

We noted probable jurisdiction to consider the constitutionality of 19 U. S. C. § 1305(a), which prohibits all persons from "importing into the United States from any foreign country . . . any obscene book, pamphlet, paper, writing, advertisement, circular, print, picture, drawing, or other representation, figure, or image on or of paper or other material, or any cast, instrument, or other article which is obscene or immoral." Pursuant to that provision, customs authorities at Los Angeles seized certain movie films, color slides, photographs, and other materials, which claimant sought to import into the United States. A complaint was filed in the United States District Court for the Central District of California for forfeiture of these items as obscene. Relying on the decision in *United States* v. *Thirty-seven Photographs*, 309 F. Supp. 36 (CD Cal. 1969), which held the statute unconstitutional on its face, the District Court dismissed the complaint. Although we subsequently reversed the decision in *United States* v. *Thirty-seven Photographs*, 402 U. S. 363 (1971), the reasoning that led us to uphold the statute is no longer viable, under the view expressed in my dissent today in *Paris Adult Theatre I* v. *Slaton, ante,* p. 73. Whatever the extent of the Federal Government's power to bar the distribution of allegedly obscene material to juveniles or the offensive exposure of such material to unconsenting adults, the statute before us is, in my view, clearly overbroad and unconstitutional on its face. See my dissent in *Miller* v. *California, ante,* p. 47. I would therefore affirm the judgment of the District Court.

COURT'S OPINION NOTES

[1] The United States brought this direct appeal under 28 U. S. C. § 1252. See *Clark* v. *Gabriel*, 393 U. S. 256, 258 (1968).

[2] On the day the complaint was dismissed, claimant filed an affidavit with the District Court stating that none of the seized materials "were imported by me for any commercial purpose but were intended to be used and possessed by me personally." In conjunction with the Government's motion to stay the order of dismissal, denied below but granted by MR. JUSTICE BRENNAN, the Government conceded it had no evidence to contradict claimant's affidavit and did not "contest the fact that this was a private importation."

[3] Act of July 31, 1912, c. 263, § 1, 37 Stat. 241.

[4] Nor can claimant rely on any other sphere of constitutionally protected privacy, such as that which encompasses the intimate medical problems of family, marriage, and motherhood. See *Paris Adult Theatre I* v. *Slaton, ante,* at 65–67, and *United States* v. *Orito, post,* at 142–143.

[5] Mr. Justice Holmes had this kind of situation in mind when he said:

"All rights tend to declare themselves absolute to their logical extreme. Yet all in fact are limited by the neighborhood of principles of policy which are other than those on which the particular right is founded, and which become strong enough to hold their own when a certain point is reached." *Hudson County Water Co.* v. *McCarter,* 209 U. S. 349, 355 (1908).

⁶ In *Caminetti* v. *United States,* 242 U. S. 470 (1917), and *Hoke* v. *United States,* 227 U. S. 308 (1913), this Court upheld the "so-called White Slave Traffic Act, which was construed to punish any person engaged in enticing a woman from one State to another for immoral ends, *whether for commercial purposes or otherwise,* . . . because it was intended to prevent the use of interstate commerce to facilitate prostitution or concubinage, and other forms of immorality." *Brooks* v. *United States,* 267 U. S. 432, 437 (1925) (emphasis added).

⁷ We further note that, while we must leave to state courts the construction of state legislation, we do have a duty to authoritatively construe federal statutes where " 'a serious doubt of constitutionality is raised' " and " 'a construction of the statute is fairly possible by which the question may be avoided.' " *United States* v. *Thirty-seven Photographs,* 402 U. S. 363, 369 (1971) (opinion of WHITE, J.), quoting from *Crowell* v. *Benson,* 285 U. S. 22, 62 (1932). If and when such a "serious doubt" is raised as to the vagueness of the words "obscene," "lewd," "lascivious," "filthy," "indecent," or "immoral" as used to describe regulated material in 19 U. S. C. § 1305 (a) and 18 U. S. C. § 1462, see *United States* v. *Orito, post,* at 140 n. 1, we are prepared to construe such terms as limiting regulated material to patently offensive representations or descriptions of that specific "hard core" sexual conduct given as examples in *Miller* v. *California, ante,* at 25. See *United States* v. *Thirty-seven Photographs, supra,* at 369–374 (opinion of WHITE, J.). Of course, Congress could always define other specific "hard core" conduct.

JUSTICE DOUGLAS'S OPINION NOTES

¹ Even the copyright power is limited by the freedoms secured by the First Amendment. *Lee* v. *Runge,* 404 U. S. 887, 892–893 (DOUGLAS, J., dissenting); Nimmer, Does Copyright Abridge the First Amendment Guarantees of Free Speech and Press?, 17 U. C. L. A. L. Rev. 1180 (1970).

² Thus, the suggestion that most of the States that had ratified the Constitution punished blasphemy or profanity, is irrelevant to our inquiry here.

³ Separating the worthwhile from the worthless has largely been a matter of individual taste because significant governmental sanctions against obscene literature are of relatively recent vintage, not having developed until the Victorian Age of the mid-19th century. N. St. John-Stevas, Obscenity and the Law 1–85 (1956). See T. Emerson, The System of Freedom of Expression 468–469 (1970); J. Paul & M. Schwartz, Federal Censorship, c. 1 (1961); Report of the Commission on Obscenity and Pornography 349–354 (1970). In this country, the first federal prohibition on obscenity was not until the Tariff Act of 1842, c. 270, § 28, 5 Stat. 566. England, which gave us the infamous Star Chamber and a history of licensing of publishing, did not raise a statutory bar to the importation of obscenity until 1853, Customs Consolidation Act, 16 & 17 Vict., c. 107, and waited until 1857 to enact a statute which banned obscene literature outright. Lord Campbell's Act, 20 & 21 Vict., c. 83.

⁴ The only colonial statute mentioning the word "obscene" was Acts and Laws of the Province of Mass. Bay, c. CV, § 8 (1712), in Mass. Bay Colony Charter & Laws 399 (1814). It did so, however, in the context of "composing, writing, printing or publishing . . . any filthy, obscene, or profane song, pamphlet, libel or mock sermon, in imitation or in mimicking of preaching, or any other part of divine worship" and must, therefore, be placed with the other colonial blasphemy laws. *E. g.,* An Act for the Punishment of divers capital and other Felonies, Conn. Acts, Laws, Charter & Articles of Confederation 66, 67 (1784); Act of 1723, c. 16, § 1, Digest of the Laws of Md. 92 (Herty 1799).

⁵ Lord Coke's De Libellis Famosis, 77 Eng. Rep. 250 (1605), for example, was the definitive statement of the common law of libel but made no mention of the misdemeanor of obscene libel.

⁶ *Ginsberg* v. *New York,* 390 U. S. 629, 655–656, 661–671 (DOUGLAS, J., dissenting).

⁷ *Ginzburg* v. *United States,* 383 U. S. 463, 491 (DOUGLAS, J., dissenting).

THE FILM "CARNAL KNOWLEDGE" IS DECLARED OBSCENE BY THE GEORGIA SUPREME COURT

Jenkins v. State, 199 S.E.2d 183 (1973)

JORDAN, Justice.

Billy Jenkins appeals his conviction and sentence for the offense of distributing obscene materials. The conviction is based on the fact that he exhibited the film Carnal Knowledge in a movie theater in Albany, Georgia.

The threshold question to be decided is whether or not the showing of the film Carnal Knowledge violates Code Ann. Ch. 26—21 prohibiting the distribution of obscene materials. The trial jury, under proper instructions from the court, has found the defendant guilty. After a review of the record and a viewing of the film by this court we affirm.

Code Ann. § 26—2101(b) provides that "Material is obscene if considered as a whole, applying community standards, its predominant appeal is to prurient interest, that is, a shameful or morbid interest in nudity, sex or excretion, and utterly without redeeming social value and if, in addition, it goes substantially beyond customary limits of candor in describing or representing such matters." The accusation charges the defendant "with the offense of distributing obscene material." The accusation without expressly referring to Code Ann. § 26—2105 is then cast in the language of the prohibited acts as defined in Code Ann. § 26—2011. The appellant contends that the accusation is defective in that it fails to include the definition of obscene materials as defined in Code Ann. § 26—2101(b). This view is adopted by the minority which seizes upon this alleged defect to hold Code Ann. § 26—2105 unconstitutional.

It is our view that a statute can provide criminal punishment without the definition of obscenity being included within that specific code section. The chapter in which Code Ann. § 26—2105 is included at its very beginning amply defines obscenity and this particular Code section, which is merely a part of the chapter, must be read in accordance with the entire chapter. This court has held that sections of the code which relate to the same subject matter shall be construed together. See Touchton v. Echols County, 211 Ga. 85, 87, 84 S.E.2d 81. It seems clear then that the definition of obscenity as set forth in the chapter applies to all of the code sections dealing with this same question.

The trial court correctly charged this definition of obscenity as the guideline for the jury to apply in this particular case. In Roth v. United States, 354 U.S. 476, 77 S.Ct. 1304, 1 L.Ed.2d 1498, it was held that "obscenity is not within the area of constitutionally protected freedom of speech or press." Memoirs v. Mass., 383 U.S. 413, 86 S.Ct. 975, 16 L.Ed.2d 1, gave a test of obscenity to the effect that it must be established that the dominant theme appeals to prurient interest, the material affronts contemporary community standards, and is utterly without redeeming social value. This test has been included in our law (Code Ann. § 26—2101(b) thus making our present statute considerably more restrictive than the new test set forth in the recent case of Miller v. California, —— U.S. ——, 93 S.Ct. 2607, 37 L.Ed.2d 419. The Miller case, supra, further held that juries can consider State or local community standards in lieu of "national standards," thereby bringing the holding of this court in Gornto v. State, 227 Ga. 46, 178 S.E.2d 894 in line with Miller, supra, on this point.

This court has held that the exhibition of an obscene motion picture is a crime involving the welfare of the public at large, since it is contrary to the standards of decency and propriety of the community as a whole. Evans Theatre Corporation v. Slaton, 227 Ga. 377, 180 S.E.2d 712. In Slaton v. Paris Adult Theater I, 228 Ga. 343, 185 S.E.2d 768 this court held that the films involved in that case were "hard core" pornography and that the commercial exhibition of such pictures is not protected by the first amendment. The Supreme Court of the United States which in effect affirmed the *Paris* case, supra, held that states have a legitimate interest in regulating commerce in obscene material and its exhibition in places of public accommodation, including "adult" theaters; further holding that the exhibition of obscene material in such places of public accommodation is not protected by any constitutional doctrine of privacy, and that a commercial theater cannot be equated with a private home. See Paris Adult Theatre I v. Slaton, -- U.S. --, 93 S.Ct. 2628, 37 L.Ed.2d 446.

We hold that the evidence in this record amply supports the verdict of guilty by the showing of the film Carnal Knowledge in violation of the definition of distributing obscene materials under our Georgia statutes.

Judgment affirmed.

All the Justices concur, except UNDERCOFLER, HAWES and GUNTER, JJ., who dissent.

GUNTER, Justice (dissenting).

The majority has today affirmed the criminal conviction of the appellant for showing the motion picture "Carnal Knowledge" to a theatre audience in Dougherty County, Georgia. The majority has held that the exhibition of this film in this "local community" is not entitled to the protection of the First Amendment as applied to Georgia and this "local community" by the Fourteenth Amendment. I am in disagreement with the majority, and I respectfully dissent. Having viewed this film with the other members of the court, I must say, quite subjectively of course, that it is inconceivable to me that this work can be relegated to that area of verbal, written, and performing expression which falls outside of the protection of the First Amendment to the Constitution of the United States. Today's majority decision has drastically narrowed the concept of the First Amendment as applied to the performing arts in Georgia and "local communities" in Georgia.

I am in disagreement with my brothers of the majority for several reasons, and I shall attempt to set them forth in this dissent.

I.

The decision of the Supreme Court of the United States in Miller v. California, -- U.S. -- 93 S.Ct. 2607, 37 L.Ed.2d 419 (decided June 21, 1973), inaugurated a new era in the continuing constitutional contest between obscenity-pornography and the First Amendment. As the Miller decision said, the history of the Supreme Court's obscenity decisions has been "somewhat tortured." at --, 93 S.Ct. at 2607. I would go one step further and say that the Supreme Court's decisions in this area, handed down during the recent and relatively short period of the First Amendment's entire history, have made it impossible for a dealer in such material to make a determination, with any degree of certainty, as to whether the material falls within the protection of the First Amendment or falls outside of its protection.

Miller gave a new definition of pornographic, unprotected material; Miller laid down basic guidelines for the trior of fact to use in determining what is protected material from what is unprotected material; Miller changed the yardstick for measuring obscene material from "national standards" to "contemporary community standards"; and Miller reiterated that if the application of its definitions, guidelines, and standards does not sufficiently protect First Amendment rights in any case, then First Amendment values are "adequately protected by the ultimate power of appellate courts to conduct an independent review of constitutional claims, when necessary."

In the case at bar the film "Carnal Knowledge" was shown by the appellant to a theatre audience in Dougherty County, Georgia; a warrant and accusation were issued against the appellant charging him with having committed a crime by showing the film; and the appellant's trial and conviction by a jury followed. All of this took place in the first four months of 1972, long before the changing of definitions, guidelines, and yardsticks of measurement by the Miller decision rendered June 21, 1973. Yet the Miller criteria have been applied by the majority in this case in affirming the appellant's conviction. That cannot be done, and for the majority to have done it in this case is, in my view, a denial of due process of law to the appellant.

In 1972 the appellant had every legal right to believe that the yardstick that he was to use in distinguishing unprotected from protected material was "national standards." The Supreme Court's opinion in Jacobellis v. Ohio, 378 U.S. 184, 84 S.Ct. 1676, 12 L.Ed.2d 793 (1964), now relegated by Miller to a mere plurality decision, said: "We thus reaffirm the position taken in Roth to the effect that the constitutional status of an allegedly obscene work must be determined on the basis of a national standard." Six Justices made up the Jacobellis majority, and not one of them gave the slightest indication that a national standard was not the yardstick to be applied.

Understandably then, appellate court judges or persons dealing in material that might be unprotected legitimately used a national standard yardstick to determine for themselves whether the material was protected or not. In the case of Feldschneider v. State, 127 Ga.App. 745, p. 749, 195 S.E.2d 184, p. 186 (1972), the Court of Appeals of Georgia said: "The trial court erred in limiting the meaning of contemporary community standards to 'the local community—to your own community.' If we were allowed to apply and be guided by the recent Gornto case by the Supreme Court of our own state, the trial court's charge would have been correct; but we are controlled by the three recent decisions of the United States Supreme Court, to wit, Jacobellis v. Manual Enterprises [Manual Enterprises, Inc. v. Day, 370 U.S. 478, 82 S.Ct. 1432, 8 L.Ed.2d 639] and Roth, supra, and consequently we hold that the trial court's charge in these two instances constituted reversable error." To the same effect is the decision in Fishman v. State, 128 Ga.App. 505, on page 508, 197 S.E.2d 467, on page 470 (1973), where a 7–2 majority of our Court of Appeals said: "The community standards to be applied are those of the national, not the immediate local community."

In January, 1972, when the motion picture "Carnal Knowledge" was exhibited by the appellant, the film had shown in the major cities of the nation, the major cities in Georgia, and in many of the cities and towns in Georgia without any contention being publicly made that it was obscene-pornographic.

"Carnal Knowledge" was reviewed in July, 1971, in the *Saturday Review,* the *Washington Post,* the *New York Daily News, Time,* the *Atlanta Constitution,* and the *Atlanta Journal.* None of these reviews gave the slightest indication that the film was obscene-pornographic. Terry Kay, *Atlanta Journal* amusements editor, concluded the review in that Georgia paper as follows: "In the end there is no real triumph for the characters. Different attitudes, perhaps, but no triumph.

"The effect is with the viewer, who—like it or not—has been stung to the quick by a prodding of human values.

"So what does 'Carnal Knowledge' tell us? Simply that we are victims, or subjects to be victimized, by the very life-system we create for ourselves.

" 'Carnal Knowledge' says it with sex. It is theatrical that way—sex being the denominator common to everyone. But it could be said about any facet of our lives.

"It is a movie that will be controversial in the heaviest sense of the word, but it is still one of the best that we have had in a long time."

In Miller, — U.S. p. —, 93 S.Ct. p. 2607, the Chief Justice of the United States said: ". . . a 'national' standard of First Amendment protection enumerated by a plurality of this court, was correctly regarded at the time of trial as limiting state prosecution under the controlling case law." However, the Chief Justice then went on to say that since the appellant in that case did not raise the "national standard" issue at the trial but only on appeal, the trial court's charge to the jury that it consider state community standards was not a constitutional error.

To me, this retroactive application of the Miller yardstick as opposed to the Jacobellis yardstick has the effect of saying that a theatre operator could rely on Jacobellis in January, 1972, in deciding whether to exhibit a film, but in April, 1972, when he was tried before a jury for exhibiting the film, it was all right for the Court and jury to completely ignore the standard established by Jacobellis and apply a different standard which had not at the time of the trial been enunciated and which would not be established by the Supreme Court of the United States until June 21, 1973.

I should add that in the present case the "national standard" issue was raised by the appellant in both the trial court and the appellate court.

The majority here today has retroactively applied the Miller "contemporary community standards" yardstick in affirming a criminal conviction, thereby depriving appellant of his legal right in January, 1972, to have applied a "national standard" yardstick in making his decision that the film "Carnal Knowledge" came within the protection of the First Amendment.

If, between the time of Jacobellis and the time of Miller, the Justices of the Supreme Court of the United States did not know what yardstick to apply, and then changed rather dramatically from one to the other, how can a theatre manager in Georgia be faulted, much less criminally convicted, for having made a decision in 1972 based on the Jacobellis national standard?

The retroactive application of Miller in this manner in this case by the majority has, in my opinion, deprived appellant of due process of law under both the Georgia and Federal Constitutions.

II.

Assuming that what I have said heretofore, to the effect that the retroactive application of local community standards in this case is constitutionally impermissible, is incorrect, and the majority today holds that I am wrong on this point, then the film "Carnal Knowledge" is, in my judgment, entitled to the protection of the First Amendment even after applying local contemporary community standards.

Miller, as noted earlier, reasserts that First Amendment values "are adequately protected by the ultimate power of appellate courts to conduct an independent review of constitutional claims when necessary." — U.S. p. —, 93 S.Ct. p. 2607.

The so-called plurality opinion in Jacobellis said 378 U.S. p. 190, 84 S.Ct. p. 1676: "Hence we reaffirm the principle that, in 'obscenity' cases as in all others involving rights derived from the First Amendment guarantees of free expression, this court cannot avoid making an independent constitutional judgment on the facts of the case as to whether the material involved is constitutionally protected. . . . We would reiterate . . . that 'the portrayal of sex, e.g., in art, literature and scientific works, is not itself sufficient reason to deny material the constitutional protection of freedom of speech and press.' . . . It follows that material dealing with sex in a manner that advocates ideas, . . . or that has literary or scientific or artistic value or any other form of social importance may not be branded as obscenity and denied the constitutional protection."

As I read the majority opinion in Miller, it approves and reaffirms these enunciations procreated into constitutional law in Jacobellis by a mere plurality of the Justices.

If there ever has been or will be a case where independent appellate review of the facts as to whether the material involved is constitutionally protected is necessary to protect First Amendment values, then the case at bar is the case.

This court has conducted an independent review. We have seen the film "Carnal Knowledge."

Four members of this Court deem it to be obscene, pornographic, unprotected material. Three members of this Court, including the writer, would hold it to be constitutionally protected material.

In Division 4 of the Miller opinion the Chief Justice said: "The dissenting Justices sound the alarm of repression . . . These doleful anticipations assume that courts cannot distinguish commerce in ideas, protected by the First Amendment, from commercial exploitation of obscene material."

My experience with this one case teaches me that the "alarm of repression" was validly sounded; it also teaches me that the Miller majority's assumption, that courts can distinguish commerce in ideas that is protected from commercial exploitation of obscene material that is not protected, is a too optimistic assumption. The instant case is the proof that is in the pudding; material is pornographic and unprotected in the subjective mind and senses of one judge; and that same material has serious literary or artistic value in the subjective mind and senses of another judge; all of which leads me to repeat that often-stated assertion by lawyers: a majority of the Justices of the Supreme Court of the United States is not final because the members of that majority are infallible,—that majority is infallible only because it is final.

If the motion picture "Carnal Knowledge" is not entitled to judicial protection under the First Amendment's umbrella, then future productions in this art form utilizing a sexual theme are destined to be obscenely soaked in the pornographic storm.

III.

The appellant's conviction should not be affirmed because he was not legally accused of having committed a crime.

A warrant was issued for the appellant for having violated Code Ann. § 26–2105. This Code Section was enacted by the Georgia legislature in 1971, and this case is the first time that this Court has given consideration to it.

This statute, as relevant in this case, provides as follows: "(a) Every person who, during the course of a . . . motion picture . . . engages in conduct which would be public indecency under section 26–2011 if performed in a public place, shall be guilty of participation in indecent exposure and upon conviction shall be punished as for a misdemeanor. (b) Every person who . . . knowingly exhibits . . . a motion picture . . . containing such conduct shall be guilty of a misdemeanor."

Code Ann. § 26–2011, our public indecency statute referred to in Code § 26–2105, is as follows: "A person commits public indecency when he performs any of the following acts in a public place and upon conviction shall be punished as for a misdemeanor: (a) An act of sexual intercourse; (b) a lewd exposure of the sexual organs; (c) a lewd appearance in a state of partial or complete nudity; (d) a lewd caress or indecent fondling of the body of another person." It is thus seen that the conduct referred to in Code Ann. § 26–2105 is "public indecency" or "indecent exposure." Code Ann. § 26–2105 does not make reference in any manner whatsoever to "obscene materials."

Prior to arraignment and trial the appellant attacked and moved to dismiss the accusation that was preferred against him based on the warrant. His contention was that the warrant and the accusation were based on the 1971 Georgia statute (Code Ann. § 26–2105), and that the 1971 Georgia statute was unconstitutional. The trial judge overruled these constitutional attacks.

In my opinion the 1971 Georgia statute is patently unconstitutional. This statute attempts to transfer the crime of public indecency into the motion picture art form. This cannot be done if the First Amendment means anything at all, and if a motion picture is a work or material that enjoys protection under the First Amendment. Conduct performed in person and in public, such as indecent exposure, is not protected by the First Amendment. Conduct portrayed in the motion picture art form is protected by the First Amendment unless the portrayal, considered in the entire context of the motion picture, lacks "serious literary, artistic, political, or scientific value" (Miller v. California standard) or is "utterly without redeeming social value" (pre-Miller v. California standard).

In other words, a single or even several acts of public indecency portrayed in a motion picture or described by the written word in a novel cannot be defined as a crime because of the protection given to motion pictures and novels as forms of expression by the First Amendment. The entire motion picture or the novel must be considered as a whole in determining whether the work is pornographic, thus falling outside of the protection of the First Amendment.

The Miller opinion says –– U.S. p. ––, 93 S.Ct. p. 2607: "State statutes designed to regulate obscene materials must be carefully limited. See Interstate Circuit, Inc. v. Dallas, supra, 390 U.S. 676, 682–685, 88 S.Ct. 1298, 20 L.Ed.2d 225 (1968)."

The 1971 Georgia statute is not "carefully limited." It says that an actor who portrays one or more acts of indecent exposure in a motion picture is guilty of having committed a crime. It further says that one who exhibits a motion picture containing such a portrayal is guilty of a crime.

I think that this 1971 Georgia statute is directly violative of the First Amendment, and I further think that it violates the Fourteenth Amendment in that it is overly broad.

The warrant in this case, and the accusation based on the warrant, charged the appellant only with having violated Code Ann. § 26–2105. In my view this statute is unconstitutional. A criminal charge cannot be founded on a void statute. Therefore, the accusation charged no crime at all, and it should have been dismissed by the trial judge when properly attacked in the trial court.

It follows that I would reverse this criminal conviction. I respectfully dissent.

HAWES, Justice (dissenting).

I join in the dissenting opinion of Mr. Justice Gunter, a classic of legal reasoning and First Amendment wisdom, and I would add nothing to what has been said were it not for my concern for the grave danger to free speech and expression inherent in the majority opinion and about which I cannot here remain silent.

Two aspects of the opinion of the majority which are of most concern to me are the following: (1) the tacit approval of small towns and hamlets as being the "community" from which the standard for obscenity is drawn; and (2) the determination by four members of this court, upon an independent appellate review, that the film Carnal Knowledge is obscene, that is, that it has no artistic or literary value and is "utterly without redeeming social value." To give approval to the first would be to place in the hands of the few the tastes and the cultural advancement of the many who are members of the greater state community and to deny in large measure the basic freedom of individuals to participate as they will in the general commerce of ideas. And to approve of the latter would be to equate realistic commentary on our sexual natures in a social context with that of obscenity, an equivalence surely belied as a matter of constitutional law and as a matter of fact. Certainly, the film under consideration here is not the kind of hard-core pornography we removed from public consumption in Slaton v. Paris Adult Theater I, 228 Ga. 343, 185 S.E.2d 768 (1971).

I add these few remarks only because I believe if the majority opinion is accepted we shall have suffered a serious injury to free speech and free expression in Georgia.

Editor's note: This decision was reversed on June 24, 1974 by the U.S. Supreme Court, which, after viewing "Carnal Knowledge," held that "the film could not . . . be found to depict sexual conduct in a patently offensive way." *Jenkins v. Georgia,* 94 S.Ct. 2750

DRAMA, DANCE, NIGHTCLUB PERFORMANCES, AND OBSCENITY

DRAMA, DANCE, NIGHTCLUB PERFORMANCES, AND OBSCENITY

FIRST AMENDMENT PROTECTION FOR A BUR-LESQUE SHOW

Adams Newark Theater Co. v. City of Newark, 120 A.2d 496 (1956)

COLIE, J. S. C.

The City of Newark, on December 16, 1955, adopted an amendment to section 8.195, article XIV, chapter 8 of the Revised Ordinances, which provides as follows:

"(a) No show, performance, exhibition or motion picture, exhibited or conducted by reason of any permit or license issued, or to be issued, under this article shall be lewd, obscene or indecent, either upon or off the stage or screen or in the place of showing; or allow or permit the conduct of any performer, employee or the audience to commit actions that shall be lewd, obscene or indecent, and the following acts or performances are hereby specifically prohibited, to wit:

"The removal by a female performer in the presence of the audience of her clothing, so as to make nude, or give the illusion of nudeness, of the lower abdomen, genital organs, buttocks or breasts;

"The exposure by a female performer in the presence of the audience, or the giving of the illusion of nudeness in the presence of the audience, of the lower abdomen, genital organs, buttocks or breasts;

"The exposure by a male performer in the presence of the audience of the genital organs or buttocks;

"The use by a performer of profane, lewd, lascivious, indecent or disgusting language;

"The performance of any dance, episode or musical entertainment which depicts sexual subjects, acts or objects offensive to public morals and decency;

"The performance of any dance, episode or musical entertainment, the purpose or effect of which is to direct the attention of the spectator to the breasts, buttocks or genital organs of the performer."

On the same date the city also adopted an amendment to section 20.7, chapter 20 of the Revised Ordinances, the precise language of which is not set forth for it is substantially as quoted from amended section 8.195 set forth above. The attack on the amended ordinances is that they are in violation of the First Amendment of the Federal Constitution and Article 1, paragraph 6 of the Constitution of this State, which provides:

"Every person may freely speak, write and publish his sentiments on all subjects, being responsible for the abuse of that right."

The rights guaranteed by the First Amendment and by our State Constitution are, beyond dispute, applicable to the commercial exhibition of plays and shows, and the type of exhibition which the plaintiffs herein stage are "shows" in every sense of the word, being so-called burlesque shows. It is beyond argument that the protection does not extend to speech which is outwardly lewd and indecent.

In the determination of the extent to which censorship may be exercised over that which is written and that which is displayed, it is now settled "that sexual life is the theme of the presentation or that the characters portray a seamy side of life and play coarse scenes or use some vulgar language does not constitute the presentation *per se* lewd and indecent. The question is whether the dominant note of the presentation is erotic allurement 'tending to excite lustful and lecherous desire,' dirt for dirt's sake only, smut and inartistic filth, with no evident purpose but 'to counsel or invite to vice or voluptuousness.' " With this language from the opinion in Adams Theatre Co. v. Keenan, 12 N.J. 267, 96 A.2d 519, 521 (1953) in mind, it is pertinent to examine the language in the amendments under review. They specifically prohibit "the exposure by a female performer in the presence of the audience, or the giving of the illusion of nudeness in the presence of the audience, of the lower abdomen, genital organs, buttocks or breasts; * * * the performance of any dance, episode, or musical entertainment which depicts sexual subjects, acts or objects offensive to public morals and decency; the performance of any dance, episode or musical entertainment, the purpose or effect of which is to direct the attention of the spectator to the breasts, buttocks or genital organs of the performer." Nudity of the lower abdomen, genital organs, buttocks or breasts is prohibited by the terms of the amendments and that prohibition is absolute no matter how incidental the nudity may be, and it utterly disregards the established rule to the effect that the acts specified may be prohibited only when the dominant note of the presentation is erotic allurement, and the same is equally true of the prohibition of any dance, episode or musical entertainment which depicts sexual subjects. For this reason, if for no other, the plaintiffs' motion for summary judgment should be granted.

There is, however, a further fault with the amendments and that is the prohibition against giving the "illusion of nudeness." This language is so nebulous as to furnish no fair criteria to theatrical producers as to what is or what is not the illusion of nudeness.

The amendments under attack constitute a flagrant attempt to prejudge specific acts as lewd and indecent, regardless of the dominant effect of the entire performance or the episode in which the prohibited act takes place.

Any one of the acts specifically prohibited by the amendments may or may not subject the producer and performers to penalties, depending upon whether or not they are performed in a context whose dominant effect is to excite lustful and lecherous desire. To paraphrase the language in Adams Theatre Co. v. Keenan, supra, the attempt by the defendant municipality is to impose a previous restraint upon the performance of certain acts which are not, *per se*, lewd or indecent. If they are indecent, and this court is not passing on that phase, the municipality is not without remedy under the existing ordinance which prohibits lewd, obscene and indecent performances.

For the reasons stated, the defendants' motions for judgment in its favor are denied and the plaintiffs' motions to set aside the amendments are granted.

LENNY BRUCE'S NIGHTCLUB MONOLOGUE IS RELUCTANTLY GIVEN FREE SPEECH PROTECTION

People v. Bruce, 202 N.E.2d 497 (1964)

PER CURIAM.

By an earlier opinion filed June 18, 1964, this court affirmed the judgment of the circuit court of Cook County entered upon a jury verdict finding the defendant herein guilty of giving an obscene performance violative of section 11–20 of the Criminal Code of 1961. (Ill.Rev.Stat. 1961, chap. 38, par. 11–20.) On June 22, 1964, the Supreme Court of the United States decided Jacobellis v. State of Ohio, 378 U.S. 184, 84 S.Ct. 1676, 12 L.Ed.2d 793, in which a movie allegedly obscene was held not to be so. On July 7, 1964, the original opinion of this court was vacated, and reargument ordered in the light of Jacobellis.

The performance here consisted of a 55-minute monologue upon numerous socially controversial subjects interspersed with such unrelated topics as the meeting of a psychotic rapist and a nymphomaniac who have both escaped from their respective institutions, defendant's intimacies with three married women, and a supposed conversation with a gas station attendant in a rest room which concludes with the suggestion that the defendant and attendant both put on contraceptives and take a picture. The testimony was that defendant also made motions .indicating masturbation and accompanied these with vulgar comments, and that persons leaving the audience were subjected to revolting questions and suggestions.

The entire performance was originally held by us to be characterized by its continual reference, by words and acts, to sexual intercourse or sexual organs in terms which ordinary adult individuals find thoroughly disgusting and revolting as well as patently offensive; that, as is evident from these brief summaries, it went beyond customary limits of candor, a fact which becomes even more apparent when the entire monologue is considered.

Our original opinion recognized defendant's right to satirize society's attitudes on contemporary social problems and to express his ideas, however bizarre, as long as the method used in doing so was not so objectionable as to render the entire performance obscene. Affirmance of the conviction was predicated upon the rule originally laid down in American Civil Liberties Union v. City of Chicago,

3 Ill.2d 334, 121 N.E.2d 585, that the obscene portions of the material must be balanced against its affirmative values to determine which predominates. We rejected defendant's argument that Roth v. United States, 354 U.S. 476, 77 S.Ct. 1304, 1 L.Ed.2d 1498, struck down this balancing test and held that material, no matter how objectionable the method of its presentation, was constitutionally privileged unless it was utterly without redeeming social importance.

It is apparent from the opinions of a majority of the court in Jacobellis that the "balancing test" rule of American Civil Liberties Union is no longer a constitutionally acceptable method of determining whether material is obscene, and it is there made clear that material having *any* social importance is constitutionally protected.

While we would not have thought that constitutional guarantees necessitate the subjection of society to the gradual deterioration of its moral fabric which this type of presentation promotes, we must concede that some of the topics commented on by defendant are of social importance. Under Jacobellis the entire performance is thereby immunized, and we are constrained to hold that the judgment of the circuit court of Cook County must be reversed and defendant discharged.

Judgment reversed.

SCHAEFER, Justice (concurring).

The majority opinion seems to indicate that so long as any elements of a monologue have social value the entire speech is protected. I believe that this is too broad a formulation of the result in the Jacobellis case. The fact that some fragments relate to matters of social importance does not, in my opinion, always immunize the whole. But the major portion of this performance, before an adult night club audience, related to social problems, and most of the objectionable passages were integral parts of the protected material. Therefore I concur.

THE CALIFORNIA SUPREME COURT DECLARES TOPLESS DANCING IS PROTECTED SPEECH

In re Giannini, 446 P.2d 535 (1968)

TOBRINER, Justice

Our ruling in this case rests on the simple proposition that a dance performed before an audience for entertainment cannot be held to violate the statutory prohibitions of indecent exposure and lewd or dissolute conduct in the absence of proof that the dance, tested in the context of contemporary community standards, appealed to the prurient interest of the audience and affronted standards of decency generally accepted in the community. We explain why we have concluded that both under principles of constitutional law and upon application of the criteria inherent in the involved statutes, conviction could stand only upon presentation of such proof. We likewise set forth our reasons for holding that the relevant community standard is that of the statewide community.

In 1965 a municipal court jury found petitioner Kelley

Iser, a "topless" dancer, and petitioner Albert Giannini, the manager of the nightclub in which she danced, guilty of violating Penal Code section 314, subdivision 1 (wilful and lewd exposure) and section 647, subdivision (a) (lewd or dissolute conduct). The appellate department of the superior court affirmed the convictions without opinion; petitioners applied unsuccessfully for transfer of the case to the Court of Appeal.

Giannini and Iser then brought this petition for habeas corpus, alleging that the sections of the Penal Code under which they were convicted are unconstitutionally vague and that the failure of the prosecution to introduce evidence of community standards as to the involved performance rendered the convictions unconstitutional.

1. *The facts.*

Petitioners were convicted of violation of section 314, subdivision 1, and section 647, subdivision (a), of the Penal Code. In relevant part, these sections read as follows: "§ 314. Every person who wilfully and lewdly * * * 1. Exposes his person, or the private parts thereof, in any public place, or in any place where there are present other persons to be offended or annoyed thereby * * * is guilty of a misdemeanor." "§ 647. Every person who commits any of the following acts shall be guilty of disorderly conduct, a misdemeanor: (a) Who solicits anyone to engage in or who engages in lewd or dissolute conduct in any public place or in any place open to the public or exposed to public view."

In support of these charges, the prosecution produced two police officers who testified to the following facts. Petitioner Giannini managed the Lighthouse Inn, a nightclub in San Pablo, California; petitioner Iser performed the "topless" dance featured at the Inn. Wearing tights and a transparent cape, Iser appeared on a spotlighted stage and performed various modern dances, including the "Swim." As part of the act, she removed the cape, exposing the upper portion of her body, and performed a dance called "Walking the Dog" to the music of a song by the same name. "Walking the Dog," according to the officers, consisted of petitioner Iser "wiggling around" for about 30 seconds on her hands and knees with her breasts exposed.

The officers testified that a large sign with the word "Topless" stood outside the club. A small sign at the entrance indicated that minors were not allowed inside; an employee of the Lighthouse Inn checked identification at the doorway. The officers further testified that petitioner Iser's performance could not be seen from outside the club. The only other evidence introduced by the prosecution consisted of photographs depicting petitioner Iser dancing; in some of the pictures her breasts were exposed.

At the conclusion of the People's case, defense counsel moved that the jury be advised to return a verdict of "not guilty" because the prosecution had failed to introduce any evidence as to a material aspect of its case, the contemporary standards of the community with respect to the type of dance at issue. Apparently concluding that the jurors represented the "community" and thus by definition would apply "community standards," the trial court denied the request.

After denial of the motion, the defense called as witnesses the owners of two San Francisco nightclubs. They testified that for several years they had continuously employed "topless" dancers who did the "Swim" and other modern dances; that between 30 and 40 other San Francisco nightclubs employed "topless" entertainers, and

that "topless nightclubs" engaged in business in Los Angeles, Santa Rosa, San Rafael, San Diego, Petaluma, Eureka, and Red Bluff. One of the owners further testified that his employees nightly performed the dance "Walking the Dog"; the other testified that the small size of the dancing platforms in his club precluded the performance of that dance.

An attorney, also testifying for the defense, stated that during "Walking the Dog" petitioner Iser wiggled her abdominal area and buttocks, that some interpreted this dance as having "sexual connotations," and that he had seen the same dance rendered on television by fully clothed performers. In addition, the defense introduced various materials generally available in the San Pablo community, such as Playboy magazine and art books, as evidence of contemporary community standards regarding bare-breasted women.

Among other instructions the trial judge charged the jury, quoting Penal Code, section 311, that: " 'Obscene' means that to the average person, applying contemporary standards the predominant appeal of the matter, taken as a whole, is to prurient interest, i.e., a shameful or morbid interest in nudity, sex, or excretion, which goes substantially beyond customary limits of candor in description or representation of such matters and is matter which is utterly without redeeming social importance."

We have seen that although defendants were found guilty of violation of the prohibition of indecent exposure in Penal Code, section 314, subdivision 1, and the prohibition of disorderly conduct in Penal Code, section 647, subdivision (a), the alleged offense occurred in the presentation of a dance before an audience. We shall point out that the performance of such a dance, like other forms of expression or communication prima facie enjoys protection under the First Amendment of the Constitution of the United States; it loses such protection upon a showing of its obscenity. To show such obscenity, however, the prosecution must introduce evidence that, applying contemporary community standards, the questioned dance appealed to the prurient interest of the audience and affronted the standards of decency accepted in the community.

In interpreting the terms "lewd" and "dissolute" as used in the statutes under which defendants were charged, the trial court held such words to be synonymous with "obscene" as used in Penal Code, section 311 which defines obscenity. Once the First Amendment protection applies to the dance as a medium of expression, and once the court charges the jury in the terms of the obscenity statute, proof that the dance, in the context of contemporary standards, appealed to the prurient interest of the audience and exceeded the customary limits of candor became essential to conviction. The absence of that proof must therefore nullify the judgment.

2. *The performance of a dance for an audience constitutes a method of expression that, in the absence of proof of obscenity, warrants the protection of the First Amendment.*

Although the United States Supreme Court has not ruled on the precise question whether the performance of a dance is potentially a form of communication protected against state intrusion by the guarantees of the First and Fourteenth Amendments to the federal Constitution, the very definition of dance describes it as an expression of emotions or ideas. Thus, "Dancing consists in the rhythmical movement of any or all parts of the body in accordance with some scheme of individual or concerted action which is expressive of emotions or ideas." (7 Encyclopaedia Britannica (1945) pp. 13–14.) The Century Dictionary and Cyclopedia defines dance as follows: "dance–A succession of more or less regularly ordered steps and movements of the body, commonly guided by rhythmical intervals of a musical accompaniment; any leaping or gliding movement with more or less regular steps and turnings, expressive of or designed to awaken some emotion. The dance is perhaps the earliest and most spontaneous mode of expressing emotion and dramatic feeling; it exists in a great variety of forms and is among some people connected with religious belief and practice, as among the Mahammedans and Hindus." (2 The Century Dictionary and Cyclopedia (1914) p. 1450.)

The Supreme Court has held that analogous media of expression, such as motion pictures, come "within the ambit of the constitutional guarantes of freedom of speech and of the press. Joseph Burstyn, Inc. v. Wilson, 343 U.S. 495, 72 S.Ct. 777, 96 L.Ed. 1098." (Jacobellis v. State of Ohio (1964) 378 U.S. 184, 187, 84 S.Ct. 1676, 1677, 12 L.Ed.2d 793 (judgment of the court per Brennan, J.); see also Flack v. Municipal Court, etc. (1967) 66 Cal.2d 981, 59 Cal.Rptr. 872, 429 P.2d 192.) "It cannot be doubted that motion pictures are a significant *medium* for the communication of ideas. They may affect public attitudes and behavior in a variety of ways, ranging * * * to the subtle shaping of thought which characterizes all artistic expression. The importance of motion pictures as an organ of public opinion is not lessened by the fact that they are designed to entertain as well as to inform." (Joseph Burstyn, Inc. v. Wilson (1952) 343 U.S. 495, 501, 72 S.Ct. 777, 780, 96 L.Ed. 1098.) (Fn. omitted; italics added.)[1]

The above analysis merely makes applicable to a particular medium the general doctrine that *all* forms of communication, not merely the expression of concrete and definite ideas, *potentially* receive First Amendment protection.[2] "We do not accede to appellee's suggestion for a free press applies only to the exposition of ideas. The line between the informing and the entertaining is too elusive for the protection of that basic right. * * * Though we see nothing of any possible value to society in these magazines, they are as much entitled to the protection of free speech as the best of literature." (Winters v. People of State of New York (1948) 333 U.S. 507, 510, 68 S.Ct. 665, 667, 92 L.Ed. 840.) "Also encompassed [within the right of freedom of speech] are amusement and entertainment as well as the exposition of ideas." (Weaver v. Jordan (1966) 64 Cal.2d 235, 242, 49 Cal.Rptr. 537, 542, 411 P.2d 289, 294.)[3]

In light of this approach, the performance of the dance indubitably represents a medium of protected expression. To take but one example, the ballet obviously typifies a form of entertainment and expression that involves communication of ideas, impressions, and feelings. Similarly, Iser's dancing, however vulgar and tawdry in content, might well involve communication to her audience. In fact, the Attorney General basically argues that Iser's dance violated the statute because it communicated improper ideas to her audience. This implicit admission of the Attorney General undermines his preliminary contention that the dance does not enjoy at least a prima facie protection of the guarantees of the First Amendment. Precisely because,

as the Attorney General points out, the performed dance primarily constitutes a form of expression and communication, it potentially merits First Amendment protections.

The prima facie applicability of the First Amendment to this medium of communication, the dance, does not fail merely because the particular form of its manifestation may be obnoxious to many persons. Although the Attorney General contends that "topless dancing," as performed in the instant case, cannot itself demonstrate any social value worthy of protection under the First Amendment, it is "as much entitled to the protection of free speech as the best of [dance]" (Winters v. New York, supra, 333 U.S. 507, 510, 68 S.Ct. 665, 667). "The line * * * is too elusive" (id.) to allow for particularized judgments as to whether each individual example of expression possesses social values meriting First Amendment protection.

Of course a conclusion that Iser's theatrical dance prima facie gains a First Amendment protection does not affect the central question presented in this case: whether her performance loses this privileged status because it is obscene. (Roth v. United States (1957) 354 U.S. 476, 77 S.Ct. 1304, 1 L.Ed.2d 1498.) As the Court of Appeal in Landau v. Fording (1966) 245 Cal.App.2d 820, 823, 54 Cal.Rptr. 177, 179, said as to the comparable medium of motion pictures, "While motion pictures, like other forms of expression, are within the ambit of the constitutional guarantees of freedom of speech and of the press (Joseph Burstyn, Inc. v. Wilson, 343 U.S. 495, 72 S.Ct. 777, 96 L.Ed. 1098), obscenity is not subject to those guarantees (Roth v. United States, 354 U.S. 476, 77 S.Ct. 1304, 1 L.Ed.2d 1498)." In short, the People's argument that, unlike other forms of dance, such as ballet, Iser's dance appeals to prurient interests, must turn on whether the performance was obscene, not on whether dance in general or "topless" dancing in particular can achieve constitutional protection.[4]

Nor can we accept the prosecution's sweeping argument that "standards required of an obscenity prosecution are inapplicable in this case" because the "conduct standing alone is clearly unlawful" and does not become lawful "because it is engaged in during an activity" which would be afforded First and Fourteenth Amendment protections. Petitioner's apparent "unlawful conduct" consisted of the baring of her breasts; the thrust of the argument presumably is that since such conduct could not be lawfully engaged in at any place and any time and under any and all circumstances it is not entitled to constitutional protection when performed in the different context of a theatrical performance.

The conduct here of course took place during a theatrical performance of a dance before an audience. We have previously explained that such a dance enjoys constitutional protection. The proper issue here therefore turns on whether the alleged unlawful conduct, which is inextricably a part of the dance, forfeits constitutional protection because of its alleged obscene nature.

To isolate the questioned conduct and to judge it in an entirely different context would be to distort the nature of this case. By fictitiously changing the manner and place of its performance the prosecution would make the conduct criminal although in the actual manner and place of its performance the conduct should be tested by constitutional standards.

Thus acts which are unlawful in a different context, circumstance, or place, may be depicted or incorporated in a stage or screen presentation and come within the protection of the First Amendment, losing that protection only if found to be obscene. Respondent's contention would automatically reject the application of the law of obscenity to the instant case. It would adjudicate Iser's conduct as if it were not performed on the stage, not a dance, and not incorporated in a form of communication. Yet the entire point of the case is that the conduct occurred in that very context.

3. *Pursuant to section 311 of the Penal Code the People must prove that, applying contemporary community standards, the expression in question appealed to the prurient interest of the audience and so exceeded customary limits of candor as to be offensive.*

As we have explained, the trial judge, quoting Penal Code, section 311, instructed the jury that " 'Obscene' means that to the average person, applying contemporary standards, the *predominant appeal* of the matter, taken as a whole, is to prurient interest, i.e., a shameful or morbid interest in nudity, sex, or excretion, *which goes substantially beyond customary limits of candor* in description or representation of such matters and is matter which is utterly without redeeming social importance." (Italics added.)

In approaching petitioners' contention that the prosecution's failure to introduce evidence of contemporary community standards constitutes reversible error, we face a preliminary question: do we apply the test of contemporary community standards to whether the predominant appeal of the matter is to "prurient interest" only or do we also apply it to whether the representation "goes substantially beyond customary limits of candor"? Clearly the Penal Code contemplates that the test of community standards applies to the question whether the *predominant appeal* of the material is to "prurient interest." The decision of the United States Supreme Court in Roth v. United States, supra, 354 U.S. 476, 77 S.Ct. 1304, 1 L.Ed.2d 1498, from which the Penal Code language emanated, clearly contemplates that test. The *Roth* opinion expresses the issue to be "whether * * *, applying contemporary community standards, the dominant theme of the material taken as a whole appeals to prurient interest." (Id. at p. 489, 77 S.Ct. at p. 1311.) Thus the *Roth* decision, in addition to the explicit textual connection in section 311 between "prurient interest" and "contemporary community standards," requires that the prurient interest of Iser's dance be judged by contemporary community standards.

The more difficult question turns on whether the reference in the section to "customery limits of candor" also contemplates a test by community standards. Although *Roth* did not list such a requirement, and the language of the Penal Code is at best ambiguous, recent decisions by the United States Supreme Court suggest an affirmative answer. In a book named "John Cleland's Memoirs of a Woman of Pleasure v. Attorney General of Com. of Massachusetts (1966) 383 U.S. 413, 418, 86 S.Ct. 975, 16 L.Ed.2d 1, a plurality opinion (Brennan and Fortas, JJ., and Warren, C. J.) modified the *Roth* test as follows: "Under this [*Roth*] definition, as elaborated in subsequent cases, three elements must coalesce: it must be established that (a) the dominant theme of the material taken as a whole appeals to a prurient interest in sex; (b) *the material is patently offensive because it affronts contemporary community standards* relating to the description or representation of sexual matters; and (c) the material is utterly

without redeeming social value."[5] (Italics added.) (See also Redrup v. State of New York (1967) 386 U.S. 767, 770–771, 87 S.Ct. 1414, 18 L.Ed.2d 515.) Moreover, Justices Harlan and Stewart, announcing the judgment of the court in Manual Enterprises, Inc. v. Day (1962) 370 U.S. 478, 82 S.Ct. 1432, 8 L.Ed.2d 639, presaged part (b) of the reassessment articulated in *Memoirs* by reversing a finding of obscenity because the materials were not "so offensive * * * as to affront current community standards of decency." (Id. at p. 482, 82 S.Ct. at p. 1434.)

In sum, a majority of the United States Supreme Court have apparently concluded that a finding of offensiveness to the accepted community standards of decency forms a prerequisite to a conclusion of obscenity. In order to conform to the Supreme Court decisions and to avoid questions of constitutionality, we interpret the words "customary limits of candor," as used in section 311 of the Penal Code, to require a showing that the material so exceeds customary limits of candor as to affront contemporary community standards of decency.

4. *The convictions must be set aside because the People failed to introduce proof of contemporary community standards.*

Having thus established a definition of obscenity, we face the question whether the People sufficiently proved all of its elements to support a conviction. We conclude the convictions must be set aside because the prosecution failed to introduce any evidence of community standards, either that Iser's conduct appealed to prurient interest or offended contemporary standards of decency.

We note at the outset the conflict of the authorities on the manner of proof of community standards. Some cases have held that the issue of obscenity can be resolved from the material or conduct itself without expert testimony or other evidence relevant to contemporary community standards. (E.g., City of Newark v. Humphres (1967) 94 N.J.Super. 384, 390–391, 228 A.2d 550; City of Chicago v. Kimmel (1964) 31 Ill.2d 202, 206, 201 N.E.2d 386; Kahm v. United States (5th Cir. 1962) 300 F.2d 78, 84–85, cert. den., 369 U.S. 859, 82 S.Ct. 949, 8 L.Ed.2d 18.) Others have held that in the absence of a showing by expert testimony that the questioned expression or conduct affronted the standards of the community, proof of obscenity failed. (Dunn v. Maryland State Board of Censors (1965) 240 Md.249, 257, 213 A.2d 751; United States v. Klaw (2d Cir. 1965) 350 F.2d 155, 167.)[6]

Relying principally on the well established doctrine that jurors should not be endowed with the prerogative of imposing their own personal standards as the test of criminality of conduct, we hold that expert testimony should be introduced to establish community standards. We cannot assume that jurors in themselves necessarily express or reflect community standards; we must achieve so far as possible the application of an objective, rather than a subjective, determination of community standards.[7] An even-handed application of the criminal law, even with evidentiary guidance (cf. In re Newbern (1960) 53 Cal.2d 786, 797, 3 Cal.Rptr. 364, 350 P.2d 116), is sufficiently difficult in an area so confusing and intricate as obscenity. To sanction convictions without expert evidence of community standards encourages the jury to condemn as obscene such conduct or material as is personally distasteful or offensive to the particular juror. (Cf. United States. v. Klaw, supra, 350 F.2d 155, 167.) "[C]ommunity standards * * * can * * * hardly be established except through experts. * * * There is no external measuring rod for obscenity. Neither, on the other hand, is its ascertainment a merely subjective reflection of the taste or moral outlook of individual jurors or individual judges. * * * Their interpretation ought not to depend solely on the necessarily limited, hit-or-miss, subjective view of what they are believed to be by the individual juror or judge. It bears repetition that the determination of obscenity is for juror or judge not on the basis of his personal upbringing or restricted reflection or particular experience of life, but on the basis of 'contemporary community standards.' " (Smith v. People of State of California (1959) 361 U.S. 147, 165, 80 S.Ct. 215, 225, 4 L.Ed.2d 205 (Frankfurter, J., concurring).)[8]

Moreover, since we designate the State of California as the relevant "community" for this case, we cannot realistically expect the trier of fact to understand intuitively how the community as a whole would react to allegedly obscene material. "Knowledge of contemporary community standards * * * is no more available to the trier of facts than the innumerable other facts which must normally be proved in an evidentiary way in many other trials." (Hudson v. United States, supra, 234 A.2d 903.) The use of "contemporary community standards" as part of the constitutional test for obscenity does not in any way indicate that a jury inevitably can accurately apply this standard without guidance; rather, the "community standard" of the entire State of California is an ascertainable, albeit ephemeral, phenomenon subject to evidentiary proof to a jury selected from a local area, just as is any other question of fact.[9]

Finally, even if the jury should be deemed to be a metaphysical embodiment of the "community," and therefore intrinsically cognizant of community standards, proof of community standards would nevertheless be indispensable to effective appellate review. An appellate court must reach an independent decision as to the obscenity of the material. (Zeitlin v. Arnebergh, supra, 59 Cal.2d 901, 908–909, 31 Cal.Rptr. 800, 383 P.2d 152, 10 A.L.R.3d 707.) Since an appellate court certainly does not in any sense compose a cross-section of the community, it cannot effectively carry out this function in the absence of evidence in the record directed toward proof of the community standard.[10]

We conclude that the judgment must be vacated for lack of evidence as to whether, applying contemporary community standards, petitioner Iser's dance appealed to the prurient interests of the audience and offended accepted standards of decency.[11] "If there is no evidence in the record upon which such a finding could be made, obviously the material involved cannot be held obscene." (Jacobellis v. State of Ohio, supra, 378 U.S. 184, 202, 84 S.Ct. 1676, 1686, 12 L.Ed.2d 793 (Warren, C. J., dissenting).) Anything to the contrary in People v. Williamson (1962) 207 Cal.App.2d 839, 847, 24 Cal.Rptr. 734, is disapproved.

5. *For purposes of determining the obscenity of the performed dance here in question, the relevant "community" is the entire State of California.*

Since we have held that the failure by the People to introduce evidence of community standards nullifies the judgment in any event, we need not technically reach the issue of the definition of the nature of the community that should measure petitioners' conduct. In order to provide guidance in the event of further prosecutions, however, we

hold that the trial judge correctly ruled that the relevant community is the State of California.

Four justices of the United States Supreme Court have pondered the question whether the First and Fourteenth Amendments require the use of a "national community" in determining whether a work is obscene, and they have split evenly on the issue: Justices Brennan and Goldberg have contended that a national standard is constitutionally compelled (Jacobellis v. State of Ohio, supra, 378 U.S. 184, 192–194, 84 S.Ct. 1676), but Chief Justice Warren and Justice Clark have reached the opposite conclusion (id. at p. 200, 84 S.Ct. 1676). In the absence of guidance from the Supreme Court, lower courts are divided: the cases support at least three standards—national (State v. Hudson County News Co. (1963) 41 N.J. 247, 265, 196 A.2d 225; Excellent Publications, Inc. v. United States (1st Cir. 1962) 309 F.2d 362, 365 (dictum)), state (McCauley v. Tropic of Cancer (1963) 20 Wis.2d 134, 149, 121 N.W.2d 545, 5 A.L.R.3d 1140), and "local" or citywide (Gent. v. State (1965) 239 Ark. 474, 393 S.W.2d 219, reversed on other grounds sub nom. Redrup v. New York, supra, 386 U.S. 767, 87 S.Ct. 1414, 18 L.Ed.2d 515).

The principal deficiency of the national standard lies in the fact that its application may well be almost unworkable in light of our holding that the People must introduce evidence relating to the standard in the chosen "community." Even if some modicum of uniformity of attitudes toward "topless" dancing pervades the entire nation, a proposition in itself doubtful, trial courts would be hard pressed, without substantially diluting the normal requirements for qualification as an expert witness, to find persons with the ability to testify knowledgeably as to that standard. (Cf. Jacobellis v. Ohio, supra, 378 U.S. 184, 200, 84 S.Ct. 1676 (Warren, C. J., dissenting); Ginzburg v. United States (1966) 383 U.S. 463, 480, 86 S.Ct. 942, 16 L.Ed.2d 31 (Black, J., dissenting).)

Nor do any theoretical propositions grounded in the First Amendment press for a national standard. Although the application of diverse local standards to test the constitutionality of permissible "political" speech would certainly be subject to question, the law of obscenity represents simply the "present critical point in the compromise between candor and shame at which the community may have arrived here and now." (United States v. Kennerley (S.D.N.Y.1913) 209 F. 119, 121 (Hand, J.).) Indeed, this compromise is inherent in elements of current definitions of obscenity, including "customary limits of candor" (Jacobellis v. Ohio, supra, 378 U.S. 184, 84 S.Ct. 1676; Pen.Code, § 311) and "patent offensiveness" (Manual Enterprises v. Day, supra, 370 U.S. 478, 482, 82 S.Ct. 1432, 8 L.Ed.2d 639). Different areas of the country, both in attitude and practice, undoubtedly do reach different compromises between "candor and shame," and we can conjure no reason for ignoring so obvious a reality. Certainly, all would agree that standards of obscenity are not immutable; they change with the character of whatever community we use for a testing ground. If we recognize and apply different standards based upon the particular time that we test the conduct or material, we should not be disturbed by different standards based upon the place of the test; geography should assume a no more troublesome role than chronology.[12]

The strongest argument in support of a national community, that a non-national standard would produce the "intolerable consequence of denying some sections of the country access to material, there deemed acceptable, which in others might be considered offensive to prevailing community standards of decency" (Manual Enterprises v. Day, supra, 370 U.S. 478, 488, 82 S.Ct. 1432, 1437, 8 L.Ed.2d 639), does not apply with any force to the instant fact situation. Evaluation of "speech" that is designed for nationwide dissemination, such as books or films, according to a non-national community standard might well unduly deter expression in the first instance and thus run afoul of First Amendment guarantees. But we need not, in the instant case, reconcile this contention with the practical problems of producing evidence of national standards. Iser's dancing is purely local in nature, a subject matter obviously not intended for nationwide dissemination. Since the decision as to whether to stage a "topless" dance rests solely on local considerations, the problem that unduly restrictive local standards may interfere with dissemination of and "access to [such] material" as books or film does not arise in the instant case.

With the alternative of using a national community eliminated, the choice lies between a statewide standard and some variant of a local community. It might be argued that the same theoretical considerations that induce a rejection of a national standard also apply to a statewide test. In particular, the compromise between "shame" and "candor" might vary within California from area to area. Moreover, the smaller the community chosen, the more likely it is that competent evidence of community standards will be available. Finally, if in the present case the prohibition mainly presumes both to protect the audience from its own alleged baseness and the local community from anticipated antisocial conduct arising from observance of the dance, as well as to save the local citizenry from toleration of the objectionable conduct, then the standard should be local. It should comprise either the area from which the audience is likely to be drawn or the area in which the citizenry may be affected by the proscribed dance.

Although these considerations are not *de minimis*, we conclude that on balance a community comprised of the entire State of California is the more appropriate. This standard avoids administrative problems in determining the exact scope of a smaller community: whether it should be city, county, individual neighborhood within a city, or whatever. Moreover, a strong policy favors uniformity in application of the state criminal law (cf. In re Lane (1962) 58 Cal.2d 99, 111, 22 Cal.Rptr. 857, 372 P.2d 897 (Gibson, C. J., concurring)); we promote this policy by assuring that application of the obscenity law in this state will be based on a uniform "community."

The writ is granted. The judgments against Giannini and Iser are set aside. They are remanded to the custody of the San Pablo Municipal Court for further proceedings, if any.

TRAYNOR, C. J., and PETERS, MOSK and SULLIVAN, JJ., concur.

BURKE, Justice (dissenting).

I dissent. I disagree with the majority that the prosecution was required to introduce expert testimony establishing contemporary community standards and that the relevant community in this case should be the entire State of California rather than the local community. No decision of the United States Supreme Court nor any statute cited by the majority compels the adoption of either rule. It is manifest that the majority's new rules will impose a difficult or impossible burden on local communities in com-

bating obscenity. They will lead to a further lessening of local control over local affairs—a further removal of the power of self-government from the local citizenry and their duly elected and selected, responsible local officials—and inevitably, a deplorable lowering of standards in many local communities to conform to lower standards elsewhere.

Mr. Justice Potter Stewart, concurring in Jacobellis v. Ohio, 378 U.S. 184, 84 S.Ct. 1676, 12 L.Ed.2d 793, noted that hardcore pornography is hard to define but that "I know it when I see it * * *." (P. 197, p. 1683 of 84 S.Ct.) And the same can be said of lewd or dissolute conduct. Here, the police officers of the small City of San Pablo thought they saw such conduct in petitioner Iser's performance; they described it to the jury from the witness stand. The jury found petitioners guilty, and on appeal the judgment was affirmed. That should have ended the controversy.

The testimony of the police officers at petitioners' trial is in my opinion amply sufficient to support the conviction. The majority conclude otherwise on the basis of their newly adopted rule that the prosecution must introduce expert testimony establishing contemporary community standards. Why is such testimony required? Because, assert the majority, "To sanction convictions without expert evidence of community standards encourages the jury to condemn as obscene such conduct or material as is personally distasteful or offensive to the particular juror." (Ante, p. 543.) "Moreover," state the majority, "since we designate the State of California as the relevant 'community' for this case, we cannot realistically expect the trier of fact to understand intuitively how the community as a whole would react to allegedly obscene material."[1] (Ante, p. 544.) And further, declare the majority, expert testimony of community standards is indispensable to effective appellate review.

These reasons are not persuasive. I agree with decisions which have expressly or impliedly concluded that a jury, properly instructed, or trial judge, is fully capable of determining whether conduct or material appeals to prurient interest and offends contemporary community standards, without expert testimony on the subject, and that such testimony is not essential to appellate review. (Kahm v. United States, 5 Cir., 300 F.2d 78, 84; People v. Pinkus, 256 A.C.A. 175, 180–181, 63 Cal.Rptr. 680; State v. Onorato, 3 Conn.Cir. 438, 216 A.2d 859, 860; City of Chicago v. Kimmel, 31 Ill.2d 202, 201 N.E.2d 386, 388.) And, as we shall see, a state standard is wholly inappropriate for judging obscenity of a local public performance such as the one in question.

Surely this court's laudable concern with the preservation of essential liberty of expression should not blind the court to the practicalities of what it is now requiring be done as a prerequisite to curtailing the spread of obscenity in California. As a result of the majority opinion, local entities of government in prosecuting what were formerly regarded as ordinary justice or municipal court lewd or dissolute conduct cases will now be faced with the difficult or impossible task of introducing expert testimony establishing a state standard. The majority state that "the 'community standard' of the entire State of California is an ascertainable, albeit ephemeral, phenomenon subject to evidentiary proof" (ante, p. 544), but the majority fail to offer any enlightenment as to how the so-called state standard is to be ascertained.

Would the toleration by a few metropolitan areas of "topless" gyrations of the type here in question establish the state standard for the more than 9,000 other cities and communities in a California? If such isolated instances of unbridled license are to be the pacemakers for all communities in the state the result can only be a collosal and catastrophic lowering of standards throughout the state. Or if most California cities and communities do not permit such performances, does this establish the state standard? Or would one strive to strike an average in determining the state standard? If 100 communities have "topless" as against 9,000 that do not, then is 1/90th "topless" to be the state standard? Chief Justice Warren and Justice Clark have expressed the belief that there is no provable "national standard" (see Jacobellis v. Ohio, supra, 378 U.S. 184, 200, 84 S.Ct. 1676, 12 L.Ed.2d 793 [dissent]),[2] and I similarly doubt that there is any provable state standard.

But even if there is such a standard, the same considerations that lead the majority to reject a national standard require the application of a local rather than state standard. The majority, in rejecting a national standard, state, "[T]he law of obscenity represents simply the 'present critical point in the compromise between candor and shame at which the community may have arrived here and now.' * * * Different areas of the country, both in attitude and practice, undoubtedly do reach different compromises between 'candor and shame,' and we can conjure no reason for ignoring so obvious a reality. Certainly, all would agree that standards of obscenity are not immutable; they change with the character of whatever community we use for a testing ground." (Ante, p. 546.) The majority further point out that the strongest argument against a non-national standard, namely that it would result in denying some sections of the country access to material, there deemed acceptable, that elsewhere might offend prevailing community standards, does not apply with any force here, since petitioner Iser's dancing is "purely local in nature, a subject matter obviously not intended for nationwide dissemination." (Ante, p. 546.) Patently, neither is her dancing intended for statewide viewing.

The majority also reject a national standard on the basis of the difficulty of obtaining qualified experts to testify regarding such a standard. A similar difficulty will exist in obtaining qualified experts to testify regarding a state standard.

It seems obvious that the imposition of such a burden in obscenity cases will result in increased permissiveness and a consequent downward trend of standards in this state. Also, as a result of the majority opinion, the high standards of many communities throughout this state will be forced downward to meet a lower level.

The only reasons advanced by the majority for concluding that a state standard is "more appropriate" are that it avoids administrative problems in determining the exact scope of a smaller community and that "a strong policy favors uniformity in application of the state criminal law * * *." (Ante, p. 547.) However, any such "administrative problem" is de minimis compared with the problem imposed by the majority upon local governmental entities of ascertaining a state standard and finding qualified experts to testify to it. In my opinion the controlling policy here should be to allow local communities the maximum control possible over local activities. If we deny this reasonable measure of local control, inevitably this court will have to bear its share of the weighty burden of having

removed one of the last remaining barriers to the spread of obscenity into our residential communities.

I would discharge the order to show cause and deny the petition.

McCOMB, J., concurs.

Rehearing denied; McCOMB, MOSK and BURKE, JJ., dissenting.

COURT'S OPINION NOTES

1. Other courts have applied these constitutional protections to various types of entertainment. In Hudson v. United States (D.C.Ct.App.1967) 234 A.2d 903, for example, the court struck down a conviction for staging obscene shows, stating that "in addition to applying to printed matter, such as books and photographs, the same standards are also extended to motion pictures, plays, and burlesque shows, which are forms of speech and prima facie expressions protected by the First Amendment." In Adams Theatre Co. v. Keenan (1953) 12 N.J. 267, 270, 96 A.2d 519, 520, the Supreme Court of New Jersey said: "The performance of a play or show, whether burlesque or other kind of theatre, is a form of speech and prima facie expression protected by the State and Federal Constitutions * * *." (See also Adams Newark Theatre Co. v. City of Newark (1956) 22 N.J. 472, 475, 126 A.2d 340.)

2. Indeed, the concepts of "potential" and prima facie First Amendment protection are becoming increasingly important in areas other than obscenity law. The restricted and literal approach to the definition of speech protected by the First Amendment is gradually being replaced by an emphasis on the interest in communication, whether or not promoted by conduct that is precisely speech. The protection of this interest depends upon a balancing process: the weighing of the interest of the state in suppressing or regulating the questioned conduct as against the opposing interest in the interchange of ideas. (Compare Brown v. State of Louisiana (1966) 383 U.S. 131, 86 S.Ct. 719, 15 L.Ed.2d 637 (opinion of Fortas, J.) with Cox v. State of Louisiana (1965) 379 U.S. 559, 85 S.Ct. 476, 13 L.Ed.2d 487, and Adderley v. State of Florida (1966) 385 U.S. 39, 87 S.Ct. 242, 17 L.Ed.2d 149. See also Bagley v. Washington Township Hospital Dist. (1966) 65 Cal.2d 499, 506–507, 55 Cal.Rptr. 401, 421 P.2d 409; People v. Woody (1964) 61 Cal.2d 716, 718, 40 Cal.Rptr. 69, 394 P.2d 813.) California's obscenity law here at issue represents merely a special, albeit well-established, example of this balancing of interests to determine whether First Amendment guarantees apply to a particular example of communication or whether sufficiently important state interests dictate a contrary result.

3. Unquestionably, these cases provide First Amendment protection for communication that in fact exhibits no special relationship to the political process. Even to the extent that it is possible, for example, to isolate and enumerate precise opinions of concepts in a Joyce or Shakespeare, the ideas they espouse might well have little apparent relevance to the political process. Yet no one could doubt that these works warrant First Amendment protection.

One rationale for this result is that, although the First Amendment is designed to protect only communication that forms the basis for workable democracy in the exchange of ideas relevant to political decisions, "[t]he line between the informing and the entertaining is too elusive"

(Winters v. New York, supra, 333 U.S. 507, 510, 68, S.Ct. 665, 667) and courts must therefore cast a wide net over all forms of communication in order to protect that which is of potential political relevance. An equally persuasive rationale, however, is that the life of the imagination and intellect is of comparable import to the preservation of the political process; the First Amendment reaches beyond protection of citizen participation in, and ultimate control over, governmental affairs and protects in addition the interest in free interchange of ideas and impressions for their own sake, for whatever benefit the individual may gain. (Cf. Kalven, The Metaphysics of the Law of Obscenity (1960) Sup. Court Rev., p. 1.) In any event, the apparent lack of relevance of the dance here at issue to any political decisions is immaterial; under either rationale the dance potentially merits First Amendment protection. Thus the First Amendment cannot be constricted into a straitjacket of protection for political expression alone. Its embrace extends to all forms of communication, including the highest: the work of art.

4. Petitioners strongly argue that the language "lewdly" in Penal Code section 314, subdivision 1, and "lewd or dissolute" in Penal Code section 647, subdivision (a), is unconstitutionally vague. At least for the present purpose of determining the alleged obscenity of a dance performed before an audience for entertainment, we interpret, as did the trial court below, the terms "lewd" and "dissolute" as identical to "obscene," a term that section 311 of the Penal Code defines with as much precision as legislatures and courts have been able to muster in this complex and confusing area. So interpreted, no vagueness objection to section 314, subdivision 1, or section 647, subdivision (a), is tenable. Mishkin v. State of New York (1966) 383 U.S. 502, 506, 86 S.Ct. 958, 16 L.Ed.2d 56.) At the same time, however, by making more specific the scope of section 314, subdivision 1, and section 647, subdivision (a), we necessarily involve ourselves in an issue of constitutional dimension: whether the prosecution has offered sufficient proof of each element of obscenity prescribed by section 311 of the Penal Code.

5. Petitioners do not so much as claim that their convictions should be set aside on the ground of the "redeeming social value" of Iser's dance. Thus we do not reach the problem of whether the dance was "utterly without redeeming social value" and we certainly do not hold that it met that test.

6. For a more complete list of authorities, see Comment, Expert Testimony in Obscenity Cases (1966) 18 Hastings L.J. 161, 170 fns. 61, 62, and 174 fn. 79.

7. In fact we rejected, in another context, final determination of obscenity by subjective reaction of the jury in Zeitlin v. Arnebergh (1963) 59 Cal.2d 901, 31 Cal.Rptr. 800, 383 P.2d 152, 10 A.L.R.3d 707. Responding to the contention that independent appellate review of the alleged obscenity of material is inappropriate because *Roth* focuses the test of obscenity on community standards and the jury by definition represents the community, this court said: "[W]e do not believe that the definition of 'obscene' material as that which 'to the average person * * * predominant appeal * * * is to prurient interest * * *.' * * * indicates that the ultimate determination of that question is always for the jury. These words fix a *standard* which is to be applied to the material; they do not designate the body which is to apply the standard. The statutory language does not inherently predicate a question for the jury; it merely frames a definition." (Id. at p. 911, at p. 806 of 31 Cal.Rptr., at p. 158 of 383 P.2d.) Similarly, in the instant case formulation of the obscenity test in terms of community standards does not suggest a ruling that the jury can reach a subjective judgment on the definition of the standard: the emphasis on the concept of "community" necessarily indicates the requirement for an objective standard.

8. Some courts that, as a general rule, require proof of community standards have held that an expression can be so patently obscene as to obviate that requirement (e.g., Womack v. United States (1961) 111 U.S.App.D.C. 8, 294 F.2d 204, 206, cert. den., 365 U.S. 859, 81 S.Ct. 826, 5 L.Ed.2d 822). In the instant case, however, we need not decide whether to adopt this exception in California. In brief, this case involves a "topless" dance shown only to adults (cf. Ginsberg v. State of New York (1968) 390 U.S. 629, 88 S.Ct. 1274, 20 L.Ed.2d 195) who knew exactly what they were going to see. Since this conduct is not so patently offensive as to violate any conceivable community standard, we need not decide whether evidence of community standards must be introduced in an extreme and unquestionable situation.

9. Although we do not minimize the difficulty in finding qualified experts for such purpose, most commentators and courts have concluded that this problem does not raise an insurmountable barrier. (Comment, Expert Testimony in Obscenity Cases (1966) 18 Hastings L.J. 161; Note, The Use of Expert Testimony in Obscenity Litigation, 1965 Wis. L.Rev. 113; United States v. Klaw, supra, 350 F.2d 155; United States v. One Carton Positive Motion Picture Film Entitled "491" (S.D.N.Y.1965) 247 F. Supp. 450; Trans-Lux Distrib. Corp. v. Maryland State Bd. of Censors (1965) 240 Md. 98, 213 A.2d 235.)

10. The only other justification sometimes offered for a holding that the prosecution need not introduce evidence of community standards rests upon an analogy to the jury's function in cases involving a determination of negligence. In a negligent homicide case, for example, the jury divines the conduct of a reasonably prudent man without expert testimony or other evidentiary assistance and then applies this standard to the proven facts. Some courts conclude from this practice that a jury also should be allowed to apply the obscenity test without proof of community standards. (E.g., Kahm v. United States, supra, 300 F.2d 78, 84.)

The analogy fails primarily for practical reasons. "Community standards" are a complex compendium of attitudes and practices pervading the geographical entity serving as the relevant "community" — in this case, the State of California. (See p. 25, infra.) A locally selected jury, without evidentiary guidance, cannot realistically be expected to appreciate this interplay sufficiently to render an accurate verdict, especially when the issue at stake is the crucial one of defining criminal conduct. (Cf. United States v. Davis (2d Cir. 1965) 353 F.2d 614, 617 (Watermann, J., dissenting).) In contrast, the jury, from their collective experience, are more likely to understand and appreciate the considerations relevant to an evaluation of how a reasonable man would act in given circumstances. That determination involves the finding of whether past conduct conformed to the historical standard of the common law. It does not embrace questions of empirical fact, such as the attitude or reaction of a geographical "community" not necessarily represented by a jury panel.

11. Although numerous cases have held that sufficiency of the evidence to support a conviction is not a proper issue on habeas corpus (In re Manchester (1949) 33 Cal.2d 740, 744, 204 P.2d 881; In re Lindley (1947) 29 Cal.2d 709, 723, 177 P.2d 918), the United States Supreme Court has declared that conviction of a crime without any evidence in the record to support the accused's guilt constitutes a denial of due process. (Garner v. State of Louisiana (1961) 368 U.S. 157, 173–174, 82 S.Ct. 248, 7 L.Ed.2d 207; Thompson v. City of Louisville (1960) 362 U.S. 199, 204, 206, 80 S.Ct. 624, 4 L.Ed.2d 654, 80 A.L.R.2d 1355.) Since the present record contains no evidence as to contemporary community standards, a crucial element in the proof of guilt, the conviction of petitioners violated due process. Hence, habeas corpus is available. (In re Harris (1961) 56 Cal.2d 879, 880, 16 Cal.Rptr. 889, 366 P.2d 305; In re Johnson (1965) 62 Cal.2d 325, 42 Cal.Rptr. 228, 398 P.2d 420; In re Waltreus (1965) 62 Cal.2d 218, 221, 42 Cal.Rptr. 9, 397 P.2d 1001.)

12. Some jurists have urged that communities differ in many respects other than toleration of alleged obscenity; yet these differences have not justified diverse standards with respect to application of constitutional guarantees such as those in criminal procedure. (See, e.g., Jacobellis v. Ohio, supra, 378 U.S. 184, 194, 84 S.Ct. 1676 (opinion of Brennan, J.) Constitutional standards of criminal procedures, however, do not, at least explicitly, take into account "community" standards. The law of obscenity, on the other hand, by definition reflects a balancing of candor and shame in the community, and it is thus quite pertinent to inquire which community's attitudes should be the touchstone of decision.

JUSTICE BURKE'S OPINION NOTES

1. Here the trial court in instructing the jury regarding obscenity stated in part that the "standards which you must apply * * * are the standards of the community, and *the smallest community which you may consider is the State of California.*" (Italics added). Although in my view the italicized statement is erroneous, petitioners do not now complain of the error. In any event, the error was or could have been raised on appeal, and habeas corpus ordinarily cannot serve as a second appeal. (In re Waltreus, 62 Cal.2d 218, 225, 42 Cal.Rptr. 9, 397 P.2d 1001: In re Winchester, 53 Cal.2d 528, 532, 2 Cal.Rptr. 296, 348 P.2d 904.)

2. In Jacobellis v. Ohio, supra, 378 U.S. 184, 192–194, 84 S.Ct. 1676, Justices Brennan and Goldberg concluded that a national standard should be applied, but the issue was not decided by a court majority.

THEATRICAL PERFORMANCE OF "THE BEARD" DOES NOT VIOLATE CALIFORNIA STATUTE WHICH MAKES IT ILLEGAL FOR ANY PERSON TO ENGAGE IN "LEWD OR DISSOLATE CONDUCT IN ANY PUBLIC PLACE" OR TO SING OR SPEAK "ANY OBSCENE SONG, BALLAD OR OTHER WORDS, IN ANY PUBLIC PLACE."

Barrows v. Municipal Court of Los Angeles Jud. Dist., 464 P.2d 483 (1970)

MOSK, Justice.

Petitioners in this proceeding are Richard Bright and Alexandra Hay, who acted in a play entitled "The Beard," Robert Barrows, who produced the play, and Robert Gist, the director. Bright and Miss Hay were charged with violating sections 647, subdivision (a), and 311.6 of the Penal Code[1] for their performances of the play and Barrows and Gist were charged with wilfully and unlawfully aiding and abetting them in committing these violations. Approximately 40 separate charges were filed against petitioners[2] and they seek a writ of prohibition to restrain respondent court from proceeding to trial.

Petitioners contend primarily that the statutes under which they are charged were not intended to apply to a live theatrical performance before an audience and that the application of the provisions to such performance violates their constitutional rights to free speech, due process and equal protection of the laws, in violation of the First and Fourteenth Amendments to the United States Constitution and article I, sections 9, 11, 13 and 21 of the California Constitution. We conclude, for the reasons hereinafter set forth, that the first of petitioners' contentions is meritorious.

The play was first performed on January 24, 1968, in Los Angeles. Petitioners were arrested before the performance on January 25 and they were rearrested after the first two performances the next day. Arrests or citations followed after numerous performances thereafter. Petitioners applied to the United States District Court for an injunction but that court, after issuing a temporary restraining order, ultimately refused permanent relief on the ground that no special circumstances justified its intervention.[3] The trial court overruled demurrers to the complaints and denied a motion to dismiss, and petitioners then sought a writ of prohibition to restrain the court from proceeding to trial. They appeal from denial of the writ.

We begin with the premise that live plays performed in a theater before an audience are entitled to the same protection under the First Amendment as motion pictures (Burton v. Municipal Court (1968) 68 Cal.2d 684, 689, 68 Cal.Rptr. 721, 441 P.2d 281), magazines (Winters v. New York (1948) 333 U.S. 507, 510, 68 S.Ct. 665, 92 L.Ed. 840), and newspapers (New York Times Co. v. Sullivan (1964) 376 U.S. 254, 265-266, 84 S.Ct. 710, 11 L.Ed.2d 686). Long before the advent of printing and motion pictures the theater constituted "a significant medium for the communication of ideas" which affected "public attitudes and behavior in a variety of ways, ranging from direct espousal of a political or social doctrine to the subtle shaping of thought which characterizes all artistic expression." (Joseph Burstyn, Inc. v. Wilson (1952) 343 U.S. 495, 501, 72 S.Ct. 777, 780, 96 L.Ed. 1098)[4]

An analysis of the background of section 647 and some related sections of the Penal Code is necessary to fully comprehend the issues before us. Section 647 is a statute designed to prohibit vagrancy. Prior to 1961, subdivision 5 of the section defined a vagrant as "[e]very lewd or dissolute person, or every person who loiters in or about public toilets in public parks." The statute was characterized by a legislative committee as "ridiculously outdated" and the committee recommended that a substantial revision of its provisions be undertaken (See Report of Assembly Interim Com. on Criminal Procedure, vol. 2, Appendix to Journal of Assembly, Reg.Sess. 1961, pp. 9, 12 et seq.) The committee approved a revision proposed by Professor Arthur H. Sherry that a statute in substantially the form of section 647, subdivision (a), be adopted in lieu of the then existing section 647, subdivision (5). Professor Sherry, in a comment on the proposal, stated that it "departs from the concept of status and deals directly with socially harmful lewd or dissolute conduct, that is, such conduct when it occurs in public view." (See Vagrants, Rogues and Vagabonds—Old Concepts in Need of Revision, 48 Cal.L.Rev. 557, 569.) The committee report quoted this comment and expressed its full concurrence in the language of the section as proposed. (Report of Assembly Interim Com. on Criminal Procedure, op. cit., p. 13.)

In the same year section 647 was revised the Legislature amended section 290 of the Penal Code. That section requires a person who has been convicted of certain sexually related offenses or who has been adjudged to be a sexual psychopath to register with the chief of police in the city in which he temporarily or permanently resides. Each change of address of a registrant must be reported within 10 days, and failure to comply with the registration requirement is a misdemeanor. The section applies automatically when a person is convicted of one of the enumerated offenses and imposes a lifelong requirement of registration and re-registration absent a court order releasing the registrant from the penalties and disabilities of his conviction under section 1203.4[5] (People v. Taylor (1960) 178 Cal.App.2d 472, 477, 3 Cal.Rptr. 186) or the issuance of a certificate of rehabilitation under sections 485.01 et seq.[6] (§ 290.5). The purpose of section 290 is to assure that persons convicted of the crimes enumerated therein shall be readily available for police surveillance at all times because the Legislature deemed them likely to commit similar offenses in the future. (Kelly v. Municipal Court (1958) 160 Cal.App.2d 38, 45, 324 P.2d 990.)

Among the persons who are required to register pursuant to section 290 are those who are convicted of rape, enticement of a female under 18 for purposes of prostitution (§ 266), incest (§ 285), sodomy (§ 286), lewd or lascivious acts upon the body of a child under 14 (§ 288), exposing one's person in a public place (§ 314) or loitering about any public toilet for the purpose of engaging in or soliciting a lewd or lascivious act (§ 647, subdivision (d). Also required to register under section 290 are those convicted of violating subdivision (a) of section 647. Section 290 was amended in 1961 in the same chapter which contained the revision of section 647. (Stats. 1961, ch. 560, §§ 2, 3.) The amendment, insofar as relevant here, substituted persons convicted under section 647, subdivision (a), as subject to the registration provisions for those convicted under former section 647, subdivision(5).

Another event of significance in 1961 was the thorough revision of the statutes relating to obscenity. (Stats.1961, ch. 2147, § 5.) These provisions are now embodied in section 311 et seq. of the Penal Code. Section 311, subdivision(a), defines the term "obscene" as meaning "that to the average person, applying contemporary standards, the predominant appeal of the matter, taken as a whole, is to prurient interest, i. e., a shameful or morbid interest in nudity, sex, or excretion, which goes substantially beyond customary limits of candor in description or representation of such matters and is matter which is utterly without redeeming social importance." The obscenity statutes largely prohibit conduct relating to the dissemination of obscene material, and there is no requirement that persons convicted of violating the obscenity laws must register as sex offenders.

These two conclusions ineluctably emerge from the foregoing analysis: first, the basic purpose of section 647 is to punish the crime of vagrancy in its various overt aspects; second, nothing in the legislative history of the section indicates that it was intended to apply to activities, such as theatrical performances, which are prima facie within the ambit of First Amendment protection.

The requirement of section 290 that persons convicted under section 647, subdivision (a), must register as sex offenders supports this view. It would be irrational to impose upon an actor in a theatrical performance or its director a lifetime requirement of registration as a sexual offender because he may have performed or aided in the performance of an act, perhaps an obscene gesture, in a play.[7] It is an errant concept we cannot attribute to the Legislature that persons convicted of such an offense will require constant police surveillance in order to prevent them from committing similar crimes against society in the future. The mere recitation of the types of crimes encompassed within the registration provisions of section 290 demonstrates that activities which enjoy prima facie protection of the First Amendment were not intended to be included within its scope. That a statute which imposes the penalty of lifetime registration as a sexual offender upon those who participate in a play, merely by reason of acts committed therein, would have an inhibiting effect upon the exercise of First Amendment rights is too evident to require elaboration.[8]

Finally a serious equal protection problem would evolve if we were to interpret section 647, subdivision (a), as respondent urges. The amendment of the obscenity statutes, section 647 and section 290, occurred in the same year and to some extent in the same enactment. Thus, the Legislature should have contemplated the effect of these statutes upon one another; yet in amending section 290 it did not require persons convicted under the obscenity laws to register as sex offenders but reiterated that those convicted under certain subdivisions of section 647 (including subdivision (a)) were required to register. It would be arbitrary and vexatious to require that persons in petitioners' position should be subject to the registration requirement, while those who have violated the laws against obscenity by selling and exhibiting obscene movies, books and pictures to minors or who employ minors for the purpose of such distribution (§§ 311.2, 311.3, 311.4) should not be subject to such a burden. Moreover, one who is found guilty under section 647, subdivision (a), because of acts committed in a live play would be covered by the registration provision, whereas a person who performed the very same act in connection with a photograph or motion picture film would not suffer this penalty.[9]

It seems evident from the foregoing that the vagrancy law, section 647, subdivision (a), was not intended to apply to live performances in a theater before an audience.

Respondents rely upon the cases of In re Giannini, supra, 69 Cal.2d 563, 72 Cal.Rptr. 655, 446 P.2d 535, and Dixon v. Municipal Court (1968) 267 Cal.App.2d 789, 73 Cal. Rptr. 587. The petitioners in *Giannini* were convicted of violating section 647, subdivision (a), by performing a dance before an audience in a nightclub. We held that the performance of a dance, whether a ballet or a lesser artistic form, warranted the protection of the First Amendment, absent proof of its obscenity, but that, in determining whether the conduct of the petitioners was lewd or dissolute, the standards to be applied were those relating to obscenity as defined in section 311, subdivision (a). (69 Cal.2d at p. 571, 72 Cal.Rptr. 655, 446 P.2d 535, fn. 4.) We did not discuss the registration requirement of section 290.

Dixon involved the application of section 647, subdivision (a), to the very play at issue here. The court, relying upon *Giannini,* held that the section was applicable to the live performance of a play in a theater but that in determining whether the acts involved could be characterized as lewd or dissolute, the standards to be applied were set forth in the law defining obscenity. The *Dixon* case recognized that conviction under section 647, subdivision (a), would subject the respondents to the registration provisions of section 290. However, the court stated that, rather than holding lewd or dissolute acts performed in a play are not proscribed, it would refrain from ascertaining whether section 290 was applicable to a conviction under section 647, subdivision (a), when it was based upon a live theatrical performance.

If section 647, subdivision (a), is applicable to a play, there is no rational basis for denying that the registration provisions of section 290 apply. There is no indication on the face of either statute that the penalties for conviction should be different if the lewd or dissolute conduct occurs, for example, in a public park, or before a theater audience. Indeed, the provisions of section 290 have been said to apply "automatically" (People v. Taylor, supra, 178 Cal.App.2d 472, 477,3 Cal.Rptr. 186) and it would require heroic judicial surgery to sever the penalty in one situation and not the other. It must be remembered that these sections were amended by the Legislature at the same time and in the same chapter and that one purpose for amending section 290 was to reflect that section 647, the vagrancy statute, had been revised. It is inconceivable that the Legislature, in amending section 290 to take cognizance of the changes in section 647, would have failed to indicate that some persons convicted under subdivision (a) were not to be subject to the registration requirement if that had been its intent.

While it is true that in *Giannini* we did not consider the applicability of the registration provisions to convictions under subdivision (a) of section 647, the decision nevertheless appears to stand for the proposition that the vagrancy section may be applied to live theatrical performances. In light of our present focus on the statutory provision, we now clarify and modify *Giannini* to that extent and hold that such performances do not fall within the purview of section 647, subdivision (a). *Dixon* is disapproved insofar as it is inconsistent with the views expressed herein.

We come, then to consideration of the question whether the prosecution of petitioners is justified under section 311.6 of the Penal Code. The section, as we have seen, makes it a misdemeanor to sing or speak "any obscene song, ballad, or other words, in any public place." It was originally enacted in 1872, at which time only the singing of obscene words was prohibited and it was illegal to do so not only in a public place but also "in any place where there are persons present to be annoyed thereby." (Deering's Ann.Code, § 311, subdivision 5.) The prohibition referring to spoken words was added to the statute in 1931 and a curious provision inserted to the effect that the section would not apply to an actor unless and until a court decided that he had violated the statute; but this dispensation was withdrawn if a complaint was filed against a manager, producer or director charging a violation of the section and the guilty words were uttered by the actor during the pendency of the complaint. (Stats.1931,ch.759, § 1.)

In 1961 the section was amended in the course of overall revision of the obscenity laws. The provision added in 1931 immunizing an actor from prosecution under certain circumstances was deleted entirely, as was the proscription against speaking or singing obscene words "in any place where there are persons present to be annoyed thereby." (Stats.1961, ch. 2147, § 5.)

In determining the definition of the word "obscene" as used in section 311.6 we turn to section 311 of the Penal Code. Section 311 and section 311.6 are both contained in chapter 7.5 of title 9 of the Penal Code. Section 311 provides, *"As used in this chapter:* (a) 'Obscene' means that to the average person, applying contemporary standards, the predominant appeal of the *matter,* taken as a whole, is to prurient interest, i. e., a shameful or morbid interest in nudity, sex, or excretion, which goes substantially beyond customary limits of candor in description or representation of such matters and is *matter* which is utterly without redeeming social importance. (b) 'Matter' means any book, magazine, newspaper, or other printed or written material or any picture, drawing, photograph, motion picture, or other pictorial representation or any statue or other figure, or any recording, transcription or mechanical, chemical or electrical reproduction or any other articles, equipment, machines or materials." (Emphasis added.)

It is readily apparent that the term "matter" as defined in subdivision (b) does not include the spoken word, and respondent so concedes. It is equally clear that the definition of obscenity in subdivision (a) refers only to certain types of "matter," as that term is defined in subdivision (b). We are, therefore, faced with the impossible task of applying a statute (section 311.6) which refers to the speaking of "obscene * * * words" although the definition of the term "obscene" (in section 311) cannot include the spoken word.[10] The Legislature specified with great particularity in subdivision (b) of section 311 what it meant by the term "matter," and it is impermissible for us to either add to this definition or subtract from it. Thus the conclusion is inescapable under these circumstances that theatrical performances are not included within the prohibition of section 311.6.[11]

This conclusion is fortified by the fact that the Legislature deleted any reference to actors in 1961 when it amended section 311.6 during the course of revising the obscenity statutes. Although this omission might under other circumstances be deemed an equivocal act, perhaps indicating that the Legislature assumed that the specific mention of actors was not necessary because plays were otherwise covered by the prohibition against obscenity, such an explanation cannot be accepted here because in the same statute the Legislature defined the coverage of the obscenity laws with precision and did not include within such definition any word which could conceivably embrace plays.

Our holding here does not suggest that acts which are independently prohibited by law may be consummated without sanction on the stage merely because they occur during the course of a theatrical play. Dramatic license would not supply indulgence for the actual murder of the villain, the rape of the heroine, or the maiming of the hero. Neither do we intend to imply, however, that conduct or speech in a theatrical production is to be judged by the same standards as conduct or speech occurring on the street or other public place. *Giannini* makes it clear that "acts which are unlawful in a different context, circumstance, or place, may be depicted or incorporated in a stage or screen presentation and come within the protection of the First Amendment, losing that protection only if found to be obscene." (69 Cal.2d at p. 572, 72 Cal.Rptr. at p. 661, 446 P.2d at p. 541.) We particularly reaffirm this portion of the decision in *Giannini*, for any more restrictive rule could annihilate in a stroke much of the modern theater and cinema. The loss to culture and to First Amendment rights would be equally tragic.

We need not point out that the Legislature may prohibit the performance of an obscene play provided that constitutional standards are met in defining obscenity. (See In re Giannini, supra, 69 Cal.2d 563, 72 Cal.Rptr. 655, 446 P.2d 535.) We hold here only that the consequences of applying section 647, subdivision (a), to acts performed in a play, the language of section 311.6 when read in the light of the definition of obscenity, and the legislative history of both sections, all indicate that the Legislature did not intend those statutes to apply to theatrical performances.

The omission appears to be commonplace; according to a recent study, only five states enjoin obscene plays and four additional jurisdictions prohibit obscene performances or presentations. (See Note (1966), 75 Yale L.J. 1364, appendix II.)

In view of the conclusions reached above, it is not necessary to discuss other contentions raised by petitioners.

The order is reversed and the court is directed to issue the writ of prohibition as prayed.

TRAYNOR, C. J., and PETERS and TOBRINER, JJ., concur.

McCOMB, Justice (dissenting).

I dissent. I would affirm the order denying a writ of prohibition, for the reasons expressed by Mr. Justice Cobey in the opinion prepared by him for the Court of Appeal, Second District, Division Three (Barrows v. Municipal Court, 2 Civ. 33328, filed May 2, 1969, certified for nonpublication).

BURKE, Justice (dissenting).

I disagree with the majority that Penal Code section 647, subdivision (a), is inapplicable to live performances in a theater before an audience. The effect of that holding is to allow acts, however obscene, to be performed on the stage with complete immunity unless they are proscribed by other statutory provisions. It is inconceivable that the Legislature intended such a result. I also do not agree with the majority that Penal Code section 311.6 is inapplicable to such performances.

Petitioners Richard Bright and Alexandra Hay were charged with violating sections 647, subdivision (a), and 311.6 for their conduct during performances of the play "The Beard." Petitioners Robert Barrows, the producer of the play, and Robert Gist, the director, were charged with aiding and abetting them in committing the violations. Respondent overruled demurrers to the complaints and denied a motion to dismiss. Petitioners then sought prohibition in the superior court to restrain respondent from proceeding to trial. They appeal from the denial of the writ.

Penal Code section 647, subdivision (a), as it read at the time in question, provided that every person "Who solicits anyone to engage in or who engages in lewd or dissolute conduct in any public place or in any place open to the public or exposed to public view" shall be guilty of disorderly conduct, a misdemeanor. Nothing in the language of the section excludes such conduct merely because it occurs during a theatrical performance before an audience.

It is implicit in In re Giannini (1968) 69 Cal.2d 563, 72 Cal.Rptr. 655, 446 P.2d 535, that the quoted subdivision may be applied to live theatrical performances, and Dixon v. Municipal Court (1968) 267 Cal.App.2d 789, 73 Cal.Rptr. 587 (hg. dan.), held that the subdivision applied to a live performance in a theater of the very play at issue here. *Dixon* stated that the asserted lewd act was a simulation of oral copulation, which was done in the course of a performance of "The Beard." The court in *Dixon* specifically considered the requirement in Penal Code section 290 that persons convicted of violating section 647, subdivision (a), register as sex offenders, which requirement is relied upon by the majority in the instant case to support its conclusion that section 647, subdivision (a), is inapplicable to live theatrical performances. The court there (at p. 792, 73 Cal.Rptr. 587) concluded, and in my opinion properly so, that it was unnecessary to decide whether the applicability of section 290 could be challenged successfully by a performer if he were convicted of violating section 647, subdivision (a). That case, like the present one, was an appeal from an order disposing of a petition for a writ of prohibition to restrain the municipal court from prosecuting the petitioners.

Dixon further declared (at p. 792, 73 Cal.Rptr. at p. 589), "It cannot be reasonably believed that the Legislature intended to allow any and all acts which are patently obscene to be committed on stages, runways or other performing areas—but this would be the effect (except as to acts specifically made criminal under other statutes; for example, sodomy) of holding section 647, subdivision (a), inapplicable. It is more logical to withhold judgment on whether section 290 could apply to a theatrical performer than to hold all persons immune from obscene performances because registration may not be apposite to their cases."

In 1969 the Legislature amended section 647 but did not change the quoted language of subdivision (a). (Stats. 1969, ch. 204, § 1; ch. 1319, § 2.) Where a statute has been construed by judicial decision, and that construction is not altered by subsequent legislation, it must be presumed that the Legislature is aware of the judicial construction and approves it. (People v. Hallner, 43 Cal.2d 715, 719, 277 P.2d 393.)

Penal Code section 311.6 provides: "Every person who knowingly sings or speaks any obscene song, ballad, or other words, in any public place is guilty of a misdemeanor." As the basis for its conclusion that the section is inapplicable to live performances before an audience, the majority point to the provision in section 311, as it read at the time in question, that "As used in this chapter [which includes § 311.6] * * * 'obscene' " has the definition there given, and the majority note that the definition there given employed the word "matter" and that the definition given for "matter" did not include the spoken word.[1] Therefore, state the majority (ante, p. 825) the court is "faced with the impossible task of applying a statute (section 311.6) which refers to the speaking of 'obscene * * * words' although the definition of the term 'obscene' (in section 311) cannot include the spoken word."

The majority thus give no effect to section 311.6 and render it meaningless. This is contrary to the cardinal rule of statutory construction that a court must, where reasonably possible, harmonize statutes and construe them so as to give force and effect to all their provisions. (See, e. g., Burks v. Poppy Construction Co., 57 Cal.2d 463, 470, 20 Cal.Rptr. 609, 370 P.2d 313; Hough v. McCarthy, 54 Cal.2d 273, 279, 5 Cal.Rptr. 668, 353 P.2d 276; cf. In re Bandmann, 51 Cal.2d 388, 393, 333 P.2d 339.)

In the light of that rule and a recent amendment to section 311, which the majority fail to consider, it is clear that the intent of the Legislature in enacting section 311 was to define the term "obscene matter"[2] rather than the word "obscene" and that the word "obscene," as used in section 311.6, when reasonably interpreted, has a meaning similar to that accorded to it by the United States Supreme Court in Roth v. United States, 354 U.S. 476, 77 S. Ct. 1304, 1 L.Ed.2d 1498 as elaborated in subsequent cases.[3] The legislative intent regarding section 311 was clarified by the 1969 amendment thereto, which, among other things, added the word "matter" following the word "obscene." The section, as it now reads, provides, "As used in this chapter: (a) 'Obscene *matter*' means * * * ." (Italics added.) Although a number of cases have indicated that section 311 defines the word "obscene" (see, e.g., In re Panchot (1968) 70 A.C. 109, 111, 73 Cal.Rptr. 689, 448 P.2d 385; In re Giannini, *supra*, 69 Cal.2d 563, 571, fn. 4, 572-574, 72 Cal.Rptr. 655, 446 P.2d 535; Zeitlin v. Arnebergh (1963) 59 Cal.2d 901, 911, 920, 31 Cal.Rptr. 800, 383 P.2d 152, 10 A.L.R.3d 707; see Dixon v. Municipal Court, *supra*, 267 Cal.App.2d 789, 791, 73 Cal.Rptr. 587), these cases preceded the 1969 amendment to section 311, which clarified the law.

That the legislature intended section 311.6 to apply to theatrical performances is also indicated by the legislative history of the section. The section, which was added in 1961 as part of an overall revision of the obscenity laws, was derived from former section 311 of the Penal Code, which was repealed in 1961 (Stats.1961, ch. 2147, § 1, p. 4427). Former section 311 was enacted in 1872, at which time the section prohibited the singing of a lewd or obscene song not only "in any public place" but also "in any place where there are persons present to be annoyed thereby." The prohibition referring to the spoken word was added in 1931 and a provision was inserted immunizing actors from prosecution under some but not all circumstances. (Stats. 1931, ch. 759, § 1, p. 1597.)[4] This provision remained in the section until the section was repealed in 1961. (See Stats. 1949, ch. 1003, § 1, p. 1848; Stats.1952, 1st Ex.Sess., ch. 23, § 4, p. 381.) The Legislature thus manifestly contemplated that former section 311

applied to actors under some circumstances, and nothing in the 1961 revision of the obscenity laws indicates a legislative intent to grant actors immunity from prosecution under section 311.6.[5] Rather the failure to include in section 311.6 the provision relating to actors indicates a legislative intent not to immunize from prosecution under any circumstances persons on the ground that they are actors. (See, generally, Baum, California's New Law on Obscene Matter, 36 State Bar J. 625,632-633.)

I would affirm the order denying the writ of prohibition.

McCOMB and SULLIVAN, JJ., concur.

Rehearing denied; McCOMB and BURKE,JJ., dissenting.

COURT'S OPINION NOTES

1. Section 647, subdivision (a), provides, "Every person who * * * solicits anyone to engage in or who engages in lewd or dissolute conduct in any public place or in any place open to the public or exposed to public view" shall be guilty of disorderly conduct, a misdemeanor.

Section 311.6 provides, "Every person who knowingly sings or speaks any obscene song, ballad, or other words, in any public place is guilty of a misdemeanor."

All references will be to the Penal Code unless otherwise noted.

2. Each petitioner was not cited after every performance. It appears that some of the complaints were based upon the performance of the play without a permit from the Los Angeles Police Commission, as required by ordinance. However, the charges based upon the failure to obtain a permit were dismissed by the trial court and we are concerned here only with the alleged violation by petitioners of sections 647, subdivision (a), and 311.6.

3. The decision was rendered by a three-judge court, with one judge dissenting. The majority opinion stated that it was doubtful the state courts would construe section 647, subdivision (a), as applicable to plays and that section 311.6 would probably be found constitutional. According to the dissenting judge, the relief petitioners sought was appropriate because both statutes were unconstitutional as applied to theatrical performances. (Barrows v. Reddin (C.D.Cal.1968) 301 F.Supp. 574.)

4. Use of the theater to depict current events, as distinguished from religious pageantry, was first attempted by Aeschylus, and refined by Euripides and later by Aristophanes who mastered comedy.

Fear of the political potential of the theater was manifest when James I published an ordinance forbidding representation of any living Christian king upon the stage. Since 1624 the lord chamberlain has had censorship control of the English theater. (See VII Ency. Soc. Sciences, 598 ff.)

5. Section 1203.4 sets forth a procedure through which a defendant who has fulfilled the conditions of his probation or has been discharged from probation may be released of the penalties and disabilities resulting from his conviction.

6. Sections 4852.01 et seq. provide that a person convicted of a felony who has been released from prison may apply for a certificate of rehabilitation and set forth the procedure for obtaining such a certificate.

7. As we shall see, the terms "lewd" and "dissolute" as used in subdivision (a) of section 647 were held in In re Giannini (1968) 69 Cal.2d 563, 571, 72 Cal.Rptr. 655, 446 P.2d 535, to be identical to the term "obscene" as

defined in section 311, subdivision (a).

8. In some states the interracial amity of Harriet Beecher Stowe's *Uncle Tom's Cabin* would have been found to be obscene. Yet today we need not be reminded that the theater has been a significant source in the development of American politics, culture, language and mores, despite what H. L. Mencken termed its frequent "florid argot." He also credited the theater with being "one of the chief sources of popular slang." (Mencken, The American Language (1938), p. 585.)

9. Section 647, subdivision (a), is limited to a public place, a place open to the public, or one exposed to public view. A private movie studio from which the public is excluded would not fit this description.

10. This anomalous situation arose because, when the Legislature revised the obscenity laws in 1961, it merely repeated the portion of section 311.6 prohibiting the speaking of obscene words, which had been in the section for many years, without taking into account the embracive definition of the term "obscene" in section 311 added the same year.

11. Admittedly, it is difficult to conceive of a situation to which section 311.6 would be applicable since there is only one definition of the term "obscene" in the Penal Code and, as stated above, it cannot apply to the spoken word.

JUSTICE BURKE'S OPINION NOTES

1. Section 311, as it read at the time in question, provided: "As used in this chapter: "(a) 'Obscene' means that to the average person, applying contemporary standards, the predominant appeal of the matter, taken as a whole, is to prurient interest, i.e., a shameful or morbid interest in nudity, sex, or excretion, which goes substantially beyond customary limits of candor in description or representation of such matters and is matter which is utterly without redeeming social importance. "(b) 'Matter' means any book, magazine, newspaper, or other printed or written material or any picture, drawing, photograph, motion picture, or other pictorial representation or any statue or other figure, or any recording, transcription or mechanical, chemical or electrical reproduction or any other articles, equipment, machines or materials. " * * * "

The section was subsequently amended. (Stats.1969, ch. 249, § 1.)

2. The terms "obscene matter" and "matter represented * * * to be obscene" are employed in various sections in the chapter that contains section 311. (See Pen. Code, §§ 311.2, 311.5, and 311.7.)

3. The United States Supreme Court "defined obscenity in *Roth* in the following terms: '[W]hether to the average person, applying contemporary community standards, the dominant theme of the material taken as a whole appeals to prurient interest.' 354 U.S., at 489, 77 S.Ct. [1304] at 1311. Under this definition, as elaborated in subsequent cases, three elements must coalesce: it must be established that (a) the dominant theme of the material taken as a whole appeals to a prurient interest in sex; (b) the material is patently offensive because it affronts contemporary community standards relating to the description or representation of sexual matters; and (c) the material is utterly without redeeming social value." (A Book Called "John Cleland's Memoirs of a Woman of Pleasure" v. Attorney General of Com. of Massachusetts, 383 U.S. 413, 418, 86

S.Ct. 975, 977, 16 L.Ed.2d 1.) "Obscene," as used in section 311.6, reasonably interpreted, has the foregoing meaning except that the words "live performance" should be substituted for the word "material."

4. The provision read: "The provision of [the subdivision prohibiting the singing or speaking of obscene songs of words under specified circumstances] shall not apply to any person participating in violation thereof only as an actor, unless and until the proper court shall have passed upon the matter and found the actor to have violated the said subdivision * * * , except where after a complaint has been filed against the owner, manager, producer or director charging a violation of said subdivision * * * , and pending the determination thereof an actor or actress utters the particular word or words complained against or other word or words of the same or similar import, in connection with such performance, act, play, drama, exhibition or entertainment." (Stats.1931, ch. 759, § 1, p. 1597.)

5. That the phrase "or in any place where there are persons present to be annoyed thereby" was omitted from section 311.6 does not show a legislative intent to exclude conduct that occurs in a theater, since the prohibitions of that section apply where the conduct occurs "in any public place" and a theater clearly appears to be such a place.

"HAIR" IS NOT OBSCENE

Southeastern Promotions, Ltd. v. City of Atlanta, Ga., 334 F. Supp. 634 (1971)

MEMORANDUM ORDER AND OPINION

EDENFIELD, District Judge.

Stripped of window-dressing and distracting side issues, the naked question in this case is whether municipal officials, solely by reason of their authority to manage a municipal civic center and auditorium, have the unfettered right to censor and monitor the types of speech, and to prescribe the types of productions, which may be performed in such a public auditorium. They do not. United States Constitution, Amendment I.

Plaintiff, a New York corporation, is in the business of promoting entertainment such as live theatrical productions. In July of 1971 its representative, Ralph Bridges, who has frequently booked productions at the Atlanta Civic Center on previous occasions, spoke with Roy Elrod, Director of the Civic Center, and requested a reservation of the Civic Center auditorium from November 23 through December 5 (excluding Thanksgiving Day) for the presentation of a musical play entitled "Hair." Elrod said he did not think "Hair" would be allowed in the Civic Center, but he apparently agreed to informally hold open the dates involved pending a ruling on the matter from the city's Municipal Buildings and Athletic Committee. In September Elrod wrote to Bridges and informed him that the Committee, which has jurisdiction over the Civic Center, denied the request to present "Hair" at the auditorium. The letter gave no reason for the denial, but Elrod orally informed Bridges, and at the hearing the Chairman of the Committee testified, that it had been the practice of the Committee to restrict the use of the auditorium to wholesome, "family type" productions, and that defendants did not think "Hair" was the proper type of entertainment for a public auditorium. According to a drama critic witness and a theatrical expert, "Hair" is a serious literary production whose theme was the exposure of the hypocrisy and pretense of the contemporary middle-age "establishment" as viewed through the eyes of the younger "hippie" generation. Both witnesses concluded that the production was not obscene or pornographic although in one scene, under subdued lighting and for a period of less than 35 seconds, certain members of the cast appear in the nude and in another scene one member of the cast is draped in or wrapped in an American flag. Both experts expressed the opinion that these two scenes were neither lewd nor unnecessary but somehow represented "freedom" and were relevant to the plot.

Plaintiff filed this action based on grounds of diversity and pursuant to 42 U.S.C.A. § 1983 (1970) on the ground that the denial by the defendants of plaintiff's right to display "Hair" constituted a prior restraint on plaintiff's freedom of speech in violation of the First Amendment. On plaintiff's motion the court temporarily restrained the defendants from leasing the auditorium to others during the dates in question pending the outcome of this lawsuit. Since no attack has been made upon the constitutionality of any state statute, a three-judge court is neither required nor proper.

The defendants in due course filed their answer and response in which they seek to raise three defenses: First, that "Hair" is obscene and pornographic and, if presented, would also violate certain criminal statutes of the State of Georgia seeking to punish indecent exposure and desecration of the flag; second, that the play not only involves "speech" within the meaning of the First Amendment but also involves actions, or "non-speech", which is not protected by that Amendment; and third, that the issues presented were not First Amendment issues but "licensing issues, their contention being that since the City operates the Civic Center, including the auditorium, not as a governmental function but in a quasi-ministerial (profit-making) capacity, the City should be allowed to prescribe the types of entertainment to be permitted or shown.

Earlier in the proceedings defendants also argued that the Director could not have leased the auditorium for the presentation of "Hair" because if he had he would have subjected himself to possible prosecution under those Georgia criminal statutes which prohibit indecent exposure[1] and desecration of the American flag.[2] The rather far-fetched implication of this argument is that since this court might make a determination that the presentation of "Hair" did not violate those Georgia statutes, it would then be interfering with threatened state criminal prosecutions—albeit against defendant Elrod himself. Such federal interference, contended defendants, might be barred by the construction of Younger v. Harris, 401 U.S. 37, 91 S.Ct. 746, 27 L.Ed.2d 669 (1971), given recently by this court in Cooley v. Endictor, Civil No. 15359 (N.D.Ga., Aug. 25, 1971), which involved the presentation of the musical play entitled "Stomp." At the hearing, however, the Director of the Civic Center denied that he had ever

been threatened with criminal prosecution or that he acted because of any threat and testified further that he knew of no state criminal statutes under which such prosecution might be conducted. This testimony clearly distinguishes Cooley v. Endictor, which otherwise might possibly have been in point.

For convenience, the court will turn first to the second defense — that theatrical productions are not "speech" protected by the First Amendment. It is true that the Supreme Court has not come face to face with this precise question, but it seems clear that live theatrical productions, no less than novels or motion pictures, are media and organs for the expression of public opinion and the propagation of ideas and critical comments and are entitled to First Amendment protection. The works of Shakespeare are no less "speech" when they are performed on stage than when they appear in print. *Accord,* LaRue v. State of California, 326 F.Supp. 348 (C.D.Cal.1971) (three-judge court); P. B. I. C., Inc. v. Byrne, 313 F.Supp. 757 (D.Mass.1970) (three-judge court), vacated and remanded to consider the question of mootness, 401 U.S. 987, 91 S.Ct. 1222, 28 L.Ed.2d 526 (1971), aff'd on remand, Civil No. 70-508-G (D. Mass., June 16, 1971), petition for cert. filed, 40 U.S.L.W. 3095 (U.S. Sept. 14, 1971) (No. 71-304). *Cf.,* Schacht v. United States, 398 U.S. 58,90 S.Ct. 1555, 26 L.Ed.2d 44 (1970).

Defendants contend, however, that "Hair" is a hybrid of "speech" and "non-speech" elements. Specifically, they say that when the actors in "Hair" appear in the nude and when an American flag is both wrapped around one actor and used to swing another, there occur "non-speech" activities which are not accorded First Amendment protection. *See* Cox v. Louisiana, 379 U.S. 536, 85 S.Ct. 453, 13 L.Ed.2d 471 (1965). The Supreme Court has held that:

" * * * [W]hen 'speech' and 'non-speech' elements are combined in the same course of conduct, a sufficiently important governmental interest in regulating the non-speech element can justify incidental limitations on First Amendment freedoms." United States v. O'Brien, 391 U.S. 367, 376, 88 S.Ct. 1673, 1678, 20 L.Ed.2d 672 (1968). Therefore, say defendants, they are permitted to more strictly regulate musical plays such as "Hair" than they may "pure" speech which is protected by the First Amendment.

The court cannot accept the proposition that stage productions may be dissected into "speech" and "non-speech" components as those terms have been used by the Supreme Court. The nonverbal elements in a theatrical production are the very ones which distinguish this form of art from literature. It may be true that First Amendment protections vary in different media, but a musical play must be deemed a unitary form of constitutionally protected expression.[3] The court concludes that the entire musical play "Hair" is speech and entitled to First Amendment protection.[4]

The next question is whether defendants are obligated to provide the facilities at the Atlanta Civic Center to plaintiff; in other words, does plaintiff have a right to present "Hair" at the Civic Center? Defendants vigorously contend that plaintiff has no such right and defendants have no such obligation. They cite Southeastern Promotions, Ltd. v. City of West Palm Beach, Fla., Civil No. 71-1461-Civ-EC (S.D.Fla., Oct. 22, 1971), which is identical in every respect with the instant case, for support. Plaintiff cites Southwest Productions, Inc. v. Freeman,

Civil No. LR-71-C-137 (E.D. Ark., Aug. 13, 1971), which is also identical in every respect with the instant case, for support. Those two cases are in clear conflict and this court agrees with Judge Eisele of Arkansas and respectfully disagrees with Senior Judge Choate of Florida.

It should be self-evident that the Atlanta Civic Center is dedicated to the public use. It was built by the taxpayers of Atlanta. It is managed by the elected and appointed representatives of those taxpayers, it is maintained by the taxpayers, and it is specifically designed to accommodate and attract the taxpayers. Still the court must inquire whether the character and purpose of the Civic Center, the nature of the activities carried on in it, and the population who take advantage of it together render it an appropriate forum for the free expression of ideas. *Accord*, Wolin v. Port of New York Authority, 392 F.2d 83, 89 (2d Cir.), cert. denied, 393 U.S. 940, 89 S.Ct. 290, 21 L.Ed.2d 275 (1968).

The Atlanta Civic Center was built by the citizens of Atlanta as a multipurpose facility for recreational, commercial and social uses. It contains a large-capacity auditorium, exhibit halls, and meeting rooms. Theatrical productions, business conventions, displays, and meetings of various kinds have been held there, and large segments of the community have frequented these events. Although the theatrical productions presented in the auditorium of the Civic Center in the past could not fairly be characterized as very controversial, political or ideological, they have tended to convey and reinforce those cherished values of many of the citizens of the "straight" world. There can be no question, then, that the Atlanta Civic Center has been a forum in which ideas, however unrevolutionary, have been expressed and communicated repeatedly over a number of years.

Decisions of the Supreme Court and the lower courts have consistently recognized that a public forum for expression must be available to *all* members of the public for the exercise of First Amendment rights. Thus it has been held that public schools,[5] public libraries,[6] public bus terminals,[7] public college newspapers,[8] public high school newspapers,[9] and public subway walls[10] are public forums in which all members of the public are entitled to exercise freedom of speech. By comparison, a public auditorium is a public forum par excellence! Since 1925 it has been settled that states and municipalities may no more interfere with freedom of speech than may the national government. Gitlow v. New York, 268 U.S. 652, 45 S.Ct. 625, 69 L.Ed. 1138 (1925). It is abundantly clear that defendants have an obligation to make the Atlantic Civic Center—a municipal auditorium—available to all for the exercise of First Amendment rights and that plaintiff may exercise those rights in the Civic Center. Plaintiff's right to do so is in no sense lessened by the fact that they might be able to go elsewhere or that they hope to make money by presenting "Hair." Bantam Books, Inc. v. Sullivan, 372 U.S. 58, 83 S.Ct. 631, 9 L.Ed.2d 584 (1963); Joseph Burstyn, Inc. v. Wilson, 343 U.S. 495, 501-502, 72 S.Ct. 777, 96 L.Ed. 1098 (1952).

We come then to defendants' argument that they are entitled, as managers of a quasi-business venture, to exercise their unfettered judgment over the content of expression in the Civic Center. They support this argument by saying that the Civic Center has an "image" for the presentation of "family-type entertainment" and that it would suffer great financial harm if it presented entertainment which did not conform to this "image." Bluntly put, defendants say they may censor. The court disagrees. Indeed, one only hopes the gentle soul of Mr. Justice Black was not hovering over this courtroom when defendants propounded this argument.

If little else is certain, it is most assuredly certain that the First Amendment unreservedly, forthrightly, and resoundingly prohibits such censorship. Even if defendants are acting with the best of intentions—and this court does not doubt that—they simply may not dictate what the public may view and what it may not. United States Servicemen's Fund v. Shands, 440 F.2d 44 (4th Cir. 1971). To be sure freedom of speech is not an absolute right. The City may set up various procedural rules so that one person cannot monopolize the Civic Center or use it for a purpose for which it is not physically suited. *See, generally,* Cox v. Louisiana, *supra.* Here, however, there has been no contention that plaintiff has not complied or will not comply with the procedural rules and technical regulations promulgated by the Civic Center.

Defendants' contention is not advanced by their attempts to characterize the grant or denial of permission to use the Civic Center as a municipal licensing function. Both Director Elrod and Chairman Cotsakis of the Municipal Buildings and Athletic Committee testified that there are absolutely no guidelines or standards whatsoever governing defendants' decisions in this regard. They resort only to their subjective feelings.[11] This is an unconstitutional method of decision and selection.

"[A] municipality may not empower its licensing officials to roam essentially at will, dispensing or withholding permission to speak, assemble, picket, or parade, according to their own opinions regarding the potential effect of the activity in question on the 'welfare', 'decency', or 'morals' of the community." Shuttlesworth v. Birmingham, 394 U.S. 147, 153, 89 S.Ct. 935, 940, 22 L.Ed.2d 162 (1969).

Defendants assert that "Hair" is obscene and therefore subject to prior restraint. Of course as the Supreme Court has so recently reaffirmed, any imposition of prior restraint upon expression bears a heavy presumption of constitutional invalidity. New York Times Co. v. United States, 403 U.S. 713, 91 S.Ct. 2140, 29 L.Ed.2d 822 (1971). Traditionally, public officials who attempt such prior restraint have been able to justify it only by showing an overwhelming contrary state interest, such as a "clear and present danger" of great violence and severe injury. Nevertheless, the Supreme Court has determined that obscenity is not entitled to First Amendment protection. Roth v. United States, *supra.* The Court has held that public officials may impose a prior restraint upon obscene motion pictures, Times Film Corp. v. Chicago, 365 U.S. 43, 81 S.Ct. 391, 5 L.Ed.2d 403 (1961), as long as certain safeguards are observed, and it would follow that the same applies to live theatrical performances.

The only evidence defendants have offered to prove that "Hair" is obscene is the libretto of the play itself and a critical quotation from a local columnist. Defendants have directed the court's attention to various foul words which appear in the libretto and have also made much of the 35 seconds of nudity. Plaintiff has offered the testimony of the expert witnesses already referred to and several reviews by theatrical critics to the effect that "Hair" is not obscene under the Supreme Court's definition of that term.[12]

Having considered the libretto and all the evidence, the

court concludes that, whatever else it may be, "Hair" is not obscene.[13] Moreover, the foul words and nudity, far from rendering "Hair" obscene, are in and of themselves constitutionally protected forms of expression which may not be censored by state action. The Supreme Court (per Mr. Justice Harlan) in Manual Enterprises v. Day, 370 U.S. 478, 490, 82 S.Ct. 1432, 1438, 8 L.Ed.2d 639 (1962), observed:

"Of course not every portrayal of male or female nudity is obscene." In Roth the Court recognized that

"The portrayal of sex, e.g., in art, literature, and scientific works, is not itself sufficient reason to deny material the constitutional protection of freedom of speech and press." 354 U.S. at 487, 77 S.Ct. at 1310.

As for foul words, the Court (again per Mr. Justice Harlan) recently held that such "obscenities" do not, standing alone, constitute obscene expression. Cohen v. California, 403 U.S. 15, 91 S.Ct. 1780, 29 L.Ed.2d 284 (1971).

Defendants also seek to justify a prior restraint by pointing to the use of the American flag as a prop in the play. As already noted, the flag is wrapped around one actor and used to swing another during the performance. Recently the Supreme Court was faced with a federal statute which prohibits an actor portraying someone in the military from wearing a military uniform as a costume if the play in which the actor appears is critical of the military. The Court reversed the conviction of an actor who had been convicted for violating this statute and held that it constituted an abridgment of the actor's First Amendment right of free speech. Schacht v. United States, *supra*. It would follow from this that the mere use of an American flag as a prop in "Hair" can in no way justify the imposition of a prior restraint on the performance of the play.

Finally, defendants contend that the 35 seconds of nudity and the use of the American flag as a prop may violate Georgia law and defendants have a right to prevent the occurrence of such violations. The statutes involved, as already mentioned, are [1970 Revision] Ga.Code Ann. § 26-2011 and [1970 Revision] Ga. Code Ann § 26-2803.

First, the court holds that the mere raising of the possibility of criminal violations does not justify the imposition of a prior restraint upon expression. *See* New York Times Co. v. United States, *supra* (concurring opinion of Mr. Justice White). Second, the court holds that the nudity and the use of the American flag as a prop do not constitute violations of those Georgia statutes. Section 26-2011 states:

"Public indecency.—A person commits public indecency when he performs any of the following acts in a public place and upon conviction shall be punished as for a misdemeanor: (a) An act of sexual intercourse; (b) A *lewd* exposure of the sexual organs; (c) A *lewd* appearance in a state of partial or complete nudity; (d) A *lewd* caress or indecent fondling of the body of another person." (Emphasis added.)

Typically, such public indecency statutes are meant to cover situations in which an unsuspecting public is subjected to certain "indecent" acts. Audiences in theatrical performances are not unsuspecting and are generally forewarned and willing. P.B.I.C., Inc. v. Byrne, *supra*. Moreover, the Georgia statute proscribes *lewd* exposure, nudity, and fondling. Mere nudity as emphasizing a theatrical theme is not lewd and does not violate Section 26-2011.[14]

Section 26-2803 states: *"Misuse of National or State*

flag.—A person who deliberately mutilates, defaces, or defiles the flag of the United States or the State of Georgia or who uses such flag or flags for commercial advertising purposes is guilty of a misdemeanor."

The mere use of an American flag as a prop in "Hair" is not a mutilation, defacement, or defilement of the flag nor does it constitute a use for commercial advertising purposes. The use of the American flag in "Hair" does not violate Section 26-2803.

SUMMARY

The evidence at the hearing was that "Hair" has been presented in over 100 American cities and 14 world capitals. Of the 100 American theaters in which "Hair" has played, approximately 30 have been municipal auditoriums, including those of Little Rock, Arkansas, Salem, Virginia, and Spartanburg, South Carolina. The Constitution of the United States commands that, as against the objections made, and upon payment of the appropriate fee, plaintiff have the opportunity to present "Hair" at the Atlanta Civic Center as well.

NOTES

1. [1970 Revision] Ga.Code Ann. § 26-2011.
2. [1970 Revision] Ga.Code Ann. § 26-2803.
3. The argument advanced by defendants could be made in any obscene movie case—yet no case has been cited referring to or accepting such a position. In a somewhat analogous vein the Supreme Court specifically rejected the old English test of judging obscenity by the effect of isolated passages and substituted a test by which a work is judged as a whole. Roth v. United States, 354 U.S. 476, 489, 77 S.Ct. 1304, 1 L.Ed.2d 1498 (1957). This standard has been explicitly adopted in the review of allegedly obscene motion pictures. Jacobellis v. Ohio, 378 U.S. 184, 84 S.Ct. 1676, 12 L.Ed.2d 793 (1964). No suggestion has ever been made by the Supreme Court that depictions of sexual conduct in motion pictures are "nonspeech" activities. It is submitted that just as *parts* of a motion picture cannot lose First Amendment protection on grounds of obscenity, so, too, *parts* of a motion picture cannot lose First Amendment protection on grounds they are "nonspeech." It is further submitted that this applies equally to live theatrical productions. In Schacht v. United States, *supra,* the Supreme Court held that an actor's First Amendment right of free speech was abridged by a statute which forbade him from wearing a military uniform as a costume in a theatrical production critical of the war in Vietnam. The late Mr. Justice Black, who wrote the opinion and who was certainly cognizant of the distinction between protected "speech" and unprotected "non-speech", did not suggest that the wearing of a military uniform in a theatrical production was "nonspeech."

4. Even if defendants' contention had some merit O'Brien held that there is a sufficiently important governmental interest in regulating "nonspeech" so as to justify incidental limitations on First Amendment rights only if the governmental regulation "is within the constitutional power of the Government; if it furthers an important or substantial governmental interest; if the governmental interest is unrelated to the suppression of free expression; and if the incidental restriction on alleged First Amendment freedoms is no greater than is essential to the further-

ance of that interest." 391 U.S. at 377, 88 S.Ct. at 1679. As will be shown, the governmental interest defendants assert is directly related to the suppression of non-obscene speech which is protected by the First Amendment. Furthermore, in response to an inquiry from the bench, counsel for defendants stated that they would not be satisfied with the excision of any "objectionable" parts from "Hair." Rather, they seek to prevent its presentation entirely because they feel it is not "family-type entertainment." Clearly defendants' "nonspeech" contention is not acceptable even if tied to *O'Brien. Accord*, LaRue v. State of California, *supra*, 326 F.Supp. at 355.

5. Tinker v. Des Moines Independent Community School District, 393 U.S. 503, 89 S.Ct. 733, 21 L.Ed.2d 731 (1969).

6. Brown v. Louisiana, 383 U.S. 131. 86 S.Ct. 719, 15 L.Ed.2d 637 (1966).

7. Wolin v. Port of New York Authority, *supra.*

8. Trujillo v. Love, 322 F.Supp. 1266 (D. Col.1971). This is to be distinguished from a public university's law school review which is neither conceived nor used as a general forum for the exchange of ideas but as a limited medium for the publication of high-quality legal articles. There is no First Amendment right to express oneself in such a publication even if the expression is related to law. Avins v. Rutgers, State University of New Jersey, 385 F.2d 151 (3d Cir. 1967).

9. Zucker v. Panitz, 299 F.Supp. 102 (S.D. N.Y.1969).

10. Kissinger v. New York City Transit Authority, 274 F.Supp. 438 (S.D.N.Y. 1967).

11. Elrod did say he also participates in an informal underground "network" of municipal auditorium managers who regularly exchange information on various types of entertainment. Many of those managers sent letters to Elrod saying "Hair" was not suitable for public auditoriums. Obviously these managers share Elrod's mistaken belief that a manager of a public auditorium is the equivalent of the Lord Chamberlain in England, censor of the stage. However, at least one manager disagreed and wrote: "Ours is a municipal auditorium—built by the people to see all types of entertainment. People who object to ["Hair"] need not attend."

12. The Court has defined obscenity as follows: "(a) [T]he dominant theme of the material taken as a whole appeals to a prurient interest in sex; (b) the material is patently offensive because it affronts contemporary community standards relating to the description or representation of sexual matter; and (c) the material is utterly without redeeming social value." A Book named "John Cleland's Memoirs of a Woman of Pleasure" v. Attorney General of Com. of Massachusetts, 383 U.S. 413, 418, 86 S.Ct. 975, 977, 16 L. Ed.2d 1 (1966).

13. The same conclusion has been reached by a three-judge federal court in Massachusetts [P.B.I.C., Inc. v. Byrne, *supra*], Judge Eisele in Arkansas [Southwest Productions, Inc. v. Freeman, *supra*], the Attorney General of Florida [The Atlanta Constitution, Oct 14, 1971, at 17-A, col. 1], and the Police Department of St. Louis, Missouri [The Atlanta Constitution, Nov. 4, 1971, at 21-A, col. 1].

14. There has been no allegation that an act of sexual intercourse occurs during the performance of "Hair."

"HAIR" IS OBSCENE

Southeastern Promotions, Inc. v. Conrad, 341 F.Supp. 465 (1972)

MEMORANDUM

FRANK W. WILSON, Chief Judge.

The plaintiff, Southeastern Promotions, Inc., seeks by this action to obtain a declaratory judgment pursuant to 28 U.S.C. §§ 2201 and 2202 regarding the plaintiff's right to lease a municipal theater or auditorium for use in presenting a commercial theatrical production known as "Hair." Jurisdiction is averred to be based upon 28 U.S.C. §§ 1332 and 1343(3) (4). The plaintiff seeks by way of relief a mandatory injunction requiring the defendants, as members of the Municipal Auditorium Board for the City of Chattanooga, Tennessee, to lease the theater or auditorium under its management to plaintiff for a specific date, the specific date now sought being Sunday, April 9, 1972, four days from the date upon which the trial in the case was concluded.

By way of response the defendants filed a motion seeking a dismissal of the complaint upon the grounds that (1) the plaintiff was without standing to maintain the lawsuit, (2) the defendants, acting in a proprietary rather than governmental capacity, cannot be required to lease the theater facility under their management, (3) the theatrical production sought to be presented by the plaintiff would violate both the ordinances of the City of Chattanooga and the laws of the State of Tennessee and would be in violation of Paragraph (1) of the standard lease requiring compliance with such laws (Exhibit No. 3), (4) the plaintiff, being a corporation and not a natural person, would have no right to maintain this action, and (5) the complaint fails to allege a cause of action.

In order to expedite the hearing of this case, action on the motion to dismiss was reserved and the defendants were ordered to file an answer. In their answer, and among other matters, the defendants contended that the theatrical production "Hair" was a violation of municipal ordinances and state laws prohibiting nudity and obscenity in public places. A trial was held upon all issues, with the issue of obscenity being tried to an advisory jury pursuant to Rule 39 (c), Federal Rules of Civil Procedure. The jury returned a verdict finding the theatrical production "Hair" obscene within the meaning of obscenity as that term relates to freedom of speech as secured by the First Amendment and further found conduct on the part of actors apart from any speech or conduct in expression of speech (symbolic speech) to be obscene conduct.

The case is now before the Court for decision of all issues raised in the plaintiff's complaint, the defendants' motion to dismiss, the defendants' answer, the record made upon the trial of the case, the advisory verdict of the jury, and the argument of counsel. By order of the Court, and without objection of the parties, the trial of this case was held shortly after the filing of the answer and this memorandum is being written immediately upon the conclusion of the trial and under the necessity of its immediate entry if the plaintiff is to have the requested date of showing four days from this date. This opinion will serve as the Court's findings of fact and conclusions of law.

The plaintiff, Southeastern Promotions, Inc., is a corporation organized under the laws of the State of New York and with its principal offices in New York City. It is engaged in the business of presenting commercial theatrical productions and has contractual relations giving it presentation rights with the theatrical group that owns and produces a theatrical production known as "Hair" and described as a "rock musical." The defendants are the duly appointed and acting members of a municipally created body known as the Board of Directors of the Memorial Auditorium. They were appointed pursuant to an ordinance of the City of Chattanooga, Tennessee, and are charged with the management and operation of the Memorial Auditorium, a municipally owned auditorium, and the Tivoli Theater, a former motion picture theater privately owned and now under lease to the City of Chattanooga.

The plaintiff has made three previous requests of the defendants for lease of the Tivoli Theater but upon each occasion the request was denied. Following the last denial this lawsuit was filed upon November 1, 1971. A hearing upon a preliminary injunction in advance of any response by the defendants was held at that time and the injunction denied. By amendment to its complaint filed March 23, 1972, the plaintiff now seeks a mandatory injunction permitting it to lease the municipal auditorium for the presenting of its theatrical production "Hair" upon the date of Sunday, April 9, 1972. No issue exists in the case but that the municipal auditorium is not scheduled for other use on that date or that the plaintiff cannot meet the conditions of the standard lease form regularly used by the defendants in leasing of the municipal auditorium other than that condition of the lease relating to compliance with the laws of the State of Tennessee and of the City of Chattanooga.

Motion to Dismiss

Turning first to the defendants' motion to dismiss, as previously stated, that motion is predicated upon a denial of standing on the part of the plaintiff corporation to maintain this action, a denial of any duty upon the defendants while acting in a proprietary capacity to lease the municipal facilities under its management, an averment of the plaintiff's inability to comply with the lease requirement that local and state law will not be violated, an averment that the plaintiff, being a corporation and not a natural person, would have no right to maintain this action, and a general averment that the complaint fails to aver any substantial federal question or constitutional issue.

With regard to the plaintiff's standing to maintain this litigation, it is the defendants' contention that the plaintiff does not propose to make any expression or theatrical presentation itself, but rather is only a booking agent having at most only a commercial interest in the presentation of "Hair." It is contended that no right of the plaintiff to freedom of speech is involved. Citing the rule that only those whose federal constitutional rights are alleged to be involved have standing to seek judicial adjudication of those rights, the defendants deny any standing in the plaintiff to assert a First Amendment violation in this lawsuit. While the undisputed evidence now bears out that the plaintiff's interest in the lawsuit is a commercial one as booking agent and promoter, and not as an owner or performer, the testimony being that it expects to net $10,000 off of a single performance in Chattanooga, the issue of standing to sue would appear to be resolved in favor of the plaintiff by the United States Supreme Court in the case of Flast v. Cohen, 392 U.S. 83, 88 S.Ct. 1942, 20 L.Ed.2d 947 (1968) wherein the Court stated: "The 'gist of the question of standing' is whether the party seeking relief has 'alleged such a personal stake in the outcome of the controversy as to assure that concrete adverseness which sharpens the presentation of issues upon which the court so largely depends for illumination of difficult constitutional questions' (citations omitted)." As stated elsewhere in that opinion, "The question of standing (i.e., in terms of constitutional limitation) is related only to whether the dispute sought to be adjudicated will be presented in an adversary context and in a form historically viewed as capable of judicial resolution." When viewed in light of these principles, it is apparent that the defendants' motion to dismiss for lack of standing on the part of the plaintiff to maintain this action must be denied.

It is next contended that although the defendant Board is a municipally created board with responsibility for management of municipally owned or leased theater and auditorium facilities, the Board's activities in this regard are of a proprietary and not of a governmental nature. It is therefore contended that leasing or not leasing these facilities is entirely optional with the Board, as would be true with a private owner. The defendants cite the following authorities in support of this proposition: Avins v. Rutgers State University of New Jersey, 3 Cir., 385 F.2d 151 (1967); Warren v. Bradley, 39 Tenn.App. 451, 284 S.W.2d 698 (1955); City of Knoxville v. Heth, 186 Tenn. 321, 210 S.W.2d 326; Miami Beach Airline Service v. Crandon, 159 Fla. 504, 32 So.2d 153; State ex rel. v. Newton, 3 Tenn.Civ.App. 93 (1912); State of Washington ex rel. Tubbs v. City of Spokane, 53 Wash.2d 35, 330 P.2d 718 (1958); State of Ohio ex rel. White v. City of Cleveland, 125 Ohio St. 230, 181 N.E. 24, 86 A.L.R. 1172; 56 Am.Jur. 2d "Municipal Corporations" § 556; and Southeastern Promotions, Ltd. v. City of Oklahoma, (Civil Action No. 72-105, D.C.W.D.Okl., Decided March 27, 1972). Generally speaking, the foregoing line of cases deals with the distinction between proprietary and governmental action and reason by analogy that proprietary action by a governmental body is to be judged by the same rules governing private proprietary action. While this line of reasoning by analogy may appear on the surface to have validity, the analogy breaks down under more careful examination. It would appear that the defendant Board in this case does act in a proprietary capacity in its management of its theater and auditorium facilities. However, whether the Board is acting in a proprietary capacity or in a governmental capacity, it is apparent that it remains a public body. It is further apparent that as a public body it could not allow men to use the auditorium but refuse under like circumstances to permit women to use it solely because they were women. It is apparent that the defendant Board could not permit persons of one religious persuasion to use the auditorium but under like circumstances refuse to permit those of another religious persuasion to use it solely because they were of another religious persuasion. The same would be true if the Board sought to discriminate upon the basis of race or national origin. Accordingly, it is apparent that whether the Board acts in a governmental capacity or in a proprietary capacity it nevertheless remains a public body, and as such it cannot differentiate or discriminate where the sole basis of that differentiation or discrimination is for some constitutionally impermissible reason. This is tacitly recognized even in the defendants' last cited case above, the recent and unreported decision of Southeastern Promotions, Ltd. v. City of Oklahoma, *supra,* wherein the Court stated, "It follows that the first part of numbered paragraph 8 of the lease contract governing the use of the Civic Music Center Hall is valid in that defendants are within their rights to decline to contract with exhibitors so long as they do not act arbitrarily."

While the Auditorium Board may lawfully deny use of its facilities unto all persons, or unto all persons for certain reasonably distinguishable types of activity, it cannot permit its use for a purpose to one person and deny its use for the same purpose to another person solely for a constitutionally impermissible reason, as for example to deny the latter person his right to freedom of speech. By way of illustration, if obscenity were the only reason advanced by the Board for denying use of its facilities and that contention of obscenity is not sustainable in fact and in law, the denial then becomes one for the constitutionally impermissible reason of denial of freedom of speech and the denial of a lease under such circumstances cannot stand.

The third ground in the defendants' motion to dismiss, namely that the theatrical production for which a lease is sought by the plaintiff would violate both ordinances of the City of Chattanooga and laws of the State of Tennessee relating to both public nudity and obscenity, raises issues of both fact and law which can only be decided after a trial on the merits of these contentions. These matters will accordingly be considered in the portion of this opinion dealing with the trial of the case on its merits.

The fourth ground in the defendants' motion to dismiss is the allegation that the plaintiff, being a corporation, cannot maintain this action. In support of this ground the defendants rely upon the case of Hague v. Committee for Industrial Organization, 307 U.S. 496, 59 S.Ct. 954, 83 L.Ed. 1423, wherein the Court stated: "Natural persons, and they alone, are entitled to the privileges and immunities which Section 1 of the Fourteenth Amendment secures for 'citizens of the United States.' Only the individual respondents may, therefore, maintain this suit." The holding in the foregoing case is inapplicable to the allegations in this case for the reason that the constitutional rights here claimed are due process, equal protection of the laws, and freedom of speech, and do not arise under the privileges and immunities clause. Corporations are considered persons within the provisions of the constitutional guarantees of due process, equal protection and freedom of speech. See Grosjean v. American Press Company, 297 U.S. 233, 56 S.Ct. 444, 80 L.Ed. 660. The fourth ground of the motion to dismiss will likewise be denied.

The fifth and final ground in the defendants' motion to dismiss is that the complaint fails to allege a federal question issue in that the defendants have not denied the plaintiff's right to speak, but at most have only denied the use of a particular forum in which to speak. It is apparent that this contention is without merit if in fact, as alleged by the plaintiff, the defendants have acted so as to deny the plaintiff equal protection of the laws, due process, and freedom of speech.

Trial on the Merits

Turning to the merits of this lawsuit, the pleadings raise essentially the issue of whether the defendant Board acted within its lawful discretion in declining to lease its theater and/or auditorium facility to the plaintiff for the reason that the plaintiff's theatrical production "Hair" would violate Paragraph (1) of the standard lease form requiring the lessee to comply with all state and local laws in its use of the leased premises. More specifically, the issue presented by the pleadings is whether the theatrical production "Hair" would violate any constitutionally valid provision of the common law of Tennessee relating to indecent exposure, gross indecency, or lewdness or would violate any constitutionally valid provision of City ordinances and State statutes which, among other matters, purport to make public nudity and obscene acts criminal offenses.[1]

This case, involving as it does the First Amendment right to freedom of speech, and the statutes and ordinances cited in the footnote asserting obscenity as a prohibited criminal offense, the issue of obscenity was severed for trial from other issues in the case and this issue was tried before the Court sitting with an advisory jury pursuant to Rule 39(c), F.R.C.P. The evidence upon the trial of the obscenity issue consisted of the full script and libretto with production notes and stage instructions (Exhibit No. 4), a recording of the sound tract of all musical numbers in the production (Exhibit No. 7), and a souvenir program (Exhibit No. 1). In addition there was received the testimony of seven witnesses who had witnessed the production "Hair," including two witnesses who attended a performance two days previous to their testimony, and an eighth witness who had not seen the production but had read the script and gave his interpretation as a drama critic. Following the completion of the evidence and the argument of counsel, the issue of obscenity was submitted to the jury upon instructions of the Court upon the issue of obscenity, as set forth in an appendix to this opinion.

After deliberation the jury returned the following verdict:

(1) We, the jury, find the theatrical production "Hair" to be *obscene* in accordance with the definition of obscene as it relates to freedom of speech under the First Amendment of the United States Constitution.

(2) We, the jury, find the theatrical production "Hair" to be *obscene* in accordance with the definition of obscenity as it relates to conduct.

After discharge of the jury further evidence was received by the Court upon issues other than obscenity, such evidence being principally with regard to the action of the Board in denying a lease of its facilities to the plaintiff and the standard form of lessees (Exhibit No. 3). Following further argument of counsel the case was submitted to the Court upon the foregoing record.

Findings of Fact

Turning first to the issue of obscenity, the script, libretto, stage instructions, musical renditions, and the testimony of the witnesses reflect the following relevant matters (It should be noted that the script, libretto, and stage instructions do not include but a small portion of the conduct hereinafter described as occurring in the play):

The souvenir program as formerly distributed in the lobby (Exhibit No. 1) identified the performers by picture and biographical information, one female performer identifying herself as follows:

"Hobbies are picking my nose, fucking, smoking dope, astro projection. All that I am or ever hope to be, I owe to my mother." It was testified that distribution of this program had now been discontinued. Prior to the opening of the play, and to the accompaniment of music appropriate to the occasion, a "tribe" of New York "street people" start gathering for the commencement of the performance. In view of the audience the performers station themselves in various places, some mingling with the audience, with a female performer taking a seated position on center stage with her legs spread wide to expose to the audience her genital area, which is covered with the design of a cherry. Thus the stage is set for all that follows. The performance then begins to the words and music of the song "Aquarius," the melody of which, if not the words, have become nationally, if not internationally, popular, according to the evidence. The theme of the song is the coming of a new age, the age of love, the age of "Aquarius." Following this one of the street people, Burger, introduces himself by various prefixes to his name, including "Up Your Burger," accompanied by an anal finger gesture and "Pittsburger," accompanied by an underarm gesture. He then removes his pants and dressed only in jockey shorts identifies his genitals by the line, "What is this God-damned thing? 3,000 pounds of Navajo jewelry? Ha! Ha! Ha!" Throwing his pants into the audience he then proceeds to mingle with the audience and, selecting a female viewer, exclaims, "I'll bet you're scared shitless."

Burger then sings a song, "Looking For My Donna," and the tribe chants a list of drugs beginning with "hashish" and ending with "Methadrine, Sex, You, WOW!" (Exhibit No. 4, p. 1-5) Another male character then sings the lyric. "SODOMY, FELLATIO, CUNNILINGUS, PEDERASTY—FATHER, WHY DO THESE WORDS SOUND SO NASTY? MASTURBATION CAN BE FUN. JOIN THE HOLY ORGY, KAMA SUTRA, EVERYONE." (Exhibit No. 4, p. 1-5)

The play then continues with action, songs, chants, and dialogue making reference by isolated words, broken sentences, rhyme, and rapid changes to such diverse subjects as love, peace, freedom, war, racism, air pollution, parents, the draft, hair, the flag, drugs, and sex. The story line gradually centers upon the character Claude and his response and the response of the tribe to his having received a draft notice. When others suggest he burn his draft card, he can only bring himself to urinate upon it. The first act ends when all performers, male and female, appear nude upon the stage, the nude scene being had without dialogue and without reference to dialogue. It is also without mention in the script. Actors simulating police then appear in the audience and announce that they are under arrest for watching this "lewd, obscene show."

The second act continues with song and dialogue to develop the story of Claude's draft status, with reference interspersed to such diverse topics as interracial love, a drug "trip," impersonation of various figures from American history,[2] religion, war, and sex. The play ends with Claude's death as a result of the draft and the street people singing the song, "Let the Sunshine In," a song the testimony reflects has likewise become popular over the Nation.

Interspersed throughout the play, as reflected in the script, is such "street language" as "ass" (Exhibit No. 4. pp. 1-20, 21 and 2-16), "fart" (Exhibit No. 4, p. 1-26), and repeated use of the words "fuck"[3] and the four letter word for excretion (Exhibit No. 4, pp. 1-7, 9 and 41). In addition, similar language and posters containing such language were used on stage but not reflected in the script.

Also, throughout the play, and not reflected in the script, are repeated acts of simulated sexual intercourse. These were testified to by every witness who had seen the play. They are often unrelated to any dialogue and accordingly could not be placed with accuracy in the script. The overwhelming evidence reflects that simulated acts of anal intercourse, frontal intercourse, heterosexual intercourse, homosexual intercourse, and group intercourse are committed throughout the play, often without reference to any dialogue, song, or story line in the play. Such acts are committed both standing up and lying down, accompanied by all the bodily movements included in such acts, all the while the actors and actresses are in close bodily contact. At one point the character Burger performs a full and complete simulation of masturbation while using a red microphone placed in his crotch to simulate his genitals. The evidence again reflects that this is unrelated to any dialogue then occurring in the play. The evidence further reflects that repeated acts of taking hold of other actors' genitals occur, again without reference to the dialogue. While three female actresses sing a song regarding interracial love, three male actors lie on the floor immediately below them repeatedly thrusting their genitals at the singers. At another point in the script (Exhibit No. 4, p. 2-22) the actor Claude pretends to have lost his penis. The action accompanying this line is to search for it in the mouths of other actors and actresses.

In support of the non-obscenity of the play "Hair" the plaintiff relies upon the contention that the simulated sexual acts consume only a small portion of the total performance time, that the nudity scene is brief and in reduced lighting, that the audience by attending consents to the play, that the play has been a financial success second only to the musical "Oklahoma," that the play has been performed in over 140 cities, that the music from the play has been upon the "Hit Parade," and that four other courts have found the play not to be obscene. Southeastern Promotions, Ltd. v. City of Atlanta, D.C., 334 F.Supp. 634 (1971); Southeastern Promotions, Ltd. v. City of Charlotte, D.C., 333 F.Supp. 345 (1971); P. B. I. C., Inc. v. Byrne, D.C., 313 F. Supp. 757 (1970); and Southwest Productions, Inc. v. Freeman, (U.S.D.C.E.D.Ark., 1971).[4]

Obscenity

The definition of legal obscenity as it relates to the First Amendment guarantee of freedom of speech is defined in the case of Roth v. United States (1957) 354 U.S. 476, 77 S.Ct.1304, 1 L.Ed.2d 1498, reh. den., 355 U.S. 852, 78 S.Ct. 8, 2 L.Ed.2d 60. The definition of obscenity in *Roth* is further amplified in Manual Enterprises, Inc. v. Day, 370 U.S. 478, 82 S.Ct. 1432, 8 L.Ed.2d 639. Although there have been numerous intervening cases in the Supreme Court dealing with obscenity, the *Roth* test of obscenity has been reaffirmed as recently as the case of Rabe v. Washington, 405 U.S. 313, 92 S.Ct. 993, 31 L.Ed. 2d 258 (Decided March 20, 1972). Having set forth that definition in the Court's charge to the jury as set forth in the appendix to this opinion, the Court will here include only a summary statement of the rule as taken from the charge.

"Thus, by way of summing up, before the theatrical production here in issue can be found to be legally obscene, these elements must coalesce; It must be established, first, that the dominant theme of the material taken as a whole appeals to a prurient interest in sex; and, second, that the material is patently offensive because it affronts contemporary community standards relating to the description or representation of sexual matters; and, third, that the material is utterly without redeeming social value." Suffice it to say that the United States Supreme

Court, unlike the English courts, does not permit the judging of a theatrical production in relevant portions in determining obscenity for the purposes of determining First Amendment freedom of speech rights. Rather, it is required that the production be judged as a whole and that it be granted First Amendment protection unless, among other matters, the production, when judged as a whole, is "utterly without redeeming social value." The latter concept has been interpreted with great strictness by the Supreme Court, with strong emphasis being placed upon the word "utterly." Furthermore, the Supreme Court has recently granted First Amendment protection to vulgar words similar to those here used. Cohen v. California, 403 U.S. 15, 91 S.Ct. 1780, 29 L.Ed.2d 284 (1971). Even apart from this, this Court could readily find, as did the jury, that substantial portions of the plaintiff's production is "utterly without redeeming social value." When required to view the production as a whole, however, including the music and those portions of the play that are not obscene, but at most only controversial, the Court cannot state that as a whole it is "utterly" without redeeming social value.

Obscenity, however, as it relates to theatrical productions, can consist of either speech or conduct or a combination of the two. It is clear to this Court that conduct, when not in the form of symbolic speech or so closely related to speech as to be illustrative thereof, is not speech and hence such conduct does not fall within the freedom of speech guarantee of the First Amendment. These matters were dealt with by the United States Supreme Court in the case of United States v. O'Brien, 391 U.S. 367, 88 S.Ct. 1673, 20 L.Ed.2d 672 (1968). That case arose out of the burning of draft cards at an anti-war demonstration. The issue presented was whether a federal statute making the knowing destruction or mutilation of a draft card a crime was an unconstitutional infringement upon the accused's right of freedom of speech. The Court, in upholding the statute from constitutional attack, stated:

"We cannot accept the view that an apparently limitless variety of conduct can be labeled 'speech' whenever the person engaging in the conduct intends thereby to express an idea. However, even on the assumption that the alleged communicative element in O'Brien's conduct is sufficient to bring into play the First Amendment, it does not necessarily follow that the destruction of a registration certificate is constitutionally protected activity. This Court has held that when 'speech' and 'nonspeech' elements are combined in the same course of conduct, a sufficiently important governmental interest in regulating the nonspeech element can justify incidental limitations on First Amendment freedoms. To characterize the quality of the governmental interest which must appear, the Court has employed a variety of descriptive terms: compelling; substantial; subordinating; paramount; cogent; strong. Whatever imprecision inheres in these terms, we think it clear that a government regulation is sufficiently justified if it is within the constitutional power of the Government; if it furthers an important or substantial governmental interest; if the governmental interest is unrelated to the suppression of free expression; and if the incidental restriction on alleged First Amendment freedoms is no greater than is essential to the furtherance of that interest. . . ."

It is further clear to this Court that conduct not within the First Amendment is not subject to the requirement that the production in which it takes place be judged as a whole, but rather that the conduct may be judged obscene or nonobscene on the basis of individual acts of conduct. It is abundantly clear that if a crime other than the crime of obscenity were committed upon the stage, the actor committing that crime could neither claim First Amendment protection nor could he require that he be judged criminal or non-criminal on the basis of the production as a whole. If a murder, rape, mayhem or crime of assault were committed upon the stage, the actor perpetrating the same could claim no First Amendment protection, nor could he require that the theatrical production as a whole be reviewed in determining the criminality of his conduct. Accordingly, it must be that when the crime of obscenity is committed upon the live stage by conduct and not by speech, or symbolic speech, no First Amendment protection attaches to that conduct and no First Amendment requirement attaches that requires the production as a whole to be reviewed in determining such criminal obscenity.

This Court is aware that a district judge dealt differently with this issue in the case of Southeastern Promotions, Ltd. v. City of Atlanta, D.C., 334 F.Supp. 634 (1971) cited above. The Court there held that a stage production cannot be disected into speech and nonspeech components. The fallacy of that position is readily apparent, however, if any crime other than the crime of obscenity were committed in the course of a live stage production. That Court would doubtless have no difficulty in disecting speech and nonspeech components if the crime committed on the stage were the crime of rape or homicide, even though called for in the script. It is a false and dangerous doctrine that the First Amendment forbids all regulation of conduct so long as that conduct masquerades under the guise of the theatrical. This Court respectfully declines to follow the rule set forth by the district judge in the Atlanta case. The same fallacy attaches to each of the cases relied upon by the plaintiff in prior adjudications of the theatrical production "Hair."

When viewed in their component parts, it is perfectly clear that the actors and actresses in the theatrical production "Hair," by their conduct, and apart from any element of speech, commit repeated acts of criminal obscenity that would be in violation of the ordinances of the City of Chattanooga and the statutes of the State of Tennessee forbidding acts of obscenity in public places. The Municipal Auditorium is a public place and the committing of live acts of simulated sexual intercourse, masturbation and mixed group nudity upon the stage before a live audience appeals to the prurient interest in sex, is patently offensive because it affronts contemporary community standards, both state and national, relating to the representation of sexual matters, and it is utterly without redeeming social value.

As regards the plaintiff's contention that the relative brevity of the sexual conduct in proportion to the total time of the play and the reduction of lighting on the scene of mixed group nudity relieves the conduct of its obscene character, these matters obviously constitute no defense to a charge of obscene conduct. These matters, on the contrary, are but proof of the plaintiff's own awareness of the obscenity of the conduct, as further evidenced by the use of an actor policeman to announce to the audience at the conclusion of the first act that they are under arrest for watching this "lewd, obscene show." Instantaneous murder is no less a crime than slow poisoning. A dimly visible robbery is no less a crime than a well lighted one.

Unlawful conduct is not rendered lawful by the wattage of the light bulb in which is it committed. Nor is it any defense that the acts other than nudity were simulated acts of sexual conduct. Simulated sexual acts are in themselves sexual conduct. Pregnancy does not have to result to establish sexual conduct.

Likewise without merit is the plaintiff's contention that its performance is protected from regulation in that it is performed before a consenting audience. If audience consent were the test of First Amendment protection, then cock fights, bull fights, and Roman gladiatorial contests could no longer be regulated or forbidden by law.

As regards the constitutional validity of the ordinances and statutes relied upon by the defendants, insofar as those ordinances and statutes make obscenity as hereinabove defined a crime, there can be no doubt of their validity. As stated in Berman v. Parker, 348 U.S. 26, 75 S.Ct. 98, 99 L.Ed. 27 (1954):

"Public safety, public health, morality, peace and quiet, law and order—these are some of the more conspicuous examples of the traditional application of the police power to municipal affairs. Yet they merely illustrate the scope of the power and do not delimit it."

Undisciplined sex is one of the most destructive forces in any society and has historically been so recognized. It is destructive of many human values and institutions, not the least of which is the family, which in turn has served as the foundation for every civilization yet known to man. Regulation of public and undisciplined sexual conduct is clearly within the police power of the state.

It is likewise equally clear that the obscenity laws relied upon by the defendants, as they relate to obscene conduct, meet the other standards laid down in United States v. O'Brien, *supra*. They further an important or substantial governmental interest, that is the suppression of public and undisciplined sexual conduct, and the protection of public morality and welfare. Their purpose is unrelated to the suppression of free speech, or, at most, they impinge upon the First Amendment freedom no more than is essential to the furtherance of that governmental interest.

As regards the ordinance forbidding nudity in public places, that, too, can meet the standards for the exercise of police power as laid down in United States v. O'Brien, *supra*, particularly when applied to mixed group nudity upon the live stage, as occurs in the theatrical production here involved. Mixed group public nudity may become the accepted community standard in this Nation. But if it does, it should be by legislative approval, not by judicial fiat in the face of legislative action to the contrary.

This Court is accordingly of the opinion that the theatrical production "Hair" contains conduct, apart from speech or symbolic speech, which would render it in violation of both the public nudity ordinances of the City of Chattanooga and the obscenity ordinances and statutes of the City and of the State of Tennessee. The defendants accordingly acted within their lawful discretion in declining to lease the Municipal Auditorium or the Tivoli Theater unto the plaintiff.

In conclusion, it is not inappropriate to note that musical, literary, and dramatic ability are scarce talents. Vulgarity, nudity, and obscenity are abundant and readily available commodities. All are good box office. The temptation to substitute the latter commodities for the former talents has become well nigh irresistible in the entertainment world in recent years. "Hair" found musical talent. It combined it with vulgarity, nudity, and obscenity to come up with a box office hit.

An order will enter dismissing this lawsuit.

JURY INSTRUCTIONS
APPENDIX

This case has its basis in the First Amendment of the Constitution of the United States. You will recall that when I summarized for you the contentions of the parties, I advised you that the plaintiff was making the contention that the defendants had discriminated against the plaintiff by denying the plaintiff a lease upon the Tivoli Theater and/or the Municipal Auditorium, and that the denial of such lease was in fact and in law a denial of the plaintiff's right of freedom of speech and of freedom of expression as secured to the plaintiff by the First Amendment and the Fourteenth Amendment of the Constitution of the United States. The First Amendment right of freedom of speech and freedom of expression extends to the plaintiff even though the plaintiff is a corporation. It is entitled to exactly the same right under the First Amendment with regard to freedom of speech and freedom of expression as would be any individual.

Upon the other hand, the defendants have denied that their action in refusing to lease the Tivoli Theater and/or the Municipal Auditorium was in violation of the plaintiff's right to freedom of expression or to the plaintiff's rights under either the First or Fourteenth Amendments of the United States Constitution. The defendants contend that the theatrical production which the plaintiff proposes to present and for which it seeks a lease is obscene and as such it accordingly is not entitled to the protection either of the First Amendment or of the Fourteenth Amendment of the United States Constitution. The issue for your decision, accordingly, has its legal basis in the First Amendment of the United States Constitution and the application of that Amendment to the facts of this case.

More particularly, the issue for your decision has its legal basis in the freedom of speech provision of the First Amendment. The relevance of referring to the Fourteenth Amendment in this regard is that the due process clause of the Fourteenth Amendment has the effect of making the provisions of the First Amendment binding upon the states and the cities and the local governments of this Nation as well as upon the Federal Government. You see, as originally adopted, the First Amendment only purported to prohibit the United States Congress from making laws abridging freedom of assembly. But with the adoption of the Fourteenth Amendment, requiring that state and local governments extend due process of law to all persons, that Amendment had the effect of making the First Amendment binding upon the states, cities, and local governments within this Nation also.

Let me read for you the First Amendment of the United States Constitution. It reads as follows: "Congress shall make no law respecting an establishment of religion, or prohibiting the free exercise thereof; or abridging the freedom of speech, or of the press; or the right of the people peaceably to assemble, and to petition the Government for a redress of grievances." Although the Amendment refers, as I have said, to the Congress, as I have further just explained to you, it is equally applicable to the government at all levels, including the State of Tennessee and the City of Chattanooga and including the defendants to this lawsuit, who, as members and officials of the Chattanooga Auditorium Board, are an arm of the City of Chattanooga and as such are subject to the prohibitions of the First Amendment.

The First Amendment as it relates to the issues in this lawsuit accordingly prohibits the defendants from taking any action which would have the effect of denying the plaintiff its right to freedom of speech as guaranteed in the First Amendment of the Constitution. You are instructed in this regard that a theatrical production as a mode of expression or as a mode of conveying ideas or entertainment is entitled to the protection of the freedom of speech provision of the First Amendment. However, freedom of speech is not an absolute or all encompassing right. By that, I mean not every form of expression may claim to be protected by the constitutional guarantee of freedom of speech. One form of expression that does not come within the protection of the First Amendment is obscenity. That is, the denial to a person of the right to express himself in a manner that falls within the legal definition of obscenity is not a violation of that person's right to freedom of speech. Accordingly, the defendants may lawfully refuse to lease either the Tivoli Theater and/or the Municipal Auditorium to the plaintiff if the theatrical production "Hair" which the plaintiff proposes to present is obscene as I shall proceed to define that word "obscene" for you.

The word "obscene" is, of course, a word in common use and is a part of our everyday language. As we use it in our everyday language and as it is defined in Webster's Dictionary, it means "foul; disgusting; offensive to chastity or to modesty; lewd." That, however, is not the definition that you must apply in testing the issue of obscenity in this case.

Now, I only point that out to you to point out that it is not the definition of legal obscenity. As I am using the word "obscene" in these instructions, it has a special, legal definition and you must apply that legal definition in deciding the issue that is for your decision in this case. The United States Supreme Court has defined (in the case of Roth v. United States, 354 U.S. 476, 77 S.Ct. 1304, 1 L.Ed.2d 1498, as amplified in Manual Enterprises, Inc. v. Day, 370 U.S. 478, 82 S.Ct. 1432, 8 L.Ed. 2d 639) the word "obscenity" as it relates to matters that do not fall within the protection of the freedom of speech provision of the First Amendment. This Court and this jury are bound by that definition and must follow that definition in making their determination in this case.

As defined by the United States Supreme Court, legal obscenity is any material to which the "average person, applying contemporary community standards, the dominant theme of the material taken as a whole appeals to prurient interest."

Let me read the definition over for you again. As defined by the United States Supreme Court, legal obscenity is any material which to "the average person, applying contemporary community standards, the dominant theme of the material taken as a whole appeals to prurient interest."

Let me now break that definition down for you into its component parts and explain for you the meaning of certain words and phrases as are used in that definition and as they have been further defined by the United States Supreme Court. You will notice that the first part of the definition refers to the average person applying contemporary community standards. The community standard here referred to is not a standard that varies from one locality to another within the Nation but rather means the contemporary national community standards.

You will notice that the second part of the definition of obscenity as established by the United States Supreme Court is that "the dominant theme of the material taken as a whole appeals to prurient interest." The phrase, "the dominant theme of the material taken as a whole," means that the theatrical production here challenged as obscene must be judged as a whole. The phrase "appeals to the prurient interest," means having a tendency to excite lustful thoughts or material that appeals to a shameful or morbid interest in sex and is utterly without redeeming social value. The material must be patently offensive in that it goes substantially beyond contemporary limits of candor in description or representation of such matters.

Thus, by way of summing up, before the theatrical production here in issue can be found to be legally obscene, these elements must coalesce: It must be established, first, that the dominant theme of the material taken as a whole appeals to a prurient interest in sex; and, second, that the material is patently offensive because it affronts contemporary community standards relating to the description or representation of sexual matters; and, third, that the material is utterly without redeeming social value.

Now, in making your determination with regard to obscenity or non-obscenity, you will not be concerned with whether the material in the play is pro-religion or anti-religion; you will not be concerned with whether the material is pro-pollution or anti-pollution; you will not be concerned with whether the material is pro-free love or anti-free love; you would not be concerned with whether it is pro-drug culture or anti-drug culture; you would not be concerned with whether it is pro-parental authority or anti-parental authority; you would not be concerned with whether it is pro-war, anti-war or whether it is pro-government or anti-government or whether it expresses popular ideas or unpopular ideas. The concept of obscenity cannot be based upon the ideas that may be expressed, whether those ideas express these concepts or not. We are not here to judge those matters but rather you want to follow the definition of obscenity as I have given it to you in these instructions. In other words, it is not a question of whether you agree or disagree with the ideas being expressed or conveyed in the theatrical production "Hair." The question is whether or not the material is obscene as I have defined that term or given you that definition.

So far in these instructions, in defining obscenity, I have been referring to speech in all of its forms, including conduct that is so closely related to speech as to be considered symbolic speech or expressive of speech. Just as speech may be obscene, likewise conduct, apart from speech or apart from conduct that is expressive of speech, may be obscene. However, there is a difference in obscenity as it refers to speech on the one hand, which I have just defined for you, and obscenity as it refers to conduct separate and apart from speech upon the other hand.

The freedom of speech provisions of the First Amendment refer to speech and not to human conduct that is not expressive of speech; that is, conduct apart from speech or conduct that is not so closely related to speech as to constitute symbolic speech as it is sometimes referred to. Since the freedom of speech provision of the First Amendment accords no protection against the regulation of human conduct by the government, whether federal, state or local, the freedom of speech provision of the First Amendment accords no protection against the regulation of obscene conduct by the various levels of government. Since the obscenity statutes and the ordinances relied upon by the defendants in this case apply to both obscene speech and to obscene conduct, then irrespective of how you may decide the issue of obscenity as it relates to the theatrical production "Hair" when considered as speech, and when considered as a whole, you should turn your attention to the conduct of the performers in the theatrical production "Hair" that is not speech or is not conduct that may be considered symbolic speech or expressive of speech and determine whether that conduct is obscene as I shall now define the word.

The definition of obscenity as it relates to conduct apart from speech is the same as the definition of obscenity as it relates to speech with two exceptions. The first exception is that since no First Amendment federal constitutional issue is involved, obscene conduct may be judged in its component parts rather than merely judging the whole conduct or merely judging the whole of the theatrical production in making your judgment regarding obscenity on the basis of conduct as a whole or of the material of the production as a whole; that is, conduct may be adjudged obscene or non-obscene either as a whole or in any of its component parts.

The second difference between the definition of obscenity as it applies to conduct rather than speech is that since no First Amendment federal constitutional issue is involved, the community standard by which the conduct is to be judged is the community standard of the State of Tennessee rather than the community standard of the Nation as a whole. Thus, obscenity as it relates to conduct apart from speech means, first, conduct that appeals to the prurient interest in sex; and, second, conduct that is patently offensive because it affronts contemporary standards. The standards here referred to being those of the state in which the conduct occurs; and, third, conduct that is utterly without redeeming social value.

In addition to the matters I have instructed you, you are further instructed with regard to the issue of obscenity that not every portrayal of male or female nudity is necessarily obscene. It depends, of course, upon the context and circumstances. The portrayal of sex in art, literature or scientific works is not of itself sufficient reason for denying material the constitutional protection of freedom of speech; and, likewise, foul words just standing alone without regard to context of the whole content do not constitute legal obscenity as I have defined that term for you.

NOTES

1. *Chattanooga Code* Sec. 25-28. *Indecent exposure and conduct.* It shall be unlawful for any person in the city to appear in a public place in a state of nudity, or to bathe in such state in the daytime in the river or any bayou or stream within the city within sight of any street or occupied premises; or to appear in public in an indecent or lewd dress, or to do any lewd, obscene or indecent act in any public place. Sec. 6-4. *Offensive, indecent entertainment.* It shall be unlawful for any person to hold, conduct or carry on, or to cause or permit to be held, conducted or carried on any motion picture exhibition or entertainment of any sort which is offensive to decency, or which is of an obscene, indecent or immoral nature, or so suggestive as to be offensive to the moral sense, or which is calculated to incite crime or riot.

Tennessee Code Annotated
Sec. 39-3003.—It shall be a misdemeanor for any person to knowingly sell, distribute, display, exhibit, possess with the intent to sell, distribute, display or exhibit; or to publish, produce or otherwise create with the intent to sell, distribute, display or exhibit any obscene material
* * * * *
The word "person" as used in this section shall include the singular and the plural and shall also mean and include any person, firm, corporation, partnership, co-partnership, association, or any other organization of any character whatsoever. Sec. 39-1013. *Sale or loan of material to minor— Indecent exhibits.* It shall be unlawful: (a) for any person knowingly to sell or loan for monetary consideration or otherwise exhibit or make available to a minor: (1) any picture, photograph, drawing, sculpture, motion picture film, or similar visual representation or image of a person, or portion of the human body, which depicts nudity, sexual conduct, excess violence, or sado-masochistic abuse, and which is harmful to minors; (2) any book, pamphlet, magazine, printed matter, however reproduced, or sound recording, which contains any matter enumerated in paragraph (1) hereof above, or which contains explicit and detailed verbal descriptions or narrative accounts of sexual excitement, sexual conduct, excess violence, or sado-masochistic abuse, and which is harmful to minors; (b) for any person knowingly to exhibit to a minor for a monetary consideration, or knowingly to sell to a minor an admission ticket or pass or otherwise to admit a minor to premises whereon there is exhibited a motion picture, show or other presentation which, in whole or in part, depicts nudity, sexual conduct, excess violence, or sadomasochistic abuse, and which is harmful to minors.

2. Lincoln is regaled with the following lyrics: "I's free now thanks to you. Massa Lincoln, emancipator of the slave, yeah, yeah, yeah! Emanci—mother fucking—pater of the slave, yeah, yeah, yeah! Emanci—mother fucking—pater of the slave, yeah, year, yeah!" With Lincoln responding, "Bang my ass . . . I ain't dying for no white man!"

3. A woman taking her departure says to the tribe, "Fuck off, kids." (Exhibit No. 4, p. 1-35). The following dialogue occurs as Claude nears his death scene: "Burger: I hate the fucking world, don't you? "Claude: I hate the fucking world, I hate the fucking winter, I hate these fucking streets. "Burger: I wish the fuck it would snow at least. "Claude: Yeah, I wish the fuck it would snow at least. "Burger: Yeah, I wish the fuck it would. "Claude: Oh, fuck! "Burger: Oh, fucky, fuck, fuck!" (Exhibit No. 4, p. 2-22)

4. This Court has no knowledge of the facts before the courts in any of the cited cases, for they make little in the way of findings of fact. Furthermore, it is apparent from the evidence in this case that the manner of presentation of "Hair" is substantially modified from time to time and place to place. The version of the play upon which the findings of fact have been made by this Court was that presented two days before the trial and five days before the writing of this opinion.

Editor's note: This decision was reversed on March 18, 1975 by the U.S. Supreme Court, which decided the case on the procedural matter of prior restraint and not on the question of obscenity. *Southeastern Promotions, Ltd. v. Conrad,* 43 LW 4365

A STATE LIQUOR CONTROL BOARD CAN PROHIBIT
PRESENTATION OF EXPLICITLY SEXUAL LIVE EN-
TERTAINMENT AND FILMS IN BARS AND TAVERNS

California v. LaRue, 409 U.S. 109 (1972)

Mr. Justice Rehnquist delivered the opinion of the Court.

Appellant Kirby is the director of the Department of Alcoholic Beverage Control, an administrative agency vested by the California Constitution with primary authority for the licensing of the sale of alcoholic beverages in that State, and with the authority to suspend or revoke any such license if it determines that its continuation would be contrary to public welfare or morals. Art. XX, § 22, California Constitution. Appellees include holders of various liquor licenses issued by appellant, and dancers at premises operated by such licensees. In 1970 the Department promulgated rules regulating the type of entertainment that might be presented in bars and nightclubs that it licensed. Appellees then brought this action in the United States District Court for the Central District of California under the provisions of 28 U. S. C. §§ 1331, 1343, 2201, 2202, and 42 U. S. C. § 1983. A three-judge court was convened in accordance with 28 U. S. C. §§ 2281 and 2284, and the majority of that court held that substantial portions of the regulations conflicted with the First and Fourteenth Amendments to the United States Constitution.[1]

Concerned with the progression in a few years' time from "topless" dancers to "bottomless" dancers and other forms of "live entertainment" in bars and nightclubs that it licensed, the Commission heard a number of witnesses on this subject at public hearings held prior to the promulgation of the rules. The majority opinion of the District Court described the testimony in these words:

> "Law enforcement agencies, counsel and owners of licensed premises and investigators for the Department testified. The story that unfolded was a sordid one, primarily relating to sexual conduct between dancers and customers. . . ." 326 F. Supp. 348, 352.

References to the transcript of the hearings submitted by the Department to the District Court indicated that in licensed establishments where "topless" and "bottomless" dancers, nude entertainers, and films displaying sexual acts were shown, numerous incidents of legitimate concern to the Department had occurred. Customers were found engaging in oral copulation with women entertainers; customers engaged in public masturbation; and customers placed rolled currency either directly into the vagina of a female entertainer, or on the bar in order that she might pick it up herself. Numerous other forms of contact between the mouths of male customers and the vaginal areas of female performers were reported to have occurred.

Prostitution occurred in and around such licensed premises, and involved some of the female dancers. Indecent exposure to young girls, attempted rape, rape itself, and assaults on police officers took place on or immediately adjacent to such premises.

At the conclusion of the evidence, the Department promulgated the regulations here challenged, imposing standards as to the type of entertainment that could be presented in bars and nightclubs that it licensed. Those portions of the regulations found to be unconstitutional by the majority of the District Court prohibited the following kinds of conduct on licensed premises:

> (a) The performance of acts, or simulated acts, of "sexual intercourse, masturbation, sodomy, bestiality, oral copulation, flagellation or any sexual acts which are prohibited by law";
> (b) The actual or simulated "touching, caressing or fondling on the breast, buttocks, anus or genitals";
> (c) The actual or simulated "displaying of the pubic hair, anus, vulva or genitals";
> (d) The permitting by a licensee of "any person to remain in or upon the licensed premises who exposes to public view any portion of his or her genitals or anus"; and, by a companion section,
> (e) The displaying of films or pictures depicting acts a live performance of which was prohibited by the regulations quoted above. Rules 143.3 and 143.4.[2]

Shortly before the effective date of the Department's regulations, appellees unsuccessfully sought discretionary review of them in both the State Court of Appeals and the Supreme Court of California. The Department then joined with appellees in requesting the three-judge District Court to decide the merits of appellees' claims that the regulations were invalid under the Federal Constitution.[3]

The District Court majority upheld the appellees' claim that the regulations in question unconstitutionally abridged the freedom of expression guaranteed to them by the First and Fourteenth Amendments to the United States Constitution. It reasoned that the state regulations had to be justified either as a prohibition of obscenity in accordance with the *Roth* line of decisions in this Court (*Roth v. United States*, 354 U. S. 476 (1957)), or else as a regulation of "conduct" having a communicative element in it under the standards laid down by this Court in *United States* v. *O'Brien*, 391 U. S. 367 (1968). Concluding that the regulations would bar some entertainment that could not be called obscene under the *Roth* line of cases, and that the governmental interest being furthered by the regulations did not meet the tests laid down in *O'Brien*, the court enjoined the enforcement of the regulations. 326 F. Supp. 348. We noted probable jurisdiction. 404 U. S. 999.

The state regulations here challenged come to us, not in the context of censoring a dramatic performance in a theater, but rather in a context of licensing bars and nightclubs to sell liquor by the drink. In *Seagram & Sons* v. *Hostetter*, 384 U. S. 35, 41 (1966), this Court said:

> "Consideration of any state law regulating intoxicating beverages must begin with the Twenty-first Amendment, the second section of which provides

that: 'The transportation or importation into any State, Territory, or possession of the United States for delivery or use therein of intoxicating liquors, in violation of the laws thereof, is hereby prohibited.' "

While the States, vested as they are with general police power, require no specific grant of authority in the Federal Constitution to legislate with respect to matters traditionally within the scope of the police power, the broad sweep of the Twenty-first Amendment has been recognized as conferring something more than the normal state authority over public health, welfare, and morals. In *Hostetter* v. *Idlewild Liquor Corp.*, 377 U. S. 324, 330 (1964), the Court reaffirmed that by reason of the Twenty-first Amendment "a State is totally unconfined by traditional Commerce Clause limitations when it restricts the importation of intoxicants destined for use, distribution, or consumption within its borders." Still earlier, the Court stated in *State Board* v. *Young's Market Co.*, 299 U. S. 59, 64 (1936):

"A classification recognized by the Twenty-first Amendment cannot be deemed forbidden by the Fourteenth."

These decisions did not go so far as to hold or say that the Twenty-first Amendment supersedes all other provisions of the United States Constitution in the area of liquor regulations. In *Wisconsin* v. *Constantineau*, 400 U. S. 433 (1971), the fundamental notice and hearing requirement of the Due Process Clause of the Fourteenth Amendment was held applicable to Wisconsin's statute providing for the public posting of names of persons who had engaged in excessive drinking. But the case for upholding state regulation in the area covered by the Twenty-first Amendment is undoubtedly strengthened by that enactment:

"Both the Twenty-first Amendment and the Commerce Clause are parts of the same Constitution. Like other provisions of the Constitution, each must be considered in the light of the other, and in the context of the issues and interests at stake in any concrete case." *Hostetter* v. *Idlewild Liquor Corp.*, 377 U. S., at 332.

A common element in the regulations struck down by the District Court appears to be the Department's conclusion that the sale of liquor by the drink and lewd or naked dancing and entertainment should not take place in bars and cocktail lounges for which it has licensing responsibility. Based on the evidence from the hearings that it cited to the District Court, and mindful of the principle that in legislative· rulemaking the agency may reason from the particular to the general, *Assigned Car Cases*, 274 U. S. 564. 583 (1927), we do not think it can be said that the Department's conclusion in this respect was an irrational one.

Appellees insist that the same results could have been accomplished by requiring that patrons already well on the way to intoxication be excluded from the licensed premises. But wide latitude as to choice of means to accomplish a permissible end must be accorded to the state agency that is itself the repository of the State's power under the Twenty-first Amendment. *Seagram & Sons* v. *Hostetter, supra*, at 48. Nothing in the record before us or in common experience compels the conclusion that either self-discipline on the part of the customer or self-regulation on the part of the bartender could have been relied upon by the Department to secure compliance with such an alternative plan of regulation. The Department's choice of a prophylactic solution instead of one that would have required its own personnel to judge individual instances of inebriation cannot, therefore, be deemed an unreasonable one under the holdings of our prior cases. *Williamson* v. *Lee Optical Co.*, 348 U. S. 483, 487–488 (1955).

We do not disagree with the District Court's determination that these regulations on their face would proscribe some forms of visual presentation that would not be found obscene under *Roth* and subsequent decisions of this Court. See, *e. g.*, *Sunshine Book Co.* v. *Summerfield*, 355 U. S. 372 (1958), rev'g *per curiam*, 101 U. S. App. D. C. 358, 249 F. 2d 114 (1957). But we do not believe that the state regulatory authority in this case was limited to either dealing with the problem it confronted within the limits of our decisions as to obscenity, or in accordance with the limits prescribed for dealing with some forms of communicative conduct in *O'Brien, supra*.

Our prior cases have held that both motion pictures and theatrical productions are within the protection of the First and Fourteenth Amendments. In *Joseph Burstyn, Inc.* v. *Wilson*, 343 U. S. 495 (1952), it was held that motion pictures are "included within the free speech and free press guaranty of the First and Fourteenth Amendments," though not "necessarily subject to the precise rules governing any other particular method of expression." *Id.*, at 502–503. In *Schacht* v. *United States*, 398 U. S. 58, 63 (1970), the Court said with respect to theatrical productions:

"An actor, like everyone else in our country, enjoys a constitutional right to freedom of speech, including the right openly to criticize the Government during a dramatic performance."

But as the mode of expression moves from the printed page to the commission of public acts that may themselves violate valid penal statutes, the scope of permissible state regulations significantly increases. States may sometimes proscribe expression that is directed to the accomplishment of an end that the State has declared to be illegal when such expression consists, in part, of "conduct" or "action," *Hughes* v. *Superior Court*, 339 U. S. 460 (1950); *Giboney* v. *Empire Storage Co.*, 336 U. S. 490 (1949).[4] In *O'Brien, supra*, the Court suggested that the extent to which "conduct" was protected by the First Amendment depended on the presence of a "communicative element," and stated:

"We cannot accept the view that an apparently limitless variety of conduct can be labeled 'speech' whenever the person engaging in the conduct intends thereby to express an idea." 391 U. S., at 376.

The substance of the regulations struck down prohibits licensed bars or nightclubs from displaying, either in the form of movies or live entertainment, "performances" that partake more of gross sexuality than of communication. While we agree that at least some of the performances to which these regulations address themselves are within the limits of the constitutional protection of freedom of expression, the critical fact is that California has not forbidden these performances across the board. It has merely proscribed such performances in establishments that it licenses to sell liquor by the drink.

Viewed in this light, we conceive the State's authority in this area to be somewhat broader than did the District Court. This is not to say that all such conduct and performance is without the protection of the First and Fourteenth Amendments. But we would poorly serve both the interests for which the State may validly seek vindication and the interests protected by the First and Fourteenth Amendments were we to insist that the sort of bacchanalian revelries that the Department sought to prevent by these liquor regulations were the constitutional equivalent of a performance by a scantily clad ballet troupe in a theater.

The Department's conclusion, embodied in these regulations, that certain sexual performances and the dispensation of liquor by the drink ought not to occur at premises that have licenses was not an irrational one. Given the added presumption in favor of the validity of the state regulation in this area that the Twenty-first Amendment requires, we cannot hold that the regulations on their face violate the Federal Constitution.[5]

The contrary holding of the District Court is therefore

Reversed.

MR. JUSTICE STEWART, concurring.

A State has broad power under the Twenty-first Amendment to specify the times, places, and circumstances where liquor may be dispensed within its borders. *Seagram & Sons* v. *Hostetter*, 384 U. S. 35; *Hostetter* v. *Idlewild Liquor Corp.*, 377 U. S. 324, 330; *Dept. of Revenue* v. *James Beam Co.*, 377 U. S. 341, 344, 346; *California* v. *Washington*, 358 U. S. 64; *Ziffrin, Inc.* v. *Reeves*, 308 U. S. 132; *Mahoney* v. *Joseph Triner Corp.*, 304 U. S. 401; *State Board* v. *Young's Market Co.*, 299 U. S. 59. I should suppose, therefore, that nobody would question the power of California to prevent the sale of liquor by the drink in places where food is not served, or where dancing is permitted, or where gasoline is sold. But here California has provided that liquor by the drink shall not be sold in places where certain grossly sexual exhibitions are performed; and that action by the State, say the appellees, violates the First and Fourteenth Amendments. I cannot agree.

Every State is prohibited by these same Amendments from invading the freedom of the press and from impinging upon the free exercise of religion. But does this mean that a State cannot provide that liquor shall not be sold in bookstores, or within 200 feet of a church? I think not. For the State would not thereby be interfering with the First Amendment activities of the church or the First Amendment business of the bookstore. It would simply be controlling the distribution of liquor, as it has every right to do under the Twenty-first Amendment. On the same premise, I cannot see how the liquor regulations now before us can be held, on their face, to violate the First and Fourteenth Amendments.*

It is upon this constitutional understanding that I join the opinion and judgment of the Court.

MR. JUSTICE DOUGLAS, dissenting.

This is an action for a declaratory judgment, challenging Rules and Regulations of the Department of Alcoholic Beverage Control of California. It is a challenge of the constitutionality of the rules on their face; no application of the rules has in fact been made to appellees by the institution of either civil or criminal proceedings. While the case meets the requirements of "case or controversy" within the meaning of Art. III of the Constitution and therefore complies with *Aetna Life Ins. Co.* v. *Haworth*, 300 U. S. 227, the case does not mark the precise impact of these Rules against licensees who sell alcoholic beverages in California. The opinion of the Court can, therefore, only deal with the Rules in the abstract.

The line which the Court draws between "expression" and "conduct" is generally accurate; and it also accurately describes in general the reach of the police power of a State when "expression" and "conduct" are closely brigaded. But we still do not know how broadly or how narrowly these Rules will be applied.

It is conceivable that a licensee might produce in a garden served by him a play—Shakespearean perhaps or one in a more modern setting—in which, for example, "fondling" in the sense of the rules appears. I cannot imagine that any such performance could constitutionally be punished or restrained, even though the police power of a State is now buttressed by the Twenty-first Amendment.[1] For, as stated by the Court, that Amendment did not supersede all other constitutional provisions "in the area of liquor regulations." Certainly a play which passes muster under the First Amendment is not made illegal because it is performed in a beer garden.

Chief Justice Hughes stated the controlling principle in *Electric Bond & Share Co.* v. *SEC*, 303 U. S. 419, 443:

"Defendants are not entitled to invoke the Federal Declaratory Judgment Act in order to obtain an advisory decree upon a hypothetical state of facts. . . . By the cross bill, defendants seek a judgment that each and every provision of the Act is unconstitutional. It presents a variety of hypothetical controversies which may never become real. We are invited to enter into a speculative inquiry for the purpose of condemning statutory provisions the effect of which in concrete situations, not yet developed, cannot now be definitely perceived. We must decline that invitation. . . ."

The same thought was expressed by Chief Justice Stone in *Federation of Labor* v. *McAdory*, 325 U. S. 450, 470–471. Some provisions of an Alabama law regulating labor relations were challenged as too vague and uncertain to meet constitutional requirements. The Chief Justice noted that state courts often construe state statutes so that in their application they are not open to constitutional objections. *Id.*, at 471. He said that for us to decide the constitutional question "by anticipating such an authoritative construction" would be either "to decide the question unnecessarily or rest our decision on the unstable foundation of our own construction of the state statute which the state court would not be bound to follow." [2] *Ibid.* He added:

> "In any event the parties are free to litigate in the state courts the validity of the statute when actually applied to any definite state of facts, with the right of appellate review in this Court. In the exercise of this Court's discretionary power to grant or withhold the declaratory judgment remedy it is of controlling significance that it is in the public interest to avoid the needless determination of constitutional questions and the needless obstruction to the domestic policy of the states by forestalling state action in construing and applying its own statutes." *Ibid.*

Those precedents suggest to me that it would have been more provident for the District Court to have declined to give a federal constitutional ruling, until and unless the generalized provisions of the rules were given particularized meaning.

MR. JUSTICE BRENNAN, dissenting.

I dissent. The California regulation at issue here clearly applies to some speech protected by the First Amendment, as applied to the States through the Due Process Clause of the Fourteenth Amendment, and also, no doubt, to some speech and conduct which are unprotected under our prior decisions. See *Memoirs* v. *Massachusetts*, 383 U. S. 413 (1966); *Roth* v. *United States*, 354 U. S. 476 (1957). The State points out, however, that the regulation does not prohibit speech directly, but speaks only to the conditions under which a license to sell liquor by the drink can be granted and retained. But as MR. JUSTICE MARSHALL carefully demonstrates in Part II of his dissenting opinion, by requiring the owner of a nightclub to forgo the exercise of certain rights guaranteed by the First Amendment, the State has imposed an unconstitutional condition on the grant of a license. See *Perry* v. *Sindermann*, 408 U. S. 593 (1972); *Sherbert* v. *Verner*, 374 U. S. 398 (1963); *Speiser* v. *Randall*, 357 U. S. 513 (1958). Nothing in the language or history of the Twenty-first Amendment authorizes the States to use their liquor licensing power as a means for the deliberate inhibition of protected, even if distasteful, forms of expression. For that reason, I would affirm the judgment of the District Court.

MR. JUSTICE MARSHALL, dissenting.

In my opinion, the District Court's judgment should be affirmed. The record in this case is not a pretty one, and it is possible that the State could constitutionally punish some of the activities described therein under a narrowly drawn scheme. But appellees challenge these regulations [1] on their face, rather than as applied to a specific course of conduct. [2] Cf. *Gooding* v. *Wilson*, 405 U. S. 518 (1972). When so viewed, I think it clear that the regulations are overbroad and therefore unconstitutional. See, *e. g.*, *Dombrowski* v. *Pfister*, 380 U. S. 479, 486 (1965). [3] Although the State's broad power to regulate the distribution of liquor and to enforce health and safety regulations is not to be doubted, that power may not be exercised in a manner that broadly stifles First Amendment freedoms. Cf. *Shelton* v. *Tucker*, 364 U. S. 479, 488 (1960). Rather,

as this Court has made clear, "[p]recision of regulation must be the touchstone" when First Amendment rights are implicated. *NAACP* v. *Button*, 371 U. S. 415, 438 (1963). Because I am convinced that these regulations lack the precision which our prior cases require, I must respectfully dissent.

I

It should be clear at the outset that California's regulatory scheme does not conform to the standards which we have previously enunciated for the control of obscenity. [4] Before this Court's decision in *Roth* v. *United States*, 354 U. S. 476 (1957), some American courts followed the rule of *Regina* v. *Hicklin*, L. R. 3 Q. B. 360 (1868), to the effect that the obscenity *vel non* of a piece of work could be judged by examining isolated aspects of it. See, *e. g.*, *United States* v. *Kennerley*, 209 F. 119 (1913); *Commonwealth* v. *Buckley*, 200 Mass. 346, 86 N. E. 910 (1909). But in *Roth* we held that "[t]he *Hicklin* test, judging obscenity by the effect of isolated passages upon the most susceptible persons, might well encompass material legitimately treating with sex, and so it must be rejected as unconstitutionally restrictive of the freedoms of speech and press." 354 U. S., at 489. Instead, we held that the material must be "taken as a whole," *ibid.*, and, when so viewed, must appeal to a prurient interest in sex, patently offend community standards relating to the depiction of sexual matters, and be utterly without redeeming social value. [5] See *Memoirs* v. *Massachusetts*, 383 U. S. 413, 418 (1966).

Obviously, the California rules do not conform to these standards. They do not require the material to be judged as a whole and do not speak to the necessity of proving prurient interest, offensiveness to community standards, or lack of redeeming social value. Instead of the contextual test approved in *Roth* and *Memoirs*, these regulations create a system of *per se* rules to be applied regardless of context: Certain acts simply may not be depicted and certain parts of the body may under no circumstances be revealed. The regulations thus treat on the same level a serious movie such as "Ulysses" and a crudely made "stag film." They ban not only obviously pornographic photographs, but also great sculpture from antiquity. [6]

Roth held 15 years ago that the suppression of serious communication was too high a price to pay in order to vindicate the State's interest in controlling obscenity, and I see no reason to modify that judgment today. Indeed, even the appellants do not seriously contend that these regulations can be justified under the *Roth-Memoirs* test. Instead, appellants argue that California's regulations do not concern the control of pornography at all. These rules, they argue, deal with *conduct* rather than with *speech* and as such are not subject to the strict limitations of the First Amendment.

To support this proposition, appellants rely primarily on *United States* v. *O'Brien*, 391 U. S. 367 (1968), which upheld the constitutionality of legislation punishing the destruction or mutilation of Selective Service certificates. *O'Brien* rejected the notion that "an apparently limitless variety of conduct can be labeled 'speech' whenever the person engaging in the conduct intends thereby to express an idea," and held that Government regulation of speech-related conduct is permissible "if it is within the constitutional power of the Government; if it furthers an important or substantial governmental interest; if the governmental interest is unrelated to the suppression of free expression; and if the incidental restriction on alleged First Amendment freedoms is no greater than is essential to the furtherance of that interest." *Id.*, at 376, 377.

While I do not quarrel with these principles as stated in the abstract, their application in this case stretches them beyond the breaking point.[7] In *O'Brien*, the Court began its discussion by noting that the statute in question "plainly does not abridge free speech on its face." Indeed, even O'Brien himself conceded that facially the statute dealt "with conduct having no connection with speech."[8] *Id.*, at 375. Here, the situation is quite different. A long line of our cases makes clear that motion pictures, unlike draft-card burning, are a form of expression entitled to prima facie First Amendment protection. "It cannot be doubted that motion pictures are a significant medium for the communication of ideas. They may affect public attitudes and behavior in a variety of ways, ranging from direct espousal of a political or social doctrine to the subtle shaping of thought which characterizes all artistic expression. The importance of motion pictures as an organ of public opinion is not lessened by the fact that they are designed to entertain as well as to inform." *Joseph Burstyn, Inc.* v. *Wilson*, 343 U. S. 495, 501 (1952) (footnote omitted). See also *Interstate Circuit, Inc.* v. *City of Dallas*, 390 U. S. 676 (1968); *Jacobellis* v. *Ohio*, 378 U. S. 184 (1964); *Pinkus* v. *Pitchess*, 429 F. 2d 416 (CA9 1970), aff'd by equally divided court *sub nom. California* v. *Pinkus*, 400 U. S. 922 (1970). Similarly, live performances and dance have, in recent years, been afforded broad prima facie First Amendment protection. See, *e. g.*, *Schacht* v. *United States*, 398 U. S. 58 (1970); *P. B. I. C., Inc.* v. *Byrne*, 313 F. Supp. 757 (Mass. 1970), vacated to consider mootness, 401 U. S. 987 (1971); *In re Giannini*, 69 Cal. 2d 563, 446 P. 2d 535 (1968), cert. denied *sub nom. California* v. *Giannini*, 395 U. S. 910 (1969).

If, as these many cases hold, movies, plays, and dance enjoy constitutional protection, it follows, ineluctably I think, that their component parts are protected as well. It is senseless to say that a play is "speech" within the meaning of the First Amendment, but that the individual gestures of the actors are "conduct" which the State may prohibit. The State may no more allow movies while punishing the "acts" of which they are composed than it may allow newspapers while punishing the "conduct" of setting type.

Of course, I do not mean to suggest that anything which occurs upon a stage is automatically immune from state regulation. No one seriously contends, for example, that an actual murder may be legally committed so long as it is called for in the script, or that an actor may inject real heroin into his veins while evading the drug laws that apply to everyone else. But once it is recognized that movies and plays enjoy prima facie First Amendment protection, the standard for reviewing state regulation of their component parts shifts dramatically. For while "[m]ere legislative preferences or beliefs respecting matters of public conven-

ience may well support regulation directed at other personal activities, [they are] insufficient to justify such as diminishes the exercise of rights so vital" as freedom of speech. *Schneider* v. *State*, 308 U. S. 147, 161 (1939). Rather, in order to restrict speech, the State must show that the speech is "used in such circumstances and [is] of such a nature as to create a clear and present danger that [it] will bring about the substantive evils that [the State] has a right to prevent." *Schenck* v. *United States*, 249 U. S. 47, 52 (1919). Cf. *Brandenburg* v. *Ohio*, 395 U. S. 444 (1969); *Dennis* v. *United States*, 341 U. S. 494 (1951).[9]

When the California regulations are measured against this stringent standard, they prove woefully inadequate. Appellants defend the rules as necessary to prevent sex crimes, drug abuse, prostitution, and a wide variety of other evils. These are precisely the same interests that have been asserted time and again before this Court as justification for laws banning frank discussion of sex and that we have consistently rejected. In fact, the empirical link between sex-related entertainment and the criminal activity popularly associated with it has never been proved and, indeed, has now been largely discredited. See, *e. g.*, Report of the Commission on Obscenity and Pornography 27 (1970); Cairns, Paul, & Wishner, Sex Censorship: The Assumptions of Anti-Obscenity Laws and the Empirical Evidence, 46 Minn. L. Rev. 1009 (1962). Yet even if one were to concede that such a link existed, it would hardly justify a broad-scale attack on First Amendment freedoms. The only way to stop murders and drug abuse is to punish them directly. But the State's interest in controlling material dealing with sex is secondary in nature.[10] It can control rape and prostitution by punishing those acts, rather than by punishing the speech that is one step removed from the feared harm.[11] Moreover, because First Amendment rights are at stake, the State must adopt this "less restrictive alternative" unless it can make a compelling demonstration that the protected activity and criminal conduct are so closely linked that only through regulation of one can the other be stopped. Cf. *United States* v. *Robel*, 389 U. S. 258, 268 (1967). As we said in *Stanley* v. *Georgia*, 394 U. S. 557, 566–567 (1969), "if the State is only concerned about printed or filmed materials inducing antisocial conduct, we believe that in the context of private consumption of ideas and information we should adhere to the view that '[a]mong free men, the deterrents ordinarily to be applied to prevent crime are education and punishment for violations of the law . . . .' *Whitney* v. *California*, 274 U. S. 357, 378 (1927) (Brandeis, J., concurring). . . . Given the present state of knowledge, the State may no more prohibit mere possession of obscene matter on the ground that it may lead to antisocial conduct than it may prohibit possession of chemistry books on the ground that they may lead to the manufacture of homemade spirits."[12]

II

It should thus be evident that under the standards previously developed by this Court, the California regulations are overbroad: They would seem to suppress not only obscenity outside the scope of the First Amendment, but also speech that is clearly protected. But California contends that these regulations do not involve suppression at all. The State claims that its rules are not regulations of obscenity, but are rather merely regulations of the sale and consumption of liquor. Appellants point out that California does not punish establishments which provide the proscribed entertainment, but only requires that they not serve alcoholic beverages on their premises. Appellants vigorously argue that such regulation falls within the State's general police power as augmented, when alcoholic beverages are involved, by the Twenty-first Amendment.[13]

I must confess that I find this argument difficult to grasp. To some extent, it seems premised on the notion that the Twenty-first Amendment authorizes the States to regulate liquor in a fashion which would otherwise be constitutionally impermissible. But the Amendment by its terms speaks only to state control of the *importation* of alcohol, and its legislative history makes clear that it was intended only to permit "dry" States to control the flow of liquor across their boundaries despite potential Commerce Clause objections.[14] See generally *Joseph E. Seagram & Sons Inc.* v. *Hostetter,* 384 U. S. 35 (1966); *Hostetter* v. *Idlewild Bon Voyage Liquor Corp.,* 377 U. S. 324 (1964). There is not a word in that history which indicates that Congress meant to tamper in any way with First Amendment rights. I submit that the framers of the Amendment would be astonished to discover that they had inadvertently enacted a *pro tanto* repealer of the rest of the Constitution. Only last Term, we held that the State's conceded power to license the distribution of intoxicating beverages did not justify use of that power in a manner that conflicted with the Equal Protection Clause. See *Moose Lodge No. 107* v. *Irvis,* 407 U. S. 163, 178–179 (1972). Cf. *Wisconsin* v. *Constantineau,* 400 U. S. 433 (1971); *Hornsby* v. *Allen,* 326 F. 2d 605 (CA5 1964), I am at a loss to understand why the Twenty-first Amendment should be thought to override the First Amendment but not the Fourteenth.

To be sure, state regulation of liquor is important, and it is deeply embedded in our history. See, *e. g., Colonnade Catering Corp.* v. *United States,* 397 U. S. 72, 77 (1970). But First Amendment values are important as well. Indeed, in the past they have been thought so important as to provide an independent restraint on every power of Government. "Freedom of press, freedom of speech, freedom of religion are in a preferred position." *Murdock* v. *Pennsylvania,* 319 U. S. 105, 115 (1943). Thus, when the Government attempted to justify a limitation on freedom of association by reference to the war power, we categorically rejected the attempt. "[The] concept of 'national defense'" we held, "cannot be deemed an end in itself, justifying any exercise of legislative power designed to promote such a goal. Implicit in the term 'national defense' is the notion of defending those values and ideals which set this Nation apart. For almost two centuries, our country has taken singular pride in the democratic ideals enshrined in its Constitution, and the most cherished of those ideals have found expression in the First Amendment. It would indeed be ironic if, in the name of national defense, we would sanction the subversion of

one of those liberties—the freedom of association—which makes the defense of the Nation worthwhile." *United States* v. *Robel,* 389 U. S., at 264. Cf. *New York Times Co.* v. *United States,* 403 U. S. 713, 716–717 (1971) (Black, J., concurring); *Home Bldg. & Loan Assn.* v. *Blaisdell,* 290 U. S. 398, 426 (1934). If the First Amendment limits the means by which our Government can ensure its very survival, then surely it must limit the State's power to control the sale of alcoholic beverages as well.

Of course, this analysis is relevant only to the extent that California has in fact encroached upon First Amendment rights. Appellants argue that no such encroachment has occurred, since appellees are free to continue providing any entertainment they choose without fear of criminal penalty. Appellants suggest that this case is somehow different because all that is at stake is the "privilege" of serving liquor by the drink.

It should be clear, however, that the absence of criminal sanctions is insufficient to immunize state regulation from constitutional attack. On the contrary, "this is only the beginning, not the end, of our inquiry." *Sherbert* v. *Verner,* 374 U. S. 398, 403–404 (1963). For "[i]t is too late in the day to doubt that the liberties of religion and expression may be infringed by the denial of or placing of conditions upon a benefit or privilege." *Id.,* at 404. As we pointed out only last Term, "[f]or at least a quarter-century, this Court has made clear that even though a person has no 'right' to a valuable governmental benefit and even though the government may deny him the benefit for any number of reasons, there are some reasons upon which the government may not rely. It may not deny a benefit to a person on a basis that infringes his constitutionally protected interests—especially, his interest in freedom of speech. For if the government could deny a benefit to a person because of his constitutionally protected speech or associations, his exercise of those freedoms would in effect be penalized and inhibited." *Perry* v. *Sindermann,* 408 U. S. 593, 597 (1972).

Thus, unconstitutional conditions on welfare benefits,[15] unemployment compensation,[16] tax exemptions,[17] public employment,[18] bar admissions,[19] and mailing privileges [20] have all been invalidated by this Court. In none of these cases were criminal penalties involved. In all of them, citizens were left free to exercise their constitutional rights so long as they were willing to give up a "gratuity" that the State had no obligation to provide. Yet in all of them, we found that the discriminatory provision of a privilege placed too great a burden on constitutional freedoms. I therefore have some difficulty in understanding why California nightclub proprietors should be singled out and informed that they alone must sacrifice their constitutional rights before gaining the "privilege" to serve liquor.

Of course, it is true that the State may in proper circumstances enact a broad regulatory scheme that incidentally restricts First Amendment rights. For example, if California prohibited the sale of alcohol altogether, I do not mean to suggest that the proprietors of theaters and bookstores would be constitutionally entitled to a special dispensation. But in that event, the classification would not be speech related and, hence, could not be rationally perceived as penalizing speech. Classifications that discriminate against the exercise of constitutional rights *per se* stand on an altogether different footing. They must be supported by a "compelling" governmental purpose and must be carefully examined to insure that the purpose is unrelated to mere hostility to the right being asserted. See, *e. g., Shapiro* v. *Thompson,* 394 U. S. 618, 634 (1969).

Moreover, not only is this classification speech related; it also discriminates between otherwise indistinguishable parties on the basis of the *content* of their speech. Thus, California nightclub owners may present live shows and movies dealing with a wide variety of topics while maintaining their licenses. But if they choose to deal with sex, they are treated quite differently. Classifications based on the content of speech have long been disfavored and must be viewed with the gravest suspicion. See, *e. g., Cox* v. *Louisiana,* 379 U. S. 536, 556–558 (1965). Whether this test is thought to derive from equal protection analysis, see *Police Department of Chicago* v. *Mosley,* 408 U. S. 92 (1972); *Niemotko* v. *Maryland,* 340 U. S. 268 (1951), or directly from the substantive constitutional provision involved, see *Cox* v. *Louisiana, supra; Schneider* v. *State,* 308 U. S. 147 (1939), the result is the same: any law that has "no other purpose . . . than to chill the assertion of constitutional rights by penalizing those who choose to exercise them . . . [is] patently unconstitutional." *United States* v. *Jackson,* 390 U. S. 570, 581 (1968).

As argued above, the constitutionally permissible purposes asserted to justify this statute are too remote to satisfy the Government's burden when First Amendment rights are at stake. See *supra,* at 131–133. It may be that the Government has an interest in suppressing lewd or "indecent" speech even when it occurs in private among consenting adults. Cf. *United States* v. *Thirty-seven Photographs,* 402 U. S. 363, 376 (1971). But cf. *Stanley* v. *Georgia,* 394 U. S. 557 (1969), but that interest must be balanced against the overriding interest of our citizens in freedom of thought and expression. Our prior decisions on obscenity set such a balance and hold that the Government may suppress expression treating with sex only if it meets the three-pronged *Roth-Memoirs* test. We have said that "[t]he door barring federal and state intrusion into this area cannot be left ajar; it must be kept tightly closed and opened only the slightest crack necessary to prevent encroachment upon more important interests." *Roth* v. *United States,* 354 U. S., at 488. Because I can see no reason why we should depart from that standard in this case, I must respectfully dissent.

COURT'S OPINION NOTES

1 Appellees in their brief here suggest that the regulations may exceed the authority conferred upon the Department as a matter of state law. As the District Court recognized, however, such a claim is not cognizable in the suit brought by these appellees under 42 U. S. C. § 1983.

2 In addition to the regulations held unconstitutional by the court below, appellees originally challenged Rule 143.2 prohibiting topless waitresses, Rule 143.3 (2) requiring certain entertainers to perform on a stage at a distance away from customers, and Rule 143.5 prohibiting any entertainment that violated local ordinances. At oral argument in that court they withdrew their objections to these rules, conceding "that topless waitresses are not within the protection of the First Amendment; that local ordinances must be independently challenged depending upon their content; and that the requirement that certain entertainers must dance on a stage is not invalid." 326 F. Supp. 348, 350–351.

3 Mr. Justice Douglas in his dissenting opinion suggests that the District Court should have declined to adjudicate the merits of appellees' contention until the appellants had given the "generalized provisions of the rules . . . particularized meaning." Since parties may not confer jurisdiction either upon this Court or the District Court by stipulation, the request of both parties in this case that the court below adjudicate the merits of the constitutional claim does not foreclose our inquiry into the existence of an "actual controversy" within the meaning of 28 U. S. C. § 2201 and Art. III, § 2, cl. 1, of the Constitution.

By pretrial stipulation, the appellees admitted they offered performances and depictions on their licensed premises that were proscribed by the challenged rules. Appellants stipulated they would take disciplinary action against the licenses of licensees violating such rules. In similar circumstances, this Court held that where a state commission had "plainly indicated" an intent to enforce an act that would affect the rights of the United States, there was a "present and concrete" controversy within the meaning of 28 U. S. C. § 2201 and of Art. III. *California Comm'n* v. *United States,* 355 U. S. 534, 539 (1958). The District Court therefore had jurisdiction of this action.

Whether this Court should develop a nonjurisdictional limitation on actions for declaratory judgments to invalidate statutes on their face is an issue not properly before us. Cf. *Ashwander* v. *Tennessee Valley Authority,* 297 U. S. 288, 341 (1936) (Brandeis, J., concurring). Certainly a number of our cases have permitted attacks on First Amendment grounds similar to those advanced by the appellees, see, *e. g., Zwickler* v. *Koota,* 389 U. S. 241 (1967); *Keyishian* v. *Board of Regents,* 385 U. S. 589 (1967); *Baggett* v. *Bullitt,* 377 U. S. 360 (1964), and we are not inclined to reconsider the procedural holdings of those cases in the absence of a request by a party to do so.

4 Similarly, States may validly limit the manner in which the First Amendment freedoms are exercised, by forbidding sound trucks in residential neighborhoods, *Kovacs* v. *Cooper,* 336 U. S. 77 (1949), and may enforce a nondiscriminatory requirement that those who would parade on a public thoroughfare first obtain a permit. *Cox* v. *New Hampshire,* 312 U. S. 569 (1941). Other state limitations on the "time, manner and place" of the exercise of First Amendment rights have been sustained. See, *e. g., Cameron* v. *Johnson,* 390 U. S. 611 (1968), and *Cox* v. *Louisiana,* 379 U. S. 559 (1965).

5 Because of the posture of this case, we have necessarily dealt with the regulations on their face, and have found them to be valid. The admonition contained in the Court's opinion in *Seagram & Sons* v. *Hostetter,* 384 U. S. 35, 52 (1966), is equally in point here: "Although it is possible that specific future applications of [the statute] may engender concrete problems of constitutional dimension, it will be time enough to consider any such problems when they arise. We deal here only with the statute on its face. And we hold that, so considered, the legislation is constitutionally valid."

*This is not to say that the Twenty-first Amendment empowers a State to act with total irrationality or invidious discrimination in controlling the distribution and dispensation of liquor within its borders. And it most assuredly is not to say that the Twenty-first Amendment necessarily overrides in its allotted area any other relevant provision of the Constitution. See *Wisconsin* v. *Constantineau,* 400 U. S. 433; *Hostetter* v. *Idlewild Liquor Corp.,* 377 U. S. 324, 329–334; *Dept. of Revenue* v. *James Beam Co.,* 377 U. S. 341.

JUSTICE DOUGLAS'S OPINION NOTES

1 Section 2 of the Twenty-first Amendment reads as follows:
"The transportation or importation into any State, Territory, or possession of the United States for delivery or use therein of intoxicating liquors, in violation of the laws thereof, is hereby prohibited."

2 Even in cases on direct appeal from a state court, when the decision below leaves unresolved questions of state law or procedure which bear on federal constitutional questions, we dismiss the appeal. *Rescue Army* v. *Municipal Court,* 331 U. S. 549.

JUSTICE MARSHALL'S OPINION NOTES

[1] Rule 143.3 (1) provides in relevant part:

"No licensee shall permit any person to perform acts of or acts which simulate:

"(a) Sexual intercourse, masturbation, sodomy, bestiality, oral copulation, flagellation or any sexual acts which are prohibited by law.

"(b) The touching, caressing or fondling on the breast, buttocks, anus or genitals.

"(c) The displaying of the pubic hair, anus, vulva or genitals."

Rule 143.4 prohibits: "The showing of film, still pictures, electronic reproduction, or other visual reproductions depicting:

"(1) Acts or simulated acts of sexual intercourse, masturbation, sodomy, bestiality, oral copulation, flagellation or any sexual acts which are prohibited by law.

"(2) Any person being touched, caressed or fondled on the breast, buttocks, anus or genitals.

"(3) Scenes wherein a person displays the vulva or the anus or the genitals.

"(4) Scenes wherein artificial devices or inanimate objects are employed to depict, or drawings are employed to portray, any of the prohibited activities described above."

[2] This is not an appropriate case for application of the abstention doctrine. Since these regulations are challenged on their face for overbreadth, no purpose would be served by awaiting a state court construction of them unless the principles announced in *Younger* v. *Harris*, 401 U. S. 37 (1971), govern. See *Zwickler* v. *Koota*, 389 U. S. 241, 248–250 (1967). Thus far, however, we have limited the applicability of *Younger* to cases where the plaintiff has an adequate remedy in a pending *criminal* prosecution. See *Younger* v. *Harris*, *supra*, at 43–44. Cf. *Douglas* v. *City of Jeannette*, 319 U. S. 157 (1943). But cf. *Berryhill* v. *Gibson*, 331 F. Supp. 122, 124 (MD Ala. 1971), probable jurisdiction noted *sub nom*. *Gibson* v. *Berryhill*. 408 U. S. 920 (1972). The California licensing provisions are, of course, civil in nature. Cf. *Hearn* v. *Short*, 327 F. Supp. 33 (SD Tex. 1971). Moreover, the *Younger* doctrine has been held to "have little force in the absence of a *pending* state proceeding." *Lake Carriers' Assn.* v. *MacMullan*, 406 U. S. 498, 509 (1972) (emphasis added). There are at present no proceedings of any kind pending against these appellees. Finally, since the *Younger* doctrine rests heavily on federal deference to state administration of its own statutes, see *Younger* v. *Harris*, *supra*, at 44–45, it is waivable by the State. Cf. *Hostetter* v. *Idlewild Bon Voyage Liquor Corp.*, 377 U. S. 324, 329 (1964). Appellants have nowhere mentioned the *Younger* doctrine in their brief before this Court, and when the case was brought to the attention of the attorney for the appellants during oral argument, he expressly eschewed reliance on it. In the court below, appellants specifically asked for a federal decision on the validity of California's regulations and stated that they did not think the court should abstain. See 326 F. Supp. 348, 351 (CD Cal. 1971).

[3] I am startled by the majority's suggestion that the regulations are constitutional on their face even though "specific future applications of [the statute] may engender concrete problems of constitutional dimension." (Quoting with approval *Joseph E. Seagram & Sons* v. *Hostetter*, 384 U. S. 35, 52 (1966). *Ante*, at 119 n. 5.) Ever since *Thornhill* v. *Alabama*, 310 U. S. 88 (1940), it has been thought that statutes which trench upon First Amendment rights are facially void even if the conduct of the party challenging them could be prohibited under a more narrowly drawn scheme. See, e. g., *Baggett* v. *Bullitt*, 377 U. S. 360, 366 (1964); *Coates* v. *City of Cincinnati*, 402 U. S. 611, 616 (1971); *NAACP* v. *Button*, 371 U. S. 415, 432–433 (1963).

Nor is it relevant that the State here "sought to prevent [bacchanalian revelries]" rather than performances by "scantily clad ballet troupe[s]." Whatever the State "sought" to do, the fact is that these regulations cover both these activities. And it should be clear that a praiseworthy legislative motive can no more rehabilitate an unconstitutional statute than an illicit motive can invalidate a proper statute.

[4] Indeed, there are some indications in the legislative history that California adopted these regulations for the specific purpose of evading those standards. Thus, Captain Robert Devin of the Los Angeles Police Department testified that the Department favored adoption of the new regulations for the following reason: "While statutory law has been available to us to regulate what was formerly considered as antisocial behavior, the federal and state judicial system has, through a series of similar decisions, effectively emasculated law enforcement in its effort to contain and to control the growth of pornography and of obscenity and of behavior that is associated with this kind of performance." See also testimony of Roy E. June, City Attorney of the City of Costa Mesa; testimony of Richard C. Hirsch, Office of Los Angeles County District Attorney. App. 117.

[5] I do not mean to suggest that this test need be rigidly applied in all situations. Different standards may be applicable when children are involved, see *Ginsberg* v. *New York*, 390 U. S. 629 (1968); when a consenting adult possesses putatively obscene material in his own home, see *Stanley* v. *Georgia*, 394 U. S. 557 (1969); or when the material by the nature of its presentation cannot be viewed as a whole, see *Rabe* v. *Washington*, 405 U. S. 313, 317 n. 2 (1972) (BURGER, C. J., concurring). Similarly, I do not mean to foreclose the possibility that even the *Roth-Memoirs* test will ultimately be found insufficient to protect First Amendment interests when consenting adults view putatively obscene material in private. Cf. *Redrup* v. *New York*, 386 U. S. 767 (1967). But cf. *United States* v. *Reidel*, 402 U. S. 351 (1971). But I do think that, at very least, *Roth-Memoirs* sets an absolute limit on the kinds of speech that can be altogether read out of the First Amendment for purposes of consenting adults.

[6] Cf. Fuller, Changing Society Puts Taste to the Test, The National Observer, June 10, 1972, p. 24: "Context is the essence of esthetic judgment . . . . There is a world of difference between Playboy and less pretentious girly magazines on the one hand, and on the other, *The Nude*, a picture selection from the whole history of art, by that fine teacher and interpreter of civilization, Kenneth Clark. People may be just as naked in one or the other, the bodies inherently just as beautiful, but the context of the former is vulgar, of the latter, esthetic.

"The same words, the same actions, that are cheap and tawdry in one book or play may contribute to the sublimity, comic universality, or tragic power of others. For a viable theory of taste, context is all."

[7] Moreover, even if the *O'Brien* test were here applicable, it is far from clear that it has been satisfied. For example, most of the evils that the State alleges are caused by appellees' performances are already punishable under California law. See n. 11, *infra*. Since the less drastic alternative of criminal prosecution is available to punish these violations, it is hard to see how "the incidental restriction on alleged First Amendment freedoms is no greater than is essential" to further the State's interest.

[8] The Court pointed out that the statute "does not distinguish between public and private destruction, and it does not punish only destruction engaged in for the purpose of expressing views . . . . A law prohibiting destruction of Selective Service certificates no more abridges free speech on its face than a motor vehicle law prohibiting the destruction of drivers' licenses, or a tax law prohibiting the destruction of books and records." 391 U. S., at 375.

[9] Of course, the State need not meet the clear and present danger test if the material in question is obscene. See *Roth* v. *United States*, 354 U. S. 476 (1957). But, as argued above, the difficulty with California's rules is that they do not conform to the *Roth* test and therefore regulate material that is not obscene. See *supra*, at 126–127.

[10] This case might be different if the State asserted a primary interest in stopping the very acts performed by these dancers and actors. However, I have serious doubts whether the State may constitutionally assert an interest in regulating any sexual act between consenting adults. Cf. *Griswold* v. *Connecticut*, 381 U. S. 479 (1965). Moreover, it is unnecessary to reach that question in this case since the State's regulations are plainly not designed to stop the acts themselves, most of which are in fact legal when done in private. Rather, the State punishes the acts only when done in public as part of a dramatic presentation. Cf. *United States* v. *O'Brien*, *supra*, at 375. It must be, therefore, that the asserted state interest stems from the effect of the acts on the audience rather than from a desire to stop the acts themselves. It should also be emphasized that this case does not present problems of an unwilling audience or of an audience composed of minors.

[11] Indeed, California already has statutes controlling virtually all of the misconduct said to flow from appellees' activities. See Calif. Penal Code § 647 (b) (Supp. 1972) (prostitution); Calif. Penal Code §§ 261, 263 (1970) (rape); Calif. Bus. & Prof. Code § 25657 (Supp. 1972) ("B-Girl" activity); Calif. Health & Safety Code §§ 11500, 11501, 11721, 11910, 11912 (1964 and Supp. 1972) (sale and use of narcotics).

[12] Of course, it is true that *Stanley* does not govern this case, since *Stanley* dealt only with the private possession of obscene materials in one's own home. But in another sense, this case is stronger than *Stanley*. In *Stanley*, we held that the State's interest in the prevention of sex crimes did not justify laws restricting possession of certain materials, even though they were conceded to be obscene. It follows *a fortiori* that this interest is insufficient when the materials are not obscene and, indeed, are constitutionally protected.

[13] The Twenty-first Amendment, in addition to repealing the Eighteenth Amendment, provides: "The transportation or importation into any State, Territory, or possession of the United States for delivery or use therein of intoxicating liquors, in violation of the laws thereof, is hereby prohibited."

[14] The text of the Amendment is based on the Webb-Kenyon Act, 37 Stat. 699, which antedated prohibition. The Act was entitled "An Act Divesting intoxicating liquors of their interstate character in certain cases," and was designed to allow "dry" States to regulate the flow of alcohol across their borders. See, *e. g., McCormick & Co.* v. *Brown*, 286 U. S. 131, 140–141 (1932); *Clark Distilling Co.* v. *Western Maryland R. Co.*, 242 U. S. 311, 324 (1917). The Twenty-first Amendment was intended to embed this principle permanently into the Constitution. As explained by its sponsor on the Senate floor "to assure the so-called dry States against the importation of intoxicating liquor into those States, it is proposed to write permanently into the Constitution a prohibition along that line.

"[T]he pending proposal will give the States that guarantee. When our Government was organized and the Constitution of the United States adopted, the States surrendered control over and regulation of interstate commerce. This proposal is restoring to the States, in effect, the right to regulate commerce respecting a single commodity—namely, intoxicating liquor." 76 Cong. Rec. 4141 (remarks of Sen. Blaine).

[15] See *Shapiro* v. *Thompson*, 394 U. S. 618 (1969). But cf. *Wyman* v. *James*, 400 U. S. 309 (1971).

[16] See *Sherbert* v. *Verner*, 374 U. S. 398 (1963).

[17] See *Speiser* v. *Randall*, 357 U. S. 513 (1958).

[18] See, *e. g., Pickering* v. *Board of Education*, 391 U. S. 563 (1968); *Keyishian* v. *Board of Regents*, 385 U. S. 589 (1967); *Baggett* v. *Bullitt*, 377 U. S. 360 (1964).

[19] See, *e. g., Baird* v. *State Bar of Arizona*, 401 U. S. 1 (1971); *Konigsberg* v. *State Bar*, 353 U. S. 252 (1957); *Schware* v. *Board of Bar Examiners*, 353 U. S. 232 (1957). But cf. *Law Students Civil Rights Research Council* v. *Wadmond*, 401 U. S. 154 (1971); *Konigsberg* v. *State Bar*, 366 U. S. 36 (1961).

[20] See, *e. g., Blount* v. *Rizzi*, 400 U. S. 410 (1971); *Hannegan* v. *Esquire Inc.*, 327 U. S. 146, 156 (1946).

OBSCENITY IN POLITICAL SPEECH

OBSCENITY IN POLITICAL SPEECH

"FUCK THE DRAFT" INSCRIBED ON THE BACK OF A
JACKET WORN IN THE LOS ANGELES COURTHOUSE
IS PROTECTED SPEECH

Cohen v. California, 403 U.S. 15 (1971)

MR. JUSTICE HARLAN delivered the opinion of the Court.

This case may seem at first blush too inconsequential to find its way into our books, but the issue it presents is of no small constitutional significance.

Appellant Paul Robert Cohen was convicted in the Los Angeles Municipal Court of violating that part of California Penal Code § 415 which prohibits "maliciously and willfully disturb[ing] the peace or quiet of any neighborhood or person . . . by . . . offensive conduct . . . ."[1] He was given 30 days' imprisonment. The facts upon which his conviction rests are detailed in the opinion of the Court of Appeal of California, Second Appellate District, as follows:

> "On April 26, 1968, the defendant was observed in the Los Angeles County Courthouse in the corridor outside of division 20 of the municipal court wearing a jacket bearing the words 'Fuck the Draft' which were plainly visible. There were women and children present in the corridor. The defendant was arrested. The defendant testified that he wore the jacket knowing that the words were on the jacket as a means of informing the public of the depth of his feelings against the Vietnam War and the draft.

> "The defendant did not engage in, nor threaten to engage in, nor did anyone as the result of his conduct in fact commit or threaten to commit any act of violence. The defendant did not make any loud or unusual noise, nor was there any evidence that he uttered any sound prior to his arrest." 1 Cal. App. 3d 94, 97–98, 81 Cal. Rptr. 503, 505 (1969).

In affirming the conviction the Court of Appeal held that "offensive conduct" means "behavior which has a tendency to provoke *others* to acts of violence or to in turn disturb the peace," and that the State had proved this element because, on the facts of this case, "[i]t was certainly reasonably foreseeable that such conduct might cause others to rise up to commit a violent act against the person of the defendant or attempt to forceably remove his jacket." 1 Cal. App. 3d, at 99–100, 81 Cal. Rptr., at 506. The California Supreme Court declined review by a divided vote.[2] We brought the case here, postponing the consideration of the question of our jurisdiction over this appeal to a hearing of the case on the merits. 399 U. S. 904. We now reverse.

The question of our jurisdiction need not detain us long. Throughout the proceedings below, Cohen consistently claimed that, as construed to apply to the facts of this case, the statute infringed his rights to freedom of expression guaranteed by the First and Fourteenth Amendments of the Federal Constitution. That contention has been rejected by the highest California state court in which review could be had. Accordingly, we are fully satisfied that Cohen has properly invoked our jurisdiction by this appeal. 28 U. S. C. § 1257 (2); *Dahnke-Walker Milling Co. v. Bondurant*, 257 U. S. 282 (1921).

I

In order to lay hands on the precise issue which this case involves, it is useful first to canvass various matters which this record does *not* present.

The conviction quite clearly rests upon the asserted offensiveness of the *words* Cohen used to convey his message to the public. The only "conduct" which the State sought to punish is the fact of communication. Thus, we deal here with a conviction resting solely upon "speech," cf. *Stromberg* v. *California*, 283 U. S. 359 (1931), not upon any separately identifiable conduct which allegedly was intended by Cohen to be perceived by others as expressive of particular views but which, on its face, does not necessarily convey any message and hence arguably could be regulated without effectively repressing Cohen's ability to express himself. Cf. *United States* v. *O'Brien*, 391 U. S. 367 (1968). Further, the State certainly lacks power to punish Cohen for the underlying content of the message the inscription conveyed. At least so long as there is no showing of an intent to incite disobedience to or disruption of the draft, Cohen could not, consistently with the First and Fourteenth Amendments, be punished for asserting the evident position on the inutility or immorality of the draft his jacket reflected. *Yates* v. *United States*, 354 U. S. 298 (1957).

Appellant's conviction, then, rests squarely upon his exercise of the "freedom of speech" protected from arbitrary governmental interference by the Constitution and can be justified, if at all, only as a valid regulation of the manner in which he exercised that freedom, not as a permissible prohibition on the substantive message it conveys. This does not end the inquiry, of course, for the First and Fourteenth Amendments have never been thought to give absolute protection to every individual to speak whenever or wherever he pleases, or to use any form of address in any circumstances that he chooses. In this vein, too, however, we think it important to note that several issues typically associated with such problems are not presented here.

In the first place, Cohen was tried under a statute applicable throughout the entire State. Any attempt to support this conviction on the ground that the statute seeks to preserve an appropriately decorous atmosphere in the courthouse where Cohen was arrested must fail in the absence of any language in the statute that would have put appellant on notice that certain kinds of otherwise permissible speech or conduct would nevertheless, under California law, not be tolerated in certain places. See *Edwards* v. *South Carolina*, 372 U. S. 229, 236–237, and n. 11 (1963). Cf. *Adderley* v. *Florida*, 385 U. S. 39 (1966). No fair reading of the phrase "offensive conduct" can be said sufficiently to inform the ordinary person that distinctions between certain locations are thereby created.[3]

In the second place, as it comes to us, this case cannot be said to fall within those relatively few categories of instances where prior decisions have established the power of government to deal more comprehensively with certain forms of individual expression simply upon a showing that such a form was employed. This is not, for example, an obscenity case. Whatever else may be necessary to give rise to the States' broader power to prohibit obscene expression, such expression must be, in some significant way, erotic. *Roth* v. *United States*, 354 U. S. 476 (1957). It cannot plausibly be maintained that this vulgar allusion to the Selective Service System would conjure up such psychic stimulation in anyone likely to be confronted with Cohen's crudely defaced jacket.

This Court has also held that the States are free to ban the simple use, without a demonstration of additional justifying circumstances, of so-called "fighting words," those personally abusive epithets which, when addressed to the ordinary citizen, are, as a matter of common knowledge, inherently likely to provoke violent reaction. *Chaplinsky* v. *New Hampshire*, 315 U. S. 568 (1942). While the four-letter word displayed by Cohen in relation to the draft is not uncommonly employed in a personally provocative fashion, in this instance it was clearly not "directed to the person of the hearer." *Cantwell* v. *Connecticut*, 310 U. S. 296, 309 (1940). No individual actually or likely to be present could reasonably have regarded the words on appellant's jacket as a direct personal insult. Nor do we have here an instance of the exercise of the State's police power to prevent a speaker from intentionally provoking a given group to hostile reaction. Cf. *Feiner* v. *New York*, 340 U. S. 315 (1951); *Terminiello* v. *Chicago*, 337 U. S. 1 (1949). There is, as noted above, no showing that anyone who saw Cohen was in fact violently aroused or that appellant intended such a result.

Finally, in arguments before this Court much has been made of the claim that Cohen's distasteful mode of expression was thrust upon unwilling or unsuspecting viewers, and that the State might therefore legitimately act as it did in order to protect the sensitive from otherwise unavoidable exposure to appellant's crude form of protest. Of course, the mere presumed presence of unwitting listeners or viewers does not serve automatically to justify curtailing all speech capable of giving offense. See, e. g., *Organization for a Better Austin* v. *Keefe*, 402 U. S. 415 (1971). While this Court has recognized that government may properly act in many situations to prohibit intrusion into the privacy of the home of unwelcome views and ideas which cannot be totally banned from the public dialogue, e. g., *Rowan* v. *Post Office Dept.*, 397 U. S. 728 (1970), we have at the same time consistently stressed that "we are often 'captives' outside the sanctuary of the home and subject to objectionable speech." *Id.*, at 738. The ability of government, consonant with the Constitution, to shut off discourse solely to protect others from hearing it is, in other words, dependent upon a showing that substantial privacy interests are being invaded in an essentially intolerable manner. Any broader view of this authority would effectively empower a majority to silence dissidents simply as a matter of personal predilections.

In this regard, persons confronted with Cohen's jacket were in a quite different posture than, say, those subjected to the raucous emissions of sound trucks blaring outside their residences. Those in the Los Angeles courthouse could effectively avoid further bombardment of their sensibilities simply by averting their eyes. And, while it may be that one has a more substantial claim to a recognizable privacy interest when walking through a courthouse corridor than, for example, strolling through Central Park, surely it is nothing like the interest in being free from unwanted expression in the confines of one's own home. Cf. *Keefe, supra.* Given the subtlety and complexity of the factors involved, if Cohen's "speech" was otherwise entitled to constitutional protection, we do not think the fact that some unwilling "listeners" in a public building may have been briefly exposed to it can serve to justify this breach of the peace conviction where, as here, there was no evidence that persons powerless to avoid appellant's conduct did in fact object to it, and where that portion of the statute upon which Cohen's conviction rests evinces no concern, either on its face or as construed by the California courts, with the special plight of the captive auditor, but, instead, indiscriminately sweeps within its prohibitions all "offensive conduct" that disturbs "any neighborhood or person." Cf. *Edwards* v. *South Carolina, supra.*[4]

II

Against this background, the issue flushed by this case stands out in bold relief. It is whether California can excise, as "offensive conduct," one particular scurrilous epithet from the public discourse, either upon the theory of the court below that its use is inherently likely to cause violent reaction or upon a more general assertion that the States, acting as guardians of public morality, may properly remove this offensive word from the public vocabulary.

The rationale of the California court is plainly untenable. At most it reflects an "undifferentiated fear or apprehension of disturbance [which] is not enough to overcome the right to freedom of expression." *Tinker* v. *Des Moines Indep. Community School Dist.*, 393 U. S. 503, 508 (1969). We have been shown no evidence that substantial numbers of citizens are standing ready to strike out physically at whoever may assault their sensibilities with execrations like that uttered by Cohen. There may be some persons about with such lawless and violent proclivities, but that is an insufficient base upon which to erect, consistently with constitutional values, a governmental power to force persons who wish to ventilate their dissident views into avoiding particular forms of expression. The argument amounts to little more than the self-defeating proposition that to avoid physical censorship of one who has not sought to provoke such a response by a hypothetical coterie of the violent and lawless, the States may more appropriately effectuate that censorship themselves. Cf. *Ashton* v. *Kentucky,* 384 U. S. 195, 200 (1966); *Cox* v. *Louisiana,* 379 U. S. 536, 550–551 (1965).

Admittedly, it is not so obvious that the First and Fourteenth Amendments must be taken to disable the States from punishing public utterance of this unseemly expletive in order to maintain what they regard as a suitable level of discourse within the body politic.[5] We think, however, that examination and reflection will reveal the shortcomings of a contrary viewpoint.

At the outset, we cannot overemphasize that, in our judgment, most situations where the State has a justifiable interest in regulating speech will fall within one or more of the various established exceptions, discussed above but not applicable here, to the usual rule that governmental bodies may not prescribe the form or content of individual expression. Equally important to our conclusion is the constitutional backdrop against which our decision must be made. The constitutional right of free expression is powerful medicine in a society as diverse and populous as ours. It is designed and intended to remove governmental restraints from the arena of public discussion, putting the decision as to what views shall be voiced largely into the hands of each of us, in the hope that use of such freedom will ultimately produce a more capable citizenry and more perfect polity and in the belief that no other approach would comport with the premise of individual dignity and choice upon which our political system rests. See *Whitney* v. *California,* 274 U. S. 357, 375–377 (1927) (Brandeis, J., concurring).

To many, the immediate consequence of this freedom may often appear to be only verbal tumult, discord, and even offensive utterance. These are, however, within established limits, in truth necessary side effects of the broader enduring values which the process of open debate permits us to achieve. That the air may at times seem filled with verbal cacophony is, in this sense not a sign of weakness but of strength. We cannot lose sight of the fact that, in what otherwise might seem a trifling and annoying instance of individual distasteful abuse of a privilege, these fundamental societal values are truly implicated. That is why "[w]holly neutral futilities . . . come under the protection of free speech as fully as do Keats' poems or Donne's sermons," *Winters* v. *New York,* 333 U. S. 507, 528 (1948) (Frankfurter, J., dissenting), and why "so long as the means are peaceful, the communication need not meet standards of acceptability," *Organization for a Better Austin* v. *Keefe,* 402 U. S. 415, 419 (1971).

Against this perception of the constitutional policies involved, we discern certain more particularized considerations that peculiarly call for reversal of this conviction. First, the principle contended for by the State seems inherently boundless. How is one to distinguish this from any other offensive word? Surely the State has no right to cleanse public debate to the point where it is grammatically palatable to the most squeamish among us. Yet no readily ascertainable general principle exists for stopping short of that result were we to affirm the judgment below. For, while the particular four-letter word being litigated here is perhaps more distasteful than most others of its genre, it is nevertheless often true that one man's vulgarity is another's lyric. Indeed, we think it is largely because governmental officials cannot make principled distinctions in this area that the Constitution leaves matters of taste and style so largely to the individual.

Additionally, we cannot overlook the fact, because it is well illustrated by the episode involved here, that much linguistic expression serves a dual communicative function: it conveys not only ideas capable of relatively precise, detached explication, but otherwise inexpressible emotions as well. In fact, words are often chosen as much for their emotive as their cognitive force. We cannot sanction the view that the Constitution, while solicitous of the cognitive content of individual speech, has little or no regard for that emotive function which, practically speaking, may often be the more important element of the overall message sought to be communicated. Indeed, as Mr. Justice Frankfurter has said, "[o]ne of the prerogatives of American citizenship is the right to criticize public men and measures—and that means not only informed and responsible criticism but the freedom to speak foolishly and without moderation." *Baumgartner* v. *United States,* 322 U. S. 665, 673–674 (1944).

Finally, and in the same vein, we cannot indulge the facile assumption that one can forbid particular words without also running a substantial risk of suppressing ideas in the process. Indeed, governments might soon seize upon the censorship of particular words as a convenient guise for banning the expression of unpopular views. We have been able, as noted above, to discern little social benefit that might result from running the risk of opening the door to such grave results.

It is, in sum, our judgment that, absent a more particularized and compelling reason for its actions, the State may not, consistently with the First and Fourteenth Amendments, make the simple public display here involved of this single four-letter expletive a criminal offense. Because that is the only arguably sustainable rationale for the conviction here at issue, the judgment below must be

Reversed.

Mr. Justice Blackmun, with whom The Chief Justice and Mr. Justice Black join.

I dissent, and I do so for two reasons:

1. Cohen's absurd and immature antic, in my view, was mainly conduct and little speech. See *Street* v. *New York,* 394 U. S. 576 (1969); *Cox* v. *Louisiana,* 379 U. S. 536, 555 (1965); *Giboney* v. *Empire Storage Co.,* 336 U. S. 490, 502 (1949). The California Court of Appeal appears so to have described it, 1 Cal. App. 3d 94, 100,

81 Cal. Rptr. 503, 507, and I cannot characterize it otherwise. Further, the case appears to me to be well within the sphere of *Chaplinsky v. New Hampshire*, 315 U. S. 568 (1942), where Mr. Justice Murphy, a known champion of First Amendment freedoms, wrote for a unanimous bench. As a consequence, this Court's agonizing over First Amendment values seems misplaced and unnecessary.

2. I am not at all certain that the California Court of Appeal's construction of § 415 is now the authoritative California construction. The Court of Appeal filed its opinion on October 22, 1969. The Supreme Court of California declined review by a four-to-three vote on December 17. See 1 Cal. App. 3d, at 104. A month later, on January 27, 1970, the State Supreme Court in another case construed § 415, evidently for the first time. *In re Bushman*, 1 Cal. 3d 767, 463 P. 2d 727. Chief Justice Traynor, who was among the dissenters to his court's refusal to take Cohen's case, wrote the majority opinion. He held that § 415 "is not unconstitutionally vague and overbroad" and further said:

> "[T]hat part of Penal Code section 415 in question here makes punishable only wilful and malicious conduct that is violent and endangers public safety and order or that creates a clear and present danger that others will engage in violence of that nature.
>
> "... [It] does not make criminal any nonviolent act unless the act incites or threatens to incite others to violence . . . ." 1 Cal. 3d, at 773–774, 463 P. 2d, at 731.

Cohen was cited in *Bushman*, 1 Cal. 3d, at 773, 463 P. 2d, at 730, but I am not convinced that its description there and *Cohen* itself are completely consistent with the "clear and present danger" standard enunciated in *Bushman*. Inasmuch as this Court does not dismiss this case, it ought to be remanded to the California Court of Appeal for reconsideration in the light of the subsequently rendered decision by the State's highest tribunal in *Bushman*.

MR. JUSTICE WHITE concurs in Paragraph 2 of MR. JUSTICE BLACKMUN's dissenting opinion.

NOTES

[1] The statute provides in full:

"Every person who maliciously and willfully disturbs the peace or quiet of any neighborhood or person, by loud or unusual noise, or by tumultuous or offensive conduct, or threatening, traducing, quarreling, challenging to fight, or fighting, or who, on the public streets of any unincorporated town, or upon the public highways in such unincorporated town, run any horse race, either for a wager or for amusement, or fire any gun or pistol in such unincorporated town, or use any vulgar, profane, or indecent language within the presence or hearing of women or children, in a loud and boisterous manner, is guilty of a misdemeanor, and upon conviction by any Court of competent jurisdiction shall be punished by fine not exceeding two hundred dollars, or by imprisonment in the County Jail for not more than ninety days, or by both fine and imprisonment, or either, at the discretion of the Court."

[2] The suggestion has been made that, in light of the supervening opinion of the California Supreme Court in *In re Bushman*, 1 Cal. 3d 767, 463 P. 2d 727 (1970), it is "not at all certain that the California Court of Appeal's construction of § 415 is now the authoritative California construction." *Post*, at 27 (BLACKMUN, J., dissenting). In the course of the *Bushman* opinion, Chief Justice Traynor stated:

"[One] may . . . be guilty of disturbing the peace through 'offensive' conduct [within the meaning of § 415] if by his actions he wilfully and maliciously incites others to violence or engages in conduct likely to incite others to violence. (*People v. Cohen* (1969) 1 Cal. App. 3d 94, 101, [81 Cal. Rptr. 503].)" 1 Cal. 3d, at 773, 463 P. 2d, at 730.

We perceive no difference of substance between the *Bushman* construction and that of the Court of Appeal, particularly in light of the *Bushman* court's approving citation of *Cohen*.

[3] It is illuminating to note what transpired when Cohen entered a courtroom in the building. He removed his jacket and stood with it folded over his arm. Meanwhile, a policeman sent the presiding judge a note suggesting that Cohen be held in contempt of court. The judge declined to do so and Cohen was arrested by the officer only after he emerged from the courtroom. App. 18–19.

[4] In fact, other portions of the same statute do make some such distinctions. For example, the statute also prohibits disturbing "the peace or quiet . . . by loud or unusual noise" and using "vulgar, profane, or indecent language within the presence or hearing of women or children, in a loud and boisterous manner." See n. 1, *supra*. This second-quoted provision in particular serves to put the actor on much fairer notice as to what is prohibited. It also buttresses our view that the "offensive conduct" portion, as construed and applied in this case, cannot legitimately be justified in this Court as designed or intended to make fine distinctions between differently situated recipients.

[5] The *amicus* urges, with some force, that this issue is not properly before us since the statute, as construed, punishes only conduct that might cause others to react violently. However, because the opinion below appears to erect a virtually irrebuttable presumption that use of this word will produce such results, the statute as thus construed appears to impose, in effect, a flat ban on the public utterance of this word. With the case in this posture, it does not seem inappropriate to inquire whether any other rationale might properly support this result. While we think it clear, for the reasons expressed above, that no statute which merely proscribes "offensive conduct" and has been construed as broadly as this one was below can subsequently be justified in this Court as discriminating between conduct that occurs in different places or that offends only certain persons, it is not so unreasonable to seek to justify its full broad sweep on an alternate rationale such as this. Because it is not so patently clear that acceptance of the justification presently under consideration would render the statute overbroad or unconstitutionally vague, and because the answer to appellee's argument seems quite clear, we do not pass on the contention that this claim is not presented on this record.

THE UNITED STATES SUPREME COURT GIVES FIRST AMENDMENT PROTECTION TO "OBSCENE" WORDS SPOKEN AT PUBLIC MEETING AND TO POLICE OFFICERS, BUT JUSTICES BURGER, BLACKMUN, POWELL, AND REHNQUIST DISSENT

Rosenfeld v. New Jersey, 408 U.S. 901 (1972)
Lewis v. City of New Orleans, 408 U.S. 913 (1972)
Brown v. Oklahoma, 408 U.S. 914 (1972)

No. 71–1044. ROSENFELD *v.* NEW JERSEY. Appeal from Super. Ct. N. J. Judgment vacated and case remanded for reconsideration in light of *Cohen v. California*, 403 U. S. 15 (1971), and *Gooding v. Wilson*, 405 U. S. 518 (1972). Reported below: See 59 N. J. 435, 283 A. 2d 535.

Mr. Chief Justice Burger, with whom Mr. Justice Blackmun and Mr. Justice Rehnquist join, dissenting.*

I am constrained to express my profound disagreement with what the Court does in these three cases on the basis of *Gooding* v. *Wilson*, 405 U. S. 518 (1972).

The important underlying aspect of these cases goes really to the function of law in preserving ordered liberty. Civilized people refrain from "taking the law into their own hands" because of a belief that the government, as their agent, will take care of the problem in an organized, orderly way with as nearly a uniform response as human skills can manage. History is replete with evidence of what happens when the law cannot or does not provide a collective response for conduct so widely regarded as impermissible and intolerable.

It is barely a century since men in parts of this country carried guns constantly because the law did not afford protection. In that setting, the words used in these cases, if directed toward such an armed civilian, could well have led to death or serious bodily injury. When we undermine the general belief that the law will give protection against fighting words and profane and abusive language such as the utterances involved in these cases, we take steps to return to the law of the jungle. These three cases, like *Gooding*, are small but symptomatic steps. If continued, this permissiveness will tend further to erode public confidence in the law—that subtle but indispensable ingredient of ordered liberty.

In Rosenfeld's case, for example, civilized people attending such a meeting with wives and children would not likely have an instantaneous, violent response, but it does not unduly tax the imagination to think that some justifiably outraged parent whose family were exposed to the foul mouthings of the speaker would "meet him outside" and, either alone or with others, resort to the 19th century's vigorous modes of dealing with such people. I cannot see these holdings as an "advance" in human liberty but rather a retrogression to what men have struggled to escape for a long time.

Mr. Justice Powell, with whom The Chief Justice and Mr. Justice Blackmun join, dissenting.

It has long been established that the First and Fourteenth Amendments prohibit the States from punishing all but the most "narrowly limited classes of speech." *Chaplinksy* v. *New Hampshire*, 315 U. S. 568, 571 (1942). The right of free speech, however, has never been held to be absolute at all times and under all circumstances. To so hold would sanction invasion of cherished personal rights and would deny the States· the power to deal with threats to public order. As the Court noted in *Chaplinsky:*

"[I]t is well understood that the right of free speech is not absolute at all times and under all circumstances. There are certain well-defined and narrowly limited classes of speech, the prevention and punishment of which have never been thought to raise any Constitutional problem. These include the lewd and obscene, the profane, the libelous, and the insulting or 'fighting' words—those which by their very utterance inflict injury or tend to

incite an immediate breach of the peace. It has been well observed that such utterances are no essential part of any exposition of ideas, and are of such slight social value as a step to truth that any benefit that may be derived from them is clearly outweighed by the social interest in order and morality. 'Resort to epithets or personal abuse is not in any proper sense communication of information or opinion safeguarded by the Constitution, and its punishment as a criminal act would raise no question under that instrument.' *Cantwell* v. *Connecticut*, 310 U. S. 296, 309–310." 315 U. S., at 571–572. (Footnotes omitted.)

This case presents an example of gross abuse of the respected privilege in this country of allowing every citizen to speak his mind. Appellant addressed a public school board meeting attended by about 150 people, approximately 40 of whom were children and 25 of whom were women. In the course of his remarks he used the adjective "m----- f------" on four occasions, to describe the teachers, the school board, the town, and his own country.

For using this language under these circumstances, appellant was prosecuted and convicted under a New Jersey statute which provides:

"Any person who utters loud and offensive or profane or indecent language in any public street or other public place, public conveyance, or place to which the public is invited ... is a disorderly person." N. J. Rev. Stat. § 2A:170–29 (1) (1971).

Prior to appellant's prosecution, the Supreme Court of New Jersey had limited the statute's coverage as follows:

"[T]he words must be spoken loudly, in a public place and must be of such a nature as to be likely to incite the hearer to an immediate breach of the peace or to be likely, in the light of the gender and age of the listener and the setting of the utterance, to affect the sensibilities of a hearer. The words must be spoken with the intent to have the above effect or with a reckless disregard of the probability of the above consequences." *State* v. *Profaci*, 56 N. J. 346, 353, 266 A. 2d 579, 583–584 (1970).

The Court today decides to vacate and remand this case for reconsideration in light of *Gooding* v. *Wilson*, 405 U. S. 518 (1972), and *Cohen* v. *California*, 403 U. S. 15 (1971). As it seems to me that neither of these cases is directly relevant, and that considerations not present in those cases are here controlling, I respectfully dissent.

Perhaps appellant's language did not constitute "fighting words" within the meaning of *Chaplinsky*. While most of those attending the school board meeting were undoubtedly outraged and offended, the good taste and restraint of such an audience may have made it unlikely that physical violence would result. Moreover, the offensive words were not directed at a specific individual. But the exception to First Amendment protection recognized in *Chaplinsky* is not limited to words whose mere utterance entails a high probability of an outbreak of physical violence. It also extends to the willful use of scurrilous language calculated to offend the sensibilities of an unwilling audience.

The Court of Appeals for the District of Columbia Circuit has addressed this issue more explicitly. Judge McGowan, writing for the court *en banc* in *Williams* v. *District of Columbia,* 136 U. S. App. D. C. 56, 419 F. 2d 638 (1969), correctly stated:

> "Apart from punishing profane or obscene words which are spoken in circumstances which create a threat of violence, the state may also have a legitimate interest in stopping one person from 'inflict[ing] injury' [*Chaplinsky* v. *New Hampshire,* 315 U. S., at 572] on others by verbally assaulting them with language which is grossly offensive because of its profane or obscene character. The fact that a person may constitutionally indulge his taste for obscenities in private does not mean that he is free to intrude them upon the attentions of others." *Id.,* at 64, 419 F. 2d, at 646.

I agree with this view that a verbal assault on an unwilling audience may be so grossly offensive and emotionally disturbing as to be the proper subject of criminal proscription, whether under a statute denominating it disorderly conduct, or, more accurately, a public nuisance. Judge McGowan further noted in *Williams:*

> "[A] breach of the peace is threatened either because the language creates a substantial risk of provoking violence, or because it is, under 'contemporary community standards,' so grossly offensive to members of the public who actually overhear it as to amount to a nuisance." *Ibid.* (Footnotes omitted.)

The Model Penal Code, proposed by the American Law Institute, also recognizes a distinction between utterances which may threaten physical violence and those which may amount to a public nuisance, recognizing that neither category falls within the protection of the First Amendment. See Model Penal Code §§ 250.2 (1)(a) and (b). (Proposed Official Draft 1962.)

The decision in *Gooding* v. *Wilson, supra,* turned largely on an application of the First Amendment overbreadth doctrine,[1] and the Court's remand order suggests that the overbreadth doctrine should be applied in this case. The consequences and the unusual character of the overbreadth doctrine have been accurately summarized in Note, The First Amendment Overbreadth Doctrine, 83 Harv. L. Rev. 844, 852 (1970):

> "[The overbreadth doctrine] results often in the wholesale invalidation of the legislature's handiwork, creating a judicial-legislative confrontation.
>
> "In the end, this departure from the normal method of judging the constitutionality of statutes must find justification in the favored status of rights to expression and association in the constitutional scheme." (Footnotes omitted.)

Because a "judicial-legislative confrontation" often results from application of the overbreadth doctrine, and because it is a departure from the normal method of judicial review,[2] it should be applied with restraint. In my view, the doctrine is not applicable in this case.

The New Jersey statute was designed to prohibit the public use of language such as that involved in this case, and certainly the State has an interest—perhaps a compelling one—in protecting non-assenting citizens from vulgar and offensive verbal assaults. A statute directed narrowly to this interest does not impinge upon the values of protected free speech. Legitimate First Amendment interests are not furthered by stretching the overbreadth doctrine to cover a case of this kind. In *Cohen* v. *California,* 403 U. S. 15 (1971), which deals with the question of what expressive activity is constitutionally punishable, Mr. Justice Harlan described the purpose of the free speech guarantee as follows:

> "It is designed and intended to remove governmental restraints from the arena of public discussion, putting the decision as to what views shall be voiced largely into the hands of each of us, in the hope that use of such freedom will ultimately produce a more capable citizenry and more perfect polity and in the belief that no other approach would comport with the premise of individual dignity and choice upon which our political system rests. See *Whitney* v. *California,* 274 U. S. 357, 375–377 (1927) (Brandeis, J., concurring)." *Id.,* at 24.

The purpose of the overbreadth doctrine is to excise statutes which have a deterrent effect on the exercise of protected speech.[3] It is difficult to believe that sustaining appellant's conviction under this statute will deter others from the exercise of legitimate First Amendment rights.[4]

The line between such rights and the type of conduct proscribed by the New Jersey statute is difficult to draw. The preservation of the right to free and robust speech is accorded high priority in our society and under the Constitution. Yet, there are other significant values. One of the hallmarks of a civilized society is the level and quality of discourse. We have witnessed in recent years a disquieting deterioration in standards of taste and civility in speech. For the increasing number of persons who derive satisfaction from vocabularies dependent upon filth and obscenities, there are abundant opportunities to gratify their debased tastes. But our free society must be flexible enough to tolerate even such a debasement provided it occurs without subjecting unwilling audiences to the type of verbal nuisance committed in this case. The shock and sense of affront, and sometimes the injury to mind and spirit, can be as great from words as from some physical attacks.

I conclude in this case that appellant's utterances fall within the proscription of the New Jersey statute, and are not protected by the First Amendment. Accordingly, I would dismiss the appeal for want of a substantial federal question.

MR. JUSTICE REHNQUIST, with whom THE CHIEF JUSTICE and MR. JUSTICE BLACKMUN join, dissenting.*

In *Lewis,* the police were engaged in making an arrest of appellant's son on grounds not challenged here. While the police were engaged in the performance of their duty, appellant intervened and ultimately addressed the police officers as "g-- d-- m----- f----- police." At that point she herself was arrested for violation of a city ordinance providing:

"It shall be unlawful and a breach of the peace for any person wantonly to curse or revile or to use obscene or opprobrious language toward or with reference to any member of the city police while in the actual performance of his duty."

In *Rosenfeld*, appellant appeared and spoke at a public school board meeting that was held in an auditorium and was attended by more than 150 men, women, and children of mixed ethnic and racial backgrounds. It was estimated that there were approximately 40 children and 25 women present at the meeting. During his speech, appellant used the adjective "m----- f-----" on four different occasions while concluding his remarks. Testimony varied as to what particular nouns were joined with this adjective, but they were said to include teachers, the community, the school system, the school board, the country, the county, and the town.

Rosenfeld was convicted under a New Jersey statute that provides:

"Any person who utters loud and offensive or profane or indecent language in any public street or other public place, public conveyance, or place to which the public is invited . . . [i]s a disorderly person." N. J. Rev. Stat. § 2A:170–29 (1) (1971).

The New Jersey Supreme Court, prior to the instant case, had placed the following limiting construction on the New Jersey statute:

"[T]he words must be spoken loudly, in a public place and must be of such a nature as to be likely to incite the hearer to an immediate breach of the peace or to be likely, in the light of the gender and age of the listener and the setting of the utterance, to affect the sensibilities of a hearer. The words must be spoken with the intent to have the above effect or with a reckless disregard of the probability of the above consequences." *State* v. *Profaci*, 56 N. J. 346, 353, 266 A. 2d 579, 583–584 (1970).

Appellant in *Brown* spoke to a large group of men and women gathered in the University of Tulsa chapel. During a question and answer period he referred to some policemen as "m----- f----- fascist pig cops" and to a particular Tulsa police officer as that "black m----- f----- pig . . . ." Brown was convicted of violating an Oklahoma statute that prohibited the utterance of "any obscene or lascivious language or word in any public place, or in the presence of females . . . ." Okla. Stat. Ann., Tit. 21, § 906 (1958).

The Court vacates and remands these cases for reconsideration in the light of *Gooding* v. *Wilson*, 405 U. S. 518 (1972), and *Cohen* v. *California*, 403 U. S. 15 (1971) (the latter decided some four months before the opinion of the New Jersey Superior Court, Appellate Division, which upheld Rosenfeld's conviction, and six months before that of the Oklahoma Court of Criminal Appeals in *Brown*).

Insofar as the Court's remand is based on *Cohen*, *supra*, for the reasons stated in MR. JUSTICE BLACKMUN's dissenting opinion in that case, *id.*, at 27, I would not deny to these States the power to punish language of the sort used here by appropriate legislation. Appellant

Lewis' words to the police officers were "fighting words," and those of appellants Rosenfeld and Brown were "lewd and obscene" and "profane" as those terms are used in *Chaplinsky* v. *New Hampshire*, 315 U. S. 568 (1942), the leading case in the field. Delineating the type of language that the States may constitutionally punish, the Court there said:

"There are certain well-defined and narrowly limited classes of speech, the prevention and punishment of which have never been thought to raise any Constitutional problems. These include the lewd and obscene, the profane, the libelous, and the insulting or 'fighting' words—those which by their very utterance inflict injury or tend to incite an immediate breach of the peace. It has been well observed that such utterances are no essential part of any exposition of ideas, and are of such slight social value as a step to truth that any benefit that may be derived from them is clearly outweighed by the social interest in order and morality. 'Resort to epithets or personal abuse is not in any proper sense communication of information or opinion safeguarded by the Constitution, and its punishment as a criminal act would raise no question under that instrument.' *Cantwell* v. *Connecticut*, 310 U. S. 296, 309–310." 315 U. S., at 571–572.

The language used by these appellants therefore clearly falls within the class of punishable utterances described in *Chaplinsky*.

Gooding v. *Wilson*, *supra*, dealt both with the type of speech that the States could constitutionally punish, and the doctrine of First Amendment overbreadth. With respect to the latter, the Court said:

"The constitutional guarantees of freedom of speech forbid the States to punish the use of words or language not within 'narrowly limited classes of speech.' *Chaplinsky* v. *New Hampshire*, 315 U. S. 568, 571 (1942). Even as to such a class, however, because 'the line between speech unconditionally guaranteed and speech which may legitimately be regulated, suppressed, or punished is finely drawn,' *Speiser* v. *Randall*, 357 U. S. 513, 525 (1958), '[i]n every case the power to regulate must be so exercised as not, in attaining a permissible end, unduly to infringe the protected freedom,' *Cantwell* v. *Connecticut*, 310 U. S. 296, 304 (1940). In other words, the statute must be carefully drawn or be authoritatively construed to punish only unprotected speech and not be susceptible of application to protected expression." *Gooding* v. *Wilson*, *supra*, at 521–522.

Unless we are to distort the doctrine of overbreadth into a verbal game of logic-chopping and sentence-parsing reminiscent of common-law pleading, it cannot fairly be said here that either the New Orleans ordinance, or the New Jersey statute as construed by the highest court of that State, could reasonably be thought "unduly to infringe the protected freedom," *Cantwell* v. *Connecticut*, 310 U. S., at 304.

I would dismiss these appeals for lack of a substantial federal question.

No. 70–5323. LEWIS v. CITY OF NEW ORLEANS. Appeal from Sup. Ct. La. Motion for leave to proceed in forma pauperis granted. Judgment vacated and case remanded for reconsideration in light of Gooding v. Wilson, 405 U. S. 518 (1972).

MR. JUSTICE POWELL, concurring in the result.

Under Chaplinsky v. New Hampshire, 315 U. S. 568 (1942), the issue in a case of this kind is whether "fighting words" were used. Here a police officer, while in the performance of his duty, was called "g-- d--- m------ f-----" police.

If these words had been addressed by one citizen to another, face to face and in a hostile manner, I would have no doubt that they would be "fighting words." But the situation may be different where such words are addressed to a police officer trained to exercise a higher degree of restraint than the average citizen. See Model Penal Code § 250.1, Comments 14 (Tent. Draft No. 13, 1961).

I see no genuine overbreadth problem in this case for the reasons stated in my dissenting opinion in Rosenfeld v. New Jersey, ante, p. 903.

I would remand for reconsideration only in light of Chaplinsky.

[For dissenting opinion of MR. CHIEF JUSTICE BURGER, see ante, p. 902.]

[For dissenting opinion of MR. JUSTICE REHNQUIST, see ante, p. 909.]

No. 71–6535. BROWN v. OKLAHOMA. Appeal from Ct. Crim. App. Okla. Motion for leave to proceed in forma pauperis granted. Judgment vacated and case remanded for reconsideration in light of Cohen v. California, 403 U. S. 15 (1971), and Gooding v. Wilson, 405 U. S. 518 (1972). Reported below: 492 P. 2d 1106.

MR. JUSTICE POWELL, concurring in the result.

The statute involved in this case is considerably broader than the statute involved in Rosenfeld v. New Jersey, ante, p. 901, and it has not been given a narrowing construction by the Oklahoma courts. Moreover, the papers filed in this case indicate that the language for which appellant was prosecuted was used in a political meeting to which appellant had been invited to present the Black Panther viewpoint. In these circumstances language of the character charged might well have been anticipated by the audience.

These factors lead me to conclude that this case is significantly different from Rosenfeld v. New Jersey, supra. I therefore concur in the Court's disposition of this case.

[For dissenting opinion of MR. CHIEF JUSTICE BURGER, see ante, p. 902.]

[For dissenting opinion of MR. JUSTICE REHNQUIST, see ante, p. 909.]

JUSTICE BURGER'S OPINION NOTE

*[This opinion applies also to No. 70–5323, Lewis v. City of New Orleans, post, p. 913, and No. 71–6535, Brown v. Oklahoma, post, p. 914.]

JUSTICE POWELL'S OPINION NOTES

[1] Insofar as the Court's decision in Gooding turns on vagueness principles, it seems inapplicable to this case. The essence of the due process vagueness concern is that no man shall be punished for violating a statute which is not "sufficiently explicit to inform those who are subject to it what conduct on their part will render them liable to its penalties . . . ." Connally v. General Construction Co., 269 U. S. 385, 391 (1926). Although the New Jersey statute involved in this case is hardly a model of clarity, it cannot reasonably be said that appellant could have been unaware that the language used under the circumstances was proscribed by the statute. Unless he was a person of infirm mentality, appellant certainly knew that his deliberate use four times of what Mr. Justice Harlan termed in Cohen a "scurrilous epithet," in the presence of a captive audience including women and children, violated the statute.

[2] See, e. g., United States v. Raines, 362 U. S. 17, 20–22 (1960).

[3] See Note, The First Amendment Overbreadth Doctrine, 83 Harv. L. Rev. 844, 853 (1970).

[4] Nor does the continued existence of the New Jersey statute, which must now be construed and applied by the New Jersey courts in light of Gooding, have the effect of deterring others in the exercise of their First Amendment rights. To remand this case with the suggestion that the overbreadth doctrine be applied accomplishes only one result: it creates the potential that appellant will receive an undeserved windfall.

I recognize, of course, that serious definitional and enforcement problems are likely to arise even where the statutes in this area are carefully drawn. Yet the inherent difficulty of the problem is not sufficient reason for legislatures and the courts to abdicate their responsibility to protect nonassenting citizens from verbal conduct which is so grossly offensive as to amount to a nuisance.

JUSTICE REHNQUIST'S OPINION NOTE

*[This opinion applies also to No. 70–5323, Lewis v. City of New Orleans, post, p. 913, and No. 71–6535, Brown v. Oklahoma, post, p. 914.]

EXPULSION OF UNIVERSITY STUDENT FOR DISTRIBUTING ON CAMPUS A NEWSPAPER "CONTAINING FORMS OF INDECENT SPEECH" IS HELD BY THE UNITED STATES SUPREME COURT AS AN IMPERMISSIBLE VIOLATION OF HER FIRST AMENDMENT FREE SPEECH RIGHTS

Papish v. University of Missouri Curators, 410 U.S. 667 (1973)

PER CURIAM.

Petitioner, a graduate student in the University of Missouri School of Journalism, was expelled for distributing on campus a newspaper "containing forms of indecent speech"[1] in violation of a bylaw of the Board of Curators. The newspaper, the Free Press Underground, had been sold on this state university campus for more than four years pursuant to an authorization obtained from the University Business Office. The particular newspaper issue in question was found to be unacceptable for two reasons. First, on the front cover the publishers had reproduced a political cartoon previously printed in another newspaper depicting policemen raping the Statue of Liberty and the Goddess of Justice. The caption under the cartoon read: ". . . With Liberty and Justice for All." Secondly, the issue contained an article entitled "M-----f----- Acquitted," which discussed the trial and acquittal on an assault charge of a New York City youth who was a member of an organization known as "Up Against the Wall, M-----f-----."

Following a hearing, the Student Conduct Committee found that petitioner had violated Paragraph B of Art. V of the General Standards of Student Conduct which requires students "to observe generally accepted standards of conduct" and specifically prohibits "indecent conduct or speech." [2] Her expulsion, after affirmance first by the Chancellor of the University and then by its Board of Curators, was made effective in the middle of the spring semester. Although she was then permitted to remain on campus until the end of the semester, she was not given credit for the one course in which she made a passing grade.[3]

After exhausting her administrative review alternatives within the University, petitioner brought an action for declaratory and injunctive relief pursuant to 42 U. S. C. § 1983 in the United States District Court for the Western District of Missouri. She claimed that her expulsion was improperly premised on activities protected by the First Amendment. The District Court denied relief. 331 F. Supp. 1321, and the Court of Appeals affirmed, one judge dissenting. 464 F. 2d 136. Rehearing *en banc* was denied by an equally divided vote of all the judges in the Eighth Circuit.

The District Court's opinion rests, in part,[4] on the conclusion that the banned issue of the newspaper was obscene. The Court of Appeals found it unnecessary to decide that question. Instead, assuming that the newspaper was not obscene and that its distribution in the community at large would be protected by the First Amendment, the court held that on a university campus "freedom of expression" could properly be "subordinated to other interests such as, for example, the conventions of decency in the use and display of language and pictures." *Id.*, at 145. The court concluded that "[t]he Constitution does not compel the University . . . [to allow] such publications as the one in litigation to be publicly sold or distributed on its open campus." *Ibid.*

This case was decided several days before we handed down *Healy* v. *James*, 408 U. S. 169 (1972), in which, while recognizing a state university's undoubted prerogative to enforce reasonable rules governing student conduct, we reaffirmed that "state colleges and universities are not enclaves immune from the sweep of the First Amendment." *Id.*, at 180. See *Tinker* v. *Des Moines Independent School District*, 393 U. S. 503 (1969). We think *Healy* makes it clear that the mere dissemination of ideas—no matter how offensive to good taste—on a state university campus may not be shut off in the name alone of "conventions of decency." Other recent prece-

dents of this Court make it equally clear that neither the political cartoon nor the headline story involved in this case can be labeled as constitutionally obscene or otherwise unprotected. *E. g., Kois* v. *Wisconsin*, 408 U. S. 229 (1972); *Gooding* v. *Wilson*, 405 U. S. 518 (1972); *Cohen* v. *California*, 403 U. S. 15 (1971).[5] There is language in the opinions below which suggests that the University's action here could be viewed as an exercise of its legitimate authority to enforce reasonable regulations as to the time, place, and manner of speech and its dissemination. While we have repeatedly approved such regulatory authority, e. g., 408 U. S., at 192–193, the facts set forth in the opinions below show clearly that petitioner was dismissed because of the disapproved *content* of the newspaper rather than the time, place, or manner of its distribution.[6]

Since the First Amendment leaves no room for the operation of a dual standard in the academic community with respect to the content of speech, and because the state University's action here cannot be justified as a nondiscriminatory application of reasonable rules governing conduct, the judgments of the courts below must be reversed. Accordingly the petition for a writ of certiorari is granted, the case is remanded to the District Court, and that court is instructed to order the University to restore to petitioner any course credits she earned for the semester in question and, unless she is barred from reinstatement for valid academic reasons, to reinstate her as a student in the graduate program.

Reversed and remanded.

Mr. Chief Justice Burger, dissenting.

I join the dissent of Justice Rehnquist which follows and add a few observations.

The present case is clearly distinguishable from the Court's prior holdings in *Cohen, Gooding,* and *Rosenfeld,* as erroneous as those holdings are.* *Cohen, Gooding,* and *Rosenfeld* dealt with prosecutions under criminal statutes which allowed the imposition of severe penalties. Unlike such traditional First Amendment cases, we deal here with rules which govern conduct on the campus of a university.

In theory, at least, a university is not merely an arena for the discussion of ideas by students and faculty; it is also an institution where individuals learn to express themselves in acceptable, civil terms. We provide that environment to the end that students may learn the self-restraint necessary to the functioning of a civilized society and understand the need for those external restraints to which we must all submit if group existence is to be tolerable.

I find it a curious—even bizarre—extension of *Cohen, Gooding,* and *Rosenfeld* to say that a university is impotent to deal with conduct such as that of the petitioner. Students are, of course, free to criticize the university, its faculty, or the Government in vigorous, or even harsh, terms. But it is not unreasonable or violative of the Constitution to subject to disciplinary action those individuals who distribute publications which are at the same time obscene and infantile. To preclude a university or college from regulating the distribution of such obscene materials does not protect the values inherent in the First Amendment; rather, it demeans those values. The anomaly of the Court's holding today is suggested by its use of the now familiar "code" abbreviation for the petitioner's foul language.

The judgment of the Court of Appeals was eminently correct. It should be affirmed.

MR. JUSTICE REHNQUIST, with whom THE CHIEF JUSTICE and MR. JUSTICE BLACKMUN join, dissenting.

We held in *Healy* v. *James*, 408 U. S. 169, 180 (1972), that "state colleges and universities are not enclaves immune from the sweep of the First Amendment." But that general proposition does not decide the concrete case now before us. *Healy* held that the public university there involved had not afforded adequate notice and hearing of the action it proposed to take with respect to the students involved. Here the Court of Appeals found, and that finding is not questioned in the Court's opinion, that "the issue arises in the context of a student dismissal, after service of written charges and after a full and fair hearing, for violation of a University rule of conduct." 464 F. 2d 136, 138.

Both because I do not believe proper exercise of our jurisdiction warrants summary reversal in a case dependent in part on assessment of the record and not squarely governed by one of our decisions, and because I have serious reservations about the result reached by the Court, I dissent from the summary disposition of this case.

I

Petitioner Papish has for many years been a graduate student at the University of Missouri. Judge Stephenson, writing for the Court of Appeals in this case, summarized her record in these words:

> "Miss Papish's academic record reveals that she was in no rush to complete the requirements for her graduate degree in Journalism. She possesses a 1958 academic degree from the University of Connecticut; she was admitted to graduate school at the University of Missouri in September in 1963; and although she attended school through the fall, winter, and summer semesters, she was, after 6 years of work, making little, if any, significant progress toward the achievement of her stated academic objective. At the time of her dismissal, Miss Papish was enrolled in a one-hour course entitled 'Research Journalism' and in a three-hour course entitled 'Ceramics 4.' In the semester immediately preceding her dismissal, she was enrolled only in 'Ceramics 3.' " 464 F. 2d, at 138 n. 2.

Whatever may have been her lack of ability or motivation in the academic area, petitioner had been active on other fronts. In the words of the Court of Appeals:

> "3. On November 1, 1967, the Faculty Committee on Student Conduct, after notice of charges and a hearing, placed Miss Papish on disciplinary probation for the remainder of her student status at the University. The basis for her probation was her violation of the general standard of student conduct . . . . This action arose out of events which took place on October 14, 1967 at a time when the University was

hosting high school seniors and their parents for the purpose of acquainting them with its educational programs and other aspects of campus life. She specifically was charged, *inter alia*, with openly distributing, on University grounds, without the permission of appropriate University personnel, two non-University publications of the Students for Democratic Society (SDS). It was alleged in the notice of charges, and apparently established at the ensuing hearing, that one of these publications, the *New Left Notes*, contained 'pornographic, indecent and obscene words, "f---," "bull s---," and "sh--s." ' The notice of charges also recites that the other publication, *The CIA at College: Into Twilight and Back*, contained 'a pornographic and indecent picture depicting two rats apparently fornicating on its cover . . . .'
>
> "4. Some two weeks prior to the incident causing her dismissal, Miss Papish was placed on academic probation because of prolonged submarginal academic progress. It was a condition of this probation that she pursue satisfactory work on her thesis, and that such work be evidenced by the completion and presentation of several completed chapters to her thesis advisor by the end of the semester. By letter dated January 31, 1969, Miss Papish was notified that her failure to comply with this special condition within the time specified would result in the termination of her candidacy for a graduate degree." *Id.*, at 138–139, nn. 3, 4.

It was in the light of this background that respondents finally expelled petitioner for the incident described in the Court's opinion. The Court fails to note, however, two findings made by the District Court with respect to the circumstances under which petitioner hawked her newspaper near the memorial tower of the University:

> "The Memorial Tower is the central unit of integrated structures dedicated to the memory of those students who died in the Armed Services in World Wars I and II. Other adjacent units include the Student Union and a Non-Sectarian chapel for prayer and meditation. Through the Memorial Arch pass parents of students, guests of the University, students, including many persons under 18 years of age and high school students." 331 F. Supp. 1321, 1325 n. 4.
>
> "The plaintiff knowingly and intentionally participated in distributing the publication to provoke a confrontation with the authorities by pandering the publication with crude, puerile, vulgar obscenities." *Id.*, at 1325.

II

I continue to adhere to the dissenting views expressed in *Rosenfeld* v. *New Jersey*, 408 U. S. 901 (1972), that the public use of the word "M----f-----" is "lewd and obscene" as those terms were used by the Court in *Chaplinsky* v. *New Hampshire*, 315 U. S. 568 (1942). There the Court said:

> "There are certain well-defined and narrowly limited classes of speech, the prevention and punishment of which have never been thought to raise

any Constitutional problem. These include the lewd and obscene, the profane, the libelous, and the insulting or 'fighting' words—those which by their very utterance inflict injury or tend to incite an immediate breach of the peace. It has been well observed that such utterances are no essential part of any exposition of ideas, and are of such slight social value as a step to truth that any benefit that may be derived from them is clearly outweighed by the social interest in order and morality." *Id.*, at 571–572.

But even were I convinced of the correctness of the Court's disposition of *Rosenfeld*, I would not think it should control the outcome of this case. It simply does not follow under any of our decisions or from the language of the First Amendment itself that because petitioner could not be criminally prosecuted by the Missouri state courts for the conduct in question, she may not therefore be expelled from the University of Missouri for the same conduct. A state university is an establishment for the purpose of educating the State's young people, supported by the tax revenues of the State's citizens. The notion that the officials lawfully charged with the governance of the university have so little control over the environment for which they are responsible that they may not prevent the public distribution of a newspaper on campus which contained the language described in the Court's opinion is quite unacceptable to me, and I would suspect would have been equally unacceptable to the Framers of the First Amendment. This is indeed a case where the observation of a unanimous Court in *Chaplinsky* that "such utterances are no essential part of any exposition of ideas, and are of such slight social value as a step to truth that any benefit that may be derived from them is clearly outweighed by the social interest in order and morality" applies with compelling force.

III

The Court cautions that "disenchantment with Miss Papish's performance, understandable as it may have been, is no justification for denial of constitutional rights." Quite so. But a wooden insistence on equating, for constitutional purposes, the authority of the State to criminally punish with its authority to exercise even a modicum of control over the university which it operates, serves neither the Constitution nor public education well. There is reason to think that the "disenchantment" of which the Court speaks may, after this decision, become widespread among taxpayers and legislators. The system of tax-supported public universities which has grown up in this country is one of its truly great accomplishments; if they are to continue to grow and thrive to serve an expanding population, they must have something more than the grudging support of taxpayers and legislators. But one can scarcely blame the latter if, told by the Court that their only function is to supply tax money for the operation of the university, the "disenchantment" may reach such a point that they doubt the game is worth the candle.

COURT'S OPINION NOTES

[1] This charge was contained in a letter from the University's Dean of Students, which is reprinted in the Court of Appeals' opinion. 464 F. 2d 136, 139 (CA8 1972).

[2] In pertinent part, the By-Law states:
"Students enrolling in the University assume an obligation and are expected by the University to conduct themselves in a manner compatible with the University's functions and missions as an educational institution. For that purpose students are required to observe generally accepted standards of conduct. . . . [I]ndecent conduct or speech . . . are examples of conduct which would contravene this standard. . . ." 464 F. 2d, at 138.

[3] Miss Papish, a 32-year-old graduate student, was admitted to the graduate school of the University in September 1963. Five and one-half years later, when the episode under consideration occurred, she was still pursuing her graduate degree. She was on "academic probation" because of "prolonged submarginal academic progress," and since November 1, 1967, she also had been on disciplinary probation for disseminating SDS literature found at a university hearing to have contained "pornographic, indecent and obscene words." This dissemination had occurred at a time when the University was host to high school seniors and their parents. 464 F. 2d, at 139 nn. 3 and 4. But disenchantment with Miss Papish's performance, understandable as it may have been, is no justification for denial of constitutional rights.

[4] Prefatorily, the District Court held that petitioner, who was a nonresident of Missouri, was powerless to complain of her dismissal because she enjoyed no "federally protected or other right to attend a state university of a state of which she is not a domiciled resident." 331 F. Supp. 1321, 1326. The Court of Appeals, because it affirmed on a different ground, deemed it "unnecessary to comment" upon this rationale. 464 F. 2d, at 141 n. 9. The District Court's reasoning is directly inconsistent with a long line of controlling decisions of this Court. See *Perry* v. *Sindermann*, 408 U. S. 593, 596–598 (1972), and the cases cited therein.

[5] Under the authority of *Gooding* and *Cohen*, we have reversed or vacated and remanded a number of cases involving the same expletive used in this newspaper headline. *Cason* v. *City of Columbus*, 409 U. S. 1053 (1972); *Rosenfeld* v. *New Jersey*, 408 U. S. 901 (1972); *Lewis* v. *City of New Orleans*, 408 U. S. 913 (1972); *Brown* v. *Oklahoma*, 408 U. S. 914 (1972). Cf. *Keefe* v. *Geanakos*, 418 F. 2d 359, 361 and n. 7 (CA1 1969).

[6] It is true, as MR. JUSTICE REHNQUIST's dissent indicates, that the District Court emphasized that the newspaper was distributed near the University's memorial tower and concluded that petitioner was engaged in "pandering." The opinion makes clear, however, that the reference to "pandering" was addressed to the content of the newspaper and to the organization on the front page of the cartoon and the headline, rather than to the manner in which the newspaper was disseminated. 331 F. Supp., at 1325, 1328, 1329, 1330, 1332. As the Court of Appeals opinion states, "[t]he facts are not in dispute." 464 F. 2d, at 138. The charge against petitioner was quite unrelated to either the place or manner of distribution. The Dean's charge stated that the "forms of speech" contained in the newspaper were "improper on the University campus." *Id.*, at 139. Moreover, the majority below quoted without disapproval petitioner's verified affidavit stating that "no disruption of the University's functions occurred in connection with the distribution." *Id.*, at 139–140. Likewise, both the dissenting opinion in the Court of Appeals and the District Court opinion refer to this same uncontroverted fact. *Id.*, at 145; 331 F. Supp., at 1328. Thus, in the absence of any disruption of campus order or interference with the rights of others, the sole issue was whether a state university could proscribe this form of expression.

JUSTICE BURGER'S OPINION NOTE

Cohen v. *California*, 403 U. S. 15, 27 (1971) (BLACKMUN, J., with whom BURGER, C. J., and Black, J., join, dissenting); *Gooding* v. *Wilson*, 405 U. S. 518, 528 (1972) (BURGER, C. J., dissenting), 534 (BLACKMUN, J., dissenting); *Rosenfeld* v. *New Jersey*, 408 U. S. 901, 902 (1972) (BURGER, C. J., dissenting), 903 (POWELL, J., dissenting), 909 (REHNQUIST, J., dissenting).

BROADCASTING AND OBSCENITY

BROADCASTING AND OBSCENITY

"THE FIELD OF BROADCAST REGULATION IS PERHAPS AN AREA AS ILL ADAPTED AS ANY FOR EMPLOYMENT OF THE *ROTH* TEST . . . . IN DETERMINING OBSCENITY IN BROADCASTING, QUESTIONABLE MATERIAL SHOULD NOT ALWAYS HAVE TO BE WEIGHED WITHIN THE CONTEXT OF EVERYTHING ELSE THAT IS PRESENTED WITH IT. BRIEF INJECTIONS OF EROTICA, PORNOGRAPHY, OR SMUT ARE ENOUGH TO SERIOUSLY PREJUDICE, IF NOT DESTROY, THE GENERAL UTILITY OF RADIO AND TELEVISION. 'THE EFFECT ON THE AVERAGE MAN OF NORMAL SENSUAL IMPULSES' TEST HARDLY SERVES TO PROTECT TOTS FROM GETTING AN EYE OR EARFUL OF SMUT WHICH THEIR PARENTS, QUITE LEGITIMATELY, MAY DESIRE THEY BE SHIELDED FROM, NOR DOES IT PROTECT THE ADULT OF TENDER SENSIBILITIES FROM BEING EXPOSED TO THAT WHICH TO HIM OR HER IS TRULY REVOLTING."

Palmetto Broadcasting Co., 33 F.C.C. 265 (1961)

BEFORE THE
FEDERAL COMMUNICATIONS COMMISSION
Washington, D.C.

In re Applications of E. G. Robinson, Jr., tr/as Palmetto Broadcasting Co. (WDKD), Kingstree, S.C. For Renewal of License and For License to Cover CP	Docket No. 13985 File No. BR–2320 Docket No. 13986 File No. BL–7852

APPEARANCES

Harry J. Daly and *Lenore Ehrig*, on behalf of Palmetto Broadcasting Co. (WDKD); and *Robert J. Rawson, P. E. Valicenti*, and *Donald L. Rushford*, on behalf of the Chief, Broadcast Bureau, Federal Communications Commission.

Initial Decision of Hearing Examiner Thomas H. Donahue

(Adopted December 8, 1961)

PRELIMINARY STATEMENT

1. On March 15, 1961, the Commission adopted an order (FCC 61–344) which stated in essence that it had reviewed the above-captioned applications in the light of correspondence with applicant and a field investigation of applicant's station, and was unable to determine that grant of the applications would serve the public interest. The order specifically pointed out that in the Commission's possession was information to the effect that one Charlie Walker had broadcast over applicant's station material that was allegedly coarse, vulgar, suggestive, and susceptible of indecent double meaning. Hearing was directed to be held at the locale of applicant's station. Five issues were designated to be heard. By memorandum opinion and order released May 4, 1961 (FCC 61–588), the Commission amended one of the issues and designated another. The issues as finally designated read:

> (1) To determine whether in its written or oral statements to the Commission with respect to the above matters, the licensee misrepresented facts to the Commission and/or was lacking in candor.
> (2) To determine whether the licensee maintained adequate control or supervision of programing material broadcast over his station during the period of his most recent license renewal.

> (3) To determine whether the licensee permitted program material to be broadcast over station WDKD on the Charlie Walker show, particularly during the period between January 1, 1960, and April 30, 1960, which program material was coarse, vulgar, suggestive, and susceptible of indecent, double meaning.
> (4) To determine the manner in which the programing broadcast by the licensee during the period of his most recent license renewal has met the needs of the areas and populations served by the station.
> (5) To determine whether, in light of the evidence adduced with respect to the foregoing issues, the licensee possesses the requisite qualifications to be a licensee of the Commission.
> (6) To determine whether, in light of the evidence adduced with respect to the foregoing issues, a grant of the above-captioned applications would serve the public interest, convenience, or necessity.

Hearing was held in Kingstree on May 31, June 1, 2, and 5, 1961. Eighteen witnesses, including Robinson, took the stand on behalf of the applicant. Ten witnesses testified on behalf of counsel for the Commission's Broadcast Bureau.

Did licensee misrepresent facts or lack candor in representing facts to the Commission

2. On May 11, 1960, the Commission sent a letter to the licensee, E. G. Robinson. In that letter reference was made to programs broadcast by Charlie Walker over WDKD, and the letter stated that in the Commission's possession were tape recordings of some of Walker's programs that were allegedly vulgar, suggestive, and susceptible of indecent double meaning. Pointing out that it was the practice of the Commission to associate complaints with station files and afford stations opportunity to submit comment, the applicant was directed to file a statement within 15 days. A copy of this letter was sent to the licensee's Washington counsel. (WDKD exhibit 3.)

3. On May 20, 1960, licensee's counsel wrote to the Commission. In that letter, counsel stated: WDKD had no knowledge of having broadcast vulgar or suggestive programs; counsel had requested the Commission's staff to be allowed to listen to tapes in the possession of the Commission but the request had been denied; counsel had been supplied with a tape of a typical Charlie Walker broadcast, but no instance of vulgarity or suggestiveness had been noted. Formal request was made that counsel be permitted to hear the tapes in the possession of the Commission and that full information concerning times and dates of the taped broadcasts, as well as the identity of the person making the charge, be provided. When such information was furnished, the letter continued, effort would be made to investigate the matter. In the meantime, concluded counsel's letter, Robinson, the licensee, had conferred with Walker who had denied knowledge of broadcasting anything vulgar or suggestive, but had nevertheless been admonished to be extremely circumspect in his broadcasts (WDKD exhibit 4).

4. On June 8, 1960, his counsel wrote Robinson. Tapes of the Charlie Walker programs in possession of the Commission had been heard. Eight excerpts from the tapes were set forth. The letter concluded with the following paragraph:

> As you can see, these are indeed suggestive and in some respects, vulgar. With the temper of the Commission being as it presently is, with Congress looking into the programing of the industry as a whole, and with the South Carolina licenses coming up for renewal in December, I believe it is necessary for you to take direct affirmative action to stop all broadcasts of this type. Further, it is my suggestion that the services of Mr. Walker be dispensed with and that you submit to the Commission, under oath, a statement indicating the action you have taken and attach thereto a statement of policy, which you should prepare and circulate among all of your employees who work on the air. This statement should clearly spell out immediate dismissal should anything off-color be detected in any broadcast. Please supply us with copies of your proposed response to the Commission so that we may check it over and offer any suggestions before its filing (WDKD exhibit 5).

5. On June 10, 1960, Robinson wrote the Commission enclosing three affidavits. In that letter Robinson stated that he had just been informed in partial detail of the contents of the taped Charlie Walker programs. In significant part, the letter continued:

> * * * These statements made by my employee, Charlie Walker, were not known to me, and I cannot help but agree that they are suggestive and, in some cases, of a vulgar nature. As a result of this information and in line with my avowed policy of maintaining a clean and decent radio station, I have unconditionally released Charlie Walker from my employ as of the date of this letter.

Repeating that he was unaware of the nature of the broadcasts, Robinson urged that the only accusation that could be leveled against him was that perhaps he "should have followed these matters more closely and should have known exactly what was going on." The letter concluded with a statement that immediately upon learning of the nature of the broadcasts, Walker had been discharged and that instructions had been issued and policy had been established insuring against such broadcasts being carried over WDKD in the future. Attached were affidavits formalizing the assertations made in the letter (WDKD exhibits 6, 7, 8, and 9).

Did applicant maintain adequate control and supervision over program material during the period of his most recent license renewal [1]

6. In this paragraph and the next six, Robinson's testimony on direct examination which appears to have bearing on the subject headnoted above is digested. He owns a small farm and a liquor store, besides his interest in the radio station.[2] The farm is operated on shares. The store is operated by a manager. Such work as he does at the farm is done from 5 to 8 a.m. From 80 to 90 percent of his time is spent on station affairs (Tr. 119–120).

7. For about a year following November 11, 1957, he was either hospitalized as a result of, or confined to his home recuperating from an automobile accident. During this period, his then assistant manager, Charles Green, looked after the radio station with some assistance from Mrs. Robinson on "inside" and "everyday" operations. Green had authority over station policy, but no major policy decisions that he could recall were made by Green (Tr. 121–124, WDKD exhibit 1).

8. The needs of WDKD's service area are identified by analyzing mail and contacting individuals and groups throughout the area. He is a member of a number of civic organizations (Tr. 127–128, 186).

9. Charlie Walker was with the station for 8 years as an announcer. Walker was on the air 4 hours a day handling the following programs: "Rise and Shine," "Grits and Gravy," "Mountain Jamboree," and "Sundown Hoedown." Walker's programs were very well received. A tremendous amount of mail was received by Walker. Sometimes a post office bag was required to carry it. He [Robinson] did not read Walker's mail (Tr. 136–138).

10. Over a period of years he talked to Walker some 8 or 10 times about "these different names that he called these different towns, what he said about me or some advertiser in a joking way," and about poking fun at his wife. In 1959 he called Walker in behind closed doors "and went over with him this and told him that I was going to have to do something about it, it just couldn't continue, and from what I knew about it, he was going to have to go." Walker asked for another chance and promised to do better. With the public behind Walker the way they were and in his position of trying to serve the public, he "went along with this thing for 3 or 4 months." He called Walker in again on May 11 when he had a notice from the Commission. He handed Walker the letter and said, "Charlie, this is it. The Commission has notified me of complaints or proof of your programs. This is it." Walker remonstrated, wanting to know the particulars of what he had done. He told Walker that he thought he could very easily find out and he called Washington counsel. When he received the Commission's letter on June 10, he called Walker in and asked him "what about it." Walker responded, "Mr. Robinson, I don't remember saying those things; however, I imagine I did, if they've got it on tape." He asked Walker for his key and discharged him on the spot. He then called a staff meeting, went over with his employees what had happened and instructed them "to see that this didn't happen in the future, nothing pertaining to this sort of stuff." Following this, he typed up a notice, circulated it and put a copy on the bulletin board, and paid a visit to his local attorney (Tr. 138–139, 142, 146–148).

11. He had never received written or oral complaints concerning the Charlie Walker program. Rev. Donald Bailey of the Presbyterian church had asked him if he would change the type of music that was being played prior to the morning devotions program and he had agreed to make the change. Prior to his accident he picked up the mail in the mornings; since then his traffic manager picks up the mail and he [Walker] routes it. He is sure that if a written complaint had been received by the station about the Walker program he would have seen it. Mrs. Robinson did tell him of one occasion when Reverend Drennan, the Methodist minister, had "said something to her about Charlie Walker." Mrs. Robinson's reply had, of course, been that not everyone likes hillbilly music and that the minister should listen to the station at other times (Tr. 155–158).

12. Staff meetings at the station are scheduled for every 2 weeks. All aspects of station operations are discussed at the meetings. Suggestions are made by Robinson to his employees and by his employees to Robinson. When applications are made for employment at WDKD, applicants are carefully screened and if employed are provided with the rules of the Commission covering their duties. He personally has direct supervision over all departments of the station. To insure against repetition of "Walkerisms," he has held meetings, posted notices on the bulletin board, circulated rules and regulations with the understanding that if anything of the type happens again, the employee responsible will be released without notice. He has installed speakers in most of the offices at the station and he tries to monitor a portion of each program throughout the day (Tr. 159, 164, 166–167).

13. Charlie Walker did a great deal of public service work. Walker helped different people obtain money for operations, for a little boy's eyeglasses, for a burned-out family.[3] Walker obtained aid for those who needed food and clothing and people with braces. Walker was assistant county chairman of a Cancer Fund Drive and raised a record amount of money. On his own time Walker would go to merchants and solicit contributions of food and clothing for the needy. On his radio programs Walker very effectively carried on a campaign for March of Dimes contributions. WDKD at different times puts on contests to obtain audience reaction to programs. A considerable mail response is received. Charlie Walker's good works were much praised not only in contest mail but to him [Robinson] personally. In talking to people throughout the service area, he found no objection to

Walker's programs. Such matters as the references Walker made to the various towns were included in these discussions, but he found no objection to this practice of Walker's and did nothing about it (Tr. 186–188, 208–211).

14. In this and the next six paragraphs Robinson's testimony on cross-examination is digested. He did have knowledge of the names Walker called the towns. Prior to filing his response to the Commission's letter of inquiry, the only knowledge he had of the unfavorable nature of Walker's broadcasts was the names Walker called the towns, what he said about him [Robinson] and what he said about different advertisers. Although he had no written policy against programs in bad taste, the subject was brought up every time a staff meeting was held and such meetings had been held, since 1956, regularly every 2 weeks and sometimes once a week. In an application filed with the Commission in May 1954 the following statement was made, "It has been the policy of this station and it will remain the policy of this station in its overall programing to offer programs that are in good taste and serve the educational, religious, and cultural background of people in and around Kingstree, South Carolina." That statement had been prepared by him on behalf of himself and his then partner, Marion Few. He did have occasion to warn and admonish Walker prior to May 1960. In 1959 as he had previously stated, he cautioned Walker several times about "those things." By "those things" he meant "Greeleyville; and Ann's Drawers for Andrews, Lake City—'City by the Lake' and all those sort of things." When asked what "those sort of things" meant, he continued, "Such as he called me 'money bags' and—I remember he said Mr. John Flagler was the only man he knew could stand up and milk a cow. * * * " He did not think the latter remark "too good" and called it to Walker's attention. Walker was employed in 1950. In 1952 Walker went into military service. Walker returned to the station in 1954. He could remember nothing prior to Walker's going into service. After Walker came out of service, particularly in 1956, "he certainly wasn't too bad about these things." Just now and then he would mention them. Walker actually got worse about them in 1959. That is when he noticed it. By "worse" he meant in calling towns by different names "and that sort of stuff" and by calling them by those names more frequently. Walker did not use any suggestive language. Walker did not use any language susceptible of indecent double meaning, that he heard. No one told him of any indecent thing Walker said. They always told about jokes Walker told and the jokes Walker told about him. They would not tell him the bad things Walker said. None of the jokes that were repeated to him had indecent double meaning. Walker's jokes were repeated to him hundreds of times. Beginning in 1959, he tried to monitor a portion of all of Walker's programs. Some of Walker's programs he monitored when he was in the hospital and at home recuperating. Other than the names of towns and that sort of thing, he never heard Walker broadcast anything objectionable. There is a speaker in the office next to his which he can hear very well. All of his employees have speakers in their offices. None of his employees ever told him that they had received complaints about Walker's programs being indecent. No advertiser ever told him that he wanted his advertising taken off the Walker program because it was indecent. As far as any minister telling him that he thought the Walker programs were coarse and suggestive, it had been brought to his attention by his wife, D. L. Taylor, and L. L. Law that Reverend Drennan had visited him at the hospital and said something about the Charlie Walker programs. He did not remember what Reverend Drennan had said and he did not remember what the people who reported the Drennan visit to him had told him Reverend Drennan had said. ("Well, sir, my condition, I'm sorry I didn't remember it.") No other minister, that he could remember, ever talked to him about the Walker programs in terms of their being indecent or susceptible of indecent double meaning. He never heard anyone comment on the indecency of the Walker programs. The names Walker called the towns were "Greasy Thrill" for Greeleyville and "Bloomersville" for Bloomville (Tr. 215, 220–233).

15. Besides the farm he had previously mentioned, he has another little farm of 52 acres that he does not cultivate. The market value of the two farms is $25,000 (Tr. 234, 236).

16. He goes to the station at 8 in the morning and stays until 12:30 p.m. He goes home for lunch and returns at 2 or 2:30 p.m. and stays there the rest of the day except when he goes into the field to service some 8 or 10 advertising accounts which he personally handles. WDKD is a daytime-only station. When he is away from the station and in his car, he makes it a practice to listen to the station although he does not keep the radio on all the time. From 1954 until he entered the hospital (in November 1957), he spent about 50 percent of his time at the station, the remainder he spent in the field selling advertising. He averaged about 6 hours a day at the station during that period (Tr. 240–242).

17. He has acted as station manager since 1953 or 1954. Prior to that time he and Few had hired a manager. This arrangement did not work out. Except for assistant managers from time to time, no one at the station (besides himself), exercises supervisory authority over programing. His first assistant manager was Charles Green who came in 1957. When Green left in 1960, Arnold Graham was made assistant manager. He has had program directors at the station. Program directors have supervision only over announcers and then not with respect to programing but with respect to quality of broadcast, being sure the announcer gives his best at all times, insuring that the announcer is checking his logs, pulling his "shows" beforehand, and filing records after completion of program. He could not remember whether Godwin had been a program director but Ashby Ward had held that position. At that time there were three announcers including Ward. Ward exercised supervision to the extent

that he helped arrange the announcers' schedules. Employees were subject to his [Robinson's] control and supervision. Mrs. Robinson is bookkeeper at the station and bears the title of "operations manager." She works with the program director, the traffic department, the continuity writer, and assists them in correcting things that might come up and things to do other than policy—"that comes to me." Mrs. Robinson's authority on programing was soley "with the program director." Mrs. Robinson and the program director would discuss different programs and then come to him. As far as instructions were concerned, she worked through the program director. No one looked to Mrs. Robinson as running the station when he was absent. Personnel would go to her with problems and "she would translate those things to me." Mrs. Robinson never brought him complaints to the effect that Charlie Walker's programs were susceptible of indecent double meaning (Tr. 243–249).

18. The second day of cross-examination continued in the following vein. In regard to his testimony that he had had discussions with Walker concerning his use of various nicknames for communities, he had learned of this practice of Walker's largely through listening to Walker over the air. The evening before his appearance that day he had jotted down everything that he could remember having heard Walker say. There were a few things that he had not previously mentioned. Walker called Olanta, S.C., "Chocolate Cake Cow Pasture"; Georgetown, "Stinkumville"; St. Stephens, "St. Step-Ins"; Lake City, "smooch me quick crossroads"; Monks Corners, "Monkey's Corners." On three separate occasions he called Walker's attention to using the phrase, "let it all hang out." He remembered hearing Walker on the air say something, he didn't catch it all, about carrying his girl to a cow pasture to relax and end up saying, "And that's right." He went to Walker immediately. Walker had no explanation. The only other terms not previously mentioned, that he could remember Walker using, was reference to himself [Walker] as "Banana Nose." When he heard Walker make such allusions he would go to him and talk to him. These discussions continued over a period of time. Walker would promise he would stop using such expressions. He thought he could recall that, as he had previously testified, he had to go back to Walker on these matters. This did not happen too often, once or twice. Walker did not use such expressions continuously; once or twice or perhaps three times, after he had talked to him. He had talked to Walker about his language over the air at least 10 times between 1954 and 1959. He could have had more or fewer discussions with Walker on the subject during that period. To his knowledge Walker used the phrase "let it all hang out," three times. He had never heard Walker use the phrase, "This is your Uncle Charlie letting it all hang out and drag in the sand." If he had heard Walker use that phrase, he thought he would have remembered it. No one, that he could recall, had ever complained to him about that language. He did not hear Walker tell the privy story. When he had confronted Walker with the digest of the privy story, Walker had said that he did not remember telling the story but wouldn't deny that he had. Walker did say that if it was on tape, he [Walker] had used the phrase. Walker's admission also applied to the Willie Tart story. He had not heard Walker broadcast the "Ain't you going to kiss me" item. No one had told him that they had heard it. People did not criticize Walker's programs to him. He could not say that he had had reports on the Willie Tart story. He could not recall that he had received such reports (Tr. 311–320, 322–327).

19. He could not recall Charlie Walker having ever been fired prior to 1960. Marion Few, his former partner, never discussed with him remarks made by Walker and did not state that they were suggestive and susceptible of indecent double meaning. Few never complained that Walker's programs were vulgar and coarse (Tr. 331–332).

20. The station's staff is composed of a general manager [Robinson], an assistant manager and commercial manager, a part-time salesman, a program director and announcer, an announcer, a chief engineer and announcer, a continuity writer, a traffic director, and a bookkeeper [Mrs. Robinson] (Tr. 342).

21. Not all of Robinson's testimony noted above squares with the testimony of other witnesses. In the following 14 paragraphs, testimony on the subject here under scrutiny at odds with Robinson's is set forth.

22. Lloyd Ashby Ward, who worked at WDKD as an announcer from September 1958 to June 1960, testified that during his tenure Robinson spent 3 to 4 hours a day at the station. Carroll Godwin, who was an announcer at WDKD from June 1952 to October 1956, estimated that Robinson spent about 3 hours a day at the station (Tr. 523, 677).

23. S. Charles Green, who was employed at the station as salesman from June 1950 to October 1953 and from January of 1957 until February 1960, testified that when he was hired the second time, on the basis of his conversations with Robinson, he thought he was being hired as assistant manager, but when he went to work at the station no announcement was made to that effect and other station employees were never notified that he held that position. Moreover, Green was employed 5 days a week from 8 in the morning until 5 in the evening in the field selling advertising. Further, Robinson never told Green that he had authority at the station during his absence or that he had authority over programing. Aside from some correspondence and the handling of a minor personnel matter, Robinson had never given Green instructions on the conduct of station affairs outside the field of sales.[4] Ward testified that when he was at the station he had no knowledge that Green was assistant manager (Tr. 638, 639–640, 671).

24. Ward testified that only three or four staff meetings were held while he was at the station. Green estimated that only five or six staff meetings were held during his second period of employment there (Tr. 523, 639).

25. Ward was employed at WDKD through June 18, 1960. He testified that no notice was posted on the bulletin board while he was there which dealt with the broadcasting of indecent material or programs not in good taste[5] (Tr. 525).

26. Ward, who it will be recalled was identified by Robinson as program director, testified that Mrs. Robinson did exercise supervisory authority over programing, did clear matters involving program content, and that he had no real authority to determine the scheduling of programs but that Mrs. Robinson almost always went along with his suggestions on such matters. While he was employed at WDKD, he was under the impression that Mrs. Robinson was second in command. Godwin also testified that the employees accepted Mrs. Robinson's authority the same as they did Mr. Robinson's (Tr. 530, 531, 542, 678).

27. In connection with Robinson's testimony concerning his knowledge of the character of Walker's broadcasts and the dearth of complaints he had received concerning those broadcasts, there is a good deal of evidence that speaks in another vein.

28. Marion L. Few testified that he was a partner and half owner with Robinson in WDKD from the time the station went on the air in 1949 until 1955 or early 1956. Walker was hired when the station went on the air and except for a period when he was in the Army, Walker was with the station during Few's entire association with the station. Walker's programs often contained suggestive and vulgar material. He often received complaints concerning the Walker programs. Nearly every time he received such a complaint, he passed it on to Robinson. Nothing was ever done in the way of improvement of the Walker programs. Although, for the most part, he had been an inactive partner in the day-to-day operation of the station, his concern over the Walker broadcasts led him, during the last 8 months of his association with the station, to increase the time he spent at the station. In 1955 or 1956 he fired Walker when he heard him broadcast the following story:

> Well, it seems that this couple had gotten married. After about three days the old boy got the first look at her feet, and he asked her why she had such big cracks between her toes. She said, "Well, you know, I got those big cracks between my big toes from walking in that Georgia mud barefooted." He said, "Are you sure that you didn't spend your time sitting in that Georgia mud?"

Walker, however, did not stay discharged. He was back at work the next day. Some 8 months later, he [Few] severed relations with Robinson and the station. The reason for this step was that Robinson was determined that Walker should be retained at the station and he [Few] was determined that he should go (Tr. 716–725, 729).

29. Bernard Smith Drennan testified that he was a minister in the South Carolina Conference of the Methodist Church and has lived in Kingstree 3½ years. He had heard Walker broadcast nicknames for the different towns and such jokes as those contained in FCC exhibit 2. (See par. 38.) Walker was a likable fellow; he did a lot of good and had a big following. He was very effective in raising money for charitable purposes. Walker got his following by the good that he did and then would inject into his programs things that were in bad taste, that people could and did object to. His children did not listen to the Charlie Walker program because they had heard his objections and respected his judgment. He had on separate occasions discussed the Charlie Walker program with both Mr. and Mrs. Robinson. Sometime the latter part of 1957 he had met Mrs. Robinson at the home of a mutual friend. He had asked her if there wasn't something that could be done about the Walker program, that he heard many complaints concerning the suggestiveness of it, and wondered how Walker got by with it and why the FCC did not do something about it. He was informed by Mrs. Robinson that Walker received more mail at the station than anyone, that his program had been monitored and the only objection raised to it had been one reference to slop jars. In early 1958 when Robinson was in the hospital recuperating from an automobile accident, he called on him frequently. Toward the end of Robinson's recuperation he and Robinson were discussing devotional programs and he asked Robinson if it were not possible to do something about the Charlie Walker show, that many people complained and did not listen to the station because of the suggestive nature of the Walker programs. He told Robinson he thought the programs were giving the community a bad name. Robinson replied that the program did get pretty rough at times, that he had not had much opportunity to listen, and that he intended to talk to Walker and do something about it. After this discussion he noticed no improvement in the Walker program. The discussion took place 2 or 3 weeks before Robinson left the hospital. The Walker program was discussed at ministerial association meetings, but opinion there was to the effect that there was nothing much the association could do about it. One objection to the Walker program he raised before the association concerned the fact that after Saturday morning devotions on WDKD, Walker would come on with a smart-aleck statement or refer to things irrelevant to devotions. No formal complaint, however, was lodged (Tr. 546–562).

30. James Kirk Lawton testified that he is pastor of the Calvary Baptist Church, Florence, S. C., and was pastor at the First Baptist Church, Kingstree, from September 1953 to October 1957. The material contained in FCC exhibit 2 was typical of the type of material he had heard on the Walker program. He discussed the Walker program with Robinson on two separate occasions. Once when Robinson's daughter was ill, he called at Robinson's home. During the course of his conversation with Robinson, talk turned to spiritual matters and he suggested that one thing that would help a great deal would be improvement in the Charlie Walker situation, pointing out that the situation was not satisfactory, not proper, that Walker's material was suggestive and indecent. Robinson made no definite commitment. Another time he called upon Robinson at the latter's office. During a discussion of matters of general interest in the community,

he again deplored the situation with respect to the Walker program and indicated hope of improvement. Following these conversations he noticed no improvement in the Walker program. Members of his congregation frequently complained to him of the vulgar, suggestive, and sexy nature of the Walker programs. The Walker programs had been discussed at ministerial meetings. It was the consensus of opinion that the organization did not want to hurt Robinson and that individually the members would appeal to Robinson and see what he could do about it. Members of his present congregation at Florence had commented to him about the Walker program the subject of these comments was the suggestive talk on the Walker program (Tr. 579–584, 586–588).

31. Green testified that when he was selling advertising for WDKD, an advertiser informed him that he did not care to use the station any longer because of the Charlie Walker programs (Tr. 642).

32. Godwin testified that when Walker was drafted he took over from Walker the handling of a program entitled, "Hymn Time." When Walker returned from the service he was again scheduled to announce the "Hymn Time" program. Godwin received some 50 letters objecting to Walker's return to the program. These objections were couched in terms of the filthy language used by Walker. Walker did handle the program for 2 or 3 days after he returned from the Army. Godwin then returned to the program. Walker frequently broadcast material that was suggestive or susceptible of indecent double meaning. An example of the type of material he had heard Walker broadcast was the following:

> * * * he and his girl friend were not on a date the night before, and they ran out of gas far out into the country, away from town. So they proceeded to walk toward town, and they walked until they were completely exhausted, then they started crawling, and crawled until finally his girl collapsed, and he crawled on.

People frequently commented to him about the content of Walker's programs. On a few occasions he had accompanied Robinson on sales trips. There was a radio in Robinson's car. On those trips he had heard, over the car radio, Walker make such comments as "let it all hang out" (Tr. 674–675, 681–686, 689, 694, 696).

33. A. E. Creamer, general manager of Sears, Roebuck, Florence, S.C., testified that he directed cancellation of Sears' advertising on the Charlie Walker program over WDKD following reports by salesmen and friends that the program was off-color, had a certain amount of vulgarity attached to it, and was not in keeping with Sears' standards of advertising (Tr. 737, 739–740).

34. T. Doug Youngblood testified that he was general manager of WFIG, Sumter, S.C., and executive secretary of the South Carolina Broadcasters Association, and had heard material broadcast by Charlie Walker over WDKD that was susceptible of indecent double meaning or was coarse and vulgar. The Walker program was discussed among members of the association in the context that it was not conducive to good broadcasting and at times downright indecent. He would not permit such programs as the Walker programs to be broadcast over his station. Programing that goes outside conventional concepts of decency does have a certain appeal. It is easy to sell smut. Pressure on competition is generated when other competitors lower standards of quality (Tr. 658, 661–662, 664–668).

35. Edward L. B. Osborne testified that he was president and general manager of WBCU, Union, S.C.; vice president of WAGS, Bishopville, S.C.; past president of the South Carolina Broadcasters Association; and had heard the Charlie Walker program on one occasion. En route to a convention he heard a program over WDKD, the contents of which he related to broadcasters at the convention and was informed, "Well, you heard the Charlie Walker show." The Walker programs have been a subject of discussion at biannual broadcasters conventions. Most broadcasters were concerned that the Walker program might hurt broadcasting. The concensus of opinion was that the program was degrading to radio in general (Tr. 749–753).

Did licensee, particularly during the period January 1–April 30, 1960, permit material to be broadcast that was coarse, vulgar, suggestive, and susceptible of indecent double meaning?

36. James Roper, operations manager and chief engineer of station WJOT, Lake City, S.C., testified that between October 27, 1959, and April 25, 1960, he taped a total of 12 or 14 broadcasts over WDKD featuring Charlie Walker. Using an Eicor tape recorder and a Hallicrafters model S–85 communications receiver, the latter was tuned to WDKD and when by listening he ascertained that it was WDKD that was in fact being received and Charlie Walker broadcasting, the recorder was attached directly to the receiver and tapes were run. All tapes were monitored after they were made. Since the tapes were not cut as quality productions but for the purpose of calling to the attention of the Commission what was going on at WDKD, their quality was not high. Of the 12 or 14 broadcasts taped, only 6 were retained; the rest were discarded. The tapes retained were all intelligible to Roper. Stored in Roper's office under lock and key for some time, they were eventually turned over to the president of WJOT. The record does not disclose the story of their custody while in the latter's possession, but it may be safely assumed that during that period they were made available to the Commission and its staff. Returned to Roper and again kept under lock and key by him, they were again taken out and monitored by Roper in the presence of a Commission investigator and the two FCC counsel who tried this hearing. The tapes then monitored were the same as those Roper had made of the WDKD broadcasts. On this latter occasion the tapes were turned over to the FCC staff. Shortly before the hearing convened, Roper and the Commission's representatives again listened to the tapes, this time to identify the tapes with the days they were broadcast. This Roper did by listening for the announcer [Walker] to make reference to a particular day or event; e.g., reference to the Monday edition of the "Jamboree" program, reference to "Founder's Day Sale," and reference to the opening of "Black River Speedway." With such identification, the sequence of program material and spot announcements as disclosed by the tapes was compared with the station's program log for the day thus selected. As an additional check, other program logs were reviewed to insure against the possibility of duplication. At this same session a transcript of the broadcasts was checked against the tapes. Roper identified FCC exhibit 2 as an accurate transcript of the contents of the tapes which he had made of the Charlie Walker broadcasts (Tr. 595–623).

37. At the outset of Roper's testimony, counsel for the applicant conceded his qualifications to take tape recordings on the theory that "Anybody can take a tape recording." Thereafter, counsel for the applicant, when FCC exhibit 2 was offered into evidence, initiated a line of interrogation apparently designed to test the bona fides of the tapes from which FCC exhibit 2 was derived. At that point the examiner reminded applicant's counsel that the tapes had been made available to applicant's counsel prior to hearing, that already in evidence was Robinson's testimony that he had confronted Walker with excerpts from the tapes and had been told in effect that if the Commission had the tapes, he [Walker] had broadcast the material, that there was then in evidence testimony of witnesses corroborating various portions of the taped material, that the tapes were readily available for audition in the hearing room, and that there were a number of people then in the hearing room who knew Walker and were familiar with his program. Considering the state of the record, applicant's counsel was asked if he believed it profitable to further pursue the subject of the authenticity of the tapes. After brief interrogation of the witness concerning voice modulation and "tape level," counsel for the applicant stated he had no objection to the receipt into evidence of the subject exhibit (Tr. 623–631).

38. Indented below is a verbatim transcript of material broadcast by Charlie Walker on October 15 and 27, 1959, January 14 and 20, 1960, and on April 25, 1960.[6] All of the indented material comes from FCC exhibit 2. Selection was made from that exhibit to avoid redundancy and to eliminate matters not actually contained in quotes. In the latter connection, however, it should be noted that the Commission's exhibit makes clear that Walker on numerous occasions not included in the material below made reference to Greeleyville as "Greasy Thrill," Andrews as "Ann's Drawers," Bloomville as "Bloomersville," and St. Stephens as "St. Step-ins."

> Next Saturday it is we gonna have the big grand opening over at the new W. P. Marshall store in Greasy Thrill and we gonna come over there and let it all hang out. Course if we let it all hang out in Greeleyville, there ain't gonna be enough room over there for nothin' else, is there?
>
> He says: "I believe that old dog of mine is a Baptist." I asked him why he thought his old dog was a Baptist and he says, "you know, Uncle Charlie, it is that he's done baptized every hub cap around Ann's drawers." "You say it is all that all the hub caps in Spring Gully is going to Heaven?"
>
> If you're goin' to see a gal over in Poston you got to go see her after it gets dark; I mean you can't go over there in the daylight. And the reason you can't go over there in the daylight is because it is that them gals around Poston are so wild, you know. They're so wild that you have to sneak up on 'em in the dark * * * And the only thing about sneaking up on 'em in the dark it is that you is liable to make a mistake: well I mean like I did one night, I thought I was sneaking up on one of dem gals from Poston and I was sneaking up on a cow. And do you know it is that I didn't even know I had a cow until it is that it swatted a fly off the end of my nose with its tail. When it swatted a fly off the end of my nose with its tail. When it swatted a fly off the end of my nose with its tail I began to get suspicious. I knew them gals in Poston couldn't do that.
>
> He was getting hard up. You ever been hard up? They tell, Uncle Charlie it is we hard up for a little bit of music right now but we ain't gonna get none. I say you take a flying bite out of my shirt tail, hear?[7]
>
> Did you hear the one about the boy and the gal in the cow pasture? He was really lovin' that gal good. Boy he was lovin' that gal good. And it is that he was getting plenty whole-hearted cooperation. He was. He was lovin' that old gal good. She was givin' him something besides lovin'. She was giving him whole-hearted cooperation. She was. And he decided that this is the gal for me; says "this is the gal I want to marry, right here." So he came right out and asked her. He says: "Darling," he says, "will you marry me?" And she says, "well I don't know." She says, "tell me do you want a home?" And he says, "honey," he says, "I'm a regular home body." And she says, "And, what about children?" And he says, "Oh," he says, "Honey, I just love children." And she says, "well," she says, "in that case," she says, "I'll marry you if you like children. We'll be in business in about six months!" [Laughter.] They gettin' a head start!
>
> It is you give me barbecued iced water and a green-eyed gal and I can go hard.
>
> Betsy says it is that not only will she flirt with dynamite, but it is that if it's single she'll propose to it. Fool, you couldn't marry no dynamite. Betsy says it is that she don't mind marrying a stick of dynamite if he's got a long fuse. A long fuse? Betsy, will you go make me some French Market coffee and cut out your trash?
>
> We's over in St. Step-ins yesterday. Had a glorious time.
>
> I get so tired of people callin' me a jackass. Them people over in St. Stephens in Russelville. They wouldn't say, "Hello, Uncle Charlie," they's say, "hello, jackass" * * * It is that so many people done called me a jackass that, I'll tell you the truth, it is that if I ain't got a saddle in the middle of my back I feel naked. All right, for everybody whose got ants in their pants, I'll tell you what you do. You make your self a big pot of French Market Coffee, and then, pour the French Market Coffee in the seat of your britches. If you got any ants in your pants that'll get rid of them. Of course, it didn't work with my red bugs, nothing ever does. I tried that to get rid of my red bugs. And my darn bugs were making mud pies out of that French Market Coffee, and throwing them at my black heads.
>
> I don't wanta save everything I get my hands on. I had my hands on something last night and I guarantee you boy I didn't want to save it * * * It is that you better believe that.
>
> You hear 'bout de gal dat had a brand new boy friend? And, well, it her brand new boy friend * * * and her brand new boy friend he had been coming over to see her a while, you know, and de gal's daddy decided that he'd better kinda lay down the law, you know, to his daughter's new boy friend, so he took the boy aside, you know, and he says, "Son," he says, "a man," he says, "a man should be the boss of his house" * * * and, he says, "I'm telling you, son, it won't take you long to find out that I'm the one who wears the pants in this family." And, the daughter's new boy friend says, "Oh, no, sir," he says, "I know that," he says, "I found it out last night, sir!" * * * And in October too, already.
>
> Bill Hyman [or Heiman] you know that works for Willie Tart in Lake City he was telling me that, he used to have some ducks, you know, used to

raise ducks, and says, "Uncle Charlie," he says, "them durn fool ducks," you know he used to have him a little patch of green peppers, you know, that hot green pepper, and he used to have it in the garden, and he said "them durn ducks would get in the garden and eat that green, and eat that hot green pepper," and says, "then it is that the ducks had to fly backwards to keep from burning up" * * * [laughter] * * * "that's right," he said, "the durn, the old duck had to get up and fly backwards to keep from barbecuing himself" * * *

I'll tell you what that Snotty Cook at that Cook Shell station in the city by the Lake in Lake City says, and I believe this is the way that Lake City was born. You see, it is that Noah built his Ark, he took all the animals on board, see, I mean, he took all the animals on board, and of course, it rained for 40 days and 40 nights, but Noah had a problem, see? Because the Ark didn't have any bathroom on it. So the only thing Noah could do, of course, was to take all the animals up on deck. But then he had a problem of how to get rid of it all, so he took a shovel and they shoveled it all over the side of the Ark into the water. So, it is that all of it settled and that's where Lake City come from.[8]

Careful drivers can have accidents. Careful boy friends can have accidents too.

I seen something last night that I wanted. I wasn't too bashful to go get it, I was just too smart. She had her husband with her. My mama didn't raise no foolish young 'uns.

That's the scientific word for happy horse crud.[9]

Why don't you get off your ding dong friend, you'll never make a million lying up in the bed looking at the ceiling.

Betsy, you're not producing, you're not. Betsy says give her time, she's not married yet. Now you know what I'm talking about.

You always drink plenty of big value coffee and you'll have enough strength to tell your girl friend no when she wants to go to the cow pasture and you want to go to prayer meetin', you know, and it is you'll have enough strength to tell 'em no. That's right.

It is that I always tell them no, not because I'm such a good boy but because it is that I ain't got enough strength to do anything else.

It is that my girl still loves me when I let 'er. See I don't let her too often because I don't wanta spoil her, see. I mean if you give women everything they want you spoil them, see. It'll break you and spoil them.

Uncle Banana Nose lettin' it all hang out * * *

I used to go with this gal that worked in that five and dime over in Greeleyville and you know it is that I'd take the gal out you know and anytime it is I'd kiss the old gal or hug her or squeeze her or tease her she'd say "Will that be all, sir?" You see that's what they say all day long at the five and dime, will that be all, sir? I broke her of that habit though. It is that I broke her of that habit. It is that I got the ole gal to where she'd quit saying, "Will that be all sir?" She started saying, "That's enough, Charlie." You gotta break 'em.

You know that Betsy goes over to Lake City every night, she does, she goes over to Lake City and they beat the devil outta her but that don't make no difference. She go back right over there again tonight. Well, I ain't never seen nobody like you, Betsy, that likes to go 13 miles just to get your rear end cut. I'll tell you what, if you want to stay home tonight I'll be glad to do it for you and save you the trip. I don't know what makes them people so rough over there. Really I don't * * * People in Lake City don't love nobody. I know because I given them several opportunities to love me and they passed it up * * * I mean them girls over there have had several opportunities and they passed it up.

You farmers better get off of it and get out there and get in at them tobacco fields. We don't want no crop failures this year. It is that we don't want any farmers to have any crop failures. I know about eight farmers' daughters that I hope like the devil that have a crop failure. [Laughter.] All I got to say they better have one! If they don't have a crop failure I'm gonna have a heart failure.

I've always been a gentleman, I sure don't go around beating up my women before I love 'em . . . Tell me, would you go around bruising up your groceries before you eat 'em? Well, that's the way I feel about them gals.[10]

If Williamsburg County was a big old house, Lanes would be the privy.

You know they always told me if you had a problem the best thing to do was to go home and sleep on it. It is. Now I'll give you just three guesses what my problem is. I'll just give you three guesses as to what my problem is. [Recorded girl's voice:] "Ain't you gonna kiss me" [Response in male voice:] "U'nh-u'nh." Well, that's my first problem right there. I get so tired of hearing that.

Old Willy Tart. You know Willy's getting kinda old now. Of course it is that he still likes to go out with the girls, but when he does it's only to refresh his memory because that's all he can do, refresh his memory. But we'll all be in the same boat one of these days, will we not?

I used to go out with a gal cause she had plenty of lovin' but now I go out with her cause she's got plenty of patience.

He was telling me, he says, "Uncle Charlie," he says, "we had 14 in the family. There was 14 of us not countin' the hogs too." He says, "There was 14 in the family," and he says "Uncle Charlie," he says, "we didn't have but one privy," he said, "one out-house, and that one out-house was sittin' on top the hill in back of the house." And he says, "do you know," he says, "in 3 years' time with all 14 in the family using it, in 3 years' time that privy was on flat ground. That family wore out that hill going back and forth. They did." He says "Uncle Charlie," he says, "they was always two of us going, two of us coming back, and one of us in there all the time, 24 hours a day." That's right, that's what he said, he says, "Uncle Charlie," he says, "that's the first time in my life I ever heard of a hole getting wore out." And you know, come to think of it, I never heard of no hole getting wore out.

You know they got a rooster down there at Frank Parsons Shell Station—a little ole bantam rooster and that bantam rooster's name is "Big Dick." And any time you go down to Frank Parsons and you wanta see that ole rooster all you gotta do is stand out there in the middle and holler "Hey Big Dick" and that ole rooster will comma running.

I can remember back when I was single boy. It is that my britches used to be wrinkled all the time too, but the reason my britches was wrinkled when I was single is because gals was always sittin' on my lap and that's why it is that my britches was always wrinkled. Man, times do change. Now what I got in 'em's wrinkled.

I got some britches at home that it is that if the crease in those britches could talk * * * my wife woulda been done killed me a long time ago (FCC exhibit 2).

Has the programing of licensee's station met the needs of the populations served during the station's most recent license renewal period

39. Kingstree, population 3,621, the county seat of Williamsburg County, population 43,807, is located in the southeastern part of South Carolina. It has a long and distinguished history dating back to 1732. The town has 3 hotels, a weekly newspaper, 2 hospitals, 2 banks, 2 high schools, 2 grade schools, 14 churches, a Carnegie library, 2 motion picture theaters, 2 parks, a considerable complement of both retail and manufacturing concerns, and a number of civic organizations. The town operates under a mayor-council-type government and maintains independent fire and police departments. Williamsburg County is largely agricultural. Over 70 percent of its area is covered by timber. There are some 6,000 farms located in the county, averaging about 70 acres per farm. Tobacco, cotton, and corn are the leading crops. The colored population of Kingstree amounts to about 44 percent of its total population. In the county about 68 percent of the population is colored [11] (WDKD exhibit 2).

40. WDKD, a daytime-only station, is the only radio station in Kingstree. Roughly speaking, radii of its 0.5-mv/m contour extend about 35 miles. All of Williamsburg County and substantial areas beyond are served by the station. Twenty-six other stations furnish 0.5-mv/m service within WDKD's 0.5-mv/m contour. Only three of these stations, however, furnish 0.5-mv/m service to as much as half of that area. Of those three, WIS, Columbia, S.C., serves the largest portion, 63.4 percent (WDKD exhibit 23).

41. WDKD's programing for the composite week covering its last renewal period, exclusive of entertainment and commercial spot announcements, may be thus briefly described. Sunday (December 14, 1958): *Religion*, one 1-hour program; *News*, five programs, total duration 32 minutes and 4 seconds. Monday (February 2, 1959): *Religion*, 2 programs, total duration 29 minutes and 12 seconds; *Agriculture*, one 4-minute 20-second program; *Sports*, 2 programs total duration 13 minutes and 52 seconds; *News*, 12 programs, total duration 1 hour 1 minute and 32 seconds; *Speech*, one 14-minute and 20-second program. Tuesday (March 10, 1959): *Public service*, one 4-minute and 20-second program ("Fire Prevention"); *Religion*, one 14-minute and 50-second program; *Agriculture*, one 4-minute and 20-second program; *Sports*, 2 programs, total duration, 13 minutes and 52 seconds; *News*, 11 programs, total duration 57 minutes and 14 seconds; *Speech*, one 14-minute and 10-second program. Wednesday (April 29, 1959): *Public service*, 2 programs ("Fire Prevention" and "Army Bandstand"), total duration 18 minutes and 50 seconds; *Religion*, one 14-minute and 20-second program; *Agriculture*, one 4-minute and 20-second program; *Sports*, 3 programs, total duration 18 minutes and 20 seconds; *News*, 13 programs, total duration 53 minutes and 30 seconds; *Speech*, one 14-minute and 20-second program. Thursday (May 21, 1959): *Public service*, one 14-minute and 30-second program (country music); *Religion*, one 14-minute and 20-second program; *Agriculture*, one 4-minute and 20-second program; *Sports*, 2 programs, total duration 13 minutes and 20 seconds; *News*, 11 programs, total duration 54 minutes and 42 seconds; *Speech*, one 14-minute and 20-second program. Friday (July 17, 1959): *Public service*, one 14-minute program ("Health Magazine"); *Religion*, one 14-minute and 30-second program; *Agriculture*, one 4-minute and 20-second program; *Sports*, 2 programs, total duration 15 minutes; *News*, 11 programs, total duration 54 minutes and 30 seconds; *Speech*, one 14-minute and 30-second program. Saturday (September 5, 1959): *Religion* 2 programs, total duration 28 minutes and 40 seconds; *Agriculture*, one 4-minute and 20-second program; *Sports*, 3 programs, total duration 1 hour 59 minutes and 40 seconds (ball game, 1 hour and 45 minutes); *News*, 11 programs, total duration 49 minutes and 40 seconds; *Speech*, one 14-minute and 20-second program [12] (FCC exhibit 3).

42. The presentation of spot announcements played a major role in WDKD's on-the-air operation during its last renewal period. Robinson in his renewal application stated that the station did not expect to present more than four spot announcements during any 14½-minute time period. This was a mistake, he testified; what he had intended to say was that not more than 4 minutes of spot announcement continuity would be included in any 14½-minute time segment (27 percent). Even this latter policy had been impossible of implementation due to the pressure from advertisers. Robinson admitted that on occasion the station presented as many as 10, 12, and 14 spot announcements during a 14½-minute time segment; that he would not be surprised if WDKD had not broadcast as many as 420 spot announcements in 1 day; that on occasion when announcers ran over the time scheduled for their programs, program material, including news, not spot announcements, were not carried to recapture time thus lost; and that announcers sometimes complained about the amount of commercial continuity they were required to present. Ward testified that it was not unusual when he was at WDKD for him to broadcast as many as 10 spot announcements in a 14½-minute time period, and that on one occasion he recalled presenting 15. Green testified that the station frequently carried more than six spot announcements during such time segments and that during sales trips he frequently heard complaints to the effect that the station was running too many spot announcements back to back and too close together (Tr. 177, 252, 254, 255, 258–262, 533, 536, 642, 644).

43. During WDKD's composite week the station carried 1,448 spot announcements.[13] This figure, while it may reflect an annual average, does not reflect the numerical peaks and concentration of spot announcements which the station frequently achieved. For example, on August 6 and 7, 1960, the station carried 448 and 475 spot announcements, respectively, on those 2 days. On October 16, 1959, the "Hymn Time" program which began at 10:10 a.m. contained spot announcements at the following intervals of time: 10:10, 10:12, 10:14, 10:18, 10:19, 10:21, 10:22, 10:23, 10:24, 10:25, 10:27, 10:28. In the time segment between 10:45 and 10:59, spot announcements were carried at 10:48, 10:49, 10:50, 10:52, 10:53, 10:54, 10:55, 10:57, and 10:58. On October 9, 1959, the program "Three B's In Music" contained commercial spots carried at 2:03, 2:04, 2:05, 2:06, 2:07, 2:08, 2:09, 2:10, 2:11, and 2:12. On the program entitled, "Spiritual Crossroads" broadcast the same day between 2:30 and 2:44:30, spots were listed at 2:32, 2:34, 2.35, 2:36, 2:37, 2:38, 2:39, 2:40, 2:41, 2:42, and 2:43. On the program, "Memory Lane," beginning at 5:15 and ending 5:29:30 also broadcast on October 9, spots were carried at 5:18, 5:20, 5:21, 5:22, 5:23, 5:24, 5:25, 5:26, 5:27, 5:28, and 5:29. On October 22, 1959, on program "Records at Random," spot announcements were

carried at 1:32, 1:34, 1:35, 1:36, 1:37, 1:38, 1:39, 1:40, 1:41, 1:42, 1:43, and 1:44. On October 10, 1959, the program "Hymn Time" included spot announcements at 10:30, 10:32:30, 10:33, 10:33:30, 10:34:30, 10:37:30, 10:38, 10:38:30, 10:39:30, 10:42, 10:42:30, 10:44. On Christmas Day 1959 on a program entitled "Christmas Music," WDKD carried commercials at the following times between 2:30 and 2:59:20: 2:31, 2:31:30, 2:32, 2:32:30, 2:33, 2:33:30, 2:34, 2:34:30, 2:35, 2:35:30, 2:36, 2:36:30, 2:38, 2:39, 2:40, 2:41, 2:42, 2:43, 2:46, 2:46:30, 2:47, 2:47:30, 2:48, 2:48:30, 2:49, 2:49:30, 2:50, 2:50:30, 2:51, 2:51:30, 2:52, 2:52:30, 2:53, 2:53:30, and 2:55; and during the time segment from 3:39:30 to 3:45 at the following times: 3:31:30, 3:32, 3:32:45, 3:33, 3:33:30, 3:34, 3:34:30, 3:36:30, 3:37, 3:37:45, 3:38, 3:38:30, 3:39, 3:39:30, 3:40:25, 3:41, 3:45 (Tr. 263, 265–267, 270, 271, 780–782, 787, and FCC exhibit 3).

44. Robinson testified that commercially, WDKD was a seasonal station, that the season ran from August to December. To offset the considerable evidence in the record reflecting the numerically high and heavily concentrated nature of WDKD's spot announcement performance, there was introduced into evidence on behalf of applicant a document entitled "Spot Announcements for a Week in February 1958, January 1959, and June 1960 (Off Season)." While the exhibit certainly demonstrates that not all of the 14½-minute time segments at WDKD during its "Off Season" were heavily saturated with spot announcements, the exhibit does show the following: For the week selected in February 1958 the station had twenty-eight 14½-minute time segments in which 5 spot announcements were carried, 9 such segments where 6 spots were carried, 8 where 7 were carried, 5 where 8 were carried, and a segment where 9 were carried. During the week in January 1959, the station had 27 segments where 5 spots were carried, 15 where 6 were carried, 7 where 7 were carried, 2 where 8 were carried, a segment where 9 were carried, and a segment where 10 were carried. During the June week in 1960, the station had 38 segments where 5 spots were carried, 27 where 6 were carried, 10 where 7 were carried, 8 where 8 were carried, 2 where 9 were carried, a segment where 10 were carried and a segment where 11 were carried (Tr. 177, 771–774, and WDKD exhibit 22).

45. A picture of how WDKD operated during a broadcast day may be obtained from the description set forth in the paragraph below, which is taken from a WDKD program log chosen at random. The day described is *June 10, 1960*, a Friday, a good day for spot sales, looking as it does to Saturday merchandising, but a day that did not fall within WDKD's so-called "peak season," August–December. (See par. 44, above.)

46. The station signed on at 5 a.m. with recorded music. At 5:03 a musical record, participating program called "Rise and Shine" came on and ran until 6.[14] During the course of that program, 17 spot announcements were presented.[15] At 6 a 4-minute, sustaining "News" program came on, followed by a spot announcement.[16] At 6:05 a musical record, participating program was presented entitled "Grits and Gravy." This program lasted until 7, but was interrupted by 19 spot announcements and at 6:30 by a 4-minute musical record, commercial program called, "Dreher Jamboree." At 7 a sponsored "News" program came on for 4½ minutes, followed by a spot announcement. At 7:05 a sponsored "S.C. News and Weather" program came on for 4 minutes.[17] At 7:09 a sponsored "Weather Report" came on for 30 seconds. At 7:10 a sponsored "Sports" program came on for 9½ minutes, followed by a spot announcement. At 7:20 a musical record, participating show entitled "Musical Timetable" was presented. This program, which ran until 8:50, was interrupted by 20 spot announcements, for 4½ minutes at 8 for news and weather and for 4½ minutes at 8:25 for a transcribed commercial message on behalf of a political candidate. At 8:50 "Dreher Jamboree" returned for 4½ minutes, followed by a spot announcement. At 8:55 a sponsored "News" program came on for 4½ minutes, followed by a spot announcement. At 9 a participating musical record program entitled "Church by the Side of Road" came on for 15 minutes. The program contained nine spot announcements. At 9:15 "Morning Devotions" was presented live, sustaining, for 14½ minutes, followed by a spot announcement. At 9:30 "Melodies for M'Lady," a musical record, sustaining show was presented for 30 minutes. During this program 16 spot announcements were broadcast. At 10 a 4½-minute, sponsored "News" program came on, followed by a spot announcement. At 10:05 "Hymn Time," a musical record, participating show, came on and continued until 10:55. This program was interrupted at 10:25 for 4½ minutes by a transcribed, commercial political message and 28 spot announcements. At 10:55 a sponsored "News and Weather" program came on for 4½ minutes, followed by a spot announcement. At 11 "Mountain Jamboree," a musical record, participating program, came on and continued until 12:20. This program was interrupted at 11:55 by a 4½-minute, sponsored program entitled "Weather and Streams," at 12 by a 4½-minute, sponsored "News" program and by 38 spot announcements. At 12:20 a 9½-minute, sponsored live, agricultural program entitled "Your Farm Agent Speaks" came on, followed by a spot announcement. At 12:30 a 4½-minute, sponsored "S.C. Market and Weather Report" came on, followed by a spot announcement. At 12:35 a 9½-minute musical record, participating program entitled "Western Startime" was presented. This program contained five spot announcements. At 12:45 a 14½-minute, sponsored "Exchange Bank News" program came on, followed by a spot announcement. At 1 a 14½-minute, sponsored program entitled "Old Trading Post," a kind of classified want ad program, was presented. This program was followed by a spot announcement. At 1:15 a 45-minute musical record, participating program, entitled "Records at Random," came on. This program included 18 spot announcements. At 2 a 30-minute musical record, participating program, entitled "Three B's in Music" was presented. Twelve spot announcements were included in this program. At 2:30 a 30-minute musical record, participating program

entitled "Spiritual Crossroads" was presented. This program included 11 spot announcements. At 3 a 1-hour musical record, participating program entitled "Platter Party" came on. This program was interrupted at 3:25 by a 4½-minute transcribed presentation on behalf of a political candidate and by 21 spot announcements. At 4 an hour-and-a-half musical record, participating program entitled "Sundown Hoedown" was presented. This program was interrupted by 36 spot announcements and by a 4½-minute, sponsored "Dreher Jamboree" program at 4:30 and by a 4½-minute, sustaining "News" program at 5. At 5:30 a 30-minute musical record, participating program entitled "Pop Tunes" was presented. This program was interrupted by 14 spot announcements and, for 4½ minutes at 5:55, by a transcribed commercial message on behalf of a political candidate. At 6 a 4½-minute, sustaining "News" program came on, followed by a spot announcement. At 6:05 a 9½-minute, sustaining "Sports" program came on, followed by a spot announcement. At 6:15 a musical record, participating program entitled "Bandstand" came on for 45 minutes. This program included 20 spot announcements. At 7 a 4½-minute, sponsored "News" program came on, followed by a spot announcement. At 7:05 a musical record, participating program called "Sunset Serenade" came on for 22 minutes. This program included six spot announcements. The station signed off at 7:27 (examiner's exhibit 1).

47. From the facts set forth in the previous paragraph, the following table may be obtained which will serve to give a bird's-eye view of how WDKD utilized the 14 hours and 27 minutes the station was on the air during the day under discussion:

News and weather	68 minutes.
Sports	19 minutes.
Transcribed political broadcasts	18 minutes.
Religion	14½ minutes.
Agriculture	9½ minutes.
Classified want ads	14½ minutes.
Musical records and commercial continuity, including 305 spot announcements.	12 hours 3½ minutes.
Total	14 hours 27 minutes.

Thus, some 17 percent of the station's broadcast day was devoted to material other than musical records and spot announcements. News and/or weather was presented 14 times during the day. On 10 occasions the program lasted 4½ minutes; twice, 4 minutes; once, 14½ minutes; and once, 30 seconds. Sports were presented twice, each program lasting 9½ minutes. There were four transcribed commercial political broadcasts, each lasting 4½ minutes. Religion, agriculture, and classified want ads were single programs.

48. The musical records played over WDKD fall into five general categories: (1) hillbilly, country, and western; (2) popular music; (3) spirituals; (4) rock-'n-roll; and (5) popular music for teenagers. This record format is designed to reach the different type listeners the station has determined the station serves, based on mail and personal interviews (Tr. 176).

49. In respect of other program categories, Robinson described WDKD's program activities at considerable length. The substance of his testimony may be thus digested: *Religion:* Years ago he adopted a policy of "religion No. 1, public service No. 2, the business will take care of itself." An hour each Sunday is set aside for church services. That hour is turned over to the local ministerial association. The association works out the scheduling of the services. The program rotates weekly from one church to another. Each morning the station also carries a 15-minute program entitled "Morning Devotions." This latter program also rotates among ministers representing various faiths. Some of the "Morning Devotions" programs are carried remote from churches, others originate in the station's studios. Further, the station also carries a tape-recorded program on Saturday morning called "Voice of Pentecost," which originates in Blaney, S.C.[18] It might be noted here that whatever the shortcomings of WDKD in other special program areas or in its overall program aspects, and notwithstanding the confusion in Robinson's testimony on the subject of religious programing, as noted below, the record does show that the station did in fact evince, during its last renewal period, a bona fide sensitivity and responsiveness to the religious needs of the community it served. *Education:* The station works closely with the schools. It cooperates in making announcements "and whatnot," with the training and industrial department of the high school, and when they have sales of light bulbs, boxes of candy, and things like that. The station supports and plugs football, basketball, and baseball games during the season and furnishes a sound truck if necessary. Robinson contacts the county superintendent and principals of the schools and offers them time for discussions "about the schools, and that sort of stuff." Announcements are made concerning preschool registration, kindergarten, and things like that.[19] *News:* The policy of the station is to have news headlines on the half hour and news on the hour. Headlines last 1 minute; news programs 5, 10, and 15 minutes. News originates from whatever information comes to the station during the day, plus information obtained from United Press wire service. Selection is made by announcers on the basis of what they believe the station's listeners would like to hear.[20] *Discussion:* "Discussion programs * * * we don't have too many of them. We ask the people to come out, and we offer time for these discussion programs, but we've had very few of them." *Talk:* The station carried very few talk programs. Locally, it is hard to get people to put on this type program. *Public service* (programs on behalf of nonprofit organizations): The station schedules all public services and cooperates with churches, schools, civic organizations, or what have you. The station refuses nobody—"We take all that stuff, put it on the air, we solicit it, we do everything we possibly can to assist those people in these public services."[21] *Agriculture:* a farm program carried live from the county agent's office is presented 5 days a week from 12:20 to 12:30 p.m. A 5-minute market report is carried

6 days a week, giving market prices taken from the UP wire service. "The Old Trading Post" is carried from 1 to 1:15, 6 days a week. This program is sponsored and designed for both farm and city people to use as a vehicle for advertising lost-and-found items and trade items, including farm equipment, cows, dogs, houses to rent, and farms for sale. During the tobacco season (August–December) the station carries daily for 15 minutes, Monday through Friday, as a part of a small network, live market reports from the tobacco sales barn at Lake City. This program is carried annually for about a 6 weeks' period. A similar program originating in Kingstree is also carried by the station. Further, reports on the tobacco market in Hemingway are received by the station by telephone and presented over WDKD in the form of spot announcements (Tr. 129–136, 167–168, 171–172, 173–175, 176, 179–184).

Evidence of community support for Robinson and his stewardship of WDKD

50. As before mentioned, 17 witnesses besides Robinson took the stand on his behalf. Who they were and the essence of what they testified to is digested in the following paragraphs.

51. *Lawrence Harry Fry* is a teacher of vocational subjects at Kingstree High School. WDKD participates in the on-the-job training aspects of the high schools' diversified occupations program. Three students have been trained at WDKD in connection with that program. WDKD for years carried a weekly program entitled "Your School Speaks," which covered various substantive areas of the schools' academic program; e.g., music, English, and history. On one or two occasions he appeared on that program. The station also carried a music program for teenagers called "Teen-Age Beat." The station taped home football games for rebroadcast and, when possible, similarly taped games away from home. Any time the school requests that an announcement be broadcast, the station is always cooperative. Charlie Walker was continually doing public service work. He recalled that Walker on one occasion came to the school and auctioned off cakes on behalf of the March of Dimes. That year Walker worked with the March of Dimes drive, and the drive raised as much, or more, money than had ever been similarly raised for that cause. Walker also aided underprivileged children. He had not listened to Walker broadcast over WDKD to any great extent. When he had listened, he had not heard anything offensive—"a joke about some individual, something like that; I mean no more than you hear on television today." In response to a question as to whether WDKD had served the needs of the community, Fry responded:

> I feel this, in my own mind, because. as I say. I've worked with it closely for the last 3 to 4 years, and I have asked them on numbers of occasions to help with some particular function that was going on at the school and also some of my students were putting on, and anything else—I've heard the statements made throughout the town: If you want something, help, call the radio station and they'll help you. I've heard that statement made all the time. And they have always cooperated a hundred percent in anything you ever asked them to do. I don't know of any time a worthwhile project they haven't helped in any way they could (Tr. 361, 362, 366–369, 370, 372, 377).

52. *Ralph Cleo Fennell* is county superintendent of education and member of the board of the Greeleyville Methodist Church. In connection with a fundraising drive for his church he, as advertising chairman, requested WDKD to carry publicity for the drive. The station carried those announcements. Charlie Walker in connection with the March of Dimes drive visited each of the classes in the Greeleyville area schools. He generated a great deal of enthusiasm among the students. They participated in the drive. The drive was a success and Walker gave the winning class a party. When because of bad weather county schools were forced to close, WDKD worked in close cooperation with the county board of education in issuing over the station early morning notices of school status. He had heard comments about the Walker programs. He was not interested in what was said. He recalled having heard Walker make references to towns by nicknames; he did not pay much attention; he was trying to listen to the announcements. He did not remember having heard Walker tell any stories. He did recall hearing him make about the best plea for a family that had been burned out that he had ever heard. The response to that plea was, he believed, great. While Walker had made some mistakes, that is past and gone. While he is condemned, he had his good side too. WDKD, in his opinion, has met the needs of the community in which it serves. In connection with the work for which he is responsible, it has certainly met those needs (Tr. 381–384, 385, 387, 388, 390, 391).

53. *Louie L. Law* is president and cashier of the Williamsburg State Bank in Kingstree, a director of the local and State tuberculosis association, on the executive council of the South Carolina Banking Association, and on the board of stewards of the Kingstree Methodist Church. He has heard the station carry material on behalf of a large number of nonprofit organizations—State, National, and local. Material on behalf of churches and the highway department he knew to be programs; the remainder could have been spot announcements. His son works at WDKD. His son went to the station through the schools' diversified occupations program. The boy, 16 years old, had difficulty in adjustment, but since employment with WDKD has been thoroughly happy. He has improved in many ways, particularly in voice, poise, and diction. Credit for the improvement goes to the Robinsons. On his own volition he went to Robinson and asked if there was anything he could do for him in connection with the instant hearing. He was present at a discussion of the hearing (then forthcoming) in Charleston, S.C., a discussion which included Mr. Lane, Mr. Taylor, and E. D. Rivers, manager of WCSC at Charleston. Mr. Rivers reported that Carroll Godwin would testify and would tell the truth. This was all that he, Law, asked; it was all that he wanted. It would be inaccurate to suggest that his call with others

upon Rivers was to suggest that Godwin not testify at the hearing as an employee of Rivers. Through Law, a document entitled "Resolution of Kingstree Business Men" was introduced. The resolution states that Robinson is a fit and proper person to operate WDKD; that he would not knowingly allow anything of an immoral nature to be broadcast over his station; that WDKD has served the county of Williamsburg and surrounding areas in a good and proper manner; that Robinson's policy is, when opportunity presents itself, to perform proper service; that Robinson should be allowed to continue management of WDKD and perform the same service as the station has performed in the past. The document is signed by two bank presidents, the county superintendent of education, chairman of the board of the local hospital, the county farm agent, the county sheriff, the county health officer, the president of the chamber of commerce, and the president of the junior chamber of commerce (Tr. 393–401, 406–409, and WDKD exhibit 12).

54. *Cornelius Graham Bass* is secretary-treasurer of the Santee Oil Co., secretary-treasurer and general manager of Services, Inc., partner and general manager of the S & P Tire Co., president of Warsaw Manufacturing Co., president of Kingstree Industrial Development Corp., chairman of the county board of education. He listens to WDKD. He advertises over WDKD. At times he requested that his advertising over the station be handled by Charlie Walker because Walker's listening audience was the largest that could be reached by any media in the area. He confirmed previous testimony relating to WDKD's cooperation with local schools. WDKD had been helpful through the use of spot announcements in obtaining for the chamber of commerce a register of potential employees for an industry which at the time was considering moving to Kingstree and subsequently did move there. Any request for time over WDKD by any Boy Scout or chamber of commerce drive he had been connected with had always met with generous response. The Lions Club used the station to promote a sale to aid underprivileged children. He listened to Charlie Walker over WDKD; whether what he heard was suggestive depended on whether you used preacher standards or the standards prevalent on radio and TV. Under his personal standards he didn't regard the Walker material as suggestive, vulgar, obscene, or indecent. He had heard material that could be considered subject to double meaning. He had heard such remarks as "that guy Charlie Walker. I just don't know how he gets away with it," made in the community during discussions of the Charlie Walker show. His testimony concerning the Walker broadcasts was based on what he had heard Walker broadcast. He had heard Walker refer to "Brown, the Clown," "Candy Man," and "Ann Drawers." He had not heard Walker make reference to taking his girl to a cow pasture. He had heard Walker make reference to "letting it all hang out" in service stations, but didn't know whether he had heard him use that phrase over the air. In his opinion WDKD has "very definitely" met the needs of the public which it serves. It would be a great loss to the area if the station were to be lost (Tr. 413–416, 419–423).

55. *Donald L. Taylor* is president of the Exchange Bank of Kingstree. The bank has advertised over WDKD for from 6 to 10 years. The board of directors conditioned their sponsorship of a 15-minute program over WDKD on Charlie Walker handling it. The program ran several years for 6 or 8 weeks during the Kingstree Tobacco Market. The bank has since then, and for several years, also sponsored another 15-minute program over WDKD. He seldom listens to radio. He does not have the time. He is a personal friend of Robinson's. Robinson is a stockholder in the bank. He went with Law and Lane to Charleston to talk to E. D. Rivers. He and Law contacted Lane to set up an appointment with Rivers. Lane introduced both him and Law to Rivers and said they were interested as to whether Godwin was antagonistic toward WDKD. Rivers took over and assured them Godwin was telling the truth. The only reason they talked to Rivers rather than Godwin was a matter of choice. There was no idea of putting pressure on anybody. In his opinion, based on his knowledge of the community and the things WDKD had done, he believes the station has served the community (Tr. 424–426, 428–431, 433, 434).

56. *James N. Hinnant* is owner of the Southern Discount Co., the principal business of which is financing and sale of automobiles. He is past chairman of the Polk National Foundation Fund for Infantile Paralysis and past chairman of the county Red Cross chapter. He has served as president of Little League Baseball; State director of the recreational association; alderman of Kingstree (two terms); on board of directors of Rotary Club; president of Royal Motors, Inc.; board member, trustee, and president of Bible Class of Methodist Church. At present he is chairman of the citizens councils of the county, on the State board from the county, and on the State executive committee. He listens to WDKD. He advertises over WDKD. Conservatively speaking, 90 percent of his advertising was placed on the Charlie Walker program at his request. This was because of Walker's extensive coverage. Through Charlie Walker the station promoted the Little League Baseball's fund drives for charities, a family that was burned out, financing the hospitalization of a boy who was a victim of that fire (in 2 or 3 days necessary funds were oversubscribed). Cancer drives and a very successful March of Dimes drive were handled by the station. In expressing his opinion of the station, the witness testified:

> I think that the greatest thing that Kingstree has and Williamsburg County has to date as a civic thing and promotional of Williamsburg County is radio station WDKD. I think they have done more than any other two or three organizations due to the facilities that they have in the promotion and progress of Williamsburg County.
>
> * * * * * * *
>
> If there is such a thing as an organization exceeding its public debt * * * to a community, they have done that * * * (Tr. 437–443).

57. *John C. Flagler* is owner and operator of 10 general merchandise stores in Williamsburg, Georgetown, and Clarendon Counties. He advertises over WDKD. He requested that his advertising be presented by Charlie Walker. He did this because Walker brought customers into his store, and he is interested in making money. He was not offended when Walker referred to him over the air as the only man in the county who could stand up and milk a cow. Whenever there was a need for fundraising or for blood donors, Walker always carried the ball. Walker was serious about such promotions and spoke from the heart. His business fell off about 20 percent after Walker left. Business is improving, but recovery is slow. He has to work hard. When Walker was on WDKD he did not have to work so hard. In his opinion, WDKD has definitely met the needs of the populations it serves, and more (Tr. 445–448).

58. *Lucius Kennedy Montgomery* is an architectural designer, a member of the Kingstree City Council, and secretary of the board of trustees of the Kingstree Methodist Church. He has been president of the Kingstree Chamber of Commerce for 7 years. WDKD has carried spot announcements on behalf of the chamber. He corroborated previous testimony concerning WDKD's role in securing an employment pool for an industry moving into Kingstree. He did not know of WDKD ever having aired a program for the chamber of commerce, but neither did he know that the chamber had ever made request for a program. In his opinion WDKD very definitely has met the needs of the areas and populations which it serves. Through this witness two exhibits were introduced; both are resolutions. Both are to the same purport as the resolution of the Kingstree businessmen. The first is entitled, "Resolution of Mayor and Council of Kingstree," and is signed by the mayor and six councilmen, one of whom is Montgomery. The second, signed by Montgomery as president and eight other members of the board of directors, is entitled "Resolution of the Chamber of Commerce" (Tr. 459–465 and WDKD exhibits 13 and 14).

59. *Weldom B. Bower* is plant manager of a branch of the Drexel Furniture Co. and is mayor of Kingstree. He has occasionally listened to WDKD. He agreed wholeheartedly with statements on behalf of the station made by previous witnesses. The station has performed excellent service in Kingstree. He has made a decision not to listen to the Charlie Walker program because of its content. He only listens to radio when he is in his car. He does not subscribe to the type of program or music that is usually heard on local radio. Unless it is something he enjoys, he turns it off. He did not listen to the radio for the Charlie Walker program. On occasion he had heard that program. He had heard material that could be interpreted as being of a suggestive nature. He could not answer as to whether the Walker program grew progressively worse. Everybody at first listened to Walker; it was an innovation, a novelty. He did not care for that type of broadcasting—its flippancy. He could not say there were obscenities; he just didn't like that kind of broadcasting. The only reference he could recall made by Walker was to "Smooch Me Quick Crossroads." He thought Walker called Andrews "Ann drawers." He had no recollection of Robinson ever aproaching him for the broadcast of material of interest to him or to the city council (Tr. 466–472).

60. *James Hugh McCutchen* is manager of the Williamsburg Livestock Co., dealing in farm machinery, and ruling elder of the Williamsburg Presbyterian Church. He has listened to WDKD and the Charlie Walker show. He had no objection to his wife or children listening to that program. He believed that he could affirm all of the testimony previously given by WDKD witnesses concerning the public-service work of WDKD. Along with supporting Red Cross and Boy and Girl Scout activities, the station had always carried church services. He did not believe that a fundraising activity could be named in which WDKD had not taken part. The station has very definitely met the needs of the area. Those it serves would be in bad shape if they did not have the station (Tr. 449–450).

61. *J. Lindwood Tyler* farms and also manages Belk's Department Store. He listens to WDKD. His store advertises over WDKD. He requested that to the extent possible the store's spots be handled by Charlie Walker. Walker had a good following and he was well accepted by many customers who would remark that they had heard Walker advertising for Belk's. He had listened to Walker's broadcasts but did not think he had heard a complete program. The civic activities of WDKD previously testified to cover his knowledge of that field and are correct. The store places so many spot announcements with WDKD it would be impossible for one announcer to handle them all. The store places as many as 60 spots over a 3-day period. He did not know whether the store carried 30-second spots or 1-minute spots. He has never been dissatisfied with the duration of the Belk's announcements. In his opinion, he believes the station has met the needs of the population and areas it serves (Tr. 452–459).

62. *Clarence P. Snowden, Jr.*, is a member of the town council of Hemingway, S.C. Through the witness an exhibit entitled "Hemingway Resolution" was introduced. This exhibit, which, except for the words "town of Hemingway" in place of "town of Kingstree" is, in its body, identical with the resolution of the Kingstree businessmen. It is signed by the mayor of Hemingway and four councilmen (Tr. 473–474, 476, and WDKD exhibit 16).

63. *T. E. Ruffin* operates department stores in Hemingway and Andrews, S.C. He advertises over WDKD 3, 4, and perhaps 5 days a week, utilizing 8 to 15 spots per day. Through this witness an exhibit entitled "Hemingway Businessmen" was introduced. The exhibit is a resolution framed to the same general purport as the other resolutions introduced into evidence by WDKD and is signed by the president of the Hemingway Merchants Association, secretary of Hemingway Merchants Association, president of Ruffin's Department Store, Inc., president of Ratcliff's Department Store, Inc., vice president of Hyman Motors, Inc., a representative of Red and White Supermarket, president of Stuckey Bros. Furniture Co., pastor of Old Johnsonville Methodist Church, vice president of Anderson State Bank, Inc., a representative of the Hemingway Home Development Co., and the principal of the Hemingway schools (Tr. 477–478, 481, 482, and WDKD exhibit 17).

64. *Leonard Grossman* is manager of the General Drygoods Store and alderman [councilman] of the town of Greeleyville, S.C. Through this witness a resolution was introduced similar in content to those previously introduced and entitled "Greeleyville Resolution." It is signed by the mayor and four councilmen of that town (Tr. 488–489 and WDKD exhibit 19).

65. *W. Frank Mishoe* is a member of the South Carolina House of Representatives. He farms and has a retail feed and seed business. He advertises over WDKD. The station carried about 20 to 25 of his spots a month. He occasionally listens to WDKD. Years ago he listened to Charlie Walker. He was not sure that he had or had not heard Walker during the last 3 years. He could not recall anything suggestive that Walker had broadcast. He did not pay that much attention to it. Through this witness an exhibit entitled "Resolution of Legislative Delegation" was introduced. In its entirety, as received, it reads:

> This is to certify that we the undersigned members of the Williamsburg County legislative delegation are of the opinion that radio station WDKD has met the commercial and civic needs of the people of Williamsburg County in the field of communications, information, and entertainment (Tr. 492–497 and WDKD exhibit 20).

66. *Woody Brooks* is president and general manager of the Brooks Veneer Co. in Andrews, S.C., and mayor of Andrews. He has listened to the Charlie Walker program perhaps a half-dozen times. His testimony on the Walker program was based on knowledge of the program thus gained. Whether what Walker broadcast was suggestive depended on the listener's frame of mind. He had heard Walker use the term "Ann drawers" and if one had the mind, that reference could be considered a little off color. He thought Walker was "sort of a nut." He seldom listened to him. He had never heard Walker talk of taking his girl to a cow pasture. He made a point to turn Walker off most of the time when he heard him. He did this not because Walker's programs were objectionable but because they were of a type he did not appreciate. He does not like country music. He had no particular objection to Walker's language. It was not only the music in the Walker programs that he objected to, but it was the entire format of the program. He did not like the " 'Uncle Willie this and that,' 'you know, boys,' that kind of jazz." He did not purport to be an expert on Walker's type of entertainment. Through this witness a document entitled "Resolution of Citizens of Andrews" was introduced. It, too, commends the general operation of WDKD and Robinson and recommends renewal of the station's license. It is signed by the mayor and the chief of police of Andrews; Reynolds, of the Reynolds Drug Co.; the president of Blakeley Bros.; the president of Hemingway Motor Co.; superintendent of schools of Andrews; and an agriculture teacher (Tr. 483–487 and WDKD exhibit 18).

67. *Roger R. Nettles* is president of Moore-Nettles Co., Inc. (wholesale sand and gravel), and member of the City Council of Lake City, S.C. Robinson had never approached him to put on programs of civic importance. Lake City recently had a bond issue of major local concern. He did request that WDKD run a local civic notice and the station carried the item. Through this witness an exhibit entitled "Resolution of Mayor of Lake City and Others" was introduced. Similar in content to the other resolutions, it was signed, besides Nettles, by the mayor of Lake City, president of the Lake City Rotary Club, worshipful master of Lake City No. 193 AFM, the president of W. Lee Flowers Co., the president of Lake City Chamber of Commerce, the president of the Council of Women's Federated Clubs of South Carolina, and the president of Lake City State Bank (Tr. 498–502 and WDKD exhibit 15).

CONCLUSIONS

1. The pivotal issue in this case is issue 3—did Robinson permit Walker to broadcast over his station material that was coarse, vulgar, suggestive, and susceptible of indecent, double meaning? Putting aside for the moment Robinson's role in the Walker broadcasts, a subject which will be treated below in connection with the second issue, the character of those broadcasts is now considered. In dealing with this matter one is faced at the outset with the free-speech implications surrounding the subject. This is so, not only because of Robinson's claims of first-amendment protection for the Walker broadcasts, but because words spoken by an individual are here involved and due regard for a precious heritage of the American people requires anyone, cast in the role of assaying the import of words spoken with a corollary responsibility to do something about them, to approach the task with an awareness that he is operating on near-sacred ground. The agency on whose behalf the examiner initially speaks, charged with the responsibility for determining the composition of traffic over the air, *NBC* v. *U.S.*, 319 U.S. 190, 216, has traditionally been most assiduous in leaning over backward to avoid exercising its authority in such fashion as to make even the slightest incursion into those liberties protected by the first amendment.

2. Robinson in his proposed findings attempts to place the Commission on the horns of a dilemma. He contends that if the Commission should find the Walker broadcasts to be obscene or indecent it would be acting ultra vires since the United States Code, 18 U.S.C. 1464, makes the broadcast of obscene and indecent material a crime, and determination of crime is for courts alone, not for administrative agencies.[22] If the Commission were to find the Walker broadcasts to be something less than obscene or indecent, claims Robinson, it would be violating the free-speech protection afforded by the first amendment.

3. The first thrust of Robinson's argument may be disposed of briefly. In doing so, it is unnecessary to attempt to draw hairline distinctions between the meaning of "coarse, vulgar, suggestive, and susceptible of indecent, double meaning" as used in the issue, and "obscene and indecent" as used in the statute. Webster's New Collegiate Dictionary (2d ed., 1951) defines "coarse" as "* * * common, of inferior quality or appearance: mean: * * * harsh, rough, or rude as opposed to delicate or dainty. * * * unrefined; vulgar: gross." "Vulgar" is defined as "* * * boorish; also offensive to good taste or refined feelings: low, coarse * * * obscene; * * * low; as a vulgar joke." "Suggestive" is defined "* * * tending to suggest what is improper, indecent, or the like." "Indecent" is defined as "not decent; specif. * * * unbecoming or unseemly; indecorous * * * morally offensive; unfit to be seen or heard." "Obscene" is defined as "* * * foul: disgusting * * * offensive to chastity or to modesty; lewd." While it might be possible to eke out from those definitions a theory that the words used in the issue are of different import than those used in the statute, such an exercise in semantics would, in the view of the examiner, smack more of logomachy than law or logic, and would be cynical treatment, indeed, of a defense seriously advanced. The examiner is as willing to brand the Walker broadcasts "obscene" and "indecent" as he is to dub them with the adjectives used in the issue. Having conceded that the broadcasts do fall within the proscriptive language of 18 U.S.C. 1464, and at the same time noting that a hearing on a radio station license renewal is in no sense a judicial proceeding looking toward the existence or nonexistence of a crime, the examiner hastens to dispose of the first thrust of Robinson's argument by pointing out that from time to time over the years the theory has been advanced before both the Commission and the courts that when a licensee's conduct has been so bad as to fall afoul of criminal sanctions, that conduct is for "eyes only" of the courts. That view has consistently been rejected by both the courts and the Commission. See *Report on Uniform Policy as to Violation by Applicants of the Laws of the United States*, 1 R.R., part 3, 495, and cases cited therein. Further, by amendment to the Communications Act, effective September 1960, Congress specifically conferred authority on the Commission to act on matters involving violation of 18 U.S.C. 1464. See page 51, infra.

4. In advancing the second front of his argument, Robinson urges that the test for obscenity set forth by the Supreme Court in *Roth* v. *U.S.*, 354 U.S. 476, must be adopted here. That test is: "Whether to the average person, applying contemporary community standards, the dominant theme of the material taken as a whole appeals to prurient interests," id. at 489.[23] Under that test, Robinson contends, the Walker material cannot be found to be obscene because: (1) Walker broadcast a great deal of material that was not of the same nature as the material quoted above and (2) the Walker broadcasts, on the whole, achieved a good deal of acceptability in the community. As will be pointed out in more detail later, contrary to Robinson's contention, the examiner is of the view that the Walker material at issue here can be found to be obscene under the test approved in *Roth*. However, the instant matter is a case of first impression and, because it is, it is important, if possible, to avoid adopting measures which ripening into precedent might unduly hamper effective radio regulation.[24] It must be conceded that the Court in the *Roth* case did apparently prescribe the test quoted above for use by the Postmaster General in determining the mailability of publications, by courts in reviewing his orders, and by State officials in enforcing State laws designed to prevent the origination, sale, advertising, and distribution of obscene writings and photographs. In the view of the examiner, however, the *Roth* case did not purport to establish the test as one that must be applied wherever or whenever a question of obscenity is to be determined.

5. In this and the following two paragraphs the examiner will attempt to explain why he does not believe the *Roth* test was intended for uniform application in all cases where a question of obscenity is involved. The *Roth* decision involved two cases, *Roth* v. *U.S.* and *Alberts* v. *California*. The one involving Roth came up following conviction for violation of a Federal statute prohibiting utilization of the U.S. mails for the dissemination of obscene matter (18 U.S.C. 1461). The other, involving Alberts, came up following conviction for violation of provisions of the California Penal Code prohibiting the authorship, publication, advertising, sale or distribution of obscene matter (West's Cal. Penal Code Ann. 1955, sec. 311). In its decision, the court did the following: It affirmed both convictions below. It unequivocally held that obscenity is not within the area of constitutionally protected speech or press. It rejected a contention that constitutional guarantees had been violated because of failure of proof below to show that the material at issue would have perceptibly created a clear and present danger of antisocial conduct or would probably have induced such conduct. It warned that sex and obscenity are not synonymous and that portrayal of sex in art, literature, and scientific works is no in itself sufficient reason to deny first-amendment protection. It warned that ceaseless vigilance is the price of retention of a fundamental liberty; that freedom of speech and press has contributed much to our free society; that the door to Federal and State intrusion into the area of free speech and press must be kept tightly closed, and opened only to the extent necessary to prevent encroachment upon more important interests; that it is vital that the standards for judging obscenity safeguard freedom of speech and press with respect to material which does not treat sex in a manner appealing to prurient interest. It rejected as unconstitutional the *Hicklin* test [25] which allowed judgment of obscenity to turn on the effect excerpts of the material at issue would have upon particularly susceptible persons. It noted with approval the test quoted in the above paragraph as employed in cases subsequent to those which employed the *Hicklin* test. It held that the courts below in their instructions to the jury had sufficiently followed the proper test. It brushed aside objections that the statutes involved were so vague as to deny due process. It concluded that, in light of its holding that obscenity is not protected by the first amendment, the contention that the Federal censorship statute unconstitutionally encroached upon powers reserved to the States and to the people was without merit. It rejected a plea by Alberts that the California statute was void as against him on the ground that his was a mail-order business and Congress had preempted the field in regulation of the mail. As the examiner reads the decision, the foregoing is what the Court held in the *Roth* case and all that it held. The Court did not say that the test therein approved for obscenity was for universal application and, significantly, in coining a short term for the Federal statute involved, it did not refer to "Federal obscenity statutes" but instead to the "Federal obscenity statute"; i.e., the one contained in the U.S. postal laws. Moreover, as the examiner will attempt to point out below, the circumstances surrounding other areas where obscenity is a problem, in and of themselves, speak firmly to the effect that the Court in *Roth* did not intend the test therein approved to be one required for application in all obscenity cases.

6. It hardly seems reasonable that the sideshow barker could publicly describe the physical attributes of his dancing girls in the same terms he might describe them in private and successfully defend against prosecution for public utterance of obscenity with proof that the *average* person was repelled, not moved by the coarseness of his "pitch." It hardly seems reasonable that a motion-picture exhibitor could or should be able to defend against on obscenity charge after intermittently interspersing in an otherwise artistic feature unrelated clips of pure erotica on the ground that the *dominant theme* of the picture viewed in its entirety did not appeal to prurient interests. It hardly seems reasonable that the huckster operating in "skid row" could seek to draw attention to his produce by raucously bawling vulgarities and defend against an obscenity charge on the ground that, considering the complex of the community and its contemporary standards, his language had no appeal to *prurient interest*. While the foregoing examples are, of course, purely hypothetical, it is certainly conceivable that such situations, or some variant of them, could occur.

7. The field of broadcast regulation is perhaps an area as ill adapted as any for employment of the *Roth* test. First, it must be remembered that, unlike the acquisition of books and pictures, broadcast material is available at the flick of a switch to young and old alike, to the sensitive and the indifferent, to the sophisticated and the credulous. Further, broadcast material is delivered on a route commonly owned by the public on a vehicle especially licensed to serve them and is received on property owned by the consignee. In short, there is a universality of utility and a public stake present in broadcasting wholly lacking in the kind of thing that was involved in *Roth*. Two hypothetical situations may serve to illustrate the disparity between the free-speech problems that were involved there and the kind that can be present in broadcasting. All hands would agree, it is supposed, that the Postmaster General would be hard put to ban the Bible from the mails. Would they not also agree that the Commission might be justified in holding that a licensee who telecast a documentary, live, in depth, of the "Song of Solomon" had not met the public-interest standard? Joyce's "Ulysses" and Lawrence's "Lady Chatterley's Lover" have both been found by the courts not to be obscene within the meaning of the postal laws, *U.S.* v. *One Book Called Ulysses*, D.C., S.D.N.Y., 5 F. Supp. 182, affirmed 2 Cir., 72 F. 2d. 705; *Grove Press, Inc.* v. *Christenberry*, 175 F. Supp. 488. However, were dramatizations of those works to be telecast with coverage, in depth, of their more lurid details (e.g., the Mollie Bloom flashbacks in pt. 3 of "Ulysses"), should not the Commission be able to seriously question the qualifications of the licensee over whose station the programs were presented? Those who believe that any prior restraint constitutes censorship and per se violation of the first amendment might wish to consider whether or not, in this latter situation, despite their views, Federal or State authority, armed with notice and in full possession of the facts concerning proposal to present such telecasts, ought not to be able successfully to seek injunction.[26] Similar hypothetical situations where it would appear free-speech problems differ profoundly in broadcasting and in the fields of letters and art might be propounded at length. The examiner is hopeful, however, that the foregoing will suffice to justify moving on to the following observations, all of which are at odds with doctrine enunciated in *Grove Press*, *id.*, at 496–497, 499, a case in which the *Roth* rule was applied and one on which Robinson also relies. In determining obscenity in broadcasting, questionable material should not always have to be weighed within the context of everything else that is presented with it. Brief injections of erotica, pornography, or smut are enough to seriously prejudice, if not destroy, the general utility of radio and television. "The effect on the average man of normal sensual impulses" test hardly serves to protect tots from getting an eye or earful of smut which their parents, quite legitimately, may desire they be shielded from, nor does it protect the adult of tender sensibilities from being exposed to that which to him or her is truly revolting. Both types of listeners and viewers have a considerable stake in broadcasting. Considering the "universality of utility" aspect of broadcasting, it would seem that whether broadcast material is in bad taste and shocks and offends substantial segments of a community might well be a perfectly proper consideration for determining whether such material is obscene. The "shamful and morbid interest in sex so pervasive as to submerge any ideas of redeeming social importance" test and the requirement that the material in question to be obscene must exceed limits of tolerance imposed by current standards of a community certainly would appear to permit a lot of broadcast material to find first-amendment protection that nevertheless would be highly offensive to large segments of a listening or viewing audience. The reaction of even minority blocs of the public are entitled to con-

sideration when public-interest judgment is made. A high degree of acceptability among literary cognoscenti as a test for obscenity seems woefully inadequate when used in connection with a medium the very nature of which is general public acceptability. Although the converse of all the foregoing propositions was found by the Court to be appropriate for application under the facts present in *Grove Press*, it appears manifest that such application in broadcast cases would be unduly restrictive to regulation in the public interest. All hands would agree, it is supposed, that the radio or television set should never require that sequestered treatment accorded the family revolver, the rat poison, or the book on love and marriage. Similar agreement may be assumed for the proposition that the dials of those sets should not have to be approached timidly and in fear of receiving offense by those of highly developed sensibilities.

8. The foregoing views are in no sense intended to suggest that under appropriate circumstances bona fide works of art, literature, or science dealing in candid fashion with subjects that may have been socially and legally taboo in some bygone period may not be aired. Nor are those views intended to suggest that the *Roth* test is not appropriate for determination of obscenity where obscenity laws are directed at books, art, or the theater. The sole purpose of the foregoing discussion is to point up the reasons behind the examiner's view that the *Roth* test was not advanced by the Supreme Court as a universal standard for determining obscenity and, of course, as a correlative to point up the lack of merit in Robinson's contention that the test must be applied here.

9. As earlier indicated, the *Roth* test can be applied to the Walker material here at issue and a conclusion reached that it is obscene. The material on its face is of such nature that only the very young or the very naive can fail to recognize in it a common vein of thinly veiled reference to the procreatory or excretory functions of man or beast or some ramification of, or appurtenance to, those functions. With the extremities of youth and credulity lopped off, the average man is left to make the test. If the testimony of those few witnesses who were interrogated about the Walker material and who indicated they knew anything about it and nevertheless found it inoffensive is discounted (see, e.g., pars. 52, 54, and 60 above) on the ground that their zeal in coming to the aid of a medium that had served them well overpowered their judgment (a conclusion the examiner is willing to reach), there is clear evidence that the average man in Kingstree and its environs found the Walker material highly objectionable. Clergymen received complaints about the Walker broadcasts (see pars. 29 and 30, above); other broadcasters feared the broadcasts would be detrimental to broadcasting (see pars. 34 and 35, above); at least one advertiser canceled his advertising over the station because of the Walker broadcasts (see par. 33, above); and a former partner of the respondent not only fired Walker because of the character of his broadcasts but left the partnership for the same reason (see par. 28, above). Of course, the average man's complaint was not couched in terms of "appealing to prurient interests," but for laymen the witnesses did pretty well in meeting the meaning of that phrase with such characterizations as "vulgar, suggestive, and sexy" (see par. 30, above); "bad taste that people could and did object to"; "the suggestiveness of it" (see par. 29, above); "filthy" (see par. 32, above); "off color"; "a certain amount of vulgarity" (see par. 33, above); "downright indecent" (see par. 34, above); and "degrading to radio" (see par. 35). Insofar as the "dominant theme" requirement of the *Roth* test is concerned, when Walker's remarkable popularity with the local advertisers is taken into account (see, e.g., pars. 54, 56, 61, and 63, above) and it is recalled that his primary function over the air, along with musical records, was to serve as filler between spot announcements, it becomes pretty apparent that his principal appeal lay in his smut and that his smut signalized, characterized, and was in fact the dominant note in his broadcasts.[27]

10. On the basis of the foregoing considerations, the examiner concludes that even under the *Roth* test the Walker broadcasts here at issue are obscene and indecent and, a fortiori, coarse, vulgar, suggestive, and susceptible of indecent double meaning. Without employing the *Roth* test, he holds the material in question obscene and indecent on its face.

11. In respect of the question posed by the second issue—whether Robinson maintained adequate control or supervision of the programs broadcast over his station—it has now become apparent that the question is rhetorical. Robinson clearly did not exercise adequate control over that aspect of his station's operation. Had he done so, the Walker material here at issue would not have been broadcast. Broadcasting licensees must assume responsibility for all material which is broadcast through their facilities, *Commission Policy on Programing*, 20 R.R. 1901. Absent intervening factors of such nature as would make licensee accountability wholly unreasonable, that principle must, by the very nature of our system of radio regulation, be maintained inviolate. Suggestions, such as Robinson advanced during the trial of this proceeding, that ill health, inadequate subordinates, extreme popularity of talent, or ignorance of the true character of the broadcast material in question, cannot be accepted as in any way relieving him of full responsibility for his station's operation.

12. When the facts set forth in paragraphs 9 to 14, 18, 19, and 28 to 35 of the above findings are carefully evaluated, it is apparent that Walker had for years been broadcasting over his station the kind of bucolic double entendre that is set out in paragraphs 28, 32, and 38 of the findings. Further, it is apparent that Robinson well knew the true character of those broadcasts. It is, therefore, clear from the correspondence between Robinson, his counsel, and the Commission (see pars. 2 to 5, above) that Robinson was attempting to palm off on the Commission representation that the Walker broadcasts were but a slight station contretemps which had been promptly corrected when its origin was called to his attention. Such a representation hardly

squares with the fact, as this record amply demonstrates, that for years he had been featuring over his station a smut artist as diskjockey. Thus, it only can be held that his representations to the Commission here under consideration were not only lacking in candor but were, under the circumstances, studied misrepresentation of fact. The question propounded by the first issue must be concluded adversely to Robinson.

13. Issue 4 inquires as to the manner in which WDKD served the needs of its community. In the *Commission's Policy on Programing* (id. at 1912–1913), the Commission after pointing out at considerable length that it was not its function to provide rigid formula for broadcast service in the public interest went on to say:

> Broadcast licensees must assume responsibility for all material which is broadcast through their facilities. This includes all programs and advertising material which they present to the public. With respect to advertising material the licensee has the additional responsibility to take all reasonable measures to eliminate any false, misleading, or deceptive matter and to avoid abuses with respect to the total amount of time devoted to advertising continuity as well as the frequency with which regular programs are interrupted for advertising messages. This duty is personal to the licensee and may not be delegated. He is obligated to bring his positive responsibility affirmatively to bear upon all who have a hand in providing broadcast matter for transmission through his facilities so as to assure the discharge of his duty to provide acceptable program schedule consonant with operating in the public interest in his community. The broadcaster is obligated to make a positive, diligent, and continuing effort, in good faith, to determine the tastes, needs, and desires of the public in his community and to provide programing to meet those needs and interests. This again, is a duty personal to the licensee and may not be avoided by delegation of the responsibility to others.

> •   •   •   •   •   •   •

> In the fulfillment of his obligation the broadcaster should consider the tastes, needs, and desires of the public he is licensed to serve in developing his programing and should exercise conscientious efforts not only to ascertain them but also to carry them out as well as he reasonably can. He should reasonably attempt to meet all such needs and interests on an equitable basis. Particular areas of interest and types of appropriate service may, of course, differ from community to community, and from time to time. However, the Commission does expect its broadcast licensees to take the necessary steps to inform themselves of the real needs and interests of the areas they serve, and to provide programing which in fact constitutes a diligent effort, in good faith, to provide for those needs and interests.

> The major element usually necessary to meet the public interest, needs, and desires of the community in which the station is located as developed by the industry, and recognized by the Commission, have included: (1) Opportunity for local self-expression, (2) the development and use of local talent, (3) programs for children, (4) religious programs, (5) educational programs, (6) public affairs programs, (7) editorialization by licensees, (8) political broadcasts, (9) agricultural programs, (10) news programs, (11) weather and market reports, (12) sport programs, (13) service to minority groups, (14) entertainment programing.

14. It has already been concluded that in one important area, insuring decency of programs, Robinson has been woefully inadequate in discharging his broadcast licensee responsibilities. Review of paragraphs 42 through 46 discloses that he has been similarly deficient in "avoid[ing] abuses with respect to the total amount of time devoted to advertising continuity as well as the frequency with which regular programs are interrupted for advertising messages."[28] As far as making a diligent and continuing effort to determine the tastes and needs of the community, the program performance of his station certainly does not reflect that the efforts Robinson put out in that regard (and he did put out some), were very fruitful. As to the 14 elements necessary to meet the interests, desires, and needs of a community, based on the record facts (see pars. 39 to 49, above), the examiner would grade WDKD's performance thus: *opportunity for local self-expression*—virtually nil as far as performance was concerned; *development of local talent*—feeble, some attention to this subject as evidenced by the station's cooperation with the schools' vocational training program; *programs for children*—nil, except for musical record programs directed at teenage audiences; *religious programs*—fully met obligation as broadcast licensee; *educational programs*—nil; *public affairs programs*—nil; *editorialization by licensee*—nil; *political broadcasts*—met obligation as broadcast licensee; *agricultural programs*—adequate discharge of licensee responsibility; *news program*—performance variable and skimpy, little attention to news in depth, standard for judgment in news selection, poor (see par. 49, above); *weather and market reports*—fully met responsibility as broadcast licensee; *sports*—met responsibility as broadcast licensee; *service to minority groups*—nil, except for musical records directed at colored audience; *entertainment programing*—adequate time devoted but scope too narrow due to reliance on recorded music. On the basis of the foregoing "report card," it follows that in the 14 categories, WDKD has "failed" in 6, "passed" in 5 (with a high mark in one—religion), and has "conditions" in 3.

15. If the foregoing marks were to be evaluated for honors in making contribution to enlargement of the American mind, Robinson would surely fail. If those marks were to be evaluated to determine whether Robinson's performance as licensee enabled his station to show adequate performance in even a majority of the above program categories, conclusion adverse to him would follow. But considerations such as the foregoing are not appropriate criteria against which WDKD's performance should be measured to obtain final response to the issue. Since at final issue here is the question of whether a man should retain a license that is the foundation of his business and since his is a regulated business, fairness dictates that the performance must be finally evaluated in terms of the performance of other licensed operations of like scope, size, and situation. This, of course, involves a purely subjective determination. It is the examiner's judgment that, excluding the fact that obscenities were broadcast over the station, WDKD's record of past performance has met the needs of the community it serves little better or little worse than most other standard broadcast stations operating under like conditions. The foregoing conclusion is about as far as the examiner can appropriately go in responding to issue 4.

16. Issues 5 and 6 are conclusionary issues and, read together, call for the examiner to make initial determination as to whether the public interest would be served by renewal of WDKD's license in the light of facts developed on the record. Before entering this final stage, the examiner should, perhaps, make perfectly clear where in his judgment the weight of the evidence lies in matters involving conflict of testimony. The only area where such conflict is significant is to be found in the clash between Robinson's testimony and the testimony of others. In all such instances the examiner holds against Robinson. The examiner has no reasonable basis to doubt the veracity of those whose testimony was at odds with that given by Robinson. He does have cause to doubt that on the stand Robinson at all times testified to the whole truth. A careful reading of Robinson's testimony as digested above will show that it is often marked by vagueness and ambivalence; a poor earnest of probity. Further, there is an immense amount of proof in this record tending to show that over a considerable period of time Walker had been broadcasting obscenities over WDKD. There is ample proof that those broadcasts had been a source of concern to many members of the community. That this concern had been made clear to Robinson on a number of occasions has been attested by several witnesses. There is no dispute that for years Robinson has been owner-manager of WDKD. Weighed against Robinson's efforts on the stand and in his correspondence with the Commission to create the impression that he was not fully aware of the character of Walker's broadcasts, such massive refutation not only destroys the point Robinson sought to make but effectively serves to impeach his credibility generally. Returning to the final issues, the pros and cons of Robinson's position will now be considered.

17. On the debit side of Robinson's ledger we find that in correspondence and at hearing, his record for candor is bad. He has lent his facilities to the broadcast of obscene material. His station, aside from the obscene matter broadcast, while it may not have differed in marked degree from the performance of other stations having similar characteristics, has carried a horrendous number of commercial spot announcements and has not approached programing to meet that complex of program needs and interests to be found in a community. Thus, there is ample basis for denying Robinson's application for renewal of station license—character deficiency and bad past operation.

18. There are, however, some considerations that militate against taking the action suggested above. The WDKD license is the foundation upon which Robinson's business and, it is presumed, his principal source of livelihood is based. To take it away would be punishment more severe in many respects than many penalties that might be assessed by a court following conviction for a crime. Such a harsh measure is to be avoided if alternative can be found.

19. The Government is not wholly without fault in this matter. Had a representative of the Department of Justice or of the Commission called upon Robinson in the early days of the Walker broadcasts and showed Walker and Robinson the provisions of 18 U.S.C. 1464 with a warning that rustic jokes with hidden meaning might well come within the purview of that law, it is inconceivable to the examiner that Robinson would have permitted those broadcasts to continue or that Walker would have wished to continue presenting them. While inaction by the Government does not form an excuse for Robinson's permitting the broadcasts to be aired, it does place one in the position of the examiner, who is also a "clerk in the same store" as those who might have taken such prophylactic action, to wonder if, under the circumstances, a little leniency toward Robinson might not be amiss to compensate for the bobble of his brethren.

20. It is apparent from the description of the town and the employment of the witnesses that Kingtree and the surrounding areas, like many other parts of the South, are engaged in the process of converting from what was once almost entirely an agricultural economy to one more balanced by business and industry. It is also apparent from the testimony of the witnesses and the record of the station operation that Robinson and WDKD are an integral part of that movement. While it is clear that in playing his role Robinson overacted his part (the Walker broadcasts and the station's "overcommercialization"), it cannot be said that Robinson's activity in this behalf was wholly without public-interest connotations.

21. Without going into a dissertation on why the gap exists and whether or not it is narrowing, the examiner feels justified in pointing out that one has only to look at standard broadcast operation in general today to appreciate that there is a considerable gap between what the Commission regards as good programing practice as stated in its *Commission Policy on Programing* and what broadcasters in general apparently believe that standard to be. As will be pointed out more fully later, the examiner does not believe that Robinson would again permit obscene matter to be aired over WDKD. Considering the hiatus between policy and performance just mentioned, it appears fair to say that at least it is highly doubtful that were the stewardship of WDKD to be altered a change for the better would result. Particularly does this observation seem warranted, when it is remembered that in one program category, religion, Robinson opened up the "spot and platter" format of his operation (sometimes euphemistically referred to in the trade as "news and music") to admit local live programing in real depth and that in four other program categories the performance of his station has been found to be adequate.

22. While Robinson did lack candor in his representations to the Commission, vis-a-vis the Walker matter, while he did exercise execrable judgment in permitting such broadcasts, and while his performance on the stand was a good deal below par, it is not the examiner's judgment that he is a venal man of evil purpose or that he is a congenital liar. Rather, Robinson is, in the examiner's judgment, typical of a type of modern American businessman. With financial success as the goal, he is in a hurry to get on with the job and more interested in results than means or methods. As far as candor is concerned in most matters, he is no different than others. However, the rules under which he plays regrettably appear to countenance misrepresentation to the Government as a kind of "white lie." It can, of course, be cogently urged that such people are precisely the kind that should not be the holders of Government franchises. On the other hand, the Commission is not in the business of reforming the morals of the American businessman. Its principal concern in the field of license qualification is selection of reliable persons who can be counted on to carry out their public-service responsibilities. A chastened malefactor is sometimes a better bet to carry out responsibilities under law than one who has not been subjected to discipline for wrongdoing. It is the examiner's belief that Robinson is now truly contrite. In this connection, it should be noted that on the stand he testified:

> * * * I have made a mistake in this thing. I'm very sorry. It hasn't happened at the station since. And I promise that it won't happen in the future (Tr. 167).

It is the examiner's opinion those words were spoken with real conviction.

23. The examiner cannot view the testimony of the 17 witnesses who testified on behalf of Robinson as being persuasive insofar as that testimony is directed to the overall merit of WDKD's performance from the public-interest standpoint. Those who have nothing to eat but rice like rice. WDKD is the only radio station for miles around. Moreover, there can be no doubt that the station is, and has been, an effective advertising medium for local merchants and in all probability an inexpensive one. Most of the witnesses who testified for Robinson had good reason to admire the station for reasons other than the quality of its programing. To the merchant, loss of inexpensive and effective aural billboard space is no less regrettable than loss of such space from a highway sign. There is, however, no blinking the fact that Robinson did marshal a formidable expression of community support for retention of his station's license. This is no matter to be lightly brushed aside. It is not now and never has been the policy of this Commission to approach its regulatory responsibility in paternalistic fashion. The wishes of local communities, as far as this examiner is aware, have always been given great weight by the FCC in the performance of its duties. In a Government such as ours, politics, in the highest sense of the term, requires such an approach to regulation. This is not to say that local desires invariably counterbalance national interest or that regulatory action may not be required in the national interest which is at odds with local desires. It does mean, in the latter case, that local sentiment has been placed in the scales with national interest and found wanting. In his final evaluation here, the examiner gives great weight to the expressions of local support collected by Robinson in defense of his license. By the same token, however, he is not unmindful that the disposition that will eventually be made of this case may have large-scale national implications in the field of broadcasting since it will reflect the policy of the Commission not only in respect of obscenity over the air but in regard to programing that misses by far measuring up to what the Commission has suggested is required to meet the public-interest standard.[29]

24. As a final consideration running in Robinson's favor, the following might be noted. The determination that will be ultimately made of this matter may also be interpreted by the industry and the public as one of a series of events signalizing abandonment by the Commission of a laissez faire policy of regulation in the field of programing and indicative of a rebirth of interest and concern by the Commission in that area of station operation. (See counsel's letter to Robinson, par. 4 of the findings.) In the complex of broadcasting in the United States, WDKD is not a large operation. If such an interpretation as that suggested is correct, it would be regrettable that the significance of the pronouncement be watered down by any conflicting interpretation to the effect that a small station is being harshly used merely as a whipping boy in a regulatory gesture.

25. The question of what to do with the applications at issue is a close one. The examiner has spent no little time and thought in considering the possibility of conditional renewal with forfeiture. Section 503(b) of the Communications Act of 1934 provides:

> (b) (1) Any licensee or permittee of a broadcast station who—
> (A) willfully or repeatedly fails to operate such station substantially as set forth in his license or permit,
> (B) willfully or repeatedly fails to observe any of the provisions of this Act or of any rule or regulation of the Commission prescribed under authority of this Act or under authority of any treaty ratified by the United States,
> (C) fails to observe any final cease and desist order issued by the Commission,
> (D) violates section 317(c) or section 509(a)(4) of this act, or
> (E) violates section 1304, 1343, or 1464 of title 18 of the United States Code,
>
> shall forfeit to the United States a sum not to exceed $1,000. Each day during which such violation occurs shall constitute a separate offense. Such forfeiture shall be in addition to any other penalty provided by this act.
> (2) No forfeiture liability under paragraph (1) of this subsection (b) shall attach unless a written notice of apparent liability shall have been issued by the Commission and such notice has been received by the licensee or permittee or the Commission shall have sent such notice by registered or certified mail to the last known address of the licensee or permittee. A licensee or permittee so notified shall be granted an opportunity to show in writing, within such reasonable period as the Commission shall by regulations prescribe, why he should not be held liable. A notice issued under this paragraph shall not be valid unless it sets forth the date, facts, and nature of the act or omission with which the licensee or permittee is charged and specifically identifies the particular provision or provisions of the law, rule, or regulation or the license, permit, or cease and desist order involved.
> (3) No forfeiture liability under paragraph (1) of this subsection (b) shall attach for any violation occurring more than one year prior to the date of issuance of the notice of apparent liability and in no event shall the forfeiture imposed for the acts or omissions set forth in any notice of apparent liability exceed $10,000.[96]

[96] Sec. 503 was amended to read as above by Public Law 86–752, approved Sept. 13, 1960, 74 Stat. 889.

The foregoing provision of the act appears to provide a good auxiliary tool for use in proceedings such as this. It might well be that the public interest would best be served here, all things considered, with ultimate disposition being made in some such fashion as the following: Payment by Robinson into the Treasury of the United States of $1,000 for each day the record shows obscenity was broadcast over his station; continuation of license on temporary basis pending Robinson filing with the Commission (1) a statement to the effect that he has read and studied the "*Commission's Policy Report on Programing*," 20 R.R. 1901, particularly those parts dealing with licensee responsibility, programing to meet a diversity of community needs and the undesirability of a station carrying an excess of commercial continuity; "section 312(a) of the Communications Act," with particular attention to subparagraph 1 of that section which, among other things, authorizes the Commission to revoke licenses for false statements knowingly made and for violations of 18 U.S.C. 1464; and "*FCC* v. *WOKO, Inc.*," 329 U.S. 223 (1946), a case involving refusal to renew a license for false information having been filed; and (2) an amended renewal application reflecting that he has, in fact, read the foregoing material in the particulars mentioned. Upon receipt of such statement and amended application, license would be renewed for a 1-year period with the understanding that at the end of that period, if the performance of the station measured up to the representations made in the amended application, license would issue for a regular term.

26. Imposition of such forfeiture sanction as that suggested above appears to be out of the question. This is so not because this proceeding fails to provide precisely the kind of situation with which Congress apparently intended section 503(b) to cope. Nor is it because of any lack of opportunity to be heard afforded Robinson. The sanction cannot be imposed because the notice provisions of sections 503(b) (2) and (3) have not been met in this proceeding. Since forfeiture law is involved, provisions must be strictly construed and procedures provided by such law scrupulously observed.

27. The examiner appears to have no alternative but to recommend grant or denial of the applications at issue. In his opinion, it would be unconscionable to permit Robinson to come off here with only token punishment for the grievous deviation he has permitted his station to make from the public-interest norm. It is also important that disposition here should stand as a warning to others that such licensee misconduct is not to be condoned. In the end, to the examiner, these considerations override those running in favor of granting the applications.

Accordingly, *It is ordered*, This 8th day of December 1961, that unless an appeal from this initial decision is taken to the Commission by any of the parties, or unless the Commission reviews the initial decision on its own motion in accordance with the provisions of section 1.153 of the rules, the applications of E. G. Robinson, Jr., tr/as Palmetto Broadcasting Co. (WDKD), Kingstree, S.C., for renewal of license and for license to cover construction permit, *Are denied*.

NOTES

[1] On the subject posed by the issue, Robinson's position appears to fall into four categories: (1) his lack of knowledge of the character of Walker's broadcasts; (2) the conventional nature of his station's organizational setup and his de facto management of all departments; (3) Walker's popularity and good works; and (4) his illness during which time the reins of management slipped from his fingers. After considerable thought, the examiner has chosen to present Robinson's testimony on the subject contemplated by the issue, in digest form, in the order in which it developed at the hearing. Only in this fashion can the full flavor of applicant's position on the matter be portrayed.

[2] In various applications filed with the Commission in the past, Robinson failed to report his ownership of the liquor store. This reporting failure, which is asserted to have been inadvertent, is the subject of a petition to amend filed during the course of hearing (Tr. 116–117).

[3] A boy whom Walker aided in getting eyeglasses, Robert McDonald, was present, with his mother, and was identified at the hearing.

[4] Although Green on occasion signed station correspondence over the title "Assistant Manager," it was merely an assumption of title on his part on the basis of his conversation with Robinson. Further, it might be here noted that Green did hold one staff meeting (Tr. 654, 655).

[5] Ward did testify that he understood that on June 13, 1960, a staff meeting was held at WDKD. He did not attend the meeting (Tr. 537).

[6] Items contained on pp. 20 and 21 were presented during the period specifically mentioned in issue 3 (Jan. 1, 1960–Apr. 30, 1960).

[7] This comment followed a story concerning a husband whose wife beat him each morning; the husband bought a bulldog and the wife beat the bulldog.

[8] At the end of this item Walker offered 10 printed copies of the lie he had just told for $1. This was followed by an offer of Bibles in exchange for coupons.

[9] This explanation followed reference to "noise distortion."

[10] This followed comment concerning Mickey Spillane beating up women before loving them since they then could not fight back.

[11] Negligible portions of the foregoing findings relating to the history and composition of Kingstree are officially noticed.

[12] Time on the air for the station during the composite week was: Sunday, 10 hours and 44½ minutes; Monday, 12 hours and 27 minutes; Tuesday, 13 hours; Wednesday, 13 hours and 12 minutes; Thursday, 14 hours and 12 minutes; Friday, 14 hours and 29½ minutes; Saturday, 13 hours and 27 minutes.

[13] Robinson in his renewal application reported the number of spot announcements carried by WDKD during the composite week as 1,077 (FCC exhibit 4).

[14] A participating program is a program the time for which is not paid for by a sponsor but in which commercial spot announcements are intermittently broadcast throughout the program.

[15] In logging the "Rise and Shine" participating program, the station, as it did with all other participating shows, followed the practice of logging the last spot announcement separately from the program, thus disassociating the spot from the participating program. There seems to be no rational basis for this practice and the examiner in the interests of brevity has counted such announcements as one of the spot announcements carried during the participating program.

[16] A sustaining program is one not paid for by a sponsor.

[17] A sponsored program, or commercial program, is a program the time for which is paid for by a sponsor. Commercial messages on behalf of the sponsor are usually carried at the beginning of the program, at the end of the program, and not infrequently during the program.

[18] Robinson at first testified that the station carried an hour-and-a-half religious program called "Hymn Time." Later he testified that this program was logged "commercial"-"entertainment." He also testified that the "Voice of Pentecost" was a 30-minute program. Introduced in applicant's behalf was an exhibit entitled "Public Service Type Programs and Announcements." This exhibit lists "Voice of Pentecost" as a 14½-minute program. Robinson testified that the station also carried on Sunday afternoons a live religious quartet originating in Lake City, S.C. Although the "Public Service Type Programs and Announcements" exhibit scrupulously lists WDKD's religious programs, it does not list any such program as the quartet. The exhibit does show, however, that the station did regularly carry, weekly, a 14½-minute program entitled "Catholic Hour" (Tr. 168–171, WDKD exhibit 10).

[19] On the whole record, it is doubtful if it can be found that WDKD carried any educational programs during its last renewal period. There is testimony in the record that educational programs may have been carried over the station in the past. (See par. 51, infra.) However, neither applicant's exhibit, "Public Service Type Programs and Announcements," nor Bureau counsel's analysis of WDKD's programing during the composite week shows any educational programs. The station did, however, from time to time carry announcements on behalf of schools within their service area (Tr. 172, WDKD exhibit 10, and FCC exhibit 3).

[20] Robinson appears to have given the station a little the best of it on regularity of news headlines and duration of news programs. Bureau counsel's analysis of applicant's composite week disclosed only three news headlines. These were carried at 1:59:30 on Wednesday, Thursday, and Friday. Moreover, reference to the time spent daily on news programs during the composite week shows little likelihood that 10- and 15-minute news programs were carried over WDKD with any such frequency as Robinson's testimony suggests. Bureau's analysis indicates that news and headlines were carried more on the order of their presentation as described in paragraph 46, infra (FCC exhibit 3).

[21] In support of Robinson's testimony here, it should be noted that applicant's exhibit "Public Service Type Programs and Announcements," which lists the programs and announcements carried by WDKD on behalf of nonprofit organizations for the year 1958, all but June, October, and November of 1959 and all but November and December of 1960 is slightly over 150 pages long, with programs and announcements listed on each page single space to an item. The examiner counted 1,880 programs of this type carried by the station during the period covered. The average in round figures is 60 per month, or roughly 2 a day. From the examiner's inspection, it would appear that virtually all of these programs were recorded and furnished by the sponsoring agency. Another exhibit of applicant's which speaks on behalf of its programing in the category under discussion is entitled "Awards Received by WDKD During Last Renewal Period." This exhibit shows that expressions of commendation were received by the station from the Army, the Thor Research Center for Better Farm Living, Navy-Marine Corps, National Guard, Crippled Children's Society, Methodist Men's Hour, U.S. Olympic Association, and U.S. Department of Agriculture (WDKD exhibits 10 and 11).

[22] Title 18 U.S.C. 1464: "Whoever utters any obscene, indecent, or profane language by means of radio communication shall be fined not more than $10,000 or imprisoned not more than two years, or both." June 25, 1948, ch. 645, 62 Stat. 769.

[23] Webster's New International Dictionary (unabridged, 2d ed., 1934) defines "prurient" in pertinent part as follows: "* * * Itching; longing; uneasy with desire or longing; of persons, having itching, morbid, or lascivious longings; of desire, curiosity, or propensity, lewd * * *."

[24] As far as the examiner has been able to ascertain, this is the first case the Federal Communications Commission has had where questionable language over the air has been at issue in a renewal proceeding. The Federal Radio Commission did have such a case, *Trinity Methodist Church South* v. *Federal Radio Commission*, 61 App. D.C. 311 (cert. den., 284 U.S. 685). Based upon his review of more recent "free speech" decisions, it is this examiner's considered opinion that there is room for doubt that the courts would now adopt the somewhat sweeping rationale of that decision.

[25] *Regina* v. *Hicklin* (1868) L.R. 3 Q.B. 360.

[26] To those who may regard the examiner's "strawmen" as falling outside the realm of possibility, let them again review the Walker anecdotes set out in pars. 28, 32, and 38, above.

[27] Webster's New International Dictionary (unabridged, 2d ed., 1934) defines "smut" in pertinent part as follows; "* * * 3. Indecent or ribald language, jests, etc.; obscenity."

[28] In this connection, it may be of interest to recall that at WDKD not only were programs interrupted by spot announcements but programs were interrupted by programs. See par. 46, above.

[29] The examiner should not depart from consideration of the testimony of Robinson's witnesses without comment on an aspect of the case upon which the Bureau lays much stress in its proposed findings. It will be noted that Louie L. Law and Donald L. Taylor both testified that they had visited the employer of one of the Bureau's witnesses, Carroll Godwin. Law testified that the purpose of the visit was to insure that Godwin was going to testify to the truth in the instant proceeding. Taylor testified that the purpose of the visit was to determine whether Godwin was antagonistic toward WDKD. (See pars. 53 and 55, above.) Moreover, it should be found here and noted, that Reverend Drennan testified that Law and Taylor, both of whom were members of his church, had called upon him and told him that if he testified in the instant matter he would hurt himself in the community and would also hurt his church (Tr. 563). The examiner does not believe that the interrogation of Law and Taylor in connection with the Godwin matter by any means developed the full story behind the visit to Godwin's employer. Further, he fully accepts the testimony of Reverend Drennan on the visit of Law and Taylor to him. He has no doubt that the fact that two of the town's leading bankers were busying themselves interviewing prospective witnesses and their employers did not make Bureau counsel's task any easier in assembling evidence with which to respond to the issues. The examiner does not believe, however, that the record will support findings that these interviews can be found to reflect unfavorably upon Robinson or that they were instituted or conducted by Law and Taylor with bad intent. Rather, they appear to be overzealous efforts inaugurated solely by Law and Taylor to help a friend and business associate who was in trouble, a course of action passively viewed by Robinson with gratitude. Proof that Robinson triggered the visits is missing. Proof, other than that which can be drawn from the circumstances themselves, that the intent of Law and Taylor in making the visits was bad is also missing. In this connection, it is important to note that neither the testimony of Godwin or Reverend Drennan appears to have in any way been inhibited by the visits. The examiner closes the door on these incidents with the observation that in his view it is poor judgment on the part of anyone not offically connected with a matter in hearing to discuss with witnesses or the employer of witnesses anything having to do with their prospective testimony. Friendship and misplaced zeal in this area could result in conduct falling within the purview of title 18, section 1505, of the United States Code, which provides in pertinent part:

> Whoever corruptly or by threats or force, or by any threatening letter or communication, endeavors to influence, intimidate, or impede any witness in any proceeding pending before any department or agency of the United States. * * *
>
> * * * * * * *
>
> Shall be fined not more than $5,000 or imprisoned not more than five years or both (June 25, 1948, ch. 645, 62 Stat. 770).

AFTER CONSIDERING COMPLAINTS THAT PACIFICA FOUNDATION FM RADIO STATIONS HAD BROADCAST OFFENSIVE PROGRAMS, THE FEDERAL COMMUNICATIONS COMMISSION DECLARES: "WE RECOGNIZE THAT AS SHOWN BY THE COMPLAINTS HERE, SUCH PROVOCATIVE PROGRAMING AS HERE INVOLVED MAY OFFEND SOME LISTENERS. BUT THIS DOES NOT MEAN THAT THOSE OFFENDED HAVE THE RIGHT, THROUGH THE COMMISSION'S LICENSING POWER, TO RULE SUCH PROGRAMING OFF THE AIRWAYS. WERE THIS THE CASE, ONLY THE WHOLLY INOFFENSIVE, THE BLAND, COULD GAIN ACCESS TO THE RADIO MICROPHONE OR TV CAMERA."

Pacifica Foundation, 36 F.C.C. 147 (1964)

BEFORE THE

FEDERAL COMMUNICATIONS COMMISSION

WASHINGTON, D.C. 20554

In re Applications of
PACIFICA FOUNDATION
For Initial License of Station KPFK (Noncommercial Educational FM), at Los Angeles, Calif. — File No. BLED-374
For Renewal of Licenses of Stations KPFA-FM and KPFB (Educational FM), at Berkeley, Calif., and Station WBAI-FM, New York, N.Y. — Files Nos. BRH-723, BRED-115, BRH-13
Consent To Transfer of Control — File No. BTC-4284

MEMORANDUM OPINION AND ORDER

(Adopted January 22, 1964)

BY THE COMMISSION: COMMISSIONER LEE CONCURRING AND ISSUING A STATEMENT.

1. The Commission has before it for consideration the above-pending applications of the listed broadcast stations licensed to Pacifica Foundation. There are three aspects to our consideration: (*a*) Certain programing issues raised by complaints; (*b*) issues of possible Communist Party affiliation of principals of Pacifica; and (*c*) a question of possible unauthorized transfer of control. We shall consider each in turn.

2. *The programing issues.*—The principal complaints are concerned with five programs: (i) a December 12, 1959, broadcast over KPFA, at 10 p.m., of certain poems by Lawrence Ferlinghetti (read by the poet himself); (ii) "The Zoo Story," a recording of the Edward Albee play broadcast over KPFK at 11 p.m., January 13, 1963; (iii) "Live and Let Live," a program broadcast over KPFK at 10:15 p.m. on January 15, 1963, in which eight homosexuals discussed their attitudes and problems; (iv) a program broadcast over KPFA at 7:15 p.m. on January 28, 1963, in which the poem, "Ballad of the Despairing Husband," was read by the author Robert Creeley; and (v) "The Kid," a program broadcast at 11 p.m. on January 8, 1963, over KPFA, which consisted of readings by Edward Pomerantz from his unfinished novel of the same name. The complaints charge that these programs were offensive or "filthy" in nature, thus raising the type of issue we recently considered in *Palmetto Bctg. Co.*, 33 FCC 483; 34 FCC 101. We shall consider the above five matters in determining whether, on an overall basis, the licensee's programing met the public-interest standard laid down in the Communications Act.[1] *Report and Statement of Policy re: Commission En Banc Programing Inquiry*, 20 Pike & Fischer R.R. 1901.

3. When the Commission receives complaints of the general nature here involved, its usual practice is to refer them to the licensee so as to afford the latter an opportunity to comment. When the Commission reviews, on an overall basis, the station's operation at the time of renewal, it thus has before it a complete file, containing all the sides of any matter which may have arisen during the license period. Specifically, with respect to the programing issue in this case, the Commission, barring the exceptions noted in the *Programing Statement* (*supra*, at p. 1909), is not concerned with individual programs—nor is it at any time concerned with matters essentially of licensee taste or judgment. Cf. *Palmetto Bctg. Co.*, *supra*, paragraph 22. As shown by the cited case, its very limited concern in this type of case is whether, upon the overall examination, some substantial pattern of operation inconsistent with the public-interest standard clearly and patently emerges. Unlike *Palmetto* where there was such a substantial pattern (id. at par. 23; see par. 7, infra), here we are dealing with a few isolated programs, presented over a 4-year period. It would thus appear that there is no substantial problem, on an overall basis, warranting further inquiry.[2] While this would normally conclude the matter, we have determined to treat the issues raised by Pacifica's response to the complaints, because we think it would serve a useful purpose, both to the industry and the public. We shall therefore turn to a more detailed consideration of the issues raised by the complaints as to these five programs. Because of Pacifica's different response to the complaints as to (i) and (iv), paragraph 2 above, we shall treat these two broadcasts separately. (See pars. 6–7, infra.)

4. There is, we think, no question but that the broadcasts of the programs, "The Zoo Story," "Live and Let Live," and "The Kid," lay well within the licensee's judgment under the public-interest standard. The situation here stands on an entirely different footing than *Palmetto*, *supra*, where the licensee had devoted a substantial period of his broadcast day to material which we found to be patently offensive—however much we weighted that standard in the licensee's favor—and as to which programing the licensee himself never asserted that it was not offensive or vulgar, *or that it served the needs of his area or had any redeeming features*. In this case, Pacifica has stated its judgment that the three above-cited programs served the public interests and specifically, the needs and interests of its listening public. Thus, it has pointed out that in its judgment, "The Zoo Story" is a "serious work of drama" by an eminent and "provocative playwright"—that it is "an honest and courageous play" which Americans "who do not live near Broadway ought to have the opportunity to hear and experience. * * *" Similarly, as to "The Kid," Pacifica states, with supporting authority, that Mr. Pomerantz is an author who has obtained notable recognition for his writings and whose readings from his unfinished novel were fully in the public interest as a serious work meriting the attention of its listeners; Pacifica further states that prior to broadcast, the tape was auditioned by one of its employees who edited out two phrases because they did not meet Pacifica's broadcast standards of good taste; and that while "certain minor swear words are used, * * * these fit well within the context of the material being read and conform to the standards of acceptability of reasonably intelligent listeners." Finally, as to the program, "Live and Let Live," Pacifica states that "so long as the program is handled in good taste, there is no reason why subjects like homosexuality should not be discussed on the air"; and that it "conscientiously believes that the American people will be better off as a result of hearing a constructive discussion of the problem rather than leaving the subject to ignorance and silence."

5. We recognize that as shown by the complaints here, such provocative programing as here involved may offend some listeners. But this does not mean that those offended have the right, through the Commission's licensing power, to rule such programing off the airwaves. Were this the case, only the wholly inoffensive, the bland, could gain access to the radio microphone or TV camera. No such drastic curtailment can be countenanced under the Constitution, the Communications Act, or the Commission's policy, which has consistently sought to insure "the maintenance of radio and television as a medium of freedom of speech and freedom of expression for the people of the Nation as a whole" (*Editorializing Report*, 13 FCC 1246, 1248). In saying this, we do not mean to indicate that those who have complained about the foregoing programs are in the wrong as to the worth of these programs and should listen to them. This is a matter solely for determination by the individual listeners. Our function, we stress, is not to pass on the merits of the program—to commend or to frown. Rather, as we stated (par. 3), it is the very limited one of assaying, at the time of renewal, whether the licensee's programing, on an overall basis, has been in the public interest and, in the context of this issue, whether he has made programing judgments reasonably related to the public interest. This does not pose a close question in the case: Pacifica's judgments as to the above programs clearly fall within the very great discretion which the act wisely vests in the licensee. In this connection, we also note that Pacifica took into account the nature of the broadcast medium when it scheduled such programing for the late evening hours (after 10 p.m., when the number of children in the listening audience is at a minimum).[3]

6. As to the Ferlinghetti and Creeley programs, the licensee asserts that in both instances, some passages did not measure up to "Pacifica's own standards of good taste." Thus, it states that it did not carefully screen the Ferlinghetti tape to see if it met its standards, "because it relied upon Mr. Ferlinghetti's national reputation and also upon the fact that the tape came to it from a reputable FM station." It acknowledges that this was a mistake in its procedures and states that "in the future, Pacifica will make its own review of all broadcasts. * * *" With respect to the Creeley passage (i.e., the poem, "Ballad of a Despairing Husband"),[4] Pacifica again states that in its judgment it should not have been broadcast. It "does not excuse the broadcast of the poem in question," but it does explain how the poem "slipped by" KPFA's drama and literature editor who auditioned the tape. It points out that prior to the offending poem, Mr. Creeley, who "has a rather flat, monotonous voice," read 18 other perfectly acceptable poems—and that the station's editor was so lulled thereby that he did not catch the few offensive words on the 19th poem. It also points out that each of the nine poems which followed was again perfectly acceptable, and that before rebroadcasting the poem on its Los Angeles station, it deleted the objectionable verse.

7. In view of the foregoing, we find no impediment to renewal on this score. We are dealing with two isolated errors in the licensee's application of its own standards—one in 1959 and the other in 1963. The explanations given for these two errors are credible. Therefore, even assuming, arguendo, that the broadcasts were inconsistent with the public-interest standard, it is clear that no unfavorable action upon the renewal applications is called for. The standard of public interest is not so rigid that an honest mistake or error on the part of a licensee results in drastic action against him where his overall record demonstrates a reasonable effort to serve the needs and interests of his community. (See note 2, supra.) Here again, this case contrasts sharply with *Palmetto*, where instead of two isolated instances, years apart, we found that the patently offensive material was broadcast for a substantial period of the station's broadcast day for many years. (See par. 3, supra.)

8. We find, therefore, that the programing matters raised with respect to the Pacifica renewals pose no bar to a grant of renewal.[5] Our holding, as is true of all such holdings in this sensitive area, is necessarily based on, and limited to, the facts of the particular case. But we have tried to stress here, as in *Palmetto*, an underlying policy—that the licensee's judgment in this freedom-of-speech area is entitled to very great weight and that the Commission, under the public-interest standard, will take action against the licensee at the time of renewal only where the facts of the particular case, established in a hearing record, flagrantly call for such action. We have done so because we are charged under the act with "promoting the larger and more effective use of radio in the public interest" (sec. 303(g)), and obviously, in the discharge of that responsibility, must take every precaution to avoid inhibiting broadcast licensees' efforts at experimenting or diversifying their programing. Such diversity of programing has been the goal of many Commission policies (e.g., multiple ownership, development of UHF, the fairness doctrine). Clearly, the Commission must remain faithful to that goal in discharging its functions in the actual area of programing itself.

9. *Communist Party affiliation issue.*—Under the public-interest standard, it is relevant and important for the Commission to determine in certain cases whether its applicants, or the principals of its applicants, for broadcast licenses or radio operator licenses are members of the Communist Party or of organizations which advocate or teach the overthrow of the Government by force or violence. Sections 307(a), 307(d), 308(b), 309, 47 U.S.C. 307(a), 307(d), 308(b), 309; *Borrow* v. *F.C.C.*, 285 F. 2d 666, 669, *cert. den.*, 366 U.S. 904; *Cronan* v. *F.C.C.*, 285 F. 2d 288 (C.A.D.C.), *cert. den.*, 366 U.S. 904; *Blumenthal* v. *F.C.C.*, 318 F. 2d 276 (C.A.D.C.), *cert. den.*, Case No. 1026, June 3, 1963; cf. *Beilan* v. *Board of Education*, 357 U.S. 399, 405; *Adler* v.

Board of Education, 342 U.S. 485, 493; *Garner* v. *Los Angeles Board*, 341 U.S. 716, 720; *Speiser* v. *Randall*, 357 U.S. 513, 527. The Commission therefore has followed a policy of inquiring as to Communist Party membership in those radio-licensing situations where it has information making such inquiry appropriate. Because of information coming to the Commission's attention from several sources, the Commission requested information from Pacifica Foundation on this score. On the basis of information obtained from Government sources, the foundation, and our own inquiry, we do not find any evidence warranting further inquiry into the qualifications in this respect of Pacifica Foundation.

10. *The unauthorized transfer of control.*—Until September 30, 1961, control of Pacifica was vested in executive members, who elected a committee of directors, who in turn elected officers and controlled the foundation's activities. On September 30, 1961, the executive membership and the committee of directors were abolished. In their place, Pacifica is controlled—pursuant to its bylaws—by a board of directors, which elects officers and controls the foundation's activities. The new bylaws which accomplished this result were appropriately reported to the Commission at the time they were adopted. However, no application for consent to a transfer of control was then filed.

11. This matter was brought to Pacifica's attention by a letter of February 7, 1963. The licensee's response of April 26, 1963, takes the position that no transfer of actual control had in fact taken place. However, in the event that the Commission deemed an application for consent to transfer of control to be necessary, Pacifica simultaneously filed such an application (BTC–4284). Pacifica argues that in actual practice, control had been in the so-called committee of directors, and that this practice had been formalized in an amendment to the bylaws of October 20, 1960, which read, in relevant part:

> Except as hereinafter provided, the powers of this corporation shall be exercised, its property controlled, and its affairs conducted by a Committee of Directors which shall consist of 21 Executive Members of this corporation.

The new board of directors, elected on September 30, 1961, was identical with the then existing committee of directors, and the officers of the foundation likewise remained the same.

12. Although the September 30, 1961, revision in the bylaws does appear to have been only the formal recognition of a development in the actual control of Pacifica which had occurred over a period of years, and although there may well be merit in Pacifica's contention that changes in the composition of its executive membership (or, for that matter, of its present board of directors) should not be regarded as transfers of control, the September 30, 1961, revision in the bylaws did transfer legal control. Prior to that date, the executive membership elected directors, who elected officers. After that date, the directors themselves have elected new directors, as well as officers. The fact that the legal control vested in the executive members did not, in practice, amount to actual control does not mean that its existence can be ignored—any more than the legal control of a 51-percent stockholder in a commercial corporation can be ignored because he fails to exercise it. See *ABC-Paramount Merger Case*, 8 Pike & Fischer R.R. 541, 619; *Press-Union Publishing Co., Inc.*, 7 Pike & Fischer R.R. 83, 96; *Universal Carloading Co.* v. *Railroad Retirement Board*, 71 F. Supp. 369.

13. On the other hand, it is clear that Pacifica did not seek to conceal or misrepresent any facts concerning those who control its affairs, and that the failure to file involved was an excusable one. We therefore grant the pending application for transfer of control.

CONCLUSION

14. In view of the foregoing, *It is ordered*, This 22d day of January 1964, that the above-entitled applications of Pacifica Foundation *Are granted* as serving the public interest, convenience, and necessity.

CONCURRING STATEMENT OF COMMISSIONER ROBERT E. LEE

I concur in the action of the Commission in granting the several applications of Pacifica Foundation. However, I feel constrained to comment on at least one program coming to our attention insofar as it may or may not reflect these stations' program policies.

Having listened carefully and painfully to a 1½-hour tape recording of a program involving self-professed homosexuals, I am convinced that the program was designed to be, and succeeded in being, contributory to nothing but sensationalism. The airing of a program dealing with sexual aberrations is not to my mind, per se, a violation of good taste nor contrary to the public interest. When these subjects are discussed by physicians and sociologists, it is conceivable that the public could benefit. But a panel of eight homosexuals discussing their experiences and past history does not approach the treatment of a delicate subject one could expect by a responsible broadcaster. A microphone in a bordello, during slack hours, could give us similar information on a related subject. Such programs, obviously designed to be lurid and to stir the public curiosity, have little place on the air.

I do not hold myself to be either a moralist or a judge of taste. Least of all do I have a clear understanding of what may constitute obscenity in broadcasting.

FOOTNOTES

[1] The Commission may also enforce the standard of sec. 1464 of title 18 (dealing with "obscene, indecent, or profane language"). See secs. 312 (a), (b); sec. 503(b)(1)(E). In our view, enforcement proceedings under sec. 1464 are not warranted, and therefore, no further consideration need be given this section.

[2] While, for reasons developed in this opinion, it is unnecessary to detail the showings here, we have examined the licensee's overall showings as to its stations' operations and find that those operations did serve the needs and interests of the licensee's areas. *Programing Statement, supra,* at pp. 1913–1916. In this connection, we have also taken into account the showing made in the letter of Apr. 16, 1963.

[3] Pacifica states that it "is sensitive to its responsibilities to its listening audience and carefully schedules for late night broadcasts those programs which may be misunderstood by children although thoroughly acceptable to an adult audience."

[4] The program containing this passage was a taped recording of Mr. Creeley's readings of selections from his poetry to students at the University of California. KPFA broadcasts many such poetry readings at the university, which are recorded by a university employee for the school's archives (and made available to the station).

[5] One other programing aspect deserves emphasis. Complaint has also been made concerning Pacifica's presentation of "far-left" programing. Pacifica has stated that it follows a policy of presenting programs covering the widest range of the political or controversial issue spectrum—from the members of the Communist Party on the left to members of the John Birch Society on the right. Again, we point out that such a policy (which must, of course, be carried out consistently with the requirements of the fairness doctrine) is within the licensee's area of programing judgment.

THE FEDERAL COMMUNICATIONS COMMISSION IMPOSES A ONE HUNDRED DOLLAR FORFEITURE ON WUHY-FM, PHILADELPHIA, FOR BROADCASTING INDECENT MATERIAL: "AND HERE IT IS CRUCIAL TO BEAR IN MIND THE DIFFERENCE BETWEEN RADIO AND OTHER MEDIA. UNLIKE A BOOK WHICH REQUIRES THE DELIBERATE ACT OF PURCHASING AND READING (OR A MOTION PICTURE WHERE ADMISSION TO PUBLIC EXHIBITION MUST BE ACTIVELY SOUGHT), BROADCASTING IS DISSEMINATED GENERALLY TO THE PUBLIC . . . UNDER CIRCUMSTANCES WHERE RECEPTION REQUIRES NO ACTIVITY OF THIS NATURE . . . . WE PROPOSE NO CHANGE FROM OUR COMMITMENT TO PROMOTING ROBUST, WIDE-OPEN DEBATE . . . . SIMPLY STATED, OUR POSITION—LIMITED TO THE FACTS OF THIS CASE—IS THAT SUCH DEBATE DOES NOT REQUIRE THAT PERSONS BEING INTERVIEWED OR STATION EMPLOYEES ON TALK PROGRAMS HAVE THE RIGHT TO BEGIN THEIR SPEECH WITH, 'S--T, MAN...', OR USE 'F----G,' OR 'MOTHER F----G' AS GRATUITOUS ADJECTIVES THROUGHOUT THEIR SPEECH. THIS FOSTERS NO DEBATE, SERVES NO SOCIAL PURPOSE, AND WOULD DRASTICALLY CURTAIL THE USEFULNESS OF RADIO FOR MILLIONS OF PEOPLE."

In Re WUHY-FM, F.C.C. 70-346 (1970)

BEFORE THE
FEDERAL COMMUNICATIONS COMMISSION
WASHINGTON, D.C. 20554

In Re
WUHY-FM, EASTERN EDUCATION RADIO,
4548 MARKET STREET, PHILADELPHIA, PA.

(Adopted April 1, 1970; Released April 3, 1970)
NOTICE OF APPARENT LIABILITY

BY THE COMMISSION: CHAIRMAN BURCH CONCURRING IN THE RESULT; COMMISSIONER COX CONCURRING IN PART AND DISSENTING IN PART AND ISSUING A STATEMENT; COMMISSIONER JOHNSON DISSENTING AND ISSUING A STATEMENT; COMMISSIONER H. REX LEE ABSENT.

1. This constitutes Notice of Apparent Liability for forfeiture pursuant to Section 503(b)(2) of the Communications Act of 1934, as amended.

2. *The facts.* Noncommercial educational radio station WUHY–FM is licensed to Eastern Education Radio, Philadelphia, Pennsylvania. On January 4, 1970, WUHY–FM broadcasted its weekly program "Cycle II" from 10:00 P.M. to 11:00 P.M.[1] This broadcast featured an interview with one Jerry Garcia, leader and member of "The Grateful Dead", a California rock and roll musical group. The interview was recorded on tape in Mr. Garcia's hotel room in New York City on Saturday afternoon, January 3, 1970. The interview was conducted by Messrs. Steve Hill and David Stupplebeen, who are both architects in the Philadelphia area, and who have been engaged from time to time on a volunteer basis by WUHY–FM to assist in programming. Mr. Robert J. Bielecki, a full-time staff engineer for WUHY–FM, was in charge of the production as a volunteer producer;

Mr. Bielecki had been allowed supervision of "Cycle II" since its inception in November of 1969. Hill and Stupplebeen returned to Philadelphia Sunday afternoon about 4:00 P.M. (January 4, 1970) with the tape of the recorded interview. Hill spent the next three or four hours editing the tape; i.e., allowing for musical selections. Mr. Bielecki, who was engaged in routine engineering duties at the time, listened to portions of the tape from time to time. Neither Hill, Bielecki, nor Stupplebeen discussed the tape with Mr. Nathan Shaw, the station manager, nor did they seek his clearance in any way; Mr. Shaw, though not at the station, could have been reached at home.

3. During the interview, about 50 minutes in length, broadcast on January 4, 1970, Mr. Garcia expressed his views on ecology, music, philosophy, and interpersonal relations. See Appendix A for the example comments on these subjects, as set forth in the licensee's letter of February 12, 1970. His comments were frequently interspersed with the words "f - - k" and "s - - t", used as adjectives, or simply as an introductory expletive or substitute for the phrase, et cetera. Examples are:

S - - t man.
I must answer the phone 900 f - - - - n' times a day, man.
Right, and it sucks it right f - - - - - g out of ya, man.
That kind of s - - t.
It's f - - - - n' rotten man. Every f - - - - n' year.
. . . this s - - t.
. . . and all that s - - t—all that s - - t.
. . . and s - - t like that.
. . . so f - - - - - g long.
Everybody knows everybody so f - - - - - g well that . . . .
S - - t.
S - - t. I gotta get down there, man.
All that s - - t.
Readily available every f - - - - - g where.
Any of that s - - t either.
Political change is so f - - - - - g slow.

4. At the conclusion of the Garcia interview, Mr. Hill presented a person known as "Crazy Max", whose real name is not known to the licensee. "Crazy Max" had been a visitor to the station, and he told Hill, while listening to the Garcia interview, that if there were time left in the program he wanted to make some remarks about computers and society. There was a short period left, and "Crazy Max" delivered his message, which also used the word "f - - k." The licensee states that Mr. Hill did not know what "Crazy Max" was going to say in detail, or how he was going to say it. It adds that "Crazy Max" will not be allowed access to the microphone again.

5. In its letter of February 12, 1970, written in response to the Commission's request for comments on the January 4th broadcast,[2] the licensee further states:

The licensee has a standing policy, known to all personnel including Mr. Bielecki, that all taped program material which contains controversial subject matter or language must be reviewed by Mr. Nathan Shaw, the station manager of WUHY–FM. Mr. Bielecki, the producer of this program, did not bring the program to Mr. Shaw's attention. Neither Mr. Shaw nor any other person in the station management heard or reviewed the program before it was aired. Mr. Bielecki has been removed as a producer because of this infraction of station policy. "Cycle II" has been suspended as a program pending licensee review of this entire matter. Internal procedures to insure against a similar incident are being strengthened.

6. *Discussion—policy.* The issue in this case is not whether WUHY–FM may present the views of Mr. Garcia or "Crazy Max" on ecology, society, computers, and so on. Clearly that decision is a matter solely within the judgment of the licensee. See Section 326 of the Communications Act of 1934, as amended. Further, we stress, as we have before, the licensee's right to present provocative or unpopular programming which may offend some listeners. *In re Renewal of Pacifica*, 36 FCC 147, 149 (1964). It would markedly disserve the public interest, were the airwaves restricted only to inoffensive, bland material. Cf. *Red Lion Broadcasting Co., Inc.* v. *F.C.C.*, 395 U.S. 367 (1969). Further, the issue here does not involve presentation of a work of art or on-the-spot coverage of a bona fide news event.[3] Rather the narrow issue is whether the licensee may present previously taped interview or talk shows where the persons intersperse or begin their speech with expressions like, "S - - t, man . . .", ". . . and s - - t like that", or ". . . 900 f - - - - n' times", ". . . right f - - - - - g out of ya", etc.

7. We believe that if we have the authority, we have a duty to act to prevent the widespread use on broadcast outlets of such expressions in the above circumstances. For, the speech involved has no redeeming social value, and is patently offensive by contemporary community standards, with very serious consequences to the "public interest in the larger and more effective use of radio" (Section 303(g)). As to the first point, it conveys no thought to begin some speech with "S - - t, man . . .", or to use "f - - - - - g" as an adjective throughout the speech. We recognize that such speech is frequently used in some settings, but it is not employed in public ones. Persons who might use it without thought in a home, job or barracks setting generally avoid its usage when on a public conveyance, elevator, when testifying in court, etc. Similarly, its use can be avoided on radio without stifling in the slightest any thought which the person wishes to convey. In this connection, we note that stations have presented thousands of persons from all walks of life in talk or interview shows, without broadcasting language of the nature here involved. However much a person may like to talk this way, he has no right to do so in public arenas, and broadcasters can clearly insist that in talk shows, persons observe the requirement of eschewing such language.

8. This brings us to the second part of the analysis—the consequence to the public interest. First, if WUHY can broadcast an interview with Mr. Garcia where he begins sentences with "S - - t, man . . .", or uses "f - - - - - g" before word after word, just because he likes to talk that way, so also can any other person on radio. Newscasters or disc jockeys could use the same expressions, as could persons, whether moderators or participants, on talk shows, on the ground that this is the way they talk and it adds flavor or emphasis to their speech.[4] But the consequences of any such widespread practice would be to undermine the usefulness of radio to millions of others. For, these expressions are patently offensive to millions of listeners. *And here it is crucial to bear in mind the difference between radio and other media.* Unlike a book which requires the deliberate act of purchasing and reading (or a motion picture where admission to public exhibition must be actively sought), broadcasting is disseminated generally to the public (Section 3(o) of the Communications Act, 47 U.S.C. 153(o)) under circumstances where reception requires no activity of this nature. Thus, it comes directly into the home and frequently without any advance warning of its content. Millions daily turn the dial from station to station. While particular stations or programs are oriented to specific audiences, the fact is that by its very nature, thousands of others not within the "intended" audience may also see or hear portions of the broadcast.[5] Further, in that audience are very large numbers of children.[6] Were this type of programming (e.g., the WUHY interview with the above described language) to become widespread, it would drastically affect the use of radio by millions of people. No one could ever know, in home or car listening, when he or his children would encounter what he would regard as the most vile expressions serving no purpose but to shock, to pander to sensationalism. Very substantial numbers would either curtail using radio or would restrict their use to but a few channels or frequencies, abandoning the present practice of turning the dial to find some appealing program. In light of the foregoing considerations we note also that it is not a question of what a majority of licensees might do but whether such material is broadcast to a significant extent by any significant number of broadcasters. In short, in our judgment, increased use along the lines of this WUHY broadcast might well correspondingly diminish the use for millions of people. It is one thing to say, as we properly did in *Pacifica*, that no segment, however large its size, may rule out the presentation of unpopular views or of language in a work of art which offends some people; and it is quite another thing to say that WUHY has the right to broadcast an interview in which Mr. Garcia begins many sentences with, "S - - t, man . . .", an expression which conveys no thought, has no redeeming social value, and in the context of broadcasting,[7] drastically curtails the usefulness of the medium for millions of people.

9. For the foregoing reasons, and specifically to prevent any emerging trend in the broadcast field which would be inconsistent with the "larger and more effective use of radio", we conclude that we have a duty to act, if we have the authority to act. We turn now to the issue of our authority.

10. *Discussion—Law (Authority).* There are two aspects of this issue. First, there is the question of the applicability of 18 U.S.C. 1464, which makes it a criminal offense to "utter any obscene, indecent, or profane language by means of radio communication." This standard, we note, is incorporated in the Communications Act. See Sections 312(a)(6) and 503(b)(1)(E), 47 U.S.C. 312(a)(6); 503(b)(1)(E). The licensee urges that the broadcast was not obscene "because it did not have a dominant appeal to prurience or sexual matters" (Letter, p. 5). We agree, and thus find that the broadcast would not necessarily come within the standard laid down in *Memoirs* v. *Massachusetts*, 383 U.S. 413, 418 (1965); see also *Jacobelli* v. *Ohio*, 378 U.S. 184, 191 (1963); *Roth* v. *United States*, 354 U.S. 476 (1956). However, we believe that the statutory term, "indecent", should be applicable, and that, in the broadcast field, the standard for its applicability should be that the material broadcast is (a) patently offensive by contemporary community standards; and (b) is utterly without redeeming social value. The Court has made clear that different rules are appropriate for different media of expression in view of their varying natures. "Each method tends to present its own peculiar problems." *Burstyn* v. *Wilson*, 343 U.S. 495, 502–503 (1951). We have set forth in par. 8, *supra*, the reasons for applicability of the above standard in defining what is indecent in the broadcast field. We think that the factors set out in par. 8 are cogent, powerful considerations for the different standard in this markedly different field.

11. There is no precedent, judicial or administrative, for this case. There have been few opinions construing 18 U.S.C. 1464 (e.g., *Duncan* v. *U.S.*, 48 F. 2d 128 (C.C.A. Or. 1931), certiorari denied 283 U.S. 863; *Gagliardo* v. *U.S.*, 366 F. 2d 720 (1966)), and none in the broadcast field here involved. The issue whether the term, "indecent", has a meaning different from "obscene" in Section 1464 was raised in *Gagliardo* (366 F. 2d at pp. 725–26) but not resolved. Support for giving it a different meaning is indicated by *U.S.* v. *Limehouse*, 285 U.S. 424 (1932) which held that the word "filthy" which was added to the postal obscenity law by amendment, now 18 U.S.C. § 1461, meant something other than "obscene, lewd, or lascivious", and permitted a prosecution of the sender of a letter which "plainly related to sexual matters" and was "coarse, vulgar, disgusting, indecent; and unquestionably filthy within the popular meaning of that term." However, in line with the principle set out above in *Burstyn*, the matter is one of first impression, and can only be definitively settled by the courts. We hold as we do, since otherwise there is nothing to prevent the development of the trend which we described in par. 8, from becoming a reality.

12. The licensee argues that the program was not indecent, because its basic subject matters ". . . are obviously decent"; "the challenged language though not essential to the meaning of the program as a whole, reflected the personality and life style of Mr. Garcia"; and "the realistic portrayal of such an interview cannot be deemed 'indecent' because the subject incidentally used strong or salty language." (Letter, p. 5). We disagree with this approach in the broadcast field. Were it followed, any newscaster or talk moderator could intersperse his broadcast with these expressions, or indeed a disc jockey could

speak of his records and related views with phrases like, "S - - t, man . . ., listen to this mother f - - - - r", on the ground that his overall broadcast was clearly decent, and that this manner of presentation reflected the "personality and life style" of the speaker, who was only "telling it like it is." The licensee itself notes that the language in question "was not essential to the presentation of the subject matter . . ." but rather was ". . . essentially gratuitous." We think that is the precise point here—namely, that the language *is* "gratuitous"—i.e., "unwarranted or [having] no reason for its existence" (Websters Collegiate Dictionary, Fifth Ed., p. 435). There is no valid basis in these circumstances for permitting its widespread use in the broadcast field, with the detrimental consequences described in par. 8, *supra.*

13. The matter could also be approached under the public interest standard of the Communications Act. Broadcast licensees must operate in the public interest (Section 315(a)), and the Commission does have authority to act to insure such operation. *Red Lion Broadcasting Co., Inc.* v. *F.C.C.* 395 U.S. 367, 380 (1969). This does not mean, of course, that the Commission could properly assess program after program, stating that one was consistent with the public interest and another was not. That would be flagrant censorship. See Section 326 of the Communications Act, 47 U.S.C. 326; *Banzhaf* v. *F.C.C.*, 132 U.S. App. D.C. 14, 27; 405 F. 2d 1082, 1095 (1968), certiorari denied, 395 U.S. 973 (1969). However, we believe that we can act under the public interest criterion in this narrow area against those who present programming such as is involved in this case. The standard for such action under the public interest criterion is the same as previously discussed—namely, that the material is patently offensive by contemporary community standards and utterly without redeeming social value. These were the standards employed in *Palmetto Broadcasting Co.*, 33 FCC 483; 34 FCC 101 (1963), affirmed on other grounds, *E. G. Robinson, Jr.* v. *F.C.C.*, 108 U.S. App. D.C. 144, 344 F. 2d 534 (1964), certiorari denied, 379 U.S. 843, where the Commission denied the application for renewal of a licensee which, inter alia, had presented smut during a substantial period of the broadcasting day.[8]

14. In sum, we hold that we have the authority to act here under Section 1464 (i.e. 503(b)(1)(E)) or under the public interest standard (Section 503(b)(1)(A)(B)—for failure to operate in the public interest as set forth in the license or to observe the requirement of Section 315(a) to operate in the public interest). Cf. *Red Lion Broadcasting Co., Inc.* v. *F.C.C.*, 395 U.S. 367, 376, n. 5. However, whether under Section 1464 or the public interest standard, the criteria for Commission action thus remains the same, in our view—namely, that the material be patently offensive and utterly without redeeming value. Finally, as we stressed before in sensitive areas like this (Report and Order on Personal Attack Rules, 8 FCC 2d 721, 725 (1968)), the Commission can appropriately act only in clear-cut, flagrant cases; doubtful or close cases are clearly to be resolved in the licensee's favor.

15. *Discussion—Application of the above principles to this case.* In view of the foregoing, little further discussion is needed on this aspect. We believe that the presentation of the Garcia material quoted in par. 3 falls clearly within the two above criteria,[9] and hence may be the subject of a forfeiture under Section 503(b)(1)(A)(B) and (E). We further find that the presentation was "willful" (503(b)(1)(A)(B)). We note that the material was taped. Further the station employees could have cautioned Mr. Garcia either at the outset or after the first few expressions to avoid using these "gratuitous" expressions; they did not do so.[10] That the material was presented without obtaining the station manager's approval—contrary to station policy—does not absolve the licensee of responsibility. See *KWK, Inc.*, 34 FCC 2d 1039, affirmed 119 U.S. App. D.C. 144, 337, F. 2d 540 (1964). Indeed, in light of the facts here, there would appear to have been gross negligence on the part of the licensee with respect to its supervisory duties.

16. We turn now to the question of the appropriate sanction. The licensee points out that this is one isolated occurrence, and that therefore the *Palmetto* decision is inapposite. We agree that there is no question of revocation or denial of license on the basis of the matter before us, even without taking into account the overall record of the station, as described in the licensee's letter, pp. 6–8. See also *In re Renewal of Pacifica*, 36 FCC 147 (1964). Rather, the issue in this case is whether to impose a forfeiture (since one of the reasons for the forfeiture provision is that it can be imposed for the isolated occurrence, such as an isolated lottery, etc.). On this issue, we note that, in view of the fact that this is largely a case of first impression, particularly as to the Section 1464 aspect, we could appropriately forego the forfeiture and simply act prospectively in this field. See, *Taft Broadcasting Co.*, 18 FCC 2d 186; *Bob Jones University*, 18 FCC 2d 8; *WBRE-TV, Inc.*, 18 FCC 2d 96. However, were we to do so, we would prevent any review of our action and in this sensitive field we have always sought to insure such reviewability. See *Red Lion Broadcasting Co., Inc.* v. *F.C.C.*, 395 U.S. 367, 376, n. 5. We believe that a most crucial peg underlying all Commission action in the programming field is the vital consideration that the courts are there to review and reverse any action which runs afoul of the First Amendment. Thus, while we think that our action is fully consistent with the law, there should clearly be the avenue of court review in a case of this nature (see Section 504(a)). Indeed, we would welcome such review, since only in that way can the pertinent standards be definitively determined. Accordingly, in light of that consideration, the new ground which we break with this decision, and the overall record of this noncommercial educational licensee, we propose to assess a forfeiture of only $100.00.

CONCLUSION

17. We conclude this discussion as we began it. We propose no change from our commitment to promoting robust, wide-open debate. *Red Lion Broadcasting Co.* v. *F.C.C.*, *supra; Pacifica Foundation, supra.* Simply stated, our position—limited to the facts of this case—is that such debate does not require that persons being interviewed or station employees on talk programs have the right to begin their speech with, "S - - t, man . . .", or use "f - - - - - g," or "mother f - - - - - g" as gratuitous adjectives throughout their speech. This fosters no debate, serves no social purpose, and would drastically curtail the usefulness of radio for millions of people. Indeed, significantly, in this case, under the licensee's policy (which was by-passed by its volunteer employees), Mr. Garcia's views would have been presented *without* the gratuitous expressions, but with them, the public would never have heard his views.

18. In view of the foregoing, we determine that, pursuant to Section 503(b)(1)(A), (B), (E) of the Communications Act of 1934, as amended, Eastern Education Radio has incurred an apparent liability of one hundred dollars ($100).

19. Eastern Education Radio is hereby notified that it has the opportunity to file with the Commission, within thirty (30) days of the date of the receipt of this Notice, a statement in writing as to why it should not be held liable, or, if liable, why the amount of liability should be reduced or remitted. Any such statement should be filed in duplicate and should contain complete details concerning the allegations heretofore made by the Commission, any justification for the violations involved, and any other information which Eastern Education Radio may desire to bring to the attention of the Commission. Statements of circumstances should be supported by copies of relevant documents where available. Upon receipt of any such reply, the Commission will determine whether the facts set forth therein are sufficient to relieve Eastern Education Radio of liability, or to justify either reduction or remission of the amount of liability. If it is unable to find that Eastern Education Radio should be relieved of liability, the Commission will issue an Order of Forfeiture and the forfeiture will be payable to the Treasurer of the United States.

20. If Eastern Education Radio does not file, within thirty (30) days of the date of receipt of this Notice, either a statement of non-liability or a statement setting forth facts and reasons why the forfeiture should be of a lesser amount, the Commission will enter an Order of Forfeiture in the amount of one hundred dollars ($100).

21. In accordance with our established procedures, we also state that if Eastern Education Radio does not wish to file a statement which denies liability and, in addition, it does not wish to await the issuance of an Order, it may, within thirty (30) days of the date of the receipt of this Notice, make payment of the forfeiture by mailing to the Commission a check, or similar instrument, in the amount of one hundred dollars ($100) drawn payable to the Treasurer of the United States.

BY DIRECTION OF THE COMMISSION,
BEN F. WAPLE, *Secretary.*

APPENDIX A

Excerpts from licensee's letter of February 12, 1970:

". . . During the interview, Mr. Garcia expressed his views on ecology, music, philosophy, and interpersonal relations. [footnote omitted] Some of Mr. Garcia's comments on these subjects are set forth below:

The problem essentially . . . the basic problem is how can you live on the planet earth without wreckin' it, right?

* * * * * * *

. . . like you know a couple of weeks ago the thing was in the paper that the headline was in the paper that there was no more clean air in the United States, period. Yeah, and it's like uh that kind of stuff is all of a sudden comin' up real fast. You know, and it's like it looks like that's the most important thing going on and that nothing else is as important as that as far as I know, that is *the* most important thing.

* * * * * * *

For example, like uh I have friends who I've known since like they started college, you know, and like now it's eight years later and you know, and they're all Ph. Ds—stuff like that. It's just coming out in those terms, uh, I know quite a few of these people who have switched their major in the last year to Ecology and that kind of s - - t, because it's like really important right. It's a big emergency going on. Okay, so—and their approach to it is generally to get together on the level of bodies of influence—that is to say, governmental s - - t, you know, things like that business and so forth, and stuff like that.

* * * * * * *

But the big thing is that it's really super, you know—it's . . . it's . . . it definitely looks bad outside man. When you fly over New York, it looks f - - - - n' rotten, man, but it's like that way every f - - - - n' where, man, you know, and like I'm from San Francisco, man, and there wasn't like five or six years ago when it was like the sky was blue, crystal clear, you know; you know and that whole thing that you hardly ever see any more, man—you know you just hardly ever see it any more.

* * * * * * *

What I'd really love to do would be live on a perfect, peaceful earth and devote all my time to music. But I can't do it man, because you just can't do that. You know, I mean it's a . . . there's a more important thing going on, that's all.

* * * * * * *

Politics is a form and music is a form and they're both ways of dealing with people, man. When you play music with people, though, you're not attacking them, you know. It isn't, it's not a competition between the two of you or the four of you or the seven of you, or however many of you. There are—it's like a cooperative effort which gets everybody high, so like that's and that's of course the thing that's really a great trip about music. It's really a great thing. It's really a good trip, right, and uh so like the things that that I've wanted to see happen and lots of other people you know it's like some way of getting people together to do things but having it be like music and not like business and not like politics, you know, uh just because that's a uh high watermark in a way. I mean it seems like people should be able to do that.

* * * * * * *

If you get together with four or five people and produce something that's greater than yourself you know, and that also doesn't only reflect your attitude, but it's like a little closer to the center because it has to do with more perceptions than your own and like for a plan to work, I think, it has to be approached on those kinds of levels and those kind of terms because uh it won't work if uh this is a planet full of people, each of whom is in a universe of his own. Everybody has to agree to give a little, and so forth, and so on."

STATEMENT OF COMMISSIONER KENNETH A. COX, CONCURRING IN PART AND DISSENTING IN PART

I agree with a good deal that is said in the Notice of Apparent Liability, but do not agree with the result reached.

I agree that broadcasting differs in significant respects from books, magazines, motion pictures and other means of communications. I agree that this may lead the courts to apply different standards in determining the degree of control which government may exercise over the content of broadcast programming. And I agree that it would be well to get this matter resolved by the courts in the near future. But I do not agree that the problem is as great as the majority say it is, or that it is likely to become endemic. I do not agree that the licensee of WUHY-FM was grossly negligent in this case or merits any more than a warning because of this incident. And I am afraid that this precedent may cause licensees not to carry programming they would otherwise have broadcast, out of fear that someone will be offended, will complain to the Commission, and the latter will find the broadcast improper. It should be noted that Cycle II has been suspended, so that whatever of value it had to offer will no longer be available to WUHY's audience.

At least the majority are now listing the words, and the usage of those words, which they regard as contrary to the public interest. I think that is desirable, although I am sure that broadcasters are going to worry about other words which they feel may be added to the list later on. And I applaud the majority for indicating that licensees will not be punished for presenting works of art or on-the-spot coverage of bona fide news events which may contain these words or others like them. I am glad they restrict their action to gratuitous use of words in circumstances where the offensive language has no redeeming social value.

However, I do not think the broadcast here involved posed a problem so serious as to justify the imposition of a sanction for the mere utterance of words. This weekly series was intended as an "underground" program dealing "with the avant-garde movement in music, publications, art, film, personalities, and other forms of social and artistic experimentation." It was presented between 10 and 11 P.M. on Sunday night, and was designed to appeal to the large college population in Philadelphia and to alienated segments of the new generation. It seems clear that a program with such a purpose—a perfectly valid one, I'm sure everyone would agree—would be different in approach and content from programs aimed at children, or women 30 to 40 years of age, or professional men, or adults generally. And it seems likely, in view of the widespread ferment among young people and their rejection of many of the standards of their parents' generation, that not only the ideas discussed but the language used to express them will sometimes be offensive to the older generation. But people who do not like the ideas or the language do not need to listen to programs of this kind. WUHY received no complaints about the broadcast here in question, nor did the Commission. However, we had received earlier complaints about the 10 to 11 P.M. time period and were monitoring the station on the night of January 4, 1970. So far as I can tell, my colleagues are the only people who have encountered this program who are greatly disturbed by it.

I agree that the language complained of is offensive to many and that it was gratuitous—that Mr. Garcia could have expressed the same ideas without using this language. However, I think it magnifies the impact of the words to set them out starkly, as the majority do in Paragraph 3 of the Notice, alone and out of context. I have not read the full transcript of the broadcast, and doubt if my colleagues have, but certainly a reading of the seven paragraphs quoted in the licensee's response gives a different perspective of the matter. While one might wish that Mr. Garcia had been able to express himself without using words which many people find offensive, it would appear that he was not trying to shock or titillate the audience. Apparently this is the way he talks—and I guess a lot of others in his generation do so, too. I find such poverty of expression depressing, and am afraid it may impair clarity of thought. My concern is not limited to the words which trouble the majority. In the seven paragraphs quoted by the licensee, Mr. Garcia uses only four words cited by the majority. But he uses the word "like" in an improper and redundant way sixteen times, and uses "man" as a word of emphasis seven times. These patterns of speech seem common among today's young. But I expect our language will survive—as it has withstood the slang and fads of generation after generation.

WUHY decided that it wanted to let Mr. Garcia communicate his views in a number of important areas to the station's audience—a decision which no one questions. At least the station was trying to do something more than play records and read wire news. Assuming the propriety of the station's program judgment, how could it have achieved its desired result without getting into trouble with the Commission? The majority suggest, in Paragraph 7, that while Mr. Garcia may talk this way in many other places, he should have been told that he cannot do so on radio. However, while I have had very limited contact with people of his age and background, I am of the impression that such an approach might not have been productive. I think one of the reasons for their use of such language is that it is *intended* to show disrespect for the standards of their elders, which they regard as outmoded, without real basis, and "irrelevant." It might have been difficult for Mr. Garcia to change his habits of speech without interfering with the flow of his ideas—or he might simply have refused to give the interview at all on those terms. Admittedly this is speculative, but

there is no way to explore these possibilities without making some assumptions—and I think mine are not unreasonable.

The only other alternative would have been to delete the offending language. The licensee, in its response to the Commission's letter of inquiry, argued persuasively that the Garcia interview was neither obscene nor profane. I am glad that the majority agree that it was not obscene, and while they do not address themselves to the issue of profanity, they certainly make no claim that the language was profane. Instead, they hold that the language was indecent, within the meaning of 18 U.S.C. 1434, which makes it a crime to "utter any obscene, indecent, or profane language by means of radio communication." The licensee argued to the contrary in its letter:

. . . Nor was the program indecent simply because certain language not normally heard in polite circles, was uttered. The basic subject matters of the program—ecology, philosophy, music—are obviously decent. The challenged language though not essential to the meaning of the program as a whole, reflected the personality and life style of Mr. Garcia. In this sense, the interview was in the nature of a documentary. The realistic portrayal of such an interview cannot be deemed "indecent" because the subject incidentally used strong or salty language. . . .

I think this position has a good deal of merit. In addition, I think that the word "indecent" in the statute may not have a clear enough meaning to satisfy the constitutional requirement that criminal statutes must put the public on notice of just precisely what conduct will constitute a violation.

Having made this contention, the licensee nonetheless said that it would not have aired the program had it been submitted for review by the station manager, as required by established station procedures. It went on to say:

Licensee would not have aired the Jerry Garcia interview because the questioned language was not essential to the presentation of the subject matter and its potential for offense was not outweighed by considerations of subject matter or artistic integrity. While the program had value in terms of subject matter and in depicting the total personality of Jerry Garcia, licensee does not believe that these values were sufficient to warrant airing the program, at least without deletion of the offending and essentially gratuitous passages.[2]

[2] Licensee does not believe that editing and deletion are an automatically acceptable solution to this kind of problem. Such deletions often damage the entire program. Moreover, they do not protect the sensibilities of the listener. Indeed such censorship may be more distracting than the deleted language itself.

A licensee is responsible for everything broadcast over its station. WUHY therefore very properly has adopted a policy that all taped program material containing "controversial subject matter or language" must be reviewed by the station manager. If those who produced and broadcast the Garcia interview had followed that procedure and the licensee had decided not to use the interview, or to do so only after deleting the language here in issue, that would have represented a licensee's efforts to discharge its responsibilities in the exercise of its own judgment. What we have here is quite a different thing. The majority are exercising government power in the area of speech. They have imposed a sanction—though admittedly a nominal one—for a single broadcast[11] containing what they, but not the licensee, regard as indecent matter. This action, binding on all licensees, is obviously far different from letting licensees make their own judgments—even if many of them would conclude, with the majority, that language of this kind should not be broadcast.

I'm afraid it has taken me a long time to get around to discussing an idea mentioned in the first sentence of the third paragraph back—the possible deletion of the offensive words. I think the licensee has pointed out some problems with this procedure in the footnote to the last quotation above. It says that bleeping out words may disrupt the program, and that it may not be too difficult for those who dislike such language to tell what was said despite the deletion—indeed, that this may actually emphasize the fact that language which the licensee apparently regards as improper had been used. It seems to me that WUHY—when put on notice that the Commission on its own motion is challenging the broadcast—is saying that it would not have broadcast the Garcia interview at all. I think that most licensees who may consider presenting similar programming in the future—that is taped material involving statements by blacks, students, or those who have dropped out of our society—will decide that if the use of words which may offend the Commission is interspersed too regularly throughout the tape to make deletion feasible, the safe course will be just not to broadcast the program. While I hold no brief for flooding the air with the views of members of these groups, I think it may be dangerous if we do not understand what they are trying to say—even if it sometimes involves the monotonous use of four letter words. Some of their complaints are probably well founded, and even if they are not, I think we need to know what troubles them and what they are talking about doing about these matters. It may be that using radio and television to help bridge the generation gap would be an example of "the larger and more effective use of radio" which the majority are so eager to preserve. If, instead, we narrow our concept of the use of radio in order to protect the sensibilities of those who seem more concerned with suppressing words and pictures they find offensive than with solving the problems that are tearing our society apart, I think we may find that the majority are wrong in stating—in Paragraph 7—that we can exercise these words from radio "without stifling in the slightest any thought which the person wishes to convey." One safe course for the timid will be simply to avoid interviewing people who can be expected to use troublesome language, or inviting them to participate in panels, or asking them to comment on current developments. This may be "safe" for the licensee but I'm not sure it will be safe for our society.

This brings me, at last, to my principal problem with the majority's decision, which is that I think they are exaggerating this problem out of all proportion. It is true that in recent months we have been receiving more complaints about the broadcast of allegedly obscene, indecent, or profane matter, but most of these involve matters outside the ambit of this ruling. That is, they deal with claims that certain records contain cryptic references to the use of drugs, that others are sexually suggestive, that the skits and blackouts on the Rowan and Martin Laugh-In are similarly suggestive, that the costumes on many variety programs are indecent, that the dances are too sensuous, that the performers are too free with each other, etc. But I think I could count on the fingers of both hands the complaints that have come to my notice which involve the gratuitous use of four letter words in situations comparable to the one in this case. This has simply not been a problem.

Nor do I agree that if we do not punish WUHY for this broadcast, there is going to be such "widespread use" of the offending words as to "drastically affect the use of radio by millions of people," because "very substantial numbers would either curtail using radio or would restrict their use to but a few channels." I just do not believe there are many broadcasters waiting eagerly to flood the country with such language on an around the clock basis in the event we were to impose no sanction here. Indeed, if the Commission had not decided to make a test case of this incident, I doubt if many people would ever have heard of it. Actually, if the majority's theory is right, they are running a rather serious risk. If the courts do not sustain their action, that would be a signal to the industry that it could freely engage in the "widespread use" of four letter words which the majority fear they are anxious to embark upon. But I don't think many of our licensees have any desire to follow such a course, nor do I believe that there is any great audience to be won by such tactics. I think most broadcasters have too high a regard for their profession and its responsibilities to fall into the patterns the majority envisage in Paragraphs 7 through 9.

Similarly, I think there is a great and clear difference between presenting an occasional late night program featuring people not on the staff of the station who use offensive language and employing newscasters and disc jockeys and allowing them to use similar expressions all day long. It is one thing to permit certain elements in society to use such language on the air so that interested members of the public can find out how they think about various problems. It is quite different to turn the operation of a station over to people who talk that way. I think this, like the more generalized claim that we are about to be inundated with indecent language, is a figment of the majority's imagination designed to justify the intrusion of governmental power into this sensitive area.

I have studied broadcasting for some time, and while I think we may expect to hear strong language on the air somewhat more often in the future as a reflection of our troubled times, I simply do not believe there is any likelihood that licensees will broadcast indecent language to such an extent that they will drive millions of listeners away from radio entirely. Broadcasters make money by attracting audiences. They have developed a number of ways to win the attention of differing segments of the total audience. I do not think that four letter words are likely to become the format of the future, since I doubt if even people who use such language themselves would regard it as enhancing a station's service.

Finally, I think it should be noted that the majority have held that someone involved in this broadcast violated a criminal statute. This means that such person or persons can be prosecuted and subjected to rather severe penalties. However, I do not think this is likely to happen because I suspect that the United States Attorney in Philadelphia has more important matters to occupy his time and that of his staff. (See my dissent in the Commission's letter addressed to Jack Straw Memorial Foundation, dated January 21, 1970. FCC 70–93.) I submit that the same thing should be true of the Federal Communications Commission.

PRELIMINARY DISSENTING OPINION OF COMMISSIONER NICHOLAS JOHNSON

"Oaths are but words, and words but wind."
—Samuel Butler, *Hudibras* (1664).

What this Commission condemns today are not words, but a culture—a lifestyle it fears because it does not understand. Most of the people in this country are under 28 years of age; over 56 million students are in our colleges and schools. Many of them will "smile" when they learn that the Federal Communications Commission, an agency of their government, has punished a radio station for broadcasting the words of Jerry Garcia, the leader of what the FCC calls a "rock and roll musical group." To call The Grateful Dead a "rock and roll musical group" is like calling the Los Angeles Philharmonic a "jug band." And that about shows "where this Commission's at."

Today the Commission simply ignores decades of First Amendment law, carefully fashioned by the Supreme Court into the recognized concepts of "vagueness" and "overbreadth," see, *e.g.*, *Zwickler v. Koota*, 389 U.S. 241, 249–50 (1967), and punishes a broadcaster for speech it describes as "indecent"—without so much as *attempting* a definition of that uncertain term. What the Commission tells the broadcaster he cannot say is anyone's guess—and therein lies the constitutional deficiency.

Today the Commission turns its back on Supreme Court precedent, see, *e.g.*, *Interstate Circuit, Inc. v. Dallas*, 390 U.S. 676 (1968), citing *Holmby Productions, Inc. v. Vaughn*, 350 U.S. 870 (1954), as well as recent federal court precedent, see, *e.g.*, *Williams v. District of Columbia*, No. 20, 927 (D.C. Cir., June 20, 1969) (en banc), which invalidated statutes with similarly vague descriptions of allegedly "indecent" speech.

Today the Commission decides that certain forms of speech and expression are "patently offensive by contemporary community

standards"—although neither the station nor the FCC received *a single complaint* about the broadcast in question, and the FCC conducted not a single survey among the relevant population groups in Philadelphia, nor compiled a single word of testimony on contemporary community standards, nor attempted even to define the relevant "community" in question.

I am aware that there *are* members of the public who are offended by some of what they hear or see on radio or television. I too am offended by much of what I hear or see on radio or television—though more often for what it fails to do than what it does. I am sympathetic to the outrage of any minority group—Black or Puritan—that feels its values are not honored by the society of which it is a part. (What the Commission decides, after all, is that the swear words of the lily-white middle class may be broadcast, but that those of the young, the poor, or the blacks may not.) There are scenes, subjects and words used on television which I would not use personally as a guest on camera. The words used here fall in that category. But I do not believe I sit here as an FCC Commissioner to enforce my moral standards upon the nation. Yet four other Commissioners do precisely that.

Furthermore, when we do go after broadcasters, I find it pathetic that we always seem to pick upon the small, community service stations like a KPFK, WBAI, KRAB, and now WUHY-FM. See, *e.g.*, *Pacifica Foundation (KPFK-FM)*, 36 F.C.C. 147 (1964); *United Federation of Teachers (WBAI-FM)*, 17 F.C.C. 2d 204 (1969); *Jack Straw Memorial Foundation (KRAB-FM)*, FCC 70–93 (released Jan. 21, 1970). It is ironic to me that of the public complaints about broadcasters' "taste" received in my office, there are probably a hundred or more about network television for every one about stations of this kind. Surely if anyone were genuinely concerned about the impact of broadcasting upon the moral values of this nation—and that impact has been considerable—he ought to consider the ABC, CBS and NBC television networks before picking on little educational FM radio stations that can scarcely afford the postage to answer our letters, let alone hire lawyers. We have plenty of complaints around this Commission involving the networks. Why are they being ignored? I shan't engage in speculation.

Today this Commission acts against a station that broadcasts 77 hours a week of locally-originated fine music, public and cultural affairs, and community-oriented programming. Ironically, the Commission censures language broadcast by the station that received one of the Corporation for Public Broadcasting's first program grants for its experimental program in participatory democracy, "Free Speech." In 1969 alone, WUHY-FM received two "major" Armstrong Awards, one of the highest achievements in radio, two awards from Sigma Delta Chi, a professional journalism group, and the Corporation for Public Broadcasting's "Public Criteria" award—the only such award given to a Philadelphia station. I do not believe it a coincidence that this Commission has often moved against the programming of innovative and experimental stations (such as KPFK, WBAI and KRAB). I do not see how licensees (particularly ones that rely on the help of talented volunteers) can develop new and creative programming concepts without approaching the line that separates the orthodox from the unconventional and controversial. I believe today's decision will deter the few innovative stations that do exist from approaching that line.

Today the Commission rules that the speech in question has "no redeeming social value," although Professor Ashley Montagu, a leading authority on the subject, believes that such speech "serves clearly definable social as well as personal purposes." A. Montagu, *The Anatomy of Swearing* 1 (1967).

Today the Commission declares that a four-letter word "conveys no thought"—and proceeds to punish a broadcaster for speech which apparently conveys so much thought that it must be banned.

Today the Commission punishes a licensee for speech in order to encourage the courts to do our work for us—forgetting that the First Amendment binds *this* agency as well as the courts. I do not believe any governmental body can stifle free speech merely to produce a "test case." We cannot, constitutionally, abdicate our responsibilities to the courts. Yet today this is what we have done.

I believe it is our responsibility to adopt precise and clear guidelines for the broadcasting industry to follow in this murky area, if we are to wade into it at all—the wisdom of which I seriously question. I believe no governmental agency can punish for the content of speech by invoking statutory prohibitions which are so broad, sweeping, vague, and potentially all-encompassing that no man can foretell when, why, or with what force the Commission will strike.

In *Joseph Burstyn, Inc. v. Wilson*, 343 U.S. 495 (1952), the Supreme Court held that the First Amendment protected motion pictures as well as normal speech. There, the Court invalidated a New York statute banning "sacrilegious" films. The Court said:

> This is far from the kind of narrow exception to freedom of expression which a state may carve out to satisfy the adverse demands of other interests of society. In seeking to apply the broad and all-inclusive definition of "sacrilegious" given by the New York courts, the censor is set adrift upon a boundless sea amid a myriad of conflicting currents of religious views, with no charts but those provided by the most vocal and powerful orthodoxies . . . . [I]t is enough to point out that the state has no legitimate interest in protecting any or all religions from views distasteful to them . . . .

If the term, "sacrilegious," is subject to the dangers of sweeping all-inclusive interpretations, what then of "indecent"? The FCC has not attempted even a "broad and all-inclusive definition" of "indecent," as the New York courts did of "sacrilegious." Rather, the FCC has cast itself adrift upon the "boundless sea" of a search for "indecency" without compass or polestar for guidance. We have only the obscure charts of the orthodox (presumably represented by a majority of Commissioners) to guide us on our way.

Groups in this country interested in civil liberties and speech freedoms should understand that the Commission today enters a new and untested area of federal censorship—censorship over the words, thoughts and ideas that can be conveyed over the most powerful medium of communication known to man: the *broadcasting* medium. To my knowledge, there are no judicial precedents, no law review articles, no FCC decisions, and no scholarly thinking that even attempt to define the standards of permissible free speech for the broadcasting medium. Should this case be appealed, therefore, these questions may be posed. All those who hold speech freedoms dear should participate. It will be regretable if the Federal Communications Bar Association, like the big broadcasting industry generally, once again proves itself to be more interested in profitable speech than free speech. We will be waiting to see if they vigorously enter an *amicus* appearance in this case.

An anonymous poet has written:

> Oh perish the use of the four- letter words
> Whose meanings are never obscure;
> The Angles and Saxons, those bawdy old birds,
> Were vulgar, obscene and impure.
> But cherish the use of the weaseling phrase
> That never says quite what you mean.
> You had better be known for your hypocrite ways
> Than vulgar, impure and obscene.
> Let your morals be loose as an alderman's vest
> If your language is always obscure.
> Today, not the act, but the word is the test
> Of vulgar, obscene and impure.

Whatever else may be said about the words we censor today, their meanings are not "obscure." I cannot say as much for the majority's standards for "indecency."

In 1601, William Shakespeare wrote in *Twelfth Night* (III, iv), "Nay, let me alone for swearing." Most of the fresh and vital cultures in our country, not the least of which are the young, have learned this lesson. This Commission has not.

I regret the double standard that causes many significant matters to lanquish in FCC files for years, which rushing other, more questionable matters to decision within days. It is extraordinary that the majority would choose to act on an issue of this consequence without even taking the time to *read*, let alone carefully consider, the full dissenting and concurring opinions of all Commissioners in this case. I may, nevertheless, take the time to prepare such a fuller opinion in the future for the record. Meanwhile, I feel it useful to put forward at least these views today, as the majority announces its decision. I dissent.

NOTES

[1] The licensee states that this is a one-hour, weekly broadcast which is "underground" in its orientation and "is concerned with the avant-garde movement in music, publications, art, film, personalities, and other forms of social and artistic experimentation." It is designed to reach youthful persons (e.g., the large college population in Philadelphia and "so-called 'alienated' segments of the new generation"—p. 1. WUHY Letter of February 12, 1970). "Cycle II" is the successor program to a similar program entitled "Feed."

[2] While the licensee states that it received no complaints concerning this January 4th broadcast (nor, we note, did the Commission), the Commission had received several complaints concerning this 10:00 P.M. slot on WUHY-FM (directed to the similar "Feed" program, which "Cycle II" succeeded in November, 1969); it therefore did monitor the broadcast, and specifically that of January 4th.

[3] In this connection, we note the licensee's apt statement of policy (pp. 5-6, Letter of February 12, 1970): "The question whether to air a program which contains controversial subject matter or language is among the most difficult a licensee is called upon to resolve. In determining whether to air any program which contains material or language which is potentially offensive or disagreeable to some listeners, licensee balances a number of considerations: The subject matter of the program: its value or relevance to the segment of listeners to which it is directed; whether the program is a work of art; whether it is a recognized classic; and whether the potentially offensive language or material is essential to the integrity of the presentation. Licensee also takes into account such factors as the time of the broadcast, the likelihood that children may be in the audience, and the necessity for appropriate cautionary announcements to listeners in advance of potentially disagreeable programming."

[4] To give but one further example, suppose a disc jockey or a moderator on a talk show for sensational or shock improvised expressions aimed at particular audiences, began using expressions such as "Listen to this mother f - - - - g person [or person]." There is no question but that such use of this vulgar term for an incestuous son is utterly without redeeming social value and, on radio, taking into account its nature (see above paragraph), patently offensive. See discussion, par. 10, *infra*.

[5] In a very real sense, the situation here is the very opposite of *Stanley v. Georgia*, 394 U.S. 557 (1969), which involved the private possession or use of obscene material.

[6] For example, the following tables point up the children's audience in the evening hours for radio and television:

Average quarter-hour radio audience of teenagers (12 to 17 years) as a percentage of all teenagers in metro area, 1969

Time	Los Angeles	New York City	Washington, D.C.
8 to 9 p.m.		16.5	16.6	14.1
9 to 10 p.m.		14.8	16.9	14.8
10 to 11 p.m.		10.5	13.8	14.1
11 to 12 midnight		4.8	6.5	10.9

Children (2 to 17 years) viewing TV as a percentage of total persons viewing based on New York and Los Angeles survey February-March

Time period	Children as percent of total			Child total (percent)
	2 to 6 years	6 to 11 years	11 to 17 years	
Sunday to Saturday, 7:30 to 9 p.m.	5	13	12	30
Sunday to Saturday, 9 to 11 p.m.	1	5	13	19
Average prime time:				
Sunday to Saturday, 11:30 to 1 a.m.	3	10	13	26
Monday to Friday, 11:30 p.m. to 1 a.m.	½	½	5	6

[7] We stress that our analysis is limited to broadcasting because of its unique nature of dissemination into millions of homes. The difference is pointed up by this very document. It is perfectly proper, in the analysis here, to use the pertinent expressions of Mr. Garcia. There is no other way to deal intelligently with the subject. But in any event, it takes a conscious act by someone interested in the subject to obtain this document and study its content.

[8] The Commission there found the programming patently offensive by contemporary community standards and no evidence that it ". . . in some way served the needs and interests of the area."

[9] There does not appear to be any factual dispute. However, the licensee has the opportunity to advance any pertinent factual questions in response to this Notice and may of course obtain a trial de novo of the matter in the district court. See Section 504(a).

[10] Indeed, one of the station participants stated at the outset of the interview, "We are going to do a lot of illegal things before this is over."

KRAB-FM, SEATTLE, IS GRANTED A ONE YEAR LICENSE RENEWAL INSTEAD OF THE CUSTOMARY THREE YEAR RENEWAL BECAUSE OF "COMPLAINTS FROM THE PUBLIC ALLEGING ON OCCASIONS PROFANE, INDECENT OR OBSCENE LANGUAGE HAS BEEN BROADCAST." TWO COMMISSIONERS DISSENT, COMMISSIONER KENNETH COX DECLARING THAT "THE MAJORITY HAVE CLEARLY ASSESSED A PENALTY HERE FOR A SINGLE BROADCAST, AND HAVE DONE SO WITHOUT CONSIDERING THE CONTEXT IN WHICH THE LANGUAGE WAS USED AND WITHOUT BEING ABLE TO DETERMINE WHETHER THE PROGRAM, AS A WHOLE, APPEALED TO PRURIENT INTEREST OR HAD OFFSETTING REDEEMING SOCIAL VALUE."

Jack Straw Memorial Foundation (KRAB-FM), 21 F.C.C.2d 833 (1970)

BEFORE THE

FEDERAL COMMUNICATIONS COMMISSION

WASHINGTON, D.C. 20554

In Re Application of
JACK STRAW MEMORIAL FOUNDATION, SEATTLE, WASH.
For Renewal of License of Radio Station KRAB-FM

JANUARY 21, 1970.

GENTLEMEN: This refers to the pending renewal application of station KRAB–FM, Seattle, Wash.

During the past license period the Commission has received complaints from the public alleging that on occasions profane, indecent, or obscene language has been broadcast by your station. In response to a Commission request you have furnished statements pertaining to your policy regarding the broadcast of such material and specific comments regarding KRAB's broadcast of a program presented by Reverend Sawyer. With respect to the Reverend Sawyer program, you state that the entire tape had not been auditioned prior to broadcast and when, during the broadcast, it became clear that the language used was contrary to your station's policy regarding material which you consider suitable broadcasting, the program was terminated.

In view of the foregoing background, we shall focus on the Reverend Sawyer matter as illustrative of the issue before the Commission. We have reviewed the pertinent portion of the Reverend Sawyer program in light of your explanatory statements and policy. We note initially that the critical consideration is not whether or not action under 18 U.S.C. 1464 is warranted. For, in any event, there is the issue of whether KRAB–FM is exercising proper supervision of its operations and specifically is following its stated policies in this area.

Thus, your station policy eschews the broadcast of "sensationalism for its own sake" and requires that speakers "observe the commonsense strictures against obscenity and libel." Your procedures require that "material which raises questions as to its merit for broadcast because of some social, moral, aesthetic, or scatological outspokenness" be referred by the program director to the station manager for audition and a determination as to whether the material should be broadcast in its entirety, in an edited version or not at all.

Any material "which inspires [the] concern" of the station manager as to its "appropriateness for broadcast" is to be reviewed by the board of directors. You report that under this system, one or two programs per month are eliminated for "obscenity, obscurantism, sensationalism, or simple boorishness." Portions of the Reverend Sawyer program were clearly contrary to your stated policy as demonstrated by KRAB's removal of the Sawyer broadcast from the air before completion. However, while we believe that in this instance there could have been a more appropriate exercise of proper licensee control in the form of compliance with your own procedures, there is no indication of any overall pattern of failure in this area of licensee responsibility.

In view of the foregoing the Commission has renewed station KRAB-FM's license for the period ending February 1, 1971. It is expected that appropriate steps will be taken by the licensee to assure implementation of stated procedures regarding the selection of broadcast material consistent with the standards which you have set forth.

Commissioners Cox and Johnson dissenting and issuing statements.

By Direction of the Commission,
Ben F. Waple, *Secretary*.

Dissenting Statement of Commissioner Kenneth A. Cox

I dissent to the majority's action in granting only a 1-year renewal for KRAB-FM. I know of nothing in the station's record that would justify imposition of this sanction.

Despite a vague reference to "complaints from the public alleging that on occasions profane, indecent, or obscene language has been broadcast," the majority comment on only one program. This was the broadcast of a portion of a 30-hour "autobiographical novel for tape" prepared by a Rev. Paul Sawyer which was aired over the station in August 1967. The Commission does not have a transcript of the program, so we have no idea of the context in which the language complained of was used. We have simply been advised that three so-called four-letter words were used—apparently several times. They are words that I do not use, and which many people find highly offensive. However, it seems clear that, under existing precedents the words as used were neither obscene nor profane. Many people might regard them as indecent—that being the third category of language prohibited by 18 U.S.C. 1464. However, that term is so indefinite that I believe it is probably unconstitutionally vague.

However, the majority do not contend that the broadcast violated 18 U.S.C. 1464—and typically the Department of Justice has not regarded this kind of usage as justifying a prosecution under the statute. Rather, my colleagues proceed on the ground that this single broadcast violated the licensee's announced policy requiring such material to be referred to the station manager for audition—and, in certain cases, to the board of directors as well. The licensee concedes that the entire Sawyer tape had not been preauditioned, and that when, during broadcast, it became clear that some of the language was contrary to station policy, the program was terminated.

I think some detail as to this single incident is necessary in order to understand what is involved here. As I understand the situation, the facts are as follows: It was suggested to Lorenzo Milam, then president of the licensee of KRAB, that the station broadcast the taped program submitted by Reverend Sawyer, the minister of the Lake Forest Park Unitarian Church, which is located in a northern suburb of Seattle. Mr. Milam auditioned portions of the tape and found the contents and the method of presentation interesting. He did not hear any objectional language in the portions which he played. The program was therefore scheduled for broadcast beginning at 10 a.m. on Saturday, August 5, 1967. Mr. Milam does not go to the station on Saturdays until after noon, but was listening to the station at home. Reverend Sawyer was at the studio to ride gain on his tape recorder, which was being used to play his tape, and the station was attended by a young woman employee. After the program had proceeded for awhile Mr. Milam heard some language which he considered objectionable. He called the station and asked either the employee in charge or Reverend Sawyer to be careful to prevent any further instances of that kind. However, he again heard language of the kind which had concerned him and so called the station a second time. He talked to Reverend Sawyer and asked him to see to it that no more such language was broadcast. Not being sure that the matter would be corrected, he then drove to the station. After discussing the matter with Reverend Sawyer and the employee in charge, it was agreed to terminate the broadcast. He and Reverend Sawyer then went on the air and discussed the tapes which had been on the air. It appears that the program was broadcast for about 2½ hours. As a result of the presentation of this program, the Commission received one complaint. The matter was investigated by an assistant U.S. attorney in Seattle. He concluded, with the concurrence of his superior, that there was no basis for prosecuting any of the parties involved in the incident.

It is Mr. Milam's position that the broadcast was not obscene or indecent, but that it was inconsistent with the station's program standards. It seems to me that any deviation from the station's policies was so slight that it should not result in the sanction imposed here.

It is desirable, of course, that licensees observe the policies they have adopted to insure service in the public interest. We have, on occasion, imposed sanctions against some who have been so lax in their supervision of staff members that extensive violations of station policy, of our rules, or of the law have occurred. But we have always exercised great care in the area of speech, indicating that we would act only where a consistent pattern of programing contrary to the public interest was involved *Palmetto Broadcasting Co.*, 33 F.C.C. 250, at 257–8 (1962); *Pacifica Foundation*, 36 F.C.C. 147, at 150 (1964).

In this case there is no such pattern, since the majority rest their action on a single program. There have been other complaints against KRAB, but the majority apparently do not regard them as of sufficient significance to be considered here—a conclusion with which I agree. I think the imposition of a sanction for one departure is not only without precedent, and in my judgment highly arbitrary, but is also likely to exert a chilling effect on licensees' freedom in programing their stations—a result the courts have sought to protect against and one which should be of grave concern to all who believe that our democracy requires the maximum possible freedom of expression.

I believe that this represents a shift in the Commission's position—one that troubles me greatly. In 1964, we granted renewals of license for KPFA-KPFB, KPFK, and WBAI, stations licensed to the Pacifica Foundation which, like KRAB, are subscriber supported rather than commercially operated. We had had those stations on deferred renewal for many months while we—and a Senate committee—investigated a number of matters. These included complaints of a number of instances in which four-letter or allegedly obscene words were broadcast. The Commission discussed these matters at length and found that they would not bar grant of a full-term renewal. As to this question, we said:

> We recognize that as shown by the complaints here, such provocative programing as here involved may offend some listeners. But this does not mean that those offended have the right, through the Commission's licensing power, to rule such programing off the airwaves. Were this the case, only the wholly inoffensive, the bland, could gain access to the radio microphone or TV camera (36 F.C.C. 147, at 149).

In 1965 the licenses for Pacifica's California stations expired. Again, the Commission had received a number of complaints about language broadcast by the stations. Our staff recommended regular renewals. However, because Pacifica had failed fully to conform to its programing policies, the Commission granted 1-year renewals—with Chairman Henry, Commissioner Loevinger, and I dissenting and voting for full-term renewals.

On March 27, 1967, after reviewing the operations of KPFA-KPFB and KPFK during their short renewal period, the Commission granted the stations regular renewals.

On February 28, 1969, we again considered applications for renewal of the licenses of Pacifica's three California stations. Again there were allegations that obscene, profane, or indecent language had been used in programing presented by the stations. The Commission considered these complaints and then, after quoting the portion of our January 1964, decision set forth above, said:

> 6. We believe that the reasoning of our January 1964 decision as quoted above is equally applicable in our consideration of the instant applications. There can be no doubt that the stations provide a unique and well received programing for a sizable segment of the population of the areas they are licensed to serve. Viewing the complaints against the overall performance of the applicant during the renewal period, we find in the listeners' complaints no impediment to a grant of the applications.

This action was taken by a vote of 5 to 2, with Commissioners Bartley and Robert E. Lee dissenting.

I think the action with respect to KRAB is inconsistent with this line of rulings with respect to the very similar operations of the Pacifica stations. The only time we gave Pacifica a 1-year renewal—which I considered improper—we had complaints with respect to five programs, not just one as is the case here. Furthermore, our staff obtained tapes of the broadcasts and summarized them for us—whereas in this case we don't have a tape or transcript and so do not know the context in which the words complained of were used.

Since joining the Commission, Chairman Burch has expressed particular concern about the broadcast of obscene or indecent language. However, in an appearance on "Meet the Press" on January 25, 1970, the following colloquy took place:

> Miss Drew. You have made it clear one of your priorities is going to be dealing with the matter of obscenity. How do you deal with obscenity without getting into censorship?
>
> Mr. Burch. You will have probably some shady areas that will be rather difficult but it seems to me, *I still think there are certain words that have no redeeming social value.* I think there are certain instances of conduct which would fall into that category.
>
> * * * * * * *
>
> Miss Drew. How would these rules work? Would you have a list of words that would be forbidden or would you have—would it be desirable for stations to tape programs ahead of time so they could be sure nothing would go wrong, or would there be certain groups that would be inadvisable for a station to put on because they are more likely than others to use an obscenity? How do you envision these rules?
>
> Mr. Burch. I don't envision it as an easy rule to apply and I am not sure it will ever end up as a rule. We had an experience of trying to draft a statement of these words that would be acceptable and those words that would be unacceptable and, aside from it being the most obscene document probably that has ever been put together by a government agency, *it was not intelligible because obviously language has to be considered in connection with the events and the acts that are taking place.* [Italic supplied.]
>
> * * * * * * *

On January 30, 1970, in a speech before the Big Brothers of the San Francisco Bay area, he recognized that:

> * * * under the guiding criteria, obscene or indecent programing is not only patently offensive by contemporary community standards but *also without redeeming social value.* [Italic supplied.]

And, again, he said that:

> Obscene programing is material which, *taken as a whole,* appeals to a prurient interest in sex. [Italic supplied.]

He also stated that the airwaves shouldn't be given over to a steady diet of bland, inoffensive material, even though controversial programing is bound to offend some, and that a pattern of smut should be treated differently than isolated occurrences.

Thus it seems to me that the Chairman has recognized that language which offends some may be broadcast without the licensee incurring any penalty (1) if, considered in context, it does not appeal to prurient interest in sex or has redeeming social value, or (2) if the broadcast is an isolated occurrence rather than part of pattern of such programing. But the majority have clearly assessed a penalty here for a single broadcast, and have done so without considering the context in which the language was used and without being able to determine whether the program, as a whole, appealed to prurient interest or had offsetting redeeming social value.

I think this departure from precedent and from recently announced principles makes this action arbitrary and capricious. It is also arbitrary because it requires observance of an undefined standard—indeed, a nonexistent standard, so far as I know. It is clear that the majority will impose a sanction for the use of the three words involved here—at least if all three are used. Of course the licensee of KRAB did not know this when it inadvertently permitted their use over the air. And what is more, other licensees do not know even now what the dangerous words are because the majority have not listed them—and I'm not going to do their work of compiling a list of forbidden words for them. And no one—probably not even the majority—knows what other words will bring down the Commission's wrath upon a licensee who permits their broadcast—regardless of frequency, context, social value, or even knowledge by the licensee that they were to be used. If a list of all the words which either offend the majority—or which they think will offend too many of the public—were ever published as banned from the air, that would clearly be prior censorship prohibited by section 326 of the Communications Act, as well as the first amendment. But failure to publish the list may have even more chilling effect upon broadcast programing, because licensees may avoid the use of many, many more words out of fear that they may be on the Commission's secret list. Licensees may reject recorded, taped, or filmed program matter even though they think it has social value. Or they may avoid coverage of on-the-spot news in the course of which participants might use language the broadcasters think may bring Commission retaliation. Or licensees may exclude from discussion, interview, or other live programing individuals or groups they fear may use proscribed language which might not be excised through the use of a tape-delay device. I do not think any of these voluntary restraints would be in the public interest.

There is a third element of arbitrariness in this case—the majority apparently have a double standard when it comes to protecting the public from language which may offend some, or many, of them. Thus far they have imposed sanctions only against the licensees of KRAB and KPFA–KPFB and KPFK, noncommercial stations which broadcast very substantial cultural and informational services for audiences which support the stations through voluntary subscriber fees. They are now considering broadcasts by noncommercial educational stations. I certainly do not favor extension of this kind of action to commercial stations—at least in situations such as we have thus far considered. But if we are going to apply such a policy to noncommercial stations, simple logic and fairness would require that it be extended to the national networks and other commercial facilities.

We have received far more complaints, for example, about matters in the "Smothers Brothers Comedy Hour" and the "Rowan and Martin Laugh-In" than have ever been lodged against KRAB or the Pacifica stations. They did not involve four letter words, but did deal with language or video matter which certain members of the public deemed obscene, indecent or profane. But I do not recall that we ever directed an inquiry to CBS or NBC. ABC once initiated a series entitled "Turn On" which was canceled after one episode because of a flood of complaints that it was offensive—but the Commission did nothing.

Commissioner Robert E. Lee recently observed an incident on the Johnny Carson show which so offended him that he called the Washington vice president of NBC. But he was satisfied with a report that some minor employee had been transferred to another assignment—though higher ranking officials of the network must have known more about this matter than Lorenzo Milam did about the language broadcast by KRAB. Of course, NBC customarily bleeps out the kind of language which has gotten KRAB and the Pacifica stations into trouble. However, it is often still possible to discern what was said. While the network's effort to do the right thing satisfies some, others still complain—as Commissioner Lee did. But the Commission did not penalize NBC. And, of course, the Smothers, Rowan and Martin, and Carson shows have all involved patterns of material that some have found offensive, rather than the limited incidents at KRAB and the Pacifica stations.

On the CBS evening news of January 5, 1970, Walter Cronkite presented two bits of filmed news coverage containing what many people regarded as profanity. One minister in Detroit forwarded a petition signed by 598 people in his area alone protesting this broadcast. I know of no action—taken or planned—against CBS.

I want to make it clear, once again, that I do not believe any action is required in any of these cases. But I do not think the Government of the United States should ignore complaints against rich and powerful commercial broadcasters and pick only on small, noncommercial broadcasters. If there is, in truth, a dangerously growing use of obscene, indecent, or profane matter on radio and television requiring the course the majority are charting here, then they should press this effort all across broadcasting. At least this would require commercial broadcasters—who have never come to the defense of KRAB and the Pacifica stations in their efforts to preserve the right to present a broad range of material not found on many other stations—to face up to the issue. They have heretofore claimed first amendment protection for their asserted right to present their views over their facilities without presenting the opposing viewpoint in accordance with our fairness doctrine and for the broadcast of cigarette commercials and lottery information—all of which positions have been rejected by the Supreme Court. More constructively, in my opinion, they have defended the right—largely at the network level—to present news, commentary, convention coverage, and documentaries without review by government as to truth or adequacy of the contents of such broadcasts. The Commission has honored these claims, subject only to observance of the fairness doctrine and inquiry in cases of substantial allegations of rigging or staging of purported news events. I think the networks and the profitable and powerful stations should recognize that if they allow the Commission to interfere with the freedom of small, unconventional

stations—on an infrequent basis and in the context of material having redeeming social value—to broadcast language that offends some, then those in our society who think that all must conform to their standards will be encouraged to seek further restrictions on broadcast programing. Their next target will quite probably be—if it isn't already—what they regard as sexually suggestive or provocative material, whether in dialogue, costume, dance, or other form.

They are likely to push on to attack matter which offends their sense of propriety as to morals, political opinion, behavior, etc. Of course the majority will assure us that they will not countenance any such extension of the doctrine implicit in their action here, but if those they apparently think they are serving are to be assured that under no circumstances will they or their children be exposed to the broadcast of single words they regard as offensive, isn't it logical to expect this constituency to demand protection against the presentation of offensive ideas or the depiction of offensive conduct. After all, the impact of ideas and the force of example are much greater than the consequences of hearing an occasional four letter word. And it is discouraging, after our nearly 200 years of democracy, that so many are so ready to silence or suppress that of which they disapprove. I do not expect any rush of commercial broadcasters to the defense of those in their industry whom they probably regard as troublemakers, but it would be encouraging to see the National Association of Broadcasters come forward instead of leaving the defense of the perimeters of freedom to the American Civil Liberties Union. I can understand the hesitancy of the industry's leaders—they are worried about estranging a substantial part of their audience, not to mention powerful Members of Congress who have spoken out on this issue. But I think the stakes in this struggle may be more important for broadcasting than most of those matters which engage the attention of the NAB.

For that matter, it is not easy for me to defend four letter words. I find them offensive in most situations, and certainly do not seek the removal of all barriers to their use in broadcasting. I would be prepared to consider serious sanctions against a station whose operations revealed a pattern of substantial, repeated use of patently offensive language in contexts involving no redeeming social value. Cf. *Palmetto Broadcasting Co.*, 33 F.C.C. 250 (1962). I might, in some circumstances, support lesser penalties for even isolated use of such language without reason or justification. But when dedicated broadcasters who try to use radio to bring a wider than ordinary range of information and entertainment to their audiences occasionally broadcast such language because in their judgment it is important in the context of the programing—or inadvertently permit its use under circumstances where their policies would normally require its deletion—I do not think it serves the public interest to penalize them. Indeed, I think to do so violates the act and the Constitution.

KRAB and the Pacifica stations are supported directly by portions of their audiences who pay subscription fees to keep them in operation—while the rest of the public can, if they wish, listen from time to time. The Commission was questioned last December by the Senate Subcommittee on Communications about the broadcast of a poem on Pacifica's Los Angeles station and the grant to Pacifica of a construction permit for a new station in Houston. Pacifica has broadcast a tape of that hearing over at least two of its stations since then, and I have received a number of letters from regular listeners to those stations. These are not sensation seekers who tune in hoping to hear salacious or smutty material, but mature people who clearly value the educational, cultural, and other programing these stations present. Many of them listen very little to other stations, and indicate that these stations mean a great deal to them. They note the occasional broadcast of language which they recognize offends some who hear it, but contend that they are more offended by the conditions which lead to the occasional use of such language in records, poems, plays, discussions, and news coverage presented over the air than by the words themselves. They do not contend that others should listen to matter the latter find offensive, but do object to attempts to interfere with the freedom of the stations to continue to broadcast programing which they value and want to continue to receive.

KRAB-FM

(Letter to Jack Straw Memorial Foundation, radio station KRAB-FM, Seattle, Wash.)

DISSENTING OPINION OF COMMISSIONER NICHOLAS JOHNSON

I fully support Commissioner Cox's detailed and thoughtful dissenting statement in this case. I, too, believe the majority's decision to give KRAB a short-term, 1-year license renewal as a punishment for the thoughts, ideas, and forms of expression used by Rev. Paul Sawyer on one of KRAB's programs is misguided and inconsistent with those fundamental principles of free speech on which our society is based. I shall have more to say at a later date about FCC censorship of allegedly indecent thoughts and language over the broadcast medium in general, and about this specific case in particular. I think it important, however, that the public understand a few brief but important facets of this case.

First, it should be made clear that the Commission today punishes a broadcaster for the content of his programing—not because he violated any public, well-defined Commission rule or statute of Congress, but because, in the broadcaster's and not the FCC's opinion, he violated his station's own internal policy. Presumably if a station had an internal policy against criticism of the Government and one of its announcers accidently violated that policy, the precedent established by the majority would seem to indicate a 1-year renewal for the offending station.

Second, although Congress has given the Commission the authority to impose sanctions for the broadcast of "obscene, profane, or indecent" language (18 U.S.C. 1464), the Commission has not even attempted to apply that statute or determine whether the words or thoughts expressed over KRAB violate those statutory guidelines. In fact, the Commission never obtained a transcript of the offending program. It has no way of knowing whether or not the speech in question occurred in a socially redeeming context. Apparently the majority's position is that certain words are per se so offensive that any consideration of the context in which they were spoken is irrelevant.

Third, the incident involved was an isolated one. Due to the length of the program (30 hours), only portions of it were auditioned by the manager, Mr. Lorenzo Milam, before broadcast. The tape was removed from the air shortly after Mr. Milam heard the offending words. The majority does not contend that the incidents complained of have occurred repeatedly, or that the language in question falls outside the protection of the Constitution or FCC rules. To penalize a licensee for an isolated incident (even if it did violate our rules, which apparently it did not), is a marked departure from established Commission policy. In *Pacifica Foundation*, 36 F.C.C. 147, 148 (1964), we said that in matters of this sort we were "not concerned with individual programs." Rather, our "very limited concern" was whether, "upon the overall examination, some substantial pattern of operation inconsistent with the public-interest standard clearly and patently emerges." We refused to take punitive action for "a few isolated programs." Our position was clear:

> The standard of public interest is not so rigid that an honest mistake or error on the part of a licensee results in drastic action against him where his overall record demonstrates a reasonable effort to serve the needs and interests of his community. (36 F.C.C. at 150.)

The majority does not even consider whether the incident involved an "honest mistake or error," as the facts clearly indicate. And KRAB's "overall record" is clearly superior to most other comparable stations.

Fourth, the public should know that KRAB is not some marginal operation which pumps out aural drivel and profit-maximizes with high rates of commercialization. KRAB–FM is a noncommercial station supported by contributions from its listeners. It devotes over 95 percent of its broadcast day to the performing arts, public affairs, news, and general educational programing. How many other stations can boast of such a record? Within recent years, this Commission has renewed the licenses of a station broadcasting 33 minutes of commercials an hour, a station that broadcast no news, and a station that defrauded advertisers out of thousands of dollars. Today the majority punishes a noncommercial station for a portion of a single program, broadcast in its attempt to provide its listeners with unconventional programing—and ignores one of the more outstanding broadcast records in the country.

Fifth, the Commission makes reference to "complaints from the public" concerning the programing of KRAB. Yet a quick check of the FCC complaints file on KRAB shows far more support than criticism. Here is a sampling of a few comments: "Fine and unusual broadcasting record of KRAB–FM," "no comparable radio programing," "urbane, sophisticated, and intellectually provocative," "programing is of extraordinary interest," "you need the freedom to broadcast important and controversial programs * * *." I do not believe any station can broadcast provocative and challenging programing without pushing at the borders of the conventional. When that happens, there will always be some who will be offended. There will always be those who would like to silence others—to blank out the ideas and thoughts they present.

That is not the American way. This Commission simply cannot respond to such pressure.

NOTES

[1] Commissioner Bartley dissented to the form of the hearing. He would have had the hearing deal with the issue of whether the license should be renewed at all. Commissioner Johnson concurred in the result.
[2] After the prehearing conference the Hearing Examiner originally designated had to withdraw from the proceeding. Examiner Ernest Nash was designated, with the consent of all parties, by Order of the Chief Hearing Examiner. (FCC 70M–1418, October 15, 1970)
[3] Friede is 30, Palmer is 24, Seymour is 25 and Wiater is also 25 years old.
[4] Words used were "balls" and "Goddamn".
[5] There was no claim of obscenity regarding this usage.
[6] New York Times, February 28, 1971.
[7] New York Times, January 23, 1971.

AFTER RECONSIDERATION THE F.C.C. GRANTS KRAB-FM A FULL THREE YEAR LICENSE RENEWAL DECLARING: "THERE IS REALLY NO QUARREL BY KRAB WITH THE STANDARD SET BY THE COMMISSION THAT BROADCASTERS SHOULD AVOID LANGUAGE THAT IS PATENTLY OFFENSIVE BY CONTEMPORARY COMMUNITY STANDARDS AND UTTERLY WITHOUT REDEEMING SOCIAL VALUE. WE CANNOT AVOID THE DIFFICULT RESULT THAT WHAT PARTICULAR LANGUAGE MAY BE UNACCEPTABLE FOR BROADCAST IS NOT SUSCEPTIBLE TO BEING REDUCED TO AN IMMUTABLE, TIME RESISTANT GLOSSARY."

The Jack Straw Memorial Foundation, 29 F.C.C.2d 334 (1971)

BEFORE THE
FEDERAL COMMUNICATIONS COMMISSION
WASHINGTON, D.C.   20554

In Re Application of
THE JACK STRAW MEMORIAL FOUNDATION
For Renewal of the License of Station
KRAB–FM, Seattle, Wash.

Docket No. 18943
File No. BRH–1430
File No. BRSCA–801

APPEARANCES

Michael H. Bader, Esq., (Haley Bader & Potts), on behalf of The Jack Straw Memorial Foundation; and *Walter C. Miller, Esq.*, on behalf of the Chief, Broadcast Bureau, Federal Communications Commission.

INITIAL DECISION OF HEARING EXAMINER ERNEST NASH

(Issued March 22, 1971; Effective date May 14, 1971, pursuant to Section 1.276 of the Commission's Rules)

INTRODUCTION

1. KRAB–FM is a non-commercial educational broadcast station operating on 107.7 mHz, Channel 299 at Seattle, Washington. It is licensed to The Jack Straw Memorial Foundation. An application for renewal of KRAB's license was filed by the licensee on November 4, 1968.

2. In a letter to the licensee dated January 21, 1970, the Commission granted a short-term renewal of KRAB's license. In its letter, the Commission said that it had received complaints from the public that profane, indecent or obscene language had been broadcast during the past license period. Referring to the station's stated policy against broadcasting obscene and libelous material, the Commission concluded that in broadcasting a program presented by Reverend Paul Sawyer, KRAB had violated its own programming policy. Commissioners Cox and Johnson issued statements dissenting from the views expressed in the Commission's letter and from the action granting the applicant a short-term rather than a full term renewal (21 FCC 2d 833).

3. KRAB filed a petition on March 20, 1970, asking that the Commission reconsider its action and grant a full 3 year renewal of its license. In response to this petition the Commission reconsidered its earlier action to the extent of offering the applicant a hearing as to whether or not it was entitled to a full-term rather than a short-term renewal (FCC 70–655, July 7, 1970). KRAB accepted the Commission's offer of a hearing and its application for renewal was thereupon designated for hearing upon the following issues: (FCC 70–873, August 19, 1970).

> (1) to determine whether KRAB–FM has exercised proper licensee responsibility in effectuating its policy regarding the suitability of material for broadcast; and
> (2) Whether in the light of issue (1), the public interest would be served by a one year or a full three-year renewal of the license of KRAB–FM.[1]

4. In its Order of Designation, the Commission also directed that the hearing examine into KRAB's handling of the Reverend Paul Sawyer broadcast, which took place in August 1967, and programs broadcast on March 9 and 10, 1969, which involved discussions with members of the San Francisco Mime Theatre. The Broadcast Bureau was also directed to give timely notice to the applicant if it intended to rely upon any other broadcasts relevant to the issues designated for the hearing.

5. On September 9, 1970, KRAB filed a Motion to Clarify and Enlarge Issues. In that Motion the applicant, among other things, requested the addition of a meritorious program issue. This request was granted and the following issue was added to the proceeding:

> to determine whether the programming of KRAB–FM has been meritorious, particularly with regard to public service programs.

(26 FCC 2d 97)
A prehearing conference was held in Washington, D.C., on September 23, 1970.[2] At that conference, the Broadcast Bureau gave written notice that it intended to rely upon a number of other programs during the course of the hearing. In this notification the Broadcast Bureau detailed the alleged obscenities which had been broadcast and gave the names of the complainants who had brought attention to these programs. As listed in the Broadcast Bureau's notification, the following programs were added to those specified by the Commission: Two programs in which the principal speaker was the Reverend James Bevel and which were broadcast during December 1967; a program with Dave Wertz broadcast 9:30 to 10:30 p.m., October 1, 1968; a program entitled "Murder at Kent State" broadcast 5:30 to 6:00 p.m., August 10, 1970.

6. Hearings were held in Seattle, Washington, on November 12, 13 and 16, 1970, and the record was closed on November 16, 1970.

FINDINGS OF FACT

1. The Jack Straw Memorial Foundation is a non-profit educational corporation organized under the laws of the State of Washington. It is the licensee of KRAB in Seattle and KBOO in Portland, Oregon. A Board of Trustees consisting of 11 members, nine of whom live in the Seattle area, are responsible for the formulation of the policies under which KRAB is operated. These policies have taken the form of written resolutions, oral understandings, or statements published in the KRAB program guides.

2. KRAB operates as a "free forum broadcast station" designed to encourage free and complete public expression. Its basic policies regarding program suitability were originally formulated by Lorenzo W. Milam who was the founder of KRAB and owned the station until he transferred it to the Jack Straw Memorial Foundation. These policies were largely oral understandings until they were reduced to writing and formally adopted by the Board of Trustees after the Commission had raised questions regarding the suitability of the content of certain programs which KRAB had broadcast.

3. KRAB is listener supported. It receives its funds in the form of contributions from listeners and has been the recipient of grants from various foundations. It operates on an annual budget of about $14,000. Most of the regular employees of the station receive little or no pay for their work. A good deal of the work needed to run the station is performed by volunteers from among its listening audience.

4. KRAB's policies as to determining whether or not a program is suitable for broadcast were related to the Commission in a transmittal made November 21, 1967, as follows:

The station will not avoid programs because of their unusualness or outspokenness. The primary criteria of broadcast standard is fairness: that the station should provide a great deal of time to speakers, writers, and thinkers from a wide variety of viewpoints. It is crucial that their material be well thought-out, meaningful, and insightful; there should be no sensationalism for its own sake.

In the case of material which raises questions as to its merit for broadcast because of some social, moral, aesthetic, or scatological outspokenness, the material shall be referred by the Program Director to the Station Manager for audition and judgement as to whether it should be broadcast entire, elided, or not at all.

If the program inspires concern on the behalf of the Station Manager as to its appropriateness for broadcast, the program shall be auditioned and passed on by the Board of Directors meeting as a whole, or by those directors appointed by the board to judge the material.

This simple procedure has worked well in the past with, perhaps, one or two programs a month being eliminated by the Station Manager or the Board or a Committee of the Board for obscenity, obscurantism, sensationalism, or simple boorishness. It relies on the judgment and good taste of the station staff, integrated with that of the Board—both with respect to programs presented and those referred to higher authority.

These standards or policies are the same ones which are in effect now and which were in effect during the broadcast of the programs which resulted in this proceeding.

5. Central to the effectuation of policies regarding programming suitability are the trustees of the Jack Straw Memorial Foundation and a group consisting of five regular employees of KRAB who audition programs for suitability. Two of these employees, the station manager Gregory Palmer, and the music director of the station, Robert L. Friede, are also trustees. The programs are pre-auditioned for suitability by Michael Wiater, the program director; Bill Seymour, the production manager; and Jane Reynolds, the production assistant as well as Friede and Palmer. Before going into the procedures which are followed, let us briefly sketch the backgrounds of these trustees and employees.

Trustees

(1) *Jonathan Gallant* is President of the Foundation and was one of its founding members. Professor Gallant teaches genetics at the University of Washington; has a PhD from Johns Hopkins University; and holds a Simon Guggenheim fellowship. He has appeared on a number of music, interview and commentary programs on KRAB.

(2) *Byron D. Coney* is a lawyer specializing in real estate and mortgage banking. He is a graduate of the University of Washington and of Harvard Law School. Mr. Coney has been secretary of the Jack Straw Memorial Foundation for three years and a Trustee since 1965. He has been a frequent participant in KRAB programs since 1963.

(3) *David Calhoun* is a native of Missoula, Montana; an honor graduate of The College of Puget Sound; manager of station KBOO, Portland, Oregon; a one time student at the University of Washington Medical School; a graduate student of literature; and a student of the organ and harpsichord. He began as a volunteer at KRAB in 1965.

(4) *David A. Roland* is an electrical engineer with degrees from the Universities of California and Washington. He holds a first-class radio telephone operators license, has worked at KRAB as a volunteer, and has been a Trustee since April, 1970.

(5) *John W. Prothero* is a research scientist at the University of Washington Medical School and holds a PhD in biophysics. He is a commentator on KRAB; a writer on scientific and social topics: an outdoors enthusiast; and a devotee of the performing arts.

(6) *Gary Margason* is a former student at San Jose State College and the University of California where he studied chemical engineering, physics, and sociology. He was one of the organizers of the Jack Straw Memorial Foundation and has served as a Trustee since 1962. He was manager of KRAB from April 1969 to January 1970. He is presently an employee of the Burke Museum and Genetics Laboratory at the University of Washington.

(7) *Michael C. Duffy* is a high school English teacher and a graduate of the University of Washington. He has produced and presented a series entitled Classic Jazz since 1963 and he has been a Trustee since 1969.

(8) *Helen H. Norton* is a housewife with interests in painting, studying and community affairs. Her community associations include President of a PTA, program director and religious education instructor for a Unitarian Fellowship and volunteer work for organizations such as Head Start, ACLU, Inter-Racial Dialogue and KRAB. She has been a Trustee since May, 1970.

(9) *Nancy Keith* is a graduate of Washington State University, a journalist and a sometime volunteer worker at KRAB. Between 1964–1967 she was program director. She has been a Trustee since 1965.

(10) *Robert L. Friede* is a graduate of Dartmouth College with a degree in anthropology. His interests lie in the field of ethnomusicology. He has been music director of KRAB since 1968 dealing chiefly with jazz, blues and rock and roll. He has sought to bring to the listeners something of the music and cultures of societies from all over the world. He was elected Treasurer and Trustee in May 1970.

(11) *Gregory L. Palmer* is a native of Seattle who attended the University of Washington. He is the present manager of KRAB.

Employees

(1) *Michael Wiater* is program director. He is a poet and an artist whose paintings have been exhibited. He has been with the English Department of the University of Washington for a number of years and is a graduate student of English. He serves as KRAB's liaison with the University community.

(2) *Bill Seymour* is production manager at KRAB. He was a student at Antioch College and he has had training and experience in the technical aspects of broadcasting. He auditions programs mainly with a view toward determining the technical quality of the recordings.

(3) *Jane Reynolds* is a student at Antioch College. She works at KRAB as part of the work-study program of her college. Her employment at KRAB is temporary. She generally auditions programs in her special fields of interest, Womens Liberation and Social Welfare. Because of her youth, she is 18 years old, Palmer post-auditions most of her work.[3]

6. Palmer has been station manager since January 1970. Preceding him in that post were Lorenzo Milam, who founded the station and served as manager until March 1968; Chuck Reinsh, who served as manager for a short period beginning in March 1968; and Gary Margason, who succeeded Reinsh and was manager until Palmer took over the job.

7. Each of the employees who auditions programs uses his or her judgment as to whether or not a program is suitable for broadcast. Each has developed expertise in certain fields and reviews programs in his fields of expertness. Besides obscenity, the auditioners look for such other matters which would affect suitability for broadcast as advocacy of law violation, boorishness, and obscurantism. If any of the four employees should have a question regarding the suitability of any material for broadcast it is discussed with Palmer, the station manager, and any problems Palmer may have as to suitability for broadcast he discusses with the Board of Trustees.

8. Palmer has a general knowledge of what is to be considered obscene so far as broadcasting is concerned. In his view, a stricter standard should apply to broadcasting than is applicable to literature or other media. He relates his standard of what constitutes obscenity to the standards of the community rather than his personal view as to what may be considered obscene. Particular standards are developed in discussions among the employees responsible for auditioning programs and among the Board of Trustees.

9. As a matter of station policy, if anyone of four particular words or their derivations should be used in a program proposed for broadcast, reference must be made to the station manager for his decision as to whether these words are to be deleted from the program before broadcast. According to Palmer, in editing programs for suitability, 99 per cent of the time when something is deleted for obscenity, it is apt to be one of these words or one of their derivations. It is not the policy of KRAB to exclude these words from all programs broadcast regardless of the context in which the words are used. Palmer has never been confronted with a situation in which an entire program had to be rejected because it was obscene. From time to time it has been found that certain words or expressions had to be deleted before broadcast in particular cases.

10. Palmer keeps abreast of current decisions and pronouncements of the Federal Communications Commission. He receives such material from the station's communications counsel. He is the principal liaison between the personnel who operate the station and the Board of Trustees.

11. A number of programs were edited and changes were made for suitability before broadcast. Palmer deleted two words from a tape entitled "The Army on Trial" because he felt that in the context in which they were used they were obscene. "Running the Bulls in Blue", a documentary produced by KRAB, was edited but mainly because of obscurities, such as crowds moving from one place to another, rather than for the deletion of obscenities. A commentary by Selma Waldman dealing with the Womens Liberation Movement contained some talk about the words men use to describe women. After a discussion with Selma Waldman, Palmer, apparently with her agreement, deleted two of the words from the broadcast. Following is a list of some other programs which were edited to remove obscenities before being broadcast over KRAB.

Comedy of Lenny Bruce
Women of the Seventies: Rights, Roles and Risks, local panel discussion
William Kunstler Speaking at the University of Washington
Stanley Crouch: Ain't no Ambulances for no Nigguhs Tonight Flying Dutchman recording
A Night in Santa Rita, Flying Dutchman recording
Pregnancy: Love it or Leave it, local panel discussion
Son of Earth Day, tape from Pacifica
The New York Panther 21 Manifesto, from Radio Free People
Vamping on the Panthers, local documentary
Commentary by Doug Miranda

12. From time to time Palmer has referred questions regarding the suitability of programming for broadcast to the Board of Trustees. For example, it became known that a group called the Seattle Liberation Front would hold a demonstration. He knew where it was going to take place and there was conveyed to Palmer the anticipation of a possibility that there would be violence. It was thought that this demonstration was important enough that the program dealing with it be broadcast live, if possible. This matter was discussed with the Board of Trustees at a meeting because of the expectation that a program dealing with the demonstration might result in the broadcast of words or expressions inconsistent with the station's standards of suitability. After consideration and discussion it was decided to broadcast the program without editing even though the tape recorders might very well pick up words or expressions not considered suitable for broadcast under the station's usual standards. There was no evidence presented at the hearing to indicate that the program did involve broadcast of any offensive words.

13. Another example of a matter of obscenity discussed with the Board of Trustees by Palmer was a proposal to remove one of the taboo words from the station's list of four. This was proposed because Friede had heard the particular word in a broadcast of a national educational television program. There was some feeling that there was no longer a need to continue the taboo against this particular word. This matter was tabled by the Board of Trustees after discussion. KRAB continues to have four taboo words. Broadcast of any of these may be permitted only after special consideration by the station manager or by the station manager in consultation with the Board of Trustees.

14. Two programs were specified for particular consideration in this proceeding by the Commission in the Order of Designation and consistent with that Order the Broadcast Bureau designated three more programs for special consideration. These programs were the broadcast by the Reverend Paul Sawyer; the interview with a member of the San Francisco Mime Theatre; the talk given by the Reverend James Bevel; the record entitled "Murder at Kent State"; and the bluegrass program hosted by Dave Wertz. These programs were alleged to have violated the station's policies in that obscenities were permitted to be broadcast. These programs and the circumstances under which they were broadcast were as follows:

Paul Sawyer Broadcast

15. At the time of the broadcast mentioned by the Commission's Order, Reverend Paul Sawyer was Minister of the Lake Forest Park Unitarian Church located in a suburb just north of Seattle. Lorenzo Milam was manager of KRAB at that time. He had come to know Sawyer through a mutual interest in sound and sound techniques. Sawyer had been a participant in some programs on KRAB and hosted a regular program dealing with sound effects.

16. Milam found out that Sawyer had been preparing a tape recorded autobiography. By the time Milam found out about it, the autobiography was about 30 hours in length. Milam listened to portions of this tape, thought it was interesting, and thought that it would be worth broadcasting on KRAB as an "autobiographic marathon". Nancy Keith and one or two other employees at KRAB listened to parts of the Sawyer autobiography. Neither Nancy Keith nor Milam recalled hearing any objectionable language in the portions of the tape which they heard. In discussing the Sawyer autobiography, some of the station personnel expressed a view that it should not be broadcast because it was dull. Nevertheless, the decision was made to go ahead with the broadcast.

17. Broadcast of the taped autobiography took place on August 5, 1967. Miss Keith was on duty at the station. Sawyer was there to handle the playing of the tape because of problems with the quality of the sound. Milam was at home. At about 9:00 a.m., he turned on the radio to listen to KRAB while eating his breakfast.

18. As Milam describes it, soon after he started listening to the autobiography, he heard a word which frightened him. Apparently, the autobiography included some descriptions of Sawyer's intimate relations with his wife. Obscenity frightens Milam, and he recognizes obscene words by the emotional response he has toward hearing them, characterized by sweating and coldness of his hands. Milam could not remember the exact word or words spoken which caused this emotional response while he was listening to the Sawyer tape. He conceded that the actual words were probably those related by the Broadcast Bureau in their Bill of Particulars or their equivalent.

19. Milam called the station and talked to Miss Keith. Miss Keith had already heard what had upset Milam and she was also quite upset. Milam told Miss Keith to talk to Sawyer. She did and Sawyer apologized saying that there would be nothing more like that on the tape. Broadcast of the tape continued but more language frightening to Milam and upsetting to Miss Keith came out. Milam called the station again and talked to Sawyer. He told Sawyer that he was threatening the station's license and he didn't want him messing around like that. Seemingly, Sawyer didn't have the same concern over the use of obscene words that Milam had, but he did give assurance that nothing else obscene was on the tape.

20. Sawyer was permitted to continue to broadcast the autobiography, but obscene words continued. This time, Milam got into his car and drove to the studio. He took the Sawyer program off the air and substituted a program of Indian music in its place.

San Francisco Mime Theatre

21. A group known as the San Francisco Mime Theatre presented some performances in Seattle about the middle of February 1969. P. J. Doyle, of the Adult Education Department of the Seattle Public Library System, attended these performances and was favorably impressed with the group. Doyle, however, was annoyed with what we considered to be an excessive use of the four-letter Anglo-Saxon verb denoting the act of sexual intercourse. Doyle's job with the library system calls upon him to use radio. He is not a professional librarian, having been a book dealer prior to coming with the library system about five or six years ago. Doyle broadcasts a regular weekly program over KRAB dealing with new book acquisitions or with books in the library's collection which have a bearing on outstanding current events. Doyle's programs are productions of the Seattle Public Library.

22. He made arrangements to interview an actor, Joseph Lamuto, who was a member of the San Francisco Mime Theatre company. Lamuto and Doyle met at the KRAB studio where the interview was taped. Although station personnel were present during the interview, it was not supervised or auditioned, as such, by a member of the station's staff.

23. Generally, the interview dealt with the Mime company's performance, but a small portion of the interview, a transcript of which is included in the record, consisted of a discussion of the consequences of using the four-letter Anglo-Saxon verb previously described. In the transcript of the interview, Doyle assures Lamuto that it is alright to say the verb and it is used about four or five times. Among other things, Lamuto illustrated his argument that people over react to this word by referring to a poem by Lawrence Ferlinghetti in which this verb is used about 20 or 25 times in such a way that it loses its usual effect, according to Lamuto. In this short discussion, Lamuto and Doyle dealt with the word and its use. It was not a discussion of the act it described and, the word was not used as epithet or expletive.

24. This interview was broadcast about two weeks after it had been taped. Prior to broadcast the tape was not auditioned by KRAB personnel nor was it edited by KRAB. Doyle had had discussions with Miss Keith regarding the standards of suitability which KRAB applied to its programs. He was aware of these standards. He considered his interview with Lamuto to have been a serious discussion about the use of the English language which had backfired. He was concerned that a program produced by the city library should get KRAB into trouble. Books which contain "four-letter words" are on the open shelves in the Seattle Public Library. Included among these are they poems of Lawrence Ferlinghetti. These books may be taken out by any holder of an adult card and an adult card may be obtained by anyone 12 years of age or older. Doyle still broadcasts his weekly program over KRAB. When he comes to words such as the one that caused problems in his interview he substitutes a "blank" and feels foolish for having to do so.

Dave Wertz

25. Dave Wertz describes himself as an amateur expert on bluegrass music. He had a program on KRAB which consisted of bluegrass music and pertinent accompanying commentary. Wertz tried to imitate the style of such well known programs of bluegrass as Nashville's Grand Ole Opry and Richmond's Old Dominion Barn Dance. Between broadcasts of music selections, Dave Wertz would tell what he called "corn country jokes".

26. When Wertz came to work for KRAB it was made clear to him that he was not to use any obscenity on the air. His type of joke does not contemplate the use of obscene words. He had no recollection of what he may have said on his broadcast of October 1968, but he had been told that someone had called to complain about the program. He may have told a few of his country stories. An example which he gave is the one about "the hillbilly whose bathroom caught on fire but fortunately the flames didn't reach the house."

Murder at Kent State

27. "Murder at Kent State" is a recording produced under the Flying Dutchman label. KRAB played three records under this label during 1970. Two of these records, after preview, were edited for obscenity and a number of words were removed before the records were broadcast. "Murder at Kent State" was also previewed before broadcast, but the same or similar words spoken on this record were not deleted prior to broadcast.

28. "Murder at Kent State" is a reading of a series of articles by Pete Hamill which appeared in the New York Post. These articles describe the incident which occurred at Kent State University in which a number of students were killed during a confrontation with the Ohio National Guard.

29. Before it was broadcast, this record was auditioned by the station manager, the program director and some of the Trustees of KRAB. The record took a total of 46 minutes to play and included about a half-dozen obscenities including an epithet directed at the Vice President of the United States.

30. KRAB played the record on August 10, 1970, several months after the incident which it describes had occurred. In playing the record without deleting the obscene or indecent language, KRAB's management was moved by the consideration that any editing would adversely affect the emotional impact of the record. It was thought that the record was newsworthy and important, particularly to the university community at the University of Washington, which was a considerable proportion of KRAB's regular audience. Since the University station had returned to broadcasting programming which did not include matters of current relevancy to the student body and faculty, KRAB felt it had an obligation to fill a void by giving the university community a program such as that represented by the recording "Murder at Kent State."

Reverend James Bevel

31. On December 9, 1967, KRAB broadcast the tape recording of a talk by Reverend James Bevel given at the University of California, Berkeley. This tape had come to KRAB from the Pacifica Foundation and the box in which it had been forwarded indicated that some deletions from the tape had been made. There were complaints to the FCC about this broadcast and the station was visited by an inspector from the Commission. This inspector asked for and was given the tape for copying. The tape was returned to KRAB. A previously scheduled broadcast of the tape for December 26, 1967, was cancelled. At that time, Lorenzo Milam, who was station manager, was out of town. Before the broadcast of December 9, 1967, the tape had been auditioned by an employee of KRAB.

32. A meeting of the Board of Trustees was held on January 2, 1968, to discuss what to do about rebroadcast of Bevel's talk. It was the unanimous decision of the Board to rebroadcast Bevel's talk, but to preface the rebroadcast with a statement by Milam describing the events which had taken place since the tape was played on December 9, 1967.

33. A transcript of the tape and a transcript of Milam's introduction were received at the hearing. An offer that the tape of these talks also be included with the record was rejected, but the Examiner did listen to the tape. Bevel's talk is largely a rambling discourse directed at what is apparently a predominately white student audience whom he considers to consist of radicals. Bevel uses certain expressions which may be described as well-known slang or vulgar references to virility: or common blasphemies or abstruse expressions which sound like they ought to be somebody's obscenity.[4] These are all listed by the Broadcast Bureau under the heading of alleged obscenities including a reference to academic "pimps to freak you off". This last quoted set of words, if it is an obscenity, is a contribution to the Examiner's education in an area where he had thought life had foreclosed all possibility of novelty.

34. Milam in his introductory remarks unleased a somewhat candid though not entirely novel evaluation of a broadcaster's feelings toward the FCC. Probably, the best way to make findings as to the tenor of the talks given by Milam and Bevel would be to quote a representative portion of each presentation. Milam's introductory statement was much shorter than Bevel's talk, but it does give an insight into the licensee's attitude which motivated it in broadcasting Bevel's talk without deletions for obscenity. Milam had the following to say:

The FCC has responsibilities to exercise care in the power of licensing of broadcast stations. The Communications Act of 1934 specifically states that the FCC shall in no way indulge in censorship of programs. The creators of that government body were wisely concerned that freedom of speech through broadcasting should in no way be curtailed. This is where the issue has been joined with Reverend James Bevel and KRAB and the local official of the FCC. In the month that we've had to stew over this event we've come to feel that this confiscation of tape was a case pure and simple, of censorship. Censorship of the cruelest form, for it created in us a deep sense of fear over the future of KRAB, the disposition of our valuable license and all the deep questions of government control. We've decided to rebroadcast the James Bevel tape. We've done so fully aware of the dangers to our permit, our broadcast license. We, and now I'm speaking for the Board of Directors of the Jack Straw Memorial Foundation which is the parent corporation of KRAB, have met and discussed at great length the possible consequences of the act of rebroadcasting of this material and we've decided that we must replay it.

The FCC in its rules has very wisely demanded that broadcast licensees should have full responsibility for the material they broadcast. They, the broadcasters alone must act on behalf of the public interest, convenience and necessity. No one else can be responsible and if the broadcaster fails in this duty he's subject to the revocation of his license. We here at KRAB feel that we would be sabotaging the public interest, convenience and necessity if we didn't play the James Bevel tape at this time. For despite his strong language, a language that is an integral part of his message, James Bevel is trying to tell us something important, trying to express a crucial view of Negro-white relations in this country. KRAB has always been a forum for the dispossessed, we've opened this frequency at 107.7 megacycles in Seattle to hundreds of different viewpoints about hundreds of different subjects. We've done this not because we agree with any one speaker, we couldn't conceivably do so, but because the miracle of free speech in this country lends itself to knowledge and understanding of so many disparate viewpoints, even those which may be offensive to us. For by understanding the hundred voices of antagonism one can and does become an active, knowing and thinking part of the democratic system. James Bevel doesn't speak for KRAB, none does really, but James Bevel is a representative of an important and sometimes frightening new force in America. By failing to play this talk KRAB would be doing a disservice to its listeners denying them a knowledge of the important forces around them. We would be saying, in effect, that the license of KRAB is more important than freedom of speech and freedom of knowledge. We

simply cannot as responsible broadcasters ignore this duty, we'd be foolish not to play the words of James Bevel.

35. Bevel spoke for about an hour. His choice of language was not such as one would expect to hear from a pulpit. His ideas were expressed in a stream of consciousness form with little attention to the niceties of rhetorical organization. To get an idea of what Bevel spoke about and how he expressed himself, it is best that we let his own words speak for him. A fair sample of what he had to say and the choice of language he made is the following:

Man is a love animal and love is an energy just like oxygen that man needs in order to act rational and when a man can inhale and breathe into his body love energy he acts rational, natural and truthful, that's why you hear the brothers saying 'acting natural'. To be natural is to consume love energy that is present in the universe and there's only one thing that can stop man from consuming and acting rational and that is if man begins to fear anything he lose the capacity to love, himself, that's the nature of the problem. Lot of folks want to argue with the chancellor, and a lot of folks want to argue with the administration, and a lot of folks want to argue with LBJ, and a lot of folks here want to argue with their mommas and their daddys and very few people here are prepared to say that the reason that the administration function as it does is that it's fearful, and very few of us here are prepared to say the reason we are here today is that we afraid that if we don't pick up a piece of paper we can't have protein. Most of us can't say that, but the realities are that we are here not because we are wise and not because we are in the pursuit of education but because we afraid not to be here. Fear, fear is a disease it's a sickness, for fear does not allow man to perceive the universe as it is because it locks man out of himself, and in the past if you ever studied literature. A lot of you jive folks studied literature and didn't even know what the hell you was doing. In class if we study literature of the past, men who live at another period when the energy was in another form, you read a story in the old testament about Adam being locked out of the Garden of Eden, man being locked out of himself, because he feared something, and when man is locked out of himself, and when he begin to fear he acts the same way, he starts hating folks. You see I get tired of walking round in this country listening to city jitterbug fascists, who call themselves radicals pretending that they're any different from the Administration, when they know damn well they're driven by fear just like the Administration, but you see fear makes man hate, what it does is make man project his contempt for himself on to other folks, and why we pretending that its the Administration that is holding up our freedom, and like we want to pretend like Reagan is holding up our freedom, and we want to pretend like Johnson is holding up our freedom, and the realities are that we hold up our own freedom because we afraid to pick up our own nuts[5] and say I'm a man here in the universe and I ain't going no goddam place, that's why we don't have freedom!

Programming and Program Policy

36. KRAB does not avoid programs because they are unusual or outspoken. Its musical programs cover a broad range from jazz to classical. Its policy in music programming is to avoid music which is broadcast by other stations in the area. Programs of oriental, pre-classical western and other types of unusual music are broadcast. KRAB also programs jazz, blues, rock, bluegrass, renaissance and baroque as well as music from foreign countries such as, Japan, Norway, Sweden, New Zealand, Korea and others.

37. KRAB broadcasts a substantial number of political programs and discussion programs not ordinarily heard on radio. In a recent primary election, more than 20 candidates were each given a half hour of time to present their views in their own way. Some candidates spoke for the half hour, others received calls from listeners, and others were interviewed. A recent referendum dealing with the State's abortion laws led KRAB to broadcast a two hour discussion moderated by a member of the staff with panelists representing both sides of the question. Religious programs have included interviews with clergymen who "speak in tongues"; the "1970 Annual Gymanfa Ganu", a Welch religious program; an interview with the Hare Krishna sect; as well as interviews with religious personages and presentation of religious programs not ordinarily heard in the Seattle area.

38. KRAB submitted 31 pages listing by title and participants its public service programs of note. Ordinarily, such lists do not tell us much about a station's programming. In this instance, however, some idea of the range of subject matter and variety of personages heard over KRAB are apparent. The following is a selection taken from KRAB's public service programming exhibit:

PICKETING IN BELLINGHAM. In March, 40 picketers protesting the war in Viet Nam were arrested and booked for disturbing the peace. A program of interviews and comments.
SHOULD COMMUNISTS BE EXPELLED FROM UNIVERSITY FACULTIES? debate between Fred Schwartz of Christian Anti-Communist Crusade and Otis Hood, Chairman of Communist Party of Massachusetts.
HAS THE COURT USURPED THE POWERS OF CONGRESS. Robert M. Hutchins.
THE CHANGING MEANING OF THE ORGANIZATION, Dr. Harry Levinson, address on industrial management and the psychological meaning of the organization of work.
EUTHANASIA, local, panel discussion.
THE WILL OF ZEUS. Stringfellow Barr discusses his book and compares the political problems of classical Greece and contemporary America.
GOLD AND THE GOLD SITUATION, panel discussion, Dr. Ernest Patty, former Pres., University of Alaska, and Pres. and Mgr. of some gold mining operations, Edward McMillan, from NB of C, Dr. Frederick B. Exner from KRAB, and John McFalls, stock consultant, local.
PEACE KEEPING UNDER THE RULE OF LAW, panel discussion on national sovereignty and the world community, Justice Earl Warren, Kenzo Takayanagi, Chairman of the Japanese Cabinet Commission on the Constitution, Senator J. William Fulbright, others.
JACQUES COUSTEAU, producer of World without Sun, lecture in Washington, D.C., on exploitation by man of natural resources.
PRODUCTION VS. REPRODUCTION, the Population Prob-

lem in the U.S. and in Calif., panel discussion, Marriner Eccles, moderator, Alice Leopold, Lewis Heilbron, Dr. Karl Brandt, others.

TRIP TO DJAKARTA, Beverly Axelrod on her meeting with Vietnamese women.

ACADEMIC FREEDOM, Arthur Flemming, President of Univ. of Ore. and former Sec. of Health, Ed., and Welfare, address, at EWSC at Cheney.

YOUNG AMERICANS FOR FREEDOM, Jack Cox, YAF State chairman for Calif., address on government errors.

A PEEK AT PIKE, documentary on Pike Street Market.

EMMETT MCLOUGHLIN: CATHOLICISM AND FREE MASONRY IN AMERICA.

POLITICAL CONDITIONS IN SOUTH AFRICA, sociology prof. Pierre van den Bergh.

TRAFFIC IN NARCOTICS, Detective Chet Sprinkle of Seattle Police Narcotics Bureau.

DR. GATCH AND THE DIET OF WORMS, Southern physician on poverty conditions.

39. As earlier stated, KRAB receives its funds from its listeners and from various foundations. It has received money for various purposes from such organizations as the Jaffe Foundation of Philadelphia, which is administered by Ambassador Walter Annenberg; the James E. Merrill Trust of New York; the Gerber Foundation; and others, including:

$10,000 from Seattle's PONCHO. PONCHO is a fund raising organization for the arts in Seattle. It made a lump sum allocation to KRAB to extend its operations. PONCHO representatives made the grant to KRAB because it "performed a very valuable and unique function as an open forum radio station through which arts needs, as well as all kinds of other social needs, local, regional needs, could be explored and examined."

$7,500 from the Corporation for Public Broadcasting. KRAB was one of 73 out of the more than 400 noncommercial radio stations in the United States to receive CPB awards. The funds were used principally for program improvement, i.e., morning show, program director, two correspondents, and general efforts to encourage news programs, documentaries, and similar programs.

$1,200 from the Washington State Arts Commission. Part of a matching fund award from the National Endowment for the Arts.

40. There were about 25 witnesses who were neither employees nor trustees of KRAB. They appeared to testify to the usefulness and excellence of KRAB's programming. These witnesses were either regular listeners to KRAB or individuals who had used the broadcast facilities either as participants in programs or on behalf of public institutions which they represented. A few witnesses had heard some of the five programs which were given particular consideration in these proceedings. There were no witnesses who appeared to support a view adverse to the station. Some of the testimony given in support of the station's usefulness to the community is given in the succeeding paragraphs.

41. Robert N. Kerr is a mechanical engineer, age 49 and a graduate of Oklahoma State University. He and his wife heard the Bevel broadcast and thought that it contained an important message for the white community. Neither he nor his wife were offended by any words used by Bevel. Kerr knew the Reverend Paul Sawyer and attended his church as well as other religious services at which Sawyer had officiated. Kerr had never heard Sawyer use obscene language or say anything that might be considered sensational. Kerr thinks Sawyer to be a person who is providing a bridge to the youth or avant garde culture. Kerr did not hear Sawyer's August 5, 1967, broadcast. However, he had heard Sawyer on other KRAB programs and never heard him broadcast anything obscene or sensational.

42. Robert M. Sprenger is a graduate student at the University of Washington where he works as a research assistant. He holds degrees in philosophy and chemistry from the University of Puget Sound. Sprenger and his wife, who is a social case worker, heard the Bevel broadcast. Neither of them was offended by anything Bevel said. Sprenger had worked as an announcer at KRAB and he was aware of the station's policies regarding program suitability.

43. Peggy L. Golberg is a house wife and mother of four children ranging in age from 12 to 23. She heard both the Sawyer and Bevel broadcasts. She remembers that she found Bevel's talk to be interesting but that she was bored by Sawyer. She does not recall hearing any language which she considered offensive. She encourages her children to listen to KRAB and she thinks the Bevel broadcast was meritorious and worth having in the Seattle area.

44. Robert W. Means is an air traffic controller who has resided in the Seattle area since he matriculated at the University of Washington in 1930. He and his wife listen to KRAB regularly. He also tapes programs for broadcast over the station. Events that he has taped have included a Ralph Nader press conference, a speech by John Howard Griffin, a speech by the former Chief of the Cuban Air Force, and a community meeting where people discussed their concern about nuclear waste material. Means had the following to say about KRAB:

One value of KRAB to the community is in the broadcasting of such diverse material as this:—some of it inspirational, some of it frightening; all of it relevant in some way to the enormous, complicated, unresolved problems of our challenged society. It has been a minor but important function of the station to open up for public discussion such edgy questions as abortion reform, treatment of criminals and in the insane, white-collar crime, changing forms of religious experience, and the like.

Of equal or greater value to me are the programs of ethnic music, book and movie reviews, commentaries from abroad or from a foreign point of view, far-ranging expeditions into American folk music, systematic explorations of the classical music catalog, and the many and varied humor programs. KRAB has been of inestimable value, putting Seattle into the forefront of American intellectual experience. This has not been accomplished by being comfortable, complacent and conformist.

45. Father John D. Lynch is Pastor of Saint Stephens Catholic Church. Prior to going to Saint Stephens, Father Lynch was the assistant at Saint James Cathedral in charge of radio and television

programs for about 11 years. He had a regular commentary program on KRAB for three years. He was free to discuss any subject and he would speak in such areas as theology, civil rights and communism. He also participated as a panelist in panel discussions on such subjects as birth control and the Bricker amendment.

46. John Stewart Edwards is a native of New Zealand and a professor of zoology at the University of Washington. He is a frequent listener to KRAB and finds that for him and his colleagues it forms a significant part of their intellectual input. He has, from time to time, heard "four-letter words" used on KRAB, but has never been offended by any such language. In that connection he expressed the following point of view:

I have heard them from time to time, yes, and if you are interested in my response to it, I would say that the response to the words as used more as epithets or as what everybody knows is used in common, everyday life, these words I find less offensive than say the kind of innuendoes, for example, on the Johnny Carson Show or on some of the popular television programs. In fact, last evening there was just such an example of what I considered an obscene innuendo on the Johnny Carson Show. I have never heard anything of that type on KRAB, although specific Anglo-Saxon four-letter words have been used mainly as epithets, which one finds used in journalism. Any reader of the New Republic or Harper's magazine will find these frequently, and I would imagine that the average listener to KRAB is more like the reader of a journal that carries these words without question these days.

47. Robert J. Block is an investment banker and real estate broker. He is a listener and has been an unsuccessful candidate for office. As a candidate, he has been offered and has used the facilities at KRAB. He has also participated in discussion programs on the station. He has never heard any program on KRAB which offended him. As he put it:

I think that their programming has been stimulating and highly useful in the rather plastic society in which we live. Nothing they have ever done has certainly offended my sensibilities.

48. Edward J. Devine was public relations assistant to the Mayor and Deputy Mayor of the city of Seattle. KRAB volunteered its facilities to cover city events. City officials were invited to appear and did appear from time to time on KRAB. Hearings of the city council were covered sometimes verbatim and broadcasts were made of events such as a Youth for Decency rally, open housing discussion, and discussion of school issues.

49. Maxine Cushing Gray is associate editor of Argus, a regional publication emphasizing politics and the arts. She listens to KRAB and she finds KRAB responsive to providing time for discussions involving the native Indian population and their problems. According to Mrs. Gray, other Seattle stations have given little, if any, time to the problems of our "native Americans".

50. Matthew Hackman is a mathematician and a member of the faculty of the University of Washington. He listens to KRAB regularly and has never heard anything offensive broadcast.

51. Fred Cordova is the director of public information for Seattle University. Seattle University is a private institution conducted by the Jesuit Fathers. It has an enrollment of over 3,000 students. Cordova has been an occasional listener to KRAB. KRAB has given coverage to campus events at Seattle University such as appearances by Mortimer Adler and Barry Goldwater; a symposium for Filipino-American youth and a symposium on Indian problems. He gave the following evaluation of the usefulness of KRAB to Seattle:

For a station like KRAB I think it is quite a necessity, if I must do a little bit of editorializing here, I think it is quite a necessity here in our city. Our media, especially in radio, is quite commercial, regardless of whether is it AM or FM, and KRAB is the only station that I know of here in the Pacific Northwest where it deviates from a normal type of programming, radio type of scheduling, and it allows, I think, good free thought on controversial as well as other urban issues that have to be aired.

52. Elsie B. Martinez is a postal clerk and a music school graduate. She listens to KRAB and has never heard anything offensive broadcast. She said,

I can turn on KRAB and I get all sorts of ethnic music, I get Bach and Scarlotti, harpsichord, get all sorts of beautiful classical music, and then I get the latest rock and roll and everything. It is very pleasant to listen to.

53. Bruce Jeffery Jones is a high school sophomore who listens regularly to KRAB as do his parents. His father is employed by the Girl Scouts and his mother is a house wife. He studies propaganda techniques at school. He listens to KRAB for its political programs, commentaries and documentaries. His listening to KRAB helps him contribute to discussion at school. He also listens to rock and roll and jazz programs. He has never heard any "four-letter words" on KRAB.

54. Mark Chaet is a student at the University of Washington studying English literature and music. He holds a third-class operators license from the FCC. He listens to KRAB and has never heard any obscenity.

55. Marcia Bayless is a high school student who holds an FCC third-class operators license. She finds KRAB to be educational and tapes of KRAB programs have been used in her school. She listens to the programs of bluegrass, jazz and classical music.

56. Robert James Bidleman is a systems analyst and Vice President of the Seattle Jazz Society. He and a good portion of the membership of the Jazz Society listen to KRAB. They can pick up jazz programming on KRAB on a continuing basis at least five days a week. No other station in the Seattle area provides as much jazz programming. He cited specific jazz programs regularly broadcast by KRAB and some of the uncommon jazz renditions heard.

57. According to William Dunlop, an assistant professor of English at the University of Washington, KRAB has the best film reviews in the area. He is particularly interested in the discussion programs which KRAB has on opera. He finds their opera reviews to be better than those of any other station.

58. Jack W. Crouse teaches art at Olympic College, a two year community college located at Bremerton. He is a listener and sub-

scriber to KRAB. He appreciates the honesty and candor which he finds on KRAB. He is the father of three children ranging in age from 14 to 20, all of whom listen to KRAB. He has heard " . . . what are conventionally called obscene words" broadcast on KRAB. He himself has never heard anything that he considers obscene, expressing the view that "obscenities are all in the minds of people, I think, and I can take virtually anything."

59. Other witnesses appeared and gave testimony supporting the views detailed above. All witnesses gave strong support for the useful and unique qualities of the station's programming.

CONCLUSIONS

1. KRAB is non-commercial, listener supported and it broadcasts a variety of programs of outstanding quality. Its programming is of a type not usually heard on radio and its appeal is directed to an audience of people with a high degree of intellectual curiosity. KRAB provides its audience with a broadcast service which is attractive and uniquely appealing. As a matter of policy, KRAB is committed to providing the Seattle area with unusual, stimulating and extraordinary programs. KRAB's programming is meritorious and the station does render an outstanding broadcast service to the area which it serves.

2. KRAB is directed by a Board of Trustees who are above average in their educational backgrounds and who represent a variety of tastes. This group is responsible for setting station policy and for exercising overall supervision over programming. It is actively involved in carrying out its duties. In order to bring its audience the type of unusual programming that its policies call for, KRAB experiments with the unique and gives time to an extraordinary variety of programs. In doing so, KRAB sometimes falls short of the expectations of its management, its audience or the licensing authority to which it is accountable for its franchise. Thus it is that this proceeding, to determine whether or not KRAB's license should be renewed for a short term of one year or a full three-year period, came about. A few of KRAB's programs involved the broadcast of words or expressions described as obscene.

3. It is not KRAB's policy to use obscene or indecent language in its broadcasts for the sensational or shock effect that such language might have. This licensee eschews obscenity, profanity, and indecency. Its procedures for clearing programs for broadcast are designed to avoid material which would give offense to the community. This proceeding was instituted because KRAB did broadcast some programs which did give offense to some members of the community in which its programs are heard. We are directed, therefore, to determine whether in broadcasting certain programs specified by the Commission and the Broadcast Bureau, KRAB violated its own standards. This determination must be made, however, in the context of standards laid down by the Commission.

4. Our most current applicable source as to the Commission's policy regarding broadcast of such offensive material is the analysis in the *Notice of Apparent Liability, In re WUHY-FM*, FCC 70-346, April 3, 1970. In its discussion in that notice, the Commission renewed its commitment to the right of licensees,

> . . . to present provocative or unpopular programming which may offend some listeners. *In re Renewal of Pacifica*, 36 FCC 147, 149 (1964). It would markedly disserve the public interest, were the airwaves restricted only to inoffensive, bland material. Cf. *Red Lion Broadcasting Co., Inc.* v. *F.C.C.*, 395 U.S. 367 (1969).

5. Taking up the matter of obscene language, the Commission did prescribe standards to guide in determining the permissible and impermissible areas. In setting these guide lines, the Commission did recognize the difficulties which arise in trying to steer a course between the censorship which the law forbids the Commission to exercise and the indecent or obscene language which the law forbids the licensee to broadcast. After relating some of the obscene and offensive language which had been broadcast by WUHY, the Commission observed that:

> 8. . . . these expressions are patently offensive to millions of listeners. *And here it is crucial to bear in mind the difference between radio and other media.* Unlike a book which requires the deliberate act of purchasing and reading (or a motion picture where admission to public exhibition must be actively sought), broadcasting is disseminated generally to the public (Section 3(o) of the Communications Act, 47 U.S.C. 153(o)) under circumstances where reception requires no activity of this nature. Thus, it comes directly into the home and frequently without any advance warning of its content. Millions daily turn the dial from station to station. While particular stations or programs are oriented to specific audiences, the fact is that by its very nature, thousands of others not within the "intended" audience may also see or hear portions of the broadcast. Further, in that audience are very large numbers of children. Were this type of programming (e.g., the WUHY interview with the above described language) to become widespread, it would drastically affect the use of radio by millions of people. No one could ever know, in home or car listening, when he or his children would encounter what he would regard as the most vile expressions serving no purpose but to shock, to pander to sensationalism. Very substantial numbers would either curtail using radio or would restrict their use to but a few channels or frequencies, abandoning the present practice of turning the dial to find some appealing program. In light of the foregoing considerations we note also that it is not a question of what a majority of licensees might do but whether such material is broadcast to a significant extent by any significant number of broadcasters. In short, in our judgment, increased use along the lines of this WUHY broadcast might well correspondingly diminish the use for millions of people. It is one thing to say, as we properly did in *Pacifica*, that no segment, however large its size, may rule out the presentation of unpopular views or of language in a work of art which offends some people; and it is quite another thing to say that WUHY has the right to broadcast an interview in which Mr. Garcia begins many sentences with, [blank], an expression which conveys no thought, has no redeeming social value, and in the context of broadcasting, drastically curtails the usefulness of the medium for millions of people.
> (Footnotes omitted.)

* * * * * * *

6. Going on to the standards to be followed, the Commission concluded that for broadcasting,

> 10. . . . we believe that the statutory term, "indecent", should be applicable, and that, in the broadcast field, the standard for its applicability should be that the material broadcast is (a) patently offensive by contemporary community standards; and (b) is utterly without redeeming social value. The Court has made clear that different rules are appropriate for different media of expression in view of their varying natures. "Each method tends to present its own peculiar problems." *Burstyn* v. *Wilson*, 343 U.S. 495, 502–503 (1951). We have set forth in par. 8, *supra*, the reasons for applicability of the above standard in defining what is indecent in the broadcast field. We think that the factors set out in par. 8 are cogent, powerful considerations for the different standard in this markedly different field.

7. A person could be a regular listener to KRAB and not hear any obscene or indecent language broadcast. The most that can be said is that a regular listener may occasionally hear some four-letter Anglo-Saxon sexual or scatological term. KRAB is not a station that presents smut regularly or frequently. There were only five programs broadcast over a period of three years which led to the controversy which resulted in this proceeding. We will consider each of these programs:

8. There is no evidence that Dave Wertz used obscene language either in the particular program specified in the Bill of Particulars or in any other of his shows. He broadcasts bluegrass music and tells the kind of stories that are associated with that type of entertainment. We conclude that telling "corny jokes" entails risk and may give some offense, but we can not conclude that Dave Wertz broadcast anything contrary to the policies of the licensee or of the Commission.

9. P. J. Doyle conducted an interview which he thought to be a serious discussion of language usage. His program was produced and presented under the auspices of the Seattle Public Library. This discussion involved the use of the one word most likely to offend if heard over the air or anywhere else.

10. Doyle's broadcast took place without prior audition by the licensee's staff or management. Doyle now knows better and he is careful about the language which is used on his program. In this instance, the question we must resolve is whether or not the licensee failed to exercise proper care by not having auditioned this program in advance of its broadcast. There is nothing in the record to show that Doyle's prior programs gave any indication that preauditioning of his program was necessary in order to avoid broadcast of material which might be offensive or otherwise in bad taste. In addition, we must bear in mind the auspices under which this program came to the station. It was, after all, produced and sponsored by the Seattle Public Library. We conclude that the licensee acted with reasonable diligence in its handling of this program. It is clear that Doyle is now aware of his responsibilities and that the material which he now broadcasts does not fall short either by the station's own standards or the standards which the Commission would have its licensee observe.

11. Reverend Paul Sawyer was known to Milam and the licensee had had some experience with Sawyer as a performer prior to broadcast of the taped autobiography which caused problems. Whether a station should broadcast anybody's autobiography for 30 hours is not our concern. What did happen was that such an "autobiographic marathon" was begun. Sawyer was not known to be a person who used obscene language. Part of the material which he planned to broadcast was auditioned and nothing heard in these auditions was obscene. When it became apparent during the actual broadcast that Sawyer's autobiography did include words or expressions which were unsuitable, his broadcast was taken off the air. We conclude that the worst that can be said regarding this incident was that it was an error in judgment which was expeditiously corrected.

12. "Murder at Kent State" and the James Bevel broadcasts bring us head on to the issue of whether a licensee may under any circumstances broadcast (a) material known to be obscene or offensive; or (b) material not considered offensive or obscene by the licensee but which might be so considered by others. In the case of the "Murder at Kent State" record, the language used included words which the licensee did consider obscene and ordinarily would not permit to be broadcast. In this case, after careful consideration, the licensee's Trustees and managerial employees decided that in their judgment use of the particular language was necessary under the circumstances involved. This is a matter of judgment which we conclude the Commission has left to licensee determination. In this case, language was not broadcast for shock or sensationalism, but rather for the purpose of presenting a vivid and accurate account of a disastrous incident in our recent history. We conclude that in this exercise of judgment, the licensee conformed to the standards prescribed by the Commission as well as its own policies regarding suitability.

13. It is too bad that Reverend James Bevel did not take a little time to organize his material. He had some very interesting and provocative ideas which some people may have lost. Reading his entire text without being forewarned to expect "dirty words" one could possibly miss some of them altogether, as indeed happened with "nuts". Bevel is an emotional and colorful speaker. But, Bevel's language was not anything like that used by Garcia and Crazy Max in the program that brought a $100.00 sanction upon WUHY-FM. Bevel's talk really comes within the scope of the concern with which the Commission was dealing in its letter of January 21, 1970, to Mr. Oliver R. Grace (FCC 70-94) rather than the more provocative WUHY-FM program. In its letter to Grace, the Commission said:

> The charge that the broadcast programs are "vulgar" or presented without "due regard for sensitivity, intelligence, and taste", is not properly cognizable by this Government agency, in light of the proscription against censorship. You will agree that there can be no Governmental arbiter of taste in the broadcast field. See *Banzhaf* v. *FCC*, 405 F 2d 1082, (C.A.D.C.), certiorari denied 395 U.S. 973, cf. *Hannegan* v. *Esquire Magazines*, 327 U.S. 146 (1946).

14. In concluding that some of the language used by the Reverend Bevel was vulgar rather than obscene, we are unavoidably treading into an area of often stormy controversy over our changing mores.

There was no real effort made to produce evidence as to the extent to which anyone in Seattle was offended by anything heard on KRAB. Neither was there any particular effort made to show that the words designated as obscene by the Broadcast Bureau were not offensive to the community. KRAB under its own policy would ordinarily avoid giving offense by avoiding the use of such language.

15. There is really no quarrel by KRAB with the standard set by the Commission that broadcasters should avoid language that is patently offensive by contemporary community standards and utterly without redeeming social value. We can not avoid the difficult result that what particular language may be unacceptable for broadcast is not susceptible to being reduced to an immutable, time resistant glossary.

16. All but one of the "obscene" words listed by the Broadcast Bureau are now to be found in Webster's New International Dictionary, 3rd Ed., 1961, G & C Merriam Co. Every one of these words, with one exception, is characterized as vulgar rather than obscene by the scholars who produced the dictionary. Our times are indeed changing. Consider what Mr. Clive Barnes, the drama critic of the New York Times recently said:

Incidentally have you noticed how the currency of swear-words, those honestly shocking oaths only to be emitted in times of intense stress, have become hopelessly devalued. A new Broadway play quite casually ran the whole lexicon, and no one seemed to notice. We appear to have overcome obscenity by incorporating it into polite conversation.[6]

17. Our recent history has been embellished by this event. "Love Story", Erich Segal's long continuing best selling novel, is now a very well attended motion picture. Our most prominent citizen saw the movie and following is a portion of a press report of what he had to say after that event:

Chatting informally this morning with newsmen about his State of the Union message, President Nixon said he had seen the movie in Camp David recently, had enjoyed it and, the President added, "I recommend it."
However, he said, he was mildly upset at the film's profanity.
He said his wife and two daughters, Tricia and Julie, had read the book and felt the "shock of the dialogue they put in the girl's mouth."
"I wasn't shocked," the President said, "I know these words, I know they use them. It's the "in" thing to do."
However, Mr. Nixon said, the dialogue "detracted from a great performance" by Ali MacGraw, who plays the female lead.
Discoursing briefly on profanity, Mr. Nixon said that swearing "has its place, but if it is used it should be used to punctuate." If profanity is overused, he said, "what you remember is the profanity and not the point."[7]

"Love Story" includes virtually every word cited by the Broadcast Bureau as obscene.

18. We can not emphasize too strongly that while KRAB did broadcast a few programs that included some language offensive to some people, they did not do so with any intent to give offense, to pander, to sensationalize, to shock, or to break down community standards. KRAB should be given credit for a real desire not to debase community standards of taste and decency. In considering their policies and their programming as an entirety, the licensee of KRAB seeks and most often attains those standards of taste and decency in programming that we should like to see reflected more often in our broadcast media.

19. We conclude that KRAB's programming, in total, is outstanding and meritorious. We conclude that the few instances in which KRAB did broadcast obscene language, either willing or unwittingly, do not justify denying grant of a full term, three-year renewal of its license.

20. Accordingly, IT IS ORDERED that unless an appeal to the Commission from this Initial Decision is taken by a party, or the Commission reviews the Initial Decision on its own motion in accordance with the provisions of Section 1.276 of the Rules, the application of The Jack Straw Memorial Foundation, for renewal of license of station KRAB–FM IS GRANTED.

FEDERAL COMMUNICATIONS COMMISSION,
ERNEST NASH, *Hearing Examiner.*

A CONVICTION FOR UTTERING OBSCENE, INDECENT, AND PROFANE LANGUAGE BY MEANS OF RADIO COMMUNICATION IS OVERTURNED, THE UNITED STATES COURT OF APPEALS, NINTH CIRCUIT, DECLARING THAT THE TRIAL JUDGE WAS IN ERROR WHEN HE INSTRUCTED THE JURY "YOU ARE TO CONCERN YOURSELF WITH WHETHER THE DEFENDANT USED OBSCENE, INDECENT, OR PROFANE LANGUAGE OVER THE RADIO. YOU ARE NOT TO CONCERN YOURSELF WITH THE REASONS OR MOTIVE FOR SUCH USE"; FURTHER, THE JUDGE WAS IN ERROR WHEN HE INSTRUCTED THE JURY: "AN OBSCENE WORD OR WORDS IS DEFINED BY THE SUPREME COURT OF THE UNITED STATES AS FOLLOWS: 'IF TO THE AVERAGE PERSON APPLYING CONTEMPORARY COMMUNITY STANDARDS, THE WORD, OR WORDS, HAVE TO DO WITH THE PRURIENT, THE LEWD OR THE LASCIVIOUS.' "

Gagliardo v. United States, 366 F.2d 720 (1966)

HAMLIN, Circuit Judge:

Dominic Gagliardo, appellant herein, was charged by indictment in the United States District Court for the District of Nevada with a violation of 18 U.S.C.§ 1464. After a jury trial he was convicted and sentenced under the Young Adult Offenders Act, 18 U.S.C. § 4209. He filed a timely appeal to this court which has jurisdiction under 28 U.S.C. § 1291.

18 U.S.C. § 1464 provides as follows:

"Whoever utters any obscene, indecent, or profane language by means of radio communication shall be fined not more than $10,000 or imprisoned not more than two years, or both."

The evidence established that at the time of the offense charged appellant was a 23-year-old male with a limited education. He had a citizens' band radio license which he operated as a hobby. Without going into the details, it is sufficient to say that a prolonged argument developed over the air between appellant and one Sartain, each broadcasting over a citizens' band radio in Las Vegas, Nevada. Sartain testified that he heard appellant make over the air certain statements which are set out in the record but which we feel need not be set out here. Suffice it to say, it was not parlor language.

Appellant contends that 18 U.S.C. § 1464 is unconstitutional under the Tenth Amendment because it is an attempt to exercise police power reserved to the states. It is well established that Congress has the power under the Commerce Clause, Article I, § 8, cl. 3 of the Constitution, to impose penal sanctions on what it considers to be morally objectionable conduct so long as "the activity sought to be regulated is 'commerce which concerns more States than one' and has a real and substantial relation to the national interest." Heart of Atlanta Motel v. United States, 379 U.S. 241, 255, 85 S.Ct. 348, 356, 13 L.Ed.2d 258 (1964). See, e.g., Katzenbach v. McClung, 379 U.S. 294, 85 S.Ct. 377, 13 L.Ed.2d 290 (1964); United States v. Darby, 312 U.S. 100, 61 S.Ct. 451, 85 L. Ed. 609 (1941); Brooks v. United States, 267 U.S. 432, 45 S.Ct. 345, 69 L.Ed. 699 (1925); Duncan v. United States, 48 F. 2d 128 (9th Cir. 1931). Cf. Roth v. United States, 354

U.S. 476, 492-493, 77 S.Ct. 1304, 1 L.Ed.2d 1498 (1957).

Appellant argues that the activities here involve wholly intrastate transmissions because the normal range of a citizens' radio transmission is from 10 to 25 miles, which would mean that transmissions from Las Vegas, Nevada, would not cross Nevada's borders and because there is no evidence in the record that the transmissions of the appellant were in fact heard outside of Nevada. There is evidence in the record, however, that transmissions of the type appellant was sending are capable of traveling beyond the Nevada border and of being heard in other states under unusual atmospheric conditions. The fact that transmissions over citizens' band radio may cross state borders, either because of unusual atmospheric conditions or because the transmitter is located near a border, justifies a conclusion that such transmissions have a substantial enough effect on interstate commerce to empower Congress to regulate all citizens' band radio. The fact that appellant's isolated transmission may not have traversed state borders is irrelevant since it is the cumulative impact on interstate commerce of all citizens' band radio transmissions which enables Congress to regulate all such transmissions. Heart of Atlanta Motel v. United States, supra, 379 U.S. at 275-277, 85 S.Ct. 348 (Black, J., concurring); Wickard v. Filburn, 317 U.S. 111, 63 S.Ct. 82, 87 L.Ed. 122 (1942). In addition, radio receivers located in Las Vegas which are designed to receive interstate transmissions may also be able to receive local citizens' band radio transmissions. The fact that some radio receivers could receive both interstate and intrastate citizens' band communications, thus inevitably creating the probability of interference with interstate communications, also brings the local transmissions within the ambit of the commerce clause. Cf. Weiss v. United States, 308 U.S. 321, 60 S.Ct. 269, 84 L.Ed. 298 (1939).

We also hold that 18 U.S.C. § 1464 does apply to all citizens' band radio communications even where it is not proven that the transmission involved did in fact cross state lines. The original prohibition against "obscene, indecent, or profane" language was enacted as section 29 of the Radio Act of 1927, c. 169, 44 Stat. 1172. It was repealed in 1934 and replaced by section 326 of the Federal Communications Act of 1934, c. 652, 48 Stat. 1091, 47 U.S.C. § 326.[1] In 1948 the last sentence of section 326 was deleted[2] and, as part of the comprehensive revision of the criminal laws under Title 18 of the United States Code, the deleted sentence became 18 U.S.C. § 1464 with slight changes in phraseology. The unqualified language of section 1464 and its predecessors indicates an intended application to all radio communications affecting interstate commerce. In addition, the jurisdiction provision of the Federal Communications Act of 1934, Title III, provides for coverage of intrastate communications affecting interstate communications, which is an explicit Congressional indication that the prohibitions of 18 U.S.C. § 1464 and its predecessors are intended to apply to transmissions over citizens' band radio. Federal Communications Act of 1934, c. 652, § 301 (d), 48 Stat. 1081 (d), 47 U.S.C. § 301(d).[3]

Other specifications of error are directed to certain jury instructions given by the court, to other instructions requested by the appellant and refused by the court, and to the action of the district judge in sending to the jury while they were deliberating certain instructions in response to a question sent by the jury to the judge. The latter action

was taken without the presence, consultation or knowledge of counsel on either side.

The government concedes that two errors occurred involving the instructions to the jury. We agree and find that each is sufficient for reversal.

The judge's secret instructions to the jury were given at the written request of a jury member who asked:[4]

"Are we to determine the *intention* of the use of profane and/or obscene language or just the use of the words over a citizen band radio." The judge responded by memo, stating that:

"You are to only concern yourself with whether the Defendant used Obscene, Indecent, or Profane language over the radio. You are not to concern yourself with the reasons or motive for such use." The giving of this instruction was prejudicial error because it directly contradicted an earlier instruction given by the trial judge, set out in the margin,[5] to the effect that specific intent was an element needed to be proved in order for the government to secure a conviction. It was also error because it was an erroneous statement of the law: the defendant's intent is a very pertinent and necessary element in a conviction for use of obscenity, see Ginzburg v. United States, 383 U.S. 463, 86 S.Ct. 969, 16 L.Ed.2d 31 (1966); Mishkin v. New York, 383 U.S. 502, 86 S.Ct. 958, 16 L.Ed. 2d 56 (1966); Smith v. People of State of California, 361 U.S. 147, 80 S.Ct. 215, 4 L.Ed.2d 205 (1959). The giving of an instruction to the jury concerning the substantive law of the trial without the presence or knowledge of counsel for both sides is error of itself, Shields v. United States, 273 U.S. 583, 47 S.Ct. 478, 71 L. Ed. 787 (1927); Ah Fook Chang v. United States, 91 F.2d 805 (9th Cir. 1937).

In its instructions the court defined obscene language as follows: "An obscene word or words is defined by the Supreme Court of the United States as follows: 'If to the average person applying contemporary community standards, the word, or words, have to do with the prurient, the lewd or the lascivious.'" Counsel for the government concedes and we agree that the above instruction was erroneous and not in accordance with the definition of obscene as given by the Supreme Court. In a book named "John Cleland's Memoirs of A Woman of Pleasure" v. Attorney General of Com. of Massachusetts, 383 U.S. 413, 418, 86 S.Ct. 975, 977, 16 L.Ed.2d 1 (1966), the Court stated: "We defined obscenity in Roth [354 U.S. 476 at 479, 77 S.Ct. 1304 at 1311 (1957)] in the following terms: '[W]hether to the average person, applying contemporary community standards, the dominant theme of the material taken as a whole appeals to prurient interest.'"

Appellant also contends that his motion of acquittal should have been granted because the language alleged to have been used was not "obscene, indecent, or profane." The government concedes, and we agree, that the language alleged to have been used can in no way be considered "obscene" because the language as a whole can not be viewed as appealing to the prurient or calculated to arouse the animal passions, but rather was made during a moment of anger. Roth v. United States, supra; A Book Named "John Cleland's Memoirs of A Woman of Pleasure" v. Attorney General of Com. of Massachusetts, supra; Duncan v. United States, 48 F.2d 128 (9th Cir. 1931).

Although the district court's instruction defining "profane" is not criticized by appellant, the government does not contend that the words used were "profane." Since the only words attributed to appellant which could even remotely be considered as being "profane" were "God damn it," which were also uttered in anger, there is no basis for holding that the language was "profane" within the meaning of the statute. See Duncan v. United States, supra.

The government's only argument is that the words used were "indecent" within the meaning of that word in section 1464. No instruction defining "indecent" was given by the district court. The government urges now that the three words—"obscene, indecent, and profane"—have different meanings and "indecent" should be defined "as including the extremely vulgar, coarse and offensive use of sexual terminology in a manner far exceeding the bounds of common decency." The government relies heavily upon United States v. Limehouse, 285 U.S. 424, 52 S.Ct. 412, 76 L.Ed. 843 (1932), which held that the word "filthy" which was added to the postal obscenity law by amendment, now 18 U.S.C. § 1461, meant something other than "obscene, lewd, or lascivious," and permitted a prosecution of the sender of a letter which "plainly related to sexual matters" and was "coarse, vulgar, disgusting, indecent; and unquestionably filthy within the popular meaning of that term."[6]

Whether this contention is or is not correct is not before us at this time. The jury should have had the word "indecent" defined for them[7]

It is for the district court in the first instance to define the word "indecent" in the event there is a second trial. Whether the definition then given is correct or whether such definition violates any constitutional standards is a matter to be determined on review. We do not reach these questions at this time inasmuch as the reversible error referred to above requires that the conviction be reversed and there is a possibility that appellant will be acquitted at a new trial if one is held.

Judgment reversed.

NOTES

1. "Sec. 326. Nothing in this Act shall be understood or construed to give the Commission the power of censorship over the radio communications or signals transmitted by any radio station, and no regulation or condition shall be promulgated or fixed by the Commission which shall interfere with the right of free speech by means of radio communication. *No person within the jurisdiction of the United States shall utter any obscene, indecent, or profane language by means of radio communication.*" (Emphasis added) The language is virtually identical with its predecessor in the Radio Act of 1927, section 29, 44 Stat. 1172.

Violations were penalized under the Federal Communications Act of 1934, c. 652, section 501, 48 Stat. 1100, 47 U.S.C. § 501.

2. The first sentence remained as 47 U.S.C. § 326.

3. "No person shall use or operate any apparatus for the transmission of energy or communications or signals by radio * * * (d) within any State when the effects of such use extend beyond the borders of said State, or when interference is caused by such use or operation with the transmission of such energy, communications, or signals from within said State to any place beyond its borders, or from any place beyond its borders to any place within said State * * * except under and in accordance with this chapter and with a license in that behalf granted under the provisions of this chapter." The same jurisdictional grant

appeared in section 1 of the Radio Act of 1927, c. 169, 44 Stat. 1162.

Pursuant to its jurisdictional grant in 47 U.S.C.§ 301, the Federal Communications Commission has promulgated regulations governing the licensing of Citizens Radio Service. 47 C.F.R. § 95 (1966). Appellant possessed a license which he apparently obtained pursuant to these regulations.

4. The jury also requested the use of a dictionary, which request was denied by the trial judge without the knowledge or presence of either counsel. We do not see how this action by the trial judge could have prejudiced appellant. See Ferrari v. United States, 244 F.2d 132 (9th Cir. 1957).

5. "In every crime, there must exist a union, or joint operation of act and intent. The burden is always upon the prosecution to prove both act and intent beyond a reasonable doubt. With respect to major crimes, such as charged in this case, specific intent must be proved before there can be a conviction. A person who knowingly does an act which the law forbids, intending with bad purpose to disobey or disregard the law, may be found to act with specific intent.

"An act is done knowingly if done voluntarily and intentionally and not because of mistake, accident or other innocent reason."

6. See Cain v. United States, 274 F.2d 598 (2d Cir. 1960); Verner v. United States, 183 F.2d 184 (9th Cir. 1950). See generally, 16 Stan.L.Rev. 463 (1964).

7. Appellant argues that obscene and indecent as used in section 1464 are synonymous. We do not agree that in Duncan v. United States, supra, the court equated "indecent with obscene." A careful reading of that case discloses that the court said that certain language quoted in the opinion was not indecent or obscene. It did not, however, define indecent or say that it meant the same as obscene.

OBSCENITY IN EDUCATION

OBSCENITY IN EDUCATION

"...THE QUESTION OF THIS CASE IS WHETHER A TEACHER MAY, FOR DEMONSTRATED EDUCATIONAL PURPOSES, QUOTE A 'DIRTY' WORD CURRENTLY USED IN ORDER TO GIVE SPECIAL OFFENSE, OR WHETHER THE SHOCK IS TOO GREAT FOR HIGH SCHOOL SENIORS TO STAND"

Keefe v. Geanokos, 418 F.2d 359 (1969)

ALDRICH, Chief Judge.

Plaintiff, who unsuccessfully sought from the district court a temporary injunction pendente lite, requests a stay, or more precisely, a temporary injunction, from us pending our determination of his appeal from the district court's refusal.[1] The matter is before us on the complaint, the answer, affidavits and exhibits introduced by both sides, certain statements of counsel, and the findings of the district court as contained in its opinion dated November 6, 1969.

The plaintiff is the head of the English department and coordinator for grades 7 through 12 for the Ipswich (Massachusetts) Public School System, with part-time duties as a teacher of English. He has tenure, pursuant to Mass.G.L. c. 71, § 41. The defendants are the members of the Ipswich School Committee.[2] Briefly, after some preliminaries, five charges were furnished the plaintiff as grounds for dismissal, and a hearing was scheduled thereon, which plaintiff seeks to enjoin as violating his civil rights. 42 U.S.C. § 1983. Jurisdiction is asserted under 28 U.S.C. § 1343(3) (4). In order to preserve the status quo, this hearing has not yet been held, and the defendants await our decision. The district court, in its opinion denying temporary relief, dealt with only one of the five charges, the third. We will hereafter refer to this as the charge.[3]

Reduced to fundamentals, the substance of plaintiff's position is that as a matter of law his conduct which forms the basis of the charge did not warrant discipline. Accordingly, he argues, there is no ground for any hearing. He divides this position into two parts. The principal one is that his conduct was within his competence as a teacher, as a matter of academic freedom, whether the defendants approved of it or not. The second is that he had been given inadequate prior warning by such regulations as were in force, particularly in the light of the totality of the circumstances known to him, that his actions would be considered improper, so that an ex post facto ruling would, itself, unsettle academic freedom. The defendants, essentially, deny plaintiff's contentions. They accept the existence of a principle of academic freedom to teach,[4] but state that it is limited to proper classroom materials as reasonably determined by the school committee in the light of perti-

nent conditions, of which they cite in particular the age of the students. Asked by the court whether a teacher has a right to say to the school committee that it is wrong if, in fact, its decision was arbitrary, counsel candidly and commendably (and correctly) responded in the affirmative. This we consider to be the present issue. In reviewing the denial of interlocutory injunctive relief, the test that we of course apply is whether there is a probability that plaintiff will prevail on the merits. Automatic Radio Mfg. Co., Inc. v. Ford Motor Co., 1 Cir., 1968, 390 F.2d 113, cert. denied 391 U.S. 914, 88 S.Ct. 1807, 20 L.Ed.2d 653.

On the opening day of school in September 1969 the plaintiff gave to each member of his senior English class a copy of the September 1969 Atlantic Monthly magazine, a publication of high reputation, and stated that the reading assignment for that night was the first article therein.[5] September was the educational number, so-called, of the Atlantic, and some 75 copies had been supplied by the school department. Plaintiff discussed the article, and a particular word that was used therein, and explained the word's origin and context, and the reasons the author had included it. The word, admittedly highly offensive, is a vulgar term for an incestuous son. Plaintiff stated that any student who felt the assignment personally distasteful could have an alternative one.

The next evening the plaintiff was called to a meeting of the school committee and asked to defend his use of the offending word. Following his explanation, a majority of the members of the committee asked him informally if he would agree not to use it again in the classroom. Plaintiff replied that he could not, in good conscience, agree. His counsel states, however, without contradiction, that in point of fact plaintiff has not used it again. No formal action was taken at this meeting. Thereafter plaintiff was suspended, as a matter of discipline, and it is now proposed that he should be discharged.[6]

The Lifton article, which we have read in its entirety, has been described as a valuable discussion of "dissent, protest, radicalism and revolt." It is in no sense pornographic. We need no supporting affidavits to find it scholarly, thoughtful and thought-provoking. The single offending word, although repeated a number of times, is not artificially introduced, but, on the contrary, is important to the development of the thesis and the conclusions of the author. Indeed, we would find it difficult to disagree with plaintiff's assertion that no proper study of the article could avoid consideration of this word. It is not possible to read the article, either in whole or in part, as an incitement to libidinous conduct, or even thoughts. If it raised the concept of incest, it was not to suggest it, but to condemn it; the word was used, by the persons described, as a superlative of opprobrium. We believe not only that the article negatived any other concept, but that an understanding of it would reject, rather than suggest, the word's use.

With regard to the word itself, we cannot think that it is unknown to many students in the last year of high school, and we might well take judicial notice of its use by young radicals and protesters from coast to coast.[7] No doubt its use genuinely offends the parents of some of the students—therein, in part, lay its relevancy to the article.

Hence the question in this case is whether a teacher may, for demonstrated educational purposes, quote a "dirty" word currently used in order to give special offense, or whether the shock is too great for high school seniors to stand. If the answer were that the students must be protected from such exposure, we would fear for their future. We do not question the good faith of the defendants in believing that some parents have been offended.[8] With the greatest of respect to such parents, their sensibilities are not the full measure of what is proper education.

We of course agree with defendants that what is to be said or read to students is not to be determined by obscenity standards for adult consumption. Ginsberg v. New York, 1968, 390 U.S. 629, 88 S.Ct. 1274, 20 L.Ed.2d 195. At the same time, the issue must be one of degree. A high school senior is not devoid of all discrimination or resistance. Furthermore, as in all other instances, the offensiveness of language and the particular propriety or impropriety is dependent on the circumstances of the utterance.

Apart from cases discussing academic freedom in the large, not surprisingly we find no decisions closely in point. The district court cited what it termed the well-reasoned opinion of the district court in Parker v. Board of Education, D.Md., 1965, 237 F.Supp. 222, aff'd 4 Cir., 348 F.2d 464, cert. denied 382 U.S. 1030, 86 S.Ct. 653, 15 L.Ed.2d 543, regarding it "strikingly similar on its facts to the instant case, in that it too involved a high school teacher challenging his dismissal from employment in a public school system because of his assigning 'Brave New World' to a class as an infringement of his claimed First Amendment right to free speech * * *." We do not find ourselves impressed by the *Parker* court's reasoning, or by the similarity of the facts. As to the latter, *Parker* was not a case where the teacher was dismissed. As the court of appeals pointed out, Parker, unlike plaintiff, did not have tenure, and his only complaint was that his contract was not renewed. With regard to the reasoning, we think it significant that the court of appeals affirmed the district court only on this distinguishing ground, and disclaimed approval of the balance of the opinion. We accept the conclusion of the court below that "some measure of public regulation of classroom speech is inherent in every provision of public education." But when we consider the facts at bar as we have elaborated them, we find it difficult not to think that its application to the present case demeans any proper concept of education. The general chilling effect of permitting such rigorous censorship is even more serious.[9]

We believe it equally probable that the plaintiff will prevail on the issue of lack of any notice that a discussion of this article with the senior class was forbidden conduct. The school regulation upon which defendants rely,[10] although unquestionably worthy, is not apposite. It does not follow that a teacher may not be on notice of impropriety from the circumstances of a case without the necessity of a regulation. In the present case, however, the circumstances would have disclosed that no less than five books, by as many authors, containing the word in question were to be found in the school library. It is hard to think that any student could walk into the library and receive a book, but that his teacher could not subject the content to serious discussion in class.

Such inconsistency on the part of the school has been regarded as fatal. Vought v. Van Buren Public Schools, E.D.Mich., 6/13/69, 38 Law Week 2034. We, too, would probably so regard it. At the same time, we prefer not to place our decision on this ground alone, lest our doing so diminish our principal holding, or lead to a bowdlerization of the school library.

Finally, we are not persuaded by the district court's conclusion that no irreparable injury is involved because the plaintiff, if successful, may recover money damages. Academic freedom is not preserved by compulsory retirement, even at full pay.

The immediate question before us is whether we should grant interlocutory relief pending appeal. This question, as defendants point out, raises the ultimate issue of the appeal itself. The matter has been extensively briefed and argued by both sides. We see no purpose in taking two bites, and believe this a case for action under Local Rule 5. The order of the district court denying an interlocutory injunction pending a decision on the merits is reversed and the case is remanded for further proceedings consistent herewith.

NOTES

1. Plaintiff did not seek a stay order from the district court pending appeal, but was excused from doing so because of the court's unavailability.

2. Two school officials are also named, but may be disregarded for purposes of this opinion.

3. The defendants agree that charges 1, 2 and 4 are dependent on charge 3. They do, however, wish to press separately charge. 5. (Insubordination). The district court did not deal with this charge, and the record does not permit us to do so. We do suspect, though, that however separate it may be, it is to some extent tied in with charge 3, and we believe that it would be better for all concerned to postpone consideration thereof until the disposition of the issue as to charge 3. We accordingly will make the same order, so far as temporary relief is concerned.

4. For a recent discussion of the cases see Developments in the Law—Academic Freedom, 81 Harv.L.Rev. 1048 (1968); cf. Wright, The Constitution on the Campus, 22 Vand.L.Rev. 1027 (1969).

5. "The Young and the Old," by Robert J. Lifton, a psychiatrist and professor at a noted medical school.

6. The question must be considered whether this suit is premature, at least so far as an injunction against holding the meeting is concerned, since conceivably the vote might be in plaintiff's favor. We intimated as much during oral argument, but defendants' counsel did not respond. Very possibly counsel recognize that dismissal is a foregone conclusion, as plaintiff suggests, or defendants feel that if, in fact, there is no cause for dismissal, they would prefer a declaratory decision in advance. Under the circumstances we accept jurisdiction as a matter of discretion.

7. *E.g.,* "Up against the wall, motherfucker."

8. It is appropriate in this connection to consider what, exactly, is the charge with which plaintiff is presently faced. "3. Use of offensive material in the classroom on September 3, 1969, and subsequently, which use would undermine public confidence and react unfavorably upon

the public school system of Ipswich * * *."

9. "Such unwarranted inhibition upon the free spirit of teachers affects not only those who, like the appellants, are immediately before the Court. It has an unmistakable tendency to chill that free play of the spirit which all teachers ought especially to cultivate and practice * * *" Frankfurter, J., concurring, in Wieman v. Updegraff, 1952, 344 U.S. 183, 194, 195, 73 S.Ct. 215, 221, 97 L.Ed. 216.

10. "1. Teachers shall use all possible care in safeguarding the health and moral welfare of their pupils, discountenancing promptly and emphatically: vandalism, falsehood, profanity, cruelty, or other form of vice." *See also,* Mass.G.L. c.71,§ 30, "Moral Education."

DISMISSAL OF HIGHSCHOOL ENGLISH TEACHER FOR ASSIGNING KURT VONNEGUT'S "WELCOME TO THE MONKEYHOUSE" CONSTITUTED AN INVASION OF HER FIRST AMENDMENT RIGHTS

Parducci v. Rutland, 316 F. Supp. 352 (1970)

JOHNSON, Chief Judge.

Plaintiff was dismissed from her position as a high school teacher in the Montgomery public schools for assigning a certain short story to her junior (eleventh grade) English classes. In her complaint, which was filed with this Court on April 27, 1970, plaintiff alleges that defendants, in ordering her dismissal, violated her First Amendment right to academic freedom and her Fourteenth Amendment right to due process of law. Plaintiff's claim for damages and request for jury trial as contained in her initial complaint were stricken by amendment. The defendants are the members of the Montgomery County Board of Education, the Superintendent of Schools of the county, the Associate Superintendent, and the Principal of plaintiff's high school. Plaintiff's request for injunctive relief is authorized under the Civil Rights Act of 1871, 42 U.S.C. § 1983. The jurisdiction of this Court is invoked pursuant to 28 U.S.C. § 1343(3) and (4).

Plaintiff was graduated with high honors from Troy State University in June, 1969. Upon graduation, she entered into a one-year contract to teach English and Spanish at Jefferson David High School in Montgomery, such contract to commence in October, 1969.

On April 21, 1970, plaintiff assigned as outside reading to her junior English classes a story, entitled "Welcome to the Monkey House." The story, a comic satire, was selected by plaintiff to give her students a better understanding of one particular genre of western literature—the short story. The story's author, Kurt Vonnegut, Jr., is a prominent contemporary writer who has published numerous short stories and novels, including *The Cat's Cradle* and a recent best seller, *Slaughter-House Five.*

The following morning, plaintiff was called to Principal Rutland's office for a conference with him and the Associate Superintendent of the school system. Both men expressed their displeasure with the content of the story, which they described as "literary garbage", and with the "philosophy" of the story, which they construed as con-

doning, if not encouraging, "the killing off of elderly people and free sex."[1] They also expressed concern over the fact that three of plaintiff's students had asked to be excused from the assignment and that several disgruntled parents had called the school to complain. They then admonished plaintiff not to teach the story in any of her classes.

Plaintiff retorted that she was bewildered by their interpretation of and attitude toward the story, that she still considered it to be a good literary work, and that, while not meaning to cause any trouble, she felt that she had a professional obligation to teach the story. The Associate Superintendent then warned plaintiff that he would have to report this incident to the Superintendent who might very well order her dismissal. Plaintiff, who by this time had become very emotionally upset, responded to this threat by tendering her resignation.

On April 27, a hearing was held before this Court on plaintiff's motion for a temporary restraining order. Although plaintiff's motion for a temporary restraining order was subsequently denied, defendants agreed at the hearing to allow plaintiff to withdraw her resignation and to accord plaintiff a hearing before the Montgomery County Board of Education on the question of dismissal.[2] The School Board hearing, in which both sides participated, was held the following day. On May 6, the School Board notified plaintiff that she had been dismissed from her job for assigning materials which had a "disruptive" effect on the school and for refusing "the counselling and advice of the school principal." The School Board also advised the plaintiff that one of the bases for her dismissal was "insubordination" by reason of a statement that she made to the Principal and Associate Superintendant that "regardless of their counselling" she "would continue to teach the eleventh grade English class at the Jeff Davis High School by the use of whatever material" she wanted "and in whatever manner" she thought best.

Having exhausted all her remedies within the school system, plaintiff immediately renewed her motion for a preliminary injunction in which she sought her immediate reinstatement as a teacher. The present submission is upon this motion, the response thereto by the defendants, the evidence taken orally before the Court, including the testimony of several witnesses and exhibits thereto, and the briefs and arguments of the parties.

At the outset, it should be made clear that plaintiff's teaching ability is not in issue. The Principal of her school has conceded that plaintiff was a good teacher and that she would have received a favorable evaluation from him at the end of the year but for the single incident which led to her dismissal.

I

Plaintiff asserts in her complaint that her dismissal for assigning "Welcome to the Monkey House" violated her First Amendment right to academic freedom.

That teachers are entitled to First Amendment freedoms is an issue no longer in dispute. "It can hardly be argued that either students or teachers shed their constitutional rights to freedom of speech or expression at the schoolhouse gate." Tinker v. Des Moines Independent Community School District, 393 U.S. 503, 506, 89 S.Ct. 733, 736, 21 L.Ed.2d 731 (1969); see Pickering v. Board of Education, etc., 391 U.S. 563, 568, 88 S.Ct. 1731, 20 L.Ed.2d 811 (1968); Pred v. Board of Public Instruction, etc., 415 F.2d 851, 855 (5th Cir. 1969). These constitutional protections are unaffected by the presence or absence of tenure under state law. McLaughlin v. Tilendis, 398 F.2d 287 (7th Cir. 1968); Johnson v. Branch, 364 F.2d 177 (4th Cir. 1966), cert. denied, 385 U.S. 1003, 87 S.Ct. 706, 17 L.Ed.2d 542 (1967).

Although academic freedom is not one of the enumerated rights of the First Amendment, the Supreme Court has on numerous occasions emphasized that the right to teach, to inquire, to evaluate and to study is fundamental to a democratic society.[3] In holding a New York loyalty oath statute unconstitutionally vague, the Court stressed the need to expose students to a robust exchange of ideas in the classroom: "Our nation is deeply committed to safeguarding academic freedom, which is of transcendant value to all of us and not merely to the teachers concerned. That freedom is therefore a special concern of the First Amendment, which does not tolerate laws that cast a pall of orthodoxy over the classroom. * * * * The classroom is peculiarly the "marketplace of ideas."[4] Furthermore, the safeguards of the First Amendment will quickly be brought into play to protect the right of academic freedom because any unwarranted invasion of this right will tend to have a chilling effect on the exercise of the right by other teachers. Cf. Wieman v. Updegraff, 344 U.S. at 194, 195, 73 S.Ct. 215 (Frankfurter, J., concurring); Pickering v. Board of Education, etc., *supra* 391 U.S. at 574, 88 S.Ct. 1731.

The right to academic freedom, however, like all other constitutional rights, is not absolute and must be balanced against the competing interests of society. This Court is keenly aware of the state's vital interest in protecting the impressionable minds of its young people from *any* form of extreme propagandism in the classroom.

"A teacher works in a sensitive area in a schoolroom. There he shapes the attitudes of young minds towards the society in which they live. In this, the state has a vital concern."[5]

While the balancing of these interests will necessarily depend on the particular facts before the Court, certain guidelines in this area were provided by the Supreme Court in Tinker v. Des Moines Independent Community School District, *supra*. The Court there observed that in order for the state to restrict the First Amendment right of a student, it must first demonstrate that:

"[T]he forbidden conduct would '*materially* and *substantially* interfere with the requirements of appropriate discipline in the operation of the school'. [Emphasis added.][6] The Court was, however, quick to caution the student that:

"[Any] conduct * * * in class or out of it, which for any reason—whether it stems from time, place or type of behavior— materially disrupts classwork or involves substantial disorder or invasion of the rights of others is, of course, not immunized by the constitutional guarantee of freedom of speech."[7]

Thus, the first question to be answered is whether "Welcome to the Monkey House" is inappropriate reading for high school juniors. While the story contains several vulgar terms and a reference to an involuntary act of sexual intercourse, the Court, having read the story very carefully, can find nothing that would render it obscene either under the standards of Roth v. United States,[8] or under the stricter standards for minors as set forth in Ginsberg v. New York.[9]

The slang words are contained in two short rhymes which are less ribald than those found in many of Shakespeare's plays. The reference in the story to an act of sexual intercourse is no more descriptive than the rape scene in Pope's "Rape of the Lock". As for the theme of the story, the Court notes that the anthology in which the story was published was reviewed by several of the popular national weekly magazines, none of which found the subject matter of any of the stories to be offensive. It appears to the Court, moreover, that the author, rather than advocating the "killing off of old people," satirizes the practice to symbolize the increasing depersonalization of man in society.

The Court's finding as to the appropriateness of the story for high school students is confirmed by the reaction of the students themselves. Rather than there being a threatened or actual substantial disruption to the educational processes of the school, the evidence reflects that the assigning of the story was greeted with apathy by most of the students. Only three of plaintiff's students asked to be excused from the assignment. On this question of whether there was a material and substantial threat of disruption, the Principal testified at the School Board hearing that there was no indication that any of plaintiff's other 87 students were planning to disrupt the normal routine of the school. This Court now specifically finds and concludes that the conduct for which plaintiff was dismissed was not such that "would materially and substantially interfere with" reasonable requirements of discipline in the school.

A recent First Circuit case lends further support to this Court's conclusion. There a high school teacher was suspended for assigning and discussing a magazine article which contained several highly offensive words. The court, finding the article to be well-written and thought-provoking, formulated the issues thusly,

"Hence the question in this case is whether a teacher may, for demonstrated educational purposes, quote a ' dirty ' word currently used in order to give special offense, or whether the shock is too great for high school seniors to stand. If the answer were that the students must be protected from such exposure, we would fear for their future. We do not question the good faith of the defendants in believing that some parents have been offended. With the greatest of respect to such parents, their sensibilities are not the full measure of what is proper education."[10]

Since the defendants have failed to show either that the assignment was inappropriate reading for high school juniors, or that it created a significant disruption to the educational processes of this school, this Court concludes that plaintiff's dismissal constituted an unwarranted invasion of her First Amendment right to academic freedom.

II

Plaintiff also alleges that she was denied "the right to use the short story in question as extra reading without a clear and concise written standard to determine which books are obscene."

The record shows that prior to plaintiff's dismissal, there was no written or announced policy at Jefferson David High School governing the selection and assignment of outside materials. One of the defendants testified at the School Board hearing that the selection of outside readings was a matter determined solely by the good taste and good judgment of the individual teacher. The only question before this Court on this point, therefore, is whether plaintiff was entitled, under the Due Process Clause, to prior notice that the conduct for which she was punished was prohibited.[11]

Our laws in this country have long recognized that no person should be punished for conduct unless such conduct has been proscribed in clear and precise terms. See Connally v. General Constr. Co., 269 U.S. 385, 391, 46 S.Ct. 126, 70 L.Ed.322 (1926). When the conduct being punished involves First Amendment rights, as is the case here, the standards for judging permissible vagueness will be even more strictly applied.[12]

In the case now before the Court, we are concerned not merely with vague standards, but with the total absence of standards. When a teacher is forced to speculate as to what conduct is permissible and what conduct is proscribed, he is apt to be overly cautious and reserved in the classroom.[13] Such a reluctance on the part of the teacher to investigate and experiment with new and different ideas is anathema to the entire concept of academic freedom.

This Court is well aware of the fact that "school officials should be given wide discretion in administering their schools" and that "courts should be reluctant to interfere with or place limits on that discretion." Such legal platitudes should not, however, be allowed to become euphemisms for "infringement upon" and "deprivations of" constitutional rights. However wide the discretion of school officials, such discretion cannot be exercised so as to arbitrarily deprive teachers of their First Amendment rights. See Johnson v. Branch, *supra*, 364 F.2d at 180. This Court cannot, on the facts of this case, find any substantial interest of the schools to be served by giving defendants unfettered discretion to decide how the First Amendment rights of teachers are to be exercised. Cf. Niemotko v. Maryland, 340 U.S. 268, 71 S.Ct. 325, 328, 95 L.Ed. 267, 280 (1951).

It should be emphasized, however, that because of the special circumstances present in this case this Court does not feel any necessity to comment upon the advisability of requiring school administrators to promulgate rules and regulations under any other circumstances.

III

The English Department at Jefferson Davis High School publishes "English Reading Lists" for the benefit of its teachers and students. Each list (the lists are compiled separately for each grade) contains the names of approximately twenty-five recommended works.

One of the recommended novels on the "Junior English Reading List" is J. D. Salinger's *Catcher in The Rye*. This novel, while undisputedly a classic in American literature, contains far more offensive and descriptive language than that found in plaintiff's assigned story. The "Senior English Reading List" contains a number of works, such as Huxley's *Brave New World* and Orwell's *1984* which have highly provocative and sophisticated themes. Furthermore, the school library contains a number of books with controversial words and philosophies.

This situation illustrates how easily arbitrary discrimination can occur when public officials are given unfettered discretion to decide what books should be taught and what books should be banned. While not questioning either the motives or good faith of the defendants, this Court finds their inconsistency to be not only enigmatic but also grossly unfair.[14]

With these several basic constitutional principles in mind it inevitably follows that the defendants in this case cannot justify the dismissal of this plaintiff under the guise of insubordination. The facts are clear that plaintiff's "insubordination" was not insubordination in any sense and was not, in reality, a reason for the School Board's action. Dickey v. Alabama State Board of Education, 273 F.Supp. 613 (D.C.).

In accordance with the foregoing, it is the order, judgment and decree of this Court that the plaintiff be reinstated as a teacher for the duration of her contract, with the same rights and privileges which attached to her status prior to her illegal suspension.

It is further ordered that plaintiff be paid her regular salary for both the period during which she was suspended and for the remaining period of her contract.

It is further ordered that defendants expunge from plaintiff's employment records and transcripts any and all references relating to her suspension and dismissal.

It is further ordered that the court costs incurred in this cause be and they are hereby taxed against the defendants.

NOTES

1. Both Mr. Rutland and Mr. Garrett later testified that neither of them was much of a reader, had any special expertise in the field of literature, or had ever taught an English course.

2. Since plaintiff was only a probationary teacher, she was not entitled under state law to a hearing before the School Board. Code of Alabama, Tit. 52 § 351 et seq.

3. See e.g., Sweezy v. New Hampshire by Wyman, 354 U.S.234, 77 S.Ct. 1203, 1 L.Ed.2d 1311 (1957); Wieman v. Updegraff, 344 U.S. 183, 73 S.Ct. 215, 97 L. Ed. 216 (1952).

4. Keyishian v. Board of Regents, etc., 385 U.S. 589, 603, 87 S.Ct. 675, 683, 17 L. Ed.2d 629 (1967). Cf. Meyer v. Nebraska, 262 U.S. 390, 43 S.Ct. 625, 67 L.Ed. 1042 (1923).

5. Shelton v. Tucker, 364 U.S. 479, 485, 81 S.Ct. 247, 250, 5 L.Ed.2d 231 (1960).

6. 393 U.S. at 509, 89 S.Ct. at 738, quoting Burnside v. Byars, 363 F.2d 744, 749 (5th Cir. 1966).

7. 393 U.S. at 513, 89 S.Ct. at 740; see Pred v. Board of Public Instruction, etc., *supra*, 415 F.2d at 859.

8. 354 U.S. 476, 77 S.Ct. 1304, 1 L.Ed.2d 1498 (1957).

9. 390 U.S. 629, 88 S.Ct. 1274, 20 L.Ed. 2d 195 (1968).

10. Keefe v. Geanakos, 418 F.2d 359, 361-362 (1st Cir. 1969).

11. Since the court has found earlier in this opinion that plaintiff's conduct was constitutionally protected, that is, was not "hard-core", she has standing to raise this Due Process question. Cf. Dombrowski v. Pfister, 380 U.S. 479, 491-492, 85 S.Ct. 1116, 14 L.Ed.2d 22 (1965).

12. NAACP v. Button, 371 U.S. 415, 432, 83 S.Ct. 328, 9 L.Ed.2d 405 (1963); Winters v. New York, 333 U.S. 507, 509-510, 68 S.Ct. 665, 92 L.Ed. 840 (1948); see Brooks v. Auburn University, 296 F. Supp. 188 (M.D.Ala.), aff'd 412 F.2d 1171 (5th Cir. 1969).

13. Cf. Keyishian v. Board of Regents, etc., *supra*, 385 U.S. at 604, 87 S.Ct. 675.

14. See Keefe v. Geanakos, *supra*, 418 F.2d at 362; Vought v. Van Buren Public Schools, 306 F.Supp. 1388, 1395-1396 (E.D.Mich.1969).

COURT FINDS FOR A DISMISSED ELEVENTH GRADE TEACHER WHO USED THE WORD "FUCK" IN THE CLASSROOM DURING A LESSON ON TABOO WORDS

Mailloux v. Kiley, 323 F.Supp. 1387 (1971)

WYZANSKI, Chief Judge.

This case involves an action by a public high school teacher against the City of Lawrence, the members of its school committee, the superintendent of its schools, and the principal of its high school. Plaintiff claims that in discharging him for his classroom conduct in connection with a taboo word the school committee deprived him of his rights under the First and Fourteenth Amendments to the United States Constitution, and that, therefore, he has a cause of action[1] under 42 U.S.C. § 1983 within this court's jurisdiction under 28 U.S.C.§ 1343 (3).

These are the facts as found by this court after a full hearing.

Defendant members of the school committee employed plaintiff to teach in the Lawrence High School for the academic year 1970-1971 at a salary of $8100. Defendant principal assigned plaintiff to teach basic English to a class of about 25 students, boys and girls 16 and 17 years of age, all in the junior class of 11th grade.

Plaintiff assigned to the class for outside reading chapters in a novel, The Thread That Runs So True, by Jesse Stuart. The novel describes an incident based on the experiences of the author as a young country school teacher in rural Kentucky. He had taken over a one-room school in which the class had been seated with boys on one side, and girls on the other side, of the room. He intermingled the sexes for seating. Some parents objected on the ground the new teacher was running a "courting school." Nowhere in the novel is there the word "fuck."

October 1, 1970, during a discussion of the book in class, some students thought the protest against changing the seating in the Kentucky classroom was ridiculous. Plaintiff said that other things today are just as ridiculous. He then introduced the subject of society and its ways, as illustrated by taboo words. He wrote the word "goo" on the board and asked the class for a definition. No one being able to define it, plaintiff said that this word did not exist in English but in another culture it might be a taboo word. He then wrote on the blackboard the word "fuck," and, in accordance with his customary teaching methods of calling for volunteers to respond to a question, asked the class in general for a definition. After a couple of minutes a boy volunteered that the word meant "sexual intercourse." Plaintiff, without using the word orally, said: "we have two words, sexual intercourse, and this word on the board * * * one * * * is acceptable by society * * * the other is not accepted. It is a taboo word." After a few minutes of discussion of other aspects of taboos, plaintiff went on to other matters.

At all times in the discussion plaintiff was in good faith pursuing what he regarded as an educational goal. He was not attempting to probe the private feelings, or attitudes, or experiences of his students, or to embarrass them.

October 2, 1970, the parent of a girl in the class, being erroneously informed that plaintiff had called upon a particular girl in the class to define the taboo word, complained to the principal. He asked Miss Horner the head of the English department to investigate the incident. Plaintiff did admit that he had written on the board the taboo word. He also said he had "probably" called upon a specific girl to define the word. But this court is persuaded by all the testimony that he did not in fact call on any girl individually and that his statement to Miss Horner, repeated later to the union, of what he "probably" did is not an accurate statement of what he actually did. At his meeting with Miss Horner, plaintiff did not refer to the novel which the class had been discussing.

After plaintiff had been interviewed by Miss Horner, defendant superintendent on October 13, 1970 suspended him for seven days with pay.

Plaintiff engaged counsel who requested a hearing before the school committee, and a bill of particulars. The committee furnished particulars alleging that: " * * * Mr. Mailloux did write a list of words on the chalkboard. One of the words was 'fuck'."

"A female student was asked to define the word 'fuck'."

"When confronted with the incident by the head of the department, Mr. Mailloux admitted that the incident was true." [This is a reference to the confrontation in Miss Horner's office.]

The committee gave plaintiff and his counsel a hearing on October 20, 1970.

October 21, 1970 the committee dismissed plaintiff on the general charge of "conduct unbecoming a teacher." It made no finding as to any specific particular.[2]

Following his discharge, plaintiff brought this action seeking temporary and permanent relief. After a two day hearing this court, regarding itself as bound by Keefe v. Geanakos 418 F.2d 359 (lst Cir.), issued on December 21, 1970 a temporary injunction ordering the defendant members of the school committee to restore plaintiff to his employment.

The total amount of salary which, but for his dismissal, plaintiff would have been paid by the City of Lawrence for his services as a teacher at the Lawrence High School from the date of his discharge to the date of his reinstatement by this court is $2,279.20. During that period plaintiff's only earnings were $311.70.

Defendants appealed and asked for a stay pending appeal. For reasons stated in Mailloux v. Kiley, 1st Cir., 436 F.2d 565 (1971), the Court of Appeals denied the stay and dismissed the appeal. This court thereafter conducted a further hearing. Upon the basis of both hearings this court makes the following additional findings.

1. The topic of taboo words had a limited relevance to the Stuart novel which plaintiff's class was discussing, but it had a high degree of relevance to the proper teaching of eleventh grade basic English even to students not expecting to go to college and therefore placed in a "low track."

2. The word "fuck" is relevant to a discussion of taboo words. Its impact effectively illustrates how taboo words function.

3. Boys and girls in an eleventh grade have a sophistication sufficient to treat the word from a serious educational viewpoint. While at first they may be surprised and self-conscious to have the word discussed, they are not likely to be embarrassed or offended.

4. Plaintiffs' writing the word did not have a disturbing effect. A class might be less disturbed by having the word written than if it had been spoken. Most students had seen the word even if they had not used it.

5. Plaintiff's calling upon the class for a volunteer to define the word was a technique that was reasonable and was in accordance with customs in plaintiff's class. It avoided implicating anyone who did not wish to participate.

6. The word "fuck" is in books in the school library.

7. In the opinion of experts of significant standing, such as members of the faculties of the Harvard University School of Education and of Massachusetts Institute of Technology, the discussion of taboo words in the eleventh grade, the way plaintiff used the word "fuck," his writing of it on the blackboard, and the inquiry he addressed to the class, were appropriate and reasonable under the circumstances and served a serious educational purpose. In the opinion of other qualified persons plaintiff's use of the word was not under the circumstances reasonable, or appropriate, or conducive to a serious educational purpose. It has not been shown what is the preponderant opinion in the teaching profession, or in that part of the profession which teaches English.

The parties have not relied upon any express regulation of the Lawrence School Committee or the Lawrence High School. The regulations set forth in an attachment to the complaint have no general or specific provisions relevant to this case.

We now turn to questions of ultimate fact and of law.

Defendant members of the school committee acted for the state when they discharged plaintiff and were therefore subject to the Fourteenth Amendment's command. Pickering v. Board of Education, 391 U.S. 563, 88 S.Ct. 1731, 20 L. Ed.2d 811; Keefe v. Geanakos, 418 F.2d 359, 1st Cir.

The Fourteenth Amendment recognizes that a public school teacher has not only a civic right to freedom of speech both outside (Pickering v. Board of Education, *supra*) and inside (See Tinker v. Des Moines Independent Community School Dist., 393 U.S. 503, 506, 89 S.Ct. 733, 21 L.Ed.2d 731) the schoolhouse, but also some measure of academic freedom as to his in-classroom teaching. Keefe v. Geanakos, *supra;* Parducci v. Rutland, 316 F.Supp. 352, M.D.Ala.

The last two cases cited upheld two kinds of academic freedom: the substantive right of a teacher to choose a teaching method which in the court's view served a demonstrated educational purpose; and the procedural right of a teacher not to be discharged for the use of a teaching method which was not proscribed by a regulation, and as to which it was not proven that he should have had notice that its use was prohibited.

Relying on those cases, plaintiff argues that both his substantive and procedural academic freedom rights, protected by the Fourteenth and First Amendments, were violated by defendant school committee when they discharged him.

The teaching methods plaintiff used were obviously not "necessary" to the proper teaching of the subject and students assigned to him, in the sense that a reference to Darwinian evolution might be thought necessary to the teaching of biology. See the concurrence of Mr. Justice Stewart in Epperson v. Arkansas, 393 U.S. 97, 116, 89 S.Ct.266, 21 L.Ed. 2d 228.

Here we have the use of teaching methods which divide professional opinion. There is substantial support from expert witnesses of undoubted competence that the discussion of taboo words was relevant to an assigned book, and, whether or not so relevant, was at least relevant to the subject of eleventh grade English, that "fuck" was an appropriate choice of an illustrative taboo word, and that writing it on the board and calling upon the class to define it were appropriate techniques. Yet there was also substantial evidence, chiefly from persons with experience as principals but also from the head of the English department at plaintiff's school, that it was inappropriate to use the particular word under the circumstances of this case. The weight of the testimony offered leads this court to make an ultimate finding that plaintiff's methods served an educational purpose, in the sense that they were relevant and had professional endorsement from experts of significant standing. But this court has not implied that the weight of opinion in the teaching profession as a whole, or the weight of opinion among English teachers as a whole, would be that plaintiff's methods were within limits that, even if they would not themselves use them, they would regard as permissible for others. To make a finding on that point would have required a more thorough sampling, especially of younger teachers, than the record offers.

Nor is this case, like *Keefe* or *Parducci,* one where the court, from its own evaluation of the teaching method used, may conclude that, even if the court would not use the method, it is plainly permissible for others to use it, at least in the absence of an express proscription.[3] *Keefe* indicated that the use in the classroom of the word "fuck" is not impermissible under all circumstances—as, for example when it appears in a book properly assigned for student reading. But a teacher who uses a taboo sexual word must take care not to transcend his legitimate professional purpose. When a male teacher asks a class of adolescent boys and girls to define a taboo sexual word the question must not go beyond asking for verbal knowledge and become a titillating probe of privacy. He must not sacrifice his dignity to join his pupils as "frére et cochon." Here, it should be stated unequivocally, there is no evidence that this plaintiff transcended legitimate professional purposes. Indeed, the court has specifically found he acted in good faith. But the risk of abuse involved in the technique of questioning students precludes this court from concluding that the method was *plainly* permissible. Too much depends on the context and the teacher's good faith.

Where, as here, a secondary school teacher chooses a teaching method that is not necessary for the proper instruction of his class, that is not shown to be regarded by the weight of opinion in his profession as permissible, that is not so transparently proper that a court can without expert testimony evaluate it as proper, but that is relevant to his subject and students and, in the opinion of experts of significant standing, serves a serious educational purpose, it is a heretofore undecided question whether the Constitution gives him any right to use the method or leaves the issue to the school authorities. Note, Developments in the Law of Academic Freedom, 81 Harv.L.Rev. 1050, Van Alstyne, The Constitutional Rights of Teachers and Professors, 1970 Duke Law Journal, p. 841.

In support of a qualified[4] right of a teacher, even at the secondary level, to use a teaching method which is relevant and in the opinion of experts of significant standing has a serious educational purpose is the central rationale of academic freedom. The Constitution recognizes that freedom in order to foster open minds, creative imaginations, and adventurous spirits. Our national belief is that the heterodox as well as the orthodox are a source of individual and of social growth. We do not confine academic freedom to conventional teachers or to those who can get a majority vote from their colleagues. Our faith is that the teacher's freedom to choose among options for which there is any substantial support will increase his intellectual vitality and his moral strength. The teacher whose responsibility has been nourished by independence, enterprise, and free choice becomes for his student a better model of the democratic citizen. His examples of applying and adapting the values of the old order to the demands and opportunities of a constantly changing world are among the most important lessons he gives to youth.

Yet the secondary school situation is distinguishable from higher levels of education. See Note, Developments in the Law of Academic Freedom, 81 Harv.L.Rev. 1045, 1050, 1098. There are constitutional considerations of magnitude which, predictably, might warrant a legal conclusion that the secondary school teacher's constitutional right in his classroom is only to be free from discriminatory religious, racial, political and like measures. Epperson v. Arkansas, *supra,* and from state action which is unreasonable, or perhaps has not even a plausible rational basis. See the concluding words in the penultimate paragraph in Mailloux v. Kiley, 1st Cir., 436 F.2d 565 (1971).

The secondary school more clearly than the college or university acts *in loco parentis* with respect to minors. It is closely governed by a school board selected by a local community. The faculty does not have the independent traditions, the broad discretion as to teaching methods, not usually the intellectual qualifications, of university professors. Among secondary school teachers there are often many persons with little experience. Some teachers and most students have limited intellectual and emotional maturity. Most parents, students, school boards, and members of the community usually expect the secondary school to concentrate on transmitting basic information, teaching "the best that is known and thought in the world," training by established techniques, and, to some extent at least, indoctrinating in the *mores* of the surrounding society. While secondary schools are not rigid disciplinary institutions, neither are they open forums in which mature adults, already habituated to social restraints, exchange ideas on a level of parity. Moreover, it cannot be accepted as a premise that the student is voluntarily in the classroom and willing to be exposed to a teaching method which, though reasonable, is not approved by the school authorities or by the weight of professional opinion. A secondary school student, unlike most college students, is usually required to attend school classes, and may have no choice as to his teacher.

Bearing in mind these competing considerations, this court rules that when a secondary school teacher uses a teaching method which he does not prove has the support of the preponderant opinion of the teaching profession or of the part of it to which he belongs, but which he merely proves is relevant to his subject and students, is regarded by experts of significant standing as serving a serious educational purpose, and was used by him in good faith the state may suspend or discharge a teacher for using that method but it may not resort to such drastic sanctions unless the state proves he was put on notice either by a regulation or otherwise that he should not use that method. This exclusively procedural protection is afforded to a teacher not because he is a state employee, or because he is a citizen, but because in his teaching capacity he is engaged in the exercise of what may plausibly be considered "vital First Amendment rights." Keyishian v. Board of Regents, 385 U.S. 489, 604, 87 S.Ct. 675, 684, 17 L.Ed.2d 629. In his teaching capacity he is not required to "guess what conduct or utterance may lose him his position," (*Ibid*). If he did not have the right to be warned before he was discharged, he might be more timid than it is in the public interest that he should be, and he might steer away from reasonable methods with which it is in the public interest to experiment. *Ibid.*

In the instant case it is not claimed that any regulation warned plaintiff not to follow the methods he chose. Nor can it be said that plaintiff should have known that his teaching methods were not permitted. There is no substantial evidence that his methods were contrary to an informal rule, to an understanding among school teachers of his school or teachers generally, to a body of disciplinary precedents, to precise canons of ethics, or to specific opinions expressed in professional journals or other publications. This was not the kind of unforeseeable outrageous conduct which all men of good will would, once their attention is called to it, immediately perceive to be forbidden. On this last point it is sufficient to refer to the testimony given by faculty members of Harvard University and M. I. T. who had prepared their students for secondary school teaching careers.

Finally, in the face of the record of judicial uncertainty in this case it cannot be held that it was self-evident that a teacher should not have used the methods followed by plaintiff. This Court, perhaps mis-reading the *Keefe* case, issued an injunction on the ground that plaintiff's conduct was, more probably than not, legally permissible. The Court of Appeals, which had before it this court's findings on the temporary injunction (which are not materially different from those now made) concluded that the temporary injunction was not such an abuse of discretion as to justify its dissolution. Mailloux v. Kiley, 1st Cir., 436 F.2d 565 (1971). We can hardly say that plaintiff should have known what was not evident to judges after taking evidence, hearing argument, and reflecting in chambers.

Inasmuch as at the time he acted plaintiff did not know, and there was no reason that he should have known, that his conduct was proscribed, it was a violation of due process for the defendants to suspend or discharge him on that account. Cf. Keyishian v. Board of Regents, Keefe v. Geanakos and Parducci v. Rutland, all *supra.*

Plaintiff, in accordance with Parducci v. Rutland, is entitled to a judgment directing:

1. All defendants to continue plaintiff in employment until the end of the academic year 1970-1971, except for good cause.

2. All defendants to expunge from their employment records and transcripts all references to plaintiff's suspension and discharge.

3. The City of Lawrence, as his employer, and the school committee members, as the persons who discharged him, to compensate him for the salary loss he suffered, $2,279.20, less his earnings, $311.70, or $1,967.50, with 6% interest from the date of the complaint December 14, 1970.

4. The City of Lawrence and the school committee members to pay costs.

The court is not unmindful that both the opinion and the judgment cover not only plaintiff's discharge without compensation but also his suspension with pay. The reason that the suspension is covered is because in the circumstances of this case the superintendent and all others treated it as a penalty. Nothing herein suggests that school authorities are not free after they have learned that the teacher is using a teaching method of which they disapprove, and which is not appropriate to the proper teaching of the subject, to suspend him until he agrees to cease using the method. See the last of Mailloux v. Kiley, 1st Cir., 436 F.2d 565 (1971).

NOTES

1. Plaintiff abandoned his contract claim.

2. Inasmuch as the committee made no finding as to whether plaintiff called upon a specific girl, this court has no need to consider whether it had substantial evidence which would have supported such a finding.

3. Perhaps, though *Keefe* and *Parducci* do not say so, the school authorities there involved were constitutionally free by express proscription to forbid the assignment of outside reading of magazine articles and novels of undoubted merit and propriety for which the teacher had not secured advance approval.

4. The so-called constitutional right is not absolute. It is akin to, and may indeed be a species of, the right to freedom of speech which is embraced by the concept of the "liberty" protected by the Fourteenth Amendment. Analytically, as distinguished from rhetorically, it is less a right than a constitutionally-recognized interest. Clearly, the teacher's right must yield to compelling public interests of greater constitutional significance. It may be that it will be held by the Supreme Court that the teacher's academic right to liberty in teaching methods in the classroom (unlike his civic right to freedom of speech) is subject to state regulatory control which is not actuated by compelling public interests but which, in the judiciary's opinion is merely "reasonable". See Epperson v. Arkansas, 393 U.S. 97, 89 S.Ct. 266, 21 L.Ed.2d 228 and Tinker v. Des Moines School Dist., 393 U.S. 503, 89 S.Ct. 733, 21 L.Ed. 2d 731. Indeed it has been suggested that state regulatory control of the classroom is entitled to prevail unless the teacher bears the heavy burden of proving that it has no rational justification, (See Mr. Justice Black dissenting in Tinker v. Des Moines School Dist., 393 U.S. 503, 519-521, 89 S.Ct. 733,), or is discriminatory on religious, racial, political, or like grounds. See Epperson v. Arkansas, 393 U.S. 97, 89 S.Ct. 266.

THE CALIFORNIA SUPREME COURT FINDS FOR A TENTH GRADE ENGLISH TEACHER NOT REHIRED BECAUSE OF HIS READING TO HIS CLASS A THEME CONTAINING LANGUAGE DEEMED "OBJECTIONABLE" BY THE PRINCIPAL, "INCLUDING A SLANG EXPRESSION FOR AN INCESTUOUS SON"

Lindros v. Governing Board of Torrance U. Sch. Dist., 510 P.2d 361 (1972)

TOBRINER, Justice.

In this case we examine Education Code section 13443,[1] which establishes the conditions under which the governing boards of local school districts may decline to rehire probationary teachers. At the end of the 1969-1970 academic year, the Governing Board of the Torrance Unified School District[2] terminated petitioner Stanley Lindros, a probationary teacher, because he read a theme to his English class which contained controversial language, and because he allegedly on one occasion allowed students to return needed books to the library without proper authorization.

For the reasons set forth below, we hold that these incidents fail to establish "cause" for termination which is reasonably "relate[d] to the welfare of the schools and pupils thereof" as required by section 13443, subdivision (d); in so doing we note that in both incidents Lindros acted in the good faith pursuit of concededly legitimate educational objectives, and that the Board demonstrated no significant adverse impact on the students or the school.

The Torrance Board employed petitioner as a tenth-grade probationary English teacher at South High School for the 1969-1970 school year. Petitioner's record attested to his eminent qualification for the position. Not only did he hold a California teacher credential but also he had studied for, or obtained, advanced degrees in philosophy, theology, and the communication arts. A Catholic priest on leave of absence from the Church, petitioner had enjoyed a wide range of experience: he had served as a parish priest, prison chaplain, resident counselor, and secondary level teacher. Nothing in the record suggests that petitioner had failed to fulfill his promise as an effective English instructor or had been unable to relate well with young people; indeed "teacher evaluation" records indicated that he proved himself "above average" in both competency in subject matter and in rapport with students.

The incident which constituted the main charge against the petitioner occurred early in the school year. In mid-October 1969 petitioner assigned his tenth-grade English classes the task of preparing a short story relating a personal emotional experience. The purpose of this assignment, as later described by petitioner, was to stress "the relationship between good creative writing and personal experience. I believe this to be the key in communicating with students and encouraging better writing."

At the request of seversl students that he present them with an example of his own work, Lindros read a short story, "The Funeral," which he originally wrote as a rough draft for a television play at Loyola University. Autobiographical in nature, the story recorded petitioner's emotions at the funeral of one of his students who, during the time Lindros taught at a predominantly black high school in Watts, died of a heroin overdose. The theme contained language later deemed objectionable by South High's principal—including a slang expression for an incestuous son. We set forth the full text below:

"The Funeral"

"I was mad, disgusted . . . tense. If Agnes hadn't reminded me I'd still be watching *Shoes of a Fisherman* at the film director's studio. But whether it was guilt or concern, I knew I should be at Ed's funeral at 2 p.m.

"The highway provided me with nothing but a blanket of mist and melancholy. Splashing past 110-th and Compton Ave. I caught sight of Greater Antioch Baptist Church just as four of my students were carrying Ed's body into the dismal looking building.

"Water dripped from the ceiling as the small choir intoned, *Come Sweet Jesus.* . . . Only the appearance of plump Rev. Black, Bible in hand, saved us from their uncoordinated efforts.

"I couldn't catch what Black was reading but it was unimportant. I was here, somber, moody, thoughtful; and all to the testimony that I as a white man did care for a young black hipe who died too young . . . too soon.

"Lloyd made it . . . Larry, Fred, Benard, Fuzzy—they were all there. Seemed like every addict in the community was on the scene with his leather jacket and shades, as if to collect . . . or to pay off to Ed. What a lineup! Sargent [sic] Masterson from Precinct 77 would have raised a brow or two at this gathering.

"Kelly had tears streaming down his face; perpetually high . . . who could blame him; deserted father, bitch mother; in and out of jail since thirteen. He shot with Ed for the last time that Saturday night.

"The wailing, so characteristic at a Black funeral did not begin until the second stanza of *I Believe,* delivered by Hessie Jones. The little Black kid next to me stared at the solitary tear that rolled down my cheek.

"Why are women so goddam hysterical? Did they really know Ed? Did they care? Were they using Ed's 'time' from their own shackles of welfare and project living? I do not know. I do not live in Watts; but I feel for them now, in their strange melodramatic way.

"Only the obituary read by Sister Maebelle shook me out of my depression. 'Ed Leavy Pollard. Born in Greenwood, Miss., 1952; Died Jan. 11, 1969. . . , She droned on in a pitifully low, uneducated tone.

"Curley, a steady shooter with Ed was moved to bellow out, 'Louder Lady, I can't hear ya.' Choresetta in the fourth pew from the front responded to this abrupt remark with a deep shaking sob. The storm grew louder. I noticed at least three leaks from the roof now. God, what a depressing hole; wet, dam [sic] pictureless, peeling paint, worn, dam pews; only the cossack of Ed,and us. 'Only us O Lord,' I thought 'but what the hell are we here for?'

"I sit here white, middleclass, secure, while the goddam system rapes these poor people of every vestage [sic] of dignity.

"Rev. Galine, a slick looking 'Tom' began the eulogy; Jeremiah was the scapegoat. First there was the woman in the back row. She was joined by three others; then another . . . and another; soon everyone in the drama had his chance to chant a response back to the Baptist Preacher; 'Oh Lord' . . . 'That's right' . . . 'I'm listnin' . . . 'Speak God.' . . . Only the periodic gasping signs (sobs) interrupted the Rev's show.

"Ed would have rolled over and grimaced if he would have heard the hysterics when David, his classmate, opened his cossack for the finale. The weeping and gnashing lasted long enough for all of us to troop past Ed and glance at his ashen, black face.

"I felt whipped out; this was a strange two hours; strange to a white who had no blackness in him; strange to a white who knew no such poverty and desperation; even stranger outside when I greeted a young Black in a Panther-like outfit: 'White-mother-fuckin Pig.' . . . "

Before reading the controversial words at the end of "The Funeral," petitioner pondered their appropriateness for the classroom, and decided in good faith that their use was permissible in some, but not all, of his classes.[3] As petitioner stated, although he recognized that "a few words in 'The Funeral' [were] not acceptable in common usage . . . [he] felt that even if one student was to give up or think less of drugs, the reason for reading the play was justified." Lindros read the young black's objectionable and defiant remark at the end of the story only in college preparatory classes, which he considered most mature; in other classes he substituted the initials "W.M.F.P." While petitioner did not preliminarily consult with school administrators as to whether he should read the story, his conduct accorded with the prevailing policy of the school that instructors could select outside instructional material. According to the hearing officer "There [was] widespread use of outside instructional material selected by the instructors and not submitted for approval." Moreover, school administrators had promulgated "no clear statement of the criteria or standards [to be] applied in selecting this material."

Furthermore, the prevailing practices and conditions at the high school strongly indicated that the inclusion of the language in a literary composition would evoke no concern. The library shelved books, readily available to students, which contained words identical to all of those found in "The Funeral"; school administrators, moreover, as part of the curriculum, had permitted instructors to take students to theatrical performances in which the lines spoken by the actors contained the same or similar words.

No disruption of classroom activities followed petitioner's reading of "The Funeral." As the hearing officer noted, "In considering the seriousness of the use of the offending material . . . these words were presented fully or by their initial letters to five classes of a total of approximately 150 students. No complaint arose from the students and none arose from the parents of these students. This will not establish that the material was appropriate for classroom use but does tend to establish that the context and manner of presentation was not nearly so startling to the students who heard it . . . as the disembodied restatement of the offending words makes it appear."

Despite this seemingly indifferent reaction, the principal of the high school learned of the incident and reprimanded Lindros. The principal counseled Lindros that the language of the short story did not accord with established classroom usage and that further use of vulgar material should be avoided; petitioner agreed to abide by this directive and signed a statement to that effect. This meeting closed the incident until the end of the school year, some eight months later, when the Torrance Board announced that it would not rehire Lindros. As both the hearing officer and the superior court later found, the reading of "The Funeral" constituted the "gravamen" of the Torrance Board's complaint against Lindros.[4]

In addition to the incident involving "The Funeral," the hearing officer found Lindros to have permitted students to leave class on one occasion without the authorization normally required by school regulations.[5] On February 6, 1970, petitioner allowed students in one class to depart a few minutes before the "sounding of the bell signalling the close of the class session." Lindros "had instructed those of his students who were in possession of a book entitled *Zorba the Greek* to depart from class early, secure the book from their lockers, and return the book to the library so that it could be redistributed when needed by the students of another English instructor. . . . It was not established that all of those students who departed were leaving to complete this errand."

After the superintendent of the Torrance School District served notice of an intention not to rehire Lindros because of the aforementioned incidents, the Board held an administrative hearing pursuant to subdivision (b) of section 13443. At this proceeding the hearing officer found that " 'The Funeral' is not within the generally accepted standard and that its use would violate the policy of the school in regard to the introduction of objectionable language into the classroom." He further found that although "[t]he school does sanction the use of literary work and current periodical material in which socially unacceptable words and phrases appear . . . [The Funeral] is not a generally accepted literary work and does not appear within a generally accepted periodical. [Petitioner's] lapse of judgment and violation of standards is a factor relating to the welfare of the students and the school." Though he found that the incident involving "The Funeral" was the "gravamen" of the complaint, the hearing officer also declared that the February 6, 1970, incident involving early dismissal of students from class constituted "cause" under section 13443.

The Torrance Board, without examining the record of the administrative hearing, adopted the hearing officer's report as its own: the Board further declared that each charge "separately and collectively" constitute[d] . . . sufficient cause not to reemploy [petitioner]."

Following the Torrance Board's final decision, Lindros petitioned the Los Angeles Superior Court for a writ of mandate under Code of Civil Procedure section 1094.5. In denying the petition the superior court declared that the language of "The Funeral" is "manifestly coarse and vulgar" and that "[p]etitioner should have known that such language by a teacher was totally unacceptable in a Tenth Grade English class." The superior court then noted that the charges relating to both "The Funeral" and the February 6, 1970, incident involving early dismissal of students "were found to be related to the welfare of the school and the pupils thereof, and the Governing Board's determination of sufficiency is conclusive." We believe that this holding cannot be sustained because petitioner's conduct did not, as a matter of law, constitute cause for termination within the meaning of Education Code section 13443. We turn now to an analysis of section 13443, and of the errors which we perceive in the superior court's denial of the writ of mandate.

I. *The question whether alleged misconduct establishes "cause" under section 13443, subdivision (d), constitutes a question of law.*

Education Code section 13443, subdivision (d) defines the conditions under which a local school board can refuse to rehire a probationary teacher. The statute provides that:

"The Governing Board's determination not to reemploy a probationary employee for the ensuing school year shall be for cause only. The determination of the Governing Board as to the sufficiency of the cause pursuant to this section shall be conclusive, but the cause shall relate solely to the welfare of the schools and the pupils thereof. . . . "

The precedents clearly establish that the question whether a particular cause for refusal to rehire relates "solely to the welfare of the schools and the pupils thereof" presents a matter of law that must be determined by the courts, and, ultimately by this court. The Board determines the *facts* and their sufficiency to support the Board's determination but the court decides whether the facts as found—in our case, the conduct of the teacher— reasonably could be said to have adversely affected the welfare of the school or its pupils.

In the fountainhead case of Griggs v. Board of Trustees (1964) 61 Cal.2d 93, 37 Cal.Rptr. 194, 389 P.2d 722, a school board refused to rehire a probationary teacher for "lack of self-restraint and tact in dealing with co-workers, pupils, and parents." (*Id.* at p. 97, 37 Cal.Rptr. at p. 197, 389 P. 2d at p. 725.) We interpreted section 13443 (then § 13444) to mean that "where there is evidence to support the board's findings of fact *and where the cause for dismissal found by the board can reasonably be said to relate to the 'welfare of the schools and pupils thereof,'* the reviewing court may not consider whether the facts found are sufficiently serious to justify dismissal." (*Id.* at p. 96, 37 Cal.Rptr. at p. 197, 389 P.2d at p. 275.) (Emphasis added.) The *Griggs* court then itself found a reasonable relationship between the "cause" (lack of tact) and the "welfare of the schools." (*Id.* at p. 97, 37 Cal.Rptr. 194, 389 P.2d 722.)

We more recently examined the division of responsibilities between courts and governing boards under section 13443 in Bekiaris v. Board of Education (1972) 6 Cal. 3d 575, 100 Cal.Rptr. 16, 493 P.2d 480. "It is to be emphasized . . . that [under section 13443] the general applicability of the rule of substantial evidence in light of the entire record does not affect the power and duty of the trial court to make an independent determination of questions having a legal character. Thus, [n]othing . . . prevents the reviewing court from determining whether the board has proceeded in excess of jurisdiction, whether there has been a fair trial, and whether the board's findings of fact are supported by substantial evidence.' [Citation.] Moreover, it is for the *court to determine whether a particular cause for dismissal 'relate[s] solely to the welfare of the schools and the pupils thereof'* as required by section 13443. [Citations.] " (*Id.* at p. 587, 100 Cal.Rptr. at p. 22, 493 P.2d at p. 486.) (Emphasis added.)

We further explained that "although the reviewing court must accept evidentiary facts shown by substantial evidence and the sufficiency of those facts to constitute a stated cause, still it remains for the court to determine *as a matter of law* whether such cause relates to the welfare of the school and its pupils and is therefore adequate under the provisions of section 13443 to justify dismissal." (*Id.* at p. 589, 100 Cal.Rptr. at p. 24, 493 P.2d at p. 488.) (Emphasis in the opinion.)

The Courts of Appeal have consistently followed this approach. Thus, the court in Blodgett v. Board of Trustees (1971) 20 Cal.App.3d 183, 97 Cal.Rptr. 406, held that refusal to rehire a probationary teacher solely because she was overweight was not a "cause" reasonably related to school welfare; the "physical condition unrelated to the plaintiff's fitness [to teach] was used as a pretext for refusing [re-employment]." (*Id.* at p. 193, 97 Cal. Rptr. at p. 412.) In Thornton v. Board of Trustees (1968) 262 Cal.App.2d 761, 68 Cal.Rptr. 842, the Court of Appeal held refusal to rehire solely because a probationary teacher was 65 years old was not "cause"[6] reasonably related to the welfare of the school.

In sum, whether particular conduct establishes cause under section 13443, poses a pure question of law. This question must be sharply distinguished from two other types of questions which arise under section 13443: (1) questions of *fact* and (2) questions as to the *sufficiency* of the "cause" to warrant dismissal in light of all the circumstances. Past cases have held that findings of fact, developed by the hearing officer and the governing board, will be upheld by the courts so long as supported by substantial evidence on the whole record. (Griggs v. Board of Trustees, *supra,* 61 Cal.2d at p. 96, 37 Cal.Rptr. 194, 389 P.2d 722.)[7] Similarly, the determination as to the "sufficiency of the cause"—whether the "cause" warrants a refusal to rehire despite the teacher's redeeming qualities as a teacher, his attitude, and the particular needs of the school district—lies solely in the discretion of the governing board *so long as* section 1344's requirement of "cause . . . relate[d] solely to the welfare of the schools and the pupils thereof . . ." has been met. (Bekiaris v. Board of Education, *supra,* 6 Cal. 3d at p. 589, 100 Cal.Rptr. 16, 24, 493 P.2d 480, 488.)

Having demonstrated that the determination of "cause" under section 13443 constitutes a question of law, we turn to an examination of that issue in light of the two charges of misconduct against petitioner Lindros.

II. *The reading of "The Funeral" did not constitute "cause" under section 13443.*

Lindros' reading of the composition did not constitute "cause" under section 13443 because, first, in presenting it to his pupils petitioner sought to pursue a bona fide educational purpose and in so doing did not adversely affect "the welfare of the schools or the pupils thereof"; second, the composition was used as teaching material without prior reasonable notice that such use would later be deemed impermissible by school authorities. We shall separately analyze each of these propositions.

A. *In reading "The Funeral" petitioner sought to pursue a bona fide educational purpose and in so doing did not adversely affect the welfare of the school or the pupils thereof.*

Erroneously applying a per se approach to the controversial epithet at the end of "The Funeral," the superior court declared that its use was "manifestly coarse and vulgar." The court, however, apparently failed to make the crucial distinction between unrestricted use of such words in the classroom and their inclusion in teaching material for a class in creative writing.

Petitioner is the first to concede that it would be "outrageous . . . if a teacher simply shouts 'mother-fucking-pigs' to his students." Obviously teachers are not to sanction the use of words as blatantly offensive as these in classroom discussion or even in the personal banter of students. But here the words were used by a character in a story; the story, in turn was presented as an example of expressive writing. The black character utters the words in "The Funeral" as a mark of his anger and disgust at a white's presence at the funeral; the words were employed for a definite literary objective. Thus, Lindros read the story to his students as part of a quite obvious teaching technique.

Many classic works seeking to capture the anger of blacks against a society that they consider inexcusably oppressive are peppered with epithets that express outrage in terms at least as violent as that used here. Malamud's "The Tenants" is a recent example; "Man-Child in a Promised Land" by Claude Brown is another. Baldwin's "The Fire Next Time," written, as it is, by a black, is the most virulent; we could cite innumerable other examples. The writer of "The Funeral" could not properly convey the fury of the young black at the apparent condescension of a white man in attending the funeral except by the use of an expletive. The outrage of the black *had* to be mirrored in language that outraged.

Lindros was obviously trying to teach his students that in writing creative compositions the author must attempt to put those words in the mouths of his characters that belong there. The blasphemous epithet must fit the emotional outburst of the speaker. To isolate the epithet and to condemn the teacher is to miss the function of expressive writing. In sum, we could not impose upon teachers of writing, as a matter of law, that they must tell and teach their students that in depicting the jargon of the ghetto, the slum, or the barrack room, characters must speak in the pedantry of Edwardian English.

The record shows that neither student nor parent complained about this use of the lurid words in Lindros' composition. The students had been exposed to identical language in books and periodicals in the school library; their teachers had taken them to dramatic productions that used these and other obnoxious terms. That the students were not "shocked" can come as no surprise.

Finally, the United States Supreme Court has recognized the widespread use of current, divergent and distasteful patterns of speech, such as those involved here; indeed, in some situations that court has accorded constitutional protection to similarly shocking and offensive language. For example, the Supreme Court recently held the phrase "fuck the draft" protected by the First Amendment when portrayed on a jacket worn in a courthouse corridor. (Cohen v. California (1971) 403 U.S. 15, 91 S.Ct. 1780, 29 L.Ed.2d 284.) Although *Cohen* involved a controversial term in expressing a political view in a public forum and is thus distinguishable from the instant situation, we note its reasoning: "How is one to distinguish this from any other offensive word? Surely the State has no right to cleanse public debate to the point where it is grammatically palatable to the most squeamish among us. Yet no readily ascertainable general principle exists for stopping short of that result were we to affirm the judgment below. For, while the particular four-letter word being litigated here is perhaps more distasteful than most others of its genre, it is nevertheless often true that one man's vulgarity is another's lyric." (Cohen v. California, *supra,* 403 U.S. at p. 25, 91 S.Ct. at p. 1788.)

Three recent cases in which the Supreme Court vacated criminal convictions for offensive speech and remanded in light of Cohen v. California, *supra,* 403 U.S. 15, 91 S.Ct. 1280, 29 L.Ed.2d 284, illustrate the same point. In Rosenfeld v. New Jersey (1972) 408 U.S. 901, 92 S.Ct. 2483, 33 L.Ed.2d 321 the defendant was convicted of disturbing the peace by indecent and offensive language; he had addressed a school board meeting, attended by some 40 children, using, on several occasions in his speech, the words "mother fucker"; in Brown v. Oklahoma (1972) 408 U.S. 914, 92 S.Ct. 2507, 33 L.Ed.2d 326, the defendant, during a speech before a group of men and women in the University of Tulsa chapel, referred to policemen as "mother fucking fascist pig cops"; in Lewis v. City of New Orleans (1972) 408 U.S. 913, 92 S.Ct. 2499, 33 L.Ed.2d 321, a mother addressed police officers who had arrested her son as "god-damned-mother-fucking-police."

These cases illustrate both the use of such speech in sections of our multifarious society and an increasing immunity from criminal sanction for such expressions. While these rulings by no means legitimize the general use of offensive language in the classroom, they do explain the background and reasons for the use of such words in literary works depicting realistically the coarse and strident forms of communication that so often attend public dialogue today.[8]

We conclude that the Board has failed to show that the inclusion of opprobrious language currently used in many subcultures, in a single composition, presented solely for teaching purposes, rises to the level of a legal cause for severance of a teacher from his employment.

B. *The reading was only a single incident in the presentation of teaching material which, although later deemed objectionable, was used in the absence of prior reasonable notice that such use would be deemed impermissible by the school authorities.*

As we have pointed out, the accepted policy at South High School permitted the selection of instructional material by teachers without submission to administrators for advanced approval. Moreover, as we have explained, books and periodicals at the school library contained language as controversial as that found in "The Funeral"; further, students with the sponsorship of their teachers attended plays in which such language was employed. In the previous section we have alluded to the unfortunate current prevalence of language as repulsive as that we face here. The record shows no specific disapproval of the use of written material containing such expressions. Under these circumstances we must conclude that petitioner acting in good faith, presented the composition to the class without prior reasonable notice that such presentation would contravene the governing policies of the high school.[9]

We do not believe that one isolated classroom usage of material later deemed objectionable by school administrators, without reasonable prior notice, can constitute "cause" for termination reasonably "relate[d] solely to the welfare of the schools and the pupils thereof." "Cause" under section 13443 requires that the teacher must have failed to exercise such reasonable judgment as would be expected of a member of his profession under the same circumstances. "Teachers, particularly in the light of their professional expertise, will normally be able to determine what kind of conduct indicates unfitness to teach. Teachers are further protected by the fact that they cannot be disciplined merely because they made a reasonable, good faith, professional judgment in the course of their employment with which higher authorities later disagreed." (Morrison v. State Board of Education (1969) 1 Cal.3d 214, 233, 82 Cal.Rptr. 175, 189, 461 P.2d 375, 389.)[10]

III. *The incident involving dismissal of students on one school day fails to establish "cause" reasonably related to the welfare of the schools and was not the true reason for the Board's refusal to rehire Lindros.*

We turn to the remaining charge that on one occasion during the school year Lindros permitted students to leave one of his classes "without proper authorization." A close review of the findings pertinent to the incident reveals that it was not conclusively established that Lindros violated any school rule, and that, in any event, the isolated *de minimis* violation charged was a mere makeweight that did not constitute the true reason for the Board's refusal to rehire Lindros.

The hearing officer's findings of fact, later adopted by both the Torrance Board and the superior court, contain ambiguities which cast doubt on the assertion that Lindros improperly dismissed his class;[11] these ambiguities strengthen our conclusion that the charge of improper dismissal of students did not trigger the action against Lindros. The record indicates that on February 6, 1970, Lindros dismissed some students for the legitimate educational purpose of returning needed copies of the book, *Zorba the Greek,* to the library. Nothing suggests that this action, by itself, violated any school rule. Although it "was not established that all of those students who departed" actually followed petitioner's instructions, Lindros could hardly be dismissed merely because he failed to prove that all of the students obeyed his instructions and went to the library after leaving his classroom. Thus the findings of fact could not support a conclusion that Lindros failed to "authorize" his students to go to the library.[12]

As the hearing officer found, however, de facto school policy required a teacher to provide a *written* authorization when sending more than five students to the library; conceivably, Lindros violated a school regulation, not by dismissing his students, but by failing on this single occasion to furnish a written "hall pass." The hearing officer's decision, however, omitted any findings about this vital fact. The findings therefore do not directly support even the conclusion that Lindros dismissed the students without proper *written* authorization. (Cf. Almaden-Santa Clara Vineyards v. Paul (1966) 239 Cal.App.2d 860, 867-868, 49 Cal.Rptr. 256.)

In any event, the record makes clear that the reading of "The Funeral" comprised the "gravamen" of the charges, and that the refusal to rehire rested upon this foundation. We are reminded here of the incisive language of Bekiaris v. Board of Education, *supra,* 6 Cal.3d 575, 592-593, 100 Cal.Rptr. 16, 26, 493 P.2d 480, 490 that "a dismissed public employee is entitled to a judicial determination of the *true* reason for his dismissal . . . " (emphasis in the original). Although *Bekiaris* condemned a dismissal involving constitutional rights, its logic equally applies in the instant situation involving statutory rights. Since both the hearing officer and superior court found that "The Funeral" comprised the "gravamen" of the complaint against petitioner, we believe that charge was the "true reason" for the refusal to rehire.[13]

Furthermore, to assume that the Torrance Board would have refused to rehire Lindros based *solely* on the incident of February 6 stretches the credible. The incident at most involved a single, unrepeated infraction of a minor regulation in mid-year, with no showing of any adverse impact on the educational process, and with no showing that it occurred by other than mere inadvertence. We doubt that the Torrance Board would have acted so harshly as to ignore Shakespeare's common sense observation that "men are men; the best sometimes forget." (Shakespeare, Othello,II (1604).[14]

Summarizing the case as a whole, we conclude that the

Board's refusal to rehire petitioner was invalid because it was not for cause reasonably related to the Welfare of the school.[15] We heed Judge Wyzanski's characterization of fundamental public policy: that education must "foster open minds, creative imagination, and adventurous spirits. Our national belief is that the heterodox as well as the orthodox are a source of individual and of social growth. We do not confine academic freedom to conventional teachers or to those who can get a majority vote from their colleagues. Our faith is that the teacher's freedom to choose among options for which there is any substantial support will increase his intellectual vitality and his moral strength. The teacher whose responsibility has been nourished by independence, enterprise, and free choice becomes for his student a better model of the democratic citizen." (Mailloux v. Kiley (D.Mass.1971) 323 F.Supp. 1387, 1391.)

The judgment of the superior court denying the writ of mandate is reversed, and the cause is remanded to the superior court for proceedings consistent with this opinion.

WRIGHT, C.J., MOSK and SULLIVAN, JJ., and ROTH, J. pro tem*, concur.

BURKE, Justice (dissenting).

I dissent. The majority have wholly emasculated the provisions of section 13443, subdivision (d), of the Education Code which, until now, assured that a local school board's decision as to the sufficiency of the cause for failing to reemploy a probationary teacher was *conclusive* and free from judicial interference. The "cause" which led defendant district to refuse to reemploy Lindros was his *classroom* use of improper, indecent language. Since the use of such language in the tenth-grade classroom obviously is a matter of relating to "the welfare of the schools and the pupils thereof," (Ed.Code, § 13443, subd. (d), the district's determination concerning the sufficiency of that cause should have been "conclusive." (*Id.*) Instead, the majority have rendered that determination wholly *inclusive,* by relying upon a variety of supposedly mitigating factors (such as Lindros' asserted "good faith") which more properly were matters of sole concern to the district in appraising the sufficiency of the cause for terminating Lindros' services. More importantly, however, and wholly apart from the particular circumstances surrounding this case, the majority's approach can be employed in future cases involving probationary teachers to undermine and defeat the clear legislative intent to vest in the local school board plenary control over these matters.

Section 13443, subdivision (d), carefully allocates the respective responsibilities of the school boards and the courts in cases involving refusals to rehire probationary teachers. That section expressly makes the governing board's determination as to the sufficiency of the cause "conclusive," so long as that cause relates to the welfare of the school or its pupils. As stated in Griggs v. Board of Trustees, 61 Cal.2d 93, 96, 37 Cal.Rptr. 194, 197, 389 P.2d 722, 725, the landmark case in this area, "Nothing in the language of section 13444 [now § 13443] prevents the reviewing court from determining whether the board has proceeded in excess of jurisdiction, whether there has been a fair trial, and whether the board's findings of fact are supported by substantial evidence. However, *where there is evidence to support the board's findings of fact and where the cause for* dismissal found by the board can reasonably

be said to relate to the 'welfare of the schools and the pupils thereof,' the reviewing court may not consider whether the facts found are sufficiently serious to justify dismissal."* (Italics added.)

In *Griggs,* the "cause" for the board's decision was the teacher's "lack of self-restraint and tact in dealing with co-workers, pupils and parents." Since substantial evidence existed to support the existence of that cause, and since that cause "is clearly a matter which relates to the welfare of the school and its pupils," this court held that "the trial court could not properly substitute its own judgment for that of the board on the question of the sufficiency of the cause for Mrs. Griggs' dismissal." (P. 97, 37 Cal.Rptr. p. 197, 389 P.2d p. 725.) I stress the fact that this court did not purport to reappraise the "good faith," "lack of significant adverse impact," or other possible mitigating factors in Mrs. Griggs' favor, unlike the majority's approach in this case, for such matters were exclusively within the domain of the school board.[1]

Subsequent cases have uniformly employed the Griggs' approach, namely, to determine only whether or not the type of conduct at issue (e.g., lack of tact) can be said to reasonably relate to the welfare of the school and its pupils. For example, in Raney v. Board of Trustees, 239 Cal.App. 2d 256, 48 Cal.Rptr. 555, the "cause" relied upon by the school board was the teacher's severe grading techniques and poor rapport with students. The court explained that were it at liberty to supervise the judgment of the board on the matter, the court "might well reach an opposite conclusion. . . . *[B]ut our theory of government gives to the school trustees, for better or for worse, an almost absolute choice either to 'hire or fire' teachers who have not yet attained tenure."* (Italics added; p. 260, 48 Cal.Rptr. p. 557.)

Similarly, in American Federation of Teachers v. San Lorenzo, etc., Sch. Dist., 276 Cal.App.2d 132, 136, 80 Cal.Rptr. 758, 760, the court held that a probationary teacher's inability to accept responsibility and inadequate supervision of students "certainly relate to the welfare of the schools and the pupils. . . ." Accordingly, the court explained that it "cannot consider whether the charges justify dismissal." (See also Governing Board v. Brennan, 18 Cal.App.3d 396, 95 Cal.Rptr. 712 [teacher advocated marijuana use]; McGlone v. Mt. Diablo Unified Sch. Dist., 3 Cal.App.3d 17, 82 Cal.Rptr. 225 [failure to supervise students]; Feist v. Rowe, 3 Cal.App.3d 404, 83 Cal.Rptr. 465.)

The two cases which reversed school board decisions in this area are not on point for they merely established that physical characteristics of a teacher, such as advanced age or obesity, cannot constitute "cause" under section 13443 since neither factor standing alone could involve the welfare of the school or students. In the instant case, on the other hand, the cause for Lindros' termination was his *classroom* use of indecent language, a matter which (like the lack of tact in *Griggs,* the severe grading techniques in *Raney,* or the inadequate supervision in *San Lorenzo*) by its very nature relates to the welfare of the school and its pupils. Of course, depending upon the underlying circumstances in each case, including the teacher's "good faith" or the lack of any "significant adverse impact," the school board might determine that particular act or impropriety is excusable and insufficient cause for refusal to reemploy. Yet that decision lies with the school board not the courts.

As I interpret section 13443, the Legislature intended to

vest the school board with sole discretion in appraising the sufficiency of the 'cause, but to assure that the cause asserted has some reasonable relation to the school and its pupils rather than pertaining solely to the teacher's private life, unrelated to school affairs. For example, a court might properly hold that a teacher's persistent refusal to obey his parents, his inability to teach his wife how to drive, his failure to keep timely dental appointments, or his intemperate language with his neighbors, were acts of a type which could not reasonably relate to the welfare of the school or its pupils under section 13443. Yet similar acts of insubordination, incompetence, tardiness or use of indecent language, when occurring in a classroom setting or otherwise affecting school affairs, clearly would meet the statutory test.

In the instant case, Lindros used language *in his classroom* which many persons deem objectionable in any context.[2] Indeed, it is well established that even permanent, tenured teachers are subject to appropriate discipline, including dismissal, on account of their classroom use of indecent or profane language. (See Board of Trustees v. Metzger, 8 Cal.3d 206, 212, 104 Cal.Rptr. 452, 501 P.2d 1172; Palo Verde, etc., Sch. Dist. v. Hensey, 9 Cal.App. 3d 967, 88 Cal.Rptr. 570.) Accordingly, the district certainly had statutory authority to refuse to reemploy Lindros for the coming year.

The majority stress such factors as Lindros' "good faith," his "bona fide educational purpose," the lack of complaints from his students, and the absence of school rules or regulations prohibiting the use of crude and vulgar language by teachers. Once again, it is apparent to me that consideration of such allegedly mitigating factors is for the school board, not the courts. If the board, in the exercise of its discretion and expertise, chooses not to reemploy a probationary teacher who uses such language, on what basis can this court interfere with that decision? Certainly there is no rule of law, statutory or otherwise, which would require advance publication of elaborate regulations and guidelines anticipating all possible infractions or misconduct which a probationary teacher might commit.[3] As the trial court pointed out, Lindros' language was "manifestly coarse and vulgar. ،... [P]etitioner should have known that such language by a teacher was totally unacceptable in a Tenth Grade English class."

The Court of Appeal, Second District, in the vacated opinion in this case written by Presiding Justice Ford (103 Cal.Rptr. 188), aptly disposed of plaintiff's contention regarding lack of notice: "There is no ironclad rule of law that regulations or rules be promulgated which specify in minute detail the various kinds of misconduct which will subject a teacher to disciplinary action. It is not unreasonable to assume that a person engaged in the profession of teaching will have a reasonable concept of generally accepted standards relating to propriety of conduct, including the avoidance of vulgarity, and will adhere to such standards in his relationship with his pupils. . . .

"Adhering to an objective standard, in the present case it was not unreasonable to determine that the plaintiff was on notice that in teaching his tenth grade English classes the art of writing a short story and in affording his students aid by using as a model a short story written by him, resort to a particular story embodying vulgarity would not serve a substantial educational purpose but would constitute a serious impropriety because of the extraneous matter of an unexemplary nature. Since manifestly inherent in such conduct was the probability of an effect adverse to the welfare of students, it was reasonable to assume that the teacher was aware that he was thereby subjecting himself to the hazard of disciplinary measures. Consequently, his contention as to the lack of adequate notice to satisfy the concept of due process is untenable."

I would conclude that the trial court properly denied mandate in this case, and, accordingly, would affirm the judgment.

McCOMB, J., concurs.

Rehearing denied; McCOMB, CLARK and BURKE, JJ., dissenting.

COURT'S OPINION NOTES

1. Except as otherwise noted, all statutory references hereinafter are to the Education Code.

Section 13443 provides probationary teachers with a panoply of procedural and substantive rights. The statute requires school administrators to give notice by March 15, with a statement of reasons, of an intent to recommend against reemployment for the following academic year. It also provides for a hearing upon request before a hearing officer appointed under Government Code section 11500 et seq., for discovery, and for a final decision by the governing board by May 15. The substantive protection afforded by the statute appears in subdivision (d) which declares in relevant part that *"The governing board's determination not to reemploy a probationary employee for the ensuing school year shall be for cause only. The determination of the governing board as to the sufficiency of the cause pursuant to this section shall be conclusive, but the cause shall relate solely to the welfare of the schools and the pupils thereof. . . ."* (Emphasis added.)

2. The Governing Board of the Torrance Unified School District will hereinafter be designated as the "Torrance Board" or "Board."

3. Although the hearing officer did not find expressly that Lindros acted in good faith in pursuit of bona fide educational purposes, we believe that such a finding is implicit in the final paragraph of the hearing officer's proposed decision: "Another relevant consideration is the problem of judgment and professionalism. It should require no argument to support the proposition that the District's Governing Board, as the ultimate employer of the teacher on behalf of the citizens of the district, has the right to control the teacher by promulgating the standards of conduct which it deems appropriate. These standards may allow broad discretion or may be explicit. Here, as is true of much in the field of education, a latitude has been allowed for the exercise of the professional judgment of the educational administrators and the teachers.

Whenever latitude for judgment is granted there will be inevitable variances in its exercise by the individuals involved. The superior may reasonably anticipate that the subordinate's exercise of judgment will vary from his own and, particularly in the case of a beginning employee, that it will be at times erroneous."

4. The superior court declared that "the substantive charge involved, as the hearing officer said, and I agree with him, the gravamen of these proceedings [was] the use of this short story, 'The Funeral,' with its coarse language at the end"; the hearing officer, however, found that the "gravamen" of the charges against Lindros included not only the reading of "The Funeral" but also use of copies

of the lyrics from the song "The Pusher" in one of Lindros' classes on January 30, 1970. These lyrics were distributed by one of Lindros' students who presented a class report on drug use. "The Pusher," according to the findings of the hearing officer, was a popular score taken from the motion picture "Easy Rider" and was at the time widely disseminated in radio broadcasts and readily available in phonographic record shops. In fact, the lyrics of "The Pusher" had been used by other instructors at South High School. The hearing officer concluded that "The Pusher" was a work of "established usage" and that its use did not constitute "cause" within the meaning of Education Code section 13443. The Torrance Board later adopted this finding as its own; thus this alleged incident of "misconduct" is not before us here. Other minor charges against petitioner—not discussed in the text—were rejected by the hearing officer or the superior court. (See fn. 5, *infra*.)

5. Lindros was originally charged with three additional isolated incidents of misconduct. First, he allegedly permitted students to write vulgar phrases on their desks and on the bulletin board on a single day in December. As to this charge, the hearing officer found that "The necessarily alleged element of permission was not established" since "[i]t was affirmatively established that [petitioner] had neither by word nor by deed caused the inscribing of these words."

In addition, Lindros was charged with, on one occasion, uttering a swear word at a fellow teacher in the presence of a third teacher. He apologized the next day. The hearing officer found that "while objectionable" this incident occurred "privately between two men in disagreement and has had no substantial impact upon the school or the pupils thereof, and therefore, does not constitute a cause not to rehire . . . within the meaning of section 13443." The Torrance Board ultimately accepted this conclusion as its own.

Finally, petitioner was charged with leaving his classroom unattended for a few minutes on a single day in October in violation of school regulations. The superior court found this allegation unsupported by substantial evidence and the Torrance Board has not challenged that determination here.

6. In 1969 the Legislature, in response to the *Thornton* holding amended Education Code section 13325 to make it apply to probationary, as well as permanent, employees (Stats.1969, ch. 795, p. 1613 § 1); section 13325 provides that upon reaching age 65 "employment shall be from year to year at the discretion of the governing board." In extending to governing boards this plenary power over probationary teachers reaching the age of 65 (Taylor v. Board of Education (1939) 31 Cal.App.2d 734, 89 P.2d 148), the Legislature impliedly recognized that the authority of governing boards is not as extensive under section 13443. (Ladd v. Board of Trustees (1972) 23 Cal.App.3d 984, 989-991, 100 Cal.Rptr. 571.)

7. Since neither party has challenged the applicability of the substantial evidence scope of review to this proceeding, we have not addressed the question whether a higher standard of review should apply.

8. "If standards of taste of future generations are to be elevated it will not be accomplished by those who seek to sweep distasteful matters under the rug, or by self-embarrassed school trustees who discharge as unfit those who would bring the problem out in the open for dis-cussion." (Oakland Unified Sch. Dist. v. Olicker (1972) 25 Cal.App.3d 1098, 1112, 102 Cal.Rptr. 421, 431 (Sims, J., concurring).) Several federal cases illustrate the serious constitutional questions which arise when school authorities seek to curb the academic freedom of teachers to employ techniques supported by substantial opinion in the teaching profession. (Keefe v. Geanakos (1st Cir. 1969) 418 F.2d 359; Parducci v. Rutland (M.D.Ala. 1970) 316 F.Supp. 352.)

9. We reject the assertion of the respondent Torrance Board that because petitioner refrained from actually reading the controversial words in question in some of his classes, he necessarily knew their use would be considered objectionable. To the contrary, Lindros' discriminating use of the controversial language in his more mature college prep classes only demonstrates his good faith effort to discern when the usage would serve a bona fide educational purpose.

10. See Oakland Unified Sch. Dist. v. Olicker (1972) 25 Cal.App. 3d 1098, 1110, 102 Cal.Rptr. 421, applying the same reasoning as to lack of notice to a teacher dismissal case under Education Code section 13403. Several federal cases, moreover, have accepted the notice argument in the context of constitutional due process and academic freedom challenges to teacher dismissals. (See Mailloux v. Kiley (D. Mass.1971) 323 F.Supp. 1387, affd. 448 F.2d 1242 (1st Cir.); Keefe v. Geanakos (1st Cir. 1969) 418 F.2d 359, 362; Webb v. Lake Mills Community School Dist. (N.D.Iowa 1972) 344 F.Supp. 791, 800-801, 804-805; Parducci v. Rutland (M.D. Ala.1970) 316 F.Supp. 352, 357; cf. President's Council, Dist. 25 v. Community School Board (2d Cir. 1972) 457 F.2d 289, 293-294.)

11. We set forth the full findings pertinent to this issue:

"F. On approximately February 6, 1970, at the close of a class session the students in the class then being instructed by respondent departed from the room with few exceptions and without being dismissed by respondent and prior to the sounding of the bell signalling the close of the class session. It was established that on this date respondent had instructed those of his students who were in possession of a book entitled "Zorba the Greek" to depart from class early, secure the book from their lockers, and return the book to the library so that it could be redistributed on the morning of February 19th when it was needed by the students of another English instructor. It was not established that all of those students who departed were leaving to complete this errand. It is contrary to school policy to permit students to be out of class during the class time without a proper pass, with the limited exception that five students at a time may be permitted to be in the hallway for the purpose of obtaining or returning books at the bookroom in the library."

12. One of petitioner's supervisors, the sole witness for the Board on the charge of early dismissal of students, testified that he observed students leave Lindros' class *without any authorization*. Petitioner's testimony contradicted that of his supervisor; petitioner attested that he authorized his students to leave class to return copies of *Zorba the Greek* to the library. Testimony of other teachers indicated that Lindros had been asked to arrange for the return of these books. Though the findings of the hearing officer (*supra*, fn. 11) contain ambiguities, apparently the hearing officer accepted petitioner's version that he *did not* dismiss his class early, but rather authorized his stu-

dents to go to the library.

13. As the superior court declared, "That brings us to what I suppose might be called *the substantive charge* involved, as the hearing officer said, and I agree with him, the *gravamen* of these proceedings, that is, the use of this short story, 'The Funeral'." (Emphasis added.) The meaning of "gravamen" is clear; "gravamen" means the "material part of a grievance, charge, etc." (Webster's New Internat. Dict. (2d ed. 1957) unabridged.)

This conclusion of the hearing officer and superior court was supported by substantial evidence. The principal of South High School testified that he would not have recommended against rehiring Lindros based solely on the alleged dismissal of students without proper authorization.

"Q: [hearing officer] 'The Funeral' was the most compelling incident?

"A: [the principal] Yes. " . . .

"Q: . . . That's not a very good question, but would you have based a recommendation of not to rehire a teacher upon an incident [of] permitting students to leave?

"A: Perhaps not."

14. We find further support for our conclusion that the gravamen for the refusal to rehire was the reading of "The Funeral" in the action of the Torrance Board itself; the Board, in effect, agreed that the incident involving "The Funeral" constituted the material complaint. Although the Board declared that the charges "separately and collectively constitute[d] . . . sufficient cause not to reemploy," the Board also accepted the position of the hearing officer that the charge relating to "The Funeral" formed the real basis for the action against petitioner. As the Board concedes, under section 13443, subdivision (c) the hearing officer conducts a hearing and prepared a proposed decision; based on the record of this hearing and the "proposed decision" the Board then makes its determination; under the Government Code the Board can *either* adopt the "proposed decision" *in its entirety* (Gov.Code,§ 11517, subd. (b)) or make further findings "upon the record" of the administrative hearing (Gov. Code. § 11517, subd. (c)). Here the Board did *not* examine the record of the administrative hearing or make further findings: accordingly it adopted the hearing officer's determination *in its entirety* under section 11517, subdivision (b)—including the finding that "The Funeral" constituted the gravamen of the complaint.

15. We therefore need not reach petitioner's other contention that his discharge was invalid on various procedural grounds as well.

JUSTICE BURKE'S OPINION NOTES

1. The majority have substantially misstated the test set forth in section 13443 and the *Griggs* case. Although correctly explaining that the role of the courts is limited to determining whether the cause for termination *relates* to the welfare of the school or its pupils (pp. 190-191), the majority purport to apply that test by inquiring whether in fact the teacher's conduct *adversely affected* the welfare of the school or its pupils. (*Id.,* at p. 186, p. 190, p. 191, pp. 191-193.) Yet the question of adverse effect is precisely the question reserved to the school board by section 13443—otherwise a court could in every case reverse the board's decision by finding that particular conduct had no "significant adverse impact" (*id*, at p. 186) on the school or its pupils.

2. Since the district's action in this case can be sustained on the basis of Lindros' improper language in his classroom, I do not reach the question whether that action could also be upheld on the independent ground that Lindros permitted unauthorized departure of students from his class.

3. The majority's reliance upon the so-called "free-speech" cases (e.g., Cohen v. California, 403 U.S. 15, 91 S.Ct. 1780, 29 L.Ed.2d 284), seems wholly misplaced, for no attempt is made to subject Lindros to criminal liability for his conduct. As conceded by the majority (p. 193), "these rulings by no means legitimize the general use of offensive language in the classroom. . . ."

INDIANAPOLIS SCHOOL REGULATIONS ON DISTRIBUTION OF LITERATURE HELD TOO VAGUE AND THE SUPPRESSION OF AN UNOFFICIAL HIGH SCHOOL NEWSPAPER HELD UNJUSTIFIED: "THE ONLY POSSIBLE QUESTION IS WHETHER THE BOARD'S EDUCATIONAL RESPONSIBILITIES JUSTIFY ITS PREVENTING THE USE BY STUDENTS IN THESE CIRCUMSTANCES OF WORDS CONSIDERED COARSE OR INDECENT. CLEARLY A UNIVERSITY CAN NOT CONSTITUTIONALLY REGULATE EXPRESSION ON THAT GROUND....ALTHOUGH THERE IS A DIFFERENCE IN MATURITY AND SOPHISTICATION BETWEEN STUDENTS AT A UNIVERSITY AND AT A HIGH SCHOOL, WE CONCLUDE THAT THE OCCASIONAL PRESENCE OF EARTHY WORDS IN THE CORN COB CURTAIN CAN NOT BE FOUND TO BE LIKELY TO CAUSE SUBSTANTIAL DISRUPTION OF SCHOOL ACTIVITY OR MATERIALLY TO IMPAIR THE ACCOMPLISHMENT OF EDUCATIONAL OBJECTIVES."

Jacobs v. Board of School Commissioners, 490 F.2d 601 (1973)

FAIRCHILD, Circuit Judge.

Defendants are officials of the Indianapolis school system. They appeal from a judgment enjoining the enforcement of certain rules governing the distribution by students of communicative written materials within the Indianapolis public school buildings and upon the grounds of such buildings. The named plaintiffs were or had been high school students when the action was started. They challenged defendants' suppression of an unofficial student newspaper, entitled the Corn Cob Curtain, in the publication and distribution of which plaintiffs had participated. The relevant rules of the Board were amended while the action was pending. The decision and judgment appealed from are reported, Jacobs v. Board of School Com'rs of City of Indianapolis, 349 F.Supp. 605 (S.D.Ind., 1972).

1. *Refusal to appoint a guardian ad litem.*

Plaintiffs were minors, represented by counsel. They alleged that activities of defendants violated their first and fourteenth amendment rights. They sued on behalf of themselves and all other high school students under defendants' jurisdiction. They primarily sought injunctive relief except that they also prayed for $150 compensatory damages and nominal or other punitive damages. Except for the prayer for damages in modest amount, plaintiffs won.

The district court denied defendants' petition for appointment of a guardian ad litem. Under the present circumstances, it is doubtful that defendants have a sufficient interest to raise this point on appeal. There is little reason to suppose that defendants would be exposed to any risk as a result of a claim that plaintiffs or class members are not bound by the judgment because there was no personal representative, next friend, or guardian ad litem. In Roberts v. Ohio Casualty Insurance Company, 256 F.2d 35 (5th Cir., 1958), relied on by defendants, and where a judgment was reversed for failure to appoint, it was the unrepresented minor who sought reversal. Nevertheless, defendants argue that the judgment should be reversed on this ground.

Rule 17(c), F.R.Civ.P., provides in part: "The court shall appoint a guardian ad litem for an infant or incompetent person not otherwise represented in an action or shall make such other order as it deems proper for the protection of the infant or incompetent person."

Defendants apparently concede that neither the appointment of a guardian ad litem nor a protective order in lieu thereof is mandatory, and neither is required if the court considers the matter and makes a judicial determination that the infant is protected without a guardian. Roberts, supra, p. 39. See Till v. Hartford Accident & Indemnity Co., 124 F.2d 405, 408 (10th Cir., 1941); Westcott v. United States Fidelity & Guaranty Co., 158 F.2d 20, 22 (4th Cir., 1946).

Here the question was argued and considered. We do not agree with defendants that the court's emphasis, in its oral ruling, on the fact that constitutional issues were presented, and that substantial monetary recovery was not sought, demonstrates a failure to decide the appropriate question. Moreover, there is nothing in the record which indicates that the minors were represented inadequately or that any party was prejudiced by the absence of a guardian ad litem. See Till and Westcott supra, and Rutland v. Sikes, 203 F.Supp. 276 (E.D. S.C., 1962), aff'd on other grounds, 311 F.2d 538 (4 Cir.), cert. denied 374 U.S. 830, 83 S.Ct.1871, 10 L.Ed.2d 1053.

2. The Constitutionality of the Board's Regulations.

During the 1971-1972 public school term, five issues of the Corn Cob Curtain were published. They contained letters, articles about politics, education, student affairs, religion, and American history, music, movie, and book reviews, poetry, and cartoons. The first four issues were distributed in Indianapolis high schools. At the time the fifth issue was ready for distribution, school authorities notified the student population that school board rules prohibit sales or solicitations on school grounds without the express prior approval of the General Superintendent. After conferring with various school officials, the named plaintiffs were informed that the Corn Cob Curtain could no longer be distributed because it contained obscene materials. Appellees refrained from distributing the fifth issue pending resolution of these issues in the courts.

At the time of the above events, Sections 11.05 and 11.06 of the Board's rules prohibited the sale or distribution of literature in the public schools without express prior approval of the General Superintendent. After the district judge stated his belief that these rules were unconstitutional prior restraints under Fujishima v. Board of Education, 460 F.2d 1355 (7th Cir., 1972), the defendants amended the rules to their present form. The disctict court held that the amended rules were unconstitutional.

The amended rules involved are set forth at 349 F.Supp. 607-609. Rule 11.05 consists of a series of numbered items or paragraphs, designated in the district court judgment as provisos. We adopt that term, and proceed to consider the arguments made by defendants with respect to them.

(a) Amended Rule 11.05, Proviso 1.1.1.3.

Reading provisos 1.1.1. and 1.1.1.3 together, they provide:

"No student shall distribute in any school any literature that is . . . either by its content or by the manner of distribution itself, productive of, or likely to produce a significant disruption of the normal educational processes, functions or purposes in any of the Indianapolis schools, or injury to others." The district court held that this rule was both vague and overbroad. We agree.

It is well established that a criminal statute is void for vagueness if its prohibitions are not clearly defined. Grayned v. City of Rockford, 408 U.S. 104, 108, 92 S.Ct. 2294, 33 L.Ed.2d 222 (1972); United States v. Dellinger, 472 F.2d 340, 355 (7th Cir., 1972), cert. denied 410 U.S. 970, 93 S.Ct. 1443, 35 L. Ed.2d 706. Vague laws are constitutionally offensive for several reasons:

"First, because we assume that man is free to steer between lawful and unlawful conduct, we insist that laws give the person of ordinary intelligence a reasonable opportunity to know what is prohibited, so that he may act accordingly. Vague laws may trap the innocent by not providing fair warning. Second, if arbitrary and discriminatory enforcement is to be prevented, laws must provide explicit standards for those who apply them. A vague law impermissibly delegates basic policy matters to policemen, judges, and juries for resolution on an ad hoc and subjective basis, with the attendant dangers of arbitrary and discriminatory application. Third, but related, where a vague statute 'abut[s] upon sensitive areas of basic First Amendment freedoms,' it 'operates to inhibit the exercise of [those] freedoms.' Uncertain meanings inevitably lead citizens to ' "steer far wider of the unlawful zone" ' . . . than if the boundaries of the forbidden areas were clearly marked.' " Grayned, supra, 408 U.S. at 108-109, 92 S.Ct. at 2299, footnotes omitted.

Here, there is no criminal statute before us. Nonetheless, a student who violates amended Rule 11.05 is subject to suspension or expulsion or other disciplinary action. Proviso 1.61. We conclude that the penalties for violation are sufficiently grievous to mandate careful scrutiny for vagueness. See generally Baggett v. Bullitt, 377 U.S. 360, 374, 84 S.Ct. 1316, 12 L.Ed.2d 377 (1964). We note the substantial danger of inadequate warnings to students, of arbitrary enforcement by teachers and principals, and of inhibition of full exercise of students' first amendment rights.

We think that proviso 1.1.1.3 is vague in defining the consequences which will make a distribution of literature unlawful. Those consequences are articulated as "a significant disruption of the normal educational processes, functions, or purposes in any of the Indianapolis schools, or injury to others." Is decorum in the lunchroom a "normal educational . . . purpose"? If an article sparks strident discussion there, is the latter a "disruption"? When does disruption become "significant"? The phrase "injury to others" is also vague. Does it mean only physical harm? Does it include hurt feelings and impairment of reputation by derogatory criticism, short of defamation, since libelous material is already covered by proviso 1.1.1.2?

Defendants argue unpersuasively that proviso 1.1.1.3 is not over-vague because of its similarity to the text of the standard by which the Supreme Court tested a precise regulation against wearing armbands in Tinker v. Des Moines School Dist., 393 U.S. 503, 514, 89 S.Ct. 733, 21 L.Ed. 2d 731.[1] It does not at all follow that the phrasing of a constitutional standard by which to decide whether a regulation infringes upon rights protected by the first amendment is sufficiently specific in a regulation to convey notice to students or people in general of what is prohibited.[2]

Proviso 1.1.1.3 is also unconstitutionally overbroad. In United States v. Dellinger, supra, 472 F.2d at 357, this court stated: "The doctrine of overbreadth applies when a statute lends itself to a substantial number of impermissible applications, such that it is capable of deterring protected conduct, when the area affected by the challenged law substantially involves first amendment interests, and when there is not a valid construction which avoids abridgement of first amendment interests." (footnotes omitted). These factors are present here.

The overbreadth stems both from the vagueness described above and from the inclusiveness of the phrase "productive of, or likely to produce" in the proviso. Expression may lead to disorder under many circumstances where the expression is not thereby deprived of first amendment protection. See Braxton v. Municipal Court, 10 Cal.3d 138, 109 Cal. Rptr. 897, 514 P.2d 697 (1973). We do not read Tinker as authorizing suppression of speech in a school building in every such circumstance where the speech does not have a sufficiently close relationship with action to be treated as action. See Dellinger, supra, 472 F.2d at 360.

Where the boundaries between prohibited and permissible conduct are ambiguous, we can not presume that the curtailment of free expression is minimized. NAACP v. Button, 371 U.S. 415, 432, 83 S.Ct. 328, 9 L.Ed.2d 405 (1963); United States v. Dellinger, supra, 472 F.2d at 356-357. Instead the plaintiffs are permitted to attack the regulation by suggesting impermissible applications without demonstrating that their own conduct "could not be regulated by a statute drawn with the requisite narrow specificity." Dombrowski v. Pfister, 380 U.S. 479, 486, 85 S.Ct. 1116, 1121, 14 L.Ed.2d 22 (1965). See Gooding v. Wilson, 405 U.S. 518, 521, 92 S.Ct. 1103, 31 L.Ed.2d 408 (1972). Proviso 1.1.1.3 at least threatens a penalty for a student who distributed a controversial pamphlet in a lunchroom resulting in robust arguments or who distributed a newspaper including derogatory but not defamatory remarks about a teacher. Absent extraordinary circumstances, the school authorities could not reasonably forecast substantial disruption of or material interference with school discipline or activities arising from such incidents. See Tinker, supra. Finally, we note that this court lacks jurisdiction to place an authoritative limiting construction upon this state regulation in contrast with the power of federal courts with respect to interpretation of federal statutes or regulations. United States v. 37 Photographs, 402 U.S. 363, 369, 91 S.Ct. 1400, 28 L.Ed.2d 822 (1971), cert. denied 403 U.S. 924, 91 S.Ct. 2221, 28 L. Ed.2d 702.

(b) *Amended Rule 11.05, Proviso 1.1.1.4.*

Reading provisos 1.1.1 and 1.1.1.4 together, they provide: "No student shall distribute in any school any literature that is . . . not written by a student, teacher, or other school employees; provided, however, that advertisements which are not in conflict with other provisions herein, and are reasonably and necessarily connected to the student publication itself shall be permitted."

We have no doubt that this rule abridges first amendment rights of plaintiffs, although not for the reason assigned by the district court. Whether the student distribution of literature be viewed as individual speech or as press publication, we think that authorship by a non-school person of the material distributed is not germane to any of the constitutional standards which must be met before conduct which is also expression can be prohibited.

Defendants suggest that student distribution of materials written by non-students and outside organizations tends to produce disorder and interference with school functions, and cite the example that "stores would undoubtedly pay students to distribute flyers advertising their products." Assuming, however, some area of possible validity, the rule is overbroad. It would prohibit use of materials written by individuals from all sorts of walks of life whose views might be thought by the students to be worthy of circulation. "Predictions about imminent disruption . . . involve judgments appropriately made on an individualized basis, not by means of broad classifications, especially those based on subject matter." Police Department of Chicago v. Mosley, 408 U.S. 92, 100, 92 S.Ct. 2286, 2293, 33 L.Ed.2d 212 (1972).

(c) *Amended Rule 11.05, Proviso 1.3.1.6.*

Literature not proscribed under 1.1.1, 1.1.1.1 to 1.1.1.4, is referred to as 'distributable literature.' (Proviso 1.1.2). Reading provisos 1.3.1 and 1.3.1.6 together, they provide:

"No distributable literature shall be distributed by any student in any school . . . unless the name of every person or organization that shall have participated in the publication is plainly written in the distributable literature itself."

In Talley v. California, 362 U.S. 60, 80 S.Ct. 536, 4 L.Ed.2d 559 (1960), the Supreme Court held invalid a city ordinance prohibiting the distribution of handbills in any place unless the handbills disclosed the names and addresses of the persons who printed, wrote, manufactured and distributed the handbills. Noting the historical importance of anonymous publications as a vehicle for criticizing oppressive practices and laws, the Court held that the broad prohibition of the ordinance violated the first amendment. Talley, supra, 63-65, 80 S. Ct. 536.[3]

Anonymous student publications perform similarly within the school community; without anonymity, fear of reprisal may deter peaceful discussion of controversial but important school rules and policies. Although the rule leaves students free to distribute anonymous literature beyond the school house gate, the question here, as in Tinker, is whether the state has demonstrated a sufficient justification for this prohibition within the school community, where students and teachers spend a significant portion of their time. See Tinker, supra, 393 U.S. 506, 89 S.Ct. 733. Defendants contend that the names of persons who have "participated in the publication" of literature must be provided so that those responsible for the publication of libelous or obscene articles can be held accountable. However, here as in Talley, the requirement is not limited to material as to which such justification might be urged. Indeed, if the regulation be read literally, l.3.l.6 applies only to literature the content of which is acceptable. School authorities could not reasonably forecast that the distribution of any type of anonymous literature within the schools would substantially disrupt or materially interfere with school activities or discipline. See *Tinker, supra,* 514, 89 S.Ct. 733.

(d) Amended Rule ll.05, Proviso l.3.l.5 and Rule ll.06.

Reading l.3.l and l.3.l.5 together, they provide:

"No distributable literature shall be distributed by any student in any school . . . in immediate exchange for money or any other thing of value . . . whether the transaction is characterized as a sale of the distributable literature, as a contribution to finance the publication or distribution of the distributable literature, or as any other transaction whereunder money or any other thing of value (or a promise of either) immediately passes to or for the direct or indirect benefit of the student who is distributing the distributable literature. . . . " Amended Rule ll.06 provides that: "No person, including students and organizations or corporations, other than the school corporation acting through its designated agents, or organizations of parents and teachers or students whose sole use of funds is for the benefit of the particular school in which they are organized or in attendance, may sell merchandise or material, collect money, or solicit funds or contributions from the students for any cause or commercial activity within any school or on its campus."

Plaintiffs suggest that these rules were adopted to accomplish indirectly that which can not be accomplished directly: the blanket prohibition of the distribution of the Corn Cob Curtain and other similar student newspapers. Plaintiffs alleged the dependence of the paper upon contributions of money for survival. It can readily be observed that a ban upon the receipt of contributions on school grounds would create financial difficulties in raising the $120 to $150 necessary to publish each edition of the Corn Cob Curtain. In Grosjean v. American Press Company, 297 U.S. 233, 56 S.Ct. 444, 80 L.Ed. 660 (1935), the Supreme Court considered the constitutionality of a Louisiana tax upon the advertising revenue of newspapers with a circulation of more than 20,000 copies per week. After finding that the effect of the tax might be to destroy both the advertising and circulation of the newspapers and noting with suspicion the form of the tax, the Court concluded that the tax was a "deliberate and calculated device . . . to limit the circulation of information to which the public is entitled," in violation of the first amendment. *Grosjean, supra,* 244, 250, 56 S.Ct. 444, 449.

Assuming, however, that the rules are not a "deliberate and calculated device" to suppress the student newspaper, it becomes necessary to analyze the justification offered by defendants. They assert the legitimacy of an interest in preventing the use of school premises "for non-school purposes—particularly commercial activities." Rule ll.06 is a general prohibition against sales of materials and solicitation of funds except for the benefit of the school. If there were any question of its intended applicability to sales by students of their unofficial newspaper, proviso l.3.l.5 makes specific application.

We have little question of the legitimacy of the interest of the school authorities in limiting or prohibiting commercial activity on school premises by persons not connected with the school, either acting directly or through students as agents. But because students have first amend-ment rights within the school, as recognized in *Tinker,* we think that the propriety of regulation of their conduct involving the exercise of protected rights must be independently justified. It is not enough to say that such activity by students is similar to commercial activity by others.

Sale of the newspaper, or other communicative material within a school, is conduct mixing both speech and non-speech elements. In order to determine whether a "sufficiently important governmental interest in regulating the non-speech element can justify incidental limitations on First Amendment freedoms," we must consider whether the regulation "is within the constitutional power of the Government; if it furthers an important or substantial governmental interest; if the governmental interest is unrelated to the suppression of free expression; and if the incidental restriction on alleged First Amendment freedoms is no greater than is essential to the furtherance of that interest." United States v. O'Brien, 391 U.S. 367, 377, 88 S.Ct. 1673, 1679, 20 L.Ed.2d 672 (1968), reh. denied 393 U.S. 900, 98 S.Ct. 63, 21 L.Ed.2d 188.

Ultimately, defendants rely on the proposition that "Commercial activities are time-consuming unnecessary distractions and are inherently disruptive of the function, order and decorum of the school."

Provisos 1.3.1.2, .3 and .4 already regulate the place and manner of distribution so as to avoid interference with others and littering. They have not been challenged here. It has not been established, in our opinion, that regulation of the place, time, and manner of distribution can not adequately serve the interests of maintaining good order and an educational atmosphere without forbidding sale and to that extent restricting the first amendment rights of plaintiffs.

(e) Amended Rule ll.05, proviso l.3.l.l.

Reading provisos 1.31 and l.3.l.l. together, they provide: No distributable literature shall be distributed by any student in any school . . . while classes are being conducted in the school in which the distribution is to be made."

It is well established that the right to use public places for expressive activity is not absolute and that "reasonable 'time, place and manner' regulations [which] may be necessary to further significant governmental interests" are constitutionally permissible. Grayned v. City of Rockford, 408 U.S. 104, 115, 92 S.Ct. 2294, 33 L.Ed.2d 222 (1972), and cases cited therein. The question here is whether the Board could reasonably forecast that the distribution of student newspapers anywhere within a school at any time while any class was being conducted would materially disrupt or interfere with school activities and discipline. See Grayned v. City of Rockford, *supra* at 118, 92 S.Ct. at 2294. In determining whether "the manner of expression is basically incompatible with the normal activity of a particular place at a particular time, . . . we must weigh heavily the fact that communication is involved [and] the regulation must be narrowly tailored to further the State's legitimate interest." Grayned v. City of Rockford, *supra* at ll6-ll7, 92 S.Ct. at 2304.

We are hampered in evaluating proviso l.3.l.l by the paucity of evidence in the record with respect to arrangements and schedules of classes in the Indianapolis secondary schools. Nonetheless, it does appear that there are periods in the morning, around noon, and in the late afternoon when although some classes are in session, substantial numbers of students are on the premises, are not involved in classroom activity, and are barred by proviso l.3.l.l from distributing and indirectly from receiving student newspapers. We conclude that the defendants have not satisfied their burden of demonstrating that the regulation banning distribution at all these times is narrowly drawn to further the state's legitimate interest in preventing material disruptions of classwork. See *Tinker, supra* 513, 89 S.Ct. 733.

3. *Defendants' claim concerning obscenity and profanity.*

Defendants' original answer averred, among other things, that plaintiffs' publications are obscene, indecent, vulgar, and profane. While the action was pending, the rules were amended so that when Rule 11.05, provisos 1.1.1 and 1.1.1.1, are read together, they provide: "No student shall distribute in any school any literature that is . . . obscene as to minors. . . . "

The district court did not directly decide defendants' claim that the existing issues of Corn Cob Curtain were obscene. Presumably the court deemed the proviso valid, for the decision indicates that the appropriate inquiry concerning obscenity would be whether future issues of the paper would be obscene as to minors. The decision, 349 F.Supp. at 610, set forth the then controlling *Roth-Memoirs* definition of obscenity, the concept of variable obscenity permitting a less exacting standard where material is directed at children, and other limitations to be regarded in making the determination.

Necessarily we observe that proviso 1.1.1.1 lacks the specific definition of sexual conduct the description of which is prohibited as now required for a valid law under Miller v. California, 413 U.S. 15, 26, 93 S.Ct. 2607, 2616, 37 L.Ed. 2d 419 (1973).

In any event, a substantial portion of defendants' brief is devoted to what it terms the most crucial issue, "whether school authorities may constitutionally and legitimately prevent and/or punish the use of defamatory, obscene and indecent language in the school house which is contrary to the moral standards of the community."

In the first place, the issues of the Corn Cob Curtain in the record are very far from obscene in the legal sense. A few earthy words relating to bodily functions and sexual intercourse are used in the copies of the newspaper in the record. Usually they appear as expletives or at some similar level. One cartoon depicts a sequence of incidents in a bathroom. This material amounts only to a very small part of the newspapers, which are tabloid size, containing eight or twelve pages. These issues contain no material which is in any significant way erotic, sexually explicit, or which could plausibly be said to appeal to the prurient interest of adult or minor. See Cohen v. California, 403 U.S. 15, 20, 91 S.Ct. 1780, 29 L.Ed.2d 284 (1971).

In *Miller, supra,* the Supreme Court limited the scope of the obscenity exception to first amendment protection to "works which depict or describe sexual conduct" and "which, taken, as a whole, appeal to the prurient interest in sex, which portray, sexual conduct in a patently offensive way, and which, taken as a whole, do not have serious literary, artistic, political or scientific value." Clearly the newspaper issues in the record do not even approach fulfillment of this definition.

Nor need we speculate about the exact effect of *Miller* on the variable obscenity concept exemplified by Ginsberg v. New York, 390 U.S. 629, 88 S.Ct. 1274, 20 L.Ed.2d 195 (1968). Making the widest conceivable allowances for differences between adults and high school students with respect to perception, maturity, or sensitivity, the material pointed to by defendants could not be said to fulfill the *Miller* definition of obscenity.

It is well established that a distinction must be drawn between obscene materials and non-obscene materials containing profanity. Cohen v. California, 403 U.S. 15, 20, 91 S.Ct. 1780, 29 L.Ed. 2d 284 (1971); Fujishima v. Board of Education, 460 F.2d 1355, 1359 n. 7 (7th Cir., 1972). The only possible question is whether the Board's educational responsibilities justify its preventing the use by students in these circumstances of words considered coarse or indecent. Clearly a university can not constitutionally regulate expression on that ground. Papish v. University of Missouri Curators, 410 U.S. 667, 93 S.Ct. 1197, 35 L.Ed.2d 618 (1973). Although there is a difference in maturity and sophistication between students at a university and at a high school, we conclude that the occasional presence of earthy words in the Corn Cob Curtain can not be found to be likely to cause substantial disruption of school activity or materially to impair the accomplishment of educational objectives. Scoville v. Board of Ed. of Joliet T.P.H.S. Dist. 204, Etc., Ill., 425 F.2d 10, 13 (7th Cir., 1970).

The injunction is broad enough to cover enforcement of the particular rules at all schools under the jurisdiction of defendants. At oral argument, plaintiffs conceded that their case was limited to the application of the rules in high schools. We therefore had no occasion to decide whether or not age difference and the like would lead to a different ruling concerning elementary schools. Should defendants apply to the district court to limit the injunction to high schools, nothing in this decision forecloses the consideration of the application on its merits.

The judgment appealed from is affirmed.

CHRISTENSEN, Senior District Judge (concurring in part and dissenting in part):

I am in general agreement with the majority opinion as it relates to the guardian ad litem problem and the invalidity of Provisos 1.1.1.4, 1.3.1.6, 1.3.1.5 and 1.3.1.1 of Rule 11.05, and Rule 11.06 of the appellant board.

I dissent, however, from those parts of the opinion holding that Rule 11.05, Proviso 1.1.1.3, is invalid for vagueness and overbreadth* and that certain language used in the Corn Cob Curtain was not "obscene as to minors" in the high school context and thus in contravention of Amended Rule 11.05, Proviso 1.1.1.1.

And I find myself in disagreement with the conclusion "that the occasional presence of earthy words in the Corn Cob Curtain cannot be found to be likely to cause substantial disruption of school activity or materially to impair the accomplishment of educational objectives". The euphemisms employed to describe contents of the publication do not fully indicate the type of language and imagery that are given rein; whether constituting the predominant part, or merely an inescapably dominating part of any particular issue, it seems clear that expressions are used which in a high school, not to mention an elementary school, would materially impair the accomplishment of educational objectives.

More likely obscene in these contexts are certain Corn Cob expressions than those involved in Papish v. University of Missouri Curators, 410 U.S. 667, 93 S. Ct. 1197, 35 L.Ed. 2d 618 (1973), would be in the setting of a university. Hence, it may not be presumptuous to suppose that when a situation is evaluated corresponding to the one we have before us the majority of that court may be inclined to accept an extrapolation of the views expressed in the dissent of the Chief Justice to the effect that preclusion of the regulation of such material by school authorities would not protect values inherent in the First Amendment but would demean them (410 U.S. at p. 672, 93 S.Ct. 1197), and those of Mr. Justice Rehnquist, with whom the Chief Justice and Mr. Justice Blackmun joined, that "insistence on equating, for constitutional purposes, the authority of the State to criminally punish with its authority to exercise even a modicum of control over the university [high school or elementary school] which it operates serves neither the Constitution nor public education well." (410 U.S. at p. 677, 93 S.Ct. at p. 1202.)

That at oral argument "plaintiffs conceded that their case was limited to the application of the rules in high schools" does not seem to me a sufficient reason for our failure to hold as to elementary schools of all places that the trial court's decision involved error. Appellees should not be permitted to waive the contentions of appellants, who have argued here both overbreadth and invalidity of the injunction. To the extent hereinabove indicated, I am of the opinion that appellants are right on both scores. And to that limited extent it appears to me that until now this court, as well as the Supreme Court, has not committed itself to an irreconcilable view.

NOTES

1. In *Tinker,* the Supreme Court held that a state may restrain students from fully exercising their first amendment rights only if it is demonstrated that the school authorities reasonably forecast substantial disruption of or material interference with school activities or discipline. *Tinker, supra* 393 U.S. at 514, 89 S.Ct. 733.

2. *E.g.,* Miller v. California, 413 U.S. 15, 26, 93 S.Ct. 2607, 2616, 37 L.Ed.2d 419 (1973).

3. We note that in the recent case of Branzburg v. Hayes, 408 U.S. 665, 680 ff, 92 S. Ct. 2646, 33 L.Ed.2d 626 (1972), the Supreme Court carefully distinguished the question of whether a newspaper reporter must respond to a grand jury subpoena from the question of whether the press could be required to publish or indiscriminately disclose all its sources.

JUDGE CHRISTENSEN'S OPINION NOTE

*No determinative difference is perceived between this rule and its rewording which the trial court thought "more apt to be constitutionally acceptable". 349 F.Supp. at pp. 611-612.

APPENDIX

The constitutions of almost all nations contain provisions guaranteeing freedom of speech and the press; about eighty-five percent of the national constitutions provide for speech and press freedoms. Unlike the First Amendment guarantees in the Bill of Rights of the United States, many of the other constitutions specifically stipulate that speech and press freedoms do not apply to materials which "offend public decency," "offend public morals," or are "contrary to morality." Representative of these constitutional provisions specifically prohibiting "immoral" or "indecent" materials are:

DOMINICAN REPUBLIC, Article 8, Section 6: "Everyone may, without prior censorship, freely express his thought in writing or by any other means of expression, graphic or oral. Whenever the thought expressed threatens the dignity and morals of persons, the public order, or the good customs of society, penalties prescribed by law shall be imposed."

GREECE, Article 14: "Any person may publish his opinion orally, in writing or in print with due adherence to the laws of the State. The press is free. Censorship and every other preventive measure is prohibited . . . . By exception, seizure after publication is permitted: (a) because of insult to the Christian religion or indecent publications manifestly offending public decency . . . . "

GUATEMALA, Article 65: "Thought may be freely expressed without prior censorship. Any person who abuses this right by acting with disregard for private life or morality, shall be held responsible before the law."

IRELAND, Article 40, Section 6: "The State guarantees liberty for the exercise of the following rights, subject to public order and morality. (i) the right of the citizens to express freely their convictions and opinions . . . . "

INDIA, Article 19: (1) All citizens have the right—(a) to freedom of speech and expression . . . .
(2) Nothing in sub-clause (a) of clause (1) shall affect the operation of any existing law, or prevent the State from making any law, in so far as such law imposes reasonable restrictions on the exercise of the right conferred by the said subclause in the interests of the sovereignty and integrity of India, the security of the State, friendly relations with foreign States, public order, decency or morality . . . . "

ITALY, Article 21: "All are entitled freely to express their thoughts by word of mouth, in writing, and by all other means of communication. The press may not be subjected to any authority or censorship . . . . Printed publications, performances and all other manifestations contrary to morality are forbidden . . . . "

MEXICO, Article 6: "The expression of ideas shall not be subject to any judicial or administrative investigation, unless it offends good morals, infringes the rights of others, incites to crime, or disturbs the public order."

NIGERIA, Article 25: (1) Every person shall be entitled to freedom of expression, including freedom to hold opinions and to receive and impart ideas and information without interference. (2) Nothing in this section shall invalidate any law that is reasonably justifiable in a democratic society (a) in the interest of defence, public safety, public order, public morality or public health . . . . "

SOUTH KOREA, Article 18: (1) All citizens shall enjoy freedom of speech and press, and freedom of assembly and association. (2) License or censorship in regard to speech and press or permit of assembly and association shall not be recognized. However, censorship in regard to motion pictures and dramatic plays may be authorized for the maintenance of public morality and social ethics."

TURKEY, Article 22: "The press is free, and shall not be subjected to censorship . . . . Freedom of the press and the obtainment of information can be restricted by law only in order to safeguard national security, or public morality, to prevent attacks on the dignity, honour and rights of individuals . . . . "

UGANDA, Article 17: "(1) Except with his own consent, no person shall be hindered in the enjoyment of his freedom of expression, that is to say, freedom to hold opinions and to receive and impart ideas and information without interference, and freedom from interference with his correspondence. (2) Nothing contained in or done under the authority of any law shall be held to be inconsistent with or in contravention of this article to the extent that the law in question makes provision, (a) that is reasonably required in the interests of national economy, the running of essential services, defence, public safety, public order, public morality or public health . . . . "

Freedom of expression constitutional guarantees, minus the references to "public morality," "public decency," and "good morals," are exemplified in the following provisions:

DENMARK, Article 77: "Any person shall be entitled to publish his thoughts in printing, in writing, and in speech, provided that he may be held answerable in a court of justice. Censorship and other preventive measures shall never again be introduced."

JAPAN, Article 21: "Freedom of assembly and association as well as speech, press and other forms of expression are guaranteed. No censorship shall be maintained, nor shall the secrecy of any means of communication be violated."

UNION OF SOVIET SOCIALIST REPUBLICS, Article 124: "In conformity with the interests of the working people, and in order to strengthen the socialist system, the citizens of the U.S.S.R. are guaranteed by law:

(a) freedom of speech;

(b) freedom of the press;

(c) freedom of assembly, including the holding of mass meetings;

(d) freedom of street processions and demonstrations . . . . "

WEST GERMANY, Article 5: "(1) Everyone has the right freely to express and to disseminate his opinion by speech, writing and pictures and freely to inform himself from generally accessible sources. Freedom of the press and freedom of reporting by radio and motion pictures are guaranteed. There shall be no censorship. (2) These rights are limited by the provisions of the general laws, the provisions of law for the protection of youth and by the right to inviolability of personal honour."

Whether or not the constitutions of the various nations include references to the protection of morality, decency, and ethics, the penal codes, postal regulations, and customs acts regulate or prohibit the distribution, sale or importation of obscene materials. For a summary of the types and degrees of censorship and regulation of obscene books, periodicals, films, and plays in various countries see *The Report of the Commission on Obscenity and Pornography* (Washington, D.C.: U.S. Government Printing Office, 1970) and volume 2 of *The Technical Report of the Commission on Obscenity and Pornography* (Washington, D.C.: Government Printing Office, 1971), which includes in-depth reports of obscenity and freedom of expression in foreign countries.

BIBLIOGRAPHY

The following annotated Bibliography is limited to books dealing directly with obscenity and the censorship of obscenity. It does not inlcude the many general works on freedom of speech and censorship. Some of the annotations include statements taken from the books themselves thus giving the reader an idea of what the author was attempting to do in the book and also an idea of the author's position on obscenity and censorship.

BOYER, Paul. *Purity in Print: The Vice-Society Movement and Book Censorship in America.* New York: Charles Scribner's Sons, 1968. 362 pp. A history of censorship in America, focusing on the nineteenth century and the first three decades of the twentieth. "My central aim," writes the author in the Introduction, "has been to place in historical perspective the so-called 'vice-socie-ties' of New York, Boston, and other cities—the organizations which were the target of so much of the censorship and anti censorship activities of the 1920s."

CHANDOS, John (ed.). *"To Deprave and Corrupt. . ."* New York: Association Press, 1962. 207 pp. A collection of essays on obscenity and censorship by journal-ists, legal scholars, and publishers, including William Lockhart, Robert McClure, Ernst van den Haag, Maurice Girodias, John Chandos, and Norman St. John-Stevas.

CLOR, Harry (ed.). *Censorship and Freedom of Expression.* Chicago: Rand McNally, 1971. 175 pp. A collection of essays by authors who, as stated in the Preface, "represent not only a variety of positions on the subject under dispute but also a variety of professions, disciplines, and experiences. Some of the authors have been active combatants on one side or the other of the obscenity conflict. The others have studied and written about the subject from the perspective of political science, religion, sex education, or psychology."

CLOR, Harry. *Obscenity and Public Morality: Censorship in a Liberal Society.* Chicago: University of Chicago Press, 1969. 315 pp. C. Herman Pritchett writes in the Preface to this book: "For Clor the crucial question is, What is the public interest in moral norms and moral character, and how is that interest best served? He argues that society must have some model of approved and unapproved, esteemed and unesteemed sexual behavior reflecting ends other than those of individual satisfaction. He believes that censorship can promote public morality by preventing or reducing the most corrupt influences, and by holding up an authoritative standard for the guidance of opinions and judgment."

CRAIG, Alec. *Above All Liberties.* London: George Allen & Unwin Ltd., 1942. 205 pp. A history of censorship of obscenity in England, plus two chapters devoted to obscenity and the law in the United States and France.

CRAIG, Alec. *The Banned Books of England and Other Countries.* London: George Allen & Unwin Ltd., 1962. 243 pp. As stated in the Introduction, "the subject of this book is the conception of literary obscenity as found in law and practice and its cultural and social effects."

CRAIG, Alec. *Suppressed Books: A History of the Conception of Literary Obscenity.* Cleveland: World Publishing Co., 1963. 285 pp. Originally published in Great Britain under the title *The Banned Books of England and Other Countries.* The American edition contains the United States District Court's 1933 *Ulysses* decision and the 1959 *Lady Chatterley's Lover* decision.

DAILY, Jay. *The Anatomy of Censorship.* New York: Marcel Dekker, Inc., 1973. 403 pp. This book, wrote the author in his Preface on June 26, 1973, "investigates the motivations of censors, governmental and voluntary, so that the conclusions should hold true whatever the changes in the field of study. Its scope is worldwide although necessarily centered in the United States. In the year spent in completing the manuscript, checking and rechecking the documentation, and preparing the final copy, the field of study has changed somewhat but not nearly so much as in the past few days. It is now evident that a new era of censorship has begun." While most of the book deals with the censorship of obscenity, a section is devoted to political, scientific, and historical orthodoxy.

DE GRAZIA, Edward. *Censorship Landmarks.* New York: R.R. Bowker, 1969. 657 pp. A collection of court decisions related to obscenity, arranged chronologically beginning with 1600-1900 cases and ending with 1960-1968 cases.

ERNST, Morris and Alexander Lindley. *The Censor Marches On: Recent Milestones in the Administration of the Obscenity Law in the United States.* New York: Double-day, Doran & Co., 1940. 346 pp. The authors state in their Preface: "Censorship has been a social phenomenon since the dawn of civilization. We shall not attempt to trace its history here. All we propose to do is to give a bird's-eye view of its manifestations during the last few decades. We shall concern ourselves mainly with telling the story of efforts to save society from sex. Taking up in turn literature, sex instruction, birth control, the stage, the movies, the radio, the graphic and plastic arts and nudism, we shall indicate how successful or unsuccessful these efforts have been, and where they have led or are leading us. Although we shall discuss court cases we shall avoid technicalities and speak the layman's language." The book includes an Appendix with court decisions on "obscene" literature, motion pictures, sex instruction, and birth control.

ERNST, Morris and William Seagle. *To the Pure . . . A Study of Obscenity and the Censor.* New York: Viking Press, 1928. 334 pp. In their Introduction the authors state: "While we are chiefly interested in obscenity as a contemporary phenomenon, in the contradictions of practice as they reveal themselves in objects, agents, means, and legal or extra-legal supports, a considerable acquaintance with historical background not only of the obscenity laws but of political and ecclesiastical censorship is essential to understand the continuing unity of purpose behind all forms of suppression." The authors focus on obscenity and the law in the United States, but also deal with the English origins of that law.

FRANK, John and Robert Hogan. *Obscenity, the Law, and the English Teacher.* Champaign, Ill.: National Council of Teachers of English, 1966. 61 pp. Contains a paper by John Frank, specialist in constitutional law, "outlining the legal basis for determining obscenity in reading materials," followed by Robert Hogan's response focusing on the "unique problems faced by teachers of English." (preface)

FRIEDMAN, Leon (ed.). *Obscenity: The Complete Oral Arguments before the Supreme Court in the Major Obscenity Cases.* New York: Chelsea House Publications, 1970. 342 pp. A collection of the oral arguments presented before the Supreme Court in such cases as *Roth v. United States, Jacobellis v. Ohio, Freedman v. Maryland, Ginzburg v. United States, Memoirs v. Massachusetts, Ginsburg v. New York,* and *Stanley v. Georgia.*

GERBER, Albert. *Sex, Pornography and Justice.* New York: Lyle Stuart, Inc., 1965. 349 pp. A history of censorship and obscenity with a discussion of English precedents and Supreme Court decisions. Includes illustrations and excerpts from once prohibited "obscene" materials.

GILMORE, Donald. *Sex Censorship and Pornography.* San Diego: Greenleaf Classics, Inc., 1969. 223 pp. This volume presents a history of censorship of pornography in the United States up to the 1957 *Roth* decision. The author states in his Introduction: "Our purpose here is a serious, in-depth study of obscenity, eroticism, pornography and censorship, and we feel that this can only be accomplished with a presentation of the material as it actually exists, without insulting the reader's intelligence with a series of dots and dashes and retouched photographs or blocked-out art."

GOLDSTEIN, Michael and Harold Kant. *Pornography and Sexual Deviance.* Berkeley: University of California Press, 1973. 194 pp. "This book," say the authors, "is the report of a research program inspired by the need for scientifically obtained data on pornography and its effects. Necessarily included in such a study is the broader area of sexual conduct and sexual attitudes.

Thus, the investigation must focus not only on erotic materials per se but also on the sexual histories of the persons selected for questioning." The authors deal with the relationships between exposure to erotic materials, sexual fantasies, and sex related crimes.

HAIGHT, Anne Lyon. *Banned Books: Informal Notes on Some Books Banned for Various Reasons at Various Times and in Various Places.* New York: R.R. Bowker, 1970. 166 pp. In the Preface of this third edition of *Banned Books* the author states: "*Banned Books* makes no pretense to exhaustiveness. It is a chronological list of books, banned from 387 B.C. into the 1960's, compiled only with the idea of showing the trend of censorship throughout the years and the change in thought and taste. . . . It is a handbook, a quick reference work which touches upon most of the famous episodes in our sorry censorship history."

HUGHES, Douglas (ed.). *Perspective on Pornography.* New York: St. Martin's Press, 1970. 223 pp. A collection of reprinted selections on pornography by Albert Moravia, Anthony Burgess, Harry Levin, Paul Goodman, George Steiner, Susan Sontag, and others.

HYDE, H. Montgomery. *A History of Pornography.* New York: Farrar, Strauss and Giroux, 1964. 246 pp. Much of this book is devoted to discussion of pornography and the law in England. The historical survey, writes the author, will "involve some consideration of the measures which different societies at different periods in history have employed to deal with it, by means of administrative action through the operation of an official or unofficial censorship, and legal action through the courts. Finally, we shall take a brief look at contemporary conditions mainly in the English speaking countries, which, while ostensibly aiming at suppressing pornography, are constantly creating and stimulating the demand for it through various media of mass communication and promoting a fruitful social climate in which it can flourish surreptitiously."

KILPATRICK, James. *The Smut Peddlers.* Garden City, N.Y.: Doubleday, Inc., 1960. 323 pp. In the words of the author in his Foreword: "This is a book about the obscenity racket and about the law of obscenity censorship as that law has emerged from courts and legislative bodies since Anthony Comstock's day. . . . There *is* a social evil in commercial pornography, and I am sympathetic toward the effort to combat it."

KRONHOUSEN, Eberhard and Phyllis Kronhausen. *Pornography and the Law,* rev. ed. New York: Ballantine Books, 1964. 416 pp. Two psychologists discuss the distinctions between erotic realism and pornography. As stated in the Foreword, they "have concentrated on the effects of erotic realism and pornography on the reader, and the way in which the creators of such material have brought these effects about." Chapters are devoted to "The Psychology of Erotic Realism," "Obscene Books and the Law," "The Psychology of Pornography"; one chapter deals with *Memoirs of Hecate County, Lady Chatterley's Lover,* and *Fanny Hill;* a final chapter is devoted to "The Erotica of Tomorrow."

KUH, Richard. *Foolish Figleaves?* New York: Macmillan Co., 1967. 368 pp. A former assistant district attorney discusses obscenity and the law, focusing especially on obscenity cases during the 1950s and 1960s.

KYLE-KEITH, Richard. *The High Price of Pornography.* Washington, D.C.: Public Affairs Press, 1961. 230 pp. The aim of this book, states the author in his Preface, is "to examine in some detail the nature and history of pornography and immorality in Western society and to find, if possible, the reasons for the upsurge in pornography which has taken place since the end of the Second World War. The corollary to this inquiry must of necessity be an examination of the various means adopted to combat the incidence of pornography." The book concludes with: "Neither law, nor moral condemnation, nor indeed voluntary community action based on moral sensibilities will have any more than temporary effect on the flood of pornography unless the moral climate itself is changed, and the community itself ceases to create the need for an evil which it professes to despise."

MURPHY, Terrence. *Censorship: Government and Obscenity.* Baltimore, Maryland: Helicon Press, 1963. 294 pp. This book, with the appropriate Imprimatur of the Catholic Church, deals with the prohibition of obscene materials as chiefly a function of the citizenry and the legislatures, not of the Supreme Court. The author asserts in a chapter devoted to "The Effects of Obscenity" that "empirical studies to date have refined and reaffirmed, within the limits of their methodology, the common sense notion that communications have effects and that in the instance of obscene material the effect is injurious. Courts and legislatures would do well to follow this common conviction and general experience of mankind."

NORWICK, Kenneth. *Pornography; The Issues and the Law.* New York: Public Affairs Committee, 1972. 28 pp. This Public Affairs Pamphlet (no. 477) is a short summary of the history of pornography censorship, including arguments for and against censorship and a review of the findings and recommendations of the Commission on Obscenity.

OBOLER, Eli. *The Fear of the Word: Censorship and Sex.* Metuchen, New Jersey: Scarecrow Press, 1974. 370 pp. This book by a librarian long concerned about censorship is well grounded in a variety of disciplines such as anthropology, psychology, philosophy, and sociology, providing the reader with a diversity of materials on the censorship of sexually oriented materials. The author deals with both the origins and the future directions of censorship.

PAUL, James and Murray Schwartz. *Federal Censorship: Obscenity in the Mail.* New York: The Free Press of Glencoe, Inc., 1961. 368 pp. "Using federal controls over the mails as the focal problem," write the authors in their Preface, "we have attempted to trace the development and to discuss the future evolution of laws designed to suppress circulation of obscene publications. We have made both general proposals for the future development of the law and particular recommendations

with respect to Postal and Customs operations—federal censorship. Our study attempts to show how these federal programs have evolved, how they have worked in the recent past, how they work today, the justification for them, and the dangers which are their price."

PERRY, Stuart. *The Indecent Publications Tribunal.* Auckland: Whitcombe and Tombs Limited, 1965. 169 pp. This book focuses on obscenity law and legislation in New Zealand.

REMBAR, Charles. *The End of Obscenity.* New York: Simon and Schuster, 1970. 528 pp. A book on the trials of *Lady Chatterley's Lover, Tropic of Cancer,* and *Fanny Hill* by an attorney who argued before the Supreme Court against their suppression.

RINGEL, William. *Obscenity Law Today.* New York: Gould Publications, 1970. 245 pp. A New York Criminal Court judge's review of obscenity and its "interplay" with the Bill of Rights; a survey of obscenity law interpreted and applied by the courts.

ROLPH, C.H. *Books in the Dock.* London: Andre Deutsch, 1969. 144 pp. A history of nineteenth and twentieth century censorship laws in Great Britain and their application to obscene materials; includes some proposals for reform.

ROLPH, C.H. (ed.). *Does Pornography Matter?* London: Routledge & Paul, 1961. 112 pp. A collection of essays on pornography as seen by several English specialists: a social anthropologist, a lawyer, a psychoanalyst, a reverend, an aesthetician, and others.

SHARP, D.C. (ed.). *Commentaries on Obscenity.* Metuchen, New Jersey: Scarecrow Press, 1970. 333 pp. An anthology of law journal articles on obscenity and the law by such scholars as Harry Kalven, Jr., William Lockhart, and Robert McClure. Much of the book deals with the 1966 *Ginzburg* decision.

ST. JOHN-STEVAS, Norman. *Obscenity and the Law.* London: Secker & Warburg, 1956. 289 pp. This book is largely devoted to obscenity in England, with short chapters dealing with censorship of obscenity in the United States and Ireland. "The chief conclusion drawn," says the author, "is that law should be invoked to suppress pornography, but should leave literary expression to be determined by prevailing standards of taste. It should draw a fundamental distinction between works written with a serious purpose and those which have no other aim save the making of money by exploiting and degrading the sexual passions."

The Supreme Court Obscenity Decisions. San Diego, Calif.: Greenleaf Classics, 1973. 271 pp. A collection of the five Supreme Court obscenity decisions of June 21, 1974.

THEISEN, Roman. *A Moral Evaluation of the American Law Regarding Literary Obscenity.* Rome: Officium Libri Catholici—Catholic Book Agency, 1957. 109 pp. This book, with the appropriate Imprimatur of the

Catholic Church, deals largely with the comparison of legal and moral questions related to obscenity. In a clear preference for the *Hicklin* test, the author states in his conclusion: "From a moral point of view a single passage in a book may be enough to arouse the lascivious thoughts and lustful desires which lead to a corruption of morals."

The Report of the Commission on Obscenity and Pornography. Washington, D.C.: U.S. Government Printing Office, 1970. 646 pp. Findings, recommendations, and reports of Commission panels; also includes dissenting opinions of some members of the Commission.

Technical Reports of the Commission on Obscenity and Pornography.
   Volume I: *Preliminary Studies.* Washington, D.C.: Government Printing Office, 1971. 198 pp.
   Volume II: *Legal Analysis.* Washington, D.C.: Government Printing Office, 1971. 241 pp.
   Volume III: *The Marketplace: The Industry.* Washington, D.C.: Government Printing Office, 1971. 208 pp.
   Volume IV: *The Marketplace: Empirical Studies.* Washington, D.C.: Government Printing Office, 1971. 288 pp.
   Volume V: *Societal Control Mechansims.* Washington, D.C.: Government Printing Office, 1971. 373 pp.
   Volume VI: *National Survey of Public Attitudes and Experience with Erotic Materials.* Washington, D.C.: Government Printing Office, 1971.
   Volume VII: *Erotica and Antisocial Behavior.* Washington, D.C.: Government Printing Office, 1971. 340 pp.
   Volume VIII: *Erotica and Social Behavior.* Washington, D.C.: Government Printing Office, 1971. 380 pp.
   Volume IX: *The Consumer and the Community.* Washington, D.C.: Government Printing Office, 1971. 480 pp.

These Technical Reports of research were "undertaken at the Commission's request and under the direction of its staff." William Lockhart, who chaired the Commission, states in the Foreword: "Although attention will initially focus on the findings and recommendations of the Commission and its four panels, the research reflected in these Technical Reports will have greater long-range importance." Each volume contains several original papers devoted to the subject of that volume.

WIDMER, Eleanor. *Freedom and Culture: Literary Censorship in the 70s.* Belmont, Calif.: Wadsworth Publishing Co., 1970. 216 pp. A collection of essays, excerpts from court opinions, and articles on literary censorship. Part One of the book is devoted to "Principles of Literary Censorship: Arguments and Counterarguments," Part Two to "Censorship and the Young," Part Three to commentaries and excerpts from court opinions dealing with the *Ulysses* case, the *Lady Chatterley* case, the *Tropic of Cancer* case, the *Fanny Hill* case, and the case of Ralph Ginzburg. The final section of the book is devoted to "The Cultural Context of American Censorship."

TABLE OF CASES

INDEX